# 1 MONTH OF
# FREE
# READING

## at
## www.ForgottenBooks.com

By purchasing this book you are eligible for one month membership to ForgottenBooks.com, giving you unlimited access to our entire collection of over 1,000,000 titles via our web site and mobile apps.

To claim your free month visit:
www.forgottenbooks.com/free962023

ISBN 978-0-260-65004-7
PIBN 10962023

# ANNUAL REPORT OF THE

# Secretary of the Treasury

ON

# THE STATE OF THE FINANCES

FOR THE FISCAL YEAR
ENDED JUNE 30

# 1922

## With Appendices

WASHINGTON
GOVERNMENT PRINTING OFFICE
1923

Treasury Department,
Document No. 2913.
*Secretary.*

# CONTENTS.

*Tables accompanying the report on the finances.*

## SECRETARIES OF THE TREASURY AND PRESIDENTS UNDER WHOM THEY SERVED.

NOTE.—Robert Morris, the first financial officer of the Government, was Superintendent of Finance from 1781 to 1784. Upon the resignation of Morris, the powers conferred upon him were transferred to the "Board of the Treasury." Those who finally accepted positions on this board were John Lewis GerVais, Samuel Osgood, and Walter LiVingston. The board served until Hamilton assumed office in 1789.

| Presidents. | Secretaries of Treasury. | Term of service. | |
|---|---|---|---|
| | | From— | To— |
| Washington............. | Alexander Hamilton, New York................ | Sept. 11,1789 | Jan. 31,1795 |
| | OliVer Wolcott, Connecticut..................... | Feb. 3,1795 | Mar. 3,1797 |
| Adams................. | OliVer Wolcott, Connecticut.................... | Mar. 4,1797 | Dec. 31,1800 |
| | Samuel Dexter, Massachusetts.................. | Jan. 1,1801 | Mar. 3,1801 |
| Jefferson............... | Samuel Dexter, Massachusetts.................. | Mar. 4,1801 | May 13,1801 |
| | Albert Gallatin, PennsylVania.................. | May 14,1801 | Mar. 3,1809 |
| Madison................ | Albert Gallatin, PennsylVania ¹..............:.... | Mar. 4,1809 | Apr. 17,1813 |
| | George W. Campbell, Tennessee................ | Feb. 9,1814 | Oct. 5,1814 |
| | Alexander J. Dallas, PennsylVania............. | Oct. 6,1814 | Oct. 21,1816 |
| | Wm. H. Crawford, Georgia...................... | Oct. 22,1816 | Mar. 3,1817 |
| Monroe................. | Wm. H. Crawford, Georgia...................... | Mar. 4,1817 | Mar. 6,1825 |
| Adams, J. Q............. | Richard Rush, PennsylVania ²................. | Mar. 7,1825 | Mar. 5,1829 |
| Jackson................ | Samuel D. Ingham, PennsylVania ³............. | Mar. 6,1829 | June 20,1831 |
| | Louis McLane, Delaware........................ | Aug. 8,1831 | May 28,1833 |
| | Wm J. Duane, PennsylVania................... | May 29,1833 | Sept. 22,1833 |
| | Roger B. Taney, Maryland ⁴.................... | Sept. 23,1833 | June 25,1834 |
| | Levi Woodbury, New Hampshire............... | July 1,1834 | Mar. 3,1837 |
| Van Buren ............. | Levi Woodbury, New Hampshire ⁵............. | Mar. 4,1837 | Mar. 3,1841 |
| Harrison ................ | Thomas Ewing, Ohio........................... | Mar. 6,1841 | Apr. 4,1841 |
| Tyler .....:............. | Thomas Ewing, Ohio ⁶......................... | Apr. 5,1841 | Sept. 11,1841 |
| | Walter Forward, PennsylVania ⁷................ | Sept. 13,1841 | Mar. 1,1843 |
| | John C. Spencer, New York ⁸.................. | Mar. 8,1843 | May 2,1844 |
| | Geo. M. Bibb, Kentucky........................ | July 4,1844 | Mar. 4,1845 |
| Polk .................... | Geo. M. Bibb, Kentucky........................ | Mar. 5,1845 | Mar. 7,1845 |
| | Robt. J. Walker, Mississippi ⁹................. | Mar. 8,1845 | Mar. 5,1849 |
| Taylor .................. | Wm M Meredith, PennsylVania................ | Mar. 8,1849 | July 9,1850 |
| Fillmore ............... | Wm M. Meredith, PennsylVania............... | July 10,1850 | July 22,1850 |
| | Thos. Corwin, Ohio............................ | July 23,1850 | Mar. 6,1853 |
| Pierce.................. | James Guthrie, Kentucky...................... | Mar. 7,1853 | Mar. 6,1857 |

¹ While holding the office of Secretary of the Treasury, Gallatin was commissioned envoy extraordinary and minister plenipotentiary April 17, 1813, with John Quincy Adams and James A. Bayard, to negotiate peace with Great Britain. On February 9, 1814, his seat as Secretary of the Treasury was declared vacant because of his absence in Europe. William Jones, of PennsylVania (Secretary of the NaVy), acted ad interim Secretary of the Treasury from April 21, 1813, to February 9, 1814.
² Rush was nominated March 5, 1825, confirmed and commissioned March 7, 1825, but did not enter upon the discharge of his duties until August 1, 1825. Samuel L. Southard, of New Jersey (Secretary of the NaVy), served as ad interim Secretary of the Treasury from March 7 to July 31, 1825.
³ Asbury Dickens (Chief Clerk), ad interim Secretary of the Treasury June 21 to August 7, 1831.
⁴ McClintock Young (Chief Clerk), ad interim Secretary of the Treasury from June 25 to 30, 1834.
⁵ McClintock Young (Chief Clerk), ad interim Secretary of the Treasury from March 4 to 5, 1841.
⁶ McClintock Young (Chief Clerk), ad interim September 13, 1841.
⁷ McClintock Young (Chief Clerk), ad interim March 1 to 7, 1843.
⁸ Spencer resigned as Secretary of the Treasury May 2, 1844; McClintock Young (Chief Clerk), ad interim from May 2 to July 3, 1844.
⁹ McClintock Young (Chief Clerk), ad interim March 6 to 7, 1849.

*Secretaries of the Treasury and Presidents under whom they served*—Continued.

| Presidents. | Secretaries of Treasury. | Term of service. | |
|---|---|---|---|
| | | *From—* | *To—* |
| Buchanan | Howell Cobb, Georgia [10] | Mar. 7, 1857 | Dec. 8, 1860 |
| | Philip F. Thomas, Maryland | Dec. 12, 1860 | Jan. 14, 1861 |
| | John A. Dix, New York | Jan. 15, 1861 | Mar. 6, 1861 |
| Lincoln | Salmon P. Chase, Ohio [11] | Mar. 7, 1861 | June 30, 1864 |
| | Wm. P. Fessenden, Maine [12] | July 5, 1864 | Mar. 3, 1865 |
| | Hugh McCulloch, Indiana | Mar. 9, 1865 | Apr. 15, 1865 |
| Johnson | Hugh McCulloch, Indiana [13] | Apr. 16, 1865 | Mar. 3, 1869 |
| Grant | Geo. S. Boutwell, Massachusetts | Mar. 12, 1869 | Mar. 16, 1873 |
| | Wm. A. Richardson, Massachusetts | Mar. 17, 1873 | June 3, 1874 |
| | Benj. H. Bristow, Kentucky [14] | June 4, 1874 | June 20, 1876 |
| | Lot M. Morrill, Maine | July 7, 1876 | Mar. 3, 1877 |
| Hayes | Lot M. Morrill, Maine | Mar. 4, 1877 | Mar. 9, 1877 |
| | John Sherman, Ohio [15] | Mar. 10, 1877 | Mar. 3, 1881 |
| Garfield | Wm. Windom, Minnesota | Mar. 8, 1881 | Sept. 19, 1881 |
| Arthur | Wm. Windom, Minnesota | Sept. 20, 1881 | Nov. 13, 1881 |
| | Chas. J. Folger, New York [16] | Nov. 14, 1881 | Sept. 4, 1884 |
| | Walter Q. Gresham, Indiana | Sept. 25, 1884 | Oct. 30, 1884 |
| | Hugh McCulloch, Indiana | Oct. 31, 1884 | Mar. 3, 1885 |
| Cleveland | Hugh McCulloch, Indiana | Mar. 4, 1885 | Mar. 7, 1885 |
| | Daniel Manning, New York | Mar. 8, 1885 | Mar. 31, 1887 |
| | Chas. S. Fairchild, New York | Apr. 1, 1887 | Mar. 3, 1889 |
| Harrison, Benj | Chas. S. Fairchild, New York | Mar. 4, 1889 | Mar. 6, 1889 |
| | Wm. Windom, Minnesota [17] | Mar. 7, 1889 | Jan. 29, 1891 |
| | Chas. Foster, Ohio | Feb. 25, 1891 | Mar. 3, 1893 |
| Cleveland | Chas. Foster, Ohio | Mar. 4, 1893 | Mar. 6, 1893 |
| | John G. Carlisle, Kentucky | Mar. 7, 1893 | Mar. 3, 1897 |
| McKinley | John G. Carlisle, Kentucky | Mar. 4, 1897 | Mar. 5, 1897 |
| | Lyman J. Gage, Illinois | Mar. 6, 1897 | Sept. 14, 1901 |
| Roosevelt | Lyman J. Gage, Illinois | Sept. 15, 1901 | Jan. 31, 1902 |
| | L. M. Shaw, Iowa | Feb. 1, 1902 | Mar. 3, 1907 |
| | George B. Cortelyou, New York | Mar. 4, 1907 | Mar. 7, 1909 |
| Taft | Franklin MacVeagh, Illinois | Mar. 8, 1909 | Mar. 5, 1913 |
| Wilson | W. G. McAdoo, New York | Mar. 6, 1913 | Dec. 15, 1918 |
| | Carter Glass, Virginia | Dec. 16, 1918 | Feb. 1, 1920 |
| | David F. Houston, Missouri | Feb. 2, 1920 | Mar. 3, 1921 |
| Harding | Andrew W. Mellon, Pennsylvania | Mar. 4, 1921 | |

[10] Isaac Toucey, of Connecticut (Secretary of the Navy), acted as Secretary of the Treasury ad interim December 10 to 12, 1860.
[11] George Harrington, District of Columbia (Assistant Secretary), ad interim July 1 to 4, 1864.
[12] George Harrington (Assistant Secretary), ad interim March 4 to 8, 1865.
[13] John F. Hartley, of Maine (Assistant Secretary), ad interim from March 5 to 11, 1869.
[14] Charles F. Conant, of New Hampshire (Assistant Secretary), ad interim June 21 to 30 [July 6], 1876.
[15] Henry E. French, of Massachusetts (Assistant Secretary), ad interim March 4 to 7, 1881.
[16] Charles E. Coon, of New York (Assistant Secretary), ad interim September 4 to 7, 1884; Henry F. French, of Massachusetts (Assistant Secretary), ad interim September 8 to 14, 1884; Charles E. Coon ad interim September 15 to 24, 1884.
[17] A. B. Nettleton, of Minnesota (Assistant Secretary), ad interim January 30 to February 24, 1891.

## · UNDERSECRETARIES OF THE TREASURY AND PRESIDENTS AND SECRETARIES UNDER WHOM THEY SERVED.

| President. | Secretary. | Undersecretary.[1] | Term of service. | |
|---|---|---|---|---|
| | | | *From—* | *To—* |
| Harding........ | Mellon.......... | S. Parker Gilbert, Jr., New Jersey..... | July  1, 1921 | ............. |

## ASSISTANTS TO THE SECRETARY OF THE TREASURY[2] AND PRESIDENTS AND SECRETARIES UNDER WHOM THEY SERVED.

| Presidents. | Secretaries. | Assistants to the Secretaries. | Term of service. | |
|---|---|---|---|---|
| | | | *From—* | *To—* |
| Washington..... | Hamilton....... | Tench Coxe, Pennsylvania............ | Sept. 11, 1789 | May  8, 1792 |
| Wilson.......... | McAdoo......... | George R. Cooksey, District of Columbia. | Mar.  6, 1917 | Mar.  4, 1921 |
| | Glass. | | | |
| | Houston. | | | |

## ASSISTANT SECRETARIES OF THE TREASURY AND PRESIDENTS AND SECRETARIES UNDER WHOM THEY SERVED.

| Presidents. | Secretaries. | Assistant Secretaries.[3] | Term of service. · | |
|---|---|---|---|---|
| | | | *From—* | *To—* |
| Taylor.......... | Meredith........ | Charles B. Penrose, Pennsylvania..... | Mar. 12, 1849 | Oct.  9, 1849 |
| | Meredith........ | Allen A. Hall, Pennsylvania.......... | Oct. 10, 1849 | Nov. 15, 1850 |
| Filmore......... | Corwin. | | | |
| | Corwin.......... | William L. Hodge, Tennessee........ | Nov. 16, 1850 | Mar. 13, 1853 |
| Pierce.......... | Guthrie. | | | |
| | Guthrie......... | Peter G. Washington, District of Columbia. | 'Mar.  4, 1853 | Mar. 12, 1857 |
| Buchanan....... | Cobb. | | | |
| | Cobb........... | Philip Clayton, Georgia.............. | Mar. 13, 1857 | Jan. 16, 1861 |
| | Thomas. | | | |
| | Dix. | | | |
| Lincoln......... | Chase........... | George Harrington, District of Columbia. | Mar..13, 1861[4] | July 11, 1865 |
| | Fessenden. | | | |
| | McCulloch. | | | |
| Johnson......... | McCulloch. | | | |
| Lincoln......... | Chase.......... | Maunsell B. Field, New York........ | Mar. 18, 1864 | June 15, 1865 |
| | Fessenden. | | | |
| | McCulloch. | | | |
| Johnson......... | McCulloch. | | | |
| Lincoln......... | Fessenden...... | William E. Chandler, New Hampshire. | Jan.  5, 1865 | Nov. 30, 1867 |
| | McCulloch. | | | |
| Johnson......... | McCulloch. | | | |

[1] Office established act June 16, 1921.
[2] Office established Sept. 2, 1789; abolished act May 8, 1792; reestablished act Mar. 3, 1917.  Appointed by the Secretary.
[3] Office established act Mar. 3, 1849; appointed by the Secretary. Act Mar. 3, 1857, made the office Presidential.
[4] Act Mar. 14. 1864, provides one additional Assistant Secretary.

*Assistant Secretaries of the Treasury and Presidents and Secretaries under whom they
served*—Continued.

| Presidents. | Secretaries. | Assistant Secretaries. | Term of service. | |
|---|---|---|---|---|
| | | | *From—* | *To—* |
| Johnson......... | McCulloch...... | John F. Hartley, Missouri............. | July 11,1865 | May 4,1875 |
| Grant........... | Boutwell. | | | |
| . | Richardson. | | | |
| | Bristow. | | | |
| Johnson......... | McCulloch...... | Edmund Cooper, Tennessee.......... | Dec. 2,1867 | May 31,1868 |
| Grant........... | Boutwell........ | WilliamA. Richardson, Massachusetts. | Mar. 20,1869 | Mar. 17,1873 |
| | Richardson..... | Frederick A. Sawyer, South Carolina.. | Mar. 8,1873 | June 11,1874 |
| | Bristow. | | | |
| | Bristow......... | Charles F. Conant, New Hampshire... | July 1,1874 | Apr. 3,1877 |
| | Morrill. | | | |
| Hayes........... | Sherman. | | | |
| Grant........... | Bristow......... | Curtis F. Burnam, Kentucky......... | Mar. 4,1875 | June 30,1876 |
| | Morrill.......... | Henry F. French, Massachusetts...... | Aug. 12,1876 | Mar. 9,1885 |
| Hayes........... | Sherman. | | | |
| Garfield......... | Windom. | | | |
| Arthur.......... | Windom. | | | |
| | Folger. | | | |
| | Gresham. | | | |
| | McCulloch. | | | |
| Cleveland....... | Manning. | | | |
| Hayes.......... | Sherman........ | Richard C. McCormick, Arizona...... | Apr. 3,1877 | Dec. 8,1877 |
| | Sherman........ | John B. Hawley, Illinois.............. | Dec. 9,1877 | Mar. 31,1880 |
| | Sherman........ | J. Kendrick Upton, New Hampshire.. | Apr. 10,1880 | Dec. 31,1881 |
| Garfield......... | Windom. | | | |
| Arthur.......... | Windom. | | | |
| | Folger. | | | |
| | Folger.......... | John C. New, Indiana................. | Feb. 28,1882 | Apr. 16,1884 |
| | Folger.......... | Charles E. Coon, New York........... | Apr. 17,1884 | Nov. 10,1885 |
| | Gresham. | | | |
| | McCulloch. | | | |
| Cleveland....... | Manning. | | | |
| | Manning........ | Charles S. Fairchild, New York....... | Mar. 14,1885 | Apr. 1,1887 |
| | Manning........ | William E. Smith, New York......... | Nov. 10,1885 | June 30,1886 |
| | Manning........ | Hugh S. Thompson, South Carolina... | July 12,1886 | Mar. 12,1889 |
| | Fairchild. | | | |
| Harrison........ | Windom. | | | |
| Cleveland....... | Fairchild........ | Isaac N. Maynard, New York......... | Apr. 6,1887 | Mar. 11,1889 |
| Harrison........ | Windom. | | | |
| | Windom........ | George H. Tichner, Illinois............ | Apr. 1,1889 | July 20,1890 |
| | Windom........ | George T. Batchelder, New York..... | Apr. 1,1889[b] | Oct. 31,1890 |
| | Windom........ | A. B. Nettleton, Minnesota........... | July 22,1890 | Dec. 1,1892 |
| | Foster. | | | |
| | Windom........ | Oliver L. Spaulding, Michigan........ | July 23,1890 | June 30,1893 |
| | Foster. | | | |
| Cleveland....... | Carlisle. | | | |
| Harrison........ | Foster.......... | Lorenzo Crounse, Nebraska........... | Apr. 27,1891 | Oct. 31,1892 |
| | Foster.......... | John H. Gear, Iowa.................... | Nov. 22,1892 | Mar. 3,1893 |
| | Foster.......... | Genio M. Lambertson, Nebraska...... | Dec. 23,1892 | Apr. 3,1893 |
| Cleveland....... | Carlisle. | | | |
| | Carlisle......... | Charles S. Hamlin, Massachusetts..... | Apr. 12,1893 | Apr. 7,1897 |
| McKinley....... | Gage. | | | |

[b] Act July 11, 1890, provides for an additional Assistant Secretary.

*Assistant Secretaries of the Treasury and Presidents and Secretaries under whom they served*—Continued.

| Presidents. | Secretaries. | Assistant Secretaries. | Term of service. | |
|---|---|---|---|---|
| | | | From— | To— |
| Cleveland | Carlisle | William E. Curtis, New York | Apr. 13, 1893 | Mar. 31, 1897 |
| McKinley | Gage. | | | |
| Cleveland | Carlisle | Scott Wike, Illinois | July 1, 1893 | May 4, 1897 |
| McKinley | Gage. | | | |
| | Gage | William B. Howell, New Jersey | Apr. 7, 1897 | Mar. 10, 1899 |
| | Gage | Oliver L. Spaulding, Michigan | Apr. 7, 1897 | Mar. 4, 1903 |
| Roosevelt | Gage. | | | |
| | Shaw. | | | |
| McKinley | Gage | Frank A. Vanderlip, Illinois | June 1, 1897 | Mar. 5, 1901 |
| | Gage | Horace A. Taylor, Wisconsin | Mar. 13, 1899 | June 3, 1906 |
| Roosevelt | Gage. | | | |
| | Shaw. | | | |
| McKinley | Gage | Milton E. Ailes, Ohio | Mar. 6, 1901 | Apr. 15, 1903 |
| Roosevelt | Gage. | | | |
| | Shaw. | | | |
| | Shaw | Robert B. Armstrong, Iowa | Mar. 5, 1903 | Mar. 5, 1905 |
| | Shaw | Charles H. Keep, New York | May 27, 1903 | Jan. 21, 1907 |
| | Shaw | James B. Reynolds, Massachusetts | Mar. 5, 1905 | Nov. 1, 1909 |
| | Cortelyou. | | | |
| Taft | MacVeagh. | | | |
| Roosevelt | Shaw | John H. Edwards, Ohio | July 1, 1906 | Mar. 15, 1908 |
| | Cortelyou. | | | |
| | Shaw | Arthur F. Statter, Oregon | Jan. 22, 1907 | Feb. 28, 1907 |
| | Cortelyou | Beekman Winthrop, New York | Apr. 23, 1907 | Mar. 6, 1909 |
| | Cortelyou | Louis A. Coolidge, Massachusetts | Mar. 17, 1908 | Apr. 10, 1909 |
| Taft | MacVeagh. | | | |
| | MacVeagh | Charles D. Norton, Illinois | Apr. 5, 1909 | June 8, 1910 |
| | MacVeagh | Charles D. Hilles, New York | Apr. 19, 1909 | Apr. 3, 1911 |
| | MacVeagh | James F. Curtis, Massachusetts | Nov. 27, 1909 | July 31, 1913 |
| Wilson | McAdoo. | | | |
| Taft | MacVeagh | A. Piatt Andrew, Massachusetts | June 8, 1910 | July 3, 1912 |
| | MacVeagh | Robert O. Bailey, Illinois | Apr. 4, 1911 | Mar. 3, 1913 |
| Wilson | McAdoo. | | | |
| Taft | MacVeagh | Sherman P. Allen, Vermont | July 20, 1912 | Sept. 30, 1913 |
| Wilson | McAdoo. | | | |
| | McAdoo | John Skelton Williams, Virginia | Mar. 24, 1913 | Feb. 2, 1914 |
| | McAdoo | Charles S. Hamlin, Massachusetts | Aug. 1, 1913 | Aug. 9, 1914 |
| | McAdoo | Byron R. Newton, New York | Oct. 1, 1913 | Oct. 1, 1917 |
| | McAdoo | William P. Malburn, Colorado | Mar. 24, 1914 | Jan. 26, 1917 |
| | McAdoo | Andrew J. Peters, Massachusetts | Aug. 17, 1914 | Mar. 15, 1917 |
| | McAdoo | Oscar T. Crosby, Virginia | Apr. 17, 1917 | Aug. 28, 1918 |
| | McAdoo | Leo S. Rowe, Pennsylvania | June 22, 1917 | Nov. 20, 1919 |
| | Glass. | | | |
| | McAdoo | James H. Moyle, Utah | Oct. 5, 1917 [a] | Aug. 26, 1921 |
| | Glass. | | | |
| | Houston. | | | |
| Harding | Mellon. | | | |
| Wilson | McAdoo | Russell C. Leffingwell, New York | Oct. 30, 1917 | July 5, 1920 |
| | Glass. | | | |
| | Houston. | | | |

[a] Act Oct. 6, 1917, provided for two additional Assistant Secretaries for duration of war and six months after.

*Assistant Secretaries of the Treasury and Presidents and Secretaries under whom they served*—Continued.

| Presidents. | Secretaries. | Assistant Secretaries. | Term of service. | |
|---|---|---|---|---|
| | | | *From—* | *To—* |
| Wilson.......... | McAdoo......... Glass. | Thomas B. Love, Texas............... | Dec. 15, 1917 | Jan. 31, 1919 |
| . . | McAdoo......... Glass. Houston. | Albert Rathbone, New York.......... | Sept. 4, 1918 | June 30, 1920 |
| | Glass............ Houston. | Jouett Shouse, Kansas................ | Mar. 5, 1919 | Nov. 15, 1920 |
| | Glass............ Houston. | Norman H. Davis, Tennessee ........ | Nov. 21, 1919 | June 14, 1920 |
| Harding......... | Houston........ Mellon. | Nicholas Kelley, New York........... | June 15, 1920 | Apr. 14, 1921 |
| Wilson.......... Harding......... | Houston........ Mellon. | S. Parker Gilbert, jr., New Jersey [1]... | July 6, 1920 | June 30, 1921 |
| Wilson.......... Harding......... | Houston........ Mellon. | Ewing Laporte, Missouri.............. | Dec. 4, 1920 | May 31, 1921 |
| Wilson.......... Harding......... | Houston........ Mellon. | Angus W. McLean, North Carolina.... | Dec. 4, 1920 | Mar. 4, 1921 |
| | Mellon.......... | Eliot Wadsworth, Massachusetts...... | Mar. 16, 1921 | .............. |
| | Mellon.......... | Edward Clifford, Illinois.............. | May 4, 1921 | .............. |
| | Mellon.......... | Elmer Dover, Washington............ | Dec. 23, 1921 | July 25, 1922 |

[1] Became Undersecretary July 1, 1921.

# ANNUAL REPORT ON THE FINANCES.

TREASURY DEPARTMENT.
*Washington, November 20, 1922.*

SIR: I have the honor to make the following report:

The 12 months which have passed since the last annual report have been marked by further liquidation and recovery from depression, and, more recently, by a substantial revival of business. Prices of commodities have risen materially and inventories generally are low, the volume of business has been mounting to higher levels, and labor throughout the country is again fully employed. The year is closing with bountiful crops, and the severe depression in agriculture has been relieved. Many of the sections which a year or so ago were in a precarious condition are to-day working out of their difficulties and gradually paying their debts. A few weak spots remain, but banking conditions generally are sound, money rates are reasonable, and there is sufficient credit available to meet all legitimate demands. The waste of war is being repaired, and even abroad there are signs of progress in reconstruction. In the Treasury the year has seen a reduction in the gross debt amounting to about $1,000,000,000, a balanced budget for the fiscal year 1922, showing a surplus of over $300,000,000 above expenditures, and substantial progress in the refunding of the short-dated debt, which has now been reduced to manageable proportions. These developments are all helpful, and afford the basis for a revival of business and industry on sound lines.

There are, however, factors operating which contain elements of uncertainty and make it difficult to determine the nature and extent of the revival which is in progress. Owing to the restrictions on immigration and the general resumption of industrial activity, the country is already suffering from a scarcity of labor which is embarrassing some lines of business and leading to higher wage scales where lower were expected a year or two ago. The railroads are suffering from undermaintenance and inadequate equipment, and are finding it difficult to move commodities to meet the demands of business, with resulting congestion in manufacture and trade and dislocation of prices. As a consequence farm products are selling too low at the farm and too high at the distributing centers. Undermaintenance is affecting other lines, and apparently is itself the underlying basis for much of the year's activity. The building trades, for example, have been fully engaged during the year in supplying the deficiencies resulting from underbuilding during the war, but with rising costs of material and labor and gradual satisfaction of demands there will surely be a tendency to reaction. There has also been unprecedented activity in the manufacture and sale of automobiles, and in the making of railroad and other equipment. These all represent efforts to meet capital requirements or to satisfy needs that were held in suspense during the war and the succeeding depression. Factors like these, however, are tending to create artificial scarcities and artificial, or at least limited, demands, and in the present unsettlement of world markets may spend themselves as the most pressing needs are met if costs become too high. Meantime the country has been accumulating gold, imported within the past two years or thereabouts, aggregating about $1,000,000,000 more than was held during the expansion of 1919–20, and this gold, itself directly inflationary, has a tendency to expand credit and to create an unnatural ease of money for purposes of expansion and speculation.

At the same time the uncertain state of Europe and the disorder of foreign currencies and the foreign exchanges have impaired the corrective forces which used to operate in normal times, and have created such unsettlement in foreign trade and so reduced the buying power of foreign countries as to destroy or endanger the foreign markets for many of our products. This has tended to keep the prices of agricultural products below the general level, while rising costs of manufacture on the other hand are tending still further to restrict foreign buying in our markets and threaten our ability to compete with manufacturers abroad. Reparations and indemnities and other intergovernmental debts are still unsettled and are contributing their share to the derangement of markets and the disorganization of international trade.

Enough forces are operating, therefore, to make us cautious in estimating the prospects for the future and take care lest we build on a false basis. Business in this country can not progress indefinitely without its foreign markets, and undue expansion now, with rising costs and artificial values, would inevitably sow the seeds of reaction and make more difficult the reestablishment of normal relationships abroad. To avoid these pitfalls we depend for the most part on the good sense and foresight of American business. The Treasury, on its part, aims above all to keep its own house in order, in the belief that a sound financial structure here will in the long run afford the best basis for extending needed assistance to Europe and for a healthful revival of domestic business on constructive lines. It has during the year made important progress in readjusting the national finances, and faces the current year with confidence that its fiscal problems can be safely met without disturbance to business and industry. I believe that if in other fields we will proceed with caution and with proper regard for the distressed condition of Europe, it will be possible to maintain our prosperity on a stable basis.

## REFUNDING THE SHORT-DATED DEBT.

The major problem of the Treasury Department during the period under review has been the refinancing of the short-dated debt. On June 30, 1921, there was still outstanding over $7,000,000,000 of debt maturing within two years, although the Treasury had already made one offering of Treasury notes in pursuance of its announced policy of distributing the short-dated debt into more convenient maturities. This early maturing debt included nearly $4,000,000,000 of Victory notes maturing May 20, 1923, almost $2,500,000,000 of Treasury certificates of indebtedness (loan and tax issues), all maturing within one year, and about $650,000,000 maturity value of war-savings certificates of the series of 1918, due January 1, 1923.

It was evident that it would not be possible to pay off all of this debt by maturity, and that most of it would have to be refunded. About $1,000,000,000 was retired during the fiscal year 1922, through the operation of the sinking fund, the reduction of the balance in the general fund, and the application of surplus revenues, leaving about $6,000,000,000 still to be refunded, an amount considerably more than the first and second Liberty loans combined. To refund this $6,000,000,000 without disturbance to business or interference with the normal activities of the people was a task of extraordinary magnitude. Moreover, it had to be undertaken without the help of the popular drives and the country-wide organization of perhaps two million persons that floated the Liberty loans during the stress of the war. The Treasury undertook to meet the problem squarely, and to finance the maturities on a straight investment basis. It therefore announced its general program early in 1921, and since then has made striking progress in its development. By October 31, 1922, about $4,000,000,000 of the $7,000,000,000 outstanding on June 30, 1921, had already been retired or refunded, and there is every assurance that if no extraordinary expenditures are permitted to intervene the remaining $3,000,000,000 can be refinanced during the balance of the current fiscal year without strain on the country's financial machinery and without disturbance to the market for outstanding securities.

*Treasury notes.*

The Treasury's program, as announced shortly after the beginning of the present administration, has involved first the gradual refunding of a large part of the early maturing debt through successive issues of Treasury notes, to mature in the years between the maturity of the Victory Liberty loan on May 20, 1923, and the maturity of the Third Liberty loan on September 15, 1928. The first offering of these notes was made on June 15, 1921, and was promptly over-subscribed. Since that date there have been five additional offerings of Treasury notes, several of them in exchange for Victory notes, and all have met with a hearty response from the investing public. The following table gives the total issues of Treasury notes to October 31, 1922:

*Issues of Treasury notes to October 31, 1922.*

| Date of issue. | Date of maturity. | Interest rate. | Amount of issue. |
|---|---|---|---|
| **1921.** | | *Per cent.* | |
| June 15 | June 15, 1924 | 5¼ | $311,191,600 |
| Sept. 15 | Sept. 15, 1924 | 5½ | 390,706,100 |
| **1922.** | | | |
| Feb. 1 | Mar. 15, 1925 | 4¾ | 601,599,500 |
| Mar. 15 | Mar. 15, 1926 | 4½ | 617,769,700 |
| June 15 | Dec. 15, 1925 | 4⅜ | 335,128,200 |
| Aug. 1 | Sept. 15, 1926 | 4¼ | 486,938,900 |
| Total | | | 2,743,334,000 |

This table shows clearly how the policy of refunding the short-dated debt into successive issues of Treasury notes in comparatively moderate amounts has made it possible to convert a substantial part of the short-dated debt into more manageable maturities, falling due at convenient intervals, and how it has enabled the Treasury at the same time to take advantage of declining interest rates to an extent which probably would not have been possible had it been under the necessity of refunding unmanageable amounts of short-dated debt at any one time. The rate of interest on Treasury notes has gradually been reduced from 5¾ per cent on the first offering of notes on June 15, 1921, to 4¼ per cent on the issue of August 1, 1922, and the investment markets have through these issues been relieved of the fear of spectacular refunding operations that would have interfered with the normal course of business.

A detailed description of the various offerings of Treasury notes is given in the article entitled "Treasury notes and certificates of indebtedness," on pages 47 to 51 of this report.

### Treasury bonds of 1947–1952.

In October, 1922, the time became appropriate for a longer-term refunding operation, and the Secretary of the Treasury accordingly announced, on October 9th, under authority of the act of Congress approved September 24, 1917, as amended, a popular offering of 4¼ per cent 25–30 year bonds, dated October 16, 1922, maturing October 15, 1952, and redeemable at par and accrued interest, in whole or in part, at the option of the United States, on and after October 15,

1947. The purpose of the offering and its relation to the refunding program appear most clearly from the Secretary's letter of October 9, 1922, to the banking institutions of the country, which is shown as Exhibit 29, on pages 171 to 173 of this report. The bonds were issued in both coupon and registered form, in denominations of $100 and upward, and the Treasury made special efforts to secure the widest possible distribution among investors throughout the country. The offering was for $500,000,000 or thereabouts, with the right reserved to the Secretary of the Treasury to allot additional bonds up to a limited amount to the extent that $4\frac{3}{4}$ per cent Victory notes or Treasury certificates of indebtedness of the series maturing December 15, 1922, were tendered in payment.

The offering met with a quick response from all sections of the country. It was the Treasury's declared intention to hold down allotments on cash subscriptions to $500,000,000, or thereabouts, and subscription books on the primary offering were accordingly closed at noon October 14, 1922. Allotments were made in full upon all cash subscriptions in amounts not exceeding $10,000 for any one subscriber. Heavy cuts were made in the larger subscriptions; only 40 per cent was allotted on subscriptions for amounts over $10,000 but not exceeding $50,000; only 30 per cent on subscriptions over $50,000 but not exceeding $100,000; only 20 per cent on subscriptions over $100,000 but not exceeding $500,000; only 15 per cent on subscriptions over $500,000 but not exceeding $1,000,000; and only 10 per cent on subscriptions over $1,000,000; with certain minimum allotments in each class. Subscriptions on the primary offering amounted to $1,399,851,900, of which $512,390,000 was allotted.

In addition to the subscriptions received on the cash offering, subscriptions aggregating $252,060,900 were received on exchange, making total subscriptions for this offering of Treasury bonds amounting to over $1,651,000,000. Subscriptions on the exchange offering, for which $4\frac{3}{4}$ per cent Victory notes or December 15 Treasury certificates were tendered in payment, were allotted in full, so that the total allotments on the offering aggregate slightly over $764,000,000.

These were the first long-time Government obligations offered to the people of the United States since the offering of the fourth Liberty loan, in September, 1918. The issue afforded a particularly favorable opportunity to holders of $4\frac{3}{4}$ per cent Victory notes to acquire a long-time Government bond on attractive terms in place of their Victory notes, which would mature or be redeemed within a few months, and it has provided for a substantial part of the heavy maturities of notes and certificates falling on December 15, reducing the amounts remaining to manageable proportions. The success of this loan has therefore meant important progress in the refunding operations, and it greatly facilitates the refunding which remains to be done.

A statement showing subscriptions and allotments by Federal reserve districts is attached as Exhibit 25, page 164. Further details are given in the official text of the offering, Department Circular No. 307, which is attached as Exhibit 28, page 168, and in the letter of the Secretary of the Treasury to the banking institutions of the country, dated October 9, 1922, which is attached as Exhibit 29, page 171.

### Retirement of Victory notes.

When the present refunding program was begun, the greatest problem was the Victory Liberty loan, which amounted to $3,913,-000,000 on June 30, 1921. A maturity of this size was too large to pay off or refund at one time, and the Treasury has therefore adopted every available means to reduce the outstanding amount in advance of maturity. To some extent this has been accomplished through purchases for the sinking fund, and to a larger extent by acceptance of Victory notes in exchange for new Treasury notes. It has also been done through calls for redemption before maturity.

On February 9, 1922, the Secretary of the Treasury announced the call for redemption on June 15, 1922, in accordance with their terms, of all outstanding Victory notes of the tax-exempt 3¾ per cent series, amounting to about $400,000,000, and at the same time offered to redeem any of these notes presented for redemption prior to June 15, 1922, at par and accrued interest to the date of such optional redemption. The terms of the call for redemption of the 3¾ per cent Victory notes are contained in Treasury Department Circular No. 277, dated February 9, 1922, which is attached as Exhibit 32, page 175, of this report.

It had been previously announced, on January 26, 1922, that the Federal reserve banks were authorized to purchase, for retirement, Victory notes at par and accrued interest direct from the holders on or before February 1, 1922, up to an aggregate principal amount of $100,000,000. The offer to purchase 4¾ per cent Victory notes at par and accrued interest was extended by successive authorizations to June 15, 1922, and on June 23, 1922, the Secretary of the Treasury announced that until further notice any 4¾ per cent Victory notes would be redeemed upon presentation by the holders at par and accrued interest to the date of such optional redemption. Provision was also made for the acceptance of Victory notes of either the 4¾ per cent or the 3¾ per cent series in coupon form at par, with an adjustment of accrued interest, in payment of income and profits taxes payable March 15, 1922. This authority was subsequently extended to cover the June 15 tax payment, and, as to the 4¾ per cent notes, to the September 15 and December 15 tax payments.

In connection with the offering of Treasury notes on June 15, 1922, the Secretary of the Treasury announced that a substantial part of the 4¾ per cent Victory notes would be called for redemption on December 15, 1922. On July 26, 1922, the formal call for redemption on December 15, 1922, of all Victory notes of the 4¾ per cent series bearing the distinguishing letters A, B, C, D, E, or F prefixed to their serial numbers, was announced, these notes having been designated by lot in the manner prescribed by the Secretary of the Treasury. The terms of the call for redemption of these notes are contained in Treasury Department Circular No. 299, which is attached as Exhibit 34, page 179, of this report.

As a result of these operations the 3¾ per cent Victory notes have all been retired and the amount of outstanding 4¾ per cent Victory notes had been reduced to $1,658,000,000, on October 31, 1922, of which $753,000,000 are called for redemption on December 15, 1922, leaving $905,000,000 to mature on May 20, 1923. By November 20, 1922, the amount of called Victory notes outstanding had been further reduced to about $715,000,000. Further retirements are in progress, with a view to reducing the amounts which will have to be refinanced at maturity or redemption.

The following table gives the amount of Victory notes of each series outstanding at various dates since the date of issue:

|  | 4¾ Victory notes. | 3¾ Victory notes. |
|---|---|---|
| Original issues | $3,822,787,900 | $672,585,100 |
| June 30, 1921 | 3,272,852,350 | 640,928,000 |
| June 30, 1922 | 1,991,183,400 | .......... |
| Oct. 31, 1922 | 1,658,846,950 | .......... |

### Treasury certificates of indebtedness.

The gradual reduction in the amount of outstanding loan and tax certificates, resulting from the refunding operations which have been in progress, appears from the following table, showing the volume of unmatured loan and tax certificates outstanding on various dates from August 31, 1919, when the public debt reached the highest point, to October 31, 1922:

| Date. | Loan and tax certificates outstanding. | Date. | Loan and tax certificates outstanding. |
|---|---|---|---|
| Aug. 31, 1919 | $3,938,295,000 | Oct. 31, 1921 | $1,932,218,000 |
| June 30, 1920 | 2,485,550,500 | June 30, 1922 | 1,754,787,500 |
| June 30, 1921 | 2,450,601,000 | Oct. 31, 1922 | 991,257,500 |

On October 16, 1922, the last of the loan certificates were retired, leaving only tax issues outstanding at the present time. The total amount outstanding is, however, abnormally small, for Victory notes, with their short maturity, have stood this year on substantially the same basis as Treasury certificates. With the gradual retirement of the remaining Victory notes it is likely that the balance will be restored and a larger share of the short-dated debt take the form of Treasury certificates.

Treasury certificates of indebtedness have continued to enjoy a broad and active investment market during the year. Every issue has been oversubscribed and favorable market conditions have enabled the Treasury to reduce the rate of interest from 5¼ per cent on the one-year certificates and 5 per cent on the six months' certificates offered in September, 1921, to 3¾ per cent on the one-year certificates offered September 15, 1922, and 3½ per cent on the six months' certificates offered June 1, 1922. A more complete description of the various issues of Treasury certificates of indebtedness and the course of certificate operations during the past year will be found in the article entitled "Treasury notes and certificates of indebtedness," on pages 47 to 51 of this report.

### The remaining short-dated debt.

At the same time with these refunding operations there have been substantial retirements of the public debt through the operation of the cumulative sinking fund and other miscellaneous public debt retirements, which are more fully described on pages 45 to 47 of this report. As a result of these retirements, current redemptions of war-savings certificates, and the refunding operations above described, the gross public debt of the United States had been reduced to $23,077,000,000 on October 31, 1922, and the short-dated debt maturing within the current fiscal year to approximately $3,000,000,000.

The next maturities fall on December 15, and include about $715,000,000 face amount of 4¾ per cent Victory notes called for redemption on that date, and about $200,000,000 of maturing tax certificates of Series TD and TD2-1922, against which the Treasury will receive in December about $275,000,000 of income and profits taxes. On January 1, 1923, the $625,000,000 of 1918 war-savings certificates become payable, and the Treasury has already announced a new offering of Treasury savings certificates with a view to refunding as much of this maturity as possible into obligations of the same general character and with the same appeal to the needs of the small investor. The Treasury is offering special facilities for the exchange of maturing war-savings certificates for the new Treasury savings certificates, and hopes in this manner to provide for a substantial part of the war-savings maturity. The only

Treasury certificates maturing in the second half of the fiscal year 1923 are about $266,000,000 on March 15, 1923, and about $273,000,000 on June 15, 1923, both of which are covered by the income and profits tax payments estimated for those dates. On May 20, 1923, the remaining $905,000,000 of 4¾ per cent Victory notes will mature according to their terms.

The maturities which thus remain and have to be refunded this year the Treasury will meet through further issues of refunding securities, on terms adjusted to the condition of the Treasury and the state of the market. The successful development of the program will depend, however, as it has in the past, upon the maintenance of a sound policy with respect to current expenditures. New or enlarged expenditures not covered by current receipts would necessitate new borrowing and embarrass the Treasury in its plans for meeting the maturities.

### Approaching public-debt maturities.

Upon the completion of this year's refunding, there will arise a new class of short-dated debt, maturing within the next five or six years and aggregating perhaps $9,500,000,000, assuming that the rest of the refunding is on a short-term basis. These maturities, consisting chiefly of third Liberty loan bonds and of Treasury notes and certificates resulting from the refunding operations of the two years past, will be spread over each year until 1928, when the third Liberty loan matures, and will be so arranged as to give free play to the policy of orderly funding and gradual liquidation which the Treasury has been following. All outstanding issues of notes and certificates maturing within this period fall due on quarterly tax payment dates, and will thus absorb any surplus revenues which may be available. This gives the best assurance of the gradual retirement of the war debt, and is perhaps the greatest advantage of the short-term refunding which the Treasury has been carrying on, for by distributing the debt over early maturities in amounts not too large to be financed each year these refunding operations have given the Treasury control over the debt and its retirement and avoided the tendency to perpetuation of the debt which would have been inherent in long-term refunding upon a comprehensive scale. Given a balanced budget and a sound policy in respect to current expenditures, similar plans can be applied to the succeeding years, with each year's surplus used to retire maturing notes and certificates. This will keep the finances clean, assure the gradual liquidation of the debt, and put the Nation in shape to meet future emergencies. It depends above all else, however, on the maintenance of strict economy in Government expenditure and a healthy surplus of receipts over expenditures each year.

ECONOMY IN GOVERNMENT EXPENDITURE.

Economy and retrenchment in Government expenditures have continued, under the leadership of the President, to be the watchwords of the whole Government, and with reduced expenditures and heavy realizations on railroad securities and other assets it proved possible to balance the budget for the fiscal year 1922 and to close the year with a surplus, amounting to about $321,000,000, on the basis of daily Treasury statements, revised. The shrinkage of about $1,100,-000,000 in cash receipts from income and profits taxes as compared with the previous year made this an unusually difficult task. That it was accomplished in the face of the unfavorable prospects that confronted the Treasury at the beginning of the year was due to the unremitting efforts of the Government departments and establishments to reduce current expenditures to the utmost consistent with proper administration. Expenditures were cut nearly $600,000,000 below the amount originally estimated, and the total was less than $3,800,000,000, as compared with over $5,500,000,000 during the previous fiscal year, or a reduction of over $1,700,000,000. A detailed statement of expenditures during the fiscal year 1922, as compared with 1921, appears on pages 109-118 of this report. The reduction in expenditures is attributable in part to the continued liquidation of war assets, for a special effort was made to realize on securities and surplus property held by the Government and about $390,000,000 was received during the year from sales of railroad equipment trust notes and the sale or collection of other securities acquired under the Federal control act or the transportation act, 1920, all of which appear in the statements for the year as deductions from expenditure rather than as receipts.

For the current fiscal year, 1923, the prospects again appeared unfavorable. At the beginning of the year the Budget estimates indicated a deficit of about $697,000,000, not including about $125,000,000 of accumulated interest on war savings certificates of the series of 1918, to be paid within the year, though properly allocable to the five-year period of their maturity. According to the most recent estimates the threatened deficit has now been reduced to about $149,000,000, or about $274,000,000 after taking into account the accumulated interest on war savings certificates. Of this improvement about $200,000,000 is due to reductions in estimated expenditure and about $350,000,000 to increased estimates of receipts largely from customs and internal-revenue taxes.

A detailed statement of estimated receipts and expenditures for the fiscal years 1923 and 1924, as compared with actual receipts and expenditures in the fiscal year 1922, appears on pages 118 to 120 of this report.

The estimates for the current year, it will be noted, include among the receipts about $225,000,000 of interest on foreign obligations, about $200,000,000 of which represents interest on the British debt to the United States, and at the same time about $300,000,000 of back taxes and about $125,000,000 of expected returns to the Treasury as a result of the gradual liquidation of the War Finance Corporation. The estimates of expenditures are based on the figures received from the Bureau of the Budget, and make no allowance for extraordinary expenditures not now authorized by law, though they do include about $200,000,000 on account of settlements with the railroads for matters arising out of Federal control or the six months' guaranty following Federal control.

To overcome the deficit by the end of the year is the end toward which the whole administration is striving. Much will be accomplished, it is hoped, through further reductions in expenditure, and there are also possibilities of further increases in receipts, as, for example, in collections of back taxes resulting from the final settlement of income and profits tax returns. This the Bureau of Internal Revenue is making special efforts to accomplish this year. Some increases may also be effected, over and above receipts already estimated, through further realization on the Government's investment in war emergency corporations, such as the War Finance Corporation, and further sales or collections of securities of various classes, particularly those of the Federal land banks and obligations of carriers acquired under Federal control or the transportation act.

### TAXATION AND REVENUE.

The revenue act of 1921 was approved November 23, 1921, and did not become effective as to its most important changes until January 1, 1922. It repealed the old excess-profits tax as of that date and as a substitute imposed a 2½ per cent additional tax on the net income of corporations. It likewise repealed most of the transportation tax and some of the nuisance taxes, and made some adjustments in the income tax, including revisions of the rates and of the exemptions. These changes have been operating during the calendar year 1922, and the Treasury is able now to form some judgment as to their reaction upon the revenues and their relations to the Federal tax system as a whole. The changes are still so recent, however, that their full effect will not be apparent until the income-tax returns based on the business of the present calendar year are filed and examined, and in these circumstances the Treasury is not prepared at the present time to recommend any general revision of the internal-revenue laws. Nor will it be necessary at this time to consider any additional taxes, for the Treasury hopes to overcome any deficiences in the revenue without recourse to new taxes.

The Treasury has already expressed its views, in the annual report for 1921, as to the direction which further tax revision should take, and in line with those general recommendations and in the light of its experience up to date with the revenue act of 1921, has some specific recommendations for revision to make at this time, particularly as to changes designed to close gaps in existing law which are causing substantial loss of revenue to the Government.   These recommendations relate chiefly to the rates of surtax and the avenues of escape now open under the law.   The higher surtax rates, which still run to 50 per cent, or a combined 58 per cent after including the normal tax, put such heavy pressure on the larger taxpayers to reduce their taxable income that these taxpayers inevitably seek every permissible means of avoiding the realization of income subject to surtax.   The result is to create an artificial situation, which is not wholesome from the point of view of business or industrial development.   At the same time it is impairing the revenues of the Government, for under existing conditions the higher surtax rates are undoubtedly operating to reduce rather than increase the revenues. This presents a problem which calls for solution, and I believe it can be solved only by relieving on the one hand the pressure for reducing taxable income, by making further readjustments of the surtax rates, and on the other hand by closing, so far as possible, the existing avenues of escape.   To attempt to close the gaps alone will not be enough, for the existing rates of surtax cause such heavy pressure for avoidance that new gaps would surely be found.   The high rates sound productive, but the fact remains that they are becoming increasingly ineffective and are yielding less and less revenue every year.   The time has come to face the facts squarely and to correct the artificial conditions which now prevail.

*Revision of the surtaxes.*

The higher rates of income surtaxes, as I have previously stated in the letter of April 30, 1921, to the chairman of the Committee on Ways and Means, "put constant pressure on taxpayers to reduce their taxable income, interfere with the transaction of business and the free flow of capital into productive enterprise, and are rapidly becoming unproductive." Developments since that time have more than confirmed these statements.   Under the revenue act of 1921 the surtaxes rise to a maximum of 50 per cent, which applies to all net incomes over $200,000, with rates on intermediate incomes graduated on this basis.   According to the best estimates available, the total yield of all surtaxes in respect to the business of the taxable year 1922 will not exceed $350,000,000, and the returns for several years have been steadily declining, from about $800,000,000 for 1919, to about $590,000,000 for 1920, and about $450,000,000 for 1921 (estimated).   The statistics of income for recent years likewise show that there has been a remarkable decline in the larger taxable incomes, at the very time that net incomes generally have been increasing. This appears most clearly from the following table:

*Table showing decline of taxable incomes over $300,000.*

| Year. | Number of returns. | | Net income. | | Dividends and interest on investments. | |
|---|---|---|---|---|---|---|
| | All classes. | Incomes over $300,000. | All classes. | Incomes over $300,000. | All classes. | Incomes over $300,000. |
| 1916................ | 437,036 | 1,296 | $6,298,577,620 | $992,972,986 | $3,217,348,030 | $706,945,738 |
| 1917................ | 3,472,890 | 1,015 | 13,652,383,207 | 731,372,153 | 3,785,557,955 | 616,119,892 |
| 1918................ | 4,425,114 | 627 | 15,924,639,355 | 401,107,868 | 3,872,234,935 | 344,111,461 |
| 1919................ | 5,332,760 | 679 | 19,859,491,448 | 440,011,589 | 3,954,553,925 | 314,984,884 |
| 1920................ | 7,259,944 | 395 | 23,735,629,183 | 246,354,585 | 4,445,145,223 | 229,052,039 |

These figures show that while net incomes of all classes during the period from 1916 to 1920 increased from $6,298,577,620 in 1916, to $23,735,629,183 in 1920, and the number of returns from 437,036 in 1916 to 7,259,944 in 1920, the number of returns of incomes over $300,000 decreased during the same period from 1,296 in 1916, to 395 in 1920, and the amount of incomes over $300,000 from $992,972,986 in 1916 to $246,354,585 in 1920. During this same period investment income of all classes increased, while in incomes over $300,000 investment income shrank from $706,945,738 in 1916 to $229,052,039 in 1920. This indicates an astounding decline in taxable incomes over $300,000 and clearly reflects the tendency of the high surtaxes to reduce taxable income. In this way the surtaxes are gradually defeating their own purpose and the high rates are becoming ineffective because of the steady disappearance of the taxable incomes to which they were intended to apply. The pressure operates in different ways, but among the means frequently used to reduce the amounts of income subject to taxation are the following:

1. Deductions of losses on sales of capital assets, with the failure to realize on capital gains;

2. Exchanges of property and securities so as to avoid taxable gains; ·

3. Tax-exempt securities; and

4. Other avenues of escape, such as the division of property, the creation of trusts, and the like.

Not all these things can be controlled by law or by regulation, and most of them lead to unnatural and frequently harmful economic results. To reach the evil the thing most necessary is the reduction of the surtax rates themselves, in order to reduce the pressure for avoidance and maintain the revenues derived from the surtax. I believe, therefore, that it would be sound policy, and at the same time most helpful to the general situation, to reduce the surtaxes to a maximum of not over 25 per cent, which would mean a combined maximum, including normal tax and surtax, of not over 33 per cent. Readjusted to this basis, the surtax rates would, in my judgment, accomplish their purpose and yield as large, or larger, revenues to the Government without the unwholesome consequences of the existing rates. The lower rates would at the same time broaden the market for Government securities, and otherwise encourage the development of productive enterprise.

Until some such readjustment is made the yield of the higher surtaxes will tend, in the ordinary course of events, to drop toward the vanishing point. The wise course is to reform the surtaxes now while the system still functions and at the same time to close, so far as possible, the gaps which now exist. On this basis the revision can be made without loss of revenue, and; in the long run, with material benefit to the revenues.

### Capital gains and losses.

A most serious gap in the existing revenue laws arises from the treatment of capital transactions. The law taxes capital gains and recognizes capital losses, but the taxpayer retains the initiative and refrains from realizing taxable gains while taking deductible losses. The situation is particularly serious under the revenue act of 1921, which limits the tax on capital gains to $12\frac{1}{2}$ per cent but puts no limit on the deduction of capital losses. This means that capital losses may entirely cancel real income, while capital gains will not be realized at all, or, if realized, are taxed at only $12\frac{1}{2}$ per cent. Under the present system the Government is being whipsawed, and the Treasury therefore strongly urges that the existing provision as to capital gains be made to apply conversely to capital losses and that the amount by which the tax may be reduced on account of losses from the sale of capital assets should not exceed $12\frac{1}{2}$ per cent of the amount of the loss. This would, to a large extent, check one of the methods widely used by taxpayers at the present time for decreasing their yearly income. The alternative is to refuse to recognize either capital gains or capital losses for income-tax purposes, and if the present situation were allowed to continue there is no doubt that it would save revenue to adopt this course. This is, in fact, the practice which has been followed in England for many years.

### Exchanges of securities.

The revenue act of 1921 provides, in section 202, for the exchange of property held for investment for other property of a like kind without the realization of taxable income. Under this section a taxpayer who purchases a bond of $1,000 which appreciates in value may exchange that bond for another bond of the value of $1,000, together with $100 in cash (the $100 in cash representing the increase in the value of the bond while held by the taxpayer), without the realization of taxable income. This provision of the act is being widely abused. Many brokers, investment houses, and bond houses have established exchange departments and are advertising that they will exchange securities for their customers in such a manner as to result in no taxable gain. Under this section, therefore, taxpayers owning securities which have appreciated in value are exchanging them for other securities and at the same time receiving a cash consideration, without the realization of taxable income, but if the securities have fallen in value since acquisition will sell them and in computing net income deduct the amount of the loss on the sale. This result is manifestly unfair and destructive of the revenues. The Treasury accordingly urges that the law be amended so as to limit the cases in which securities may be exchanged for other securities, without the realization of taxable income, to those cases where the exchange is in connection with the reorganization, consolidation, or merger of one or more corporations.

### *Tax-exempt securities.*

The most outstanding avenue of escape from the surtax exists in the form of tax-exempt securities, which under our constitutional system may be issued without restriction by the States and their political subdivisions and agencies. The Federal Government may likewise issue securities wholly exempt from taxation, State and Federal, but since the first Liberty loan has followed the policy of issuing its bonds, notes, and certificates without exemptions from Federal surtaxes, except in minor amounts and for limited periods. Under the provisions of the Federal farm loan act, however, the Federal land banks and joint stock land banks are still authorized to issue, and are issuing in large blocks, bonds exempt from all Federal, State, and local taxation, and the State and muncipal governments are constantly adding to the outstanding volume of their securities, all on a tax-exempt basis. The exemption which gives value to these securities is, of course, the exemption from the Federal income surtax, and as matters now stand, the Federal Government, while denying itself the advantage of the exemption from the surtaxes in selling its own securities, in effect provides a subsidy, at its own expense, to the State and municipal governments, the Federal and joint stock land banks and other agencies issuing tax-exempt securities, through the exemption from Federal income surtaxes which these tax-exempt securities enjoy. For this exemption the Federal Government gets no compensating advantage, and the effect of the exemption is to provide a perfect means of escape from Federal surtaxes which is naturally most valuable to the wealthiest investor, and especially to one who is not engaged in business and is, therefore, free to convert his investments into tax-exempt securities and thus avoid paying income tax.

The volume of fully tax-exempt securities, according to the best estimates available, is now approaching $11,000,000,000 and has recently been increasing at the rate of about $1,000,000,000 a year. With these securities available for investment, fully exempt as they are from Federal income surtaxes, investors who would normally put their surplus funds into productive enterprise, are automatically driven under the pressure of high surtax rates into investment in tax-exempt securities, with the result that the Federal Government loses the revenue, business and industry lose the capital, and funds badly needed for productive purposes are diverted into unproductive and frequently wasteful public expenditure. This is a situation which can not be permitted to continue without grave danger to our economic structure, as well as to our system of taxation, and the Treasury has accordingly been urging for some time the adoption of a constitutional amendment restricting further issues of tax-exempt securities as the only practicable means of correcting the evil. (See Exhibit 87, page 318, for letter of January 16, 1922, from the Secretary of the Treasury to the Chairman of the Committee on Ways and Means, with accompanying papers.) Even a constitutional amendment would apply only to future issues of securities, but once the amendment is adopted outstanding issues of tax-exempt securities will gradually eliminate themselves, and as they become scarcer should so increase in market value as to destroy or at least impair their value for tax-exempt purposes. An analysis of outstanding issues of State and municipal bonds indicates that 50 per cent, or thereabouts, will mature within the next 20 years, so that within a measurable period after the adoption of a constitutional amendment restricting further issues of tax-exempt securities the situation would, to a large extent, be under control.

A constitutional amendment, satisfactory to the Treasury and approved by the Attorney General, has already been proposed by joint resolution favorably reported to the last session of Congress by the Committee on Ways and Means. This amendment would apply equally, and without discrimination, to the Federal Government, on the one hand, and the State and municipal governments, on the other hand, and would in effect put an end to future issues of tax-exempt securities, making it possible, for the Federal Government, to tax income from future issues by or under authority of the several States if, as, and to the extent that it taxes future issues of Federal securities, and, for the State governments, to tax income from future issues of Federal securities if, as, and to the extent that they tax future issues of their own securities. The amendment, which appears in H. J. Res. 314,°reads as follows:

## ARTICLE —.

SECTION 1. The United States shall have power to lay and collect taxes on income derived from securities issued, after the ratification of this article, by or under the authority of any State, but without discrimination against income derived from such securities and in favor of income derived from securities issued, after the ratification of this article, by or under the authority of the United States or any other State.

SEC. 2. Each State shall have power to lay and collect taxes on income derived by its residents from securities issued, after the ratification of this article, by or under the authority of the United States; but without discrimination against income derived from such securities and in favor of income derived from securities issued, after the ratification of this article, by or under the authority of such State.

The Treasury most earnestly urges that this amendment be promptly adopted and submitted to the States for their approval.

### Administrative changes.

Other administrative changes should be made in the law with·a view to closing up miscellaneous avenues of escape and improving the collection of the revenues. There should also be an indefinite appropriation for refunds of taxes illegally or erroneously collected, in order to facilitate the adjustment and payment of claims. Appropriations of this character already exist for the payment of customs refunds and drawbacks, and similar provision for internal revenue refunds would avoid the necessity for frequent deficiency appropriations, and incidentally save the embarrassment arising from the allowance of refunds in cases where no appropriation is available for payment.

### No additional taxes.

The changes herein recommended will not decrease the revenues, and in the long run should bring larger returns to the Treasury. No additional taxes, therefore, are necessary on this account, and the Treasury is not recommending any new taxes at this time to meet indicated deficiencies in the revenue. It is still impossible to tell with certainty whether the present year will close without a deficit, but enough has already been accomplished to reduce materially the deficit appearing from the estimates presented at the beginning of the year. The latest figures show increased receipts from all sources, including particularly customs and internal taxes, aggregating about $350,000,000, and, on the other hand, decreased expenditures of about $200,000,000, making a net gain for Budget purposes of about $550,000,000. The present year, moreover, presents extraordinary circumstances, including, as it does, many overhanging items, both of receipts and expenditure, which are not subject to administrative control and, since they depend upon extraneous conditions, are difficult, and sometimes almost impossible, to forecast. Under such conditions and with the progress that has already been made in bringing the Budget for the year into balance, the Treasury does not believe it necessary to impose at this time any additional taxes for the purpose of supplementing the revenues.

The probabilities are that reductions in expenditure will not overcome all of the deficit indicated by the estimates. The Treasury believes, however, that given relatively stable conditions in the markets and in the business world it will be possible to meet the rest of the deficit by increased receipts, arising, on the one hand, from further realization on securities and other surplus assets of the Government and, on the other, from increased collections of income and profits taxes in respect to prior years. To this end the Treasury is making exceptional efforts this year to dispose of the accumulation of income and profits tax returns covering 1917 and subsequent years, in the hope that by this means it will be able to make substantial further collections of back taxes. There are also indications, which have so far as possible been taken into account in the estimates already submitted, of increased collections of income taxes as a result of the improvement in business during the calendar year 1922. The extent of this improvement, and its effect on the revenues, will not, of course, be disclosed until March 15, 1923, when the first installment of income taxes for the taxable year 1922 becomes payable, but any additional receipts on that account will help to reduce any deficit that may still remain in the current revenues.

#### OBLIGATIONS OF FOREIGN GOVERNMENTS.

The obligations of various foreign governments held by the Treasury on November 15, 1922, aggregated $10,045,282,026.60, principal amount, and may be classified as follows:

(1) $9,386,311,178.10 representing loans made by the Secretary of the Treasury, with the approval of the President, under the Liberty bonds acts.

(2) $574,876,884.95 received from the Secretary of War and the Secretary of the Navy on account of sales of surplus war material under the act of July 9, 1918.

(3) $84,093,963.55 received from the American Relief Administration on account of relief supplies furnished under the act of February 25, 1919.

In addition to the above, the United States Grain Corporation, the entire stock of which is owned by this Government, holds obligations of various foreign governments amounting to $56,858,802.49. It is expected that these obligations, which were acquired by the Grain

Corporation on account of sales of flour for relief purposes under the act of March 30, 1920, will also be turned over to the Treasury Department for custody upon the completion of the pending liquidation of that corporation. Notes of the Polish Government amounting to about $24,000,000 are also held by the War Department and the United States Shipping Board. It is understood that these obligations were received on account of sales of surplus war material by the former and transportation services by the latter, and that the amounts may be subject to further adjustment.

A detailed statement of the foreign obligations now held by the Treasury and by the United States Grain Corporation, showing also the interest accrued and remaining unpaid as of the last interest payment dates, is given as Exhibit 77, page 281.

The following statement shows the credits established under the Liberty bond acts (after deducting credits withdrawn), as at the close of business on November 15, 1922:

| Country. | Credits established. | Cash advanced. | Other charges against credits. | Balance under established credits. |
|---|---|---|---|---|
| Belgium | $349,214,467.89 | $349,214,467.89 | | |
| Cuba | 10,000,000.00 | 10,000,000.00 | | |
| Czechoslovakia | 67,329,041.10 | 61,974,041.10 | | $5,355,000.00 |
| France | 2,997,477,800.00 | 2,997,477,800.00 | | |
| Great Britain | 4,277,000,000.00 | 4,277,000,000.00 | | |
| Greece | 48,236,629.05 | 15,000,000.00 | $33,236,629.05 | |
| Italy | 1,648,034,050.90 | 1,648,034,050.90 | | |
| Liberia | 26,000.00 | 26,000.00 | | |
| Rumania | 25,000,000.00 | 25,000,000.00 | | |
| Russia | 187,729,750.00 | 187,729,750.00 | | |
| Serbia | 26,780,465.56 | 26,780,465.56 | | |
| Total | 9,636,828,204.50 | 9,598,236,575.45 | 33,236,629.05 | 5,355,000.00 |

The balance of the credit which was granted to the Czecho-Slovak Republic to assist that Government in the repatriation of its troops from Siberia was $6,072,834.36 at the beginning of the fiscal year 1922. The movement of these troops was carried out by the War Department and the Shipping Board, and on May 29, 1922, the Czecho-Slovak Republic used $717,834.36 out of this credit to reimburse the Shipping Board for its services. The balance to the credit of that Republic is now $5,355,000, and whatever may remain after all payments to the War Department have been completed will be withdrawn.

It is not contemplated that any further advances will be made by the Treasury against the credits in favor of Greece. The nature of these credits was described in last year's annual report.

The following statement shows the amount of advances which have been repaid up to November 15, 1922:

| Country. | To Nov. 15, 1921. | Nov. 16, 1921, to Nov. 15, 1922. | Total. |
|---|---|---|---|
| Belgium | $1,522,901.66 | $440,552.83 | $1,963,454.49 |
| Cuba | 1,425,000.00 | 834,500.00 | 2,259,500.00 |
| France | 46,714,861.81 | 17,357,868.04 | 64,072,729.85 |
| Great Britain | 110,681,641.56 | 30,500,000.00 | 141,181,641.56 |
| Rumania | 1,794,180.48 | | 1,794,180.48 |
| Serbia | 605,326.34 | 48,564.63 | 653,890.97 |
| Total | 162,743,911.85 | 49,181,485.50 | 211,925,397.35 |

The $30,500,000 repaid by the British Government during the past year was on account of the obligations of that Government given for purchases of silver under the Pittman Act, according to the special arrangement made regarding these obligations.

The repayments made by the Governments of Belgium and Serbia and substantially all of those made by France during the past year represent the unused balances of advances made by the Treasury to those Governments and turned over by them to the Commission for Relief in Belgium and to the American Relief Commission to be expended for relief purposes. These unused balances were returned to the Treasury to be applied as payments on account of the principal of the obligations of the respective Governments.

No repayments of principal have been made on any of the obligations acquired under the acts of July 9, 1918, February 25, 1919, or March 30, 1920.

The following table shows the amount of interest paid on foreign obligations acquired by the Treasury under the Liberty bond acts:

| Country. | To Nov. 15, 1921. | Nov. 16, 1921, to Nov. 15, 1922. | Total. |
|---|---|---|---|
| Belgium | $10,907,281.55 | | $10,907,281.55 |
| Cuba | 1,442,922.91 | $416,810.23 | 1,859,733.14 |
| Czechoslovakia | 304,178.09 | | 304,178.09 |
| France | 129,570,376.13 | | 129,570,376.13 |
| Great Britain | 247,844,685.50 | 103,812,500.00 | 351,657,185.50 |
| Greece | 1,159,153.34 | | 1,159,153.34 |
| Italy | 57,598,852.62 | | 57,598,852.62 |
| Liberia | 861.10 | | 861.10 |
| Rumania | 263,313.74 | | 263,313.74 |
| Russia | 4,872,811.50 | 2,612,744.46 | 7,485,555.96 |
| Serbia | 636,059.14 | | 636,059.14 |
| Total | 454,600,495.62 | 106,842,054.69 | 561,442,550.31 |

Great Britain's interest payments during the past year were made as follows:

| Date of payment. | Interest on obligations given for Pittman silver advances. | Interest on other obligations. | Total. |
|---|---|---|---|
| Apr. 15, 1922 | $1,372,500.00 | ................ | $1,372,500.00 |
| May 15, 1922 | 915,000.00 | ................ | 915,000.00 |
| Oct. 16, 1922 | 915,000.00 | $50,000,000.00 | 50,915,000.00 |
| Nov. 15, 1922 | 610,000.00 | 50,000,000.00 | 50,610,000.00 |
| Total | 3,812,500.00 | 100,000,000.00 | 103,812,500.00 |

On page 58 of the Annual Report of the Secretary of the Treasury for the fiscal year 1920, reference was made to two special funds arising out of the liquidation of certain property of the Russian Government and held for Russia by the Secretary of the Treasury, aggregating $2,143,601.07. On August 3, 1922, these funds were applied (1) to cancel the unpaid balance of the interest, amounting to $1,808,-506, which became due on Russian obligations, May 15, 1918; and (2) as part payment of the unpaid balance of the interest due November 15, 1918. Most of the funds which the Treasury has received in payment of interest on Russian obligations represent the proceeds of liquidation of the financial affairs of the Russian Government in this country. Copies of a letter dated May 23, 1922, from the Secretary of State and the reply of the Secretary of the Treasury, dated June 2, 1922, in regard to the loans of this Government to Russia and the liquidation of the affairs of the Russian Government in this country, are attached as Exhibit 79, page 283.

The following statement shows the amount of interest paid by each foreign government on obligations acquired under the act of July 9, 1918, on account of sales of surplus war material:

| Country. | To Nov. 15, 1921. | Nov. 16, 1921, to Nov. 15, 1922. | Total. |
|---|---|---|---|
| Belgium | $2,797,351.40 | $1,379,429.06 | $4,176,780.46 |
| France | 20,038,719.13 | 20,859,564.43 | 40,898,283.56 |
| Latvia | 126,266.19 | ................ | 126,266.19 |
| Poland | 1,290,620.78 | ................ | 1,290,620.78 |
| Russia | 10,179.87 | 40,580.43 | 50,760.30 |
| Total | 24,263,137.37 | 22,279,573.92 | 46,542,711.29 |

The only interest payment received to date on foreign obligations acquired under the act of February 25, 1919, was one of $181,017.17 on Russian obligations, which was paid on August 5, 1922.

The Treasury understands that no interest has been paid on the obligations held by the United States Grain Corporation, acquired under the act of March 30, 1920.

The following statement by the Secretary of the Treasury, regarding the status of the obligations of foreign governments held by the United States, and particularly the origin of the indebtedness of the British Government to the United States, was made public on August 24, 1922:

A number of inquiries have been received, as a result of statements recently published, with respect to the exact status of the obligations of foreign governments held by the United States. Especial attention has been directed to the origin of the indebtedness of the British Government amounting to about $4,135,000,000. It has been said that this liability was not incurred for the British Government, but for the other allies, and that the United States, in making the original arrangements, had insisted in substance that though the other allies were to use the money borrowed, it was only on British security that the United States was prepared to lend it. It is apparent from the inquiries which have reached the Treasury Department that it is supposed that this, in substance, is the explanation of the existing indebtedness of Great Britain.

In answer to these inquiries, it should be said that the obligations of foreign governments, in question, had their origin almost entirely in purchases made in the United States, and the advances by the United States Government were for the purpose of covering payments for these purchases by the Allies.

The statement that the United States Government virtually insisted upon a guaranty by the British Government of amounts advanced to the other allies is evidently based upon a misapprehension. Instead of insisting upon a guaranty, or any transaction of that nature, the United States Government took the position that it would make advances to each Government to cover the purchases made by that Government and would not require any Government to give obligations for advances made to cover the purchases of any other Government. Thus, the advances to the British Government, evidenced by its obligations, were made to cover its own purchases, and advances were made to the other allies to cover their purchases.

The nature of the arrangements is shown by a memorandum which the Secretary of the Treasury, in June, 1918, handed to the British ambassador, as follows:

So far as the purchases of the allied Governments for war purposes within the United States and its Territories and insular possessions are concerned it is the expectation of the Secretary of the Treasury to continue as heretofore the advances necessary to enable the financing of such approved purchases. The Secretary of the Treasury quite agrees with what he understands to be the views of the Chancellor of the Exchequer that advances shall be made to each allied Government for the commodities purchased in the United States by or for it and that no allied Government should be required to give its obligations for such purposes when merely serving as a conduit for the supply of the materials so purchased to another allied Government. Any other course would indeed be incompatible with what the Secretary of the Treasury deems a cardinal principle which should be followed in respect to such advances, namely, that the allied Government for the use of which the commodity is purchased must give its own obligation therefor and the obligation of any other allied Government can not be accepted by the United States as an equivalent.

It is well to further quote from a memorandum handed to the British ambassador in June, 1920, by the Secretary of the Treasury, in regard to these loans as follows:

It has been at all times the view of the United States Treasury that questions regarding the indebtedness of the Government of the United Kingdom of Great Britain and Ireland to the United States Government and the funding of such indebtedness had no relation either to questions arising concerning the war loans of the United States and of the United Kingdom to other Governments or to questions regarding the reparation payments of the central Empires of Europe. These views were expressed to the representatives of the British Treasury constantly during the period when the United States Government was making loans to the Government of the United Kingdom and since that time in Washington, in Paris, and in London.

From these two statements it appears to be quite clear that the respective borrowing nations each gave their own obligations for the money advanced by the United States and that no guaranty of the obligations of one borrowing nation was asked from any other nation. This is the understanding of the Treasury as to the status of the foreign obligations growing out of the war now held by the United States.

*Austrian relief.*—The United States Government holds one of a series of Austrian Government bonds designated as "Relief Series B of 1920," which was issued by that Government in connection with food purchased on credit from the United States Grain Corporation for relief purposes. The principal amount of this obligation is $24,055,708.92. A copy is attached as Exhibit 78, page 282. The other bonds of "Relief Series B of 1920" outstanding are held by various European nations. This series of bonds, according to the express terms thereof, is a first lien upon all the assets and revenues of Austria. Her assets and revenues are also subject to claims of certain foreign governments on account of reparations and costs of armies of occupation. Measures for the financial and economic reconstruction of Austria have for some time been the subject of considerable discussion between the principal governments interested in the Austrian situation. The proposed plan of Austrian rehabilitation contemplates that all Governments having claims against Austria on account of relief, reparation, or costs of armies of occupation shall extend the time of payment thereof and suspend their liens on Austrian assets for a period of 20 years, so that such assets may be available as security for new external credits. In order that this Government might cooperate in this respect with the other governments having claims against Austria, the following joint resolution was passed by the Congress and approved by the President on April 6, 1922:

Whereas the economic structure of Austria is approaching collapse and great numbers of the people of Austria are, in consequence, in imminent danger of starvation and threatened by diseases growing out of extreme privation and starvation; and

Whereas this Government wishes to cooperate in relieving Austria from the immediate burden created by her outstanding debts: Therefore be it

*Resolved by the Senate and House of Representatives of the United States of America in Congress assembled,* That the Secretary of the Treasury is hereby authorized to extend, for a period not to exceed twenty-five years, the time of payment of the principal and interest of the debt incurred by Austria for the purchase of flour from the United States Grain Corporation, and to release Austrian assets pledged for the payment of such loan, in whole or in part, as may in the judgment of the Secretary of the Treasury be necessary for the accomplishment of the purposes of this resolution: *Provided, however,* That substantially all the other creditor nations, to wit, Czechoslovakia, Denmark, France, Great Britain, Greece, Holland, Italy, Norway, Rumania, Sweden, Switzerland, and Yugoslavia shall take action with regard to their respective claims against Austria similar to that herein set forth. The Secretary of the Treasury shall be authorized to decide when this proviso has been substantially complied with.

The Secretary of the Treasury has not yet been requested to take formal action under the above resolution, but stands ready to act when occasion arises and its conditions are met. On August 7, 1922, the Reparation Commission released from reparation claims for a period of 20 years certain revenues of the Austrian Government in order that they might be used as security for a new Austrian bank of issue. In this connection the United States Government informed the Austrian Government that it was prepared, within the limits of the resolution of April 6, 1922, to suspend its priority in respect to Austrian assets and revenues to the extent necessary for this purpose.

### WORLD WAR FOREIGN DEBT COMMISSION.

The World War Foreign Debt Commission was created by the act of February 9, 1922, entitled "An act to create a commission authorized under certain conditions to refund or convert obligations of foreign Governments held by the United States of America, and for other purposes," the text of which is as follows:

*Be it enacted by the Senate and House of Representatives of the United States of America in Congress assembled*, That a World War Foreign Debt Commission is hereby created consisting of five members, one of whom shall be the Secretary of the Treasury, who shall serve as chairman, and four of whom shall be appointed by the President, by and with the advice and consent of the Senate.

SEC. 2. That, subject to the approval of the President, the commission created by section 1 is hereby authorized to refund or convert, and to extend the time of payment of the principal or the interest, or both, of any obligation of any foreign Government now held by the United States of America, or any obligation of any foreign Government hereafter received by the United States of America (including obligations held by the United States Grain Corporation, the War Department, the Navy Department, or the American Relief Administration), arising out of the World War, into bonds or other obligations of such foreign Government in substitution for the bonds or other obligations of such Government now or hereafter held by the United States of America, in such form and of such terms, conditions, date or dates of maturity, and rate or rates of interest, and with such security, if any, as shall be deemed for the best interests of the United States of America: *Provided*, That nothing contained in this act shall be construed to authorize or empower the commission to extend the time of maturity of any such bonds or other obligations due the United States of America by any foreign Government beyond June 15, 1947, or to fix the rate of interest at less than 4½ per centum per annum: *Provided further*, That when the bond or other obligation of any such Government has been refunded or converted as herein provided, the authority of the commission over such refunded or converted bond or other obligation shall cease.

SEC. 3. That this act shall not be construed to authorize the exchange of bonds or other obligations of any foreign Government for those of any other foreign Government, or cancellation of any part of such indebtedness except through payment thereof.

SEC. 4. That the authority granted by this act shall cease and determine at the end of three years from the date of the passage of this act.

SEC. 5. That the annual report of this commission shall be included in the annual report of the Secretary of the Treasury on the state of the finances, but said commission shall immediately transmit to the Congress copies of any refunding agreements entered into, with the approval of the President, by each foreign Government upon the completion of the authority granted under this act.

Approved, February 9, 1922.

The act provides that the Secretary of the Treasury shall be one of the members of the commission and serve as its chairman. As the other four members of the commission, the President appointed on February 21, 1922, Charles E. Hughes, Secretary of State; Herbert C. Hoover, Secretary of Commerce; Reed Smoot, United States Senator; and Theodore E. Burton, Member of the House of Representatives. On February 28, 1922, the Senate confirmed the appointments of Secretary Hughes and Secretary Hoover, and on April 11, 1922, confirmed the appointments of Senator Smoot and Congressman Burton.

The organization and first meeting of the commission was held on April 18, 1922. Eliot Wadsworth, Assistant Secretary of the Treasury, was appointed secretary of the commission, and the following resolution was adopted:

*Resolved*, That the Secretary of State be requested to inform each of the Governments whose obligations, arising out of the World War, are held by the United States, including obligations held by the United States Grain Corporation, the War Department, the Navy Department, or the American Relief Administration, of the organization of the World War Foreign Debt Commission pursuant to the act of Congress approved February 9, 1922, and that the commission desires to receive any proposals or representations which the said Government may wish to make for the settlement or refunding of its obligations under the provisions of the act.

In accordance with this resolution the Secretary of State instructed the diplomatic representatives of this Government at the capitals of each of the foreign Governments indebted to the United States, with the exception of Armenia, Austria, Cuba, Greece, Liberia, Nicaragua, and Russia, to communicate to the respective Governments to which they were accredited the text of the resolution and of the act. This action was not taken in respect to the Governments above named for the following reasons:

Armenia, Greece, and Russia: In none of these countries is there a Government recognized by the United States.

Austria: Congress passed on April 6, 1922, a joint resolution giving the Secretary of the Treasury special authority to deal with the Austrian debt.

Cuba: Interest and installments of principal are being regularly paid and no refunding is required.

Liberia: An act authorizing a new loan, from the proceeds of which the existing loan will be repaid in full, has already been passed by the House of Representatives pursuant to request of the Department of State, and is now pending before the Senate.

Nicaragua: This debt is regarded as already in funded form.

In response to the invitation of this Government the following countries have designated representatives to negotiate with the commission: Belgium, Czechoslovakia, Finland, France, Great Britain, Hungary, Poland, Rumania, and Serbia.

. The commission held further meetings on June 1 and 30, July 27, August 10, and September 29, 1922.

In July, 1922, the French Government sent a special mission, headed by Mr. Jean V. Parmentier, director of the movement of funds of the French treasury, to the United States to discuss with the commission the French debt to this Government. Mr. Parmentier, upon his arrival, placed in the hands of the commission certain data relating to the financial and economic situation of France. He explained to the commission the position of his Government in respect to the funding of its debt to the United States, stating that he had been designated by the French Government to afford the commission complete information as to the financial condition of his Government, but that the latter did not consider it possible at the present time to enter into any definite engagements for a funding or settlement of its debt. He further stated that it was his Government's desire to postpone for an indefinite period consideration of this matter, until the financial situation of France should become more clear, particularly as to reparation receipts from Germany. The commission's position on the subject was explained to Mr. Parmentier, and especially its desire that a funding of the French debt should take place in the near future. On August 17, 1922, Mr. Parmentier informed the chairman of the commission that he had been keeping his Government informed of the progress made in the negotiations and that he had received a cable instructing him to return for a full discussion with his Government of the situation as it had developed. The chairman replied that in his view it could only be beneficial if Mr. Parmentier should in person discuss with his Government the negotiations which had taken place between him and the commission. Mr. Parmentier returned to France shortly after this conference.

Announcement was made by the Government of Great Britain on July 17, 1922, that a special delegation would proceed to the United States early in September to negotiate terms for the funding of the British debt to the United States. The British Embassy in Washington subsequently reported that the delegation would sail on October 18 for New York, headed by Sir Robert Horne, Chancellor of the Exchequer, who would be accompanied by Mr. Montagu Collet Norman, Governor of the Bank of England, as second delegate. With the recent change of government in England, however, the departure of a delegation has been postponed pending the holding of the elections in that country.

Great Britain has paid $100,000,000 as interest on her obligations to the United States during the current fiscal year, $50,000,000 on October 16, 1922, and $50,000,000 on November 15, 1922, in addition to the payments under the special agreement as to silver advances.

The Italian Government has stated that it is prepared to send a special commission to this country to negotiate with the commission.

The Rumánian Government has sent a special delegation to the United States to negotiate with the commission.

The commission has had discussions of a preliminary nature with a few of the other debtor governments, but no definite funding agreements have yet been entered into.

Statistical information has been and is being compiled and analyzed with a view to ascertaining the financial and economic conditions of the various debtor nations. The commission is hopeful that after the British debt to the United States has been refunded, which is expected to take place shortly, substantial progress will be made in concluding refunding arrangements with the other debtor nations.

### BUREAU OF INTERNAL REVENUE.[1]

Internal-revenue collections for the fiscal year ended June 30, 1922, aggregated $3,197,451,083, compared with $4,595,357,061.95 for the fiscal year ended June 30, 1921, a decrease of $1,397,905,978. 95, or about 30 per cent. This decrease in collections is due principally to a decrease of $1,141,219,208.90 in receipts from income and profits taxes, which aggregated $2,086,918,464.85 for the fiscal year 1922, as compared with $3,228,137,673.75 for the fiscal year 1921.

The collections made during the first six months of the fiscal year 1922 included the third and fourth installments of income and profits taxes on incomes of the calendar year 1920, returns for which were made under the provisions of the revenue act of 1918. The collections made during the last six months of the fiscal year included the first and second installments of income and profits taxes on incomes of the calendar year 1921, returns for which were made under the provisions of the revenue act of 1921. The provisions of these two acts with respect to the computation of net income and the credits which may be applied against income in computing the tax are substantially different. There was, in addition, a considerable shrinkage of income in 1921 as compared with 1920.

---

[1] The figures concerning internal-revenue receipts as here given differ from figures carried in other Treasury statements showing the financial condition of the Government, because the former represent collections by internal-revenue officers throughout the country, including deposits by postmasters of amounts received from sale of internal-revenue documentary stamps, while the latter represent the deposits of these collections in the Treasury or depositaries during the fiscal year concerned, the differences being due to the fact that some of the collections in the latter part of the fiscal year can not be deposited, or are not reported to the Treasury as deposited, until after June 30th, thus carrying them into the following fiscal year as recorded in the statements showing the condition of the Treasury. (See Department Circular No. 176, par. 25.)

There are still large numbers of unaudited income tax returns which must be disposed of before the work can be brought to a current basis. From 1918 to 1921, inclusive, millions of complicated income and profits tax returns were received in the bureau, and it was unable to audit the returns as rapidly as they came in. The result was a vast accumulation. Complicated questions of law and accounting, involving in some cases millions of dollars, have to be decided before the tax liability of some of the largest taxpayers can be determined. In many cases the returns of different corporations must be consolidated. In other cases it is necessary to arrive at the value of property paid into a corporation for shares of stock at the date of organization in order to ascertain the correct amount of invested capital, and in numerous cases it is necessary to determine the valuations of natural resources as of March 1, 1913, for the purpose of determining the correct amount of depletion for the tax years in question. The settlement of these questions necessarily consumes time. The collection of back taxes, furthermore, has been delayed by the provision of the revenue act of 1921 which gives taxpayers a right to an appeal and hearing prior to the assessment of taxes found to be due upon the examination of returns filed for prior years, for taxpayers in hundreds of cases have filed appeals with the Committee on Appeals and Review. Every effort is being made to dispose of these accumulated appeals. The Committee on Appeals and Review has been considerably enlarged and a special committee on appeals and review has been created to handle the appeals from additional assessments of taxes for the year 1917. It is believed that by March, 1923, the accumulated appeals will have been disposed of and that after that time the appeals can be disposed of currently.

Everything possible is being done to expedite the auditing of returns filed for prior years and the closing of these cases. The Income Tax Unit is, as rapidly as is consistent with careful consideration, examining the returns filed for prior years and assessing additional taxes shown to be due. It is hoped, in view of the special efforts being made to close cases pending in the bureau, that the accumulation may be disposed of by the end of the fiscal year 1923, and that from then on the bureau will be able to audit the returns as rapidly as they come in and keep its work on a current basis.

A survey of the work in the Income Tax Unit last fall disclosed that the prompt audit of returns was being seriously delayed by the accumulation of claims which in large part offset the audit of returns and the assessment of additional taxes, since in practically all cases an assessment resulted in a claim which had to be adjusted before the tax was collectible. Precedence was accordingly given to claims work, the decentralization of that work was carried to completion, duplication of review was eliminated, and a number of changes in the procedure were made. As a result, the adjustment of claims has made available for collection the additional taxes held up by claims for abatement and claims for credit.

The number of claims on hand has been reduced materially during the year. The 163,000 income and excess-profits tax claims on hand in October, 1921, were reduced to 106,000 on June 30, 1922. The 167,405 claims adjusted during the year involved $332,479,-050.60, of which 139,631, involving $182,371,597.88, were allowed, and 27,774, involving $150,107,452.72, were rejected.

Under an appropriation made by Congress in December, 1921, with a view to facilitating the settlement of pending claims, the personnel has been increased during the year as follows: The consolidated returns division, 200 auditors; the natural resources division and the amortization division, 75 engineers; the field service, 600 auditors and 120 clerks; and the bureau in Washington, 100 clerks. These employees have been trained and are now rendering valuable assistance to the bureau. The classes in tax law and accountancy have had an enrollment of 2,872 employees, and the correspondence courses for field employees 1,700. Competent auditors and attorneys, regular employees of the bureau, have rendered most valuable service outside of office hours in the training of these and other employees.

During the fiscal year ended June 30, 1922, an aggregate of 954,731 income and profits returns were audited. Of these 717,879 were individual and partnership returns and 236,852 were corporation returns. On office audits (those made without field examination) $22,736,236.26 additional tax was assessed on individual and partnership returns and $56,943,624.71 was assessed on corporation returns. There were 24,868 field investigations on individuals and partnerships as a result of which $28,885,736.49 in additional tax was assessed. There were also 14,088 field investigations of corporation reports resulting in additional assessments of $78,717,066.69. The total assessments on all back income taxes for the fiscal year ended June 30, 1922, were $187,282,664.15.

During the quarter ended September 30, 1922, the number of income returns audited was 448,809, as compared with 319,561 for the preceding quarter. As a result of these audits, the amount of additional back taxes assessed for this quarter exceeded the amount assessed for the preceding quarter by $5,777,739.70. During the quarter ended June 30, 1922, there was made available for collection the amount of $15,438,873.69 in back taxes through the rejection in whole or in part of claims for abatement and claims for credit. During the quarter ended September 30, 1922, there was made available for collection from this source back taxes aggregating $30,504,271.16, or almost twice the amount assessed in the previous quarter.

The follówing table indicates approximately the condition of the work of the income tax unit of the bureau on August 31, 1922:

*Condition of work, income-tax unit, August 31, 1922.*

| Class and year. | Total returns to be audited and reaudited.[1] | Returns audited. | | Balance to be audited. | |
|---|---|---|---|---|---|
| | | Number. | Per cent | Number. | Per cent. |
| Personal: | | | | | |
| 1917 | 860,000 | 846,538 | 98 | 13,462 | 2 |
| 1918 | 725,000 | 703,584 | 97 | 21,416 | 3 |
| 1919 | 860,000 | 832,238 | 97 | 27,762 | 3 |
| 1920 | 890,000 | 161,113 | 18 | 728,887 | 82 |
| 1921 | 890,000 | | | 890,000 | 100 |
| Total | 4,225,000 | 2,543,473 | 60 | 1,681,527 | 40 |
| Corporation: | | | | | |
| 1917 | 366,600 | 330,010 | 90 | 36,590 | 10 |
| 1918 | 380,386 | 319,720 | 84 | 60,666 | 16 |
| 1919 | 375,922 | 214,058 | 57 | 161,864 | 43 |
| 1920 | 358,000 | 63,477 | 18 | 294,523 | 82 |
| 1921 | 350,000 | 750 | | 349,250 | 100 |
| Total | 1,830,908 | 928,015 | 51 | 902,893 | 49 |
| Grand total | 6,055,908 | 3,471,488 | 57 | 2,584,420 | 43 |

[1] These figures include all returns filed and, in addition, a number of cases thrown back into audit by the filing of claims. These reaudits together with delinquent returns still being received from the collector's office, account for the differences in the number of returns filed in this report as compared with the report of the Secretary for 1921.

The above table shows that the audit of the personal income-tax returns for the years prior to 1920 is practically complete. The showing on corporation-tax returns is less favorable. These returns are difficult to audit and much remains to be done before the work will be current.

During the fiscal year ended June 30, 1922, a total of 162,404 delinquent income taxpayers were discovered and 408,920 verifications were made of income-tax returns filed on Forms 1040-A (net income under $5,000). These investigations resulted in the discovery of $15,549,436 additional tax. For the same period 244,354 delinquent miscellaneous taxpayers were discovered and 143,120 miscellaneous tax returns were verified. These investigations resulted in the discovery of $31,340,172 additional tax.

During the entire fiscal year the total revenue producing investigations made by field deputy collectors resulted in the assessment and collection of $56,791,914. During the fiscal year ended June 30, 1921, $39,976,126 was assessed and collected from this source. The average amount collected and reported for assessment per deputy increased from $15,634 in 1921 to $23,901 in 1922.

Estate-tax collections for the fiscal year aggregated $139,418,846.04, compared with $154,043,260.39 for the preceding fiscal year. The total number of estate-tax returns filed during the year was 13,192, showing a tax liability of $114,614,189.56. As the result of field examinations and division audit, additional tax liability amounting to $13,645,598.29 was disclosed.

A table showing the general sources of internal revenue from 1863 to 1922 is included in this report as Table M, page 498.

### Prohibition and narcotic enforcement.

The prohibition unit of the Bureau of Internal Revenue, charged with the enforcement of the national prohibition act, promulgated new regulations during the fiscal year 1922, with a view to bringing about a better enforcement of the act. A complete reorganization of the unit has resulted in expediting the handling of permits, and a new specially designed paper has been adopted to check the counterfeiting of withdrawal permits and physicians' prescription blanks. Additional restrictions have made the transportation of liquor by automobile trucks more difficult. The unit has endeavored to enforce more effectively the provisions of Title III, designed to insure for legitimate industry a sufficient supply of alcohol. The manufacture and sale of industrial alcohol have been carefully regulated, and the conversion of this alcohol into beverage is less common than formerly. Withdrawals of liquor from bonded warehouses have been greatly reduced and the current monthly withdrawals apparently represent the normal nonbeverage requirements of the country. The principal sources of liquor for beverage purposes at the present time are smuggling and the manufacture of illicitly distilled whisky.

All distilled spirits hitherto stored in distillery, general and special bonded warehouses, are being concentrated into a small number of warehouses. The liquor will there be more secure from loss by theft and casualty, and the cost to the Government of guarding the bonded warehouses will be diminished.

The Harrison Narcotic Act has been as strictly enforced as the limited appropriations available have permitted. There has been an increase of 65 per cent in the number of violations reported over the previous year. Without any appreciable increase in the investigating force, there has, however, been an increase of approximately 100 per cent in the convictions secured, demonstrating thereby the effectiveness of the force.

### CUSTOMS.[1]

Customs receipts for the fiscal year 1922 were $357,544,712 and not only exceeded the receipts for the previous fiscal year by $49,519,610, but were larger than for any previous year in the Government's history. The next largest sum, $333,683,445, was collected in the fiscal year 1910. Customs refunds during the year amounted, however, to

---

[1] Figures for custom refunds and the cost of operating the customs service are on the basis of reports of collectors of customs and therefore do not agree with the figures shown on page 114, which are on the basis of warrants issued (net).

$37,132,197.80, an increase of $13,871,155.02 over the previous year, when they aggregated $23,261,042.78. The increase in customs receipts for the fiscal year 1922 as compared with the fiscal year 1921 was, in the main, due to the emergency tariff act, approved May 27, 1921, which not only increased the rate of duty on numerous articles over those provided in the tariff act of 1913, but imposed duties on many articles which had been on the free list.

While the emergency tariff act, in removing many articles from the free list, increased customs receipts, it materially added to the work of the service. The antidumping provisions particularly involved much additional work, and other special provisions increased the burdens imposed on the service. The new tariff bill, H. R. 7456, which was pending in Congress during the entire period of the fiscal year 1922 and was enacted into law on September 21, 1922, also required much extra work, for while the bill was in Congress the customs service, at the request of the respective committees of the House and Senate having the bill in charge, was constantly engaged in gathering and furnishing to the committee data in regard to the foreign and domestic values of various kinds of merchandise.

The urgent deficiency act approved August 24, 1921, carried a special appropriation of $100,000 for the customs service. This appropriation was made for the purpose of securing data as to the American values of merchandise, and a special organization was created to do the work. In connection with this organization, it was deemed advisable by the Treasury Department to make temporary details from the customs service of about 60 of its most experienced officers and a number of men were withdrawn from the special agency service for the same purpose.

Notwithstanding the increased volume of work resulting from the enactment of the emergency tariff act and the investigations made in connection with the gathering of data for the Congress, the cost of operating the customs service for the fiscal year 1922 was $11,174,369 as compared with $11,227,905 for the fiscal year 1921, a decline of $53,536.

It is estimated that the customs revenue for the fiscal year 1923, most of which falls under the new tariff act, will be about $450,000,000, or in excess of any previous year. While the total cost of collecting this revenue will necessarily be somewhat greater than for the fiscal year 1922, it is expected that the relative cost of collection will be reduced.

### THE DOMESTIC CREDIT SITUATION.

Loan liquidation, the outstanding feature of banking development during the preceding year, continued during the greater part of the 12-months period ending October 31, 1922. At the same time money rates declined materially, until about August of this year, and commercial banks accumulated a supply of free funds and increased their investments in Government and corporate securities. During the latter part of the period, however, the gradual advance in prices, together with the increasing volume of business and of trading in stocks and bonds, has been reflected in an increasing volume of bank loans, and in somewhat higher rates for money. Early in 1922 the decline of wholesale commodity prices had come to a stop, and the general price index this year records a slow rise, manifested first in the prices of farm products and gradually spreading to other classes of products, especially coal, iron, and steel.

The principal changes in the loans and investments of about 800 weekly reporting member banks in the larger cities during the past year are shown in the following table:

[In millions of dollars.]

|  | Nov. 2, 1921. | Jan. 4, 1922. | June 28, 1922. | Nov. 1, 1922. | Change during year. | |
|---|---|---|---|---|---|---|
|  |  |  |  |  | Amount. | Per cent. |
| Loans and discounts...................... | 11, 398 | 11, 206 | 10, 783 | 11, 275 | −123 | −1.08 |
| Investments............................ | 3, 451 | 3, 565 | 4, 405 | 4, 539 | +1,088 | +31.53 |
| Total loans and investments........ | 14, 849 | 14, 771 | 15, 188 | 15, 814 | +965 | +6.50 |
| Borrowings from Federal reserve banks... | 767 | 647 | 165 | 341 | −426 | −55.54 |

The liquidation of loans during 1920 and 1921 occurred largely in the industrial centers, but beginning early in the current year there has been gradual liquidation of so-called "frozen loans" in the agricultural districts. The upward tendency of prices of farm products, which in 1921 had fallen relatively far below the prices of other groups of commodities, has helped the farmers and those dependent upon them to liquidate their indebtedness. The Stock Growers Finance Corporation, formed during the summer of 1921 to meet the emergency then existing, has been able to discontinue operations, and the War Finance Corporation, operating under the agricultural credits act, has found that payments on maturing obligations this fall have greatly exceeded new loans. In other lines, foreign accounts are being gradually liquidated, so that concerns which were themselves borrowing in order to carry these accounts have been able to pay off a part of their loans. Moreover, many industrial concerns, taking advantage of the favorable investment market, have issued long-term securities, and in many cases have used the proceeds to discharge or reduce their indebtedness to banks.

Loans secured by Government obligations have declined during the period, and commercial loans have shown an almost continuous decline until within recent weeks, when the pressure of fall demands became evident. There has been, on the other hand, a steady increase in loans secured by corporate stocks and bonds since March of this year, reflecting the increased activity of the security markets.

The abundance of free funds arising from the increase in deposits and the reduction in loans has brought about a considerable change in the character of the earning assets of the banks. After paying off their indebtedness to the Federal reserve banks, member banks were faced with the problem of finding satisfactory investment for their accumulating funds or the alternative of letting them lie unproductive. The weekly reporting member banks accordingly increased their investments about $1,088,000,000 between November 2, 1921, and November 1, 1922. On November 1, 1922, about 29 per cent of the active funds of these banks were invested in securities, compared with 23 per cent a year earlier. The increasing importance of investments is shown even more strikingly when they are compared with commercial loans, which are the bulk of "all other loans and discounts" in the weekly statements of the 800 reporting member banks. About a year ago the reporting banks held $44 of securities for every $100 of commercial loans, while at present (November 1, 1922) security holdings are $63 for every $100 of commercial loans. For reporting member banks in New York City, where liquidation of commercial loans during the year was relatively larger than elsewhere, the ratio between security holdings and commercial loans has increased from 46 to nearly 79 per cent.

It is notable that more than four-fifths of the total increase in investments of the reporting member banks consists of Government securities. United States bonds, largely Liberty bonds, show an increase of nearly $600,000,000 for the period and Treasury notes an increase of $537,000,000, while Victory notes, partly through exchange for Treasury notes and partly by retirement, fell off $133,000,000. This employment of surplus funds in the purchase of United States securities by member banks reflects their own investment policy and is a natural result of the abnormal accumulation of funds in their hands. It does not represent any change in policy on the part of the Treasury, which has continued during the year to sell its securities on an investment basis, with a view to their distribution among real investors rather than among the banks.

A feature of the banking situation has been the rapid increase in demand and time deposits during the current year. The changes which have occurred in the deposits of reporting member banks during the past year are shown in the following table:

[In millions of dollars.]

| | Nov. 2, 1921. | Jan. 4, 1922. | June 28, 1922. | Nov. 1, 1922. | Change during year. | |
| --- | --- | --- | --- | --- | --- | --- |
| | | | | | Amount. | Per cent. |
| Demand deposits (net)................... | 10,180 | 10,416 | 11,124 | 11,188 | +1,008 | +9.90 |
| Time deposits............................ | 2,988 | 3,011 | 3,380 | 3,642 | +654 | +21.89 |
| Government deposits...................... | 258 | 257 | 124 | 222 | −36 | −13.95 |
| Total............................... | 13,426 | 13,684 | 14,628 | 15,052 | +1,626 | +12.11 |

Demand and time deposits of the weekly reporting member banks reached their low point on September 21, 1921, at $12,749,000,000, and had increased $2,081,000,000 by November 1, 1922. The volume of these deposits is now in excess of the high point reached during the period of inflation in 1919 and 1920, and it is notable that the increase during the past year has occurred in spite of an actual decline in loans and discounts of the same banks. While the increase in demand deposits of these banks from November 2, 1921, to November 1, 1922, was $1,008,000,000, there was a decrease of $123,000,000 in loans and discounts during the same period. This may be accounted for largely by the increase in investments, the increase in the gold supply as a result of gold imports, the decline in Government deposits, and the reduction in the volume of Federal reserve notes outstanding during the first half of the year.

The change in general credit conditions has been reflected in a reduction in discounts and other earning assets of the Federal reserve banks, and more recently by a moderate increase under the pressure of fall demands. The changes which have occurred in the condition of the Federal reserve banks during the period under review are shown in the following table:

[In millions of dollars.]

| | Nov. 2, 1921. | Jan. 4, 1922. | June 28, 1922. | Nov. 1, 1922. | Changes during year. | |
| --- | --- | --- | --- | --- | --- | --- |
| | | | | | Amount. | Per cent. |
| Discounts | 1,260 | 1,113 | 469 | 588 | −672 | −53.33 |
| Purchased bills | 87 | 127 | 154 | 261 | +174 | +200.00 |
| United States securities | 202 | 231 | 557 | 360 | +158 | +78.22 |
| Total | 1,549 | 1,471 | 1,180 | 1,209 | −340 | −21.95 |
| Total reserves | 2,946 | 3,010 | 3,148 | 3,212 | +266 | +9.03 |
| Federal reserve notes in actual circulation. | 2,408 | 2,405 | 2,124 | 2,309 | −99 | −4.11 |

The low point for the period in discounts was reached on July 26, 1922, when they amounted to only $380,000,000. Since August the Federal reserve banks have been offered an increasing amount of paper for rediscount. This amount undoubtedly would have been greater had not the Federal reserve banks become heavy purchasers of acceptances, thus indirectly supplying additional credits. The continued importations of gold have also enabled member banks to reduce their borrowings from the Federal reserve banks to a lower level than otherwise could have been done.

The Federal reserve banks, following their own investment policy, showed substantial increases in their investments in Government securities during the first half of the present calendar year. On June 28, 1922, the amount of these holdings, including Pittman Act certificates, was $557,000,000, as compared with $231,000,000 on

January 4. The proportion of Government securities to the total earning assets of the reserve banks during that six-month period rose from about 16 per cent to 47 per cent, notwithstanding the redemption of $39,000,000 Pittman certificates. From June 28 to November 1 of this year, however, the reserve bank holdings of Government securities have declined by about $197,000,000 to $360,000,000, including Pittman Act certificates.

The decline in Federal reserve notes which was noted during 1921 continued until June 14, 1922, when the amount in circulation was $2,123,000,000. There has been an increase since that date, amounting to $186,000,000, as improved industrial conditions have created a demand for additional currency. Between November 2, 1921, and November 1, 1922, the ratio of total reserves to combined deposit and Federal reserve note liabilities of the Federal reserve banks increased from 71 to 76, accounted for largely by continued importations of gold.

Every Federal reserve district has been able to meet its own credit requirements during the year without resorting to assistance from other districts. Inter-Federal reserve bank loans were all paid off during the latter part of 1921, and since the middle of last December no Federal reserve bank has been obliged to rediscount paper with other Federal reserve banks.

The course of money rates in the New York market, because of easier credit conditions, continued downward during the greater part of the period, though within recent weeks there has been a noticeable turn, as may be seen from the following table showing the range of rates each month since October, 1921, for call loans, commercial paper, and bankers' acceptances:

| Date. | Call loans. | | 4 to 6 months commercial paper. | | 60 to 90 day bankers' acceptances. | |
|---|---|---|---|---|---|---|
| | High. | Low. | High. | Low. | High. | Low. |
| 1921. | *Per cent.* | *Per cent.* | *Per cent.* | *Per cent.* | *Per cent.* | *Per cent.* |
| October | 6 | 4 | 5¾ | 5½ | 4⅞ | 4½ |
| November | 6 | 4 | 5¾ | 5 | 4⅜ | 4¼ |
| December | 6 | 4½ | 5¼ | 5 | 4⅜ | 4⅛ |
| 1922. | | | | | | |
| January | 6 | 3 | 5¼ | 4¾ | 4¼ | 4 |
| February | 6 | 4 | 5 | 4¾ | 4⅛ | 4 |
| March | 5½ | 3 | 5 | 4½ | 4⅛ | 3½ |
| April | 5 | 3½ | 4¾ | 4½ | 3⅝ | 3¼ |
| May | 5 | 3 | 4½ | 4¼ | 3⅜ | 3⅛ |
| June | 5½ | 2¾ | 4¼ | 4 | 3⅜ | 3 |
| July | 5 | 2¾ | 4 | 3¾ | 3⅛ | 2⅞ |
| August | 5 | 3 | 4 | 3¾ | 3⅛ | 3 |
| September | 6 | 3½ | 4½ | 3¾ | 3⅜ | 3 |
| October | 6 | 4 | 4½ | 4¼ | 4 | 3⅜ |

The discount rates of Federal reserve banks have been further reduced during the past 12 months, as appears from the following table, which gives the rates of the 12 banks at the high point, on November 1, 1921, and on November 1, 1922:

| District. | High point. | Nov. 1, 1921. | Nov. 1, 1922. | Decrease from high point. |
|---|---|---|---|---|
| | Per cent. | Per cent. | Per cent. | Per cent. |
| Boston | 7 | 5 | 4 | 3 |
| New York | 7 | 5 | 4 | 3 |
| Philadelphia | 6 | 5 | 4½ | 1½ |
| Cleveland | 6 | 5½ | 4½ | 1½ |
| Richmond | 6 | 6 | 4½ | 1½ |
| Atlanta | 7 | 6 | 4½ | 2½ |
| Chicago | 7 | 6 | 4½ | 2½ |
| St. Louis | 6 | 6 | 4½ | 1½ |
| Minneapolis | 7 | 6 | 4½ | 2½ |
| Kansas City | 6 | 6 | 4½ | 1½ |
| Dallas | 7 | 6 | 4½ | 2½ |
| San Francisco | 6 | 5½ | 4 | 2 |

### THE WAR FINANCE CORPORATION AND ITS OPERATIONS.

At the time of the last annual report, the machinery for administering the agricultural credits act had just been organized throughout the United States. Thirty-three loan agencies had been established in the various agricultural and live-stock districts, banking institutions had become familiar with the powers and purposes of the corporation, and the flow of credit to the farmers and stockmen had begun to gain momentum. From the first of November, 1921, to the end of February, 1922, the loans authorized by the corporation averaged approximately $2,000,000 a day.

The corporation's activities have been conducted on a nation-wide scale. To November 10, 1922, it made or approved advances for agricultural and live-stock purposes aggregating approximately $430,000,-000 in 37 States. The loans authorized on live stock in the West total $90,000,000; on cotton in the South, $81,847,000; on grain in the Northwest, Middle West, and Southwest, $36,790,000; on peanuts in Virginia, $2,044,000; on tobacco in Kentucky, Indiana, and Ohio, as well as in North Carolina and neighboring States, $40,000,000; on rice in California and Arkansas, $9,750,000; on sugar beets in Colorado and Utah, $9,996,000; on other agricultural commodities, $2,000,000; and for general agricultural purposes, $157,518,000. These loans have reached the farmers and stockmen through approximately 4,400 banks, through 33 cooperative marketing associations having a total membership of about three-quarters of a million, and through 100 live-stock loan companies. In addition, the corporation, since January, 1921, has authorized advances totaling $53,000,000 to assist in financing exports, including $6,000,000 on grain, $3,250,000 on tobacco, $35,750,000 on cotton, and $3,100,000 on other agricultural products.

When the agricultural credits act was passed, the situation in the agricultural and live-stock districts was decidedly acute. Farmers and stockmen generally were in a desperate plight. Breeding herds were being sacrificed on a wholesale scale. Immature stock was being sent to the block, and cotton, corn, and other agricultural commodities commanded prices that were discouragingly low. Forced liquidation and hasty selling impaired the farmer's buying power, and this, in turn, brought about a reduced for demand for the products of industry. Bank deposits were being drawn down, reserves were depleted, loans could not be collected, and the stability of our whole agricultural and banking structure was seriously threatened.

In January of this year the effect of the activities of the corporation began to be felt on a considerable scale. Conditions took a turn for the better and a progressive improvement set in. The corporation's loans strengthened the banking situation in the country districts and relieved the necessity of forced liquidation. They put the banks in position not only to carry their farmer customers for a longer period but also to make new advances, and were a vital factor in bringing about a marked improvement in the whole economic situation. In fact at no time in our history has there been an improvement so rapid and extensive as that which has taken place during the past 18 months.

Because the corporation was able, under the authority granted by the Congress, to harmonize its activities with the needs of the various sections of the country and to direct its efforts toward the restoration of more normal conditions throughout the Nation, the beneficial effects of its operations rapidly became cumulative. Corn and hogs, sheep and cattle, wheat and cotton, and most other staple agricultural commodities are sold in national markets, and the strengthening of each weak spot in the situation was helpful everywhere. The relief of the cotton growers and the restoration of their buying power aided not only the South but the North and West, whence the cotton planter draws his supplies of various kinds. A return of confidence to the corn-belt farmer meant a better market for feeder stock from the ranges of the West. When the farmers of the Northwest were put in position to continue their operations a better market for cotton goods was opened up, with resulting benefit to the cotton grower. In spite of local difficulties here and there and unsatisfactory markets for some commodities, the improved prices for farm products and the increased purchasing power in the farming districts led to a general revival of business within a few months. Repayments began to flow into the corporation; and in the course of orderly liquidation there has been a substantial reduction in its bank loans, practically all its advances to cooperative marketing associations during the past season have been liquidated, and large repayments have been made on its live-stock loans.

A special feature of the work of the corporation during the past year was the financing of cooperative marketing associations. The growth of the cooperative movement is one of the most encouraging developments in the marketing of agricultural products in recent years, for it promises to bring about definite and far-reaching improvements in our whole system of distributing farm commodities. Many new associations have been organized for the handling of cotton, wheat, tobacco, rice, and other staple products, and they have made considerable progress in developing facilities for uniform grading and classification, thus insuring more efficient handling and furnishing a better basis for credit. They have also erected machinery which will greatly facilitate the gradual, orderly marketing of many of our great staple commodities.

The relations of the War Finance Corporation with cooperative marketing associations have been satisfactory. In general, they have conducted their operations in a businesslike way and have willingly met the corporation's requirements and regulations.

While the corporation has approved loans aggregating $113,000,000 to cooperative marketing associations to assist in financing the orderly marketing of the 1922 crops, only a portion of this amount will be used. These associations, for the most part, have already demonstrated their ability to conduct their business on a sound basis, and the banks, not only in the districts immediately concerned, but also in the large financial centers, are showing a decided interest in supplying them with funds. In fact, banks all over the country have made and are making large sums available to cooperative organizations.

Although by June the acute phases of the agricultural crisis had passed and there had been a steady decline in the demands upon the corporation for assistance, it was apparent that the steadying effect of its activities was still needed. Under the circumstances, Congress, by an act approved June 10, 1922, extended until June 30, 1923, the period during which the corporation may make loans. The law as it now stands, therefore, contemplates that the corporation will cease active operations at the close of the current fiscal year.

The War Finance Corporation is a temporary agency. Its highly centralized form of organization, with concentrated power and resources, was well suited to the grave crisis of 1920–21. But it is entirely unsuited to the permanent banking structure of the Nation. Now that the emergency has been met for the most part, appropriate action should be taken to adapt the machinery of finance to the permanent needs of our basic agricultural activities—needs which have been greatly emphasized by the experiences of the past two years.

### AGRICULTURAL. CREDITS.

Agricultural conditions have steadily improved since the collapse of the world market for farm products in 1920 and 1921, though there are still many evidences that the prices of farm products are out of line as compared with manufactured goods. Forced sales by the farmers in order to meet maturing obligations have generally ceased, and the marketing of agricultural products has resumed a more orderly course. The administration has done its utmost to relieve the situation, and the Federal Reserve Board, the Federal reserve banks, and the War Finance Corporation have been rendering every possible assistance, especially to farmers and live-stock growers, in financing the growing and marketing of their products. The Federal land banks, moreover, have been functioning to the limit of their capacity and have made loans on farm lands at the rate of over $200,000,000 during the year. The War Finance Corporation has provided substantial relief under the so-called agricultural credits act, approved August 24, 1921, and is still engaged in operations. It must be recognized as an emergency agency, however, and will not under the law continue in active business after this fiscal year.

Active consideration is accordingly being given to more permanent measures of relief, with particular reference to the provision of better facilities for distribution and marketing, and credits of intermediate length. In all of these measures the administration is taking an active interest. Some months ago, moreover, the Joint Commission of Agricultural Inquiry made an investigation of the agricultural situation, as related to the banking and financial resources of the country, recommending that further provision be made for intermediate agricultural credits ranging from six months to three years, and the Treasury Department, the Federal Reserve Board, and the War Finance Corporation have all been cooperating in an effort to work out some satisfactory plan. I am inclined to believe that for the most part the situation can be met through existing banking facilities, with the help of the Federal reserve banks, and perhaps some extension of rediscounts, under proper regulations of the Federal Reserve Board, to cover agricultural paper running as long as nine months. For all practical purposes this should provide for everything except the live-stock industry, and because of its peculiar nature I believe it would be helpful to provide, under Federal supervision, for the organization of live-stock loan companies equipped to handle this business.

The farmer's difficulty now is not so much lack of credits as it is lack of markets, and recovery of markets depends rather more on world conditions than on domestic credits. The war and the reaction which followed the war brought about an extreme disorganization of commerce and industry all over the world. This country has already made an important recovery, and there have been substantial advances in the prices of the principal agricultural products, in consequence of which the condition of the farmer has greatly improved. The prices of agricultural products, however, are still out of gear, and there must be further readjustments and better facilities for distribution before the farmer's position can be fully restored. There can be no doubt that one of the first conditions of sound recovery in the country as a whole is the restoration of the purchasing power of the farmer, the impairment of which had so much to do with the last depression in business.

## FEDERAL FARM LOAN SYSTEM.

The greatest activity in the history of the farm loan system characterized the period from November 1, 1921, to November 1, 1922. The Federal land banks during that period made loans to 70,993 farmers, totaling $219,780,649, and sold to the investing public Federal farm loan bonds aggregating $278,150,000. By the 1st of May of the present year the banks had overcome the congestion in business which resulted from their long suspension during litigation, and from the generally depressed condition of the early part of 1921, and since that time have been able to give immediate attention to current demands. The sale of Federal farm loan bonds has exceeded the needs of the banks for lending purposes, and consequently the Federal land banks have repurchased up to date $69,650,000 face amount of the bonds held by the Treasury, thereby reducing the Treasury's holdings to $113,385,000. The Federal land banks made these repurchases pursuant to the provisions of the law under which the Treasury originally acquired the bonds, but without any call from the Treasury, as the Secretary has wanted to avoid any pressure on the banks or any interference with the flow of funds to meet the needs of agriculture. As a matter of fact the Federal land banks themselves advised that the repurchases would not interfere with their lending operations, and on that basis the Treasury accepted the repayments, believing it to be desirable, as market conditions permit, to liquidate the Government's holdings of these securities.

### Condition of Federal land banks.

During the 12 months' period ending October 31, 1922, the sum of $2,333,890 was paid to the Treasury for the retirement of Government stock in the Federal land banks, leaving the Government's present holdings of stock in the several banks at $4,264,880. The present rate of progress indicates that within the next 12 months, two, and probably four, of the Federal land banks will have retired all of their stock owned by the Government. The Federal farm loan system is therefore rapidly approaching a condition which meets the original intention that it should be a mutual organization operated under Government supervision and control, with the capital stock supplied by the borrowing farmers and not by the Government.

The following consolidated statement of condition of the 12 Federal land banks at the close of business October 31, 1922, shows the development of the Federal farm loan system, and the volume of the farm loan bonds and farm mortgages outstanding.

### ASSETS.

| | |
|---|---:|
| Net mortgage loans | [1] $605,987,214.04 |
| Accrued interest on mortgage loans (not matured) | 10,921,559.80 |
| U. S. Government bonds and securities | 67,688,829.51 |
| Accrued interest on bonds and securities (not matured) | 523,720.54 |
| Farm loan bonds on hand (unsold) | 2,595,925.00 |
| Accrued interest on farm loan bonds on hand (not matured) | 26,511.18 |
| Other accrued interest (uncollected) | 12,840.64 |
| Notes receivable, acceptances, etc | 373,719.03 |
| Cash on hand and in banks | 11,672,006.39 |
| Accounts receivable | 86,726.21 |
| Installments matured (in process of collection) | 1,049,351.43 |
| Banking houses | 489,393.63 |
| Furniture and fixtures | 166,733.50 |
| Other assets | 1,055,351.56 |
| Total assets | 702,649,882.46 |

### LIABILITIES.

| | | |
|---|---:|---:|
| Capital stock: | | |
| United States Government | $4,264,880.00 | |
| National farm loan associations | 30,866,995.00 | |
| Borrowers through agents | 119,965.00 | |
| Individual subscribers | 4,890.00 | |
| Total capital stock | | 35,256,730.00 |
| Reserve (from earnings) | | 2,532,500.00 |
| Surplus (from earnings) | | 300,000.00 |
| Farm loan bonds authorized and issued | | 641,208,375.00 |
| Accrued interest on farm loan bonds (not matured) | | 14,328,140.69 |
| U. S. Government deposits | | |
| Notes payable | | 2,200,000.00 |
| Due borrowers on uncompleted loans | | 311,202.95 |
| Amortization installments paid in advance | | 896,977.20 |
| Matured interest on farm loan bonds (coupons not presented) | | 139,783.07 |
| Reserved for dividends unpaid | | 86,877.53 |
| Other liabilities | | 918,417.62 |
| Undivided profits | | 4,470,878.40 |
| Total liabilities | | 702,649,882.46 |

### MEMORANDA.

| | |
|---|---:|
| Net earnings to Oct. 31, 1922 | 11,786,591.94 |

[1] Unpledged mortgages (gross), $13,316,762.62.

Less:

| | | |
|---|---:|---:|
| Dividends paid to Oct. 31, 1922 | $4,022,141.74 | |
| Carried to suspense account to Oct. 31, 1922 | 379,790.27 | |
| Other charges to Oct. 31, 1922 | 81,281.53 | |
| | | $4,483,213.54 |
| Carried to surplus account to Oct. 31, 1922 | $300,000.00 | |
| Carried to reserve account to Oct. 31, 1922 | 2,532,500.00 | |
| Undivided profits Oct. 31, 1922 | 4,470,878.40 | |
| Total reserve and undivided profits Oct. 31, 1922 | | 7,303,378.40 |
| Capital stock originally subscribed by U. S. Government | | 8,892,130.00 |
| Amount of Government stock retired to Oct. 31, 1922 | | 4,627,250.00 |
| Capital stock held by U. S. Government Oct. 31, 1922 | | 4,264,880.00 |

## *Joint stock land banks.*

The activities of the joint stock land banks during the past year have likewise been greater than during any previous year, and the number of joint stock land banks has increased from 26 to 61 since the previous report of the Secretary of the Treasury. In view of the rapid increase in the activities of these institutions and their growing output of tax-free bonds, it is appropriate to suggest again the question as to the continued existence of this branch of the system, and as to the economic soundness of the policy of granting tax exemption privileges to private enterprise organized for individual profit. The Treasury has heretofore recommended that as to future issues of joint stock land bank bonds the tax exemption provisions should be repealed, and it reiterates that recommendation in the belief that it is bad public policy to grant tax exemptions, amounting in substance to a subsidy from the Federal Government, to private enterprise of this character.

### FARMERS' SEED-GRAIN LOANS.

Under a provision incorporated in the agricultural appropriation act of 1921, approved May 31, 1920, and in accordance with the circular issued thereunder by the Treasury Department and the Department of Agriculture, entitled "Joint Circular No. 6," the Treasury Department, during the past year, has continued to release those farmers whose crops were failures, as defined in the act, from repayment of the amounts borrowed from the Government for the purchase of seed wheat. The Treasury has also made additional collections on account of repayments of farmers' seed grain loans not released by the act of May 31, 1920, payments of interest on loans, and contributions to the guaranty funds.

The following table shows the number and amount of the loans, the amount released, the amount of principal collected, the amount of interest collected, contributions to the guaranty funds, and the balance of principal outstanding uncollected as of September 30, 1922, the latest date for which figures are available:

| Federal land bank. | Number of loans. | Amount loaned. | Principal collected. | Principal released. | Balance of principal uncollected. | Interest collected. | Guaranty funds. |
|---|---|---|---|---|---|---|---|
| Wichita | 8,282 | $1,891,132.75 | $1,365,750.99 | $183,132.34 | $342,249.42 | $75,243.53 | $246,414.45 |
| St. Paul | 1,138 | 358,370.45 | 67,031.02 | 205,416.74 | 85,922.69 | 1,764.88 | 443.20 |
| Spokane | 6,149 | 1,951,379.50 | 10,361.03 | 1,249,703.50 | 691,314.97 | 478.30 | 24.15 |
| Total | 15,569 | 4,200,882.70 | 1,443,143.04 | 1,638,252.58 | 1,119,487.08 | 77,486.71 | 246,881.80 |

### PUBLIC DEBT TRANSACTIONS.

At the beginning of the fiscal year the amount of the interest-bearing debt outstanding was $23,737,304,180.37. During the year, new issues aggregated $5,911,260,119.74, redemptions aggregated $6,914,141,312.66, the amount transferred to matured debt aggregated $23,387,400, and the amount outstanding on June 30, 1922, was $22,711,035,587.45, a reduction of $1,026,268,592.92. The principal issues were Treasury certificates of indebtedness, $3,905,090,000, and Treasury notes, $1,935,404,750. The principal redemptions were maturing certificates of indebtedness, $4,766,854,950, and retirements of Victory notes, amounting to $1,907,976,250, through redemption, purchase or exchange for other securities. Further details concerning these transactions appear elsewhere in this report under the headings, "Refunding the short-dated debt," "Treasury notes and certificates of indebtedness," "Treasury Bonds," "Government savings securities," and in Exhibits 1 to 25 on pages 126 to 164. These exhibits also show exchange transactions, in connection with which securities amounting to $4,516,877,930 were issued, and securities amounting to $4,537,140,830 retired. The difference of $20,262,900 between the amount issued and the amount retired represents items in transit or deliverable on June 30, 1921, and June 30, 1922.

The consolidated statement appearing as Exhibit 21 on page 158 of this report shows all transactions in the five war loans from the date of their respective issues to June 30, 1922. This statement gives some idea of the magnitude of the work undertaken by the Treasury organization and the Federal reserve banks as fiscal agents of the United States. For purposes of issues 198,509,510 pieces of Liberty bonds and Victory notes, having a face value of $66,290,850,000, have been delivered by the Bureau of Engraving and Printing; 93,571,658 pieces, amounting to $21,432,924,700, have been delivered by the department on original cash subscriptions; 65,259,868 pieces (including securities issuable on June 30, 1922) have been issued and 112,614,685 retired on account of exchanges, conversions, transfers, etc., amounting to $26,962,942,650. There have been redemptions of 3,284,366 pieces, amounting to $4,345,519,350, leaving 42,932,475 pieces, amounting to $17,087,405,350, outstanding on June 30, 1922.

During the year various Treasury Department regulations governing transactions in Liberty bonds and Victory notes were revised. (See Exhibits 41, 42, 43, 44, 45, and 80, pages 193, 194, 195, 196, and 287.)

*Cumulative sinking fund.*

During the fiscal year $274,516,965.89 became available for the purchase of Liberty bonds and Victory notes for the cumulative sinking fund established by section 6 of the Victory Liberty loan act, approved March 3, 1919. This amount consisted of the primary credit of $253,404,864.87, a balance of $1,385,434.16, brought forward from the previous fiscal year, and the secondary credit of $19,726,666.86, representing interest for the fiscal year 1922 on securities purchased for the sinking fund. In this connection the following public announcement was made on August 14, 1922: "The Secretary of the Treasury announces that the second fiscal year's operations under the cumulative sinking fund established by the act approved March 3, 1919, were completed June 30, 1922, and that $275,896,000 face amount of Liberty bonds and Victory notes were purchased and retired for account of the sinking fund during the fiscal year. The total principal cost of the bonds and notes purchased was $274,481,902.16." This left an unexpended balance amounting to $35,063.73 to be carried over into the fiscal year 1923. It is estimated that during the fiscal year 1923 a total of $283,838,800 will be available for the sinking fund, and that during the fiscal year 1924 a total of $298,872,000 will become available. Details concerning the securities purchased during the fiscal year 1922, together with cumulative totals of all securities purchased for the cumulative sinking fund, are shown in the following table:

| Title. | Par amount. | Principal cost. |
| --- | --- | --- |
| First 3½'s | $11,000.00 | $11,000.00 |
| First 4¼'s | 16,850.00 | 16,850.00 |
| Second 4¼'s | 109,000.00 | 109,000.00 |
| Third 4¼'s | 17,208,500.00 | 17,208,092.00 |
| Fourth 4¼'s | 240,650.00 | 240,650.00 |
| Victory 4¾'s | 211,017,000.00 | 209,973,819.00 |
| Victory 3¾'s | 47,293,000.00 | 46,922,491.16 |
| Total, fiscal year | 275,896,000.00 | 274,481,902.16 |
| Cumulative total to June 30, 1922 | 537,146,250.00 | 529,326,478.66 |

*Five per cent bond-purchase fund.*

In connection with its refunding operations, the Treasury made further purchases of Victory notes during the year under section 15 of the second Liberty bond act, as amended, on account of the so-called bond-purchase fund, as follows:

| Title. | Par amount. | Principal cost. |
| --- | --- | --- |
| Victory 4¾'s | $112,661,000.00 | $111,741,075.07 |
| Victory 3¾'s | 17,859,000.00 | 17,727,631.41 |
| Total | 130,520,000.00 | 129,468,706.48 |

As the provision of the law providing for these purchases expired by limitation on July 2, 1922, there will be no more transactions in the bond-purchase fund. During the whole time that the fund was in operation, securities with an aggregate face value of $1,965,791,450 were purchased, at an aggregate principal cost of $1,876,413,174.59 Accrued interest paid amounted to $23,226,476.66.

*Bonds purchased from franchise tax paid by Federal reserve banks.*

The net earnings derived by the United States from Federal reserve banks as franchise tax amounted to $59,974,465.64 for the calendar year 1921 and were applied to the purchase of Liberty bonds and Victory notes as follows:

| Title. | Par amount. | Principal cost. |
|---|---|---|
| Third 4¼'s. | $50,885,000.00 | $50,504,357.13 |
| Victory 4¾'s. | 8,707,000.00 | 8,727,236.72 |
| Victory 3¾'s. | 741,000.00 | 742,865.89 |
| Total, fiscal year 1922 | 60,333,000.00 | 59,974,459.74 |

The aggregate value of securities retired from franchise-tax payments through the fiscal year 1922 is as follows:

| | |
|---|---|
| Fiscal year 1918. | $1,134,234.48 |
| Fiscal year 1920 | 2,922,450.00 |
| Fiscal year 1921 | 60,724,500.00 |
| Fiscal year 1922 | 60,333,000.00 |
| Total | 125,114,184.48 |

*Bonds purchased from repayments of foreign loans.*

The following statement concerning bonds purchased from repayments of foreign loans was issued on August 14, 1922:

The Secretary of the Treasury announces that during the fiscal year ended June 30, 1922, $64,837,900 face amount of Liberty bonds were purchased and retired by the Treasury out of repayments of principal by foreign governments. These purchases were made pursuant to section 3 of the second Liberty bond act, as amended, which provides that the Secretary of the Treasury is authorized to apply any payments received from foreign governments on account of the principal of their obligations to the redemption or purchase at not more than par and accrued interest of any outstanding Liberty bonds. The foreign repayments from which the purchases in question were made comprise $32,511,994.26 of repayments by the French Government; $30,500,000 by the British Government on obligations deemed to have been given on account of Pittman silver; $878,500 by the Cuban Government; $440,-552.83 by the Belgian Government; $48,564.63 by the Serbian Government; a total of $64,379,611.72 of repayments. For the most part, these payments were on special account, or by way of adjustment of accounts, and should not be taken to indicate that any general program of repayment of the foreign obligations has begun.

The Liberty bonds retired on this account were third 4¼'s, and the total principal cost was $64,367,997.22.

The following table shows the aggregate of bonds purchased from repayments of foreign loans during the fiscal years 1919 to 1922:

| Title. | Par amount. | Principal cost. |
|---|---|---|
| Second 4¼'s: | | |
| Fiscal year 1921..................................................... | $2,145,950.00 | $1,891,891.61 |
| Third 4¼'s: | | |
| Fiscal year 1919.................................................... | 7,921,700.00 | 7,569,976.52 |
| Fiscal year 1920.................................................... | 70,154,950.00 | 66,520,512.76 |
| Fiscal year 1921.................................................... | 44,365,550.00 | 41,349,313.27 |
| Fiscal year 1922.................................................... | 64,837,900.00 | 64,367,997.22 |
| Fourth 4¼'s: | | |
| Fiscal year 1920.................................................... | 2,514,950.00 | 2,230,482.32 |
| Fiscal year 1921.................................................... | 27,427,800.00 | 27,427,800.00 |
| Total: | | |
| Fiscal year 1919.................................................... | 7,921,700.00 | 7,569,976.52 |
| Fiscal year 1920.................................................... | 72,669,900.00 | 68,750,995.08 |
| Fiscal year 1921.................................................... | 73,939,300.00 | 70,669,004.88 |
| Fiscal year 1922.................................................... | 64,837,900.00 | 64,367,997.22 |
| Grand total...................................................... | 219,368,800.00 | 211,357,973.70 |

All the bonds purchased have been canceled and retired and the public debt reduced in corresponding amounts.

*Bonds and notes retired on miscellaneous accounts.*

During the fiscal year ended June 30, 1922, retirements of Liberty bonds and Victory notes received in payment of estate and inheritance taxes, forfeitures to the United States, gifts, and miscellaneous receipts, were as follows:

| Issue. | Estate or inheritance taxes. | For-feitures. | Gifts. | Miscella-neous receipts. |
|---|---|---|---|---|
| First 3½'s........................................................ | | $60,400 | $700 | $100 |
| First 4's.......................................................... | | 200 | | 100 |
| First 4¼'s........................................................ | $322,000 | 2,150 | 50 | |
| Second 4's........................................................ | | 650 | | |
| Second 4¼'s...................................................... | 5,677,250 | 49,050 | 50 | 87,000 |
| Third 4¼'s........................................................ | 4,829,100 | 6,650 | 50 | 50 |
| Fourth 4¼'s....................................................... | 9,202,150 | 18,250 | 500 | 200 |
| Victory 4¾'s...................................................... | 814,800 | 2,500 | 550 | 163,650 |
| Total, fiscal year 1922............................... | 20,845,300 | 139,850 | 1,900 | 251,100 |
| Cumulative total to June 30, 1922............................ | 50,666,350 | 178,850 | 15,250 | 380,200 |

### TREASURY NOTES AND CERTIFICATES OF INDEBTEDNESS.

From November 15, 1921, to November 15, 1922, seven issues of certificates of indebtedness, aggregating $1,424,697,000, were sold by the Treasury. Subscriptions in each case were closed on the day of issue, with heavy oversubscriptions recorded. During the same period four offerings of Treasury notes were made, on which total allotments amounted to $2,041,451,200.

The last annual report of the Secretary of the Treasury covered Treasury note and Treasury certificate operations through the offerings of November 1, 1921. The next issue was the usual quarterly operation incident to the December 15 payment of income and profits taxes and the maturity on December 15 of nearly $390,000,000 of tax certificates. Semiannual interest on the first Liberty loan and the Victory Liberty loan fell due on the same date. Two series of tax certificates were offered, both dated December 15, 1921, one bearing $4\frac{1}{4}$ per cent interest and maturing in six months, on June 15, 1922, the other bearing $4\frac{1}{2}$ per cent interest and maturing in one year, on December 15, 1922. The combined offering, which was for $250,000,000, or thereabouts, met with a prompt response from the investing public, and subscriptions were nearly five times the offering, aggregating $1,183,102,000. The total amount of subscriptions allotted was $308,447,000, of which $64,903,000 was for the June 15, 1922, maturity and $243,544,000 for the December 15, 1922, maturity.

On January 26, 1922, the Treasury announced an offering of $4\frac{3}{4}$ per cent short-term Treasury notes, designated Series A–1925, dated February 1, 1922, and due March 15, 1925. The offering was made to cover the Treasury's current requirements, including the maturity of about $250,000,000 of Treasury certificates on February 16, 1922, and at the same time to provide in part for refunding the Victory notes maturing May 20, 1923. The offering was for $400,000,000, or thereabouts, with the right reserved to the Secretary of the Treasury to allot additional notes up to one-half that amount to the extent that payment was tendered in either $3\frac{3}{4}$ or $4\frac{3}{4}$ per cent Victory notes. The offering was heavily oversubscribed, total subscriptions aggregating $1,249,965,300. The amount allotted was $601,599,500, including $200,000,000 on subscriptions for which payment was tendered in Victory notes.

The next offering of certificates was announced for March 15, 1922, the first quarterly tax payment date of the calendar year 1922. Treasury certificates amounting to about $530,000,000 were maturing on that date, with about $52,000,000 more due on April 1, 1922. There was also payable on March 15, 1922, about $107,000,000 of interest on the public debt. To provide for the cash requirements remaining after the collection of income and profits taxes and other ordinary revenues, an issue of one-year tax certificates, amounting to $250,000,000, or thereabouts, was offered on March 15, 1922, bearing $4\frac{1}{4}$ per cent interest and maturing March 15, 1923. This rate was 1 per cent less than the rate six months earlier on certificates of similar maturity. Total subscriptions for the offering amounted to $674,830,500, of which $266,250,000 was allotted. For the same date announcement was made of an offering of $4\frac{3}{4}$ per cent Treasury notes, designated Series A–1926, dated March 15, 1922, due March 15, 1926. These notes were offered only in exchange for $4\frac{3}{4}$ per cent Victory notes, and no fixed amount was announced for the issue.

Subscriptions received before the close of business March 15, 1922, amounted to $617,769,700, and were allotted in full.

To meet the current needs of the Treasury, including an interest payment of about $135,000,000 on the fourth Liberty loan, an issue of loan certificates for $150,000,000, or thereabouts, was announced for April 15, 1922, bearing 3½ per cent interest and maturing on October 16, 1922. Notwithstanding the fact that the rate of interest was the lowest since September, 1917, and three-fourths of 1 per cent lower than the rate on the last issue of similar maturity, the issue was promptly oversubscribed, and subscriptions aggregated $309,212,000, or more than double the offering. No allotment was made on over-subscriptions, total allotments being $150,000,000. To anticipate the heavy payments due on June 15, 1922, an offering of tax certificates was made on June 1, 1922, in the amount of $200,000,000, or there-abouts, bearing 3½ per cent interest and maturing December 15, 1922. Certificates maturing June 15, 1922, and 3¾ per cent Victory notes were accepted at par, with an adjustment of accrued interest, in pay-ment for certificates of this issue. The offering met with a quick response, and subscriptions, which closed at noon on the day of issue, amounted to $383,541,500. No allotment was made on over-subscriptions, and total allotments, therefore, amounted to $200,-000,000. On June 15, 1922, the date of the second quarterly pay-ment of income and profits taxes, there were payable about $380,-000,000 of maturing Treasury certificates of indebtedness, about $250,000,000 of 3¾ per cent Victory notes called for redemption, and about $125,000,000 of interest on the public debt. To meet these payments an offering was made on June 15, 1922, of one-year 3¾ per cent tax certificates due June 15, 1923, coupled with an offering of three and one-half year 4⅜ per cent Treasury notes, designated Series B–1925, due December 15, 1925, which was intended to provide further for the refunding of the Victory Liberty loan. The rate of interest carried by the certificates was one-half of 1 per cent lower than the rate three months earlier on certificates of similar maturity, and the rate on the Treasury notes was three-eighths of 1 per cent lower than the rate on the March 15 issue of Treasury notes. The subscriptions received for the certificates aggregated $469,797,-000, as against an offering of $250,000,000, or thereabouts, and the amount allotted was $273,000,000. No fixed amount was announced for the issue of Treasury notes, which were offered only in exchange for 4¾ per cent Victory notes, and the books on the offering were kept open for two weeks in order to give holders of 4¾ per cent Victory notes throughout the country ample opportunity to make the exchange. Subscriptions received before the closing of the books on June 22, 1922, amounted in all to $335,141,300 and were allotted in full. The terms of the combined offering were set forth in a letter of the Secretary of the Treasury accompanying the announcement of the offering, dated June 8, 1922, which is attached as Exhibit 38, page 188.

In connection with the maturity, on August 1, 1922, of about $250,000,000 of Treasury certificates and the call for the redemption of about half of the outstanding 4¾ per cent Victory notes which went out on July 26, 1922, an offering was made for August 1 of 4¼ per cent Treasury notes, designated Series B–1926, due September 15, 1926. This rate marked a further reduction of one-eighth of 1 per cent from the rate offered on the last previous issue of Treasury notes six weeks earlier. The amount of the offering was $300,000,000, or thereabouts, with the right reserved to the Secretary of the Treasury to allot a limited amount of additional notes to the extent that payment was tendered in 4¾ per cent Victory notes. Subscriptions on the primary offering aggregated $1,236,-861,450, or more than four times the offering, and of this amount $345,425,000 was allotted. The amount of exchanges of 4¾ per cent Victory notes for the new notes was $141,515,700, making the aggregate allotment for the issue $486,940,200. The terms of the offering and the position of the Treasury at the time were outlined in a circular letter to the banks and trust companies of the country dated July 26, 1922, which is attached as Exhibit 40, page 191.

The offering on September 15, 1922, the third quarterly income tax date of the calendar year, consisted of one-year 3¾ per cent tax certificates. The offering was for $200,000,000, or thereabouts, and subscriptions, which closed at noon the day of issue, amounted to $570,476,500, of which $227,000,000 was allotted.

Substantial progress has been made during the past year in the retirement of Pittman Act certificates. The policy of the Treasury has been to retire each month an amount equivalent to the amount of silver certificates made available as a result of the coinage of silver dollars, and in addition to retire from time to time out of the general fund amounts of certificates not required to secure issues of Federal reserve bank notes. The amount of Pittman Act certificates outstanding was thus reduced from $215,875,000 on June 30, 1921, to $74,000,000 on June 30, 1922. By October 31, 1922, it had been reduced to $38,000,000.

Further details concerning certificates of indebtedness and Treasury notes will be found in Exhibits 1 to 40, pages 126–191, and in Tables A to G, pages 458 to 478. A summary of all issues of certificates of indebtedness from the beginning of the war to October 31, 1922, is given in Table G, page 476. The official circulars announcing the various offerings of Treasury notes, and loan and tax certificates, together with offers to redeem before maturity at the option of the holders, issued since the annual report of the

Secretary of the Treasury for 1921, are attached as Exhibits 35 to 39, pages 184 to 189, and Exhibits 46 to 60, pages 205–215.

The aggregate amount of certificates issued from the beginning of the war to October 31, 1922, was $54,671,462,309. Of this total, $21,422,925,500 represent loan certificates, $12,412,625,000 were sold in anticipation of income and profits taxes, and $20,835,911,809 comprise special issues. The following table gives in detail the unmatured Treasury certificates of indebtedness and Treasury notes outstanding on October 31, 1922:

*Unmatured Treasury certificates of indebtedness and Treasury notes outstanding October 31, 1922.*

| Detail. | Interest. | Date. | Due. | Amount. | |
|---|---|---|---|---|---|
| Certificates of indebtedness: | | | | | |
| Tax— | *Per cent.* | | | | |
| Series TD-1922 | 4½ | Dec. 15, 1921 | Dec. 15, 1922 | $166,945,500 | |
| Series TD2-1922 | 3½ | June 1, 1922 | Dec. 15, 1922 | 58,062,000 | |
| Series TM-1923 | 4¼ | Mar. 15, 1922 | Mar. 15, 1923 | 266,250,000 | |
| Series TJ-1923 | 3¾ | June 15, 1922 | June 15, 1923 | 273,000,000 | |
| Series TS-1923 | 3¾ | Sept. 15, 1922 | Sept. 15, 1923 | 227,000,000 | |
| | | | | | $991,257,500 |
| Pittman Act | 2 | (1) | (2) | | 38,000,000 |
| Treasury notes: | | | | | |
| Series A-1924 | 5¾ | June 15, 1921 | June 15, 1924 | 311,191,600 | |
| Series B-1924 | 5½ | Sept. 15, 1921 | Sept. 15, 1924 | 390,706,100 | |
| Series A-1925 | 4¾ | Feb. 1, 1922 | Mar. 15, 1925 | 601,599,500 | |
| Series B-1925 | 4¾ | June 15, 1922 | Dec. 15, 1925 | 335,128,200 | |
| Series A-1926 | 4¾ | Mar. 15, 1922 | Mar. 15, 1926 | 617,769,700 | |
| Series B-1926 | 4¼ | Aug. 1, 1922 | Sept. 15, 1926 | 486,938,900 | |
| | | | | | 2,743,334,000 |
| Total | | | | | 3,772,591,500 |

[1] Various dates, 1918–19.
[2] 1 year from date of issue or renewal.

## GOVERNMENT SAVINGS SECURITIES.

The sale of Government savings securities has continued throughout the year with results which clearly demonstrate the usefulness and increasing attractiveness of this class of securities. The various offerings of savings securities have given to all classes of people, no matter how small their means, an opportunity to invest in the obligations of their Government, and more important still, the publicity given to these offerings has carried the message of economy and thrift into every city, town, and hamlet in the country, and there are few homes in which the securities, in greater or lesser amounts, may not be found. First issued in 1917, as one of the means of meeting the financial requirements of the World War, the continued sale of these securities has been of material aid to the Government in the financing of its current requirements, and at the same time has increased the prosperity and well-being of those who have saved and bought them.

To meet the changing demand for securities of this class there have been substantial changes in the character and terms of the securities offered.   The first offering in 1917 included the 25 cent thrift stamp and the $5 war-savings stamp.   In 1919 Treasury savings certificates of the $100 and $1,000 denominations were offered, with the addition in 1921 of the $1 Treasury savings stamp and the $25 Treasury savings certificate.   With the exception of the 25 cent and $1 stamp, sold at face value and noninterest bearing, these securities were issued in yearly series, at prices which increased from month to month during each calendar year, and yielded to the purchasers interest at about 4 per cent per annum for the average period to maturity, and a lower rate if redeemed before maturity.

The necessity of keeping constantly before the small investor a security adapted to his needs and at the same time giving an interest yield sufficiently large to be attractive, led to the offering of a new issue of Treasury savings certificates on December 15, 1921, under a plan whereby each certificate issued should mature five years from the date of its issue, instead of at a uniform maturity date as was the case with previous issues.   The certificates were offered on a discount basis, as formerly, but at flat issue prices which would yield interest at the rate of about 4½ per cent, compounded semiannually, if held to maturity, and about 3½ per cent, compounded semiannually, if redeemed before maturity.   At the same time arrangements were made to coordinate postal savings and Treasury savings operations and to inaugurate a peace-time savings movement under which the Post Office Department and the Treasury would join to advance postal savings for the deposit of savings and Treasury ·savings certificates for investment.

The Secretary of the Treasury announced the new issue of Treasury savings certificates and the unified savings program in the following statement, which was issued on December 14, 1921:

The Treasury Department offers for sale to the public, beginning December 15, 1921, a new issue of Treasury savings certificates in denominations of $25, $100, and $1,000 (maturity value).   The new certificates are issued on a discount basis, as in the past, but are offered for sale at flat issue prices instead of at prices which increase from month to month.   The prices for the new issue, until further notice, will be as follows: $20 for the $25 certificate, $80 for the $100 certificate, and $800 for the $1,000 certificate.

The certificates mature five years from the date of issue in each case, instead of at a uniform maturity date, and if held to maturity yield interest at the rate of about 4½ per cent per annum compounded semiannually.   The certificates are redeemable before maturity at the redemption values stated on the backs of the certificates, upon presentation and surrender to the Treasury Department, Washington, and in that event yield interest at the rate of about 3½ per cent per annum, compounded semi-annually.   The $25 certificate bears the portrait head of Theodore Roosevelt, the $100 certificate that of Washington, and the $1,000 certificate that of Lincoln.   The new certificates are issued only in registered form, in order to afford protection against loss and theft, and will be recorded on the books of the Treasury Department in Washington.   The name and address of the owner and the date of issue will be inscribed on each certificate by the issuing agent at the time of issue.   The terms of the certificates have been much simplified as compared with previous issues, and the offering is on a basis which should prove particularly attractive to small investors.

The limit of holdings has been increased by the act of Congress approved November 23, 1921, from $1,000 to $5,000, and it is now possible therefore to hold Treasury (war) savings certificates of any one series up to an aggregate maturity value not exceeding $5,000. This change makes the certificates attractive for the investment of trust funds and the surplus funds of labor, fraternal, church and similar organizations which seek an investment of intermediate length, with absolute safety and a satisfactory income return.

The new certificates are on sale at about 4,000 post offices throughout the country beginning December 15, 1921, and may also be obtained at the Federal reserve banks and such banks and other agencies as may qualify for the purpose.

Treasury savings stamps in the $1 denomination, noninterest bearing, will continue on sale at post offices and other agencies until further notice, as a convenience to those who wish to accumulate the purchase price of the new certificates through stamps.

The new offering means that postal savings and Treasury savings activities have now been coordinated into one peace-time savings program under which the Post Office Department and the Treasury will join to advance postal savings for the deposit of savings and Treasury savings certificates for investment. The consolidation of postal savings and Treasury savings facilities into a single Government savings system preserves and improves the best features of each. The plan is designed to stimulate the accumulation of savings by accepting deposits in amounts of $1 or more through the postal savings banks which are being conducted in the post offices, and to encourage investment by offering Treasury savings certificates on more attractive terms, in convenient denominations, both for direct sale and on conversion of postal savings deposits. In order that Government savings facilities may be available throughout the country, the Post Office Department is now extending postal savings to many additional post offices, and the new issue of Treasury savings certificates has already been distributed to several thousand post offices. The sale will gradually be extended to other post offices as the demand broadens. Postal savings deposits may be exchanged at postal savings offices for Treasury savings certificates, and interest will be allowed on deposits withdrawn for this purpose at the current postal savings rate for each full month up to the first day of the month in which the exchange is made.

The small war-time Treasury securities, comprising the 25-cent thrift stamp and the $5 war-savings stamp, are accordingly being discontinued, effective December 31, 1921, but the thrift stamps outstanding will be accepted at face value for the new Treasury savings securities or will be redeemed at face value in cash at post offices. The main reliance for the accumulation of small savings for investment in Treasury savings certificates will henceforth be postal savings deposits, and now that special provision has been made for the conversion of these deposits, the Government has a unified and effective savings system, with the 10-cent postal savings stamp, postal savings deposits from $1 upward, and $1 Treasury savings stamp and the $25, $100, and $1,000 Treasury savings certificates.

In undertaking this movement for peace-time savings the Government looks forward with confidence to the renewed cooperation of all helpful agencies. There can be no question about the need for saving, nor of this country's capacity to save. By offering a uniform and comprehensive means of accumulating and investing money, the Government hopes to furnish an incentive for saving, to encourage savings and investment in Government securities, and at the same time to stimulate savings activities generally. An active response to the Government's savings movement should accomplish three main objects: it will aid the Government in the current financing of its requirements; it will make for greater national prosperity; and it will increase the personal happiness and individual welfare of those who save.

In its savings activities in the past, the Government has received the hearty support of many agencies and organizations interested in savings, including the American

Federation of Labor, industries and other employers, teachers, bankers, postmasters, and public officials throughout the country. With their continued cooperation, the unified Government savings program will be assured of success.

The terms of the new issue thus announced appear in Department Circular No. 270, dated December 15, 1921, attached hereto as Exhibit 61, page 215. The regulations governing the surrender of 1921 war savings securities held by authorized agents were set forth in Department Circular No. 271, dated December 20, 1921, attached hereto as Exhibit 68, page 242. At about the same time, Department Circular No. 178, dated January 15, 1920, relative to holdings of United States Treasury (war) savings certificates in excess of the legal limit, was amended by a circular dated December 15, 1921, for the purpose of covering the increase in the limitation of holdings from $1,000 (maturity value) to $5,000 (maturity value), authorized by the act of Congress approved November 23, 1921. A copy of the amended circular is attached as Exhibit 67, page 241. The regulations further defining the rights of holders of Treasury savings certificates of all issues and series and setting forth the terms and conditions upon which such certificates will be payable in case of the death or disability of the owner, as contained in Department Circular No. 149, were further amended and supplemented by a revised circular dated August 1, 1922, attached hereto as Exhibit 69, page 246. The regulations further defining the rights of War-Savings Certificates of all issues and series have likewise been revised by Department Circular No. 108, as amended and supplemented November 9, 1922, attached hereto as Exhibit 94, page 351.

In order to facilitate the conversion of postal savings deposits into Treasury savings certificates, the board of trustees of the Postal Savings System, at a meeting held December 7, 1921, adopted the following resolution:

*Resolved,* That if and to the extent that postal savings deposits are withdrawn to purchase United States Treasury savings securities through the Post Office Department, interest shall be allowed on the deposits thus withdrawn at the going rate allowed on postal savings deposits (now 2 per cent per annum) from the first day of the month following the date when such deposits were made up to the first day of the month in which such withdrawal and purchase are effected.

Instructions to postmasters to put this resolution into effect on January 1, 1922, were issued by the Director of the Postal Savings System on December 21, 1921, and provisions to this effect have been inserted in the Treasury Department circulars offering Treasury savings certificates.

In carrying out the plan to coordinate the savings activities of the Treasury and Post Office Departments, the Savings Division of the Treasury, heretofore charged with the duty of promoting the sale of Treasury savings securities, has been reorganized under the title

"United States Government Savings System." Moreover, the Director of Savings, a Treasury official, has been elected secretary of the board of trustees of the Postal Savings System, thus bringing the savings organizations of both departments into harmony. The duties of the old savings organization were threefold, viz: (1) To develop and protect the secondary market for all issues of Government securities, (2) to sell Government savings securities, (3) to develop in the people of the country, through education in the principles of economy and thrift, habits of regular saving and investment in United States Government savings securities. Under the reorganization practically all of the purely educational work previously conducted for the purpose of inculcating habits of economy and thrift has been abandoned, and the whole effort of the new organization, as well as the small sales organization maintained in the fiscal agency departments of the 12 Federal reserve banks, has been directed towards the conduct of an intensive campaign to sell the Government's savings securities. As heretofore the Postal System has been the chief sales agency. In furtherance of this campaign the advantages offered by the Postal Savings System for deposit of savings and Treasury savings certificates for investment have constantly been kept before the people through display advertisements in newspapers (including foreign language papers), periodicals, and magazines, by means of descriptive posters and circulars distributed broadcast throughout the country, including a house-to-house distribution to practically every home through the letter carriers, and through news articles released to the city and country press. That this campaign has been successful is demonstrated by the following table showing the cash receipts from the sale of Treasury (war) savings securities, by months, from the time they were first placed on sale in December, 1917, up to and including the month of October, 1922. It will be observed that the receipts in the first 10 months of 1922 are more than five times greater than the receipts in the entire year 1921. This is convincing evidence of the country's capacity to save and its responsiveness to the opportunities made available for this purpose.

| Month. | 1917 | 1918 | 1919 | 1920 | 1921 | 1922 |
|---|---|---|---|---|---|---|
| January | | $24,559,722.15 | $70,996,041.14 | $8,987,462.59 | $2,646,396.88 | $8,896,071.56 |
| February | | 41,148,244.22 | 15,816,539.27 | 5,221,213.48 | 3,324,164.22 | 8,693,242.30 |
| March | | 53,967,864.49 | 10,143,081.68 | 6,063,359.22 | 2,838,416.58 | 9,880,942.69 |
| April | | 60,972,984.12 | 9,572,728.48 | 4,815,437.69 | 2,471,904.05 | 10,749,347.94 |
| May | | 57,956,640.12 | 6,558,198.33 | 3,552,962.19 | 1,682,606.72 | 10,542,156.31 |
| June | | 58,250,485.00 | 5,269,535.51 | 3,107,909.72 | 1,481,271.98 | 12,059,050.88 |
| July | | 211,417,942.61 | 5,176,865.12 | 2,359,274.53 | 1,403,106.07 | 14,183,629.47 |
| August | | 129,044,200.62 | 6,201,164.07 | 2,231,509.77 | 1,321,198.52 | 11,544,404.78 |
| September | | 97,614,581.48 | 6,111,944.78 | 1,814,705.89 | 1,083,602.12 | 13,661,364.60 |
| October | | 89,084,097.31 | 7,316,467.60 | 1,589,750.48 | 1,209,074.50 | 18,763,085.89 |
| November | | 73,689,846.00 | 8,020,436.67 | 1,912,967.05 | 1,285,573.34 | |
| December | $10,236,451.32 | 63,970,813.47 | 9,124,292.13 | 1,934,452.46 | 2,245,408.97 | |
| Total | 10,236,451.32 | 961,677,421.59 | 160,307,294.78 | 43,891,005.07 | 22,992,723.95 | 118,973,296.42 |

## Increase in price of Treasury savings certificates.

In order to meet changing investment conditions and take advantage of the gradual decline in interest rates, the Treasury increased the selling price of Treasury savings certificates, effective October 1, 1922, from $80 to $82 for a $100 certificate, with like increases for the other denominations. For this purpose the issue of December 15, 1921, was withdrawn from sale and replaced by a new issue dated September 30, 1922, similar to the old issue in all respects except price. At the same time the $1 Treasury savings stamp was discontinued and withdrawn from sale. The Secretary of the Treasury announced the changes in a public statement on September 16, 1922, reading as follows:

The Treasury announces that effective October 1, 1922, the issue prices of Treasury savings certificates will increase to $20.50 for the $25 certificate, $82 for the $100 certificate, and $820 for the $1,000 certificate. At the new prices Treasury savings certificates will yield about 4 per cent compounded semiannually if held to maturity and about 3 per cent simple interest if redeemed before maturity. The new certificates will be dated September 30, 1922, in order to distinguish them from the certificates now on sale, which are dated December 15, 1921. The current issue of certificates, which is being sold at $20 for a $25 certificate, $80 for a $100 certificate, and $800 for a $1,000 certificate, will continue on sale until the close of business September 30, 1922, and will then be withdrawn from sale in favor of the new certificates. Treasury savings stamps, noninterest bearing, which are now on sale in the denomination of $1, will likewise be withdrawn from sale at the close of business September 30, 1922.

The current issue of Treasury savings certificates was first placed on sale December 15 1921, and since that date certificates up to about $115,000,000 (maturity value) have been sold. Sales have been running at the rate of about $15,000,000 maturity value per month and there is every evidence that the certificates have proven increasingly attractive to investors. With sales satisfactorily established on a going basis and with the improvement that has taken place in the investment markets, the time has come to readjust the interest basis on which the certificates are sold and the Treasury has accordingly decided to make the increase in price which is now announced. At the new prices the certificates should continue to be highly attractive to investors, particularly small investors who desire to save systematically, and the Treasury looks forward with confidence to the continued cooperation of all helpful agencies in promoting their sale.

Apart from the change in price the new certificates will correspond in all essential respects to the certificates now on sale. Each certificate matures five years from the date of its issue, but may be redeemed at the option of the holder at any time after issue, at the value indicated on the back of the certificate. The certificates are issued only in registered form, in order to afford protection against loss and theft, and are exempt from the normal Federal income tax and from all State and local taxation (except estate or inheritance taxes). The aggregate amount of Treasury savings certificates of any one series that may be held by any one person at any one time is limited to $5,000 maturity value, and for this purpose the certificates issued within any one calendar year, whatever the issue or the issue price, constitute one series.

Treasury savings certificates of all denominations may be purchased at post offices throughout the country, at banks and other agencies, or from the Federal reserve banks and branches, and mail applications addressed direct to the Treasurer of the United States, Washington, D. C., will receive prompt attention.

The terms of the new certificates thus announced appear in Department Circular No. 301, dated September 30, 1922, attached hereto as Exhibit 62, page 224. The regulations governing the surrender of the December 15, 1921, issue of Treasury savings certificates and of Treasury savings stamps and Treasury savings cards held by authorized agents were set forth in Treasury Department Circular No. 302, dated September 30, 1922, attached hereto as Exhibit 70, page 265. (See also Exhibit 66, page 240.)

*Redemption and exchange of 1918 war-savings certificates.*

The Treasury announced on November 15, 1922, its plans for handling the war-savings certificates of the series of 1918 which mature on January 1, 1923, to the amount of about $625,000,000. For the convenience of holders of these certificates, it is offering special facilities, first, for their exchange into the new Treasury savings certificates, with provision for advance exchanges beginning November 15, 1922, and second, special facilities for cash redemption on and after January 1, 1923, with provision for presentation in advance for redemption as of that date. Post offices and banking institutions throughout the United States have received full information as to the provisions for redemption and exchange, and will be in a position to extend all possible assistance to their customers.

Beginning November 15, 1922, holders of 1918 war-savings certificates can exchange them at maturity value for Treasury savings certificates dated January 1, 1923' and at the same time can get advance payment of any cash difference by taking the largest amount of Treasury savings certificates that their war-savings certificates, taken at maturity value, will cover. Exchanges after January 15, 1923, with any necessary cash adjustments, will be made as of the date of exchange. Holders will not be able to make cash redemption of their certificates before maturity, but beginning November 15, 1922, may present them in advance for redemption as of January 1, 1923, and in that event will receive on or about January 1, 1923, checks payable to their order covering the redemption value. Registered war-savings certificates must be presented to the post office where registered, but unregistered certificates are being received for redemption or exchange at any money-order post office, any Federal reserve bank or branch, or the Treasury at Washington. Banking institutions generally are handling these transactions for their customers, and holders of maturing certificates are urged to present their certificates, so far as possible, through their own banks and trust companies.

The arrangements covering redemptions and exchanges, and the regulations governing the presentation and surrender of maturing certificates, appear in greater detail in (1) the Secretary's letter of

November 13, 1922, to the banking institutions of the country,
attached hereto as Exhibit 64, page 236; (2) the official circular (No.
308) as to redemption and exchange of war-savings certificates,
series of 1918, attached hereto as Exhibit 63, page 233; (3) Department Circular No. 310 as to redemption and exchange of Treasury
savings certificates, series of 1918, attached hereto as Exhibit 95,
page 358; and (4) the official form (P. D. 750), attached hereto as
Exhibit 65, page 238, which provides an application blank for either
redemptions or exchanges, and in that connection gives examples of
what holders of 1918 war-savings stamps can get by exchanging their
stamps for the new Treasury savings certificates.

MARKET PRICES OF LIBERTY BONDS AND VICTORY NOTES.

The rise in the market prices of Liberty bonds and Victory notes
continued until about September, 1922, every issue having reached
or exceeded par by July. There has since been some reaction,
owing to the pressure of commercial demands and somewhat higher
rates for money, but all issues are still selling within a point or two
of par in the market. The average increase in Liberty bond prices to
date since the low point reached in 1920 has been about 15 points,
or an increase in market value of approximately $2,500,000,000,
based on the amount outstanding at the present time.

The following table gives the low points reached by Liberty bonds
and Victory notes, and the closing quotations on July 15 and December 15, 1920, July 15 and December 15, 1921, and on the 15th of
each month from January to November, 1922:

*Market prices of Liberty bonds and Victory notes.*

| Date. | First 3½'s. | First 4's. | First 4¼'s. | Second 4's. | Second 4¼'s. | Third 4¼'s. | Fourth 4¼'s. | Victory 4¾'s. | Victory 3¾'s. |
|---|---|---|---|---|---|---|---|---|---|
| Low point................... | [1] $86.30 | [2] $83.00 | [3] $84.00 | [4] $81.70 | [4] $82.00 | [5] $86.00 | [4] $82.54 | [4] $94.82 | [4] $94.72 |
| **1920.** | | | | | | | | | |
| July 15...................... | 91.02 | 86.10 | 86.44 | 85.26 | 85.42 | 88.88 | 85.68 | 95.92 | 95.90 |
| Dec. 15...................... | 90.12 | 86.02 | 86.12 | 85.10 | 85.36 | 87.90 | 85.90 | 95.00 | 95.00 |
| **1921.** | | | | | | | | | |
| July 15...................... | 86.50 | 87.12 | 87.34 | 86.92 | 87.02 | 91.16 | 87.16 | 98.32 | 98.32 |
| Dec. 15...................... | 95.10 | 97.30 | 97.40 | 96.84 | 97.04 | 98.14 | 97.42 | 100.02 | 100.02 |
| **1922.** | | | | | | | | | |
| Jan. 16...................... | 96.60 | 97.70 | 97.80 | 97.60 | 97.60 | 97.84 | 97.78 | 100.18 | 100.20 |
| Feb. 15...................... | 96.94 | 96.34 | 96.86 | 96.02 | 96.76 | 97.56 | 97.20 | 100.16 | 99.98 |
| Mar. 15...................... | 96.72 | 97.20 | 97.32 | 97.26 | 97.30 | 98.56 | 97.50 | 100.66 | 100.04 |
| Apr. 15...................... | 99.86 | 99.70 | 99.86 | 99.50 | 99.72 | 99.92 | 99.94 | 100.74 | 100.02 |
| May 15...................... | 99.20 | 99.60 | 99.76 | 99.40 | 99.52 | 99.90 | 99.90 | 100.60 | 100.02 |
| June 15...................... | 100.18 | 100.00 | 100.02 | 99.90 | 99.98 | 99.98 | 100.06 | 100.56 | 100.00 |
| July 15...................... | 100.80 | 100.70 | 100.82 | 100.48 | 100.52 | 100.34 | 100.92 | 100.54 | ......... |
| Aug. 15...................... | 100.80 | 101.22 | 101.16 | 100.50 | 100.46 | 100.48 | 101.20 | [6] 100.82 | ......... |
| Sept. 15...................... | 101.20 | 100.80 | 100.64 | 100.20 | 100.18 | 100.34 | 100.66 | [6] 100.74 | ......... |
| Oct. 16...................... | 100.84 | 100.00 | 99.34 | 100.00 | 99.18 | 99.30 | 99.14 | [6] 100.20 | ......... |
| Nov. 15...................... | 100.22 | 98.10 | 98.34 | 97.90 | 97.98 | 98.38 | 98.30 | [6] 100.30 | ......... |

[1] July 9, 1921.   [2] May 19, 1920.   [3] May 18, 1920.   [4] May 20, 1920.   [5] Dec. 21, 1920.   [6] Uncalled Victory 4¾'s.

The improvement in the market prices of Liberty bonds has without doubt been sustained by the successful development of the Treasury's program for the orderly funding and gradual liquidation of the short-dated debt. Fundamentally, however, the appreciation of Liberty bonds has been due to lower rates for money and lower prices for commodities, which inevitably bring better prices for fixed income securities of the highest class; and, contrariwise, with slightly higher rates for money and higher prices for commodities, it is only natural that there should be some fluctuations in the prices for Liberty bonds. Prices of bonds have a close relation to money rates. When funds are scarce and rates high, bonds sell at prices sufficiently low that the yield may be commensurate with prevailing market rates of interest. On the other hand, when funds are more plentiful and rates low, bonds sell at correspondingly higher prices and lower yields. The changes in the money and investment markets have thus been reflected in the yields on Liberty bonds and Victory notes as well as in their market prices. The following table shows the average monthly yield of Liberty bonds and Victory notes for July and December, 1920, July and December, 1921, and for each month from January to October, 1922:

*Yield on Liberty bonds and Victory notes.*[1]

| Date. | First 3½'s. | First 4's. | First 4¼'s. | First-second 4¼'s. | Second 4's. | Second 4¼'s. | Third 4¼'s. | Fourth 4¼'s. | Victory 4¾'s. | Victory 3¾'s. |
|---|---|---|---|---|---|---|---|---|---|---|
| **1920.** | *Per ct.* | *Per ct.* | *Per ct.* | *Per ct.* | *Per ct.* | *Per ct.* | *Per ct.* | *Per ct.* | *Per ct.* | *Per ct.* |
| July | 4.049 | 4.959 | 5.221 | 4.546 | 5.129 | 5.399 | 5.959 | 5.523 | 6.383 | 5.360 |
| December | 4.117 | 4.974 | 5.248 | 4.594 | 5.164 | 5.437 | 6.296 | 5.556 | 6.919 | 5.896 |
| **1921.** | | | | | | | | | | |
| July | 4.359 | 4.863 | 5.129 | 4.429 | 4.989 | 5.258 | 5.771 | 5.390 | 5.681 | 4.670 |
| December | 3.804 | 4.185 | 4.440 | 4.372 | 4.237 | 4.485 | 4.657 | 4.491 | 4.707 | 3.707 |
| **1922.** | | | | | | | | | | |
| January | 3.717 | 4.169 | 4.420 | 4.327 | 4.215 | 4.464 | 4.665 | 4.480 | 4.626 | 3.627 |
| February | 3.724 | 4.218 | 4.471 | 4.321 | 4.260 | 4.510 | 4.712 | 4.529 | 4.569 | 3.667 |
| March | 3.660 | 4.146 | 4.397 | 4.322 | 4.175 | 4.424 | 4.473 | 4.431 | 3.821 | 3.584 |
| April | 3.541 | 4.031 | 4.278 | 4.273 | 4.048 | 4.296 | 4.319 | 4.280 | 3.539 | 3.500 |
| May | 3.530 | 4.015 | 4.262 | 4.244 | 4.030 | 4.277 | 4.272 | 4.258 | 3.639 | 3.343 |
| June | 3.496 | 3.998 | 4.245 | 4.220 | 4.004 | 4.251 | 4.244 | 4.240 | 3.508 | ........ |
| July | 3.459 | 3.948 | 4.190 | 4.144 | 3.971 | 4.214 | 4.166 | 4.171 | 3.431 | ........ |
| August | 3.446 | 3.937 | 4.181 | 4.177 | 3.971 | 4.218 | 4.160 | 4.162 | [2] 3.678 | ........ |
| September | 3.436 | 3.965 | 4.215 | 4.213 | 3.991 | 4.239 | 4.208 | 4.208 | [2] 3.703 | ........ |
| October | 3.456 | 4.049 | 4.295 | 4.193 | 4.062 | 4.309 | 4.369 | 4.305 | [2] 4.170 | ........ |

[1] Computed by the Government actuary.    [2] Uncalled Victory 4¾'s.

With the reduction which has taken place in commercial loans there has been a substantial decline during the past year in the amount of Government securities held as collateral for loans by both reporting member banks and Federal reserve banks, though the last few weeks have seen some increases in these loans. Even now, however, the amount of Government securities thus held as collateral is only about one-half of the amount held a year ago. On the other hand, reporting member banks and Federal reserve banks, following their own investment policies, have greatly increased their investments in Liberty bonds, Victory notes, and Treasury notes during the same period. The amounts owned by reporting member banks increased from about $913,000,000 on November 2, 1921, to about $1,910,000,000 on November 1, 1922; and the amount owned by Federal reserve banks increased from $16,000,000 on November 2, 1921, to $246,000,000 on May 3, 1922, from which point it has been reduced to $156,000,000 by November 15, 1922. The holdings of reporting member banks by October 11, 1922, had fallen $34,000,000 from the high of $1,807,000,000 reached on September 6, 1922, but by November 1, 1922, their aggregate holdings had increased to $1,910,000,000, largely as a result of allotments on the October 16th issue of Treasury bonds. The following table gives the amount of Liberty bonds, Victory notes, and Treasury notes owned and held as collateral by the weekly reporting member banks and the Federal reserve banks at various dates:

*Liberty bonds, Victory notes and Treasury notes owned and held to secure loans.*

[Amounts in millions of dollars.]

| Date. | Liberty bonds, Victory notes, and Treasury notes outstanding. | Weekly reporting member banks.[1] | | | | Federal reserve banks.[1] | | | |
|---|---|---|---|---|---|---|---|---|---|
| | | Owned.[2] | Held as collateral.[3] | Total. | Per cent of amount outstanding. | Owned.[2] | Held as collateral. | Total. | Per cent of amount outstanding. |
| **1919.** | | | | | | | | | |
| Dec. 31............. | 20,240 | 876 | 1,294 | 2,170 | 10.72 | 2 | 1,070 | 1,072 | 5.30 |
| **1920.** | | | | | | | | | |
| June 30............. | [1] 19,582 | 808 | 1,023 | 1,831 | 9.35 | 2 | 938 | 940 | 4.80 |
| Oct. 31............. | 19,528 | 801 | 912 | 1,713 | 8.77 | 2 | 964 | 966 | 4.95 |
| Dec. 31............. | 19,512 | 851 | 909 | 1,760 | 9.02 | 2 | 953 | 955 | 4.89 |
| **1921.** | | | | | | | | | |
| June 30............. | 19,460 | 883 | 672 | 1,555 | 7.99 | 12 | 609 | 621 | 3.19 |
| Oct. 31............. | 19,573 | 913 | 546 | 1,459 | 7.45 | 16 | 436 | 452 | 2.31 |
| Dec. 31............. | 19,457 | 977 | 513 | 1,490 | 7.66 | 41 | 438 | 479 | 2.46 |
| **1922.** | | | | | | | | | |
| Jan. 31............. | 19,421 | 1,237 | 450 | 1,687 | 8.69 | 71 | 324 | 395 | 2.03 |
| Feb. 28............. | 19,776 | 1,148 | 427 | 1,575 | 7.96 | 144 | 271 | 415 | 2.10 |
| Mar. 31............. | 19,712 | 1,210 | 394 | 1,604 | 8.14 | 181 | 225 | 406 | 2.06 |
| Apr. 30............. | 19,661 | 1,347 | 346 | 1,693 | 8.61 | 246 | 178 | 424 | 2.16 |
| May 31............. | 19,608 | 1,442 | 317 | 1,759 | 8.97 | 228 | 161 | 389 | 1.98 |
| June 30............. | 19,319 | 1,571 | 285 | 1,856 | 9.61 | 208 | 172 | 380 | 1.97 |
| July 31............. | 19,319 | 1,742 | 257 | 1,999 | 10.35 | 182 | 123 | 305 | 1.58 |
| Aug. 31............. | 19,663 | 1,793 | 259 | 2,052 | 10.44 | 178 | 128 | 306 | 1.56 |
| Sept. 30............. | 19,620 | 1,766 | 261 | 2,027 | 10.33 | 213 | 133 | 346 | 1.76 |
| Oct. 31............. | [4] 20,180 | [4] 1,910 | [4] 292 | 2,202 | 10.91 | [4] 175 | [4] 267 | 442 | 2.19 |

[1] These figures are available for a given day each week and are taken for the dates nearest those given at the left of the table.
[2] Partly estimated.
[3] Includes a few loans secured by certificates of indebtedness.
[4] Includes Treasury bonds of 1947-52.

### DEPOSITS OF GOVERNMENT FUNDS.

During the fiscal year ended June 30, 1922, deposits of Government funds were maintained with the following depositaries, in addition to the Treasurer of the United States: Federal reserve banks and branches (which also act as fiscal agents of the United States); special depositaries; Federal land banks; national bank depositaries, both general and limited; foreign depositaries and insular depositaries, including the treasurer of the Philippine Islands. Statements indicating the numbers of such depositaries by classes and the amounts of public moneys held by them, on the basis of daily Treasury statements, revised, at the end of the fiscal year 1921 and at the end of the fiscal year 1922, are shown in the abstract of report of the Division of Deposits on page 439. The regulations governing the deposit of public moneys were revised during the year, and appear in Department Circular No. 176, as amended and supplemented May 15, 1922, attached hereto as Exhibit 96, page 362.

The fiscal year 1922 was marked by further retrenchment in deposits of Government funds. Deposits with Federal reserve banks and their branches necessarily show considerable variation from day to day because of the great volume of Government business transacted by such banks in the performance of their depositary and fiscal agency functions. Deposits with special depositaries under the Liberty loan acts are also subject to great variation substantially in direct proportion to the refunding operations of the Treasury, inasmuch as the only deposits in which depositaries of this class participate are deposits of public moneys arising from such sales of bonds, notes, or Treasury certificates of indebtedness of the United States as under the terms of the official offering may be paid for by credit. The resulting deposits are withdrawn from the banks from time to time as needed to meet current disbursements of the Government, and, generally speaking, the greater part of the deposits arising from any given sale of Government securities are withdrawn within a period averaging three or four weeks after the deposit. Deposits with Federal land banks under the provisions of section 32 of the act approved July 17, 1916, as amended July 1, 1921, are temporary only, and while the deposits made during the fiscal year 1922 aggregated $11,-250,000, all of them had been repaid to the Treasury prior to June 30, 1922.

As a result of the continued application of the Treasury's established policy of designating and maintaining balances with general national-bank depositaries only at points where actually necessary for the performance of some essential Government business and of limiting such balances to the minimum required to provide for the amount and character of the Government business transacted, further important progress was made during the fiscal year 1922 in reducing the number of such depositaries and the balances carried therewith to the credit of the Treasurer of the United States. On June 30, 1921, there were 533 general national-bank depositaries with total fixed balances of $9,990,500, while on June 30, 1922, there were but 335 general national-bank depositaries with total fixed balances of $8,804,500, a net reduction of 198 in the number of depositaries and $1,186,000 in the amount of the fixed balances.  A recapitulation of all changes affecting the general national-bank depositary system of the Government during the period under review is as follows: General depositaries discontinued, 221; general depositaries designated, 23; fixed balances reduced, 67; fixed balances increased, 44.

During the same period the Treasury further developed its policy of designating limited national-bank depositaries of public moneys for the sole purpose of receiving deposits made by United States courts and their officers and by postmasters for credit to their official checking accounts.  These depositaries are not authorized to accept any other deposits and hold no funds to the credit of the Treasurer of the United States.  On June 30, 1921, there were 187 limited national-bank depositaries, while by June 30, 1922, the number of such depositaries had increased to 845.  On June 30, 1922, the amount held by these depositaries and general depositaries to the credit of Government officers, other than the Treasurer of the United States, was $16,169,825.24, as against $16,036,064.70 at the end of the preceding fiscal year, on the basis of daily Treasury statements, revised.  National-bank depositaries are required by Treasury regulations to pay interest at the rate of 2 per cent per annum on daily balances carried to the credit of the Treasurer of the United States and to the credit of Government officers other than the Treasurer of the United States, so that the designation of limited national-bank depositaries places on an interest-bearing basis the funds maintained by United States courts and their officers and local postmasters throughout the country in the form of official checking accounts, thus producing a substantial revenue which would not otherwise be received by the Government.  Furthermore, the funds in question have the benefit of the supervision given by the Treasury to depositary banks and the collateral security pledged by such depositaries.

During the fiscal year ended June 30, 1922, the Treasury continued to maintain foreign depositaries of public moneys in France, Great Britain, Italy, Belgium, and Haiti.  The balances with such depositaries, however, to the credit of the Treasurer of the United States and to the credit of other Government officers, on the basis of daily Treasury statements, revised, were reduced from $52,258,530.78 on June 30, 1921, to $1,222,951.03 on June 30, 1922.  Public Resolution No. 61, Sixty-Seventh Congress, approved June 19, 1922, gives the Secretary of the Treasury authority to designate depositaries of public moneys in foreign countries and in the Territories and insular possessions of the United States, thus enabling the Treasury to designate and retain such depositaries where necessary for the transaction of the Government's business.  Previous legislation on this subject was limited both as to duration and scope.

Since June 1, 1913, Government depositaries have been required to pay interest at the rate of 2 per cent per annum on daily balances. The amounts received from this source, exclusive of special depositaries under the Liberty loan acts, for the past 10 years are as follows:

*Interest on Government deposits.*

| | | | |
|---|---|---|---|
| 1913....................... | $122,218.89 | 1918..................... | $1,134,569.09 |
| 1914..................... | 1,409,426.07 | 1919..................... | 5,507,742.43 |
| 1915..................... | 1,222,706.93 | 1920..................... | 1,865,975.76 |
| 1916..................... | 791,671.45 | 1921..................... | [1] 2,580,746.84 |
| 1917..................... | 703,771.76 | 1922..................... | [2] 796,871.71 |

[1] Amended figures.      [2] Incomplete and subject to revision.

Special depositaries of public moneys are also required by Treasury regulations to pay interest on daily deposits at the rate of 2 per cent per annum. The interest received on these deposits during the fiscal year ended June 30, 1922, was $5,957,918.35. The total amount received from April 24, 1917, to June 30, 1922, was $52,850,291.73. This is shown by semiannual periods and Federal reserve districts in the following statement:

*Interest collected to June 30, 1922, by Federal reserve districts, on deposits in special depositaries on account of sales of Liberty bonds, Victory notes, Treasury notes, and certificates of indebtedness, and income and profits tax payments under acts of April 24, 1917, September 24, 1917, April 4, 1918, September 24, 1918, July 9, 1918, and March 3, 1919.*

| Federal reserve district. | Apr. 24 to June 30, 1917. | July 1 to Dec. 31, 1917. | Jan. 1 to June 30, 1918. | July 1 to Dec. 31, 1918. |
|---|---|---|---|---|
| Boston............................... | $5,340.47 | $495,044.28 | $757,345.98 | $1,138,915.47 |
| New York............................. | 338,480.60 | 2,418,335.72 | 2,486,301.63 | 6,720,162.97 |
| Philadelphia.......................... | 1,044.64 | 200,276.04 | 557,068.79 | 1,059,668.15 |
| Cleveland............................. | | 290,482.56 | 803,219.84 | 872,392.10 |
| Richmond............................. | | 81,252.94 | 128,860.72 | 109,503.64 |
| Atlanta............................... | 252.06 | 28,189.21 | 96,086.74 | 144,165.99 |
| New Orleans branch............... | | 26,332.71 | 60,320.38 | 79,005.33 |
| Chicago.............................. | 9,023.53 | 300,428.59 | 658,048.19 | 974,334.63 |
| St. Louis.............................. | | 56,412.34 | 268,726.24 | 403,488.76 |
| Minneapolis.......................... | | 32,520.68 | 158,309.21 | 164,790.29 |
| Kansas City........................... | | 39,634.27 | 150,897.61 | 332,145.49 |
| Dallas................................ | 1,353.62 | 35,888.58 | 80,191.52 | 268,329.88 |
| San Francisco......................... | 2,726.51 | 137,996.92 | 208,486.34 | 377,421.12 |
| Total........................... | 358,221.43 | 4,142,794.84 | 6,423,863.19 | 12,644,323.82 |

| Federal reserve district. | Jan. 1 to June 30, 1919. | July 1 to Dec. 31, 1919. | Jan. 1 to June 30, 1920. | July 1 to Dec. 31, 1920. |
|---|---|---|---|---|
| Boston............................... | $733,967.20 | $563,524.88 | $254,689.51 | $131,904.55 |
| New York............................. | 2,968,858.77 | 3,336,357.90 | 1,887,688.21 | 837,038.64 |
| Philadelphia.......................... | 596,436.23 | 529,102.81 | 171,509.48 | 123,242.32 |
| Cleveland............................. | 696,750.48 | 530,146.39 | 352,082.30 | 98,743.63 |
| Richmond............................. | 242,735.18 | 555,390.68 | 140,635.35 | 29,202.82 |
| Atlanta............................... | 203,550.98 | 153,908.04 | 82,811.99 | 17,182.07 |
| New Orleans branch............... | 88,140.55 | 40,666.90 | 61,682.62 | 23,774.93 |
| Chicago.............................. | 1,107,399.81 | 817,172.84 | 355,685.31 | 159,607.51 |
| St. Louis.............................. | 369,783.56 | 264,058.53 | 100,947.90 | 45,418.04 |
| Minneapolis.......................... | 311,793.53 | 171,863.85 | 104,223.41 | 19,254.89 |
| Kansas City........................... | 309,106.79 | 159,047.57 | 95,489.75 | 49,622.84 |
| Dallas................................ | 132,651.09 | 182,127.50 | 118,843.58 | 15,256.09 |
| San Francisco......................... | 590,811.02 | 246,486.13 | 182,833.46 | 97,164.11 |
| Total........................... | 8,351,885.19 | 7,549,854.02 | 3,909,122.87 | 1,647,417.44 |

*Interest collected to June 30, 1922, by Federal reserve districts, etc.*—Continued.

| Federal reserve district. | Jan. 1 to June 30, 1921. | July 1 to Dec. 31, 1921. | Jan. 1 to June 30, 1922. | Total. |
|---|---|---|---|---|
| Boston | $197,098.16 | $229,145.55 | $293,199.36 | $4,800,075.41 |
| New York | 905,079.42 | 1,382,584.79 | 1,130,984.88 | 24,411,873.53 |
| Philadelphia | 203,114.68 | 296,937.77 | 196,007.92 | 3,934,408.83 |
| Cleveland | 170,999.61 | 339,829.56 | 208,690.66 | 4,363,342.13 |
| Richmond | 61,321.73 | 53,373.59 | 105,497.31 | 1,507,773.96 |
| Atlanta | 16,393.10 | 20,544.91 | 44,474.72 | 807,559.81 |
| New Orleans branch | 5,417.03 | 10,288.39 | 24,339.61 | 419,968.45 |
| Chicago | 87,765.18 | 356,846.54 | 412,204.08 | 5,238,516.21 |
| St. Louis | 55,839.57 | 93,306.68 | 109,287.53 | 1,767,269.15 |
| Minneapolis | 39,930.85 | 74,455.39 | 63,793.12 | 1,150,935.22 |
| Kansas City | 40,237.12 | 63,463.86 | 69,799.89 | 1,309,445.19 |
| Dallas | 17,151.75 | 49,760.21 | 71,030.98 | 972,584.80 |
| San Francisco | 64,542.38 | 103,123.90 | 154,947.15 | 2,166,539.04 |
| Total | 1,864,890.58 | 3,073,661.14 | 2,884,257.21 | 52,850,291.73 |

## SECURITIES OWNED BY THE UNITED STATES GOVERNMENT.

The aggregate amount of securities owned by the United States Government on June 30, 1922, as reported to the Treasury and shown in detail in Exhibit 76, on page 277, was $11,057,052,849.92, as against a total of $11,326,731,680.72 at the close of the previous fiscal year, a net decrease of $269,678,830.80, due principally to sales during the fiscal year of $263,258,750 face amount of equipment trust gold notes acquired by the Director General of Railroads pursuant to the Federal control act approved March 21, 1918, as amended, and the act approved November 19, 1919. For descriptive purposes, the securities owned on June 30, 1922, may be divided into five main classes, namely: (1) foreign obligations, $10,045,393,404.64, principal amount; (2) capital stock of war emergency corporations, $327,492,835.92, par amount, after deducting cash deposited with the Treasurer of the United States to the credit of such corporations; (3) railroad securities, $456,505,129.93, principal amount; (4) Federal land bank securities $142,899,880; and (5) miscellaneous securities, $84,761,599.43. Interest accrued and unpaid is not included in the figures.

The foreign obligations, in the aggregate amount of $10,045,393,404.64, include (*a*) loans to foreign Governments under authority of the acts approved April 24, 1917, and September 24, 1917, as amended (on the basis of cash advances less repayments of principal), $9,386,422,556.14; (*b*) foreign obligations received from the Secretary of War and the Secretary of the Navy on account of sales of surplus war supplies, $574,876,884.95; and (*c*) foreign obligations received from the American Relief Administration on account of relief pursuant to the act approved February 25, 1919, $84,093,963.55. The total of these obligations on June 30, 1922, was $38,523,801.95 less than on June 30, 1921, as a result of repayments by foreign Governments on the principal of their obligations, pursuant to special agreements or on adjustment of accounts.

The stock of war emergency corporations owned by the United States, amounting in the aggregate to $327,492,835.92, after deducting cash deposited to their credit with the Treasurer of the United States, includes the capital stock of the United States Shipping Board Emergency Fleet Corporation, the Hoboken Manufacturers' Railroad Company, the United States Housing Corporation, the United States Sugar Equalization Board (Inc.), the United States Grain Corporation, the United States Spruce Production Corporation, and the War Finance Corporation. The total increase in this class of securities during the fiscal year 1922 was $58,942,459.35, which results first, from a reduction of about $94,000,000 in the balance with the Treasurer to the credit of the War Finance Corporation, operating as an offset against the amount of the outstanding capital stock of this corporation; second, a reduction of $25,000,000 in the outstanding capital stock of the United States Grain Corporation effected on October 17, 1921; and, third, payments received from the Housing Corporation.

The railroad securities, amounting in the aggregate to $456,505,-129.93, consist of (a) the obligations of carriers acquired under section 7 of the Federal control act approved March 21, 1918, as amended (exclusive of obligations of carriers acquired by the Director General of Railroads from the operating revenues of carriers under the provisions of section 12 of the above-mentioned act), $55,867,000; (b) equipment trust gold notes acquired by the Director General of Railroads pursuant to the Federal control act approved March 21, 1918, as amended, and the act approved November 19, 1919, to provide for the reimbursement of the United States for motive power, cars, and other equipment ordered for carriers under Federal control, $49,999,800; (c) obligations of carriers acquired pursuant to section 207 of the transportation act approved February 28, 1920, through the funding of indebtedness of the carriers to the United States on account of matters arising out of Federal control, $116,646,500; and (d) the obligations of carriers acquired pursuant to section 210 of the transportation act approved February 28, 1920, as amended (loans to railroads from the $300,000,000 revolving fund provided under section 210), $233,991,829.93.

The holdings of railroad securities decreased during the fiscal year $223,933,523.74, due principally to sales of $263,258,750 face amount of equipment trust gold notes of carrier corporations described in (b) above. The sales were made all at par and accrued interest, and the proceeds, pursuant to section 202 of the transportation act, have been covered into the Treasury to the credit of the appropriation "Federal control of transportation systems," becoming available for use by the Director General of Railroads in the settlement of matters growing out of Federal control.

The Federal land bank securities, in the aggregate face amount of $142,899,880, consist of (a) capital stock of the 12 Federal land banks still owned by the United States, $4,264,880, and (b) Federal farm loan bonds acquired pursuant to the act approved January 18, 1918, as extended by the joint resolution approved May 26, 1920, aggregating $138,635,000. During the fiscal year 1922 repayments were made by the Federal land banks on their capital stock owned by the United States, amounting in the aggregate to $2,435,795. The holdings of farm loan bonds decreased $44,400,000 on account of repurchases by the Federal land banks of their bonds acquired by the United States pursuant to the above-mentioned provisions of law. On June 30, 1922, the holdings of farm loan bonds consisted of $136,885,000 4½ per cent bonds (the same figure as on June 30, 1921), and $1,750,000 principal amount of 5 per cent bonds, which is $44,400,000 less than on June 30, 1921, due to repurchases above mentioned.

The miscellaneous securities reported, amounting in the aggregate to $84,761,599.43, consist of (a) securities received by the Secretary of War on account of sales of surplus war supplies, $29,138,771.32; (b) securities received by the Secretary of the Navy on account of sales of surplus property, $9,870,377.78; (c) securities received by the United States Shipping Board on account of sales of ships, etc., $38,752,450.33; and (d) capital stock of the Panama Railroad Co., $7,000,000. The decrease in the amount of miscellaneous securities from $104,089,768.89, as of June 30, 1921, is due principally to a decrease in securities held by the United States Shipping Board, amounting to $29,023,452.14, which represents, for the most part, sales of securities by the board.

During the fiscal year 1922 the Sugar Equalization Board (Inc.), whose capital stock of $5,000,000 par amount is owned by the United States, deposited its cash assets which, on June 30, 1922, amounted to $14,369,856.84, to the credit of the board with the Treasurer of the United States. The capital stock of the United States Spruce Production Corporation, amounting to $10,000,000, was added to the statement during the fiscal year, while deposits of the corporation with the Treasurer of the United States, carried as an offset, amounted on June 30, 1922, to $3,457,806.55. The capital stock of the Panama Railroad Company, in the amount of $7,000,000, was also added to the statement of securities during the fiscal year 1922.

The securities reported by the Treasury as owned by the United States are held in safekeeping by the Treasurer of the United States and the Federal reserve banks and branches to the extent that they have been turned over to the Treasury. Many of the securities, however, though reported to the Treasury and carried in the statement, are still held by other departments and agencies of the Government, but the aggregate amounts so held are relatively small as compared with the total.

### RAILROADS.

During the past year the Treasury has continued to make payments to railroads under the transportation act of 1920. These payments have been made in accordance with certificates issued by the Interstate Commerce Commission under the following sections of the act:

Section 204: For reimbursement of deficits of the so-called "shortline" railroads during Federal control.

Section 209: For the guaranty of net railway operating income during the six months' period immediately following the termination of Federal control on March 1, 1920.

Section 210: For new loans.

Copies of the above sections, as amended, will be found on pages 215–222, inclusive, of the annual report of the Secretary of the Treasury for the fiscal year ended June 30, 1921.

*Section 204.*

In making payments under this section the Treasury is required, upon request of the President, to deduct from the amount certified to be due to the carrier the amount certified to be due from the carrier to the President, as operator of the transportation systems under Federal control, and payable to his agent, the Director General of Railroads. From November 15, 1921, to November 15, 1922, $1,949,180.72 was paid under section 204; $1,928,586.44 to the carriers directly, and $20,594.28 to the Director General. The Interstate Commerce Commission estimates the total amount payable under this section at $15,204,272.57. Of this sum $5,139,550.45 in the aggregate had been paid up to November 15, 1922; $4,166,954.51 directly to the carriers, and $972,595.94 to the Director General. It is expected that about $8,000,000 of the remainder will be certified for payment during the balance of the present fiscal year.

A statement showing partial and final payments to carriers under section 204 of the act, together with the deductions therefrom, for the period from November 15, 1921, to November 15, 1922, is attached as Exhibit 73, page 272.

*Section 209.*

From November 15, 1921, to November 15, 1922, $19,622,039.83 was paid to carriers under this section. According to estimates of the Interstate Commerce Commission, the total amount payable under section 209 will aggregate $535,000,000. Of this amount, $450,090,803.59

in the aggregate had been paid up to November 15, 1922, leaving an estimated balance of $84,909,196.41 still payable, of which it is expected that $75,000,000 will be certified for payment during the remainder of the present fiscal year. Final payments have been made to 105 carriers out of 676 accepting the guaranty.

A statement showing partial and final payments to carriers under this section from November 15, 1921, to November 15, 1922, is attached as Exhibit 74, page 273.

## Section 210.

An appropriation of $300,000,000 was provided by section 210 of the transportation act of 1920, as a revolving fund for loans to railroads and for paying judgments, decrees, and awards rendered against the Director General of Railroads. The loans made by the Treasury to railroads under this section from November 15, 1921, to November 15, 1922, aggregated $58,419,450. Of this amount, $33,740,000 represented funds advanced to meet maturing loans previously made under section 210. Repayments during the same period amounted to $77,425,512.14, of which $41,253,142.14 represented payments in advance of maturity.

Total loans made to railroads from the fund, up to and including November 15, 1922, amounted to $317,886,667, while advances to the director general for the purposes specified amounted to $17,999,997.97, making total expenditures under this section $335,886,664.97. At the same time receipts on account of the fund aggregated $121,309,226.47, of which $22,624,681.00 represented interest collected and $98,684,545.47 repayments of principal. The balance to the credit of the fund at the close of business on November 15, 1922, was $85.422,561.50. Since the passage of the transportation act 84 railroads have availed themselves of the opportunity to borrow under section 210.

During the year between November 15, 1921, and November 15, 1922, four railroads paid their loans in full, and twenty-six roads reduced their loans. A few of the railroads defaulted in interest payments on their loans, and one—the Atlanta, Birmingham & Atlantic Railway Co.—defaulted on an installment of the principal. This road went into receivership in February, 1921, about six months after a loan of $200,000 (since reduced to $180,000) had been made to it under section 210.

The following is a list of the carriers in default on their payments, as of November 15, 1922:

Atlanta, Birmingham & Atlantic Ry. Co.:
    Interest due Feb. 1, 1922.............................. $5,400.00
    Interest due Aug. 1, 1922.............................  5,400.00
    Principal due Aug. 13, 1922........................... 20,000.00
    Interest due Aug. 13, 1922............................     39.13
                                                        ———————— $30,839.13

Kansas City, Mexico & Orient R. R. Co.: (Receiver)

Balance of interest due June 1, 1922............................... $42,095.83

Virginia Southern R. R. Co.:

Interest due July 1, 1922........................................... 1,140.00

Waterloo, Cedar Falls & Northern Ry. Co.:

Interest due Apr. 15, 1922........................................ 37,800.00

Interest due Oct. 15, 1922........................................ 37,800.00

Wichita Northwestern Ry. Co.:

Interest due Dec. 1, 1921.............................. $9,700.20

Interest due June 1, 1922.............................. 11,452.50

                                                         21,152.70

Total......................................................... 170,827.66

A statement showing the amount of loans outstanding on November 15, 1921; loans made between November 15, 1921, and November 15, 1922; and loans outstanding on November 15, 1922, is attached as Exhibit 75, page 275.

CHECKING ACCOUNTS OF GOVERNMENT CORPORATIONS AND AGENCIES.

The United States Shipping Board Emergency Fleet Corporation, the United States Housing Corporation, the War Finance Corporation, the United States Grain Corporation, the Russian Bureau of the War Trade Board, the several Federal land banks, the Railroad Administration, the United States Sugar Equalization Board (Inc.), and the United States Spruce Production Corporation have maintained checking balances with the Treasurer of the United States during the year, in the manner outlined in previous annual reports of the Secretary of the Treasury. The two last-named accounts have been transferred to the Treasurer since the last annual report.

The following table shows the amount of checks on these accounts paid by the Treasurer from the dates of the establishment of the account to October 31, 1922, and the balances on deposit with the Treasurer on the latter date:

| | Checks paid by the Treasurer of the United States. | Period. | Balances with the Treasurer of the United States, Oct. 31, 1922. |
|---|---|---|---|
| Emergency Fleet Corporation........ | $6,947,051,355.78 | Feb. 28, 1918, to Oct. 31, 1922. | $54,727,519.83 |
| United States Housing Corporation... | 146,851,143.97 | July 27, 1918, to Oct. 31, 1922. | 1,265,529.15 |
| War Finance Corporation............. | 3,362,331,338.71 | June 2, 1918, to Oct. 31, 1922. | 298,226,852.86 |
| United States Grain Corporation...... | 933,967,229.41 | Oct. 31, 1918, to Feb. 2, 1922.. | (¹) |
| Russian Bureau of the War Trade Board. | 13,333,773.99 | Nov. 30, 1918, to Sept. 28, 1920. | (²) |
| Federal land banks.................. | 17,237,642.21 | June 2, 1920, to Oct. 31, 1922.. | 328.00 |
| Railroad Administration............. | 1,832,743,323.12 | Apr. 13, 1918, to Oct. 31, 1922. | 34,161,815.42 |
| United States Sugar Equalization Board (Inc.). | .................... | Apr. 7, 1922, to Oct. 31, 1922.. | 15,279,636.52 |
| United States Spruce Production Corporation. | 25,000.00 | Dec. 20, 1921, to Oct. 31, 1922. | 3,951,525.15 |
| Total.......................... | 13,253,540,807.19 | .......................... | 407,613,206.93 |

¹ Closed Feb. 2, 1922.                             ² Closed Sept. 28, 1920.

The plans worked out by the Treasury for handling these accounts have operated to the entire satisfaction of all concerned. The result has been to assure absolute security to the funds, and to save withdrawals of large amounts from the Treasury until actually needed to pay obligations of the Government, thus reducing the amount of Government borrowings with a consequent saving in interest charges.

### GOLD.

Although gold imports have continued heavy during the past year, they have been considerably lower than during the preceding year, as appears from the following table, which gives the imports and exports of gold for the fiscal years 1921 and 1922, and from July 1, 1922, to October 31, 1922:

| | Fiscal year 1921. | Fiscal year 1922. | July 1 to Oct. 31, 1922. |
|---|---|---|---|
| Gold imports | $638,559,805 | $468,318,273 | $107,409,326 |
| Gold exports | 133,537,902 | 27,345,282 | 20,589,769 |
| Net imports | 505,021,903 | 440,972,991 | 86,819,557 |

Total imports during the fiscal year 1922 showed a reduction of $170,241,532 as compared with imports during the previous 12 months. The principal imports during the fiscal year came from the following countries:

| | |
|---|---|
| France | $129,650,473 |
| England | 124,503,143 |
| Sweden | 55,294,298 |
| Germany | 19,924,893 |
| Canada | 19,509,099 |
| Denmark | 18,924,110 |
| British India | 14,863,765 |
| British Oceania | 13,011,302 |

Exports of gold between July 1, 1921, and June 30, 1922, were relatively unimportant, aggregating only $27,345,282, of which $10,025,595 went to Hongkong, $5,519,339 to British India, and $5,305,513 to Mexico.

Among the factors which have contributed to the reduction in gold imports are: (1) the decline in this country's so-called favorable balance of trade; (2) the gradual exhaustion of the supply of foreign gold available for export; (3) the cessation of gold importations by the Federal reserve banks (during the fiscal year 1921 over $100,000,000 in gold previously held for their account by the Bank of England was transferred to this country); (4) a reduction in foreign gold production, due largely to strikes; (5) the increased absorption of gold by India and other far eastern countries; and (6) the increase in the volume of foreign securities sold to American investors.

The country's stock of gold has been further augmented by gold production in the United States. During the calendar year 1921 the amount produced in this country was $50,067,300, or slightly less than during the previous year. It is estimated that the production for the first half of 1922 was at about the same rate. The amount of gold coin and bullion consumed in the industrial arts during 1921, however, is estimated at about $23,000,000, exclusive of old material reworked, leaving an estimated net addition of about $27,000,000 to the monetary stock from domestic production. The monetary stock of gold, as shown in the monthly circulation statements, has been increased by the inclusion since January 1, 1922, of gold bullion and foreign gold coin held by the Federal reserve banks and agents. Previously gold bullion and foreign gold coin were not included in the monetary stock unless actually held by the Treasury.

The total stock of monetary gold in the United States increased approximately $487,000,000 between July 1, 1921, and June 30, 1922, as compared with $589,000,000 during the previous 12 months, with about $117,000,000 additional by October 31, 1922, so that at present the stock is more than double the stock in 1913. It is estimated that at the present time the United States holds from 45 to 50 per cent of the world's stock of monetary gold, as compared with about 23 per cent prior to the outbreak of the war in 1914. The changes in the monetary stock of gold in this country since 1913 are shown in the following table:

| July 1— | Stock of monetary gold in United States (in millions of dollars). | Per cent of amount in 1913. |
|---|---|---|
| 1913 | 1,871 | 100 |
| 1914 | 1,891 | 101 |
| 1915 | 1,986 | 106 |
| 1916 | 2,450 | 131 |
| 1917 | 3,019 | 161 |
| 1918 | 3,076 | 164 |
| 1919 | 3,113 | 166 |
| 1920 | 2,709 | 145 |
| 1921 | 3,298 | 176 |
| 1922 | 3,785 | 202 |
| 1922 (Oct. 31) | 3,902 | 209 |

As in previous years, practically all of the gold imported during the past 12 months has found its way into the Federal reserve banks. Between July 1, 1921, and June 30, 1922, the gold holdings of the Federal reserve banks increased from about $2,462,000,000 to about $3,021,000,000, or 22.7 per cent, as compared with an increase of 24.9 per cent during the previous 12 months. There has been a further increase of $57,000,000 from July 1 to October 31, 1922, and at the present time approximately 78.9 per cent of the monetary stock of gold in the United States is included in the reserves of the Federal reserve banks.

The following table gives in millions of dollars the monetary stock of gold in the country on the first day of each month and the gold holdings of the Federal reserve banks about the first of each month since July 1, 1921:

[In millions of dollars.]

| Date. | Stock of monetary gold in United States. | Total gold holdings of Federal reserve banks. |
|---|---|---|
| **1921.** | | |
| July | 3,298 | 2,462 |
| August | 3,259 | 2,553 |
| September | 3,449 | 2,641 |
| October | 3,524 | 2,726 |
| November | 3,575 | 2,800 |
| December | 3,616 | 2,849 |
| **1922.** | | |
| January | 3,657 | 2,870 |
| February | 3,681 | 2,912 |
| March | 3,721 | 2,951 |
| April | 3,751 | 2,975 |
| May | 3,767 | 2,995 |
| June | 3,774 | 3,008 |
| July | 3,785 | 3,021 |
| August | 3,825 | 3,071 |
| September | 3,859 | 3,063 |
| October | 3,874 | 3,089 |
| November | 3,902 | 3,078 |
| Per cent increase from July 1, 1921, to Oct. 31, 1922 | 18.3 | 25.0 |

The Treasury has within the past year resumed the payment of gold without demand and has thus done everything within its power to restore the free and unrestricted circulation of gold. On March 18, 1922, the Secretary of the Treasury issued the following statement:

The Secretary of the Treasury announces that the Treasury has now resumed payments of gold certificates in ordinary course of business without demand, and that the Federal reserve banks throughout the country will be guided by a similar policy in making current payments for Government account. This action removes the last artificial restriction upon gold payments in this country, though gold has at all times during and since the war been freely paid out by the Treasury and the Federal reserve banks whenever demanded in payment of gold obligations.

This marks a return to the traditional policy of the United States of paying out gold certificates freely with other forms of currency, and a compliance with the spirit, as well as the letter, of the act of March 14, 1900, as amended, under which the Secretary of the Treasury is charged with the duty of maintaining the parity of all forms of money with gold.

Although gold certificates have been paid out freely by the Treasurer since March of this year, and to some extent by the Federal reserve banks in making current payments for Government account, there has been no increase in the amount held outside of the Treasury. The certificates which have been issued by the Federal reserve banks have come from their own holdings or have been obtained by exchanging gold certificates of large denominations for those of smaller denominations more suitable for use in everyday transactions. In this way the amount of gold certificates in circulation outside of the Federal reserve banks has materially increased without requiring the setting aside of additional gold as security therefor.

Under the law one-third of the gold held against gold certificates must be in the form of coin. In anticipation of an increase in the amount of gold certificates outstanding, and in order to build up the reserve stocks of the Treasury and the Federal reserve banks, the coinage of gold has been resumed at the mints. Between April 1 and November 1 of this year the amount of gold coin held in the Treasury increased by about $80,000,000 and the amount held over and above the one-third requirement against gold certificates outstanding increased from about $32,000,000 to about $119,000,000.

Coincident with the resumption of current payments in gold certificates and the coinage of gold was the resumption of the printing of gold certificates. As gold certificates had been made legal tender in 1919, the new certificates carry the legend, "This certificate is a legal tender in the amount thereof in payment of all debts and dues public and private. Acts of March 14, 1900, as amended and December 24, 1919."

No change has taken place with regard to the Treasury's attitude toward gold of Soviet origin, which, in accordance with the advice of the Department of State, is not accepted when tendered at United States mints and assay offices.

### SILVER.

Purchases of domestic silver, pursuant to the so-called Pittman Act, approved April 23, 1918, continued throughout the year, and aggregated 56,636,809 fine ounces from June 30, 1921, to June 30, 1922, inclusive. Additional purchases, amounting to 22,649,070 ounces, had been made by October 31, 1922, so that by that date 140,011,576 fine ounces of silver had been purchased out of approximately 209,000,000 ounces melted under the act. Purchases by months during the period under review were as follows:

| | Ounces. | | Ounces. |
|---|---|---|---|
| 1921—July | 4,670,119 | 1922—March | 5,370,980 |
| August | 4,913,614 | April | 8,117,748 |
| September | 3,471,436 | May | 4,122,400 |
| October | 5,917,997 | June | 5,204,750 |
| November | 3,447,000 | July | 2,841,000 |
| December | 5,424,025 | August | 8,325,000 |
| 1922—January | 2,532,000 | September | 4,377,445 |
| February | 3,444,740 | October | 7,105,625 |

Under the terms of the Pittman Act 270,232,722 silver dollars were melted, and by October 31, 1922, 144,671,473 had been recoined, the greater part of which is held to secure outstanding silver certificates.

This has greatly increased the accumulated coin in the mints, and their storage capacity will be severely taxed by the continued coinage and further accumulation of standard silver dollars for this purpose.

In accordance with the terms of the so-called Pittman Act, all purchases of silver thereunder are being made at the fixed price of $1 per fine ounce. The price of foreign silver, or silver which .can not qualify for purchase under the act, has been subject to various influences during the year, although the fluctuations have not covered as wide a range as in the years immediately preceding. The average monthly price of fine bar silver in New York during the past year is shown in the following table:

| | Price per ounce. | | Price per ounce. |
|---|---|---|---|
| 1921—July.................... | $0. 60798 | 1922—March................. | $0. 64838 |
| August.................. | . 62070 | April................... | . 67055 |
| September.............. | . 66235 | May................... | .71623 |
| October................ | .71373 | June................... | .71604 |
| November.............. | . 68470 | July.................... | . 70693 |
| December.............. | . 66250 | August................. | . 69819 |
| 1922—January................ | .65853 | September.............. | . 69888 |
| February.............. | . 65696 | October................ | . 68405 |

During the period the price of silver reached its highest point on May 22, 1922, when it was $0.741875 per fine ounce and its lowest point on July 1 and 2, 1921, when it was $0.59125 per fine ounce.

### THE MINTS.

The coinage executed by the mints at Philadelphia, Denver, and San Francisco during the fiscal year 1922 consisted principally of double eagles and standard silver dollars. The coinage of gold, which was resumed during the year, resulted in the minting of approximately $53,000,000 in double eagles. Small amounts of minor coins were struck in order to clean up partially completed lots. The accumulation of subsidiary and minor coin now in the Treasury and Federal reserve banks, it is expected, will be sufficient to last throughout the coming calendar year and will preclude the necessity of manufacturing coins of small denominations for some time to come. In addition to the manufacture of United States coins, the coinage executed for foreign countries amounted to 11,916,030 pieces. The Mint Service purchased during the fiscal year under review gold valued at $540,629,997.69.

### SOLDIERS' BONUS.

On September 19, 1922, the President vetoed H. R. 10874, the bill to provide for a soldiers' bonus or so-called adjusted compensation for veterans of the World War, and the Senate subsequently sustained the veto.

During the consideration of the measure the Secretary expressed his views with regard to the bonus in two letters, dated January 24 and March 11, 1922, to the chairman of the Committee on Ways and Means of the House of Representatives, emphasizing particularly the financial difficulties it would have involved. These letters are included herein as Exhibit 90, page 329, and Exhibit 92, page 340, respectively.

On February 16, 1922, the President stated his stand in opposition to bonus legislation, unless a sales tax should be enacted or some other provision made for raising the needed revenues, by letter to the chairman of the Committee on Ways and Means, which appears herein as Exhibit 91, page 339. A copy of the President's message vetoing the bill as subsequently passed by the Congress, is likewise included herein as Exhibit 93, page 347.

### HOSPITALIZATION.

The consultants appointed by the Secretary of the Treasury under the act of March 4, 1921, which provided for additional hospital facilities for the veterans of the World War, have already completed and turned over to the United States Veterans' Bureau the following hospitals:

| | Bed capacity. |
|---|---|
| Fort Logan H. Roots, Little Rock, Ark | 270 |
| Lake City, Fla | 100 |
| Prescott, Ariz | 422 |
| Fort McKenzie, Wyo | 245 |
| Fort Walla Walla, Wash | 165 |
| Bronx, New York City | 1,011 |
| Fort Bayard, N. Mex | 250 |
| Perryville, Md | 300 |
| Rutland, Mass | 220 |
| Augusta, Ga | 265 |
| Total | 3,248 |

It is estimated that the following additional hospitals will be completed and turned over to the Veterans' Bureau within the present fiscal year:

| | Bed capacity. |
|---|---|
| Milwaukee, Wis | 612 |
| Dayton, Ohio | 306 |
| Marion, Ind | 80 |
| Oteen, N. C | 200 |
| Palo Alto, Calif | 500 |
| Tuskegee, Ala | 596 |
| St. Louis, Mo | 250 |
| Total | 2,544 |

This leaves the tuberculosis hospitals at Chelsea, N. Y., and Aspinwall, Pa., still to be completed, making a total of 6,265 beds provided for out of this appropriation.

In order that no deficit should be created in the funds allowed by Congress under the act of March 4, 1921, a contingency which might have arisen if the whole building program had been started at once, it was necessary to delay two of the hospitals called for in the original program until it was certain that (1) all the buildings contemplated could be completed under the allotments made for them, and (2) in case additions to institutions made necessary increased central facilities that could not be foreseen at the beginning, there would be money in reserve for these new requirements. The work on the first 18 hospitals, however, has progressed so near to completion that it is now possible to proceed with the tuberculosis hospital at Chelsea, N. Y. Some delay was occasioned at the Chelsea Hospital, however, by an existing agreement between the Treasury and the Veterans' Bureau for a combined investment at the hospital there to create a 500-bed institution, and the plans were drawn and submitted to the contractors for bids with this understanding. After abiding by this joint arrangement for three months, however, the Veterans' Bureau withdrew from the agreement. It was then necessary to readjust the plans, and ask for new bids on part of the work, in order that a hospital of such size as could be undertaken would come within the limit of the funds provided by Public Act 384. As the final plans for Chelsea required more money than had been contemplated, it made necessary a modification of the plans for the hospital at Aspinwall, Pa., but these adjustments have now been completed and work at the Aspinwall institution will be started as soon as it is certain what funds can be released for it.

The final report of the activities under the act of March 4, 1921 (Public, No. 384), is nearing completion, and it is hoped will be ready before long to be submitted to Congress. This report will not only give a statement of the hospitals built under the act, but will show the studies which the consultants made preliminary to giving their advice on the location, size, and character of these hospitals. These studies indicate a method of approach to a problem which had never been faced by any Government before, that is, the long-time hospitalization of ex-soldiers for diseases contracted during their service. There are also included charts showing the distribution of population, the general relation of drafted men to population, the number of disabled men that may be expected from the age group drafted into the Army, and from diseases acknowledged as traceable to service, the present equipment in the way of hospitals in the United States, with analyses by district and State, the prospective future hospital demand, an analysis of transportation facilities, the relation of hospital care to domiciliary care, the number of beds of different types required, the standard floor plans of modern types of buildings with elevations of finished structure, etc., the future use of these hospitals, and the relation of these studies to the attempted Federal plan for hospitalization on which the work of the future may be based.

During the year several changes were made in the administration of the work connected with the care of the veterans, all tending toward greater centralization. The United States Veterans' Bureau was established by the act of August 9, 1921, and the Federal Board of Hospitalization created by Executive order in November, 1921. By the Executive order of April 29, 1922, all Public Health hospitals caring for sick and disabled veterans of the World War were transferred to the Veterans' Bureau, as were all supplies in the purveying depots of the Public Health Service purchased from funds allotted by the Director of the Veterans' Bureau, together with all supplies transferred to the Public Health Service for the use of veterans by the War and Navy Departments and other Government agencies. These changes have somewhat complicated the task of the Treasury in carrying out the provisions of the act of March 4, 1921, but through the cooperation of all concerned the work is progressing satisfactorily.

Copies of all standard plans prepared for the consultants by the Supervising Architect's Office and by the architects of the National Home for Disabled Volunteer Soldiers have been furnished to the United States Veterans' Bureau for such use as it may deem advisable, and in this way a saving of time in the construction of other hospital projects has been effected.

At the time that these hospitals were begun the construction cost was above that of normal times, and it has steadily risen since that time, especially during the last eight or nine months.

The following resolution was adopted by the National Tuberculosis Association on May 6, 1922:

Whereas, one of the results of the recent war has been the necessity that the United States Government provide hospital care for a very large number of ex-service men suffering, not only from injuries, but from a number of chronic diseases, including tuberculosis, nephritis, diabetes, and mental diseases, and

Whereas, the Secretary of the Treasury has provided, through a board of consultants and its advisory committee, representing national voluntary health bodies, a carefully studied and comprehensive Federal hospital program. Therefore, be it

Resolved, That this Association hereby expresses its hearty approval and appreciation of the action of the Secretary of the Treasury and of the work of the board of consultants which he appointed.

Thanks are due to the National Tuberculosis Association, the National Committee for Mental Hygiene, the United States Veterans' Bureau, the Federal Board of Hospitalization, the National Home for Disabled Volunteer Soldiers, the War Department, the Navy Department, the Catholic Hospital Association, and the principal and trustees of the Tuskegee Normal and Industrial Institute for their cooperation and help in the progress of this work of hospitalization.

A detailed statement showing hospitals completed and in process of construction on November 13, 1922, will be found as Exhibit No. 89, on page 328.

### PUBLIC HEALTH.

The policy undertaken last year of stationing officers in various ports of Europe, as well as in ports of Mexico, South America, and the Orient, for the purpose of assisting in the enforcement of the United States quarantine regulations, has proved of signal advantage, and will be extended where necessary. The Federal quarantine facilities will, however, require further improvement and extension in order to provide proper protection against the introduction of various diseases.

The Public Health Service has maintained during the year its interstate relationships, with satisfactory results: plague-suppressive measures have been continued at New Orleans, Galveston, Beaumont, and San Francisco, and rodent surveys have also been continued in other parts of the United States to determine the possible presence of plague.

In connection with the work for the prevention of venereal diseases, 16 institutes were held during the year. These were attended by more than 6,000 persons from all parts of the United States. The meetings proved of great value. Both the number and character of the attendance showed the intelligent interest of the country in this branch of public health work.

The research work of the service has made progress and could be extended with great advantage into other fields, notably cancer and tuberculosis.

The collection and dissemination of information regarding the prevalence of disease, and the publication of Public Health Reports and other statistical data have continued as heretofore.

No epidemic of serious proportions has occurred in the United States during the past year. Unless the present disturbed economic and industrial conditions in Europe improve, however, it is possible that there will be an increase in the prevalence of certain diseases, and it is more than ever important that the Public Health Service have sufficient facilities to provide protection against the introduction of epidemic diseases into this country.

A radical change in the hospital work of this service took place during the year. Forty-seven hospitals acquired since the war and operating for the care of the disabled veterans were transferred to the

United States Veterans' Bureau by the Executive order of April 29, 1922.[1] This definitely terminated the responsibility of the Public Health Service for providing medical care and treatment to veterans. The hospital work of the service thus resumes the status which existed previous to 1919. The number of beneficiaries other than veterans has, however, increased very much since that time and this increase promises to continue. The 24 hospitals remaining under the operation of the Public Health Service, moreover, have received only slight repairs during the stress of emergency work, when they were constantly filled to capacity. No extensive enlargements were possible and the establishments require general rehabilitation and, in many instances, reconstruction along more modern lines.

Numerous requests have been received from other branches of the Government that the Public Health Service make medical examinations of persons entering the Government service, as well as periodic examinations of those already employed, and provide facilities for the prompt relief of injuries sustained in line of duty, as is contemplated under the employees' compensation act. The industrial medical service, begun among employees of the Public Health Service early in the past year, has accordingly been extended to other Government departments. This service has attempted to eliminate unnecessary absenteeism from sickness and other causes in the same manner as has been done by private industrial concerns. As an example of what can be accomplished by this means, the records of one department where it has been in operation show a marked decrease in the daily average of absences from all causes.

With the transfer of the hospitals to the United States Veterans' Bureau there was, of course, a large reduction in the personnel of the Public Health Service both in Washington and in the field. There are 900 commissioned reserve officers of the Public Health Service now serving in the United States Veterans' Bureau. These changes in the personnel of the Public Health Service have made necessary certain readjustments which are still in progress and which will not be completed for some months to come.

## PUBLIC BUILDINGS.

During the past year construction costs have not permitted any general resumption of the construction of public buildings under authorizations heretofore made. Nevertheless, in every instance where local conditions appeared favorable bids have been solicited by public advertisement and, when acceptable proposals have been received, contracts have been made, and building operations promptly

---

[1] See Exhibit 88, page 325.

begun. During the same period the activities of the Supervising Architect's Office have been concentrated effectively upon the work of designing and constructing hospital buildings for the care of veterans of the World War. The construction of public buildings proper, and of hospitals for the Public Health Service and Veterans' Bureau, including additional facilities for hospitalization at plants already established, is shown in detail in the abstract of the report of the Supervising Architect's Office, which accompanies this report, pages 413 to 418. In this abstract will also be found statements showing the public building work authorized by Congress, the financial operations of the Supervising Architect's Office for the fiscal year ended June 30, 1922, and a classification of buildings, by titles, with expenditures for each class, prepared pursuant to the act approved June 6, 1900 (31 Stat. 592).

## National Archives Building.

The urgent need for a suitable building in Washington for the preservation of the archives of the Government is beyond question, and recommendations that provision be made therefor have been urged upon the attention of Congress from time to time by the Secretaries of the Treasury in their reports upon the state of the finances. The accumulation of war records has aggravated the situation, and the need for additional storage facilities is becoming more and more pressing. The construction of such a building, moreover, would release for other purposes much valuable space in the executive departments and independent establishments which is now taken up with records and files. Many of the Government's records, though their loss would be irreparable, are now stored in nonfireproof buildings, where they are in constant jeopardy. An estimate of the appropriation necessary to acquire a suitable site, centrally located, has again been submitted by the Treasury, and it is hoped that favorable action will be taken at an early date.

## Contractors' war claims.

In examining contractors' war claims the available clerical force that could be assigned to that duty was augmented by the detail to Washington for the period allowed by law of such superintendents of construction as could be spared. In the absence of legislation authorizing further detail of superintendents of construction to aid in this work, it became necessary to reassign those employees to the field, and the settlement of claims has thus been more or less hampered by the lack of an adequate force. A summary of the claims filed and a statement of their status as of June 30, 1922, appear on page 417 in the abstract of the report of the Supervising Architect's Office.

## Post-office buildings.

As the increase of the postal business bears so definite a relation to the economic growth of the country, it is not surprising to find that there are at the present time many localities where the facilities for handling the mails have become inadequate, and where the continued use of Federal buildings constructed many years ago involves a great sacrifice of time and efficiency. It is hoped that Congress in the near future will authorize such remedial measures as may be necessary to provide for the situation, particularly in certain larger cities where the Government is confronted with serious difficulties in its efforts to give efficient mail service. It is also recommended that Congress consider the advisability of eliminating from any post-office building program the construction of post-office buildings in small communities where the interests of the community, as well as the interest of the Government, are effectively served by having the postal business carried on in rented quarters. In such small communities the interest on investment, upkeep, operating expenses, and depreciation of a Government-owned building are out of all proportion to the benefits derived either by the Government or the public.

The policy suggested, taken in connection with the present practice of using standardized types of post-office buildings, would promote economies in Government operations.

### BUREAU OF WAR RISK INSURANCE.

The Bureau of War Risk Insurance continued as a part of the Treasury Department during the early part of the fiscal year until the passage of the Sweet bill, on August 9, 1921, when it was merged into the newly created United States Veterans' Bureau. The Bureau of War Risk Insurance was originally established September 2, 1914, for the purpose of providing adequate facilities for insurance of the commerce of this country against the risks of war, and, after our entry into the war, grew to be one of the largest bureaus of the Treasury, having 5,025 employees on the date of its disconnection from the department.

### SOLDIERS' AND SAILORS' CIVIL RELIEF BONDS.

During the past year the United States Veterans' Bureau, in cooperation with the Treasury and the Comptroller General, instituted measures looking toward final settlement with life insurance companies and associations which continued insurance for members of the Military and Naval Establishments of the United States under guaranty by the Government, as authorized by the act approved March 8, 1918, entitled, "Soldiers' and sailors' civil relief act." United States bonds, known as "Soldiers' and sailors' civil relief bonds," had been issued from time to time to the insurers in connection with this guaranty, according to the general plan described in the .communication from the Director of the Budget to the President and by the President transmitted to the Speaker of the House of Representatives, under date of May 6, 1922, which reads, in part, as follows:

Article IV of the act of March 8, 1918, provided in effect that the Bureau of War Risk Insurance would under certain circumstances guarantee payment of premiums owing by persons in the military or naval service on policies of life insurance to the companies in which such policies were taken out. The purpose of this article was to prevent the lapsation of such policies for nonpayment of premiums while the insured was in the military or naval service. It is provided by section 408 of said article that the Secretary of the Treasury should within a certain time deliver to the proper officer of each insurance company bonds of the United States to be held by such insurance companies as a pledge for the payment of unpaid premiums owing by such persons in the military or naval service. It is provided by section 412 of that article that at the expiration of one year after the termination of the war there should be an account stated between each insurer and the United States. And section 413 provides that the balance in favor of the insurer should in each case be paid to the insurer by the United States upon the surrender by the insurer of the bonds delivered to it from time to time by the Secretary of the Treasury.

In the third deficiency appropriation act for the fiscal year 1922, approved July 1, 1922, Congress granted the authority and appropriation requested, and in due course final settlements will be made and the outstanding bonds will be retired. It is expected that the transactions will be completely closed by the end of the present calendar year.

Total issues of United States bonds as guaranties for payment of premiums under the act in question amounted to $195,500. By June 30, 1922, $144,600 had been retired, and accordingly there were outstanding on that date $50,900. It is understood that the amount appropriated by Congress, $25,000, will be sufficient to cover net losses to the United States on this account, and permit the retirement of the bonds which remain outstanding.

### THE COAST GUARD.

The results of the operations of the Coast Guard during the year have been most gratifying. The total number of persons saved or rescued from peril was 2,954, or 1,333 more than in 1921. The number of persons on board vessels assisted was 14,531. The instances of lives saved and vessels assisted numbered 2,224, and the instances of miscellaneous assistance rendered by the various agencies of the service numbered 1,535, a total of 3,759 as against 2,788 for the year 1921. The value of vessels (including cargoes) assisted during the year was $35,346,765.

In the interest of the enforcement of the laws of the United States, 21,586 vessels were boarded and examined during the year by units of this service.

The other duties with which the Coast Guard is charged, aside from those pertaining directly to the conservation of life and property from shipwreck, include: International service of ice observation and ice patrol, conducted under the terms of the international convention for the safety of life at sea; winter cruising for the better protection of shipping during the stormy season from December 1 to March 31; the patrol of the waters of the North Pacific Ocean, Bering Sea, and southeastern Alaska; enforcement of the rules and regulations governing the anchorage and movements of vessels in the navigable waters of the United States; the removal of derelicts and other floating dangers from the paths of navigation; the enforcement of the customs, navigation, and motor-boat laws of the United States; patrolling and supervising regattas and marine parades; the examination of applicants for "certificated lifeboat men," under the seamen's act; rendering medical aid to deep-sea fishermen, etc. The purpose of the patrol of the waters of the North Pacific Ocean, Bering Sea, and Southeastern Alaska is to enforce, (1) the convention of July 7, 1911, between the United States, Great Britain, Russia, and Japan; (2) the act of August 24, 1912, for the protection of the fur seal and the sea otter; and (3) the laws and regulations for the protection of game, fisheries, and fur-bearing animals of Alaska.

Splendid service was rendered by the Coast Guard last spring during and after the devastating floods which swept the valleys of the Ohio and Mississippi Rivers, and their tributaries, inundating vast areas of land and causing widespread destruction. The department dispatched the Coast Guard Cutters *Kankakee* and *Yocona* to what appeared to be the best points of vantage in the flooded territory, and also called on members of the four Coast Guard stations at and in the vicinity of Chicago, Ill., for assistance. Through the labors of those assigned to this expedition and their cooperation with local and other relief agencies at work in the flooded regions, tons of foodstuffs were transported and hundreds of persons were rescued from positions of peril and taken to places of safety, with their live stock, household goods, and other belongings. When the flood had subsided, the *Yocona* made a cruise in the lower Mississippi and picked up 300 refugees, with their personal effects, and returned them to their homes. The cutter on this cruise also collected more than 1,000 head of live stock, which were delivered to the owners. The work of the Coast Guard in this connection has elicited warm praise from the affected territories.

The Secretary of the Treasury awarded 30 life-saving medals of honor of the second class (silver) during the year, under the provisions of law, in recognition of bravery exhibited in the rescue or attempted rescue of persons in danger of drowning.

The attention of Congress is invited to the remarks in the Annual Report for 1921 concerning the provisions for promotion in the commissioned grades of the Coast Guard. The bill to correct the harmful situation occasioned by the slow and limited promotion of the commissioned personnel is still pending in Congress. It has progressed to the point of a favorable report by the Committee on Interstate and Foreign Commerce of the House of Representatives, and the Treasury ventures to urge again that it be enacted into law.

### BUREAU OF ENGRAVING AND PRINTING.

The Bureau of Engraving and Printing delivered within the year 416,820,113 sheets of engraved securities and other Government paper of all kinds, a decrease from the previous year of 21,874,711 sheets. The face value of perfect sheets delivered amounted to $14,915,115,872.08, a decrease of $7,726,447,806.63 as compared with the fiscal year 1921.

The number of employees was reduced from 6,950 on July 1, 1921, to 5,683 on June 30, 1922, exclusive of 346 on indefinite furlough, showing a net reduction of 1,267 for the year.

### NEW CURRENCY DESIGNS.

In the last report to Congress reference was made to the plans of the Treasury for the revision of the designs for paper currency. Problems have arisen in connection with the preparation of the models which have called for further study during the year, but progress is now being made and it is expected that within the current year new designs will be developed which will meet with general approval from both the protective and the artistic viewpoints.

### INTER-AMERICAN HIGH COMMISSION.

The United States section of the Inter-American High Commission remained under the jurisdiction of the Secretary of the Treasury during only a part of the fiscal year 1922. It had become manifest that the work of the commission was more closely related to the Department of Commerce than to the Treasury Department. At the request of the Secretary of the Treasury, therefore, the President relieved him of the chairmanship of the section, and on November 17, 1921, designated the Secretary of Commerce as chairman, the Secretary of the Treasury remaining as honorary chairman.

The attention of the section during the period when the Secretary of the Treasury was chairman was concentrated on two subjects: (1) the exchanges between the American Republics and (2) the compilation of accurate and complete data on financial conditions in the

American Republics. The United States section invited the other sections of the commission to collaborate on a survey of the various factors affecting directly or indirectly the course of exchange between the American countries. At the time of the change in direction of the section's work, meetings of all the sections had been scheduled, and several of them were held before the end of the calendar year 1921. An account of the conclusions reached by these meetings and the recommendations made will be found in the report of the present chairman of the section.

Revision of the economic and financial reports prepared by the United States section continued during the first half of the fiscal year. These reports were consulted by an increasing number of financial and commercial representatives, as well as by the members of the group committees. They are based in large part upon official economic, financial, and commercial reports and represent an attempt to assemble available data covering the several Republics on such topics as the national debt, systems of banking and currency, the budget, sources of revenue, and objects of expenditures.

#### DISTRICT OF COLUMBIA TEACHERS' RETIREMENT FUND.

Pursuant to the provisions of the act of January 15, 1920, as amended, there was placed to the credit of the District of Columbia teachers' retirement fund $217,356.92 during the fiscal year 1922. Upon the advice of the Commissioners of the District of Columbia, Liberty bonds, aggregating $236,300, face amount, were purchased during the year for the fund. This brings the face amount of the investments held by the Treasurer for this fund up to $463,750, consisting entirely of 4¼ per cent Liberty bonds. In addition to these bonds there was an unexpended balance of $21,897.36, including funds for investment with the Treasurer on June 30, 1922.

#### UNITED STATES GOVERNMENT LIFE INSURANCE FUND.

Under the provisions of section 18 of the act approved December 24, 1919, the Secretary of the Treasury is authorized to invest and reinvest in interest-bearing obligations of the United States all moneys received in payment of premiums on converted insurance in excess of the amount required for authorized payments or reserve. The administration of the fund is vested in the Director of the United States Veterans' Bureau, and investments are made by the Secretary from time to time upon the basis of reports received from the director as to the amounts available for investment. All investments through the fiscal year 1922 are in Liberty bonds bearing 4¼ per cent interest, and on June 30, 1922, amounted in the aggregate to $60,077,650, face amount, of which $25,625,750 were purchased during the fiscal year 1922. The securities so purchased are held in trust by the Secretary of the Treasury for account of the fund, and are verified from time to time through reports to the Director. The following statement shows the holdings of the fund by loans, as of June 30, 1922:

|  | Par value. |
|---|---|
| First Liberty loan converted 4¼ per cent bonds | $5,584,600 |
| Second Liberty loan converted 4¼ per cent bonds | 16,932,400 |
| Fourth Liberty loan 4¼ per cent bonds | 37,560,650 |
| Total | 60,077,650 |

### THE CIVIL-SERVICE RETIREMENT AND DISABILITY FUND.

Section 8 of the act of May 22, 1920, requires the Secretary of the Treasury to cause deductions to be withheld from all specific appropriations for salaries or compensation of those employees of the Government to whom the act applies, equal to 2½ per cent of such employees' basic pay or compensation, and to transfer the amounts so ascertained on the books of the Treasury to the credit of the "Civil-service retirement and disability fund" which is appropriated for the payment of annuities, refunds, and allowances as provided in the act. The Secretary of the Treasury is further directed to invest from time to time in interest-bearing securities of the United States such portions of the civil-service retirement and disability fund as in his judgment may not be immediately required for the payment of the annuities, etc., the income derived from such investments to constitute a part of the fund. Under these provisions $17,984,250, face amount, Liberty loan bonds had been purchased up to the close of business June 30, 1922, of which $8,120,000 consists of second Liberty loan converted 4¼ per cent bonds, and $9,864,250 of fourth Liberty loan 4¼ per cent bonds. These bonds are all registered in the name of the Secretary of the Treasury for account of the civil-service retirement and disability fund, and are held in safe-keeping by the Division of Loans and Currency of the Secretary's office. The earnings on investments and reinvestments to June 30, 1922, amounted to $649,399.14.

Under the provisions of section 4 of the act, the administration of the fund is vested in the Commissioner of Pensions, under the direction of the Secretary of the Interior. Section 16 of the act requires the Board of Actuaries, one of whom is the Government Actuary, to report annually upon the actual operations of the act, and invests this Board of Actuaries with authority to recommend to the Commissioner of Pensions such changes as in its judgment may be necessary to protect the public interest and maintain the system upon a sound financial basis.

## SURETY BONDS.

On June 30, 1922, there were 32 surety companies holding certificates of authority issued by the Secretary of the Treasury to execute bonds running to the United States, as provided in the act of Congress of August 13, 1894, and the amendment of March 23, 1910. There were also four companies organized in foreign countries, operating through branch offices in the United States, which were authorized to act only as reinsurers on bonds and other undertakings running to the United States. During the current fiscal year four new companies have qualified to transact business with the United States, and the certificate of authority of one company has been revoked.

The regulations applicable to surety companies authorized to do business with the Government, as originally embodied in Treasury Department Circular No. 54, issued under date of September 21, 1910, have been revised during the period under review, and are now in harmony with the insurance laws of the several States. A copy of this circular appears as Exhibit 82 in this report, page 308.

There appears to be an almost constant increase in the number of indemnity and surety bonds running in favor of the United States. The number of bonds executed annually is approximately 200,000 These bonds have to be examined and approved as to sureties by the Treasury Department, with the exception of certain bonds involved in the operation of the Postal Service, bonds of alien emigrants, and some other miscellaneous bonds in which the Treasury has only an indirect interest. During the past ten years the number of bonding companies which have received certificates of authority from the Secretary of the Treasury to execute bonds running to the United States has more than doubled, and the work imposed by law in the audit of the financial reports of the companies has correspondingly increased. This additional work has had to be performed by means of details from other organizations, the statutory provisions for clerical assistance proving insufficient each year.

The experience of the Treasury in dealing with insolvent bonding companies has clearly shown that the present method of supervision over bonding companies and the control of data relating to bonds executed by them is not adequate, and that the public interest would be better served by centralized control of the entire bonding work of the Federal Government in one office, which would be a clearing house for all bonds executed in favor of the United States. The records of this office would show the number, class, and character of all bonds outstanding and executed by each company, and this data would materially aid the Government in the preparation and filing of claims against insolvent surety companies. Under the present method, with the bonding work scattered through the Federal service and each department and office acting independently, without centralized recording, it is almost impossible to state all claims. There are now pending for settlement Government claims against such companies amounting to about one million dollars. All told, about 35 companies have become insolvent, merged with other companies, or voluntarily retired from business during the history of corporate suretyship on Federal bonds, and of this number about 15 have gone into liquidation by reason of insolvency.

The General Accounting Office is the natural office to take over this work and establish the centralized control and records, and the Treasury has accordingly given its approval to the proposed transfer of the surety bond work now performed by the Treasury to the Comptroller General of the United States. This will require legislation, and it is understood that the Comptroller General has already prepared a bill for submission to Congress which it is hoped will receive early and favorable consideration.

### TREASURY ORGANIZATION.

The principal changes in Treasury organization during the past year were: (1) The creation of a Budget and Improvement Committee for the preparation and examination of Treasury estimates of appropriations and for the improvement of administrative methods and procedure within the Treasury; (2) the establishment of a Bureau of Supply to act as a central purchasing agency in and for the Treasury; and (3) the transfer on May 1, 1922, of 47 operating hospitals, with a total bed capacity of about 17,500, containing approximately 13,000 patients, and a total operating personnel of about 11,500, from the Public Health Service to the United States Veterans' Bureau by Executive Order dated April 29, 1922. This transfer completed the consolidation of all activities with respect to the veterans' relief in the United States Veterans' Bureau and relieved the Public Health Service of all responsibility for providing medical care and treatment of veterans.

### Budget and Improvement Committee.

Concurrently with the establishment of the Bureau of the Budget in the latter part of June, 1921, the President announced his determination to reduce Government expenditures to the minimum amount consistent with proper administration, and called upon all branches of the Government to cooperate in improving business methods and eliminating waste. The Treasury Department, through its budget officer and his assistants, has done its utmost to carry out this program, and with highly gratifying results. On July 1, 1921, the Bureau of the Budget, by direction of the President, called upon the head of each department to examine carefully into its needs for the fiscal year 1922 to determine what part of the funds already appropriated were indispensable in carrying on the work of the department, the remaining portion of each appropriation to be set apart as a general reserve. As a result of the survey of the Treasury Department, there was set aside in the general reserve $9,079,208.34. Subsequently reserves aggregating $596,210.25 were added, and from time to time reserves amounting in all to $4,716,044.76 were released leaving a net general reserve of $4,959,373.83, which may be regarded as the Treasury's savings for the year. In addition, deferred expenditures on account of appropriations for construction of buildings, acquisition of sites, etc., amounted to $20,941,287.40.

On July 8, 1922, a budget and improvement committee was appointed to assist in the preparation and examination of Treasury estimates for appropriations, and to study existing procedure within the department with the view of improving methods of work and bringing about a more effective organization. (See Exhibit 85, page 316.)

The committee first took up the department estimates for the fiscal year 1924. Each member was assigned to one or more bureaus or offices and was charged with the special study of its activities and requirements. Subsequently the estimates for each bureau or office were considered in detail by the entire committee in conference with responsible officials, and each item was subjected to the test of whether, in view of the urgent necessity for economy, it was absolutely necessary that the full amount requested be included in the estimates. The recommendations of the committee were reviewed by the budget officer, and the department estimates as finally approved and submitted to the Bureau of the Budget were in the aggregate $18,336,647.75 less than those originally submitted by the various bureaus and offices.

Although the department estimates for the fiscal year 1923 had been carefully revised before submission and the appropriations made by Congress were much below the estimates, heads of bureaus and offices were called upon at the beginning of the fiscal year to make a survey with the view of ascertaining whether any part of the appropriations made might be set apart as a departmental reserve to be used only for urgent needs arising later in the year and then only on the approval of the Secretary. Estimates submitted by the heads of bureaus and offices as to the amounts which might be thus set aside amounted to $233,701.80. After review of the needs of all bureaus and offices by the budget and improvement committee in conference with the responsible officials, additional reserves of $914,585.50 were set up making a total of $1,148,287.30 for the year 1923.

Aside from its work in connection with estimates, the budget and improvement committee will conduct a continuous study of the organization and business methods of the department with the view of inaugurating improvements wherever possible. From time to time special subjects are referred to it for investigation, and other subjects the committee takes up on its own motion.

## Bureau of Supply.

Under the provisions of Treasury Department Circular No. 283, dated March 28, 1922, a bureau of supply was established in the Treasury Department, effective as of April 1, 1922. The bureau was given powers broad enough to cover the purchase of material and supplies for all bureaus, divisions, offices, and services in the Treasury Department in Washington and in the field, except the Bureau of Engraving and Printing and the purchase of distinctive paper for Government securities.

The order of June 16, 1922, supplementing Circular No. 283, directed that the bureaus concerned detail to the bureau of supply such clerical and other personnel as were devoting any substantial part of their time to the purchase, handling, or distribution of supplies, or to the keeping of records in connection therewith. This order further directed that such appropriations or parts of appropriations as provided for the purchase of supplies should be allotted to the bureau of supply. The first definite step toward effecting this centralization was taken on July 1, 1922, when the supply functions formerly conducted by the chief clerk and appropriations incident thereto, were transferred to the bureau of supply. Similar action was taken between July 1 and September 30, 1922, by the following: Division of Printing and Stationery, Division of Bookkeeping and Warrants, office of the Treasurer of the United States, Bureau of Internal Revenue, office of the Commissioner of the Public Debt, and the Public Health Service.

The work of this bureau is carried on entirely by employees detailed from the various offices of the Treasury from which the supply functions have been transferred. The 76 employees now on detail consist of clerks, messengers, and laborers. This number may be slightly increased when all of the supply functions of the several Treasury offices have been taken over, but it is expected that as soon as the organization is further perfected the work can be carried on with less personnel than heretofore.

In addition to the ultimate reduction in personnel, it is expected that economies will be effected mainly in three ways: (1) By consolidating stocks and surplus supplies; (2) by standardizing certain supplies to permit purchase in large quantities; and (3) by centralizing accounting, thereby enabling the department to pay vouchers promptly and so benefit by taking cash discounts whenever available.

A copy of Department Circular No. 283 of March 28, 1922, is attached as Exhibit 83, page 313, and the supplemental department order of June 16, 1922, as Exhibit 84, page 314.

### General Supply Committee.

During the fiscal year 1922, the General Supply Committee executed 811 contracts covering 12,792 separate items. The purchases for the fiscal year amounted to $6,777,022.89, including $685,097.35 for supplies purchased by the departments from surplus property held by the committee. The decrease from the amount purchased in the fiscal year 1921 is due chiefly to generally lower prices. In order to benefit by the descending scale of prices, many short-term contracts were executed, instead of the customary contracts for the period of a year. Whenever possible, a clause was inserted in the long-term contracts guaranteeing to the Government the benefit of any reduction in price, and where this clause was not inserted a reduction was often granted when the attention of the contractors was called to the variance between market and contract prices.

Estimates of their requirements for a given period were obtained from the Government departments and establishments in Washington, and better prices were secured by soliciting proposals for furnishing these quantities as a whole at f. o. b. rates. Previously, the term contracts under which purchases were made had provided for the delivery, within the storeroom doors of the departments, of such amounts as should be called for from time to time, with no agreement for any definite quantity. With uncertainty as to the quantities removed, and the cost of delivering the supplies eliminated, it is possible to obtain contracts at much lower prices. Substantial economy will result, therefore, from the ability to purchase ordinary supplies used in Washington in definite quantities with specified dates of delivery, and from the storing and distributing of such supplies from a central warehouse.

Surplus property.—Surplus property valued at $1,138,700.35 was transferred to the committee, of which $685,097.35 was reissued to other departments. The proceeds of sales of unserviceable and obsolete equipment amounted to $79,595.35. The invoice value of surplus property on hand July 1, 1922, was approximately $2,000,000.

During the fiscal year the department received 17,081 typewriters, and 3,263 of these have already been overhauled and reissued to other branches of the Government all over the United States. About $330,000 worth of miscellaneous stationery was received from the Navy Department out of its surplus stock in various depots, and about 10 per cent of this stock has already been reissued to departments in the District of Columbia.

Attention is called to the necessity for proper storage space for surplus property at present kept in temporary wooden buildings at East Potomac Park. These buildings, intended for use as temporary barracks, are highly inflammable and poorly suited for storage. Constant work and expenditure is required to maintain them in condition to avoid serious damage to their contents.

A statement showing the progress of the reissuance of surplus property, as provided for under the Executive order of December 3, 1918, is given on page 453.

*Proposal for a central purchasing agency.*—The work of the General Supply Committee has demonstrated that it is now opportune to establish a central purchasing agency for the Government as a whole, so that economies may be effected by taking advantage of seasonal reductions, favorable trade conditions, purchasing in large quantities. from manufacturers, and prompt discounting of bills. The cost of such a central agency would not be great, and it is recommended that. this matter be given early consideration.

### PERSONNEL.

After the transfer to the General Accounting Office of 2,372 employees at the close of the last fiscal year, the aggregate personnel of the Treasury on July 1, 1921, was 77,924. By the end of the fiscal year 1922, the number had been further reduced by 17,615 to 60,309. The following table shows the number of employees in the departmental and field services of the Treasury on July 1, 1921, and on June 30, 1922:

|  | July 1, 1921. | June 30, 1922. | Decrease. |
|---|---|---|---|
| Departmental service: |  |  |  |
| Public Health | 703 | 248 | 455 |
| War Risk | 4,793 | .......... | 4,793 |
| Others | 20,388 | 19,346 | 1,042 |
| Total | 25,884 | 19,594 | 6,290 |
| Field service: |  |  |  |
| Public Health | 22,375 | [1] 9,110 | 13,265 |
| War Risk | 302 | .......... | 302 |
| Others | 29,363 | 31,605 | [2] 2,242 |
| Total | 52,040 | 40,715 | 11,325 |
| Total in Treasury | 77,924 | 60,309 | 17,615 |

[1] Includes 4,166 receiving $1 per year.          [2] Increase.

On August 9, 1921, the entire personnel of the Bureau of War Risk Insurance, then numbering 5,025, was transferred to the newly created United States Veterans' Bureau. A further reduction in the number of employees in both the departmental and field services. occurred on May 1, 1922, when 11,077 employees of the Public

Health Service were also transferred to the Veterans' Bureau. Other reductions effected in the offices of the Treasurer, the chief clerk of the Treasury, the Bureau of Engraving and Printing, and the Division of Loans and Currency brought the number of employees in the departmental service down to 19,594 on July 1, 1922. Between that date and September 30, 1922, there has been a further decrease of 688 employees. A classified statement of the number of employees in the departmental service of the Treasury at the close of each month from July, 1921, to September, 1922, will be found as Exhibit 86, page 317.

The increase of 2,242 employees in the field services during the year was largely in the Internal Revenue Service, and is accounted for by the number of additional agents necessary to enforce the national prohibition act, and additional field auditors in connection with the audit of income-tax returns. By September 30, 1922, the personnel of the field services had been increased to a total of 41,081, the greater part of this increase being in the Internal Revenue Service.

### RETIREMENT OF CIVIL SERVICE EMPLOYEES.

On June 7, 1922, the President by Executive order extended the provisions of the retirement act to include certain unclassified employees receiving $600 or more per annum; and on June 17, 1922, Congress passed an amendment to the retirement act extending its provisions to include certain unclassified employees receiving less than $600 per annum, thereby enabling the department to retire a large number of employees of these classes who had reached the retirement age and to replace them with younger and more active persons. At the same time the act permits the department to give employees in these groups who have become old in the service something upon which to live after retirement. The retirement act was further amended on September 22, 1922, by an act extending its provisions, with certain modifications, to include employees 55 years of age or over who have served for a total period of not less than 15 years and who shall become involuntarily separated from the service before reaching the retirement age, unless removed for cause on charges of misconduct or delinquency preferred against them.

In this connection attention is invited to the suggestions made in the Annual Report of the Secretary of the Treasury for the year 1921: (1) that the age limit for retirement should be lowered from 70 years to not more than 68 years, and (2) that the annuities granted under the retirement act should be increased. The present annuities are not sufficient in themselves to support with any degree of comfort those who are retired, and I believe that somewhat more liberal provisions would be justified.

The following table shows the number of persons retired from the service in the Treasury Department, their combined salaries, the number to whom annuities have been granted, and the amounts of annuities for the period from July 1, 1921, to September 30, 1922:

| Employees retired. | Departmental service. | | Field service. | |
|---|---|---|---|---|
| | Number. | Salaries. | Number. | Salaries. |
| On account of age.................................... | 107 | $152,255.00 | 165 | $208,677.00 |
| On account of age (piece rate)........................ | 29 | 64,218.03 | [1] 19 | ............. |
| On account of total disability......................... | 31 | 39,320.00 | 23 | 37,360 00 |
| On account of total disability (piece rate)............. | 9 | 14,539.71 | ........ | ........ |
| Total........................................ | 176 | 270,332.74 | 207 | 246,037.00 |

[1] Employees retired who received fees, the amount of which is not readily obtainable.

RECAPITULATION.

| | Departmental service. | Field service. |
|---|---|---|
| Number granted annuities........................................ | 157 | 140 |
| Number not granted annuities.................................... | 5 | 11 |
| Number of applications pending before Pension Bureau........................ | 12 | 42 |
| Number of applications not received............................. | 2 | 12 |
| Number died before making application............................ | ........... | 2 |
| Total........................................................ | 176 | 207 |
| Amount of annuities granted.................................... | $91,335 87 | $73,963.41 |

### ADMISSION TO PRACTICE BEFORE THE TREASURY DEPARTMENT.

Treasury Department Circular No. 230, governing the recognition of attorneys and agents to practice before the department, originally issued February 15, 1921, was revised and reissued April 25, 1922 (Exhibit 81, p. 298), with a number of important changes, the necessity for which had been demonstrated by experience.

Under the regulations as amended all applications for enrollment must be individual, and all practice before the department must be as individuals or as partnerships. Corporations cannot be enrolled, and officers or employees of a corporation who are enrolled as individuals are not permitted to act for the corporation in representing claimants and others before the department. This is in accordance with the general rule of legal practice, and is intended to give the department the benefit of the sense of personal responsibility which does not attach to the corporate form of doing business. In addition to the restrictions imposed by section 190, Revised Statutes, no former officer or employee of the Treasury Department is permitted to appear in a representative capacity before the department in any matter to which he gave actual personal consideration or as to the facts of which he had actual personal knowledge while in the service of the department. Advertising by enrolled attorneys or agents is required to be limited to the name and address of the attorney or agent and a brief description of his practice, with a mention of any special field of practice, if desired. Advertisements which describe the capacity or ability of an attorney or agent or which are so worded as to imply official capacity or connection with the Government, or advertising or solicitation which makes any suggestion of previous connection with the department or acquaintance with its officials or employees, or any reference to the fact of enrollment, are specifically forbidden. The solicitation of business by circulars, advertisements, or other means, including communications or interviews not warranted by previous or personal relations with the person addressed, is forbidden. While contingent fees may be proper in some cases before the department, they are not looked upon with favor and may be made the ground of suspension or disbarment. Both their reasonableness in view of the service rendered and all the attendant circumstances are made a proper subject of inquiry by the department.

These amendments to the regulations were designed to establish a standard of conduct for enrolled attorneys and agents equal to that established by bar associations or by associations of public accountants. The revised regulations have met with the approval of those attorneys and accountants who subscribe to the codes of ethics of their professions, and the department has received their active support and assistance in detecting and bringing to account enrolled attorneys or agents who have violated the regulations.

The committee on enrollment and disbarment of attorneys and agents was enlarged and reorganized on January 1, 1922. The reorganized committee has met twice each week, or oftener when necessary, for the purpose of passing on applications for enrollment and considering complaints against persons already enrolled.

During the fiscal year under review, 4,866 applications for enrollment as attorneys and agents were approved and 81 applications were rejected. Two enrolled attorneys were disbarred from practice before the department and one enrolled agent was suspended for a period of 90 days. Applications for enrollment are still being received at the rate of several hundred each month.

### PANAMA CANAL.

The general fund of the Treasury was charged during the fiscal year 1922 with $3,687,362.85 on account of the Panama Canal, including $2,791,035.40 for maintenance and construction work and $896,327.45 for fortifications and miscellaneous expenditures. The general fund was credited during the year with $12,049,660.65 of receipts from tolls, etc., making an excess of receipts for the year of $8,362,297.80. The total amount expended for canal construction, fortifications, maintenance, and operation, together with the amount of interest paid on Panama Canal loans up to the close of the fiscal year 1922, is shown in the following table:

| Year. | Construction, maintenance, and operation. | Fortifications. | Total. | Interest paid on Panama Canal loans. |
|---|---|---|---|---|
| 1903 | $9,985.00 | .............. | $9,985.00 | .............. |
| 1904 | 50,164,500.00 | .............. | 50,164,500.00 | .............. |
| 1905 | 3,918,819.83 | .............. | 3,918,819.83 | .............. |
| 1906 | 19,379,373.71 | .............. | 19,379,373.71 | .............. |
| 1907 | 27,198,618.71 | .............. | 27,198,618.71 | .............. |
| 1908 | 38,093,929.04 | .............. | 38,093,929.04 | $785,268.00 |
| 1909 | 31,419,442.41 | .............. | 31,419,442.41 | 1,319,076.58 |
| 1910 | 33,911,673.37 | .............. | 33,911,673.37 | 1,692,166.40 |
| 1911 | 36,604,569.02 | $465,034.44 | 37,069,603.46 | 1,691,107.20 |
| 1912 | 34,285,276.50 | 1,036,091.08 | 35,321,367.58 | 3,000,669.60 |
| 1913 | 39,917,866.71 | 1,823,491.32 | 41,741,358.03 | 3,201,055.81 |
| 1914 | 31,452,359.61 | 3,376,900.85 | 34,829,260.46 | 3,194,105.95 |
| 1915 | 24,427,107.29 | 4,767,605.38 | 29,194,712.67 | 3,199,385.05 |
| 1916 | 14,638,194.78 | 2,868,341.97 | 17,506,536.75 | 3,189,024.79 |
| 1917 | 15,949,262.47 | 3,313,532.55 | 19,262,795.02 | 3,103,250.67 |
| 1918 | 17,299,762.56 | 3,487,862.36 | 20,787,624.92 | 2,976,476.55 |
| 1919 | 10,704,409.74 | 1,561,364.74 | 12,265,774.48 | 2,984,888.33 |
| 1920 | 6,031,463.72 | 3,433,592.82 | 9,465,056.54 | 3,040,872.89 |
| 1921 | 16,230,390.79 | 2,088,007.66 | 18,318,398.45 | 2,994,776.66 |
| 1922 | 2,791,035.40 | 896,327.45 | 3,687,362.85 | 2,995,398.14 |
| Total | 454,428,040.66 | 29,118,152.62 | 483,546,193.28 | 39,367,522.62 |

## FINANCES.

### Condition of the Treasury, June 30, 1922.

General fund:

In Treasury offices—

| | | |
|---|---|---|
| Gold | $200,336,149.90 | |
| Standard silver dollars | 7,927,172.00 | |
| United States notes | 4,145,964.00 | |
| Federal reserve notes | 1,878,289.00 | |
| National-bank notes | 234,352.00 | |
| Subsidiary silver coin | 17,747,501.85 | |
| Minor coin | 3,620,013.33 | |
| Silver bullion (at cost) | 44,284,867.40 | |
| Unclassified (unassorted currency, etc.) | 3,283,342.53 | |
| Public debt paid, awaiting reimbursement | 503,020.03 | |
| | | $283,960,672.04 |
| In Federal reserve banks | 33,091,888.68 | |
| In transit | 21,991,600.88 | |
| | | 55,083,489.56 |
| In special depositaries— | | |
| Account of sales of Treasury notes and certificates of indebtedness | | 146,476,840.69 |
| In national-bank depositaries— | | |
| To credit of Treasurer of the United States | 7,832,260.63 | |
| To credit of other Government officers | 16,169,825.24 | |
| In transit | 2,129,381.31 | |
| | | 26,131,467.18 |

General fund—Continued.
In treasury of Philippine Islands—

| | | | |
|---|---|---|---|
| To credit of Treasurer of the United States | $4, 417, 7 7. 43 | | |
| In transit.............................. | 554. 05 | | |
| | | $4, 418, 311. 48 | |
| In foreign depositaries— | | | |
| To credit of Treasurer of the United States | 700, 619. 43 | | |
| To credit of other Government officers... | 521, 190. 60 | | |
| In transit.............................. | 1, 141. 00 | | |
| | | 1, 222, 951. 03 | |
| | | 517, 293, 731. 98 | |

Deduct current liabilities—

| | | | |
|---|---|---|---|
| Federal reserve note 5 per cent fund........ | $179, 138, 539. 55 | | |
| Less notes in process of redemption............ | 679, 432. 50 | | |
| | | 178, 459, 107. 05 | |
| Federal reserve bank note 5 per cent fund.. | 7, 445, 646. 55 | | |
| Less notes in process of redemption.......... | 1, 030, 273. 00 | | |
| | | 6, 415, 373. 55 | |
| National-bank note 5 per cent fund........ | 29, 791, 025. 87 | | |
| Less notes in process of redemption.......... | 15, 540, 014. 63 | | |
| | | 14, 251, 011. 24 | |
| Treasurer's checks outstanding.......... | | 447, 858. 57 | |
| Post Office Department balance......... | | 12, 427, 459. 46 | |
| Board of trustees, Postal Savings System balance.............................. | | 7, 103, 734. 69 | |
| Balance to credit of postmasters, clerks of courts, disbursing officers, etc.......... | | 28, 902, 135. 42 | |
| Undistributed assets of insolvent national banks................................ | | 1, 931, 759. 56 | |
| Retirement of additional circulating notes, act of May 30, 1908............. | | 31, 080. 00 | |
| Miscellaneous redemption accounts....... | | 3, 197, 276. 59 | |
| | | | 253, 166, 796. 13 |

| | |
|---|---|
| Balance in the Treasury June 30, 1922, as per statement of the public debt of the United States Government.. | 264, 126, 935. 85 |

The following is a brief summary of the net change in the general fund balances between June 30, 1921, and June 30, 1922:

General fund balances:

| | |
|---|---|
| Balance per daily Treasury statement, June 30, 1921·......... | $549, 678, 105. 76 |
| Deduct net excess of expenditures over receipts in June reports subsequently received....................................... | 16, 779, 775. 99 |
| Net balance June 30, 1921................................. | 532, 898, 329. 77 |
| Excess of ordinary receipts over expenditures chargeable against ordinary receipts in the fiscal year 1922..................... | 321, 047, 216. 40 |
| Total to be accounted for................................ | 853, 945, 546. 17 |

14263—FI 1922——7

General fund balances—Continued.

| | |
|---|---|
| Public debt retirements from surplus revenue.................. | $321,047,216.40 |
| (This is additional to $422,352,950 sinking fund and other debt retirements chargeable against ordinary receipts.) | |
| Public debt retirements from decrease in net balance in the general fund............................................. | 268,771,393.92 |
| Balance in the Treasury June 30, 1922, as per statement of the public debt of the United States Government................. | 264,126,935.85 |
| Total................................................... | 853,945,546.17 |

*United States notes (greenbacks).*—The redemptions of United States notes unfit for circulation during the year amounted to $339,348,000. An equal amount was issued in order to maintain the outstanding aggregate of the notes as required by law.

*Gold reserve fund.*—There were no redemptions of United States notes for gold from the reserve fund during the year. This fund remains at $152,979,025.63, or the same amount as at the close of the previous fiscal year.

*Trust funds.*—The following table shows the trust funds held for the redemption of the notes and certificates for which they are respectively pledged:

| | | | |
|---|---|---|---|
| Gold coin and bullion.... | $695,000,469 | Gold certificates outstanding..................... | $985,163,129 |
| Silver dollars....:........ | 304,066,593 | Less amount in the Treasury.............. | 290,162,660 |
| Silver dollars, 1890....... | 1,510,543 | | |
| | | Net............... | 695,000,469 |
| | | Silver certificates outstanding............... | 305,653,163 |
| | | Less amount in the Treasury.............. | 1,586,570 |
| | | Net............... | 304,066,593 |
| | | Treasury notes (1890) outstanding............... | 1,510,543 |
| | | Less amount in the Treasury.............. | ............. |
| | | Net............... | 1,510,543 |
| Total.............. | 1,000,577,605 | Total.............. | 1,000,577.605 |

*Gold fund, Federal Reserve Board.*—The balance to the credit of the gold fund of the Federal Reserve Board on June 30, 1922, amounted to $2,108,886,911.43, an increase of $571,030,015.98 over the amount to the credit of this fund on June 30, 1921.

*The public debt.*—The gross public debt of the United States at the close of the fiscal year 1922 amounted to $22,964,079,190.58. This is shown in detail in Exhibit 1, page 126, and Table A, page 458.

## Receipts and expenditures, on cash basis.

The following statements summarize cash receipts and expenditures during the fiscal year 1922, and the estimated receipts and expenditures for the fiscal years 1923 and 1924 on the basis of the latest information received from the Bureau of the Budget and the various departments and establishments of the Government:

*Summary of receipts and expenditures on the basis of daily Treasury statements.*

| | Actual, fiscal year 1922. | Estimated, fiscal year 1923. | Estimated, fiscal year 1924. |
|---|---|---|---|
| Net balance in the general fund at the beginning of fiscal year | $549,678,106 | $272,105,513 | $272,105,501 |
| Receipts: | | | |
|   Ordinary | 4,109,104,151 | 3,429,862,959 | 3,361,812,359 |
|   Public debt [1] | 3,866,865,652 | 4,456,687,400 | 1,475,075,532 |
|     Total | 8,525,647,909 | 8,158,655,872 | 5,108,993,392 |
| Expenditures: | | | |
|   Ordinary | 3,372,607,900 | [2] 3,373,712,871 | 2,835,746,234 |
|   Public debt chargeable against ordinary receipts | 422,694,600 | 330,088,800 | 345,097,000 |
|   Other public debt [1] | 4,458,239,896 | 4,182,748,700 | 1,656,044,600 |
|   Net balance in the general fund at close of fiscal year | 272,105,513 | 272,105,501 | 272,105,558 |
|     Total | 8,525,647,909 | 8,158,655,872 | 5,108,993,392 |
| POSTAL SERVICE. | | | |
| Postal receipts | 484,853,540 | 528,494,271 | 585,605,591 |
| Postal expenditures | 545,666,532 | 559,996,841 | 584,653,151 |
| Deficiency in postal receipts | 60,812,992 | 31,502,570 | .......... |
| Surplus of postal receipts | .......... | .......... | 952,440 |

[1] Other public debt expenditures and public debt receipts, as shown in this statement, do not include Treasury certificates issued and retired within the same fiscal year.

[2] Includes $125,000,000 of accumulated interest on war-saving certificates, series of 1918, to be paid during the fiscal year 1923, though properly allocable to the full five years of their life and not simply to the fiscal year 1923.

NOTE.—The postal deficiency for 1922, the estimated postal deficiency for 1923, and the estimated surplus of postal receipts for 1924, shown above, are included in the general classification of ordinary expenditures and estimated ordinary expenditures under the Post Office Department on p. 119.

Cash receipts and expenditures are shown in more detail in the following tables:

*Receipts and expenditures for the fiscal years 1921 and 1922, and estimated receipts and expenditures for the fiscal years 1923 and 1924.*

[On the basis of daily Treasury statements.]

| | Fiscal year 1921. | Fiscal year 1922. | Fiscal year 1923. | Fiscal year 1924. |
|---|---|---|---|---|
| **RECEIPTS.** | | | | |
| Ordinary: | | | | |
| Customs | $308,564,391.00 | $356,443,387.18 | $450,000,000.00 | $425,000,000.00 |
| Internal revenue— | | | | |
| Income and profits taxes | $3,206,046,157.74 | $2,008,128,192.63 | $1,500,0,000.00 | $1,500,000,000.00 |
| Miscellaneous internal revenue | 1,390,380,823.28 | 1,145,125,064.11 | 900,00,000.00 | 925,000,000.00 |
| ...us revenue | 4,586,426,981.02 | 3,213,253,256.79 | 2,400,000,000.00 | 2,425,000,000.00 |
| Sales of public lands | 1,530,439.42 | 895,391.22 | 725,000.00 | 600,000.00 |
| Federal ... bank franchise tax | 60,724,742.27 | 59,974,465.64 | 10,000,000.00 | 10,000,000.00 |
| Interest on foreign obligations | 31,142,982.51 | 27,715,040.79 | 224,737,965.00 | 222,761,045.00 |
| Repayments of foreign obligations | 83,678,223.38 | 49,114,107.46 | 31,250,00.00 | 31,225,000.00 |
| Sale of surplus war supplies | 183,692,848.69 | 89,321,255.06 | 83,510,000.00 | 27,812,000.00 |
| Retirement of capital stock of ...in Corporation | 100,000,000.00 | 25,000,000.00 | | |
| Panama Canal | 12,280,741.79 | 11,747,092.47 | 13,924,000.00 | 14,224,000.00 |
| Other miscellaneous | 246,891,610.83 | 275,640,154.33 | 215,715,994.00 | 205,190,314.00 |
| | 719,911,588.59 | 539,407,505.97 | 579,862,959.00 | 511,812,359.00 |
| Total ordinary receipts | 5,624,932,960.91 | 4,109,104,150.94 | 3,429,862,959.00 | 3,361,812,359.00 |
| **EXPENDITURES.** | | | | |
| ...ry | 5,115,927,689.30 | 3,372,607,889.84 | 3,373,712,871.00 | 2,835,746,234.00 |
| Public debt expenditures ...able against ordinary ...: | | | | |
| Sinking fund | 261,100,250.00 | 276,046,000.00 | 283,838,800.00 | 298,572,000.00 |
| Purchases of ...his from foreign repayments | 73,939,300.00 | 64,837,900.00 | 31,250,000.00 | 31,225,000.00 |
| Redemptions of ...his and notes from ... taxes | 26,348,950.00 | 21,084,850.00 | 5,000,000.00 | 5,000,000.00 |
| Retirements from Federal reserve bank franchise tax receipts | 60,724,500.00 | 60,333,000.00 | 10,000,000.00 | 10,000,000.00 |

| | | | | | |
|---|---|---|---|---|---|
| Forfeitures, gifts, etc. | 422,113,000.00 | 392,850.00 | 422,694,600.00 | 339,088,800.00 | 345,097,000.00 |
| Total ordinary expenditures (including debt redemptions chargeable against ordinary receipts) | 5,538,040,680.30 | | 3,735,302,499.84 | 3,763,891,671.00 | 3,189,843,234.09 |
| Excess of ordinary receipts over total expenditures chargeable against ordinary receipts | 86,882,271.61 | | 313,891,651.10 | | 180,969,125.00 |
| Excess of total expenditures chargeable against ordinary receipts over ordinary receipts | | | | 271,588,712.00 | |

[1] For details see Exhibits 71 and 72, pp. 267 and 270.

[2] For details see pp. 119 and 120.

[3] Includes $125,000,000 of accumulated interest on war-savings certificates, series of 1918, to be paid during the fiscal year 1923, though properly allocable to the full five years of their life and not simply to the fiscal year 1923.

Public debt expenditures and receipts in fiscal year 1922 and estimates for fiscal years 1923 and 1924.

[On basis of daily Treasury statements.]

| | Fiscal year 1922. | Fiscal year 1923. | Fiscal year 1924. |
|---|---|---|---|
| EXPENDITURES. | | | |
| Certificates of indebtedness: | | | |
| Loan and tax | $2,450,843,500 | $1,754,787,500 | $1,250,000,000 |
| Pittman Act | 141,875,000 | 74,000,000 | |
| Special | 32,854,458 | | |
| Victory notes | 1,968,139,250 | 1,989,000,000 | 1 115,000,000 |
| Treasury notes | | | 311,191,600 |
| War savings securities: | | | |
| Series 1918 | | 2,540,000,000 | 3 5,500,000 |
| Series 1919 | 86,120,704 | 5,000,000 | 49,400,000 |
| All other series | | 15,000,000 | 20,000,000 |
| Liberty bond retirements | 153,791,640 | 75,000,000 | 335,000,000 |
| Retirements of Federal reserve bank notes and national-bank notes | 107,251,870 | 89,000,000 | 15,000,000 |
| Old debt items | 58,122 | 50,000 | 50,000 |
| Total public debt expenditures | 1,880,934,495 | 4,512,887,500 | 2,001,141,600 |
| Deduct debt expenditures chargeable against ordinary receipts: | | | |
| Sinking fund | $276,946,000 | $283,828,800 | $298,872,000 |
| Purchase of Liberty bonds from foreign repayments | 64,837,900 | 31,230,000 | 31,225,000 |
| Redemption of bonds and notes from estate taxes | 21,084,850 | 5,000,000 | 5,000,000 |
| Retirements from Federal reserve bank franchise tax receipts | 60,333,000 | 10,000,000 | 10,000,000 |
| Retirements from gifts, forfeitures, etc | 392,850 | | |
| | 422,694,600 | 330,088,800 | 345,097,000 |
| | 4,458,239,896 | 4,182,748,700 | 1,656,044,600 |
| RECEIPTS. | | | |
| Treasury savings securities | 69,368,775 | 121,000,000 | 100,000,000 |
| Deposits to retire Federal reserve bank notes and national-bank notes | 107,183,227 | 89,000,000 | 15,000,000 |
| New issues of securities, including Treasury bonds, notes and certificates | 3,690,313,650 | 4,246,687,400 | 1,360,075,532 |
| Total public-debt receipts | 3,866,865,652 | 4,456,687,400 | 1,475,075,532 |
| Excess of public debt retirements over the retirements chargeable against ordinary receipts | 591,374,244 | | 180,969,068 |
| Excess of public debt issues over redemptions chargeable against public debt receipts due to indicated deficit in ordinary receipts | | 272,938,700 | |
| | 4,458,239,896 | 4,182,748,700 | 1,656,044,600 |

1 Estimated amount of Victory notes that will not be presented for redemption until the fiscal year 1924.

2 Exclusive of $125,000,000 of accumulated interest on war savings certificates, series of 1918, to be paid during the fiscal year 1923, though properly allowable to the full 5 years of their life and not simply to the fiscal year 1923; this has been included as interest on the public debt under ordinary expenditures.

3 Estimated amount of war savings certificates, series of 1918, that will not be presented for redemption until the fiscal year 1924.

NOTE.—Other public debt expenditures and public-debt receipts, as shown in this statement, do not include Treasury certificates issued and retired within the same fiscal year.

Preliminary statement showing classified expenditures of the Government for the period from July 1, 1921, to June 30, 1922.

[For comparative figures and total expenditures for the fiscal year 1921 see Exhibit 71, p. 267.]

[On the basis of daily Treasury statements.]

| | July, 1921. | August, 1921. | September, 1921. | October, 1921. | November, 1921. | December, 1921. | January, 1922. |
|---|---|---|---|---|---|---|---|
| Legislative establishment. | $1,511,592.44 | $1,584,542.18 | $1,326,052.32 | $1,309,919.32 | $1,574,229.43 | $1,640,682.18 | $1,105,270.72 |
| Executive proper. | 21,669.69 | 17,194.15 | 18,138.58 | 17,591.06 | 17,155.80 | 21,555.59 | 19,980.11 |
| State Department. | 883,043.77 | 475,224.93 | 689,864.33 | 575,747.43 | 681,497.02 | 1,056,832.98 | 490,781.52 |
| Treasury Department. | 43,970,001.93 | 24,386,133.63 | 12,297,032.90 | 10,088,422.59 | 33,018,535.50 | 19,820,916.96 | 22,578,602.45 |
| War Department. | 59,211,762.32 | 48,335,998.99 | 34,865,066.83 | 33,570,966.76 | 36,611,671.99 | 31,899,932.11 | 34,303,085.06 |
| Department of Justice. | 1,399,221.44 | 1,227,207.37 | 1,302,551.39 | 1,603,655.76 | 1,488,967.86 | 1,505,296.00 | 1,500,007.97 |
| Post Office Department. | 8,352,387.68 | 256,645.24 | 15,267,044.51 | 291,083.60 | 10,175,218.56 | 240,987.74 | 328,608.32 |
| Navy Department. | 56,522,307.28 | 46,089,184.62 | 44,878,756.55 | 38,357,833.79 | 43,156,907.59 | 40,938,995.27 | 39,941,085.00 |
| Interior Department. | 27,577,664.15 | 29,089,169.20 | 29,222,767.48 | 28,157,151.11 | 27,701,577.18 | 29,430,688.33 | 31,031,478.79 |
| Department of Agriculture. | 9,892,270.95 | 14,970,408.67 | 15,919,840.35 | 15,922,722.42 | 15,321,312.61 | 12,657,488.21 | 12,747,894.13 |
| Department of Commerce. | 2,077,831.61 | 1,470,401.33 | 2,248,840.65 | 1,443,872.49 | 1,834,789.50 | 1,871,710.44 | 1,579,576.76 |
| Department of Labor. | 807,328.50 | 315,940.90 | 402,612.77 | 1,525,885.86 | 590,518.69 | 383,016.20 | 535,488.01 |
| Veterans' Bureau[1]. | | 26,218,309.95 | 35,135,439.22 | 37,033,115.48 | 37,291,490.88 | 39,006,755.44 | 37,012,283.50 |
| ⟨…⟩ Sites ⟨…⟩ Board | 32,709,742.35 | 11,040,032.73 | 8,034,356.20 | 11,616,152.07 | 7,788,404.95 | 8,957,529.93 | 5,510,503.70 |
| Federal control of transportation act, 1920. | 17,290,144.94 | 56,090,592.42 | 9,244,880.02 | [2] 44,665,865.99 | [2] 8,222,122.26 | [2] 27,812,538.90 | [2] 42,950,185.15 |
| War Finance Corporation. | [2] 1,013,689.77 | [2] 772,460.73 | [3] 31,183,088.11 | 6,760,099.81 | 25,807,203.88 | 19,750,336.92 | 39,315,917.27 |
| Grain Corporation. | | | | [3] 25,000,000.00 | | | 4,000,000.00 |
| Other independent offices and commissions. | 14,885,125.39 | 7,520,602.81 | 360,694.88 | [4] 69,995.17 | 2,934,233.26 | 1,689,134.98 | 3,629,535.40 |
| District of Columbia. | 2,630,641.91 | 1,624,415.44 | 1,395,525.25 | 2,165,647.29 | 2,014,845.55 | 2,160,538.60 | 3,516,736.01 |
| Interest on public debt. | 43,854,045.11 | 17,740,165.93 | 85,729,897.64 | 130,203,694.69 | 86,541,015.25 | 144,170,489.21 | 37,087,981.07 |
| Total. | 322,583,091.69 | 288,478,309.76 | 267,050,942.76 | 301,666,709.99 | 326,307,453.24 | 329,299,383.24 | 231,334,610.64 |
| Deduct unclassified repayments, etc. | 897,565.48 | [4] 2,208,312.90 | 1,249,770.36 | [2] 2,332,851.51 | 2,081,608.87 | [4] 165,657.60 | 356,222.29 |
| Total. | 321,685,526.21 | 290,686,622.66 | 265,801,172.40 | 304,001,561.50 | 324,225,844.37 | 329,467,395.84 | 230,978,388.35 |
| Panama Canal. | 133,043.03 | 471,224.63 | 722,760.39 | 156,394.35 | 257,532.35 | 298,355.02 | 265,506.81 |
| Total ordinary. | 321,818,569.24 | 291,157,847.34 | 266,523,932.79 | 304,157,955.85 | 324,483,376.72 | 329,765,750.86 | 231,246,895.16 |

[1] Payments on account of veterans' relief made prior to Aug. 11, 1921, by the War Risk Insurance Bureau are included under Treasury Department, while similar payments made prior to that date by the Federal Board for Vocational Education are included under other independent offices and commissions. During the fiscal year 1922, allotments for veterans' relief have been made to the Treasury Department in the amount of $26,350,668.66, to the War Department in the amount of $4,866,383.40, and to the Navy Department in the amount of $529,237.84, but expenditures under these allotments appear as expenditures of the respective departments and not of the Veterans' Bureau.

[2] Deduct, excess of credits.

[3] $25,000,000 of this amount represents reduction in capital stock of United States Grain Corporation effected Oct. 17, 1921, and is reflected in an increase of receipts in an equal amount (see note, p. 2, daily Treasury statement for Oct. 18, 1921).

[4] Add.

*Preliminary statement showing classified expenditures of the Government for the period from July 1, 1921, to June 30, 1922—Continued.*

| | July, 1921 | August, 1921 | September, 1921 | October, 1921 | November, 1921 | December, 1921 | January, 1922 |
|---|---|---|---|---|---|---|---|
| **Public debt:** | | | | | | | |
| Public debt ( ...tes ...the against ...inary | | | | | | | |
| receipts— | | | | | | | |
| Sinking fund | $57,578,000.00 | $23,397,000.00 | $91,000.00 | $57,289,100.00 | $36,888,900.00 | $52,802,700.00 | $29,503,100.00 |
| Purchases of Liberty bonds from foreign repayments | 518,700.00 | | | | 13,800.00 | 15,614,850.00 | 432,400.00 |
| Redemption of ...bds and notes from ...see ...the tax | 2,298,350.00 | 1,807,050.00 | 1,793,000.00 | 2,021,800.00 | 2,483,250.00 | 1,823,200.00 | 1,950,550.00 |
| Retirements from Federal ...r...e bank ...the tax | | | | | | 2,619,000.00 | 4,435,000.00 |
| Retirements from gifts, forfei...ts, and other ...ts | 3,600.00 | 4,500.00 | 4,900.00 | 650.00 | 3,350.00 | 5,000.00 | 2,550.00 |
| Total public debt expenditures chargeable against ordinary receipts | 60,398,650.00 | 25,298,550.00 | 1,888,900.00 | 59,311,550.00 | 39,389,300.00 | 72,864,750.00 | 36,323,600.00 |
| Total expenditures (public debt and ordinary) chargeable against ordinary receipts | 382,217,219.24 | 316,456,397.34 | 268,412,832.79 | 363,469,505.85 | 363,872,676.72 | 402,630,500.86 | 267,570,495.16 |
| Other public debt expenditures | 169,880,077.44 | 212,220,683.22 | 1,171,953,843.53 | 487,082,650.47 | 49,330,859.06 | 728,210,930.98 | 23,504,456.34 |
| Total public debt (see items below) | 230,284,727.44 | 237,519,233.22 | 1,173,842,743.53 | 546,394,200.47 | 88,720,159.06 | 801,075,683.98 | 59,828,056.34 |
| **...tion, public debt:** | | | | | | | |
| ...ts of ...bts ...bd | 156,517,000.00 | 169,111,000.00 | 1,051,903,590.00 | 457,571,000.00 | 29,851,000.00 | 704,667,000.00 | 7,012,500.00 |
| Treasury (War) ...ngs securities renewed | 8,825,772.44 | 9,077,647.28 | 8,643,853.53 | 8,874,220.47 | 8,045,299.06 | 8,307,610.98 | 7,475,905.58 |
| Old ...bt ...bd | 2,420.00 | 2,920.94 | 3,680.00 | 1,500.00 | 5,390.00 | 2,120.00 | 800.76 |
| First Liberty bonds | 31,850.00 | 17,200.00 | 10,650.00 | 33,450.00 | 20,500.00 | 21,150.00 | 42,500.00 |
| Second ...ty bonds | 692,350.00 | 616,850.00 | 615,800.00 | 534,550.00 | 396,290.00 | 504,900.00 | 629,200.00 |
| Third Liberty ...ds | 1,001,900.00 | 376,800.00 | 396,350.00 | 553,750.00 | 630,460.00 | 16,003,500.00 | 866,350.00 |
| Fourth Liberty ...bds | 1,030,950.00 | 808,100.00 | 713,050.00 | 819,650.00 | 1,354,300.00 | 820,700.00 | 745,400.00 |
| Victory notes retired | 57,642,200.00 | 60,117,600.00 | 97,085,650.00 | 63,820,200.00 | 36,977,850.00 | 60,019,050.00 | 34,579,500.00 |
| ...al ...ates and F...ral reserve bank notes retired | 4,540,885.00 | 7,391,115.00 | 14,490,360.00 | 14,185,930.00 | 11,429,180.00 | 10,729,650.00 | 8,475,900.00 |
| Total public debt | 230,284,727.44 | 237,519,233.22 | 1,173,842,743.53 | 546,394,200.47 | 88,720,159.06 | 801,075,683.98 | 59,828,056.34 |

| | February, 1922 | March, 1922 | April, 1922 | May, 1922 | June, 1922 | Total July 1, 1921, to June 30, 1922 |
|---|---|---|---|---|---|---|
| Legislative proper | $1,328,612.72 | $1,498,513.13 | $1,429,309.55 | $1,464,276.04 | $1,315,112.84 | $7,786,12.87 |
| Executive proper | 15,010.13 | 17,381.54 | 16,456.23 | 19,863.72 | 16,683.76 | 218,690.36 |
| State Department | 871,695.51 | 407,581.36 | 1,270,229.92 | 834,454.40 | 1,429,618.53 | 9,414,61.70 |
| ...ry Department | 12,896,146.87 | 18,661,045.72 | 46,616,328.83 | 20,940,889.07 | 29,138,333.27 | 294,414,289.72 |
| War Department | 30,125,848.01 | 42,398,305.03 | 35,241,287.96 | 37,412,073.30 | 30,754,720.03 | 454,730,717.67 |
| ...t of ... Ino. | 1,461,411.18 | 1,784,328.40 | 1,545,893.05 | 1,670,713.87 | 1,396,634.29 | 17,888,825.58 |
| Post Office Department | 10,387,934.25 | 8,331,513.48 | 269,193.01 | 369,335.44 | 13,460,410.00 | 67,730,361.83 |
| Navy Department | 32,288,614.07 | 31,689,920.15 | 23,481,074.86 | 32,426,773.51 | 46,203,741.15 | 476,775,193.84 |
| Department of ... | 26,583,016.01 | 30,708,353.35 | 23,476,503.28 | 27,139,605.52 | 30,909,191.66 | 1,097,166.11 |
| Department of ... | 8,859,688.21 | 11,027,071.35 | 8,447,461.35 | 9,545,941.38 | 7,884,889.47 | 142,695,844.10 |
| Veterans' ... | 2,573,788.96 | 705,027.62 | 1,723,124.21 | 1,738,861.59 | 1,901,189.70 | 21,688,044.86 |
| ...ing Board | 2,532,645.12 | 569,577.69 | 493,986.65 | 336,625.72 | 713,845.46 | 81.57 |
| Federal ... and transportation act, 1920 | 39,985,647.38 | 39,707,387.92 | 33,670,447.19 | 36,629,151.41 | 39,121,601.31 | 400,691,609.68 |
| War Finance ... | 4,458,041.09 | 3,049,877.15 | [2] 6,632,197.07 | [2] 21,878,074.19 | 2,571,363.21 | 87,205,732.12 |
| Sugar Equalization Board | [2] 50,088,964.20 | 9,077,389.99 | 43,537,901.60 | [2] 18,970,664.91 | 5,085,574.82 | [2,4] 133,469,450.82 |
| ... and commissions | 30,407,311.37 | 24,339,987.73 | 1,068,462.62 | 21,970,417.11 | [2] 16,029,787.63 | 94,428,001.01 |
| Int of C... | 3,000,000.00 | | | | [3] 200,000.00 | [3] 32,000,000.00 |
| | 1,710,169.86 | 2,013,882.46 | [2] 14,369,856.84 | [2] 709,773.68 | 1,532,274.28 | [2] 15,279,636.52 |
| | 1,921,411.26 | 2,126,531.68 | 4,522,351.72 | 1,588,256.19 | 2,650,496.25 | 43,871,656.40 |
| | | | 4,803,334.75 | 1,942,377.26 | | 23,962,521.25 |
| Int on public debt | 22,847,969.73 | 99,700,420.41 | 121,822,074.35 | 86,584,434.39 | 114,718,581.28 | 991,000,759.24 |
| Total | 182,057,987.53 | 327,874,306.16 | 240,203,644.78 | 237,129,697.12 | 314,644,463.66 | 3,368,632,555.57 |
| Deduct unclassified repayments, etc | [5] 6,988.45 | 2,079,756.46 | [2] 2,190,821.65 | [4] 816,056.36 | 825,076.42 | [4] 232,088.39 |
| Total | 182,064,975.98 | 325,794,549.70 | 242,394,466.43 | 237,945,753.48 | 313,818,387.24 | 3,368,884,644.16 |
| Panama Canal | 140,965.87 | 160,387.08 | 166,495.39 | 15,723.40 | 234,042.95 | 3,025,421.32 |
| Purchase of obligations of foreign Governments | | | | | 717,834.36 | 717,834.36 |
| Total ordinary | 182,205,931.85 | 325,954,936.78 | 242,560,961.82 | 237,961,476.88 | 314,770,264.55 | 3,372,607,899.84 |

[1] ... prior to Aug. 11, 19... by the War Risk ... War ...
... veterans' ... have in ... to the ... of the ...
[2] Deduct, ... of $529,237.84, ...
[3] ... see note, p. 2, ...
[4] A ... held ... (... 17, 1921, ...) ... by the ... administration, representing proceeds of sale of ... approved Nov. 19, 1919, and have been further reduced by ... under the Federal control act or transportation act, 1920.
[5] ... equipment ... trust ... acquired ... at ... of the ... of ... $123,783,487.75 up to June 30, 192... on account of ... of receipts in an equal

Preliminary statement showing classified expenditures of the Government for the period from July 1, 1921, to June 30, 1922—Continued.

| | February, 1922. | March, 1922. | April, 1922. | May, 1922. | June, 1922. | Total July 1, 1921, to June 30, 1922. |
|---|---|---|---|---|---|---|
| **Public debt:** | | | | | | |
| Public debt expenditures chargeable against ordinary receipts— | | | | | | |
| Sinking fund | $910,200.00 | | $10,000,000.00 | $19,680,000.00 | $17,586,000.00 | $276,046,000.00 |
| Purchases of Liberty bonds from foreign payments | | $1,799,300.00 | 745,050.00 | 1,559,450.00 | 18,578,150.00 | 64,837,900.00 |
| Redemption of bonds and notes from estate taxes | 2,157,350.00 | 24,299,000.00 | 24,613,000.00 | 2,349,300.00 | 553,500.00 | 21,084,850.00 |
| Retirements from Federal reserve bank franchise tax receipts | 2,057,000.00 | | | | 10,700.00 | 60,333,000.00 |
| Retirements from gifts, forfeitures, and other miscellaneous receipts | 60,500.00 | 14,100.00 | 25,800.00 | 13,600.00 | 254,300.00 | 392,350.00 |
| Total public debt expenditures chargeable against ordinary receipts | 5,185,050.00 | 26,062,400.00 | 35,386,850.00 | 23,602,350.00 | 36,982,650.00 | 422,694,600.00 |
| Total expenditures (public debt and ordinary) chargeable against ordinary receipts | 187,390,981.85 | 352,017,336.78 | 277,947,811.52 | 261,563,826.88 | 351,752,914.55 | 3,795,302,499.84 |
| Other public debt expenditures | 516,906,539.57 | 1,676,029,251.31 | 95,886,177.33 | 47,976,222.93 | 1,429,544,204.75 | 6,608,531,896.93 |
| Total public debt (see items below) | 522,091,589.57 | 1,702,091,651.31 | 131,273,027.33 | 71,578,572.93 | 1,466,526,854.75 | 7,031,226,496.93 |
| **Recapitulation,** [illegible] | | | | | | |
| [illegible] | 264,193,500.00 | 1,011,477,000.00 | 61,313,000.00 | 9,978,000.00 | 852,270,000.00 | 4,775,864,950.00 |
| [illegible] | 6,256,759.10 | 5,960,511.31 | 5,252,527.33 | 4,972,452.93 | 4,428,144.52 | 86,120,704.53 |
| [illegible] retired | 7,830.47 | 6,940.00 | 11,300.00 | 4,370.00 | 8,860.23 | 55,122.40 |
| First [illegible] | 96,400.00 | 59,100.00 | 28,950.00 | 13,500.00 | 38,950.00 | 413,600.00 |
| Second Liberty [illegible] | 407,350.00 | 450,000.00 | 223,100.00 | 537,700.00 | 417,200.00 | 6,015,150.00 |
| Third Liberty [illegible] retired | 476,800.00 | 24,495,000.00 | 34,831,900.00 | 22,223,450.00 | 35,912,750.00 | 137,788,400.00 |
| Fourth Liberty [illegible] | 1,096,000.00 | 692,150.00 | 297,400.00 | 788,650.00 | 435,100.00 | 9,574,450.00 |
| Victory [illegible] | 243,923,450.00 | 648,498,150.00 | 23,082,700.00 | 26,701,250.00 | 565,711,650.00 | 1,908,139,250.00 |
| [illegible] notes retired | 5,663,500.00 | 10,452,800.00 | 6,233,150.00 | 6,359,200.00 | 7,301,200.00 | 107,251,870.00 |
| Total public debt | 522,091,589.57 | 1,702,091,651.31 | 131,273,027.33 | 71,578,572.93 | 1,466,526,854.75 | 7,031,226,496.93 |

NOTE.—Because of legislation establishing revolving funds and providing for the reimbursement of appropriations, commented upon in the annual report of the Secretary of the Treasury for the fiscal year 1919, p. 126 ff., the gross expenditures in the case of some departments and agencies, notably the War Department, the Railroad Administration, and the Shipping Board, have been considerably larger than above stated. This statement does not include expenditures on account of the Postal Service other than salaries and expenses of the Post Office Department in Washington, postal deficiencies, and items appropriated by Congress payable from the general fund of the Treasury.

## Receipts and expenditures, on warrant basis.

The following comparison of receipts and expenditures is on the basis of warrants issued (net) and includes unexpended balances to the credit of disbursing officers at the end of the year, but not expenditures under such unexpended balances at the beginning of the year:

*Comparison of receipts, fiscal years 1922 and 1921, on the basis of warrants issued (net).*

|  | 1922 | 1921 | Increase, 1922. | Decrease, 1922. |
|---|---|---|---|---|
| Customs............... | $357,544,712.40 | $308,025,102.17 | $49,519,610.23 | ................. |
| Internal revenue: |  |  |  |  |
| Income and profits taxes. | 2,086,918,464.85 | 3,228,137,673.75 | ................. | $1,141,219,208.90 |
| Miscellaneous............ | 1,121,239,843.45 | 1,351,835,935.31 | ................. | 230,596,091.86 |
| Sales of public lands........ | 895,391.22 | 1,530,439.42 | ................. | 635,048.20 |
| Alaska fund............... | 136,053.10 | 174,329.90 | ................. | 38,276.80 |
| Assessments on Federal reserve banks for salaries, etc. | 3,067,169.36 | 4,819,339.72 | ................. | 1,752,170.36 |
| Assessments on national banks for expenses of examiners............. | 2,012,600.00 | 1,583,037.11 | 429,562.89 | ................. |
| Consular fees............. | 6,707,058.72 | 5,676,850.61 | 1,030,208.11 | ................. |
| Customs fees, fines, penalties, services of officers, etc. | 1,032,589.34 | 1,173,285.63 | ................. | 140,696.29 |
| Commerce collections........ | 239,432.57 | 305,904.84 | ................. | 66,472.27 |
| Donation of royalty on machine guns............. | ................. | 520,266.12 | ................. | 520,266.12 |
| Depredations on public lands. | 60,149.90 | 68,646.25 | ................. | 8,496.35 |
| Deposits for surveying public lands............... | 68,461.03 | 62,324.51 | 6,136.52 | ................. |
| District of Columbia general receipts............... | 14,777,218.19 | 14,439,985.93 | 337,232.26 | ................. |
| District of Columbia sources. | 457,798.25 | 561,106.29 | ................. | 103,308.04 |
| Discount on bonds, notes, and certificates purchased...... | 3,436,145.91 | 10,675,194.55 | ................. | 7,239,048.64 |
| Earnings on radio service.... | 369,735.67 | 666,371.84 | ................. | 296,636.17 |
| Federal land banks, liquidation of capital stock........ | 1,057,830.00 | 954,835.00 | 102,995.00 | ................. |
| Food Administration........ | ................. | 37,078,988.55 | ................. | 37,078,988.55 |
| Forest Service, cooperative fund...................... | 1,394,826.71 | 1,946,041.18 | ................. | 551,214.47 |
| Fees on letters patent........ | 2,875,013.15 | 2,696,502.46 | 178,510.69 | ................. |
| Forest reserve fund.......... | 5,125,668.20 | 2,591,297.93 | 2,534,370.27 | ................. |
| Franchise tax (surplus earnings of Federal reserve banks)................. | 59,974,465.64 | 60,724,742.27 | ................. | 750,276.63 |
| Funds contributed for river and harbor improvements.. | 2,930,051.68 | 3,774,947.68 | ................. | 844,896.00 |
| Gain by exchange............ | 7,245,624.49 | 19,008.08 | 7,226,616.41 | ................. |
| Grain Corporation, decrease of capital stock............ | 25,000,000.00 | 100,000,000.00 | ................. | 75,000,000.00 |
| Housing Corporation, operations and disposal of properties................... | 4,523,207.53 | 4,240,055.17 | 283,152.36 | ................. |
| Farm loan bonds: |  |  |  |  |
| Principal.................. | 44,400,000.00 | ................. | 44,400,000.00 | ................. |
| Interest.................. | 8,611,170.08 | 8,306,075.00 | 305,095.08 | ................. |
| Foreign loans: |  |  |  |  |
| Principal.................. | 49,114,107.46 | 83,678,223.38 | ................. | 34,564,115.92 |
| Interest.................. | 6,607,723.54 | 18,327,306.91 | ................. | 11,719,583.37 |
| Interest on foreign obligation, sale of surplus property, War Department..... | 21,107,317.25 | 12,701,508.93 | 8,405,808.32 | ................. |
| Interest on public deposits... | 7,388,278.07 | 5,668,852.42 | 1,719,425.65 | ................. |
| Interest on loans to railroad companies............... | [1] 3,000.00 | [2] 84,000.00 | ................. | 81,000.00 |
| Interest on advance payments to contractors....... | 14,300.29 | 667,383.05 | ................. | 653,082.76 |
| Immigrant fund.............. | 2,517,823.19 | 5,767,893.69 | ................. | 3,250,070.50 |
| Judicial fees, fines, penalties, etc.................. | 5,132,937.71 | 4,382,676.51 | 750,261.20 | ................. |
| Land fees................. | 1,139,880.25 | 1,753,759.83 | ................. | 613,879.58 |

[1] Exclusive of $12,906,960.89 interest received on account of loans to railroads under section 210 of the transportation act of 1920, and $27,324,181.14 interest collected under the provisions of the Federal control act of Mar. 21, 1918, which amounts were credited, respectively, to the revolving funds, "Loans to railroads" and "Federal control of transportation systems."

[2] Exclusive of $4,369,607.49 interest received on account of loans to railroads under sec. 210 of the transportation act of 1920, and $26,415,163.88 interest collected under the provisions of the Federal control act of Mar. 21, 1918, which amounts were credited, respectively, to the revolving funds, "Loans to railroads" and "Federal control of transportation systems."

Comparison of receipts, fiscal years 1922 and 1921, on the basis of warrants issued
(net)—Continued.

|  | 1922 | 1921 | Increase, 1922. | Decrease, 1922. |
|---|---|---|---|---|
| Naval petroleum reserve lands, oil leasing act...... | $2, 016, 104. 81 | $3, 117, 600. 00 | .................. | $1, 101, 495. 19 |
| Navy hospital and clothing funds, fines, forfeitures, etc. | 12, 547, 632. 58 | 2, 474, 577. 79 | $10, 073, 054. 79 | .................. |
| Naturalization fees........... | 657, 190. 00 | 912, 601. 16 | .................. | 255, 411. 16 |
| Oil-leasing act receipts: |  |  |  |  |
| Future productions...... | 5, 505, 418. 35 | 1, 414, 567. 69 | 4, 090, 850. 66 | .................. |
| Past productions........ | 765, 707. 42 | 5, 193, 548. 55 | .................. | 4, 427, 841. 13 |
| Oregon and California land-grant fund................ | 252, 426. 74 | 363, 802. 04 | .................. | 111, 375. 30 |
| Passport fees............... | 1, 265, 202. 03 | 1, 172, 705. 64 | 92, 496. 39 | .................. |
| Profits on coinage, bullion deposits, etc............. | 21, 660, 921. 07 | 12, 610, 210. 05 | 9, 050, 711. 02 | .................. |
| Payment by German Government under terms of armistice............... | 4, 403, 655. 52 | 11, 154, 467. 22 | .................. | 6, 750, 811. 70 |
| Proceeds of town sites, etc... | 18, 645. 08 | 32, 343. 93 | .................. | 13, 698. 85 |
| Proceeds of seal and fox skins. | 292, 998. 87 | 1, 024, 886. 81 | .................. | 731, 887. 94 |
| Panama Canal tolls, etc...... | 12, 049, 660. 65 | 11, 914, 361. 32 | 135, 299. 33 | .................. |
| Rent of public buildings (war)...................... | 548, 454. 59 | 935, 301. 39 | .................. | 386, 846. 80 |
| Revenues of national parks... | 377, 809. 72 | 384, 276. 18 | .................. | 6, 466. 46 |
| Return of advances to reclamation fund................ | 1, 000, 000. 00 | 1, 000, 000. 00 | .................. | .................. |
| Rent of public buildings, grounds, etc.............. | 682, 684. 94 | 1, 083, 000. 85 | .................. | 400, 315. 91 |
| Reimbursement on account of expenditures made for Indian tribes............. | 3, 127. 73 | 33, 729. 48 | .................. | 30, 601. 75 |
| Sale of war supplies, War Department............... | 78, 268, 106. 20 | 181, 598, 778. 78 | .................. | 103, 330, 672. 58 |
| Sale of explosive plant, Nitro, W. Va.................... | .................. | 700, 000. 00 | .................. | 700, 000. 00 |
| Sales of ordnance materials, etc. (war).............. | 33, 959. 72 | 169, 049. 92 | .................. | 135, 090. 20 |
| Sales of war supplies, Navy Department............... | 11, 048, 530. 93 | 1, 804, 337. 37 | 9, 244, 193. 56 | .................. |
| Sales of naval vessels........ | .................. | 74, 953. 04 | .................. | 74, 953. 04 |
| Surplus postal revenues, prior years................ | 81, 494. 18 | .................. | 81, 494. 18 | .................. |
| Sales of Government property | 22, 838, 951. 33 | 356, 550. 78 | 22, 482, 400. 55 | .................. |
| Sales of lands and buildings.. | 102, 186. 49 | 246, 260. 00 | .................. | 144, 073. 51 |
| Sales to Indians............. | 126, 454. 74 | 383, 246. 87 | .................. | 256, 792. 13 |
| Tax on circulation of national banks.................... | 4, 537, 773. 70 | 4, 799, 615. 73 | .................. | 261, 842. 03 |
| Work done by War Department...................... | 898, 554. 29 | 344, 784. 23 | 553, 770. 06 | .................. |
| Miscellaneous............... | 10, 796, 991. 32 | 6, 671, 097. 43 | 4, 125, 893 89 | .................. |
| TRUST FUNDS. |  |  |  |  |
| Department of State: |  |  |  |  |
| Miscellaneous trust funds. | 16, 045. 73 | 335, 211. 57 | .................. | 319, 165. 84 |
| Treasury Department: |  |  |  |  |
| Miscellaneous trust funds. | 2, 433. 81 | .................. | 2, 433. 81 | .................. |
| War Department: |  |  |  |  |
| Army deposit funds...... | 372. 00 | 158, 248. 70 | .................. | 157, 876. 70 |
| Soldiers' Home permanent fund........... | 2, 446, 908. 78 | 821, 009 01 | 1, 625, 899. 77 | .................. |
| Preservation of birthplace of Abraham Lincoln................. | 2, 040. 00 | 2, 040. 00 | .................. | .................. |
| Miscellaneous trust funds. | 35. 00 | .................. | 35. 00 | .................. |
| Navy Department: |  |  |  |  |
| Navy deposit fund...... | 249, 218. 39 | 98, 986. 40 | 150, 231. 99 | .................. |
| Marine Corps deposit fund................. | 1, 005, 127. 56 | 102, 689. 37 | 902, 438. 19 | .................. |
| Navy pension fund....... | 7, 188. 13 | 2, 863. 53 | 4, 324. 60 | .................. |
| Interior Department: |  |  |  |  |
| Proceeds of Indian lands.. | 758, 728. 39 | 1, 319, 516. 82 | .................. | 560, 788. 43 |
| Indian moneys, proceeds of labor............... | 22, 294, 874. 18 | 20, 443, 157. 66 | 1, 851, 716. 52 | .................. |
| Miscellaneous trust funds. | 1, 185, 826. 22 | 909, 301. 27 | 276, 524. 95 | .................. |
| Personal funds of patients, St. Elizabeths Hospital............... | 207, 352. 80 | 210, 934. 26 | .................. | 3, 581. 46 |
| Pension money, St. Elizabeths Hospital......... | 73, 918. 24 | 74, 075. 27 | .................. | 157. 03 |
| Veterans' Bureau: |  |  |  |  |
| Premium on converted war-risk insurance..... | 26, 007, 398. 63 | 22, 051, 782. 65 | 3, 955, 615. 98 | .................. |

*Comparison of receipts,' fiscal years 1922 and 1921, on the basis of warrants issued (net)—*Continued.

| | 1922 | 1921 | Increase, 1922. | Decrease, 1922. |
|---|---|---|---|---|
| TRUST FUNDS—continued. | | | | |
| District of Columbia: | | | | |
| Miscellaneous trust fund deposits.............. | $921,862.90 | $826,234.80 | $95,628.10 | ................ |
| Washington redemption fund.................. | 189,381.89 | 148,826.20 | 40,555.69 | ................ |
| Police and firemen's relief fund.................. | 192,891.47 | 161,168.67 | 31,722.80 | ................ |
| Other trust funds........ | 70,847.83 | 26,253.68 | 44,594.15 | ................ |
| Teachers' retirement fund deductions....... | 202,782.64 | 192,847.75 | 9,934.89 | ................ |
| Total............... | 4,103,741,926.79 | 5,585,475,693.85 | 186,150,805.86 | $1,667,884,572.92 |
| Deduct moneys covered by warrant in year subsequent to the deposit thereof....... | 146,592.21 | 1,105,240.83 | ................ | 958,648.62 |
| | 4,103,595,334.58 | 5,584,370,453.02 | 186,150,805.86 | 1,666,925,924.30 |
| Add moneys received in fiscal year but not covered by warrant................. | 1,196.46 | 146,592.21 | ................ | 145,395.75 |
| Total ordinary receipts. | 4,103,596,531.04 | 5,584,517,045.23 | 186,150,805.86 | 1,667,071,320.05 |
| Public debt: | | | | |
| Fourth Liberty loan..... | ................ | [1] 2,213.00 | 2,213.00 | ................ |
| Victory Liberty loan..... | [1] 1,300.00 | [1] 12,730.00 | ................ | [1] 11,430.00 |
| Treasury notes........... | 1,935,404,750.00 | 311,191,600.00 | 1,624,213,150.00 | ................ |
| Certificates of indebtedness................... | 3,905,090,000.00 | 8,486,964,950.00 | ................ | 4,581,874,950.00 |
| Treasury (war) savings securities............... | 70,325,625.10 | 26,418,352.19 | 43,907,272.91 | ................ |
| Postal-savings bonds..... | 112,200.00 | 178,880.00 | ................ | 66,680.00 |
| Bank-note fund.......... | 107,086,627.50 | 40,186,945.00 | 66,899,682.50 | ................ |
| Total public debt receipts................ | 6,018,017,902.60 | 8,864,925,784.19 | 1,735,022,318.41 | 4,581,930,200.00 |
| Total receipts, exclusive of postal........ | 10,121,614,433.64 | 14,449,442,829.42 | 1,921,173,124.27 | 6,249,001,520.05 |
| Postal revenues............ | 484,853,540.71 | 463,491,274.70 | 21,362,266.01 | ................ |
| Total receipts, including postal........... | 10,606,467,974.35 | 14,912,934,104.12 | 1,942,535,390.28 | 6,249,001,520.05 |

[1] Counter entries.

*Comparison of expenditures, fiscal years 1922 and 1921, on the basis of warrants issued (net).*

| | 1922 | 1921 | Increase, 1922. | Decrease, 1922. |
|---|---|---|---|---|
| LEGISLATIVE ESTABLISHMENT. | | | | |
| United States Senate......... | $2,365,567.19 | $2,470,110.61 | ................ | $104,543.42 |
| House of Representatives.... | 6,047,115.58 | 6,618,808.00 | ................ | 571,692.42 |
| Legislative, miscellaneous.... | 424,314.41 | 106,307.27 | $318,007.14 | ................ |
| Botanic Garden.............. | 84,899.76 | 82,933.65 | 1,966.11 | ................ |
| Library of Congress.......... | 822,600.70 | 886,625.78 | ................ | 64,025.08 |
| Public Printer............... | 6,981,425.05 | 8,316,080.91 | ................ | 1,334,655.86 |
| Total, legislative establishment............. | 16,725,922.69 | 18,480,866.22 | 319,973.25 | 2,074,916.78 |
| EXECUTIVE OFFICE. | | | | |
| Salaries and expenses, Executive office................. | 216,534.74 | 210,891.25 | 5,643.49 | ................ |
| INDEPENDENT BUREAUS AND OFFICES. | | | | |
| Alaska relief funds.......... | 14,877.22 | 14,093.06 | 784.16 | ................ |
| Alien Property Custodian.... | 363,965.02 | 462,235.74 | ................ | 98,270.72 |
| Anthracite and Bituminous Coal Commission........... | .68 | 24,141.72 | ................ | 24,141.04 |

*Comparison of expenditures, fiscal years 1922 and 1921, on the basis of warrants issued (net)—Continued.*

| | 1922 | 1921 | Increase, 1922. | Decrease, 1922. |
|---|---|---|---|---|
| **INDEPENDENT BUREAUS AND OFFICES**—continued. | | | | |
| Arlington Memorial Amphitheater Commission........ | [1] $5,083.85 | $50.00 | .................. | $5,133.85 |
| Board of Mediation and Conciliation.................... | 6,657.29 | 20,945.97 | .................. | 14,288.68 |
| Bureau of Efficiency......... | 139,667.78 | 144,528.13 | .................. | 4,860.35 |
| Capital Issues Committee.... | .............. | 23.78 | .................. | 23.78 |
| Civil Service Commission..... | 665,978.64 | 659,088.14 | $6,890.50 | .............. |
| Commission of Fine Arts..... | 10,544.95 | 10,602.46 | .................. | 57.51 |
| Committee on Public Information................. | [1] 18,214.37 | 64,523.52 | .................. | 82,737.89 |
| Council of National Defense.. | 1,248.69 | 66,636.05 | .................. | 65,387.36 |
| Employees' Compensation Commission................ | 2,689,005.88 | 2,529,334.29 | 159,671.59 | .............. |
| European food relief.......... | 107,746.17 | 1,658,829.74 | .................. | 1,551,083.57 |
| Federal Board for Vocational Education........... | [2] 18,567,989.79 | [3] 104,672,029.43 | .................. | 86,104,039.64 |
| Federal Power Commission.. | 36,992.53 | 21,526.99 | 15,465.54 | .............. |
| Federal Reserve Board...... | 4,456,034.44 | 4,493,633.34 | .................. | 37,598.90 |
| Federal Trade Commission... | 953,537.94 | 1,010,327.37 | .................. | 56,789.43 |
| General Accounting Office.... | 2,537,374.25 | [4] | 2,537,374.25 | .............. |
| Housing Corporation........ | 1,387,240.06 | 1,322,237.63 | 65,002.43 | .............. |
| Interdepartmental Social Hygiene Board............. | 412,468.16 | 932,609.70 | .................. | 520,141.54 |
| Interstate Commerce Commission................... | 5,391,271.55 | 6,097,061.30 | .................. | 705,789.75 |
| Miscellaneous items......... | 743,049.03 | 9,149.82 | 733,899.21 | .............. |
| National Advisory Committee for Aeronautics..... | 175,034.55 | 184,600.52 | .................. | 9,565.97 |
| National security and defense, Executive.......... | 2,905.24 | 14,303.90 | .................. | 11,398.66 |
| Railroads................... | [1] 125,232,444.02 | 739,019,362.64 | .................. | 864,251,806.66 |
| Railroad Labor Board....... | 402,611.91 | 385,094.78 | 17,517.13 | .............. |
| Rock Creek and Potomac Parkway Commission..... | 220,408.10 | 140,619.56 | 79,788.54 | .............. |
| Smithsonian Institution and National Museum......... | 835,497.54 | 896,508.27 | .................. | 61,010.73 |
| State, War, and Navy Department Buildings....... | 1,639,607.86 | 2,204,713.55 | .................. | 565,105.69 |
| Temporary government for West Indian Islands....... | 343,440.00 | 343,440.00 | .................. | .............. |
| U. S. Food and Fuel Administrations.................. | 610.96 | [1] 249,375.95 | 249,986.91 | .............. |
| U. S. Pilgrim Tercentenary Commission............... | 157,354.30 | 242,645.70 | .................. | 85,291.40 |
| U. S. Shipping Board........ | 86,145,816.32 | 92,886,783.88 | .................. | 6,740,967.56 |
| U. S. Tariff Commission..... | 318,612.55 | 311,629.55 | 6,983.00 | .............. |
| U. S. Veterans' Bureau: [5] | | | | |
| Salaries and expenses.... | 5,666,158.24 | ([5]) | 5,666,158.24 | ............... |
| Medical and hospital services.............. | 38,007,874.77 | ([5]) | 38,007,874.77 | .............. |
| Military and naval compensation............. | 117,891,438.53 | ([5]) | 117,891,438.53 | .............. |
| Military and naval family allowance.............. | 882,190.36 | ([5]) | 882,190.36 | .............. |
| Miscellaneous items...... | [1] 3.92 | ([5]) | .................. | 3.92 |
| Special funds— | | | | |
| Military and naval insurance.......... | 75,645,628.49 | ([5]) | 75,645,628.49 | .............. |
| Miscellaneous special funds.............. | 529,196.00 | ([5]) | 529,196.00 | .............. |
| Government life insurance fund (trust fund)— | | | | |
| Investments......... | 22,563,224.84 | ([5]) | 24,101,176.87 | .............. |
| Expenses........... | 2,882,151.63 | ([5]) | 1,344,199.60 | .............. |
| Vocational rehabilitation [6] | 164,510,136.09 | ([5]) | 164,510,136.09 | .............. |
| Increase of compensation. | 2,134,908.70 | ([5]) | 2,134,908.70 | .............. |
| War Industries Board........ | 139.34 | 1,963.75 | .................. | 1,824.41 |
| War Trade Board............. | 146.48 | [1] 1,121,701.03 | .................. | [1] 1,121,847.51 |
| Total, independent bureaus and offices...... | 434,184,996.71 | 959,474,197.30 | 434,586,270.91 | 959,875,471.50 |

[1] Excess of repayments, deduct.
[2] Includes $14,299,213.62 expenditures under "Vocational rehabilitation," now under Veterans' Bureau.
[3] Includes $101,049,138.97 expenditures under "Vocational rehabilitation," now under Veterans' Bureau.
[4] For expenditures of accounting offices prior to creation of the General Accounting Office (July 1, 1921) see accounting offices under Treasury Department, p. 115.
[5] For expenditures prior to creation of Veterans' Bureau (Aug. 9, 1921) see Bureau of War Risk Insurance under Treasury Department, p. 115.
[6] For expenditures prior to Aug. 9, 1921, see Federal Board for Vocational Education, above.

Comparison of expenditures, fiscal years 1922 and 1921, on the basis of warrants issued (net)—Continued.

| | 1922 | 1921 | Increase, 1922. | Decrease, 1922. |
|---|---|---|---|---|
| DISTRICT OF COLUMBIA. | | | | |
| Salaries and expenses........ | $21,478,256.98 | $20,877,085.79 | $601,171.19 | ............... |
| Special funds: | | | | |
| Water department....... | 700,993.40 | 846,832.35 | ............... | $145,838.95 |
| Washington aqueduct.... | 200,253.91 | 186,260.08 | 13,993.83 | ............... |
| Miscellaneous special funds | 56,511.11 | 8,873.67 | 47,637.44 | ............... |
| Trust funds: | | | | |
| Miscellaneous trust-fund deposits............... | 842,825.03 | 798,484.91 | 44,340.12 | ............... |
| Washington redemption fund............... | 183,187.04 | 156,733.29 | 26,453.75 | ............... |
| Policemen and firemen's relief fund............. | 199,158.86 | 169,581.69 | 29,577.17 | ............... |
| Teachers' retirement fund— | | | | |
| Investments........ | 249,500.00 | 160,000.00 | 89,500.00 | ............... |
| Current expenses..... | 7,275.00 | 26,393.92 | ............... | 19,118.92 |
| Other trust funds....... | 71,224.27 | 12,013.84 | 59,210.43 | ............... |
| Total, District of Columbia................ | 23,989,185.60 | 23,242,259.54 | 911,883.93 | 164,957.87 |
| DEPARTMENT OF AGRICULTURE. | | | | |
| Salaries...................... | 6,339,316.73 | 6,242,868.99 | 96,447.74 | ............... |
| Miscellaneous................ | 881,212.47 | 912,758.90 | ............... | 31,546.43 |
| Farmers' seed-grain loans.... | 859,358.52 | 1,953,124.68 | ............... | 1,093,766.16 |
| Stimulating agriculture and distribution of products.... | 578.08 | 6,872.35 | ............... | 6,294.27 |
| Office of Farm Mangagement, expenses................... | 295,937.29 | 294,410.85 | 1,526.44 | ............... |
| Bureau of Animal Industry, expenses................... | 5,087,261.28 | 4,182,966.93 | 904,294.35 | ............... |
| Bureau of Plant Industry, expenses................... | 2,519,598.79 | 2,477,744.79 | 41,854.00 | ............... |
| Forest Service, expenses..... | 4,615,979.83 | 4,892,006.77 | ............... | 276,026.94 |
| Bureau of Chemistry, expenses................... | 920,948.42 | 913,637.92 | 7,310.50 | ............... |
| Bureau of Soils, expenses..... | 298,465.38 | 440,257.79 | ............... | 141,792.41 |
| Bureau of Entomology, expenses................... | 1,652,137.49 | 1,202,400.88 | 449,736.61 | ............... |
| Bureau of Biological Survey, expenses................... | 750,583.97 | 741,053.22 | 9,530.75 | ............... |
| Division of Publications, expenses................... | 126,725.53 | 122,760.48 | 3,965.05 | ............... |
| States Relations Service, expenses................... | 3,104,651.73 | 3,112,941.70 | ............... | 8,289.97 |
| Bureau of Public Roads, expenses................... | 433,098.24 | 404,089.25 | 29,008.99 | ............... |
| Bureau of Markets and Crop Estimates, expenses....... | 2,251,356.20 | 2,063,839.10 | 187,517.10 | ............... |
| Federal Horticultural Board. | 728,501.03 | 649,420.72 | 79,080.31 | ............... |
| Procuring nitrate of soda..... | 24,070.10 | 9,155,873.62 | ............... | 9,131,803.52 |
| Weather Bureau, expenses... | 1,565,831.53 | 1,532,492.10 | 33,339.43 | ............... |
| Lands for protection of watersheds and streams.......... | 830,785.27 | 1,179,472.82 | ............... | 348,687.55 |
| Road construction........... | 95,084,057.74 | 62,498,203.00 | 32,585,854.74 | ............... |
| Increase of compensation..... | 3,236,838.34 | 3,012,856.60 | 223,981.74 | ............... |
| Enforcement of insecticide act, general expenses...... | 105,095.40 | 108,047.63 | ............... | 2,952.23 |
| Cooperative agricultural extension work............... | 5,474,049.50 | 5,031,577.73 | 442,471.77 | ............... |
| Meat inspection, Bureau of Animal Industry.......... | 3,713,692.37 | 3,653,315.06 | 60,377.31 | ............... |
| Special funds. | | | | |
| Cooperative work, Forest Service................. | 1,525,993.61 | 2,197,977.24 | ............... | 671,983.63 |
| Payments to States and Territories from national forest funds..... | 1,023,083.81 | 1,180,063.13 | ............... | 156,979.32 |
| Other special funds...... | 535,254.04 | 436,662.83 | 98,591.21 | ............... |
| Total, Department of Agriculture.......... | 143,984,462.69 | 120,599,697.08 | 35,254,888.04 | 11,870,122.43 |

*Comparison of expenditures, fiscal years 1922 and 1921, on the basis of warrants issued (net)—Continued.*

|  | 1922 | 1921 | Increase, 1922. | Decrease, 1922. |
|---|---|---|---|---|
| **DEPARTMENT OF COMMERCE.** | | | | |
| Office of the Secretary....... | $359,926.44 | $367,276.86 | .................. | $7,350.42 |
| Bureau of Foreign and Domestic Commerce.......... | 1,160,266.47 | 850,577.23 | $309,689.24 | .................. |
| Bureau of the Census........ | 2,764,445.10 | 6,257,455.53 | .................. | 3,493,010.43 |
| Steamboat Inspection Service | 838,534.23 | 968,636.58 | .................. | 130,102.35 |
| Bureau of Navigation........ | 297,780.39 | 316,760.58 | .................. | 18,980.19 |
| Bureau of Standards........ | 1,753,577.93 | 1,634,649.52 | 118,928.41 | .................. |
| Bureau of Lighthouses...... | 9,062,763.72 | 9,719,309.48 | .................. | 656,545.76 |
| Coast and Geodetic Survey... | 1,690,489.43 | 1,925,361.92 | .................. | 234,872.49 |
| Bureau of Fisheries.......... | 1,153,938.04 | 1,324,461.04 | .................. | 170,523.00 |
| Increase of compensation..... | 2,009,791.04 | 2,519,707.52 | .................. | 509,916.48 |
| Miscellaneous................ | 78,634.20 | 8,392.79 | 70,241.41 | .................. |
| Total, Department of Commerce.......... | 21,170,146.99 | 25,892,589.05 | 498,859.06 | 5,221,301.12 |
| **DEPARTMENT OF THE INTERIOR.** | | | | |
| Interior civil: | | | | |
| Office of the Secretary.... | 1,153,194.11 | 1,161,429.22 | .................. | 8,235.11 |
| General Land Office..... | 706,231.93 | 685,746.83 | 20,485.10 | .................. |
| Public Land Service..... | 4,406,340.45 | 2,599,199.20 | 1,807,141.25 | .................. |
| Indian Office............. | 289,794.67 | 292,647.16 | .................. | 2,852.49 |
| Pension Office............ | 1,297,349.13 | 1,260,905.68 | 36,443.45 | .................. |
| Civil-service retirement and disability fund— | | | | |
| Investments.......... | 9,283,138.54 | 8,000,000.00 | 1,190,605.64 | ................. |
| Current expenses..... | 6,179,618.39 | 3,100,000.00 | 3,172,151.29 | .................. |
| Construction and operation of railroads in Alaska................ | 4,358,171.51 | 9,560,868.11 | .................. | 5,202,696.60 |
| Patent Office............ | 1,839,625.10 | 1,669,385.70 | 170,239.40 | .................. |
| Bureau of Education..... | 559,727.76 | 487,410.21 | 72,317.55 | ..~.............. |
| Colleges for agriculture and mechanic arts.....~. | 2,500,000.00 | 2,500,000.00 | .................. | .................. |
| Office of Architect, Capitol................ | 758,420.94 | 705,384.42 | 53,036.52 | .................. |
| Reclamation Service..... | 151,074.08 | 122,513.01 | 28,561.07 | .................. |
| Reclamation special fund. | 4,794,782.17 | 5,950,300.54 | .................. | 1,155,518.37 |
| Geological Survey....... | 1,580,337.01 | 1,623,156.18 | .................. | 42,819.17 |
| Bureau of Mines......... | 1,686,473.63 | 1,473,995.16 | 212,478.47 | .................. |
| Adjustment and payment of mineral claims, act of Mar. 2, 1919...... | 596,556.14 | 2,158,666.27 | .................. | 1,562,110.13 |
| National parks........... | 1,531,280.43 | 1,181,875.99 | 349,404.44 | .................. |
| Beneficiaries............. | 1,843,342.61 | 1,735,455.67 | 107,886.94 | .................. |
| Territorial governments.. | 32,980.62 | 103,862.34 | .................. | 70,881.72 |
| Increase of compensation. | 1,875,528.06 | 2,266,726.68 | .................. | 391,198.62 |
| Miscellaneous............ | 154,800.80 | 165,395.02 | .................. | 10,594.22 |
| Total, Interior civil..... | 47,578,768.08 | 48,804,923.39 | 7,220,751.12 | 8,446,906.43 |
| Indian affairs: | | | | |
| Current and contingent expenses............... | 1,074,556.92 | 1,444,109.65 | .................. | 369,552.73 |
| Fulfilling treaty stipulations.................. | 678,471.70 | 595,190.15 | 83,281.55 | ............... |
| Miscellaneous supports... | 636,986.07 | 700,258.19 | .................. | 63,272.12 |
| Interest on Indian trust funds.................. | 1,139,292.57 | 1,129,733.11 | 9,559.46 | .................. |
| Support of Indian schools. | 4,447,881.09 | 4,788,118.33 | .................. | 340,237.24 |
| Miscellaneous expense.... | 3,926,242.18 | 4,570,048.21 | .................. | 643,806.03 |
| Trust funds.............. | 26,596,982.55 | 28,243,349.96 | .................. | 1,646,367.41 |
| Total, Indian affairs.... | 38,500,413.08 | 41,470,807.60 | 92,841.01 | 3,063,235.53 |
| Pensions: | | | | |
| Army pensions.......... | 243,807,151.41 | 251,394,689.21 | .................. | 7,587,537.80 |
| Navy pensions.......... | 8,441,828.42 | 8,886,899.71 | .................. | 445,071.29 |
| Fees of examining surgeons, etc.............. | 327,867.87 | 329,827.21 | .................. | 1,959.34 |
| Total pensions........ | 252,576,847.70 | 260,611,416.13 | .................. | 8,034,568.43 |
| Total, Interior Department, including pensions and Indian affairs ................ | 338,656,028.86 | 350,887.147.12 | 7,313,592.13 | 19,544,710.39 |

*Comparison of expenditures, fiscal years 1922 and 1921, on the basis of warrants issued (net)—Continued.*

| | 1922 | 1921 | Increase, 1922. | Decrease, 1922. |
|---|---|---|---|---|
| **DEPARTMENT OF JUSTICE.** | | | | |
| Department of Justice proper: | | | | |
| Salaries and expenses..... | $1,057,833.73 | $1,028,912.59 | $28,921.14 | .................. |
| Detection and prosecution of crimes.......... | 1,768,955.10 | 2,320,732.87 | .................. | $551,777.77 |
| Increase of compensation. | 766,473.66 | 778,755.81 | .................. | 12,282.15 |
| Judicial: | | | | |
| Courts, salaries and expenses................. | 8,420,327.49 | 8,530,511.74 | .................. | 110,184.25 |
| Fees of jurors and witnesses................. | 2,440,732.19 | 2,351,201.72 | 89,530.47 | .................. |
| Support of prisoners...... | 1,308,687.23 | 953,425.88 | 355,261.35 | .................. |
| Penitentiaries............ | 1,392,647.39 | 1,494,075.81 | .................. | 101,428.42 |
| Miscellaneous............ | 694,626.76 | 189,834.11 | 504,792.65 | .................. |
| Total Department of Justice.............. | 17,850,283.55 | 17,647,450.53 | 978,505.61 | 775,672.59 |
| **DEPARTMENT OF LABOR.** | | | | |
| Office of the Secretary........ | 354,942.97 | 452,301.46 | .................. | 97,358.49 |
| Bureau of Labor Statistics.... | 233,208.71 | 257,144.12 | .................. | 23,935.41 |
| Bureau of Immigration....... | 3,658,199.33 | 4,348,302.03 | .................. | 690,102.70 |
| Bureau of Naturalization..... | 690,033.08 | 668,668.71 | 21,364.37 | .................. |
| Children's Bureau........... | 467,741.43 | 254,677.04 | 213,064.39 | .................. |
| Women's Bureau............ | 75,422.27 | 82,645.00 | .................. | 7,222.73 |
| Increase of compensation..... | 534,937.57 | 616,655.95 | .................. | 81,718.38 |
| Miscellaneous................ | 215,117.03 | 360,462.57 | .................. | 145,345.54 |
| Total, Department of Labor................ | 6,229,602.39 | 7,040,856.88 | 234,428.76 | 1,045,683.25 |
| **NAVY DEPARTMENT.** | | | | |
| Salaries and contingent expenses (civil).............. | 2,098,140.89 | 2,794,203.86 | .................. | 696,062.97 |
| Office of the Secretary, miscellaneous items........... | [1] 544,956.98 | 271,433.60 | .................. | 816,390.58 |
| Pay, miscellaneous........... | 11,115,051.21 | 4,872,031.43 | 6,243,019.78 | .................. |
| Bureau of Navigation: | | | | |
| Outfits on first enlistment | 8,121,868.49 | 20,989,827.74 | .................. | 12,867,959.25 |
| Transportation........... | 8,844,916.53 | 10,407,766.80 | .................. | 1,562,850.27 |
| Other items............. | 6,571,945.18 | 6,788,898.27 | .................. | 216,953.09 |
| Bureau of Engineering....... | 20,190,116.15 | 33,459,963.90 | .................. | 13,269,847.75 |
| Bureau of Construction and Repair.................... | 23,211,239.75 | 34,534,125.31 | .................. | 11,322,885.56 |
| Bureau of Ordnance: | | | | |
| New batteries for ships of the Navy........... | 4,202,364.35 | 10,008,641.17 | .................. | 5,806,276.82 |
| Ordnance and ordnance stores................. | 13,071,539.86 | 21,350,918.58 | .................. | 8,279,378.72 |
| Other items............. | [1] 621,775.18 | 12,707,091.45 | .................. | 13,328,866.63 |
| Bureau of Supply and Accounts: | | | | |
| Pay of the Navy......... | 170,660,523.38 | 169,455,338.82 | 1,205,184.56 | .................. |
| Provisions.............. | 41,156,957.40 | 49,830,671.68 | .................. | 8,673,714.28 |
| Fuel and transportation.. | 81,242,658.30 | 29,357,476.39 | 51,885,181.91 | .................. |
| Freight................. | 18,878,419.12 | 6,851,076.89 | 12,027,342.23 | .................. |
| Maintenance............ | 10,035,594.87 | 10,712,989.27 | .................. | 677,394.40 |
| Naval supply account fund................... | 32,694,233.17 | 226,623,334.57 | .................. | 193,929,101.40 |
| Clothing and small stores special fund............ | 42,159,900.61 | 6,542,791.79 | 35,617,108.82 | .................. |
| Navy allotments, trust fund................... | 1,118,152.88 | 5,970,387.96 | .................. | 4,852,235.08 |
| Other items............. | 194,525.50 | 1,178,181.26 | .................. | 983,655.76 |
| Bureau of Medicine and Surgery..................... | 6,000,990.66 | 6,265,573.51 | .................. | 264,582.85 |
| Bureau of Yards and Docks.. | 19,873,216.56 | 25,159,861.48 | .................. | 5,286,644.92 |
| Bureau of Aeronautics....... | 13,611,862.96 | 24,633,529.86 | .................. | 11,021,666.90 |
| Naval Academy.............. | 2,457,827.55 | 2,477,347.99 | .................. | 19,520.44 |
| Marine Corps: | | | | |
| Pay................... | 23,807,665.74 | 16,188,164.63 | 7,619,501.11 | .................. |
| Maintenance............ | 9,060,819.54 | 16,303,316.27 | .................. | 7,242,496.73 |
| Other items............. | 2,579,916.64 | 2,808,878.71 | .................. | 228,962.07 |
| Increase of the Navy....... | 143,028,025.57 | 202,469,924.00 | .................. | 59,441,898.43 |
| General account of advances. | [1] 257,189,984.59 | [1] 333,660,373.64 | .................. | [1] 76,470,389.05 |
| Miscellaneous.............. | 732,133.83 | 776,011.43 | .................. | 43,877.60 |
| Increase of compensation, Navy Department, including Naval Establishment... | 430,922.68 | 19,741,260.23 | .................. | 19,310,337.55 |
| Total, Navy Department.................. | 458,794,812.62 | 647,870,645.21 | 114,597,338.41 | 303,673,171.00 |

[1] Excess of repayments, deduct.

14263—FI 1922——8

*Comparison of expenditures, fiscal years 1922 and 1921, on the basis of warrants issued (net)*—Continued.

| | 1922 | 1921 | Increase, 1922. | Decrease, 1922. |
|---|---|---|---|---|
| POST OFFICE DEPARTMENT. | | | | |
| Salaries......................... | $3,220,085.87 | $2,397,129.12 | $822,956.75 | .................. |
| Deficiency in postal revenues.. | 64,346,234.52 | 130,128,458.02 | .................. | $65,782,223.50 |
| Miscellaneous expenses....... | 257,750.22 | 1,518,401.90 | .................. | 1,260,651.68 |
| Total, Post Office Department............ | 67,824,070.61 | 134,043,989.04 | 822,956.75 | 67,042,875.18 |
| Federal control of telegraph and telephone systems..... | 613.20 | 1,195,708.79 | .................. | 1,195,095.59 |
| STATE DEPARTMENT. | | | | |
| Salaries and expenses........ | 1,495,235.31 | 1,313,265.94 | 181,969.37 | .................. |
| Foreign intercourse........... | 8,864,356.16 | 7,210,625.33 | 1,653,730.83 | .................. |
| Total, State Department................. | 10,359,591.47 | 8,523,891.27 | 1,835,700.20 | .................. |
| TREASURY DEPARTMENT. | | | | |
| Office of the Secretary....... | 93,878.62 | 71,333.68 | 22,544.94 | .................. |
| Office of the chief clerk and superintendent............. | 988,756.07 | 959,930.45 | 28,825.62 | .................. |
| Office of Commissioner of Accounts and Deposits....... | 5,850.00 | .................. | 5,850.00 | .................. |
| Division of Bookkeeping and Warrants.................. | ⁷ 1,016,980.76 | ⁷ 632,409.70 | 384,571.06 | .................. |
| Division of Deposits.......... | 15,427.73 | .................. | 15,427.73 | .................. |
| Public Debt Service.......... | 5,210,650.41 | 14,124,283.78 | .................. | 8,913,633.37 |
| Division of Appointments.... | 46,709.14 | 40,417.00 | 6,292.14 | .................. |
| Division of Printing and Stationery.................... | 361,845.02 | 767,910.54 | .................. | 406,065.52 |
| Division of Mail and Files.... | 15,476.59 | 12,211.13 | 3,265.46 | .................. |
| Office of disbursing clerk..... | 27,093.88 | 26,836.94 | 256.94 | .................. |
| Customs service: | | | | |
| Administrative salaries.. | 60,829.70 | 67,459.52 | .................. | 6,629.82 |
| Collecting the revenue from customs.......... | 10,876,122.74 | 10,813,748.57 | 62,374.17 | .................. |
| Miscellaneous expenses... | 245,656.84 | 93,514.80 | 152,142.04 | .................. |
| Refunds, debentures, drawbacks, etc........ | 36,588,098.60 | 23,508,903.43 | 13,079,195.17 | .................. |
| Special funds............ | 833.87 | 3,597.96 | .................. | 2,764.09 |
| Bureau of the Budget........ | 115,325.20 | 5,000.00 | 110,325.20 | .................. |
| Federal Farm Loan Bureau.. | 233,787.01 | 208,416.75 | 25,370.26 | .................. |
| Office of Treasurer of the United States.............. | 1,629,428.86 | 1,599,334.86 | 30,094.00 | .................. |
| Office of Comptroller of the Currency.................. | 2,290,745.84 | 1,843,651.14 | 447,094.70 | .................. |
| Internal Revenue Service: | | | | |
| Administrative salaries... | 661,245.05 | 619,459.91 | 41,785.14 | .................. |
| Collecting the revenue.... | 33,175,784.19 | 32,524,619.99 | 651,164.20 | .................. |
| Enforcement of narcotic and prohibition acts.... | 7,224,417.93 | 6,819,486.23 | 404,931.70 | .................. |
| Miscellaneous expenses... | 37,800.21 | 78,423.07 | .................. | 40,622.86 |
| Refunds, debentures, drawbacks, etc........ | 51,095,516.07 | 30,420,052.56 | 20,675,463.51 | .................. |
| Special funds............ | 352,111.92 | 3,944,135.00 | .................. | 3,592,023.08 |
| Coast Guard................ | 12,096,434.57 | 12,456,317.06 | .................. | 359,882.49 |
| Coast Guard allotments, trust fund...................... | 55,913.86 | 349,086.01 | .................. | 293,172.15 |
| Bureau of Engraving and Printing: | | | | |
| Administrative salaries and miscellaneous items. | 225,326.91 | 235,179.00 | .................. | 9,852.09 |
| Compensation of employees..................... | 2,252,288.72 | 2,187,915.79 | 64,372.93 | .................. |
| Materials and miscellaneous expenses.......... | 1,353,234.84 | 1,385,500.49 | .................. | 32,265.65 |
| Plate printing............ | 1,793,731.90 | 1,764,175.48 | 29,556.42 | .................. |
| Secret Service.............. | 396,821.32 | 377,753.59 | 19,067.73 | .................. |
| Public Health Service: | | | | |
| Administrative salaries and miscellaneous items. | 2,283,881.15 | 2,758,354.32 | .................. | 474,473.17 |
| Hospital construction.... | 3,044,656.61 | 3,718,509.47 | .................. | 673,852.86 |
| Medical and hospital services................ | 27,299,595.84 | 35,437,847.37 | .................. | 8,138,251.53 |
| Pay of commissioned officers, pharmacists, acting assistant surgeons, and other employees.............. | 2,072,110.53 | 2,108,691.15 | .................. | 36,580.62 |

⁷ Includes $536,057.01 for 1922, and $72,032.20 for 1921, charges on silver dollar bullion sold under Pittman Act.

*Comparison of expenditures, fiscal years 1922 and 1921, on the basis of warrants issued (net)—Continued.*

| | 1922 | 1921 | Increase, 1922. | Decrease, 1922. |
|---|---|---|---|---|
| TREASURY DEPARTMENT—continued. | | | | |
| Public Health Service—Con. | | | | |
| Pay of personnel and maintenance of hospitals.................. | $4,264,185.34 | $10,179,750.06 | ................. | $5,915,564.72 |
| Mints and assay offices...... | 1,183,826.99 | 1,489,619.11 | ................. | 305,792.12 |
| Bureau of War Risk Insurance [8] (now U. S. Veterans' Bureau): | | | | |
| Salaries and expenses..... | 31,886.67 | 9,553,867.07 | ................. | 9,521,980.40 |
| Medical and hospital services................ | 1,438,906.29 | 4,989,765.46 | ................. | 3,550,859.17 |
| Military and naval compensation.............. | 8,137,465.39 | 127,416,407.31 | ................. | 119,278,941.92 |
| Military and naval family allowance.............. | 271,506.37 | 14,855,449.26 | ................. | 14,583,942.89 |
| Miscellaneous items...... | 2.25 | [1] 9,811.65 | $9,813.90 | ................. |
| Special funds— | | | | |
| Military and naval insurance.......... | 7,746,754.10 | 75,852,541.96 | ................. | 68,105,787.86 |
| Miscellaneous special funds.............. | [1] 56,486.43 | 8,949.06 | ................. | 65,435.49 |
| Trust fund— | | | | |
| Government life insurance fund (investments)......... | 2,015,094.52 | 20,558,946.94 | ................. | 18,543,852.42 |
| Government life insurance fund (expenses).............. | 400,938.20 | 2,526,624.08 | ................. | 2,125,685.88 |
| Public buildings: | | | | |
| Office of Supervising Architect.............. | 201,701.31 | 202,344.03 | ................. | 642.72 |
| Public buildings, construction and rent...... | 2,123,192.67 | 2,413,269.11 | ................. | 290,076.44 |
| Hospitals................. | 74,022.19 | 313,278.54 | ................. | 239,256.35 |
| Quarantine stations...... | 173,757.14 | 1,802,616.96 | ................. | 1,628,859.82 |
| Repairs, equipment, and general expenses....... | 11,380,719.19 | 4,405,499.27 | 6,975,219.92 | ................. |
| Operating expenses...... | 7,123,643.52 | 6,728,257.66 | 395,385.86 | ................. |
| American Printing House for the Blind............. | 50,000.00 | 50,000.00 | ................. | ................. |
| Increase of compensation..... | 12,080,284.14 | 14,154,309.10 | ................. | 2,074,024.96 |
| Miscellaneous............... | [1] 478,162.89 | [1] 609,749.06 | 131,586.17 | ................. |
| Accounting offices........... | ([9]) | 3,407,596.08 | ................. | 3,407,596.08 |
| Total Treasury Department............ | 263,407,605.46 | 492,253,997.09 | 43,771,976.91 | 272,618,368.54 |
| WAR DEPARTMENT. | | | | |
| Military activities: | | | | |
| War Department proper, salaries................ | 5,027,817.90 | 6,498,091.55 | ................. | 1,470,273.65 |
| Finance Department..... | 843,270.09 | 5,882,908.53 | ................. | 5,039,638.44 |
| Pay of the Army......... | 50,692,348.10 | 421,437,334.23 | ................. | 370,744,986.13 |
| Army allotments, trust fund............... | [1] 95,416.62 | 2,920,087.82 | ................. | 3,015,504.44 |
| Quartermaster Corps— | | | | |
| General appropriations................ | 118,066,698.74 | [1] 191,328,068.60 | 309,394,767.34 | ................. |
| Barracks and quarters................ | 6,907,380.34 | 7,136,013.15 | ................. | 228,632.81 |
| Construction and repair of hospitals.... | 790,712.14 | 3,277,127.56 | ................. | 2,486,415.42 |
| Inland and port storage and shipping facilities........... | 4,864,996.95 | 27,488,520.67 | ................. | 22,623,523.72 |
| Supplies, equipment, etc., Reserve Officers' Training Corps | 2,414,054.41 | 3,710,205.20 | ................. | 1,296,150.79 |
| Roads, walks, wharves, and drainage.......... | 2,107,703.21 | 4,573,673.51 | ................. | 2,465,970.30 |
| Subsistence of the Army.............. | 14,345,209.58 | ([10]) | 14,345,209.58 | ................. |

[1] Excess of repayments, deduct.
[8] Expenditures for 1922 to Aug. 9, 1921; see U. S. Veterans' Bureau, p. 110, for expenditures subsequent to such date.
[9] See General Accounting Office, p. 110, for expenditures for 1922.
[10] Paid from "General appropriations, Quartermaster Corps," in 1921.

*Comparison of expenditures, fiscal years 1922 and 1921, on the basis of warrants issued (net)—Continued.*

|  | 1922 | 1921 | Increase, 1922. | Decrease, 1922. |
|---|---|---|---|---|
| WAR DEPARTMENT—contd. | | | | |
| Military activities—Contd. | | | | |
| Quartermaster Corps - Continued. | | | | |
| Supplies, services, and transportation. | $36,604,281.77 | $23,794,210.94 | $12,810,070.83 | ................ |
| Miscellaneous items.. | 10,717,046.09 | 4,647,611.36 | 6,069,434.73 | ................ |
| Signal Service............. | 2,172,988.60 | 3,789,448.99 | ................ | $1,616,460.39 |
| Air Service............... | 23,363,506.89 | 34,135,867.99 | ................ | 10,772,361.10 |
| Medical Department..... | 2,396,466.70 | 6,827,102.64 | ................ | 4,430,635.94 |
| Bureau of Insular Affairs. | 2,168.38 | 1 512.70 | 2,681.08 | ................ |
| Engineer Department.... | 12,284,961.12 | 1 33,538,743.81 | 45,823,704.93 | ................ |
| Fortifications, etc., Panama Canal............. | 896,327.45 | 2,088,007.06 | ................ | 1,191,679.61 |
| Ordnance Department— | | | | |
| Ordnance service..... | 2,326,575.50 | 7,101,291.30 | ................ | 4,774,715.80 |
| Ordnance stores and supplies............ | 249,201.35 | 4,762,412.95 | ................ | 4,513,211.60 |
| Ammunition........ | 3,826,221.52 | 6,589,177.58 | ................ | 2,762,956.06 |
| Automatic rifles and manufacture of arms............. | 1,946,040.12 | 12,449,912.01 | ................ | 10,503,871.89 |
| Nitrate plants........ | 1,035,788.26 | 7,822,208.20 | ................ | 6,786,419.94 |
| Armament of fortifications............. | 5,388,075.98 | 45,259,017.08 | ................ | 39,870,941.10 |
| Arsenals............. | 1,755,022.63 | 3,657,895.71 | ................ | 1,902,873.08 |
| Ordnance storage facilities............. | 802,880.85 | 4,581,484.43 | ................ | 3,778,603.58 |
| Other items under Ordnance Department............... | 1 69,835.07 | 1 309,124.94 | . | 1 239,289.87 |
| Tank Service........ | 329,050.64 | 280,588.01 | 48,462.63 | ................ |
| Chemical Warfare Service | 2,334,932.92 | 1,873,592.57 | 461,340.35 | ................ |
| National Guard......... | 20,818,741.09 | 7,970,815.42 | 12,847,925.67 | ................ |
| Military Academy....... | 2,445,842.29 | 1,410,967.17 | 1,034,875.12 | ................ |
| Miscellaneous military... | 2,031,877.00 | 1,657,318.50 | 374,558.50 | ................ |
| Vocational training of soldiers................. | 749,899.30 | 3,855,419.08 | ................ | 3,105,519.78 |
| Increase of compensation, Military Establishment. | 6,303,550.28 | 15,985,116.24 | ................ | 9,681,565.96 |
| Army account of advances | 1 12,597,672.15 | 20,603,527.39 | ................ | 33,201,199.54 |
| Total, military activities.................. | 334,078,714.35 | 478,890,504.79 | 403,213,030.76 | $48,024,821.20 |
| Nonmilitary activities: | | | | |
| Public buildings and grounds................ | 849,857.06 | 897,598.77 | ................ | 47,741.71 |
| National cemeteries— | | | | |
| Disposition of remains of officers, soldiers, and civil employees.......... | 5,512,671.37 | 11,927,974.02 | ................ | 6,415,302.65 |
| Other items under national cemeteries | 383,689.20 | 473,992.65 | ................ | 90,303.45 |
| National military parks.. | 151,627.12 | 189,776.80 | ................ | 38,149.68 |
| National homes for disabled volunteer soldiers— | | | | |
| Medical and hospital services........... | 2,053,435.76 | 4,570,000.00 | ................ | 2,516,564.24 |
| Care and maintenance | 8,776,588.69 | 6,313,478.65 | 2,463,110.04 | ................ |
| Monuments............. | 22,441.80 | 55,445.67 | ................ | 33,003.87 |
| War claims and relief acts. | 1,059,013.84 | 375,744.83 | 683,269.01 | ................ |
| Artificial limbs, trusses, and appliances for disabled soldiers.......... | 48,411.80 | 138,725.96 | ................ | 90,314.16 |
| Miscellaneous war, civil.. | 928,133.02 | 1,340,529.72 | ................ | 412,396.70 |
| Increase of compensation, civil................... | 1,181,952.79 | 1,456,101.78 | ................ | 274,148.99 |
| Panama Canal, operation and maintenance....... | 2,791,035.40 | 16,230,390.79 | ................ | 13,439,355.39 |
| Trust funds— | | | | |
| Pay of the Army deposit fund......... | 7,434.65 | 1 2,159,271.52 | 2,166,706.17 | ................ |
| Soldiers' Home permanent fund....... | 948,515.51 | 1,271,876.21 | ................ | 323,360.70 |
| Preservation of birthplace of Abraham Lincoln............ | 2,500.00 | 1,700.00 | 800.00 | ................ |

1 Excess of repayments, deduct.

*Comparison of expenditures, fiscal years 1922 and 1921, on the basis of warrants issued (net)—Continued.*

| | 1922 | 1921 | Increase, 1922. | Decrease, 1922. |
|---|---|---|---|---|
| WAR DEPARTMENT—cont'd. | | | | |
| Nonmilitary activities—Con. | | | | |
| Rivers and harbors— | | | | |
| Improving rivers..... | $37,079,036.52 | $45,602,287.93 | ................. | $8,523,251.41 |
| Improving harbors... | 2,881,657.37 | 9,496,071.31 | ................. | 6,614,413.94 |
| Special funds for rivers and harbors.. | 3,301,733.37 | 3,721,963.06 | ................. | 420,229.69 |
| Total, nonmilitary activities......... | 67,979,735.27 | 101,904,386.63 | $5,313,885.22 | 39,238,536.58 |
| Total, War Department............ | 402,058,449.62 | 580,794,891.42 | 408,526,915.98 | 587,263,357.78 |
| SPECIAL ACCOUNTS. | | | | |
| Purchase of obligations of foreign Governments...... | 717,834.36 | 73,896,697.44 | ................. | 73,178,863.08 |
| Purchase of farm loan bonds.. | [1] 175,133.04 | 8,600,000.00 | ................. | 8,775,133.04 |
| Interest on the public debt.. | 989,485,409.93 | 996,676,803.75 | ................. | 7,191,393.82 |
| Premium on the public debt. | 142,311.51 | ................. | 142,311.51 | ................. |
| | 990,170,422.76 | 1,079,173,501.19 | 142,311.51 | 89,145,389.94 |
| | 3,195,622,729.96 | 4,467,332,578.98 | 1,049,801,244.94 | 2,321,511,093.96 |
| Deduct repayments received in fiscal year but not covered by warrant............ | 6,085.41 | 68,202.86 | ................. | 62,117.45 |
| | 3,195,616,644.55 | 4,467,264,376.12 | 1,049,801,244.94 | 2,321,448,976.51 |
| Add repayments covered by warrant in fiscal year subsequent to the deposit thereof..................... | 68,202.86 | 1,449,091.98 | ................. | 1,380,889.12 |
| Total, ordinary warrant expenditures......... | 3,195,684,847.41 | 4,468,713,468.10 | 1,049,801,244.94 | 2,322,829,865.63 |
| Adjustments to the general fund— | | | | |
| Add— | | | | |
| Disbursing officers' credits, etc., at beginning of fiscal year | 769,363,200.53 | 1,400,194,821.10 | ................. | 630,831,620.57 |
| Unpaid warrants at beginning of fiscal year................ | 21,584,162.21 | 16,756,579.65 | 4,827,582.56 | ................. |
| | 3,986,632,210.15 | 5,885,664,868.85 | 1,054,628,827.50 | 2,953,661,486.20 |
| Deduct— | | | | |
| Disbursing officers' credits, etc., at close of fiscal year.. | 624,470,588.44 | 769,363,200.53 | ................. | 144,892,612.09 |
| Unpaid warrants at close of fiscal year.. | 1,965,257.07 | 21,584,162.21 | ................. | 19,618,905.14 |
| | 626,435,845.51 | 790,947,362.74 | ................. | 164,511,517.23 |
| Total ordinary cash expenditures..... | [11] 3,360,196,364.64 | [11] 5,094,717,506.11 | 1,054,628,827.50 | 2,789,149,968.97 |
| PUBLIC DEBT. | | | | |
| First Liberty loan, at 3½ per cent................... | 72,200.00 | 150.00 | 72,050.00 | ................. |
| First Liberty loan, converted at 4 per cent................ | 300.00 | 550.00 | ................. | 250.00 |
| First Liberty loan, converted at 4¼ per cent......·....... | 342,550.00 | 199,300.00 | 143,250.00 | ................. |
| Second Liberty loan.......... | 650.00 | 1,000.00 | ................. | 350.00 |
| Second Liberty loan, converted at 4¼ per cent....... | 5,938,850.00 | 8,769,450.00 | ................. | 2,830,600.00 |
| Third Liberty loan.......... | 137,772,300.00 | 51,155,500.00 | $86,616,800.00 | ................. |
| Fourth Liberty loan.......... | 9,476,600.00 | 39,499,250.00 | ................. | 30,022,650.00 |
| Victory Liberty loan......... | 1,907,986,250.00 | 332,587,450.00 | 1,575,398,800.00 | ................. |

[1] Excess of payments, deduct.
[11] Exclusive of public debt retirements chargeable against ordinary receipts during 1922 of $422,352,950 and during 1921 of $422,393,350, which amounts are included in this table under public debt expenditures.

*Comparison of expenditures, fiscal years 1922 and 1921, on the basis of warrants issued (net)—Continued.*

| | 1922 | 1921 | Increase, 1922. | Decrease, 1922. |
|---|---|---|---|---|
| PUBLIC DEBT—continued. | | | | |
| Loan of 1908–1918............ | $50,620.00 | $143,200.00 | .................. | $92,580.00 |
| Certificates of indebtedness, various issues............ | 4,775,873,950.00 | 8,552,216,500.00 | .................. | 3,776,342,550.00 |
| Treasury (war) savings securities.................. | 85,415,860.52 | 159,731,963.18 | .................. | 74,316,102.66 |
| Bank-note fund.............. | 107,251,870.00 | 37,460,631.00 | $69,791,239.00 | .................. |
| Funded loan of 1907.......... | 6,200.00 | 3,600.00 | 2,600.00 | .................. |
| Miscellaneous redemptions... | 1,262.40 | 5,469.69 | .................. | 4,207.29 |
| Total public debt expenditures........... | 7,030,189,462.92 | 9,181,774,013.87 | 1,732,024,739.00 | ·3·883,609,289.95 |
| Total cash expenditures, exclusive of postal... | 10,390,385,827.56 | 14,276,491,519.98 | 2,786,653,566.50 | 6,672,759,258.92 |
| Postal Service, payable from postal revenues............ | 484,853,540.71 | 463,491,274.70 | 21,362,266.01 | .................. |
| Total expenditure, including postal........ | 10,875,239,368.27 | 14,739,982,794.68 | 2,808,015,832.51 | 6,672,759,258.92 |

The following table shows estimates of receipts and expenditures for the fiscal years 1923 and 1924 compared with classified receipts and expenditures (warrant basis) for the fiscal year 1922:

*Comparison of estimated receipts, fiscal years 1923 and 1924, with actual receipts for the fiscal year 1922 on the basis of warrants issued (net).*

| | Estimated, 1924. | Estimated, 1923. | Actual, 1922. |
|---|---|---|---|
| Receipts (ordinary): | | | |
| Customs........● ..................... | $425,000,650.00 | $450,000,000.00 | $357,544,712.40 |
| Internal revenue— | | | |
| Income and profits taxes................. | 1,500,000,000.00 | 1,500,000,000.00 | 2,086,918,464.85 |
| Miscellaneous internal revenue............ | 925,000,000.00 | 900,000,000.00 | 1,121,239,843.45 |
| Sales of public lands........................... | 600,000.00 | 725,000.00 | 895,391.22 |
| Miscellaneous receipts— | | | |
| Assessments on Federal reserve and national banks........................... | 2,000,000.00 | 2,000,000.00 | 5,079,769.36 |
| Consular fees........................... | 4,600,000.00 | 4,600,000.00 | 6,712,979.11 |
| District of Columbia............... | 17,256,500.00 | 17,985,315.00 | 14,777,218.19 |
| Federal reserve bank franchise tax........ | 10,000,000.00 | 10,000,000.00 | 59,974,465.64 |
| Farm loan bonds— | | | |
| Principal............................ | 25,000,000.00 | 25,000,000.00 | 44,400,000.00 |
| Interest............................ | 3,909,825.00 | 5,034,825.00 | 8,611,170.08 |
| Foreign loans— | | | |
| Principal repayments................ | 31,225,000.00 | 31,250,000.00 | 49,114,107.46 |
| Interest............................ | 222,761,045.00 | 224,737,965.00 | 6,607,723.54 |
| Interest on foreign obligations, sale of surplus property by War Department........ | .................... | .................... | 21,107,317.25 |
| Interest on public deposits (Treasury).... | 3,000,000.00 | 3,972,500.00 | 7,388,278.07 |
| Naval hospital fund, fines, forfeitures, etc. | 1,378,000.00 | 1,378,000.00 | 12,547,632.58 |
| Oil leasing act receipts................... | 9,000,000.00 | 9,000,000.00 | 8,337,480.25 |
| Panama Canal tolls, etc................... | 14,224,000.00 | 13,924,000.00 | 12,049,660.75 |
| Profits on coinage, bullion deposits, etc... | 10,000,000.00 | 17,000,000.00 | 21,660,921.07 |
| Sale of war supplies— | | | |
| War Department..................... | 25,800,000.00 | 70,000,000.00 | 78,268,106.20 |
| Navy Department.................... | 1,000,000.00 | 12,000,000.00 | 11,048,530.93 |
| Sale of Government property............... | 7,592,410.00 | 12,345,325.00 | 22,838,951.33 |
| Tax on circulation of national banks...... | 3,877,773.00 | 4,111,523.00 | 4,537,773.70 |
| Trust fund receipts— | | | |
| Indian moneys, proceeds of labor..... | 20,000,000.00 | 20,000,000.00 | 22,294,874.18 |
| Premiums on converted war-risk insurance.......................... | 33,733,848.00 | 31,183,640.00 | 26,007,398.63 |
| Other trust fund receipts.............. | 11,585,331.00 | 10,012,882.00 | 9,637,308.51 |
| Other miscellaneous receipts............. | 53,268,627.00 | 53,601,984.00 | 84,141,848.04 |
| | 3,361,812,359.00 | 3,429,862,959.00 | 4,103,741,926.79 |
| Adjustment to the general fund: Decrease in uncovered moneys on June 30, 1922, under such amount on June 30, 1921............ | .................... | .................... | 145,395.75 |
| Total ordinary receipts, exclusive of postal revenues···························· | 3,361,812,359.00 | 3,429,862,959.00 | 4,103,596,531.04 |

*Comparison of estimated expenditures, fiscal years 1923 and 1924, with actual expenditures for the fiscal year 1922, on the basis of warrants issued (net).*

| | Estimated, 1924. | Estimated, 1923. | Actual, 1922. |
|---|---|---|---|
| Expenditures (ordinary): | | | |
| Legislative | $14,139,128.00 | $14,289,364.00 | $16,725,922.69 |
| Executive Office | 378,280.00 | 364,360.00 | 216,534.74 |
| Independent offices— | | | |
| Alien Property Custodian | 275,000.00 | 300,000.00 | 363,965.02 |
| Alaska relief funds | 20,000.00 | 20,000.00 | 14,877.22 |
| Anthracite and Bituminous Coal Commission | 10,000.00 | 190,000.00 | .68 |
| Arlington Memorial Bridge Commission | 10,000.00 | 12,000.00 | |
| Board of Mediation and Conciliation | | | 6,657.29 |
| Bureau of Efficiency | 141,850.00 | 149,050.00 | 139,667.78 |
| Civil Service Commission | 864,197.00 | 760,000.00 | 665,978.64 |
| Commission of Fine Arts | 5,937.00 | 6,417.00 | 10,544.95 |
| | | | [1] 18,214.37 |
| Committee on Public Information | | | 1,248.69 |
| Council of National Defense | | | 2,689,005.88 |
| Employees' Compensation Commission | 3,160,000.00 | 3,075,000.00 | 18,567,989.79 |
| Federal Board for Vocational Education | 6,146,187.00 | 5,604,530.00 | |
| Federal Fuel Distribution | | 100,000.00 | |
| Federal Narcotic Control Board | | 2,500.00 | |
| Federal Power Commission | 59,903.00 | 60,000.00 | 36,992.53 |
| Federal Reserve Board | | | 4,456,034.14 |
| Federal Trade Commission | 940,000.00 | 900,000.00 | 953,537.94 |
| General Accounting Office | 2,994,000.00 | 3,500,000.00 | 2,537,374.25 |
| Grant Memorial Commission | 1,800.00 | | |
| Lincoln Memorial Commission | 3,600.00 | | |
| Perry's Victory Memorial Commission | 75,000.00 | | |
| United States Housing Corporation | 814,250.00 | 971,900.00 | 1,387,240.06 |
| Interdepartmental Social Hygiene Board | | | 412,468.16 |
| Interstate Commerce Commission | 4,468,000.00 | 5,200,000.00 | 5,391,271.55 |
| Interstate Governmental Commission, Colorado River | | 10,000.00 | |
| National Advisory Committee for Aeronautics | 250,000.00 | 215,000.00 | 175,034.55 |
| Railroads | 40,183,847.00 | 234,960,000.00 | [1] 125,232,444.02 |
| Railroad Labor Board | 330,000.00 | 335,000.00 | 402,611.91 |
| Smithsonian Institution | 620,000.00 | 736,000.00 | 835,497.54 |
| State, War, and Navy Department Buildings | 2,196,000.00 | 2,705,000.00 | 1,639,607.86 |
| Tariff Commission | 650,000.00 | 340,000.00 | 318,612.55 |
| U. S. Geographic Board | 2,000.00 | 1,000.00 | |
| U. S. Shipping Board | 30,385,000.00 | 38,508,515.00 | 86,145,816.32 |
| U. S. Veterans' Bureau | [2] 451,573,000.00 | [2] 464,184,959.00 | [2] 408,149,678.89 |
| War Finance Corporation | [1] 60,000,000.00 | [1] 125,000,000.00 | |
| Miscellaneous items | | | 1,570,715.77 |
| District of Columbia | 23,800,000.00 | 24,800,000.00 | 23,739,685.60 |
| Departmental— | | | |
| Department of Agriculture | 154,100,440.00 | 156,586,899.00 | 143,984,462.69 |
| Department of Commerce | 18,678,000.00 | 21,495,000.00 | 21,170,146.99 |
| Interior Department— | | | |
| Civil | 35,996,953.00 | 38,375,511.00 | 38,295,629.54 |
| Indian Service | 32,920,000.00 | 32,132,000.00 | 38,500,413.08 |
| Pensions (includes examining fees) | 250,924,000.00 | 275,758,000.00 | 252,576,847.70 |
| Department of Justice | 18,329,000.00 | 18,364,484.00 | 17,850,283.55 |
| Department of Labor | 5,983,775.00 | 6,770,120.00 | 6,229,602.39 |
| Navy Department— | | | |
| Pay of the Navy | 119,000,000.00 | 120,800,000.09 | 170,660,523.38 |
| Increase of the Navy | 29,000,000.00 | 53,200,000.00 | 143,028,025.57 |
| Marine Corps | 24,990,000.00 | 25,749,748.00 | 35,448,401.92 |
| All other | 149,030,637.00 | 149,442,521.00 | 109,657,861.75 |
| Post Office Department, including postal deficiencies, but excluding Postal Service payable from postal revenue | [1] 952,440.00 | [3] 31,517,170.00 | 67,824,070.61 |
| State Department | 15,245,724.00 | 15,960,089.00 | 10,359,591.47 |
| Treasury Department— | | | |
| Refunds of revenue | 37,709,093.00 | 141,421,090.00 | 87,683,614.67 |
| Collecting the revenue | 48,978,933.00 | 50,238,623.00 | 44,051,906.93 |
| Public buildings, construction, repairs, equipment, and operation | 11,031,360.00 | 22,289,620.00 | 21,077,036.02 |
| All other | 56,837,148.00 | 69,989,794.00 | [4] 109,264,966.15 |

[1] Excess of repayments, deduct.
[2] Exclusive of Army, Navy, and Marine Corps allotments of pay.
[3] Includes $14,600 additional compensation payable from Treasury.
[4] Includes expenditures of $17,970,972.84 under Bureau of War Risk Insurance (Now U. S. Veterans Bureau) to Aug. 9, 1921.

*Comparison of estimated expenditures, fiscal years 1923 and 1924, with actual expenditures for the fiscal year 1922, on the basis of warrants issued (net).—Continued.*

| | Estimated, 1924. | Estimated, 1923. | Actual, 1922. |
|---|---|---|---|
| Expenditures (ordinary)—Continued. | | | |
| Departmental—Continued. | | | |
| War Department— | | | |
| Pay of the Army...................... | $123,748,830.00 | $128,000,000.00 | $50,692,348.10 |
| Panama Canal, operation and maintenance........................... | 6,340,000.00 | 6,900,000.00 | 2,791,035.40 |
| Rivers and harbors................. | 40,000,000.00 | 48,000,000.00 | 43,262,427.26 |
| All other........................... | 146,737,802.00 | 150,038,598.00 | 305,312,638.86 |
| Interest on the public debt......................... | 950,000,000.00 | 1 1,100,000,000.00 | 989,485,409.93 |
| Investment of trust funds: | | | |
| Government life insurance fund............... | 30,417,000.00 | 27,183,000.00 | 24,578,319.36 |
| Civil service retirement and disability fund.... | 6,000,000.00 | 6,000,000.00 | 9,283,138.54 |
| District of Columbia teachers' retirement fund. | 200,000.00 | 200,000.00 | 249,500.00 |
| Federal control of telephone and telegraph systems.................................. | | | 613.20 |
| Total.................................... | 2,835,746,234.00 | 3,373,712,871.00 | 3,195,622,729.96 |
| Adjustments to the general fund— | | | |
| Decrease of uncovered repayments on June 30, 1922, under such amount on June 30, 1921........................ | | | 62,117.45 |
| Decrease in book credits of disbursing officers and agencies with the Treasurer on June 30, 1922, under such amount on June 30, 1921........................ | | | 144,892,612.09 |
| Decrease in amount of unpaid warrants on June 30, 1922, under such amount on June 30, 1921........................ | | | 19,618,905.14 |
| Total ordinary cash expenditures..... | 2,835,746,234.00 | 3,373,712,871.00 | 3,360,196,364.64 |
| Public debt retirements chargeable against ordinary receipts: | | | |
| Sinking fund............................. | 298,872,000.00 | 283,838,800.00 | 275,896,000.00 |
| Purchases of Liberty bonds from foreign repayments................................. | 31,225,000.00 | 31,250,000.00 | 64,837,900.00 |
| Bonds and notes received for Federal estate taxes................................... | 5,000,000.00 | 5,000,000.00 | 20,893,200.00 |
| Redemptions from Federal reserve bank franchise tax receipts...................... | 10,000,000.00 | 10,000,000.00 | 60,333,000.00 |
| Forfeitures, gifts, etc. | | | 392,850.00 |
| Total public debt retirements chargeable against ordinary receipts.................. | 345,097,000.00 | 330,088,800.00 | 422,352,950.00 |
| Total expenditures chargeable against ordinary receipts...................................... | 3,180,843,234.00 | 3,703,801,671.00 | 3,782,549,314.64 |
| Excess of ordinary receipts over total expenditures chargeable against ordinary receipts....... | 180,969,125.00 | | 321,047,216.40 |
| Excess of total expenditures chargeable against ordinary receipts over ordinary receipts........ | | 273,938,712.00 | |

[1] Includes $125,000,000 of accumulated interest on war-savings certificates, series of 1918, to be paid during the fiscal year 1923, though properly allocable to the full five years of their life and not simply to the fiscal year 1923.

*Estimated internal-revenue receipts under revenue act approved November 23, 1921.*

| Source of revenue. | Fiscal year 1923. | Fiscal year 1924. |
|---|---|---|
| Income tax: | | |
| Individual.................................................... | $700,000,000 | $700,000,000 |
| Corporation................................................. | 375,000,000 | 600,000,000 |
| Profits tax.................................................... | 125,000,000 | ................ |
| Back taxes.................................................... | 300,000,000 | 200,000,000 |
| Total income and profits tax........................... | 1,500,000,000 | 1,500,000,000 |
| Miscellaneous internal revenue (see details below)....................... | 900,000,000 | 925,000,000 |
| Total internal revenue.......................... | 2,400,000,000 | 2,425,000,000 |
| Miscellaneous internal revenue: | | |
| Estate tax.................................................... | 145,000,000 | 150,000,000 |
| Telegraph and telephone.................................. | 30,000,000 | 30,000,000 |
| Alcoholic spirits, etc..................................... | 35,000,000 | 33,000,000 |
| Beverages (nonalcoholic)— | | |
| Cereal beverages...................................... | 6,000,000 | 7,000,000 |
| Fruit juices and soft drinks........................ | 1,000,000 | 1,000,000 |
| Fountain sirups..................................... | 5,000,000 | 6,000,000 |
| Carbonic acid gas................................... | 2,000,000 | 2,000,000 |
| Tobacco and tobacco manufactures....................... | 300,000,000 | 300,000,000 |
| Admissions and dues...................................... | 65,000,000 | 70,000,000 |
| Automobiles, trucks, parts, etc........................... | 123,000,000 | 128,000,000 |
| Cameras and lenses....................................... | 1,000,000 | 1,000,000 |
| Photographic films and plates............................ | 100,000 | 100,000 |
| Candy........................................................ | 9,000,000 | 10,000,000 |
| Firearms, shells, etc...................................... | 5,000,000 | 6,000,000 |
| Hunting knives, dirk knives, daggers, etc................ | 15,000 | 15,000 |
| Smokers' articles.......................................... | 175,000 | 175,000 |
| Automatic vending machines, etc......................... | 100,000 | 100,000 |
| Liveries, hunting garments, etc........................... | 300,000 | 400,000 |
| Yachts and motor boats (sale)............................ | 350,000 | 400,000 |
| Art works................................................... | 700,000 | 700,000 |
| Carpets, rugs, trunks, valises, etc....................... | 1,000,000 | 1,250,000 |
| Jewelry, watches, clocks, etc............................. | 18,000,000 | 22,000,000 |
| Corporation capital stock................................. | 82,000,000 | 85,000,000 |
| Stamp taxes, including playing cards..................... | 55,000,000 | 56,000,000 |
| Oleomargarine, adulterated and process butter, etc...... | 3,000,000 | 3,000,000 |
| Miscellaneous taxes, including occupational taxes and receipts under national prohibition and narcotic laws..................... | 12,260,000 | 11,860,000 |
| Total........................................ | 900,000,000 | 925,000,000 |

*Estimates of miscellaneous receipts for the fiscal years 1923 and 1924, by various departments and establishments of the Government.*

| | 1923 | 1924 |
|---|---|---|
| Legislative establishment............................................. | $439,468.00 | $462,800.00 |
| Executive Office..................................................... | 1,000.00 | 1,000.00 |
| State Department..................................................... | 6,104,300.00 | 6,130,300.00 |
| Treasury Department................................................ | 38,504,778.00 | 29,018,992.00 |
| War Department (includes sale of surplus war supplies)............. | 89,384,947.00 | 38,465,703.00 |
| Department of Justice................................................ | 11,590,700.00 | 13,380,700.00 |
| Navy Department.................................................... | 18,572,000.00 | 6,148,000.00 |
| Interior Department.................................................. | 39,415,519.00 | 39,706,587.00 |
| Department of Agriculture............................................ | 7,217,800.00 | 7,247,000.00 |
| Department of Commerce............................................. | 3,259,050.00 | 3,578,500.00 |
| Department of Labor................................................. | 4,297,200.00 | 4,347,200.00 |
| United States Veterans' Bureau...................................... | 34,483,640.00 | 38,717,148.00 |
| Repurchases of Federal farm loan bonds............................. | 25,000,000.00 | 25,000,000.00 |
| United States Housing Corporation.................................. | 3,453,000.00 | 4,011,000.00 |
| Other independent offices and commissions.......................... | 242,277.00 | 130,884.00 |
| District of Columbia................................................. | 17,985,315.00 | 17,256,500.00 |
| Panama Canal....................................................... | 13,924,000.00 | 14,224,000.00 |
| Federal reserve bank franchise tax receipts.......................... | 10,000,000.00 | 10,000,000.00 |
| Interest on foreign obligations...................................... | 224,737,965.00 | 222,761,045.00 |
| Repayments of foreign obligations.................................. | 31,250,000.00 | 31,225,000.00 |
| Total estimated miscellaneous receipts......................... | 579,862,959.00 | 511,812,359.00 |

*Estimates for 1924 and appropriations for 1923.*

APPROPRIATIONS FOR 1923.

Appropriations made for the fiscal year 1923 and for prior years
during the first session of the Sixty-seventh Congress from July
13, 1921, and the second session of the Sixty-seventh Congress to
Nov. 1, 1922, including revised estimated permanent and indefinite appropriations, and appropriations for the Postal Service
payable from postal revenues.................................. $4,250,678,595.66

Deduct:

| | | |
|---|---|---|
| Postal Service for 1923 payable from the postal revenues.......................... | $564,524,766.50 | |
| Postal deficiencies of prior years, payable from postal revenues.................... | 8,003,431.14 | |
| Deficiencies and supplements for prior years. | 403,911,707.19 | |
| | | 976,439,904.83 |

Total appropriations for 1923, exclusive of deficiencies and
Postal Service payable from postal revenues, and excluding also the railroad guaranty, repayments under revolving
fund appropriations, repayments to appropriations, and
appropriations of unexpended balances.................. 3,274,238,690.83

Comparison of the estimates for 1924 with the appropriations for
1923 shows a decrease in the 1924 estimates of $195,298,359.14, as
exhibited in the table following, without, however, including in the
figures for 1923 the railroad guaranty, repayments under revolving
fund appropriations, repayments to appropriations, and appropriations of unexpended balances, the effect of which on the appropriations for that year is shown on pages 47 to 49 of the report for the
fiscal year 1920, but after including in the 1923 figures $125,000,000
of accumulated interest on war-savings certificates, series of 1918, to
be paid during the fiscal year 1923, though properly allocable to the
full five years of their life and not simply to the fiscal year 1923.

*Estimates of appropriations for 1924 compared with appropriations for 1923.*

[Excluding Postal Service payable from the postal revenues.]

| Department, etc. | 1924 estimates, including permanent annual. | 1923 appropriations, including revised permanent annual. | Increase, 1924 estimates over 1923 appropriations (+), decrease (−). |
|---|---|---|---|
| Legislative | $14,418,912.60 | $14,504,164.95 | −$85,252.35 |
| Executive Office | 407,850.00 | 396,595.00 | +11,255.00 |
| Independent offices: | | | |
| Alien Property Custodian | 281,200.00 | 370,000.00 | −88,800.00 |
| Arlington Memorial Bridge Commission | | 25,000.00 | −25,000.00 |
| Bureau of Efficiency | 145,000.00 | 152,200.00 | −7,200.00 |
| Civil Service Commission | 877,295.00 | 807,911.00 | +69,384.00 |
| Commission of Fine Arts | 6,000.00 | 6,480.00 | −480.00 |
| Employees' Compensation Commission | 2,432,740.00 | 2,660,306.00 | −227,566.00 |
| Federal Board for Vocational Education | 6,427,000.00 | 5,932,000.00 | +495,000.00 |
| Federal Fuel Distribution Office | | 150,000.00 | −150,000.00 |
| Federal Trade Commission | 955,000.00 | 955,600.00 | −600.00 |
| General Accounting Office | 3,361,163.00 | 3,922,418.00 | −561,255.00 |
| Housing Corporation | 870,450.00 | 1,056,425.00 | −185,975.00 |
| Interstate Commerce Commission | 4,514,500.00 | 5,361,462.00 | −846,962.00 |
| Interstate Governmental Commission, Colorado River | | 10,000.00 | −10,000.00 |
| National Advisory Committee for Aeronautics | 260,000.00 | 225,600.00 | +34,400.00 |
| Railroad Labor Board | 340,000.00 | 350,000.00 | −10,000.00 |
| Smithsonian Institution and National Museum | 654,000.00 | 791,564.00 | −137,564.00 |
| State, War, and Navy Department Buildings | 1,707,230.00 | 3,360,890.00 | −1,653,660.00 |
| Federal Narcotic Control Board | 2,500.00 | | +2,500.00 |
| Federal Power Commission | 59,495.74 | | +59,495.74 |
| Grant Memorial Commission | 1,800.00 | | +1,800.00 |
| Lincoln Memorial Commission | 3,600.00 | | +3,600.00 |
| Perry's Victory Memorial Commission | 99,185.00 | | +99,185.00 |
| Tariff Commission | 700,000.00 | 345,000.00 | +355,000.00 |
| United States Coal Commission | | 200,000.00 | −200,000.00 |
| United States Geographic Board | 2,000.00 | 1,000.00 | +1,000.00 |
| United States Shipping Board | 50,411,500.00 | 100,459,000.00 | −50,047,500.00 |
| United States Veterans' Bureau— | | | |
| Salaries and miscellaneous | 55,363,000.00 | 39,009,454.65 | +16,353,545.35 |
| Military and naval compensation | 118,450,000.00 | 160,000,000.00 | −41,550,000.00 |
| Military and naval insurance | 90,000,000.00 | (1) | +90,000,000.00 |
| Medical and hospital facilities and services | 52,000,000.00 | 76,658,680.00 | −24,658,680.00 |
| Vocational rehabilitation | 124,500,000.00 | 146,409,188.80 | −21,909,188.80 |
| Indigent in Alaska, special fund | 20,000.00 | 25,000.00 | −5,000.00 |
| District of Columbia | 25,043,973.00 | 25,971,090.80 | −927,117.80 |
| Department of Agriculture | 81,251,613.00 | 62,412,036.00 | +18,839,577.00 |
| Department of Commerce | 19,715,535.00 | 20,618,496.20 | −902,961.20 |
| Department of the Interior: | | | |
| Civil | 28,884,447.00 | 39,607,973.43 | −10,723,526.43 |
| Pensions and Pension Office | 253,350,000.00 | 254,246,191.67 | −896,191.67 |
| Indian Service | 33,973,305.00 | 34,071,052.00 | −97,747.00 |
| Department of Justice | 18,751,056.00 | 18,631,205.00 | +119,851.00 |
| Department of Labor | 6,203,556.00 | 7,490,188.11 | −1,286,632.11 |
| Navy Department: | | | |
| Pay of the Navy | 121,446,892.00 | 121,745,426.00 | −298,534.00 |
| Provisions, maintenance, freight, fuel, and transportation | 42,774,000.00 | 46,553,615.00 | −3,779,615.00 |
| Marine Corps | 25,516,005.00 | 26,346,748.00 | −830,743.00 |
| Increase of the Navy, scrapping of naval vessels, and construction and repair of vessels | 40,985,000.00 | 28,500,000.00 | +12,485,000.00 |
| Other items under Navy Department | 66,212,128.00 | 75,178,476.25 | −8,966,348.25 |
| Post Office Department (exclusive of Postal Service) | | 14,600.00 | −14,600.00 |
| State Department: | | | |
| Proper | 1,124,940.00 | 1,185,033.00 | −60,093.00 |
| Foreign intercourse | 13,933,297.79 | 9,910,167.66 | +4,023,130.13 |
| Treasury Department: | | | |
| Collecting the revenue | 49,729,690.00 | 50,933,380.00 | −1,203,690.00 |
| Refunds, drawbacks, etc., of revenue | 37,484,093.41 | 36,636,700.00 | +847,393.41 |
| Public buildings, construction | 566,750.00 | 1,102,000.00 | −535,250.00 |
| Public buildings, operating expenses, repairs, equipment, etc | 9,270,070.00 | 8,932,750.00 | +337,320.00 |
| Other items under Treasury Department | 51,838,258.87 | 63,022,435.44 | −11,184,176.57 |
| War Department: | | | |
| Military activities— | | | |
| Pay of the Army | 123,752,497.00 | 128,122,581.00 | −4,370,084.00 |
| Quartermaster Corps, subsistence, supplies, transportation, etc., of the Army | 63,085,764.00 | 63,498,468.67 | −412,704.67 |

[1] Expenditures for 1923 are being paid from balance of $43,000,000 appropriation made Oct. 6, 1917, augmented by premium receipts.

*Estimates of appropriations for 1924 compared with appropriations for 1923*—Continued.

| Department, etc. | 1924 estimates, including permanent annual. | 1923 appropriations, including revised permanent annual. | Increase, 1924 estimates over 1923 appropriations (+), decrease (−). |
|---|---|---|---|
| War Department—Continued. | | | |
| Military activities—Continued. | | | |
| National Guard............................ | $33,992,222.00 | $25,885,200.00 | +$8,107,022.00 |
| Other military activities................... | 43,453,717.00 | 53,130,605.28 | −9,676,888.28 |
| Nonmilitary activities— | | | |
| Rivers and harbors........................ | 46,599,531.00 | 63,358,261.00 | −16,758,730.00 |
| Soldiers' homes.......................... | 5,964,500.00 | 7,116,800.00 | −1,152,300.00 |
| Panama Canal, operation and maintenance | 6,889,105.28 | 4,131,234.00 | +2,757,871.28 |
| Other nonmilitary activities.............. | 2,779,964.00 | 1,651,236.92 | +1,128,727.08 |
| Interest on public debt........................... | 950,000,000.00 | ²1,100,000,000.00 | −150,000,000.00 |
| Sinking fund....................... | 298,872,000.00 | 283,838,800.00 | +15,033,200.00 |
| Other public debt retirements chargeable against ordinary receipts............................... | 46,225,000.00 | 46,250,000.00 | −25,000.00 |
| Total, excluding Postal Service payable from the postal revenues.................. | 3,078,940,331.69 | 3,274,238,690.83 | −195,298,359.14 |

² Includes $125,000,000 of accumulated interest on war-saving certificates, series of 1918, to be paid during the fiscal year 1923 though properly allocable to the full five years of their life and not simply to the fiscal year 1923.

Attention is respectfully invited to the attached abstracts of the annual reports of the various bureaus and divisions of the Treasury Department and to the tables and exhibits accompanying the report on the finances.

A. W. MELLON,
*Secretary of the Treasury.*

To the SPEAKER OF THE HOUSE OF REPRESENTATIVES.

# EXHIBITS ACCOMPANYING THE REPORT ON THE FINANCES.

125

# EXHIBITS.

## Exhibit 1.

### STATEMENT OF THE PUBLIC DEBT OF THE UNITED STATES, JUNE 30, 1922.

| Detail. | Amount issued. | Amount retired. | Amount outstanding. | |
|---|---|---|---|---|
| **INTEREST-BEARING DEBT.** | | | | |
| Bonds: | | | | |
| 2 per cent consols of 1930 | $646,250,150.00 | $46,526,100.00 | $599,724,050.00 | |
| 4 per cent loan of 1925 | 162,315,400.00 | 43,825,500.00 | 118,489,900.00 | |
| 2 per cent Panamas of 1916–1936 | 54,631,980.00 | 5,677,800.00 | 48,954,180.00 | |
| 2 per cent Panamas of 1918–1938 | 30,000,000.00 | 4,052,600.00 | 25,947,400.00 | |
| 3 per cent Panamas of 1961 | 50,000,000.00 | | 50,000,000.00 | |
| 3 per cent conversion bonds of 1946–47 | 28,894,500.00 | | 28,894,500.00 | |
| 2¼ per cent postal savings bonds (first to twenty-second series) | 11,889,440.00 | | 11,880,440.00 | $883,840,470.00 |
| First Liberty loan: | | | | |
| 3½ per cent bonds of 1932–1947 | 1,089,455,550.00 | 37,611,800.00 | $1,410,002,050.00 | |
| Converted 4 per cent bonds of 1932–1947 | | | 12,523,500.00 | |
| Converted 4¼ per cent bonds of 1932–1947 | | | 535,826,050.00 | |
| Second converted 4¼ per cent bonds of 1932–1947 | | | 3,492,150.00 | 1,951,843,750.00 |
| Second Liberty loan: | | | | |
| 4 per cent bonds of 1927–1942 | 3,807,865,000.00 | 497,267,960.00 | 54,420,800.00 | |
| Converted 4¼ per cent bonds of 1927–1942 | | | 3,256,176,250.00 | 3,310,597,050.00 |
| Third Liberty loan— | | | | |
| 4¼ per cent bonds of 1928 | 4,175,650,050.00 | 701,862,050.00 | 3,473,788,000.00 | |
| Fourth Liberty loan— | | | | |
| 4¼ per cent bonds of 1933–1938 | 6,964,581,100.00 | 619,197,350.00 | 6,345,383,750.00 | 15,081,612,550.00 |
| Notes: | | | | |
| Victory Liberty loan— | | | | |
| 4¾ per cent notes of 1922–23 | 4,495,373,000.00 | 2,504,189,600.00 | 1,991,183,400.00 | 1,991,183,400.00 |
| Treasury notes— | | | | |
| Series A–1924 | 311,191,600.00 | | 311,191,600.00 | |
| Series B–1924 | 380,706,100.00 | | 380,706,100.00 | |
| Series A–1925 | 601,599,500.00 | | 601,599,500.00 | |
| Series A–1926 | 617,769,700.00 | | 617,769,700.00 | |
| Series B–1925 | 325,329,450.00 | | 325,329,450.00 | |
| Certificates of indebtedness: | | | | |
| Tax— | | | | |
| Series TS–1922 | 182,871,000.00 | | 182,871,000.00 | |
| Series TS2–1922 | 179,691,500.00 | | 179,691,500.00 | |
| Series TD–1922 | 243,544,000.00 | | 243,544,000.00 | |
| Series TM–1923 | 266,250,000.00 | | 266,250,000.00 | 2,246,396,350.00 |

| Item | | | | | |
|---|---|---|---|---|---|
| Series TD2-1922 | 200,000,000.00 | | 200,000,000.00 | 1,345,356,500.00 | 1,828,787,500.00 |
| Series TJ-1923 | 273,000,000.00 | | 273,000,000.00 | | |
| Loan— | | | | | |
| Series B-1922 | 259,471,500.00 | 40,500.00 | 259,431,000.00 | 409,431,000.00 | |
| Series D-1922 | 150,000,000.00 | | 150,000,000.00 | 74,000,000.00 | |
| Pittman Act | 239,375,000.00 | 185,375,000.00 | 74,000,000.00 | | |
| Treasury (war) savings securities: [2] | | | | | |
| Treasury (war) savings certificates, Series 1918 | 1,022,105,582.16 | 506,233,735.13 | | 515,871,847.03 | 679,015,317.45 |
| Treasury (war) savings certificates, Series 1919 | 102,642,803.39 | 48,244,989.20 | | 54,397,934.19 | |
| Treasury (war) savings certificates, Series 1920 | 43,668,495.58 | 18,629,261.37 | | 25,039,234.21 | |
| Treasury (war) savings certificates, Series 1921 | 22,079,899.23 | 6,796,349.62 | | 15,283,549.61 | |
| Treasury savings certificates, Series 1921, issue of Dec. 15, 1921 | 1,942,809.33 | 141,340.00 | | 1,801,469.33 | |
| Treasury savings certificates, Series 1922, issue of Dec. 15, 1921 | 59,542,732.58 | 1,315,860.00 | | 58,226,872.58 | |
| Thrift and Treasury savings stamps, unclassified sales, etc | 9,019,270.75 | 624,860.25 | | 8,394,410.50 | |
| Total interest-bearing debt outstanding | | | | | 22,711,035,587.45 |
| **MATURED DEBT ON WHICH INTEREST HAS CEASED—PAYABLE ON PRESENTATION.** | | | | | |
| Funded loan of 1891, continued at 2 per cent, called for redemption May 18, 1900, matured Aug. 18, 1900 | | | | 1,000.00 | |
| Funded loan of 1891, matured Sept. 2, 1891 | | | | 19,800.00 | |
| Loan of 1904, matured Feb. 2, 1904 | | | | 13,050.00 | |
| Funded loan of 1907, matured July 2, 1907 | | | | 374,600.00 | |
| Refunding certificates, matured July 1, 1907 | | | | 10,270.00 | |
| Old debt matured at various dates prior to Jan. 1, 1861, and other items of debt matured at various dates subsequent to Jan. 1, 1861 | | | | 893,720.26 | |
| Certificates of indebtedness, at various dates, matured | | | | 9,000,000.00 | |
| Loan of 1898 | | | | 326,010.00 | |
| Victory Liberty loan 3¾ per cent notes of 1922-23 | | | | 14,669,400.00 | |
| Total matured debt outstanding on which interest has ceased | | | | | 25,250,880.36 |
| **DEBT BEARING NO INTEREST—PAYABLE ON PRESENTATION.** | | | | | |
| Obligations required to be reissued when redeemed: | | | | | |
| United States notes | | | 346,681,016.00 | 193,701,990.37 | |
| Less gold reserve | | | 152,979,025.61 | | |
| Obligations that will be retired on presentation: | | | | | |
| Old demand notes | | | | 53,012.50 | |
| National bank notes and Federal reserve bank notes assumed by the United States on deposit of lawful money for their retirement | | | | 32,039,351.50 | |
| Fractional currency | | | | 1,993,368.50 | |
| Total debt bearing no interest outstanding | | | | | 227,792,722.87 |
| Total gross debt [3] | | | | | 22,964,079,190.58 |

See p. 128 for footnotes.

Statement of the public debt of the United States, June 30, 1922—Continued.

| Detail. | Amount issued. | Amount retired. | | Amount outstanding. |
|---|---|---|---|---|
| DEBT BEARING NO INTEREST—PAYABLE ON PRESENTATION—continued. | | | | |
| Old ... Past obligations, etc.: | | | | |
| Matured interest obligations ... thing | | | | $82,145,120.55 |
| 1918 ... ased (partly estimated) on war savings securities, series of | | | | 117,113,167.32 |
| 1919 ... Past accrued (partly ... | | | | 8,967,146.18 |
| Discount accrued (partly ... ased) on war savings securities, series of 1920 ⁴ | | | | 2,805,074.49 |
| Treasury warrants and ... nds outstanding | | | | 1,965,257.07 |
| Disbursing officers' ... heks outstanding | | | | 83,467,094.88 |
| | | | | $296,463,860.49 |
| Balance held by the Treasury of the United States as per daily Treasury statement for June 30, 1922 | | | | 23,260,543,061.07 |
| Deduct: | | | | |
| Net excess of disbursements over receipts in June reports subsequently received | | | | 272,105,512.63 |
| | | | | 7,978,576.78 |
| | | | | 284,126,935.85 |
| Net debt, including matured interest obligations, etc., June 30, 1922 ⁵ | | | | 22,993,416,115.22 |

¹ Includes $14,609,400 ... Very 3¾ per cent notes shown ... der " ... alled debt on which ' ... Past has ... end."
² ... nds issued of the ... ses of 1918, 1919, and 1920 are on basis of reports of sales; amount issued of the ... ses of 1921 ... kept new issue) is on basis of cash ... pts by United States, and ... hales ... pts from sales of ... Trift stamps and ... lury savings stamps. ... nts issued of the ... ses of 1921 and 1922, new ... se, are on basis of cash receipts from sales of ... United States, plus accrued ... ust, and ... title ... pts from sales of Treasury savings stamps; the amount outstanding being the net ... ion ... tue. by Treasurer, United States, ... debt June 30, 1922, on the basis of daily Treasury statements was $22,963,381,706.31 and the net ... unt of ... Ino debt redemptions and receipts in ... nat, etc., ⁴ The total gross ... ⁴ ... dnt calculated on basis of exact ... ront at rate of 4 per cent per annum compounded quarterly, with the all ... ance for ash ... emptions to ... da. was $997,482.27.
⁵ No deduction is made on account of ... gns of foreign ... nts or other investments.

NOTE.—Issues of sol ... dir and sailors' civil relief bonds not included in the above. Total issue to June 30, 1922, was $195,500, of which $144,600 has been retired.

*Detail of outstanding interest-bearing issues as shown above, June 30, 1922.*

| Title. | Authorizing act. | Rate of interest. | Date of issue. | When redeemable or payable. | Interest payable. |
|---|---|---|---|---|---|
| Pre-war loans: | | *Per cent.* | | | |
| Consols of 1930 | Mar. 14, 1900 | 2 | Apr. 1, 1900 | Payable after Apr. 1, 1930 | Jan. 1, Apr. 1, July 1, Oct. 1. |
| Loan of 1925 | Jan. 14, 1875 | 4 | Feb. 1, 1895 | Payable after Feb. 1, 1925 | Feb 1, May 1, Aug. 1, Nov. 1. |
| Panama Canal loan, 1936 | June 28, 1902, and Dec. 21, 1905. | 2 | Aug. 1, 1906 | Redeemable after Aug. 1, 1916. Payable Aug. 1, 1936 | Do. |
| Panama Canal loan, 1938 | do | 2 | Nov. 1, 1908 | Redeemable after Nov. 1, 1918. Payable Nov. 1, 1938 | Do. |
| Panama Canal loan, 1961 | Aug. 5, 1909, Feb. 4, 1910, and Mar. 2, 1911. | 3 | June 1, 1911 | Payable June 1, 1961 | Mar. 1, June 1, Sept. 1, Dec. 1. |
| Conversion bonds | Dec. 23, 1913 | 3 | Jan. 1, 1916–17 | Payable 30 years from date of issue. | Jan. 1, Apr. 1, July 1, Oct. 1. |
| Postal savings bonds (first to twenty-second series). | June 25, 1910 | 2½ | Jan. 1, July 1, 1911–1922. | Redeemable 1 year from date of issue. Payable 20 years from date of issue. | Jan. 1, July 1. |
| War loans: | | | | | |
| First Liberty loan— | | | | | |
| 3½ per cent bonds of 1932–1947 | Apr. 24, 1917 | 3½ | June 15, 1917 | Redeemable on or after June 15, 1932. Payable June 15, 1947. | June 15, Dec. 15. |
| Converted 4 per cent bonds of 1932–1947 | Apr. 24, 1917, Sept. 24, 1917 | 4 | Nov. 15, 1917 | do | Do. |
| Converted 4¼ per cent bonds of 1932–1947 | Apr. 24, 1917, Sept. 24, 1917, as amended. | 4¼ | May 9, 1918 | do | Do. |
| Second converted 4¼ per cent bonds of 1932–1947. | do | 4¼ | Oct. 24, 1918 | do | Do. |
| Second Liberty loan— | | | | | |
| 4 per cent bonds of 1927–1942 | Sept. 24, 1917 | 4 | Nov. 15, 1917 | Redeemable on or after Nov. 15, 1927. Payable Nov. 15, 1942 | May 15, Nov. 15. |
| Converted 4¼ per cent bonds of 1927–1942 | Sept. 24, 1917, as amended | 4¼ | May 9, 1918 | do | Do. |
| Third Liberty loan— | | | | | |
| 4¼ per cent bonds of 1928 | do | 4¼ | do | Payable Sept. 15, 1928 | Mar. 15, Sept. 15. |
| Fourth Liberty loan— | | | | | |
| 4¼ per cent bonds of 1933–1938 | do | 4¼ | Oct. 24, 1918 | Redeemable on or after Oct. 15, 1933. Payable Oct. 15, 1938 | Apr. 15, Oct. 15. |
| Victory Liberty loan— | | | | | |
| 4¾ per cent Victory notes of 1922–23 | do | 4¾ | May 20, 1919 | Redeemable June 15, or Dec. 15, 1922. Payable May 20, 1923 | June 15, Dec. 15. |
| Treasury notes: | | | | | |
| Series A–1924 | do | 5¾ | June 15, 1921 | June 15, 1924 | Do. |
| Series B–1924 | do | 5½ | Sept. 15, 1921 | Sept. 15, 1924 | Mar. 15, Sept. 15. |
| Series A–1925 | do | 4¾ | Feb. 1, 1922 | Mar. 15, 1925 | Do. |
| Series A–1926 | do | 4¾ | Mar. 15, 1922 | Mar. 15, 1926 | Do. |
| Series B–1925 | do | 4⅜ | June 15, 1922 | Dec. 15, 1925 | June 15, Dec. 15. |
| Certificates of indebtedness: | | | | | |
| Tax— | | | | | |
| Series TS–1922 | do | 5¼ | Sept. 15, 1921 | Sept. 15, 1922 | Mar. 15, Sept. 15. |
| Series TS 2–1922 | do | 4½ | Nov. 1, 1921 | do | May 1, Sept. 15. |
| Series TD–1922 | do | 4½ | Dec. 15, 1921 | Dec. 15, 1922 | June 15, Dec. 15. |

*Detail of outstanding interest-bearing issues as shown above, June 30, 1922—Continued.*

| Title. | Authorizing act. | Rate of interest. | Date of issue. | When redeemable or payable. | Interest payable. |
|---|---|---|---|---|---|
| | | *Per cent.* | | | |
| Certificates of [1] indebtedness—Continued. | | | | | |
| Tax—Continued. | | | | | |
| Series TM-1923 | Sept. 24, 1917, as amended | 4¼ | Mar. 15, 1922 | Mar. 15, 1923 | Mar. 15, Sept. 15. |
| Series TD 2-1922 | do | 3¾ | June 1, 1922 | Dec. 15, 1922 | At maturity. |
| Series TS 1923 | do | 3¾ | June 15, 1922 | June 15, 1923 | June 15, Dec. 15. |
| Loan— | | | | | |
| Series B-1922 | do | 5¾ | Aug. 1, 1921 | Aug. 1, 1922 | Feb. 1, Aug. 1. |
| Series D-1922 | do | 3¾ | Apr. 15, 1921 | Oct. 16, 1922 | At maturity. |
| Pittman Act | Sept. 24, 1917, as amended, and Apr. 23, 1918. | 2 | Various dates, 1918-19. | One year from date of issue or renewal. | Jan. 1, July 1. |
| Treasury (war) savings securities | Sept. 24, 1917, as amended | [2] 4 | Jan. 2, 1918 | Jan. 1, 1923 | At maturity. |
| | | | Jan. 2, 1919 | Payable Jan. 1, 1924. | |
| | | | Jan. 2, 1920 | Payable Jan. 1, 1925. | |
| | | | Jan. 1921 | Payable Jan. 1, 1926. | |
| | | | Various dates from Dec. 15, 1921. | Five years from date of issue. | |
| Treasury savings certificates, new issue | do | [2] 4¼ | | | |
| Soldiers' and sailors' civil relief bonds | Mar. 8, 1918 | 3¾ | July 1, 1918 | Mature July 1, 1928; may be called 1 year after termination of war. | Jan. 1, July 1. |

[1] If held to maturity, war savings securities yield interest at rate of 4 per cent per annum compounded quarterly to maturity on the average period to maturity on the average issue price. Thrift stamps and Treasury savings stamps do not bear interest.
[2] Treasury savings certificates, new issue, yield interest at 4¼ per cent per annum, compounded semiannually, if held to maturity. The certificates mature five years from date of issue, but may be redeemed before maturity to yield about 3¾ per cent compounded semiannually.

## Exhibit 2.

### PRELIMINARY STATEMENT OF THE PUBLIC DEBT OCTOBER 31, 1922.

[On the basis of daily Treasury statements.]

Bonds:

| | | |
|---|---|---|
| Consols of 1930 | $599,724,050.00 | |
| Loan of 1925 | 118,489,900.00 | |
| Panama's of 1916–1936 | 48,954,180.00 | |
| Panama's of 1918–1938 | 25,947,400.00 | |
| Panama's of 1961 | 50,000,000.00 | |
| Conversion Bonds | 28,894,500.00 | |
| Postal Savings Bonds | 11,851,000.00 | |
| | | $883,861,030.00 |
| First Liberty Loan | 1,948,790,350.00 | |
| Second Liberty Loan | 3,284,350,100.00 | |
| Third Liberty Loan | 3,459,496,850.00 | |
| Fourth Liberty Loan | 6,343,039,100.00 | |
| | | 15,035,676,400.00 |
| Treasury bonds of 1947–1952 | | 742,496,494.64 |
| Total bonds | | 16,662,033,924.64 |

Notes:

| | | |
|---|---|---|
| Victory Liberty Loan—4¾ per cent— | | |
| Called for redemption Dec. 15, 1922 | 753,175,850.00 | |
| Maturing May 20, 1923 | 905,671,100.00 | |
| | | 1,658,846,950.00 |
| Treasury notes— | | |
| Series A–1924 | 311,191,600.00 | |
| Series B–1924 | 390,706,100.00 | |
| Series A–1925 | 601,599,500.00 | |
| Series B–1925 | 335,128,200.00 | |
| Series A–1926 | 617,769,700.00 | |
| Series B–1926 | 486,938,900.00 | |
| | | 2,743,334,000.00 |

Treasury Certificates:

| | | |
|---|---|---|
| Tax | 991,257,500.00 | |
| Pittman Act | 38,000,000.00 | |
| | | 1,029,257,500.00 |
| War Savings Securities (net cash receipts) | 609,286,908.90 | |
| Treasury Savings Securities (net redemption value of certificates outstanding) | 114,068,064.19 | |
| | | 723,354,973.09 |

| | |
|---|---|
| Total interest-bearing debt | 22,816,827,347.73 |
| Debt on which interest has ceased | 23,317,990.26 |
| Noninterest-bearing debt | 237,638,597.87 |
| Total gross debt | 23,077,783,935.86 |

## EXHIBIT 3.

## LIBERTY BONDS, VICTORY NOTES, TREASURY NOTES, AND CERTIFICATES OF INDEBTEDNESS OUTSTANDING (INCLUDING ISSUABLE BUT UNDELIVERED SECURITIES) BY DENOMINATIONS, JUNE 30, 1922.

| | $50. | $100. | $500. | $1,000. | $5,000. | $10,000. | $50,000. | $100,000. | Total. | Total number of pieces. |
|---|---|---|---|---|---|---|---|---|---|---|
| **First Liberty loan:** | | | | | | | | | | |
| First 3½'s— | | | | | | | | | | |
| upon obds. | $30,239,050 | $38,566,200 | $48,612,500 | $950,520,000 | $22,710,000 | $91,460,000 | $63,250,000 | $140,500,000 | $1,067,937,750 | 2,038,188 |
| ected this. | | 3,111,800 | 3,482,500 | 17,550,000 | | | | | 342,064,300 | 71,991 |
| First 4's— | | | | | | | | | | |
| Coupon bonds | 1,623,700 | 1,290,100 | 430,000 | 722,000 | 70,000 | 70,000 | 100,000 | | 4,185,800 | 46,858 |
| Registered bonds | 215,200 | 2,312,500 | 1,819,000 | 2,591,000 | 530,000 | 770,000 | | | 8,337,700 | 33,843 |
| First 4¼'s— | | | | | | | | | | |
| Coupon bonds | 34,517,900 | 63,901,900 | 57,042,000 | 155,571,000 | 30,735,000 | 56,250,000 | 7,850,000 | 16,700,000 | 397,017,800 | 1,600,804 |
| Registered bonds | 1,661,550 | 10,602,700 | 16,933,000 | 38,911,000 | 16,260,000 | 19,890,000 | | | 128,808,250 | 217,600 |
| First second 4¼'s— | | | | | | | | | | |
| upon bonds | 144,800 | 227,400 | 271,500 | 1,849,000 | 210,000 | 410,000 | | | 2,612,700 | 7,145 |
| Registered bonds | 25,350 | 106,600 | 126,500 | 311,000 | 130,000 | 180,000 | | | 879,450 | 2,181 |
| Total | 68,427,550 | 119,109,200 | 128,707,000 | 1,167,625,000 | 70,645,000 | 169,030,000 | 71,200,000 | 157,200,000 | 1,951,843,750 | 4,018,610 |
| **Second Liberty loan:** | | | | | | | | | | |
| Second 4's— | | | | | | | | | | |
| Coupon bonds | 6,744,900 | 5,472,900 | 2,064,500 | 6,233,000 | 805,000 | 1,440,000 | | 400,000 | 22,730,300 | 200,264 |
| Registered bonds | 2,039,700 | 6,636,300 | 5,462,500 | 8,967,000 | 2,905,000 | 3,480,000 | 1,800,000 | | 31,690,500 | 128,018 |
| Second 4¼'s— | | | | | | | | | | |
| Coupon bonds | 117,298,400 | 207,431,500 | 203,957,000 | 972,081,000 | 265,530,000 | 819,270,000 | 32,500,000 | 196,500,000 | 2,585,567,900 | 5,935,311 |
| Registered bonds | 6,456,450 | 30,972,400 | 51,061,500 | 140,793,000 | 68,025,000 | 124,300,000 | | | 670,608,350 | 710,819 |
| Total | 132,539,450 | 250,513,100 | 262,545,500 | 1,128,044,000 | 337,265,000 | 948,490,000 | 54,300,000 | 196,900,000 | 3,310,597,050 | 6,974,412 |
| **Third Liberty loan, third 4¼'s:** | | | | | | | | | | |
| Coupon bonds | 209,859,050 | 317,550,200 | 257,211,500 | 1,000,103,000 | 215,995,000 | 750,730,000 | 43,550,000 | 196,100,000 | 2,751,448,750 | 9,005,481 |
| Registered bonds | 14,921,950 | 63,221,300 | 78,198,000 | 167,093,000 | 60,175,000 | 99,080,000 | | | 722,339,250 | 1,278,916 |
| Total | 224,781,000 | 380,771,500 | 335,409,500 | 1,167,196,000 | 276,170,000 | 849,810,000 | 43,550,000 | 196,100,000 | 3,473,788,000 | 10,284,397 |
| **Fourth Liberty loan, fourth 4¼'s:** | | | | | | | | | | |
| Coupon bonds | 238,111,850 | 426,310,900 | 360,123,500 | 1,654,531,000 | 497,760,000 | 1,663,710,000 | 87,350,000 | 538,000,000 | 4,840,547,250 | 11,666,047 |
| Registered bonds | 21,167,300 | 97,187,700 | 115,665,500 | 294,081,000 | 123,775,000 | 227,610,000 | | | 1,504,836,500 | 1,975,278 |
| Total | 259,279,150 | 523,498,600 | 475,789,000 | 1,948,612,000 | 621,535,000 | 1,891,320,000 | 87,350,000 | 538,000,000 | 6,345,383,750 | 13,641,325 |

|  |  |  |  |  |  |  |  |  |  |  |
|---|--:|--:|--:|--:|--:|--:|--:|--:|--:|--:|
| **Victory Liberty loan:** |  |  |  |  |  |  |  |  |  |  |
| Victory 4¾'s— |  |  |  |  |  |  |  |  |  |  |
| Coupon notes | 163,692,450 | 269,929,800 | 203,073,000 | 608,198,000 | 105,835,000 | 211,100,000 | 13,850,000 | 22,500,000 | 1,561,828,250 | 7,029,768 |
| Registered notes | 7,024,450 | 49,508,700 | 73,971,000 | 178,451,000 | 45,570,000 | 38,450,000 |  |  | 429,355,150 | 975,460 |
| Victory 3¾'s— |  |  |  |  |  |  |  |  |  |  |
| Coupon notes | 57,750 | 144,100 | 277,500 | 4,119,000 | 1,665,000 | 3,270,000 | 50,000 | 3,600,000 | [1] 9,533,350 | 7,930 |
| Registered notes | 1,350 | 8,200 | 11,500 | 285,000 | 320,000 | 800,000 |  |  | [1] 5,076,050 | 598 |
| Total | 170,776,000 | 319,590,800 | 277,333,000 | 791,053,000 | 153,390,000 | 253,620,000 | 13,900,000 | 26,100,000 | [2] 2,005,792,800 | 8,013,756 |
| **Treasury notes:** |  |  |  |  |  |  |  |  |  |  |
| A–1924, 5¼ per cent |  | 1,995,600 | 11,450,000 | 55,196,000 | 49,550,000 | 85,700,000 |  | 108,300,000 | 311,191,600 | 117,415 |
| B–1924, 5¼ per cent |  | 1,214,100 | 9,340,000 | 46,882,000 | 53,060,000 | 131,210,000 |  | 149,100,000 | 390,706,100 | 102,727 |
| A–1925, 4¼ per cent |  | 1,272,000 | 8,499,500 | 51,198,000 | 68,490,000 | 182,540,000 |  | 289,600,000 | 601,599,500 | 115,765 |
| B–1925, 4¼ per cent |  | 1,538,200 | 4,135,500 | 27,962,000 | 20,125,000 | 79,870,000 |  | 165,100,000 | [3] 325,329,450 | 68,278 |
| A–1926, 4¼ per cent |  | 3,936,700 | 7,845,000 | 72,148,000 | 42,930,000 | 171,810,000 |  | 319,100,000 | 617,769,700 | 156,163 |
| Total |  | 10,256,600 | 41,170,000 | 253,386,000 | 233,155,000 | 651,130,000 |  | 1,031,200,000 | [3] 2,246,596,350 | 560,348 |
| **Certificates of indebtedness:** |  |  |  |  |  |  |  |  |  |  |
| Loan issues |  |  | 7,693,000 | 33,879,000 | 52,620,000 | 130,840,000 |  | 185,600,000 | [4] 410,632,000 | 74,729 |
| Tax issues |  |  | 22,872,000 | 107,507,000 | 171,065,000 | 406,030,000 |  | 644,900,000 | [5] 1,353,158,500 | 234,516 |
| Pittman 2 per cent |  |  |  |  |  |  |  |  | 74,000,000 |  |
| Total |  |  | 30,565,000 | 141,386,000 | 223,685,000 | 536,870,000 |  | 830,500,000 | [6] 1,837,790,500 | 309,245 |
| Grand total | 855,803,150 | 1,603,739,800 | 1,551,519,000 | 6,597,232,000 | 1,915,845,000 | 5,300,270,000 | 270,300,000 | 2,976,000,000 | [7] 21,171,792,200 | 43,802,093 |

[1] Matured obligations.

[2] Includes $14,609,400 matured Victory notes.

[3] Includes $26,296,750 Treasury notes issuable against completed payments, the denominations of which are unavailable.

[4] Includes $1,201,000 matured certificates of indebtedness.

[5] Includes $7,892,000 matured certificates of indebtedness, also $784,500 certificates of indebtedness undelivered, the denominations of which are unavailable.

[6] Includes $74,000,000 Pittman certificates not shown by denominations; $784,500 undelivered certificates of indebtedness the denominations of which are unavailable and $9,003,000 matured certificates of indebtedness.

[7] See notes (²), (⁵), and (⁶) above.

## Exhibit 4.

## REGISTERED LIBERTY BONDS AND VICTORY NOTES OUTSTANDING AND INTEREST PAYABLE, FISCAL YEAR ENDED JUNE 30, 1922.

|  | First 3½'s. | First 4's. | First 4¼'s. | First 2d 4¼'s. | Second 4's. | Second 4¼'s. |
|---|---|---|---|---|---|---|
| Outstanding June 30, 1921 | $321,215,000.00 | $10,154,100.00 | $123,470,050.00 | $1,032,550.00 | $39,996,150.00 | $669,498,950.00 |
| Net increase in registration | $20,849,300.00 | | $5,338,200.00 | | | $1,109,400.00 |
| Net decrease in ............ June 30, ... | $342,064,300.00 | $1,816,400.00 | | $153,100.00 | $8,305,650.00 | |
| .............. June 30, 19.. | | $8,337,700.00 | $128,808,250.00 | $879,450.00 | $31,690,500.00 | $670,608,350.00 |
| Interest paid during fiscal year | $11,498,072.25 | $370,682.00 | $5,403,677.85 | $39,488.32 | $1,545,187.00 | $28,651,124.83 |
| Number of accounts: | | | | | | |
| June 30, 1921 | 32,496 | 27,384 | 129,564 | 1,529 | 119,046 | 386,280 |
| June 30, 1922 | 29,330 | 22,482 | 123,094 | 1,361 | 90,204 | 370,695 |
| Net ...crease in number of accounts | 3,166 | 4,902 | 6,470 | 168 | 28,842 | 15,585 |
| Number of checks drawn | 61,493 | 49,297 | 252,049 | 2,872 | 209,929 | 761,121 |

|  | Third 4¼'s. | Fourth 4¼'s. | Victory 4¾'s. | Victory 3¾'s. | Total. |
|---|---|---|---|---|---|
| ........ June 30, 1921 | $801,851,250.00 | $1,444,906,650.00 | $630,933,950.00 | $74,695,650.00 | $4,117,754,300.00 |
| Net increase in ...... | | $59,929,850.00 | | | $87,226,750.00 |
| Net ...... decrease in ...... | $79,512,000.00 | | $201,578,800.00 | *$69,619,600.00 | $360,985,550.00 |
| Outstanding June 30, 1922 | $722,339,220.00 | $1,504,836,500.00 | $429,355,150.00 | *$5,076,050.00 | $3,843,995,500.00 |
| Interest payable during fiscal year | $3,448,826.71 | $62,644,846.96 | $25,134,668.01 | *$1,200,070.62 | $169,936,634.55 |
| Number of accounts: | | | | | |
| June 30, 1921 | 842,171 | 1,218,630 | 627,053 | 1,492 | 3,385,645 |
| June 30, 1922 | 755,742 | 1,080,673 | 537,694 | 497 | 3,011,772 |
| Net ...... increase in number of accounts | 86,429 | 137,957 | 89,359 | 945 | 373,873 |
| Number of ...... drawn | 1,632,460 | 2,332,172 | 1,159,402 | *1,387 | 6,462,182 |

¹ Matured.

* Covers but one dividend—Dec. 15, 1921.

EXHIBIT 5.

## ISSUES AND RETIREMENTS OF PRE-WAR LOANS, UNMATURED, FISCAL YEAR ENDED JUNE 30, 1922.

| | Consols of 1930. | | | 4 per cent loan of 1925. | | | 2 per cent Panama's of 1916–1936. | | | 2 per cent Panama's of 1918–1938. | | |
|---|---|---|---|---|---|---|---|---|---|---|---|---|
| | Registered. | Coupon. | Total. | Registered. | Coupon. | Total. | Registered. | Coupon. | Total. | Registered. | Coupon. | Total. |
| Outstanding June 30, 1921 | $598,532,300 | $1,191,750 | $599,724,050 | $108,863,950 | $9,625,950 | $118,489,900 | $48,948,140 | $6,040 | $48,954,180 | $25,875,720 | $71,680 | $25,947,400 |
| Issued on account of: | | | | | | | | | | | | |
| Exchange for coupon bonds | 115,950 | | 115,950 | 1,309,800 | | 1,309,800 | 40 | | 40 | 200 | | 200 |
| Exchange for mutilated bonds | | | | 500 | | 500 | | | | | | |
| Transfer of ownership | 26,962,950 | | 26,962,950 | 13,154,900 | | 13,154,900 | 1,538,420 | | 1,538,420 | 1,081,940 | | 1,081,940 |
| Claims settlements | | | | 4,500 | | 4,500 | | | | | | |
| Total issued | 27,078,900 | | 27,078,900 | 14,469,700 | | 14,469,700 | 1,538,460 | | 1,538,460 | 1,082,140 | | 1,082,140 |
| Retired on account of: | | | | | | | | | | | | |
| Exchange for registered bonds | | 115,950 | 115,950 | | 1,309,800 | 1,309,800 | | 40 | 40 | | 200 | 200 |
| Exchange for mutilated bonds | | | | 500 | | 500 | | | | | | |
| Transfer of ownership | 26,962,950 | | 26,962,950 | 13,154,900 | | 13,154,900 | 1,538,420 | | 1,538,420 | 1,081,940 | | 1,081,940 |
| Claims settlements | | | | 4,500 | | 4,500 | | | | | | |
| Total retired | 26,962,950 | 115,950 | 27,078,900 | 13,159,900 | 1,309,800 | 14,469,700 | 1,538,420 | 40 | 1,538,460 | 1,081,940 | 200 | 1,082,140 |
| Outstanding June 30, 1922 | 598,648,250 | 1,075,800 | 599,724,050 | 110,173,750 | 8,316,150 | 118,489,900 | 48,948,180 | 6,000 | 48,954,180 | 25,875,920 | 71,480 | 25,947,400 |

Issues and retirements of pre-war loans, unmatured, fiscal year ended June 30, 1922—Continued.

| | 3 per cent Panama's of 1961. | | | 3 per cent conversion bonds. | | | 2¼ per cent postal savings. | | | Total pre-war loans. | | |
|---|---|---|---|---|---|---|---|---|---|---|---|---|
| | Registered. | Coupon. | Total. | Registered. | Coupon. | Total. | Registered. | Coupon. | Total. | Registered. | Coupon. | Total. |
| Outstanding June 30, 1921 | $43,994,400 | $6,005,600 | $50,000,000 | $8,903,400 | $19,995,100 | $28,894,500 | $11,233,020 | $485,220 | $11,718,240 | $846,355,930 | $37,372,340 | $883,728,270 |
| **Issued on account of:** | | | | | | | | | | | | |
| Cash subscriptions | | | | | | | 108,480 | 3,720 | 112,200 | 108,480 | 3,720 | 112,200 |
| Exchange for coupon bonds | 92,700 | | 92,700 | 1,256,000 | | 1,256,000 | 80,440 | | 80,440 | 2,855,130 | | 2,855,130 |
| Exchange for mutilated bonds | 9,000 | | 9,000 | | | | 1,000 | | 1,000 | 10,500 | | 10,500 |
| Transfer of ownership | 5,333,100 | | 5,333,100 | 1,392,200 | | 1,392,200 | 762,600 | | 762,600 | 50,226,110 | | 50,226,110 |
| Claims settlements | 1,500 | | 1,500 | | | | 5,640 | | 5,640 | 11,640 | | 11,640 |
| Total issued | 5,436,300 | | 5,436,300 | 2,648,200 | | 2,648,200 | 958,160 | 3,720 | 961,880 | 53,211,880 | 3,720 | 53,215,580 |
| **Retired on account of:** | | | | | | | | | | | | |
| Exchange for registered bonds | | 92,700 | 92,700 | | 1,256,000 | 1,256,000 | | | | | 2,855,130 | 2,855,130 |
| Exchange for mutilated bonds | 9,000 | | 9,000 | | | | | 80,440 | 80,440 | 10,500 | | 10,500 |
| Transfer of ownership | 5,333,100 | | 5,333,100 | 1,392,200 | | 1,392,200 | 762,600 | | 762,600 | 50,226,110 | | 50,226,110 |
| Claims settlements | 500 | 1,000 | 1,500 | | | | 5,640 | | 5,640 | 10,640 | 1,000 | 11,640 |
| Total retired | 5,342,600 | 93,700 | 5,436,300 | 1,392,200 | 1,256,000 | 2,648,200 | 769,240 | 80,440 | 849,680 | 50,247,250 | 2,856,130 | 53,103,380 |
| Outstanding June 30, 1922 | 44,088,100 | 5,911,900 | 50,000,000 | 10,164,400 | 18,730,100 | 28,894,500 | 11,421,940 | 408,500 | 11,830,440 | 849,320,540 | 34,519,930 | 883,840,470 |

## EXHIBIT 6.

### ISSUES AND RETIREMENTS, FIRST LIBERTY LOAN, FISCAL YEAR ENDED JUNE 30, 1922.

First Liberty loan of 1932–1947.

| Detail. | 3¼'s. | | | 4's. | | 4¼'s. | | Second converted 4¼'s. | | Total. |
|---|---|---|---|---|---|---|---|---|---|---|
| | Interim certificates. | Registered. | Coupon. | Registered. | Coupon. | Registered. | Coupon. | Registered. | Coupon. | |
| Gross securities outstanding and issuable June 30, 1921. | $372,050 | $321,215,000 | $1,088,487,200 | $10,154,100 | $7,823,700 | $123,470,050 | $397,238,050 | $1,032,550 | $2,459,600 | $1,952,257,300 |
| Plus permanent bonds on consignment. | | | | | | | 328,400 | | | 328,400 |
| Less securities issuable. | | | | | 1,650 | | 19,650 | | 2,100 | 23,400 |
| Net securities outstanding June 30, 1921. | 372,050 | 321,215,000 | 1,088,487,200 | 10,154,100 | 7,827,050 | 123,470,050 | 397,546,800 | 1,032,550 | 2,457,500 | 1,952,562,300 |
| Securities issued during fiscal year upon— | | | | | | | | | | |
| Surrender, interim certificates. | | | 103,600 | | | | | | | 103,600 |
| Conversion. | | | | | | 669,200 | 4,801,950 | | | 5,471,150 |
| Exchange— | | | | | | | | | | |
| Registered for coupon. | | | 36,687,900 | | 695,350 | | 9,386,050 | | 161,750 | 46,931,050 |
| Coupon for registered. | | 59,581,100 | | 1,200 | | 14,863,350 | | 10,800 | | 74,456,450 |
| Of denominations. | | | 28,841,950 | | 278,000 | | 57,300,400 | | 395,250 | 86,815,600 |
| Temporary for permanent. | | | | | 1,595,850 | | 2,722,300 | | 126,000 | 4,444,150 |
| Mutilated for perfect. | | 300 | 16,200 | 1,000 | 750 | 2,700 | 14,950 | | | 35,900 |
| Transfer of ownership. | | 20,442,000 | | 1,400 | | 4,290,900 | | 9,300 | | 24,743,600 |
| Claims settlements. | | 59,200 | 2,900 | 15,250 | 1,800 | 40,150 | 6,750 | 1,000 | | 127,050 |
| Total. | | 80,082,600 | 65,652,550 | 18,850 | 2,571,750 | 19,866,300 | 74,232,400 | 21,100 | 683,000 | 243,128,550 |
| Securities retired during fiscal year: | | | | | | | | | | |
| Account of reissue— | | | | | | | | | | |
| Surrender, interim certificates. | 104,100 | | | | | | | | | 104,100 |
| Conversion. | | | | 1,077,500 | 4,381,500 | | | | | 5,459,000 |
| Exchange— | | | | | | | | | | |
| Registered for coupon. | | 38,770,900 | | 740,100 | | 10,097,300 | | 163,900 | | 49,772,200 |
| Coupon for registered. | | | 59,581,100 | | 1,200 | | 14,863,350 | | 10,800 | 74,456,450 |
| Of denominations. | | | 28,841,950 | | 278,000 | | 57,300,400 | | 395,250 | 86,815,600 |
| Temporary for permanent. | | | | | 1,597,550 | | 3,050,900 | | 123,900 | 4,772,350 |
| Mutilated for perfect. | | 300 | 16,200 | 1,000 | 750 | 2,700 | 14,950 | | | 35,900 |

Issues and retirements, first Liberty loan, fiscal year ended June 30, 1922—Continued.

First Liberty loan of 1932-1947.

| Detail. | Interim certificates. | 3½'s. | | 4's. | | 4¼'s. | | Second converted 4¼'s. | | Total. |
|---|---|---|---|---|---|---|---|---|---|---|
| | | Registered. | Coupon. | Registered. | Coupon. | Registered. | Coupon. | Registered. | Coupon. | |
| Securities retired during fiscal year—Continued. | | | | | | | | | | |
| Account of reissue—Continued. | | | | | | | | | | |
| Transfer of ownership | | $20,442,000 | $53,000 | $1,400 | | $4,290,900 | | $9,300 | | $24,743,600 |
| Claims settlements | | 9,100 | | 15,250 | $1,800 | 40,700 | $6,200 | 1,000 | | 127,050 |
| Total | $104,100 | 59,222,300 | 88,492,250 | 1,835,250 | 6,260,800 | 14,431,600 | 75,235,800 | 174,200 | $529,950 | 246,286,250 |
| Account of redemption— | | | | | | | | | | |
| Purchases through sinking fund | | 11,000 | | | | 16,800 | 50 | | | 27,850 |
| Received for Federal estate taxes | | | | | | 79,700 | 242,300 | | | 322,000 |
| Forfeitures | | | 60,400 | | 200 | | 2,150 | | | 62,750 |
| Gifts | | | 700 | | | | 50 | | | 750 |
| Miscellaneous receipts | | | 100 | | 100 | | | | | 200 |
| Total | | 11,000 | 61,200 | | 300 | 96,500 | 244,550 | | | 413,550 |
| Total retirements (for reissue and redemption) | 104,100 | 59,233,300 | 88,553,450 | 1,835,250 | 6,261,100 | 14,528,100 | 75,480,350 | 174,200 | 529,950 | 246,699,800 |
| Securities outstanding, June 30, 1922: | | | | | | | | | | |
| Permanent bonds | 267,950 | 342,064,300 | 1,065,586,300 | 8,337,700 | 1,730,800 | 128,808,250 | 395,117,250 | 879,450 | 2,591,650 | 1,945,383,650 |
| Temporary bonds | | | | | 2,406,900 | | 1,181,600 | | 18,900 | 3,607,400 |
| Issuable | | | 2,083,500 | | 48,100 | | 718,950 | | 2,150 | 2,852,700 |
| Total securities outstanding and issuable June 30, 1922 | 267,950 | 342,064,300 | 1,067,669,800 | 8,337,700 | 4,185,800 | 128,808,250 | 397,017,800 | 879,450 | 2,612,700 | 1,951,843,750 |

## Exhibit 7.

### ISSUES AND RETIREMENTS, SECOND LIBERTY LOAN, FISCAL YEAR ENDED JUNE 30, 1922.

| Detail. | Second Liberty loan of 1927–1942. | | | | Total. |
|---|---|---|---|---|---|
| | 4's. | | 4¼'s. | | |
| | Registered. | Coupon. | Registered. | Coupon. | |
| Gross securities outstanding and issuable June 30, 1921 | $39,996,150 | $37,874,000 | $669,498,950 | $2,569,150,950 | $3,316,520,050 |
| Plus permanent bonds on consignment | | | | 147,950 | 147,950 |
| Less securities issuable | | 2,650 | | 96,600 | 99,250 |
| Net securities outstanding June 30, 1921 | 39,996,150 | 37,871,350 | 669,498,950 | 2,569,202,300 | 3,316,568,750 |
| Securities issued during fiscal year upon— | | | | | |
| Conversion | | | 2,847,000 | 20,668,150 | 23,515,150 |
| Exchange— | | | | | |
| Registered for coupon | | 3,998,050 | | 65,282,400 | 69,280,450 |
| Coupon for registered | 12,350 | | 66,709,650 | | 66,722,000 |
| Of denominations | | 1,309,650 | | 313,647,500 | 314,957,150 |
| Temporary for permanent | | 7,007,300 | | 13,510,000 | 20,517,300 |
| Mutilated for perfect | 8,450 | 4,350 | 5,800 | 221,500 | 240,100 |
| Transfer of ownership | 25,850 | | 26,633,850 | | 26,659,700 |
| Claims settlements | 92,100 | 7,250 | 224,750 | 16,750 | 340,850 |
| Total | 138,750 | 12,326,600 | 96,421,050 | 413,346,300 | 522,232,700 |
| Securities retired during fiscal year: | | | | | |
| Account of reissue— | | | | | |
| Conversion | 4,021,650 | 19,427,050 | | | 23,448,700 |
| Exchange— | | | | | |
| Registered for coupon | 4,296,350 | | 67,765,300 | | 72,061,650 |
| Coupon for registered | | 12,350 | | 66,709,650 | 66,722,000 |
| Of denominations | | 1,309,650 | | 313,647,500 | 314,957,150 |
| Temporary for permanent | | 7,014,100 | | 13,659,200 | 20,673,300 |
| Mutilated for perfect | 8,450 | 4,350 | 5,800 | 221,500 | 240,100 |
| Transfer of ownership | 25,850 | | 26,633,850 | | 26,659,700 |
| Claims settlements | 92,100 | 7,250 | 210,850 | 30,650 | 340,850 |
| Total | 8,444,400 | 27,774,750 | 94,615,800 | 394,268,500 | 525,103,450 |
| Account of redemption— | | | | | |
| Purchases through sinking fund | | | 108,300 | 700 | 109,000 |
| Received for Federal estate taxes | | | 587,550 | 5,089,700 | 5,677,250 |
| Forfeitures | | 650 | | 49,050 | 49,700 |
| Gifts | | | | 50 | 50 |
| Miscellaneous receipts | | | | 87,000 | 87,000 |
| Total | | 650 | 695,850 | 5,226,500 | 5,923,000 |
| Total retirements (for reissue and redemption) | 8,444,400 | 27,775,400 | 95,311,650 | 399,495,000 | 531,026,450 |
| Securities outstanding June 30, 1922: | | | | | |
| Permanent bonds | 31,690,500 | 12,518,750 | 670,608,350 | 2,577,608,500 | 3,292,426,100 |
| Temporary bonds | | 9,903,800 | | 5,445,100 | 15,348,900 |
| Issuable | | 307,750 | | 2,514,300 | 2,822,050 |
| Total securities outstanding and issuable June 30, 1922. | 31,690,500 | 22,730,300 | 670,608,350 | 2,585,567,900 | 3,310,597,050 |

## Exhibit 8.

## ISSUES AND RETIREMENTS, THIRD AND FOURTH LIBERTY LOANS, FISCAL YEAR ENDED JUNE 30, 1922.

| Detail. | Third Liberty loan of 1928. | | | Fourth Liberty loan of 1933–1938. | | |
|---|---|---|---|---|---|---|
| | Registered. | Coupon. | Total. | Registered. | Coupon. | Total. |
| Gross securities outstanding and issuable June 30, 1921 | $801,851,250 | $2,809,704,000 | $3,611,555,250 | $1,444,906,650 | $4,909,938,850 | $6,354,845,500 |
| Less securities issuable | | 67,250 | 67,250 | | 1,367,800 | 1,367,800 |
| Plus permanent bonds on consignment | | | | | | |
| Net securities outstanding June 30, 1921 | 801,851,250 | 2,809,771,250 | 3,611,622,500 | 1,444,906,650 | 4,908,571,050 | 6,353,477,700 |
| Securities issued during fiscal year upon— | | | | | | |
| Exchange— | | | | | | |
| Registered for coupon | | 106,070,050 | 106,070,050 | | 114,027,200 | 114,027,200 |
| Coupon for registered | 71,035,100 | | 71,035,100 | 181,203,650 | | 181,203,650 |
| Of denominations | | 387,596,150 | 387,596,150 | | 550,923,050 | 550,923,050 |
| Temporary for permanent | | 38,959,400 | 38,959,400 | | 183,151,300 | 183,151,300 |
| Mutilated for perfect | 30,000 | 456,600 | 486,600 | 67,300 | 158,500 | 225,800 |
| Transfer of ownership | 19,117,400 | | 19,117,400 | 43,716,000 | | 43,716,000 |
| Claims settlements | 432,800 | 41,250 | 474,050 | 699,450 | 335,000 | 1,034,450 |
| Total | 90,615,300 | 533,123,450 | 623,738,750 | 225,686,400 | 848,585,050 | 1,074,281,450 |
| Securities ... ... during fiscal year: | | | | | | |
| ... of reissue— | | | | | | |
| Exchange— | | | | | | |
| Registered for ... in | 110,103,950 | | 110,103,950 | 120,192,650 | | 120,192,650 |
| Coupon for registered | | 71,035,100 | 71,035,100 | | 181,203,650 | 181,203,650 |
| Of denominations | | 387,597,150 | 387,597,150 | | 550,944,550 | 550,944,550 |
| Temporary for permanent | | 39,037,950 | 39,037,950 | | 183,813,250 | 183,813,250 |
| Mutilated for perfect | 30,000 | 456,600 | 486,600 | 67,300 | 158,500 | 225,800 |
| Transfer of ownership | 19,117,400 | | 19,117,400 | 43,716,000 | | 43,716,000 |
| Claims ... | 420,150 | 53,900 | 474,050 | 710,400 | 324,050 | 1,034,450 |
| Total | 129,671,500 | 498,180,700 | 627,852,200 | 164,686,350 | 914,444,000 | 1,079,130,350 |
| Account of redemption— | | | | | | |
| Purchased through— | | | | | | |
| Sinking fund | 1,973,700 | 15,234,800 | 17,208,500 | 240,200 | 450 | 240,650 |
| Proceeds of repayments of loans to foreign governments | 38,123,000 | 26,714,900 | 64,837,900 | | | |
| Franchise tax receipts | | 50,885,000 | 50,885,000 | | | |
| Received for Federal estate taxes | 359,100 | 4,470,000 | 4,829,100 | 829,600 | 8,372,550 | 9,202,150 |
| Forfeitures | | 6,650 | 6,650 | | 18,250 | 18,250 |

| | 50 50 | 50 50 | 50 50 | 400 | 100 200 | 500 200 |
|---|---|---|---|---|---|---|
| Gifts | | | | | | |
| Miscellaneous receipts | | | | | | |
| Total | 40,455,800 | 97,311,450 | 137,767,250 | 1,070,200 | 8,391,550 | 9,461,750 |
| Total retirements (for reissue and redemption) | 170,127,300 | 595,492,150 | 765,619,450 | 165,756,550 | 922,835,550 | 1,088,592,100 |
| Securities outstanding June 30, 1922: | | | | | | |
| Permanent bonds | 722,339,250 | 2,719,956,100 | 3,442,295,350 | 1,504,836,500 | 4,779,735,550 | 6,284,572,050 |
| Temporary bonds | | 27,446,450 | 27,446,450 | | 54,595,000 | 54,595,000 |
| Issuable June 30, 1922 | | 4,046,200 | 4,046,200 | | 6,216,700 | 6,216,700 |
| Total securities outstanding and issuable June 30, 1922 | 722,339,250 | 2,751,448,750 | 3,473,788,000 | 1,504,836,500 | 4,840,547,250 | 6,345,383,750 |

## EXHIBIT 9.

### ISSUES AND RETIREMENTS, VICTORY LIBERTY LOAN, FISCAL YEAR ENDED JUNE 30, 1922.

| Detail. | Victory Liberty loan of 1922–23. | | | | Total. |
|---|---|---|---|---|---|
| | 4¾'s. | | 3¾'s. | | |
| | Registered. | Coupon. | Registered. | Coupon. | |
| Gross securities outstanding and issuable June 30, 1921 | $630,933,950 | $2,641,908,400 | $74,695,650 | $566,232,350 | $3,913,770,350 |
| Less securities issuable | | 71,200 | | | 71,200 |
| Net securities outstanding June 30, 1921 | 630,933,950 | 2,641,837,200 | 74,695,650 | 566,232,350 | 3,913,699,150 |
| Securities issued during fiscal year upon— | | | | | |
| Original subscription | | [1] 1,300 | | | [1] 1,300 |
| Conversion | 1,747,550 | 210,281,300 | 56,800 | 18,941,800 | 231,027,450 |
| Exchange— | | | | | |
| Registered for coupon | | 139,080,250 | | 19,117,500 | 158,197,750 |
| Coupon for registered | 29,865,000 | | 2,234,650 | | 32,099,650 |
| Of denominations | | 513,464,700 | | 17,082,300 | 530,547,000 |
| Mutilated for perfect | 38,550 | 36,950 | 300 | | 75,800 |
| Transfer of ownership | 13,586,750 | | 1,332,200 | | 14,918,950 |
| Claims settlements | 461,350 | 81,650 | | 1,300,000 | 1,843,000 |
| Total | 45,699,200 | 862,943,550 | 3,623,950 | 56,441,600 | 968,708,300 |
| Securities retired during fiscal year: | | | | | |
| Account of reissue— | | | | | |
| Conversion | 171,800 | 18,826,800 | 4,833,550 | 207,124,100 | 230,956,250 |
| Exchange— | | | | | |
| Registered for coupon | 144,421,550 | | 19,117,500 | | 163,539,050 |
| Coupon for registered | | 29,865,000 | | 2,234,650 | 32,099,650 |
| Of denominations | | 513,464,700 | | 17,082,300 | 530,547,000 |
| Mutilated for perfect | 38,550 | 36,950 | | | 75,800 |
| Transfer of ownership | 13,586,750 | | 1,332,200 | | 14,918,950 |
| Claims settlements | 477,300 | 65,700 | 1,300,000 | | 1,843,000 |
| Total | 158,695,950 | 562,259,150 | 26,583,550 | 226,441,050 | 973,979,700 |
| Account of redemption· | | | | | |
| Purchased through— | | | | | |
| Sinking fund | | 211,017,000 | | 47,293,000 | 258,310,000 |
| Bond purchase fund | | 112,661,000 | | 17,859,000 | 130,520,000 |
| Franchise tax receipts | | 8,707,000 | | 741,000 | 9,448,000 |
| Proceeds of Treasury notes | 1,489,600 | 6,598,150 | 6,700 | 10,100 | 8,104,550 |
| Received for Federal estate taxes | 70,050 | 744,750 | | | 814,800 |
| Forfeitures | | 2,500 | | | 2,500 |
| Gifts | | 550 | | | 550 |
| Miscellaneous receipts | | 163,650 | | | 163,650 |
| Victory notes redeemed— | | | | | |
| In exchange for Treasury notes— | | | | | |
| Series A–1925 | 8,047,150 | 181,873,000 | 1,490,000 | 8,729,500 | 200,139,650 |
| Series A–1926 | 63,670,650 | 554,099,050 | | | 617,769,700 |
| Series B–1925 | 15,304,600 | 310,024,900 | | | 325,329,500 |
| In pursuance of call of 3¾ per cent notes— | | | | | |
| Redemptions prior to June 15, 1922 | | | 24,825,800 | 111,245,650 | 136,071,450 |
| Redemptions as of June 15, 1922 | | | 20,337,500 | 191,460,300 | 211,797,800 |
| In exchange for certificates of indebtedness— | | | | | |
| Series TD2–1922 | | | | 216,500 | 216,500 |
| Series TJ–1923 | | | | 7,790,500 | 7,790,500 |
| Received for Federal income and profits taxes | | 143,100 | | 1,354,000 | 1,497,100 |
| Total | 88,582,050 | 1,386,034,650 | 46,660,000 | 386,699,550 | 1,907,976,250 |
| Total retirements (for reissue and redemption) | 247,278,000 | 1,948,293,800 | 73,243,550 | 613,140,600 | 2,881,955,950 |
| Securities outstanding June 30, 1922 | 429,355,150 | 1,556,486,950 | 5,076,050 | 9,533,350 | 2,000,451,500 |
| Issuable, June 30, 1922 | | 5,341,300 | | | 5,341,300 |
| Total securities outstanding and issuable, June 30, 1922 | 429,355,150 | 1,561,828,250 | 5,076,050 | 9,533,350 | 2,005,792,800 |

[1] Counter entry; deduct.

## Exhibit 10.

## TREASURY NOTES ISSUED, RETIRED, AND OUTSTANDING, FISCAL YEAR 1922.

| Title. | Outstanding June 30, 1921. | Issued on subscriptions. | Issued and retired on account of— | | Outstanding June 30, 1922. |
|---|---|---|---|---|---|
| | | | Denominational exchange. | Transfer between Federal reserve banks. | |
| Treasury notes: | | | | | |
| Series A-1924 | $311,191,600 | | $37,320,700 | $22,343,700 | $311,191,600 |
| Series B-1924 | | $390,706,100 | 41,176,300 | 54,226,600 | 390,706,100 |
| Series A-1925 | | 601,599,500 | 49,552,400 | 82,277,500 | 601,599,500 |
| Series B-1925 | | 325,329,450 | ¹ 3,566,500 | 4,000,000 | ¹ 325,329,450 |
| Series A-1926 | | 617,769,700 | 25,185,800 | 21,084,500 | 617,769,700 |
| Total | 311,191,600 | 1,935,404,750 | 156,801,700 | 183,932,300 | 2,246,596,350 |

¹ Includes $2,000 issuable on exchange.

## EXHIBIT 11.

## LOAN AND TAX CERTIFICATES OF INDEBTEDNESS ISSUED, RETIRED, AND OUTSTANDING, FISCAL YEAR 1922.

| Title. | Outstanding June 30, 1921. | Issued on subscriptions. | Retired by redemptions. | Issued and retired on account of— Denominational exchange. | Transfer between Federal reserve banks. | Outstanding June 30, 1922. |
|---|---|---|---|---|---|---|
| Certificates of indebtedness: | | | | | | |
| Loan issues— | | | | | | |
| Matured— | | | | | | |
| Mar. 20, 1918.... | $500 | | | | | $500 |
| Apr. 10, 1918.... | 10,000 | | $10,000 | | | 500 |
| Series IV-A..... | 500 | | | | | 2,000 |
| Series IV-B..... | 2,000 | | | | | 5,500 |
| Series IV-C..... | 5,500 | | | | | 3,500 |
| Series IV-D..... | 3,500 | | | | | |
| Series IV-E..... | 1,000 | | 1,000 | | | |
| Series V-A...... | 1,500 | | 1,500 | | | |
| Series V-B...... | 1,000 | | | | | 1,000 |
| Series V-F...... | 1,000 | | 1, | | | |
| Series C-1920.... | 3,500 | | 3, | | | 500 |
| Series E-1920.... | 4,000 | | 4, | | | |
| Series F-1920.... | 500 | | | | | 1,000 |
| Series G-1920.... | 26,000 | | 25, | | | 500 |
| Series H-1920... | 10,000 | | 9, | | | |
| Series A-1921.... | 25,500 | | 25, | | | |
| Series B-1921.... | 34,000 | | 34, | | | 24,500 |
| Series D-1921.... | 1,143,000 | | 1,118, | | | 1,500 |
| Series E-1921.... | 76,000 | | 74 | | | 76,500 |
| Series C-1921.... | 155,492,500 | | 155,416,000 | | | 407,500 |
| Series F-1921.... | 192,026,500 | | 191,619,000 | | | 17,500 |
| Series G-1921.... | 128,886,500 | | 128,869,000 | | | 39,000 |
| Series H-1921.... | 190,511,500 | | 190,472,500 | | | 471,000 |
| Series A-1922.... | 256,170,000 | | 255,699,000 | $8,929,000 | $11,340,500 | 148,500 |
| Series C-1922.... | | $51,796,000 | 51,647,500 | 4,759,500 | 8,271,000 | |
| Unmatured— | | | | | | |
| Series B-1922.... | | 259,471,500 | 40,500 | 32,501,500 | 56,271,000 | 259,431,000 |
| Series D-1922.... | | 150,000,000 | | 13,461,000 | 58,734,500 | 150,000,000 |
| Total loan issues........ | 924,436,000 | 461,267,500 | 975,071,500 | 59,651,000 | 134,617,000 | 410,632,000 |
| Tax issues— | | | | | | |
| Matured— | | | | | | |
| Jan. 2, 1918...... | 2,000 | | | | | 2,000 |
| Aug. 20, 1918.... | 26,500 | | 5,000 | | | 21,500 |
| Series T-2....... | 27,500 | | 27,500 | | | |
| Series T-8....... | 10,000 | | 8,000 | | | 2,000 |
| Series T-10...... | 33,500 | | 16,500 | | | 17,000 |
| Series TM3-1920. | 3,000 | | 3,000 | | | |
| Series TJ-1920.. | 41,500 | | 37,500 | | | 4,000 |
| Series TD-1920.. | 190,500 | | 119,000 | | | 71,500 |
| Series TM4-1920. | 5,000 | | 1,000 | | | 4,000 |
| Series TM-1921.. | 198,000 | | 196,500 | | | 1,500 |
| Series TJ-1921.. | 5,400,000 | | 5,361,000 | | | 39,000 |
| Series TM2-1921. | 149,000 | | 133,500 | | | 15,500 |
| Series TM3-1921. | 10,000 | | 9,000 | | | 1,000 |
| Series TM4-1921. | 193,500 | | 189,500 | | | 4,000 |
| Series TJ2-1921.. | 1,605,000 | | 1,604,000 | | | 1,000 |
| Series TS-1921.. | 341,969,500 | | 341,870,000 | | | 99,500 |
| Series TD-1921.. | 389,557,500 | | 389,242,500 | | | 315,000 |
| Series TS2-1921. | 193,302,000 | | 193,294,000 | | | 8,000 |
| Series TM-1922.. | 288,501,000 | | 287,759,000 | 8,780,500 | 8,690,000 | 742,000 |
| Series TJ-1922.. | 314,184,000 | | 309,482,000 | 14,203,000 | 34,201,000 | 4,702,000 |
| Series TM2-1922. | | 116,891,000 | 116,801,500 | 14,549,000 | 8,086,500 | 89,500 |
| Series TM3-1922. | | 124,572,000 | 124,262,500 | 8,077,000 | 8,694,500 | 309,500 |
| Series TJ2-1922.. | | 64,903,000 | 63,550,500 | 6,980,000 | 16,095,000 | 1,352,500 |
| Unmatured— | | | | | | |
| Series TS-1922.. | | 182,871,000 | | 14,885,500 | 21,258,000 | 182,871,000 |
| Series TS2-1922. | | 179,691,500 | | 30,201,000 | 43,848,000 | 179,691,500 |
| Series TD-1922.. | | 243,544,000 | | 28,494,500 | 47,118,000 | 243,544,000 |
| Series TM-1923.. | | 266,250,000 | | 22,305,500 | 55,596,500 | 266,250,000 |
| Series TD2-1922. | | 200,000,000 | | 5,380,000 | 51,783,500 | 200,000,000 |
| Series TJ-1923... | | 273,000,000 | | 4,244,000 | 43,212,500 | 273,000,000 |
| Total tax issues........ | 1,535,409,000 | 1,651,722,500 | 1,833,973,000 | 158,100,000 | 338,583,500 | 1,353,158,500 |
| Grand total... | 2,459,845,000 | 2,112,990,000 | 2,809,044,500 | 217,751,000 | 473,200,500 | 1,763,790,500 |

## EXHIBIT 12.

### ISSUES AND RETIREMENTS OF TREASURY (WAR) SAVINGS SECURITIES, FISCAL YEAR ENDED JUNE 30, 1922.

| Detail. | Series. | | | | New issue. | | Thrift and Treasury savings stamps, unclassified sales, etc. | Total. |
|---|---|---|---|---|---|---|---|---|
| | 1918 | 1919 | 1920 | 1921 | 1921 | 1922 | | |
| **Securities** outstanding June 30, 1921 [1], Accrued interest liabilities (actual and contingent) | $580,175,584.02 | $62,490,941.33 | $28,925,797.06 | $11,865,447.91 | | | $10,647,640.00 | $694,105,410.37 |
| | 95,273,993.11 | 6,640,184.50 | | | | | | 101,914,177.61 |
| Total value of outstanding securities June 30, 1921 | 675,449,577.13 | 69,131,125.88 | 28,925,797.06 | 11,865,447.91 | | | 10,647,640.00 | 796,019,587.98 |
| Issued during fiscal year 1922 | [2]3,134.82 | [2]4,065.30 | 1,657,712.29 | 9,060,172.66 | [2]$1,942,809.33 | [3]$59,542,732.58 | [2]1,571,757.00 | 79,654,469.74 |
| Retired during fiscal year 1922: Reimbursements to agents for unsold securities | 2,352.20 | 462.80 | 14,569.64 | 251,072.00 | 141,340.00 | 1,315,860.00 | 60,245.50 | 328,702.14 |
| Redemptions | 64,298,249.97 | 8,088,479.09 | 5,559,765.50 | 5,390,998.96 | | | 621,227.00 | 85,415,860.52 |
| Total | 64,300,602.17 | 8,088,941.89 | 5,574,275.14 | 5,642,070.96 | 141,340.00 | 1,315,860.00 | 681,472.50 | 85,744,562.66 |
| **Securities** outstanding June 30, 1922 [4], Accrued interest liabilities (actual and contingent) | 515,871,847.03 | 54,307,934.19 | 25,039,234.21 | 15,283,549.61 | [3]1,801,469.33 | [3]58,226,872.58 | 8,394,410.50 | 679,015,317.45 |
| | 117,113,167.32 | 8,967,146.18 | 2,896,074.49 | (⁵) | | | | 128,886,387.99 |
| Total value of outstanding securities June 30, 1922 | 632,985,014.35 | 63,365,080.37 | 27,845,308.70 | 15,283,549.61 | 1,801,469.33 | 58,226,872.58 | 8,394,410.50 | 807,901,705.44 |

[1] Series 1918 and 1919 were on basis of sales reports; series 1920 and 1921 were on basis of Treasurer's net cash receipts.
[2] Deduct adjustments in sales reports subsequent to June 30, 1921.
[3] Net redemption value; includes accrued discount, which has been charged by Treasurer as interest payment and credited as a public debt receipt.
[4] Series 1918, 1919, and 1920 are on basis of sales reports; series 1921, 1921 (new issue), and 1922 (new issue) are on basis of Treasurer's net cash receipts.
[5] Figures not available for computation of accrued discount.

EXHIBIT 13.

LIBERTY BONDS, VICTORY NOTES, TREASURY NOTES, AND CERTIFICATES OF INDEBTEDNESS DELIVERED AND RETIRED DURING THE FISCAL YEAR 1922 AND OUTSTANDING ON JUNE 30, 1922.

| Loan or series. | June 30, 1921. | | Delivered. | Retired. | June 30, 1922. | |
|---|---|---|---|---|---|---|
| | Outstanding. | Unissued securities held by Federal reserve banks. | | | Unissued securities held by Federal reserve banks. | Outstanding. |
| First | | | | | | |
| 3 per cent titles | $372,050 | $1,550 | $92,186,500 | $105,650 | | $267,950 |
| 3¾ per cent upon obls | 1,088,487,200 | 6,780,900 | 83,402,700 | | $15,375,600 | 1,065,586,300 |
| 4 per cent obls | 321,215,000 | | 89,082,600 | 59,233,300 | | 342,064,300 |
| 4 per cent 1 pon bonds | 7,827,050 | 36,313,700 | 1,953,000 | 12,199,950 | 29,756,100 | 4,137,700 |
| 4¼ per cent 4 per cent old obls | 10,154,100 | | 18,550 | 1,835,250 | | 8,337,700 |
| 4¼ per cent upon bonds | 397,545,800 | 199,544,400 | 68,600,200 | 119,092,200 | 158,400,350 | 396,298,850 |
| 4¼ per cent 4½ per cent old bonds | 123,470,050 | 6,106,150 | 16,024,350 | 17,092,300 | | 128,808,250 |
| Second 1 and 4½ per cent upon bonds | 2,457,500 | 599,700 | 642,960 | 293,450 | 796,100 | 2,610,550 |
| Second 1 and 4½ per cent registered obls | 1,032,550 | 1,331,500 | 1,329,500 | 175,100 | | 879,450 |
| Second loan: | | | | | | |
| 4 per cent upon obls | 37,571,350 | 64,575,950 | 4,935,550 | 49,592,250 | 44,368,050 | 22,852,550 |
| 4 per cent old obls | 39,996,150 | | 138,750 | 8,444,400 | | 31,690,500 |
| 4½ per cent upon bonds | 2,569,202,300 | 255,263,550 | 305,246,050 | 335,983,100 | 213,725,200 | 2,583,053,600 |
| Converted 4½ per cent | 660,498,950 | 6,177,600 | 94,773,300 | 99,841,500 | | 670,608,350 |
| Third liberty loan: | | | | | | |
| 4¼ per cent upon bonds | 2,809,771,250 | 686,193,900 | 358,783,700 | 807,749,950 | 298,696,350 | 2,817,852,550 |
| 4¼ per cent old obls | 801,851,250 | 16,851,450 | 77,971,300 | 174,334,750 | | 722,339,250 |
| Fourth loan: | | | | | | |
| 4¼ per cent old obls | 4,908,571,050 | 549,210,350 | 535,561,350 | 855,372,050 | 303,639,150 | 4,834,330,550 |
| 4¼ per cent old obls | 1,444,906,650 | 11,573,650 | 221,888,250 | 173,331,450 | | 1,504,836,500 |
| Victory Liberty loan: | | | | | | |
| 4¼ per cent 1 rpn | 2,641,537,200 | 114,435,150 | 755,932,450 | 1,536,070,200 | 119,047,550 | 1,556,486,950 |
| 4¼ per cent old bns | 639,933,950 | 23,021,250 | 15,872,350 | 340,422,400 | | 429,335,150 |
| 3¾ per cent upon ries, matured | 556,232,350 | 107,418,600 | 53,999,150 | 686,489,650 | 31,630,100 | 9,533,350 |
| 3¾ per cent old notes, matured | 74,685,650 | 9,686,450 | 417,036,850 | 62,269,200 | | 5,076,050 |
| Loan es— | | | | | | |
| Matured prior to June 30, 1921 | 1,319,000 | | | 1,308,000 | | 41,000 |
| Matured between July 1, 1921, and June 30, 1922— | | | | | | |
| Series C–1921 | 152,936,000 | 38,621,000 | | 191,480,500 | | 76,500 |
| Series G–1921 | 187,408,500 | 37,688,000 | | 224,689,000 | | 407,500 |
| Series G–1921 | 122,950,500 | 39,035,000 | | 161,963,000 | | 17,500 |
| Series H–1921 | 185,262,500 | 40,390,500 | | 225,614,000 | | 39,000 |
| Series A–1922 | 253,249,000 | 46,531,000 | 9,100,000 | 308,409,000 | | 471,000 |
| Series 1922 | | | 99,316,000 | 99,167,500 | | 148,500 |

Series B-1922.
Series D-1922.

Tax...

Series TD-1921.
Series TS2-1921.
Series TM-1922.
Series TJ-1922.
Series TM2-1922.
Series TJ2-1922.

Series TS-1922.
Series TS2-1922.
Series TD-1922.
Series TM-1923.
Series TD2-1922.
Series...

Pittman War...
Special War...
Special...
Series A-1924.
Series B-1924.
Series...
Series B-1925.
Series...

Total...

Issuable items on exchange:
Liberty loans.
Treasury notes.

Issuable items on original subscriptions (denominations unavailable):
Certificates of indebtedness.
Treasury notes.

Total issuable...

Total...

1 Consignment securities.
2 Includes shipments to Federal reserve banks for stock.
3 Includes unissued stock returned by Federal reserve banks.
4 Counter entry; deduct.
5 Includes $9,063,000 on which interest has ceased (certificates of indebtedness). Includes $14,609,400 on which interest has ceased (Victory 3¾'s).
6 Deducted from unissued securities held by Federal reserve banks and added to "outstanding," thus reconciling this statement with the public debt statement.

## Exhibit 14.

### RETIREMENTS OF PRE-WAR LOANS, MATURED, FISCAL YEAR ENDED JUNE 30, 1922.

| Detail. | Outstanding June 30, 1921. | Redeemed. | Outstanding June 30, 1922 |
|---|---|---|---|
| Funded loan of 1891, continued at 2 per cent, called for redemption May 18, 1900 | $1,000.00 | ............ | $1,000.00 |
| Funded loan of 1891, matured Sept. 2, 1891 | 19,800.00 | ............ | 19,800.00 |
| Loan of 1904, matured Feb. 2, 1904 | 13,050.00 | ............ | 13,050.00 |
| Funded loan of 1907, matured July 2, 1907 | 380,800.00 | $6,200.00 | 374,600.00 |
| Refunding certificates, matured July 1, 1907 | 10,350.00 | 80.00 | 10,270.00 |
| Old debt matured at various dates prior to July 1, 1891 | 893,960.26 | 240.00 | 893,720.26 |
| Loan of 1908–1918 | 376,660.00 | 50,620.00 | 326,040.00 |
| Total | 1,695,620.26 | 57,140.00 | 1,638,480.26 |

## Exhibit 15.

### ISSUES AND RETIREMENTS OF DEBT BEARING NO INTEREST, FISCAL YEAR ENDED JUNE 30, 1922.

| Detail. | Outstanding June 30, 1921. | Issued. | Retired. | Outstanding June 30, 1922. |
|---|---|---|---|---|
| Old demand notes | $53,012.50 | .................... | .................... | $53,012.50 |
| United States notes........ $346,681,016.00 | | | | |
| Less gold reserve.. 152,979,025.63 | | | | |
| | 193,701,990.37 | $339,348,000.00 | $339,348,000.00 | 193,701,990.37 |
| National bank notes—redemption account | 32,204,594.00 | 107,086,627.50 | 107,251,870.00 | 32,039,351.50 |
| Fractional currency | 1,999,310.90 | .................... | 942.40 | 1,908,368.50 |
| Total | 227,958,907.77 | 446,434,627.50 | 446,600,812.40 | 227,792,722.87 |

EXHIBIT 16.

PUBLIC DEBT OF THE UNITED STATES—RECAPITULATION OF ISSUES AND RETIREMENTS, FISCAL YEAR ENDED JUNE 30, 1922.

| Detail. | Interest-bearing debt. | | | | | | Matured debt. | Debt bearing no interest. | Total gross debt. |
|---|---|---|---|---|---|---|---|---|---|
| | Pre-war loans. | Treasury (war) savings securities. | Certificates of indebtedness. | Treasury notes. | Liberty bonds and Victory notes. | Total interest-bearing. | | | |
| Outstanding June 30, 1921 | $383,728,270 | $694,105,410.37 | $2,609,330,450 | $311,191,600 | $19,148,948,430 | $22,737,304,180.37 | $10,939,620.26 | $227,958,907.77 | $23,976,202,708.40 |
| Plus permanent bonds on consignment | | | | | 543,600 | 543,600.00 | | | 543,600.00 |
| Less securities issuable, June 30, 1921 | | | | | ¹ 1,561,650 | ¹ 1,561,650.00 | | | ¹ 1,561,650.00 |
| Net securities outstanding, June 30, 1921 | 383,728,270 | 694,105,410.37 | 2,609,330,450 | 311,191,600 | 19,147,930,400 | 23,736,286,130.37 | 10,939,620.26 | 227,958,907.77 | 23,975,184,658.40 |
| Issued on account of: | | | | | | | | | |
| Original subscription | 112,200 | 70,654,469.74 | ³ 3,905,000,000 | ² 1,935,404,750 | ² 1,300 | 5,911,260,119.74 | | | 5,911,260,119.74 |
| Receipts of ... money | | | | | | | | 107,086,627.50 | 107,086,627.50 |
| Interim ...es surrendered | | | | | 103,600 | 103,600.00 | | | 103,600.00 |
| Exchange of registered for coupon | | | | | 260,013,750 | 260,013,750.00 | | | 260,013,750.00 |
| Exchange of ...upon for registered | 2,855,130 | | | | 494,506,500 | 494,506,600.00 | | | 494,506,600.00 |
| Exchange of denominations | | | | | 425,516,850 | 428,371,980.00 | | | 428,371,980.00 |
| Exchange of ...ary for permanent | | | ⁴ 690,951,500 | ⁵ 340,732,000 | 1,870,838,950 | 2,902,522,450.00 | | | 2,902,522,450.00 |
| Exchange of ...ited for perfect | | | | | 247,072,130 | 247,072,150.00 | | | 247,072,150.00 |
| Transfer of ownership | 10,500 | | | | 1,064,200 | 1,074,700.00 | | | 1,074,700.00 |
| Settlement of claims | 50,226,110 | | | | 129,155,650 | 179,381,760.00 | | | 179,381,760.00 |
| United States notes reissued | 11,640 | | | | 3,819,400 | 3,831,040.00 | | 339,348,000.00 | 339,348,000.00 |
| Total | 53,215,580 | 70,654,469.74 | 4,596,041,500 | 2,276,136,750 | 3,432,089,750 | 10,428,138,049.74 | 339,348,000.00 | 446,434,627.50 | 10,874,572,677.24 |
| Retired through— | | | | | | | | | |
| Reissues on account of— | | | | | | | | | |
| Interim ...tes surrendered | | | | | 104,100 | 104,100.00 | | | 104,100.00 |
| Conversion | | | | | 259,863,950 | 259,863,950.00 | | | 259,863,950.00 |
| Exchange of registered for coupon | | | | | 515,669,500 | 515,669,500.00 | | | 515,669,500.00 |

¹ Deduct.
² Includes $784,500 on ... with definitive ...tes ... issued against interim receipts outstanding.
³ Includes $26,298,750 on ... ...ich definitive certificates were undelivered against interim receipts outstanding.
⁴ ...tes $473,200,500 exchanges ...en Federal reserve banks.
⁵ ...tes $183,932,300 exchanges ...en Federal reserve banks.

*Public debt of the United States—Recapitulation of issues and retirements, fiscal year ended June 30, 1922—Continued.*

| Detail | Interest-bearing debt. | | | | | | Matured debt. | Debt bearing no interest. | Total gross debt. |
| --- | --- | --- | --- | --- | --- | --- | --- | --- | --- |
| | Pre-war loans. | Treasury (war) savings securities. | Certificates of indebtedness. | Treasury notes. | Liberty bonds and Victory notes. | Total interest-bearing. | | | |
| Retired through—Continued. | | | | | | | | | |
| Reissues on amnt of—Contd. | | | | | | | | | |
| Exchange of upon for registered. | $2,855,130 | | | | $425,516,850 | $428,371,980.00 | | | $428,371,980.00 |
| Exchange of denominations. | | | a $690,951,500 | b $340,734,000 | 1,870,861,450 | 2,902,546,950.00 | | | 2,902,546,950.00 |
| Exchange of temporary for permanent. | | | | | 246,296,850 | 246,296,850.00 | | | 246,296,850.00 |
| Exchange of mutilated for perfect. | 10,500 | | | | 1,064,200 | 1,074,700.00 | | | 1,074,700.00 |
| Transfer of ownership. | 50,226,110 | | | | 129,155,650 | 179,381,760.00 | | | 179,381,760.00 |
| ment of claims. | 11,640 | | | | 3,819,400 | 3,831,040.00 | | | 3,831,040.00 |
| United States notes. | | | | | | | | $339,348,000.00 | 339,348,000.00 |
| Total retired on account of reissues. | 53,103,380 | | 690,951,500 | 340,734,000 | 3,452,351,950 | 4,537,140,830.00 | | 339,348,000.00 | 4,876,488,830.00 |
| Redemption on account of— | | | | | | | | | |
| Sinking fund. | | | | | 275,896,000 | 275,896,000.00 | | | 275,896,000.00 |
| Bond purchase fund. | | | | | 130,520,000 | 130,520,000.00 | | | 130,520,000.00 |
| Repayments of loans to foreign governments. | | | | | 64,837,900 | 64,837,900.00 | | | 64,837,900.00 |
| Franchise tax of Federal reserve banks. | | | | | 60,333,000 | 60,333,000.00 | | | 60,333,000.00 |
| Proceeds of Treasury notes. | | | | | 8,104,550 | 8,104,550.00 | | | 8,104,550.00 |
| Received for Federal estate taxes. | | | | | 20,845,300 | 20,845,300.00 | | | 20,845,300.00 |
| Forfeitures. | | | | | 139,850 | 139,850.00 | | | 139,850.00 |
| Gifts. | | | | | 1,900 | 1,900.00 | | | 1,900.00 |
| ... elpis. | | | | | 251,100 | 251,100.00 | | | 251,100.00 |
| Very notes. | | | | | 1,500,612,200 | 1,500,612,200.00 | | | 1,500,612,200.00 |
| Reimbursements to agents for paid int. | | $328,702.14 | | | | 328,702.14 | | | 328,702.14 |
| National and Federal reserve bank notes. | | | | | | | | 107,252,812.40 | 107,252,812.40 |
| Notes and c- at holders' option. | | 85,415,860.52 | 4,766,854,950 | | | 4,852,270,810.52 | $9,076,140.00 | | 4,861,346,950.52 |
| Total retired on account of redemption. | | 85,744,562.66 | 4,766,854,950 | | 2,061,541,800 | 6,914,141,312.66 | 9,076,140.00 | 107,252,812.40 | 7,030,470,265.06 |
| Total retired. | 53,103,380 | 85,744,562.66 | 5,457,806,450 | 340,734,000 | 5,513,893,750 | 11,451,282,142.66 | 9,076,140.00 | 446,600,812.40 | 11,906,959,095.06 |

| | | | | | | | | |
|---|---|---|---|---|---|---|---|---|
| Securities outstanding (net) June 30, 1922 | 883,840,470 | 679,015,317.45 | 1,837,565,500 | 2,246,594,350 | 17,066,126,400 | 22,713,142,037.45 | 1,863,480.26 | 227,792,722.87 | 22,942,798,240.58 |
| Securities issuable June 30, 1922 | | | | 2,000 | 21,278,950 | 21,280,950.00 | | | 21,280,950.00 |
| Securities outstanding and issuable June 30, 1922 | 883,840,470 | 679,015,317.45 | 1,837,565,500 | 2,246,596,350 | 17,087,405,350 | 22,734,422,987.45 | 1,863,480.26 | 227,792,722.87 | 22,964,079,190.58 |
| Adjustment of interest-bearing debt matured during year | | | ¹ 8,778,000 | | ¹ 14,609,400 | ¹ 23,387,400.00 | 23,387,400.00 | | |
| Outstanding June 30, 1922 | 883,840,470 | 679,015,317.45 | 1,828,787,500 | 2,246,596,350 | 17,072,795,950 | 22,711,035,587.45 | 25,250,880.26 | 227,792,722.87 | 22,964,079,190.58 |

¹ Deduct.
⁴ Includes $473,200,500 exchanges between Federal reserve banks.
⁵ Includes $183,952,300 exchanges between Federal reserve banks.

## EXHIBIT 17.

LIBERTY BONDS, VICTORY NOTES, TREASURY NOTES, AND CERTIFICATES OF INDEBTEDNESS ISSUED AND RETIRED DURING THE FISCAL YEAR 1922 AND OUTSTANDING ON JUNE 30, 1922, BY DENOMINATIONS.

| Detail. | $50 | $100 | $500 | $1,000 | $5,000 | $10,000 | $50,000 | $100,000 | Total. | Total number of pieces. |
|---|---|---|---|---|---|---|---|---|---|---|
| **Outstanding June 30, 1921:** | | | | | | | | | | |
| Interim certificates | $109,250 | $122,300 | $34,500 | $61,000 | $35,000 | $10,000 | | | $372,050 | 3,546 |
| Liberty issues in coupon form | 1,066,186,956 | 1,720,105,600 | 1,364,864,500 | 6,482,062,000 | 1,206,265,000 | 3,190,380,000 | | $1,149,000,000 | 15,029,804,050 | 48,296,865 |
| Liberty issues in registered form | 61,336,200 | 289,380,600 | 382,583,500 | 905,169,000 | 386,285,000 | 664,700,000 | $289,300,000 | 997,300,000 | 4,117,754,300 | 6,048,069 |
| Certificates of indebtedness | | | 71,618,000 | 279,880,000 | 352,605,000 | 682,380,000 | | | ¹2,632,512,450 | 1,572,308 |
| Treasury notes | | | 10,354,500 | 48,188,000 | 46,375,000 | 73,690,000 | | 118,100,000 | 298,923,500 | 108,882 |
| Total | 1,127,652,400 | 2,021,804,500 | 1,829,455,000 | 7,715,360,000 | 1,971,505,000 | 4,611,160,000 | 289,300,000 | 2,264,400,000 | 22,079,366,350 | 55,029,670 |
| **On hand in Federal reserve banks (consignment stock) June 30, 1921:** | | | | | | | | | | |
| Interim certificates | 150 | 400 | | 1,000 | | | | | 1,550 | 8 |
| Liberty issues in coupon form | 81,311,200 | 95,028,500 | 174,240,500 | 943,471,000 | 305,075,000 | 422,150,000 | | 32,990,000 | 2,022,276,200 | 3,981,691 |
| Liberty issues in registered form | 96,750 | 256,700 | 1,007,000 | 2,172,000 | 5,795,000 | 11,440,000 | 21,100,000 | | 74,767,450 | 11,742 |
| Certificates of indebtedness | | | 26,582,000 | 79,747,000 | 101,980,000 | 148,540,000 | | 152,990,000 | 509,749,000 | 169,690 |
| Treasury notes | | | 4,191,000 | 13,989,000 | 20,455,000 | 36,380,000 | | 14,100,000 | 91,394,100 | 53,032 |
| Total | 81,408,100 | 98,564,700 | 206,020,500 | 1,039,380,000 | 433,305,000 | 618,510,000 | 21,100,000 | 199,900,000 | 2,698,188,300 | 4,216,163 |
| **Securities issued during fiscal year:** | | | | | | | | | | |
| Liberty issues in coupon form | 38,710,150 | 60,716,700 | 40,500,500 | 348,109,000 | 210,535,000 | 1,450,000,000 | | 188,700,000 | 2,154,870,850 | 2,057,646 |
| Liberty issues in registered form | 2,803,200 | 16,387,700 | 26,212,500 | 80,935,000 | 38,635,000 | 97,090,000 | | | 488,703,400 | 386,194 |
| Certificates of indebtedness | | | 72,943,000 | 291,327,000 | 441,980,000 | 927,290,000 | 24,650,000 | 1,245,890,000 | ¹4,774,380,000 | 630,911 |
| Treasury notes | | | 61,685,000 | 302,568,000 | 310,760,000 | 729,500,000 | | 1,148,600,000 | 2,567,367,500 | 715,054 |
| Total | 41,513,350 | 97,356,900 | 201,341,500 | 1,035,960,000 | 1,002,510,000 | 3,203,760,000 | 24,650,000 | 2,598,100,000 | 9,985,291,750 | 3,789,805 |
| Total to be accounted for | 1,250,573,850 | 2,217,726,100 | 2,236,817,000 | 9,790,700,000 | 3,407,320,000 | 8,433,430,000 | 335,050,000 | 5,050,400,000 | 34,762,846,400 | 63,035,638 |
| **Securities retired during fiscal year:** | | | | | | | | | | |
| Interim certificates | 30,050 | 39,600 | 9,000 | 12,000 | 15,000 | | | | 105,650 | 1,030 |
| Liberty issues in coupon form | 345,131,800 | 490,964,300 | 343,215,500 | 1,941,367,000 | 401,995,000 | 1,247,070,000 | | 256,300,000 | 4,769,743,600 | 14,645,183 |
| Liberty issues in registered form | 10,742,850 | 52,336,800 | 63,072,000 | 152,233,000 | 70,615,000 | 167,180,000 | 64,750,000 | | 837,229,650 | 1,051,301 |
| Certificates of indebtedness | | | 119,189,000 | 437,064,000 | 562,575,000 | 1,036,590,000 | | 1,392,600,000 | ³5,514,847,450 | 1,905,939 |
| Treasury notes | | | 6,605,500 | 24,820,000 | 37,645,000 | 24,840,000 | | 23,700,000 | 120,080,900 | 72,985 |
| Total | 355,904,700 | 545,811,100 | 532,091,000 | 2,555,496,000 | 1,072,845,000 | 2,475,680,000 | 64,750,000 | 1,672,600,000 | 11,242,007,250 | 16,676,438 |

| | | | | | | | | | |
|---|---|---|---|---|---|---|---|---|---|
| **On hand in Federal reserve banks (consignment stock) June 30, 1922:** | | | | | | | | | |
| Liberty issues in coupon form | 39,033,850 | 63,117,200 | 104,735,500 | 486,388,000 | 203,805,000 | 318,260,000 | | 175,900,000 | 1,215,344,550 | 2,180,395 |
| Certificates of indebtedness | | 6,021,100 | 21,389,000 | 72,504,000 | 110,305,000 | 184,660,000 | | | 594,758,000 | 157,588 |
| Treasury notes | | | 28,457,500 | 86,540,000 | 106,790,000 | 163,600,000 | | 225,900,000 | 617,308,600 | 243,643 |
| Total | 39,033,850 | 69,138,300 | 154,582,000 | 645,432,000 | 420,900,000 | 666,520,000 | | 401,800,000 | 2,397,411,150 | 2,681,606 |
| **Outstanding June 30, 1922:** | | | | | | | | | |
| Interim certificates | 79,350 | 83,100 | 25,500 | 50,000 | 20,000 | 10,000 | | | 287,950 | 2,524 |
| Liberty issues in coupon form | 802,037,650 | 1,328,789,300 | 1,131,654,000 | 5,345,887,000 | 1,116,315,000 | 3,497,200,000 | | 1,114,300,000 | 13,221,862,950 | 37,510,624 |
| Liberty issues in registered form | 53,513,300 | 263,666,200 | 346,731,000 | 849,063,000 | 340,400,000 | 606,020,000 | 270,300,000 | 830,500,000 | 3,843,995,500 | 5,394,704 |
| Certificates of indebtedness | | | 30,565,000 | 141,386,000 | 223,685,000 | 536,870,000 | | | [4]1,837,006,000 | 4,309,402 |
| Treasury notes | | 10,256,100 | 41,168,500 | 233,386,000 | 233,155,000 | 651,130,000 | | 1,031,200,000 | [2]2,229,295,600 | 560,340 |
| Total | 855,630,300 | 1,602,776,700 | 1,550,144,000 | 6,589,772,000 | 1,913,575,000 | 5,291,230,000 | 270,300,000 | 2,976,000,000 | [1]21,123,428,000 | 43,777,394 |
| Total as above accounted for | 1,250,573,850 | 2,217,726,100 | 2,236,817,000 | 9,790,700,000 | 3,407,320,000 | 8,433,430,000 | 335,050,000 | 5,050,400,000 | [3]34,762,846,400 | 63,035,638 |
| Amount outstanding as above | | | | | | | | | 21,123,428,000 | |
| **Plus items issuable:** | | | | | | | | | |
| Liberty issues in coupon form (on exchange) | | | | | | | | | 21,278,950 | |
| Treasury notes (on exchange) | | | | | | | | | 2,000 | |
| Treasury notes (full-paid subscription) | | | | | | | | | 26,298,750 | |
| Certificates of indebtedness (full-paid subscription) | | | | | | | | | 784,500 | |
| Total outstanding and issuable | | | | | | | | | [5]21,171,792,200 | |

[1] Includes 460 pieces, par value $248,729,450, denominations unavailable, chiefly special certificates.
[2] Includes 94 pieces, par value $1,792,100,000, denominations unavailable, chiefly special certificates.
[3] Includes 397 pieces, par value $1,966,829,450, denominations unavailable, chiefly special certificates.
[4] Includes 157 pieces, par value $74,000,000, denominations unavailable, chiefly special certificates.
[5] Includes $9,003,000 matured certificates of indebtedness, $14,609,400 matured Victory 3¾'s.

EXHIBIT 18.

## LIBERTY BONDS, VICTORY NOTES, TREASURY NOTES, AND CERTIFICATES OF INDEBTEDNESS RECEIVED AND DELIVERED DURING THE FISCAL YEAR 1922 AND ON HAND ON JUNE 30, 1922, BY DENOMINATIONS.

| Detail. | $50. | $100. | $500. | $1,000. | $5,000. | $10,000. | $50,000. | $100,000. | Total. | Total number of pieces. |
|---|---|---|---|---|---|---|---|---|---|---|
| **Stock in vault June 30, 1921:** | | | | | | | | | | |
| Liberty issues in coupon form | $432,155,850 | $423,427,900 | $359,468,000 | $1,989,851,000 | $369,610,000 | $1,161,250,000 | | | $5,226,762,000 | 15,867,230 |
| Liberty issues in registered form | 58,491,900 | 120,088,500 | 16,795,500 | 673,431,000 | 602,670,000 | 1,128,880,000 | $1,788,700,000 | $2,142,700,000 | 6,597,383,400 | 3,153,280 |
| Certificates of indebtedness | | 5,473,900 | 10,312,000 | 44,995,000 | 74,035,000 | 217,200,000 | | 544,300,000 | 897,325,500 | 120,556 |
| Treasury notes | | | | 137,537,000 | 32,225,000 | 89,240,000 | | 10,000,000 | 342,287,900 | 228,944 |
| **Received from Bureau of Engraving and Printing during fiscal year:** | | | | | | | | | | |
| Liberty issues in coupon form | 25,050,000 | 47,700,000 | 19,000,000 | 238,000,000 | 23,000,000 | 672,000,000 | | | 1,034,750,000 | 1,325,800 |
| Liberty issues in registered form | 100,000 | 9,400,000 | 8,000,000 | 39,000,000 | 52,500,000 | 5,000,000 | | | 129,000,000 | 162,200 |
| Certificates of indebtedness | | 22,500,000 | 117,250,000 | 423,500,000 | 607,500,000 | 1,240,000,000 | 5,000,000 | 1,810,000,000 | 4,225,750,000 | 927,100 |
| Treasury notes | | | 105,000,000 | 460,000,000 | 567,500,000 | 1,017,000,000 | | 1,600,000,000 | 3,749,500,000 | 1,118,700 |
| **Restored to stock during fiscal year:** | | | | | | | | | | |
| Liberty issues in coupon form | 5,400,100 | 10,874,500 | 33,933,500 | 321,172,000 | 35,245,000 | 74,390,000 | | | 481,005,100 | 620,273 |
| Liberty issues in registered form | ¹116,750 | ¹41,600 | ¹1,195,000 | ¹1,191,000 | | 2,430,000 | | | ¹21,134,350 | ¹2,203 |
| Certificates of indebtedness | | 545,000 | 4,048,000 | 2,400,000 | 1,500,000 | 1,500,000 | ¹5,400,000 | ¹10,800,000 | 5,900,000 | ¹2,950 |
| Treasury notes | | | | 15,567,000 | 22,200,000 | 4,300,000 | | 1,300,000 | 47,900,000 | 33,936 |
| Total to be accounted for | 521,181,100 | 597,301,700 | 793,700,500 | 4,341,202,000 | 2,861,425,000 | 5,638,330,000 | 1,788,300,000 | 6,165,000,000 | 22,706,440,300 | 23,558,776 |
| **Delivered to register for destruction:** | | | | | | | | | | |
| Liberty issues in coupon form | 1,474,500 | 3,313,200 | 15,654,000 | 190,527,000 | 257,575,000 | 105,050,000 | | | 468,843,700 | 336,272 |
| Liberty issues in registered form | 50,450 | 186,100 | 186,500 | 3,357,000 | 55,975,000 | 303,090,000 | | | 302,655,050 | 30,205 |
| Certificates of indebtedness | | | 27,692,500 | 78,095,000 | 118,295,000 | | 52,650,000 | 85,200,000 | 1,238,572,500 | 194,562 |
| Treasury notes | | | | | | | | 711,400,000 | | |
| **Delivered for issue:** | | | | | | | | | | |
| Liberty issues in coupon form | 38,710,150 | 66,716,700 | 40,500,000 | 348,109,000 | 210,835,000 | 1,450,000,000 | | 188,700,000 | 2,154,870,850 | 2,057,646 |
| Liberty issues in registered form | 2,803,200 | 16,387,700 | 26,212,500 | 93,985,000 | 38,935,000 | 97,060,000 | | | 488,703,400 | 386,194 |
| Certificates of indebtedness | | 14,252,500 | 72,943,000 | 291,327,000 | 441,989,000 | 927,200,000 | 24,650,000 | ¹1,248,100,000 | ²2,982,250,000 | ¹630,817 |
| Treasury notes | | | 61,696,000 | 302,569,000 | 310,766,000 | 729,500,000 | | 1,148,600,000 | 2,567,367,500 | 715,054 |
| **Delivered for specimens:** | | | | | | | | | | |
| Certificates of indebtedness | | | | 2,000 | 15,000 | 40,000 | | 300,000 | 357,000 | 12 |
| Treasury notes | | | | | 5,000 | 20,000 | | 100,000 | 125,000 | 4 |
| **Stock in vault June 30, 1922:** | | | | | | | | | | |
| Liberty issues in coupon form | 422,421,300 | 411,972,500 | 356,247,500 | 2,001,087,000 | 459,445,000 | 457,630,000 | | 520,100,000 | 4,108,803,300 | 15,419,385 |
| Liberty issues in registered form | 55,721,500 | 70,200,600 | 101,494,500 | 619,928,000 | 558,200,000 | 929,350,000 | | | 5,913,900,600 | 2,896,888 |
| Certificates of indebtedness | | 14,266,400 | 33,410,000 | 101,471,000 | 150,745,000 | 228,370,000 | 1,711,000,000 | 1,988,000,000 | 907,796,000 | 225,215 |
| Treasury notes | | | 57,674,000 | 310,475,000 | 285,660,000 | 411,020,000 | | 383,800,000 | 1,572,195,400 | 666,522 |
| Total accounted for | 521,181,100 | 597,301,700 | 793,700,500 | 4,341,202,000 | 2,861,425,000 | 5,638,330,000 | 1,788,300,000 | 6,165,000,000 | 22,706,440,300 | 23,558,776 |

¹ Counter entry.   ² Deduct.

* Does not include 94 pieces, special certificates, value $1,792,100,000.

Exhibit 19.

## LIBERTY BONDS AND VICTORY NOTES—DENOMINATIONAL EXCHANGES OF COUPON BONDS, SHOWING NET INCREASES AND DECREASES FROM APRIL 6, 1917, TO JUNE 30, 1922.

| Detail. | First 3½'s. | First 4's. | First 4¼'s. | First-second 4¼'s. | Second 4's. | Second 4¼'s. | Third 4¼'s. | Fourth 4¼'s. | Victory 4¾'s. | Victory 3¾'s. | Total. |
|---|---|---|---|---|---|---|---|---|---|---|---|
| **Original deliveries (including those on conversion):** | | | | | | | | | | | |
| $50 | $100,064,050 | $98,935,000 | $60,484,400 | $297,200 | $383,289,600 | $241,381,950 | $701,958,600 | $864,615,800 | $415,100,900 | $601,050 | $2,969,728,550 |
| $100 | 122,360,100 | 124,104,700 | 98,674,300 | 399,300 | 444,724,000 | 353,392,600 | 720,302,600 | 1,025,791,800 | 565,920,500 | 1,604,100 | 3,457,274,000 |
| $500 | 97,735,000 | 84,207,000 | 77,409,000 | 259,500 | 239,212,000 | 284,071,000 | 379,896,500 | 519,188,000 | 352,530,500 | 3,157,000 | 2,127,686,500 |
| $1,000 | 949,310,000 | 164,524,000 | 181,080,000 | 1,222,000 | 1,593,870,000 | 1,515,637,000 | 1,384,390,000 | 2,384,269,000 | 1,308,080,000 | 346,554,000 | 9,825,956,000 |
| $5,000 | | 13,045,000 | 19,225,000 | 105,000 | 239,585,000 | 259,305,000 | 206,125,000 | 449,650,000 | 257,555,000 | 54,985,000 | 1,499,580,000 |
| $10,000 | | 13,460,000 | 19,500,000 | 160,000 | 460,390,000 | 552,900,000 | 408,610,000 | 1,044,450,000 | 486,330,000 | 233,220,000 | 3,219,220,000 |
| Total | 1,269,490,150 | 498,275,700 | 456,372,700 | 2,443,000 | 3,449,270,600 | 3,206,707,550 | 3,801,280,700 | 6,287,964,600 | 3,385,516,900 | 640,121,150 | 22,997,443,050 |
| **Surrendered for denominational exchange:** | | | | | | | | | | | |
| $50 | 62,237,950 | 22,369,950 | 20,232,400 | 100,150 | 104,322,700 | 105,016,400 | 416,607,250 | 523,207,900 | 274,316,750 | 480,000 | 1,528,891,450 |
| $100 | 63,430,600 | 15,923,000 | 30,834,400 | 164,100 | 86,835,800 | 130,922,800 | 348,935,700 | 530,452,300 | 301,534,000 | 1,181,600 | 1,500,214,300 |
| $500 | 34,849,500 | 2,453,000 | 16,432,000 | 95,000 | 24,849,500 | 65,120,000 | 102,419,500 | 148,713,700 | 109,006,500 | 1,654,000 | 505,592,500 |
| $1,000 | 14,402,000 | 4,044,000 | 36,515,000 | 219,000 | 41,221,000 | 352,827,000 | 460,197,000 | 703,695,000 | 428,147,000 | 99,642,000 | 2,141,210,000 |
| $5,000 | | 2,590,000 | 6,835,000 | 25,000 | 49,980,000 | 92,830,000 | 108,050,000 | 198,465,000 | 116,065,000 | 20,110,000 | 592,950,000 |
| $10,000 | | 2,600,000 | 5,390,000 | 60,000 | 69,760,000 | 147,270,000 | 176,230,000 | 372,190,000 | 142,050,000 | 88,160,000 | 1,003,710,000 |
| Total | 174,920,050 | 49,979,950 | 116,538,800 | 663,250 | 376,969,000 | 893,986,200 | 1,612,439,450 | 2,464,724,700 | 1,371,119,250 | 211,227,600 | 7,272,568,250 |
| **Issued on denominational exchange:** | | | | | | | | | | | |
| $50 | 10,780,550 | 3,867,350 | 1,208,600 | 1,250 | 28,033,700 | 14,127,000 | 68,373,450 | 80,547,800 | 45,021,250 | 87,700 | 252,053,650 |
| $100 | 5,846,500 | 2,923,100 | 2,449,700 | 2,000 | 28,810,800 | 18,788,200 | 37,674,500 | 73,314,400 | 38,079,000 | 271,900 | 208,160,100 |
| $500 | 15,815,000 | 4,782,500 | 8,472,500 | 122,000 | 28,599,500 | 34,812,000 | 55,589,500 | 87,808,500 | 53,625,000 | 758,000 | 290,384,500 |
| $1,000 | 142,478,000 | 35,202,000 | 52,533,000 | 308,000 | 202,580,000 | 361,559,000 | 825,662,000 | 1,215,784,000 | 599,669,000 | 97,730,000 | 3,533,505,000 |
| $5,000 | | 1,985,000 | 13,715,000 | 10,000 | 37,075,000 | 88,800,000 | 130,605,000 | 218,810,000 | 148,705,000 | 18,220,000 | 657,925,000 |
| $10,000 | | 1,220,000 | 38,160,000 | 220,000 | 51,870,000 | 375,900,000 | 494,530,000 | 788,460,000 | 486,020,000 | 94,160,000 | 2,330,540,000 |
| Total | 174,920,050 | 49,979,950 | 116,538,800 | 663,250 | 376,969,000 | 893,986,200 | 1,612,439,450 | 2,464,724,700 | 1,371,119,250 | 211,227,600 | 7,272,568,250 |

*Liberty bonds and Victory notes—Denominational exchanges of coupon bonds, showing net increases and decreases from April 6, 1917, to June 30, 1922—Continued.*

| Detail. | First 3½'s. | First 4's. | First 4¼'s. | First-second 4¼'s. | Second 4's. | Second 4¼'s. | Third 4¼'s. | Fourth 4¼'s. | Victory 4¾'s. | Victory 3¾'s. | Total. |
|---|---|---|---|---|---|---|---|---|---|---|---|
| Decrease on denominational exchange: | | | | | | | | | | | |
| $50 | $51,457,400 | $18,502,600 | $19,023,800 | $98,900 | $76,289,000 | $90,889,400 | $348,228,800 | $442,660,100 | $229,295,500 | $392,300 | $1,276,837,800 |
| $100 | 57,584,100 | 12,999,900 | 28,384,700 | 162,100 | 58,025,000 | 112,134,700 | 311,261,200 | 447,137,900 | 263,455,000 | 910,300 | 1,292,054,900 |
| $500 | 19,034,500 | | 7,939,500 | 20,000 | | 30,308,000 | 46,830,000 | 60,907,500 | 55,381,500 | 896,000 | 221,337,000 |
| $1,000 | | | | 30,000 | | 118,468,000 | 63,942,000 | 133,271,000 | 1,180,000 | 1,912,000 | 318,803,000 |
| $5,000 | | 615,000 | | 20,000 | 12,970,000 | 15,725,000 | 3,880,000 | 3,065,000 | | 1,890,000 | 38,165,000 |
| $10,000 | | 1,380,000 | | 10,000 | 19,270,000 | 26,950,000 | | | | | 47,610,000 |
| Total | 128,076,000 | 33,497,500 | 55,368,000 | 341,000 | 166,554,000 | 394,475,100 | 774,142,000 | 1,087,041,500 | 549,312,000 | 6,000,600 | 3,194,807,700 |
| Increase on denominational exchange: | | | | | | | | | | | |
| $50 | | | | | | | | | | | |
| $100 | | | | | | 100 | | | | 600 | 700 |
| $500 | | 2,329,500 | | 47,000 | 3,730,000 | | | 2,500 | | | 6,129,000 |
| $1,000 | 128,076,000 | 31,158,000 | 15,718,000 | 119,000 | 161,359,000 | 127,200,000 | 429,407,000 | 645,359,000 | 172,702,000 | | 1,711,098,000 |
| $5,000 | | 10,000 | 6,880,000 | 5,000 | 65,000 | 11,695,000 | 26,435,000 | 25,410,000 | 32,640,000 | | 103,140,000 |
| $10,000 | | | 32,770,000 | 170,000 | 1,380,000 | 255,580,000 | 318,300,000 | 416,270,000 | 343,970,000 | 6,000,000 | 1,374,440,000 |
| Total | 128,076,000 | 33,497,500 | 55,368,000 | 341,000 | 166,554,000 | 394,475,100 | 774,142,000 | 1,087,041,500 | 549,312,000 | 6,000,600 | 3,194,807,700 |

## Exhibit 20.

### LIBERTY BOND AND VICTORY NOTE CONVERSIONS FROM NOVEMBER 15, 1917, TO JUNE 30, 1922.

| Issue. | Original issue. | Issued on conversion. | Converted into— | | | | | | Redeemed to June 30, 1922. | Outstanding June 30, 1922. |
|---|---|---|---|---|---|---|---|---|---|---|
| | | | First 4's. | First 4¼'s. | First second 4¼'s. | Second 4¼'s. | Victory 3¾'s. | Victory 4¾'s. | | |
| First 3½'s | [1] $1,989,455,550 | | $568,318,450 | $7,570,550 | $3,492,150 | | | | $72,350 | $1,410,002,050 |
| First 4's | | $568,318,450 | | 540,276,100 | | | | | 15,518,850 | 12,523,500 |
| First 4¼'s | | 547,846,650 | | | | | | | 22,020,600 | 525,826,050 |
| First second 4¼'s | | 3,492,150 | | | | | | | | 3,492,150 |
| Second 4's | 3,807,865,000 | | | | | $3,674,384,850 | | | 79,059,350 | 54,420,800 |
| Second 4¼'s | | 3,674,384,850 | | | | | | | 418,208,600 | 3,256,176,250 |
| Third 4¼'s | 4,175,650,050 | | | | | | | | 701,862,050 | 3,473,788,000 |
| Fourth 4¼'s | 6,964,581,100 | | | | | | | | 619,197,350 | 6,345,383,750 |
| Victory 3¾'s | 672,585,100 | 424,666,750 | | | | | | $505,068,900 | 577,573,550 | [2] 14,609,400 |
| Victory 4¾'s | 3,822,787,900 | 505,068,900 | | | | | $424,666,750 | | 1,912,006,650 | 1,991,183,400 |
| Total | 21,432,924,700 | 5,723,777,750 | 568,318,450 | 547,846,650 | 3,492,150 | 3,674,384,850 | 424,666,750 | 505,068,900 | 4,345,519,350 | 17,087,405,350 |

[1] Includes full-paid interim certificates not exchanged for 3½ per cent bonds.

[2] Now included in matured debt.

## EXHIBIT 21.

## RECAPITULATION OF LIBERTY BONDS AND VICTORY NOTES ISSUED AND RETIRED FROM APRIL 6, 1917, TO JUNE 30, 1922, AND AMOUNT OUTSTANDING JUNE 30, 1922.

| Detail. | Pieces. | Amount. |
|---|---|---|
| I. Delivered by the Bureau of Engraving and Printing to the Division of Loans and Currency: | | |
| First Liberty loan— | | |
| 3½ per cent full-paid interim certificates...................... | 5,676,950 | $4,130,200,000 |
| 3½ per cent coupon bonds.................................... | 5,518,000 | 1,745,250,000 |
| 3½ per cent registered bonds................................ | 632,500 | 1,300,000,000 |
| Converted 4 per cent temporary coupon bonds.............. | 4,720,000 | 820,000,000 |
| Converted 4 per cent permanent coupon bonds............. | 470,750 | 87,750,000 |
| Converted 4 per cent registered bonds...................... | 526,000 | 492,700,000 |
| Converted 4¼ per cent temporary coupon bonds............ | 5,575,000 | 950,000,000 |
| Converted 4¼ per cent permanent coupon bonds............ | 2,895,500 | 932,500,000 |
| Converted 4¼ per cent registered bonds.................... | 449,560 | 1,000,250,000 |
| Second converted 4¼ per cent temporary bonds............ | 130,200 | 3,200,000 |
| Second converted 4¼ per cent permanent coupon bonds..... | 17,300 | 9,050,000 |
| Second converted 4¼ per cent registered bonds............. | 47,530 | 38,565,000 |
| Second Liberty loan— | | |
| 4 per cent temporary coupon bonds......................... | 15,968,000 | 4,630,250,000 |
| 4 per cent permanent coupon bonds........................ | 1,156,500 | 240,000,000 |
| 4 per cent registered bonds................................ | 1,415,000 | 1,750,000,000 |
| Converted 4¼ per cent temporary coupon bonds............ | 13,552,000 | 3,77,500,000 |
| Converted 4¼ per cent permanent coupon bonds........... | 9,131,000 | 3,82,350,000 |
| Converted 4¼ per cent registered bonds.................... | 1,355,160 | 1,80g,190,000 |
| Third Liberty loan— | | |
| 4¼ per cent temporary coupon bonds....................... | 25,368,000 | 4,704,150,000 |
| 4¼ per cent permanent coupon bonds...................... | 18,858,000 | 4,709,425,000 |
| 4¼ per cent registered bonds.............................. | 2,028,550 | 1,661,270,000 |
| Fourth Liberty loan— | | |
| 4¼ per cent temporary coupon bonds....................... | 35,883,000 | 7,89,000,000 |
| 4¼ per cent permanent coupon bonds...................... | 18,289,600 | 7,18,600,000 |
| 4¼ per cent registered bonds.............................. | 3,432,550 | 2,596,050,000 |
| Victory Liberty loan— | | |
| 3¾ per cent coupon notes.................................. | 1,490,800 | 2,327,400,000 |
| 3¾ per cent registered notes............................... | 76,060 | 777,280,000 |
| 4¾ per cent coupon notes.................................. | 22,121,200 | 5,558,100,000 |
| 4¾ per cent registered notes............................... | 1,674,800 | 1,312,820,000 |
| Total............................................. | 198,509,510 | 66,290,850,000 |
| Less unissued stocks— | | |
| 1. On hand June 30, 1922— | | |
| a. With Division of Loans and Currency............. | 18,326,643 | 10,024,743,050 |
| b. With Federal reserve banks....................... | 2,180,395 | 1,215,344,550 |
| Total........................................... | 20,507,038 | 11,240,087,600 |
| 2. Excess stocks delivered to register for retirement— | | |
| a. By Division of Loans and Currency................ | 12,685,856 | 4,160,658,650 |
| b. By Federal reserve banks.......................... | 6,509,713 | 2,515,515,350 |
| Total........................................... | 19,195,569 | 6,676,174,000 |
| Total deductions................................. | 39,702,607 | 17,916,261,600 |
| Total to be accounted for (see Item V)........... | 158,806,903 | 48,374,588,400 |
| II. Deliveries from stock by Division of Loans and Currency: | | |
| 1. Against an equal face amount of cash received into the Treasury on account of original subscriptions— | | |
| First Liberty loan................................. | 3,703,986 | 1,989,455,550 |
| Second Liberty loan............................... | 14,938,073 | 3,807,865,000 |
| Third Liberty loan................................ | 24,406,982 | 4,175,650,050 |
| Fourth Liberty loan............................... | 33,024,445 | 6,964,581,100 |
| Victory Liberty loan.............................. | 17,498,172 | 4,495,373,000 |
| Total........................................... | 93,571,658 | 21,432,924,700 |
| 2. Against an equal par amount of securities surrendered— | | |
| a. On exchange of denominations..................... | 5,919,032 | 4,837,752,900 |
| b. On exchange of coupon for registered.............. | 2,727,286 | 2,916,191,300 |
| c. On exchange of registered for coupon.............. | 1,541,304 | 1,158,318,050 |
| d. On transfer....................................... | 520,239 | 467,426,050 |
| e. On mixed cases................................... | 589 | 1,946,300 |
| f. On account of mutilations......................... | 3,242 | 1,339,600 |
| g. On conversion (does not include 4 per cent bonds delivered against interims)............................ | 15,053,251 | 5,249,822,850 |
| h. On exchange of temporary for permanent.............. | 31,941,341 | 10,314,015,100 |
| i. On coupon error.................................. | 27 | 17,800 |
| j. On exchange of interim certificates................ | 7,501,966 | 1,985,057,750 |
| Total........................................... | 65,206,277 | 26,931,887,700 |

*Recapitulation of Liberty bonds and Victory notes issued and retired from April 6, 1917, to June 30, 1922, and amount outstanding June 30, 1922—*Continued.

| Detail. | Pieces. | Amount. |
|---|---|---|
| II. Deliveries from stock by Division of Loans and Currency—Contd. | | |
| 3. For adjudicated claims for replacements..................... | 28,968 | $9,776,000 |
| Total accounted for............................... | 158,806,903 | 48,374,588,400 |
| III. Received for retirement and cancellation: | | |
| 1. For redemption accounts— | | |
| *a.* Bond purchase fund............................... | 1,730,091 | 1,965,791,450 |
| *b.* Cumulative sinking fund........................... | 376,508 | 537,146,250 |
| *c.* Repayment of foreign loans....................... | 149,621 | 219,368,800 |
| *d.* Franchise tax, Federal reserve banks............. | 35,909 | 63,255,450 |
| *e.* Estate and inheritance taxes..................... | 40,914 | 50,666,350 |
| *f.* Gifts and forfeitures............................. | 720 | 194,100 |
| *g.* Miscellaneous receipts........................... | 392 | 380,200 |
| *h.* Redemptions of Victory notes other than included above | 950,211 | 1,508,716,750 |
| Total......................... | 3,284,366 | 4,345,519,350 |
| 2. For reissue of an equal par amount— | | |
| *a.* On exchange of denominations..................... | 43,499,315 | 4,837,775,400 |
| *b.* On exchange of coupon for registered............. | 5,636,738 | 2,916,191,300 |
| *c.* On exchange of registered for coupon............. | 1,754,947 | 1,179,481,050 |
| *d.* On transfer..................................... | 859,656 | 407,426,050 |
| *e.* On mixed cases.................................. | 1,972 | 1,946,300 |
| *f.* On account of mutilations....................... | 3,258 | 1,339,600 |
| *g.* On conversion.................................... | 16,965,091 | 5,249,860,500 |
| *h.* On exchange of temporary for permanent......... | 40,406,303 | 10,314,070,400 |
| *i.* On coupon error................................ | 27 | 17,800 |
| *j.* On exchange of interim certificates.............. | 3,470,568 | 1,985,058,250 |
| Total......................... | 112,597,875 | 26,953,166,650 |
| 3. Securities lost or destroyed in lieu of which other securities issued in replacement (covered by insurance or bonds of indemnity)..................................... | 16,810 | 9,776,000 |
| Total received and lost or destroyed............... | 115,899,051 | 31,308,462,000 |
| IV. Outstanding June 30, 1922: | | |
| 1. First Liberty loan 3½ per cent full paid interim certificates.... | 2,524 | 267,950 |
| 2. First Liberty loan 3½ per cent bonds..................... | 2,105,326 | 1,407,650,600 |
| 3. First Liberty loan converted 4 per cent bonds............. | 80,509 | 12,475,400 |
| 4. First Liberty loan converted 4¼ per cent bonds.......... | 1,817,452 | 525,107,100 |
| 5. First Liberty loan second converted 4¼ per cent bonds....... | 9,312 | 3,490,000 |
| 6. Second Liberty loan 4 per cent bonds.................... | 327,587 | 54,113,050 |
| 7. Second Liberty loan converted 4¼ per cent bonds........... | 6,643,497 | 3,253,661,950 |
| 8. Third Liberty loan 4¼ per cent bonds.................... | 10,279,392 | 3,469,741,800 |
| 9. Fourth Liberty loan 4¼ per cent bonds.................... | 13,633,600 | 6,339,167,050 |
| 10. Victory Liberty loan 3¾ per cent notes................... | 8,528 | 14,609,400 |
| 11. Victory Liberty loan 4¾ per cent notes................... | 8,000,125 | 1,985,842,100 |
| Total outstanding............................... | 42,907,852 | 17,066,126,400 |
| V. Total received for retirement and cancellation, and outstanding..... | 158,806,903 | 48,374,588,400 |
| VI. Reconciliation with public debt statement: | | |
| Outstanding as above................................ | 42,907,852 | 17,066,126,400 |
| Plus issuable on exchanges........................... | 24,623 | 21,278,950 |
| Total as shown on public debt statement................. | 42,932,475 | 17,087,405,350 |

## EXHIBIT 22.

### LOAN AND TAX CERTIFICATES OF INDEBTEDNESS ISSUED THROUGH EACH FEDERAL RESERVE BANK FROM JULY 1, 1921, TO OCTOBER 31, 1922.

| Authorizing act and series. | Date of issue. | Date of maturity. | Rate. | Total amount. | Federal reserve bank. | | | | | |
|---|---|---|---|---|---|---|---|---|---|---|
| | | | | | Boston. | New York. | Philadelphia. | Cleveland. | Richmond. | Atlanta. |
| Loan certificates of 1922: | | | | | | | | | | |
| Sept. 24, 1917, as amended Apr. 4, 1918, and Mar. 3, 1919— | | | Per cent. | | | | | | | |
| Series B-1922 | Aug. 1, 1921 | Aug. 1, 1922 | 5½ | $259,471,500 | $21,068,500 | $99,622,500 | $30,336,500 | $19,370,000 | $7,865,000 | $6,949,500 |
| Series C-1922 | Nov. 1, 1921 | Apr. 1, 1922 | 4¼ | 51,796,000 | 2,410,000 | 13,813,000 | 3,652,000 | 7,984,000 | 1,649,500 | 1,290,500 |
| Series D-1922 | Apr. 15, 1922 | Oct. 16, 1922 | 3½ | 150,000,000 | 12,990,000 | 50,880,000 | 10,590,000 | 13,590,000 | 5,190,000 | 4,380,000 |
| Total loan certificates | | | | 461,267,500 | 36,468,500 | 164,315,500 | 44,578,500 | 40,944,000 | 14,704,500 | 12,620,000 |
| Issued in anticipation of income and profits taxes, 1922: | | | | | | | | | | |
| Sept. 24, 1917, as amended— | | | | | | | | | | |
| Series TM2-1922 | Aug. 1, 1921 | Mar. 15, 1922 | 5¼ | 116,891,000 | 9,101,500 | 47,263,500 | 9,033,500 | 11,295,000 | 3,746,000 | 1,812,500 |
| Series TS-1922 | Sept. 15, 1921 | Sept. 15, 1922 | 5¼ | 182,871,000 | 10,921,500 | 80,057,500 | 12,081,500 | 13,320,000 | 4,665,000 | 1,617,500 |
| Series TM3-1922 | Sept. 15, 1921 | Mar. 15, 1922 | 5 | 124,572,000 | 8,692,000 | 48,422,500 | 8,191,500 | 10,100,000 | 2,550,500 | 2,793,500 |
| Series TS2-1922 | Nov. 1, 1921 | Sept. 15, 1922 | 4½ | 179,691,500 | 17,002,500 | 66,495,000 | 17,476,500 | 14,283,000 | 6,619,000 | 5,547,500 |
| Series TJ2-1922 | Dec. 15, 1921 | June 15, 1922 | 4¼ | 64,903,000 | 3,100,500 | 18,471,500 | 3,707,000 | 10,300,000 | 2,799,500 | 1,826,500 |
| Series TD-1922 | Dec. 15, 1921 | Dec. 15, 1922 | 4½ | 243,544,000 | 20,696,000 | 94,098,500 | 25,888,500 | 20,700,000 | 6,996,500 | 6,853,500 |
| Series TD2-1922 | June 1, 1922 | Dec. 15, 1922 | 3½ | 200,000,000 | 17,320,000 | 67,840,000 | 14,120,000 | 18,120,000 | 6,920,000 | 5,840,000 |
| Issued in anticipation of income and profits taxes, 1923: | | | | | | | | | | |
| Sept. 24, 1917, as amended— | | | | | | | | | | |
| Series TM-1923 | Mar. 15, 1922 | Mar. 15, 1923 | 4¼ | 266,250,000 | 21,650,000 | 101,050,000 | 17,650,000 | 22,650,000 | 8,650,000 | 7,300,000 |
| Series TJ-1923 | June 15, 1922 | June 15, 1923 | 3¾ | 273,000,000 | 21,650,000 | 107,800,000 | 17,650,000 | 22,650,000 | 8,650,000 | 7,300,000 |
| Series TS-1923 | Sept. 15, 1922 | Sept. 15, 1923 | 3¾ | 227,000,000 | 17,320,000 | 94,840,000 | 14,120,000 | 18,120,000 | 6,920,000 | 5,840,000 |
| Total tax certificates | | | | 1,878,722,500 | 147,451,000 | 726,338,500 | 139,918,500 | 161,538,000 | 58,516,500 | 46,731,000 |
| Grand total loan and tax certificates | | | | 2,339,990,000 | 183,922,500 | 890,654,000 | 184,497,000 | 202,482,000 | 73,221,000 | 59,351,000 |

| Authorizing act and series. | Date of issue. | Date of maturity. | Rate. | Federal reserve bank. | | | | | |
|---|---|---|---|---|---|---|---|---|---|
| | | | | Chicago. | St. Louis. | Minneapolis. | Kansas City. | Dallas. | San Francisco. |
| | | | *Per cent.* | | | | | | |
| Loan certificates of 1922: Sept. 24, 1917, as amended Apr. 4, 1918, and Mar. 3, 1919— | | | | | | | | | |
| Series B-1922............... | Aug. 1, 1921 | Aug. 1, 1922 | 5¼ | $26,127,500 | $9,233,500 | $7,709,000 | $9,883,500 | $5,289,500 | $16,016,500 |
| Series C-1922............... | Nov. 1, 1921 | Apr. 1, 1922 | 4¼ | 8,062,300 | 2,218,500 | 1,550,000 | 1,725,000 | 1,541,000 | 5,900,000 |
| Series D-1922............... | Apr. 15, 1922 | Oct. 16, 1922 | 3¾ | 21,000,000 | 6,000,000 | 5,190,000 | 6,000,000 | 3,600,000 | 10,590,000 |
| Total loan certificates......... | | | | 55,190,000 | 17,452,000 | 14,449,000 | 17,608,500 | 10,430,500 | 32,506,500 |
| Issued in ⬛⬛⬛ of · ⬛⬛ one and profits ⬛⬛⬛⬛ ⬛⬛ ⬛⬛— Sept. 24, 1917, as ⬛⬛ | | | | | | | | | |
| Series TM2-1922........ | Aug. 1, 1921 | Mar. 15, 1922 | 5¼ | 17,636,000 | 3,695,000 | 2,689,000 | 2,516,500 | 2,489,000 | 5,643,500 |
| Series TS-1922......... | Sept. 15, 1921 | Sept. 15, 1922 | 5¼ | 26,778,500 | 6,145,500 | 3,500,000 | 6,705,000 | 3,979,000 | 13,100,000 |
| Series TM3-1922........ | Sept. 15, 1921 | Mar. 15, 1922 | 5 | 15,856,000 | 3,035,500 | 3,420,000 | 5,632,000 | 5,278,500 | 10,600,000 |
| Series TS2-1922........ | Nov. 1, 1921 | Sept. 15, 1922 | 4¼ | 21,288,000 | 6,638,500 | 5,730,000 | 6,475,000 | 3,586,500 | 8,550,000 |
| | Dec. 15, 1921 | June 15, 1922 | 4¼ | 9,877,500 | 2,411,500 | 1,450,000 | 2,069,000 | 2,605,000 | 6,285,000 |
| Series TD-1922........ | Dec. 15, 1921 | Dec. 15, 1922 | 4¼ | 27,318,500 | 8,611,500 | 7,442,500 | 2,493,500 | 4,175,000 | 12,270,000 |
| Series ... ⬛⬛⬛ 1922........ | June 1, 1922 | Dec. 15, 1922 | 3¾ | 28,000,000 | 8,000,000 | 6,920,000 | 8,000,000 | 4,800,000 | 14,120,000 |
| Issued in ⬛⬛⬛ of ⬛⬛ one and profits tax, 1923: Sept. 24, 1917, as ⬛⬛—1 | | | | | | | | | |
| Series TM-1923......... | Mar. 15, 1922 | Mar. 15, 1923 | 4¼ | 35,000,000 | 10,000,000 | 8,650,000 | 10,000,000 | 6,000,000 | 17,650,000 |
| Series TJ-1923......... | June 15, 1922 | June 15, 1923 | 3¾ | 35,000,000 | 10,000,000 | 8,630,000 | 10,000,000 | 6,000,000 | 17,650,000 |
| Series TS-1923......... | Sept. 15, 1922 | Sept. 15, 1923 | 3½ | 28,000,000 | 8,000,000 | 6,920,000 | 8,000,000 | 4,800,000 | 14,120,000 |
| Total tax certificates........ | | | | 244,754,500 | 66,537,500 | 55,371,500 | 67,891,000 | 43,713,000 | 119,958,500 |
| Grand total loan and tax certificates........ | | | | 299,944,500 | 83,989,500 | 69,820,500 | 85,499,500 | 54,143,500 | 152,465,000 |

## EXHIBIT 23.

### LOAN AND TAX CERTIFICATES OF INDEBTEDNESS ISSUED THROUGH EACH FEDERAL RESERVE BANK FROM APRIL 6, 1917, TO OCTOBER 31, 1922.

[In thousands of dollars.]

**Issued in anticipation of loans.**

| Federal reserve bank | First loan | Second loan | Third loan | Fourth loan | Victory loan | Series 1920 | Series 1921 | Series 1922 | Total |
|---|---|---|---|---|---|---|---|---|---|
| Boston | $57,367 | $132,044 | $214,417 | $381,153 | $475,792 | $188,176 | $105,076 | $57,677 | $1,611,702 |
| New York | 460,462 | 1,467,543 | 1,255,308 | 1,680,989 | 2,255,145 | 959,163 | 539,979 | 264,270 | 8,882,859 |
| Philadelphia | 43,400 | 89,132 | 196,500 | 316,020 | 420,335 | 145,544 | 100,530 | 70,336 | 1,381,797 |
| Cleveland | 58,900 | 182,513 | 238,034 | 440,599 | 554,761 | 174,479 | 121,767 | 64,244 | 1,835,267 |
| Richmond | 13,703 | 40,014 | 75,829 | 117,983 | 187,497 | 48,864 | 35,814 | 22,319 | 542,023 |
| Atlanta | 13,305 | 32,135 | 79,573 | 114,857 | 143,312 | 72,428 | 21,098 | 16,192 | 492,900 |
| Chicago | 77,693 | 138,597 | 325,355 | 663,204 | 963,416 | 278,575 | 157,360 | 85,179 | 2,679,379 |
| St. Louis | 32,745 | 45,700 | 133,584 | 185,963 | 245,288 | 84,738 | 50,955 | 28,249 | 808,222 |
| Minneapolis | 14,600 | 29,471 | 89,350 | 127,560 | 218,881 | 73,113 | 25,221 | 21,439 | 599,635 |
| Kansas City | 30,300 | 38,039 | 128,524 | 176,895 | 187,745 | 81,875 | 44,845 | 25,984 | 714,178 |
| Dallas | 18,225 | 39,347 | 90,925 | 83,320 | 101,546 | 77,638 | 18,783 | 14,502 | 444,235 |
| San Francisco | 36,900 | 85,958 | 172,791 | 305,020 | 390,475 | 168,052 | 93,872 | 47,047 | 1,300,115 |
| Treasury | 10,605 | | 11,895 | 65,316 | 23,397 | 7,400 | 12,000 | | 130,613 |
| Total | 888,205 | 2,320,493 | 3,012,085 | 4,659,820 | 6,157,590 | 2,360,045 | 1,327,250 | 717,438 | 21,422,926 |

**Issued in anticipation of taxes.**

| Federal reserve bank | Series 1918 | Series 1919 | Series 1920 | Series 1921 | Series 1922 | Series 1923 | Total | Grand total |
|---|---|---|---|---|---|---|---|---|
| Boston | $63,260 | $256,912 | $157,623 | $127,678 | $129,969 | $60,620 | $846,062 | $2,457,764 |
| New York | 831,473 | 1,451,852 | 1,358,566 | 822,994 | 663,992 | 303,680 | 5,462,567 | 14,345,426 |
| Philadelphia | 95,537 | 141,002 | 191,939 | 135,318 | 156,178 | 49,420 | 769,394 | 2,151,191 |
| Cleveland | 255,452 | 435,440 | 246,367 | 194,631 | 165,684 | 63,420 | 1,390,394 | 3,225,661 |
| Richmond | 20,822 | 92,519 | 64,261 | 54,652 | 52,672 | 24,223 | 309,446 | 851,469 |
| Atlanta | 13,006 | 71,414 | 79,129 | 25,639 | 32,527 | 20,440 | 242,146 | 735,046 |
| Chicago | 162,934 | 463,807 | 395,438 | 182,606 | 201,066 | 98,000 | 1,503,851 | 4,183,220 |
| St. Louis | 22,703 | 75,522 | 98,585 | 60,029 | 59,813 | 28,000 | 344,652 | 1,152,874 |
| Minneapolis | 11,398 | 51,650 | 63,788 | 26,890 | 40,683 | 24,220 | 218,599 | 818,234 |
| Kansas City | 21,037 | 41,984 | 69,996 | 56,257 | 58,518 | 28,000 | 275,792 | 989,970 |
| Dallas | 28,951 | 61,940 | 88,671 | 24,440 | 34,017 | 16,800 | 254,819 | 699,054 |
| San Francisco | 47,831 | 166,157 | 199,031 | 123,430 | 99,739 | 49,420 | 685,608 | 1,985,723 |
| Treasury | | 44,588 | 34,645 | 40,063 | | | 119,296 | 249,909 |
| Total | 1,624,404 | 3,354,787 | 3,078,030 | 1,873,997 | 1,715,158 | 766,250 | 12,412,626 | 33,835,552 |

# Exhibit 24.

## TREASURY NOTES ISSUED THROUGH EACH FEDERAL RESERVE BANK AND THE TREASURY DEPARTMENT FROM JUNE 15, 1921, TO OCTOBER 31, 1922.

| Authorizing act and series. | Date of issue. | Date of maturity. | Rate. | Total amount. | Federal reserve bank. | | | | | |
|---|---|---|---|---|---|---|---|---|---|---|
| | | | | | Boston. | New York. | Philadelphia. | Cleveland. | Richmond. | Atlanta. |
| Sept. 24, 1917, as amended: | | | *Per ct.* | | | | | | | |
| Series A-1924 | June 15, 1921 | June 15, 1924 | 5¾ | $311,191,600 | $22,905,000 | $157,225,200 | $45,509,500 | $21,175,200 | $8,698,500 | $2,169,900 |
| Series B-1924 | Sept. 15, 1921 | Sept. 15, 1924 | 5½ | 390,706,100 | 37,423,400 | 146,615,100 | 40,597,200 | 36,500,000 | 14,249,000 | 5,934,000 |
| Series A-1925 | Feb. 1, 1922 | Mar. 15, 1925 | 4¾ | [1] 601,599,500 | 51,960,000 | 254,213,300 | 45,865,900 | 40,305,000 | 14,966,300 | 11,743,900 |
| Series B-1925 | June 15, 1922 | Dec. 15, 1925 | 4⅝ | [2] 335,141,300 | 11,158,200 | 173,914,300 | 20,128,800 | 24,162,300 | 4,549,600 | 2,707,800 |
| Series A-1926 | Mar. 15, 1922 | Mar. 15, 1926 | 4¾ | [2] 617,769,700 | 51,093,800 | 314,059,200 | 47,904,000 | 49,795,000 | 13,252,200 | 4,114,500 |
| Series B-1926 | Aug. 1, 1922 | Sept. 15, 1926 | 4¼ | [3] 486,940,200 | 37,096,600 | 196,949,300 | 32,759,500 | 45,573,000 | 13,763,800 | 11,391,200 |
| Total | | | | 2,743,348,400 | 211,637,000 | 1,242,976,400 | 232,764,900 | 217,510,500 | 69,479,400 | 38,061,300 |

| Authorizing act and series. | Date of issue. | Date of maturity. | Rate. | Federal reserve bank. | | | | | | Treasury Department. |
|---|---|---|---|---|---|---|---|---|---|---|
| | | | | Chicago. | St. Louis. | Minneapolis. | Kansas City. | Dallas. | San Francisco. | |
| Sept. 24, 1917, as amended: | | | *Per ct.* | | | | | | | |
| Series A-1924 | June 15, 1921 | June 15, 1924 | 5¾ | $20,650,200 | $9,740,100 | $5,301,100 | $5,346,500 | $4,058,600 | $8,411,800 | |
| Series B-1924 | Sept. 15, 1921 | Sept. 15, 1924 | 5½ | 43,210,700 | 16,212,500 | 13,840,000 | 11,674,500 | 5,449,000 | 19,000,000 | |
| Series A-1925 | Feb. 1, 1922 | Mar. 15, 1925 | 4¾ | 84,145,300 | 17,384,200 | 15,199,800 | 21,697,500 | 9,840,500 | 34,278,500 | |
| Series B-1925 | June 15, 1922 | Dec. 15, 1925 | 4⅝ | 48,138,600 | 12,250,000 | 6,350,900 | 16,125,400 | 4,292,200 | 11,363,200 | |
| Series A-1926 | Mar. 15, 1922 | Mar. 15, 1926 | 4¾ | 65,964,800 | 20,745,000 | 7,747,300 | 9,909,900 | 2,004,000 | 31,180,000 | |
| Series B-1926 | Aug. 1, 1922 | Sept. 15, 1926 | 4¼ | 59,107,200 | 17,061,500 | 13,503,000 | 14,677,500 | 8,455,700 | 34,824,000 | $1,777,900 |
| Total | | | | 321,216,800 | 93,393,300 | 61,942,100 | 79,431,300 | 34,100,000 | 139,057,500 | 1,777,900 |

[1] Includes $200,000,000 allotted in exchange for Victory notes.
[2] Issued only in exchange for 4¾ per cent Victory notes.
[3] Includes $141,515,700 allotted in exchange for Victory notes.

## EXHIBIT 25.

### TREASURY BONDS OF 1947-1952, SUBSCRIPTIONS AND ALLOTMENTS (UNREVISED), BY FEDERAL RESERVE DISTRICTS.

| | Total. | Boston. | New York. | Philadelphia. | Cleveland. | Richmond. | Atlanta. |
|---|---|---|---|---|---|---|---|
| Cash subscriptions received | $1,399,851,900 | $113,390,400 | $567,994,100 | $103,788,500 | $100,355,300 | $37,070,800 | $29,668,100 |
| Cash subscriptions allotted: | | | | | | | |
| $10,000 or less (in full) | 327,559,600 | 49,015,900 | 109,261,700 | 32,523,900 | 27,785,000 | 15,865,900 | 10,077,400 |
| $10,100 to $50,000 (40 per cent) | 29,718,200 | 3,025,200 | 9,874,300 | 3,478,000 | 2,192,000 | 1,072,900 | 1,234,400 |
| $50,100 to $100,000 (30 per cent) | 23,714,500 | 2,844,600 | 9,822,400 | 2,031,800 | 1,488,000 | 534,300 | 483,800 |
| $100,100 to $500,000 (20 per cent) | 52,648,600 | 4,906,800 | 23,396,000 | 4,087,400 | 3,335,000 | 1,602,700 | 1,560,000 |
| $500,100 to $1,000,000 (15 per cent) | 30,301,500 | 1,632,500 | 16,355,700 | 1,767,500 | 1,850,000 | 1,120,000 | 262,500 |
| Over $1,000,000 (10 per cent) | 48,447,600 | 1,275,300 | 29,702,000 | 2,592,600 | 3,550,000 | 150,000 | 550,000 |
| Total cash subscriptions allotted | 512,390,000 | 62,700,300 | 198,382,100 | 46,454,200 | 40,200,000 | 20,345,800 | 14,158,100 |
| Allotments on exchanges for— | | | | | | | |
| Victory notes | (1) | (1) | 71,397,600 | 5,821,600 | (1) | 3,402,700 | 1,864,000 |
| Certificates of indebtedness | (1) | (1) | 75,192,000 | 1,724,000 | (1) | 259,500 | 586,000 |
| Total | 252,060,900 | 19,508,400 | 146,589,600 | 7,545,600 | 18,210,700 | 3,662,200 | 2,450,000 |
| Total allotments | 764,450,900 | 82,208,700 | 344,971,700 | 54,029,800 | 58,410,700 | 24,008,000 | 16,608,100 |

| | Chicago. | St. Louis. | Minneapolis. | Kansas City. | Dallas. | San Francisco. | Treasury. |
|---|---|---|---|---|---|---|---|
| Cash subscriptions received | $134,942,800 | $55,300,100 | $33,369,300 | $40,564,900 | $16,076,800 | $67,390,800 | |
| Cash subscriptions allotted: | | | | | | | |
| $10,000 or less (in full) | 34,705,300 | 24,625,200 | 5,522,600 | 5,954,100 | 2,900,300 | 9,322,300 | |
| $10,100 to $50,000 (40 per cent) | 3,544,400 | 1,633,200 | 399,200 | 1,016,200 | 379,400 | 1,879,000 | |
| $50,100 to $100,000 (30 per cent) | 2,219,000 | 1,737,600 | 346,500 | 752,500 | 529,500 | 921,500 | |
| $100,100 to $500,000 (20 per cent) | 5,660,000 | 1,719,600 | 1,004,000 | 1,632,700 | 980,000 | 2,553,000 | |
| $500,100 to $1,000,000 (15 per cent) | 3,808,800 | 562,500 | 600,000 | 991,500 | 300,000 | 1,047,500 | |
| Over $1,000,000 (10 per cent) | 3,112,500 | 966,700 | 1,679,400 | 1,350,000 | 350,000 | 3,169,100 | |
| Total cash subscriptions allotted | 52,992,000 | 31,244,200 | 9,551,700 | 12,000,000 | 5,439,200 | 18,802,400 | |
| Allotments on exchanges for— | | | | | | | |
| Victory notes | 13,691,800 | 5,529,800 | 1,530,500 | 4,449,200 | 728,100 | 9,865,400 | 1,886,000 |
| Certificates of indebtedness | 8,429,000 | 1,567,500 | 712,000 | 771,500 | 1,034,000 | 2,887,500 | 962,100 |
| Total | 22,120,800 | 7,097,300 | 2,242,500 | 5,270,700 | 1,762,100 | 12,752,900 | 2,848,100 |
| Total allotments | 75,112,800 | 38,341,500 | 11,794,200 | 17,270,700 | 7,201,300 | 31,645,300 | 2,848,100 |

1 Data not available.

## EXHIBIT 26.

### BRIEF DESCRIPTION OF LIBERTY BONDS AND VICTORY NOTES.

*Form and Denominations.*—Liberty Bonds and Victory Notes are issued in both coupon and registered form in the following denominations: Coupon, $50, $100, $500, $1,000, $5,000, $10,000; registered $50, $100, $500, $1,000, $5,000, $10,000, $50,000, $100,000; except that the First 3½'s are not issued in coupon form in denominations of $5,000 and $10,000, nor in registered form in the denomination of $50.

*3½ per cent Liberty Bonds exempt from Federal, State, and local taxation.*—Such bonds are exempt, both as to principal and interest, from all taxation (except estate or inheritance taxes) now or hereafter imposed by the United States, any State, or any of the possessions of the United States, or by any local taxing authority.

*4 per cent and 4¼ per cent Liberty Bonds and 4¾ per cent Victory Notes exempt from State and local taxation and from normal Federal income tax.*—Such bonds and notes are exempt, both as to principal and interest, from all taxation now or hereafter imposed by the United States, any State, or any of the possessions of the United States, or by any local taxing authority, except (a) estate or inheritance taxes, and (b) graduated additional income taxes, commonly known as surtaxes, and excess-profits and war-profits taxes, now or hereafter imposed by the United States, upon the income or profits of individuals, partnerships, associations, or corporations.

*4 per cent and 4¼ per cent Liberty Bonds also entitled to limited exemptions from Federal income surtaxes and profits taxes.*—Pursuant to the consolidation (effective January 1, 1921) made by the Revenue Act of 1921, and the proclamation of the President which fixed July 2, 1921, as the date of the termination of the war, such bonds are entitled to limited exemptions from graduated additional income taxes, commonly known as surtaxes, and excess-profits and war-profits taxes, now or hereafter imposed by the United States, upon the income or profits of individuals, partnerships, associations, or corporations, in respect to the interest on principal amounts thereof, as follows:

During the life of the obligations—

$5,000 in the aggregate of First 4's, First 4¼'s, First Second 4¼'s, Second 4's, Second 4¼'s, Third 4¼'s, Fourth 4¼'s, Treasury bonds of 1947–52, Treasury certificates of indebtedness, and Treasury (war) savings certificates.

Until July 2, 1923—

$30,000 of First Second 4¼'s.

$125,000 in the aggregate of First 4's, First 4¼'s, First Second 4¼'s, Second 4's, Second 4¼'s, Third 4¼'s, and Fourth 4¼'s.

From July 2, 1923, to July 2, 1926—

$50,000 in the aggregate of First 4's, First 4¼'s, First Second 4¼'s, Second 4's, Second 4¼'s, Third 4¼'s, and Fourth 4¼'s.

*All Bonds and Notes exempt from taxes in hands of foreign holders.*—Bonds and notes of the United States are, while beneficially owned by a nonresident alien individual, or a foreign corporation, partnership, or association, not engaged in business in the United States, exempt, both as to principal and interest, from any and all taxation now or hereafter imposed by the United States, any State, or any of the possessions of the United States, or by any local taxing authority.

*4¼ per cent Liberty Bonds and 4¾ per cent Victory Notes receivable at par in payment of Federal estate and inheritance taxes.*—All such bonds and notes which have been owned by any person continuously for at least six months prior to the date of his death and which upon such date constitute part of his estate are receivable by the United States at par and accrued interest in payment of Federal estate or inheritance taxes.

*Victory Notes receivable in payment of income and profits taxes.*— 4¾ per cent Victory Notes are receivable at par, with an adjustment of accrued interest; in payment of income and profits taxes payable December 15, 1922; uncalled 4¾ per cent Victory Notes will likewise be receivable in payment of income and profits taxes payable March 15, 1923.

*2½ per cent Cumulative Sinking Fund.*—For the fiscal year beginning July 1, 1920, and for each fiscal year thereafter until all Liberty Bonds and Victory Notes are retired, the Victory Liberty Loan Act appropriates, out of any money in the Treasury not otherwise appropriated, for the purpose of a sinking fund, an amount equal to the sum of (1) 2½ per cent of the aggregate amount of such bonds and notes outstanding on July 1, 1920, less an amount equal to the par amount of any obligations of foreign Governments held by the United States on that date, and (2) the interest which would have been payable during the fiscal year for which the appropriation is made on the bonds and notes purchased, redeemed, or paid out of the sinking fund during such year or in previous years.

*Conversion Privileges.*—First 4's are convertible into First 4¼'s. Second 4's are convertible into Second 4¼'s. No other conversion privileges are outstanding.

---

The principal and interest of all Liberty Bonds and Victory Notes are payable in United States gold coin of the present standard of value.

Liberty Bonds and Victory Notes are issued under authority of the acts of Congress approved April 24, 1917, September 24, 1917, April 4, 1918, July 9, 1918, September 24, 1918, and March 3, 1919, and pursuant to official Treasury Department circulars, from which these statements are summarized and to which they are subject.

Exhibit 27.

### BRIEF DESCRIPTION OF TREASURY BONDS, NOTES, CERTIFICATES OF INDEBTEDNESS, AND SAVINGS CERTIFICATES.

*Form and denominations.*—Treasury Bonds of 1947-52 are issued in both coupon and registered form in the following denominations: Coupon, $100, $500, $1,000, $5,000, $10,000; registered, $100, $500, $1,000, $5,000, $10,000, $50,000, $100,000.

Treasury Notes are issued only in coupon form, and in the following denominations: $100, $500, $1,000, $5,000, $10,000, $100,000.

Treasury Certificates of Indebtedness are issued only in coupon form, and in the following denominations: $500, $1,000, $5,000, $10,000, $100,000.

Treasury Savings Certificates are issued only in registered form, with maturity values of $25, $100, $1,000.

*Treasury Bonds, Treasury Notes, Treasury Certificates of Indebtedness, and Treasury Savings Certificates, exempt from State and local taxation and from normal Federal income tax.*—All such bonds, notes, and certificates are exempt, both as to principal and interest, from all taxation now or hereafter imposed by the United States, any State, or any of the possessions of the United States, or by any local taxing authority, except (a) estate or inheritance taxes, and (b) graduated additional income taxes, commonly known as surtaxes, and excess-profits and war-profits taxes, now or hereafter imposed by the United States, upon the income or profits of individuals, partnerships, associations, or corporations. The interest on an amount of 4 and 4¼ per cent Liberty Bonds, Treasury Bonds, Treasury Certificates of Indebtedness, and Treasury (War) Savings Certificates, the principal of which does not exceed in the aggregate $5,000, owned by any individual, partnership, association, or corporation, shall be exempt from the taxes provided for in subdivision (b) above.

*All Bonds, Notes, and Certificates of Indebtedness exempt from taxes in hands of foreign holders.*—Bonds, notes, and certificates of indebtedness of the United States are, while beneficially owned by a nonresident alien individual, or a foreign corporation, partnership, or association, not engaged in business in the United States, exempt, both as to principal and interest, from any and all taxation now or hereafter imposed by the United States, any State, or any of the possessions of the United States, or by any local taxing authority.

*Treasury Bonds and Treasury Notes bearing interest at a higher rate than 4 per cent per annum, receivable at par in payment of Federal estate and inheritance taxes.*—All such bonds and notes which have been owned by any person continuously for at least six months prior to the date of his death and which upon such date constitute part of his estate are receivable by the United States at par and accrued interest in payment of Federal estate or inheritance taxes.

*Treasury Notes and Certificates of Indebtedness receivable in payment of income and profits taxes.*—Treasury Notes are receivable at par, with an adjustment of accrued interest, during such time and under such rules and regulations as shall be prescribed or approved by the Secretary of the Treasury, in payment of income and profits taxes payable at or within six months before the maturity of the notes.

Treasury Certificates of Indebtedness are upon similar terms and conditions acceptable in payment of income and profits taxes payable at the maturity of the certificates.

*Treasury (War) Savings Certificates of any one series not to be held to an amount exceeding $5,000 (maturity value).*—Any one person at any one time may hold Treasury (War) Savings Certificates of any one series to an aggregate amount not exceeding $5,000 (maturity value).

---

The principal and interest of Treasury bonds, notes, and certificates of indebtedness are payable in United States gold coin of the present standard of value.

Treasury Bonds, Treasury Notes, Treasury Certificates of Indebtedness, and Treasury (War) Savings Certificates are issued under authority of the acts of Congress approved April 24, 1917, September 24, 1917, April 4, 1918, July 9, 1918, September 24, 1918, March 3, 1919, and November 23, 1921, and pursuant to official Treasury Deparment circulars, from which these statements are summarized and to which they are subject.

## EXHIBIT 28.

[Department Circular No. 307.   Loans and Currency.]

**UNITED STATES OF AMERICA—FOUR AND ONE-QUARTER PER CENT TREASURY BONDS OF 1947–1952, DATED AND BEARING INTEREST FROM OCTOBER 16, 1922, DUE OCTOBER 15, 1952. REDEEMABLE AT THE OPTION OF THE UNITED STATES AT PAR AND ACCRUED INTEREST ON AND AFTER OCTOBER 15, 1947. INTEREST PAYABLE APRIL 15 AND OCTOBER 15.**

The Secretary of the Treasury invites subscriptions, at par and accrued interest, from the people of the United States, for four and one-quarter per cent Treasury bonds of 1947–1952, of an issue of gold bonds of the United States authorized by the Act of Congress approved September 24, 1917, as amended.   The amount of the offering will be $500,000,000, or thereabouts, with the right reserved to the Secretary of the Treasury to allot additional bonds up to a limited amount to the extent that 4¾ per cent Victory notes or Treasury certificates of indebtedness of Series TD or TD2–1922 are tendered in payment.

### DESCRIPTION OF BONDS.

The bonds will be dated October 16, 1922, and will bear interest from that date at the rate of four and one-quarter per cent per annum payable April 15 and October 15 in each year, on a semiannual basis.   The bonds will mature October 15, 1952, but may be redeemed at the option of the United States on and after October 15, 1947, in whole or in part, at par and accrued interest, on any interest day or days, on four months' notice of redemption given in such manner as the Secretary of the Treasury shall prescribe.   In case of partial redemption the bonds to be redeemed will be determined by such method as may be prescribed by the Secretary of the Treasury. From the date of redemption designated in any such notice, interest on the bonds called for redemption shall cease.   The principal and interest of the bonds will be payable in United States gold coin of the present standard of value.

Bearer bonds with interest coupons attached will be issued in denominations of $100, $500, $1,000, $5,000, and $10,000. Bonds registered as to principal and interest will be issued in denominations of $100, $500, $1,000, $5,000, $10,000, $50,000, and $100,000. Provision will be made for the interchange of bonds of different denominations and of coupon and registered bonds and for the transfer of registered bonds, without charge by the United States, under rules and regulations prescribed by the Secretary of the Treasury.

The bonds shall be exempt, both as to principal and interest, from all taxation now or hereafter imposed by the United States, any State, or any of the possessions of the United States, or by any local taxing authority, except (a) estate or inheritance taxes, and (b) graduated additional income taxes, commonly known as surtaxes, and excess-profits and war-profits taxes, now or hereafter imposed by the United States, upon the income or profits of individuals, partnerships, associations, or corporations. The interest on an amount of bonds and certificates authorized by said act approved September 24, 1917, and amendments thereto, the principal of which does not exceed in the aggregate $5,000, owned by any individual, partnership, association, or corporation, shall be exempt from the taxes provided for in clause (b) above.

Any of the bonds which have been owned by any person continuously for at least six months prior to the date of his death, and which upon such date constitute part of his estate, shall, under rules and regulations prescribed by the Secretary of the Treasury, be receivable by the United States at par and accrued interest in payment of any estate or inheritance taxes imposed by the United States, under or by virtue of any present or future law upon such estate or the inheritance thereof. The bonds will be acceptable to secure deposits of public moneys, but do not bear the circulation privilege and are not entitled to any privilege of conversion.

### APPLICATION, ALLOTMENT, AND PAYMENT.

Applications will be received at the Federal Reserve Banks, as fiscal agents of the United States. Banking institutions generally will handle applications for subscribers, but only the Federal Reserve Banks are authorized to act as official agencies.

Within the limitation on the amount of the offering, applications from any one subscriber for an amount of bonds not exceeding $10,000 will be allotted in full, and allotments thereon may be made upon application. Applications for amounts in excess of $10,000 will be received subject to allotment. The right is reserved to reject any subscription for an amount in excess of $10,000, and to allot less than the amount of bonds applied for and to close the subscriptions at any time without notice. The Secretary of the Treasury also reserves the right to make allotment in full upon applications for smaller amounts, and to make reduced allotments upon, or to reject, applications for larger amounts, and to make classified allotments and allotments upon a graduated scale; and his action in these respects will be final.

Payment at par and accrued interest for any bonds allotted must be made on or before October 16, 1922, or on later allotment; provided, however, that persons who desire to make payment in instal-

ments may pay 50 per cent on October 16, 1922, or on later allotment, and the balance on November 15, 1922, with accrued interest
to that date on the deferred instalment. Any qualified depositary
will be permitted to make payment by credit for bonds allotted to
it for itself and its customers up to any amount for which it shall be
qualified in excess of existing deposits, when so notified by the Federal
Reserve Bank of its district, except upon subscriptions for which
Victory notes or Treasury certificates of indebtedness of Series TD or
TD2-1922 are tendered in payment. Treasury certificates of indebtedness of Series D-1922, maturing October 16, 1922, of Series TD-1922
and TD2-1922, both maturing December 15, 1922 (with any unmatured coupons attached), and Victory notes of the 4¾ per cent series,
whether or not called for redemption, will be accepted at the Federal
Reserve Banks at par, with an adjustment of accrued interest, as of
October 16, 1922, in payment for any Treasury bonds of 1947-1952
now offered which shall be subscribed for and allotted. Victory
notes in coupon form must have all unmatured coupons attached,
and if in registered form must be duly assigned to the Secretary of the
Treasury for redemption, in accordance with the general regulations
of the Treasury Department governing assignments. Payments
must be made when and as herein provided under penalty of forfeiture of any instalment previously paid and of all right and interest
in the bonds allotted.

As fiscal agents of the United States, Federal Reserve Banks are
authorized and requested to receive subscriptions and to make
allotments thereon on the basis and up to the amounts indicated
by the Secretary of the Treasury to the Federal Reserve Banks of
the respective districts. Allotment notices will be sent out promptly
upon allotment, and the basis of allotment will be publicly announced.

### FURTHER DETAILS.

Bonds will be delivered promptly after allotment and upon payment, and coupon bonds may be delivered prior to October 16, 1922,
to subscribers for amounts not in excess of $10,000 who make pay-
ment in full upon allotment. The Federal Reserve Banks may issue
interim receipts pending delivery of the definitive bonds.

Further details may be announced by the Secretary of the Treasury from time to time, information as to which, as well as forms for
application, may be obtained from the Treasury Department,
Division of Loans and Currency, Washington, D. C., or from any
Federal Reserve Bank.

A. W. MELLON,
*Secretary of the Treasury.*

TREASURY DEPARTMENT,
  OFFICE OF THE SECRETARY,
      *October 9, 1922.*

To THE INVESTOR:

Almost any banking institution in the United States will handle your subscription
for you, or you may make subscription direct to the Federal Reserve Bank of your
district. Your special attention is invited to the terms of subscription and allotment
as stated above, and to the fact that 4¾ per cent Victory notes and Treasury certificates of Series TD or TD2-1922 may be tendered in payment. Application blanks
may be obtained upon application from the Treasury Department, Division of Loans
and Currency, Washington, D. C., or any Federal Reserve Bank or branch.

EXHIBIT 29.

**LETTER OF SECRETARY OF THE TREASURY, DATED OCTOBER 9, 1922, TO BANKING INSTITUTIONS, ACCOMPANYING THE OFFERING OF FOUR AND ONE-QUARTER PER CENT TREASURY BONDS OF 1947-1952, DATED OCTOBER 16, 1922.**

OCTOBER 9, 1922.

DEAR SIR: I am sending you herewith a copy of the official Treasury Department Circular [1] announcing the offering of 4¼ per cent Treasury bonds of 1947–52 for which subscription books open to-day. The offering is for $500,000,000, or thereabouts, with the right reserved to the Secretary of the Treasury to allot additional bonds to the extent that 4¾ per cent Victory notes or Treasury certificates maturing December 15th are tendered in payment.

The new bonds will be 25/30 year bonds, dated October 16, 1922, maturing October 15, 1952, and redeemable at the option of the United States on and after October 15, 1947. The bonds will be issued in both coupon and registered form, in denominations of $100 and upwards. Applications will be received through the Federal Reserve Banks, and the Treasury is prepared to make deliveries promptly upon allotment and payment. Subject to the limitations on the amount of the offering, allotments will be made in full, in the order of receipt of application, upon subscriptions for amounts not exceeding $10,000 for any one subscriber, and upon subscriptions for which either 4¾ per cent Victory notes or Treasury certificates maturing December 15th are tendered in payment. Other applications for amounts exceeding $10,000 for any one subscriber will be received subject to allotment.

This is a refunding issue, and it affords a particularly favorable opportunity to holders of 4¾ per cent Victory notes to acquire a long-time Government bond on attractive terms in place of Victory notes which will mature or be redeemed within the next few months. I am, therefore, addressing this letter to the heads of all banking institutions in the country, and asking you to provide every possible facility for investing in the new bonds. I hope that you will also make a special effort to bring the offering to the attention of your customers, large and small, for it is the Treasury's desire to secure the widest possible distribution of the bonds among investors.

I think you will be interested in this connection to know what has already been accomplished in the refunding of the short-dated debt, and what still remains to be done. On April 30, 1921, when the Treasury first announced its refunding program, the gross public debt, on the basis of daily Treasury statements, amounted to about $24,000,000,000, of which over $7,500,000,000 was maturing within about two years. On September 30, 1922, the total gross debt on the same basis stood at about $22,800,000,000, and of the early maturing debt about $4,000,000,000 had already been retired or refunded, chiefly into short-term Treasury notes with maturities spread over the next four fiscal years. There will fall due this fiscal year about $1,100,000,000 of Treasury certificates of indebtedness, about $625,000,000 maturity value of War-Savings Certificates of the Series of 1918, and about $1,800,000,000 of Victory notes. Of the

---

[1] See Exhibit 28, p. 168.

Treasury certificates, about $48,000,000 represents Pittman Act certificates which will be retired this year through the recoinage of silver bullion, while about $100,000,000 of loan certificates maturing October 16, 1922, will be paid out of funds already in hand. The retirement of these certificates will leave only tax certificates outstanding, and it will in any event continue to be desirable, with income and profits tax payments as large as they are, for the Treasury to have outstanding at least $1,000,000,000 of tax certificates in amounts and with maturities conforming to the quarterly tax payments. This correspondingly reduces the amount of necessary refunding into other securities.

After October 16, 1922, the next maturities fall on December 15th, and include about $870,000,000 face amount of 4¾ per cent Victory notes called for redemption, and about $420,000,000 of maturing tax certificates of Series TD and TD2–1922, against which the Treasury will receive in December about $250,000,000 of income and profits taxes. On January 1, 1923, the $625,000,000 of War-Savings Certificates become payable, but the Treasury has already announced, as you know, a new offering of Treasury Savings Certificates with a view to refunding as much as possible of the maturity into obligations of the same general character and with the same appeal to the needs of the small investor. The Treasury will shortly announce special facilities for the exchange of maturing War-Savings Certificates for the new Treasury Savings Certificates, and plans in this manner to provide for a substantial part of the War-Savings maturity. The only Treasury certificates maturing in the second half of the fiscal year 1923 are about $266,000,000 on March 15, 1923, and about $273,000,000 on June 15, 1923, both of which are covered by the income and profits tax payments estimated for those dates. On May 20, 1923, the remaining $930,000,000 of 4¾ per cent Victory notes will mature according to their terms.

The maturities which remain and have to be refunded the Treasury will meet through issues of refunding securities, properly adjusted to market conditions, and I believe it will be able to meet them, as it has in the past, without disturbance to the markets and without strain on the financial machinery. During the course of the refunding operations which have been in progress the Treasury has issued from time to time Treasury certificates of indebtedness, Treasury notes and Treasury Savings Certificates, all relatively short-term. These operations have been successful and have been accomplished without disturbance to the market for outstanding securities. With the announcement of the bonds now offered, the Treasury is adding to its list a refunding issue of long-time bonds, on a basis which should prove particularly attractive to investors. These bonds will provide, through exchanges and otherwise, for a substantial part of the heavy maturities falling on December 15th, and the success of the offering will leave only a normal amount of financing to be placed on that date.

It is four years since the Treasury has offered to the people of the United States an issue of long-time Government bonds. During that period it has been financing itself on a short-term basis, and it has succeeded, with your cooperation, in placing with investors throughout the country a great volume of Treasury certificates and Treasury notes. Now that the time has come for a longer-term operation, I am looking forward with confidence to your continued support, and hope that, as with previous offerings of Government securities, you will give your best efforts to the distribution of the new Treasury bonds among investors.

Cordially yours,

A. W. MELLON,
*Secretary of the Treasury.*

To THE PRESIDENT OF THE BANK-
ING INSTITUTION ADDRESSED.

## EXHIBIT 30.

[Treasury Department, Loans and Currency, Form P. D. 736.]

### APPLICATION FOR 4¼ PER CENT TREASURY BONDS OF 1947-52.

Date: October....................

To the SECRETARY OF THE TREASURY.

The undersigned hereby applies for $.......... face amount of United States of America Four and One Quarter Per Cent Treasury Bonds of 1947–52, and agrees to make payment at par for any bonds allotted upon this application, with accrued interest from October 16, 1922, all in accordance with the provisions of Treasury Department Circular No. 307, dated October 9, 1922.

Payment for bonds allotted upon this application will be made in the manner indicated below:

| | | |
|---|---|---|
| ☐ Cash | | ☐ Treasury Certificates, Series D-1922. |
| ☐ Victory 4¾'s, (Coupon) | | ☐ Treasury Certificates, Series TD-1922. |
| ☐ Victory 4¾'s, (Registered) | | ☐ Treasury Certificates, Series TD2-1922. |

(If payment is to be made in more than one of the above forms, the amount to be tendered in each should be indicated opposite the respective items.).

**There** is transmitted herewith, in { full / partial } payment for the bonds applied for,

(Strike out one.)

..........*. $..........., in ...........................................................

(Describe remittance. If Victory notes or Treasury certificates are presented, they should be scheduled on the reverse of this form.)

**The undersigned** desires { coupon / registered } bonds of the denominations indicated below:

(Strike out class not desired.)

| Number of pieces | Denomination | Par amount |
|---|---|---|
| .......... | $100 | .......... |
| | 500 | .......... |
| | 1,000 | .......... |
| | 5,000 | .......... |
| .......... | 10,000 | .......... |
| .......... | * 50,000 | .......... |
| .......... | * 100,000 | .......... |

Total face amount,......................... $.........

(Which must agree with amount of bonds applied for)

* Registered bonds only.

INSTRUCTIONS WITH RESPECT TO REGISTERED BONDS.

| | |
|---|---|
| To be filled in only if Registered bonds are desired. | Registered bonds are to be inscribed in the name of ................<br>Post Office Address: ....................................<br>　　　　　　　　　　　　　　(Street and number)<br>...................... ....................<br>　　(City or town)　　　　　　　(State) |

Autograph signature of applicant: ..............................

\* Post Office Address: ......................................
　　　　　　　　　(Street and number.)

...................... ..................
　　　(City or town)　　　　　　(State)

\* Unless otherwise indicated below, the Treasury Bonds of 1947–52 issued upon this application will be forwarded to the address of the applicant as above given.

Special delivery instructions, if any: ............................
...........................................

This application should be transmitted through the subscriber's own bank, or other agency acting in his behalf, or it may be presented direct to the Federal Reserve Bank of his district, or a branch thereof, or to the Treasury Department, Division of Loans and Currency, Washington, D. C.

### EXHIBIT 31.

**LETTER OF SECRETARY OF THE TREASURY TO HOLDERS OF VICTORY NOTES, ACCOMPANYING THE OFFERING OF FOUR AND ONE-QUARTER PER CENT TREASURY BONDS OF 1947–1952, DATED OCTOBER 16, 1922.**

OCTOBER 9, 1922.

DEAR SIR: I am sending you herewith a copy of the official Treasury Department Circular [1] announcing the new offering of $4\frac{1}{4}$ per cent Treasury bonds of 1947–1952. The subscription books open to-day, and $4\frac{3}{4}$ per cent Victory notes, whether or not called for redemption, and Treasury Certificates of the series maturing December 15, 1922, will be accepted in payment, on the terms stated in the circular. The new bonds will be 25/30 year bonds, dated October 16, 1922, maturing October 15, 1952, and redeemable at the option of the United States on and after October 15, 1947. The bonds will be issued in both coupon and registered form, in denominations of $100 and upwards. The Treasury is prepared to make deliveries promptly upon allotment and payment.

This offering of Treasury bonds affords a particularly favorable opportunity to holders of $4\frac{3}{4}$ per cent Victory notes to acquire a long-time Government bond on attractive terms in place of Victory notes which will mature or be redeemed within the next few months. All $4\frac{3}{4}$ per cent Victory notes bearing the distinguishing letters A, B, C, D, E, or F prefixed to their serial numbers have, as you know, been called for redemption on December 15, 1922, and will cease to bear interest on that date, while the remaining $4\frac{3}{4}$ per cent Victory notes mature on May 20, 1923, according to their terms. Victory notes tendered in payment, if in registered form, must be duly assigned to "The Secretary of the Treasury for redemption," before some officer authorized to witness assignments of United States registered bonds, in accordance with the general regulations of the Treasury Department governing assignments. Coupon Victory notes must have the December 15, 1922, and May 20, 1923, coupons attached.

---

[1] See Exhibit 28, p. 168.

Holders of Victory notes who wish to invest in the new bonds should make prompt application through their own banks, or, if desired, direct to the Federal Reserve Bank of the district.

Very truly yours,

A. W. MELLON,
*Secretary of the Treasury.*

To THE HOLDER OF VICTORY NOTES ADDRESSED.

EXHIBIT 32.

[Department Circular No. 277. Public Debt.]

**REDEMPTION OF 3¾ PER CENT VICTORY NOTES BEFORE MATURITY.**

TREASURY DEPARTMENT,
OFFICE OF THE SECRETARY,
*Washington, February 9, 1922.*

*To Holders of Victory Notes and Others Concerned:*

The Secretary of the Treasury hereby gives notice that, in order to facilitate the refunding of the Victory Liberty Loan, all Victory notes of the 3¾ per cent series are called for redemption on June 15, 1922, and may be redeemed before that date at the option of the holder, upon the terms and conditions and subject to the rules and regulations hereinafter prescribed.

1. *Call for Redemption of 3¾ per cent Victory Notes.*—All of the 3¾ per cent series of United States of America Convertible Gold Notes of 1922–23, otherwise known as 3¾ per cent Victory notes, are hereby called for redemption on June 15, 1922, pursuant to the provision for redemption contained in the notes and in Treasury Department Circular No. 138, dated April 21, 1919, under which the notes were originally issued. Interest on all Victory notes of the 3¾ per cent series will cease on said redemption date, June 15, 1922. Holders of the notes hereby called for redemption, upon presentation and surrender thereof as hereinafter provided, will be entitled to have the notes redeemed and paid at par, with an adjustment of accrued interest, on said redemption date. Accrued interest to said date will be covered as to coupon notes by the coupons due June 15, 1922, which should be detached and collected in ordinary course when due, and as to registered notes will be covered by interest checks in the usual manner.

2. *Suspension and Termination of Victory Note Conversion Privilege.*—In view of the call for the redemption of all 3¾ per cent Victory notes on June 15, 1922, and pursuant to the provisions of said Treasury Department Circular No. 138, the privilege of conversion of Victory notes of either series into Victory notes of the other series is hereby suspended from February 9, 1922, to June 15, 1922, both inclusive, and on June 15, 1922, will terminate. Victory notes accordingly cease to be interconvertible, effective February 9, 1922, and on and after that date no conversions of the notes may be made.

3. *Presentation and Surrender for Redemption.*—(*a*) *Coupon Notes.* Any 3¾ per cent Victory notes in coupon form should be presented and surrendered for redemption to the Treasurer of the United States in Washington, or to any Federal Reserve Bank or branch, and must have the coupons due December 15, 1922, and May 20, 1923, attached. The notes must be delivered in every case at the expense and risk of

the holder, and should be accompanied by appropriate written advice (see Form P. D. 590, hereto attached). In the event that notes are presented for redemption with the December 15, 1922, or May 20, 1923, coupons detached, the notes will nevertheless be redeemed, but the full face amount of any missing coupons will be deducted. The amounts so deducted will be held in the Treasury to provide for the redemption of such missing coupons as may subsequently be presented.

(b) *Registered Notes.* Any 3¾ per cent Victory notes in registered form must be duly assigned to the Secretary of the Treasury for redemption, in accordance with the general regulations of the Treasury Department governing assignments, and should be presented to the Secretary of the Treasury, Division of Loans and Currency, Washington, or to any Federal Reserve Bank or branch thereof. The notes must be delivered at the expense and risk of the holder, and should be accompanied by appropriate written advice (see Form P. D. 591, hereto attached). Unless instructions are received to the contrary, remittance covering payment will be sent to the last address of record of the registered holder of the surrendered notes. In case it is desired to have payment of registered notes thus presented for redemption made to anyone other than the registered holder, the notes may be assigned to "The Secretary of the Treasury for redemption for account of _____."

(Here insert the name and address of the payee desired.)

. (c) *Presentation Prior to June 15, 1922.* In order to facilitate payment of the notes hereby called for redemption, any 3¾ per cent Victory notes may be presented and surrendered in the manner herein prescribed at any time in advance of June 15, 1922, for redemption and payment on that date.

4. *Redemption of 3¾ per cent Victory Notes Before June 15, 1922, at Holder's Option.*—In order to meet the convenience of Victory note holders and facilitate the redemption of 3¾ per cent Victory notes, the Federal Reserve Banks and the Treasurer of the United States have been authorized, effective this date, to redeem before June 15, 1922, at the option of the holder, at par and accrued interest to the date of optional redemption, any of the 3¾ per cent Victory notes hereby called for redemption. Any holder who desires to effect redemption in accordance herewith prior to June 15, 1922, should make written request therefor and should present and surrender the notes in the manner provided in paragraph 3 hereof, except that coupon notes must in that event have all unmatured coupons attached, including the coupons due June 15, 1922. Appropriate forms of written request will be found in Forms P. D. 590 and 591, hereto attached.

5. *Miscellaneous.*—Any further information which may be desired as to the redemption of Victory notes under this circular may be obtained from the Treasury Department, Division of Loans and Currency, or from any Federal Reserve Bank or branch. The Secretary of the Treasury may at any time or from time to time prescribe supplemental or amendatory rules and regulations on the matters covered by this circular.

A. W. MELLON,<br>
*Secretary of the Treasury.*

TREASURY DEPARTMENT,
Division of Loans and Currency.
Form P. D. 590.

FORM OF ADVICE TO ACCOMPANY 3¾ PER CENT VICTORY NOTES IN <u>COUPON</u> FORM PRE-
SENTED FOR REDEMPTION.

To the FEDERAL RESERVE BANK OF................

or

To the TREASURER OF THE UNITED STATES, *Washington, D. C.:*

Pursuant to Department Circular No. 277, dated February 9, 1922, the undersigned presents and surrenders herewith for redemption $................, face amount, 3¾ per cent Victory notes in coupon form, with coupons due December 15, 1922, and May 20, 1923, attached, as follows:

| Number of notes. | Denomination. | Serial numbers of notes. | Face amount. |
|---|---|---|---|
| .................... | $50 | ................................................... | ............ |
| .................... | 100 | ................................................... | ............ |
| .................... | 500 | ................................................... | ............ |
| .................... | 1,000 | ................................................... | ............ |
| .................... | 5,000 | ................................................... | ............ |
| .................... | 10,000 | ................................................... | ............ |
| Total......... | ............ | ................................................... | ............ |

and requests that remittance covering payment therefor be forwarded to the undersigned at the address indicated below.

(Signature) .......................................

(Address in full)............................

(Date) ....................       ....................

---

### REQUEST FOR REDEMPTION PRIOR TO JUNE 15, 1922.

[To be used only in the event applicant elects to exercise option of prior redemption.]

In connection with the foregoing, the undersigned requests immediate redemption of the above-described Victory notes prior to June 15, 1922, at par and accrued interest to date of such optional redemption. In addition to the coupons dated December 15, 1922, and May 20, 1923, the notes surrendered have attached thereto coupons dated June 15, 1922.

(Signature) .........................................

14263—FI 1922——12

TREASURY DEPARTMENT,
Division of Loans and Currency.
 Form P. D. 591.

FORM OF ADVICE TO ACCOMPANY 3¾ PER CENT VICTORY NOTES IN <u>REGISTERED</u> FORM PRE-
SENTED FOR REDEMPTION.

To the FEDERAL RESERVE BANK OF ...............
    or
To the SECRETARY OF THE TREASURY,
   *Division of Loans and Currency,*
     *Washington, D. C.:*

 Pursuant to Department Circular No. 277, dated February 9, 1922, the undersigned
presents and surrenders herewith for redemption $.............., face amount, 3¾ per
cent Victory notes in registered form, duly assigned to the ''Secretary of the Treasury
for redemption,'' as follows:

| Number of notes. | Denomination. | Serial numbers of notes. | Face amount. |
|---|---|---|---|
| .................... | $50 | ................................................................ | ................ |
| .................... | 100 | ................................................................ | ................ |
| .................... | 500 | ................................................................ | ................ |
| .................... | 1,000 | ................................................................ | ................ |
| .................... | 5,000 | ................................................................ | ................ |
| .................... | 10,000 | ................................................................ | ................ |
| .................... | 50,000 | ................................................................ | ................ |
| .................... | 100,000 | ................................................................ | ................ |
| Total......... | ............... | ................................................................ | ................ |

and requests that remittance covering payment therefor be forwarded to the undersigned at the address indicated below.
     (Signature).......................................

     (Address in full)..............................

(Date)....................       .....................

REQUEST FOR REDEMPTION PRIOR TO JUNE 15, 1922.

[To be used only in the event applicant elects to exercise option of prior redemption.]

 In connection with the foregoing, the undersigned requests immediate redemption
of the above-described Victory notes prior to June 15, 1922, at par and accrued interest
to the date of such optional redemption.
     (Signature).......................................

## EXHIBIT 33.

[Supplement to Department Circular No. 277 of February 9, 1922. Public Debt.]

### REDEMPTION OF 3¾ PER CENT VICTORY NOTES BEFORE MATURITY.

TREASURY DEPARTMENT,
OFFICE OF THE SECRETARY,
*Washington, May 5, 1922.*

*To Holders of Victory Notes and Others Concerned:*

Treasury Department Circular No. 277, dated February 9, 1922, calling 3¾ per cent Victory notes for redemption before maturity, is hereby amended and supplemented as follows:

*Redemption of registered 3¾ per cent Victory notes on June 15, 1922, or before that date at holder's option.*—Inasmuch as 3¾ per cent Victory notes are called for redemption on June 15, 1922, the transfer books for the registered notes of this issue will not be closed on May 15, 1922, and the usual semiannual interest checks will not be prepared and mailed by the Treasury Department on June 15, 1922, to the registered holders of record. Accrued interest on such notes to June 15, 1922, or, if presented for redemption prior to that date, to the date of optional redemption, will be paid by the Federal Reserve Banks or the Treasurer of the United States simultaneously with the payment on account of principal.

A. W. MELLON,
*Secretary of the Treasury.*

## EXHIBIT 34.

[Department Circular No. 299. Public Debt.]

### PARTIAL REDEMPTION OF 4¾ PER CENT VICTORY NOTES BEFORE MATURITY.

TREASURY DEPARTMENT,
OFFICE OF THE SECRETARY,
*Washington, July 26, 1922.*

*To Holders of 4¾ Per Cent Victory Notes and Others Concerned:*

The Secretary of the Treasury hereby gives notice that, in order to facilitate the refunding of the Victory Liberty Loan and provide for the retirement of part of the outstanding notes before maturity, all 4¾ per cent Victory notes which bear the distinguishing letters A, B, C, D, E, or F, prefixed to their serial numbers, are called for redemption on December 15, 1922, and may be surrendered for redemption before that date at the option of the holder, upon the terms and conditions and subject to the rules and regulations hereinafter prescribed:

1. *Call for Redemption.*—All 4¾ per cent Victory notes, otherwise known as United States of America Gold Notes of 1922–23, which bear the distinguishing letters A, B, C, D, E, or F, prefixed to their serial numbers, having been designated for the purpose by lot in the manner prescribed by the Secretary of the Treasury, are called for redemption on December 15, 1922, pursuant to the provision for redemption contained in the notes and in Treasury Department

Circular No. 138, dated April 21, 1919, under which the notes were originally issued. Interest on all the 4¾ per cent Victory notes thus called for redemption will cease on said redemption date, December 15, 1922. Holders of the notes hereby called for redemption, upon presentation and surrender thereof as hereinafter provided, will be entitled to have the notes redeemed and paid at par, with an adjustment of accrued interest, on said redemption date. Accrued interest to said date will be covered as to coupon notes by the coupons due December 15, 1922, which should be detached and collected in ordinary course when due, and as to registered notes will be covered by interest payments to be made simultaneously with the payments on account of principal. The transfer books for registered notes hereby called for redemption will not close on November 15, 1922, but will remain open until December 15, 1922. Victory notes of the 4¾ per cent series bearing the distinguishing letters G, H, I, J, K, or L, prefixed to their serial numbers, are not in any manner affected by this call for redemption, and will become due and payable as to principal on May 20, 1923, according to their terms.

2. *Presentation and Surrender for Redemption.*—(a) *Coupon Notes.* Any 4¾ per cent Victory notes in coupon form which are called for redemption hereunder should be presented and surrendered for redemption to the Treasurer of the United States in Washington, or to any Federal Reserve Bank or branch, and must have the coupons due May 20, 1923, attached. The notes must be delivered in every case at the expense and risk of the holder, and should be accompanied by appropriate written advice (see Form P. D. 726, hereto attached). In the event that any notes are presented for redemption with the May 20, 1923, coupon detached, the notes will nevertheless be redeemed, but the full face amount of any such missing coupons will be deducted. The amounts so deducted will be held in the Treasury to provide for the redemption of such missing coupons, if subsequently presented.

(b) *Registered Notes.*—Any 4¾ per cent Victory notes in registered form which are called for redemption hereunder should be duly assigned to "The Secretary of the Treasury for redemption," in accordance with the general regulations of the Treasury Department governing assignments, and should be presented and surrendered for redemption to the Treasury Department, Division of Loans and Currency, Washington, D. C., or to any Federal Reserve Bank or branch. The notes must be delivered at the expense and risk of the holder, and should be accompanied by appropriate written advice (see Form P. D. 727, hereto attached). If assignment for redemption is made by the registered owner, payment of principal and interest to the date of redemption will be made to the registered owner at his last address of record, unless written instructions to the contrary are received from the registered owner. If assignment for redemption is made by an assignee holding under proper assignment from the registered owner, payment of principal and interest to the date of redemption will be made to such assignee at the address specified in the form of advice. Assignments in blank, or other assignments having the same effect, will also be recognized, and in that event payment will be made to the person surrendering the notes for redemption, since under such assignments the notes become in effect payable to bearer. In case it is desired to have payment of registered notes presented for redemption made to someone other than the registered owner, without intermediate assignments, the notes may be assigned to "The Secretary of the Treasury for redemption for account of _____," but as-

(Here insert name and address of payee desired.)

signments in this form must be completed before acknowledgment and not left in blank.

(c) *Presentation Prior to December 15, 1922.*—In order to facilitate payment of the notes hereby called for redemption, any such $4\frac{3}{4}$ per cent Victory notes may be presented and surrendered in the manner herein prescribed at any time in advance of December 15, 1922, for redemption and payment on that date with interest to such redemption date.

3. *Redemption of Called $4\frac{3}{4}$ Per Cent Victory Notes Before December 15, 1922, at Holder's Option.*—In order to meet the convenience of Victory note holders and facilitate the redemption of called $4\frac{3}{4}$ per cent Victory notes, the Federal Reserve Banks and the Treasurer of the United States have been authorized, effective this date, to redeem at any time before December 15, 1922, at the option of the holder, at par and accrued interest to the date of optional redemption, any of the $4\frac{3}{4}$ per cent Victory notes hereby called for redemption. Any holder who desires to surrender his notes in accordance herewith for redemption prior to December 15, 1922, should make appropriate written request therefor and should present and surrender the notes in the manner provided in paragraph 2 hereof, except that coupon notes must in that event have all unmatured coupons attached, including the coupons due December 15, 1922. Appropriate forms of written request will be found in Forms P. D. 726 and 727, hereto attached.

4. *Miscellaneous.*—Any further information which may be desired as to the redemption of Victory notes under this circular may be obtained from the Treasury Department, Division of Loans and Currency, Washington, D. C., or from any Federal Reserve Bank or branch. The Secretary of the Treasury may at any time or from time to time prescribe supplemental or amendatory rules and regulations governing the matters covered by this circular.

A. W. MELLON,<br>*Secretary of the Treasury.*

TREASURY DEPARTMENT.
DIVISION OF LOANS AND CURRENCY.
   Form P. D. 726.

## FORM OF ADVICE TO ACCOMPANY 4¾ PER CENT VICTORY NOTES IN <u>COUPON</u> FORM PRESENTED FOR REDEMPTION.

To the Federal Reserve Bank of ................,
                          or
Treasurer of the United States, *Washington, D. C.:*

Pursuant to the provisions of Treasury Department Circular No. 299, dated July 26, 1922, the undersigned presents and surrenders herewith for redemption $........ face amount, of 4¾ per cent Victory notes in coupon form, with coupon due May 20, 1923, attached, as follows:

| Number of notes. | Denomination. | Serial numbers of notes. | Face amount. |
|---|---|---|---|
| ..................... | $50 | ................................................ | ................ |
| ..................... | 100 | ................................................ | ................ |
| ..................... | 500 | ................................................ | ................ |
| ..................... | 1,000 | ................................................ | ................ |
| ..................... | 5,000 | ................................................ | ................ |
| ..................... | 10,000 | ................................................ | ................ |
| Total......... | ............ | ................................................ | ................ |

and requests that remittance covering payment therefor be forwarded to the undersigned at the address indicated below.

(Signature) .......................................
(Address in full) .............................

(Date) ....................          .....................

---

### REQUEST FOR REDEMPTION PRIOR TO DECEMBER 15, 1922.

[To be used only in the event applicant elects to exercise option of prior redemption.]

In connection with the foregoing, the undersigned requests immediate redemption of the above-described Victory notes prior to December 15, 1922, at par and accrued interest to date of such optional redemption. In addition to the coupon dated May 20, 1923, the notes surrendered have attached thereto the coupon dated December 15, 1922.

(Signature) .......................................

(Date) ....................

TREASURY DEPARTMENT,
DIVISION OF LOANS AND CURRENCY.
Form P. D. 727.

### FORM OF ADVICE TO ACCOMPANY 4¾ PER CENT VICTORY NOTES IN REGISTERED FORM PRESENTED FOR REDEMPTION.

To THE FEDERAL RESERVE BANK OF.................,
or
TREASURY DEPARTMENT, *Division of Loans and Currency, Washington, D. C.:*

Pursuant to the provisions of Treasury Department Circular No. 299, dated July 26, 1922, the undersigned presents and surrenders herewith for redemption $............., face amount, of 4¾ per cent Victory notes in registered form, inscribed in the name of ....................................... and duly assigned to "The Secretary of the Treasury for redemption," as follows:

| Number of notes. | Denomination. | Serial numbers of notes. | Face amount. |
|---|---|---|---|
| ...................... | $50 | .......................................................... | .................. |
| ...................... | 100 | .......................................................... | .................. |
| ...................... | 500 | .......................................................... | .................. |
| ...................... | 1,000 | .......................................................... | .................. |
| ...................... | 5,000 | .......................................................... | .................. |
| ...................... | 10,000 | .......................................................... | .................. |
| ...................... | 50,000 | .......................................................... | .................. |
| ...................... | 100,000 | .......................................................... | .................. |
| Total......... | .................. | .......................................................... | .................. |

and requests that remittance covering payment therefor be forwarded to the undersigned at the address indicated below.

(Signature) .........................................
(Address in full) ...............................
(Date) ....................          ....................

_____

#### REQUEST FOR REDEMPTION PRIOR TO DECEMBER 15, 1922.

[To be used only in the event applicant elects to exercise option of prior redemption.]

In connection with the foregoing, the undersigned requests immediate redemption of the above-described Victory notes prior to December 15, 1922, at par and accrued interest to the date of such optional redemption.

(Signature) .........................................
(Date) ....................

EXHIBIT 35.

[Department Circular No. 276. Loans and Currency.]

**UNITED STATES OF AMERICA—FOUR AND THREE-QUARTERS PER CENT TREASURY NOTES. SERIES A-1925, DATED AND BEARING INTEREST FROM FEBRUARY 1, 1922, DUE MARCH 15, 1925.**

The Secretary of the Treasury offers for subscription, at par and accrued interest, through the Federal Reserve Banks, Treasury notes of Series A-1925, of an issue of gold notes of the United States authorized by the Act of Congress approved September 24, 1917, as amended. The notes will be dated and bear interest from February 1, 1922, will be payable March 15, 1925, and will bear interest at the rate of four and three-quarters per cent per annum    e September 15, 1922, and thereafter semiannually on March 15 and September 15 in each year.

Applications will be received at the Federal Reserve Banks.

Bearer notes with interest coupons attached will be issued in denominations of $100, $500, $1,000, $5,000, $10,000, and $100,000. The notes are not subject to call for redemption before maturity, and will not be issued in registered form. The principal and interest of the notes will be payable in United States gold coin of the present standard of value.

The notes of said series shall be exempt, both as to principal and interest, from all taxation now or hereafter imposed by the United States, any State, or any of the possessions of the United States, or by any local taxing authority, except (a) estate or inheritance taxes, and (b) graduated additional income taxes, commonly known as surtaxes, and excess-profits and war-profits taxes, now or hereafter imposed by the United States, upon the income or profits of individuals, partnerships, associations, or corporations.

Notes of this series will be accepted at par, with an adjustment of accrued interest, during such time and under such rules and regulations as shall be prescribed or approved by the Secretary of the Treasury, in payment of income and profits taxes payable at or within six months before the maturity of the notes. Any of the notes which have been owned by any person continuously for at least six months prior to the date of his death, and which upon such date constitute part of his estate, shall, under rules and regulations prescribed by the Secretary of the Treasury, be receivable by the United States at par and accrued interest in payment of any estate or inheritance taxes imposed by the United States, under or by virtue of any present or future law upon such estate or the inheritance thereof. The notes of this series will be acceptable to secure deposits of public moneys, but do not bear the circulation privilege.

The right is reserved to reject any subscription and to allot less than the amount of notes applied for and to close the subscriptions at any time without notice. Payment at par and accrued interest for notes allotted must be made on or before February 1, 1922, or on later allotment. After allotment and upon payment Federal Reserve Banks may issue interim receipts pending delivery of the definitive notes. Any qualified depositary will be permitted to make payment by credit for notes allotted to it for itself and its customers up to any amount for which it shall be qualified in excess of existing deposits, when so notified by the Federal Reserve Bank of its district. Treasury certificates of indebtedness of Series A–1922, maturing February 16, 1922, with any unmatured interest coupons attached, and Victory notes of either the 4¾ per cent or the 3¾ per cent series, will be accepted at the Federal Reserve Banks at par, with an adjustment of accrued interest, in payment for any Treasury notes of the Series A–1925 now offered which shall be subscribed for and allotted. Victory notes in coupon form must have all unmatured coupons attached, and if in registered form must be duly assigned to the Secretary of the Treasury for redemption, in accordance with the general regulations of the Treasury Department governing assignments.

The amount of the offering will be $400,000,000, or thereabouts, with the right reserved to the Secretary of the Treasury to allot additional notes up to one-half that amount, to the extent that payment is tendered in Victory notes pursuant to this circular. As fiscal agents of the United States, Federal Reserve Banks are authorized and requested to receive subscriptions and to make allotments thereon on the basis and up to the amounts indicated by the Secretary of the Treasury to the Federal Reserve Banks of the respective districts.

A. W. MELLON,
*Secretary of the Treasury.*

TREASURY DEPARTMENT
OFFICE OF THE SECRETARY,
*January 26, 1922.*

TO THE INVESTOR:

Almost any banking institution in the United States will handle your subscription for you, or you may make subscription direct to the Federal Reserve Bank of your district. Your special attention is invited to the terms of subscription and allotment as stated above. If you desire to purchase notes of the above issue after the subscriptions close, or notes of any outstanding issue, you should make application to your own bank, or if it can not obtain them for you, to the Federal Reserve Bank of your district.

## EXHIBIT 36.

[Department Circular No. 280. Loans and Currency.]

**UNITED STATES OF AMERICA—FOUR AND THREE-QUARTERS PER CENT TREASURY NOTES. SERIES A–1926, DATED AND BEARING INTEREST FROM MARCH 15, 1922, DUE MARCH 15, 1926. OFFERED ONLY IN EXCHANGE FOR 4¾ PER CENT VICTORY NOTES.**

The Secretary of the Treasury offers for subscription, at par, through the Federal Reserve Banks, in exchange for 4¾ per cent Victory notes, Treasury notes of Series A–1926, of an issue of gold notes of the United States authorized by the act of Congress approved September 24, 1917, as amended. The notes will be dated and bear interest from March 15, 1922, will be payable March 15, 1926, and will bear interest at the rate of four and three-quarters per cent per annum payable semiannually on September 15 and March 15 in each year.

Applications will be received at the Federal Reserve Banks.

Bearer notes with interest coupons attached will be issued in denominations of $100, $500, $1,000, $5,000, $10,000, and $100,000. The notes are not subject to call for redemption before maturity, and will not be issued in registered form. The principal and interest of the notes will be payable in United States gold coin of the present standard of value.

The notes of said series shall be exempt, both as to principal and interest, from all taxation now or hereafter imposed by the United States, any State, or any of the possessions of the United States, or by any local taxing authority, except (a) estate or inheritance taxes, and (b) graduated additional income taxes, commonly known as surtaxes, and excess-profits and war-profits taxes, now or hereafter imposed by the United States, upon the income or profits of individuals, partnerships, associations, or corporations.

Notes of this series will be accepted at par, with an adjustment of accrued interest, during such time and under such rules and regulations as shall be prescribed or approved by the Secretary of the Treasury, in payment of income and profits taxes payable at or within six months before the maturity of the notes. Any of the notes which have been owned by any person continuously for at least six months prior to the date of his death, and which upon such date constitute part of his estate, shall, under rules and regulations prescribed by the Secretary of the Treasury, be receivable by the United States at par and accrued interest in payment of any estate or inheritance taxes imposed by the United States, under or by virtue of any present or future law upon such estate or the inheritance thereof. The notes of this series will be acceptable to secure deposits of public moneys, but do not bear the circulation privilege.

The right is reserved to reject any subscription and to allot less than the amount of notes applied for and to close the subscriptions at any time without notice. Payment for notes allotted must be made on or before March 15, 1922, or on later allotment, in Victory notes of the 4¾ per cent series, which will be accepted at the Federal Reserve Banks at par, with an adjustment of accrued interest. Victory notes in coupon form must have all unmatured coupons attached, and if in registered form must be duly assigned to the Secretary of the Treasury for redemption, in accordance with the general regulations of the Treasury Department governing assignments. Interest adjustments will be made as of March 15, 1922, and accrued interest to that date on Victory notes accepted in payment will be paid in cash through the Federal Reserve Banks. Payment for the notes now offered can not be made in cash or by credit. After allotment and upon payment Federal Reserve Banks may issue interim receipts pending delivery of the definitive notes.

As fiscal agents of the United States, Federal Reserve Banks are authorized and requested to receive subscriptions and to make allotments in full in the order of the receipt of applications up to the amounts indicated by the Secretary of the Treasury to the Federal Reserve Banks of the respective districts.

A. W. MELLON,
*Secretary of the Treasury.*

TREASURY DEPARTMENT,
OFFICE OF THE SECRETARY,
*March 9, 1922.*

To THE INVESTOR:

Almost any banking institution in the United States will handle the exchange for you, or you may make application direct to the Federal Reserve Bank of your district. Your special attention is invited to the terms of subscription and allotment as stated above, and to the fact that the notes of Series A–1926 are offered only in exchange for 4¾ per cent Victory notes. If you should desire to purchase notes of the above issue after the subscriptions close, or notes of any outstanding issue, you should make application to your own bank, or if it can not obtain them for you, to the Federal Reserve Bank of your district.

## ⟋ Exhibit 37.

[Department Circular No. 292.  Loans and Currency.]

**UNITED STATES OF AMERICA—FOUR AND THREE-EIGHTHS PER CENT TREASURY NOTES.  SERIES B-1925, DATED AND BEARING INTEREST FROM JUNE 15, 1922, DUE DECEMBER 15, 1925. OFFERED ONLY IN EXCHANGE FOR 4¾ PER CENT VICTORY NOTES.**

The Secretary of the Treasury offers for subscription, at par, through the Federal Reserve Banks, in exchange for 4¾ per cent Victory notes, a limited amount of Treasury notes of Series B-1925, of an issue of gold notes of the United States authorized by the act of Congress approved September 24, 1917, as amended.  The notes will be dated and bear interest from June 15, 1922, will be payable December 15, 1925, and will bear interest at the rate of four and three-eighths per cent per annum payable semiannually on December 15 and June 15 in each year.

Applications will be received at the Federal Reserve Banks.

Bearer notes with interest coupons attached will be issued in denominations of $100, $500, $1,000, $5,000, $10,000, and $100,000. The notes are not subject to call for redemption before maturity, and will not be issued in registered form.  The principal and interest of the notes will be payable in United States gold coin of the present standard of value.

The notes of said series shall be exempt, both as to principal and interest, from all taxation now or hereafter imposed by the United States, any State, or any of the possessions of the United States, or by any local taxing authority, except (a) estate or inheritance taxes, and (b) graduated additional income taxes, commonly known as surtaxes, and excess-profits and war-profits taxes, now or hereafter imposed by the United States, upon the income or profits of individuals, partnerships, associations, or corporations.

Notes of this series will be accepted at par, with an adjustment of accrued interest, during such time and under such rules and regulations as shall be prescribed or approved by the Secretary of the Treasury, in payment of income and profits taxes payable at or within six months before the maturity of the notes.  Any of the notes which have been owned by any person continuously for at least six months prior to the date of his death, and which upon such date constitute part of his estate, shall, under rules and regulations prescribed by the Secretary of the Treasury, be receivable by the United States at par and accrued interest in payment of any estate or inheritance taxes imposed by the United States, under or by virtue of any present or future law upon such estate or the inheritance thereof.  The notes of this series will be acceptable to secure deposits of public moneys, but do not bear the circulation privilege.

The right is reserved to reject any subscription and to allot less than the amount of notes applied for and to close the subscriptions at any time without notice.  Payment for notes allotted must be made on or before June 15, 1922, or on later allotment, in Victory notes of the 4¾ per cent series, which will be accepted at the Federal Reserve Banks at par, without adjustments of accrued interest, as of June 15, 1922.  Victory notes in coupon form must have interest coupons attached maturing December 15, 1922, and May 20, 1923, but interest coupons maturing June 15, 1922. must be detached and collected in ordinary course when due. Victory notes in registered form must be duly assigned to the Secretary of the Treasury for redemption, in accordance with the general regulations of the Treasury Department governing assignments. After allotment and upon payment Federal Reserve Banks may issue interim receipts pending delivery of the definitive notes. Payment for the notes now offered can not be made in cash or by credit, nor will Treasury certificates of indebtedness of any series be accepted in payment.

As fiscal agents of the United States, Federal Reserve Banks are authorized and requested to receive subscriptions and to make allotments in full in the order of the receipt of applications up to the amounts indicated by the Secretary of the Treasury to the Federal Reserve Banks of the respective districts.

A. W. MELLON,
*Secretary of the Treasury.*

TREASURY DEPARTMENT,
OFFICE OF THE SECRETARY,
*June 8, 1922.*

TO THE INVESTOR:

Almost any banking institution in the United States will handle the exchange for you, or you may make application direct to the Federal Reserve Bank of your district. Your special attention is invited to the terms of subscription and allotment as stated above, and to the fact that the notes of Series B-1925 are offered only in exchange for 4¾ per cent Victory notes. If you should desire to purchase notes of the above issue after the subscriptions close, or notes of any outstanding issue, you should make application to your own bank, or if it can not obtain them for you, to the Federal Reserve Bank of your district.

EXHIBIT 38.

**LETTER OF SECRETARY OF THE TREASURY TO HOLDERS OF FOUR AND THREE-QUARTERS PER CENT VICTORY NOTES, ACCOMPANYING THE OFFERING OF TREASURY NOTES OF SERIES B-1925, DATED JUNE 15, 1922.**

JUNE 8, 1922.

DEAR SIR: As a holder of 4¾ per cent Victory notes, you will, I believe, be interested in the inclosed Treasury Department Circular No. 292,[1] dated June 8, 1922, announcing an issue of United States Treasury notes of Series B-1925, which are offered only in exchange for 4¾ per cent Victory notes. Treasury notes of Series B-1925 will be dated June 15, 1922, will be payable December 15, 1925, and will bear interest at the rate of 4⅜ per cent per annum, payable semiannually on December 15 and June 15 in each year. The new notes are issued only in coupon form, in denominations of $100 and upwards. As you know, 4¾ per cent Victory notes mature on May 20, 1923, but may be called for redemption in whole or in part, at the option of the United States, on December 15, 1922, and it is the Treasury's intention to call a substantial amount for redemption on that date. This offering of Treasury notes, therefore, affords an opportunity to holders of 4¾ per cent Victory notes to acquire by exchange a new obligation of the United States running for three and a half years at an attractive rate of interest, in place of Victory notes which will be payable either December 15, 1922, or May 20, 1923, depending upon the call for redemption.

---

[1] See Exhibit 37, p, 187.

Almost any banking institution in the United States will handle the exchange for you, or you may make application direct to the Federal Reserve Bank of your district. Victory notes tendered in exchange, if in registered form, must be duly assigned to "The Secretary of the Treasury for redemption," before some officer authorized to witness assignments of United States registered bonds and notes, in accordance with the general regulations of the Treasury Department governing assignments. Coupon Victory notes must have the December 15, 1922, and May 20, 1923, coupons attached, but the June 15, 1922, coupons should be detached and collected in ordinary course. No adjustments of interest will be necessary in any case, since exchanges will be made as of June 15, 1922, and interest due on that date will be paid in ordinary course.

As you will notice from the circular, the right is reserved to reject any subscription and to allot less than the amount of notes applied for and to close the subscriptions at any time without notice. You should therefore, if you desire to make the exchange, make prompt application for the new notes through your own bank, or direct to the Federal Reserve Bank of your district, and make arrangements, preferably through your own bank, for the surrender to the Federal Reserve Bank of the 4¾ per cent Victory notes tendered in exchange.

Very truly yours,

A. W. MELLON,
*Secretary of the Treasury.*

To the Holder of 4¾ per cent
Victory Notes Addressed.

## Exhibit 39.

[Department Circular No. 298. Loans and Currency.]

**UNITED STATES OF AMERICA—FOUR AND ONE-QUARTER PER CENT TREASURY NOTES. SERIES B-1926, DATED AND BEARING INTEREST FROM AUGUST 1, 1922, DUE SEPTEMBER 15, 1926.**

The Secretary of the Treasury offers for subscription, at par and accrued interest, through the Federal Reserve Banks, Treasury notes of Series B-1926, of an issue of gold notes of the United States authorized by the Act of Congress approved September 24, 1917, as amended. The notes will be dated and bear interest from August 1, 1922, will be payable September 15, 1926, and will bear interest at the rate of four and one-quarter per cent per annum payable March 15, 1923, and thereafter semi-annually on September 15 and March 15 in each year.

Applications will be received at the Federal Reserve Banks.

Bearer notes with interest coupons attached will be issued in denominations of $100, $500, $1,000, $5,000, $10,000, and $100,000. The notes are not subject to call for redemption before maturity, and will not be issued in registered form. The principal and interest of the notes will be payable in United States gold coin of the present standard of value.

The notes of said series shall be exempt, both as to principal and interest, from all taxation now or hereafter imposed by the United States, any State, or any of the possessions of the United States, or by any local taxing authority, except (a) estate or inheritance taxes, and (b) graduated additional income taxes, commonly known as surtaxes, and excess-profits and war-profits taxes, now or hereafter imposed by the United States, upon the income or profits of individuals, partnerships, associations, or corporations.

Notes of this series will be accepted at par, with an adjustment of accrued interest, during such time and under such rules and regulations as shall be prescribed or approved by the Secretary of the Treasury, in payment of income and profits taxes payable at or within six months before the maturity of the notes. Any of the notes which have been owned by any person continuously for at least six months prior to the date of his death, and which upon such date constitute part of his estate, shall, under rules and regulations prescribed by the Secretary of the Treasury, be receivable by the United States at par and accrued interest in payment of any estate or inheritance taxes imposed by the United States, under or by virtue of any present or future law upon such estate or the inheritance thereof. The notes of this series will be acceptable to secure deposits of public moneys, but do not bear the circulation privilege.

The right is reserved to reject any subscription and to allot less than the amount of notes applied for and to close the subscriptions at any time without notice. Payment at par and accrued interest for notes allotted must be made on or before August 1, 1922, or on later allotment. After allotment and upon payment Federal Reserve Banks may issue interim receipts pending delivery of the definitive notes. Any qualified depositary will be permitted to make payment by credit for notes allotted to it for itself and its customers up to any amount for which it shall be qualified in excess of existing deposits, when so notified by the Federal Reserve Bank of its district. Treasury certificates of indebtedness of Series B-1922, maturing August 1, 1922, and Victory notes of the 4¾ per cent series will be accepted at the Federal Reserve Banks at par, with an adjustment of accrued interest, in payment for any Treasury notes of the Series B-1926 now offered which shall be subscribed for and allotted. Victory notes in coupon form must have all unmatured coupons attached, and if in registered form must be duly assigned to the Secretary of the Treasury for redemption, in accordance with the general regulations of the Treasury Department governing assignments.

The amount of the offering will be $300,000,000, or thereabouts, with the right reserved to the Secretary of the Treasury to allot additional notes to the extent that payment is tendered in Victory notes pursuant to this circular. As fiscal agents of the United States, Federal Reserve Banks are authorized and requested to receive subscriptions and to make allotments thereon on the basis and up to the amounts indicated by the Secretary of the Treasury to the Federal Reserve Banks of the respective districts.

A. W. MELLON,
*Secretary of the Treasury.*

TREASURY DEPARTMENT,
 OFFICE OF THE SECRETARY,
 *July 26, 1922.*
To THE INVESTOR:

Almost any banking institution in the United States will handle your subscription for you, or you may make subscription direct to the Federal Reserve Bank of your district. Your special attention is invited to the terms of subscription and allotment as stated above, and to the fact that 4¾ per cent Victory notes may be tendered in payment. If you desire to purchase notes of the above issue after the subscriptions close, or notes of any outstanding issue, you should make application to your own bank, or if it can not obtain them for you, to the Federal Reserve Bank of your district.

## EXHIBIT 40.

**LETTER OF SECRETARY OF THE TREASURY, DATED JULY 26, 1922, TO BANKS AND TRUST COMPANIES, ACCOMPANYING THE OFFERING OF TREASURY NOTES OF SERIES B-1926, DATED AUGUST 1, 1922.**

JULY 26, 1922.

DEAR SIR: The Treasury is announcing to-day a call for the redemption on December 15, 1922, of about half of the 4¾ per cent Victory notes which remain outstanding, and at the same time is offering on the usual terms a new issue of $300,000,000, or thereabouts, of short-term Treasury notes bearing interest at 4¼ per cent, with provision for additional allotments up to a limited amount in exchange for 4¾ per cent Victory notes.

These two operations mark an important further step in the development of the Treasury's refunding program, and I am sending this letter to the president of every banking institution in the country in order to draw attention to the significance of the announcements and ask the cooperation of the banks in affording to their customers ample facilities for investing in the new notes. The call for the partial redemption of 4¾ per cent Victory notes affects about $1,000,000,000 face amount of notes, and makes the notes thus called for redemption payable on December 15, 1922, leaving the balance of the Victory Liberty Loan to mature on May 20, 1923, according to its terms. The notes called for redemption bear the distinguishing letters A, B, C, D, E, or F prefixed to their serial numbers, and can thus be readily distinguished from the notes not affected by the call. Copies of the official circulars will come to you from the Federal Reserve Bank of your district and additional copies may be obtained upon application.

The notes now offered for subscription are designated Treasury notes of Series B-1926, are dated August 1, 1922, will mature September 15, 1926, and will not be subject to call for redemption before maturity. The amount of the offering is $300,000,000, or thereabouts, but the Secretary of the Treasury reserves the right to allot additional notes up to a limited amount to the extent that 4¾ per cent Victory notes are tendered in payment. Subscriptions may be closed at any time without notice, and the right is reserved to reject any subscription and to allot less than the amount applied for. Holders of outstanding 4¾ per cent Victory notes, whether or not called for redemption, thus have an opportunity now, within the limitations of the offering, to exchange their notes for new securities of the Government bearing interest at 4¼ per cent and running for a period of over three years after Victory notes would mature or be redeemed. Applications for the Treasury notes now offered will be received in regular course through the several Federal Reserve Banks, as fiscal agents of the United States, from which further particulars concerning the offering may be obtained. This is the fourth exchange offering which the Treasury has made in order to facilitate the refunding of the Victory Liberty Loan, and on this offering, as on previous offerings, I hope that banks and trust companies throughout the country will extend to their customers every possible assistance in effecting exchanges.

The Treasury's program for dealing with the short-dated debt of the Government has now progressed to such a point that I believe it is worth while to recite what has already been accomplished and call attention to what remains to be done within the current fiscal year. On April 30, 1921, when the situation was first outlined in my letter of that date to the Chairman of the Committee on Ways and Means, the gross public debt, on the basis of daily Treasury Statements, amounted to about $23,995,000,000, of which over $7,500,000,000 was short-dated debt maturing within about two years, made up of over $4,050,000,000 in Victory notes, over $2,800,-000,000 in Treasury certificates of indebtedness. and about $650,-000,000 in War Savings Certificates. By June 30, 1922, the gross public debt had been reduced to about $22,963,000,000, a reduction of about $1,032,000,000 during the period of 14 months. This reduction has taken place, for the most part, in the short-dated debt, and has been accomplished through the operation of the sinking fund and other public debt expenditures chargeable against ordinary receipts, the application of surplus revenues to the retirement of debt, and the reduction of the balance in the general fund. At the same time the Treasury has been engaged, through its refunding operations, in distributing substantial amounts of the remaining short-dated debt into more convenient maturities, and in this manner has refunded about $2,250,000,000 of early maturing debt into Treasury notes of various series maturing in 1924, 1925, and 1926. As a result of these operations the amount of outstanding Victory notes has been reduced from over $4,050,000,000 on April 30, 1921, to about $1,990,000,000 on June 30, 1922, and the amount of outstanding Treasury certificates from over $2,800,000,000 to about $1,825,000,000. In addition there are about $625,000,000 of War Savings Certificates of the Series of 1918 which become payable on January 1, 1923, so that on June 30, 1922, there still remained outstanding about $4,440,000,000 of short-dated debt, all of which matures in the current fiscal year.

The refunding of this debt, most of which will have to be accomplished within the next ten months, presents a problem of first importance. The $300,000,000, or thereabouts, of Treasury notes offered for subscription on the usual terms will provide for the Treasury certificates maturing August 1 and for the Treasury's remaining cash requirements between now and September 15, 1922, while the offering to allot additional notes in exchange for 4¾ per cent Victory notes should accomplish the refunding of some more of the Victory Liberty Loan and correspondingly reduce the amount of Victory notes to be provided for upon redemption or maturity. At the same time the call for the redemption of about half of the outstanding Victory notes before maturity will make that much of the Victory Loan payable on December 15 of this year, and enable the Treasury to deal with it before maturity by appropriate refunding loans. This will mean that by January 1, 1923, the outstanding Victory notes will have been reduced to about $1,000,000,000, or, in other words, a manageable maturity which can be dealt with as opportunity offers without spectacular refunding operations that would upset the security markets and disturb the course of business and industry.

The current offering of notes is thus an essential part of the refunding program on which the Treasury is engaged, and the banking institutions of the country by extending their facilities for the exchange of outstanding 4¾ per cent Victory notes for the new notes will be performing an important service for the country as well as for their customers.

Cordially yours,                    A. W. MELLON, *Secretary.*

TO THE PRESIDENT OF THE BANK OR TRUST COMPANY ADDRESSED.

## EXHIBIT 41.

[Third Supplement to Department Circular No 141 of September 15, 1919. Loans and Currency.]

### SUPPLEMENTAL RULES AND REGULATIONS CONCERNING TRANSACTIONS IN LIBERTY BONDS AND VICTORY NOTES.

TREASURY DEPARTMENT,
OFFICE OF THE SECRETARY,
*Washington, March 2, 1922.*

1. Treasury Department Circular No. 141, dated September 15, 1919, prescribing rules and regulations governing transactions in Liberty bonds and Victory notes, as amended by the Supplement dated April 30, 1920, is hereby further amended by striking out paragraph 27 thereof, as amended by said supplement, and inserting in lieu thereof a new paragraph 27, reading as follows:

#### TRANSPORTATION CHARGES AND RISKS ON BONDS AND NOTES.

· 27. Transportation charges and risks upon bonds and notes presented to the Treasury Department, Washington, or a Federal Reserve Bank, for exchange or transfer, or for other transactions included within the scope of this circular, must be borne by the holders of the bonds or notes presented, and the bonds or notes must be delivered to the Treasury Department or the Federal Reserve Bank with all transportation charges prepaid. Registered bonds and notes to be delivered upon exchange or transfer, or otherwise, unless delivered in person to the registered owner or his duly authorized representative, will be delivered by registered mail without expense to, but at the risk of, the registered owner, except that such registered bonds or notes will be delivered by express collect at the risk and expense of the registered owner if written request for such delivery be made. Coupon bonds and notes to be delivered upon exchange or otherwise, unless delivered in person to the owner or his duly authorized representative, will be delivered at the owner's risk and expense, and will be delivered by express collect unless complete arrangements for delivery by registered mail insured have been made by the owner prior to the shipment of the bonds or notes to be delivered. Holders of bonds and notes are advised to consult with their own banks and trust companies in cases where transactions involve the transportation of coupon bonds or notes, for arrangements may be made as between Federal Reserve Banks and incorporated banks and trust companies for the transportation of such coupon bonds and notes to and from Federal Reserve Banks by registered mail insured, the charges in each case to be paid by the respective holders and to be remitted by the incorporated banks and trust companies to the Federal Reserve Banks. Similar arrangements for the transportation of coupon bonds and notes by registered mail insured may be effected when transactions are submitted direct to the Treasury Department, Washington, information as to which may be obtained, upon application, from the Treasury Department, Division of Loans and Currency. Transportation charges and risks on bonds and notes transmitted between Federal Reserve Banks and the Treasury Department under the provisions of this circular will be borne by the United States. Registered bonds and notes assigned in blank, and registered bonds and notes assigned to the Secretary of the Treasury for exchange for coupon bonds/notes, without instructions restricting delivery, lack the protection which registration affords, and will therefore be regarded, for the purposes of this paragraph, as in effect coupon bonds and notes.

2. Notwithstanding the provisions of Treasury Department Circular No. 137, dated March 7, 1919, as amended and supplemented June 10 and November 1, 1919, the provisions of said paragraph 27, as thus amended, shall apply to and govern transactions involving the conversion of 4 per cent bonds of the First Liberty Loan Converted and the Second Liberty Loan.

3. Nothing herein contained shall be deemed to modify or affect the provisions of Treasury Department Circular No. 164, dated December 15, 1919, as amended and supplemented March 13 and

August 27, 1920, as to transportation charges and risks in connection with exchanges and conversions of coupon Liberty bonds in temporary form.

4. The Secretary of the Treasury may withdraw or amend at any time or from time to time all or any of the provisions of this supplemental circular.

A. W. MELLON,
*Secretary of the Treasury.*

EXHIBIT 42.

[Supplement to Department Circular No. 225. Loans and Currency.]

**RECEIPT OF LIBERTY BONDS, VICTORY NOTES, AND TREASURY NOTES FOR ESTATE OR INHERITANCE TAXES.**

TREASURY DEPARTMENT,
OFFICE OF THE SECRETARY,
*Washington, June 30, 1922.*

1. The provisions of Department Circular No. 225, dated January 31, 1921, prescribing regulations governing the receipt of Liberty bonds and Victory notes for Federal estate or inheritance taxes are hereby extended and made applicable to Treasury notes of the United States now or hereafter issued under authority of Section 18 of the Second Liberty Bond Act, as amended and supplemented, bearing interest at a higher rate than 4 per centum per annum, and any such Treasury notes shall accordingly be receivable by the United States at par and accrued interest in payment of any estate or inheritance taxes imposed by the United States, under or by virtue of any present or future law, upon the same terms and conditions as provided in said Department Circular No. 225, dated January 31, 1921, with respect to the acceptance of Liberty bonds and Victory notes bearing interest at a higher rate than 4 per centum per annum.

2. The issues of Treasury notes at this date outstanding, bearing interest at a higher rate than 4 per centum per annum, are:

| Description. | Date of issue. | Short title. |
|---|---|---|
| (a) 5¾ per cent notes, payable June 15, 1924................................ | June 15, 1921 | Series A-1924. |
| (b) 5¼ per cent notes, payable Sept. 15, 1924................................ | Sept. 15, 1921 | Series B-1924. |
| (c) 4½ per cent notes, payable Mar. 15, 1925................................ | Feb. 1, 1922 | Series A-1925. |
| (d) 4¾ per cent notes, payable Mar. 15, 1926................................ | Mar. 15, 1922 | Series A-1926. |
| (e) 4¾ per cent notes, payable Dec. 15, 1925................................ | June 15, 1922 | Series B-1925. |

3. For the calculation of accrued interest on the current coupons of Treasury notes tendered in payment of estate or inheritance taxes under this circular, the method outlined in Exhibit B to Department Circular No. 225, dated January 31, 1921, should be followed. Interest tables at the various rates borne by Treasury notes may be obtained from the Treasury Department, Division of Loans and Currency, Washington. The interest tables appropriate for use in connection with the issues of Treasury notes at present outstanding are as follows:

Form General 1017, for Series A-1924 (interest dates June 15 and December 15).

Form General 1016, for Series B-1924 (interest dates March 15 and September 15).

Form L. & C. 369, for Series A–1925 prior to September 15, 1922 (interest during this period is on annual 365-day basis).

Form L. & C. 435, for Series A–1925 subsequent to September 15, 1922 (interest dates March 15 and September 15).

Form L. & C. 435, for Series A–1926 (interest dates March 15 and September 15).

Interest tables or decimals for computing interest as may be required for other or future issues may be obtained from the Treasury Department, Division of Loans and Currency, Washington, upon request.

A. W. MELLON,
*Secretary of the Treasury.*

## EXHIBIT 43.

[Fourth Supplement to Department Circular No. 141 of September 15, 1919. Loans and Currency.]

**SUPPLEMENTAL RULES AND REGULATIONS CONCERNING TRANSACTIONS IN VICTORY NOTES.**

TREASURY DEPARTMENT,
OFFICE OF THE SECRETARY,
*Washington, July 26, 1922.*

1. In accordance with the provisions of Treasury Department Circular No. 138, dated April 21, 1919, the provisions of Treasury Department Circular No. 141, dated September 15, 1919, prescribing rules and regulations governing transactions in Liberty bonds and Victory notes, are hereby modified with respect to transactions in $4\frac{3}{4}$ per cent Victory notes, as follows:

2. Pursuant to the call for redemption on December 15, 1922, of all $4\frac{3}{4}$ per cent Victory notes which bear the distinguishing letters A, B, C, D, E, or·F, prefixed to their serial numbers, as provided in Treasury Department Circular No. 299, dated July 26, 1922, the outstanding $4\frac{3}{4}$ per cent Victory notes are thrown into two separate and distinct classes, *first*, notes bearing the distinguishing letters A, B, C, D, E, or F, which are called for redemption on December 15, 1922, and, *second*, notes bearing the distinguishing letters G, H, I, J, K, or L, which are not called for redemption and will mature May 20, 1923, according to their terms. Effective this date, the Treasury Department, and the Federal Reserve Banks as fiscal agents of the United States, will observe this division between called and uncalled notes in all transactions affecting $4\frac{3}{4}$ per cent Victory notes, including transactions involving exchanges of denomination, exchanges of coupon notes for registered notes, exchanges of registered notes for coupon notes, and transfers of registered notes. Deliveries of $4\frac{3}{4}$ per cent Victory notes upon exchange or transfer will accordingly be made henceforth in notes bearing distinguishing letters within the same block as the notes surrendered for exchange or transfer; that is to say, against notes bearing the distinguishing letters A, B, C, D, E, or F, deliveries will be made of notes bearing distinguishing letters A, B, C, D, E, or F, and against notes bearing the distinguishing letters G, H, I, J, K, or L, deliveries will be made of notes bearing distinguishing letters G, H, I, J, K, or L.

A., W. MELLON,
*Secretary of the Treasury.*

EXHIBIT 44.

[Fifth Supplement to Department Circular No. 141 of September 15, 1919. Loans and Currency.]

## SUPPLEMENTAL RULES AND REGULATIONS CONCERNING TRANSACTIONS IN LIBERTY BONDS AND VICTORY NOTES.

TREASURY DEPARTMENT,
OFFICE OF THE SECRETARY,
*Washington, July 28, 1922.*

1. Paragraph 14 of Treasury Department Circular No. 141, dated September 15, 1919, as heretofore amended and supplemented, governing transactions in Liberty bonds and Victory notes, is hereby amended to read as follows:

14. *Assignments from minors.*—Bonds or notes registered in the name of a minor without more, or in the name of a minor by a natural guardian, as, for example, "John Jones, minor, by Henry Jones, natural guardian," or in the name of a legal guardian for a minor, may be assigned during minority only by the guardian legally appointed by a court of competent jurisdiction, or otherwise legally qualified, or pursuant to order or decree of a court of competent jurisdiction; provided, however, that in cases where such bonds or notes have been purchased by the natural guardian of the minor out of his own funds as a gift to the minor, or otherwise purchased for the benefit of the minor and registered in the name of the minor without more, or in the name of the minor by such natural guardian, as, for example, "John Jones, minor, by Henry Smith, guardian," and the entire gross value of the minor's estate, both real and personal, does not exceed $500, assignments by the natural guardian for transfer or for exchange into coupon bonds or notes, or for redemption, may be recognized upon presentation of proof satisfactory to the Secretary of the Treasury that the proceeds of the bonds or notes so assigned are necessary and are to be used for the support or education of the minor. The Secretary of the Treasury may also require in any such case a bond of indemnity with satisfactory sureties. In the event that bonds or notes are registered in the name of a natural guardian for a minor, designated either as natural guardian or guardian, as, for instance, "John Jones, guardian of Henry Jones, a minor," or "John Jones, natural guardian of Henry Jones, a minor," or a substantially similar form, assignments by the natural guardian of the minor when executed under his representative title in the same form as set forth in the registration will be recognized by the Treasury Department without requiring proof of his appointment or authority to act; provided, however, that no assignment by any such natural guardian to himself individually will be recognized unless accompanied by a duly authenticated copy of an order or decree of a court of competent jurisdiction specifically authorizing the assignment, in accordance with the provisions of Treasury Department Circular No. 147, dated July 22, 1919. Any provisions of Treasury Department Circular No. 182, dated February 14, 1920, inconsistent herewith, are to that extent hereby superseded. No assignment of any such bonds or notes by the legal or natural guardian of the minor for exchange, or for transfer to any person other than the ward, or for redemption, will be recognized after notice of the termination of the guardianship or of the attainment of majority by the ward, unless the ward joins in such assignment.

A. W. MELLON,
*Secretary of the Treasury.*

EXHIBIT 45.

[Department Circular No. 288. Public Debt.]

## REGULATIONS IN REGARD TO LOST, STOLEN, DESTROYED, MUTILATED, AND DEFACED UNITED STATES BONDS AND NOTES.

TREASURY DEPARTMENT,
OFFICE OF THE SECRETARY,
*Washington, D. C., May 15, 1922.*

The following statutes of the United States relate to lost, stolen, destroyed, mutilated, and defaced United States bonds and notes, and claims for relief arising in connection therewith:

Whenever it appears to the Secretary of the Treasury, by clear and unequivocal proof, that any interest-bearing bond of the United States has, without bad faith upon the part of the owner, been destroyed, wholly or in part, or so defaced as to impair its value to the owner, and such bond is identified by number and description, the Secretary of the Treasury shall, under such regulations and with such restrictions as to time and retention for security or otherwise as he may prescribe, issue a duplicate thereof, having the same time to run, bearing like interest as the bond so proved to have been destroyed or defaced, and so marked as to show the original number of the bond destroyed and the date thereof. But when such destroyed or defaced bonds appear to have been of such a class or series as has been or may, before such application, be called in for redemption, instead of issuing duplicates thereof, they shall be paid, with such interest only as would have been paid if they had been presented in accordance with such call. (Sec. 3702, Revised Statutes.)

The owner of such destroyed or defaced bond shall surrender the same, or so much thereof as may remain, and shall file in the Treasury a bond in a penal sum of double the amount of the destroyed or defaced bond, and the interest which would accrue thereon until the principal becomes due and payable, with two good and sufficient sureties, residents of the United States, to be approved by the Secretary of the Treasury, with condition to indemnify and save harmless the United States from any claim upon such destroyed or defaced bond. (Sec. 3703, Revised Statutes.)

Whenever it is proved to the Secretary of the Treasury, by clear and satisfactory evidence, that any duly registered bond of the United States, bearing interest, issued for valuable consideration in pursuance of law, has been lost or destroyed, so that the same is not held by any person as his own property, the Secretary shall issue a duplicate of such registered bond, of like amount, and bearing like interest and marked in the like manner as the bond so proved to be lost or destroyed. (Sec. 3704, Revised Statutes.)

The owner of such missing bond shall first file in the Treasury a bond in a penal sum equal to the amount of such missing bond, and the interest which would accrue thereon, until the principal thereof becomes due and payable, with two good and sufficient sureties, residents of the United States, to be approved by the Secretary of the Treasury, with condition to indemnify and save harmless the United States from any claim because of the lost or destroyed bond. (Sec. 3705, Revised Statutes.)

Whenever any recognizance, stipulation, bond, or undertaking conditioned for the faithful performance of any duty, or for doing or refraining from doing anything in such recognizance, stipulation, bond, or undertaking specified, is by the laws of the United States required or permitted to be given with one surety or with two or more sureties, the execution of the same or the guaranteeing of the performance of the condition thereof shall be sufficient when executed or guaranteed solely by a corporation incorporated under the laws of the United States, or of any State having power to guarantee the fidelity of persons holding positions of public or private trust, and to execute and guarantee bonds and undertakings in judicial proceedings: *Provided*, That such recognizance, stipulation, bond, or undertaking be approved by the head of department, court, judge, officer, board, or body executive, legislative, or judicial required to approve or accept the same. But no officer or person having the approval of any bond shall exact that it shall be furnished by a guaranty company or by any particular guaranty company. (Act Aug. 13, 1894, sec. 1; 28 Stat. 279.) See also sections 2–8 of the same statute, as amended by the Act approved March 23, 1910.

The word "bond" or "bonds" where it appears in sections 8, 9, 10, 14, and 15 of this Act as amended, and sections 3702, 3703, 3704, and 3705 of the Revised Statutes, and section 5200 of the Revised Statutes as amended, but in such sections only, shall be deemed to include notes issued under this section. (Sec. 18(*d*), Second Liberty Bond Act as amended.)

Whoever shall make or cause to be made, or present or cause to be presented, for payment or approval, to or by any person or officer in the civil, military, or naval service of the United States, any claim upon or against the Government of the United States, or any department or officer thereof, knowing such claim to be false, fictitious, or fraudulent; or whoever, for the purpose of obtaining or aiding to obtain the payment or approval of such claim, shall make or use, or cause to be made or used, any false bill, receipt, voucher, roll, account, claim, certificate, affidavit, or deposition, knowing the same to contain any fraudulent or fictitious statement or entry; or whoever shall enter into any agreement, combination, or conspiracy to defraud the Government of the United States, or any department or officer thereof, by obtaining or aiding to obtain the payment or allowance of any false or fraudulent claim; or whoever, having charge, possession, custody, or control of any money or other public property used or to be used in the military or naval service, with intent to defraud the United States or willfully to conceal such money or other property, shall deliver or cause to be delivered, to any other person having authority to receive the same, any amount of such money or other property less than that for which he received a certificate or took a receipt; or whoever, being authorized to make or deliver any certificate, voucher, receipt, or other paper certifying the receipt of arms, ammunition, provisions, clothing, or other property so used or to be used, shall make or deliver the same to any other person without a full knowledge of the truth of the facts stated therein, and with intent to defraud the United States, shall be fined not more than five thousand dollars, or imprisoned not more than five years, or both. (Sec. 35, Penal Code of the United States, approved March 4, 1909.)

## COUPON BONDS AND NOTES.

1. *Coupon bonds or notes lost or stolen.*—The Treasury Department can grant no relief on account of lost or stolen coupon bonds or notes. United States bonds and notes in coupon form are payable to bearer, and title thereto passes by delivery, without indorsement and without notice to the Treasury Department. Under generally recognized principles of law an innocent purchaser for value without notice before maturity acquires good title to coupon bonds or notes even though reported lost or stolen, and no proof of ownership is required when coupon bonds or notes are presented in regular course to the Treasury Department, or its designated agencies, for payment, exchange, or conversion. The Treasury Department assumes no responsibility whatever with respect to coupon bonds or notes reported lost or stolen and enters no stoppages or caveats against their payment, exchange, or conversion. This is the long-established policy of the Treasury, and is in accordance with the following public announcement made by the Secretary of the Treasury on April 27, 1867, and reaffirmed and republished from time to time as to United States bonds and notes in coupon form reported lost or stolen:

> In consequence of the increasing trouble, wholly without practical benefit, arising from notices which are constantly received at the Department respecting the loss of coupon bonds, which are payable to bearer, and of Treasury notes issued and remaining in blank at the time of loss, it becomes necessary to give this public notice, that the Government can not protect, and will not undertake to protect, the owners of such bonds and notes against the consequences of their own fault or misfortune.
>
> Hereafter all bonds, notes, and coupons, payable to bearer, and Treasury notes issued and remaining in blank, will be paid to the party presenting them in pursuance of the regulations of the Department, in the course of regular business; and no attention will be paid to caveats which may be filed for the purpose of preventing such payment.

The Treasury Department does not undertake to furnish any information with respect to the presentation of coupon bonds or notes reported lost or stolen, but it will, wherever possible, in order to assist in tracing lost or stolen securities, furnish, upon appropriate written inquiry, such information as may be available in the Department as to whether or not bonds or notes reported lost or stolen have already been presented, and if already presented, as to the source from which they were received. United States coupon bonds and notes are customarily handled in the regular course of business without reference to serial number, and in most cases, therefore, it is improbable that any information will be available as to the source from which received.

2. *Coupon bonds or notes destroyed or materially defaced.*—In case of the destruction, wholly or in part, or the material defacement, of

a coupon bond or note, the Treasury may grant relief, upon application of the owner, in accordance with the provisions of sections 3702–3703 of the Revised Statutes, above quoted. Reports of the destruction or defacement of coupon bonds or notes should be made to the Treasury Department, Division of Loans and Currency, Washington, D. C., or to the Federal Reserve Bank of the district, and the exact description of the bond or note should be furnished. If only partially destroyed, defaced, or mutilated, the portion or portions remaining should be carefully packed to avoid further mutilation and delivered or forwarded with the report. Upon receipt of the report full information with respect to procedure and proof required for relief will be furnished together with application and affidavit forms. The claimant, who must be the owner, will be required to establish to the satisfaction of the Secretary of the Treasury by clear and unequivocal proof, (1) the complete identification of the bond or note, by loan (issue and series), denomination, serial number, and coupons, if any, attached; (2) his ownership thereof; (3) the destruction or defacement of the bond or note, and that it was without bad faith on his part. This proof should include affidavits by the claimant and all other persons having knowledge of the facts, which must be supported, with respect to each person making such an affidavit, by the affidavits of two responsible and disinterested persons who are in no manner related to the claimant, and who should, wherever possible, be officers of the United States or executive officers of incorporated banks or trust companies, identifying the affiant and showing that he is a person known to them and whose statements, as set forth in his affidavit, are worthy of the confidence and consideration of the Treasury Department. No proof should be submitted until full instructions and blank forms are received from the Treasury Department or the Federal Reserve Bank. All evidence should be filed with the Treasury Department, Division of Loans and Currency, Washington, D. C., or with the Federal Reserve Bank to which the destruction or defacement was reported. If, upon receipt and examination of the evidence by the department, it appears that relief may be granted under the provisions of the statutes, a form of bond of indemnity will be furnished to the claimant by the Department for execution, with good and sufficient surety satisfactory to the Secretary of the Treasury, in a penal sum of double the amount of the principal of the bond or note, and the interest which would accrue thereon to maturity. Upon return of the bond of indemnity, duly executed, and its approval by the Secretary of the Treasury, the relief authorized will be granted. In no event should a bond of indemnity be submitted until called for by the Department, and it should be submitted then only on the prescribed form furnished for the purpose. If relief is granted on account of destroyed, defaced, or mutilated bonds other than Liberty bonds, registered bonds only will be issued, coupon bonds of such issues not being available. If the bonds or notes as to which relief is granted have matured or have been called for earlier redemption, relief will take the form of payment thereof, with interest to maturity or the redemption date, as the case may be.

3. *Coupon bonds or notes with immaterial defacements or mutilations.*—If the defacement or mutilation of a coupon bond or note appears to be immaterial or is so slight that the bond or note may be

fully and completely identified, and the missing fragments could not by any possibility form the basis of a claim against the United States, the Treasury Department may grant relief without a bond of indemnity, upon the filing of satisfactory proof in affidavit form as to ownership and the circumstances of defacement or mutilation. The defaced or mutilated bond or note should in such cases be presented to the Treasury Department, Division of Loans and Currency, Washington, D. C., or to the Federal Reserve Bank of the district, and full instructions regarding procedure for the granting of relief will then be furnished.

### INTEREST COUPONS.

4. *Lost, stolen, or destroyed interest coupons.*—The Treasury Department can not grant relief on account of interest coupons which have been lost, stolen, or destroyed after being detached from United States bonds or notes, or on account of interest coupons attached to bonds or notes lost or stolen. The Treasury Department assumes no responsibility whatever with respect to interest coupons which have been reported lost or stolen, or detached coupons which have been reported destroyed, and it enters no stoppages or caveats against their payment. The Treasury, moreover, does not undertake to furnish any information with respect to the presentation of interest coupons, though it will, wherever possible, in order to assist in tracing lost or stolen securities, furnish, upon appropriate written inquiry, such information as may be available in the Department as to whether or not coupons reported lost, stolen, or destroyed have already been presented. Interest coupons from United States coupon bonds and notes, however, are customarily handled in the regular course of business without reference to serial number, and in most cases, therefore, it will be impossible to give any information as to the source from which received. In cases where interest coupons have been partially destroyed, mutilated, or defaced, but the remaining portions can be identified as to amount, due date, and serial number, and the missing fragments could not by any possibility form the basis of a claim against the United States, relief may be granted upon the surrender of the remaining portions of the coupons to the Treasurer of the United States, Washington, D. C., accompanied by satisfactory proof in affidavit form as to the ownership of the coupons and the circumstances of their partial destruction, mutilation, or defacement.

### REGISTERED BONDS AND NOTES.

5. *Registered bonds or notes lost, stolen, or destroyed.*—In case of the loss, theft, or destruction of a registered bond or note, the Treasury Department may grant relief upon proper application, subject to the provisions of sections 3704–3705 of the Revised Statutes, above quoted, and of these regulations. Pending the granting of relief interest will continue to be drawn payable to the order of the registered owner even though the bond or note has been reported lost, stolen, or destroyed, subject, however, to any assignments thereon. Upon discovery of the loss, theft, or destruction, report should immediately be made of the facts, with a full description of the bonds and notes and of any assignments thereon, to the Treasury Department,

Division of Loans and Currency, Washington, D. C., with the request that a caveat be entered on the records of the Department against the transfer, exchange, or payment thereof. This report should follow, in substance, the following form:

(Date) -------------------

To the SECRETARY OF THE TREASURY,
　　　DIVISION OF LOANS AND CURRENCY,
　　　　　　　　Washington, D. C.

The following United States bonds/notes were_____
　　　　　　　　　　　　　　　　　　(Briefly state particulars.)

--------------------- on or about ---------------------.
　　　　　　　　　　　　　　　(Date.)

| Title of loan. | Denomination. | Serial number. | Inscribed in name of— | Assigned to (if assigned in blank or for exchange for coupon bonds/notes, so state): |
|---|---|---|---|---|
| | | | | |
| | | | | |
| | | | | |

Please enter caveat(s) against the transfer, exchange, or payment thereof, and advise me as to the procedure for relief.

(Signature) -------------------------------

(Address) -------------------------------

6. *Registered bonds or notes bearing no assignments and lost, stolen, or destroyed.*—Upon receipt of a report of the loss, theft, or destruction of registered bonds or notes bearing no assignments a caveat against the transfer, exchange or payment thereof will be entered on the records of the Treasury Department, and full information will be furnished to the registered owner with respect to the procedure for securing relief, together with the necessary forms for the purpose. The claimant, who in cases arising under this paragraph should be the registered owner of record or his recognized representative, will be required to establish to the satisfaction of the Secretary of the Treasury, by clear and satisfactory evidence, (1) the complete identification of the registered bond or note by loan (issue and series), denomination, serial number, and inscription; (2) his ownership thereof; and (3) that the registered bond or note has been lost, stolen, or destroyed so that the same is not held by any person as his own property. The proof should include affidavits by the claimant and other persons having knowledge of the facts, which must be supported, with respect to each person making such an affidavit, by the affidavits of two responsible and disinterested persons who are in no manner related to the claimant and who should, wherever possible, be officers of the United States or executive officers of incorporated banks or trust companies, identifying the affiant and showing that he is a person known to them and whose statements, as set forth in his affidavit, are worthy of the confidence and consideration of the Treasury Department. No evidence should be submitted until full

instructions and blank forms are received from the Treasury Department or the Federal Reserve Bank of the district. If, upon receipt and examination of the evidence by the Department, it appears that relief may be granted under the provisions of the statutes, a form of bond of indemnity will be furnished to the claimant for execution, with good and sufficient surety satisfactory to the Secretary of the Treasury, in a penal sum of the amount of the principal of the bond or note and the interest which would accrue thereon to maturity. Upon return of the bond of indemnity, duly executed, and its approval by the Secretary of the Treasury, the relief authorized will be granted. In no event should a bond of indemnity be submitted until called for by the Department, and it should be submitted then only on the prescribed form furnished for the purpose. If relief is granted, new bonds or notes will be issued inscribed in the same manner as those lost, stolen, or destroyed, except that if the lost, stolen, or destroyed bonds or notes have matured or have been called for earlier redemption, relief will take the form of payment thereof. In cases of lost or stolen registered bonds or notes relief will not be granted until the expiration of six months from the time of the alleged loss or theft.

7. *Registered bonds or notes bearing specific assignments and lost, stolen, or destroyed.*—Upon receipt of a report of the loss, theft, or destruction of registered bonds or notes bearing specific assignments, a caveat against the transfer, exchange, or payment thereof will be entered on the records of the Treasury Department, and the procedure for securing relief will be the same as provided in paragraph 6 hereof for registered bonds and notes bearing no assignments, except that if the ownership of such bonds or notes has passed from the registered owner of record by assignment, the owner of the bond or note at the time of loss, theft, or destruction should present the claim and should give the required bond of indemnity. If relief is granted, the new bonds or notes will be issued, however, in the name of the registered owner of record, from whom the claimant, if not himself the registered owner, should secure an appropriate assignment or power of attorney. In the event that the relief granted takes the form of payment of the bonds or notes, the claimant should likewise secure an appropriate assignment or power of attorney from the registered owner of record. In order to avoid later difficulties, claimants on account of registered bonds or notes assigned to them and subsequently lost, stolen, or destroyed, should procure immediately from the registered owner of record a power of attorney to assign the bonds or notes and to collect the interest thereon. (Appropriate forms for this purpose may be obtained from the Treasury Department, Washington, D. C., or the Federal Reserve Bank of the district.) In this connection attention is called to the fact that a power of attorney to sell and assign a United States registered bond or note does not authorize an assignment to the attorney himself unless specific authority therefor is contained in the power of attorney.

8. *Registered bonds or notes assigned in blank or for exchange, and lost, stolen, or destroyed.*—Registered bonds or notes assigned in blank, or bearing assignments for exchange for coupon bonds or notes without instructions restricting delivery, are in effect payable to bearer, since title thereto may pass by delivery without further assignment or indorsement. The Treasury Department can accordingly grant no

relief on account of the loss or theft of bonds or notes so assigned, and will not enter caveats against their transfer, exchange, or payment, if reported lost or stolen. The Treasury Department assumes no responsibility with respect to bonds or notes so assigned, but if notified of their loss or theft will make appropriate notations on its records, and, in the event that the bonds or notes thereafter are received for transfer, exchange, or payment, may require the person presenting such bonds or notes to submit evidence showing whether or not he is a bona fide holder in due course. If it appears that the person presenting the bonds or notes is not a bona fide holder in due course, the Department may withhold transfer, exchange, and payment, and in any event it will notify the registered owner of the result of the inquiry. In case bonds or notes so assigned are destroyed or defaced, relief will be given upon application in proper form on substantially the same terms and conditions as prescribed in paragraph 2 hereof for coupon bonds or notes destroyed or defaced, except that the bond of indemnity shall be in the penal sum of the amount of the principal of the bonds or notes and the interest which would accrue thereon to maturity. The owner of the bonds or notes at the time of destruction or defacement should present the claim, and should give the required bond of indemnity. If relief is granted, the new bonds or notes will be issued, however, in the name of the registered owner of record, from whom the claimant, if not himself the registered owner, should secure an appropriate assignment or power of attorney, as indicated in paragraph 7 hereof.

9. *Registered bonds and notes with immaterial defacements and mutilations.*—If the defacement or mutilation of a registered bond or note appears to be immaterial or is so slight that the bond or note may be fully and completely identified, and the missing fragments could not by any possibility form the basis of a claim against the United States, the Treasury Department may grant relief without a bond of indemnity, upon the filing of satisfactory proof in affidavit form as to ownership and the circumstances of defacement or mutilation. The defaced or mutilated registered bond or note should in such cases be presented to the Treasury Department, Division of Loans and Currency, Washington, D. C., or to the Federal Reserve Bank of the district, and full instructions regarding procedure for the granting of relief will then be furnished.

10. *Recovery of registered bonds or notes reported lost, stolen, or destroyed.*—When registered bonds or notes previously reported lost, stolen, or destroyed, are recovered, the Treasury Department, Division of Loans and Currency, Washington, D. C., should be immediately notified in order that the caveats (or notations) placed against the bonds or notes may be removed. The report of recovery, with request for removal of the caveat (or notation), should be made over the signature of the registered owner of record, or of the recognized representative of such registered owner, and should specifically describe the bonds or notes recovered. If the registered bonds or notes at the time of loss, theft, or destruction were assigned and a caveat (or notation) was entered at the request of the assignee or in his behalf, the report of recovery, with request for the removal of the caveat (or notation), should be made over the signature of the assignee or his recognized representative.

## BONDS OF INDEMNITY.

11. The Secretary of the Treasury reserves the right before granting relief in any case under these regulations to require a bond of indemnity, with satisfactory surety, even though the filing of a bond of indemnity is not specifically provided for hereunder. The requirements of the Treasury Department with respect to the acceptance of individual and corporate sureties on bonds of indemnity given in accordance with the requirements of this circular are set forth in the prescribed form of bond of indemnity.

## TREASURY CERTIFICATES OF INDEBTEDNESS.

12. The foregoing regulations, in so far as applicable thereto. likewise govern relief in case of the loss, theft, defacement, mutilation, or destruction of Treasury certificates of indebtedness, or of any interest coupons appertaining thereto. Treasury certificates of indebtedness of the issues regularly sold to the public are payable to bearer, and for the purposes of this circular stand on the same basis as United States coupon bonds and notes.

## TREASURY (WAR) SAVINGS SECURITIES.

13. Regulations governing relief in case of the loss, theft, defacement, mutilation, or destruction of Treasury (war) savings securities are not embodied in this circular, but are set forth in Treasury Department Circulars No. 108, dated January 21, 1918, and No. 149, dated July 31, 1919, respectively, as amended and supplemented, to which those interested are referred.

## MISCELLANEOUS.

14. All communications relating to matters covered by this circular, as well as requests for forms for use in connection with applications for relief hereunder, should be addressed to the Treasury Department, Division of Loans and Currency, Washington, D. C., or, if desired, to the Federal Reserve Bank of the district.

15. This circular supersedes the general regulations promulgated by Treasury Department Document 2740, dated July 1, 1915, known as the regulations in relation to United States bonds, in so far as such regulations relate to lost, stolen, mutilated, defaced, or destroyed bonds, as well as paragraphs 23 and 24 of Treasury Department Circular No. 141, dated September 15, 1919.

16. The Secretary of the Treasury may at any time or from time to time make any further or any supplemental or amendatory rules and regulations governing the matters covered in this circular, subject, however, to the provisions of sections 3702, 3703, 3704, and 3705 of the Revised Statutes of the United States.

A. W. MELLON.
*Secretary of the Treasury.*

EXHIBIT 46.

[Department Circular No 268. Loans and Currency.]

**UNITED STATES OF AMERICA—TREASURY CERTIFICATES OF INDEBTEDNESS, DATED AND BEARING INTEREST FROM DECEMBER 15, 1921. SERIES T J2-1922, 4¼ PER CENT, DUE JUNE 15, 1922. SERIES T D-1922, 4½ PER CENT, DUE DECEMBER 15, 1922.**

The Secretary of the Treasury, under the authority of the act approved September 24, 1917, as amended, offers for subscription, at par and accrued interest, through the Federal Reserve Banks, Treasury certificates of indebtedness, in two series, both dated and bearing interest from December 15, 1921, the certificates of Series T J2-1922 being payable on June 15, 1922, with interest at the rate of four and one-quarter per cent per annum semiannually, and the certificates of Series T D-1922 being payable on December 15, 1922, with interest at the rate of four and one-half per cent per annum, payable semiannually.

Applications will be received at the Federal Reserve Banks.

Bearer certificates will be issued in denominations of $500, $1,000, $5,000, $10,000, and $100,000. The certificates of Series T J2-1922 will have one interest coupon attached, payable June 15, 1922, and the certificates of Series T D-1922 two interest coupons attached, payable June 15, 1922, and December 15, 1922.

The certificates of said series shall be exempt, both as to principal and interest, from all taxation now or hereafter imposed by the United States, any State, or any of the possessions of the United States, or by any local taxing authority, except (a) estate or inheritance taxes, and (b) graduated additional income taxes, commonly known as surtaxes, and excess-profits and war-profits taxes, now or hereafter imposed by the United States, upon the income or profits of individuals, partnerships, associations, or corporations. The interest on an amount of bonds and certificates authorized by said act approved September 24, 1917, and amendments thereto, the principal of which does not exceed in the aggregate $5,000, owned by any individual, partnership, association, or corporation, shall be exempt from the taxes provided for in clause (b) above.

The certificates of these series will be accepted at par, with an adjustment of accrued interest, during such time and under such rules and regulations as shall be prescribed or approved by the Secretary of the Treasury, in payment of income and profits taxes payable at the maturity of the certificates. The certificates of these series do not bear the circulation privilege.

The right is reserved to reject any subscription and to allot less than the amount of certificates of either or both series applied for and to close the subscriptions as to either or both series at any time without notice. Payment at par and accrued interest for certificates allotted must be made on or before December 15, 1921, or on later allotment. After allotment and upon payment Federal Reserve Banks may issue interim receipts pending delivery of the definitive certificates. Any qualified depositary will be permitted to make payment by credit for certificates allotted to it for itself and its customers up to any amount for which it shall be qualified in excess of existing deposits, when so notified by the Federal Reserve Bank of its district. Treasury certificates of indebtedness of Series T D-

1921, maturing December 15, 1921, will be accepted at par, with an adjustment of accrued interest, in payment for any certificates of the Series T J2–1922 or T D–1922 now offered which shall be subscribed for and allotted.

As fiscal agents of the United States, Federal Reserve Banks are authorized and requested to receive subscriptions and to make allotments on the basis and up to the amounts indicated by the Secretary of the Treasury to the Federal Reserve Banks of the respective districts.

A. W. MELLON,<br>
Secretary of the Treasury.

TREASURY DEPARTMENT,
OFFICE OF THE SECRETARY,
December 12, 1921.

To THE INVESTOR:

Almost any banking institution in the United States will handle your subscription for you, or you may make subscription direct to the Federal Reserve Bank of your district. Your special attention is invited to the terms of subscription and allotment as stated above. If you desire to purchase certificates of the above issues after the subscriptions close, or certificates of any outstanding issue, you should make application to your own bank, or if it can not obtain them for you, to the Federal Reserve Bank of your district.

⊥          EXHIBIT 47.

[Department Circular No. 279.  Loans and Currency.]

**UNITED STATES OF AMERICA—FOUR AND ONE-QUARTER PER CENT TREASURY CERTIFICATES OF INDEBTEDNESS. SERIES TM–1923, DATED AND BEARING INTEREST FROM MARCH 15, 1922, DUE MARCH 15, 1923.**

The Secretary of the Treasury, under the authority of the act approved September 24, 1917, as amended, offers for subscription, at par and accrued interest, through the Federal Reserve Banks, Treasury certificates of indebtedness, Series TM–1923, dated and bearing interest from March 15, 1922, payable March 15, 1923, with interest at the rate of four and one-quarter per cent per annum, payable semiannually.

Applications will be received at the Federal Reserve Banks.

Bearer certificates will be issued in denominations of $500, $1,000, $5,000, $10,000, and $100,000. The certificates will have two interest coupons attached, payable September 15, 1922, and March 15, 1923.

The certificates of said series shall be exempt, both as to principal and interest, from all taxation now or hereafter imposed by the United States, any State, or any of the possessions of the United States, or by any local taxing authority, except (a) estate or inheritance taxes, and (b) graduated additional income taxes, commonly known as surtaxes, and excess-profits and war-profits taxes, now or hereafter imposed by the United States, upon the income or profits of individuals, partnerships, associations, or corporations. The interest on an amount of bonds and certificates authorized by said act approved September 24, 1917, and amendments thereto, the principal of which does not exceed in the aggregate $5,000, owned by any individual, partnership, association, or corporation, shall be exempt from the taxes provided for in clause (b) above.

Certificates of this series will be accepted at par, with an adjustment of accrued interest, during such time and under such rules and regulations as shall be prescribed or approved by the Secretary of the Treasury, in payment of income and profits taxes payable at the maturity of the certificates. The certificates do not bear the circulation privilege.

The right is reserved to reject any subscription and to allot less than the amount of certificates applied for and to close the subscriptions at any time without notice. Payment at par and accrued interest for certificates allotted must be made on or before March 15, 1922, or on later allotment. After allotment and upon payment Federal Reserve Banks may issue interim receipts pending delivery of the definitive certificates. Any qualified depositary will be permitted to make payment by credit for certificates allotted to it for itself and its customers up to any amount for which it shall be qualified in excess of existing deposits, when so notified by the Federal Reserve Bank of its district. Treasury certificates of indebtedness of Series TM–1922, Series TM2–1922, and Series TM3–1922, all maturing March 15, 1922, and Series C–1922, maturing April 1, 1922, with any unmatured interest coupons attached, will be accepted at par, with an adjustment of accrued interest, in payment for any certificates of the Series TM–1923 now offered which shall be subscribed for and allotted.

As fiscal agents of the United States, Federal Reserve Banks are authorized and requested to receive subscriptions and to make allotments on the basis and up to the amounts indicated by the Secretary of the Treasury to the Federal Reserve Banks of the respective districts.

A. W. MELLON,
*Secretary of the Treasury.*

TREASURY DEPARTMENT,
OFFICE OF THE SECRETARY,
*March 9, 1922.*

TO THE INVESTOR:

Almost any banking institution in the United States will handle your subscription for you, or you may make subscription direct to the Federal Reserve Bank of your district. Your special attention is invited to the terms of subscription and allotment as stated above. If you desire to purchase certificates of the above issue after the subscriptions close, or certificates of any outstanding issue, you should make application to your own bank, or, if it can not obtain them for you, to the Federal Reserve Bank of your district.

## EXHIBIT 48.

[Department Circular No. 285. Loans and Currency.]

**UNITED STATES OF AMERICA—THREE AND ONE-HALF PER CENT TREASURY CERTIFICATES OF INDEBTEDNESS. SERIES D–1922, DATED AND BEARING INTEREST FROM APRIL 15, 1922, DUE OCTOBER 16, 1922.**

The Secretary of the Treasury, under the authority of the act approved September 24, 1917, as amended, offers for subscription, at par and accrued interest, through the Federal Reserve Banks, Treasury certificates of indebtedness, Series D–1922, dated and bearing interest from April 15, 1922, payable October 16, 1922, with interest at the rate of three and one-half per cent per annum.

Applications will be received at the Federal Reserve Banks.

Bearer certificates will be issued in denominations of $500, $1,000, $5,000, $10,000, and $100,000. The certificates will have one interest coupon attached, payable October 16, 1922.

The certificates of said series shall be exempt, both as to principal and interest, from all taxation now or hereafter imposed by the United States, any State, or any of the possessions of the United States, or by any local taxing authority, except (a) estate or inheritance taxes, and (b) graduated additional income taxes, commonly known as surtaxes, and excess-profits and war-profits taxes, now or hereafter imposed by the United States, upon the income or profits of individuals, partnerships, associations, or corporations. The interest on an amount of bonds and certificates authorized by said act approved September 24, 1917, and amendments thereto, the principal of which does not exceed in the aggregate $5,000, owned by any individual, partnership, association, or corporation, shall be exempt from the taxes provided for in clause (b) above.

The certificates of this series do not bear the circulation privilege and will not be accepted in payment of taxes.

The right is reserved to reject any subscription and to allot less than the amount of certificates applied for and to close the subscriptions at any time without notice. Payment at par and accrued interest for certificates allotted must be made on or before April 15, 1922, or on later allotment. After allotment and upon payment Federal Reserve Banks may issue interim receipts pending delivery of the definitive certificates. Any qualified depositary will be permitted to make payment by credit for certificates allotted to it for itself and its customers up to any amount for which it shall be qualified in excess of existing deposits, when so notified by the Federal Reserve Bank of its district.

As fiscal agents of the United States, Federal Reserve Banks are authorized and requested to receive subscriptions and to make allotments on the basis and up to the amounts indicated by the Secretary of the Treasury to the Federal Reserve Banks of the respective districts.

A. W. MELLON,
*Secretary of the Treasury.*

TREASURY DEPARTMENT,
OFFICE OF THE SECRETARY,
*April 12, 1922.*

TO THE INVESTOR:

Almost any banking institution in the United States will handle your subscription for you, or you may make subscription direct to the Federal Reserve Bank of your district. Your special attention is invited to the terms of subscription and allotment as stated above. If you desire to purchase certificates of the above issue after the subscriptions close, or certificates of any outstanding issue, you should make application to your own bank, or if it can not obtain them for you, to the Federal Reserve Bank of your district.

## EXHIBIT 49.

[Department Circular No. 291. Loans and Currency.]

### UNITED STATES OF AMERICA—THREE AND ONE-HALF PER CENT TREASURY CERTIFICATES OF INDEBTEDNESS. SERIES TD2-1922, DATED AND BEARING INTEREST FROM JUNE 1, 1922, DUE DECEMBER 15, 1922.

The Secretary of the Treasury, under the authority of the act approved September 24, 1917, as amended, offers for subscription, at par and accrued interest, through the Federal Reserve Banks, Treasury certificates of indebtedness, Series TD2–1922, dated and bearing interest from June 1, 1922, payable December 15, 1922, with interest at the rate of three and one-half per cent per annum.

Applications will be received at the Federal Reserve Banks.

Bearer certificates will be issued in denominations of $500, $1,000, $5,000, $10,000, and $100,000. The certificates will have one interest coupon attached, payable December 15, 1922.

The certificates of said series shall be exempt, both as to principal and interest, from all taxation now or hereafter imposed by the United States, any State, or any of the possessions of the United States, or by any local taxing authority, except (a) estate or inheritance taxes, and (b) graduated additional income taxes, commonly known as surtaxes, and excess-profits and war-profits taxes, now or hereafter imposed by the United States, upon the income or profits of individuals, partnerships, associations, or corporations. The interest on an amount of bonds and certificates authorized by said act approved September 24, 1917, and amendments thereto, the principal of which does not exceed in the aggregate $5,000, owned by any individual, partnership, association, or corporation, shall be exempt from the taxes provided for in clause (b) above.

The certificates of this series will be accepted at par, with an adjustment of accrued interest, during such time and under such rules and regulations as shall be prescribed or approved by the Secretary of the Treasury, in payment of income and profits taxes payable at the maturity of the certificates. The certificates do not bear the circulation privilege.

The right is reserved to reject any subscription and to allot less than the amount of certificates applied for and to close the subscriptions at any time without notice. Payment at par and accrued interest for certificates allotted must be made on or before June 1, 1922, or on later allotment. After allotment and upon payment Federal Reserve Banks may issue interim receipts pending delivery of the definitive certificates. Any qualified depositary will be permitted to make payment by credit for certificates allotted to it for itself and its customers up to any amount for which it shall be qualified in excess of existing deposits, when so notified by the Federal Reserve Bank of its district. Treasury certificates of indebtedness of Series TJ–1922 and Series TJ2–1922, both maturing June 15, 1922, with any unmatured interest coupons attached, and Victory notes of the 3¾ per cent series (which have been called for redemption on June 15, 1922), will be accepted at par, with an adjustment of accrued interest, in payment for any certificates of the Series TD2–1922 now offered which shall be subscribed for and allotted. Victory notes of the 3¾ per cent series in coupon form must have all unmatured coupons attached, and if in registered form must be duly assigned to the Secretary of the Treasury for redemption, in accordance with the general regulations of the Treasury Department governing assignments.

As fiscal agents of the United States, Federal Reserve Banks are authorized and requested to receive subscriptions and to make allotments on the basis and up to the amounts indicated by the Secretary of the Treasury to the Federal Reserve Banks of the respective districts.

A. W. MELLON,
*Secretary of the Treasury.*

TREASURY DEPARTMENT,
OFFICE OF THE SECRETARY,
*May 26, 1922.*

To THE INVESTOR:

Almost any banking institution in the United States will handle your subscription for you, or you may make subscription direct to the Federal Reserve Bank of your district. Your special attention is invited to the terms of subscription and allotment as stated above. If you desire to purchase certificates of the above issue after the subscriptions close, or certificates of any outstanding issue, you should make application to your own bank, or, if it can not obtain them for you, to the Federal Reserve Bank of your district.

## Exhibit 50.

[Department Circular No. 293. Loans and Currency.]

**UNITED STATES OF AMERICA—THREE AND THREE-QUARTERS PER CENT TREASURY CERTIFICATES OF INDEBTEDNESS. SERIES TJ-1923, DATED AND BEARING INTEREST FROM JUNE 15, 1922, DUE JUNE 15, 1923.**

The Secretary of the Treasury, under the authority of the act approved September 24, 1917, as amended, offers for subscription, at par and accrued interest, through the Federal Reserve Banks, Treasury certificates of indebtedness, Series TJ–1923, dated and bearing interest from June 15, 1922, payable June 15, 1923, with interest at the rate of three and three-quarters per cent per annum, payable semiannually.

Applications will be received at the Federal Reserve Banks.

Bearer certificates will be issued in denominations of $500, $1,000, $5,000, $10,000, and $100,000. The certificates will have two interest coupons attached, payable December 15, 1922, and June 15, 1923.

The certificates of said series shall be exempt, both as to principal and interest, from all taxation now or hereafter imposed by the United States, any State, or any of the possessions of the United States, or by any local taxing authority, except (*a*) estate or inheritance taxes, and (*b*) graduated additional income taxes, commonly known as surtaxes, and excess-profits and war-profits taxes, now or hereafter imposed by the United States, upon the income or profits of individuals, partnerships, associations, or corporations. The interest on an amount of bonds and certificates authorized by said act approved September 24, 1917, and amendments thereto, the principal of which does not exceed in the aggregate $5,000, owned by any individual, partnership, association, or corporation, shall be exempt from the taxes provided for in clause (*b*) above.

The certificates of this series will be accepted at par, with an adjustment of accrued interest, during such time and under such rules and regulations as shall be prescribed or approved by the Secretary of the Treasury, in payment of income and profits taxes payable at the maturity of the certificates. The certificates do not bear the circulation privilege.

The right is reserved to reject any subscription and to allot less than the amount of certificates applied for and to close the subscriptions at any time without notice. Payment at par and accrued interest for certificates allotted must be made on or before June 15, 1922, or on later allotment. After allotment and upon payment Federal Reserve Banks may issue interim receipts pending delivery of the definitive certificates. Any qualified depositary will be permitted to make payment by credit for certificates allotted to it for itself and its customers up to any amount for which it shall be qualified in excess of existing deposits, when so notified by the Federal Reserve Bank of its district. Treasury certificates of indebtedness of Series TJ–1922 and Series TJ2–1922, both maturing June 15, 1922, and Series B–1922, maturing August 1, 1922, with any unmatured interest coupons attached, and Victory notes of the $3\frac{3}{4}$ per cent series (which have been called for redemption on June 15, 1922), will be accepted at par, with an adjustment of accrued interest, in payment for any certificates of the Series TJ–1923 now offered which shall be subscribed for and allotted. Victory notes of the $3\frac{3}{4}$ per cent series in coupon form must have all unmatured coupons attached, and if in registered form must be duly assigned to the Secretary of the Treasury for redemption, in accordance with the general regulations of the Treasury Department governing assignments.

As fiscal agents of the United States, Federal Reserve Banks are authorized and requested to receive subscriptions and to make allotments on the basis and up to the amounts indicated by the Secretary of the Treasury to the Federal Reserve Banks of the respective districts.

A. W. MELLON,
*Secretary of the Treasury.*

TREASURY DEPARTMENT,
OFFICE OF THE SECRETARY,
*June 8, 1922.*

TO THE INVESTOR:

Almost any banking institution in the United States will handle your subscription for you, or you may make subscription direct to the Federal Reserve Bank of your district. Your special attention is invited to the terms of subscription and allotment as stated above. If you desire to purchase certificates of the above issue after the subscriptions close, or certificates of any outstanding issue, you should make application to your own bank, or, if it can not obtain them for you, to the Federal Reserve Bank of your district.

EXHIBIT 51.

[Department Circular No. 306.   Loans and Currency.]

## UNITED STATES OF AMERICA—THREE AND THREE-QUARTERS PER CENT TREASURY CERTIFICATES OF INDEBTEDNESS. SERIES TS–1923, DATED AND BEARING INTEREST FROM SEPTEMBER 15, 1922, DUE SEPTEMBER 15, 1923.

The Secretary of the Treasury, under the authority of the act approved September 24, 1917, as amended, offers for subscription, at par and accrued interest, through the Federal Reserve Banks, Treasury certificates of indebtedness, Series TS–1923, dated and bearing interest from September 15, 1922, payable September 15, 1923, with interest at the rate of three and three-quarters per cent per annum payable semiannually.

Applications will be received at the Federal Reserve Banks.

Bearer certificates will be issued in denominations of $500, $1,000, $5,000, $10,000, and $100,000.   The certificates will have two interest coupons attached, payable March 15, 1923, and September 15, 1923.

The certificates of said series shall be exempt, both as to principal and interest, from all taxation now or hereafter imposed by the United States, any State, or any of the possessions of the United States, or by any local taxing authority, except (a) estate or inheritance taxes, and (b) graduated additional income taxes, commonly known as surtaxes, and excess-profits and war-profits taxes, now or hereafter imposed by the United States, upon the income or profits of individuals, partnerships, associations, or corporations. The interest on an amount of bonds and certificates authorized by said act approved September 24, 1917, and amendments thereto, the principal of which does not exceed in the aggregate $5,000, owned by any individual, partnership, association, or corporation, shall be exempt from the taxes provided for in clause (b) above.

The certificates of this series will be accepted at par, with an adjustment of accrued interest, during such time and under such rules and regulations as shall be prescribed or approved by the Secretary of the Treasury, in payment of income and profits taxes payable at the maturity of the certificates.   The certificates do not bear the circulation privilege.

The right is reserved to reject any subscription and to allot less than the amount of certificates applied for and to close the subscriptions at any time without notice.   Payment at par and accrued interest for certificates allotted must be made on or before September 15, 1922, or on later allotment.   After allotment and upon payment Federal Reserve Banks may issue interim receipts pending delivery of the definitive certificates.   Any qualified depositary will be permitted to make payment by credit for certificates allotted to it for itself and its customers up to any amount for which it shall be qualified in excess of existing deposits, when so notified by the Federal Reserve Bank of its district.   Treasury certificates of indebtedness of Series TS–1922 and Series TS2–1922, both maturing September 15, 1922, and Series D–1922, maturing October 16, 1922, with any unmatured interest coupons attached, will be accepted at par, with an adjustment of accrued interest, in payment for any certificates of the Series TS–1923 now offered which shall be subscribed for and allotted.

As fiscal agents of the United States, Federal Reserve Banks are authorized and requested to receive subscriptions and to make allotments on the basis and up to the amounts indicated by the Secretary of the Treasury to the Federal Reserve Banks of the respective districts.

A. W. MELLON,
*Secretary of the Treasury.*

TREASURY DEPARTMENT,
OFFICE OF THE SECRETARY,
*September 11, 1922.*

To THE-INVESTOR:

Almost any banking institution in the United States will handle your subscription for you, or you may make subscription direct to the Federal Reserve Bank of your district. Your special attention is invited to the terms of subscription and allotment as stated above. If you desire to purchase certificates of the above issue after the subscriptions close, or certificates of any outstanding issue, you should make application to your own bank, or, if it can not obtain them for you, to the Federal Reserve Bank of your district.

## EXHIBIT 52.

### OFFER TO REDEEM BEFORE MATURITY, TREASURY CERTIFICATES OF INDEBTEDNESS, SERIES TD-1921.

Secretary Mellon announced that he has authorized' the Federal Reserve Banks on and after Friday, November 25, 1921, and until further notice, to redeem in cash before December 15, 1921, at the holders' option, at par and accrued interest to the date of such optional redemption, Treasury certificates of indebtedness of Series TD-1921, dated December 15, 1920, maturing December 15, 1921.

## EXHIBIT 53.

### OFFER TO REDEEM BEFORE MATURITY, TREASURY CERTIFICATES OF INDEBTEDNESS, SERIES A-1922.

Secretary Mellon announced that he has authorized the Federal Reserve Banks on and after Monday, January 16, 1922, and until further notice, to redeem in cash before February 16, 1922, at the holders' option, at par and accrued interest to the date of such optional redemption, Treasury certificates of indebtedness of Series A-1922, dated May 16, 1921, maturing February 16, 1922.

## EXHIBIT 54.

### OFFER TO REDEEM BEFORE MATURITY, TREASURY CERTIFICATES OF INDEBTEDNESS, SERIES TM-1922, TM2-1922, AND TM3-1922.

Secretary Mellon announced that he has authorized the Federal Reserve Banks on and after Thursday, February 23, 1922, and until further notice, to redeem in cash before March 15, 1922, at the holders' option, at par and accrued interest to date of such optional redemption, Treasury certificates of indebtedness of Series TM-1922, dated March 15, 1921, Series TM2-1922, dated August 1, 1921, and Series TM3-1922, dated September 15, 1921, all maturing March 15, 1922.

## Exhibit 55.

**OFFER TO REDEEM BEFORE MATURITY, TREASURY CERTIFICATES OF INDEBTEDNESS, SERIES C-1922.**

Secretary Mellon announced that he has authorized the Federal Reserve Banks on and after Tuesday, March 21, 1922, and until further notice, to redeem in cash before April 1, 1922, at the holders' option, at par and accrued interest to date of such optional redemption, Treasury certificates of indebtedness of Series C–1922, dated November 1, 1921, maturing April 1, 1922.

## Exhibit 56.

**OFFER TO REDEEM BEFORE MATURITY, TREASURY CERTIFICATES OF INDEBTEDNESS, SERIES TJ-1922 AND TJ2-1922.**

Secretary Mellon announced that he has authorized the Federal Reserve Banks on and after Tuesday, May 23, 1922, and until further notice, to redeem in cash before June 15, 1922, at the holders' option, at par and accrued interest to date of such optional redemption, Treasury certificates of indebtedness of Series TJ–1922, dated June 15, 1921, and Series TJ2–1922, dated December 15, 1921, both maturing June 15, 1922.

## Exhibit 57.

**OFFER TO REDEEM BEFORE MATURITY, TREASURY CERTIFICATES OF INDEBTEDNESS, SERIES B-1922.**

Secretary Mellon announced that he has authorized the Federal Reserve Banks on and after Saturday, July 15, 1922, and until further notice, to redeem in cash before August 1, 1922, at the holders' option, at par and accrued interest to date of such optional redemption, Treasury certificates of indebtedness of Series B–1922, dated August 1, 1921, maturing August 1, 1922.

## Exhibit 58.

**OFFER TO REDEEM BEFORE MATURITY, TREASURY CERTIFICATES OF INDEBTEDNESS, SERIES TS-1922 AND TS2-1922.**

Secretary Mellon announced that he has authorized the Federal Reserve Banks on and after Wednesday, August 23, 1922, and until further notice, to redeem in cash before September 15, 1922, at the holders' option, at par and accrued interest to date of such optional redemption, Treasury certificates of indebtedness of Series TS–1922, dated September 15, 1921, and Series TS2–1922, dated November 1, 1921, both maturing September 15, 1922.

## Exhibit 59.

**OFFER TO REDEEM BEFORE MATURITY, TREASURY CERTIFICATES OF INDEBTEDNESS, SERIES D-1922.**

Secretary Mellon announced that he has authorized the Federal Reserve Banks on and after Monday, September 25, 1922, and until further notice, to redeem in cash before October 16, 1922, at the holders' option, at par and accrued interest to date of such optional redemption, Treasury certificates of indebtedness of Series D–1922, dated April 15, 1922, maturing October 16, 1922.

## Exhibit 60.

### OFFER TO REDEEM BEFORE MATURITY, TREASURY CERTIFICATES OF INDEBTEDNESS, SERIES TD-1922 AND TD2-1922.

Secretary Mellon announces that he has authorized the Federal Reserve Banks on and after Monday, October 23, 1922, and until further notice, to redeem in cash before December 15, 1922, at the holder's option, at par and accrued interest to the date of optional redemption, Treasury certificates of indebtedness of Series TD-1922, dated December 15, 1921, and Series TD2-1922, dated June 15, 1922, both maturing December 15, 1922.

The Secretary at the same time called attention to the general offer announced by the Treasury on July 26, 1922, in connection with the call for the redemption of 4¾ per cent Victory notes, under which the Federal Reserve Banks are authorized to redeem before December 15, 1922, at the holder's option, at par and accrued interest to the date of optional redemption, any called Victory notes which may be presented for prior redemption. Pursuant to the notice of redemption then given, all 4¾ per cent Victory notes bearing the distinguishing letters A, B, C, D, E, or F, prefixed to their serial numbers, are called for redemption on December 15, 1922, and from that date cease to bear interest.

## Exhibit 61.

[Department Circular No. 270. Public Debt.]

### UNITED STATES OF AMERICA—TREASURY SAVINGS CERTIFICATES, NEW ISSUE.

TREASURY DEPARTMENT,
OFFICE OF THE SECRETARY,
*December 15, 1921.*

#### OFFERING OF TREASURY SAVINGS CERTIFICATES, NEW ISSUE.

1. Under authority of Section 6 of the Act of Congress approved September 24, 1917, as amended and supplemented, the Secretary of the Treasury offers for sale to the people of the United States, beginning December 15, 1921, an issue of United States War-Savings Certificates, to be known as Treasury Savings Certificates, New Issue. Payment for or on account of Treasury Savings Certificates issued hereunder may be evidenced by Treasury Savings Stamps affixed to Treasury Savings Cards, as hereinafter provided. It shall not be lawful for any one person at any one time to hold United States Treasury (War) Savings Certificates of any one series to an aggregate amount exceeding $5,000 (maturity value). The sum of United States Treasury (War) Savings Certificates of all series and issues outstanding shall not at any one time exceed in the aggregate $4,000,000,000 (maturity value). The Treasury Savings Certificates issued within any one calendar year shall constitute a separate series, under the serial designation of the year of issue. Treasury Savings Certificates, New Issue, issued during the calendar year 1922 shall constitute the Series of 1922, and certificates issued during December, 1921, shall be included in the Series of 1921 of United States Treasury (War) Savings Certificates.

DESCRIPTION OF TREASURY SAVINGS CERTIFICATES, NEW ISSUE.

2. *Form and Denominations.*—Treasury Savings Certificates, New Issue, will be issued only in registered form, in denominations, of $25, $100, and $1,000 (maturity value), and will bear the name and address of the owner and the date of issue, which shall be inscribed thereon by the issuing agent at the time of issue. At the time of issue of each such certificate the registration stub attached thereto shall be executed in the same manner by the issuing agent, and shall be detached and forwarded in the manner hereinafter directed for transmission to the Treasury Department at Washington. The registration stubs will remain at the Treasury Department at Washington and will constitute the basis for the Department's record of the registered ownership of the certificates. In addition to the registration stub above described, each certificate will be provided with an additional or duplicate stub, which shall be executed at the same time and in the same manner as the original registration stub and retained by issuing post offices in such manner as the Postmaster General shall direct, and by Federal Reserve Banks and other issuing agents subject to the order of the Secretary of the Treasury. The certificates will mature five years from the date of issue in each case, and will be redeemable before maturity at the option of the owner. The certificates, at the issue prices hereinafter named, y e d about 4½ per cent per annum, compounded semiannually, if held to maturity, and about 3½ per cent per annum, compounded semiannually, if redeemed before maturity. The certificates will not be transferable, and will be payable only to the owner named thereon except in case of death or disability of the owner and in such case will be payable as provided in regulations prescribed by the Secretary of the Treasury. The certificates will not be valid unless the owner's name and address and the date of issue are duly inscribed thereon by an authorized agent at the time of issue. Treasury Savings Certificates, New Issue, are dated December 15, 1921, and will bear the facsimile signature of the Secretary of the Treasury.

3. *Issue prices.*—Treasury Savings Certificates, New Issue, are offered until further notice at the following fiat issue prices:

| Denomination (maturity value). | Issue price. |
| --- | --- |
| $25 | $20 |
| 100 | 80 |
| 1,000 | 800 |

4. *Tax exemption.*—Treasury Savings Certificates, New Issue, shall be exempt, both as to principal and interest, from all taxation now or hereafter imposed by the United States, any State, or any of the possessions of the United States, or by any local taxing authority, except (a) estate or inheritance taxes, and (b) graduated additional income taxes, commonly known as surtaxes, and excess-profits and war-profits taxes, now or hereafter imposed by the United States, upon the income or profits of individuals, partnerships, associations, or corporations. The interest on an amount of bonds and certificates authorized by said Act approved September 24, 1917, and amendments thereto, the principal of which does not exceed in the aggregate $5,000, owned by any individual, partnership, association, or corporation, shall be exempt from the taxes provided for in clause (b) above.

5. *Payment at maturity.*—Owners of Treasury Savings Certificates, New Issue, will be entitled to receive at or after maturity, five years

from the date of issue thereof, the respective face amounts as stated thereon, upon presentation and surrender of the certificates by mail or otherwise at the Office of the Secretary of the Treasury, Division of Loans and Currency, Washington, and upon compliance with all other provisions thereof, provided the form of demand for payment appearing on the back thereof shall be properly signed by the owner in the presence of, and duly certified by, a United States postmaster (who should also affix the official postmark of his office), an executive officer of an incorporated bank or trust company (who should also affix the corporate seal of the bank or trust company), or any other person duly designated by the Secretary of the Treasury for the purpose.   In case of the death or disability of the owner, a special form of demand for payment prescribed by the Secretary of the Treasury must be duly executed.

6. *Payment prior to maturity.*—The owner of a Treasury Savings Certificate, New Issue, at his option, will be entitled to receive, prior to maturity, the lesser amount indicated for the respective months following purchase in the following tables (and in the similar table appearing on the back of the certificate) with respect to certificates of the denomination concerned.   Payment prior to maturity of the amount payable in respect of any such certificate will be made upon presentation, surrender, and demand made as aforesaid in paragraph 5 hereof, at the Office of the Secretary of the Treasury, Division of Loans and Currency, Washington, and upon compliance with all other provisions thereof.

*Tables showing how Treasury Savings Certificates, New Issue, increase in value during successive months following purchase.*

DENOMINATION OF $25.—ISSUE PRICE, $20.

| Month. | First year. | Second year. | Third year. | Fourth year. | Fifth year. |
|---|---|---|---|---|---|
| First | $20.00 | $20.70 | $21.45 | $22.20 | $23.00 |
| Second | 20.05 | 20.75 | 21.50 | 22.25 | 23.05 |
| Third | 20.10 | 20.80 | 21.55 | 22.30 | 23.10 |
| Fourth | 20.15 | 20.85 | 21.60 | 22.35 | 23.15 |
| Fifth | 20.20 | 20.90 | 21.65 | 22.40 | 23.20 |
| Sixth | 20.25 | 20.95 | 21.70 | 22.45 | 23.25 |
| Seventh | 20.35 | 21.05 | 21.80 | 22.60 | 23.40 |
| Eighth | 20.40 | 21.10 | 21.85 | 22.65 | 23.45 |
| Ninth | 20.45 | 21.15 | 21.90 | 22.70 | 23.50 |
| Tenth | 20.50 | 21.20 | 21.95 | 22.75 | 23.55 |
| Eleventh | 20.55 | 21.25 | 22.00 | 22.80 | 23.60 |
| Twelfth | 20.60 | 21.30 | 22.05 | 22.85 | 23.65 |
| At maturity, 5 years from date of issue | | | | | 25.00 |

DENOMINATION OF $100.—ISSUE PRICE, $80.

| Month. | First year. | Second year. | Third year. | Fourth year. | Fifth year. |
|---|---|---|---|---|---|
| First | $80.00 | $82.80 | $85.80 | $88.80 | $92.00 |
| Second | 80.20 | 83.00 | 86.00 | 89.00 | 92.20 |
| Third | 80.40 | 83.20 | 86.20 | 89.20 | 92.40 |
| Fourth | 80.60 | 83.40 | 86.40 | 89.40 | 92.60 |
| Fifth | 80.80 | 83.60 | 86.60 | 89.60 | 92.80 |
| Sixth | 81.00 | 83.80 | 86.80 | 89.80 | 93.00 |
| Seventh | 81.40 | 84.20 | 87.20 | 90.40 | 93.60 |
| Eighth | 81.60 | 84.40 | 87.40 | 90.60 | 93.80 |
| Ninth | 81.80 | 84.60 | 87.60 | 90.80 | 94.00 |
| Tenth | 82.00 | 84.80 | 87.80 | 91.00 | 94.20 |
| Eleventh | 82.20 | 85.00 | 88.00 | 91.20 | 94.40 |
| Twelfth | 82.40 | 85.20 | 88.20 | 91.40 | 94.60 |
| At maturity, 5 years from date of issue | | | | | 100.00 |

*Tables showing how Treasury Savings Certificates, New Issue, increase in value during successive months following purchase—*Continued.

DENOMINATION OF $1,000.—ISSUE PRICE, $800.

| Month. | First year. | Second year. | Third year. | Fourth year. | Fifth year. |
|---|---|---|---|---|---|
| First........................... | $800 | $828 | $858 | $888 | $920 |
| Second.......................... | 802 | 830 | 860 | 890 | 922 |
| Third........................... | 804 | 832 | 862 | 892 | 924 |
| Fourth.......................... | 806 | 834 | 864 | 894 | 926 |
| Fifth........................... | 808 | 836 | 866 | 896 | 928 |
| Sixth........................... | 810 | 838 | 868 | 898 | 930 |
| Seventh......................... | 814 | 842 | 872 | 904 | 936 |
| Eighth.......................... | 816 | 844 | 874 | 906 | 938 |
| Ninth........................... | 818 | 846 | 876 | 908 | 940 |
| Tenth........................... | 820 | 848 | 878 | 910 | 942 |
| Eleventh........................ | 822 | 850 | 880 | 912 | 944 |
| Twelfth......................... | 824 | 852 | 882 | 914 | 946 |
| At maturity, 5 years from date of issue........................ | | | | | 1,000 |

7. *Exchanges of denominations.*—Treasury Savings Certificates, New Issue, may be exchanged at the Treasury Department, Washington (but not at the Federal Reserve Banks, post offices, or other agencies), for Treasury Savings Certificates of the same issue and series with the same date of issue and date of maturity and inscribed in the same name but in other authorized denominations to the same aggregate maturity value.

TRANSMISSION OF REGISTRATION STUBS.

8. *Transmission of registration stubs by post offices.*—The original registration stubs detached from Treasury Savings Certificates, New Issue, sold by post offices, shall be attached to the accounts of sales of such certificates rendered to the Third Assistant Postmaster General, Division of Stamps, and forwarded by the Third Assistant Postmaster General to the Secretary of the Treasury, Division of Loans and Currency, Washington, so as to reach the Treasury Department not later than the calendar month succeeding the month in which the certificates are sold.

9. *Transmission of registration stubs by other issuing agents.*—The original registration stubs detached from Treasury Savings Certificates, New Issue, sold by other issuing agents, shall be forwarded to the Federal Reserve Bank from which such certificates were obtained, with the monthly accounts of such agents. The Federal Reserve Bank receiving such stubs will see that a registration stub is at hand for each such certificate reported sold and will forward such stubs, together with the original registration stubs detached from all Treasury Savings Certificates issued and sold by it, to the Secretary of the Treasury, Division of Loans and Currency, Washington, monthly, so as to reach the Treasury Department not later than the calendar month succeeding the month in which the certificates are sold. The original registration stubs detached from Treasury Savings Certificates sold by the Treasurer of the United States shall be forwarded to the Secretary of the Treasury, Division of Loans and Currency, monthly, so as to reach that division not later than the calendar month succeeding the month in which the certificates are sold.

## TREASURY SAVINGS STAMPS AND CARDS.

10. Until further notice United States Treasury Savings Stamps having a face value of $1 each may be purchased at face value, and United States Treasury Savings Cards may be obtained without cost, at any authorized agency for the sale of Treasury Savings Certificates, New Issue. Treasury Savings Stamps must be affixed to Treasury Savings Cards, and when so affixed will be accepted at face value on account of the purchase price of Treasury Savings Certificates, New Issue, in any denomination, upon presentation at a post office or other authorized agency, provided, that at the same time the holder of the Treasury Savings Card shall pay any difference between the aggregate face amount of the stamps affixed to the card and the issue price of the Certificate. Treasury Savings Stamps are intended primarily for accumulation on Treasury Savings Cards in lots of 20 stamps, on account of the purchase price of a $25 Treasury Savings Certificate. Treasury Savings Stamps can not be registered, do not bear interest, and are not intended for direct redemption in cash. No relief can be given for Treasury Savings Stamps lost, stolen, or destroyed.

### AGENCIES FOR SALE.

11. United States Treasury Savings Certificates, New Issue, in all denominations may be purchased at the Treasury Department, Washington, at the Federal Reserve Banks, and from incorporated banks and trust companies and others which have duly qualified as collateral agents, and in such denominations as may be prescribed by the Secretary of the Treasury at post offices of the first and second class, and such other post offices as the Postmaster General may designate for the purpose. Until further notice United States Treasury Savings Stamps may be purchased and United States Treasury Savings Cards may be obtained without cost at any authorized agency for the sale of Treasury Savings Certificates, New Issue. Sales of all Treasury Savings Securities or Stamps by cash agents or by sales stations will cease at the close of business on December 31, 1921, and neither cash agents nor sale stations will be permitted to obtain Treasury Savings Certificates, New Issue, for sale. Sales by the Treasury Department, the Federal Reserve Banks, incorporated banks and trust companies and other duly qualified collateral agents, and post offices will be governed, subject to the provisions of this circular, by the same regulations, *mutatis mutandis*, as prescribed for the year 1921 under Treasury Department Circular No. 216, dated December 15, 1920, except that collateral agents will not be required to render an account and transmit the proceeds of sales made during each calendar month until the twentieth day of the succeeding month. Collateral agents already duly qualified to a sufficient amount will not be required to file anew formal applications or pledge agreements and may act as collateral agents for the sale of Treasury Savings Securities hereunder without further application; and by the receipt or sale of Treasury Savings Certificates, New Issue, or of Treasury Savings Stamps after December 31, 1921, such collateral agents will be conclusively presumed to have assented to all the terms and provisions of this circular and to the retention of any collateral security pledged or to be pledged as collateral security hereunder. Copies of Forms

L. & C. 356, 357, and 358, with regard to collateral agents, revised to cover Treasury Savings Certificates, New Issue, are appended to this circular as exhibits, and additional copies may be obtained upon application from the Federal Reserve Banks and the Treasury Department, Division of Loans and Currency, Washington.

### CONVERSION OF POSTAL SAVINGS DEPOSITS.

12. Payment for Treasury Savings Certificates, New Issue, when purchased at post offices with postal savings facilities, may be made with Postal Savings deposits, and interest upon deposits withdrawn for this purpose will be allowed at the current postal savings rate, in accordance with regulations prescribed by the Postmaster General, from the first day of the month following the date of deposit to the first day of the month in which such purchase is made.

### UNITED STATES THRIFT STAMPS AND THRIFT CARDS.

13. The sale of United States Thrift Stamps and the distribution of United States Thrift Cards will cease at the close of business on December 31, 1921. On and after January 3, 1922, Thrift Stamps then outstanding will be accepted at their face value of 25 cents on account of the purchase price of Treasury Savings Stamps and of Treasury Savings Certificates, New Issue, in any denomination, or, at the option of the holder, may be redeemed at face value in cash upon presentation and surrender to the Treasury Department Washington, any Federal Reserve Bank, or any authorized post office.

### TREASURY SAVINGS CERTIFICATES, SERIES OF 1918, 1919, 1920, AND 1921.

14. The issue and sale of Treasury Savings Certificates, Series of 1921, for cash or in exchange for Treasury Savings Stamps will cease at the close of business on December 31, 1921. The issue of such certificates after that date in exchange for United States War-Savings Certificates, Series of 1921, with War-Savings Certificate Stamps, Series of 1921, affixed, to the same aggregate maturity value, will be continued until further notice at the Treasury Department, Washington, upon the same terms and conditions, *mutatis mutandis,* as heretofore provided for the exchange of such securities of the Series of 1920, by Treasury Department Circular No. 217, dated December 15, 1920, to which reference is hereby made. The issue of Treasury Savings Certificates of the Series of 1918, 1919, and 1920, in exchange for War-Savings Certificates of the same series, respectively, will be continued until further notice upon the same terms and conditions as heretofore prescribed, except that after December 31, 1921, such issue will only be made at the Treasury Department, Washington; *Provided, however,* That when registered War-Savings Certificates of any series are surrendered for such exchange, presentation and surrender must be made through the post office of registration. War-Savings Certificates presented for such exchange must in each case be accompanied by a request for exchange on Form General 1020, when registered certificates are surrendered, or Form General 1021, when unregistered certificates are surrendered. Copies of these forms may be obtained at Federal Reserve Banks, duly qualified post offices, and the Treasury Department, Division of Loans and Currency, Washington.

## MISCELLANEOUS PROVISIONS.

15. Treasury Savings Certificates are not receivable as security for deposits of public moneys and do not bear the circulation privilege.

16. The Secretary of the Treasury may at any time withdraw this circular as a whole or make from time to time any supplemental or amendatory regulations which shall not modify or impair the terms and conditions of Treasury Savings Certificates issued hereunder. The Secretary of the Treasury may at any time withdraw Treasury Savings Certificates or Treasury Savings Stamps from sale, refuse to issue or to permit to be issued any Treasury Savings cards, and refuse to sell or to permit to be sold any such certificates or stamps to any person, firm, corporation, or association.

17. The provisions of Treasury Department Circular No. 149, as revised June 25, 1921, further defining the rights of holders of Treasury Savings Certificates, will apply to and govern, subject to the provisions of this circular, the rights of holders of Treasury Savings Certificates, New Issue, issued hereunder, except that in paragraphs V, VI, XI, and XIV of said circular No. 149, the figure "5,000" shall be substituted for the figure "1,000." The provisions of Treasury Department Circular No. 178, dated January 15, 1920, as amended and supplemented, with respect to holdings of United States War-Savings Certificates in excess of the legal limit apply to and govern Treasury Savings Certificates issued hereunder, subject to the provisions of this circular.

18. Further details may be announced by the Secretary of the Treasury from time to time, information as to which will be promptly furnished to Federal Reserve Banks, to postmasters, and to other agents.

A. W. MELLON,
*Secretary of the Treasury.*

TREASURY DEPARTMENT.
Loans and Currency.
Form L. & C. 356 (Revised, 1922).

### PLEDGE AGREEMENT.

To the FEDERAL RESERVE BANK OF ....................
*As Fiscal Agent of the United States:*

The undersigned desires to become a collateral agent for the issue and sale of Treasury Savings Certificates, New Issue, and Treasury Savings Stamps, in accordance with the provisions of Treasury Department Circular No. 270, dated December 15, 1921, as from time to time amended and supplemented, and to obtain, from time to time, for sale to the public, as provided in said circular, Treasury Savings Certificates, New Issue, and Treasury Savings Stamps, in the aggregate amount of $.......... (such Treasury Savings Certificates to be taken for this purpose at the maturity value thereof, and such Treasury Savings Stamps at $1 each), and, as and when such certificates and stamps shall be sold and accounted and paid for, to obtain in lieu thereof, from time to time thereafter, additional Treasury Savings Certificates, New Issue (at maturity value), and Treasury Savings Stamps (at $1 each), up to but not exceeding at any one time the total amount stated above.

The undersigned agrees that none of such certificates and stamps obtained by the undersigned shall be sold and disposed of otherwise than as provided in said circular, and further agrees faithfully to perform all other obligations to be performed by collateral agents as therein and herein provided.

The undersigned agrees, in accordance with the provisions of Treasury Department Circular No. 270, dated December 15, 1921, before or upon delivery to the undersigned of Treasury Savings Certificates, New Issue, and Treasury Savings Stamps, in the aggregate amount stated above, to deliver to such Federal Reserve Bank (or to a custodian designated by it), and to pledge with such Federal Reserve Bank, in negotiable form, and in the case of coupon bonds, with all unmatured coupons attached, the following-described bonds and other securities, of the classes described in subdivisions (a), (b), and (c) of Treasury Department Circular No. 92, dated April 17, 1919, authorized to be deposited as collateral security under the terms of said Treasury Department Circular No. 270:

| Description of security. | Collateral value. |
|---|---|
| | $.............. |
| | .............. |
| | .............. |
| | .............. |
| | .............. |
| | .............. |
| | .............. |
| | .............. |
| | .............. |
| | .............. |
| Total collateral value.......................................... | ..............; |

to be held by such Federal Reserve Bank, as Fiscal Agent of the United States, as collateral security for the faithful performance of the obligations of the undersigned, now or hereafter from time to time arising, as a collateral agent for the issue and sale of Treasury Savings Certificates, New Issue, and Treasury Savings Stamps, in accordance with the provisions of said Treasury Department Circular No. 270, and of any supplemental or amendatory regulations made from time to time as therein provided; the undersigned, however, so long as not in default hereunder, to be entitled to collect from time to time and to retain any and all interest upon the above-described collateral security.

In case of any default in the performance of any of the obligations of the undersigned as collateral agent for the sale of Treasury Savings Certificates, New Issue, or Treasury Savings Stamps hereunder or under said Treasury Department Circular No 270, dated December 15, 1921, said Federal Reserve Bank shall have full power to collect said collateral security or any part thereof then matured, or to sell, assign, and transfer said collateral security or any part thereof without notice, at public or private sale, free from any equity of redemption and without appraisement or valuation, and after deducting all legal and other costs, attorney's fees, and expenses for collection, sale, and delivery, to apply the proceeds of such sale or collection, in whole or in part, to the satisfaction of any damages, demands, or deficiency arising by reason of such default, as said Federal Reserve Bank may deem best. The undersigned hereby for ......self, heirs, administrators, executors, successors, and assigns, ratifies and confirms whatever said Federal Reserve Bank may do by virtue of these presents.

Upon delivery to the undersigned of any Treasury Savings Certificates, New Issue, or Treasury Savings Stamps, desired to be obtained hereunder, this Pledge Agreement shall come into full force and effect, and the undersigned shall become a collateral agent as aforesaid.

In witness whereof, the undersigned has caused this agreement to be executed under seal by the officer below named thereunto duly authorized by action of its governing board.

Dated.................... 192..

(Corporate Seal.)             (Signature in full)...............................

                    By ...............................................
                              (Authorized signature required.)

                    (Address, number and street).....................

                         (City or town) .....................

                              (County) ................

                              (State) ...............

TREASURY DEPARTMENT.
Loans and Currency.
Form L. & C. 357 (Revised, 1922).

Name...................................,

       Street and Number.........................,

           City or Town.........................,

              County.........................,

                 State......................

Your pledge agreement on Form L. & C. 356 (Revised, 1922) has been approved and you are hereby appointed a collateral agent for the sale of Treasury Savings Certificates, New Issue, and Treasury Savings Stamps, subject to the provisions of Treasury Department Circular No. 270, dated December 15, 1921, as from time to time amended and supplemented.

              Federal Reserve Bank of...............................,

                                 *Fiscal Agent of the United States,*

                 By...........................,

                                   *Governor.*

Dated....................192..

(Original to be issued to agent, duplicate to be forwarded to the Secretary of the Treasury, Division of Loans and Currency, and triplicate to be retained by Federal Reserve Bank.)

TREASURY DEPARTMENT.
Loans and Currency.
Form L. & C. 358 (Revised, 1922).

                                       Serial No.....

MONTHLY ACCOUNT OF SALES OF TREASURY SAVINGS CERTIFICATES, NEW ISSUE, AND TREASURY SAVINGS STAMPS, BY COLLATERAL AGENT.

To Federal Reserve Bank of..............,

    The undersigned hereby renders the following account of transactions in Treasury Savings Certificates, New Issue, and Treasury Savings Stamps, from ..............

192.., to .............., 192.., both inclusive:

*Stock account.*

| | Number of pieces. | | | |
| --- | --- | --- | --- | --- |
| | Treasury Savings Certificates. | | | Treasury Savings Stamps. |
| | Denomination, $25. | Denomination, $100. | Denomination, $1,000. | |
| On hand at close of preceding month... | .............. | .............. | .............. | .............. |
| Obtained during month............... | .............. | .............. | .............. | .............. |
| Total........................ | .............. | .............. | .............. | .............. |
| Sales during month.................. | .............. | .............. | .............. | .............. |
| Unsold stock returned............... | .............. | .............. | .............. | .............. |
| Net total on hand................ | .............. | .............. | .............. | .............. |

*Gross amount due in respect of sales.*

|  | Number of pieces. | Issue price. | Total issue value. |
|---|---|---|---|
| Treasury Savings Certificates..{$25 denomination........... | | | |
| $100 denomination......... | | | |
| $1,000 denomination........ | | | |
| Treasury Savings Stamps............... | | $1.00 | |
| Total............... | | | |

The undersigned herewith remits for credit to its account the following:

| | | |
|---|---|---|
| Currency................. Bank drafts or checks drawn upon the Federal Reserve Bank, or upon any member bank, payable to the order of "Federal Reserve Bank of........................ as Fiscal Agent of the United States," as follows: | $ | |
| Treasury Savings Cards with Treasury Savings Stamps affixed, received in exchange for Treasury Savings Certificates, stamps taken at $1 each............... Thrift Cards with Thrift Stamps affixed, received in exchange for Treasury Savings Certificates or Treasury Savings Stamps, Thrift Stamps taken at 25 cents each................. | | |

Remarks ..................................................................

.............................................................................

.............................................................................

.............................................................................

.............................................................................

(Signed)....._(Name of Collateral Agent.)_

By ...._(Official signature required.)_

(Address, number, and street) ....................

(City or town) .................

(County)...........

(State)...........

NOTE 1.—A similar account must be rendered on or before the 20th day of each month.

NOTE 2.—No medium of payment other than above provided will be accepted by any Federal Reserve Bank, except at its own risk, and no agent shall be entitled to credit, in respect of any payment to be made by check or draft, except when such draft shall have been collected by the Federal Reserve Bank, as fiscal agent of the United States.

## EXHIBIT 62.

[Department Circular No. 301. Public Debt.]

## UNITED STATES OF AMERICA—NEW OFFERING OF TREASURY SAVINGS CERTIFICATES.

TREASURY DEPARTMENT,
OFFICE OF THE SECRETARY,
*September 30, 1922.*

NEW OFFERING OF TREASURY SAVINGS CERTIFICATES.

1. Under authority of Section 6 of the Act of Congress approved September 24, 1917, as amended and supplemented, the Secretary of the Treasury offers for sale to the people of the United States, beginning October 1, 1922, an issue of United States War-Savings

Certificates, to be known as Treasury Savings Certificates and to be dated September 30, 1922. Pursuant to the provisions of Treasury Department Circular No. 270, dated December 15, 1921, Treasury Savings Certificates, New Issue, offered thereunder, and Treasury Savings Stamps, are hereby withdrawn from sale at the close of business September 30, 1922, and the sale of such Treasury Savings Certificates, New Issue, and of Treasury Savings Stamps, and the distribution of Treasury Savings Cards will cease at the close of business on that date. Treasury Savings Certificates, New Issue, issued during the calendar year 1922, and Treasury Savings Certificates which may be issued hereunder during the calendar year 1922, constitute the Series of 1922 of Treasury Savings Certificates. It shall not be lawful for any one person at any one time to hold United States Treasury (War) Savings Certificates of any one series to an aggregate amount exceeding $5,000 (maturity value). The sum of United States Treasury (War) Savings Certificates of all series and issues outstanding shall not at any one time exceed in the aggregate $4,000,000,000 (maturity value). The Treasury Savings Certificates issued within any one calendar year shall constitute a separate series, under the serial designation of the year of issue.

## DESCRIPTION OF CERTIFICATES.

2. *Form and Denominations.*—Treasury Savings Certificates will be issued only in registered form, in denominations of $25, $100, and $1,000 (maturity value), and will bear the name and address of the owner and the date of issue, which shall be inscribed thereon by the issuing agent at the time of issue. At the time of issue of each such certificate the registration stub attached thereto shall be executed in the same manner by the issuing agent, and shall be detached and forwarded in the manner hereinafter directed for transmission to the Treasury Department at Washington. The registration stubs will remain at the Treasury Department at Washington and will constitute the basis for the Department's record of the registered ownership of the certificates. In addition to the registration stub above described, each certificate will be provided with an additional or duplicate stub, which shall be executed at the same time and in the same manner as the original registration stub and retained by issuing post offices in such manner as the Postmaster General shall direct, and by Federal Reserve Banks and other issuing agents subject to the order of the Secretary of the Treasury. The certificates will mature five years from the date of issue in each case, and will be redeemable before maturity at the option of the owner. The certificates, at the issue prices hereinafter named, yield about 4 per cent per annum, compounded semiannually, if held to maturity, and about 3 per cent per annum, simple interest, if redeemed before maturity. The certificates will not be transferable, and will be payable only to the owner named thereon except in case of death or disability of the owner and in such case will be payable, or, in the case of the death of the owner prior to maturity, the certificate may be reissued to the person entitled thereto, as provided in regulations prescribed by the Secretary of the Treasury. (See Treasury Department Circular No. 149, Revised, of August 1, 1922.) The certificates will not be valid unless the owner's name and address and the date of issue are duly

inscribed thereon by an authorized agent at the time of issue. Treasury Savings Certificates issued hereunder will bear the facsimile signature of the Secretary of the Treasury.

3. *Issue prices.*—Treasury Savings Certificates are offered hereunder, until further notice, at the following flat issue prices:

| Denomination (maturity value): | Issue price. |
|---|---|
| $25 | $20. 50 |
| 100 | 82 |
| 1,000 | 820 |

4. *Tax exemption.*—Treasury Savings Certificates shall be exempt, both as to principal and interest, from all taxation now or hereafter imposed by the United States, any State, or any of the possessions of the United States, or by any local taxing authority, except (*a*) estate or inheritance taxes, and (*b*) graduated additional income taxes, commonly known as surtaxes, and excess-profits and war-profits taxes, now or hereafter imposed by the United States, upon the income or profits of individuals, partnerships, associations, or corporations. The interest on an amount of bonds and certificates authorized by said Act approved September 24, 1917, and amendments thereto, the principal of which does not exceed in the aggregate $5,000, owned by any individual, partnership, association, or corporation, shall be exempt from the taxes provided for in clause (*b*) above.

5. *Payment at maturity.*—Owners of Treasury Savings Certificates issued hereunder will be entitled to receive at or after maturity, five years from the date of issue thereof, the respective face amounts as stated thereon, upon presentation and surrender of the certificates by mail or otherwise at the Office of the Secretary of the Treasury, Division of Loans and Currency, Washington, D. C., and upon compliance with all other provisions thereof, provided the form of demand for payment appearing on the back thereof shall be properly signed by the owner in the presence of, and duly certified by, a United States postmaster (who should also affix the official postmark of his office), an executive officer of an incorporated bank or trust company (who should also affix the corporate seal of the bank or trust company), or any other person duly designated by the Secretary of the Treasury for the purpose. In case of the death or disability of the owner, a special form of demand for payment prescribed by the Secretary of the Treasury must be duly executed.

6. *Payment prior to maturity.*—Owners of Treasury Savings Certificates issued hereunder, at their option, will be entitled to receive, prior to maturity, the lesser amount indicated for the respective months following issue in the following tables (and in the similar table appearing on the back of the certificate) with respect to certificates of the denomination concerned. Payment prior to maturity of the amount payable in respect of any such certificate will be made upon presentation, surrender, and demand made as aforesaid in paragraph 5 hereof, at the Office of the Secretary of the Treasury, Division of Loans and Currency, Washington, D. C., and upon compliance with all other provisions thereof.

*Tables showing how Treasury Savings Certificates, issued hereunder; increase in value during successive months following issue.*

DENOMINATION $25.—ISSUE PRICE $20.50.

| Month. | First year. | Second year. | Third year. | Fourth year. | Fifth year. |
|---|---|---|---|---|---|
| First | $20.50 | $21.10 | $21.70 | $22.30 | $22.90 |
| Second | 20.55 | 21.15 | 21.75 | 22.35 | 22.95 |
| Third | 20.60 | 21.20 | 21.80 | 22.40 | 23.00 |
| Fourth | 20.65 | 21.25 | 21.85 | 22.45 | 23.05 |
| Fifth | 20.70 | 21.30 | 21.90 | 22.50 | 23.10 |
| Sixth | 20.75 | 21.35 | 21.95 | 22.55 | 23.15 |
| Seventh | 20.80 | 21.40 | 22.00 | 22.60 | 23.20 |
| Eighth | 20.85 | 21.45 | 22.05 | 22.65 | 23.25 |
| Ninth | 20.90 | 21.50 | 22.10 | 22.70 | 23.30 |
| Tenth | 20.95 | 21.55 | 22.15 | 22.75 | 23.35 |
| Eleventh | 21.00 | 21.60 | 22.20 | 22.80 | 23.40 |
| Twelfth | 21.05 | 21.65 | 22.25 | 22.85 | 23.45 |
| At maturity, 5 years from date of issue | | | | | 25.00 |

DENOMINATION OF $100.—ISSUE PRICE $82.

| Month. | First year. | Second year. | Third year. | Fourth year. | Fifth year. |
|---|---|---|---|---|---|
| First | $82.00 | $84.40 | $86.80 | $89.20 | $91.60 |
| Second | 82.20 | 84.60 | 87.00 | 89.40 | 91.80 |
| Third | 82.40 | 84.80 | 87.20 | 89.60 | 92.00 |
| Fourth | 82.60 | 85.00 | 87.40 | 89.80 | 92.20 |
| Fifth | 82.80 | 85.20 | 87.60 | 90.00 | 92.40 |
| Sixth | 83.00 | 85.40 | 87.80 | 90.20 | 92.60 |
| Seventh | 83.20 | 85.60 | 88.00 | 90.40 | 92.80 |
| Eighth | 83.40 | 85.80 | 88.20 | 90.60 | 93.00 |
| Ninth | 83.60 | 86.00 | 88.40 | 90.80 | 93.20 |
| Tenth | 83.80 | 86.20 | 88.60 | 91.00 | 93.40 |
| Eleventh | 84.00 | 86.40 | 88.80 | 91.20 | 93.60 |
| Twelfth | 84.20 | 86.60 | 89.00 | 91.40 | 93.80 |
| At maturity, 5 years from date of issue | | | | | 100.00 |

DENOMINATION OF $1,000.—ISSUE PRICE $820.

| Month. | First year. | Second year. | Third year. | Fourth year. | Fifth year. |
|---|---|---|---|---|---|
| First | $820 | $844 | $868 | $892 | $916 |
| Second | 822 | 846 | 870 | 894 | 918 |
| Third | 824 | 848 | 872 | 896 | 920 |
| Fourth | 826 | 850 | 874 | 898 | 922 |
| Fifth | 828 | 852 | 876 | 900 | 924 |
| Sixth | 830 | 854 | 878 | 902 | 926 |
| Seventh | 832 | 856 | 880 | 904 | 928 |
| Eighth | 834 | 858 | 882 | 906 | 930 |
| Ninth | 836 | 860 | 884 | 908 | 932 |
| Tenth | 838 | 862 | 886 | 910 | 934 |
| Eleventh | 840 | 864 | 888 | 912 | 936 |
| Twelfth | 842 | 866 | 890 | 914 | 938 |
| At maturity, 5 years from date of issue | | | | | 1,000 |

7. *Exchanges of denominations.*—Treasury Savings Certificates may be exchanged at the Treasury Department, Division of Loans and Currency, Washington (but not at Federal Reserve Banks, post offices, or other agencies), for Treasury Savings Certificates of the same issue and series with the same date of issue and date of maturity and inscribed in the same name but in other authorized denominations to the same aggregate maturity value.

### TRANSMISSION OF REGISTRATION STUBS.

8. *Transmission of registration stubs by post offices.*—The original registration stubs detached from Treasury Savings Certificates sold by post offices shall be attached to the accounts of sales of such certificates rendered to the Third Assistant Postmaster General, Division of Stamps, and forwarded by the Third Assistant Postmaster General to the Treasury Department, Division of Loans and Currency, Washington, D. C., so as to reach the Treasury Department not later than the calendar month succeeding the month in which the certificates are sold.

9. *Transmission of registration stubs by other issuing agents.*—The original registration stubs detached from Treasury Savings Certificates sold by other issuing agents shall be forwarded to the Federal Reserve Bank from which such certificates were obtained, with the monthly accounts of such agents. The Federal Reserve Bank receiving such stubs will see that a registration stub is at hand for each such certificate reported sold and will forward such stubs, together with the original registration stubs detached from all Treasury Savings Certificates issued and sold by it, to the Treasury Department, Division of Loans and Currency, Washington, D. C., so as to reach the Treasury Department not later than the calendar month succeeding the month in which the certificates are sold. The original registration stubs detached from Treasury Savings Certificates sold by the Treasurer of the United States shall be forwarded to the Treasury Department, Division of Loans and Currency, Washington, D. C., so as to reach that division not later than the calendar month succeeding the month in which the certificates are sold.

### TREASURY SAVINGS STAMPS AND CARDS AND THRIFT STAMPS.

10. On and after October 1, 1922, United States Treasury Savings Stamps and Thrift Stamps then outstanding will be accepted at their face value of $1 per stamp for Treasury Savings Stamps and 25 cents per stamp for Thrift Stamps on account of the purchase price of Treasury Savings Certificates offered hereunder, in any denomination, or, at the option of the holder, may be redeemed at face value in cash upon presentation and surrender to the Treasury Department, Office of the Treasurer of the United States, Washington, D. C.. any Federal Reserve Bank, or any authorized post office.

### AGENCIES FOR SALE.

11. United States Treasury Savings Certificates offered hereunder, in all denominations may be purchased at the Treasury Department, Washington, D. C., at the Federal Reserve Banks, and from incorporated banks and trust companies and others which have duly qualified as collateral agents, and in such denominations as may be prescribed by the Secretary of the Treasury at post offices of the first and second class, and such other post offices as the Postmaster General may designate for the purpose. Sales by the Treasury Department, the Federal Reserve Banks, incorporated banks and trust companies and other duly qualified collateral agents, and post offices will be

governed, subject to the provisions of this circular, by the same regulations, *mutatis mutandis*, as prescribed for the year 1922 under Treasury Department Circular No. 216, dated December 15, 1920, as modified and extended by Treasury Department Circular No. 270, dated December 15, 1921. Collateral agents already duly qualified to a sufficient amount will not be required to file anew formal applications or pledge agreements and may act as collateral agents for the sale of Treasury Savings Certificates hereunder without further application; and by the receipt or sale of Treasury Savings Certificates offered hereunder, such collateral agents will be conclusively presumed to have assented to all the terms and provisions of this circular and to the retention of any collateral security pledged or to be pledged as collateral security hereunder. Copies of Forms L. & C. 356, 357, and 358, with regard to collateral agents, revised to cover the Treasury Savings Certificates offered hereunder, are appended to this circular as exhibits, and additional copies may be obtained upon application from the Federal Reserve Banks and the Treasury Department, Division of Loans and Currency, Washington, D. C.

### CONVERSION OF POSTAL SAVINGS DEPOSITS.

12. Payment for Treasury Savings Certificates, when purchased at post offices having postal savings facilities, may be made with Postal Savings deposits, and interest withdrawn for this purpose will be allowed at the current postal savings rate, in accordance with regulations prescribed by the Postmaster General, from the first day of the month following the date of deposit to the first day of the month in which such purchase is made.

### MISCELLANEOUS PROVISIONS.

13. Treasury Savings Certificates are not receivable as security for deposits of public moneys and do not bear the circulation privilege.

14. The Secretary of the Treasury may at any time withdraw this circular as a whole or make from time to time any supplemental or amendatory regulations which shall not modify or impair the terms and conditions of Treasury Savings Certificates issued hereunder. The Secretary of the Treasury may at any time withdraw the Treasury Savings Certificates offered hereunder from sale, or refuse to sell or to permit to be sold any such certificates to any person, firm, corporation, or association.

15. The provisions of Treasury Department Circular No. 149, as revised August 1, 1922, further defining the rights of holders of Treasury Savings Certificates, will apply to and govern, subject to the provisions of this circular, the rights of holders of Treasury Savings Certificates, issued hereunder. The provisions of Treasury Department Circular No. 178, dated January 15, 1920, as amended and supplemented, with respect to holdings of United States War-Savings Certificates in excess of the legal limit apply to and govern Treasury Savings Certificates issued hereunder, subject to the provisions of this circular.

16. Nothing herein contained shall be deemed to annul or revoke the provisions of paragraph 14 of Treasury Department Circular No. 270, dated December 15, 1921, with respect to the issue of Treasury

Savings Certificates, Series of 1918, 1919, 1920, and 1921, respectively, in exchange for War-Savings Certificates of the same series, but the provisions of said paragraph shall remain in full force and effect until further notice, except that in no event will War-Savings Certificates of either of said series be accepted in exchange for Treasury Savings Certificates of the same series after the maturity thereof.

17. Regulations governing the surrender of unsold Treasury Savings Certificates, New Issue, unsold Treasury Savings Stamps and unissued Treasury Savings Cards are contained in Treasury Department Circular No. 302, dated September 30, 1922, to which reference is hereby made.

18. Further details may be announced by the Secretary of the Treasury from time to time, information as to which will be promptly furnished to Federal Reserve Banks, to postmasters, and to other agents.

A. W. MELLON,<br>Secretary of the Treasury.

TREASURY DEPARTMENT.
Loans and Currency.
Form L. & C 356 (Revised, 1922).

PLEDGE AGREEMENT.

To the FEDERAL RESERVE BANK OF ....................,
    *As Fiscal Agent of the United States:*

The undersigned desires to become a collateral agent for the issue and sale of Treasury Savings Certificates, in accordance with the provisions of Treasury Department Circular No. 301, dated September 30, 1922, as from time to time amended and supplemented, and to obtain, from time to time, for sale to the public, as provided in said circular, Treasury Savings Certificates in the aggregate amount of $......... (such Treasury Savings Certificates to be taken for this purpose at the maturity value thereof), and, as and when such certificates shall be sold and accounted and paid for, to obtain in lieu thereof, from time to time thereafter, additional Treasury Savings Certificates (at maturity value) up to but not exceeding at any one time the total amount stated above.

The undersigned agrees that none of such certificates obtained by the undersigned shall be sold and disposed of otherwise than as provided in said circular, and further agrees faithfully to perform all other obligations to be performed by collateral agents as therein and herein provided.

The undersigned agrees, in accordance with the provisions of Treasury Department Circular No. 301, dated September 30, 1922, before or upon delivery to the undersigned of Treasury Savings Certificates in the aggregate amount stated above, to deliver to such Federal Reserve Bank (or to a custodian designated by it), and to pledge with such Federal Reserve Bank, in negotiable form, and in the case of coupon bonds, with all unmatured coupons attached, the following-described bonds and other securities, of the classes described in subdivisions (a), (b), and (c) of Treasury Department Circular No. 92, dated April 17, 1919, authorized to be deposited as collateral security under the terms of said Treasury Department Circular No. 301:

| Description of security. | Collateral value. |
|---|---|
| ............................................................ | $............... |
| ............................................................ | ............... |
| ............................................................ | ............... |
| ............................................................ | ............... |
| ............................................................ | ............... |
| ............................................................ | ............... |
| ............................................................ | ............... |
| ............................................................ | ............... |
| ............................................................ | ............... |
| Total collateral value........................................ | ...............; |

ιο be held by such Federal Reserve Bank, as Fiscal Agent of the United States, as collateral security for the faithful performance of the obligations of the undersigned, now or hereafter from time to time arising, as a collateral agent for the issue and sale of Treasury Savings Certificates in accordance with the provisions of said Treasury Department Circular No. 301, and of any supplemental or amendatory regulations made from time to time as therein provided; the undersigned, however, so long as not in default hereunder, to be entitled to collect from time to time and to retain any and all interest upon the above-described collateral security.

In case of any default in the performance of any of the obligations of the undersigned as collateral agent for the sale of Treasury Savings Certificates hereunder or under said Treasury Department Circular No. 301, dated September 30, 1922, said Federal Reserve Bank shall have full power to collect said collateral security or any part thereof then matured, or to sell. assign, and transfer said collateral security or any part thereof without notice, at public or private sale, free from any equity of redemption and without appraisement or valuation, and after deducting all legal and other costs, attorney's fees, and expenses for collection, sale. and delivery, to apply the proceeds of such sale or collection, in whole or in part, to the satisfaction of any damages, demands, or deficiency arising by reason of such default, as said Federal Reserve Bank may deem best. The undersigned hereby for ......self, heirs, administrators, .executors, successors, and assigns, ratifies and confirms whatever said Federal Reserve Bank may do by virtue of these presents.

Upon delivery to the undersigned of any Treasury Savings Certificates desired to be obtained hereunder, this Pledge Agreement shall come into full force and effect, and the undersigned shall become a collateral agent as aforesaid.

In witness whereof, the undersigned has caused this agreement to be executed under seal by the officer below named thereunto duly authorized by action of its governing board.

Dated ...................., 192..
(Corporate Seal.)                (Signature in full) ...............................
                                 By ..............................................
                                        (Authorized signature required.)
                                 (Address, number and street) .....................
                                            (City or town) ................
                                                 (County) ............
                                                  (State) ............

TREASURY DEPARTMENT.
Loans and Currency.
Form L. & C. 357 (Revised, 1922).
Name ...............................,
   Street and Number..............,
      City or Town ................,
         County.................,
            State................

Your pledge agreement on Form L. & C. 356 (Revised, 1922) has been approved and you are hereby appointed a collateral agent for the sale of Treasury Savings Certificates, subject to the provisions of Treasury Department Circular No. 301, dated September 30, 1922, as from time to time amended and supplemented.

Federal Reserve Bank of ...............................,
                                 *Fiscal Agent of the United States,*
                                 By ..............................,
                                             *Governor.*

Dated ...................., 192..

(Original to be issued to agent, duplicate to be forwarded to the Treasury Department, Division of Loans and Currency, and triplicate to be retained by Federal Reserve Bank.)

TREASURY DEPARTMENT.
Loans and Currency.
Form L. & C. 358 (Revised, 1922).

Serial No. ....

### MONTHLY ACCOUNT OF SALES OF TREASURY SAVINGS CERTIFICATES BY COLLATERAL AGENT.

To Federal Reserve Bank of ................,

The undersigned hereby renders the following account of transactions in Treasury Savings Certificates from .............., 192....., to .............., 192...., both inclusive:

*Stock account.*

|  | Number of pieces, Treasury Savings Certificates. | | |
|---|---|---|---|
|  | Denomination, $25. | Denomination, $100. | Denomination, $1,000. |
| On hand at close of preceding month.................... | .............. | .............. | .............. |
| Obtained during month.............................. | .............. | .............. | .............. |
| Total.. ................................ | .............. | .............. | .............. |
| Sales during month................................ | .............. | .............. | .............. |
| Unsold stock returned.............................. | .............. | .............. | .............. |
| Net total on hand.................................. | .............. | .............. | .............. |

*Gross amount due in respect of sales.*

|  | Number of pieces. | Issue price. | Total issue value. |
|---|---|---|---|
| Treasury Savings Certificates.. {$25 denomination............ | .............. | .............. | .............. |
| $100 denomination........... | .............. | .............. | .............. |
| $1,000 denomination... ...... | .............. | .............. | .............. |
| Total....... ............................. | .............. | .............. | .............. |

The undersigned herewith remits for credit to its account the following:

| Currency...................................................... | $.............. | ........ |
|---|---|---|
| Bank drafts or checks drawn upon the Federal Reserve Bank, or upon any member bank, payable to the order of "Federal Reserve Bank of ...................., as Fiscal Agent of the United States," as follows: | | |
| ................................................................ | .............. | ........ |
| ................................................................ | .............. | ........ |
| Treasury Savings Cards with Treasury Savings Stamps affixed, received in exchange for Treasury Savings Certificates, stamps taken at $1 each............. | .............. | ........ |
| Thrift Cards with Thrift Stamps affixed, received in exchange for Treasury Savings Certificaes, Thrift Stamps taken at 25 cents each...................... | .............. | ........ |

Remarks.................................................................
........................................................................
........................................................................
........................................................................
........................................................................

(Signed) ..............................

(Name of Collateral Agent.)

By ...............................

(Official signature required.)

(Address, number and street) ....................

(City or town) ................

(County) ............

(State) ............

NOTE 1.—A similar account must be rendered on or before the 20th day of each month.

NOTE 2.—No medium of payment other than above provided will be accepted by any Federal Reserve Bank except at its own risk, and no agent shall be entitled to credit, in respect of any payment to be made by check or draft, except when such draft shall have been collected by the Federal Reserve Bank, as fiscal agent of the United States.

EXHIBIT 63.

[Department Circular No. 308.  Public Debt.]

## REDEMPTION AND EXCHANGE OF WAR-SAVINGS CERTIFICATES, SERIES OF 1918.

TREASURY DEPARTMENT,
OFFICE OF THE SECRETARY,
*Washington, November 9, 1922.*

*To Holders of War-Savings Certificates of the Series of 1918, Post-masters, Federal Reserve Banks, and Others Concerned:*

United States War-Savings Certificates of the Series of 1918 become due and payable January 1, 1923, according to their terms. The Secretary of the Treasury offers special facilities for their redemption and exchange, as follows:

1. *General.*—Holders of War-Savings Certificates, Series of 1918, will be entitled to receive on or after January 1, 1923, $5.00 for each War-Savings Stamp of the Series of 1918 then affixed thereto. Certificates having registered stamps affixed are payable only at the post office where registered. Unregistered certificates are payable at any money-order post office or at the Treasury Department in Washington, and will likewise be accepted for payment at the Federal Reserve Banks and their branches, acting as fiscal agents of the United States. Holders may, on or after January 1, 1923, redeem their certificates in cash, at maturity value, or beginning November 15, 1922, may exchange them, at maturity value, with any necessary adjustments in cash, for Treasury Savings Certificates, Series of 1923, issued pursuant to Treasury Department Circular No. 301, dated September 30, 1922. Certificates presented for either redemption or exchange must be duly receipted in the name inscribed thereon, or, in the event of the death or disability of the owner, in the name of the person authorized to receive payment under the provisions of Treasury Department Circular No. 108, dated January 21, 1918, as amended and supplemented. Banking institutions generally will handle redemptions and exchanges for their customers, but the only official agencies are the post offices, the Federal Reserve Banks and branches, and the Treasury Department at Washington, except that duly qualified collateral agents for the issue and sale of Treasury Savings Certificates may make exchanges of unregistered War-Savings Certificates for Treasury Savings Certificates.

2 *Cash redemption.*—Holders desiring cash redemption must present their certificates, at their own expense and risk, to the post office where registered in the case of registered certificates, or to any money-order post office, Federal Reserve Bank or branch, or the Treasurer of the United States, at Washington, D. C., in the case of unregistered certificates. Holders will facilitate redemption by presenting unregistered certificates through their own banks, for recognized banking institutions generally will receive such certificates for collection, for account of the holders, or may cash unregistered certificates for the holders and get cash reimbursement therefor, at maturity value, on or after January 1, 1923, upon surrender of the certificates, duly receipted as herein provided, to the Federal Reserve Bank of the district.

(a) *Presentation before maturity.*—In order to facilitate redemptions of maturing certificates holders are offered the privilege, beginning November 15, 1922, of surrendering their certificates, receipted as of January 1, 1923, to the post office where registered in the case of registered certificates, or to any money-order post office, Federal Reserve Bank or branch, or the Treasurer of the United States, in the case of unregistered certificates, for redemption as of January 1, 1923. Postmasters receiving certificates in advance of January 1, 1923, for redemption on that date as herein provided, will transmit the certificates appropriately scheduled, and in the case of registered certificates with appropriate certification as to discharge of registration, to the nearest Federal Reserve Bank or branch. Payment for all certificates thus presented, including certificates presented direct to Federal Reserve Banks and branches or the Treasurer for redemption as of January 1, 1923, will be made by check payable to the order of the holder, which will be mailed to reach him on or about January 1, 1923.

(b) *Presentation at or after maturity.*—Cash redemption will be made only as of January 1, 1923, or on later surrender. Certificates presented on or after January 1, 1923, should be receipted as of the date of presentation. The Treasurer of the United States and the Federal Reserve Banks and branches will be prepared to make payment of matured certificates immediately upon presentation. Post offices are not required to make payment until ten days after receiving written demand therefor, but wherever practicable will waive this requirement and make payment at an earlier date. Payment of certificates surrendered through banks will be made to the bank through which presented, while payment of certificates presented direct to post offices, Federal Reserve Banks and branches, or the Treasurer of the United States will be made direct to the holder.

3. *Exchange for Treasury Savings Certificates.*—Holders desiring to exchange their War Savings Certificates for Treasury Savings Certificates must present their certificates, at their own expense and risk, to the post office where registered in the case of registered certificates, or to any money-order post office, Federal Reserve Bank or branch, or the Treasurer of the United States at Washington, in the case of unregistered certificates. Duly qualified collateral agents for the issue and sale of Treasury Savings Certificates may receive unregistered War-Savings Certificates, Series of 1918, in exchange for Treasury Savings Certificates, and will be entitled to credit, at maturity value, in their accounts with the Federal Reserve Bank of the district, for War-Savings Certificates received in exchange, duly receipted as herein provided, upon surrender to the Federal Reserve Bank. Collateral agents may make cash adjustments in connection with such exchanges, as herein provided, accounting therefor to the Federal Reserve Bank.

(a) *Presentation between November 15, 1922, and January 15, 1923.*—Exchanges of War-Savings Certificates, Series of 1918, for Treasury Savings Certificates, Series of 1923, will be made as of January 1, 1923, upon applications filed between November 15, 1922, and January 15, 1923, accompanied by the War-Savings Certificates to be exchanged, duly receipted as herein provided. Treasury Savings Certificates dated January 1, 1923, will be delivered promptly upon exchange, registered in the name and address requested by the holder of the surrendered War-Savings Certificates. Cash adjustments, if in favor of the United States, must be made upon exchange, or if in favor of the applicant, will be made as of January 1, 1923, except that in all cases where the applicant takes the maximum amount of Treasury Savings Certificates covered by the maturity value of the War-Savings Certificates surrendered, immediate payment will be made of any cash difference. Treasury Savings Certificates will not in any event be redeemable before the date of issue stated thereon.

(b) *After January 15, 1923.*—Exchanges after January 15, 1923, will be made as of the date of presentation and surrender. The Treasury Savings Certificates issued upon such exchange will be dated and carry interest from the date of the exchange, and will be registered in the name and address requested by the holder of the surrendered War-Savings Certificates. All cash adjustments on such exchanges, whether in favor of the United States or in favor of the applicant, will be made at the time of the exchange.

4. *Further Details*—(a) *Forms.*—In presenting War-Savings Certificates, Series of 1918, for redemption or exchange, whether in advance of January 1, 1923, or on or after that date, holders may use Form P. D. 750, copies of which may be obtained upon application from any post office, any Federal Reserve Bank or branch, or the Treasury Department, Washington, D. C. A copy of this form, giving examples of exchanges of War-Savings Certificates for Treasury Savings Certificates, is attached to this circular as an exhibit.[1]

(b) *Procedure in case of death or disability of the owner.*—The provisions of Treasury Department Circular No. 108, dated January 21, 1918, as amended and supplemented, further define the rights of holders of War-Savings Certificates and subject to the provisions hereof will govern the presentation and surrender of certificates for redemption or exchange in the event of the death or disability of the owner. Where certificates are inscribed in the name of a deceased owner and the estate is being administered in a court of competent jurisdiction, the certificates should be receipted by the legal representative of the estate and accompanied by a certificate of his appointment or by duly certified copies of the letters testamentary or letters of administration, as the case may be. Certificates inscribed in the names of minors should be receipted by the legal guardian, or, if there is no guardian, by the minor himself if of sufficient competency and understanding to sign the receipt and comprehend the nature thereof, or, if not of sufficient competency and understanding, receipted for the minor by the parent or natural guardian with whom the minor resides. Holders may obtain further information as to the provisions of the circular from their own banks or post offices.

(c) *Limitation of holdings.*—Under the provisions of Section 6 of the Act of Congress approved September 24, 1917, as amended, it is not lawful for any one person at any one time to hold War-Savings Certificates of the Series of 1918, to an aggregate amount exceeding $5,000 (maturity value). Holders may, however, redeem their excess holdings in accordance with the provisions of Treasury Department Circular No. 178, dated January 15, 1920, as amended and supplemented.

(d) *Further information.*—Any further information which may be desired as to the redemption or exchange of War-Savings Certificates

---

[1] See Exhibit 65, p. 238.

of the Series of 1918 may be obtained from post offices, Federal Reserve Banks and branches, or the Treasury Department, Division of Loans and Currency, Washington, D. C.

5. The Secretary of the Treasury may at any time or from time to time prescribe supplemental or amendatory rules and regulations governing the redemption and exchange of War-Savings Certificates, Series of 1918.

A. W. MELLON,
*Secretary of the Treasury.*

EXHIBIT 64.

**LETTER OF SECRETARY OF THE TREASURY, DATED NOVEMBER 13, 1922, TO BANKS AND TRUST COMPANIES AS TO REDEMPTION AND EXCHANGE OF WAR-SAVINGS CERTIFICATES OF THE SERIES OF 1918.**

NOVEMBER 13, 1922.

DEAR SIR: About $625,000,000, maturity value, of War-Savings Certificates of the Series of 1918 become due and payable January 1, 1923, according to their terms. These certificates are in the hands of millions of holders throughout the United States, and for their convenience the Treasury is offering special facilities for cash redemption or exchange into Treasury Savings Certificates of the Series of 1923, including provision for presentation before January 1, 1923. The Treasury believes that banking institutions generally will wish to assist their customers in making redemptions and exchanges, and I am writing you this letter in order to outline the principal features of the Treasury's plans for dealing with the maturing certificates. In this connection I am enclosing copies of the official form of Request for Redemption or Exchange (Form P. D. 750), and the official Treasury Department Circular (No. 308) setting forth the regulations which govern redemption and exchange. Additional copies of the form and circular may be obtained upon application from the Federal Reserve Banks, which will also be prepared to furnish information covering specific cases which may arise.

Holders of War-Savings Certificates of the Series of 1918 may either redeem their certificates for cash on or after January 1, 1923, or may exchange them at maturity value for the new Treasury Savings Certificates of the Series of 1923, which will be issued immediately under date of January 1, 1923, when the old certificates are presented between November 15, 1922, and January 15, 1923. Holders who take all the Treasury Savings Certificates on such exchange that their maturing War-Savings Certificates will purchase will also get immediate payment of any cash due them on the exchange. Exchanges after January 15, 1923, with any necessary adjustments in cash, will be made as of the date of the exchange. In order to facilitate redemptions of certificates which holders desire to redeem in cash, the Treasury also offers the privilege of advance presentation of the certificates for redemption as of January 1, 1923, checks covering the maturity value of the certificates thus surrendered to be drawn payable to the order of the holder and mailed, by Federal Reserve Banks and branches or the Treasury Department, as the case may be, so as to reach the holder on or about January 1, 1923.

Banks throughout the United States can greatly facilitate these transactions by extending all possible aid to their customers in effecting redemptions and exchanges. Recognized banking institutions which cash unregistered certificates for their customers may get cash reimbursement therefor, on or after January 1, 1923, from the Federal Reserve Bank of the district upon surrender of the certificates to the Federal Reserve Bank, duly receipted as provided in the official circular, and both the Treasury and the Federal Reserve Banks will in other respects endeavor to extend every facility for the handling of redemptions and exchanges through the banks. Collateral agents for the issue and sale of Treasury Savings Certificates will also be permitted to receive unregistered War-Savings Certificates on the usual terms in exchange for the new certificates, accounting to the Federal Reserve Banks for any cash adjustments.

The Treasury Savings Certificates offered in exchange give holders of maturing War-Savings Certificates an opportunity to reinvest their money in a similar United States Government security having all the advantages of War-Savings Certificates and many other attractive features. At present prices, Treasury Savings Certificates are issued at $20.50 for a $25 certificate, $82 for a $100 certificate, and $820 for a $1,000 certificate, maturing in each case five years from the date of issue, and yield about 4 per cent interest, compounded semiannually if held to maturity. Certificates having January 1, 1923, as the date of issue will thus mature on January 1, 1928, and may be redeemed before that date in accordance with their terms at the redemption values stated on the backs of the certificates, to yield about 3 per cent simple interest. The Treasury Savings Certificates now offered are issued under the provisions of Treasury Department Circular No. 301, dated September 30, 1922, will be registered on the books of the Treasury Department at Washington in order to protect the owner against loss or theft, and are exempt from the normal Federal income tax and from all State and local taxation (except estate or inheritance taxes). Any one person, that is to say, any individual (which includes each member of a family, adults and minors), as well as any firm, corporation, or association, may hold Treasury Savings Certificates of any one series to an aggregate amount not exceeding $5,000, maturity value.

The wide distribution which War-Savings Certificates had during the war was due in large measure to the splendid cooperation of the banks of the country, and now that the time has arrived for the redemption and refunding of the largest issue outstanding, the Treasury looks forward with confidence to the continued cooperation and support of the banks in the furtherance of its plans for dealing with the maturity. This is a matter in which the banks can render effective patriotic service to the Government and at the same time give valuable assistance to their own customers, by extending all their facilities for the cashing of the maturing certificates and their exchange for new certificates.

Cordially yours,

A. W. MELLON,
*Secretary.*

To the PRESIDENT OF THE BANKING INSTITUTION ADDRESSED.

Inclosures: Form P. D. 750, Treasury Department Circular No. 308, dated November 9, 1922.

## Exhibit 65.

### FORM OF REQUEST FOR REDEMPTION OR EXCHANGE OF WAR-SAVINGS CERTIFICATES, SERIES OF 1918.

(Form P. D 750).

*Important.*—War-Savings Certificates due January 1, 1923, may be presented at any time on or after November 15, 1922, for immediate exchange or for payment at maturity. Registered certificates must be presented at the post office of registration; other certificates may be presented through the applicant's own bank or trust company, or at any money-order post office, at any Federal Reserve Bank or branch, or to the Treasurer of the United States, Washington, D. C.

---

Cash redemptions of certificates will be made only as of January 1, 1923, or upon later surrender.

Exchanges for Treasury Savings Certificates, Series of 1923, will be made as of January 1, 1923, upon applications presented between November 15, 1922, and January 15, 1923, and new certificates dated January 1, 1923, will be delivered promptly upon surrender. Exchanges after January 15, 1923, will be made as of the date of surrender. Immediate payment will be made of any cash difference due you on exchange if you take the largest amount of Treasury Savings Certificates you can get for your surrendered War-Savings Certificates: in all other cases the cash difference due you will be paid as of January 1, 1923, or upon later surrender. Any cash difference due from you must accompany the application. (See examples on other side )

---

*To the Secretary of the Treasury, Washington, D. C.:*

The undersigned presents herewith—

............. War-Savings Stamps affixed to War-Savings Cer-
(How many.)
tificates, duly receipted in the name inscribed thereon, having
an aggregate maturity value of............................ $.............
Cash, to the amount of........................................ $.............
(To be applied on exchange for Treasury Savings Certificates, see examples 2 on other side.)

Total.................................................... $.............

And requests:

Cash, in the amount of....................................... $.............
(To be paid to the bank through which presented; otherwise to the applicant direct.)
Treasury Savings Certificates, having a maturity value of
$..............., as described below,[1] at an aggregate issue
price of.................................................... $.............
(Issue prices: $20.50 for a $25 certificate; $82 for a $100 certificate; and $820 for a $1,000 certificate.)

Total (which must agree with total given above)............ $.............

[1] Issue Treasury Savings Certificates, Series of 1923, as follows:

| NAME IN WHICH TREASURY SAVINGS CERTIFICATES ARE TO BE ISSUED. | POST-OFFICE ADDRESS. | NUMBER DESIRED. | DENOMINATION. | MATURITY VALUE. | ISSUE PRICE. |
|---|---|---|---|---|---|
| | | | | | |
| | | | | | |
| | | | | | |
| | | | | | |

.............................................
(Signature of applicant.)
.............................................
(Number.)          (Street.)
.............................................
(Town or city.)          (State.)

If registered War-Savings Certificates are surrendered, the postmaster must execute the following form:

[POST-OFFICE STAMP.] I hereby certify that registration cards covering the registration of ............War-Savings Stamps, Series of 1918, being all the registered (How many.) stamps surrendered with this application, are on file in this office, and that such cards have been marked "Paid." I am satisfied that the applicant who signed this request is the registered owner of the registered certificates surrendered herewith (or the authorized payee in case of death or disability.)

.............................................
(Signature of postmaster.)

.............................................
(Post office.)                    (State.)

[SEE OTHER SIDE FOR FURTHER DETAILS.]

*Exchange your War-Savings Certificates for the new Treasury Savings Certificates.*

War-Savings Certificates, Series of 1918, mature January 1, 1923, when $5 will be payable for each War-Savings Stamp, Series of 1918, then affixed thereto. The certificates may be redeemed in cash on or after January 1, 1923, or may be

EXCHANGED AT ANY TIME ON OR AFTER NOVEMBER 15, 1922, FOR TREASURY SAVINGS CERTIFICATES.

Treasury Savings Certificates are issued in denominations of $25, $100, and $1,000 (maturity value), and sold on a discount basis for $20.50, $82, and $820, respectively. The certificates mature five years from the date of issue, or may be redeemed at any time on demand, and at these prices yield 4 per cent interest per annum, compounded semiannually, if held to maturity, or 3 per cent simple interest if redeemed before maturity. The certificates are registered on the books of the Treasury Department, which protects the owner against loss or theft, and are exempt from the normal Federal income tax and from all State, county, and local taxation (except estate or inheritance taxes). Any one person—that is to say, an individual (including each member of a family, adults and minors), firm, corporation, or association—may hold Treasury Savings Certificates of any one series to an aggregate amount not exceeding $5,000 (maturity value) at any one time.

Exchanges of War-Savings Certificates for Treasury Savings Certificates, Series of 1923, will be made as of January 1, 1923, upon applications filed between November 15, 1922, and January 15, 1923, and new certificates dated January 1, 1923, will be delivered promptly upon surrender. Exchanges after January 15, 1923, will be made as of the date of surrender. War-Savings Certificates will be received by post offices, Federal Reserve Banks and branches, and the Treasury in advance of January 1, 1923, for redemption on that date, payment to be made by check to the order of the holder, which will be mailed so far as possible to reach the applicant on or about January 1, 1923.

WHAT YOU CAN GET BY EXCHANGING YOUR WAR-SAVINGS CERTIFICATES.

| MATURITY VALUE OF WAR-SAVINGS STAMPS SURRENDERED. | EXAMPLE NO. | TREASURY SAVINGS CERTIFICATES IN EXCHANGE. | | CASH AD-JUSTMENT DUE YOU. | CASH AD-JUSTMENT TO BE PAID BY YOU. |
|---|---|---|---|---|---|
| | | *Maturity value.* | *Issue price.* | | |
| $1,000 | Example 1 | $1,200@ | $984.00 | $16.00 | ..... |
| | Example 2 | 1,225@ | 1,004.50 | ..... | $4.50 |
| | Example 3 | 1,000@ | 820.00 | 180.00 | ..... |
| $500 | Example 1 | 600@ | 492.00 | 8.00 | ..... |
| | Example 2 | 625@ | 512.50 | ..... | 12.50 |
| | Example 3 | 500@ | 410.00 | 90.00 | ..... |
| $100 | Example 1 | 100@ | 82.00 | 18.00 | ..... |
| | Example 2 | 125@ | 102.50 | ..... | 2.50 |
| | Example 3 | 75@ | 61.50 | 38.50 | ..... |
| $50 | Example 1 | 50@ | 41.00 | 9.00 | ..... |
| | Example 2 | 75@ | 61.50 | ..... | 11.50 |
| | Example 3 | 25@ | 20.50 | 29.50 | ..... |
| $25 | Example 1 | 25@ | 20.50 | 4.50 | ..... |
| | Example 2 | 50@ | 41.00 | ..... | 16 00 |

These examples may be applied to other maturity values in the same relation. The cash adjustments due the United States, as in the examples numbered 2, must be paid in all cases at the time of exchange. Cash adjustments due the applicant will be paid on January 1, 1923, or upon later exchange, except that immediate payment of the cash difference will be made wherever the applicant takes the largest possible amount of Treasury Savings Certificates for his maturing War-Savings Certificates, as in the examples numbered 1. It will be noted that in no case will the cash differences payable to applicants before January 1, 1923, exceed $20, since a cash difference of $20.50 would make it possible to buy another Treasury Savings Certificate, and the applicant must take the full amount of Treasury Savings Certificates in order to get advance payment of the cash difference. Cash differences in cases like the examples numbered 3 will not be paid before January 1, 1923.

*Consult your bank or your postmaster.*

EXHIBIT 66.

**PLACARD RELATING TO THE EXCHANGE OF WAR-SAVINGS CERTIFICATES FOR NEW TREASURY SAVINGS CERTIFICATES.**

*Exchange your 1918 War-Savings Certificates for the new Treasury Savings Certificates.*

The United States Treasury offers you an opportunity to renew your investment.

War-Savings Certificates, Series of 1918, mature January 1, 1923, when $5 will be payable for each War-Savings Stamp, Series of 1918, then affixed thereto. The certificates may be redeemed in cash on or after January 1, 1923, or may be exchanged at any time on or after November 15, 1922, for Treasury Savings Certificates.

Exchanges of War-Savings Certificates for Treasury Savings Certificates, Series of 1923, will be made as of January 1, 1923, upon applications filed between November 15, 1922, and January 15, 1923, and new certificates dated January 1, 1923, will be delivered promptly upon exchange. Exchanges after January 15, 1923, will be made as of the date of surrender.

Present your War-Savings Certificates through your own bank or trust company, or direct to your post office, any Federal Reserve Bank or branch, or the Treasurer of the United States at Washington. Registered certificates must be presented to the post office where registered. War-Savings Certificates will also be received in advance of January 1, 1923, for redemption on that date, payment to be made by check to the order of the holder, which will be mailed so far as possible to reach him on or about January 1, 1923.

Treasury Savings Certificates are issued in denominations of $25, $100, and $1,000 (maturity value), and sold for $20.50, $82, and $820, respectively. The certificates mature five years from the date of issue, or may be redeemed at any time on demand, and at these prices yield about 4 per cent interest per annum compounded semiannually, if held to maturity, or about 3 per cent simple interest if redeemed before maturity. The certificates are registered on the books of the Treasury Department, which protects the owner against loss or theft, and are exempt from the normal Federal income tax and from all State, county, and local taxation (except estate or inheritance taxes). Any one person—that is to say, any individual (including each member of a family, adults and minors), or any firm, corporation, or association—may hold Treasury Savings Certificates of any one series to an aggregate amount not exceeding $5,000 (maturity value) at any one time.

*Consult your bank or your postmaster.*

A. W. MELLON,
*Secretary of the Treasury.*

NOVEMBER 15, 1922.
T. S. S.—22–22.

EXHIBIT 67.

[Supplement to Department Circular No. 178 of January 15, 1920. Loans and Currency.]

**HOLDINGS OF UNITED STATES TREASURY (WAR) SAVINGS CERTIFICATES IN EXCESS OF LEGAL LIMIT.**

TREASURY DEPARTMENT,
OFFICE OF THE SECRETARY,
*Washington, December 15, 1921.*

*To Holders of United States War-Savings Certificates and Treasury Savings Certificates, and Others Concerned:*

1. Under the provisions of section 6 of the act of Congress approved September 24, 1917, as amended by section 1402 of the Revenue Act of 1921, approved November 23, 1921, it is not lawful for any one person at any one time to hold United States Treasury (War) Savings Certificates of any one series, of whatever issue or denomination, to an aggregate amount exceeding $5,000, maturity value. The term "Treasury (War) Savings Certificates," as used herein, includes War-Savings Certificates, payments for or on account of which are evidenced by War-Savings Stamps, and Treasury Savings Certificates, issued in denominations of $25, $100, and $1,000, maturity value. Treasury Department Circular No. 178, dated January 15, 1920, is accordingly amended, effective November 23, 1921, by changing the limitation of holdings specified throughout such circular from $1,000.

maturity value, to $5,000, maturity value. For the purpose of determining whether the limitation on the holdings of United States Treasury (War) Savings Certificates, Series of 1921, by any one person has been exceeded, War-Savings Certificates, Series of 1921, and Treasury Savings Certificates, Series of 1921, issued at any time during the calendar year 1921, and Treasury Savings Certificates, New Issue, issued during December, 1921, shall all be included within the Series of 1921 of United States Treasury (War) Savings Certificates. Treasury Savings Certificates, New Issue, issued during the calendar year 1922 shall constitute the Series of 1922, and such certificates issued within any subsequent calendar year shall constitute a separate series under the serial designation of the year of issue. Treasury Savings Stamps, of the face value of $1 each and noninterest-bearing, are not included within any series of Treasury (War) Savings Certificates for the purposes of this circular.

2. By virtue of said act approved November 23, 1921, any one person may hold Treasury (War) Savings Certificates of any one series to an amount not exceeding $5,000, maturity value, whether acquired prior or subsequent to November 23, 1921. The amendment does not operate retroactively, however, as to cases in which War-Savings Certificates or Treasury Savings Certificates in excess of $1,000, maturity value, were surrendered and final settlement made before November 23, 1921, pursuant to the law then in force, and such cases can not be reopened.

A. W. MELLON,<br>
Secretary of the Treasury.

EXHIBIT 68.

[Department Circular No. 271. Public Debt.]

**SURRENDER OF WAR-SAVINGS CERTIFICATES AND STAMPS, SERIES OF 1921, TREASURY SAVINGS CERTIFICATES, SERIES OF 1921, TREASURY SAVINGS STAMPS, AND THRIFT STAMPS, HELD BY AUTHORIZED AGENTS AND SALES STATIONS.**

TREASURY DEPARTMENT,<br>
OFFICE OF THE SECRETARY,<br>
Washington, December 20, 1921.

*To agents and sales stations for the sale of War-Savings Certificates and Stamps, Series of 1921, agents for the sale of Treasury Savings Certificates, Series of 1921, Federal Reserve Banks, and others concerned:*

1. *General provisions.*—The sale of United States War-Savings Certificates and Stamps, Series of 1921, of United States Treasury Savings Certificates, Series of 1921, and of United States Thrift Stamps, will cease at the close of business on December 31, 1921. The term "Treasury Savings Certificates, Series of 1921," where it appears in this circular, shall be deemed to mean Treasury Savings Certificates, Series of 1921, issued pursuant to Treasury Department Circular No. 215, dated December 15, 1920, and not Treasury Savings Certificates, New Issue, of whatever series. Rules and regulations governing agencies for the distribution and sale, beginning December 15, 1921, of Treasury Savings Certificates, New Issue, and of Treasury Savings Stamps, are prescribed in Treasury Department Circular No. 270, dated December 15, 1921. As announced in said Circular, all cash agents and sales stations for the issue and sale of Treasury (War) Sav-

ings securities are discontinued, effective December 31, 1921, except as provided in paragraph 3 hereof. The sale of War-Savings Stamps of all series and the sale of Thrift Stamps are absolutely discontinued, effective December 31, 1921.

## SALES STATIONS.

2. Every sales station is required to surrender all War-Savings Certificates and Stamps, Series of 1921, Treasury Savings Stamps, and Thrift Stamps remaining in its hands unsold at the close of business on December 31, 1921, to an incorporated bank or trust company in the Federal Reserve district in which it is located, on or before January 20, 1922, or to the Federal Reserve Bank of the district on or before January 31, 1922. Federal Reserve Banks and incorporated banks and trust companies are hereby authorized to receive such certificates and stamps so surrendered and to make cash reimbursement in each case to the sales station for War-Savings Stamps so surrendered at the rate of $4.24 for each stamp, for Treasury Savings Stamps so surrendered at the rate of $1 for each stamp, and for Thrift Stamps so surrendered at the rate of 25 cents for each stamp. The surrender of such certificates and stamps by a sales station may be accepted by the Federal Reserve Bank or an incorporated bank or trust company only upon presentation by such sales station of its sales station identification card, or other satisfactory evidence of its designation as a sales station for the issue and sale of War-Savings Certificates and Stamps. Any incorporated bank or trust company so receiving War-Savings Certificates and Stamps, Series of 1921, Treasury Savings Stamps, or Thrift Stamps must deliver such certificates and stamps on or before January 31, 1922, to the Federal Reserve Bank of its district, together with a schedule setting forth the names of the authorized sales stations from which the stamps have been received and the number and kind of stamps received from each sales station. On receipt thereof the Federal Reserve Bank, as fiscal agent of the United States, will make cash reimbursement to such incorporated bank or trust company for the War-Savings Stamps so surrendered at the rate of $4.24 for each stamp, for the Treasury Savings Stamps so surrendered at the rate of $1 for each stamp, and for the Thrift Stamps so surrendered at the rate of 25 cents for each stamp. No Federal Reserve Bank or incorporated bank or trust company shall accept from any one sales station the surrender of War-Savings Stamps, Series of 1921, in excess of $5,000 (maturity value), without special authority from the Secretary of the Treasury.

## CASH AGENTS.

3. Every cash agent is required to surrender, on or before January 31, 1922, to the Federal Reserve Bank from which the certificates and stamps were obtained, all Treasury Savings Certificates, Series of 1921, War-Savings Certificates and Stamps, Series of 1921, Treasury Savings Stamps, and Thrift Stamps held by such agent for issue and sale to the public and remaining unsold at the close of business December 31, 1921: *Provided, however,* That any cash agent who shall have sold Treasury Savings Certificates, Series of 1921, under an approved partial-payment plan which calls for payments after December 31, 1921, with the final installment on or before September 30,

1922, will be permitted to surrender unsold stocks of such Treasury Savings Certificates until October 31, 1922. Upon any such surrender each such cash agent will be entitled to cash reimbursement, for Treasury Savings Certificates and War-Savings Stamps so surrendered at a rate equivalent to the current redemption value thereof during the month in which such surrender is made, not later than the month in which the certificates or stamps are required to be surrendered, for Treasury Savings Stamps so surrendered at the rate of $1 for each stamp, and for Thrift Stamps so surrendered at the rate of 25 cents for each stamp. No Federal Reserve Bank shall accept from any cash agent the surrender of War-Savings Stamps, Series of 1921, and Treasury Savings Certificates, Series of 1921, to an aggregate maturity value in excess of the agent's authority to hold, without special authority therefor from the Secretary of the Treasury.

### COLLATERAL AGENTS.

4. Every collateral agent is required to surrender, on or before January 31, 1922, to the Federal Reserve Bank from which the certificates and stamps were obtained, all Treasury Savings Certificates, Series of 1921, War-Savings Certificates and Stamps, Series of 1921, and Thrift Stamps, not sold before the close of business December 31, 1921, and upon such surrender shall receive appropriate credit for the certificates and stamps surrendered in its account with the Federal Reserve Bank. Every collateral agent which does not undertake the sale of Treasury Savings Certificates, New Issue, is required to surrender, and any other collateral agent at its option may surrender, unsold Treasury Savings Stamps remaining in its hands at the close of business on December 31, 1921, and upon such surrender shall receive appropriate credit for the stamps surrendered in its account with the Federal Reserve Bank.

### POST OFFICES.

5. Post offices will be required to surrender all Treasury Savings Certificates, Series of 1921, War-Savings Certificates and Stamps Series of 1921, and Thrift Stamps held by them for sale and remaining in their hands unsold at the close of business on December 31, 1921, and all duplicate registration stubs for Treasury Savings Certificates, Series of 1921, issued by them during the calendar year 1921, in accordance with instructions issued by the Postmaster General. No post office shall accept the surrender of any unissued Treasury Savings Certificates, War-Savings Certificates and Stamps, or Thrift Stamps from any agent or sales station for the sale of War-Savings Certificates or Treasury Savings Certificates other than a postal agent; but nothing herein contained shall be deemed to prevent the redemption by post offices, in regular course, of War-Savings Certificates or Thrift Stamps acquired or held by agents or sales stations on their own account.

## SURRENDER OF DUPLICATE REGISTRATION STUBS FROM TREASURY SAVINGS CERTIFICATES.

6. Every cash or collateral agent which qualified for the issue and sale of Treasury Savings Certificates, Series of 1921, is required, on or before November 30, 1922, to surrender all duplicate registration stubs from Treasury Savings Certificates, Series of 1921, issued by such agent, to the Federal Reserve Bank from which such certificates were obtained.

## SURRENDER OF BLANK WAR-SAVINGS CERTIFICATES, SERIES OF 1921, AND THRIFT CARDS.

7. Every cash or collateral agent and sales station shall surrender all blank War-Savings Certificates, Series of 1921, and may surrender all blank Thrift Cards, held by it unissued at the close of business on December 31, 1921, at the same time and in the same manner as the War-Savings Stamps, Series of 1921, surrendered by it in accordance with this circular: *Provided, however,* That no credit will be given nor reimbursement made for blank certificates or cards so surrendered.

## FEDERAL RESERVE BANKS.

8. United States Treasury Savings Certificates, Series of 1918, 1919, 1920, and 1921, will cease to be issued by Federal Reserve Banks in exchange for War-Savings Certificates of corresponding series at the close of business on December 31, 1921. On or before February 10, 1922, Federal Reserve Banks will forward to the Register of the Treasury, Washington, all Treasury Savings Certificates, Series of 1918, 1919, 1920, and 1921, War-Savings Certificates and Stamps, Series of 1921, and Thrift Stamps remaining in their hands unissued and unsold on such date. Federal Reserve Banks will forward to the Register of the Treasury, Washington, on or before November 10, 1922, all Treasury Savings Certificates, Series of 1921, permitted to be surrendered by cash agents until October 31, 1922, pursuant to paragraph 3 hereof. Federal Reserve Banks will also forward to the Secretary of the Treasury, Division of Loans and Currency, Washington, on or before December 10, 1922, all duplicate registration stubs from Treasury Savings Certificates, Series of 1921, surrendered by cash or collateral agents pursuant to paragraph 6 hereof.

## MISCELLANEOUS PROVISIONS.

9. The provisions of this circular as to the surrender of Treasury Savings Certificates, Series of 1918, 1919, 1920, and 1921, War-Savings Certificates and Stamps, Series of 1921, United States Treasury Savings Stamps, and United States Thrift Stamps, apply only to unissued certificates and stamps, and to duly authorized agents and sales stations, and in the case of cash or collateral agents, apply only to such certificates and stamps as were obtained by such agents from the Federal Reserve Bank to which they are presented for surrender. No incorporated bank or trust company is

authorized hereunder to accept the surrender of any such certificates or stamps from any one other than a duly authorized sales station for the sale thereof, and no Federal Reserve Bank is authorized hereunder to accept the surrender of any Treasury Savings Certificates, War-Savings Certificates and Stamps, Treasury Savings Stamps, or Thrift Stamps, from any cash or collateral agent which were not obtained from it by such agent: *Provided, however,* That Federal Reserve Banks are authorized to accept War-Savings Certificates and Stamps, Treasury Savings Stamps, and Thrift Stamps from incorporated banks and trust companies, in accordance with the provisions of paragraph 2 hereof. Except as herein otherwise specifically provided in paragraph 3, no Federal Reserve Bank is authorized hereunder to accept the surrender of any certificates or stamps (except blank War-Savings Certificates and Thrift Cards) presented to it after January 31, 1922, without special authority therefor in each case from the Secretary of the Treasury.

10. All cases in which Treasury Savings Certificates, Series of 1921, War-Savings Stamps, Series of 1921, Treasury Savings Stamps, or Thrift Stamps are presented for surrender hereunder contrary to the provisions of this circular should be promptly referred to the Secretary of the Treasury, Division of Loans and Currency, Washington, for further instructions.

11. The Secretary of the Treasury may at any time withdraw this circular as a whole, or amend from time to time any of the provisions thereof, and may, from time to time, make any supplemental or amendatory regulations which shall not modify or impair the terms and conditions of United States Treasury (War) Savings securities, of whatever issue or denomination, issued in pursuance of the act of September 24, 1917, as amended and supplemented.

A. W. MELLON,
*Secretary of the Treasury.*

## EXHIBIT 69.

[Department Circular No. 149, Revised.  Public Debt.]

### REGULATIONS CONCERNING UNITED STATES TREASURY SAVINGS CERTIFICATES.

TREASURY DEPARTMENT,
OFFICE OF THE SECRETARY,
*Washington, August 1, 1922.*

*To Holders of Treasury Savings Certificates, and Others Concerned:*

Treasury Department Circular No. 149, Revised, dated June 25, 1921, as heretofore amended and extended, is hereby amended to read as follows:

The following Treasury Department regulations further define the rights of holders of Treasury Savings Certificates of all issues and series, issued under authority of the act approved September 24, 1917, as amended and supplemented, and determine the terms and conditions upon which such certificates will be payable in case of the death or disability of the owner:

# I.

## CERTIFICATES NOT TRANSFERABLE.

Treasury Savings Certificates are not transferable and are payable only to the owner named thereon except in case of the death or disability of the owner and in such case will be payable or may be reissued as hereinafter provided.

# II.

## PAYMENT.

1. Owners of Treasury Savings Certificates will be entitled to receive, at or after maturity thereof, the respective face amounts as stated thereon, or at their option will be entitled to receive, prior to maturity, the lesser amounts indicated for the respective months following purchase in the table printed on the back of each certificate with respect to certificates of the denomination concerned. Payment will be made in each case upon presentation and surrender of the certificates by mail or otherwise at the Treasury Department, Division of Loans and Currency, Washington, D. C., and upon compliance with all other provisions thereof, provided the form of demand for payment appearing on the back thereof shall be properly signed by the owner in the presence of, and duly certified by, a United States postmaster (who should also affix the official postmark of his office), an executive officer of an incorporated bank or trust company (who should also affix the corporate seal of the bank or trust company), or any other person duly designated by the Secretary of the Treasury for the purpose. In case of the death of the owner, the form of demand for payment on the back of the certificate should not be executed, but the special procedure hereinafter prescribed must be followed.

2. Treasury Savings Certificates will not bear interest after maturity and accordingly should be promptly presented for payment at maturity.

# III.

## TAX EXEMPTION.

Treasury Savings Certificates shall be exempt, both as to principal and interest, from all taxation now or hereafter imposed by the United States, any State, or any of the possessions of the United States, or by any local taxing authority, except (a) estate or inheritance taxes, and (b) graduated additional income taxes, commonly known as surtaxes, and excess-profits and war-profits taxes, now or hereafter imposed by the United States, upon the income or profits of individuals, partnerships, associations, or corporations. The interest on an amount of bonds and certificates authorized by the act approved September 24, 1917, and amendments thereto, the principal of which does not exceed in the aggregate $5,000, owned by any individual, partnership, association, or corporation, shall be exempt from the taxes provided for in clause (b) above.

## IV.

### LOST, STOLEN, OR DESTROYED CERTIFICATES.

In the event of the loss, theft, or destruction of a Treasury Savings Certificate duly issued and registered in accordance with the regulations and instructions governing issue and registration, the registered owner may apply to the Treasury Department, Division of Loans and Currency, Washington, D. C., on Form L. & C. 275, hereto annexed, either for the issuance of a duplicate certificate or for the payment of the original certificate. On being satisfied of the facts as to loss, theft, or destruction, the Secretary of the Treasury will, after not less than three months have elapsed from the time of application, issue to the registered owner a duplicate certificate or make payment of the original certificate, but no duplicate certificate will be issued after maturity of the original. Any duplicate certificate so issued shall be marked "duplicate," but shall receive a new number and bear a notation of the number of the original certificate. Appropriate notation of the issue of the duplicate certificate or payment of the original certificate will be made on the registration records of the Treasury Department. The Secretary of the Treasury may, in special cases where he deems the facts warrant such action, require the claimant to give a bond of indemnity, with approved surety or sureties, against any claim that may thereafter be made on the original certificate. The duplicate certificate when issued shall stand for all purposes in the place and stead of the original lost, stolen, or destroyed certificate. After the issuance of a duplicate certificate, or the payment of the original certificate, the original shall cease to have validity for any purpose, and if recovered shall be surrendered to the Treasury Department, Division of Loans and Currency, Washington, D. C., for cancellation.

## V.

### CREDITORS' RIGHTS.

Payment of Treasury Savings Certificates will be made to the owner named thereon, notwithstanding any lien, attachment, trustee process, garnishment, judgment, receivership, levy, execution, order, decree, or similar process of law, equity, or in bankruptcy directed against the owner thereof, but nothing herein contained shall excuse the owner from full compliance with, or performance of, any lawful judgment, order, or decree of a court of competent jurisdiction with reference to disposition of the proceeds of the certificate. Neither the United States of America nor any officer or employee thereof shall be a proper or necessary party to any suit or action with reference to such certificate or the proceeds thereof or be bound by any judgment, order, or decree rendered or entered therein.

## VI.

### HOLDING OF TREASURY SAVINGS CERTIFICATES BY CORPORATIONS, UNINCORPORATED ASSOCIATIONS, PARTNERSHIPS, AND JOINT STOCK COMPANIES.

1. Treasury Savings Certificates may be issued and registered in the name of a corporation, unincorporated association, partnership, or joint stock company, and should bear an appropriate notation in the space provided thereon for the name of the owner, indicating whether the owner is a corporation, unincorporated association, partnership, or joint stock company. Payment of such certificates will ordinarily be made by check payable to the order of the corporation, unincorporated association, partnership, or joint stock company. No designation may be made on the certificate or registration stub of an officer or agent to receive payment on behalf of a corporation, unincorporated association, partnership, or joint stock company.

2. In the case of a certificate registered in the name of a corporation, unincorporated association, or joint stock company, the demand for payment must be signed in the name of the corporation, association, or joint stock company by a duly authorized officer of such corporation, association, or joint stock company; for example, "X Company, by John Jones, President." The fact that the demand for payment on such certificates is signed and duly certified in accordance with Section II hereof will, in general, be accepted as sufficient proof that the person signing the demand for payment in such cases is duly authorized to execute the demand on behalf of the corporation, association, or joint stock company; provided, however, that the officer before whom the demand for payment is signed and by whom it is certified shall in no case be the officer signing the demand for payment.

3. In the case of a certificate registered in the name of a partnership, the demand for payment should be signed in the firm name by one of the partners as a member of the firm; for example, "Smith and Jones, by John Jones, a member of the firm." In such cases the fact that the demand for payment is signed and duly certified in accordance with Section II hereof will, in general, be accepted as sufficient proof that the person signing the demand for payment is a member of the firm.

4. In case payment of a certificate registered in the name of a partnership is demanded by an agent of the partnership, the demand for payment must be signed in the firm name by such person as agent; for example, "Smith and Jones, by Henry White, agent," and the certificate must be accompanied by a duly executed power of attorney signed by all the partners, authorizing such person to demand and receive payment of the certificate on behalf of the partnership.

## VII.

### FIDUCIARIES.

Treasury Savings Certificates may be issued and registered in the names of fiduciaries in their representative capacities, and should be inscribed in the names of such fiduciaries, followed by as complete as possible a description of the capacity in which they hold the certificates. Payment of any such certificate will, in general, be made to such fiduciary without further proof of his authority than the fact that the demand for payment on the certificates is duly signed by him and duly certified in accordance with Section II hereof. The demand for payment in such cases should be signed by the fiduciary in the same manner as his name and designation as fiduciary appear on the face of the certificate. In the event of the death or disqualification of such fiduciary, payment or reissue may be made, in the discretion of the Secretary of the Treasury, to the person or persons in his opinion beneficially entitled thereto. In determining whether the $5,000 limitation on the holdings of any one person has been exceeded, the full maturity value of Treasury (War) Savings Certificates of any one series held for the benefit of such person in the name of a fiduciary or fiduciaries shall be added to the full maturity value of Treasury (War) Savings Certificates, of the same series, of whatever issue or denomination, held by such person in his own name, and the sum must not exceed $5,000 (maturity value). Certificates so registered will not, however, be considered a part of the holdings of the fiduciary so as to diminish the $5,000 (maturity value) of certificates of any one series which he may own in his own right.

## VIII.

### TREASURY SAVINGS CERTIFICATES ISSUED TO TWO PERSONS.

Treasury Savings Certificates may be issued and registered in the names of two persons (but not more than two) in the alternative, as, for instance, "John Jones OR Mary Jones." Such certificates will be payable to either person named thereon without requiring the signature of the other person and to the survivor of them without proof of the other person's death, and upon payment to either person the other shall cease to have any interest therein. No other form of registration in the names of two persons is authorized, except to the extent permitted by Sections VII and XI of this circular. When certificates are issued in the alternative, the names and addresses of both persons shall be inscribed on the certificates and on the registration stubs. In determining whether the $5,000 limitation on the holdings of any one person has been exceeded, the full maturity value of Treasury (War) Savings Certificates of any one series, of whatever issue or denomination, held with any other person shall be added to the full maturity value of such certificates held individually, and the sum must not exceed $5,000 (maturity value) of the same series.

## IX.

### INFANT HOLDERS OF TREASURY SAVINGS CERTIFICATES.

1. Treasury Savings Certificates may be issued and registered in the name of an infant.
2. If a guardian of the property has, to the knowledge of the Secretary of the Treasury, been appointed for an infant owner of a Treasury

Savings Certificate, payment of the certificate will be made only to such guardian, upon presentation of proof satisfactory to the Secretary of the Treasury of his appointment and qualification. In general, such proof should consist of a certificate of the proper court or a certified copy of the order of the court appointing such guardian, showing the appointment and qualification of the guardian, and that such appointment is still in full force and effect. In each case, the certificate of the court should be dated not more than three months prior to the date of the presentation of such Treasury Savings Certificate to the Treasury Department for payment.

3. If no guardian of the property has, to the knowledge of the Secretary of the Treasury, been appointed for an infant owner of a Treasury Savings Certificate, payment of such certificate will be made direct to such infant owner, provided such infant is, at the time payment of such certificate is demanded, of sufficient competency and understanding, in the opinion of the Secretary of the Treasury to sign his name to the demand and to comprehend the nature thereof. In general, the fact that the demand for payment has been signed by the infant and duly certified in accordance with Section II hereof, will be accepted as sufficient proof of such competency and understanding on the part of such infant. In the event that such infant is not, in the opinion of the Secretary of the Treasury, of such competency and understanding, payment will be made to either parent of the infant with whom the infant resides, or, in the event that such infant resides with neither parent, then to the person with whom such infant resides. In making demand for payment, the representative shall sign the infant's name as well as the name of such representative. Application should be made on Form L. & C. 277, hereto annexed.

4. Issuance of a duplicate for, or payment of, a lost, stolen, or destroyed certificate which has been registered in the name of an infant will be made to the infant or to a representative, as hereinbefore provided, upon compliance with the regulations respecting lost, stolen, or destroyed certificates, contained in Section IV hereof.

## X.

### DISABILITY OF HOLDERS OF TREASURY SAVINGS CERTIFICATES.

1. Payment of a Treasury Savings Certificate held by a person who has been legally declared to be incompetent to manage his affairs and for whose estate a conservator or other legally constituted representative has been appointed by a court of competent jurisdiction, to the knowledge of the Secretary of the Treasury, will be made only to such conservator or other legal representative, upon the presentation of proof satisfactory to the Secretary of the Treasury of his appointment and qualification. In general, such proof should consist of a certificate of the proper court or a certified copy of the order of the court appointing such conservator or other legal representative showing the appointment and qualification of such conservator or other legal representative and that such appointment is still in full force and effect. In each case, the certificate of the court should be dated not more than three months prior to the date of the presentation of such Treasury Savings Certificate to the Treasury Department for payment.

2. In general, the fact that the demand for payment on a Treasury Savings Certificate has been signed and duly certified in accordance with Section II hereof, will be accepted as sufficient proof of the competency and understanding of the person signing the demand for payment.

## XI.

### REGISTRATION OF TREASURY SAVINGS CERTIFICATES IN FAVOR OF BENEFICIARY.

1. Treasury Savings Certificates may be issued and registered payable to a single designated beneficiary in case of death of the registered owner, as, for instance, "John Smith, payable on death to Mary Smith." In that event the issuing agent shall at the time of issue inscribe on the certificate and on the registration stub the words "Payable on death to ———," inserting the name and address of the beneficiary. Such certificates will be payable to the registered owner during his lifetime, and to the beneficiary upon death of the registered owner, provided the beneficiary be then living. In that case the beneficiary will be entitled either to reissue or to payment of the certificate, at his option. Application should be made on Form L. & C. 274, hereto annexed. Reissue of a certificate registered payable to a beneficiary will be made only in the name of such beneficiary and only where upon reissue the beneficiary will not hold Treasury (War) Savings Certificates of the same series to an aggregate amount exceeding $5,000 (maturity value). If the beneficiary shall predecease the registered owner, the certificate will be payable to the owner as though such beneficial registration had not been made. Second registration in favor of another beneficiary, or change of beneficiary, will not be permitted.

2. Should the beneficiary die after the death of the registered owner, but before payment of the certificate, the regulations covering payment or reissue of certificates held by a deceased owner shall govern the payment or reissue of the certificate as though the beneficiary were such deceased owner.

## XII.

### PAYMENT OR REISSUE OF TREASURY SAVINGS CERTIFICATE HELD BY DECEASED OWNER.

In the case of the death of the registered owner of a Treasury Savings Certificate (other than a certificate registered payable to a beneficiary), payment will be made, or at their election the certificate will be reissued, to the persons and in the manner hereinafter provided:

(a) If the decedent leave a will which is duly admitted to probate, or die intestate and the estate of such decedent is administered in a court of competent jurisdiction, payment of such certificate will be made only to the duly appointed representative of the estate, and reissue will be made only at his request. Application for payment or reissue of the certificate should be made on Form L. & C. 279, hereto annexed Administration will be required prior to payment or reissue of a Treasury Savings Certificate in all cases where the gross personal estate of the deceased owner exceeds $500 in value, unless it appears to the satisfaction of the Secretary of the Treasury that administration of the estate of such decedent is not required in the State of the decedent's domicile.

(b) In case no legal representative of the decedent's estate is appointed and either the gross personal estate does not exceed $500 in value or it appears to the satisfaction of the Secretary of the Treasury that administration of the estate of such decedent is not required in the State of the decedent's domicile, the certificate will be paid or reissued to and on the demand of the persons equitably entitled thereto in the opinion of the Secretary of the Treasury, in the following order of classes:

First. The certificate will be paid to the creditor for the reasonable funeral expenses, expenses of the last illness, or other preferred claims against the decedent's estate, or person paying such creditor, to the extent of such preferred claims. Application should be made on Form L. & C. 273, hereto annexed.

Second. The certificate will be paid or reissued to the husband, wife, or next of kin of the deceased, in the following order of preference:

(1) Husband or wife;
(2) Child or children;
(3) Father;
(4) Mother;
(5) Any other of the next of kin of the deceased;

provided, however, that nothing herein contained shall require the payment or reissue of a single certificate to more than one person. Application should be made upon Form L. & C. 276, hereto annexed.

(c) In case the gross personal estate of the decedent exceeds $500 in value, and it is claimed that administration of the estate is not required in the State of the decedent's domicile, the application for payment or reissue of the Treasury Savings Certificates owned by the decedent must be accompanied by an agreement by all of the legal heirs of the decedent who are of lawful age and competent and by the legally appointed guardians or conservators of any minor or incompetent heirs, duly acknowledged under oath before a notary public or other officer authorized by law to administer oaths, showing that such persons constitute all the legal heirs of the estate of the decedent or their legally appointed representatives; that all debts owing by the decedent have been paid; that administration of the estate of the decedent is not required in the State of the decedent's domicile, and that all of such heirs or their legal representatives have agreed on the distribution of the estate and consent to payment or reissue of the Treasury Savings Certificates being made to the claimant who executes the application. Such agreement must also be accompanied by the affidavits of two disinterested persons, preferably public officers of the United States or executive officers of incorporated banks or trust companies, showing that the affiants are responsible persons known to them, whose statements are worthy of the confidence of the Treasury Department. The Secretary of the Treasury may further require in special cases an affidavit or certificate from a practicing attorney or judicial officer of the State of the decedent's domicile, showing that administration of the estate of the decedent is not required in such State, and referring specifically to any statutes or any judicial decisions of the courts of such State under which exemption from administration is claimed.

## XIII.

### REISSUE.

1. In case of the reissue of a Treasury Savings Certificate pursuant to the provisions hereof, the original certificate will be retired and a new certificate of the same issue, series, denomination, date of issue, and maturity, but bearing a new serial number and inscribed and registered in the name of the person entitled to reissue of the original certificate, will be issued and registered. Reissue of certificates may be effected only at the Treasury Department, Division of Loans and Currency, Washington, D. C., on application duly executed by the person entitled to demand reissue of the certificate on the form prescribed for such purpose.

2. A Treasury Savings Certificate registered payable to a single designated beneficiary in case of death of the registered owner may be reissued in the name of such beneficiary on the death of the registered owner in accordance with the provisions of Section XI hereof.

3. A Treasury Savings Certificate registered in the name of a decedent may be reissued to the person entitled, in accordance with the provisions of Section XII hereof.

4. In no case will a Treasury Savings Certificate be reissued in the name of any person, if upon such reissue such person will hold Treasury (War) Savings Certificates of the same series to an aggregate amount exceeding $5,000 (maturity value).

## XIV.

### INHERITANCE TAXES.

Payment or reissue of Treasury Savings Certificates will be made without any deduction for inheritance, estate, or transfer taxes, either State or Federal, on death of a deceased owner; and no claim shall lie against the United States or any officer or employee thereof for failure to deduct or withhold any such tax. The person to whom payment or reissue of the certificates is made shall be liable for all such taxes, if any shall be due, and the lien thereof shall attach to the proceeds of the certificates in his hands.

## XV.

### CHANGE OF NAME.

In case the name of the owner of a Treasury Savings Certificate has, since the issuance of the certificate, been changed by marriage or by order or decree of court, the Secretary of the Treasury, upon being satisfied of the identity of the person, will accept the owner's demand for payment, provided both the new and the original name are signed.

## XVI.

### LIMITATION IN AMOUNT.

Under the provisions of section 6 of the act of Congress approved September 24, 1917, as amended and supplemented, it is not lawful for any one person at any one time to hold Treasury (War) Savings Certificates of any one series (of whatever issue or denomination) to an aggregate amount exceeding $5,000 (maturity value). As to each series, the issue of Treasury Savings Certificates and the issue of War-Savings Certificates are included within the same series of Treasury (War) Savings Certificates for the purpose of determining whether the limitation on the holdings of any one person has been exceeded. For further regulations governing holdings of Treasury (War) Savings Certificates in excess of the legal limit, see Treasury Department Circular No. 178, dated January 15, 1920, as amended and supplemented.

## XVII.

### ADMINISTRATION.

1. The administration of the foregoing regulations shall be in accordance with such forms and administrative regulations and instructions as the Secretary of the Treasury shall from time to time prescribe. The Secretary of the Treasury may in any case accept as sufficient proof of the identity or of the competency and understanding of the person making demand for payment or reissue, the fact that the demand has been signed in the presence of and duly certified by a United States postmaster, an executive officer of an incorporated bank or trust company, or any other person duly designated by the Secretary of the Treasury for the purpose.

2. The Secretary of the Treasury may make, from time to time, any further or supplemental or amendatory regulations which shall not modify or impair the terms and conditions of Treasury Savings Certificates issued pursuant to the act of Congress approved September 24, 1917, as amended and supplemented.

A. W. MELLON,
*Secretary of the Treasury.*

TREASURY DEPARTMENT –
DIVISION OF LOANS AND CURRENCY
Form L & C 273
Ed. 5,000—Aug. 1-22

APPLICATION OF UNDERTAKER, DOCTOR, OR OTHER PREFERRED CREDITOR FOR PAYMENT OF TREASURY SAVINGS CERTIFICATES.

This application should not be executed if letters of administration or letters testamentary have been issued upon the estate of the deceased, in which event Form L & C 279 should be filled out, and forwarded, with the Treasury Savings Certificates and certified copies of such letters or a duly executed certificate of appointment of such legal representative, to the Treasury Department, Division of Loans and Currency, Washington, D. C.

STATE OF ............................... } ss:
COUNTY OF............................... }

................................., being duly sworn, deposes and says:
          (Name of claimant.)
I am the ..................................................
(Undertaker who buried—Doctor who attended in last illness—Person who paid such undertaker or doctor.)
.................................. who died intestate at ......................, on the·
          (Name of deceased.)                              (Place of death.)
...... day of .........., 19.., leaving the following-described Treasury Savings Certificates, transmitted herewith:

| SERIES. | DENOMINA-TION. | SERIAL NUMBER. | NAME AND ADDRESS OF REGISTERED OWNER AS THEY APPEAR ON THE CERTIFICATE. |
|---|---|---|---|
| | | | |
| | | | |
| | | | |
| | | | |
| | | | |
| | | | |
| | | | |

The gross personal estate of the decedent, including War-Savings Certificates and Treasury Savings Certificates, does not exceed $.........., to the best of my knowl edge and belief. Administration of the estate of the deceased has not been asked for or granted, and to the best of my knowledge and belief will not be asked for or granted. The reasonable charge for said services rendered is $.........., as evidenced by the bill hereto attached. I have ........................................ On the
(State whether payment his been received in part, and if so, the amount thereof.)
next page is a certificate by a near relative of deceased to the accuracy of this claim. I hereby make demand for the payment of $.......... from the proceeds of the above-described Treasury Savings Certificates held by the deceased, to which payment I am entitled under the regulations prescribed by the Secretary of the Treasury.

.............................................
(Signature.)
Witness............................ Address...............................
(A witness is not required unless applicant signs by X mark.) (Number.) (Street.)
Address...........................  ........................................
(City.) (State.)

Subscribed and sworn to before me by the above-named claimant this ...... day of .........., 19.....

.........................................
[OFFICIAL SEAL.]                                         *Notary Public.*

My commission expires ................, 19...

This application must be sworn to before a notary public, or other officer authorized by law to administer oaths, and unless authenticated by the official impression seal of the officer should be accompanied by a certificate from the proper official, showing that the officer was in commission on the date of the acknowledgment.

It must further be acknowledged on the following form by the applicant in the presence of, and duly certified by, a United States postmaster (who should also affix the official postmark of his office), an executive officer of an incorporated bank or trust company (who should also affix the corporate seal of the bank or trust company), or any other person duly designated by the Secretary of the Treasury for the purpose.
Personally appeared before me..............................., known
(Name of applicant.)
or proved to me to be............................... the original owner
(Undertaker who buried—Doctor who attended in last illness—Person who paid such undertaker or doctor.)
whose name is inscribed on said certificates, and acknowledged the within demand to be his free act and deed.
Witness my hand and official designation:

.........................................
(Signature of attesting officer.)
[SEAL OR STAMP.]
...............................
(Official designation.)
Dated at..........................., 19...

CERTIFICATE BY A NEAR RELATIVE OF DECEASED AS TO ACCURACY OF PREFERRED CLAIM.

..............................., 19..
I hereby certify that the bill submitted by......................................
for the sum of $.......... for ......................................
(Funeral, medical, or other preferred.)
expenses of......................................, deceased, is correct and just and
(Name of owner of certificate.)
remains unpaid.

.........................................
(Signature or X mark.)
.........................................
(Relationship.)
Address...........................
(Number.) (Street.)
.........................................
(City.) (State.)
Witness......................................
(A witness is not required unless applicant signs by X mark.)
Address......................................

The Treasury Savings Certificates must be forwarded with this application.

TREASURY DEPARTMENT
DIVISION OF LOANS AND CURRENCY
Form L & C 274
Ed. 5,000—Aug. 1-22

APPLICATION BY BENEFICIARY FOR PAYMENT OR REISSUE OF TREASURY SAVINGS CERTIFICATES.

STATE OF..............................
COUNTY OF.............................}ss:

...........................(Name of applicant.).........., being duly sworn, deposes and says:

I am the identical person designated on the following-described Treasury Savings Certificates, transmitted herewith, as beneficiary thereof in case of death of the registered owner, to wit:

| SERIES. | DENOMINA-TION. | SERIAL NUMBER. | NAME AND ADDRESS AS THEY APPEAR ON THE CERTIFICATE. |
|---|---|---|---|
| .......... | .......... | .......... | Registered Owner................................ |
| .......... | .......... | .......... | ................................ |
| .......... | .......... | .......... | Beneficiary................................ |
| .......... | .......... | .......... | ................................ |

The registered owner thereof was........................................, who
(Name of registered owner.)
died at ...................., on ...................., 19..; and the decedent's resi-
(Place of death.)         (Date of death.)
dence at the date of his death was........................................
(Number.)   (Street.)   (Town or city.)   (State.)

Hereto attached is a certificate of death of said registered owner, issued by the public authorities of the place of death.

(Strike out if no public certificate is issued in the community and see that the affidavit of death on the next page is properly executed.)

I am the person entitled to payment of the above-described certificates, and hereby make demand for { payment / reissue } thereof to me. The decedent's estate does not hold, and

(Strike out method not desired.)

in case of such reissuance I shall not hold, Treasury (War) Savings Certificates of any one series, of whatever issue or denomination, to an aggregate amount exceeding $5,000, maturity value.

Witness................................           ................................
(A witness is not required unless appli-           (Signature or X mark of applicant.)
cant signs by X mark.)

Address............................           Address........................
                                                  (Number.)         (Street.)
                                              ................................
Subscribed and sworn to before me this .......... day of ...................., 19..
[OFFICIAL SEAL.]                              ................................
                                                            Notary Public.
My commission expires...................., 19..

This application must be sworn to before a notary public, or other officer authorized by law to administer oaths, and unless authenticated by the official impression seal of the officer should be accompanied by a certificate from the proper official, showing that the officer was in commission on the date of the acknowledgment.

It must further be acknowledged on the following form by the applicant in the presence of, and duly certified by, a United States postmaster (who should also affix the official postmark of his office), an executive officer of an incorporated bank or trust company (who should also affix the corporate seal of the bank or trust company), or any other person duly designated by the Secretary of the Treasury for the purpose.

Personally appeared before me ................................, known
(Name of applicant.)
or proved to me to be the designated beneficiary of the within-described certificates, and acknowledged the within demand to be his free act and deed.

Witness my hand and official designation:

[SEAL OR STAMP.]                              ................................
                                              (Signature of attesting officer.)
                                              ................................
                                              (Official designation.)
Dated at ...................., 19..
14263—FI 1922——17

## AFFIDAVIT OF DEATH OF DECEASED OWNER.

(To be used only when the authorities of the place of death do not issue a death certificate.)

STATE OF ................................ }ss:
COUNTY OF ..............................

Personally appeared before me ...................... and ......................
residents of the .................. of ...................., county of ..................
State of.................., who, being severally sworn, declare, each for himself,
that they were acquainted with the said decedent, and know that he is deceased;
that they know the claimant to be the identical person designated as beneficiary
of the above-described Treasury Savings Certificates in case of the death of the registered owner thereof; and further, that they have no interest directly or indirectly
in this claim.

...............................         ...............................
(Signature.)                               (Address.)

...............................         ...............................
(Signature.)                               (Address.)

Subscribed and sworn to before me this .......... day of ...................., 19..

[OFFICIAL SEAL.]                           ...............................
                                                 *Notary Public.*

My commission expires ...................., 19..

This affidavit must be sworn to before a notary public, or other officer authorized by law to administer
oaths, and unless authenticated by the official impression seal of the officer should be accompanied by a
certificate from the proper official, showing that the officer was in commission on the date of the acknowledgment.

The Treasury savings certificates must be forwarded with this application.

-----

TREASURY DEPARTMENT
DIVISION OF LOANS AND CURRENCY
Form L & C 275
Ed. 10,000—Aug. 1-22

## APPLICATION FOR THE ISSUE OF DUPLICATES OR FOR PAYMENT OF LOST, STOLEN, OR DESTROYED TREASURY SAVINGS CERTIFICATES.

STATE OF ................................ }ss:
COUNTY OF..............................

........................................., being duly sworn, deposes and says:
(Name of applicant.)

I am the original owner of the following-described Treasury Savings Certificates:

| SERIES. | DENOMINA-TION. | SERIAL NUMBER. | NAME AND ADDRESS OF REGISTERED OWNER AS THEY APPEAR ON THE CERTIFICATE. |
|---------|----------------|----------------|------------------------------------------------------------------------|
| ............... | ............... | ............... | ............................................................ |
| ............... | ............... | ............... | ............................................................ |
| ............... | ............... | ............... | ............................................................ |
| ............... | ............... | ............... | ............................................................ |

which have been ............................... in the following manner:
(Lost, stolen, or destroyed.)

State fully every material fact and circumstance as to the loss, theft, or destruction of the above-described certificates, showing where the certificates were placed or last seen; whether under lock and key;
whether accessible to persons other than the owner; in case of theft, what is known of the identity of the
thief and what steps have been taken to recover the certificates; in case of loss, how it occurred and whether
thorough search has been made; in case of destruction, how it occurred, whether any portions of the certificates remain, and how the fact of destruction is known. If any portions of the certificates remain, they
should be carefully packed and forwarded with this application. In case the certificates were accessible
to any person other than the applicant at the time of the alleged loss, theft, or destruction, an affidavit by
such person should be presented setting forth his knowledge of the existence of the certificates and of the
fact of their loss, theft, or destruction. In case it is not possible to procure such affidavits the affidavit of
the applicant should state why such affidavits are not presented.

............................................................................
............................................................................
............................................................................
............................................................................
............................................................................

Annexed hereto is an affidavit of a responsible person to whom I am well known,
which sets forth his belief that the statements herein are worthy of the confidence
of the Treasury Department.

I hereby make demand for payment (or duplicates) of the above-described certifi-
(Strike out method not desired.)
cates, to which I am entitled under the regulations prescribed by the Secretary of
the Treasury. I do not hold Treasury (War) Savings Certificates of any one series,
of whatever issue or denomination, to an aggregate amount exceeding $5,000, maturity
value.

Witness..................................  ........................................
(A witness is not required unless applicant  (Signature of applicant.)
signs by X mark )

Address..............................  Address ..................................
(Number.)         (Street.)

........................................
(Town or city.)      (State.)

Subscribed and sworn to before me this .......... day of ................, 19

[OFFICIAL SEAL.]

........................................
*Notary Public.*

My commission expires..................., 19

This application must be sworn to before a notary public, or other officer authorized by law to administer
oaths, and unless authenticated by the official impression seal of the officer should be accompanied by a
certificate from the proper official, showing that the officer was in commission on the date of the acknowledgment.

If payment is demanded, the application must further be acknowledged on the
following form by the applicant in the presence of, and duly certified by, a United
States postmaster (who should also affix the official postmark of his office), an executive
officer of an incorporated bank or trust company (who should also affix the corporate
seal of the bank or trust company), or any other person duly designated by the Secretary of the Treasury for the purpose.

Personally appeared before me ..........................., known or proved
(Name of applicant.)
to me to be the original owner whose name is inscribed on the within-described certificates, and acknowledged the within demand to be his free act and deed.
Witness my hand and official designation:

........................................
(Signature of attesting officer.)

[SEAL OR STAMP.]

........................................
(Official designation.)

Dated at ..........................., 19

( *This affidavit must be executed by a responsible person to whom the applicant is well known, preferably an officer
of the United States, or an executive officer of an incorporated bank or trust company.*)

STATE OF .............................. ⎫
⎬ *ss:*
COUNTY OF .............................. ⎭

........................................, being duly sworn, deposes and says:
I have known ........................., who is the identical person
named in the above application, for .......... years, and I believe his statements in
the within affidavit to be worthy of the confidence of the Treasury Department.

........................................
(Signature of deponent.)

Address ..................................
(Number.)         (Street.)

........................................
(Town or city.)      (State.)

Subscribed and sworn to before me this .......... day of ..................., 19

[OFFICIAL SEAL.]

........................................
*Notary Public.*

My commission expires ..................., 19

This affidavit must be sworn to before a notary public, or other officer authorized by law to administer oaths, and unless authenticated by the official impression seal of the officer should be accompanied
by a certificate from the proper official showing that the officer was in commission on the date of the
acknowledgment.

TREASURY DEPARTMENT
DIVISION OF LOANS AND CURRENCY
Form L. & C. 276
Ed. 25,000—Aug. 1-22.

APPLICATION FOR PAYMENT OR REISSUE OF TREASURY SAVINGS CERTIFICATES HELD
BY DECEASED OWNER TO PERSON OTHER THAN A DULY APPOINTED LEGAL REPRE-
SENTATIVE OR PREFERRED CREDITOR.

(See instructions on page 3 of this form.)

STATE OF............................ } ss:
COUNTY OF............................

........................................, being duly sworn, deposes and says:
(Name of applicant.)

I reside at ...................., and am ................................, of......
(Residence of applicant.)          (Relationship to decedent, if any.)

........................., deceased. Said decedent died on the ..............
(Name of owner of certificates.)                                (Date of death.)
day of ...................., 19.., at ...................., and was at the time
                                        (Place of death.)
of death legally domiciled at ...................., county of ...................,
State of .................... No executor or administrator of said decedent has
been appointed by any court. The funeral expenses and expenses of last illness
have been paid by ..............................., as evidenced by the attached
receipted bills, out of funds of the estate (or out of personal funds).
                    (Strike out words not applicable.)
To the best of my knowledge and belief said decedent was at the time of his death
the owner of the following-described Treasury Savings Certificates, transmitted
herewith:

| SERIES. | DENOMI-NATION. | SERIAL NUMBER. | NAME AND ADDRESS OF REGISTERED OWNER AS THEY APPEAR ON THE CERTIFICATE. |
|---------|----------------|----------------|-----------------------------------------------------------------------|
| ...... | ...... | ...... | ................................................. |
| ...... | ...... | ...... | ................................................. |
| ...... | ...... | ...... | ................................................. |
| ...... | ...... | ...... | ................................................. |
| ...... | ...... | ...... | ................................................. |
| ...... | ...... | ...... | ................................................. |
| ...... | ...... | ...... | ................................................. |
| ...... | ...... | ...... | ................................................. |

Hereto attached is a certificate of death issued by the public authorities.
(Strike out if no public certificate is issued in the community and see that affidavit of death on next
page is properly executed.)
The value of the gross personal estate of the decedent, including War-Savings
Certificates and Treasury Savings Certificates, to the best of my knowledge and
belief, does not exceed $..........;
(If the gross personal estate exceeds $500, the procedure prescribed in paragraph 2 of Instructions must
be followed.)
To the best of my knowledge and belief the deceased left no will, and adminis-
tration of his estate has not been and will not be asked for or granted.
Said decedent left surviving only the following near relatives:

Extreme care must be taken to see that all information is fully given, in accordance with attached instructions; if the space provided below is inadequate, additional sheets may be prepared and made a
part of this application.

........................    ....................    ......    ........................
        (Name.)                  (Relationship.)         (Age.)          (Address.)

........................    ....................    ......    ........................
        (Name.)                  (Relationship.)         (Age.)          (Address.)

........................    ....................    ......    ........................
        (Name.)                  (Relationship.)         (Age.)          (Address.)

........................    ....................    ......    ........................
        (Name.)                  (Relationship.)         (Age.)          (Address.)

........................    ....................    ......    ........................
        (Name.)                  (Relationship.)         (Age.)          (Address.)

I do not know of any other person who claims to be entitled to payment of Treasury Savings Certificates standing in the name of said decedent, except the following: (If none, insert "None.")

.................................................................................

I am the person entitled to payment of the above-described certificates, and hereby make demand for $\left\{\begin{matrix}\text{payment}\\\text{reissue}\end{matrix}\right\}$ thereof to me. Decedent's estate does not hold, and in
(Strike out method not desired.)
case of such reissuance I shall not hold, Treasury (War) Savings Certificates of any one series, of whatever issue or denomination, to an aggregate amount exceeding $5,000, maturity value.

Witness.................................... ................................
         (A witness is not required unless applicant        (Signature or X mark of applicant.)
         signs by X mark.)

Address................................    Address ..............................
                               (Number.)      (Street.)

                                       ..............................
                                       (Town or city.)   (State.)

Subscribed and sworn to before me this ...... day of .........., 19..

[OFFICIAL SEAL.]              ..............................

My commission expires .........., 19..           *Notary Public.*

---

This application must be sworn to before a notary public, or other officer authorized by law to administer oaths, and unless authenticated by the official impression seal of the officer should be accompanied by a certificate from the proper official, showing that the officer was in commission on the date of the acknowledgment.

It must further be acknowledged on the following form by the applicant in the presence of, and duly certified by, a United States postmaster (who should also affix the official postmark of his office), an executive officer of an incorporated bank or trust company (who should also affix the corporate seal of the bank or trust company), or any other person duly designated by the Secretary of the Treasury for the purpose.

Personally appeared before me ............................., known or proved
                                    (Name of applicant.)

to me to be ............................. of the original owner whose name is in-
             (State connection with original owner.)
scribed on the within-described certificates, and acknowledged the above demand to be his free act and deed
Witness my hand and official designation:

                             ..............................

[SEAL OR STAMP]            (Signature of attesting officer.)

                             ..............................

Dated at .............................., 19..      (Official designation).

#### AFFIDAVIT OF DEATH OF DECEASED OWNER.

To be used only when the authorities of the place of death do not issue a death certificate.

STATE OF.................................⎫
                                   ⎬ ss:
COUNTY OF..............................⎭

Personally appeared before me............................. and ......... .........

................residents of the .................... of ....................,

county of....................State of ....................., who, being severally sworn, declare, each for himself, that they were acquainted with the said decedent, and know that he is deceased; that they know the claimant to be the identical person

named in the foregoing application and related to said decedent as a<sub>b</sub>ove stated, and
further, that they have no interest directly or indirectly in this claim.

................................    ..............................
      (Signature.)         (Address.)

................................    ..............................
      (Signature.)         (Address.)

Subscribed and sworn to before me this ...... day of .........., 19..

[OFFICIAL SEAL]

................................

My commission expires .........., 19..          *Notary Public.*

This affidavit must be sworn to before a notary public, or other officer authorized by law to administer oaths, and unless authenticated by the official impression seal of the officer should be accompanied by a certificate from the proper official, showing that the officer was in commission on the date of the acknowledgment.

### INSTRUCTIONS.

1. This blank must be used only when there is no administration of the estate in any court, and claims of all preferred creditors have been paid.

2. Pursuant to section XII of Treasury Department Circular No. 149, Revised, dated August 1, 1922, in all cases where the gross personal estate of the deceased owner exceeds $500 in value, administration will be required before payment or reissue of a Treasury Savings Certificate will be made unless it appears to the satisfaction of the Secretary of the Treasury that administration of the estate of such decedent is not required in the State of the decedent's domicile. If the gross personal estate of the deceased owner exceeds $500 in value and it is claimed that administration of the estate is not required in the State of the decedent's domicile, this application must be accompanied by an agreement by all the legal heirs of the decedent who are of lawful age and competent and by the legally appointed guardians or conservators of any minor or incompetent heirs, duly acknowledged under oath before a notary public or other officer authorized by law to administer oaths, showing that such persons constitute all the legal heirs of the estate of the decedent or their legally appointed representatives; that all debts owing by the decedent have been paid; that administration of the estate of the decedent is not required in the State of the decedent's domicile, and that all such heirs or their legal representatives have agreed on the distribution of the estate and consent to payment or reissue of the Treasury Savings Certificates being made to the claimant who executes this application. Such agreement must also be accompanied by the affidavits of two disinterested persons, preferably public officers of the United States or executive officers of incorporated banks or trust companies, showing that the affiants are responsible persons known to them, whose statements are worthy of the confidence of the Treasury Department. The Secretary of the Treasury may further require in special cases an affidavit or certificate from a practicing attorney or judicial officer of the State of the decedent's domicile showing that administration of the estate of the decedent is not required in such State, and referring specifically to any statutes or any judicial decisions of the courts of such State under which exemption from administration is claimed.

3. The application should state whether the decedent left surviving a widow or widower, child or children, or child or children of a deceased child; whether a guardian or guardians have been appointed in case any of such children are minors; and whether decedent left surviving a father or mother, or both, giving all names and addresses.

4. The application should state whether funeral expenses and physician's services during last illness have been paid; if so, by whom, and whether from personal funds or funds belonging to the estate. Receipted bills of undertaker and doctor should be attached and must agree with the affidavit in all cases. If such expenses have not been paid, the fact should be clearly stated.

5. If no official death certificate is attached, the affidavit of two disinterested persons having personal knowledge of decedent's death as printed on page 3 must be furnished.

6. If two or more persons are equally entitled to payment or reissue as next of kin under the regulations, the application should be executed by such claimants jointly, or should be accompanied by a waiver of all right, title, and interest in the Treasury Savings Certificates payment or reissue of which is requested, executed by such persons as do not join in the application.

7. Any additional facts must be stated, a knowledge of which is necessary in order that payment of the amount due the estate of the deceased owner may be made in accordance with the regulations of the Secretary of the Treasury (Treasury Department Circular No. 149, Revised, dated August 1, 1922, and any subsequent regulations in force).

8. THE TREASURY SAVINGS CERTIFICATES MUST BE FORWARDED WITH THIS APPLICATION.

TREASURY DEPARTMENT
DIVISION OF LOANS AND CURRENCY
Form L & C 277
Ed. 5,000—Aug. 1-22

### APPLICATION BY PARENT OR PERSON WITH WHOM INFANT RESIDES FOR PAYMENT OF TREASURY SAVINGS CERTIFICATES REGISTERED IN NAME OF INFANT.

STATE OF .............................⎱
⎰ *ss:*
COUNTY OF.............................⎰

.............................., being duly sworn, deposes and says:

I am the............................of...........................................
  (Father, mother, or person with whom infant resides.)

who is an infant, ...............years of age, and resides at.......................
                                              (Number.)   (Street.)

......................................................, with........................; that said
  (Town or city.)                  (State.)

infant owns the following-described Treasury Savings Certificates, transmitted herewith:

| .SERIES. | DENOMI-NATION. | SERIAL NUMBER. | NAME AND ADDRESS OF REGISTERED OWNER AS THEY APPEAR ON THE CERTIFICATE. |
|---|---|---|---|
| ............... | ............... | ............... | ................................................................ |
| ............... | ............... | ............... | ................................................................ |
| ............... | ............... | ............... | ................................................................ |
| ............... | ............... | ............... | ................................................................ |
| ............... | ............... | ............... | ................................................................ |

Said infant is not of sufficient competency and understanding to sign his name to the demand for payment printed on said certificates and to understand the nature thereof, and by reason of that fact I hereby make demand for payment of said certificates to me on behalf of said infant. Said infant does not hold Treasury (War) Savings Certificates of any one series to an aggregate amount exceeding $5,000, maturity value. No guardian of the property of said infant has been appointed by any court or otherwise.

.............................
           (Infant's name.)

Witness....................................
 (A witness is not required unless applicant signs by X mark.)

.............................
(Signature or X mark of applicant).

Address...................................

Address.......................
        (Number.)    (Street.)

.............................
  (Town or city.)      (State.)

Subscribed and sworn to before me this......day of.........., 19

[OFFICIAL SEAL.]

.............................
                   *Notary Public.*

My commission expires.........., 192

This application must be sworn to before a notary public, or other officer authorized by law to administer oaths, and unless authenticated by the official impression seal of the officer should be accompanied by a certificate from the proper official, showing that the officer was in commission on the date of the acknowledgment.

It must further be acknowledged on the following form by the applicant in the presence of, and duly certified by, a United States postmaster (who should also affix the official postmark of his office), an executive officer of an incorporated bank or trust company (who should also affix the corporate seal of the bank or trust company), or any other person duly designated by the Secretary of the Treasury for the purpose.

Personally appeared before me.............................., known or proved
(Name of payee.)
to me to be..............................of the original infant owner whose name
(State connection with original owner.)
is inscribed on the within-described certificates, and acknowledged the within demand to be his free act and deed.

I hereby certify that in my opinion said.............................. is not of
(Name of infant.)
sufficient competency and understanding to sign his name to the demand for payment and to comprehend the nature thereof.

Witness my hand and official designation:

.............................
(Signature of attesting officer.)

[SEAL OR STAMP ]

.............................
(Official designation.

Dated at.............................., 192...

The Treasury Savings Certificates must be forwarded with this application.

----

TREASURY DEPARTMENT
DIVISION OF LOANS AND CURRENCY
Form L & C 279
Ed. 35,000—Aug. 1-22

APPLICATION OF EXECUTOR OR ADMINISTRATOR FOR PAYMENT OR REISSUE OF TREASURY SAVINGS CERTIFICATES.

I am the {executor / administrator} of the estate of .............................., who died
(Name of deceased.)
at .................... on the ...... day of ..........., 19  , leaving the following-
(Place of death.)
described Treasury Savings Certificates, transmitted herewith:

| SERIES. | DENOMINATION. | SERIAL NUMBER. | NAME AND ADDRESS OF REGISTERED OWNER AS THEY APPEAR ON THE CERTIFICATE. |
|---------|---------------|----------------|----------------------------------------------------------------------|
| ........ | ............ | ............ | ...................................................... |
| ........ | ............ | ............ | ...................................................... |
| ........ | ............ | ............ | ...................................................... |
| ........ | ............ | ............ | ...................................................... |
| ........ | ............ | ............ | ...................................................... |

Attached hereto is a court certificate showing my appointment and qualification as {executor / administrator} of said estate.

(If the appointment of the executor or administrator is dated more than one year prior to the receipt of this application in the Department, the certificate must be dated not more than three months prior to such receipt, and must show that the appointment is still in full force and effect and has not been revoked.)

The decedent's estate does not hold Treasury (War) Savings Certificates of any one series, of whatever issue or denomination, to an aggregate amount exceeding $5,000, maturity value.

I hereby demand payment of the above-described Treasury Savings Certificates.

*Or*— (Strike out method not desired.)

I hereby demand reissue of the above-described Treasury Savings Certificates to
.............................., residing at ...................., ....................,
(Name in which to be reissued.)     (Number and street.)     (Town or city.)

..................., who will not after such reissuance hold Treasury (War) Savings
........(State.)
Certificates of any one series to an aggregate amount exceeding $5,000, maturity value.
...................                   ...................................
    (Date.)                                      (Signature of applicant.)
                                    No. and street ..........................

                                    Town or city...........:.............

                                         State......................

Personally appeared before me ............................., known or proved
                                          (Name of applicant.)
to me to be the{executor   }of the estate of the original owner whose name is
               {administrator}
inscribed on the within-described certificates, and signed the within demand, acknowl-
edging it to be his free act and deed.
Witness my hand and official designation:

                                    ...................................
                                         (Signature of attesting officer )
[SEAL OR STAMP]
                                    .................................
                                         (Official designation.)
Dated at .............................., 19..

The within application and demand must be properly signed by the applicant in
the presence of, and duly certified by, a United States postmaster (who should also
affix the official postmark of his office), an executive officer of an incorporated bank
or trust company (who should also affix the corporate seal of the bank or trust company), or any other person duly designated by the Secretary of the Treasury for the
purpose.
The Treasury savings certificates must be forwarded with this application.

## Exhibit 70.

[Department Circular No. 302. Public Debt.]

**SURRENDER OF TREASURY SAVINGS CERTIFICATES, NEW ISSUE,
TREASURY SAVINGS STAMPS AND TREASURY SAVINGS CARDS
HELD BY AUTHORIZED AGENTS.**

TREASURY DEPARTMENT,
OFFICE OF THE SECRETARY,
*Washington, September 30, 1922.*

*To Agents for the Sale of Treasury Savings Certificates, New Issue,
Federal Reserve Banks, and Others Concerned:*

1. *General provisions.*—Pursuant to the provisions of Treasury
Department Circular No. 301, dated September 30, 1922, the sale of
United States Treasury Savings Certificates, New Issue, offered under
the provisions of Treasury Department Circular No. 270, dated December 15, 1921, and the sale of United States Treasury Savings Stamps
and the distribution of United States Treasury Savings Cards will
cease at the close of business on September 30, 1922. The Treasury
Savings Certificates thus withdrawn from sale are hereinafter called
Treasury Savings Certificates, New Issue.

2. *Collateral Agents.*—Every collateral agent is required to surrender, on or before October 31, 1922, to the Federal Reserve Bank
from which such certificates and stamps were obtained, all Treasury
Savings Certificates, New Issue, and Treasury Savings Stamps not
sold before the close of business September 30, 1922, and upon such
surrender shall receive appropriate credit for the certificates and
stamps surrendered in its account with the Federal Reserve Bank.
Every collateral agent will also surrender, to the Federal Reserve

Bank from which such cards were obtained, all Treasury Savings Cards remaining in its hands unissued at the close of business September 30, 1922.

3. *Post Offices.*—Post offices will be required to surrender all Treasury Savings Certificates, New Issue, and Treasury Savings Stamps held by them for sale and remaining in their hands unsold at the close of business on September 30, 1922, and all Treasury Savings Cards remaining in their hands unissued at the close of business on such date, in accordance with instructions issued by the Postmaster General. No post office shall accept the surrender of any unsold Treasury Savings Certificates, New Issue, or Treasury Savings Stamps from any agent for the sale thereof other than a postal agent; but nothing herein contained shall be deemed to prevent the redemption by post offices, as hereinafter provided, of Treasury Savings Stamps at the face value thereof.

4. *Federal Reserve Banks.*—On or before October 31, 1922, Federal Reserve Banks will forward to the Register of the Treasury, Washington, D. C., all Treasury Savings Certificates, New Issue, and Treasury Savings Stamps remaining in their hands unsold at the close of business September 30, 1922. Federal Reserve Banks will forward to the Register of the Treasury, Washington, D. C., on or before November 30, 1922, all Treasury Savings Certificates, New Issue, and Treasury Savings Stamps surrendered to them by collateral agents pursuant to paragraph 2 hereof. Federal Reserve Banks will receive special instructions as to the disposition of Treasury Savings Cards remaining in their hands unissued at the close of business September 30, 1922, or surrendered to them by collateral agents pursuant to paragraph 2 hereof.

5. *Redemption of Treasury Savings Stamps.*—On and after October 1, 1922, Treasury Savings Stamps then outstanding will be accepted at their face value of $1 per stamp on account of the purchase price of Treasury Savings Certificates, issued pursuant to Treasury Department Circular No. 301, dated September 30, 1922, in any denomination, or, at the option of the holder, may be redeemed at such face value in cash upon presentation and surrender at the office of the Treasurer of the United States, Washington, D. C., any Federal Reserve Bank or any authorized post office.

6. The Secretary of the Treasury may at any time withdraw this circular as a whole or amend from time to time any of the provisions thereof, and may from time to time make any supplemental or amendatory regulations which shall not modify or impair the terms and conditions of United States Treasury (War) Savings securities, of whatever issue or denomination, issued in pursuance of the act of September 24, 1917, as amended and supplemented.

A. W. MELLON,<br>
*Secretary of the Treasury.*

EXHIBIT 71.

## CASH EXPENDITURES OF THE GOVERNMENT FOR THE FISCAL YEARS 1917 TO 1922, INCLUSIVE, AS PUBLISHED IN DAILY TREASURY STATEMENTS, CLASSIFIED ACCORDING TO DEPARTMENTS AND ESTABLISHMENTS.

[Because of legislation establishing revolving funds and providing for the reimbursement of appropriations, commented upon in the Annual Report of the Secretary of the Treasury for the fiscal year 1919, p. 126 ff., the gross expenditures in the case of some departments and agencies, notably the War Department, the Railroad Administration, and the Shipping Board, have been considerably larger than here stated. This statement does not include expenditures on account of the Postal Service other than salaries and expenses of the Post Office Department in Washington, postal deficiencies, and items appropriated by Congress payable from the general fund of the Treasury.]

| | Fiscal year 1917 (revised). | Fiscal year 1918. | Fiscal year 1919. | Fiscal year 1920. | Fiscal year 1921. | Fiscal year 1922. |
|---|---|---|---|---|---|---|
| Ordinary: | | | | | | |
| Legislative [1] | $15,092,373.97 | $15,525,506.72 | $17,90,106.24 | $19,327,708.72 | $18,92,65.17 | $17,68,87 |
| Executive proper [1] | 1,280,494.85 | 9,662,847.53 | 17,467,82.03 | 6,675,517.58 | 210,656.79 | 218,690.36 |
| State Department | 6,169,316.41 | 909 | 20,766,90.14 | 13,596,024.42 | 8,780,796.84 | 9,465,571.70 |
| Treasury | 8,294,313.65 | 4,850,687,186.88 | 227,277,92.81 | 322,315,627.43 | 488,66,83.10 | 294,414,389.72 |
| War | 358,158,361.12 | 18 | 8,15,717.86 | 1,610,587,380.88 | 1,101,615,013.32 | 434,730,717.67 |
| Post Office | 10,566,401.25 | 4,173, | | 50,914,398.18 | 17,206,418.03 | 17,888,928.38 |
| Navy | 1,895,578.21 | 1,278,840,486.50 | 2,412,250.05 | 736,021,4.43 | 135,39,108.17 | 67,730,61.83 |
| Interior Department | 239,632,756.63 | | 2,002,310,785.02 | | 630,373,835.58 | 476,775,193.74 |
| Department of Agriculture | 216,415,516.48 | 42,870, | 88,283,627.61 | 279,244,60.87 | 357,314,933.01 | 341,097,66.11 |
| Department of Commerce | 29,547,234.01 | 12,83 | 39,86,454.41 | 65,546,203.14 | 119,337,759.41 | 142,695,444.10 |
| Department of Labor [3] | 11,689,792.94 | 5, | 15,89,814.30 | 30,910,737.75 | 30,325,761.55 | 21,688,011.86 |
| Veterans' Bureau [3] | 3,852,111.34 | | 12,942,558.75 | 5,415,358.40 | 8,502,509.55 | 627,471.57 |
| Federal Control of Railroads, sums and trans- | 14,291,282.96 | 770,681,550.83 | 1,820,606,870.90 | 530,565,649.61 | 130,723,26.26 | 400,691,699.68 |
| War Risk Insurance act, 1920 | | 1 | 38 795,274.60 | 4 1,036,672,157.53 | 2 730,711,69.98 | 5,6 139,469,190.82 |
| | | 14,99,168.33 | 2 846.92 | 7 8,472,196.61 | 5 2,028,152.12 | 94,425,001.01 |

[1] In the fiscal years 1921 and 1922 the salaries made in reimbursement of ... the Railroad Administration on ... by Railroad ... during Federal control, Post Office Department are included in ...

[2] Owing to ... the Post Office Department and the Railroad Administration, Deposit of this ... Risk Insurance ... During the fiscal year 1922 ... rate ... prior to the date by the Federal Board for Vocational Education are included in the amount of $1,366,383.40, and to the Navy Department in the ... $529,217.81, but ... $288,399,222.46 payments on the ... of the Director General of Railroads, to July 15, 19.

[4] Deduct excess of ...

[5] The railroad ... by $296,636,606.26 up to June 30, 1922, on ... by the Railroad ... up to June 30, 1922, on account of the Federal ... approved Mr. 21, 1918, as amended Nov. 19, 919, and have at the Federal control or ... by $121,783,487.75

[7] Deduct ... rights of War ... of War ... of its holdings of United States ... (See note 2, p. 2, daily Treasury statement for June 30, 191.)

Cash expenditures of the Government for the fiscal years 1917 to 1922, inclusive, as published in daily Treasury statements, classified according to departments and establishments—Continued.

[Because of legislation establishing revolving funds and providing for the reimbursement of appropriations, commented upon in the Annual Report of the Secretary of the Treasury for the fiscal year 1919, p. 126 ff., the gross expenditures in the case of some departments and agencies, notably the War Department, the Railroad Administration, and the Shipping Board, have been considerably larger than here stated. This statement does not include expenditures on account of the Postal Service other than salaries and expenses of the Post Office Department in Washington, postal deficiencies, and items appropriated by Congress payable from the general fund of the Treasury.]

| | Fiscal year 1917 (revised). | Fiscal year 1918. | Fiscal year 1919. | Fiscal year 1920. | Fiscal year 1921. | Fiscal year 1922. |
|---|---|---|---|---|---|---|
| **Ordinary—Continued.** | | | | | | |
| Grain Corporation | | | $57,338,207.08 | [8] $350,328,494.70 | [9] $90,353,411.42 | [10] $22,000,000.00 |
| Sugar Equalization Board | | | | | | [5] 15,279,636.52 |
| Food and Fuel Administrations | $7,58,8.88 | $4,89,896.40 | | | | |
| Other independent offices and commissions [1] | 13,681,8.39 | 17,714,740.06 | 75,375,899.41 | 59,469,305.17 | 119,942,516.73 | 43,871,656.40 |
| District of Columbia | 24,742,0.68 | | 16,014,105.80 | 19,987,808.41 | 22,715,138.60 | 23,962,521.25 |
| Interest on public debt | | 189,743,277.14 | 619,215,569.17 | 1,020,251,622.28 | 999,144,731.35 | 991,000,759.24 |
| Total | 1,66,88,650.77 | 7,87,96,704.60 | 14,534,953,678.78 | 5,945,397,399.94 | 5,009,710,854.74 | 3,368,632,555.57 |
| Deduct unclassified repayments, etc. | [11] 150,273.43 | [11] 26,469,620.31 | [11] 985,060.84 | 4,399,847.00 | [11] 292,583.14 | [11] 292,088.59 |
| Total | 1,66,08,926.20 | 7,84,86,324.91 | 14,935,848,739.62 | 5,940,997,552.94 | 5,008,783,261.60 | 3,368,984,644.16 |
| Panama Canal | 19,782,509.32 | 19,298,099.30 | 13,195,522.37 | 11,365,714.01 | 16,461,409.47 | 3,025,421.32 |
| Payment for West Indian islands | 25,000,000.00 | | | | | |
| Purchase of obligations of foreign Governments | 885,000,000.00 | 4,734,029,750.00 | 3,479,255,265.56 | 421,337,028.09 | 73,896,697.44 | 717,834.36 |
| Purchase of Federal farm loan bonds | | 65,018,296.93 | 96,580,427.48 | 29,643,546.17 | 16,781,320.79 | |
| Subscription to stock, Federal land banks | 8,880,315.00 | | | | | |
| Total ordinary | 1,977,681,750.52 | 12,696,702,471.14 | 18,514,879,955.03 | 6,403,343,841.21 | 5,115,927,689.30 | 3,372,607,899.84 |
| **Public debt:** | | | | | | |
| Public debt expenditures chargeable against ordinary receipts— | | | | | | |
| Sinking fund | | | | | 261,100,250.00 | 276,046,000.00 |
| Purchases of Liberty bonds from foreign repayments | | | 7,921,700.00 | 72,669,900.00 | 73,939,300.00 | 64,837,900.00 |
| Redemption of bonds and notes from estate taxes | | | 93,050.00 | 3,141,050.00 | 207,348,950.00 | 21,084,850.00 |
| Retirements from Federal reserve bank franchise tax receipts | | | | 2,922,450.00 | 60,724,500.00 | 60,333,000.00 |
| Retirements from gifts, forfeitures, and other miscellaneous receipts | | 1,134,234.48 | | 12,950.00 | 168,500.00 | 392,850.00 |
| Total public debt expenditures chargeable against ordinary receipts | | 1,134,234.48 | 8,014,750.00 | 78,746,350.00 | 422,281,500.00 | 422,694,600.00 |
| Total expenditures (public debt and ordinary) chargeable against ordinary receipts | 1,977,681,750.52 | 12,697,836,705.62 | 18,522,894,705.03 | 6,482,090,191.21 | 5,538,209,189.30 | 3,795,302,499.84 |

| | | | | | |
|---|---|---|---|---|---|
| Other public debt expenditures | 677,544,782.25 | 7,213,555,218.81 | 16,318,491,810.41 | 16,959,293,373.62 | 8,759,745,670.69 | 6,608,531,896.93 |
| Total public debt (see items below) | 677,544,782.25 | 7,214,689,453.29 | 16,326,506,560.41 | 17,038,039,723.62 | 9,182,027,170.69 | 7,031,226,496.93 |

RECAPITULATION, PUBLIC DEBT.

| | | | | | |
|---|---|---|---|---|---|
| Certificates of indebtedness redeemed | 632,572,268.00 | 7,096,312,732.00 | 15,538,78,900.00 | 15,589,117,458.53 | 8,552,225,500.00 | 4,775,864,950.00 |
| ...ry (...) savings ...es ...emed | | 2,727,345.96 | 131,519,529.91 | 200,982,934.62 | 160,256,308.19 | 86,120,701.53 |
| Old debt ...this. | 18,398.75 | 20,650.33 | 63,029,583.00 | 209,165.97 | 152,361.50 | 58,122.40 |
| One-year Treasury notes ...ed (sec. 18, Federal reserve act, ...ed Dec. 23, 1913) | 4,390,000.00 | 27,362,000.00 | 19,150,000.00 | | | |
| Fit Liberty bonds ...ed | | 656,000.00 | 4,003,050.00 | 32,336,700.00 | 202,650.00 | 413,600.00 |
| Send ...arty ...nls ...tired | | 61,050,000.00 | 180,351,000.00 | 241,144,200.00 | 8,703,400.00 | 6,015,150.00 |
| ...ird Liberty obnds ...ed | | 14,935,500.00 | 201,655,700.00 | 296,300,800.00 | 51,172,350.00 | 137,788,400.00 |
| ...lth ...bilty obds ...tired | | | 165,000,000.00 | 405,222,800.00 | 39,414,450.00 | 9,574,450.00 |
| Vary notes retired | | | | 249,001,500.00 | 332,439,450.00 | 1,908,139,250.00 |
| ...al bank notes and Federal reserve bank notes re-tired | 40,564,115.50 | 21,625,225.00 | 23,718,797.50 | 23,424,161.50 | 37,460,701.00 | 107,251,870.00 |
| Total public debt | 677,544,782.25 | 7,214,689,453.29 | 16,326,506,560.41 | 17,038,069,723.62 | 9,182,027,170.69 | 7,031,226,496.93 |

1 In the fiscal years 1921 and 1922 changes were made in classification of expenditures between legislative establishment, executive proper, and other independent offices and commissions, which account for most of the differences as compared with expenditures for other fiscal years.
2 Deduct excess of credits.
8 Includes $350,000,000 applied by United States Grain Corporation to reduction of capital stock and reflected in "Miscellaneous receipts for fiscal year 1920." (See note 1, p. 2, daily Treasury statement for June 30, 1920.)
9 Net expenditure after taking into account credits and $100,000,000 applied to reduction in capital stock of United States Grain Corporation.
10 $25,000,000 of this amount represents reduction in capital stock of United States Grain Corporation effected Oct. 17, 1921, and is reflected in an increase of receipts in an equal amount. (See note, p. 2, daily Treasury statement for Oct. 18, 1921.)
11 Add.

EXHIBIT 72.

## ORDINARY RECEIPTS AND EXPENDITURES CHARGEABLE AGAINST ORDINARY RECEIPTS FROM APRIL 6, 1917, TO OCTOBER 31, 1922, ON THE BASIS OF DAILY TREASURY STATEMENTS.

RECEIPTS.

| | Customs. | Income and profits tax. | Miscellaneous internal revenue. | Miscellaneous revenue, including Panama Canal. | Total. |
|---|---|---|---|---|---|
| April 6, 1917, to June 30, 1917 | $65,210,500.96 | $326,996,757.77 | $142,391,206.47 | $32,930,241.89 | $567,438,7 .00 |
| Fiscal year 1918 | 179,998,383.49 | 2,314,006,291.84 | 872,028,020.27 | 295,556,160.10 | 3,664,582,864.70 |
| Fiscal year 1919 | 184,457,867.39 | 3,018,783,647.29 | 1,296,501,291.67 | 652,514,290.08 | 5,152,257,136.43 |
| Fiscal year 1920 | 322,902,650.39 | 3,944,949,287.75 | 1,460,082,286.91 | 966,631,163.83 | 6,694,565,388.88 |
| July, 1920 | 30,694,297.30 | 64,917,691.90 | 107,69 917.32 | 27,081,618.93 | 230,366,525.45 |
| August, 1920 | 29,327,518.83 | 59,551,871.46 | 144,710,931.31 | 164,910,344.05 | 398,400,645.68 |
| September, 1920 | 24,036,208.77 | 716,183,757.45 | 147,314,343.27 | 23,712,762.32 | 911,307,071.81 |
| October, 1920 | 25,599,595.60 | 55,683,825.49 | 122,805,403.43 | 15,944,980.45 | 225,031,804.97 |
| November, 1920 | 21,894,850.58 | 61,193,604.70 | 124,808,247.10 | 67,474,100.57 | 274,420,812.25 |
| December, 1920 | 18,551,794.65 | 670,671,179.54 | 122,664,468.74 | 120,098,964.39 | 931,989,897.32 |
| January, 1921 | 17,485,532.78 | 54,223,322.41 | 111,432,952.10 | 34,180,441.81 | 217,328,249.10 |
| February, 1921 | 21,152,665.92 | 70,511, 7. | 111,699,939.74 | 45,299,962.09 | 218,503,614.78 |
| March, 1921 | 29,203,977.43 | 727,543,549.04 | 95,807,254.03 | 69,012,822.22 | 921,027,602.72 |
| April, 1921 | 40,417,183.94 | 108,380,023.20 | 90,985,753.69 | 56,385,799.99 | 296,170,695.82 |
| May, 1921 | 25,485,133.15 | 52,262,908.39 | 94,812,476.67 | 51,145,880.68 | 223,706,388.89 |
| June, 1921 | 24,722,632.05 | 564,920,472.13 | 115,617,135.85 | 44,756,912.09 | 750,017,152.12 |
| Total for fiscal year 1921 | 308,564,391.00 | 3,206,046,157.74 | 1,380,379,823.28 | 719,942,988.89 | 5,624,932,960.91 |
| July, 1921 | 19,756,200.37 | 47,156,908.02 | 110,984,768.44 | 31,120,487.96 | 220,068,454.79 |
| August, 1921 | 26,449,062.28 | 47,439,706.64 | 136,780,512.99 | 31,773,994.92 | 242,443,186.83 |
| September, 1921 | 23,356,692.08 | 537,492,412.86 | 116,626,602.53 | 11,852,492.61 | 689,328,280.08 |
| October, 1921 | 26,408,043.05 | 47,986,607.45 | 112,873,295.45 | 50,579,545.39 | 237,847,511.34 |
| November, 1921 | 24,843,122.17 | 35,366,755.18 | 104,737,183.52 | 30,535,782.07 | 195,492,842.94 |
| December, 1921 | 26,155,151.35 | 523,973,741.40 | 106,733,179.06 | 83,430,728.98 | 740,292,801.39 |
| January, 1922 | 27,251,033.11 | 45,628,859.72 | 85,429,053.20 | 32,691,806.92 | 191,000,7:2.95 |
| February, 1922 | 33,634,742.85 | 33,266,712.41 | 81,5 6,576.99 | 27,289,412.43 | 175,651,444.68 |
| March, 1922 | 40,298,428.44 | 391,362,045.17 | 83,671, 99.87 | 33,415, 9. | 550,757,683.19 |
| April, 1922 | 33,893,780.52 | 33,363,133.13 | 64,963,637.15 | 65,789,089.94 | 197,919,640.74 |
| May, 1922 | 33,578,214.90 | 27,603,368.96 | 61,394,6 7.60 | 81,799,529.20 | 205,375,740.66 |
| June, 1922 | 38,891,826.06 | 295,327,941.74 | 79,416,746.71 | 59,123,296.54 | 472,935,811.35 |
| Total for fiscal year 1922 | 356,443,387.18 | 2,068,128,192.08 | 1,145,125,064.11 | 539,407,606.97 | 4,109,104,150.94 |
| July, 1922 | 37,491,580.74 | 32,108,600.98 | 82,477,791.80 | 52,898,535.05 | 204,976,518.57 |
| August, 1922 | 39,012,088.99 | 23,817,137.63 | 114,984,312.55 | 38,964,603.30 | 216,777,979.47 |
| September, 1922 | 53,135,385.46 | 286,535,255.48 | 81,283,050.14 | 33,854,990.45 | 454,988,681.53 |
| October, 1922 | 40,135,835.81 | 26,721,825.01 | 79,717,916.77 | 154,663,538.18 | 301,239,415.77 |
| Total July 1 to Oct. 31, 1922 | 169,774,911.00 | 369,182,819.10 | 358,463,071.26 | 249,381,363.98 | 1,177,802,195.34 |
| Grand total | 1,587,352,091.41 | 15,248,063,194.17 | 6,664,970,763.97 | 3,490,357,354.74 | 26,960,683,404.29 |

EXPENDITURES.

| | Ordinary, exclusive of purchase of obligations of foreign governments. | Purchase of obligations of foreign governments. | Public debt retirements chargeable against ordinary receipts. | Total expenditures chargeable against ordinary receipts. | Excess of receipts (+), or excess of expenditures (−). |
|---|---|---|---|---|---|
| April 6, 1917, to June 30, 1917 | $330,896,628.55 | $885,000,000.00 | | $1,215,886,628.55 | −$648,447,921.46 |
| Fiscal year 1918 | 7,998,672,721.14 | 4,738,029,750.00 | $1,134,234.48 | 12,697,836,705.62 | −9,033,253,840.92 |
| Fiscal year 1919 | 15,935,624,669.47 | 3,479,255,265.56 | 8,014,750.00 | 18,522,894,705.03 | −13,370,637,558.60 |
| Fiscal year 1920 | 5,982,006,813.12 | 421,337,028.09 | 78,746,350.00 | 6,452,090,191.21 | +212,475,197.67 |
| July, 1920 | 295,561,839.31 | 11,000,000.00 | 7,667,100.00 | 314,168,939.31 | −83,802,413.86 |
| August, 1920 | 417,101,594.56 | 30,469,467.89 | 2,453,200.00 | 450,024,262.43 | −51,623,696.77 |
| September, 1920 | 481,044,489.25 | 15,732,165.64 | 37,161,950.00 | 533,038,604.89 | +277,368,466.82 |
| October, 1920 | 426,497,372.37 | | 5,318,700.00 | 431,816,072.37 | −211,781,267.40 |
| November, 1920 | 426,092,313.00 | | 12,894,650.00 | 438,986,963.00 | −163,566,150.75 |
| December, 1920 | 404,575,091.03 | | 3,744,600.00 | 408,319,691.03 | +523,669,706.29 |
| January, 1921 | 388,179,272.33 | | | 473,614,322.33 | −236,298,073.23 |
| February, 1921 | 351,102,030.45 | | 55,376,350.00 | 406,478,380.45 | −157,914,765.67 |
| March, 1921 | 519,78,297.00 | | 85,435,050.00 | 588,489,010.91 | +333,135,591.81 |
| April, 1921 | 494,091,189.49 | 16,695,063.91 | 52,012,650.00 | 530,406,299.49 | −234,235,623.67 |
| May, 1921 | 368,450,545.01 | | 36,315,100.00 | 418,295,045.01 | −194,588,646.12 |
| June, 1921 | 469,613,938.06 | | 49,944,500.00 | 543,671,608.06 | +206,345,544.06 |
| Total for fiscal year 1921 | 5,042,030,991.86 | 73,896,697.44 | 422,251,500.00 | 5,538,299,189.30 | +86,723,771.61 |
| July, 1921 | 291,818,569.24 | | 60,398,650.00 | 382,217,219.24 | −173,148,764.41 |
| August, 1921 | 291,157,847.34 | | 25,298,550.00 | 316,456,397.34 | −74,013,210.51 |
| September, 1921 | 266,523,932.79 | | 1,888,900.00 | 268,412,832.79 | +420,915,427.29 |
| October, 1921 | 304,157,955.85 | | 59,311,550.00 | 363,449,505.85 | −125,621,994.51 |
| November, 1921 | 324,483,376.72 | | 39,389,300.00 | 363,872,676.72 | −168,399,833.78 |
| December, 1921 | 329,765,750.86 | | 72,364,750.00 | 402,630,500.86 | +337,662,300.53 |
| January, 1922 | 231,246,893.85 | | 36,323,600.00 | 267,570,495.16 | −76,549,742.21 |
| February, 1922 | 182,205,931.85 | | 5,185,050.00 | 187,380,981.85 | −11,719,537.17 |
| March, 1922 | 325,954,936.78 | | 26,062,400.00 | 352,017,336.78 | +198,740,346.41 |
| April, 1922 | 242,560,961.82 | | 35,386,850.00 | 277,947,811.82 | −80,028,171.08 |
| May, 1922 | 237,961,476.88 | | 23,602,350.00 | 261,563,826.88 | −55,188,066.22 |
| June, 1922 | 314,052,430.19 | 717,834.36 | 36,962,650.00 | 351,752,914.55 | +121,182,896.80 |
| Total for fiscal year 1922 | 3,371,880,065.48 | 717,834.36 | 422,694,000.00 | 3,795,302,499.84 | +313,801,651.10 |
| July, 1922 | 218,696,870.97 | | 6,900,850.00 | 225,497,720.97 | −20,521,202.40 |
| August, 1922 | 218,025,762.25 | | 3,529,750.00 | 221,535,512.25 | −4,777,942.78 |
| September, 1922 | 304,132,012.53 | | 42,079,550.00 | 347,111,562.53 | +107,697,119.00 |
| October, 1922 | 411,109,750.05 | | 54,787,500.00 | 465,897,250.05 | −164,657,834.28 |
| Total July 1 to Oct. 31, 1922 | 1,151,964,395.80 | | 108,097,650.00 | 1,260,062,045.80 | −82,259,850.46 |
| Grand total | 38,873,076,305.42 | 9,598,236,575.45 | 1,010,969,084.48 | 49,512,281,965.35 | −22,521,598,361.06 |

¹ Net.

## Exhibit 73.

**PAYMENTS TO CARRIERS FROM NOVEMBER 16, 1921, TO NOVEMBER 15, 1922, INCLUSIVE, PROVIDED FOR IN SECTION 204 OF THE TRANSPORTATION ACT OF 1920, AS AMENDED, FOR THE REIMBURSEMENT OF DEFICITS ON ACCOUNT OF FEDERAL CONTROL.**

| Carrier. | Partial. | Final. | Deductions.[1] | Total certified. |
|---|---|---|---|---|
| Apalachicola Northern R. R. Co.................... | .............. | $3,763.97 | ............ | $3,763.97 |
| Arizona & Swansea R. R. Co...................... | .............. | 15,296.34 | ............ | 15,296.34 |
| Bridgton & Saco River R. R. Co.................. | .............. | 15,359.93 | ............ | 15,359.93 |
| Bristol R. R. Co.............................. | .............. | 729.31 | ............ | 729.31 |
| Blytheville, Leachville & Arkansas Southern R. R. Co............................. | .............. | 29,892.09 | $3,697.73 | 29,892.09 |
| Bullfrog Goldfield R. R. Co..................... | .............. | 15,144.79 | ............ | 15,144.79 |
| Butler County R. R. Co......................... | .............. | 18,078.37 | 364.67 | 18,078.37 |
| Cazenovia Southern R. R. Co.................... | .............. | 7,187.52 | ............ | 7,187.52 |
| Chesapeake Western Ry......................... | .............. | 11,040.05 | ............ | 11,040.05 |
| Chicago Tunnel Co............................ | .............. | 22,747.33 | ............ | 22,747.33 |
| Chicago Warehouse & Terminal Co ............. | .............. | 64,246.10 | ............ | 64,246.10 |
| Colorado Springs & Cripple Creek District Ry. Co., receiver................................ | .............. | 284,321.42 | ............ | 284,321.42 |
| Elwood, Anderson & Lapelle R. R. Co........... | .............. | 15,693.35 | ............ | 15,693.35 |
| Emmitsburg R. R. Co.......................... | .............. | 2,998.07 | ............ | 2,998.07 |
| Fernwood, Columbia & Gulf R. R. Co........... | .............. | 46,478.60 | ............ | 46,478.60 |
| Fulton Chain Railway Co....................... | .............. | 3,881.06 | ............ | 3,881.06 |
| Georgia Coast & Piedmont R. R. Co............. | .............. | 23,126.96 | ............ | 23,126.96 |
| Glenmora & Western Ry. Co.................... | .............. | 10,917.04 | 169.86 | 10,917.04 |
| Illinois Northern Ry........................... | .............. | 202,509.43 | 736.46 | 202,509.43 |
| Intermountain Ry. Co.......................... | .............. | 20,739.20 | ............ | 20,739.20 |
| Jefferson & Northwestern Ry. Co............... | .............. | 4,983.55 | 4,256.09 | 4,983.55 |
| Kentwood & Eastern Ry. Co.................... | .............. | 8,764.96 | ............ | 8,764.96 |
| Kentwood, Greenburg & Southwestern R. R Co. | .............. | 52,423.22 | ............ | 52,423.22 |
| Knoxville, Sevierville & Eastern Ry. Co., receiver.. | .............. | 5,009.25 | ............ | 5,009.25 |
| La Salle & Bureau County R. R. Co............. | .............. | 13,414.14 | 841.08 | 13,414.14 |
| Lawndale Ry. & Industrial Co.................. | .............. | 2,730.98 | ............ | 2,730.98 |
| Leetonia Ry. Co.............................. | .............. | 44,831.32 | ............ | 44,831.32 |
| Little Rock, Maumelle & Western R. R. Co., receiver................................. | .............. | 24,433.76 | 2,651.85 | 24,433.76 |
| Lime Rock R R. Co........................... | .............. | 10,441.91 | ............ | 10,441.91 |
| Lufkin, Hemphill & Gulf Ry. Co............... | .............. | 6,517.07 | ............ | 6,517.07 |
| Madison Southern Ry. Co....................... | .............. | 5,953.10 | ............ | 5,953.10 |
| Manchester & Oneida Ry. Co.................... | .............. | 6,327.14 | 4,779 44 | 6,327.14 |
| Mansfield Ry. & Transportation Co.............. | .............. | 14,802.09 | ............ | 14,802.09 |
| Millers Creek R. R. Co......................... | .............. | 50,237.97 | ............ | 50,237.97 |
| Milltown Air Line Ry.......................... | .............. | 14,959.72 | 440.00 | 14,959.72 |
| Moscow, Camden & San Augustine R. R. Co..... | .............. | 7,168.23 | 85.50 | 7,168.23 |
| Nacogdoches & Southeastern R. R. Co........... | .............. | 18,498.53 | 235.15 | 18,498.53 |
| Neame, Carson & Southern R. R. Co............. | .............. | 39,188.86 | ............ | 39,188.86 |
| Nevada-California-Oregon Ry................... | .............. | 50,015.76 | 59 17 | 50,015.76 |
| New Castle & Ohio River Ry. Co................ | .............. | 1,128.29 | ............ | 1,128.29 |
| Northampton & Bath R. R. Co.................. | .............. | 121,911.41 | ............ | 121,911.41 |
| Ocean Shore R. R............................. | .............. | 63,322.30 | ............ | 63,322.30 |
| Okmulgee Northern Ry. Co..................... | .............. | 15,684.26 | ............ | 15,684.26 |
| Owasco River Ry.............................. | .............. | 21,740.17 | ............ | 21,740.17 |
| Paris & Mount Pleasant R. R. Co., receiver....... | .............. | 1,748.47 | 1,748.47 | 1,748.47 |
| Raquette Lake Ry............................. | .............. | 9,717.82 | ............ | 9,717.82 |
| Salina Northern R. R. Co., receiver.............. | .............. | 3,840.26 | ............ | 3,840.26 |
| Sandy River & Rangeley Lakes R. R. Co......... | .............. | 52,585.11 | ............ | 52,585.11 |
| San Joaquin & Eastern R. R. Co................ | .............. | 53,741.34 | ............ | 53,741.34 |
| Silverton Northern R. R. Co.................... | .............. | 20,845.16 | ............ | 20,845.16 |
| South Buffalo Ry. Co.......................... | .............. | 196,175.57 | ............ | 196,175.57 |
| South San Francisco Belt Ry................... | .............. | 29,590.87 | ............ | 29,590.87 |
| Spokane & British Columbia Ry. Co............. | .............. | 14,289.87 | ............ | 14,289.87 |
| Statenville Ry. Co............................ | .............. | 7,178.03 | 528.81 | 7,178.03 |
| Susquehanna & New York R. R. Co.............. | .............. | 20,271.48 | ............ | 20,271.48 |
| St. John & Ophir R. R. Co..................... | .............. | 17,977.70 | ............ | 17,977.70 |
| United Verde & Pacific Ry. Co.................. | .............. | 34,533.15 | ............ | 34,533.15 |
| Ursina & North Fork Ry. Co.................... | .............. | 3,094.98 | ............ | 3,094.98 |
| Ventura County Ry. Co......................... | .............. | 17,456.32 | ............ | 17,456.32 |
| Wabash, Chester & Western R. R. Co........... | .............. | 37,939.95 | ............ | 37,939.95 |
| Waterville Ry. Co............................ | .............. | 9,671.53 | ............ | 9,671.53 |
| Wyandotte Southern R. R. Co.................. | .............. | 10,388.98 | ............ | 10,388.98 |
| Total....................... | .............. | 1,959,685.51 | ............ | 1,959,685.51 |
| Less refund of overpayments— | | | | |
| Franklin & Pittsylvania R. R. Co.. | $1,223.18 | | | |
| Montana Western Ry. Co.......... | 2,233.90 | | | |
| Georgia, Florida & Alabama Ry. Co. | 7,047.71 | | | |
| | .............. | 10,504.79 | ............ | 10,504.79 |
| Payments from Nov. 16, 1921, to Nov. 15, 1922, inclusive.......................... | | 1,949,180.72 | 20,594 28 | 1,949,180.72 |
| Payments to Nov. 15, 1921, inclusive.......... | $2,177,651.41 | 1,012,718 32 | 952,001.66 | 3,190,369.73 |
| Total payments to Nov. 15, 1922, inclusive... | 2,177,651.41 | 2,961,899.04 | 972,595.94 | 5,139,550.45 |

[1] Amount due from the carrier to the President (as operator of the transportation systems under Federal control) on account of traffic balances or other indebtedness.

## EXHIBIT 74.

**PAYMENTS TO CARRIERS FROM NOVEMBER 16, 1921, TO NOVEMBER 15, 1922, INCLUSIVE, UNDER THE GUARANTY PROVIDED FOR IN SECTION 209 OF THE TRANSPORTATION ACT OF 1920, AS AMENDED.**

| Carrier. | Advances. | Partial. | Final.[1] | Total. |
|---|---|---|---|---|
| Alabama Central Ry. | | | $2,246.20 | $2,246.20 |
| Alabama & Mississippi R. R. Co., receiver. | | | 16,543.61 | 16,543.61 |
| Alton & Southern R. R. Co. | | $100,000.00 | | 100,000.00 |
| Apalachicola Northern R. R. Co. | | | 14,802.29 | 14,802.29 |
| Aransas Harbor Terminal Ry. | | | 18,093.95 | 18,093.95 |
| Bennettsville & Cheraw R. R. Co. | | | 6,319.94 | 6,319.94 |
| Bloomsburg & Sullivan R. R. Co. | | | 2,961.03 | 2,961.03 |
| Bridgton & Saco River R. R. Co. | | | 2,995.70 | 2,995.70 |
| Brownwood North & South Ry. Co. | | | 1,051.27 | 1,051.27 |
| Buffalo, Rochester & Pittsburgh Ry. Co. | | | 222,364.47 | 222,364.47 |
| Bullfrog Goldfield R. R. Co. | | | 14,454.88 | 14,454.88 |
| Carolina & Tennessee Southern Ry. Co. | | | 4,434.82 | 4,434.82 |
| Central Vermont Ry. Co. | | | 40,148.63 | 40,148.63 |
| Central West Virginia & Southern R. R. Co. | | | 8,574.89 | 8,574.89 |
| Charleston Terminal Co. | | | 10,351.89 | 10,351.89 |
| Chesapeake Western Ry. | | | 6,804.15 | 6,804.15 |
| Chicago & Eastern Illinois R. R. Co., receiver. | | | 723,982.56 | 723,982.56 |
| Chicago Junction Ry. Co. | | | 315,319.54 | 315,319.54 |
| Chicago, Milwaukee & St. Paul Ry. Co. | | | 676,636.00 | 676,636.00 |
| Chicago & North Western Ry. Co. | | | 3,733,520.55 | 3,733,520.55 |
| Chicago, Peoria & St. Louis R. R. Co. | | 55,000.00 | 78,372.69 | 133,372.69 |
| Chicago, Rock Island & Pacific Ry. Co. | | 1,000,000.00 | | 1,000,000.00 |
| Chicago, St. Paul, Minneapolis & Omaha Ry. Co. | | | 368,096.82 | 368,096.82 |
| Chicago Tunnel Co. | | | 16,812.53 | 16,812.53 |
| Chicago Warehouse & Terminal Co. | | | 46,806.40 | 46,806.40 |
| Colorado Springs & Cripple Creek District Ry. Co., receiver. | | | 170,921.69 | 170,921.69 |
| Danville & Western Ry. Co. | | | 37,548.74 | 37,548.74 |
| Deering Southwestern Ry. | | | 3,623.67 | 3,623.67 |
| Denison & Pacific Suburban Ry. Co. | | | 340.86 | 340.86 |
| Denver & Rio Grande R. R. Co., receiver. | | | 477,953.32 | 477,953.32 |
| Detroit, Bay City & Western R. R. Co. | | | 13,313.36 | 13,313.36 |
| Detroit & Mackinac Ry. Co. | | | 61,678.28 | 61,678.28 |
| Duluth, South Shore & Atlantic Ry. Co. | | | 178,459.94 | 178,459.94 |
| Durham & Southern R. R. Co. | | | 70,166.99 | 70,166.99 |
| El Paso & Southwestern Co. | | 500,000.00 | 691,408.32 | 1,191,408.32 |
| Emmitsburg R. R. Co. | | | 2,497.62 | 2,497.62 |
| Fernwood, Columbia & Gulf R. R. Co. | | | 12,480.05 | 12,480.05 |
| Flint River & Northeastern R. R. Co. | | | 1,238.91 | 1,238.91 |
| Fort Smith, Subiaco & Rock Island R. R. Co. | | | 5,059.23 | 5,059.23 |
| Fort Worth & Rio Grande Ry. Co. | | | 41,885.67 | 41,885.67 |
| Galveston Wharf Co. | | | 31,742.96 | 31,742.96 |
| Georgia, Florida & Alabama Ry. Co. | | | 15,450.03 | 15,450.03 |
| Georgia Northern Ry. Co. | | | 1,632.37 | 1,632.37 |
| Georgia Southern & Florida Ry. Co. | | | 366,737.96 | 366,737.96 |
| Gulf, Florida & Alabama Ry. Co., receiver. | | | 6,684.92 | 6,684.92 |
| Illinois Central R. R. Co. and its subsidiaries. | | | 1,313,078.57 | 1,313,078.57 |
| International & Great Northern Ry. Co., receiver. | | 528,010.15 | | 528,010.15 |
| Jefferson & Northwestern Ry. Co. | | | 18,362.49 | 18,362.49 |
| Kansas City, Clinton & Springfield Ry. Co. | | | 31,228.29 | 31,228.29 |
| Kansas City, Mexico & Orient Ry. Co. of Texas. | | | 84,715.19 | 84,715.19 |
| Kansas City, Mexico & Orient R. R. Co., receiver. | | | 32,904.17 | 32,904.17 |
| Lake Erie & Western R. R. Co. | | | 140,918.65 | 140,918.65 |
| La Salle & Bureau County R. R. Co. | | | 375.09 | 375.09 |
| Lehigh & Hudson River Ry. Co. | | | 184,750.94 | 184,750.94 |
| Liberty-White R. R. Co., receiver. | | | 8,104.28 | 8,104.28 |
| Louisiana Railway & Navigation Co. | | 102,626.94 | | 102,626.94 |
| Lufkin, Hemphill & Gulf Ry. Co. | | | 10,851.76 | 10,851.76 |
| Manchester & Oneida Ry. Co. | | | 5,486.80 | 5,486.80 |
| Marion & Southern R. R. Co. | | | 2,923.72 | 2,923.72 |
| Middle Tennessee R. R. Co. | | | 20,864.90 | 20,864.90 |
| Middletown & Unionville R. R. Co. | | | 10,303.90 | 10,303.90 |
| Mineral Range R. R. Co. | | | 123,167.95 | 123,167.95 |
| Minneapolis & Eastern Ry. Co. | | | 2,139.63 | 2,139.63 |

[1] Amounts in this column represent balances due and paid after taking into account advances and partial payments previously made.

*Payments to carriers from November 16, 1921, to November 15, 1922, inclusive, under the guaranty provided for in section 209 of the transportation act of 1920, as amended—Continued.*

| Carrier. | Advances. | Partial. | Final.[1] | Total. |
|---|---|---|---|---|
| Minneapolis, St. Paul & Sault Ste. Marie Ry. Co. | - | | $592, 467. 82 | $592, 467. 82 |
| Mississippi Central R. R. Co. | | | 38, 581. 46 | 38, 581. 46 |
| Mississippi Eastern Ry. Co. | | | 4, 494. 77 | 4, 494. 77 |
| Mobile & Ohio R. R. Co. | | | 605, 735. 85 | 605, 735. 85 |
| Montana Western Ry. Co. | | | 4, 019. 21 | 4, 019. 21 |
| New Orleans Great Northern R. R. Co. | | | 131, 055. 93 | 131, 055. 93 |
| New York, Ontario & Western Ry. Co. | | | 95, 010. 33 | 95, 010. 33 |
| Oil Fields' Short Line R. R. Co. | | | 11, 588. 35 | 11, 588. 35 |
| Owasco River Ry. | | | 5, 200. 42 | 5, 200. 42 |
| Pacific Coast R. R. Co. | | | 2, 342. 79 | 2, 342. 79 |
| Pacific Coast Ry. Co. | | | 21, 558. 36 | 21, 558. 36 |
| Paris & Mount Pleasant R. R. Co., receiver. | | $5, 000. 00 | 6, 105. 81 | 11, 105. 81 |
| Peoria & Pekin Union Ry. Co. | | | 83, 829. 87 | 83, 829. 87 |
| Philadelphia & Reading Ry. Co. | | | 1, 656, 060. 80 | 1, 656, 060. 80 |
| Port Bolivar Iron Ore Ry. Co. | | 4, 000. 00 | | 4, 000. 00 |
| Port St. Joe Dock & Terminal Ry. Co. | | | 1, 410. 22 | 1, 410. 22 |
| Quanah, Acme & Pacific Ry. Co. | | | 17, 226. 86 | 17, 226. 86 |
| Rapid City, Black Hills & Western R. R. Co. | | | 8, 685. 30 | 8, 685. 30 |
| Raritan River R. R. Co. | | | 24, 305. 19 | 24, 305. 19 |
| Rock Island Southern Ry. Co. | | | 58, 711. 84 | 58, 711. 84 |
| Salina Northern R. R. Co., receivers | | 8, 000. 00 | 14, 086. 24 | 22, 086. 24 |
| San Antonio & Aransas Pass Ry Co. | | | 81, 354. 39 | 81, 354. 39 |
| Sandy River & Rangeley Lakes R. R. | | | 26, 534. 07 | 26, 534. 07 |
| Santa Maria Valley R. R. Co. | | | 10, 513. 78 | 10, 513. 78 |
| Seaboard Air Line Ry Co. | | 300, 000. 00 | | 300, 000. 00 |
| Sioux City Terminal Ry. Co. | | | 21, 623. 22 | 21, 623. 22 |
| St. Louis-San Francisco Ry. Co. | | | 855, 449. 76 | 855, 449. 76 |
| St. Louis, San Francisco & Texas Ry. Co. | | | 114, 967. 63 | 114, 967. 63 |
| Stanley Merrill & Phillips Ry. Co. | | | 32, 482. 71 | 32, 482. 71 |
| Susquehanna & New York R. R. Co. | | | 29, 950. 61 | 29, 950. 61 |
| Tennessee, Alabama & Georgia R. R. Co., receiver. | | | 40, 359. 66 | 40, 359. 66 |
| Terminal Railroad Association of St. Louis. | | | 278, 960. 75 | 278, 960. 75 |
| Texas Midland R. R. | | | 58, 367. 54 | 58, 367. 54 |
| Texas & Pacific Ry. Co., receivers. | | 500, 000. 00 | 298, 041. 77 | 798, 041. 77 |
| Tonopah & Goldfield R. R. Co. | | | 16, 683. 34 | 16, 683. 34 |
| Trans-Mississippi Terminal R. R. Co. | | | 21, 950. 23 | 21, 950. 23 |
| Ulster & Delaware R. R. Co. | | | 69, 450. 00 | 69, 450. 00 |
| Ursina & North Fork Ry. Co. | | | 4, 150. 90 | 4, 150. 90 |
| Wabash Ry. Co. | | | 618, 287. 71 | 618, 287. 71 |
| Washington & Choctaw Ry. Co. | | | 2, 201. 99 | 2, 201. 99 |
| Waterville Ry. Co. | | | 938. 59 | 938. 59 |
| Western Allegheny R. R. Co. | | | 39, 226. 17 | 39, 226. 17 |
| Woodstock Ry. Co. | | | 7, 123. 47 | 7, 123. 47 |
| Total. | | | 16, 523, 791. 74 | 19, 626, 428. 83 |
| Less— Refund of overpayment by Paris & Great Northern R. R. Co. | | | 4, 389. 00 | 4, 389. 00 |
| Payments to above carriers from Nov. 16, 1921, to Nov. 15, 1922, inclusive. | | 3, 102, 637. 09 | 16, 519, 402. 74 | 19, 622, 039. 83 |
| Payments to Nov. 15, 1921, inclusive. | $263, 935, 874. 00 | 165, 827, 775. 05 | 705, 114. 71 | 430, 468, 763. 76 |
| Total payments to Nov. 15, 1922, inclusive. | 263, 935, 874. 00 | 168, 930, 412. 14 | 17, 224, 517. 45 | 450, 090, 803. 59 |

[1] Amounts in this column represent balances due and paid after taking into account advances and partial payments previously made.

## Exhibit 75.

**LOANS TO CARRIERS UNDER SECTION 210 OF THE TRANSPORTATION ACT OF 1920, AS AMENDED, AND REPAYMENTS ON SUCH LOANS FROM NOVEMBER 16, 1921, TO NOVEMBER 15, 1922, INCLUSIVE, WITH LOANS OUTSTANDING NOVEMBER 15, 1921, AND NOVEMBER 15, 1922.**

| Carrier. | Loans outstanding Nov. 15, 1921. | Loans made from Nov. 16, 1921, to Nov. 15, 1922. | Repayments from Nov. 16, 1921, to Nov. 15, 1922. | Loans outstanding Nov. 15, 1922. |
|---|---|---|---|---|
| Akron, Canton & Youngstown Ry. Co... | $212,000.00 | .............. | .............. | $212,000.00 |
| Alabama, Tennessee & Northern R. R. Corp.................. | 90,000.00 | $399,000.00 | $13,750.00 | 475,250.00 |
| Alabama & Vicksburg Ry. Co............. | 1,394,000.00 | .............. | .............. | 1,394,000.00 |
| Ann Arbor R. R. Co.................. | 590,000.00 | .............. | 80,000.00 | 510,000.00 |
| Aransas Harbor Terminal Ry.... | 50,000.00 | .............. | .............. | 50,000.00 |
| Atlanta, Birmingham & Atlantic Ry.Co.. | 180,000.00 | .............. | .............. | 180,000.00 |
| Baltimore & Ohio R. R. Co.......... | 3,000,000.00 | .............. | .............. | 3,000,000.00 |
| Bangor & Aroostook R. R. Co........... | 196,000.00 | .............. | 16,000.00 | 180,000.00 |
| Birmingham & Northwestern Ry. Co.... | .............. | 75,000.00 | .............. | 75,000.00 |
| Boston & Maine R. R................ | 14,705,479.00 | 5,000,000.00 | 5,000,000.00 | 14,705,479.00 |
| Buffalo, Rochester & Pittsburgh Ry. Co.. | 1,000,000.00 | .............. | .............. | 1,000,000.00 |
| Cambria & Indiana R. R. Co........... | 250,000.00 | .............. | 250,000.00 | .............. |
| Carolina, Clinchfield & Ohio Ry. Co...... | 3,000,000.00 | 6,000,000.00 | 1,000,000.00 | 8,000,000.00 |
| Central of Georgia Ry. Co............. | 237,900.00 | .............. | 15,860.00 | 222,040.00 |
| Central New England Ry. Co............. | 300,000.00 | .............. | .............. | 300,000.00 |
| Central Vermont Ry. Co............. | 193,000.00 | .............. | 13,000.00 | 180,000.00 |
| Charles City Western Ry. Co........... | 140,000.00 | .............. | .............. | 140,000.00 |
| Chesapeake & Ohio Rv. Co............. | 6,428,000.00 | 2,669,000.00 | 1,023,976.03 | 8,073,023.97 |
| Chicago & Eastern Illinois R. R. Co., Receiver. | 785,000.00 | .............. | .............. | 785,000.00 |
| Chicago Great Western R. R. Co........... | 2,445,373.00 | 240,000.00 | 240,000.00 | 2,445,373.00 |
| Chicago, Indianapolis & Louisville Ry. Co. | 155,000.00 | .............. | .............. | 155,000.00 |
| Chicago, Milwaukee & St. Paul Ry. Co... | 35,340,000.00 | 25,000,000.00 | 25,340,000.00 | 35,000,000.00 |
| Chicago, Rock Island & Pacific Ry. Co... | 9,862,000.00 | .............. | .............. | 9,862,000.00 |
| Chicago & Western Indiana R. R. Co.... | 7,911,000.00 | .............. | 94,000.00 | 7,817,000.00 |
| Cisco & Northeastern Ry. Co........... | .............. | 216,450.00 | .............. | 236,450.00 |
| Cowlitz, Chehalis & Cascade Ry. Co...... | .............. | 45,000.00 | .............. | 45,000.00 |
| Cumberland & Manchester R. R. Co..... | 375,000.00 | .............. | .............. | 375,000.00 |
| Des Moines & Central Iowa R. R. (formerly the Inter-Urban Ry. Co.)......... | 633,500.00 | .............. | .............. | 633,500.00 |
| Erie R. R. Co................ | 11,574,450.00 | .............. | .............. | 11,574,450.00 |
| Evansville, Indianapolis & Terre Haute Ry. Co... | 150,000.00 | 250,000.00 | .............. | 400,000.00 |
| Fernwood, Columbia & Gulf R. R. Co.... | 33,000.00 | .............. | .............. | 33,000.00 |
| Flemingsburg & Northern R. R. Co..... | 7,250.00 | .............. | .............. | 7,250.00 |
| Fort Do ge, Des Moines & Southern R. R. Co d.................... | 200,000.00 | .............. | .............. | 200,000.00 |
| Fort Smith & Western R. R. Co., Receiver of the.................... | 156,000.00 | .............. | .............. | 156,000.00 |
| Gainesville & Northwestern R. R. Co.... | .............. | 75,000.00 | .............. | 75,000.00 |
| Georgia & Florida Ry., Receivers of.... | 792,000.00 | .............. | .............. | 792,000.00 |
| Great Northern Ry. Co................ | 18,362,000.00 | .............. | 16,620,000.00 | 1,742,000.00 |
| Greene County R. R. Co............. | 60,000.00 | .............. | 6,000.00 | 54,000.00 |
| Gulf, Mobile & Northern R. R. Co...... | 515,000.00 | 918,500.00 | .............. | 1,433,500.00 |
| Hocking Valley Ry. Co.................. | 1,053,000.00 | 612,000.00 | .............. | 1,665,000.00 |
| Illinois Central R. R. Co............ | 4,144,000.00 | .............. | 296,000.00 | 3,848,000.00 |
| Indiana Harbor Belt R. R. Co......... | 579,000.00 | .............. | 165,000.00 | 414,000.00 |
| International & Great Northern Ry. Co., Receiver of.................. | 194,300.00 | .............. | 38,860.00 | 155,440.00 |
| Kansas City, Mexico & Orient R. R. Co., Receiver of.................... | 2,500,000.00 | 2,500,000.00 | 2,500,000.00 | 2,500,000.00 |
| Kansas City Terminal Ry. Co............. | 580,000.00 | .............. | .............. | 580,000.00 |
| Lake Erie, Franklin & Clarion R. R. Co.. | 25,000.00 | .............. | 2,500.00 | 22,500.00 |
| Long Island R. R. Co.............. | 719,000.00 | .............. | 219,000.00 | 500,000.00 |
| Louisville & Jeffersonville Bridge & R. R. Co. .................... | 162,000.00 | .............. | .............. | 162,000.00 |
| Maine Central R. R. Co.............. | 2,373,000.00 | .............. | .............. | 2,373,000.00 |
| Minneapolis & St. Louis R. R. Co........ | 1,382,000.00 | .............. | .............. | 1,382,000.00 |
| Missouri, Kansas & Texas Ry. Co. of Texas, Receiver of.............. | 450,000.00 | .............. | 30,000.00 | 420,000.00 |
| Missouri & North Arkansas Ry. Co...... | .............. | 3,500,000.00 | .............. | 3,500,000.00 |
| Missouri Pacific R. R. Co............. | 5,709,760.00 | .............. | 80,000.00 | 5,629,760.00 |
| National Railway Service Corporation: | | | | |
| Baltimore & Ohio R. R. Co......... | 5,026,666.67 | .............. | 520,000.00 | 4,506,666.67 |
| Bangor & Aroostook R. R. Co....... | 53,100.00 | .............. | 5,810.00 | 47,790.00 |
| Chicago, Rock Island & Pacific Ry. Co. | 1,568,540.00 | .............. | 7,497.96 | 1,561,042.04 |
| Minneapolis & St. Louis R. R. Co.... | 386,190.00 | .............. | 1,846.08 | 384,343.92 |
| New Orleans, Texas & Mexico R. R. Co...... | 926,000.00 | .............. | 95,793.12 | 830,206.88 |
| Wheeling & Lake Erie Ry. Co....... | 3,304,000.00 | .............. | 15,793.95 | 3,288,206.05 |

*Loans to carriers under section 210 of the transportation act of 1920, as amended, and repayments on such loans from November 16, 1921, to November 15, 1922, inclusive. with loans outstanding November 15, 1921, and November 15, 1922—Continued.*

| Carrier. | Loans outstanding Nov. 15, 1921. | Loans made from Nov. 15, 1921, to Nov. 15, 1922. | Repayments from Nov. 16, 1921, to Nov. 15, 1922. | Loans outstanding Nov. 15, 1922. |
|---|---|---|---|---|
| New Orleans, Texas & Mexico R. R. Co.. | $234,000.00 | | $234,000.00 | |
| New York Central R. R. Co | 26,775,000.00 | | 3,785,000.00 | $22,990,000.00 |
| New York, New Haven & Hartford R. R. Co | 16,530,000.00 | $2,900,000.00 | 100,000.00 | 19,330,000.00 |
| Norfolk Southern R. R. Co | 261,000.00 | 1,050,000.00 | 11,100.00 | 1,299,900.00 |
| Northern Pacific Ry. Co | 6,000,000.00 | | 6,000,000.00 | |
| Pennsylvania R. R. Co | 12,480,000.00 | | 12,480,000.00 | |
| Peoria & Pekin Union Ry. Co | 1,799,000.00 | | 2,000.00 | 1,797,000.00 |
| Rutland R. R. Co | 61,000.00 | | | 61,000.00 |
| Salt Lake & Utah R. R. Co | 984,300.00 | | 80,300.00 | 904,000.00 |
| Seaboard Air Line Ry. Co | 8,558,900.00 | 139,500.00 | | 8,698,400.00 |
| Seaboard-Bay Line Co | | 4,400,000.00 | | 4,400,000.00 |
| Shearwood Ry. Co | 29,000.00 | | | 29,000.00 |
| Tampa Northern R. R. Co | 100,000.00 | | | 100,000.00 |
| Tennessee Central Ry. Co | | 1,500,000.00 | | 1,500,000.00 |
| Terminal Railroad Association of St. Louis | 896,925.00 | | 896,925.00 | |
| Toledo, St. Louis & Western R. R. Co., Receiver of | 692,000.00 | | 46,000.00 | 646,000.00 |
| Trans-Mississippi Terminal R. R. Co | 1,000,000.00 | | | 1,000,000.00 |
| Virginia Blue Ridge Ry. Co | 106,000.00 | | | 106,000.00 |
| Virginia Southern R. R. Co | 38,000.00 | | | 38,000.00 |
| Virginian Ry. Co., The | 2,000,000.00 | | | 2,000,000.00 |
| Waterloo, Cedar Falls & Northern Ry. Co. | 1,260,000.00 | | | 1,260,000.00 |
| Western Maryland Ry. Co | 2,772,800.00 | 650,000.00 | 100,000.00 | 3,322,800.00 |
| Wheeling & Lake Erie Ry. Co | 2,700,000.00 | 260,000.00 | | 2,960,000.00 |
| Wilmington, Brunswick & Southern R. R. Co | 90,000.00 | | | 90,000.00 |
| Wichita Northwestern Ry. Co | 381,750.00 | | | 381,750.00 |
| Total | 238,208,183.67 | 58,419,450.00 | 77,425,512.14 | 219,202,121.53 |
| Loans and repayments to Nov. 15, 1921, inclusive | | 259,467,217.00 | 21,259,033.33 | |
| Total loans and repayments to Nov. 15, 1922, inclusive | | 317,886,667.00 | 98,684,545.47 | |

## EXHIBIT 76.

### SECURITIES OWNED BY THE UNITED STATES GOVERNMENT.

[Compiled from latest reports received by the Treasury, June 30, 1922.]

Obligations of foreign governments, under authority of acts approved Apr. 24, 1917, and Sept. 24, 1917, as amended (on basis of cash advances, less repayments of principal):

| | | |
|---|---:|---:|
| Belgium | $347,251,013.40 | |
| Cuba | 7,740,500.00 | |
| Czechoslovakia | 61,974,041.10 | |
| France | 2,933,516,448.19 | |
| Great Britain | 4,135,818,358.44 | |
| Greece | 15,000,000.00 | |
| Italy | 1,648,034,050.90 | |
| Liberia | 26,000.00 | |
| Rumania | 23,205,819.52 | |
| Russia | 187,729,750.00 | |
| Serbia | 26,126,574.59 | |
| Total | | $9,386,422,556.14 |

Foreign obligations received from the Secretary of War on account of sale of surplus war supplies:

| | | |
|---|---:|---:|
| Belgium | 29,872,732.54 | |
| Czechoslovakia | 20,612,300.11 | |
| Esthonia | 12,213,377.88 | |
| France | 407,341,145.01 | |
| Latvia | 2,521,869.32 | |
| Lithuania | 4,159,491.96 | |
| Nicaragua | 170,585.35 | |
| Poland | 57,411,894.41 | |
| Rumania | 12,922,675.42 | |
| Russia | 406,082.30 | |
| Serbs, Croats, and Slovenes | 24,978,020.99 | |
| Total | | 572,610,175.29 |

Foreign obligations received from the Secretary of the Navy on account of sale of surplus war supplies:

| | | |
|---|---:|---:|
| Poland | | 2,263,709.66 |

Foreign obligations received from the American Relief Administration on account of relief, pursuant to act approved Feb. 25, 1919:

| | | |
|---|---:|---:|
| Armenia | 8,028,412.15 | |
| Czechoslovakia | 6,428,089.19 | |
| Esthonia | 1,785,767.72 | |
| Finland | 8,281,926.17 | |
| Latvia | 2,610,417.82 | |
| Lithuania | 822,136.07 | |
| Poland | 51,671,749.36 | |
| Russia | 4,465,465.07 | |
| Total | | 84,093,963.55 |

Capital stock of war emergency corporations:

| | | |
|---|---:|---:|
| Capital stock of the Emergency Fleet Corporation | | 50,000,000.00 |
| Capital stock of the Hoboken Manufacturers R. R. Co | | 400,000.00 |
| Capital stock of the Housing Corporation, issued | 70,000,000.00 | |
| Less amount retired plus cash deposits covered into Treasury under act approved July 11, 1919 | 15,927,735.11 | |
| | | 54,072,264.89 |
| Capital stock of the Sugar Equalization Board (Inc.) | 5,000,000.00 | |
| Offset by cash deposited with Treasurer United States to credit of the board | 14,369,856.84 | |
| Capital stock of the United States Grain Corporation authorized and issued | 500,000,000.00 | |
| Less amount retired | 475,000,000.00 | |
| Capital stock of the United States Spruce Production Corporation | 10,000,000.00 | |
| Less cash deposited with the Treasurer of the United States to the credit of the corporation | 3,457,806.55 | |
| | | 25,000,000.00 |
| Capital stock of the War Finance Corporation, authorized and issued | 500,000,000.00 | |
| Less cash deposited with the Treasurer of the United States to credit of War Finance Corporation | 308,521,622.42 | |
| | | 6,542,193.45 |
| | | 191,478,377.58 |

Obligations of carriers acquired under section 7 of the Federal control act, approved Mar. 21, 1918, as amended: [1]

| | | |
|---|---:|---:|
| Boston & Maine R. R. | 26,165,000.00 | |
| Minneapolis & St. Louis R. R. Co | 750,000.00 | |
| Missouri, Kansas & Texas Ry. of Texas, receiver of the | 52,000.00 | |
| New York Central R. R. Co | 6,500,000.00 | |
| Pennsylvania R. R. Co | 20,000,000.00 | |
| Pittsburgh & Lake Erie R. R. Co | 500,000.00 | |
| Seaboard Air Line Ry. Co | 1,850,000.00 | |
| Washington, Brandywine & Point Lookout R. R. Co | 50,000.00 | |
| Total | | 55,867,000.00 |

[1] This amount does not include securities purchased by the Director General of Railroads under the provisions of section 12 of the Federal control act, approved Mar. 21, 1918.

Equipment trust 6 per cent gold notes, acquired by Director General of Railroads pursuant to Federal control act of Mar. 21, 1918, as amended, and act approved Nov. 19, 1919, to provide for the reimbursement of the United States for motive power, cars, and other equipment ordered for carriers under Federal control:[1]

| | |
|---|---|
| Ann Arbor R. R. Co | $228,800.00 |
| Atlanta, Birmingham & Atlantic Ry. Co | 917,000.00 |
| Baltimore & Ohio R. R. Co | 5,142,800.00 |
| Boston & Maine R. R | 5,904,600.00 |
| Carolina, Clinchfield & Ohio Ry | 1,794,000.00 |
| Charleston & Western Carolina Ry. Co | 227,500.00 |
| Chicago & Alton R. R. Co | 525,200.00 |
| Chicago & Eastern Illinois R. R. Co | 213,200.00 |
| Chicago, Indianapolis & Louisville Ry. Co | 300,300.00 |
| Chicago Great Western R. R. Co | 188,500.00 |
| Chicago, Milwaukee & St. Paul Ry. Co | 4,751,500.00 |
| Chicago & Western Indiana R. R. Co | 80,600.00 |
| Detroit, Toledo & Ironton R. R. Co | 244,400.00 |
| Detroit & Toledo Shore Line R. R. Co | 144,300.00 |
| Erie R. R. Co | 1,301,300.00 |
| Grand Trunk Ry. of Canada | 258,700.00 |
| Grand Trunk Western Ry. Co | 894,400.00 |
| Hocking Valley Ry. Co | 819,000.00 |
| Kansas City Southern Ry. Co | 275,600.00 |
| Maine Central R. R. Co | 347,100.00 |
| Minneapolis & St. Louis R. R. Co | 436,800.00 |
| Missouri, Kansas & Texas Ry. Co | 365,300.00 |
| Missouri Pacific R. R. Co | 3,008,200.00 |
| Mobile & Ohio R. R. Co | 175,500.00 |
| Morgantown & Kingwood R. R. Co | 2,254,200.00 |
| New York, New Haven & Hartford R. R. Co | 1,285,700.00 |
| Norfolk Southern R. R. Co | 114,400.00 |
| Northwestern Pacific R. R. Co | 79,300.00 |
| Pere Marquette Ry. Co | 2,918,500.00 |
| Rutland R. R. Co | 107,900.00 |
| Seaboard Air Line Ry. Co | 1,430,000.00 |
| Southern Ry Co | 2,974,400.00 |
| Spokane, Portland & Seattle Ry. Co | 253,500.00 |
| St. Louis-San Francisco Ry. Co | 4,156,100.00 |
| Texas & Pacific Ry. Co | 691,600.00 |
| Toledo, St. Louis & Western R. R. Co | 341,900.00 |
| Wabash R. R. Co | 3,273,400.00 |
| Western Maryland Ry. Co | 248,300.00 |
| Wheeling & Lake Erie Ry. Co | 1,326,000.00 |

Total........................................ $49,999,800.00

Obligations of carriers acquired pursuant to section 207 of the transportation act approved Feb. 28, 1920, as amended:

| | |
|---|---|
| Ann Arbor R. R. Co | 550,000.00 |
| Baltimore & Ohio R. R. Co | 9,000,000.00 |
| Bangor & Aroostook R. R. Co | 325,000.00 |
| Chicago & Eastern Illinois R. R. Co | 3,425,000.00 |
| Chicago, Milwaukee & St. Paul Ry. Co | 20,000,000.00 |
| Erie R. R. Co | 8,250,000.00 |
| Gulf, Mobile & Northern R. R. Co | 480,000.00 |
| International & Great Northern Ry. Co | 2,400,000.00 |
| Missouri Pacific R. R. Co | 3,000,000.00 |
| New York, Chicago & St. Louis R. R. Co | 1,000,000.00 |
| New York, New Haven & Hartford R. R. Co | 64,316,500.00 |
| St. Louis-San Francisco Ry. Co | 3,000,000.00 |
| Wheeling & Lake Erie Ry. Co | 900,000.00 |

Total........................................ 116,646,500.00

Obligations of carriers acquired pursuant to section 210 of the transportation act approved Feb. 28, 1920, as amended:

| | |
|---|---|
| Akron, Canton & Youngstown Ry. Co | 212,000.00 |
| Alabama, Tennessee & Northern R. R. Corporation | 475,250.00 |
| Alabama & Vicksburg Ry. Co | 1,394,000.00 |
| Ann Arbor R. R. Co | 550,000.00 |
| Aransas Harbor Terminal Ry | 50,000.00 |
| Atlanta, Birmingham & Atlantic Ry. Co | 180,000.00 |
| Baltimore & Ohio R. R. Co | 3,000,000.00 |
| Bangor & Aroostook R. R. Co | 184,000.00 |
| Birmingham & Northwestern Ry. Co | 75,000.00 |
| Boston & Maine R. R | 14,705,479.00 |
| Buffalo, Rochester & Pittsburgh Ry. Co | 1,000,600.00 |
| Carolina, Clinchfield & Ohio Ry | 8,000,000.00 |
| Central of Georgia R. R. Co | 222,040.00 |
| Central New England Ry. Co | 300,000.00 |
| Central Vermont Ry. Co | 193,000.00 |
| Charles City Western Ry. Co | 140,000.00 |
| Chesapeake & Ohio Ry. Co | 9,097,000.00 |
| Chicago & Eastern Illinois R. R. Co., receiver of | 785,000.00 |
| Chicago Great Western R. R. Co | 2,445,373.00 |
| Chicago, Indianapolis & Louisville Ry. Co | 155,000.00 |
| Chicago, Milwaukee & St. Paul Ry. Co | 35,000,000.00 |

[1] The notes are in series which mature, respectively, on the 15th day of January in various years up to 1935.

Obligations of carriers acquired pursuant to section 210 of the transportation act approved Feb. 28, 1920, as amended—Continued.

| | |
|---|---:|
| Chicago, Rock Island & Pacific Ry. Co...: | $9,862,000.00 |
| Chicago & Western Indiana R. R. Co | 7,817,000.00 |
| Cisco & Northeastern Ry. Co | 152,863.00 |
| Cowlitz, Chehalis & Cascade Ry. Co | 45,000.00 |
| Cumberland & Manchester R. R. Co | 375,000.00 |
| Des Moines & Central Iowa R. R., formerly the Inter-Urban Railway Co | 633,500.00 |
| Erie R. R. Co | 11,574,450.00 |
| Evansville, Indianapolis & Terre Haute Ry. Co | 400,000.00 |
| Fernwood, Columbia & Gulf R. R. Co | 33,000.00 |
| Flemingsburg & Northern R. R. Co | 7,250.00 |
| Fort Dodge, Des Moines & Southern R. R. Co | 200,000.00 |
| Fort Smith & Western R. R. Co, receiver of the | 156,000.00 |
| Gainesville & Northwestern R. R. Co | 75,000.00 |
| Georgia & Florida Ry., receivers of | 792,000.00 |
| Great Northern Ry Co | 3,362,000.00 |
| Greene County R. R Co | 60,000.00 |
| Gulf, Mobile & Northern R. R. Co | 1,433,500.00 |
| Hocking Valley Ry. Co | 1,665,000.00 |
| Illinois Central R. R. Co | 4,144,000.00 |
| Indiana Harbor Belt R. R. Co | 579,000.00 |
| International & Great Northern Ry. Co., receiver of | 194,300.00 |
| Kansas City, Mexico & Orient R. R. Co., receiver of the | 2,500,000.00 |
| Kansas City Terminal Ry. Co | 580,000.00 |
| Lake Erie, Franklin & Clarion R. R. Co | 23,750.00 |
| Long Island R. R. Co | 500,000.00 |
| Louisville & Jeffersonville Bridge and R. R. Co | 162,000.00 |
| Maine Central R. R. Co | 2,373,000.00 |
| Minneapolis & St. Louis R. R. Co | 1,382,000.00 |
| Missouri, Kansas & Texas Ry. Co. of Texas, receiver of the | 450,000.00 |
| Missouri & North Arkansas Ry. Co | 3,500,000.00 |
| Missouri Pacific R. R. Co | 5,629,760.00 |
| National Ry. Service Corp | 10,825,289.93 |
| New Orleans, Texas & Mexico Ry. Co | 234,000.00 |
| New York Central R. R. Co | 24,785,000.00 |
| New York, New Haven & Hartford R. R. Co | 19,430,000.00 |
| Norfolk Southern R. R. Co | 1,299,900.00 |
| Pennsylvania R. R. Co | 12,480,000.00 |
| Peoria & Pekin Union Ry. Co | 1,797,000.00 |
| Rutland R. R. Co | 61,000.00 |
| Salt Lake & Utah R. R. Co | 904,000.00 |
| Seaboard Air Line Ry. Co | 8,698,400.00 |
| Seaboard Bay Line Co | 2,200,000.00 |
| Shearwood Ry. Co | 29,000.00 |
| Tampa Northern R. R. Co | 100,000.00 |
| Terminal R. R. Association of St. Louis | 519,175.50 |
| Toledo, St. Louis & Western R. R. Co., receiver of | 646,000.00 |
| Trans-Mississippi Terminal R. R. Co | 1,000,000.00 |
| Virginia Blue Ridge Ry. Co | 105,000.00 |
| Virginian Ry. Co | 2,000,000.00 |
| Virginia Southern R. R. Co | 38,000.00 |
| Waterloo, Cedar Falls & Northern Ry. Co | 1,260,000.00 |
| Western Maryland Ry. Co | 3,322,800.00 |
| Wheeling & Lake Erie Ry. Co | 2,960,000.00 |
| Wichita, Northwestern Ry. Co | 381,750.00 |
| Wilmington, Brunswick & Southern R. R. Co | 90,000.00 |

| | |
|---|---:|
| Total | $233,991,829.93 |
| Capital stock of the Panama R. R. Co | 7,000,000.00 |

Capital stock of Federal land banks, on basis of purchases, less repayments to date:

| | |
|---|---:|
| Springfield, Mass | 689,985.00 |
| Baltimore, Md | 630,035.00 |
| Columbia, S. C | 429,510.00 |
| Louisville, Ky | 325,435.00 |
| New Orleans, La | 410,465.00 |
| St. Louis, Mo | 321,635.00 |
| St. Paul, Minn | 150,965.00 |
| Omaha, Nebr | 44,740.00 |
| Wichita, Kans | 356,035.00 |
| Houston, Tex | 177,885.00 |
| Berkeley, Calif | 601,110.00 |
| Spokane, Wash | 127,080.00 |

| | |
|---|---:|
| Total | 4,264,880.00 |

Federal farm loan bonds, acquired pursuant to act approved Jan. 18, 1918, as extended by joint resolution approved May 26, 1920:

| | |
|---|---:|
| Federal farm loan 4½ per cent bonds | 136,885,000.00 |
| Federal farm loan 5 per cent bonds | 1,750,000.00 |

| | |
|---|---:|
| Total | 138,635,000.00 |
| Securities received by the Secretary of War on account of sales of surplus war supplies | 29,138,771.32 |
| Securities received by the Secretary of the Navy on account of sales of surplus property | 9,870,377.78 |
| Securities received by the United States Shipping Board on account of sales of ships, etc | 38,752,450.33 |

| | |
|---|---:|
| Grand total | $11,057,052,849.92 |

Amount due the United States from the central branch of the Union Pacific R. R. on account of bonds issued (Pacific R. R. aid bonds, acts approved July 1, 1862, July 2, 1864, and May 7, 1878):

| | |
|---|---|
| Principal................................................................... | $1,600,000.00 |
| Interest.................................................................... | 1,940,373.55 |
| Total...................................................................... | 3,540,373.55 |

NOTE.—This statement is made up on the basis of the face value of the securities therein described as received by the United States, with due regard for repayments. To the extent that the securities are not held in the custody of the Treasury, the statement is made up from reports received from other Government departments and establishments. The statement does not include securities which the United States holds as collateral, or as the result of the investment of trust funds (as, for example, securities held for account of the Alien Property Custodian, the United States Government life insurance fund, and other similar trust funds).

## EXHIBIT 77.

### OBLIGATIONS OF FOREIGN GOVERNMENTS HELD BY THE UNITED STATES, TOGETHER WITH INTEREST ACCRUED AND REMAINING UNPAID THEREON AS OF THE LAST INTEREST PERIOD PRIOR TO OR ENDING WITH NOVEMBER 15, 1922.

| Country. | Obligations acquired under Liberty bond acts. | | Obligations acquired from sales of surplus war material (act of July 9, 1918). | | Obligations acquired by American relief administration on account of relief (act of Feb. 25, 1919). | | Obligations held by United States Grain Corporation on account of sales of flour (act of Mar. 30, 1920). | | Total. | | Total indebtedness. |
|---|---|---|---|---|---|---|---|---|---|---|---|
| | Principal. | Interest (including interest due Nov. 15, 1922). | Principal. | Interest. | Principal. | Interest. | Principal. | Interest. | Principal. | Interest. | |
| Armenia | | | | | $8,028,412.15 | $1,204,261.83 | $3,931,505.34 | $472,995.05 | $11,959,917.49 | $1,677,256.88 | $13,637,174.37 |
| Austria | | | | | | | 24,055,708.92 | 2,886,685.08 | 24,055,708.92 | 2,886,685.08 | 26,942,394.00 |
| Belgium | $347,251,013.40 | $60,073,383.65 | $29,872,732.54 | [1][2] | | | | | 377,123,745.94 | 60,073,383.65 | 437,197,129.59 |
| Cuba | 7,740,500.00 | [3] | | | | | | | 7,740,500.00 | [2] | 7,740,500.00 |
| Czechoslovakia | 61,974,041.10 | 10,136,141.81 | 20,612,300.11 | 2,939,392.88 | 6,428,089.19 | 964,213.33 | 2,873,238.25 | 344,788.60 | 91,857,668.65 | 14,404,536.67 | 106,292,205.32 |
| Esthonia | | | 12,213,377.88 | 1,832,006.70 | 1,785,767.72 | 257,618.96 | | | 13,999,145.60 | 2,089,625.66 | 16,088,771.26 |
| Finland | | | | | 8,281,926.17 | 1,012,436.10 | | | 8,281,926.17 | 1,012,436.10 | 9,294,362.27 |
| France | 2,933,405,070.15 | 503,386,035.61 | 407,341,145.01 | [2] | | | | | 3,340,746,215.16 | 503,386,035.61 | 3,844,132,250.77 |
| Great Britain | 4,135,818,358.44 | 611,044,201.85 | | | | | | | 4,135,818,358.44 | 611,044,201.85 | 4,746,862,560.29 [4] |
| Greece | 15,000,000.00 | 750,000.00 | | | | | | | 15,000,000.00 | 750,000.00 | 15,750,000.00 |
| Italy | 1,648,034,050.90 | 284,681,434.61 | | | | | 1,685,835.61 | 202,300.28 | 1,648,034,050.90 | 284,681,434.61 | 1,932,715,485.51 |
| Latvia | | | 2,521,869.32 | 232,014.20 | 2,610,417.82 | 391,562.67 | | | 5,132,287.14 | 643,576.87 | 5,775,864.01 |
| Liberia | 26,000.00 | 3,518.85 | | | | | | | 26,000.00 | 3,518.85 | 29,518.85 |
| Lithuania | | | 4,159,491.96 | 623,923.80 | 822,136.07 | 123,320.40 | | | 4,981,628.03 | 747,244.20 | 5,729,872.23 |
| Nicaragua | | | | | | | | | 170,585.35 | [1] | 170,585.35 |
| Poland | | | 59,678,604.07 | 7,042,817.10 | 51,671,749.36 | 7,750,762.41 | 24,312,514.37 | 2,825,229.50 | 135,662,867.80 | 17,618,809.01 | 153,281,676.81 |
| Rumania | 23,205,819.52 | 3,925,703.00 | 12,922,675.42 | 1,938,401.34 | | | | | 36,128,494.94 | 5,864,104.34 | 41,992,599.28 |
| Russia | 187,729,750.00 | 39,214,326.16 | 406,082.30 | 10,152.06 | 4,465,465.07 | 488,192.56 | | | 192,601,297.37 | 39,712,670.78 | 232,313,968.15 |
| Serbia | 26,126,574.59 | 4,611,738.14 | 24,978,020.99 | 3,382,349.78 | | | | | 51,104,595.58 | 7,994,087.92 | 59,098,683.50 |
| Total | 9,386,311,178.10 | 1,517,826,483.68 | 574,876,884.95 | 18,041,057.86 | 84,093,963.55 | 12,192,363.31 | 56,858,802.49 | 6,731,998.51 | 10,102,140,829.00 | 1,554,791,908.36 | 11,656,932,737.45 |

[1] No interest due on Nicaraguan notes until maturity, as is also the case of certain Belgian obligations aggregating $2,284,151.40.

[2] Interest has been paid as it became due.

[3] Includes $61,000,000 of British obligations which were given for Pittman silver advances and for which an agreement for payment has been made.

[4] Great Britain paid $50,000,000 on October 16, 1922, and $0,000,000 on November 15, 1922, on account of interest on other than Pittman silver obligations.

## Exhibit 78.

### SPECIMEN OF OBLIGATION OF AUSTRIA.

Obligation of the Government of Austria—Twenty Four Million Sixty Six Thousand Seven Hundred Ninety Eight Dollars and Fifty Six Cents ($24,066,798.56).—Relief Series B of Nineteen Hundred and Twenty.—No. I.

The Government of Austria for value received, promises to pay to the Government of the United States of America, or assigns, on the First Day of January, Nineteen Hundred and Twenty-Five, the principal sum of Twenty Four Million Sixty-Six Thousand Seven Hundred Ninety Eight Dollars and Fifty-Six Cents ($24,066,798.56), on which interest will be paid half yearly at the rate of six per cent (6%) per annum from date of this obligation to the date of payment. Both the principal and the interest of this obligation will be paid in gold coin of the United States of America, of the standard weight and fineness existing at the date of this obligation at the Treasury of the United States of America in the city of Washington, District of Columbia, or at the option of the holder, at the Sub-Treasury of the United States of America in the City of New York.

The principal and interest of this obligation will be paid without deduction for and will be exempt from any and all tax and/or charge, present and future, imposed by authority of the Government of Austria or its possessions, or by any political or taxing authority within Austria.

This obligation is one of a series of obligations of similar tenor but in different amounts and payable in different currencies, all maturing on the first day of January Nineteen Hundred and Twenty-Five, designated as "Relief Series B of 1920".

The Government of Austria agrees that no payment will be made upon or in respect of any of the obligations of said Series issued by the Government of Austria before, at or after, maturity, whether for principal or for interest, unless a similar payment shall simultaneously be made upon all obligations of the said Series issued by the Government of Austria in proportion to the respective obligations of said Series.

Pursuant to the powers conferred upon it, the Reparation Commission has authorized the Austrian Government, under the control of the Austrian Section of the Reparation Commission, to issue the present series of bonds, which shall be a first charge upon all the assets and revenues of Austria, and shall have a priority over costs of reparation under the Treaty of Saint-Germain, or under any treaty or agreement supplementary thereto, or under arrangements concluded between Austria and the Allied and Associated Powers during the Armistice signed on November 3rd, 1918, without prejudice to the obligations of Austria to pay the expenses of the Armies of Occupation, of the Reparation Commission and of restitution, and to make deliveries and payments in kind under the Treaty of Saint-Germain (except under Article 181, and Paragraph 19 of Annex II of Part VIII) and under any protocols or agreements in force to the extent to which such deliveries may be required by the Reparation Commission or, in accordance with the provision of the said Treaty, protocols or agreements, by an interested Power.

IN WITNESS WHEREOF the Government of Austria has caused this obligation to be executed and its official seal attached by Dr. Richard Reisch, Secretary of State for Finances duly authorized and empowered for that purpose.

Dated September 4, 1920.

Signed for the Government of Austria

WITNESS:

| (Sgd) | Dr. SIMON | (Sgd) | REISCH |
| | | | *Secretary of State for Finances.* |
| (Sgd) | Dr. SCHULLER | (Sgd) | Dr. WLADIMER BECK |
| (SEAL) | | | *President of the Audit Office.* |

Countersigned for the Austrian Section of the Reparation Commission.

(Sgd)  H. KLOBUKOWSKI            (Sgd)  SCARAMANGA

(Notation on back of obligation:)

The aforegoing obligation has been taken from the Government of Austria in payment of food commodities sold by the United States Grain Corporation to the Government of Austria.

The United States Grain Corporation finds that the Government of Austria is entitled to an allowance amounting to Eleven Thousand and Eighty-nine Dollars Sixty-Four Cents ($11,089.64) for damaged flour on the steamship "Gudvun", and that the aforegoing obligation should be credited in the said amount.

UNITED STATES GRAIN CORPORATION
(Signed)  EDW. M. FLESH
*Vice-President and Treasurer.*

Dated at New York, N. Y., November 4th, 1920.

## EXHIBIT 79.

**LETTER FROM THE SECRETARY OF STATE CONCERNING THE LIQUIDATION OF RUSSIAN OBLIGATIONS IN THE UNITED STATES, AND THE REPLY OF THE SECRETARY OF THE TREASURY.**

DEPARTMENT OF STATE,
*Washington, May 23, 1922.*

MY DEAR MR. SECRETARY: I desire to refer to the arrangements made toward the close of 1917 for the liquidation of the financial business of Russia in this country, following the fall of the last recognized Russian Government.

It appears from the files of the State Department, and from published records, that the extraordinarily difficult task of dealing with the Russian financial situation in this country under the circumstances indicated was undertaken jointly by the State and Treasury Departments in cooperation with Mr. Boris Bakhmeteff, representing the last recognized Russian Government, and that contracts then outstanding with American manufacturers to the value of more than $102,000,000 were successfully liquidated with funds of the Russian Government amounting to much less than that sum. It is the understanding of the State Department that this process of liquidation has now been brought to a practical conclusion, and that such business as remains is in process of orderly settlement.

Having regard to recent public discussion of the subject, may I ask that you confirm these facts and furnish any additional information from the records of the Treasury Department which you may consider helpful to a public understanding of the matter?

I am, my dear Mr. Mellon,

Very sincerely yours,

(Sgd)   CHARLES E. HUGHES..

----

TREASURY DEPARTMENT,
*Washington, June 2, 1922.*

MY DEAR MR. SECRETARY: I received your letter of May 23, 1922, regarding the liquidation of the Russian Government's financial obli-gations in this country after the fall of the last recognized Russian Government.

The facts set forth in your letter are in accord with the information possessed by the Treasury on the subject, and I am glad to avail myself of your suggestion to furnish any additional information from the Treasury's records that may be considered helpful to a public understanding of the matter.

It appears that under the authority of the Liberty Bond Acts the Secretary of the Treasury, with the approval of the President, made certain loans to the Provisional Government of Russia for the purpose of more effectually providing for the national security and defense and prosecuting the war. The net amount of the loans so made is $187,729,750. Although a credit of $100,000,000 was established by the Treasury in favor of the Russian Government on May 16, 1917, the first loan to that Government was not actually made until July 6, 1917, and was in the amount of $35,000,000. No loans were made by the Treasury to the Russian Government after the fall of the Provisional Government early in November, 1917, with the exception of an advance of $1,329,750 on November 15, 1917, the proceeds of which were simultaneously applied by the Russians to the payment of interest to the Government of the United States.

The funds advanced by the Treasury in making the above loans were used solely for the purchase of obligations of the Russian Government in accordance with the Liberty Bond Acts, in the same manner as with other foreign governments, and the funds so paid for these obligations became the funds of the Russian Government. All of the obligations thus purchased are signed in the name of the Provisional Government of Russia by Mr. Boris Bakhmeteff who was the representative of that Government designated to the Treasury by the Department of State as being authorized to sign them in the name and on behalf of that Government.

In connection with the loans so made to the Russian Government, the latter rendered reports to the Treasury of its expenditures. These reports cover the period from April 6, 1917, the date of the United States Government's entry into the war, to March 4, 1921, and show total expenditures for that period of about $231,000,000. The principal items of such expenditures appear to have been munitions, including remounts; exchange and cotton purchases, and other supplies. It would seem clear that only a comparatively small portion of the total expenditures of the Russian Government in this country during the period referred to was made from funds advanced by the United States Treasury, in view of the fact that it appears from the reports filed by the Russian representatives with this Department that of the $187,729,750 so loaned about $125,000,000 was transferred by the Russian Ambassador to the account of the Russian Ministry of Finance at Petrograd and only the balance of about $62,000,000 was retained by the Russian Ambassador for expenditure in this country.

According to information shown by the Treasury records, the Russian Government's financial situation in this country at the time of the fall of the Provisional Government in November, 1917, was, in a general way, as follows:

Its bank balances then on hand amounted to about $56,000,000. The Russian Ambassador has estimated that about $10,000,000 thereof represented the balance remaining from this Government's loans to Russia, and that the rest of such funds consisted of moneys derived from other sources, such as British credits and loans made by private bankers in this country. At this time the Russian Government also had a large amount of property in the United States, consisting mainly of war supplies. Apart from its indebtedness to the United States Government on account of the loans above mentioned, the Russian Government's financial obligations in the United States arose principally out of contracts for supplies and certain private loans issued in this country. The contractual liabilities amounted to about $102,000,000, and the total principal amount of such private loans was $86,000,000. In these circumstances, the Department of State and the Treasury considered it advisable to enter into arrangements with the Russian Ambassador with a view to effecting such an application of the Russian Government's available assets in this country that the interests of the American manufacturers and contractors and of the United States Government would be protected. In accordance with these arrangements, the Russian Ambassador deposited about $47,000,000 of the $56,000,000 cash above referred to with the National City Bank of New York in a so-called liquidation account, subject to his disposition. This money was to be devoted to the general liquidation of Russian obligations in this country. The balance of approximately $9,000,000 was placed in special accounts with that bank to be used for certain specific purposes. These funds also were subject to the Ambassador's disposition. Pursuant to an understanding had with the National City Bank, however, no withdrawals were to be made from the liquidation account without the bank's first notifying the Treasury and ascertaining whether it objected to the particular disbursement proposed.

It further appears that from December 1, 1917, when the liquidation account was opened, to March 4, 1921, when the account was closed, additional deposits were made therein, aggregating a total amount of about $29,000,000. The funds so deposited resulted chiefly from the sale of Russian property in this country and the charter hire from certain Russian ships. This made the total deposits in the liquidation account aggregate about $76,000,000, and the total disbursements from this account for the period in question also amounted to about $76,000,000. From the reports of the Russian representatives, it appears that these disbursements were made for supplies, transportation, storage, inspection, interest on loans made by the United States Government and on private loans floated in this country, salaries and upkeep of the Russian Embassy and consulates and other Russian institutions in the United States, and various miscellaneous purposes. It is further shown by such reports that payments on contracts for supplies amounted to approximately $36,000,000, and that about $10,000,000 was expended for interest on said loans. It will be noted that these two items alone are greatly in excess of the portion of the liquidation funds estimated by the Russian Ambassador to have been derived from American Government loans.

From the pertinent records, it appears that the settlement of the contracts outstanding in this country at the time of the fall of the Provisional Government was effected by the Russian Ambassador in cooperation with representatives of the Department of State, of the Treasury, and of the War Industries Board, with the result that the outstanding contracts were settled by payment, cancellation, and other means, without loss to American contractors. This settlement, I should say, may well be regarded as a noteworthy achievement in view of the extent of the liabilities involved in such contracts and the comparatively limited amount of cash available here to the Russian Government for use in respect thereto.

On February 14, 1921, the Treasury was informed by the Russian representatives that the liquidation of the outstanding liabilities of the Provisional Government of Russia in regard to contracts placed in the United States had been for the most part completed, and an arrangement was thereupon entered into whereby the liquidation account as such was closed out March 4, 1921, and the balance therein, amounting to $70,426.34, paid to the Treasurer of the United States and applied on account of interest due and payable on Russian obligations held by the United States. It was agreed by the Russian representatives, however, that sums which might still accrue to them from the remaining business of liquidation which would, prior to the closing out of the liquidation account, have been payable into that account, should likewise be applied on interest due on said obligations. Such sums to the aggregate amount of $337,766.73 have actually been paid since March 4, 1921, by the Russian representatives to the Treasurer of the United States and applied on interest due on the Russian obligations. It is the understanding of the Treasury that the funds so paid were realized chiefly from further sales of the Russian Government's property.

As you are aware, all of the information above given with respect to loans made by this Government to Russia, and the greater part of the data set forth in regard to the liquidation of the Russian Government's financial obligations in this country after the fall of the Provisional Government, have heretofore been made public in various reports and other documents. Attention is particularly called to the Annual Report of the Secretary of the Treasury for the fiscal year 1920; the testimony of Mr. Polk, then the Under Secretary of State, and of Mr. Leffingwell, a former Assistant Secretary of the Treasury, before the House Committee on Expenditures in the State Department on June 26 to September 8, 1919, in connection with House Resolution 132; the correspondence between the Russian Ambassador and the Department of State read before the subcommittee of the Senate Committee on Foreign Relations during the second session of the 66th Congress at the hearing on Senate Resolution 263 and printed on pages 501–504 of Senate Report 526, dated April 14, 1920; the hearings on House Resolution 635 before the Committee on Foreign

SECRETARY OF THE TREASURY.

Affairs of the House, 66th Congress, third session; Senate Document No. 86, 67th Congress, second session, entitled "Loans to Foreign Governments"; the testimony of former Secretary of the Treasury Houston and former Assistant Secretary of the Treasury Kelley before the Senate Committee on the Judiciary on February 2 to February 7, 1921; and the letter dated February 25, 1921, from Secretary Houston in response to Senate Resolution 417, printed in the Congressional Record for February 26, 1921.

In addition to reports showing the Russian Government's expenditures since the entry of the United States Government into the war, the Russian Embassy has filed with the Treasury Department detailed reports and statements, with explanatory memoranda, in respect to the liquidation by such Embassy, after the fall of the Provisional Government, of the Russian Government's obligations in the United States out of that Government's assets in this country, and I understand that the Russian representatives have shown every disposition to make all possible information available to the Treasury.

Sincerely yours,

(Signed) A. W. MELLON, *Secretary.*

Honorable CHARLES E. HUGHES,
*Secretary of State.*

EXHIBIT 80.

[Department Circular No. 154 (revised). Chief Clerk.]

## ACCEPTANCE OF UNITED STATES BONDS AND NOTES AS SECURITY IN LIEU OF SURETY OR SURETIES ON PENAL BONDS.

TREASURY DEPARTMENT,
OFFICE OF THE SECRETARY,
*Washington, May 15, 1922.*

*To Bond-Approving Officers, the Treasurer of the United States, Federal Reserve Banks, and Others Concerned:*

Treasury Department Circular No. 154, dated June 30, 1919, is hereby amended and supplemented so as to read as follows:

The following rules and regulations are prescribed for carrying into effect Section 1329 of the Revenue Act of 1921, approved November 23, 1921, which provides as follows:

SEC. 1329. That wherever by the laws of the United States or regulations made pursuant thereto, any person is required to furnish any recognizance, stipulation, bond, guaranty, or undertaking, hereinafter called "penal bond," with surety or sureties, such person may, in lieu of such surety or sureties, deposit as security with the official having authority to approve such penal bond, United States Liberty bonds or other bonds or notes of the United States in a sum equal at their par value to the amount of such penal bond required to be furnished, together with an agreement authorizing such official to collect or sell such bonds or notes so deposited in case of any default in the performance of any of the conditions or stipulations of such penal bond. The acceptance of such United States bonds or notes in lieu of surety or sureties required by law shall have the same force and effect as individual or corporate sureties, or certified checks, bank drafts, post-office money orders, or cash, for the penalty or amount of such penal bond. The bonds or notes deposited hereunder and such other United States bonds or notes as may be substituted therefor from time to time as such security, may be deposited with the Treasurer of the United States, a Federal reserve bank, or other depositary duly designated for that purpose by the Secretary, which shall issue receipt therefor, describing such bonds or notes so deposited. As soon as security for the performance of such penal bond is no longer necessary, such bonds or notes so deposited, shall be returned to the depositor: *Provided,* That in case a person or persons supplying a contractor with labor or material as provided by the Act of Congress, approved February 24, 1905 (33 Stat. 811), entitled "An Act to amend an Act approved August thirteenth, eighteen hundred and ninety-four, entitled 'An Act for the protection of persons furnishing materials and labor for the construction of public works,'" shall file with the obligee, at any time after a default in the performance of any contract subject to said Acts, the application and affidavit therein provided, the obligee shall not deliver to the obligor the deposited bonds or notes nor any surplus proceeds thereof until the expiration of the time limited by said Acts for the institution of suit by such person or persons, and, in case suit shall be instituted within such time, shall hold said bonds or notes or proceeds subject to the order of the court having jurisdiction thereof: *Provided further.* That nothing herein contained shall affect or impair the priority of the claim of the United States against the bonds or notes deposited or any right or remedy granted by said Acts or by this section to the United States for default upon any obligation of said penal bond: *Provided further.* That all laws inconsistent with this section are hereby so modified as to conform to the provisions hereof: *And provided further*, That nothing contained herein shall affect the authority of courts over the security, where such bonds are taken as security in judicial proceedings, or the authority of any administrative officer of the United States to receive United States bonds for security in cases authorized by existing laws. The Secretary may prescribe rules and regulations necessary and proper for carrying this section into effect.

### I. ACCEPTANCE OF BONDS AND NOTES BY BOND-APPROVING OFFICERS.

1. Any individual, partnership, or corporation required by the laws of the United States or regulations made pursuant thereto to furnish any recognizance, stipulation, bond, guaranty, or undertaking (hereinafter called penal bond), with surety or sureties, may, in lieu of such surety or sureties, deposit as security with the official having authority to approve such penal bond (hereinafter called the bond-approving officer), United States Liberty bonds, Victory notes, or other United States bonds or notes in a sum equal at their par value to the amount of the penal bond required to be furnished, together with a power of attorney and agreement in the form hereinafter prescribed, authorizing the bond-approving officer to collect or sell such bonds or notes so deposited in case of any default in the performance of any of the conditions or stipulations of such penal bond. The acceptance of such United States bonds or notes in lieu of surety or sureties required by law shall have the same force and effect as individual or corporate sureties, or certified checks, bank drafts, post-office money orders, or cash, for the penalty or amount of such penal bond. The term "bond-approving officer," where it appears in this circular, shall be deemed to include the officer's successors in office. Treasury certificates of indebtedness are not acceptable under said Section 1329 of the Revenue Act of 1921 as security in lieu of surety or sureties.

2. The individual, partnership, or corporation required to furnish any penal bond, who deposits United States bonds or notes as security in lieu of surety or sureties in accordance with the provisions of this circular, must be the owner of the bonds or notes deposited, and is hereinafter called the obligor. United States bonds or notes may be deposited with bond-approving officers pursuant to the provisions of this circular in either coupon or registered form. Coupon bonds or notes shall have attached thereto all coupons unmatured at the date of such deposit, and all matured coupons should be detached. Registered bonds or notes must be registered in the name of the obligor, and duly assigned, at or before the date of such deposit, either to the bond-approving officer with whom they are deposited or his administrative superior, or in blank, in accordance with the regulations of the Treasury Department in relation to United States

bonds. (See Treasury Department Circular No. 141, dated September 15, 1919, as amended and supplemented.)

3. The United States bonds or notes to be deposited must in every case be delivered to the bond-approving officer at the obligor's risk and expense. Coupon bonds or notes and registered bonds or notes assigned in blank or for exchange for coupon bonds or notes cannot safely be forwarded by registered mail unless insured by the obligor against risk of loss in transit. Registered bonds or notes, unless assigned in blank or for exchange for coupon bonds or notes, need not be so insured when forwarded by registered mail, unless the obligor so elects. The bond-approving officer shall issue a receipt in duplicate, substantially in Form A, hereto attached, for the United States bonds or notes so deposited, the original of the receipt to be given to the obligor and the duplicate to be retained by the bond-approving officer for his files.

4. At the time of the deposit of any United States bonds or notes with a bond-approving officer in accordance with the provisions of this circular, the obligor shall deliver to the bond-approving officer a duly executed power of attorney and agreement, in favor of the bond-approving officer, authorizing such officer to collect or sell such bonds or notes so deposited in case of any default in the performance of any of the conditions or stipulations of the penal bond, and to apply the proceeds of such sale or collection, in whole or in part, to the satisfaction of any damages, demands, or deficiency arising by reason of such default. The power of attorney and agreement shall be, in the case of an individual, substantially in Form C, hereto attached; in the case of a partnership, substantially in Form D, hereto attached; and in the case of a corporation, substantially in Form E, hereto attached.

5. In connection with the acceptance of United States bonds or notes hereunder as security in lieu of surety or sureties, bond-approving officers must satisfy themselves as to the ownership of the bonds or notes deposited and the sufficiency of the power of attorney and agreement, and in the case of registered bonds or notes, as to the regularity of the assignments as well, and, in general, that the deposit is made in conformity with the provisions of this circular.

6. Any obligor who deposits United States bonds or notes in accordance with the provisions of this circular may, upon written application to and with the approval of the bond-approving officer, substitute for the bonds or notes so deposited (a) other United States bonds or notes in a sum equal at their par value to not less than the par amount of the United States bonds or notes to be withdrawn, upon compliance with all the provisions of this circular applicable to an original deposit of United States bonds or notes in lieu of surety or sureties, or (b) a penal bond with surety or sureties or such other security as may be allowed by law. The bonds or notes withdrawn shall be returned in the manner hereinafter provided for the return of bonds and notes deposited.

## II. DEPOSITS OF BONDS AND NOTES BY BOND-APPROVING OFFICERS WITH DEPOSITORIES.

7. United States bonds and notes deposited with bond-approving officers as security in accordance with the provisions of this circular,

14263—FI 1922——19

and such other United States bonds or notes as may be substituted therefor from time to time as such security, may be deposited by bond-approving officers with the Treasurer of the United States, a Federal Reserve Bank or any branch Federal Reserve Bank having the requisite facilities, or other depository duly designated for that purpose by the Secretary of the Treasury; provided, however, that bond-approving officers shall deposit with the Treasurer of the United States all United States bonds and notes received by them in the District of Columbia pursuant to the provisions of this circular. Depositaries of public moneys are not authorized to act as depositories for United States bonds or notes accepted under this circular, unless specifically designated for that purpose by the Secretary of the Treasury. Any authorized depository receiving deposits of United States bonds or notes from bond-approving officers in accordance with this circular shall give receipt therefor in duplicate, describing the bonds or notes so deposited, substantially in Form B, hereto attached, the original to be delivered to the bond-approving officer and the duplicate to be retained by the depository for its own files. The bond-approving officer will hold the original receipt subject to the instructions of his administrative superior. United States bonds or notes so deposited with an authorized depository may be withdrawn only by or on the written order of the bond-approving officer.

8. United States bonds and notes accepted by bond-approving officers from obligors under this circular, and not deposited by them with authorized depositories, will be held at the risk of the respective bond-approving officers, subject to such regulations and instructions as may be prescribed for their guidance by their respective administrative superiors. Coupon bonds or notes and registered bonds or notes assigned in blank or for exchange for coupon bonds or notes are in effect bearer obligations and must be kept in safe custody at peril; registered bonds or notes not assigned in blank or for exchange for coupon bonds or notes must also be kept in safe custody, but in the event of loss or destruction may be replaced upon compliance with the provisions of law and the regulations of the Treasury Department applicable thereto.

9. Bond-approving officers desiring to deposit United States bonds or notes received by them with authorized depositories must deliver such bonds or notes to the depository, without risk or expense to the depository. Coupon bonds or notes and registered bonds or notes assigned in blank or for exchange for coupon bonds or notes can not safely be shipped by registered mail unless covered by insurance. Registered bonds or notes not assigned in blank or for exchange for coupon bonds or notes may be forwarded by registered mail uninsured.

## III. RETURN OR OTHER DISPOSITION OF BONDS AND NOTES DEPOSITED.

10. The obligor shall be entitled to receive the interest accruing upon United States bonds or notes deposited in accordance with this circular, in the absence of any default in the performance of any of the conditions or stipulations of the penal bond. The interest on any registered bonds or notes which the obligor is entitled to receive hereunder will be paid by check in regular course to the registered holder. The coupons for any interest on coupon bonds or notes

which the obligor is entitled to receive hereunder will, upon written application from the obligor to the bond-approving officer, be detached, as they mature, from the bonds or notes deposited and forwarded to the obligor at the obligor's risk and expense, either by the bond-approving officer or upon his written order by the depository with which the bonds or notes may be deposited, or, at the direction of the bond-approving officer, collected by the depository and check therefor forwarded to the obligor. In the absence of written application therefor by the obligor, coupons for interest on coupon bonds or notes to which the obligor may be entitled hereunder shall remain attached to the bonds or notes deposited, subject to the provisions of this circular.

11. As soon as security for the performance of the penal bond is no longer necessary, the United States bonds or notes deposited in lieu of surety or sureties on such penal bond, together with the power of attorney and agreement accompanying such bonds or notes, shall be returned to the obligor by the bond-approving officer, without application therefor from the obligor. The determination of the question whether security is any longer necessary for the performance of the penal bond shall rest with the bond-approving officer and such other officers as shall have jurisdiction in the premises under the provisions of law and administrative regulations which may be applicable; provided, however, that in case a person or persons supplying labor or material as provided by the Act of Congress, approved February 24, 1905 (33 Stat. 811), entitled "An Act to amend an Act approved August 13, 1894, entitled 'An Act for the protection of persons furnishing materials and labor for the construction of public works,'" shall file with the obligee, at any time after a default in the performance of any contract subject to said Acts, the application and affidavit therein provided, neither the obligee nor the bond-approving officer shall deliver to the obligor the deposited bonds or notes or any surplus proceeds thereof until the expiration of the time limited by said Acts for the institution of suit by such person or persons (viz., one year from the date of final settlement of the contract for the performance of which the bonds or notes were pledged), and, in case suit shall be instituted within such time, shall hold said bonds or notes or proceeds subject to the order of the court having jurisdiction thereof; provided, further, that nothing herein contained shall affect. or impair the priority of the claim of the United States against the bonds or notes deposited or any right or remedy granted by said Acts or under this circular to the United States for default upon any obligation of said penal bond.

12. Bonds or notes to be returned to the obligor will be forwarded at the obligor's risk and expense, either by the bond-approving officer, or upon his written order by the depository with which the bonds or notes may be deposited, and unless delivered direct to the obligor, will be forwarded, in the absence of other written instructions and remittance to cover expenses, by express, collect, except that registered bonds or notes not assigned in blank or for exchange for coupon bonds or notes may be forwarded by registered mail, uninsured. Registered bonds or notes assigned to the bond-approving officer or his administrative superior shall be reassigned to the obligor before their return.

13. Any obligor who desires to withdraw a portion only of the bonds or notes deposited, by reason of reduction in liability under the penal bond, shall make written application for such withdrawal to the bond-approving officer, who shall, if he approve such application, return such portion of the bonds or notes to the obligor.

14. Upon the complete or partial return to the obligor of bonds or notes deposited as security under the provisions of this circular, the bond-approving officer shall require from the obligor a receipt in duplicate, substantially in Form G, hereto attached, and shall further require the obligor, in case of complete return, to surrender the original receipt on Form A.

## IV. FORM OF PENAL BONDS WITH UNITED STATES BONDS OR NOTES AS SECURITY.

15. Penal bonds on which United States bonds or notes are accepted as security in lieu of surety or sureties may be substantially in Form F, hereto attached. Administrative offices of the Government may, however, use other forms of penal bonds appropriate to the work of their respective offices, provided that upon the execution of the penal bond the principal shall indorse on the face thereof and sign the following statement:

The United States bonds/notes described in the annexed schedule are hereby pledged as security for the performance and fulfillment of the foregoing undertaking in accordance with Section 1329 of the Revenue Act of 1921, approved November 23, 1921, and Treasury Department Circular No. 154, dated May 15, 1922.

..................................................
                                    *Principal on the above bond.*

16. Nothing contained in this circular shall be construed as modifying the existing practice or duties of administrative offices in handling penal bonds, except to the extent made necessary under the terms of this circular, by reason of the acceptance of United States bonds or notes as security in lieu of surety or sureties thereon.

## V. SPECIAL PROVISIONS.

17. *General Supply Committee.*—United States bonds and notes deposited to guarantee proposals or bids submitted to the General Supply Committee, or as security for the performance or fulfillment of contracts made through said committee, shall either be delivered in person or forwarded by registered mail at the obligor's risk and expense to the Chief Clerk of the Treasury Department, who shall deposit said bonds or notes with the Treasurer of the United States against receipts therefor to be issued in triplicate. The original and duplicate of the receipt shall in each case be delivered to the Chief Clerk of the Treasury Department, who shall retain the original receipt and transmit the duplicate to the Director of Supplies, Treasury Department, Washington. Bonds or notes thus deposited may be withdrawn only by or on the written order of the Director of Supplies, countersigned by the Chief Clerk of the Treasury Department, and the surrender of the original and duplicate receipt. In no instance should United States bonds or notes be forwarded to the General Supply Committee with the proposal or contract forms.

Coupon bonds or notes and registered bonds or notes assigned in blank or for exchange for coupon bonds or notes forwarded by registered mail should be insured by the obligor against risk of loss in transit. Registered bonds or notes not assigned in blank or for exchange for coupon bonds or notes need not be insured against loss in transit, unless the obligor so elects. The regulations prescribed in sections 2, 4, and 11 of this circular with respect to the assignment of registered bonds or notes, the power of attorney and agreement to accompany the bonds or notes, the substitution of other bonds or notes, and the return of bonds or notes to the obligors, shall apply to all United States bonds or notes accepted by the General Supply Committee as guarantees on proposals or as security for the performance of contracts made by such committee. Bonds or notes tendered by unsuccessful bidders will be returned promptly.

18. *Collectors of customs.*—The acceptance by collectors of customs of United States bonds or notes in lieu of surety or sureties on penal bonds shall be governed by the general rules and regulations contained in this circular, except as modified with the approval of the Secretary of the Treasury to cover special cases.

19. *Collectors of internal revenue.*—Special instructions for the guidance of collectors of internal revenue in accepting United States bonds or notes in lieu of surety or sureties on penal bonds will be issued through the office of the Commissioner of Internal Revenue, upon the approval of the Secretary of the Treasury.

20. *Other Departments and establishments.*—Bond-approving officers of other Departments and establishments of the Government accepting Liberty bonds, Victory notes, or other United States bonds or notes in lieu of surety or sureties under the provisions of Section 1329 of the Revenue Act of 1921, shall be governed by the provisions of this circular. This circular may be modified or amended only upon the approval of the Secretary of the Treasury.

### VI. OTHER DETAILS.

21. Nothing contained in this circular shall affect the authority of courts over the security when United States bonds or notes are taken as security in judicial proceedings, or the authority of any administrative officer of the United States to receive United States bonds or notes for security in cases authorized by provisions of law other than Section 1329 of the Revenue Act of 1921, approved November 23, 1921.

22. The Secretary of the Treasury may withdraw or amend at any time or from time to time any or all of the foregoing rules and regulations, subject, however, to the provisions of Section 1329 of the Revenue Act of 1921, approved November 23, 1921.

A. W. MELLON,
*Secretary of the Treasury.*

## Form A.

.................................................
                (City.)       (State.)       (Date.)

The undersigned hereby acknowledges receipt of the United States bonds/notes
hereinafter described, deposited as security in lieu of surety or sureties on ..........
.............................., filed with ............................................
  (Description of penal bond.)              (Department or establishment.)
.............................., through ....................... for ...............
                      (Bureau or office.)       (Description of
.............. * Said bonds/notes are registered in the name of...............
obligation secured.)
........................, and are assigned to .....................................
                            (State form of assignment.)

| Title of bonds/notes. | Coupon or registered. | Total face amount. | Denomination. | Serial number. | Interest dates. |
|---|---|---|---|---|---|
| ............ | ............ | ............ | ............ | ............ | ............ |
| ............ | ............ | ............ | ............ | ............ | ............ |
| ............ | ............ | ............ | ............ | ............ | ............ |
| ............ | ............ | ............ | ............ | ............ | ............ |

This receipt is executed in duplicate, and the original must be surrendered by the
obligor before the above-described bonds or notes deposited are returned to him.   This
receipt is not assignable.

.................................................
        *(Signature and official title of Bond-Approving Officer.)*

* This information to be furnished only in case of registered bonds/notes.

---

## Form B.

.................................................
                (City.)       (State.)       (Date.)

The undersigned hereby acknowledges receipt from ........................, of
                (Name and official title of bond-approving officer.)
the United States bonds/notes hereinafter described, deposited by .............., as
                            (Name of obligor.)
security in lieu of surety or sureties on ...................................., filed
                    (Description of penal bond.)
with ............................., through ............................,
  (Department or establishment.)         (Bureau or office.)
for ............................. *Said bonds/notes are registered in the name of
  (Description of obligation secured.)
......................, and are assigned to ......................................
                      (State form of assignment.)

| Title of bonds/notes. | Coupon or registered. | Total face amount. | Denomination. | Serial number. | Interest dates. |
|---|---|---|---|---|---|
| ............ | ............ | ............ | ............ | ............ | ............ |
| ............ | ............ | ............ | ............ | ............ | ............ |
| ............ | ............ | ............ | ............ | ............ | ............ |
| ............ | ............ | ............ | ............ | ............ | ............ |

The above-described bonds/notes will be returned only to or on the written order
of said bond-approving officer or his successor in office, upon presentation and surrender of the original of this receipt.   This receipt is executed in duplicate and is
not assignable.

.................................................
                  *(Signature of Depository.)*

* This information to be furnished only in case of registered bonds/notes.

## Form C.

### POWER OF ATTORNEY AND AGREEMENT.

#### (For individual.)

Know all men by these presents, that I, the undersigned, of .........., do hereby constitute and appoint ................, and his successors in office, as my attorney,

(Name and official title of bond-approving officer.)

for me and in my name to collect or to sell, assign, and transfer certain United States Liberty bonds, Victory notes, or other United States bonds or notes, described as follows: ..................................................................

.............................................................................

..........................................................................

such bonds/notes having been deposited by me, pursuant to authority conferred by Section 1329 of the Revenue Act of 1921, approved November 23, 1921, and subject to the provisions thereof and of Treasury Department Circular No. 154, dated May 15, 1922, as security for the faithful performance of any and all of the conditions or stipulations of a certain obligation entered into by me with the United States, under date of ................., which is hereby made a part hereof, and I agree that, in case of any default in the performance of any of the conditions and stipulations of such undertaking, my said attorney shall have full power to collect said bonds/notes or any part thereof, or to sell, assign, and transfer said bonds/notes or any part thereof, without notice, at public or private sale, free from any equity of redemption and without appraisement or valuation, notice and right to redeem being waived, and to apply the proceeds of such sale or collection, in whole or in part, to the satisfaction of any damages, demands, or deficiency arising by reason of such default, as my said attorney may deem best.

And I hereby for myself, my heirs, executors, administrators, and assigns, ratify and confirm whatever my said attorney shall do by virtue of these presents.

In witness whereof, I have hereunto set my hand and seal this ...... day of .........., 19..

.................................................. [SEAL.]

Before me, the undersigned, a notary public within and for the county of........
................, in the State of ........................(or the District of Columbia), personally appeared the above-named ..................... and acknowledged the execution of the foregoing power of attorney.

Witness my hand and notarial seal this ...... day of .........., 19..

[Notarial seal.] ........................................

*Notary Public.*

---

## Form D.

### POWER OF ATTORNEY AND AGREEMENT.

#### (For partnership.)

Know all men by these presents, that we, the undersigned, carrying on business in partnership together under the firm name and style of ..................., of ......
.............., do, and each of us does, hereby constitute and appoint............

(Name and official title of bond-approving officer.)

.................................., and his successors in office, as the attorney of us and each of us, and of our said firm of ..................., in the name or names and on behalf of us and our said firm, to collect, or to sell, assign, and transfer certain United States Liberty bonds, Victory notes, or other United States bonds or notes, described as follows:

.............................................................................

..........................................................................,

such bonds/notes having been deposited by us, pursuant to authority conferred by Section 1329 of the Revenue Act of 1921, approved November 23, 1921, and subject to the provisions thereof and of Treasury Department Circular No. 154, dated May 15, 1922, as security for the faithful performance of any and all of the conditions or stipulations of a certain obligation entered into by us with the United States, under date of ................., which is hereby made a part hereof, and we agree that, in case of any default in the performance of any of the conditions and stipulations of such undertaking, our said attorney shall have full power to collect said bonds/notes or any part thereof, or to sell, assign, and transfer said bonds/notes or any part thereof without notice, at public or private sale, free from any equity of redemption and without appraisement or valuation, notice and right to redeem being waived, and to apply the proceeds of such sale or collection, in whole or in part, to the satisfaction of any damages, demands, or deficiency arising by reason of such default, as our said attorney may deem best.

And we hereby for ourselves, our heirs, executors, administrators, and assigns, ratify and confirm whatever our said attorney shall do by virtue of these presents.

In witness whereof, we have hereunto set our hands and seals this ...... day of .........., 19..

........................................... [SEAL.]
........................................... [SEAL.]

Before me, the undersigned, a notary public within and for the county of .........., in the State of .......... (or the District of Columbia), personally appeared the above-named ...................., partners doing business under the firm name and style of...................., and acknowledged the execution of the foregoing power of attorney.

Witness my hand and notarial seal this .......... day of .........., 19..

[Notarial seal.] ....................................
                                         *Notary Public.*

---

FORM E.

POWER OF ATTORNEY AND AGREEMENT.

(For corporation.)

Know all men by these presents, that .........., a corporation duly incorporated under the laws of the State of .........., and having its principal office in the city of .........., State of .........., in pursuance of a resolution of the board of directors of said corporation, passed on the ...... day of .........., 19.., a duly certified copy of which resolution is hereto attached, does hereby constitute and appoint ..........................................., and his successors in office, as attorney
(Name and official title of bond-approving officer.)
for said corporation, for and in the name of said corporation to collect or to sell, assign, and transfer certain United States Liberty bonds, Victory notes, or other United States bonds or notes, described as follows:....................................
..........................................................................

....such bonds/notes having been deposited by it, pursuant to authority conferred by Section 1329 of the Revenue Act of 1921, approved November 23, 1921, and subject to the provisions thereof and of Treasury Department Circular No. 154, dated May 15, 1922, as security for the faithful performance of any and all of the conditions or stipulations of a certain obligation entered into by it with the United States, under date of ........., which is hereby made a part hereof, and the undersigned agrees that, in case of any default in the performance of any of the conditions and stipulations of such undertaking, its said attorney shall have full power to collect said bonds/notes or any part thereof, or to sell, assign, and transfer said bonds/notes or any part thereof without notice, at public or private sale, free from any equity of redemption and without appraisement or valuation, notice and right to redeem being waived, and to apply the proceeds of such sale or collection, in whole or in part, to the satisfaction of any damages, demands, or deficiency arising by reason of such default, as its said attorney may deem best.

And said corporation hereby for itself, its successors and assigns, ratifies and confirms whatever its said attorney shall do by virtue of these presents.

In witness whereof, the .........., the corporation hereinabove named, by ...................., duly authorized to act in the premises, has executed this
(Name and title of officer.)
instrument and caused the seal of the corporation to be hereto affixed this.......... day of .........., 19..

[Corporate seal.]
                    By ...........................................

Before me, the undersigned, a notary public, within and for the county of .......... in the State of .......... (or the District of Columbia), personally appeared........
                                              (Name and
.......... and for and in behalf of said .........., corporation, acknowledged
title of officer.)
the execution of the foregoing power of attorney.

Witness my hand and notarial seal this ...... day of .........., 19..

[Notarial seal.] ....................................
                                         *Notary Public.*

## Form F.

FORM OF PENAL BOND FOR EXECUTION BY INDIVIDUALS, PARTNERSHIPS, OR CORPORATIONS WHERE UNITED STATES BONDS OR NOTES ARE ACCEPTED AS SECURITY IN LIEU OF SURETY OR SURETIES.

Know all men by these presents, that .........., of the city of .........., and State of .........., as obligor, ...... held and firmly bound unto the United States of America, in the penal sum of .......... dollars ($......), lawful money of the United States, for the payment of which sum, well and truly to be made to the United States, without relief from valuation or appraisement laws,..........bind, .........., .......... heirs, executors, administrators, successors, and assigns firmly by these presents.

The condition of the above obligation is such that ................................
(Insert conditions and stipulations appropriate to the penal bond.)

The above-bounden obligor, in order the more fully to secure the United States in the payment of the aforementioned sum, hereby pledges as security therefor bonds/notes of the United States in the principal sum of ................ dollars ($..........), which said bonds/notes are numbered serially and are in the denominations and amounts, and are otherwise more particularly described as follows: ......
...........................................................................................
.........................................................................................,
which said bonds/notes have this day been deposited with ........................
(Name and official title of bond-approving officer.)
and his receipt taken therefor.

Contemporaneously herewith the undersigned has also executed and delivered a power of attorney and agreement in favor of.................................................,
(Name and official title of bond-approving officer.)
authorizing and empowering said officer as such attorney to collect or sell the above-described bonds/notes so deposited, or any part thereof, in case of any default in the performance of any of the above-named conditions or stipulations.

In witness whereof, this bond has been signed, sealed, and delivered by the above-named obligor, this ...... day of .........., 19..

.......................................... [SEAL.]
.......................................... [SEAL.]

Signed, sealed, and delivered in the presence of:
...........................................
...........................................

--------

## Form G.

RECEIPT BY OBLIGOR ON RETURN OF BONDS OR NOTES.

.............., .............., ..............
(City.)    (State.)    (Date.)

The undersigned hereby acknowledges receipt of the United States bonds/notes hereinafter described, deposited with .............................. as security
(Name and official title of bond-approving officer.)
in lieu of surety or sureties on ........................ filed with ....................
(Description of penal bond.)    (Department or establishment.)
through .........................., for ........................................
(Bureau or office.)    (Description of obligation secured.)
*Said bonds/notes are registered in the name of ........................ and are assigned to ................................................................
(State form of assignment.)

| Title of bonds/notes. | Coupon or registered. | Total face amount. | Denomination. | Serial number. | Interest dates. |
|---|---|---|---|---|---|
| .................. | .......... | .......... | .............. | .............. | .............. |
| .................. | .......... | .......... | .............. | .............. | .............. |
| .................. | .......... | .......... | .............. | .............. | .............. |
| .................. | .......... | .......... | .............. | .............. | .............. |

This receipt is executed in duplicate.

..........................................
(Signature of Obligor.)

*This information to be furnished only in case of registered bonds/notes.

## EXHIBIT 81.

[Department Circular No. 230. Chief Clerk.]

**LAWS AND REGULATIONS GOVERNING THE RECOGNITION OF ATTORNEYS, AGENTS AND OTHER PERSONS REPRESENTING CLAIMANTS AND OTHERS BEFORE THE TREASURY DEPARTMENT AND OFFICES THEREOF.**

TREASURY DEPARTMENT,
OFFICE OF THE SECRETARY,
*Washington, April 25, 1922.*

The following statutes relate to the recognition of attorneys, agents and other persons representing claimants and others before the Treasury Department and offices thereof:

That the Secretary of the Treasury may prescribe rules and regulations governing the recognition of agents, attorneys, and other persons representing claimants before his Department, and may require of such persons, agents and attorneys, before being recognized as representatives of claimants, that they shall show that they are of good character and in good repute, possessed of the necessary qualifications to enable them to render such claimants valuable service, and otherwise competent to advise and assist such claimants in the presentation of their cases. And such Secretary may after due notice and opportunity for hearing suspend, and disbar from further practice before his Department any such person, agent, or attorney shown to be incompetent, disreputable, or who refuses to comply with the said rules and regulations, or who shall with intent to defraud, in any manner willfully and knowingly deceive, mislead, or threaten any claimant or prospective claimant, by word, circular, letter, or by advertisement. (Act of July 7, 1884, 23 Stat., 258.)

Whoever, being an officer of the United States, or a person holding any place of trust or profit, or discharging any official function under, or in connection with, any Executive Department of the Government of the United States, or under the Senate or House of Representatives of the United States, shall act as an agent or attorney for prosecuting any claim against the United States, or in any manner, or by any means, otherwise than in discharge of his proper official duties, shall aid or assist in the prosecution or support of any such claim, or receive any gratuity, or any share of or interest in any claim from any claimant against the United States, with intent to aid or assist, or in consideration of having aided or assisted, in the prosecution of such claim, shall be fined not more than five thousand dollars, or imprisoned not more than one year, or both. (Act of March 4, 1909, sec. 109, 35 Stat., 1107.)

It shall not be lawful for any person appointed after the first day of June, one thousand eight hundred and seventy-two, as an officer, clerk, or employé in any of the Departments, to act as counsel, attorney, or agent for prosecuting any claim against the United States which was pending in either of said Departments while he was such officer, clerk, or employé, nor in any manner, nor by any means, to aid in the prosecution of any such claim, within two years next after he shall have ceased to be such officer, clerk, or employé. (Sec. 190, Revised Statutes.)

That it shall be unlawful for any person who, as a commissioned officer of the Army, or officer or employee of the United States, has at any time since April 6, 1917, been employed in any Bureau of the Government and in such employment been engaged on behalf of the United States in procuring or assisting to procure supplies for the Military Establishment, or who has been engaged in the settlement or adjustment of contracts or agreements for the procurement of supplies for the Military Establishment, within two years next after his discharge or other separation from the service of the Government, to solicit employment in the presentation or to aid or assist for compensation in the prosecution of claims against the United States arising out of any contracts or agreements for the procurement of supplies for said Bureau, which were pending or entered into while the said officer or employee was associated therewith. A violation of this provision of this chapter shall be punished by a fine of not more than $10,000 or imprisonment for not more than one year, or both. (Act of July 11, 1919, 41 Stat., 131.)

That section five hundred and fifty-eight of the Code of Law for the District of Columbia, relating to notaries public, be amended by adding at the end of said section the following: "*Provided,* That the appointment of any person as such notary public, or the acceptance of his commission as such, or the performance of the duties there-

---

[1] Effective April 25, 1922. This circular supersedes Treasury Department Circular No 230, dated February 15, 1921, as amended June 7, 1921, July 1, 1921, and December 23, 1921.

under, shall not disqualify or prevent such person from representing clients before any of the Departments of the United States Government in the District of Columbia or elsewhere, provided such person so appointed as a notary public who appears to practice or represent clients before any such Department is not otherwise engaged in Government employ, and shall be admitted by the heads of such Departments to practice therein in accordance with the rules and regulations prescribed for other persons or attorneys who are admitted to practice therein: *And provided further,* That no notary public shall be authorized to take acknowledgments, administer oaths, certify papers, or perform any official acts in connection with matters in which he is employed as counsel, attorney, or agent or in which he may be in any way interested before any of the Departments aforesaid." (Act of June 29, 1906, 34 Stat., 622. Held by 26 Opinions of Attorney General, 236, to apply to all notaries who may practice before the Departments.)

The head of each Department is authorized to prescribe regulations, not inconsistent with law, for the government of his Department, the conduct of its officers and clerks, the distribution and performance of its business, and the custody, use, and preservation of the records, papers, and property appertaining to it. (Sec. 161, Revised Statutes.)

Pursuant to the authority contained in the above-quoted statutory provisions, the following rules and regulations are prescribed:

1. *Committee on Enrollment and Disbarment.*—(*a*) A committee on enrollment and disbarment is hereby created, consisting of the Chief Clerk of the Treasury Department, who shall be a member *ex officio,* and six other members, one of whom shall be detailed from the office of the Secretary of the Treasury and shall act as chairman, three from the office of the Commissioner of Internal Revenue, and one each from the office of the Solicitor of the Treasury and the Division of Customs. The Chief Clerk of the Treasury Department shall have custody of all papers, records, rolls, etc., belonging to the committee, and shall, in the absence of the designated chairman, act as chairman. The members of the committee shall serve for the calendar year and shall perform the duties herein prescribed in addition to their other duties. The committee shall meet regularly on the first Tuesday of each month, if a business day, and shall meet specially on other days at the call of the chairman. Four members shall constitute a quorum.

(*b*) The committee shall receive and consider applications to be recognized as attorney, agent or other representative before the Treasury Department or offices thereof; receive complaints against those enrolled; conduct hearings, make inquiries, perform other duties as prescribed herein, and do all things necessary in the matter of proceedings for the enrollment, discipline, suspension or disbarment of attorneys, agents or other representatives, pursuant to these regulations; and it shall submit its recommendations therein to the Secretary of the Treasury for approval.

2. *Applications for enrollment.*—Applicants for enrollment pursuant to these regulations shall submit to the Secretary of the Treasury an application, properly executed, on Form 23 attached hereto. Applications in any other form will not be considered. The statements contained in the application must be verified by the applicant. The applicant must also take the oath of allegiance, and to support the Constitution of the United States as required by section 3478, Revised Statutes. A person who can not take the oath of allegiance, and to support the Constitution of the United States, can not be enrolled. Members of the bar of a court of record will apply for enrollment as attorneys; all others will apply for enrollment as agents. The Secretary of the Treasury may in any case require

other and further evidence of qualification. Applicants will be notified of the approval or disapproval of their applications. All applications for enrollment must be individual, and individuals who practice as partners should apply for enrollment as individuals and not in the partnership name. An individual who has been enrolled may, however, represent claimants and others before the Treasury Department in the name of a partnership of which he is a member or with which he is otherwise regularly connected. Except as hereinafter provided in paragraph 3, a corporation can not be enrolled and attorneys or agents will not be permitted to practice before the Treasury Department for account of a corporation which represents claimants and others in the prosecution of business before the Treasury Department. Persons applying for enrollment who propose to act for such a corporation in the prosecution of claims and other business before the Treasury Department, will be subject to rejection, and enrolled attorneys or agents who act for a corporation in representing claimants and others in the prosecution of claims and other business will be subject to suspension from practice, as to such claims or business.

3. *Customhouse brokers.*—(a) The act of June 10, 1910 (36 Stat., 464, T. D. 30789), provides in part that persons, copartnerships, associations, joint-stock associations, and corporations may be licensed as customhouse brokers by the collector or chief officer of customs at any port of entry or delivery to transact business as such customhouse broker in the collection district in which such license is issued. Customhouse brokers so licensed require no further enrollment under these regulations for the transaction of business within their respective collection districts, but for the representation of a claimant before the Treasury Department in the city of Washington application for enrollment as attorney or agent must be made in conformity with the requirements of the preceding paragraph, and otherwise in accordance with these regulations, except that if a customhouse broker, so licensed in a collection district, is a copartnership, association, joint-stock association, or corporation, its claims or other business may be prosecuted in its name before the department in the city of Washington by an accredited member or representative, who must, however, be first duly enrolled in accordance herewith.

(b) The provisions of sections (b) and (c) of paragraph 6 hereof shall apply to customhouse brokers only as to the application to themselves of designations which might imply official capacity or connection, and as to solicitation of claims or business before the Treasury Department and suggestion of previous connection with the Treasury Department or acquaintance with its officers or employees.

4. *Restriction of right to be heard to parties and enrolled attorneys and agents.*—(a) The committee on enrollment and disbarment shall maintain in the office of the Chief Clerk, Treasury Department, a roll of attorneys and agents entitled to practice before the Treasury Department. It shall likewise maintain lists of those whose applications for enrollment have been rejected and those who have been suspended or disbarred. The Chief Clerk shall furnish copies of said roll and lists, with such additions thereto or subtractions therefrom as may be made from time to time, to the several bureaus, offices

and divisions of the Treasury Department, and upon request may furnish information as to whether or not any person is enrolled as an attorney or agent before the Treasury Department.

(b) All bureaus, offices and divisions of the Treasury Department are hereby prohibited from recognizing or dealing with anyone appearing as attorney or agent unless the name of such attorney or agent appears upon the list of those entitled to practice before the Treasury Department, provided, however, that the head of any bureau, office or division may, in his discretion, temporarily recognize such representative pending action upon his application for enrollment, provided his name does not appear on the list of those whose application for enrollment have been rejected or on the list of those who have been suspended or disbarred. It shall be the duty of the several bureaus, offices and divisions of the Treasury Department to ascertain in each case whether the name of one appearing before them in a representative capacity appears on the roll of those entitled to practice, whether such representative has been suspended or disbarred, and whether he is ineligible under section (c) of this paragraph or under section 190 of the Revised Statutes. Nothing herein contained shall preclude individual parties or members of firms, or officers of corporations, or authorized employees of firms or corporations, from appearing, upon proper identification, as representatives of their own interests or of their respective firms or corporations in any matter before the department in which such person, firm or corporation is concerned as a principal; but attorneys, counsel, solicitors, accountants and other agents for such persons, firms or corporations must be enrolled.

(c) No attorney or agent shall be permitted to appear in a representative capacity before the Treasury Department, or any of the bureaus, offices, units, divisions, subdivisions or other agencies thereof, in regard to any claim, application for reaudit, refund, abatement or reduction in tax assessed, or any other matter, to which he gave actual personal consideration, or as to the facts of which he had actual personal knowledge, while in the service of the Treasury Department.

The foregoing regulation is in addition to the inhibition contained in section 190 of the Revised Statutes of the United States, and does not authorize the appearance of an attorney or agent in the prosecution of any claim that would be prohibited by that section.

5. *Suspension and disbarment proceedings.*—(a) If any officer or employee of the Treasury Department, whether in the city of Washington or elsewhere, has reason to believe, or if the complaint is made to him, that an enrolled attorney or agent has violated any provision of the laws and regulations governing practice before the Treasury Department or otherwise engaged in improper practice, he shall promptly make written report thereof through the proper channels to the committee on enrollment and disbarment. The committee may, on the basis of any such complaint, upon its own motion, or otherwise upon reasonable cause, institute proceedings for suspension or disbarment against any enrolled attorney or agent. Notice thereof, signed by the Secretary or Undersecretary of the Treasury, shall be sent by mail to such attorney or agent at the address under which he is enrolled, and such notice shall state the charge or charges made, and give the place and time of hearing, which shall be not less

than thirty nor more than forty days from the date of mailing the notice. The respondent may file with the committee an answer in duplicate, which shall be verified, at least five full days before the time of the hearing, and the complainant may, in the discretion of the committee, be furnished with the duplicate thereof. The committee may, in its discretion, extend the time for answer, or postpone the date of hearing, or adjourn any hearing from time to time as may be necessary. An enrolled attorney or agent against whom proceedings for suspension or disbarment have been instituted as herein provided may, subject to the approval of the Secretary of the Treasury, be suspended for the time being from practice before the Treasury Department, pending the conclusion of the proceedings.

(b) The committee shall conduct hearings according to such rules of procedure as it shall determine, and may receive evidence in such form as it may deem proper. The respondent may be represented by counsel. The testimony of witnesses may, in the discretion of the committee, be required to be under oath, and may be stenographically reported and transcribed. Depositions for use at a hearing may, with the approval of the committee, be taken by either party upon oral or written interrogatories before any officer duly authorized to administer an oath for general purposes, upon ten days' written notice if the deposition is to be taken within the District of Columbia, and upon twenty days' written notice if it is to be taken elsewhere. When a deposition is taken upon written interrogatories, any cross-examination shall be upon written interrogatories. Copies of such written interrogatories shall be served with the notice, and copies of any written cross-interrogatories shall be mailed to the opposing party or his counsel at least ten days before the time of taking the deposition.

(c) The committee shall, promptly after the conclusion of the hearing, or, if the respondent does not appear in person for the hearing, promptly after the date set therefor, submit to the Secretary of the Treasury a copy of the notice of hearing, the complaint, answer (if any), the record of the hearing (if any), and any written findings of fact by a majority of the committee, together with a recommendation either that the charges be dismissed, or that the respondent be reprimanded, suspended for a given period of time, or disbarred. The findings and recommendation shall be signed by all members of the committee agreeing thereto. Members of the committee dissenting therefrom shall submit statements of their reasons therefor. If any members of the committee were not present at the hearing the fact shall be stated.

(d) Upon the suspension or disbarment of an attorney or agent, notice thereof shall be given by the committee to the heads of all bureaus, offices and divisions of the Treasury Department and to the other branches of the Government, and, unless duly reinstated, such person shall not thereafter be recognized as an attorney or agent in any claim or other matter before the Treasury Department or any office thereof.

6. *Causes for rejection, suspension or disbarment.*—(a) The Secretary of the Treasury may, as herein provided, suspend or disbar any enrolled attorney or agent shown to be incompetent or disreputable, or who refuses to comply with these rules and regulations, or who shall with intent to defraud, in any manner willfully and knowingly

deceive, mislead, or threaten any claimant or prospective claimant, by word, circular or letter, or by advertisement. It shall be the duty of every attorney and agent to use the utmost diligence in furnishing evidence required in matters presented to the Treasury Department, and the use of any means whereby the final settlement of a claim or other business pending before the Treasury Department is unjustifiably delayed may be sufficient cause for suspension or disbarment. If any enrolled attorney or agent shall knowingly employ as correspondent or subagent in any matter pending before the Treasury Department a person who is at the time denied enrollment, or suspended or disbarred from practice before the department, such attorney or agent himself may be suspended or disbarred.

(b) Advertising by enrolled attorneys or agents which describes their capacity or ability to render service as enrolled attorneys or agents is forbidden. Letterheads, business cards, and insertions in directories, newspapers, trade journals, or other publications should set forth only the name and address of the attorney or agent and a brief description of his practice. The description should not do more than state the nature of the attorney's or agent's business, that is to say, whether he practices as an attorney, accountant or agent, and, if desired, any special field of service or practice covered. The use by attorneys, agents or others of adjectives or other terms which might imply official capacity or connection with the Government or any of its departments, is specifically forbidden.

(c) The solicitation of claims or other business as attorney or agent for others before the Treasury Department by circulars, advertisements or other means, including personal letters, communications or interviews not warranted by previous business or personal relations with the persons addressed, is forbidden. *Advertising or solicitation, which makes any suggestion of previous connection with the Treasury Department or acquaintance with its officials or employees, or any reference to the fact of enrollment, is specifically forbidden.*

(d) Statements or implications to the effect that an attorney or agent is in position by reason of past experience, past official connection, or personal association with the Treasury Department or any officials or employees thereof, directly or indirectly to influence the disposition of business in the Treasury Department, and statements, or implications to the effect that the agent or attorney is able to obtain information or consideration that is not available to the public in regard to such business, are forbidden.

(e) While contingent fees may be proper in some cases before the department, they are not generally looked upon with favor and may be made the ground of suspension or disbarment. Both their reasonableness in view of the services rendered and all the attendant circumstances are a proper subject of inquiry by the department. The Commissioner of Internal Revenue or the head of any other Treasury bureau or division of the Secretary's office may at any stage of a pending proceeding require an attorney or agent to make full disclosure as to what inducements, if any, were held out by him to procure his employment and whether the business is being handled on a contingent basis, and, if so, the arrangement regarding compensation.

(f) Violation of any of the foregoing regulations is declared cause for suspension or disbarment of any attorney or agent enrolled to practice before the Treasury Department, while violation thereof by any person applying for enrollment as attorney or agent will be cause for rejection of his application.

(g) Upon notification that an attorney or agent enrolled in the Treasury Department has been disbarred from practice before some other branch of the Government, the committee shall forthwith send to such attorney or agent, in the same manner as prescribed for notice of hearing, an order signed by the Secretary of the Treasury to show cause within thirty days why he should not be disbarred from practice before the Treasury Department; and thereafter the committee shall proceed in such case in the same manner as if-a notice of hearing had been sent.

(h) The above enumeration of causes for rejection, disbarment or suspension shall not exclude other causes which the Secretary may reasonably deem sufficient in any case.

7. *Authority to prosecute claims; delivery of checks, drafts and warrants.*—(a) A power of attorney from the principal in proper form may be required of attorneys or agents by heads of bureaus, offices and divisions, in any case. *In the prosecution of claims involving payments to be made by the United States, proper powers of attorney shall always be filed before an attorney or agent is recognized.* No power of attorney shall be recognized which is filed after settlement made by the accounting officers, even though the settlement certificate may not yet have issued, unless such power of attorney recites that the principal is fully cognizant of such settlement and of the balance found due.

(b) In all cases originally filed in the Treasury Department and audited and allowed by the accounting officers, payable from appropriations thereafter to be made by Congress, the drafts, warrants or checks issued for the proceeds of such claims shall be made to the order of the claimant, and may be delivered to the attorney or agent legally authorized to prosecute the same, upon his filing in the department, after the allowance of the claim, the ascertainment of the amount due, and its submission to Congress for an appropriation, written authority executed in proper legal form for delivery of such draft, warrant or check. The authority so filed shall describe the claim by the number of certificate of settlement, the amount allowed, the title of appropriation from which to be paid, the date when submitted to Congress, and the number of the executive document in which it is contained. Drafts, warrants or checks issued for the proceeds of other like cases audited and allowed by the accounting officers but which are to be paid from appropriations available at the time of allowance shall also be made to the order of the claimant and may be delivered to the attorney or agent filing written authority, executed in proper legal form, to receive them. The Secretary of the Treasury reserves the right, however, in any case to send any draft, warrant or check to the claimant direct. (See also paragraph 9 hereof.)

(c) Drafts, warrants or checks issued in payment of amounts allowed by Congress in favor of corporations and individuals and appropriated for in private or special acts, and for the payment of all other claims presented directly to Congress and prosecuted before its committees, shall be made to the order of claimants and delivered to them in person or mailed to their actual post-office addresses.

(d) Drafts, warrants or checks issued in payment of judgments rendered by the Court of Claims, United States courts, or other courts shall be made to the order of the judgment creditor and delivered to or sent in care of the attorney certified by the court to be the attorney of record upon his filing in the department written authority, executed in proper legal form, after the date of the rendition of the judgment, for such disposition of such draft, warrant or check.

(e) When judgments of the Court of Claims, United States courts, or other courts are paid by the United States, a notice of such payment, giving number, class, and date of the draft, warrant or check, and amount paid, will be sent by the Treasury Department to the clerk of the court in which the judgment was entered in order that payment may be entered on the docket of the court.

8. *Substitution of attorneys or agents and revocation of authority.*— (a) Substitution of attorneys or agents may be effected only on the written consent of the attorney or agent of record, his principal, and the attorney or agent whom it is desired to substitute, and in all cases only with the assent of the head of the bureau, office or division concerned; provided that where the power of attorney under which an attorney or agent of record is acting expressly confers the power of substitution, such attorney or agent, if in good standing before the department, may, by a duly executed instrument, substitute another in his stead, such other, however, to be recognized as the attorney or agent only with the assent of the head of the bureau, office or division concerned.

(b) If a firm dissolve, or those associated as attorneys or agents by virtue of a power of attorney contest the right of either to receive a draft, warrant or check, the principal only shall thereafter be recognized, unless the members or survivors of such firm, or the associates in such power of attorney, file a proper agreement showing which of such members, survivors or associates may continue to prosecute the matter and may receive a draft, warrant or check; and in no case shall a final settlement of the matter or action toward the transmission of a draft, warrant or check to the principal be delayed more than sixty days by reason of the failure to file such agreement.

(c) The revocation by a principal or his legal representatives of authority to prosecute a matter will not be effective, so far as the Treasury Department is concerned, without the assent of the head of the bureau, office or division before which the matter is pending. Where a matter has been suspended pending the furnishing of evidence for which a call has been made on an attorney or agent, failure to take action thereon within three months from the date of suspension may be deemed by the administrative officer before whom the case is pending cause for revocation of the authority of such attorney or agent without further notice to him.

9. In the settlement of claims of officers, soldiers, sailors and marines, or their representatives, and all other like claims for pay and allowances within the jurisdiction of the General Accounting Office, the draft, warrant or check for the full amount found due shall be delivered to the payee in person or sent to his bona fide post-office address (residence or place of business) in accordance with the provisions of the act of June 6, 1900 (31 Stat., 637).

10. This circular supersedes the regulations promulgated by Treasury Department Circular No. 230 of February 15, 1921, as amended

June 7, July 1, and December 23, 1921, relating to the recognition of attorneys, agents and others.

11. These regulations shall apply to attorneys, agents and others representing claimants and others before the Treasury Department in the city of Washington or elsewhere, with the exception as to custom-house brokers set forth in paragraph 3, and shall be effective from and after the twenty-fifth day of April, 1922. This circular shall apply to all unsettled matters then pending in this department, or which may thereafter be presented or referred to the department or offices thereof for adjudication, and shall be applicable to all those now enrolled to practice before the Treasury Department as attorney or agent, provided that nothing herein contained shall be construed to abrogate any rules or orders of the General Accounting Office relating to the fees of attorneys, agents or others, or to require those now enrolled again to apply to be enrolled.

12. The Secretary of the Treasury may withdraw or amend at any time or from time to time all or any of the foregoing rules and regulations, with or without previous notice, and may make such special orders as he may deem proper in any case.

A. W. MELLON,<br>
Secretary of the Treasury.

---

TREASURY DEPARTMENT,
CHIEF CLERK.
Form 23. (Revised April 25, 1922.)

APPLICATION FOR ADMISSION TO PRACTICE BEFORE THE TREASURY DEPARTMENT.

The Honorable
THE SECRETARY OF THE TREASURY.
SIR:
I, ..................................................................................
residing at ........................................................................
with my office at..................................................................
hereby apply for enrollment to be recognized as.................................
(Attorney or agent.)
to represent others before the Treasury Department.

1. I am a citizen of the United States (if naturalized, state where and when: Place ..................... Date.....................), and the date of my birth is....
...................... "

2. I am a member of the bar of.................................................
and attach hereto a certificate to that effect from said court. ·
I am now in active practice and in good standing in said court.

3.¹ I am................................engaged in business under the name of
(State nature of business.)
.................................................and familiar with the laws, rules and regulations of the Treasury Department. I am qualified to act as the representative of others and render them valuable service, particularly in matters relating to....
......................................because of my education, training and business experience, which have been as follows: (State in chronological order, giving dates.)
Preliminary education:   ·                                       Dates.
....................................................................................
....................................................................................

Professional or technical education:
....................................................................................
....................................................................................
....................................................................................

¹ Paragraph 3 should be filled in only by persons applying for enrollment as agent.

Practical business experience:

..............................................................................................
..............................................................................................
..............................................................................................
..............................................................................................

Professional or technical experience:

..............................................................................................
..............................................................................................
..............................................................................................

Particular qualifications rendering applicant competent to advise and assist claimants in presentation of their cases:

..............................................................................................
..............................................................................................
..............................................................................................
..............................................................................................

4. I have never been rejected, suspended or disbarred from appearing as attorney or agent, or in any other representative capacity, before any branch of the Federal or any State Government or municipality, or any court. (State details of any exception.)........................................................................

..............................................................................................

5. I have never been an officer or employee of the United States.
I have been an officer or employee of the United States as follows: (State office or employment, with dates of appointment and separation.)...........................

..............................................................................................

6. I have read and noted Treasury Department Circular No. 230, dated April 25, 1922, and particularly paragraph 6 thereof.
7. I have made no previous application to be recognized as attorney or agent before the Treasury Department. (State details of any exception.)........................

..............................................................................................

8.[2] I,..............................................., do solemnly swear (or affirm) that the statements contained in the foregoing application are true and correct; that I will support and defend the Constitution of the United States against all enemies, foreign and domestic; that I will bear true faith and allegiance to the same; that I take this obligation freely without any mental reservation or purpose of evasion; and that if authorized to represent others before the Treasury Department I will at all times conduct myself strictly in compliance with the laws and regulations governing practice before the Department. So help me God.

(Name)........................................
(Address)......................................

Subscribed and sworn to before me this......day of.........., 192..
(Signature of officer)..........................................
(Official title).................................................

[Impress seal here.]

### CERTIFICATES OF CHARACTER.[3]

| I hereby certify that I have known the within-named...................... ...................since............; (Year.) that during all that time I have known him to be of good moral character and worthy of the trust and confidence of claimants and of the Treasury Department. | I hereby certify that I have known the within-named.................... ...................since............, (Year.) that during all that time I have known him to be of good moral character and worthy of the trust and confidence of claimants and of the Treasury Department. |
|---|---|
| ................................. (Name and address of person not related to applicant.) ........................... (Date.) | ................................. (Name and address of person not related to applicant.) ........................... (Date.) |

[1] NOTE.—This oath may be taken before any justice of the peace, notary public, or other person who is legally authorized to administer an oath in the State, Territory or District where the application is executed. The seal of the officer administering the oath must be affixed, or if he has no seal, his official character must be duly certified under seal.
[2] Leave certificates blank if a member of the bar.

WASHINGTON, ....................., 192..

The attached application of...................................................
for enrollment to be recognized as....................to represent others before the
Treasury Department has been examined, and after consideration it is recommended
that the application be...........................................................
...........................................................................

................................., Chairman.

.................................

.................................

.................................

.................................

.................................

Approved by the Secretary.          *Committee on Enrollment and Disbarment,*
(See Schedule No....)                              *Treasury Department.*

## Exhibit 82.

[Department Circular No. 297. Section of Surety Bonds, Division of Appointments.]

**REGULATIONS APPLICABLE TO SURETY COMPANIES DOING BUSINESS WITH THE UNITED STATES UNDER THE ACT OF CONGRESS APPROVED AUGUST 13, 1894, AS AMENDED BY THE ACT OF CONGRESS OF MARCH 23, 1910.**

TREASURY DEPARTMENT,
OFFICE OF THE SECRETARY,
*Washington, July 5, 1922.*

1. The following regulations will govern the issuance by the Secretary of the Treasury of certificates of authority to bonding companies to do business with the United States as sureties on recognizances, stipulations, bonds, and undertakings, hereinafter sometimes called obligations, under the provisions of the Act of Congress of August 13, 1894, as amended by the Act of Congress of March 23, 1910, and the acceptance of such obligations from such companies so long as they continue to hold said certificates of authority.

2. *Application for certificate of authority.*—Every company applying for such a certificate of authority will be required to submit to the Secretary of the Treasury an application in writing signed by its President and Secretary, and accompanied by the following papers:

(*a*) A certified copy of its charter or articles of incorporation, together with the certificate of the Insurance Commissioner, or other proper officer of the State under whose laws the company was organized, showing that it is fully and legally incorporated and organized under the laws of said State, and is authorized to transact and is transacting therein a fidelity and surety business, and the period during which it has been engaged in the transaction of such business.

(*b*) A copy of its by-laws, certified by the Secretary or Assistant Secretary of the company, and a certificate of either of such officers as to the election of its officers and directors.

(*c*) A list, signed and sworn to by its Secretary or Assistant Secretary, and by its Treasurer or Assistant Treasurer, of the names and post-office addresses of its stockholders; the number of shares held by each; the amount paid in on account of capital, and the amount, if any, paid in as surplus.

(*d*) A full statement, verified, signed, and sworn to by its President and Secretary, in such form as the Secretary of the Treasury may prescribe, showing its assets and liabilities and such other information respecting its business as may be required.

3. *Issuance of certificates of authority.*—If, from the evidence submitted in the manner and form herein required, the Secretary of the Treasury shall be satisfied that such company has authority under its charter or articles of incorporation to do the business provided for by the Acts above referred to, and if the Secretary of the Treasury shall be satisfied from such company's financial statement and from any further evidence or information he may require, and from such examination of the company, at its own expense, as he may cause to be made, that such company has a capital fully paid up in cash of not less than $250,000, is solvent and financially and otherwise qualified to do the business provided for in said Acts, and is able to keep and perform its contracts, he will, subject to the further conditions herein contained, issue a certificate of authority to such company, under the seal of the Treasury Department, to qualify as surety on obligations permitted or required by the laws of the United States, to be given with one or more sureties, for a term expiring on the last day of April next following. A new certificate of authority shall, so long as the company remains qualified under the law and these regulations, be issued annually on the first day of May.

4. *Deposits.*—No such company will be granted authority to do business under the provisions of the Acts above referred to unless it shall have and maintain on deposit with the Insurance Commissioner, or other proper financial officer, of the State in which it is incorporated, or of any other State of the United States, for the protection of all its policyholders in the United States, legal investments having a current market value of not less than $100,000.

5. *Business.*—Such company must engage in the business of fidelity insurance and suretyship, whether or not also making contracts of insurance in one or more of the classes generally known as casualty risks, but shall not be engaged in any other classes of insurance or any other business. It must be the intention of every such company to engage actively in the execution of fidelity and surety bonds running to the United States.

6. *Regulations.*—Every company now or hereafter authorized to do business under the Acts of Congress above referred to shall be subject to the following regulations:

7. *Investment of capital and assets.*—The cash capital and other funds of every such company must be safely invested in accordance with the laws of the State in which it is incorporated, and subject to the following general restrictions:

No part of any of said cash capital, or of any other assets or funds of any such company shall be invested in or loaned on its own stock. No part of said cash capital, or of any other assets or funds shall be loaned unless such loan shall be secured by mortgage on unencumbered improved or productive real estate within the United States, such loan not to exceed sixty per centum of the current market value of the mortgaged premises; or by the pledge of bonds or stocks or other evidences of indebtedness, such loan at no time to be in excess of ninety per centum of the current market value of the securities pledged; or by pledge of bonds or other evidences of indebtedness of the United States, the market value of which is equal to at least the amount loaned thereon. No part of the capital of any such company shall be or remain invested in or loaned upon any security or real estate subject to any prior lien.

The foregoing general restrictions shall not apply to assets acquired as salvage, if they are being liquidated with reasonable promptness.

8. *Financial reports.*—Every such company will be required to file with the Secretary of the Treasury, on or before the last day of January of each year, a statement of its financial condition made up as of the close of the preceding calendar year upon the annual statement blank adopted by the National Convention of Insurance Commissioners, signed and sworn to by its President and Secretary. On or before the last day of July of each year every such company will be required to file with the Secretary of the Treasury a financial statement as of June 30, on the form required by the National Convention of Insurance Commissioners, signed and sworn to by its President and Secretary, consisting of income and disbursements, assets, liabilities, and jurat, exhibit of premiums, underwriting and investment exhibits, Schedule E, Schedule A, part 1, Schedule of Mortgage Loans made and paid off during the period of statement, Schedule C, part 1, Schedule D, parts 1 and 2 (excluding interest and dividend items), Schedule F, salvage assets, and Schedule of Deposits. On or before the last days of April and October of each year every such company will be required to file a financial statement with the Secretary of the Treasury as of the last day of the preceding month, on the form adopted by the National Convention of Insurance Commissioners, signed and sworn to by its President and Secretary, consisting of income and disbursements, assets, liabilities, and jurat, and an underwriting and investment exhibit.

Every such company shall furnish such other exhibits or information, and in such manner as the Secretary of the Treasury may at any time require.

9. *Valuation of assets.*—In determining the financial condition of every such company, its assets and liabilities will be computed on the basis recommended by the National Convention of Insurance Commissioners so far as practicable and consistent with these regulations. Credit will be allowed for reinsurance in all classes of risks, subject in case of fidelity and surety risks, to the limitations contained in paragraph 12, section "a," provided that the reinsuring company is (1) any company authorized by the Secretary of the Treasury, or (2) any company described in subsections 2 and 3 of paragraph 12, section "a" and authorized under its charter to reinsure the classes of risks for which credit for reinsurance is claimed by the ceding company, and provided further, that any such reinsuring company shall meet all other requirements imposed on reinsuring companies by said paragraph 12, section "a."

The Secretary of the Treasury may in his discretion value the assets or other securities of such companies in accordance with the best information obtainable.

10. *Limitation of risk.*—Except as herein provided, no company having authority, under the Acts of Congress above referred to, to do business with the United States, shall be accepted as sole surety on any obligation under this Department, which shall execute any obligation on behalf of any individual, firm, association, or corporation, whether or not the United States is interested as a party thereto,

the penal sum of which is greater than ten per centum of the paid up capital and surplus of such company.

11. Two or more companies may be accepted as sureties on any obligation under this Department, the penal sum of which does not exceed the limitation herein prescribed of their aggregate qualifying power, as fixed and determined by the Secretary of the Treasury. In such cases each company shall limit its liability, in terms, upon the face of the bond, to a definite specified amount, such amount to be in all cases, however, within the limitations herein prescribed. In cases where the law specially requires it, such obligation shall be executed by the principal and sureties jointly and severally.

12. The limitation herein prescribed shall not apply to any obligation when the liability in excess of the company's qualifying power, as fixed and determined by the Secretary of the Treasury, is protected as follows:

(a) In respect to obligations running to the United States, by reinsurance, effected simultaneously with the execution and delivery of the original obligation, or within forty-five days thereafter, of such excess with any company holding a certificate of authority from the Secretary of the Treasury. In respect to obligations not running to the United States, by reinsurance, effected simultaneously with the execution and delivery of the original obligation, or within forty-five days thereafter, of such excess with (1) any company holding a certificate of authority from the Secretary of the Treasury, (2) with any company organized under the laws of the United States, or of any State thereof, authorized under its charter to reinsure fidelity and surety risks, and having a capital stock paid up in cash of not less than $250,000, or (3) any company of any foreign country holding a license from any State of the United States to do business in such State, authorized under its charter and such license to reinsure fidelity and surety risks, and having a deposit capital in this country of not less than $250,000 available to all its policyholders and creditors in the United States; provided, that any such reinsuring company as is described in (2) or (3) shall file with the Secretary of the Treasury a certified copy of its charter or articles of incorporation, and, if it is a company of a foreign country, also a certified copy of its license to do business in the State which has granted such license; and provided further, that any such reinsuring company shall file on or before the first day of March of each year with the Secretary of the Treasury such statement as he may require for the purpose of determining whether it has a capital stock or deposit capital, as the case may be, in accordance with the foregoing requirements, and whether it is solvent and able to keep and perform its contracts. No credit, however, will be allowed the ceding company for reinsurance ceded in excess of ten per centum of the reinsuring company's capital and surplus.

(b) By the deposit with it in pledge, or by conveyance to it in trust, for its protection, of property the current market value of which is at least equal to the liability in excess of the company's qualifying power.

(c) In case such obligation was incurred on behalf of or on account of a fiduciary holding property in a trust capacity, by a joint control agreement which provides that the whole or a sufficient portion of the property so held may not be disposed of or pledged in any way without the consent of the insuring company.

13. In determining the limitation herein prescribed, the full penalty of the obligation will be regarded as the liability, and no offset will be allowed on account of any estimate of risk which is less than such full penalty, except in the following cases:

(a) Appeal bonds; in which case the liability will be regarded as the amount of the judgment appealed from, plus ten per cent of said amount to cover interest and costs.

(b) Bonds of executors, administrators, trustees, guardians,. and other fiduciaries, where the penalty of the bond or other obligation is fixed in excess of the estimated value of the estate; in which cases the estimated value of the estate, upon which the penalty of the bond was fixed, will be regarded as the liability.

(c) Credit will also be allowed for indemnifying agreements executed by sole heirs or beneficiaries of an estate releasing the surety from liability.

(d) Contract bonds given in excess of the amount of the contract; in which cases the amount of the contract will be regarded as the liability.

(e) Bonds for banks or trust companies as principals, conditioned to repay moneys on deposit, whereby any law or decree of a court, the amount to be deposited shall be less than the penalty of the bond; in which cases the maximum amount on deposit at any one time will be regarded as the liability.

14. *Schedules of single risks.*—During the months of January, April, July, and October of each year every company will be required to report to the Secretary of the Treasury every obligation which it has assumed during the three months immediately preceding, the penal sum of which is greater than ten per centum of its paid up capital and surplus, together with a full statement of the facts which tend to bring it within the provisions of these regulations, on a form suitable for the purpose.

15. The amount of paid up capital and surplus of any such company shall be determined from the financial and other statements of such company filed with the Secretary of the Treasury as herein provided, or by reports of examinations made by the Insurance Departments of the several States, or by such examination of such company, at its own expense, as the Secretary of the Treasury may deem necessary or proper.

16. A statement showing the capital, surplus, and qualifying power of the various companies authorized under these regulations will be published semiannually, as of June 30th and December 31st of each year, such publication to be made as soon as practicable following the examination of the statements above referred to. If the Secretary of the Treasury shall make any changes in the annual or semiannual statement of any company, he shall, before issuing such publication, give the company due notice thereof.

17. Whenever, in the judgment of the Secretary of the Treasury, any such company is no longer sufficient security, he shall revoke its certificate of authority.

18. The Secretary of the Treasury may amend or supplement these regulations at any time.

19. The foregoing regulations supersede all previous regulations relating to the same subject.

A. W. MELLON, *Secretary.*

EXHIBIT 83.

[Department Circular No. 283. Chief Clerk.]

## ORDER ESTABLISHING CENTRALIZED PURCHASING FOR THE TREASURY DEPARTMENT.

TREASURY DEPARTMENT,
OFFICE OF THE SECRETARY,
*Washington, March 28, 1922.*

*To All Officers of the Treasury Department and Others Concerned:*

1. There is hereby created and established a Bureau of Supply in and for the Treasury Department. The officer in charge will be known as the Director of Supply and will be detailed from a bureau or division of the Treasury Department.

2. The Bureau of Supply is assigned for administrative purposes to the Assistant Secretary in charge of foreign loans and miscellaneous.

3. The Bureau of Supply will assume on April 1, 1922, or as soon thereafter as practicable, all functions relating to the actual purchase of material and supplies now exercised by offices, divisions, services, and bureaus (hereinafter referred to as bureaus) in the Treasury Department in Washington and in the field, except as hereinafter provided. The Bureau of Engraving and Printing is not included in this order, because of existing statutes. These functions will be taken over gradually, and no bureau in Washington or in the field shall cease its present purchasing operations until specifically so instructed.

The Bureau of Supply will take over such storerooms within the Department as can be efficiently used for common distribution of supplies.

4. All requisitions for material and supplies will be prepared by the Consuming Bureaus and must show the appropriation from which payment is to be made, the necessity of the purchase, and such other details as may be required by the Bureau of Supply, including specifications if necessary.

All requisitions made by Consuming Bureaus to be paid for from appropriations under their control will be submitted by such bureaus to the Bureau of Supply.

All other requisitions will be submitted to the Bureau of Supply through the office having control of the appropriation and must be approved by such office.

The head of the office controlling the appropriation from which purchases are to be made, or his duly authorized representatives, will be responsible for the legality and necessity of procurement and, subject to the approval of the Director of Supply, for the inspection of material upon delivery. They will prepare vouchers for payment and certify upon such vouchers that the articles were secured in accordance with the law, have been received in good condition and in the quality and quantity specified; that prices charged are just, reasonable and in accordance with the order or contract.

The heads of the Consuming Bureaus will be charged with the duty of anticipating their requirements so as to permit of orderly and economical procurement, and yet avoid having public funds tied up in surplus stocks.

They will, when requested, co-ordinate their requirements with those of other bureaus and submit them at designated periods to permit of combined purchase and inspection, interchangeability or standardization of supplies and limitations in types, grades, and varieties.

5. The Director of Supply will be responsible for the prompt, efficient, economical and legal manner of procurement. All orders or contracts for supplies involving an expenditure of $100 or more will be approved by the Assistant Secretary in charge of the bureau concerned, but for supplies involving an expenditure of less than $100, the order or contract may be approved by the Director of Supply.

Copies of all orders and contracts shall be furnished to the bureaus concerned.

The Director of Supply will conduct all business relations with contractors in respect to orders and contracts, with the exception that inspecting offices may correspond directly with contractors on matters of inspection only, furnishing copies of such correspondence to the Director of Supply.

The Director of Supply will be responsible for the inspection of articles purchased for stock to be delivered at common storerooms under his supervision in Washington and may call upon the Consuming Bureaus for assistance.

6. This order does not supersede or modify any of the provisions of Department Circular No. 3, dated October 8, 1915, prescribing regulations for the conduct of the General Supply Committee. The functions of that Committee will be performed as at present, except that supervision now exercised by the Chief Clerk will hereafter be undertaken by the Director of Supply.

A. W. MELLON,<br>Secretary of the Treasury.

EXHIBIT 84.

TREASURY DEPARTMENT,<br>Washington, June 16, 1922.

**ORDER SUPPLEMENTING CIRCULAR NO. 283, ESTABLISHING CENTRALIZED PURCHASING FOR THE TREASURY DEPARTMENT.**

*To all Officers of the Treasury Department and Others Concerned:*

Pursuant to and supplementing the provisions of Department Circular 283 of March 28, 1922, you are hereby notified and directed as follows:

Upon receipt of notice from the Office of the Secretary, you will assign for duty in the Bureau of Supply, such clerical and other personnel under your control as devote any substantial part of their time to the purchase, handling or distribution of supplies, or keeping records pertaining to such work. Should any question arise as to the personnel to be so transferred, such question shall be referred to the Office of the Secretary for determination.

The pay and status of personnel assigned to duty with the Bureau of Supply shall not be changed except with the approval of the Director of that Bureau. Vacancies occurring in the personnel of the Bureau of Supply shall be filled upon recommendation of the Director.

Except as may be in conflict with existing law, you will transfer to the Bureau of Supply such of the following as it may select, viz: storerooms, material, equipment and supplies, including telephone and motor vehicles now being used within the Department for the procurement, storage and distribution of supplies.

An inventory shall be furnished the Bureau of Supply of all material, equipment and supplies, transferred thereto, and receipts therefor will be issued to the transferring office. The inventory submitted must be on forms approved by the Director.

All records required to complete pending transactions relative to purchase and distribution of supplies shall be transferred to the Bureau of Supply.

Simultaneously with the transfer provided for in paragraph two of this order all appropriations or parts of appropriations, contingent, miscellaneous and otherwise, except those for the Bureau of Engraving and Printing and for distinctive paper for all classes of securities and currency, made and provided for the purchase of supplies for the offices, bureaus and divisions of the Treasury Department shall be transferred in whole or in part and, upon transfer, be available to the Bureau of Supply, to be used to procure supplies strictly in accordance with the terms and for the purposes set forth in the various items of appropriations.

The Director of Supply will furnish monthly to all offices concerned statements of balances of such appropriations or parts of appropriations transferred under the provisions of the preceding paragraph. Copies of purchase orders will be furnished requiring offices only when supplies purchased are to be delivered direct to user from contractor.

The Bureau af Supply will make all contracts involving an expenditure of funds allotted to said Bureau.

Payments for purchases of supplies will be made by the disbursing clerk of the Department, upon vouchers properly approved by the Director of Supply.

The Director of Supply will determine upon methods and forms to be used in requisitioning supplies by bureaus, divisions and field activities of the Department.

All provisions of Department Circular 283 in conflict with this order are hereby rescinded.

A. W. MELLON,
*Secretary of the Treasury.*

EXHIBIT 85.

**LETTER OF THE SECRETARY OF THE TREASURY APPOINTING A BUDGET AND IMPROVEMENT COMMITTEE FOR THE TREASURY DEPARTMENT.**

JULY 8, 1922.

Messrs. S. R. JACOBS, *Deputy Commissioner of the Public Debt, (Chairman);*

W. N. THOMPSON, *Assistant to the Under Secretary;*

CHARLES H. FULLAWAY, *Associate Director, Savings Division;*

C. R. SCHOENEMAN, *War Loan Staff;*

D. S. BLISS, *Bureau of Internal Revenue;*

FRANK A. BIRGFELD, *Superintendent Accounts Division, Office of Supervising Architect;*

W. O. WOODS, *Bureau of Internal Revenue;*

L. C. MARTIN, *Chief, Division of Mail and Files.*

A. M. WHEELER, *Public Health Service.*

GENTLEMEN: You are hereby appointed a Budget and Improvement Committee for the Treasury Department, to be responsible, under the direction of the Budget Officer and Under Secretary of the Treasury, for the preparation and examination of Treasury estimates of appropriations and for the improvement of administrative methods and procedure within the Treasury Department.

In connection with the estimates of appropriations it is expected that you will assist the Budget Officer of the Treasury Department, designated under Section 214 of the Budget and Accounting Act, approved June 10, 1921, and that in cooperation with the budget officer of each bureau or division you will, as a Committee, consider the estimates for all Treasury Department offices, individually and as a whole, and make appropriate recommendations for the revision of the estimates, where that appears to be necessary or desirable in the interest of the proper administration of the Department. In this capacity your Committee will supersede the Assistant Budget Officers of the Treasury Department who were designated about a year ago and functioned as a Budget Committee in connection with the estimates for the fiscal year 1923.

The efficient and economical conduct of the Department's business, above all other things, is a determining factor in the achievement of reduced estimates, for in large measure decreased operating costs must be accomplished through the elimination of duplicated effort and the application of the most practicable and efficient methods of work. To this end your Committee is charged with the duty of studying existing procedure within the various Bureaus and offices of the Department and of conducting such investigations therein as may be necessary, with a view to the introduction of improved methods of work and more effective Departmental organization. It is expected that to this end your Committee will hold stated meetings and feel free to call upon the heads of Treasury offices for such information as may be desired, and that after study and investigation, appropriate recommendations will be made to the Secretary from time to time for changes in methods of work or procedure.

It is my desire to place the Treasury Department on the most businesslike basis, and I hope that with the cooperation of all concerned and diligent effort on the part of your Committee an important advance can be made in this direction.

Very truly yours. (Signed) A. W. MELLON,
*Secretary.*

## Exhibit 86.

Number of employees in the Treasury Department in Washington, by months, from July 31, 1921, to September 30, 1922, inclusive.

| Bureau or office. | 1921 | | | | | | 1922 | | | | | | | | |
|---|---|---|---|---|---|---|---|---|---|---|---|---|---|---|---|
| | July 31. | Aug. 31. | Sept. 30. | Oct. 31. | Nov. 30. | Dec. 31. | Jan. 31. | Feb. 28. | Mar. 31. | Apr. 30. | May 31. | June 30. | July 31. | Aug. 31. | Sept. 30. |
| Secretary's office | 34 | 35 | 34 | 34 | 33 | 33 | 34 | 34 | 34 | 34 | 34 | 34 | 28 | 24 | 25 |
| Chief clerk's office | 1,178 | 1,189 | 1,192 | 1,185 | 1,168 | 1,163 | 1,160 | 1,164 | 1,177 | 1,173 | 1,160 | 1,020 | 723 | 720 | 715 |
| Division of Appointments | 35 | 34 | 34 | 33 | 34 | 34 | 34 | 33 | 34 | 34 | 34 | 34 | 35 | 35 | 34 |
| Division of Bookkeeping and Warrants | 90 | 91 | 91 | 90 | 90 | 87 | 87 | 87 | 85 | 85 | 85 | 85 | 80 | 79 | 79 |
| Division of ____ | 51 | 52 | 51 | 52 | 47 | 47 | 48 | 49 | 51 | 50 | 51 | 51 | 51 | 51 | 42 |
| Division of ____ | 8 | 8 | 8 | 8 | 8 | 8 | 8 | 8 | 8 | 8 | 8 | 8 | 9 | 9 | 8 |
| Division of Loans and Currency | 2,043 | 2,026 | 1,850 | 1,841 | 1,806 | 1,824 | 1,799 | 1,789 | 1,779 | 1,771 | 1,751 | 1,724 | 1,521 | 1,531 | 1,517 |
| Division of Mail and Files | 14 | 13 | 13 | 13 | 13 | 12 | 13 | 13 | 13 | 13 | 13 | 13 | 13 | 13 | 13 |
| Division of Printing and Stationery | 45 | 43 | 42 | 43 | 42 | 42 | 42 | 41 | 42 | 42 | 42 | 42 | 42 | 41 | 42 |
| Savings Division | 18 | 18 | 19 | 17 | 18 | 17 | 17 | 18 | 17 | 16 | 16 | 11 | 15 | 15 | 16 |
| Secret Service Division | 11 | 11 | 11 | 11 | 11 | 11 | 11 | 11 | 11 | 11 | 11 | 11 | 13 | 13 | 13 |
| Bond roll (miscellaneous) | 33 | 37 | 35 | 37 | 38 | 37 | 42 | 44 | 48 | 49 | 49 | 50 | 48 | 53 | 52 |
| Comptroller of the currency | 80 | 81 | 80 | 80 | 81 | 81 | 81 | 81 | 81 | 82 | 80 | 81 | 82 | 79 | 79 |
| United States Coast Guard | 217 | 222 | 227 | 227 | 226 | 226 | 228 | 228 | 225 | 224 | 225 | 211 | 201 | 200 | 198 |
| Disbursing clerk's office | 17 | 17 | 17 | 17 | 17 | 16 | 17 | 17 | 17 | 17 | 16 | 16 | 19 | 19 | 19 |
| Bureau of Engraving and Printing | 6,581 | 6,488 | 6,459 | 6,419 | 6,397 | 6,377 | 6,361 | 6,345 | 6,309 | 6,233 | 6,113 | 6,029 | 5,974 | 5,556 | 5,634 |
| Federal Farm Loan Bureau | 62 | 62 | 63 | 62 | 62 | 62 | 68 | 67 | 68 | 68 | 69 | 69 | 67 | 69 | 70 |
| Internal Revenue Bureau | 6,960 | 6,929 | 7,016 | 6,999 | 7,002 | 7,011 | 7,006 | 7,063 | 7,107 | 7,147 | 7,192 | 7,191 | 7,252 | 7,228 | 7,208 |
| Mint Bureau | 13 | 13 | 14 | 14 | 13 | 13 | 13 | 13 | 13 | 13 | 13 | 13 | 13 | 13 | 13 |
| Public Health Bureau | 633 | 619 | 607 | 600 | 582 | 583 | 579 | 571 | 571 | 565 | 221 | 225 | 238 | 277 | 275 |
| Office of the Register of the Treasury | 932 | 915 | 901 | 886 | 875 | 878 | 877 | 875 | 879 | 867 | 940 | 956 | 1,134 | 1,087 | 1,121 |
| Supervising Architect's Office | 246 | 262 | 287 | 270 | 257 | 261 | 256 | 258 | 257 | 255 | 249 | 243 | 248 | 236 | 223 |
| Office of the Treasurer of the United States | 1,252 | 1,239 | 1,212 | 1,220 | 1,215 | 1,206 | 1,186 | 1,179 | 1,172 | 1,169 | 1,108 | 1,089 | 1,091 | 1,113 | 1,101 |
| Bureau of War Risk Insurance [1] | 5,025 | | | | | | | | | | | | | | |
| Bureau of the Budget [2] | 16 | 18 | 23 | 26 | 23 | 24 | 25 | 27 | 27 | 29 | 31 | 36 | 37 | 37 | 36 |
| Office of the Commissioner of Accounts and Deposits [3] | 1 | 1 | 1 | 1 | 1 | 1 | 1 | 1 | 1 | 1 | 1 | 1 | 5 | 5 | 5 |
| Office of the Commissioner of the Public Debt [4] | | | 24 | 49 | 44 | 45 | 48 | 46 | 46 | 45 | 45 | 45 | 60 | 60 | 62 |
| Division of Public Debt, Accounts and Audit [4] | | | 142 | 142 | 141 | 140 | 142 | 142 | 142 | 142 | 141 | 138 | 139 | 139 | 111 |
| Public debt (miscellaneous) | | | | | | | | | | | | | 25 | 22 | 22 |
| General Supply Committee [5] | | | | | | | | | | | | 140 | 140 | 138 | 136 |
| Total | 25,596 | 20,424 | 20,453 | 20,375 | 20,243 | 20,239 | 20,181 | 20,209 | 20,212 | 20,143 | 19,703 | 19,571 | 19,303 | 18,662 | 18,911 |

[1] Transferred to the United States Veterans' Bureau, act of Aug. 9, 1921.
[2] Created by act of June 10, 1921.
[3] Act of June 16, 1921, effective July 1, 1921.
[4] Transferred from Division of Loans and Currency, Sept. 1, 1921.
[5] Transferred from chief clerk's office, June 15, 1922.

EXHIBIT 87.

## LETTER OF THE SECRETARY OF THE TREASURY RELATIVE TO TAX-EXEMPT SECURITIES, JANUARY 16, 1922.

JANUARY 16, 1922.

DEAR MR. CHAIRMAN: I am glad, in accordance with the request of the Committee, to present the Treasury's views as to the issuance of tax-exempt securities and the latest available information as to the amounts now outstanding and their effects upon the revenues and the investment markets. The problem presented by these issues of tax-free securities is of growing importance and I think that it deserves the most serious attention.

The views of the Treasury on the subject, and its suggestions as to possible remedies, have already been set forth in my letter to you of April 30, 1921,[1] and in my letter of September 23, 1921,[1] to the Chairman of the Committee on Banking and Currency of the House of Representatives, a copy of which I sent to you with my letter of September 23, 1921. Copies of these letters are attached for ready reference. The further views of the Treasury have been indicated to some extent in my letter of November 4, 1921, to you, and in the Under Secretary's letter of November 10th to the Chairman of the Committee on Banking and Currency, copies of which are enclosed.

Since these letters the President, in his address to Congress on December 6, 1921, has emphasized the importance of action in the matter in the following words:

There are a full score of topics concerning which it would be becoming to address you, and on which I hope to make report at a later time. I have alluded to the things requiring your earlier attention. However, I can not end this limited address without a suggested amendment to the organic law.

Many of us belong to that school of thought which is hesitant about altering the fundamental law. I think our tax problems, the tendency of wealth to seek nontaxable investment, and the menacing increase of public debt, Federal, State, and municipal—all justify a proposal to change the Constitution so as to end the issue of nontaxable bonds. No action can change the status of the many billions outstanding, but we can guard against future encouragement of capital's paralysis, while a halt in the growth of public indebtedness would be beneficial throughout our whole land.

Such a change in the Constitution must be thoroughly considered before submission. There ought to be known what influence it will have on the inevitable refunding of our vast national debt, how it will operate on the necessary refunding of State and municipal debt, how the advantages of Nation over State and municipality, or the contrary, may be avoided. Clearly the States would not ratify to their own apparent disadvantage. I suggest the consideration because the drift of wealth into nontaxable securities is hindering the flow of large capital to our industries, manufacturing, agricultural, and carrying, until we are discouraging the very activities which make our wealth.

I should also like to call to your attention the statement as to the decline in taxable income, particularly from investments, which appeared in my Annual Report for 1921, on pages 20–21, as follows:

The Injurious Effect of High Rates on the Revenues.

The actual effect of the high surtaxes can readily be seen in the statistics published by the Bureau of Internal Revenue.

The following table shows in comparative form, for the years 1916 to 1919, inclusive, the total number of returns of all classes and the returns of incomes over $300,000; the total net income in the same way, and also the investment income:

---

[1] See Annual Report of the Secretary of the Treasury, 1921, pp. 349 and 379

*Table showing decline of taxable incomes over $300,000.*

| | Number of returns. | | Net income. | | Income from dividends, interest, and Investments. | |
|---|---|---|---|---|---|---|
| | All classes. | Incomes over $300,000. | All classes. | Incomes over $300,000. | All classes. | Incomes over $300,000. |
| 1916 | 437,036 | 1,296 | $6,298,577,620 | $992,972,986 | $3,217,348,030 | $706,945,733 |
| 1917 | 3,472,890 | 1,015 | 13,652,383,207 | 731,372,153 | 3,785,557,955 | 616,119,892 |
| 1918 | 4,425,114 | 627 | 15,924,639,355 | 401,107,868 | 3,872,234,935 | 344,111,461 |
| 1919 | 5,332,760 | 679 | 19,859,491,448 | 440,011,589 | 3,954,553,925 | 314,984,884 |

The years under consideration, 1916 to 1919, inclusive, were, on the whole, years of unexampled prosperity, and of earnings and profits beyond those ever known before in any like period in the history of the country. Notwithstanding this, and while the total income of all classes increased, at the same time there was a striking decrease in taxable incomes of $300,000 and over—the drop being from $992,972,986 in 1916 to $440,011,589 in 1919.

The effect of the high surtaxes in the other brackets is apparent from a brief study of the statistics regarding taxable investment income.

In the bracket "Incomes of $300,000 and over," the taxable investment income declined from $746,614,591 in 1916 to $328,360,613 in 1919; in the bracket "$100,000 to $300,000," the decline was from $602,853,543 in 1916 to $427,910,905 in 1919; and in the bracket "$60,000 to $100,000," the decline was from $366,614,917 in 1916 to $323,743,874 in 1919.

If we take the taxable income from interest, exclusive of interest on Government obligations, the decline is still more striking, the figures being as follows:

Incomes, $300,000 and over:
```
    1916.................................................... $165,733,900
    1917....................................................  111,468,127
    1918....................................................   74,610,507
    1919....................................................   60,087,093
```
Incomes, $100,000 to $300,000:
```
    1916....................................................  158,870,428
    1917....................................................  119,539,786
    1918....................................................   91,030,392
    1919....................................................   91,467,182
```
Incomes, $60,000 to $100,000:
```
    1916....................................................   93,280,583
    1917....................................................   75,375,484
    1918....................................................   65,784,062
    1919....................................................   68,814,933
```

The foregoing brackets represent the incomes subject to surtaxes under the revenue act of 1918, respectively, at 63 to 65 per cent, 52 to 60 per cent, and 29 to 48 per cent. To these figures should be added the normal tax of 8 per cent in order to find the total tax obligation.

In view of these figures, is it not clear that these high surtax rates are rapidly ceasing to be productive of revenue to the Government? And is it not equally clear that their effect has been to divert into unproductive channels not merely the income on the old investments, but to force a large part of the old investment capital into unproductive channels?

I attach for the further information of the Committee in this connection the following tables which have been prepared by the Government Actuary:

1. Estimate of the total amount of wholly tax-exempt securities outstanding January 1, 1922.

2. Table showing advantage of investing in tax-free securities as compared with a like investment in taxable securities.

3. Estimate of revenue loss to Federal Government through wholly tax-exempt securities outstanding January 1, 1922.

According to reports, there were issued during the calendar year 1921 fully tax-exempt securities of States and municipalities to the aggregate amount of about $1,100,000,000, and the indications are that further issues will follow during the current year in substantial volume. Fully tax-exempt land bank bonds, Federal and Joint Stock, to an amount exceeding $100,000,000, were also issued during 1921, and further issues are in prospect. The Federal Government, on the other hand, has adopted the policy of not issuing fully tax-exempt obligations of its own, and its current offerings must be sold in competition with the fully tax-exempt offerings of States and cities.

The most important consideration is that the existence of the growing mass of tax-exempt securities, coupled with the extremely high surtax rates still imposed by law, tends to drive persons of large income more and more to invest in wholly exempt securities issued and still being issued by States and municipalities and heretofore issued by the Federal Government. The result is to impair the revenues of the Federal Government and to pervert the surtaxes, so that instead of raising revenue they frequently operate rather to encourage investment in wholly tax-exempt securities, and even to encourage the issue of such securities by States and municipalities. This process tends to divert investment funds from the development of productive enterprises, transportation, housing, and the like, into non-productive or wasteful State or municipal expenditures, and forces both the Federal Government and those engaged in business and industry to compete with wholly tax-exempt issues and on that account to pay higher rates of interest.

The greatest value of the full exemption from taxation arises, of course, from the exemption it confers in respect to Federal income surtaxes, and the constantly increasing volume of tax-free securities therefore constitutes a real menace to the revenues of the Federal Government. At the same time it makes the high surtaxes operate as inducements to investment in non-productive public indebtedness and is gradually destroying them as revenue producers. As a consequence, the yield of the surtaxes is dwindling and there is a premium on the issue of bonds of States and cities. In the last analysis this is at the expense of the Federal Government, and it is having a most unfortunate and far-reaching effect upon the development of the whole country, because of the diversion of wealth from productive enterprise.

The problem is one of exceptional difficulty, and it is not easy to point to a practicable remedy. But the problem is none the less real, and it is important to do whatever can be done to meet it. One angle of approach is through the proposed Constitutional amendment; another is through the revision of the surtax rates to remove the heavy premium on tax-free securities. It will be helpful to the whole situation if the matter may have early consideration by the Committee, with a view to appropriate action.

Sincerely yours,

(Signed)          A. W. MELLON, *Secretary.*

Hon. JOSEPH W. FORDNEY,
      *Chairman, Committee on Ways and Means,*
         *House of Representatives, Washington, D. C.*

JANUARY 12, 1922.

Memorandum for Secretary:
(In re tax-exempt securities.)

The Bureau of the Census reports that for the years 1913 and 1919, the total indebtedness of the States was as follows:

1913............................................................... $422,796,525
1919............................................................... 744,582,933

This would indicate a total indebtedness of the States, as of January 1, 1920, of about $775,000,000.

The Bureau of the Census reported the total indebtedness of County and minor civil divisions of the States, which includes all cities, towns, etc., as of 1913, at $4,075,152,-904. This included $3,475,954,353 exclusive of Sinking Fund assets. This indebtedness probably increased by January 1, 1920, to about $5,595,000,000. That is, the total indebtedness of the States and their minor civil divisions as of January 1, 1920, was about $6,370,000,000.

According to the financial press, about $672,000,000 of new indebtedness was added during the year 1920, and about $1,100,000,000 for the year 1921. This would make the total indebtedness of the States and minor political subdivisions thereof as of January 1, 1922, $8,142,000,000.

From this the estimated total tax-free securities outstanding, as of January 1, 1922, may be tabulated as follows:

State, County, and minor political subdivisions of the States....... $8,142,000,000
U. S. tax-free bonds (net outstanding)............................. 2,184,000,000
Federal Farm Loan Bonds (net outstanding)......................... 284,000,000
Bonds of Insular possessions (net outstanding)[1].................. 50,000,000

Total.................................................. 10,660,000,000

This estimate may be fairly taken as a maximum, as no allowance is made in the computation for any debt maturing since July 1st, 1919.

(Sgd.)     Jos. S. McCoy
*Government Actuary.*

JANUARY 14, 1922.

Memorandum for Secretary:
Loss to Government through tax-free securities.

Estimated total of all tax-free securities issued in the United States,
outstanding January 1, 1922...................................... $10,660,000,000

Of this amount it is probable that say $5,660,000,000 is held by Corporations, such as Insurance, Surety and Bonding companies, Banks and Trust companies, etc., which are required to retain certain reserves. Many States require these reserves held by concerns doing business therein to be in the form of local state and municipal securities. A taxable security to yield the same revenue, after paying a tax of $12\frac{1}{2}\%$, as does a 5% tax-exempt security, must yield 5.714%. That is, on an investment of $100,000 by a corporation, the advantage of a tax-free investment would be $714.00 per year, as compared with a taxable investment. As a large percentage of insurance, banking and surety companies are required to invest in these tax-free securities, they would still be obliged to invest in them if they were taxable, so it would seem safe to say that, if they were all made taxable, the gain to the Federal Government in tax from corporation-held tax-exempt securities would be not in excess of $35,000,000 per annum. We must also remember that all commercial stocks are now tax-exempt in the hands of corporations, without materially reducing their taxes. Of the remaining $5,000,000,-000 in tax-exempt securities, held by individuals, partnerships and abroad, it is safe to say that upon about $2,500,000,000 the gain in tax would be nil, and that upon the remaining $2,500,000,000, about $85,000,000. That is, if all tax-exempt securities outstanding January 1, 1922, were made taxable, the gross increase in revenue to the Government would be approximately $120,000,000.

There is little doubt that under these conditions the future investor in what are now tax-exempt securities, would demand that they bear a higher rate of interest or be sold at a discount, sufficient at least to meet this tax.

(Sgd.)     Jos. S. McCoy
*Government Actuary.*

---

[1] Philippine Islands, Hawaii and Porto Rico.

JANUARY 14, 1922.

ADVANTAGE OF INVESTING IN TAX-FREE SECURITIES AS COMPARED WITH A LIKE INVEST-
MENT IN TAXABLE SECURITIES.

I. In each case $40,000 is assumed to be invested in a tax-free 5% security and by comparison in a taxable stock bearing the necessary rate of interest so as to yield the same income, after paying the income tax of the existing law.

| Net income of investor exclusive of that from the above investment. | Net income of investor from the above investment, after paying income tax on same. | | Tax—Surtax on dividends. | Income from taxable stock before paying tax. | Necessary rate of interest of taxable security. |
|---|---|---|---|---|---|
| | With tax-free security. | With taxable stock. | | | |
| $4,000 | $2,000 | $2,000 | $0.00 | $2,000.00 | 5.00% |
| 16,000 | 2,000 | 2,000 | 105.26 | 2,105.26 | 5.26% |
| 28,000 | 2,000 | 2,000 | 272.73 | 2,272.73 | 5.68% |
| 40,000 | 2,000 | 2,000 | 439.02 | 2,439.02 | 6.10% |
| 60,000 | 2,000 | 2,000 | 777.78 | 2,777.78 | 6.94% |
| 80,000 | 2,000 | 2,000 | 1,225.81 | 3,225.81 | 8.00% |
| 100,000 | 2,000 | 2,000 | 1,846.15 | 3,846.15 | 9.62% |
| 200,000 | 2,000 | 2,000 | 2,000.00 | 4,000.00 | 10.00% |
| 500,000 | 2,000 | 2,000 | 2,000.00 | 4,000.00 | 10.00% |
| 1,000,000 | 2,000 | 2,000 | 2,000.00 | 4,000.00 | 10.00% |

II. Advantage of investing in a tax-free security, as compared with any other form of investment when the income is subject to both normal and surtax, such as a mortgage, commercial bond, etc.:

In each case $40,000 is assumed to be invested in a tax-free security, and by comparison, the same amount in the other form of investment, yielding the necessary rate of profit, so as to give the same income after paying the income tax of the existing law. The investor is assumed to be married, without dependents.

| Net income of investor exclusive of that from the above investment. | Net income of investor from the above investment, after paying income tax on same. | | Total tax on receipts from above investment | Income from taxable security before paying tax. | Necessary rate of interest of taxable security. |
|---|---|---|---|---|---|
| | With tax-free security. | With taxable security. | | | |
| $500 | $2,000 | $2,000 | $0.00 | $2,000.00 | 5.00% |
| 4,000 | 2,000 | 2,000 | 80.00 | 2,080.00 | 5.20% |
| 16,000 | 2,000 | 2,000 | 265.26 | 2,265.26 | 5.66% |
| 28,000 | 2,000 | 2,000 | 432.73 | 2,432.73 | 6.08% |
| 40,000 | 2,000 | 2,000 | 599.02 | 2,599.02 | 6.50% |
| 60,000 | 2,000 | 2,000 | 937.78 | 2,937.78 | 7.34% |
| 80,000 | 2,000 | 2,000 | 1,385.81 | 3,385.81 | 8.46% |
| 100,000 | 2,000 | 2,000 | 2,006.15 | 4,006.15 | 10.02% |
| 200,000 | 2,000 | 2,000 | 2,160.00 | 4,160.00 | 10.40% |
| 500,000 | 2,000 | 2,000 | 2,160.00 | 4,160.00 | 10.40% |
| 1,000,000 | 2,000 | 2,000 | 2,160.00 | 4,160.00 | 10.40% |

From these tables it is observed that there is an advantage to the investor in tax-exempt securities yielding a 5% income, as compared with an investment of the same sum in the stock of a corporation where the return from that stock is less than from 5% to 10%, depending upon the taxable net income of the investor. In case of an investment of the same sum in a mortgage, corporate bond, or other completely taxable form of investment the advantage exists, unless this latter investment yields from 5% to 10.40%, depending upon the net income.

Where the amount invested is greater than $40,000, the upper limit will be the same, but the advantage will be somewhat extended where the net income from other sources is small or comparatively small, as is shown in the table following.

*Investment of $1,000,000 in a 5 per cent tax-exempt security as compared with the investment of the same sum in commercial stocks.*

| Net income of investor exclusive of that from the above investment. | Net income of investor from the above investment, after paying income tax on same. | | Tax—Surtax on dividends. | Income from taxable stock before paying tax. | Necessary rate of interest of taxable security. |
|---|---|---|---|---|---|
| | With tax-free security. | With taxable stock. | | | |
| $4,000 | $50,000 | $50,000 | $7,611.11 | $57,611.11 | 5.76% |
| 16,000 | 50,000 | 50,000 | 13,111.11 | 63,111.11 | 6.31% |
| 28,000 | 50,000 | 50,000 | 20,037.74 | 70,037.74 | 7.00% |
| 40,000 | 50,000 | 50,000 | 28,923.08 | 78,923.08 | 7.89% |
| 60,000 | 50,000 | 50,000 | 38,076.92 | 88,076.92 | 8.81% |
| 80,000 | 50,000 | 50,000 | 44,509.80 | 94,509.80 | 9.45% |
| 100,000 | 50,000 | 50,000 | 47,058.82 | 97,058.82 | 9.71% |
| 200,000 | 50,000 | 50,000 | 50,000 | 100,000.00 | 10.00% |
| 500,000 | 50,000 | 50,000 | 50,000 | 100,000.00 | 10.00% |
| 1,000,000 | 50,000 | 50,000 | 50,000 | 100,000.00 | 10.00% |

The letter from the Secretary of the Treasury, dated November 4, 1921, to which reference is made in the above letter was as follows:

NOVEMBER 4, 1921.

DEAR MR. CHAIRMAN: I received your letter of October 27, 1921, with the enclosed copy of the Joint Resolution introduced by Mr. McFadden (H. J. Res. 211), proposing an amendment to the Constitution of the United States to restrict the further issuance of tax-exempt securities. This amendment is in the form suggested by the Treasury in my letter of September 23, 1921, to Congressman McFadden, a copy of which is enclosed for your information. This letter outlines the Treasury's general views with regard to the proposed Constitutional amendment.

I think it would be helpful if the present Congress, as a part of the tax revision program, would take some action to propose to the States a Constitutional amendment to restrict future issues of tax-exempt securities, and that the amendment in the form introduced by Mr. McFadden merits the serious consideration of the Committee on Ways and Means. At the least, it offers the basis for a thoroughgoing treatment of the tax-exempt security problem. The existence of the present great mass of about $10,000,000,000 of fully tax-exempt securities, with the prospect of continued issues of tax-exempt securities unless some restrictive amendment is adopted, necessarily tends to defeat the surtaxes imposed by the revenue laws, while the combined effect of the high surtaxes and the unlimited volume of tax-exempt securities is inevitably to divert capital which would otherwise be employed in productive enterprise into relatively unproductive public expenditure. I believe that there would be nothing in the long run more helpful to the recovery of business and industry in the country, and at the same time nothing better calculated to protect the Government's own revenues, than a revised system of taxation which not only moderates the surtaxes but also takes steps to stop the diversion of investment funds into tax-exempt securities.

Very truly yours,

(Signed)     A. W. MELLON, *Secretary.*

Hon. JOSEPH W. FORDNEY,
  *Chairman, Committee on Ways and Means,*
    *House of Representatives, Washington, D. C.*
1 enclosure.

The letter from the Undersecretary of the Treasury, dated November 10, 1921, to which reference is made in the Secretary's letter of January 16, 1922, was as follows:

NOVEMBER 10, 1921.

MY DEAR CONGRESSMAN: I received your letter of November 2, 1921, with the enclosed copy of the Joint Resolution (H. J. Res. 211), which you introduced on October 25th, proposing an amendment to the Constitution of the United States to restrict further issues of tax-exempt securities. I had already noted that this Joint Resolution followed the draft submitted with the Secretary's letter of September 23rd. In response to the request of the Chairman of the Committee on Ways and Means, to which the Joint Resolution was referred, the Secretary has now expressed his further views in the matter in a letter to the Committee dated November 4, 1921,[1] a copy of which is enclosed for your information.

I have examined the suggested substitute resolution enclosed with your letter of November 2nd, and have several comments. I should say that the chief objection to the substitute was a practical one, namely, that it includes provisions with respect to the taxation of salaries of public officials of the several States and of the political subdivisions thereof which would tend to create opposition to the Constitutional amendment as a whole, entirely out of proportion to the benefits to be derived from this particular change. It may be that the salaries of such officials ought to be subject to the Federal income tax, and undoubtedly the present situation results in some discrimination in favor of State and municipal officials as against Federal officials and other individuals. It will be exceedingly difficult in any circumstances, however, to get three-fourths of the States to ratify a Constitutional amendment to restrict the further issue of tax-exempt securities, and to add to these difficulties by giving the State and local officials who are likely to be most active in the several States a definite personal interest against the amendment might easily defeat the whole proposition. It may also be said that notwithstanding the present discrimination in favor of State and local officials, the tax-exempt status of their salaries results, after all, in only a slight increase in their compensation, and that for the most part the State and local officials are not so highly paid as to make this extra compensation any crying evil. In other words, while the proposed substitute may be entirely right in theory as to salaries of State and local officials, and conversely as to Federal officials in respect of State and local taxation, as a practical matter this feature of it would probably endanger the really important part of the amendment.

The substitute also inserts in the form of a proviso the condition that incomes derived from securities issued by or under the authority of the United States must be taxed by the United States before the United States has power to tax incomes from securities issued by or under the authority of the several States, and makes the same change with respect to the taxation by the States of incomes derived from securities issued by or under the authority of the United States. The provision as to taxation by the States has been altered, moreover, so as to remove the limitation to "residents thereof" in the two places where it appeared in the Secretary's draft, and under both provisos "incomes derived from all securities" issued by themselves after the ratification of the amendment would have to be taxed before there would be power on the part of the Federal taxing authorities, or State and local taxing authorities, as the case might be, to tax incomes derived from securities issued by the other. The word "all" would seem to be unnecessarily restrictive, and the omission of the limitation of the taxing power of the States to incomes derived by "residents thereof" might open up securities issued by or under the authority of the Federal Government to double taxation by the States. I am therefore inclined to believe that the phraseology of the amendment proposed by H J. Res. 211 is better, in that it makes more clear the reciprocal character of the change and gives better protection against discrimination. The intent of the conditions is to insure that there will be mutuality, and this is provided for best by words like "if, when and as" or "in the same manner and to the same extent that." As a matter of fact there is much to be said for making even H. J. Res. 211 more clear in this respect and using the words "if, when and as" or "in the same manner and to the same extent that" or other similar words. If the condition is stated simply in the form of a proviso, the power to tax might arise in favor of the Federal or State Governments from the mere fact of taxation of their own securities, though the taxation were not in any proper sense mutual, or were even discriminatory. It might thus be said, for example, that incomes from 4 and 4½ per cent Liberty bonds are now "taxed by the United States," in that the Federal income surtaxes and profits taxes apply to such incomes, subject to certain limited exemptions.

Very truly yours,

(Signed)     S. P. GILBERT, Jr.

Hon. LOUIS T. McFADDEN,
   *Chairman, Committee on Banking and Currency,*
   *House of Representatives, Washington, D. C.*

---

[1] See page 323.

## Exhibit 88.

### EXECUTIVE ORDER TRANSFERRING CERTAIN HOSPITALS FROM THE PUBLIC HEALTH SERVICE TO THE VETERANS' BUREAU.

Whereas, Section 9 of the Act of Congress entitled "An Act to Establish a Veterans' Bureau and to improve the facilities and service of such Bureau, and further to amend and modify the War Risk Insurance Act," approved August 9, 1921, provides that—

SECTION 9. The director, subject to the general directions of the President, shall be responsible for the proper examination, medical care, treatment, hospitalization, dispensary, and convalescent care, necessary and reasonable after care, welfare of, nursing, vocational training, and such other services as may be necessary in the carrying out of the provisions of this Act, and for that purpose is hereby authorized to utilize the now existing or future facilities of the United States Public Health Service, the War Department, the Navy Department, the Interior Department, the National Homes for Disabled Volunteer Soldiers, and such other governmental facilities as may be made available for the purposes set forth in this Act; and such governmental agencies are hereby authorized and directed to furnish such facilities, including personnel, equipment, medical, surgical, and hospital services and supplies as the director may deem necessary and advisable in carrying out the provisions of this Act, in addition to such governmental facilities as are hereby made available, * * *

And whereas said Section 9 further provides that:

In the event that there is not sufficient Government Hospital and other facilities for the proper medical care and treatment of beneficiaries under this Act, and the director deems it necessary and advisable to secure additional Government facilities, he may, within the limits of appropriations made for carrying out the provisions of this paragraph, and with the approval of the President, improve or extend existing governmental facilities or acquire additional facilities by purchase or otherwise. Such new property and structures as may be so improved, extended, or acquired shall become part of the permanent equipment of the Veterans' Bureau or of some one of the now existing agencies of the Government, including the War Department, Navy Department, Interior Department, Treasury Department, the National Homes for Disabled Volunteer Soldiers, in such a way as will best serve the present emergency, taking into consideration the future services to be rendered the veterans of the World War, including the beneficiaries under this Act.

Now, therefore, By virtue of the authority vested in me by said law, I direct that the following specifically described hospitals now under the supervision of the United States Public Health Service and operated for hospital or sanatoria or other uses for sick and disabled former soldiers, sailors and marines, are hereby transferred to the United States Veterans' Bureau and shall on and after the effective date hereof operate under the supervision, management and control of the Director of the United States Veterans' Bureau:

No. 13 Southern Infirmary Annex, Mobile, Alabama.
No. 14 Annex to New Orleans Marine Hospital, Algiers, La.
No. 24 Palo Alto, California.
No. 25 Houston, Texas.
No. 26 Greenville, South Carolina.
No. 27 Alexandria, Louisiana.
No. 23 Dansville, New York.
No. 29 Norfolk, Virginia (Sewell's Point).
No. 30 Chicago, Illinois (4629 Drexel Boulevard).
No. 30 Chicago, Illinois (Annex–7535 Stoney Island Avenue)
No. 31 Corpus Christi, Texas.
No. 32 Washington, D. C. (2650 Wisconsin Avenue).
No. 33 Jacksonville, Florida.
No. 34 East Norfolk, Massachusetts.
No. 35 St. Louis, Missouri (5900 Arsenal).
No. 36 Boston, Massachusetts (Parker Hill).

No. 37 Waukesha, Wisconsin.
No. 38 New York, New York (345 West 50th Street).
No. 39 Hoboken, Pennsylvania.
No. 40 Cape May, New Jersey.
No. 41 New Haven, Connecticut.
No. 42 Perryville, Maryland.
No. 44 West Roxbury, Massachusetts.
No. 45 Biltmore, North Carolina.
No. 46 Deming, New Mexico.
No. 47 Markleton, Pennsylvania.
No. 48 Atlanta, Georgia.
No. 49 Philadelphia, Pennsylvania (Gray's Ferry Road & 24th St.).
No. 50 Whipple Barracks, Arizona.
No. 51 Tucson, Arizona.
No. 52 Boise, Idaho.
No. 53 Dwight, Illinois.
No. 54 Arrowhead Springs, California.
No. 55 Fort Bayard, New Mexico.
No. 56 Fort McHenry, Baltimore, Maryland.
No. 57 Knoxville, Iowa.
No. 58 New Orleans, Louisiana (439 Flood St.).
No. 59 Tacoma, Washington.
No. 60 Oteen, North Carolina.
No. 61 Fox Hills, Staten Island, N. Y.
No. 62 Augusta, Georgia.
No. 63 Lake City, Florida.
No. 64 Camp Kearny, California.
No. 66 St. Paul, Minnesota (Dayton & Virginia Avenue).
No. 67 Kansas City, Missouri (11th and Harrison Streets).
No. 68 Minneapolis, Minnesota (914 Elliott Avenue).
No. 69 Newport, Kentucky.
No. 71 Sterling Junction, Massachusetts.
No. 72 Helena, Montana (Fort William Henry Harrison).
No. 73 Chicago, Illinois (Annex to U. S. Veterans' Hospital 30).
No. 74 Gulfport, Mississippi.
No. 75 Colfax, Iowa.
No. 76 Edward Hines, Jr. Hospital (Maywood, Illinois).
No. 77 Portland, Oregon.
No. 78 North Little Rock, Arkansas (Fort Logan H. Roots).
No. 79 Dawson Springs, Kentucky.
No. 80 Fort Lyon, Colorado, and the Purveying Depot at Perryville, Maryland.

I hereby direct that the following hospitals now under construction by the Treasury Department or projected under existing law shall, when and as each is completed, be transferred to the United states Veterans' Bureau, and shall on and after the respective dates of such transfer be operated under the supervision, management and control of the Director of the United States Veterans' Bureau.

Fort McKenzie, Sheridan, Wyoming.
Fort Walla Walla, Walla Walla, Washington.
Excelsior Springs, Excelsior Springs, Missouri.
Catholic Orphan Asylum (Bronx) New York.
Central New England Sanitorium, Rutland, Massachusetts.
Hospital at Tuskegee, Alabama.
Hospital in Western Pennsylvania.
Hospital on Jefferson Barracks Reservation, St. Louis, Missouri.
Hospital in Metropolitan District, New York.

All facilities, property and equipment now in the possession of the United States Public Health Service in the hospitals above mentioned and all supplies in said hospitals and in the purveying depots at Perryville and North Chicago purchased from funds allotted to said Service by the Director of the United States Veterans' Bureau are hereby transferred to the United States Veterans' Bureau.

It is hereby directed that the Surgeon General of the United States Public Health Service, the Director of the United States Veterans' Bureau and the Director of the Bureau of the Budget, shall each designate a representative to form a Board, which Board shall allocate to the United States Veterans' Bureau and to the United States Public Health Service, with due regard to their respective present and future needs, all supplies transferred to the United States Public Health Service by the War Department, Navy Department or other governmental agencies, in accordance with law, and said Board shall also allocate to the United States Veterans' Bureau and to the United States Public Health Service the buildings and facilities at the Purveying Depot at North Chicago, Illinois, according to their respective needs.

All leases, contracts and other obligations and instrumentalities of the United States Public Health Service in the District of Columbia or elsewhere and all records, files, documents, correspondence and other papers relating to the service rendered by the United States Public Health Service in the operation of the hospitals and purveying depots hereby transferred or relating to the medical examination, assignment to hospitals, and treatment of persons who are now or who have been patients and beneficiaries of the United States Veterans' Bureau are hereby transferred to the United States Veterans' Bureau as of the effective date of this Order.

The Secretary of the Treasury, with due regard to the needs of the United States Public Health Service, shall authorize and direct the Surgeon General of the United States Public Health Service to detail to the United States Veterans' Bureau for duty until released by the Director of the Bureau, the commissioned personnel now on duty at the hospitals and purveying depots above mentioned and such other commissioned personnel as may be required for the operation of the Veterans' Hospitals and purveying depots, provided that the regular commissioned officers of the United States Public Health Service shall be subject to recall in the discretion of the Surgeon General of that Service. Such other personnel of the United States Public Health Service as are now paid from funds allotted by the Director of the United States Veterans' Bureau shall, subject to the approval of the Director of the Bureau, be transferred and given appointment in the United States Veterans' Bureau in the manner prescribed by Civil Service laws and regulations.

So that the transfer herein directed may be made with minimum inconvenience this order shall be construed to allow administrative adjustments hereunder to be made effective May 1, 1922.

This order shall not be construed as in any way limiting or curtailing the authority conferred by existing law whereby the Director of the United States Veterans' Bureau may utilize the now existing or future facilities of the United States Public Health Service, the War Department, the Navy Department, the Interior Department, the National Homes for Disabled Volunteer Soldiers, or such other governmental facilities as may be made available for the use of the United States Veterans' Bureau.

(Signed)      WARREN G. HARDING.

THE WHITE HOUSE, *April 29, 1922.*

## Exhibit 89.

HOSPITALS COMPLETED AND IN COURSE OF CONSTRUCTION, NOVEMBER 13, 1922.

| Hospital. | Allotted. | Number of beds contemplated. | Type. | Completion of hospitals. | Remarks. |
|---|---|---|---|---|---|
| Provisional Hospital No. 2, Fort Logan H. Roots, Little Rock, Ark. | $250,000.00 | 270 | N. P....... | June 6, 1922 | Completed and transferred to U. S. V. B. |
| U. S. V. H. No. 27, Alexandria, La. | 59,516.17 | None. | T. B........ | .....do........ | Do. |
| U. S. V. H. No. 63, Lake City, Fla. | 272,000.00 | 100 | T. B....... | Aug. 25, 1922 | Do. |
| U. S. V. H. No. 50, Prescott, Ariz. (Whipple Barracks). | 577,000.00 | 422 | T. B....... | July 12, 1922 | Do. |
| Fort McKenzie, Wyo......... | 177,000.00 | 245 | N. P....... | June 7, 1922 | Do. |
| Provisional Hospital No. 1, Fort Walla Walla, Wash. | 450,000.00 | 165 | T. B....... | July 13, 1922 | Do. |
| U. S. V. H. No. 81, Bronx, New York City. | 3,485,000.00 | 1,011 | N. P....... | July 26, 1922 | Do. |
| U. S. V. H. No. 55, Fort Bayard, N. Mex. | 992,500.00 | 250 | T. B....... | July 11, 1922 | Do. |
| U. S. V. H. No. 42, Perryville, Md. | 483,000.00 | 300 | N. P....... | .....do........ | Do. |
| Provisional Hospital No. 4, Rutland, Mass. | 815,000.00 | 220 | T. B....... | Sept. —, 1922 | Do. |
| U. S. V. H. No. 62, Augusta, Ga. | 870,783.00 | 265 | N. P....... | Oct. 10, 1922 | 98½ per cent complete; contract. |
| N. H. D. V. S., Milwaukee, Wis. | 1,400,000.00 | 612 | T. B....... | Jan. 1, 1923 | 95 per cent complete; contract. |
| N. H. D. V. S., Dayton, Ohio. | 750,000.00 | 306 | T. B....... | .....do........ | 96 per cent complete; contract. |
| N. H. D. V. S., Marion, Ind.. | 100,000.00 | 80 | N. P....... | .....do........ | 95 per cent complete; contract. |
| U. S. V. H. No. 60, Otéen, N. C. | 458,000.00 | 200 | N. P....... | Jan. —, 1923[1] | 76 per cent complete; contract. |
| U. S. V. H. No. 24, Palo Alto, Calif. | 1,303,619.65 | 515 | N. P....... | Dec. —, 1922 | 83½ per cent complete; contract. |
| Negro hospital, Tuskegee, Ala. | 1,985,000.00 | 302 / 294 | T. B....... / N. P....... | }Feb. —, 1923 | 82 per cent complete; contract. |
| St. Louis, Mo. (Jefferson Barracks). | 1,265,000.00 | 250 | General.... | Mar. 1, 1923 | 56 per cent complete; contract. |
| Chelsea, N. Y. (metropolitan district). | 1,000,000.00 | 236 | T. B....... | June 23, 1923 | Contract awarded Oct. 23, 1922, for two wings of infirmary. |
| Aspinwall, Pa................ | 1,000,000.00 | 120 | T. B....... | ............ | Preparing plans for advertisement. |
| N. H. D. V. S.—Quarters..... | 54,630.30 | None. | ............ | ............ | |
| Dayton—Nurses' quarters. | | | | Jan. 1, 1923 | 75 per cent complete; contract. |
| Officers' quarters. | | | T. B....... | ....do........ | 50 per cent complete; contract. |
| Milwaukee—Nurses' quarters. | | | | | 45 per cent complete; contract. |
| Officers' quarters. | | | T. B....... | .....do........ | 50 per cent complete; contract. |
| Marion—Officers' quarters. | | | N. P....... | .....do........ | 50 per cent complete; contract. |
| Marine Hospital No. 5, Chicago, Ill. | 972.17 | None. | ............ | ............ | Work contracted for by Public Health Service prior to hospital program. |
| N. H. D. V. S., Battle Mountain, Hot Springs, S. Dak. | 977.02 | None. | ............ | ............ | Architects' fees for projected work; discontinued. |
| N. H. D. V. S., Leavenworth, Kans. | 16,601.76 | None. | ............ | ............ | Do. |
| Equipment................... | 600,000.00 | None. | ............ | ............ | |
| Totals................. | 18,366,600.07 | 6,163 | 2,933 T. B.. / 2,980 N. P.. / 250 general. | ............ | |

[1] Probably.

## Exhibit 90.

**LETTER FROM THE SECRETARY OF THE TREASURY TO THE CHAIRMAN OF THE COMMITTEE ON WAYS AND MEANS, JANUARY 24, 1922, WITH RESPECT TO THE SOLDIERS' BONUS.**

Treasury Department,
Office of the Secretary,
*Washington, January 24, 1922.*

Dear Mr. Chairman: I received your letter of January 21, 1922, and am glad, in accordance with your request, to present the latest figures as to the probable receipts and expenditures of the Government for the fiscal years 1922 and 1923, and to indicate in that connection what public debt operations the Treasury will have to carry on between now and June 30, 1923, in order to finance its current requirements and provide for maturing obligations. I am at the same time transmitting for your information the four attached statements as to receipts and expenditures and the public debt.

It appears from these statements that for 1922 the budget estimates indicate a deficit of over 24 million dollars, and for 1923 a deficit of over 167 million dollars. These figures make no allowance for expenditures not covered by the budget, as, for example, 50 million dollars already requested by the United States Shipping Board for the settlement of claims, 7 million dollars to be spent by the United States Grain Corporation on account of Russian relief under the act approved December 22, 1921, $5,000,000 to be paid as the 1923 installment under the treaty with Colombia, and a possible 50 millions on account of additional compensation to Government employees, a total of 112 millions, chiefly for 1923. The results of the first half of the fiscal year 1922, after making due allowance for extraordinary items, indicate that the budget estimates for the year are substantially correct. It is still too early to say whether deficits can be avoided, but it is almost certain that in neither 1922 nor 1923 will there be any surplus. At any rate, it is clear that in order to balance the budget, expenditures must be still further reduced, rather than increased, and that the net reductions below the budget figures within the two years must aggregate about 300 million dollars in order to overcome the indicated deficits. At the same time the Government faces a heavy shrinkage in receipts, and internal-revenue collections in particular are subject to great uncertainty. As a matter of fact, in view of the depression in business, there is grave doubt whether the estimates of receipts which appear in the budget can be realized, and up to date the shrinkage has rather more than kept pace with the shrinkage in expenditures. It is clear that under these conditions there is no room for new or extraordinary expenditures, and that if new items should be added which are not included in the budget, it would be necessary to make simultaneous provision for the taxes to meet them.

One of the chief factors in the gradual return to normal conditions throughout the country has been the marked reduction in Federal expenditures which has already occurred, and this has in turn permitted the lightening of the burden of taxation. What has been accomplished along these lines within less than a year, through the cooperation of the Congress and the Executive, makes a concrete record of achievement in economy which is worthy of our highest efforts to maintain. The economies effected, moreover, have been made without stinting in any way the relief of disabled veterans of the late war, for the figures show that the Federal Government spent for this purpose in the fiscal year 1921 about 380 million dollars and will spend for the same purpose in the fiscal year 1922, and again in the fiscal year 1923, about 450 millions a year, or more than will be spent for any other one purpose except interest on the public debt.

The overshadowing problem of the Treasury at this time, of course, is the handling of the public debt, and particularly the conduct of the refunding operations which will be necessary within the next year and a half on a scale unprecedented in times of peace. Some progress has been made in these operations, but the great bulk of the refunding still remains to be done. The gross public debt of the Government on December 31, 1921, on the basis of daily Treasury statements, amounted to $23,438,984,351, of which almost 6½ billion dollars falls due within the next 16 months, over 3½ billions of it in the form of Victory notes, which mature May 20, 1923, about $2,200,000,000 in the form of Treasury certificates, which mature at various dates within a year, and nearly 700 millions in the form of war savings certificates, which mature January 1, 1923, or may be redeemed before that time. The refunding of this vast maturity will require the Treasury's constant attention from now on. Altogether it makes up an amount almost as large as the Fourth Liberty Loan, and considerably more than the First and Second Liberty Loans combined. The Liberty Loans were floated during the stress of war, through great popular drives and with the help of a country-wide Liberty Loan organization that comprised perhaps 2 million persons. To conduct refunding operations on a similar scale in time of peace, to the amount of 6½ billions of dollars, is a task of unparalleled magnitude, and it is of the utmost importance to the general welfare that it be accomplished without disturbance to business or interference with the normal activities of the people. This can not be done if the refunding is embarrassed by other operations.

The greatest problem is the Victory Liberty Loan, which amounted to $3,548,000,000 on December 31, 1921. A maturity of this size is too large to pay off or refund at one time, and it is accordingly necessary that the Treasury should adopt every means at its command to reduce the outstanding amount in advance of maturity. To this end it will be the Treasury's policy to continue to issue short-term notes from time to time when market conditions are favorable and to use the proceeds to effect the retirement of Victory notes, accomplishing this, if they can not be had otherwise, through the redemption of part of the notes before maturity. It will likewise be the policy, so far as possible, to apply the sinking fund and other special funds available for the retirement of debt to the purchase or redemption of Victory notes. The $2,200,000,000 of Treasury certificates outstanding and the $700,000,000, or thereabouts, of war savings certificates raise similar problems and will likewise require refunding operations on a large scale during the next year and a half. The Treasury has already placed on sale, on December 15, 1921, a new issue of Treasury savings certificates, which is designed to provide in part for the outstanding savings certificates to be redeemed. It is clear, however, that an important part of the maturity on January 1, 1923, will have to be refunded, at least temporarily, into other obligations. The bulk of the Treasury certificates of indebtedness will also have to be refunded, probably into other Treasury certificates, for it is almost necessary, while Government expenditures are so large and tax payments so heavy, to float a substantial amount of Treasury certificates in order to carry on current operations without money strain.

If the situation continues to develop in an orderly way, and no complications are introduced in the form of extraordinary expenditure which would force new borrowings, the Treasury expects to be able to proceed with the program already outlined, and such other refunding operations as may prove to be advisable, within the limits of its existing authority and without interference with the business of the country or disturbance to the investment markets. The time is coming, perhaps in the near future, when it will be possible to undertake refunding operations for a longer term with a view to the distribution of the debt among investors on a more permanent basis. It is important in this connection, however, not to overlook one special characteristic of the Treasury's public debt operations since August 31, 1919, when the gross debt reached its peak, namely, that the operations since that date have been accompanied by gradual but steady debt retirement and that even the refunding operations now in prospect will not increase the public debt. Generally speaking, the Treasury has been floating a constantly decreasing total volume of securities and its borrowings have accordingly not taken new money or absorbed funds that would otherwise go into business. If the Government, on the other hand, were increasing the public debt, quite different problems would arise. Treasury offerings would then take up new money and there would be danger of inflation, of higher rates for money, and of strain on the investment markets, with consequent prejudice to the Government's own inevitable refunding operations and to business and industry generally. The whole character of the operations would be altered.

The estimates which have been given as to the prospects for the fiscal years 1922 and 1923 and the program which has been outlined for the refunding of the short-dated debt do not make allowance for any extraordinary expenditures within the next few years for a soldiers' bonus or so-called adjusted compensation for veterans of the World War. The figures show that there will be no available surplus, but more probably a deficit, and that with the enormous refunding operations which the Treasury has to conduct it would be dangerous in the extreme to attempt to finance the expenditures involved in the bonus through new borrowings. The position of the Treasury remains unchanged, but if there is to be a soldiers' bonus, it is clear that it must be provided for through taxation, and through taxation, in addition to the taxes imposed by existing law.

It is difficult to estimate how much additional taxation would be necessary, for the last bonus bill considered was S. 506, reported by the Committee on Finance of the Senate on June 20, 1921. From the report of the committee and the estimates of the Government Actuary it would appear that the total cost of the bonus under this bill would be about $3,330,000,000, of which at least $850,000,000 would fall in the first two years of its operation, with varying amounts over intervening years and an ultimate payment in the twentieth year of over

$2,114,000,000. The minimum cost would apparently be about
$1,560,000,000, in case substantially all the veterans should take the
cash plan, and the maximum cost about $5,250,000,000, in case sub-
stantially all of the veterans should elect to take the certificate plan
in lieu of cash. If an unexpectedly large proportion of the veterans
should choose cash, the cost within the first two years might run
well over $1,000,000,000. It would seem reasonably certain, how-
ever, that at least one-half would elect the cash-payment plan, in
which event the cost in the first two years would be about $850,000,000
and the total cost would fall between the two extremes, or at about
$3,330,000,000. These estimates take no account of expenses of
administration or the possible cost of vocational training aid, farm
or home aid, or land settlement aid to veterans who elect such benefits,
which would involve substantial additional cost. The expenditures
involved, moreover, would be in addition to already substantial
expenditures on account of veterans of the World War, chiefly for
relief to disabled veterans, which amount to about $450,000,000 a
year according to the estimates for 1922 and 1923. The Government's obligation to the disabled veterans is continuing and para-
mount, and heavy expenditures for their relief will be necessary for
many years to come.

On the most conservative estimates, therefore, the cost of a soldiers'
bonus in the first two years would probably be not less than
$850,000,000. This would necessitate additional tax levies to a corre-
sponding amount during the same period. The taxes already in force
are too onerous for the country's good and are having an unfortunate
effect on business and industry. The field of taxation, moreover, has
already been so thoroughly covered, owing to the extraordinary
revenue needs growing out of the war, that it is exceedingly difficult
to discover new taxes that could properly be levied to yield as much
as 850 millions within two years. In these circumstances, should
Congress determine to adopt the policy of paying a soldiers' bonus,
it would become necessary to impose general taxes on broad classes
of articles or transactions in order to pay it. For such taxes, in their
nature of wide application, much might be said as substitutes for
existing taxes, but the Treasury would hesitate to recommend them
as additional taxes, except to meet some extraordinary purpose.

Whatever additional taxes might be levied, provision for them
would have to be made in the same bill with the bonus. The budget
system is now firmly established, and the budget already submitted
has pointed out the relation between receipts and expenditures for
this year and next year. If the Congress decides to authorize large
expenditures outside of the budget, it is fundamental that it should
make simultaneous provision for the additional taxes necessary to
meet them.

It is also well to keep in mind that no indirect means of financing
the bonus could make it any less an expense that will have to be
borne in the long run by the taxpayer. Thus it would be futile, as
well as unwise, to attempt to provide for the bonus through the use
of the principal or interest of the foreign obligations held by the
United States or through the sale of any such obligations to the public.
For the most part, the foreign obligations are still in the form of
demand obligations and it is impossible in the present state of inter--

national finance and in advance of funding arrangements to estimate what may be collected on them in the near future by way of principal or interest. The obligations are not in shape, moreover, to sell to the public, and to offer them to investors with the guaranty of this Government would seriously interfere with our own refunding operations, upset the security markets, and in the long run prove more expensive to this Government than would the sale of its own direct obligations. At the same time, it would enormously complicate the international situation and certainly embarrass the funding negotiations. Even if enough could be realized on the foreign debt in time to pay the bonus, it would accomplish nothing to set it aside for that purpose. As the law now stands, and in justice to the millions of Liberty bond holders, the Government is bound to apply any principal payments by foreign Governments, as well as any proceeds of sale, to the retirement of outstanding Liberty bonds, about 10 billions of which were issued in the first instance to provide for the advances to foreign Governments. Interest collected on the foreign obligations should likewise go to provide for the interest on Liberty bonds, and it has been the Treasury's plan in the funding to adjust the dates and amounts of the interest payments as nearly as may be to the interest payments on our own bonds. In any event, it is clear that if the proceeds of the foreign obligations should be applied to different purposes, the Government of the United States to that extent would have to provide for payment of the principal and interest of the Liberty bonds from other sources, which means that the people would have to pay taxes for this purpose that would otherwise be unnecessary. The plan to use the foreign obligations to pay a soldiers' bonus, therefore, would still leave the burden on the shoulders of the American taxpayer.

I have made this extended analysis of the country's financial position and of the Treasury's plans and prospects for 1922 and 1923 in order that the Congress may have before it in definite form the facts as to what financial consequences the soldiers' bonus would entail and what added burdens it would inevitably place upon the country.

I am sending a copy of this letter to Senator McCumber, for the information of the Committee on Finance of the Senate.

Very truly yours,

A. W. MELLON,
*Secretary of the Treasury.*

Hon. J. W. FORDNEY,
*Chairman, Committee on Ways and Means,*
*House of Representatives.*

## Exhibit A.

Receipts and expenditures for the fiscal year 1921, and estimated receipts and expenditures for the fiscal years 1922 and 1923.[1]

[On the basis of daily Treasury statements.]

| | Fiscal year 1921. | Fiscal year 1922. | Fiscal year 1923. |
|---|---|---|---|
| **RECEIPTS.** | | | |
| Ordinary: | | | |
| Customs | $308,564,391.00 | $275,000,000.00 | $330,000,000.00 |
| Internal revenue— | | | |
| Income and profits taxes | $3,206,046,157.74 | $2,110,000,000.00 | $1,715,000,000.00 |
| Miscellaneous internal revenue | 1,390,380,823.28 | 1,104,500,000.00 | 896,000,00.00 |
| | 4,596,426,981.02 | 3,214,500,000.00 | 2,611,000,000.00 |
| Miscellaneous revenue— | | | |
| Sales of public lands | 1,530,439.42 | 1,500,000.00 | 1,060,000.00 |
| Federal reserve bank franchise tax | 60,724,742.27 | 60,000,000.00 | 30,00,000.00 |
| Interest on foreign obligations | 31,142,982.51 | 25,000,000.00 | 25,00,000.00 |
| Repayments of foreign obligations | 83,678,223.38 | 30,500,000.00 | 30,00,000.00 |
| Sale of surplus war supplies | 133,692,848.69 | 141,200,000.00 | 100,00,000.00 |
| Retirement of capital stock of Grain Corporation | 100,000,000.00 | 25,000,000.00 | 7,00,000.00 |
| Panama Canal | 12,280,741.79 | 11,760,000.00 | 13,315,000.00 |
| Other miscellaneous | 246,891,610.83 | 183,993,663.00 | 196,87,750.00 |
| Total ordinary receipts | 719,941,588.89 | 478,953,663.00 | 404,182,750.00 |
| | 5,624,932,960.91 | 3,968,433,663.00 | 3,345,182,750.00 |
| **EXPENDITURES.** | | | |
| Ordinary | 5,115,927,689.30 | 3,604,980,166.00 | 3,143,415,927.00 |
| Public debt expenditures chargeable against ordinary receipts: | | | |
| Sinking fund | 261,100,250.00 | 272,442,200.00 | 283,538,800.00 |
| Purchases of Liberty bonds from foreign repayments | 73,939,300.00 | 30,500,300.00 | 30,500,000.00 |
| Redemptions of bonds and notes received for estate taxes | 26,348,950.00 | 25,000,000.00 | 25,000,000.00 |
| Retirements from Federal reserve bank franchise tax receipts | 60,724,500.00 | 60,000,000.00 | 30,000,000.00 |
| | 422,113,000.00 | 387,942,200.00 | 369,338,800.00 |
| Total ordinary expenditures (including public debt expenditures chargeable against ordinary receipts) | 5,538,040,689.30 | 3,992,922,366.00 | 3,512,754,727.00 |
| Excess of receipts over expenditures | 86,892,271.61 | ............ | ............ |
| Excess of expenditures over receipts | ............ | 24,468,703.00 | 167,571,977.00 |

[1] On same basis as given in Annual Report of the Secretary of the Treasury for 1921 and in the Budget for 1923. The estimates do not include expenditures not covered by the Budget, as, for example, $50,000,000 requested by United States Shipping Board for settlement of claims, $7,000,000 to be spent by United States Grain Corporation on account of Russian relief under act approved December 22, 1921, $5,000,000 to be paid as the 1923 installment under the treaty with Colombia, and a possible $50,000,000 on account of additional compensation to Government employees.

## EXHIBIT B.

Preliminary statement showing classified receipts and expenditures of the Government from July 1, 1921, to December 31, 1921, with comparative figures for the fiscal year 1921.

[On the basis of daily Treasury statements.]

| | July 1 to Sept. 30, 1921. | Oct. 1 to Dec. 31, 1921. | Total July 1 to Dec. 31, 1921. | July 1 to Sept. 30, 1920. | Oct. 1 to Dec. 31, 1920. | Total July 1 to Dec. 31, 1920. | Jan. 1 to Mar. 31, 1921. | Apr. 1 to June 30, 1921. | Total July 1, 1920, to June 30, 1921. |
|---|---|---|---|---|---|---|---|---|---|
| **RECEIPTS.** | | | | | | | | | |
| Ordinary: | | | | | | | | | |
| Customs | $69,602,044.73 | $77,406,316.57 | $147,008,361.30 | $84,058,024.90 | $66,039,240.83 | $150,097,265.73 | $67,842,176.13 | $90,624,949.14 | $308,564,391.00 |
| Internal revenue— | | | | | | | | | |
| Income and profits tax | 632,089,027.52 | 607,327,104.03 | 1,239,416,131.55 | 840,653,320.81 | 787,550,609.73 | 1,628,203,930.54 | 852,277,918.48 | 725,564,308.72 | 3,206,046,157.74 |
| Miscellaneous internal revenue | 304,401,943.96 | 324,343,658.63 | 628,745,602.59 | 399,726,191.93 | 370,333,119.27 | 770,064,311.20 | 318,900,145.87 | 301,416,366.21 | 1,390,380,823.28 |
| Miscellaneous revenue | 71,902,681.12 | 161,352,750.52 | 233,255,431.64 | 214,542,816.77 | 209,909,310.39 | 415,452,127.16 | 142,840,433.13 | 149,368,281.81 | 707,660,847.10 |
| Panama Canal tolls, etc. | 2,844,204.37 | 3,193,325.92 | 6,037,530.29 | 1,993,908.53 | 2,607,734.32 | 3,701,642.85 | 5,658,757.99 | 2,920,310.95 | 12,280,741.79 |
| Total | 1,140,839,901.70 | 1,173,623,155.67 | 2,314,463,057.37 | 1,540,074,262.94 | 1,427,445,014.54 | 2,967,519,277.48 | 1,387,519,466.60 | 1,269,894,216.83 | 5,624,932,960.91 |
| Excess of ordinary receipts over ordinary expenditures. | 261,339,552.33 | 215,216,072.24 | 476,555,624.57 | 289,224,706.29 | 170,280,238.14 | 459,504,944.43 | 111,761,802.91 | 62,261,475.73 | 509,005,271.61 |
| Excess of ordinary expenditures over ordinary receipts. | | | | | | | | | |
| Excess of ordinary receipts over total expenditures (public debt and ordinary) chargeable against ordinary reciepts. | 173,753,452.33 | 43,650,472.24 | 217,403,924.57 | 241,942,456.29 | 148,322,288.14 | 390,264,744.43 | 81,062,247.09 | 222,478,725.73 | 86,723,771.61 |
| Excess of total expenditures (public debt and ordinary) chargeable against ordinary receipts over ordinary receipts. | | | | | | | | | |
| **EXPENDITURES.** | | | | | | | | | |
| Ordinary: | | | | | | | | | |
| Legislative establishment | 4,422,186.94 | 4,524,830.93 | 8,947,017.87 | 4,927,391.02 | 4,905,522.01 | 9,832,913.03 | 4,803,483.14 | 4,346,169.00 | 18,982,565.17 |
| Executive proper | 57,002.42 | 56,302.45 | 113,304.87 | 34,853.70 | 50,913.84 | 105,767.54 | 49,260.76 | 55,028.49 | 210,056.79 |
| State Department | 2,048,133.03 | 2,314,077.43 | 4,362,210.46 | 2,322,749.39 | 1,827,909.99 | 4,150,659.38 | 2,242,427.40 | 2,388,010.06 | 8,780,796.84 |
| Treasury Department | 80,412,168.46 | 62,922,875.05 | 143,335,043.51 | 96,985,410.39 | 82,724,463.76 | 178,822,823.96 | 181,790,347.00 | 128,023,532.15 | 488,636,833.10 |
| War Department | 142,412,828.14 | 104,082,370.14 | 246,495,198.28 | 274,365,883.97 | 268,402,413.76 | 542,367,823.20 | 307,518,350.95 | 251,728,789.17 | 1,101,615,013.32 |
| Department of Justice | 3,928,980.20 | 4,526,859.62 | 8,455,839.82 | 3,958,629.16 | 4,183,089.23 | 8,141,718.39 | 4,425,703.15 | 4,638,996.49 | 17,206,418.03 |
| Post Office Department | 23,876,077.43 | 10,707,289.90 | 34,583,367.33 | 1,407,168.05 | 10,602,201.47 | 12,009,369.52 | 25,956,317.37 | 97,393,421.28 | 135,350,108.17 |

*Preliminary statement showing classified receipts and expenditures of the Government from July 1, 1921, to December 31, 1921, with comparative figures for the fiscal year 1921—Continued.*

| | July 1 to Sept. 30, 1921. | Oct. 1 to Dec. 31, 1921. | Total July 1 to Dec. 31, 1921. | July 1 to Sept. 30, 1920. | Oct. 1 to Dec. 31, 1920. | Total July 1 to Dec. 31, 1920. | Jan. 1 to Mar. 31, 1921. | Apr. 1 to June 30, 1921. | Total July 1, 1920, to June 30, 1921. |
|---|---|---|---|---|---|---|---|---|---|
| **RECEIPTS—continued.** | | | | | | | | | |
| **Ordinary—Continued.** | | | | | | | | | |
| Navy Department | $148,290,248.45 | $122,453,736.65 | $270,743,985.10 | $161,294,823.36 | $166,805,503.61 | $328,100,326.97 | $177,462,791.62 | $144,810,716.99 | $650,373,835.58 |
| Interior Department | 85,889,600.83 | 85,289,416.67 | 171,179,017.50 | 87,118,246.55 | 82,244,026.35 | 169,362,272.90 | 82,520,943.00 | 105,931,677.11 | 357,814,893.01 |
| Department of Agriculture | 40,281,388.97 | 43,901,523.24 | 84,182,912.21 | 33,993,228.76 | 28,975,392.46 | 62,968,621.22 | 32,494,508.75 | 24,374,629.44 | 119,837,759.41 |
| Department of Commerce | 6,306,073.59 | 5,140,372.43 | 11,446,446.02 | 10,768,625.62 | 7,150,964.20 | 17,919,589.82 | 6,966,718.38 | 5,942,463.35 | 30,828,761.55 |
| Department of Labor | 1,525,882.17 | 1,499,420.75 | 3,025,302.92 | 2,153,500.97 | 2,783,299.26 | 4,936,890.23 | 1,977,409.34 | 1,588,149.98 | 8,502,509.55 |
| ... Bureau | 61,353,749.17 | 113,331,361.80 | 174,685,110.97 | | | | | | |
| United States Shipping Board | 51,784,131.28 | 28,362,086.95 | 80,146,218.31 | 33,983,454.67 | 61,402,975.86 | 95,389,430.53 | 2,225,335.06 | 33,108,502.67 | 130,723,268.26 |
| Federal control of transportation systems and ... act, 1920. | 82,615,617.38 | ² 80,710,527.15 | ¹ 1,906,090.23 | 193,585,743.50 | 185,186,288.24 | 378,770,031.74 | 214,217,272.44 | 137,724,365.80 | 730,711,669.98 |
| War ... | ² 32,974,288.61 | 52,317,690.61 | 19,343,432.00 | 22,238,355.21 | ² 23,510,031.64 | ¹ 1,271,676.43 | ⁶ 6,367,886.74 | ¹⁴ 14,388,888.95 | ² 22,028,452.12 |
| Other ... and ... offices | | 25,000,000.00 | 25,000,000.00 | 90,353,411.42 | 90,353,411.42 | 90,353,411.42 | | | 90,353,411.42 |
| ... | 22,665,823.08 | 6,214,363.41 | 28,880,186.49 | 19,985,573.71 | 25,218,136.75 | 45,081,710.46 | 34,341,012.22 | 40,519,794.05 | 119,942,516.73 |
| ... | 5,651,582.60 | 6,350,051.44 | 12,001,654.04 | 5,015,212.98 | 5,899,200.35 | 10,914,413.31 | 5,226,571.18 | 6,573,874.11 | 22,715,158.60 |
| District of ... | 147,324,108.68 | 360,915,199.15 | 508,239,307.83 | 136,351,254.07 | 342,067,610.37 | 478,418,864.44 | 171,906,101.93 | 348,819,764.98 | 999,144,731.35 |
| Total | 878,112,344.21 | 957,275,501.47 | 1,835,387,845.68 | 1,180,081,991.37 | 256,293,010.25 | 2,436,375,001.62 | 1,249,756,856.95 | 1,323,578,996.17 | 5,009,710,854.74 |
| Deduct unclassified repayments, etc. | ⁶ 60,977.06 | ² 419,300.24 | ⁶ 480,277.30 | ⁶ 898,151.75 | 8,457,743.6⁵ | 7,559,591.88 | ² 2,571,299.54 | ⁴ 4,065,699.20 | 922,593.14 |
| Total | 878,173,321.27 | 957,694,801.71 | 1,835,868,122.98 | 1,180,980,143.12 | 247,835,266.62 | 2,428,815,409.74 | 1,252,328,156.49 | 1,327,644,695.37 | 5,008,788,261.60 |
| Panama Canal | 1,327,028.10 | 712,281.72 | 2,039,309.82 | 2,965,341.14 | 3,063,590.56 | 6,028,931.70 | 3,923,480.58 | 4,510,997.19 | 16,461,409.47 |
| Purchase of obligations of foreign Governments | | | | 57,201,633.53 | | 57,201,633.53 | | | 73,896,697.44 |
| Purchase of Federal farm loan bonds | | | | 9,702,438.86 | 6,265,919.22 | 15,968,358.08 | 812,962.71 | | 16,781,320.79 |
| Total ordinary | 879,500,349.37 | 968,407,083.43 | 1,837,907,432.80 | 1,250,849,556.65 | 257,164,776.40 | 2,508,014,333.05 | 1,275,757,663.69 | 1,332,155,692.56 | 5,115,927,689.30 |
| **Public debt expenditures chargeable against ordinary receipts:** | | | | | | | | | |
| Sinking fund | 81,066,000.00 | 146,980,700.00 | 228,046,700.00 | 5,261,250.00 | 15,129,000.00 | 20,390,250.00 | 124,956,000.00 | 115,754,000.00 | 261,100,250.00 |
| Purchases of Liberty bonds from foreign repayments | 518,700.00 | 15,628,650.00 | 16,147,350.00 | 38,002,050.00 | 2,028,250.00 | 40,030,300.00 | 475,000.00 | 33,434,000.00 | 73,939,300.00 |
| Redemptions of bonds and notes from estate taxes | 5,988,400.00 | 6,328,250.00 | 12,316,650.00 | 4,017,900.00 | 4,666,700.00 | 8,684,600.00 | 6,657,650.00 | 11,006,700.00 | 26,348,950.00 |

| | | | | | | | | |
|---|---|---|---|---|---|---|---|---|
| Retirements from Federal reserve bank franchise tax receipts | | 2,619,000.00 | | | 60,724,500.00 | | | 60,724,500.00 |
| Retirements from gifts, forfeitures, and other miscellaneous receipts | 13,000.00 | 9,000.00 | 22,000.00 | 1,050.00 | 134,000.00 | 135,050.00 | 10,900.00 | 22,550.00 | 168,500.00 |
| Total public debt expenditures chargeable against ordinary receipts | 87,586,100.00 | 171,565,600.00 | 259,151,700.00 | 47,282,250.00 | 21,957,950.00 | 69,240,200.00 | 192,824,050.00 | 160,217,250.00 | 422,281,500.00 |
| Total expenditures (public debt and ordinary) chargeable against ordinary receipts | 967,086,449.37 | 1,129,972,683.43 | 2,097,059,132.80 | 1,298,131,806.65 | 1,279,122,726.40 | 2,577,254,533.05 | 1,468,581,713.69 | 1,492,372,942.56 | 5,538,209,189.30 |

1 Payments on account of veterans' relief made prior to Aug. 11, 1921, by the War Risk Insurance Bureau are included under "Treasury Department," while similar payments made prior to that date by the Federal Board for Vocational Education are included under "Other independent offices and commissions."

2 Deduct excess of credits.

3 The expenditures on account of "Federal control of transportation systems and transportation act, 1920," above, have been reduced during the period from July 1 to Dec. 31, 1921, by $142,374,992.85 on account of deposits to the credit of the appropriation for "Federal control of transportation systems" of the proceeds of sales of equipment trust notes acquired under the Federal control act approved Mar. 21, 1918, as amended, and the act approved Nov. 19, 1919.

4 Represents reduction in capital stock of United States Grain Corporation effected Oct. 17, 1921, and reflected in "Miscellaneous receipts" in an equal amount. (See note 2, page 2, of daily Treasury statement for Oct. 18, 1921.)

5 Add.

NOTE.—Because of legislation establishing revolving funds and providing for the reimbursement of appropriations, commented upon in the Annual Report of the Secretary of the Treasury for the fiscal year 1919, p. 126 ff, the gross expenditures in the case of some departments and agencies, notably the War Department, the Railroad Administration, and the Shipping Board, have been considerably larger than above stated. This statement does not include expenditures on account of the Postal Service other than salaries and expenses of the Post Office Department in Washington, postal deficiencies, and items appropriated by Congress payable from the general fund of the Treasury.

## Exhibit C.

### PRELIMINARY STATEMENT OF THE PUBLIC DEBT ON DECEMBER 31, 1921.

[On the basis of daily Treasury statements.]

Total gross debt before deduction of the balance held by the Treasurer free of current obligations, and without any deduction on account of obligations of foreign Governments or other investments, was as follows:

Bonds:

| | | |
|---|---:|---:|
| Consols of 1930 | $599, 724, 050. 00 | |
| Loan of 1925 | 118, 489, 900. 00 | |
| Panama's of 1916–1936 | 48, 954, 180. 00 | |
| Panama's of 1918–1938 | 25, 947, 400. 00 | |
| Panama's of 1961 | 50, 000, 000. 00 | |
| Conversion bonds | 28, 894, 500. 00 | |
| Postal savings bonds | 11, 774, 020. 00 | |
| | | $883, 784, 050. 00 |
| First Liberty loan | 1, 952, 123, 150. 00 | |
| Second Liberty loan | 3, 313, 261, 100. 00 | |
| Third Liberty loan | 3, 592, 593, 750. 00 | |
| Fourth Liberty loan | 6, 349, 411, 400. 00 | |
| | | 15, 207, 389, 400. 00 |
| Total bonds | | 16, 091, 173, 450. 00 |
| Notes: | | |
| Victory Liberty loan | | 3, 548, 289, 500. 00 |
| Treasury notes— | | |
| Series A–1924 | 311, 191, 600. 00 | |
| Series B–1924 | 390, 706, 100. 00 | |
| | | 701, 897, 700. 00 |
| Treasury certificates: | | |
| Tax | 1, 515, 157, 500. 00 | |
| Loan | 567, 437, 500. 00 | |
| Pittman Act | 113, 000, 000. 00 | |
| | | 2, 195, 595, 000. 00 |
| Treasury (war) savings securities (net cash receipts) | | 651, 844, 374. 27 |
| Total interest-bearing debt | | 23, 188, 800, 024. 27 |
| Debt on which interest has ceased | | 11, 867, 140. 26 |
| Noninterest-bearing debt | | 238, 317, 186. 83 |
| Total gross debt | | 23, 438, 984, 351. 36 |

## Exhibit D.

*Statement showing comparative figures as to short-dated public debt, June 30, 1920, to December 31, 1921.*

[On the basis of daily Treasury statements, adjusted to include accrued discount on Treasury (war) savings securities.]

| | June 30, 1920. | Dec. 31, 1920. | June 30, 1921. | Dec. 31, 1921. |
|---|---:|---:|---:|---:|
| Maturities before June 30, 1923: | | | | |
| Victory notes (mature May 20, 1923) | $4, 246, 385, 530. 00 | $4, 225, 970, 755. 00 | $3, 913, 933, 350. 00 | $3,548,289,500.00 |
| Treasury certificates (maturing within a year)— | | | | |
| Loan and tax | 2, 485, 552, 500. 00 | 2, 300, 656, 000. 00 | 2, 450, 843, 500. 00 | 2, 082, 595, 000. 00 |
| Pittman Act and special issues | 283, 375, 000. 00 | 292, 229, 450. 00 | 248, 729, 450. 00 | 113, 000, 000. 00 |
| Treasury (war) savings securities, series of 1918 (net cash receipts plus accrued discount to respective dates) | 758, 996, 409. 08 | 702, 520, 765. 18 | 675, 449, 577. 13 | [1] 644, 090, 608. 33 |
| | 7, 774, 309, 439. 08 | 7, 521, 376, 970. 18 | 7, 288, 955, 877. 13 | 6, 387, 975, 108. 33 |

[1] Partly estimated. The estimated additional discount to accrue on Treasury (war) savings securities of the series of 1918 to Jan. 1, 1923, is about $19,000,000, which should be added in computing the amount of the maturity.

*Statement showing comparative figures as to short-dated public debt, June 30, 1920, to December 31, 1921—Continued.*

|  | June 30, 1920. | Dec. 31, 1920. | June 30, 1921. | Dec. 31, 1921. |
|---|---|---|---|---|
| Maturities after June 30, 1923: |  |  |  |  |
| Treasury notes.................... | ................... | ................ | $311,191,600 00 | $701,897,700 00 |
| Treasury (war) savings securities (net cash receipts plus accrued discount to respective dates) series of 1919, 1920, and 1921, maturing, respectively, on Jan. 1, 1924, Jan. 1, 1925, Jan. 1, 1926, and later dates... | $143,172,726.64 | $143,524,063.78 | 120,570,010.89 | [1] 118,662,982.07 |
| Total...................... | [1] 7,917,482,165.72 | 7,664,901,023.96 | 7,720,717,487.98 | 7,208,535,790.40 |

[1] Partly estimated. The estimated additional discount to accrue on Treasury (war) savings securities of the series of 1918 to Jan. 1, 1923, is about $19,000,000, which should be added in computing the amount of the maturity.

## EXHIBIT 91.

**LETTER FROM THE PRESIDENT TO THE CHAIRMAN OF THE COMMITTEE ON WAYS AND MEANS, DATED FEBRUARY 16, 1922, WITH RESPECT TO THE SOLDIERS' BONUS.**

FEBRUARY 16, 1922.

MY DEAR MR. FORDNEY: In accordance with the promise made to yourself and your associates on the Senate and House Committees, charged with the responsibility of formulating the proposed bonus legislation, I have carefully looked into the program of taxation which has been suggested. In addition thereto I have made inquiry into the feasibility of issuing either short-time Treasury notes or long-time bonds to meet the financial obligations which the proposed legislation will impose. It is not possible to commend to you either of the plans suggested.

It continues to be my best judgment that any compensation legislation enacted at this time ought to carry with it the provisions for raising the needed revenues, and I find myself unable to suggest any commendable plan other than that of a general sales tax. Such a tax will distribute the cost of rewarding the ex-service men in such a manner that it will be borne by all the people whom they served, and does not commit the Government to class imposition of taxes or the resumption of the burdens recently repealed, the maintenance of which can be justified only by a great war emergency.

It is fully realized how great is the difficulty which confronts the Congress in solving this difficult problem. I am aware of the strong sentiment in Congress in favor of this adjusted compensation. I have spoken approvingly myself, always with the reservation that the bestowal shall be made when it may be done without such injury to the country as will nullify the benefits to the ex-service men themselves which this expression of gratitude is designed to bestow.

It is not an agreeable thing to suggest that action be postponed again, but, frankly, I do not find myself favorable to the piece-meal payment plan, which is manifestly designed to avoid embarrassment to the Treasury. The long drawn out payments will not afford an effective helpfulness to the service men.

We have no serious problem in beginning the allotments of public lands and the immediate issue of paid-up insurance. The real difficulty lies in the payment of the cash bonus. Rather than provide that the maximum cash payments shall extend over a period of two and one-half years, it would be a vastly better bestowal if we could await the day when we may safely undertake to pay at once in full, so that the award may be turned to real advantage.

Inasmuch as the Treasury is to be called upon to meet more than six billion dollars of maturing obligations in the sixteen months immediately before us, it is not possible to recommend the issue of several hundred millions of additional short-time notes. Further excessive borrowing would likely undo all that has been accomplished in readjusting interest rates and stabilizing the financial world, both vitally essential to the resumption of industrial and commercial activities.

Granting that it is not fair to oppose any proposed plan without offering a substitute, let me repeat that I believe the American people will accept the levy of a general sales tax to meet the proposed bonus payments, and we should contribute thereby no added difficulties to the problems of readjustment. If Congress will not adopt such a plan, it would be wise to let the legislation go over until there is a situation which will justify the large outlay. We are driving for large economies, we are pushing the disposition of surplus war property, and have other transactions under consideration which ought to prove a great relief to the Federal Treasury. It is not consistent to enact legislation in anticipation of these things, but it would be a prudent plan to await the developments, and I can see in such a postponement no lack of regard for the service men in whom all the American people are so genuinely interested. I take it that the ex-service men themselves are no less concerned than others about the restoration of business and the return to abundant employment. Those of their wounded or sick comrades, who were impaired by their war service, are being cared for with the most liberal generosity the nation can bestow. There are here and there exceptional cases of neglect, and attending complaint, but we are seeking them out and correcting with all possible speed. It has not been possible to meet all the demands for special hospitalization but we are building to that end, without counting the cost. We are expending $400,000,000 a year in compensation, hospitalization and rehabilitation. These things are recited to reassure you that such delay as will enable Congress to act in prudence for the common good, will have no suggestion of unmindfulness or ingratitude.

Very truly yours,

WARREN G. HARDING.

Hon. JOSEPH W. FORDNEY,
*House of Representatives, Washington, D. C.*

EXHIBIT 92.

**LETTER FROM THE SECRETARY OF THE TREASURY TO THE CHAIRMAN OF THE COMMITTEE ON WAYS AND MEANS, MARCH 11, 1922, WITH RESPECT TO THE SOLDIERS' BONUS.**

TREASURY DEPARTMENT,
OFFICE OF THE SECRETARY,
*Washington, March 11, 1922.*

DEAR MR. CHAIRMAN: I received the letter of March 8, 1922, with the inclosed copies of H. R. 10769, from the Committee on Ways and Means, and, in accordance with the suggestion that the Committee would be glad to have the Treasury's comment thereon, have examined the proposed bill to r de for a soldiers' bonus or so-called adjusted compensation for veterans of the World War. I have considered the bill particularly from the point of view of its probable cost, and in that connection have obtained from the Government actuary, and submit herewith, the best available estimates as to the cost of the several plans. I notice that the bill carries no appropriation, but merely an authorization of appropriation, which will mean, of course, that no moneys could be paid under it by the Treasury unless further legislation should make an actual appropriation. I notice further that the bill makes no provision whatever for raising additional revenue to meet the cost of the bonus to the Government.

In my letter to you of January 24, 1922, I indicated that the Government faced a probable deficit, on the basis of the budget estimates, of perhaps $300,000,000 during this and the next fiscal year, and that if Congress should decide to adopt the policy of paying a soldiers' bonus it would be necessary at the same time to provide the additional taxes to meet it. On the basis of the bill then under consideration I estimated that the minimum cost of the bonus for the first two years would amount to about $850,000,000, and that it might amount to over a billion dollars if enough of the veterans should choose cash. Since that time the President, in his letter of February 16, 1922, has advised that it continued to be his best judgment that any bonus legislation should carry with it the provisions for raising the needed revenues, that he found himself unable to suggest any commendable plan other than a general sales tax, and that if Congress should not wish to adopt such a plan it would be wise to let the legislation go over.

The bill now in question (H. R. 10769) has presumably been framed with a view to reducing the apparent cost of the measure to the Government, and with that purpose in mind has eliminated the cash bonus, except for a limited number of ex-service men who served for so short a time that their total adjusted pay on a cash basis would not amount to more than $50. The total cost of this provision, it is estimated, would be about $16,000,000. The bill retains, however, the other four of the five bonus plans, including farm and home aid, land settlement aid, and vocational training. It provides, as the principal bonus plan, for so-called adjusted-service certificates which amount, in effect, to paid-up endowment insurance policies issued by the Government, to mature at the end of twenty years, or earlier upon the death of the veteran. The maturity value of these policies is calculated on the basis of the so-called adjusted service credit (which corresponds roughly to the adjusted service pay that would have been allowed under the cash bonus plan), plus an increase of 25 per cent, with interest on the combined figure at the rate of $4\frac{1}{2}$ per cent per annum compounded annually for twenty years. The adjusted-service certificates would be non-negotiable, and there is no provision for direct policy loans by the Government until after September 30, 1925, but in the meantime national and State banks and trust companies are authorized to make loans to holders of certificates up to 50 per cent of the adjusted-service credit plus interest thereon at the stated rate to the date of the loan.

As to veterans who borrow on their certificates from the banks and fail to repay the loans within six months after maturity or before September 30, 1925, the bill provides that the Government must redeem the certificates in cash upon demand, between May 30 and October 15, 1925, at 80 per cent of the adjusted service credit plus interest thereon at the stated rate to the date of redemption, and apply the proceeds of such redemption, first, to the payment of the bank loan with principal and interest, and then any balance to the veteran or his beneficiary. After September 30, 1925, the bill provides for direct loans on the certificates from the Government. The bill makes no provision whatever for sinking fund, amortization or other reserves against either the liability that would be thrown upon the Government in 1925, or against the liability on the certificates at the end of twenty years, nor does it make any provision for the payments which would accrue in ordinary course from year to year on account of the death of veterans.

The direct cost to the Government of a bill carrying these provisions for about 4,500,000 ex-service men is almost impossible to estimate because of the uncertainty as to which of the plans will be chosen, and in what proportions. With the cash bonus eliminated, except to the extent of payments of $50 or less, the provision of the bill that offers the nearest approach to cash is the plan for farm and home aid, under which the veterans would be able to get, beginning January 1, 1923, for the purpose of purchasing, improving, or making payments on a city or suburban home or farm, the full amount of cash that would have been payable on a cash bonus, increased by 40 per cent. The plan for land settlement aid provides for the development of reclamation projects and for allowances to veterans who elect it. These two plans offer so many attractive possibilities to veterans, as well as to persons interested in the development of home building, reclamation, and other projects, that their cost during the first few years of the operation of the bill is sure to be substantial. It is impossible, of course, to estimate what proportion of the veterans will choose these plans as distinguished from the certificate plan and the vocational training plan, but the Government actuary has prepared tables of estimated cost on the assumption that 70 per cent will choose the certificate plan, 23 per cent the farm and home aid plan, 5 per cent the vocational training plan, and 2 per cent the land settlement plan.

In the calculations as to the cost of the certificate plan, it is assumed that half of the veterans will borrow on their certificates from the banks and default on their loans, in view of the attractive provisions for cash redemption in case of default. The table showing the estimated direct cost of the bill on this basis for the twenty-year period from 1923 to 1943 is attached as Exhibit 1. A further table showing in detail the cost of the certificate plan on the same basis, as to the 70 per cent of the veterans taking certificates, is also attached as Exhibit 2. It appears from these tables that on the basis assumed by the actuary the total direct cost to the Government in the fiscal year 1923 would be $289,954,000; in the fiscal year 1924, $216,440,000; in the fiscal year 1925, $128,013,000; and in the fiscal year 1926, for the most part by October 15, 1925, when the adjusted service certificates used as security for bank loans would have to be redeemed, $615,822,000. This would mean total payments within about three and one-half years of over $1,200,000,000. These estimates take no account of amortization or other reserves against certificates to remain outstanding after the fiscal year 1926, which would add at least $40,000,000 a year to the current charges, or of possible additional costs under the land settlement plan if the reclamation projects therein authorized should be carried through. It is estimated that about $100,000,000 per annum would be required after 1923 if these reclamation projects should be pressed.

In order that the Committee may have full information as to the possible cost of the bill to the Government, there is also inclosed a table, designated Exhibit 3, which indicates the total cost of each of the plans in case all of the veterans should choose one plan but makes no attempt to estimate what plans the veterans would choose. It appears from this table that if all the veterans should choose the certificate plan the total face value of the certificates would amount to over $4,500,000,000, distributed over 20 years and that if all the veterans should choose the farm and home aid plan the total cost would amount to $2,093,000,000, within the next 2 or 3 years. There is attached a further table, designated Exhibit 4, which gives in further detail the estimates as to the maximum cost each year to the Government under each of the optional plans, with no allowance, however, for direct borrowing from the Government under the certificate plan.

These tables show one thing clearly, namely, that no one can even approximately estimate the direct cash cost of the proposed bill to the Government for the next few years, and that by January 1, 1926, it will probably cost over $1,200,000,000 and may cost very much more if enough veterans should elect to take farm and home aid.

Apart from the direct cost of the bill, a most serious feature is the provision for bank loans upon adjusted service certificates during the period between its passage and September 30, 1925. The effect of this provision is to transfer the cost of policy loans from the Government to the banks, and to place in the banks, to the extent that the ex-service men are able to obtain loans from them, a mass of unliquid, nonnegotiable paper upon which the banks will be unable to realize until 1925. The result would be frozen bank loans and inflation of currency and credit. To the extent that the banks are obliged to make loans on adjusted service certificates, their ability to take care of the demands of business and industry will be correspondingly reduced, and even though the paper accrued by the certificates may not be eligible for rediscount at the Federal Reserve Banks, the indirect result is certain to be increased borrowings by member banks from the Federal Reserve Banks in order to provide the funds for carrying the paper until it is either repaid by the borrower or redeemed by the Government in 1925. Needless to say, paper which is secured by nonnegotiable collateral, and which may not be repaid for three years, is not desirable paper for commercial banks to hold. A table prepared by the Government actuary, designated Exhibit 5 (p. 135), is hereto attached to show the estimated possible loans by banks under this provision.

From the point of view of the Treasury, the most serious aspect of these loans on adjusted service certificates is the fact that the loans would be floated at the banks on the credit of the United States. The plan in substance, therefore, involves a dangerous abuse of the

Government's credit, for it contemplates the issue of a vast amou.1t of Government obligations which are nonnegotiable and have no present realizable value unless pledged with banks, in which event the obligations become, in effect, two or three year notes, which the Government would be obliged to pay off in 1925 upon default by the veterans. This practically means that cash payments on adjusted service certificates would be financed for the next three years through a forced loan from the banks. This is borrowing on the credit of the United States fully as much as if the loans were made direct by the United States and financed by direct borrowings on Government bonds, notes, or certificates of indebtedness. In fact, from the point of view of the banking system and the general financial situation, it would be far better if a bonus is to be financed by borrowing, for the Government to resort to direct borrowing and to provide for direct policy loans on adjusted service certificates from the outset than to attempt to avoid direct cost to the Government for the time being, at the expense of both the banking system and the Government's credit.

If Congress concludes to adopt a soldiers' bonus with paid-up endowment insurance as its chief feature, the direct or regular way would be to authorize insurance certificates with provisions for direct policy loans and the amortization or other reserves that would be required as a matter of sound business policy. A certificate plan on this basis, if chosen by all ex-service men eligible to elect it, would, according to the best available estimates, mean an aggregate liability of about $4,500,000,000, and on the basis of a 20-year maturity would involve the following current charges each year for the next 20 years: (1) the payments necessary each year on account of the maturity of certificates by death, averaging about $40,000,000 a year; (2) amortization payments, computed at 4 per cent compounded annually, calculated to provide within 20 years for the whole liability, averaging about $123,000,000 a year; and (3) provision for direct policy loans from the Government on about the same basis as is customarily allowed by life insurance companies, in an amount that would probably average not less than $200,000,000 a year for the first two or three years of the operation of the plan. On this basis an insurance plan, standing by itself, would cost at the minimum about $400,000,000 a year for the next few years.

The necessity of amortization if an insurance plan is to be adopted becomes clear upon an examination of the outstanding public debt. The heaviest payments under an insurance plan would fall in the same period when the longer-term Liberty bonds become due, for on a 20-year basis the certificates would mature in 1942, if the bonus bill should be passed this year. The fourth Liberty loan, which amounts to over $6,300,000,000, matures in 1938; the second Liberty loan, which amounts to over $3,300,000,000, matures in 1942; and the first Liberty loan, which amounts to almost $2,000,000,000, matures in 1947. With these heavy maturities of the public debt, aggregating about $11,600,000,000, it would be highly imprudent to lay up another maturity of between $3,000,000,000 and $4,000,000,000 in the same period without making provision for its amortization in the meantime.

It is clear from these estimates that whatever form the soldiers' bonus may take, whether it contemplates a thoroughgoing insurance plan or follows the outlines of the bill which is now pending, it will cost from $300,000,000 to $400,000,000 for the next three or four years, and may involve continuing liabilities thereafter of over $200,000,000 a year until 1943. It is impossible to avoid the cost if a bonus is to be adopted, and it is both dangerous and unwise to attempt to avoid it for the time being by throwing the burden upon the banks of the country and piling up for the Treasury an accumulated liability which, in 1925, may amount to over $600,000,000. There is no way by which the American taxpayer can avoid the burden, and if a bonus is to be imposed it is far better for all concerned that it be placed upon a direct and definite basis and paid for each year out of current revenue. To do this at the present time will necessarily mean the imposition of additional taxes for the purpose.

Very truly yours,

A. W. MELLON, *Secretary.*

Hon. J. W. FORDNEY,
*Chairman Committee on Ways and Means,*
*House of Representatives, Washington, D. C.*

EXHIBIT 1.

*Cost to the Government on the basis of 70 per cent choosing the certificate plan, 23 per cent the farm and home aid plan, 5 per cent vocational training, and 2 per cent the land-settlement plan.*

| Fiscal year. | Cash. | Certificate plan. | Vocational training. | Farm and home aid. | Land settlement. | Total. |
|---|---|---|---|---|---|---|
| 1923 | $16,000,000 | $20,604,000 | $63,350,000 | $200,000,000 | (¹) | $289,954,000 |
| 1924 | | 26,440,000 | 40,000,000 | 150,000,000 | | 216,440,000 |
| 1925 | | 26,713,000 | 1,300,000 | 100,000,000 | | 128,013,000 |
| 1926 | | 554,532,000 | | 31,390,000 | $29,900,000 | 615,822,000 |
| 1927 | | 52,936,000 | | | | 52,936,000 |
| 1928 | | 52,046,000 | | | | 52,046,000 |
| 1929 | | 77,233,000 | | | | 77,233,000 |
| 1930 | | 52,415,000 | | | | 52,415,000 |
| 1931 | | 47,675,000 | | | | 47,675,000 |
| 1932 | | 37,932,000 | | | | 37,932,000 |
| 1933 | | 38,265,000 | | | | 38,265,000 |
| 1934 | | 33,600,000 | | | | 33,600,000 |
| 1935 | | 54,004,000 | | | | 54,004,000 |
| 1936 | | 34,448,000 | | | | 34,448,000 |
| 1937 | | 35,003,000 | | | | 35,003,000 |
| 1938 | | 35,593,000 | | | | 35,593,000 |
| 1939 | | 31,333,000 | | | | 31,333,000 |
| 1940 | | 22,144,000 | | | | 22,144,000 |
| 1941 | | −16,895,000 | | | | −16,895,000 |
| 1942 | | −15,749,000 | | | | −15,749,000 |
| 1943 | | 1,173,528,000 | | | | 1,173,528,000 |
| Total | | 2,379,800,000 | 104,650,000 | 481,390,000 | 29,900,000 | 2,995,740,000 |

¹ To this should be added probably $100,000,000 per annum after 1923, if this scheme is to be carried through.

## Exhibit 2.

*Cost of certificate plan. based on 70 per cent taking certificates and 50 per cent of these borrowing and in default (35 per cent of total possible certificates).*

| Fiscal year. | Face of loans made during year. | Repayment on account of loans (principal only). | Payment by Government on account of maturity. | Payment on account of default in loans. | Total payment by Government. |
|---|---|---|---|---|---|
| 1923 | [1] $41,320,000 | | $26,604,000 | | $26,604,000 |
| 1924 | [1] 182,750,775 | | 26,440,000 | | 26,440,000 |
| 1925 | [1] 58,150,000 | | 26,713,000 | | 26,713,000 |
| 1926 | 50,000,000 | | 26,826,000 | $477,706,000 | 554,532,000 |
| 1927 | 50,000,000 | $24,000,000 | 26,936,000 | | 52,936,000 |
| 1928 | 50,000,000 | 25,000,000 | 27,046,000 | | 52,046,000 |
| 1929 | 100,000,000 | 50,000,000 | 27,233,000 | | 77,233,000 |
| 1930 | 100,000,000 | 75,000,000 | 27,415,000 | | 52,415,000 |
| 1931 | 100,000,000 | 80,000,000 | 27,675,000 | | 47,675,000 |
| 1932 | 100,000,000 | 90,000,000 | 27,932,000 | | 37,932,000 |
| 1933 | 100,000,000 | 90,000,000 | 28,265,000 | | 38,265,000 |
| 1934 | 100,000,000 | 95,000,000 | 28,600,000 | | 33,600,000 |
| 1935 | 125,000,000 | 100,000,000 | 29,004,000 | | 54,004,000 |
| 1936 | 125,000,000 | 120,000,000 | 29,448,000 | | 34,448,000 |
| 1937 | 125,000,000 | 120,000,000 | 30,003,000 | | 35,003,000 |
| 1938 | 130,000,000 | 125,000,000 | 30,593,000 | | 35,593,000 |
| 1939 | 130,000,000 | 130,000,000 | 31,333,000 | | 31,333,000 |
| 1940 | 130,000,000 | 140,000,000 | 32,144,000 | | 22,144,000 |
| 1941 | 140,000,000 | 190,000,000 | 33,105,000 | | −16,895,000 |
| 1942 | 150,000,000 | 200,000,000 | 34,251,000 | | −15,749,000 |
| 1943 | | | 1,173,528,000 | | 1,173,528,000 |
| Total | | | | | 2,379,800,000 |

[1] To banks.

## Exhibit 3.

*Maximum cost to Government.*

Cash payment of all bonuses not in excess of $50 .................... $16,000,000
Certificate plan (on base of all choosing certificates):
    Net cash base .......................................... 1,495,000,000
    Add 25 per cent ....................................... 373,750,000

    Gross cash base ....................................... 1,868,750,000
Improved at 4½ per cent interest compounded annually for 20 years, face of certificates ........................................... 4,506,890,500

Vocational training (on base of all choosing):
    Cash base ............................................. 1,495,000,000
    Add 40 per cent ....................................... 598,000,000

    Total ................................................. 2,093,000,000
Total possible for fiscal year 1923: 181 days×$1.75×4,000,000 ...... 1,267,000,000

Farm and home aid (on base of all choosing):
    Cash base ............................................. 1,495,000,000
    Add 40 per cent ....................................... 598,000,000

    Total ................................................. 2,093,000,000

Land settlement:
    Cash base ............................................. 1,495,000,000
    Possible cost to Government ............................ 18,562,500,000
    (Cash bonus base as 8 per cent of total cost.)

EXHIBIT 4.

*Maximum cost to Government under each of the plans in H. R. 10769.*

[No allowance for borrowing.]

| Fiscal year. | Cash. | Certificate plan, on account of— | | Vocational training. | Farm and home aid. | Land settlement. |
|---|---|---|---|---|---|---|
| | | Death. | Maturity. | | | |
| 1923 | $16,000,000 | $38,006,000 | | $1,267,000,000 | $1,000,000,000 | |
| 1924 | | 38,057,000 | | 826,000,000 | 1,046,500,000 | |
| 1925 | | 38,162,000 | | | 46,500,000 | $495,000,000 |
| 1926 | | 38,323,000 | | | | 500,000,000 |
| 1927 | | 38,480,000 | | | | 500,000,000 |
| 1928 | | 38,637,000 | | | | |
| 1929 | | 38,904,000 | | | | |
| 1930 | | 39,164,000 | | | | |
| 1931 | | 39,535,000 | | | | |
| 1932 | | 39,903,000 | | | | |
| 1933 | | 40,379,000 | | | | |
| 1934 | | 40,857,000 | | | | |
| 1935 | | 41,434,000 | | | | |
| 1936 | | 42,069,000 | | | | |
| 1937 | | 42,862,000 | | | | |
| 1938 | | 43,704,000 | | | | |
| 1939 | | 44,762,000 | | | | |
| 1940 | | 45,920,000 | | | | |
| 1941 | | 47,293,000 | | | | |
| 1942 | | 48,930,000 | | | | |
| 1943 | | | | | | |
| Total | 16,000,000 | 825,381,000 | $3,681,509,500 | 2,093,000,000 | 2,093,000,000 | 1,495,000,000 |

EXHIBIT 5.

*Maximum loans by banks.*

[All veterans taking certificate plan and borrowing.]

| Fiscal year. | Loans. | Repayment | Default. |
|---|---|---|---|
| 1923 | $187,784,375 | $87,784,375 | |
| 1924 | 612,202,500 | 100,000,000 | |
| 1925 | | 212,215,625 | |
| Total | 799,986,875 | 400,000,000 | $399,986,875 |

| | | |
|---|---|---|
| 80 per cent of value Oct. 1, 1925, of certificates of defaulted loans | | $662,437,600 |
| Principal of defaulted loans | $399,986,875 | |
| Interest (estimated) | 47,998,425 | |
| | | 447,985,300 |
| Additional payment to veterans | | 214,452,300 |
| Maximum cash payment on account of default in loans to banks | | 662,437,600 |

EXHIBIT 93.

**MESSAGE OF THE PRESIDENT VETOING H. R. 10874, A BILL "TO PROVIDE ADJUSTED COMPENSATION FOR THE VETERANS OF THE WORLD WAR, AND FOR OTHER PURPOSES."**

THE WHITE HOUSE,
*Washington, September 19, 1922.*

*To the House of Representatives:*

Herewith is returned, without approval H. R. 10874, a bill "to provide adjusted compensation for the veterans of the World War, and for other purposes."

With the avowed purpose of the bill to give expression of a nation's gratitude to those who served in its defense in the world war I am in accord, but to its provisions I do not subscribe. The United States never will cease to be grateful, it cannot and never will cease giving expression to that gratitude.

In legislating for what is called adjusted compensation Congress fails, first of all, to provide the revenue from which the bestowal is to be paid. Moreover, it establishes the very dangerous precedent of creating a treasury covenant to pay which puts a burden, variously estimated between four and five billions, upon the American people, not to discharge an obligation, which the government always must pay, but to bestow a bonus which the soldiers themselves, while serving in the world war, did not expect.

It is not to be denied that the nation has certain very binding obligations to those of its defenders who made real sacrifices in the world war, and who left the armies injured, disabled or diseased, so that they could not resume their places in the normal activities of life. These obligations are being gladly and generously met. Perhaps there are here and there inefficiencies and injustices, and some distressing instances of neglect, but they are all unintentional, and every energy is being directed to their earliest possible correction. In meeting this obligation there is no complaint about the heavy cost. In the current fiscal year we are expending $510,000,000 on hospitalization and care of sick and wounded, on compensation and vocational training for the disabled, and for insurance. The figures do not include the more than $35,000,000, in process of expenditure on hospital construction. The estimates for the year to follow are approximately $470,000,000, and the figures may need to be made larger. Though the peak in hospitalization may have passed, there is a growth in domicilization, and the discharge in full of our obligations to the diseased, disabled, or dependent who have a right to the government's care, with insurance-liability added, will probably reach a total sum in excess of $25,000,000,000.

More than 99,000 veterans are now enrolled in some of the 445 different courses in vocational training. Fifty-four thousand of them are in schools or colleges, more than 38,000 are in industrial establishments, and a few more than 6,000 are being trained in schools operated by the Veterans' Bureau.

Approximately nineteen thousand have completed their courses and have employment in all cases where they desire it, and 53,000 have deferred for the present time their acceptance of training. The number eligible under the law may reach close to 400,000, and facilities will continue to be afforded, unmindful of the necessary cost, until every obligation is fulfilled.

Two hundred and seventy-six thousand patients have been hospitalized, more than a quarter of a million discharged, and 25,678 patients are in our hospitals today.

Four hundred and sixteen thousand awards of compensation have been made on account of death or disability, and $480,000,000 have been paid to disabled men or their dependent relatives. One hundred and seventy-five thousand disabled ex-service men are now receiving compensation along with medical or hospital care where needed, and a quarter of a million checks go out monthly in distributing the eight-million dollar payment on indisputable obligations.

I recite the figures to remind the Congress how generously and how properly it has opened the treasury doors to discharge the obligations of the nation to those to whom it indisputably owes compensation and care. Though undying gratitude is the need of every one who served, it is not to be said that a material bestowal is an obligation to those who emerged from the great conflict not only unharmed, but physically, mentally and spiritually richer for the great experience. If an obligation were to be admitted, it would be to charge the adjusted compensation bill with inadequacy and stinginess wholly unbecoming our republic. Such a bestowal, to be worth while, must be generous and without apology. Clearly the bill returned herewith takes cognizance of the inability of the government wisely to bestow, and says, in substance, "we do not have the cash, we do not believe in a tax levy to meet the situation, but here is our note, you may have our credit for half its worth." This is not compensation, but rather a pledge by the Congress, while the Executive Branch of the government is left to provide for payments falling due in ever increasing amounts.

When the bill was under consideration in the House I expressed the conviction that any grant of bonus ought to provide the means of paying it, and I was unable to suggest any plan other than that of a general sales tax. Such a plan was unacceptable to the Congress, and the bill has been enacted without even a suggested means of meeting the cost. Indeed, the cost is not definitely known, either for the immediate future, or in the ultimate settlement. The treasury estimates, based on what seems the most likely exercise of the options, figures the direct cost at approximately $145,000,000 for 1923, $225,000,000 for 1924, $114,000,000 for 1925, $312,000,000 for 1926, making a total of $795,000,000 for the first four years of its operation, and a total cost in excess of $4,000,000,000. No estimate of the large indirect cost ever had been made. The certificate plan sets up no reserve against the ultimate liability. The plan avoids any considerable direct outlay by the government during the earlier years of the bill's proposed operations, but the loans on the certificates would be floated on the credit of the nation. This is borrowing on the nation's credit just as truly as though the loans were made by direct government borrowing, and involves a dangerous abuse of public credit. Moreover, the certificate plan of payment is little less than certified inability of the government to pay, and invites a practice on sacrificial barter which I cannot sanction.

It is worth remembering that the public credit is founded on the popular belief in the defensibility of public expenditure, as well as the government's ability to pay. Loans come from every rank in life, and our heavy tax burdens reach, directly or indirectly, every element in our citizenship. To add one-sixth of the total sum of our public debt for a distribution among less than five millions out of one hundred and ten millions, whether inspired by grateful sentiment or political expediency, would undermine the confidence on which our credit is builded, and establish the precedent of distributing public funds whenever the proposal and the numbers affected make it seem politically appealing to do so.

Congress clearly appraised the danger of borrowing directly to finance a bestowal which is without obligation, and manifestly recognized the financial problems with which the nation is confronted.

Our maturing promises to pay within the current fiscal year amount to approximately $4,000,000,000, most of which will have to be refunded. Within the next six years more than $10,000,000,000 of debt will mature, and will have to be financed. These outstanding and maturing obligations are difficult enough to meet without the complication of added borrowings, every one of which threatens higher interest, and delays the adjustment to stable government financing and the diminution of federal taxes to the defensible cost of government.

It is sometimes thoughtlessly urged that it is a simple thing for the rich republic to add four billions to its indebtedness. This impression comes from the readiness of the public response to the government's appeal for funds amid the stress of war. It is to be remembered that in the war everybody was ready to give his all. Let us not recall the comparatively few exceptions. Citizens of every degree of competence loaned and sacrificed, precisely in the same spirit that our armed forces went out for service. The war spirit impelled. To a war necessity there was but one answer, but a peace bestowal on the ex-service men, as though the supreme offering could be paid for with cash, is a perversion of public funds, a reversal of the policy which exalted patriotic service in the past, and suggests that future defense is to be inspired by compensation rather than consciousness of duty to flag and country.

The pressing problem of the government is that of diminishing our burdens, rather than adding thereto. It is the problem of the world. War inflations and war expenditures have unbalanced budgets and added to indebtedness until the whole world is staggering under the load. We have been driving in every direction to curtail our expenditures and establish economies without impairing the essentials of governmental activities. It has been a difficult and unpopular task. It is vastly more applauded to expend than to deny. After nearly a year and a quarter of insistence and persuasion, with a concerted drive to reduce government expenditures in every quarter possible, it would wipe out everything thus far accomplished to add now this proposed burden, and it would rend the commitment to economy and saving so essential to our future welfare.

The financial problems of the government are too little heeded until we are face to face with a great emergency. The diminishing income of the government, due to the receding tides of business and attending incomes, has been overlooked momentarily, but cannot be long ignored. The latest budget figures for the current fiscal year show an estimated deficit of more than $650,000,000, and a further deficit for the year succeeding, even after counting upon all interest collections on foreign indebtedness which the government is likely to receive. To add to our pledges to pay, except as necessity compels, must seem no less than governmental folly. Inevitably it means increased taxation, which Congress was unwilling to levy for the purposes of this bill, and will turn us from the course toward economy so essential to promote the activities which contribute to common welfare.

It is to be remembered that the United States played no self-seeking part in the world war, and pursued an unselfish policy after the cause was won. We demanded no reparation for the cost involved, no payments out of which obligations to our soldiers could be met. I have not magnified the willing outlay in behalf of those to whom we have a sacred obligation.   It is essential to remember that a more than four-billion-dollar pledge to the able-bodied ex-service men now will not diminish the later obligation which will have to be met when the younger veterans of today shall contribute to the rolls of the aged, indigent and dependent.   It is as inevitable as that the years will pass, that pension provision for world war veterans will be made, as it has been made for those who served in previous war.   It will cost more billions than I venture to suggest.   There will be justification when the need is apparent, and a rational financial policy today is necessary to make the nation ready for the expenditure which is certain to be required in the coming years.   The contemplation of such a policy is in accord with the established practice of the nation, and puts the service men of the world war on the same plane as the millions of men who fought the previous battles of the republic.

I confess a regret that I must sound a note of disappointment to the many ex-service men who have the impression that it is as simple a matter for the government to bestow billions in peace as it was to expend billions in war.   I regret to stand between them and the pitiably small compensation proposed.   I dislike to be out of accord with the majority of Congress which has voted the bestowal.   The simple truth is that this bill proposes a government obligation of more than four billions without a provision of funds for the extraordinary expenditure, which the Executive Branch of the government must finance in the face of difficult financial problems, and the complete defeat of our commitment to effect economies.   I would rather appeal, therefore, to the candid reflections of Congress and the country, and to the ex-service men in particular, as to the course better suited to further the welfare of our country.   These ex-soldiers who served so gallantly in war, and who are to be so conspicuous in the progress of the republic in the half century before us, must know that nations can only survive where taxation is restrained from the limits of oppression, where the public treasury is locked against class legislation, but ever open to public necessity and prepared to meet all essential obligations.   Such a policy makes a better country for which to fight, or to have fought, and affords a surer abiding place in which to live and attain.

WARREN G. HARDING.

EXHIBIT 94.

[Department Circular No. 108 (Revised).  Loans and Currency.]

## REGULATIONS FURTHER DEFINING RIGHTS OF HOLDERS OF WAR-SAVINGS CERTIFICATES.

TREASURY DEPARTMENT.<br>OFFICE OF THE SECRETARY,<br>Washington, November 9, 1922.

*To holders of War-Savings Certificates and others concerned:*

Treasury Department Circular No. 108, dated January 21, 1918, as heretofore amended and supplemented, is hereby amended and supplemented to read as follows:

The following Treasury Department regulations further define the rights of holders of War-Savings Certificates of all issues and series, issued under the authority of the act approved September 24, 1917, as amended and supplemented, and set forth the terms and conditions upon which such certificates will be payable in case of the death or disability of the owner:

## I.

### CERTIFICATES NOT PRESENTED AT MATURITY.

War-Savings Certificates shall not bear interest after maturity.

## II.

### LOST OR DESTROYED CERTIFICATES.

A War-Savings Certificate which has been lost or destroyed will not be paid nor will a duplicate thereof be issued, unless the certificate has been registered in accordance with the regulations and instructions issued by the Postmaster General. In the event of the loss or destruction of a registered certificate, the registrant may apply to the post office where the certificate was registered, on forms prescribed by the Postmaster General, either for the issuance of a duplicate certificate or for the payment thereof. On being satisfied of the facts as to loss or destruction, the Secretary of the Treasury will, after not less than three months have elapsed from the time of application, authorize payment, or the issuance to the registered owner of a duplicate certificate, to be so marked, on which shall be noted the number of registered stamps affixed to the original certificate, with the proper notations of registration. Such certificate shall receive a new registration number. The Secretary of the Treasury may in special cases. where he deems the facts warrant such action, require the claimant to give a bond of indemnity with approved sureties against any claim that may thereafter be made on the old certificate. The duplicate certificate when issued shall stand in the place and stead of the original lost or destroyed certificate for all purposes. After the issuance of a duplicate certificate, the original shall cease to have validity for any purpose, and if recovered shall be returned to the post office of registration for cancellation. No duplicate certificate will be issued after maturity of the original.

## III.

### CREDITORS' RIGHTS.

Payment of registered or unregistered certificates shall be made to the owner named thereon notwithstanding any lien, attachment, trustee process, garnishment, judgment, receivership, levy, execution, order, decree, or similar process of law, equity, or in bankruptcy directed against the owner thereof, but nothing herein contained shall excuse the owner from full compliance with, or performance of, any lawful judgment, order, or decree of a court of competent jurisdiction with reference to disposition of the proceeds of the certificate. Collection of the certificate by the owner pursuant to such judgment, order, or decree will be deemed a payment received on behalf of the owner and not for any other person within the language of the receipt printed on the certificate, notwithstanding that the owner is, by such judgment, order, or decree, required to pay the proceeds to another person. Neither the United States of America nor any officer or employee thereof shall be a proper or necessary party to any suit or action with reference to such certificate or the proceeds thereof nor be bound by any judgment, order, or decree rendered or entered therein.

## IV.

#### HOLDING OF CERTIFICATES BY CORPORATIONS, PARTNERSHIPS, AND OTHERS.

1. War-Savings Certificates may be issued in the name of and held by corporations, partnerships, associations, or joint stock companies and may be registered by such holders.

2. Payment of a certificate registered in the name of a corporation, partnership, association, or joint stock company shall be made to any officer or agent designated on the registration card to receive payment or to any other officer or agent presenting proof satisfactory to the Secretary of the Treasury of his or her authority to receive payment.

## V.

#### FIDUCIARIES.

Certificates shall not be issued or registered in the names of fiduciaries in their representative capacities. Should any such certificate be issued or registered, it will be deemed to be held by the person named thereon in his or her individual capacity, and all words of description or of representative capacity shall be disregarded.

## VI.

#### CERTIFICATES ISSUED TO TWO PERSONS.

War-Savings Certificates may be issued and may be registered in the names of two persons (but not more than two) in the alternative, as, for instance, "John Jones OR Mary Jones." Such certificates shall be payable to either person named thereon without requiring the signature of the other person and to the survivor of them without proof of the other person's death, and upon payment to either person the other shall cease to have any interest therein. No other form of certificate in the names of two persons is authorized. In registering certificates issued in the alternative both persons named thereon shall fill out registration cards. In determining whether the $5,000 (maturity value) limitation on the holdings of a single person has been exceeded, the full maturity value of certificates, of any one series, held with any other person shall be added to the full maturity value of certificates, of the same series, held individually, and the sum must not exceed $5,000 (maturity value).

## VII.

#### INFANT HOLDERS OF WAR-SAVINGS CERTIFICATES.

1. A War-Savings Certificate held by an infant who is capable of filling out and signing a registration card may be registered by such infant.

14263—FI 1922——23

2. A War-Savings Certificate held by an infant who is incapable of filling out and signing a registration card may be registered in the name of such infant by one of such infant's parents or by a duly appointed guardian for such infant or by a person with whom such infant resides, the name of the infant to be signed by the representative, as, for instance, "Mary Smith by John Smith, her father."

3. If a guardian of the property has, to the knowledge of the postmaster from whom payment is demanded, been appointed for an infant holder of a War-Savings Certificate, payment of the certificate, whether registered or unregistered, shall be made only to such guardian.

4. If an infant holder of a War-Savings Certificate (registered or unregistered) for whom no such guardian has been appointed, to the knowledge of the postmaster, is, at the time payment of such certificate is demanded, of sufficient competency and understanding, in the opinion of the postmaster, to sign his or her name to the receipt and to comprehend the nature thereof, payment shall be made directly to such infant owner. In the event that such infant is not, in the opinion of the postmaster, of such competency and understanding, payment shall be made to either parent of the infant with whom the infant resides, or, in the event that such infant resides with neither parent, then to the person with whom such infant resides. In receipting for the money, the representative shall sign the infant's name as well as the name of such representative.

5. Issuance of a duplicate for, or payment of, a lost or destroyed certificate which has been registered in the name of an infant shall be to the infant or to a representative, as hereinabove provided, upon compliance with the regulations respecting lost or destroyed certificates.

## VIII.

### DISABILITY OF HOLDERS OF CERTIFICATES.

1. Certificates held by persons legally declared to be incompetent to manage their affairs, and for whose estate a conservator or other legally constituted representative has been appointed by a court of competent jurisdiction, to the knowledge of the postmaster from whom payment is demanded, shall be paid to such conservator or legal representative.

2. Certificates held by persons not legally declared to be incompetent to manage their affairs, who, by reason of infirmity or for other reasons satisfactory to the postmaster from whom payment is demanded, can not appear in person to demand payment of his or her certificates, may be paid to a representative upon compliance by the owner with instructions prescribed by the Postmaster General.

3. Certificates held by persons under any other disability shall be paid only to the holders of the certificates, except as provided in the case of infancy.

## IX.

### REGISTRATION OF CERTIFICATES IN FAVOR OF BENEFICIARY.

1. Certificates may be registered payable to a single designated beneficiary in case of death of the owner, as, for instance, "John Smith, payable on death to Mary Smith." Such certificates will be

payable to the registered owner during his lifetime, and to the beneficiary upon death of the registered owner, provided the beneficiary be then living. In that case the beneficiary will be entitled either to reissue or to payment of the certificate, at his option. Reissue of a certificate registered payable to a beneficiary will be made only in the name of such beneficiary and only where upon reissue the beneficiary will not hold Treasury (War) Savings Certificates of the same series to an aggregate amount exceeding $5,000 (maturity value). If the beneficiary shall predecease the registered owner, the certificate will be payable to the owner as though such beneficial registration had not been made. Second registration in favor of another beneficiary, or change of beneficiary, will not be permitted.

2. Such a certificate may also be registered by the beneficiary upon the beneficiary's signing a registration card and complying with the other requirements for registration of the certificate. Unless registered by the beneficiary, the United States will not be liable, in respect of any beneficiary certificate, if payment or reissue upon the death of the owner be made to a person not the true beneficiary thereof.

3. Should the beneficiary die after the death of the registered owner but before payment of the certificate, the regulations covering the payment or reissue of certificates held by a deceased owner shall govern the payment or reissue of the certificate as though the beneficiary were such deceased owner.

4. The right to designate a beneficiary shall extend only to registered certificates.

## X.

### PAYMENT OR REISSUE OF WAR-SAVINGS CERTIFICATES HELD BY DECEASED OWNER.

In the case of the death of the owner of a War-Savings Certificate (other than a certificate registered payable to a beneficiary), payment will be made, or at their election the certificate will be reissued, to the persons and in the manner hereinafter provided:

1. If the decedent leave a will which is duly admitted to probate, or die intestate and the estate of such decedent is administered in a court of competent jurisdiction, payment of such certificate will be made only to the duly appointed representative of the estate, and reissue will be made only at his request. Administration will be required prior to payment or reissue of a War-Savings Certificate in all cases where the gross personal estate of the deceased owner exceeds $500 in value, unless it appears to the satisfaction of the Secretary of the Treasury that administration of the estate of such decedent is not required in the State of the decedent's domicile.

2. In case no legal representative of the decedent's estate is appointed and either the gross personal estate does not exceed $500 in value or it appears to the satisfaction of the Secretary of the Treasury that administration of the estate of such decedent is not required in the State of the decedent's domicile, the certificate will be paid or reissued to and on the demand of persons equitably entitled thereto in the opinion of the Secretary of the Treasury, in the following order of classes:

First. The certificate will be paid to the creditor for the reasonable funeral expenses, expenses of the last illness, or other preferred claims against the decedent's estate, or person paying such creditor, to the extent of such preferred claims.

Second. The certificate will be paid or reissued to the husband, wife, or next of kin of the deceased in the following order of preference:

      (1) Husband or wife;
      (2) Child or children;
      (3) Father;
      (4) Mother;
      (5) Any other of the next of kin of the deceased;

provided, however, that nothing herein contained shall require the payment or reissue of a single certificate to more than one person.

3. In case the gross personal estate of the decedent exceeds $500 in value, and it is claimed that administration of the estate is not required in the State of the decedent's domicile, the application for payment or reissue of the War-Savings Certificates owned by the decedent must be accompanied by an agreement by all of the legal heirs of the decedent who are of lawful age and competent and by the legally appointed guardians or conservators of any minor or incompetent heirs, duly acknowledge under oath before a notary public or other officer authorized by law to administer oaths, showing that such persons constitute all the legal heirs of the estate of the decedent or their legally appointed representatives; that all debts owing by the decedent have been paid; that administration of the estate of the decedent is not required in the State of the decedent's domicile, and that all of such heirs or their legal representatives have agreed on the distribution of the estate and consent to payment or reissue of the War-Savings Certificates being made to the claimant who executes the application. Such agreement must also be accompanied by the affidavits of two disinterested persons, preferably public officers of the United States or executive officers of incorporated banks or trust companies, showing that the affiants are responsible persons known to them, whose statements are worthy of the confidence of the Treasury Department. The Secretary of the Treasury may further require in special cases an affidavit or certificate from a practicing attorney or judicial officer of the State of the decedent's domicile, showing that administration of the estate of the decedent is not required in such State, and referring specifically to any statutes or any judicial decisions of the courts of such State under which exemption from administration is claimed.

4. In case of the reissue of a War-Savings Certificate pursuant to the provisions of paragraph IX or X hereof, the original certificate will be retired and a new certificate or certificates of the same series with the same aggregate number of stamps affixed, but bearing a new serial number and inscribed in the name of the person entitled to the reissue of the original certificate, will be issued. Reissue of certificates may be effected only at the Treasury Department, Division of Loans and Currency, Washington, D. C., on application duly executed by the person entitled to demand reissue of the certificate on the form prescribed for such purpose. Registered certificates must, however, be presented through the post office of registration. In no case will a War-Savings Certificate be reissued in the name of any person, if upon such reissue such person will hold

Treasury (War) Savings Certificates of the same series to an aggregate amount exceeding $5,000 (maturity value).

## XI.

### SIGNING RECEIPT.

Whenever, pursuant to these regulations, payment of a certificate is made to a person not the original owner thereof, the receipt printed on the certificate need not be signed, but such person shall sign a receipt, which shall be pasted on the certificate over the receipt printed thereon, as follows:

Received $      in payment hereof, I hereby certify that I am the identical person entitled to payment of this certificate under the regulations prescribed by the Secretary of the Treasury, in lieu of the original owner named above, and that said original owner (or his estate) does not hold War-Savings Certificates, of any one series, to an aggregate amount exceeding Five Thousand Dollars (maturity value).

.............................                    ...............................
              (Date.)                                        (Signature of payee.)

## XII.

### INHERITANCE TAXES.

Payment of the certificate will be made without any deduction for inheritance, estate, or transfer taxes on death of a deceased owner, either State or Federal, and no claim shall lie against the United States or any officer or employee thereof for failure to deduct or withhold any such tax. The person to whom payment of the certificate is made shall be liable for all such taxes, if any shall be due, and the lien thereof shall attach to the proceeds of the certificate in his or her hands.

## XIII.

### CHANGE OF NAME.

Where the owner of a certificate has since the issuance of the certificate changed his or her name by marriage or by order or decree of court, the postmaster shall accept the receipt of the owner signed in his or her own new name, as well as in his or her original name, upon being satisfied of the identity of the person.

## XIV.

### LIMITATION IN AMOUNT.

If it shall appear that any person has received certificates issued to such person by way of gift, bonus, dividend, or in any other lawful manner except the purchase thereof by such person, whereby he or she holds certificates, of any one series, in excess of an aggregate of $5,000 (maturity value), the excess amount of certificates shall be immediately surrendered at a money-order post office and shall be paid at their then value. In any other case, if it shall appear at the time a certificate is presented for payment that the person presenting the same holds certificates, of the same series, to an aggregate amount exceeding $5,000 (maturity value), the postmaster shall refuse payment of all certificates in excess of such amount and shall demand surrender of certificates held by such owner until the holdings of such owner are reduced to $5,000 (maturity value). The postmaster shall make appropriate notation on certificates so surrendered, and shall forward such certificates to the Third Assistant Postmaster General for transmission to the Secretary of the Treasury. Such certificates shall have no validity for any purpose. Nothing herein contained shall prevent the payment of a certificate of a deceased owner to the person entitled thereto under these regulations, without regard to the amount of certificates already owned by such payee, unless it shall appear that such deceased owner held certificates, of the same series, to an aggregate amount exceeding $5,000 (maturity value), in which case only $5,000 (maturity value), for any one series, shall be paid, and the excess shall be taken up in accordance with the foregoing.

## XV.

### ADMINISTRATION.

The administration of the foregoing regulations shall be in accordance with such forms and administrative regulations and instructions and through such assistants or subordinates as the Postmaster General shall from time to time prescribe, and in accordance with regulations issued or to be issued by the Secretary of the Treasury.

The right is reserved to make, from time to time, any further or supplemental or amendatory regulations which shall not modify or impair the terms and conditions of War-Savings Certificates issued or to be issued in pursuance of the act of Congress approved September 24, 1917, as amended and supplemented.

A. W. MELLON,
*Secretary of the Treasury.*

EXHIBIT 95.

[Department Circular No. 310. Public Debt ]

### REDEMPTION AND EXCHANGE OF TREASURY SAVINGS CERTIFICATES, SERIES OF 1918.

TREASURY DEPARTMENT,
OFFICE OF THE SECRETARY,
*Washington, November 15, 1922.*

*To Owners of Treasury Savings Certificates of the Series of 1918, and Others Concerned:*

United States Treasury Savings Certificates of the Series of 1918 become due and payable January 1, 1923, according to their terms. Treasury Savings Certificates of the Series of 1918 are all in registered form, and bear on their face the title "United States War Savings Certificates, Treasury Savings Certificate Issue." The Secretary of the Treasury offers special facilities for their redemption and exchange, as follows:

1. *General.*—Registered owners of Treasury Savings Certificates, Series of 1918, will be entitled to receive on or after January 1, 1923, One Hundred Dollars ($100) for each such certificate. Certificates

are payable and must be presented and surrendered (by mail or otherwise) at the office of the Secretary of the Treasury, Division of Loans and Currency, Washington, D. C. Owners may, on or after January 1, 1923, redeem their certificates in cash at maturity value, or, beginning November 15, 1922, may exchange them at maturity value, with any necessary adjustments in cash, for Treasury Savings Certificates, Series of 1923, issued pursuant to Treasury Department Circular No. 301, dated September 30, 1922, and inscribed in the same name or in such other name or names as the owner may request. The demand for payment appearing on the back of each certificate presented for either redemption or exchange must be properly signed by the owner in the presence of and duly certified by a United States postmaster (who should affix the official postmark of his office), an executive officer of an incorporated bank or trust company (who should affix the corporate seal of the bank or trust company), or any other person duly designated by the Secretary of the Treasury for the purpose. In the event of the death or disability of the owner, the demand for payment shall be executed by the person authorized to receive payment under the provisions of Treasury Department Circular No. 149 Revised, dated August 1, 1922.

2. *Cash Redemption—*

(a) *Presentation before maturity.*—In order to facilitate redemptions of maturing certificates, owners are offered the privilege, beginning November 15, 1922, of surrendering their certificates in advance, for redemption as of January 1, 1923. Payment for all certificates thus presented will be made by check payable to the order of the registered owner, which will be mailed to reach him on or about January 1, 1923.

(b) *Presentation at or after maturity.*—Cash redemption will be made only as of January 1, 1923, or on later surrender. Payment will be made by check payable to the order of the registered owner.

3. *Exchange for Treasury Savings Certificates, Series of 1923—*

(a) *Presentation between November 15, 1922, and January 15, 1923.*—Exchanges of Treasury Savings Certificates, Series of 1918, for Treasury Savings Certificates, Series of 1923, will be made as of January 1, 1923, upon applications filed between November 15, 1922, and January 15, 1923, accompanied by the Treasury Savings Certificates to be exchanged, as herein provided. Treasury Savings Certificates dated January 1, 1923, will be delivered promptly upon exchange, registered in the name and address requested by the owner of the surrendered Treasury Savings Certificates. Cash adjustments, if in favor of the United States, must be made upon exchange, or if in favor of the applicant, will be made as of January 1, 1923, except that in all cases where the applicant takes the maximum amount of Treasury Savings Certificates covered by the maturity value of the Treasury Savings Certificates surrendered, prompt payment will be made of any cash difference. The Treasury Savings Certificates, Series of 1923, issued upon exchange, will not in any event be redeemable before the date of issue stated thereon.

(b) *After January 15, 1923.*—Exchanges after January 15, 1923, will be made as of the date of receipt at the Treasury Department. The Treasury Savings Certificates issued upon such exchange will be dated and carry interest from the date of the exchange, and will be registered in the name and address requested by the holder of the surrendered Treasury Savings Certificates. All cash adjustments on such exchanges, whether in favor of the United States or in favor of the applicant, will be made at the time of the exchange.

4. *Further Details*—

(a) *Forms*.—In presenting Treasury Savings Certificates, Series of 1918, for redemption or exchange, whether in advance of January 1, 1923, or on or after that date, holders may use Form P. D. 751, copies of which may be obtained upon application from the Treasury Department, Division of Loans and Currency, Washington, D. C. A copy of this form will be found on the reverse side of this circular.

(b) *Procedure in case of death or disability of the owner*.—The provisions of Treasury Department Circular No. 149 Revised, dated August 1, 1922, further define the rights of holders of Treasury Savings Certificates and will govern the presentation and surrender of certificates for redemption or exchange in the event of the death or disability of the owner.

(c) *Further information*.—Any further information which may be desired as to the redemption or exchange of Treasury Savings Certificates of the Series of 1918 may be obtained from post offices, Federal Reserve Banks and branches, or the Treasury Department, Division of Loans and Currency, Washington, D. C.

5. The Secretary of the Treasury may at any time or from time to time prescribe supplemental or amendatory rules and regulations governing the redemption and exchange of Treasury Savings Certificates, Series of 1918.

A. W. MELLON,
*Secretary of the Treasury.*

TREASURY DEPARTMENT,
LOANS AND CURRENCY
Form P. D. 751.
Ed. 7,500—Nov. 15–22.

REQUEST FOR REDEMPTION OR EXCHANGE OF TREASURY SAVINGS CERTIFICATES,
SERIES OF 1918.

*IMPORTANT:* TREASURY SAVINGS CERTIFICATES DUE JANUARY 1, 1923, MAY BE PRE-
SENTED AT ANY TIME ON OR AFTER NOVEMBER 15, 1922, FOR IMMEDIATE EXCHANGE
OR FOR PAYMENT AT MATURITY. CERTIFICATES MUST BE PRESENTED TO THE TREAS-
URY DEPARTMENT, DIVISION OF LOANS AND CURRENCY, WASHINGTON, D. C.

*To the Secretary of the Treasury, Division of Loans and Currency, Washington, D. C.*
THE UNDERSIGNED PRESENTS HEREWITH—
.......... Treasury Savings Certificates, Series of 1918, with the
demand for payment thereon properly executed, having an
aggregate maturity value of................................... $..........
Cash, to the amount of........................................... $..........
(To be applied on exchange for Treasury Savings Certificates, series of 1923; see
examples 2 below.)

TOTAL............................................... $..........
AND REQUESTS—
Cash, in the amount of......................................... $..........
Treasury Savings Certificates, Series of 1923, having a maturity
value of $.........., as described below,* at an aggregate issue
price of............................................. $..........
(Issue prices: $20.50 for a $25 certificate; $82 for a $100 certificate; and $820 for
a $1,000 certificate.)

TOTAL (which must agree with total given above)......... $..........

*Issue Treasury Savings Certificates, Series of 1923, as follows:

| NAME IN WHICH TREASURY SAV- INGS CERTIFI- CATES ARE TO BE ISSUED | POST OFFICE ADDRESS | NUMBER DESIRED | DENOMINA- TION | MATURITY VALUE | ISSUE PRICE |
|---|---|---|---|---|---|
| ............ | ............ | ............ | ............ | ............ | ............ |
| ............ | ............ | ............ | ............ | ............ | ............ |
| ............ | ............ | ............ | ............ | ............ | ............ |

....................................
(Signature of applicant)

....................................
(Number)          (Street)

....................................
(Town or city)          (State)

| MATURITY VALUE OF TREASURY SAVINGS CERTIFICATES SURRENDERED. | EXAMPLE NO. | TREASURY SAVINGS CERTIFICATES, SERIES OF 1923, IN EXCHANGE. | | CASH ADJUSTMENT DUE YOU. | CASH ADJUSTMENT TO BE PAID BY YOU. |
|---|---|---|---|---|---|
| | | *Maturity Value.* | *Issue Price.* | | |
| | Example 1.... | $1,200 @ | $984.00 | $16.00 | ............ |
| $1,000................ | Example 2.... | 1,225 @ | 1,004.50 | ............ | $4.50 |
| | Example 3.... | 1,000 @ | 820.00 | 180.00 | ............ |
| | Example 1.... | $600 @ | $492.00 | $8.00 | ............ |
| $500.................... | Example 2.... | 625 @ | 512.50 | ............ | $12.50 |
| | Example 3.... | 500 @ | 410.00 | 90.00 | ............ |
| | Example 1.... | $100 @ | $82.00 | $18.00 | ............ |
| $100.................... | Example 2.... | 125 @ | 102.50 | ............ | $2.50 |
| | Example 3.... | 75 @ | 61.50 | 38.50 | ............ |

These examples may be applied to other maturity values in the same relation. The cash adjustments due the United States, as in the examples numbered 2, must be paid in all cases at the time of exchange. Cash adjustments due the applicant will be paid on January 1, 1923, or upon later exchange, except that prompt payment of the cash difference will be made wherever the applicant takes the largest possible amount of Treasury Savings Certificates for his maturing Treasury Savings Certificates, as in the examples numbered 1. It will be noted that in no case will the cash differences payable to applicants before January 1, 1923, exceed $20, since a cash difference of $20.50 would make it possible to buy another Treasury Savings Certificate, and the applicant must take the full amount of Treasury Savings Certificates in order to get advance payment of the cash difference. Cash differences in cases like the examples numbered 3 will not be paid before January 1, 1923.

EXHIBIT 96.

[Department Circular No. 176 amended and supplemented. Accounts and Deposits.]

**REGULATIONS GOVERNING DEPOSITS OF PUBLIC MONEYS AND PAYMENT OF GOVERNMENT WARRANTS AND CHECKS.**

TREASURY DEPARTMENT,
OFFICE OF THE SECRETARY,
*Washington, May 15, 1922:*

*To the Treasurer of the United States, Federal Reserve Banks and Branches, National Bank Depositaries, Special Depositaries of Public Moneys, Collectors of Internal Revenue, Collectors of Customs, Receivers of Public Moneys, Depository Postmasters, Marshals and Clerks of Courts, all other Officers or Agents of the United States engaged in collecting, depositing, or transmitting public moneys, and others concerned:*

I. DEPOSIT OF PUBLIC MONEYS.

1. This circular governs deposits of public moneys with the Treasurer of the United States, Federal Reserve Banks and branches, and National bank depositaries. All deposits of public moneys hereunder shall be for credit to the account of the Treasurer of the United States, except deposits with National bank depositaries to the credit of official checking accounts of Government officers. The term "Federal Reserve Bank"

where it appears in this circular, unless otherwise indicated by the context, includes branch Federal Reserve Banks with which deposits are authorized to be made. The term "general National bank depositaries" means depositaries with authority to accept deposits for credit in the Treasurer's general account, and the term "limited National bank depositaries" means depositaries with authority to accept deposits only for credit in official checking accounts of Government officers with such depositaries. The term "National bank depositaries" where it appears in this circular, unless otherwise indicated by the context, includes both general National bank depositaries and limited National bank depositaries. All collectors, receivers of public moneys of every description, and other persons having public money to pay to the United States, are hereinafter sometimes called "depositors of public moneys."

### GENERAL PROVISIONS AS TO DEPOSITARIES.

2. *Classes of depositaries.*—The established policy of the Treasury Department is to designate and maintain balances with general National bank depositaries of public moneys only at points where a depositary is necessary to meet the requirements of Government officers for cash for pay-roll or other expenditures, or to receive deposits of cash from depositors of public moneys for credit to the account of the Treasurer of the United States, and then only if there is no Federal Reserve Bank or branch located at or near the point. National banks may, however, be designated by the Secretary of the Treasury to be limited depositaries of public moneys, for the sole purpose of receiving, up to specified maximum amounts, deposits made by United States courts and their officers, by postmasters, and in special cases by other duly authorized Government officers for credit to their official checking accounts with such depositaries. National bank depositaries must qualify, before receiving deposits, by pledging as collateral security for such deposits, including interest thereon, securities of the classes described in paragraph 31 hereof, to an amount, taken at the rates therein provided, at least equal to the deposits. Limited National bank depositaries designated under this circular are not authorized to accept any other deposits hereunder. Deposits arising from the proceeds of sales of bonds, notes, and Treasury certificates of indebtedness of the United States, and the payment of income and profits taxes, may be made from time to time with special depositaries of public moneys under the act of Congress approved September 24, 1917, as amended and supplemented. Deposits of public moneys are also maintained with the several Federal Reserve Banks, pursuant to the provisions of section 15 of the Federal Reserve Act, as amended, and the act approved May 29, 1920, providing for the discontinuance of the subtreasuries.

3. *Special depositaries.*—Any incorporated bank or trust company in the United States desiring to participate in deposits of public moneys arising from the sale of bonds, notes, or Treasury certificates of indebtedness of the United States, or from the payment of income or profits taxes, under section 8 of the act approved September 24, 1917, as amended and supplemented, may make application for designation as a special depositary of public moneys to the Federal Reserve Bank of its district, pursuant to Treasury Department Circular No.

92 of April 17, 1919, as from time to time amended and supplemented. Detailed regulations governing such depositaries are prescribed in said circular, to which reference is hereby made. The provisions of this circular do not apply to or govern special depositaries under said circular, and such depositaries are not, by virtue of any such designation or their qualification thereunder, authorized to accept deposits hereunder from collectors or other depositors of public moneys for credit to the account of the Treasurer of the United States, or to the official checking accounts of Government officers.

### GENERAL PROVISIONS AS TO DEPOSITS.

4. *Cash deposits.*—All cash received by collectors of internal revenue, collectors of customs, depository postmasters, and other depositors of public moneys shall be deposited, if the depositor is located in the same city with a Federal Reserve Bank or branch, with such Federal Reserve Bank or branch, and in other cases with the general National bank depositary or depositaries located in the same city or town with the depositor: *Provided, however,* That if there is no general National bank depositary located in the same city or town with the depositor, all cash shall be forwarded to the Federal Reserve Bank of the district or the nearest branch thereof: *And provided further,* That depositors located in the District of Columbia shall make deposits of cash direct with the Treasurer of the United States. Payments made by postal or express money order shall be handled, subject to collection, in the same manner as cash.

For regulations governing the deposit of cash returning unexpended balances to the Treasury, see Treasury Department Circular No. 281, dated March 20, 1922.

5. *Checks and drafts.*—Checks and drafts received by collectors of internal revenue, collectors of customs, depository postmasters, and other depositors of public moneys shall be deposited as hereinafter provided. All checks and drafts received by any Government officer are received subject to collection, and in the event that any check or draft can not be collected or is lost or destroyed before collection, appropriate action must be taken by the depositor in the same manner as if the check or draft had not been received. Payments made by check or draft are not effective unless and until the check or draft has been actually collected and paid. Remittance of a bank draft by the drawee bank is conditional payment only and the item is not deemed collected and paid unless and until the draft so tendered is paid. All checks and drafts received in payment of obligations to the United States must be payable unconditionally in money. Checks or drafts payable in exchange at the option of the drawee will not be accepted. Drafts shall be handled hereunder in the same manner as checks, and the term "checks" where it appears in this circular, will, unless otherwise indicated by the context, be deemed to include drafts.

6. *Certificates of deposit.*—Certificates of deposit shall be issued, until further notice, on the following forms: Internal Revenue, Form 15; Customs, Form 1¾; Public Lands, Surveys, and miscellaneous deposits requiring triplicate set, Form 1A; Army, Navy, Judiciary, Indian, Sales of Treasury Savings securities by Federal Reserve Banks, and general, Form 1; Proceeds of Collections (Treas-

urer of the United States), Form 5396; Transfer of funds, Form 12; Surplus Money Order Funds, Form 6594; Surplus Postal Funds, Form 6598; Postal Savings Funds, Form 6549; deposits for disbursing officers' official checking accounts with Treasurer of United States, and Secretary's special deposit account, Form 6599; and Sales of Treasury Savings securities by Postmasters, Form 1312. The act of Congress approved March 6, 1920, provides that all patent fees shall be paid to the Commissioner of Patents, who shall deposit them directly with the Treasurer of the United States. Accordingly other depositaries will not accept deposits of patent fees. In every case certificates of deposit shall be dated by the depositary and the date on the certificate shall be the same as that of the transcript of the Treasurer's account in which the amount is credited. Certificates of deposit should be numbered but not dated by the depositor when prepared by him. All certificates must be signed by a duly authorized officer of the depositary. The original of each certificate of deposit (unless other specific instructions are given) shall be transmitted to the Treasurer of the United States, with the transcript on Form 17, on which the credit appears. The other certificates of deposit in the set should be disposed of in accordance with the instructions which appear on the certificate (or in case the certificate contains no instructions, in accordance with the provisions of Department Circular No. 12, as amended and supplemented May 15, 1922), and one copy may be retained by the depositary for its own records. Federal Reserve Banks and branches should see that the face of each certificate in any set of certificates of deposit covering in whole or in part items other than cash for which credit is given in the Treasurer's account before actual collection, bears a legend reading as follows: "This certificate of deposit issued subject to deduction for uncollectible items." It is of the utmost importance that certificates of deposit be properly issued, and in this connection depositaries should give special attention to two points, viz: (1) The name and title (if any) of the depositor, as *John Doe, receiver of public moneys*, or, in cases where the deposit is made by one person for account of another person, *John Doe, receiver of public moneys, through Richard Roe;* and (2) the account or purpose for which the deposit is received, as *Sales of public lands*, or *Sales of Treasury Savings securities* (with a notation of the series), should be clearly indicated in order to enable the Treasury Department to classify the deposit and credit the proper receipt account at the same time that the depositary is charged with the amount of the deposit. Certificates should not read on account of "Miscellaneous Receipts" only, but the specific source of receipt should also be definitely stated. Depositaries receiving deposits of internal revenue receipts are particularly requested to use great care in specifying upon the face of certificates of deposit on Form 15 deposits of "Income and Profits Taxes" separate and distinct in each case from deposits of "Miscellaneous Internal Revenue Collections" (formerly called "Ordinary"). It is not necessary, however, to make any further separation of classes of internal revenue deposits on the face of certificates of deposit on Form 15. In view of the great number of collections made by clerks of court on account of fines and costs, depositaries may issue one set of certificates only for all such deposits made in any one day by such officers, provided the clerk furnishes a consolidated statement to be attached to the original certificate showing the court cases with name and amount deposited in each case as fines and costs.   In no case shall a duplicate or second set of certificates be issued without special authority of the Secretary of the Treasury, unless and until the entire original set has been canceled.   But copies of any certificate in a set, except the original, may be furnished on request, provided each such copy is plainly stamped across the face in large letters "Copy."   If an error is discovered after the original has been mailed, the Treasurer of the United States should be notified at once in order that proper correction may be made.   Certificates of deposit issued for deposits representing the return of unexpended balances should be drawn in accordance with the requirements of Treasury Department Circular No. 281, dated March 20, 1922.

7. *Unauthorized receipt or use of public money.*—Section 96 of the act of Congress approved March 4, 1909, provides the following penalties for the unauthorized receipt or use of public money:

Every banker, broker, or other person not an authorized depositary of public moneys, who shall knowingly receive from any disbursing officer, or collector of internal revenue, or other agent of the United States, any public money on deposit, or by way of loan or accommodation, with or without interest, or otherwise than in payment of a debt against the United States, or shall use, transfer, convert, appropriate, or apply any portion of the public money for any purpose not prescribed by law; and every president, cashier, teller, director, or other officer of any bank or banking association who shall violate any provision of this section is guilty of embezzlement of the public money so deposited, loaned, transferred, used, converted, appropriated, or applied, and shall be fined not more than the amount embezzled, or imprisoned not more than ten years, or both.

### GENERAL PROVISIONS AS TO DEPOSIT OF CHECKS.

8. *Deposit of checks.*—Unless and until otherwise directed by the Secretary of the Treasury, all checks and drafts received by collectors of internal revenue, collectors of customs, depository postmasters, and other depositors of public moneys (except checks for deposit in authorized official checking accounts maintained by Government officers with National bank depositaries) shall be deposited pursuant to the following instructions:

9. *Deposit of checks with Federal Reserve Banks and branches.*— Except as otherwise hereinafter provided, all checks, whether certified or uncertified, and whether or not drawn on banks or trust companies located in the same city with the depositor, including checks for deposit to the official credit of the depositor with the Treasurer of the United States, shall be forwarded for deposit each day (unless specific instructions for different procedure are given with the approval of the Secretary of the Treasury) to the Federal Reserve Bank of the district in which the depositor's head office is located (or in case the head office is located in the same city with a branch Federal Reserve Bank, to such branch Federal Reserve Bank): *Provided, however,* That depositors located in the District of Columbia shall, and in special cases other depositors may, make deposits hereunder direct with the Treasurer of the United States: *And provided, further,* That checks drawn on the Treasurer of the United States for deposit to the official credit of the depositor may in all cases be deposited direct with the Treasurer.   Specific instructions may be given by the Secretary of the Treasury in certain instances for the

deposit of checks with Federal Reserve Banks of other districts, or with branch Federal Reserve Banks. Government officers having deputies located away from the head office will make the necessary arrangements for the deposit of checks received by such deputies with the Federal Reserve Bank or branch with which the officer himself makes deposits hereunder, for credit in the name of the officer for whom the deputy acts, unless otherwise directed by the Secretary of the Treasury, or, if there is a Federal Reserve Bank or branch in the same city with the office of the deputy, with such Federal Reserve Bank or branch in like manner.

For regulations governing the deposit of checks returning unexpended balances, see Treasury Department Circular No. 281, dated March 20, 1922.

10. *Classification of items for deposit.*—Items forwarded to the Federal Reserve Bank or branch for deposit and collection in accordance herewith should first be sorted into two principal groups as follows:

(*a*) Items drawn on banks and trust companies located in the same city with the Federal Reserve Bank or branch with which the deposit is made, and

(*b*) Items drawn on banks and trust companies located outside of the city in which is located the Federal Reserve Bank or branch with which the deposit is made.

Collectors of internal revenue will make further classification of checks forwarded by them for deposit in accordance with paragraph 14 hereof.

The several groups shall each be accompanied by a separate letter of transmittal or draft certificate of deposit (to consist of a full set in proper form, to be dated and signed by the Federal Reserve Bank, not by the depositor), and such letter of transmittal or draft certificate of deposit must, in all cases, specify the account or purpose for which the deposit is received. (See special instructions below to collectors of internal revenue, collectors of customs, and postmasters, paragraphs 14, 17, and 20 hereof, respectively.)

Apart from this classification, all items which return to the Treasury unexpended balances from funds advanced upon accountable warrants issued upon requisitions, or received as a transfer of funds from an officer to whom the funds were originally advanced, should be separated from all other deposits in accordance with Treasury Department Circular No. 281, dated March 20, 1922, which should be consulted for detailed regulations regarding the manner of making such deposits.

11. *Indorsement, transmission, and collection of checks.*—The depositor should stamp on the face of each check deposited the words: "This check is in payment of an obligation to the United States and must be paid at par. No protest," followed by his name and title. The Federal Reserve Bank will make an effort to collect every check on these terms. If the bank on which a check is drawn for any reason does not pay it at par, it will be returned to the depositor in the same manner as a bad check. A check is not paid by the bank on which it is drawn if the bank tenders in payment a bank draft which for any reason is not paid. All checks forwarded by depositors to Federal Reserve Banks should be indorsed: "Pay to

the order of the Federal Reserve Bank of ---------------------
                                     (Insert name of city in which Federal

-----------------------------------------------------------------
Reserve Bank, not branch, is located.)
for credit to the Treasurer of the United States, ----------------,
                                              (Date.)
                                                            ,,
-----------------------------------------------------------------'
                     (Signature or stamp of depositor.)

(See special instructions to collectors of internal revenue, para-graph 15.) *The checks must in all cases be forwarded by registered mail.* Inasmuch as the indorsement is specific, it is not necessary that checks be insured. Depositors must, however, retain a record of the checks forwarded, so that if any check is lost payment may be immediately stopped and a duplicate secured. Necessary expenses for postage and registration charges should be borne by such appropriation as may be available and must not in any event be deducted from the amount of the deposit. (See special instructions to collectors of internal revenue, collectors of customs, and postmasters, below.) If the depositor has no appropriation available to pay such charges, he should make prompt report to the Secretary of the Treasury, Division of Deposits, and request instructions. When transmitting checks to a Federal Reserve Bank, the depositor should request such bank to issue certificates of deposits on the appropriate form and dispose of the certificates in the set in accordance with instructions which appear thereon.

12. *Uncollected and lost checks.*—In the event that any check for which a certificate of deposit has been issued is not paid for any reason by the bank on which it is drawn, such check, if recovered by the Federal Reserve Bank, will be immediately returned to the depositor, who will give receipt therefor on the reverse of Form 5504 (see page 15), showing the date, number, and amount of each certificate of deposit in which the amount of the unpaid check (or checks) was included, and the class of the deposit, as "Income and Profits Taxes," or "Miscellaneous Internal Revenue," etc. In case the unpaid item is not recovered by the Federal Reserve Bank, the depositor will, nevertheless, upon request of the Federal Reserve Bank, give receipt on Form 5504 as above, making a notation of the circumstances on the reverse of the form and indicating the reason why the check itself was not returned. The depositor will in either case adjust his accounts accordingly and proceed to collect the amount involved in the item as if no check had been received. In case an exchange draft tendered by the bank on which the check is drawn is not paid for any reason, the check itself is not considered paid and the depositor will proceed accordingly. In case of failure for any reason to collect checks forwarded for collection by the Treasurer of the United States or checks deposited by regional and sub-offices of the United States Veterans Bureau, such checks if recovered by the Federal Reserve Bank should be returned to the Cashier, Office of the Treasurer, United States, with duplicate debit voucher on Form 5315, and the original Form 5315 transmitted with the transcript in support of the charge for such returned items in all cases where the Treasurer's account has already been credited therefor. In case the unpaid item or items are not recovered by the Federal Reserve Banks, a notation of the circumstances should be

made on the reverse of Form 5315. In the event that any check for which a certificate of deposit has been given is reported lost after deposit, the Federal Reserve Bank will notify the depositor, who will request the drawer to stop payment thereon and forward a duplicate check. The depositor will give to the Federal Reserve Bank a statement on the reverse side of Form 5504 (page 15) appropriately changed for the purpose, showing the date, number, and amount of each certificate of deposit in which the amount of the lost check (or checks) was included, the class of the deposit, and that he has requested the drawer of the check to stop payment. The depositor will then adjust his accounts accordingly, and if a duplicate check is not received in due course, he will proceed to make collection as if no check had been received. When the drawer makes payment for either a bad check or lost check, the depositor will treat it in his accounts as new business and make deposit of the amount with the Federal Reserve Bank in the usual manner; except that whenever payment is made for either a bad check or lost check before receipt on Form 5504 has been given, the new payment should be forwarded to the Federal Reserve Bank in lieu of the original item.

FOR SPECIAL ATTENTION OF COLLECTORS OF INTERNAL REVENUE.

13. *Deposit of checks with Federal Reserve Banks and branches.*— All checks, whether certified or uncertified, and whether or not drawn on banks or trust companies located in the same city with the collector, received by collectors of internal revenue (hereinafter in this title called collectors) and their deputies in payment of internal revenue taxes, including income and profits taxes, shall be forwarded for deposit each day by collectors, unless otherwise specifically instructed by the Secretary of the Treasury, to the Federal Reserve Bank of the district in which the collector's head office is located (or, in case the head office is located in the same city with a branch Federal Reserve Bank, to such branch Federal Reserve Bank) in accordance with paragraph 9 hereof. Specific instructions may be given by the Secretary of the Treasury in certain instances for the deposit of checks with Federal Reserve Banks of other districts or branch Federal Reserve Banks. Collectors will make the necessary arrangements for deposits by their deputies in accordance with the provisions of this paragraph and of said paragraph 9.

14. *Classification of checks for deposit.*—Checks forwarded to the Federal Reserve Bank in accordance herewith may be inclosed under one outer wrapper, but must be separated into the following classes in addition to the groups specified in paragraph 10:

(a) Checks received exclusively in payment of income and profits taxes, inclosed in a separate package containing an inner wrapper or label plainly marked "Income and Profits Tax Checks only."

(b) All other checks received (in whole or in part) in payment of other internal revenue taxes, inclosed in a separate package containing an inner wrapper or label plainly marked "Miscellaneous Internal Revenue Collections."

Collectors of internal revenue should, whenever practicable, arrange each class of checks so forwarded into groups pursuant to paragraph 10 hereof. Each such group of checks must be accompanied by a draft certificate of deposit (original, duplicate, and triplicate, in proper form, to be dated and signed by the Federal Reserve Bank, not by the collector), and such draft certificate of deposit must, in all cases, specify the amount of the deposit representing "Income and Profits Taxes" separate and distinct from the amount representing "Miscellaneous Internal Revenue Collections" (formerly called "Ordinary").

15. *Indorsement, transmission, and collection of checks.*—The collector should stamp, indorse, and transmit such checks in accordance with paragraph 11 hereof, adding to the indorsement, the notation "Income and Profits Taxes" or "Miscellaneous Internal Revenue Collections," as the case may be. Collectors are authorized by the Commissioner of Internal Revenue to incur any necessary expense for postage and registration charges from the appropriation "Collecting the Internal Revenue." When transmitting the checks to the Federal Reserve Bank, the collector should request the Federal Reserve Bank to issue certificates of deposit on Form 15 in his name, and to send the duplicate and triplicate of the certificates of deposit to his office, for disposition in accordance with the instructions which appear on the margin of the certificate.

16. *Uncollected and lost checks.*—In the event that any check is returned unpaid for any reason, or reported lost after deposit, the collector will proceed in accordance with paragraph 12 hereof. If any taxpayer should fail to make good any such check after demand, the collector should proceed to collect the taxes by the usual methods, as though no check had been received.

FOR SPECIAL ATTENTION OF COLLECTORS OF CUSTOMS.

17. *Deposit of checks with Federal Reserve Banks and branches.*—All checks, whether certified or uncertified, and whether or not drawn on banks and trust companies located in the same city with the collector, received by collectors of customs (hereinafter in this title called collectors), shall be forwarded for deposit each day by collectors, unless otherwise specifically instructed by the Secretary of the Treasury, to the Federal Reserve Bank of the district in which the collector's head office is located (or, in case the head office is located in the same city with a branch Federal Reserve Bank, to such branch Federal Reserve Bank) in accordance with paragraph 9 hereof. Specific instructions may be given by the Secretary of the Treasury in certain instances for the deposit of checks with Federal Reserve Banks of other districts or branch Federal Reserve Banks. Collectors will make the necessary arrangements for deposits by their deputies in accordance with the provisions of this paragraph and of said paragraph 9. Checks forwarded to the Federal Reserve Bank in accordance herewith should be arranged in groups as required by paragraph 10 hereof and each such group of checks must be accompanied by a draft certificate of deposit (to consist of a full set, in proper form, to be dated and signed by the Federal Reserve Bank, not by the collector). Such draft certificate of deposit must, in all cases, specify .the amounts of the deposits representing collections for the Treasury Department, Department of Commerce, and Department of Labor, separate and distinct from each other, and must make such further specification within each Department as shall be required.

18. *Indorsement, transmission, and collection of checks.*—The collector should stamp, indorse, and transmit all checks in accordance

SECRETARY OF THE TREASURY. 371

with paragraph 11 hereof. Collectors are authorized to incur any necessary expense for postage and registration charges from the appropriation "Collecting the Revenue from Customs." When transmitting the checks to the Federal Reserve Bank, the collector should request the Federal Reserve Bank to issue certificates of deposit on Form 1¾ in his name, and to make disposition of the certificates in the set in accordance with the instructions which appear on the certificates.

19. *Uncollected and lost checks.*—In the event that any check is returned unpaid for any reason, or is reported lost after deposit, the collector will proceed in accordance with paragraph 12 hereof.

### FOR SPECIAL ATTENTION OF POSTMASTERS.

20. *Deposit of checks with Federal Reserve Banks and branches.*— All checks received by State depository postmasters representing surplus postal funds, surplus money-order funds, and receipts from sales of Treasury Savings securities (except to the extent that surplus postal funds and surplus money-order funds may be required by the depository postmaster for authorized postal expenditures, or for the redemption of War-Savings Certificates, Thrift Stamps, or Treasury Savings Stamps), whether or not such checks are drawn on banks and trust companies located in the same city with the postmaster, shall be forwarded for deposit each day, unless specific instructions are given for deposit elsewhere, to the Federal Reserve Bank of the district in which the State depository post office is located (or, in case the post office is located in the same city with a branch Federal Reserve Bank, to such branch Federal Reserve Bank), in accordance with the provisions of paragraph 9 hereof. Specific instructions may be given by the Secretary of the Treasury in certain instances for the deposit of checks with Federal Reserve Banks of other districts or branch Federal Reserve Banks. The postmaster at Washington, D. C., will make deposits hereunder with the Treasurer of the United States direct. Checks forwarded to the Federal Reserve Bank in accordance herewith should be arranged in groups as required by paragraph 10 hereof and each such group of checks must be accompanied by a draft certificate of deposit (to consist of a full set, in proper form, to be signed, dated, and completed by the Federal Reserve Bank), and such draft certificate of deposit must, in all cases, make such specification as shall be required of postmasters by the Postmaster General and by the instructions appearing on the certificate. The depository postmaster should stamp, indorse, and transmit the checks in accordance with paragraph 11 hereof. An appropriate statement should be added to the indorsement showing whether the deposit is made on account of surplus postal funds, surplus money-order funds, or receipts from sales of Treasury Savings securities. When transmitting the checks to the Federal Reserve Bank, the postmaster should request the Federal Reserve Bank to issue certificates of deposit on the appropriate form in his name, and to make disposition of the certificates in the set in accordance with the instructions which appear on the certificates.

21. *Uncollected and lost checks.*—In the event that any check is returned unpaid for any reason or is reported lost after deposit, the postmaster will proceed in accordance with paragraph 12 hereof

## OTHER DEPOSITORS OF PUBLIC MONEYS.

22. All checks received by other depositors of public moneys will be stamped, indorsed, transmitted, and deposited with Federal Reserve Banks and their branches in accordance with the provisions of paragraphs 8 to 12 hereof, inclusive.

## FOR SPECIAL ATTENTION OF OFFICERS OF UNITED STATES COURTS AND UNITED STATES ATTORNEYS.

23. United States attorneys, marshals, and clerks of United States courts, who receive public moneys accruing to the United States from fines, penalties, and forfeitures, fees, costs, forfeitures of recognizances, moneys arising from unclaimed wages and effects of seamen that have remained in the registry of the courts for more than six years, unclaimed moneys remaining in court registry five years or longer, debts due the United States, interest on such debts, sales of public property, or from any other sources, except as stated below, will deposit the same in accordance with paragraphs 4 and 8 to 12 hereof, inclusive. Moneys collected in cases for violation of customs, navigation, equipment of motor boats, steamboat-inspection, immigration, and Chinese exclusion laws should be paid to the collector of customs in the district or port in which the case arose. Fines for importation of opium or having opium in possession under the act of February 9, 1909, amended January 17, 1914, should also be paid to the collector of customs. Moneys collected in criminal cases under the internal revenue laws, including fines for making smoking opium under law of January 17, 1914, or under the anti-narcotic act of December 17, 1914, should be paid to the collector of internal revenue in the district in which the case arose. But fines arising from violation of section 240, Criminal Code, and fines arising from violation of the national prohibition act should be deposited by the clerk of court collecting them to the credit of the Treasurer of the United States. Moneys collected as damages on account of trespass on the National Forests should be paid to the fiscal agent of the Forest Service district in which the case arose. The fines and costs in such cases should be deposited to the credit of the Treasurer of the United States. Fines collected under sections 52 and 53, Criminal Code (setting fire to timber on public lands or failing to extinguish same), should be paid to the proper county officer for the public-school fund of the county where the land is situated, but costs should be deposited to the credit of the Treasurer of the United States. Moneys collected in Indian suits involving rentals, leasing, damages, etc., of Indian property or allotments for use of the particular Indian owners, should be paid to the disbursing officer for the agency having jurisdiction over them; costs should be deposited to the credit of the Treasurer of the United States. Moneys (including costs) collected in civil or criminal post-office cases should be transmitted to the Solicitor of the Treasury by draft or check made payable to the order of the Treasurer of the United States.

## FOR SPECIAL ATTENTION OF FEDERAL RESERVE BANKS.

24. *General provisions.*—Federal Reserve Banks and branches will be expected to remain open during usual banking hours for the purpose of receiving deposits hereunder. Federal Reserve Banks

and branches will not receive deposits by postmasters or United States courts or their officers for credit in their official checking accounts unless specifically authorized by the Secretary of the Treasury to accept such deposits.

25. *Collection and credit.*—Federal Reserve Banks will give credit for items deposited for credit in the Treasurer's general account on the following basis: Federal Reserve Banks are expected to arrange for payments of calls on balances with special depositaries and payments on subscriptions for Treasury notes and certificates of indebtedness and other Government securities offered for sale through the Federal Reserve Banks, in funds that will be immediately available on the due date, and are accordingly expected to give immediate credit on the due date for such amounts in the Treasurer's account: *Provided, however,* That when cash payments for Treasury notes and certificates and other Government securities are made in funds not immediately available on the date of issue, the Federal Reserve Banks will be expected to collect accrued interest thereon at the coupon rate up to the date on which the funds become available, and to give credit therefor in the Treasurer's account on that date. Federal Reserve Banks are likewise expected to give credit in the Treasurer's account on the date of deposit for all items payable in Federal Reserve funds or other immediately available funds, and for all items classified in group (a) of paragraph 10 hereof, which are received early enough to be cleared on the day of receipt. In no case should credit in the Treasurer's general account be deferred more than one day for items classified in group (a) of paragraph 10, except that credit may be deferred for two days for items which can not be cleared in less than two days. Certificates of deposit for the full amount of all such items received from any depositors of public moneys should be issued at the time of credit in the Treasurer's general account.

Federal Reserve Banks are requested to give credit for items classified in group (b) of paragraph 10 hereof on the basis of the average time of collection, which should be agreed upon in each case between the Federal Reserve Bank and the Treasury, and which should not exceed five days. Certificates of deposit for such items should be issued at the time of credit in the Treasurer's account. Any Federal Reserve Bank instead of following this procedure may, by special arrangement with the Treasury, credit the Treasurer's general account each day for collections in accordance with its established time schedule, entering such credits in the transcripts of the general account as "Unclassified Receipts" until the last item of the deposit has been so credited. The certificate of deposit should then be issued and the total amount of the deposit credited, with corresponding charge in the transcript against the "Unclassified Receipts" previously credited. Federal Reserve Banks following this alternative procedure will be expected to sort items received under group (b) in accordance with the time schedules to be applied, and are requested to expedite to the utmost collection and credit in order to avoid holding the accounts of depositors in suspense.

Federal Reserve Banks are authorized to send checks deposited for credit to the Treasurer's general account which have been properly stamped in accordance with paragraph 11 hereof direct to the drawee bank for payment. The Federal Reserve Banks will exercise all possible precautions in presenting such checks for payment, and where there is any doubt of the solvency of the drawee bank will, if practicable, make presentation over the counter. If Federal Reserve Banks elect to send such checks to other banks for collection, they will be held responsible for any failure or other delinquency of the bank or banks through which the items are sent for collection.

26. *Uncollected and lost checks.*—In the event that any checks for which a certificate of deposit has been given are not paid for any reason by the drawee bank, the check or checks, if recovered by the Federal Reserve Bank, should be promptly returned to the depositor, who will give a receipt therefor on the reverse of Form 5504, page 15. This receipt must show the date, number, and amount of each certificate of deposit in which the amount of the unpaid check (or checks) was included, and the class of the deposit, as "Income and Profits Taxes," or "Miscellaneous Internal Revenue," etc. In case the unpaid item or items are not recovered by the Federal Reserve Bank the depositor will nevertheless upon request of the Federal Reserve Bank give receipt on Form 5504, as above, making a notation of the circumstances on the reverse of the form. In either event, the Federal Reserve Bank, upon obtaining such a receipt from the depositor, will immediately charge the amount, with appropriate description, in its current transcript of the Treasurer's account on Form 17, and forward therewith in support of the entry the receipt given by the depositor with a debit voucher, both on Form 5504, a supply of which has been forwarded by the Treasury Department to each Federal Reserve Bank for this purpose. In case of checks forwarded for collection by the Treasurer of the United States and checks deposited by regional and sub-offices of the United States Veterans Bureau which are not paid for any reason by the drawee bank, the check or checks, if recovered by the Federal Reserve Bank should be returned to the Cashier, Office of the Treasurer, United States, with duplicate debit voucher, Form 5315, and the original Form 5315 transmitted with the transcript to support the charge in all cases where the Treasurer's account has already been credited. In case the unpaid item or items are not recovered by the Federal Reserve Bank a notation of the circumstances should be made on the reverse of Form 5315.

If a check credited in the Federal Reserve Bank's collection account should be lost or returned unpaid, and no certificate of deposit has been issued therefor, the amount thereof should be charged to the collection account, and the check, if recovered by the Federal Reserve Bank, returned to the depositor.

A check is not considered paid within the meaning of this circular if the exchange draft covering it which is tendered by the drawee bank is not paid. In case the exchange draft is not paid because of insolvency of the bank on which it is drawn, the draft should be retained by the Federal Reserve Bank as the basis for a claim, and the Federal Reserve Bank will be expected in ordinary course to file claim thereon for account of the Treasurer, though dividends on claims so filed should be accepted only upon specific authority from the Secretary of the Treasury.

In the event that any checks for which a certificate of deposit has been given are lost after deposit, the depositor should be promptly notified and requested to have payment stopped thereon. The depositor will state on the reverse of Form 5504, appropriately marked for the purpose, the date, number, and amount of each certificate of deposit in which the amount of the lost check (or checks) was included, the class of deposit, and that the drawer of the check has been requested to stop payment thereon. The Federal Reserve Bank, upon obtaining such a statement from the depositor, will immediately charge the amount, with appropriate description, in its current transcript of the Treasurer's account on Form 17 and forward therewith in support of the entry the depositor's statement with debit voucher, both on Form 5504.

27. *Certificates of deposit.*—Federal Reserve Banks are requested to use great care to observe the depositor's classification of deposits and to see that all certificates of deposit are duly executed in accordance with paragraph 6 hereof. The date inserted on the certificate of deposit by the Federal Reserve Bank must, in all cases, be the same as the date of the transcript in which the amount is credited. Certificates of deposit should be numbered by the depositor if prepared by him, but in the event that the depositor fails to number the certificate the Federal Reserve Banks will supply a number. Certificates of deposit on Form 15 for deposits of internal revenue collections must specify on the face thereof deposits of "Income and Profits Taxes" separate and distinct in each case from deposits of "Miscellaneous Internal Revenue Collections" (formerly called "Ordinary"). Certificates of deposit on Form 1¾ for customs collections must specify upon the face thereof deposits representing collections for the Treasury Department, Department of Commerce, and Department of Labor separate and distinct from each other, and make such further specification within each department as may be indicated by the collector. All copies of the certificate of deposit (duplicate, triplicate, etc.) must bear the same date and must not be delivered to the depositor prior to such date.

Certificates of deposit issued for deposits representing the return of unexpended balances should be drawn in accordance with the requirements of Treasury Department Circular No. 281, dated March 20, 1922.

28. *Checks drawn on banks outside district.*—Checks received by Federal Reserve Banks in accordance with this circular which are drawn on banks in other Federal Reserve districts should be collected in the usual manner and should not be charged in the Treasurer's general account as transfers of funds to other Federal Reserve Banks.

FOR SPECIAL ATTENTION OF NATIONAL BANK DEPOSITARIES.

29. *General provisions.*—General National bank depositaries are not authorized to maintain any collection account for deposits of public moneys, but are required to give immediate credit in the Treasurer's account and to issue certificates of deposit for the full amount of all public moneys deposited with them for credit in the Treasurer's account in accordance with this circular. Except pursuant to specific instructions to that effect from the Secretary of the Treasury, no deposits of checks or drafts shall be accepted hereunder by National bank depositaries for credit to the account of the Treasurer of the

United States, but deposits of cash and postal or express money orders only may be made in accordance with paragraph 4 hereof.

30. *Excess balances.*—Each general National bank depositary, whenever it holds funds to the credit of the Treasurer of the United States in excess of its fixed balance, shall make immediate transfer of such excess funds to the Federal Reserve Bank of its district for credit to the Treasurer's general account in funds available for immediate credit by such Federal Reserve Bank: *Provided, however,* That such transfers may also be made with the consent of the Federal Reserve Bank of the district to a branch of such Federal Reserve Bank. National bank depositaries, whenever they hold funds to the credit of the official checking accounts of United States courts or their officers and of postmasters, pursuant to paragraph 32 hereof, in excess of the collateral value of the security deposited therefor, shall promptly report the facts to the Secretary of the Treasury, Division of Deposits, and deposit additional security with the Treasurer of the United States to cover such deposits.

31. *Collateral security for deposits with National bank depositaries.*—Until further notice, securities of the following classes, and no others, will be accepted as security for deposits hereunder with National bank depositaries, and at the rates below provided:

(a) Bonds, notes, and Treasury certificates of indebtedness of the United States, of any issue, including outstanding interim certificates or receipts for payments therefor; all at par.

(b) Bonds of the Federal Land Banks, bonds of the War Finance Corporation, bonds of Porto Rico and the District of Columbia, and bonds and certificates of indebtedness of the Philippine Islands; all at par.

(c) The $3\frac{1}{2}$ per cent bonds of the Territory of Hawaii at 90 per cent of market value; and other bonds of said Territory at market value, not to exceed par.

All securities to be pledged as collateral security for such deposits must be deposited with the Treasurer of the United States accompanied by a letter stating distinctly the purpose for which deposited. When registered bonds or notes are to be deposited as collateral security hereunder, such bonds must be assigned to the Treasurer of the United States in trust for the bank by an officer of the bank, duly authorized by resolution of its board of directors to make such assignment, and the assignment must be duly acknowledged pursuant to the regulations of the Secretary of the Treasury governing assignments of registered bonds and notes. A certified copy of the resolution of the board of directors must accompany the bonds or notes when forwarded to the Treasurer of the United States.

32. *Court and post-office funds, etc.*—Limited National bank depositaries designated for the sole purpose of receiving deposits made by United States courts and their officers and by postmasters for credit to their official checking accounts, are not authorized to receive deposits hereunder for credit to the account of the Treasurer of the United States. Such depositaries are required to forward to the Treasurer of the United States at the end of each week, and at the end of each month, a report on Form 18 showing the aggregate amounts of such deposits, and to the Secretary of the Treasury, Division of Deposits, at the end of each week, a report on Form 7, showing in detail the deposits to the credit of the local postmaster

and United States courts and their officers. General National bank depositaries authorized to accept deposits by United States courts and their officers and by postmasters for credit to their official checking accounts are required to report daily to the Treasurer of the United States on line 12 of Form 17 the aggregate amounts of such deposits and to report on Form 7 at the end of each week to the Secretary of the Treasury, Division of Deposits, showing such deposits in detail. Bankruptcy funds and postal savings deposits should not be included in these reports.

33. *Interest on deposits.*—Each National bank depositary will be required to pay interest at the rate of 2 per cent per annum on daily balances, including deposits specified in paragraph 32 hereof. Interest will be calculated on an actual days' basis, and shall be paid semi-annually on January 1 and July 1 in each year, 1 per cent for each six months' period. Reports on Form 5407 must be submitted to the Treasurer of the United States not later than January 15 and July 15, respectively, accompanied by payment of the amount due, in the form of a draft on the Federal Reserve Bank of the district in which the depositary is located.

34. *Restoration of depleted balances.*—Whenever the balance to the credit of the Treasurer of the United States in any general National bank depositary is reduced by the cashing of Government warrants and checks below the amount fixed by the Secretary of the Treasury, the balance will be immediately restored upon the receipt by the Treasurer of the United States of a request from the depositary bank, either by wire prepaid or by letter. Such requests must be in the form and in accordance with instructions prescribed by the Treasurer of the United States. (See Treasurer's circulars dated December 1, 1920, and April 30, 1921, copies of which will be furnished on request.) The Treasurer of the United States will restore balances in either of the following methods, as may be desired by the bank; (1) by directing the appropriate Federal Reserve Bank by wire to credit the bank's reserve account, or (2) by placing funds to the bank's credit by wire with its correspondent in any city where a Federal Reserve Bank or branch is located. Immediately upon making such transfer the Treasurer will advise the bank, by wire prepaid, of the credit. No funds will be transferred, however, to a depositary bank in advance of the actual reduction of the Treasurer's balance or in anticipation of the future cashing of Government obligations.

## II. Payment of Government Warrants and Checks.

35. *Federal Reserve Banks and branches.*—Federal Reserve Banks and branches will make arrangements to cash Government warrants and checks drawn on the Treasurer of the United States for disbursing officers of the War Department and Navy Department, and other Government officers, provided that satisfactory identification of the officers shall be furnished. The Treasurer will upon special request advise Federal Reserve Banks and branches as to whether the balances to the credit of disbursing officers are sufficient for payment of the checks presented. Each Federal Reserve Bank and branch will cash Government warrants and checks drawn on the Treasurer of the United States when they are presented and properly

indorsed by responsible incorporated banks and trust companies who guarantee all prior indorsements thereon, including the indorsement of the drawer when the check is drawn in his favor. Warrants and checks cashed by Federal Reserve Banks and branches shall be charged to the account of the Treasurer of the United States, subject to examination and payment by the Treasurer. Federal Reserve Banks and branches will not be expected to cash Government warrants and checks presented direct to the bank by the general public.

36. *National bank depositaries.*—Each general National bank depositary with a fixed balance to the credit of the Treasurer of the United States will cash Government warrants and checks drawn on the Treasurer of the United States when they are presented and properly indorsed by responsible holders who guarantee all prior indorsements thereon, including the indorsement of the drawer when the check is drawn in his favor. Warrants and checks so cashed may be charged to the account of the Treasurer of the United States, subject to examination and payment by the Treasurer. General National bank depositaries are not required, however, to charge Government warrants and checks cashed by them in the account of the Treasurer of the United States, except in special cases where checks drawn on the Treasurer of the United States are deposited for the official credit of the drawer or the credit of other Government officers in the account of the Treasurer of the United States.

37. *Payment by Treasurer.*—The Treasurer of the United States reserves the usual right of the drawee to examine, when received, all Government warrants and checks cashed by Federal Reserve Banks and branches and general National bank depositaries, and to refuse payment thereon. The Treasurer will handle all such items received by him on the following basis: (1) Immediate return will be made of any warrant or check, payment of which is refused on account of forged signature of drawer, insufficient funds, stoppage of payment, or any material defect discovered upon first examination, in all of which cases the transit account of the remitting bank will be charged with the amount of the returned warrant or check and the remitting bank will be expected to give immediate credit therefor in the Treasurer's account. (2) In the event that any warrant or check which has been paid by the Treasurer is subsequently found to bear a forged indorsement, or to have been raised, or to bear any other material alteration or defect which was not discoverable upon first examination, a photographic copy of the warrant or check will be forwarded to the remitting bank and its transit account will be charged with the amount by the Treasurer, but the remitting bank will not be expected to give credit in the Treasurer's account for items of this class until it has received reimbursement therefor. (3) In cases of warrants or checks bearing a forged signature of the drawer, not discovered upon first examination by the Treasurer, and in other cases where the Treasurer's right to reclaim is in question, the warrants or checks will be forwarded to the remitting bank as collection items and taken up by the Treasurer when credited, with no intermediate charge in the account of the remitting bank.

Three years after the close of the fiscal year (ending June 30) in which they are drawn, warrants, Treasurer's checks, and disbursing officer's checks are *not* payable by the Treasurer of the United States, but should be sent to the Secretary of the Treasury, Division of Bookkeeping and Warrants, for payment from the "Outstanding Liabilities" appropriation; provided, however, that this restriction does not apply to checks for interest on United States bonds, District of Columbia, Philippine, and Porto Rican bonds, to checks drawn by the Comptroller of the Currency in payment of dividends of failed banks, or to checks drawn by the Treasurer of the United States Soldiers' Home at Washington, D. C., which are payable without limit as to time; and, provided, further, that checks drawn by a receiver of public moneys or by a register, United States Land Office, may be paid by the Treasurer within five years after the close of the fiscal year in which they are drawn.

38. *Checks on Assistant Treasurers.*—Checks drawn on Assistant Treasurers of the United States, whose offices have been discontinued under the provisions of the act approved May 29, 1920, should be forwarded for payment to the Treasurer of the United States in the same manner as other checks of Government disbursing officers.

### OTHER PROVISIONS.

39. All previous regulations and instructions inconsistent herewith are hereby superseded, including, so far as inconsistent herewith, the provisions of Treasury Department Circulars No. 5, dated April 6, 1916, No. 105, dated December 27, 1917, and No. 144, dated May 20, 1919, and the provisions of the first edition of this circular issued under date of December 31, 1919.

40. Except as herein otherwise provided, nothing contained in this circular shall be deemed to affect deposits by postmasters to the credit of their official checking accounts, the deposit of court funds by United States courts and their officers, or the deposit of Postal Savings funds, in-cases where such deposits are not for credit by the depositary in the account of the Treasurer of the United States. Unless specifically extended thereto by the Secretary of the Treasury, nothing contained in this circular shall be deemed to apply to or govern the deposit of public moneys in Federal land banks or joint stock land banks under the act approved July 17, 1916, as amended.

41. The provisions of this circular do not apply to or govern the deposit of public moneys outside of the continental United States, except to the extent specifically extended by the Secretary of the Treasury from time to time. Reference is made to the provisions of Treasury Department Circular No. 194, as amended and supplemented May 4, 1922, for special regulations applicable to the Philippine Islands.

42. The Secretary of the Treasury may withdraw or amend at any time or from time to time any or all of the provisions of this circular.

A. W. Mellon,
*Secretary of the Treasury.*

FORM 5504,
(*Formerly Form N.*)

[Obverse.]

Group as
paid checks.

First sort.
General ledger section.

Second sort.
Symbol ......

Treasurer's office.          DEBIT VOUCHER.          Form 5504.

........................................., 192..

.............................. of ..............................
(Name of Federal Reserve Bank or branch.)

Debit has been made this day in transcript of Treasurer's general account for uncollectible checks deposited by .......... in payment of .......... and returned to the depositor as unpaid, as per receipt on reverse hereof, (or lost checks, as per description on reverse hereof) in the amount of $.....................................

..........................
*Cashier.*

NOTE.—Forward with transcript in support of entry.

[Reverse.]

*Received........................, 192.., from..................................
(Name of Federal Reserve Bank or branch.)

of.............., uncollectible (lost) checks amounting to $.............., which amount was included in certificates of deposit issued by said bank as follows:

| Certificate No. | Date of certificate. | Total amount of certificate. | Classification of deposit (as income and profits taxes, miscellaneous internal revenue, customs, miscellaneous receipts, official checking account, surplus postal funds, surplus money-order funds, Treasury Savings securities, etc.). | Amount of uncollectible (lost) checks included in each certificate. |
|---|---|---|---|---|
|  |  |  |  |  |
|  |  |  |  |  |

Total, $............

.............. District of ..............          ....................................
(Signature and title of depositor.)

*If voucher covers lost checks, give appropriate description of circumstances instead of receipt.

# ABSTRACTS OF REPORTS OF BUREAUS AND DIVISIONS.

381

# ABSTRACTS OF REPORTS OF BUREAUS AND DIVISIONS.

The following is a summary of the reports of the various bureaus and divisions of the Treasury Department:

## TREASURER OF THE UNITED STATES.

On the basis of daily Treasury statements, revised, the total ordinary receipts from all sources (exclusive of postal revenues) during the fiscal year 1922 were $4,103,596,531.04, a decrease of $1,480,-920,514.19 as compared with the fiscal year 1921. Total cash expenditures chargeable against ordinary receipts during the year amounted to $3,782,549,314.64, a decrease of $1,734,730,041.47 as compared with the previous fiscal year. The net result for the year was an excess of ordinary receipts over total expenditures chargeable against ordinary receipts of $321,047,216.40.

Disbursements made on account of the Panama Canal, exclusive of fortifications, during the fiscal year 1922 on the basis of warrants drawn (not cash expenditures) were $2,791,035.40, while receipts from tolls, etc., were $12,049,660.65, leaving a net excess of receipts over warrants drawn of $9,258,625.25.

Receipts and expenditures on account of the principal of the public debt during the fiscal year 1922 are shown in the following statement:

```
Receipts on account of—
    Postal savings bonds.....................................      $112,200.00
    National-bank notes and Federal reserve bank notes..........    107,086,627.50
    Certificates of indebtedness.................................  3,905,090,000.00
    Victory Liberty loan (counter entry).........................          1,300.00
    Treasury notes...............................................  1,935,404,750.00
    Treasury (war) savings securities............................     70,325,625.10
                                                                  _____
        Total....................................................  6,018,017,902.60
Expenditures on account of—
    Certificates of indebtedness...............  $4,775,873,950.00
    Treasury (war) savings securities..........      85,415,860.52
    Old debt items retired......................         58,082.40
    First Liberty bonds..........................        415,050.00
    Second Liberty bonds.........................      5,939,500.00
    Third Liberty bonds..........................    137,772,300.00
    Fourth Liberty bonds.........................      9,476,600.00
    Victory notes................................  1,907,986,250.00
    National-bank notes and Federal reserve
      bank notes retired.........................    107,251,870.00
                                                  _____
        Total....................................................  7,030,189,462.92
    Net excess of expenditures (representing debt retirement).  1,012,171,560.32
```

383

The retirements of the debt were effected as follows:

From—

| | |
|---|---:|
| Cumulative sinking fund | $275, 896, 000. 00 |
| Purchases from repayments of foreign loans | 64, 837, 900. 00 |
| Receipts from estate taxes | 20, 893, 200. 00 |
| Purchases from franchise tax receipts (Federal reserve banks).. | 60, 333, 000. 00 |
| Forfeitures to the United States and miscellaneous receipts... | 390, 950. 00 |
| Gifts to the United States | 1, 900. 00 |
| Total | 422, 352, 950. 00 |
| Surplus of ordinary receipts over expenditures chargeable against ordinary receipts | 321, 047, 216. 40 |
| Reduction in net balance in general fund between June 30, 1921, and June 30, 1922 | 268, 771, 393. 92 |
| Total | 1, 012, 171, 560. 32 |

The gold in the Treasury continued to increase during the entire fiscal year and on June 30, 1922, amounted to $3,157,202,555.96, which was held on the following accounts: Reserve fund, $152,979,-025.63; trust funds (for the redemption of gold certificates in actual circulation), $695,000,469; gold fund of Federal Reserve Board, $2,108,886,911.43; and general fund $200,336,149.90, of which $178,-459,107.05 was held for redemption of Federal reserve notes.

At the close of the fiscal year 1921 the balance in the gold fund of the Federal Reserve Board was $1,537,856,895.45. During the fiscal year 1922 the deposits therein were $2,421,691,036.13, and the withdrawals $1,850,661,020.15, leaving a balance on June 30, 1922, of $2,108,886,911.43.

There was on deposit in designated depositaries, at the close of the fiscal year 1922, $209,210,382.70 of public moneys, exclusive of items in transit, distributed as follows:

Depositaries:

| | |
|---|---:|
| In Federal reserve banks | $33, 091, 888. 68 |
| In special depositaries | 146, 476, 840. 69 |
| In national banks | 24, 002, 085. 87 |
| In foreign depositaries | 1, 221, 810. 03 |
| In treasury of Philippine Islands | 4, 417, 757. 43 |
| Total | 209, 210, 382. 70 |

On June 30, 1922, United States bonds and certificates of indebtedness in the custody of the Treasurer pledged to secure bank circulation amounted to $818,765,000, of which $84,218,700 was on account of Federal reserve bank notes. United States bonds and other securities held to secure public deposits in national banks amounted to $41,569,989 on that date, and securities held for the safekeeping of deposits in postal savings depositaries amounted to $103,352,227.50.

There were no redemptions of United States notes from the reserve fund during the fiscal year 1922. National-bank notes presented for redemption during the fiscal year amounted to $624,309,160, or 83.4 per cent of the average amount outstanding. National-bank notes assorted and delivered amounted to $622,260,032.50, of which $8,006,740 were fit for use and were returned to the respective banks of issue for further circulation. There were also presented for redemption Federal reserve notes amounting to $68,455,037.50, and Federal reserve bank notes amounting to $157,600,425.50, none of which were fit for further circulation.

Canceled and uncanceled Federal reserve notes amounting to $2,127,406,150 were received from Federal reserve banks and branches for credit to the accounts of Federal reserve agents. Such notes are received, counted, and delivered by the National Bank Redemption Agency, but are settled for between the Federal reserve banks and the agents either directly or by adjustments in their redemption funds, and are therefore not taken into the cash of the National Bank Redemption Agency.

The pieces of United States paper currency issued during the fiscal year 1922 numbered 463,877,378, with a value of $944,044,000, an increase over the fiscal year 1921 of 145,035,374 pieces and of $386,768,000 in value. Redemptions aggregated 418,767,973 pieces, with a value of $651,720,961, as against 284,785,175 pieces, with a value of $1,058,831,173 in the fiscal year 1921. The pieces outstanding on June 30, 1922, numbered 379,394,013, with a value of $1,639,007,851, against 334,284,603 pieces, with a value of $1,346,-684,812 outstanding on June 30, 1921. This increase results from (1) the extension of facilities for making redemptions and replacements of worn and unfit currency through Federal reserve banks and branch Federal reserve banks, (2) the resumption of the issue of gold certificates, and (3) the issue of silver certificates against silver dollars coined to replace those broken up and sold under provisions of the act of April 23, 1918.

Shipments of currency from the Treasury in Washington to Treasury offices and to banks during the fiscal year 1922 amounted to $673,877,498, as against $460,015,189 during the fiscal year 1921.

## COMPTROLLER OF THE CURRENCY.

### National bank charters.

The act of February 25, 1863, providing for the establishment of the national banking system, stipulated that every association formed pursuant to that act should "have succession" for the period named in the articles of association, not, however, exceeding 20 years from the passage of the act.

This act was repealed and a revised banking law enacted June 3, 1864, providing, among other things, that every association "shall have succession for the period of twenty years from its organization."

Under the act of 1863 charters were issued to some 456 associations, of which 54 were organized for less than 20 years, and in consequence expired by limitation prior to July, 1882. Such of these banks as were in existence and desired to continue in business were compelled to reorganize, as it was not until July 12, 1882, that the act was passed authorizing extensions of charters of banks which had reached the close of their corporate existence. This act provided for the extension of the "period of succession" for a term of not more than 20 years from the expiration of the period named in the bank's articles of association.

To effect extension it was necessary for each association; first, to secure the written consent of shareholders owning two-thirds of the stock, the consent to be certified to the Comptroller of the Currency for the board of directors under seal of the association, by the president or cashier; second, to have a special examination to determine the condition of the bank, approval of the extension being contingent upon the bank's condition at that time; third, to permit dissenting shareholders to withdraw, and receive the value of their shares; fourth, to require that circulating notes issued subsequent to extension should "bear such device as shall make them readily distinguishable" from circulating notes theretofore issued, and further require at the end of three years from extension a deposit of lawful money to provide for the redemption of all notes issued prior to extension and outstanding at the end of this three-year period.

In 1902 many national banks rounded out their second period of succession, and on April 12 of that year an act was approved authorizing, for an additional period of 20 years, the extension of the charters of all banks which had been extended under the act of 1882 in the same manner provided in the act granting the first extension.

Whatever may have been the motive actuating Congress in requiring that circulating notes issued by the banks subsequent to the extension of their charters (under the acts of 1882 and 1902) should be of designs distinguishing them from prior issues, experience developed the fact that this requirement resulted in an unnecessary and enormous expense both to the banks and to the Government—to the banks in the cost of new plates and to the Government in the cost of distinctive paper and in the printing of the notes. Between July 12, 1882, and June 30, 1922, the charters of 4,333 associations were extended under the act of 1882, and 1,512 were extended for the second period of 20 years under the act of 1902. The expense to the banks for the plates for the new designs of notes was approximately $1,000,000 and to the Government for paper, printing, etc., about $500,000.

At various times the Comptrollers of the Currency recommended the repeal of the law providing for new designs for the notes issued under these conditions, but no consideration was given to the question until it was formally brought to the attention of the Committees on Banking and Currency of the present Congress.

In his annual report to Congress in December, 1921, the present Comptroller of the Currency submitted for consideration two bills. One provided for the extension of the charters, for an additional period of 20 years, of banks whose charters had been extended under both the act of 1882 and the act of 1902, and in the manner provided by the act of 1882, except that shareholders were to be accorded the option of giving their written consent or their vote to extend at a meeting called to consider the question. Provision was also made in the bill for the repeal of the law requiring new plates for the printing of notes after the extension of the charter.

The alternative bill, the one that was recommended by the comptroller, granted national banking associations perpetual succession. This bill conferred upon the shareholders of any bank the privilege of withdrawing within 30 days after the termination of 20 years of its existence, i. e., 20 years from the date of the last extension of its charter.

The House passed the bill granting banks perpetual succession, but the Senate amended the bill by fixing 99 years as the period of succession. In conference the Senate amendment was agreed to, the House accepted the report of the conferees, and the bill, as amended, was approved by the President on July 1, 1922. The act repeals all laws or parts of laws relating to extension for a period of 20 years, and amends the second section of section 5136, United States Revised Statutes, relating to the corporate powers of national banks, to read as follows:

Sec. 2. That all acts or parts of acts providing for the extension of the period of succession of national banking associations for twenty years are hereby repealed, and the provisions of paragraph second of section 5136, Revised Statutes, as herein amended shall apply to all national banking associations now organized and operating under any law of the United States.

As will be observed, the law automatically extended for 99 years the period of succession of all banks organized and operating on July 1, 1922, and granted to all banks organized after that date succession for 99 years from date of organization. It will also be noted that the act makes no provision for the withdrawal of shareholders as was provided in the extension acts of 1882 and 1902, although a provision to that effect was incorporated in the bill for perpetual succession as originally submitted and recommended by the Comptroller of the Currency.

As national banks having the required capital and surplus, located in States the laws of which permit the exercise of fiduciary powers by State financial institutions, may be permitted to exercise such powers, and as trusts are often in perpetuity or for very long periods, it follows that banks having perpetual succession can most satisfactorily accept such trusts. This was the principal reason actuating the comptroller in urging favorable consideration of the bill for perpetual succession. In that connection the attention of Congress was called to the fact that the laws of some 23 States provide for or permit perpetual succession of banks or other corporations authorized to exercise fiduciary powers.

The comptroller has issued certificates under the new law to each of those banks which was organized and in operation on the date of the passage of the act, extending its corporate existence for a full period of 99 years, unless it should be sooner dissolved by the act of its shareholders owning two-thirds of its stock, or unless its franchise should become forfeited by reason of violation of law, or unless it should be terminated by act of Congress hereafter enacted.

Of the 12,230 national banks that have been chartered since the beginning of the national banking system 8,274 were in existence on June 30, 1922. Various causes contributed to the retirement of the remaining 3,956 from the system; 3,269 went into voluntary liquidation, 608 failed and were placed in charge of receivers, while 79 were consolidated with other national banks under the act of November 7, 1918. It appears further that 456 national banking associations were chartered under the original bank act of 1863, of which 226 are still in operation; 7,441 under the act of 1864; 10 under the gold-currency act of 1870; and 4,323 under the act of 1900. .

On June 30, 1922, the 8,274 national banks in existence had an authorized capital of $1,315,476,565, and total circulation outstanding of $758,202,027, of which $732,585,640 was secured by United States bonds and $25,616,387 by deposits of lawful money in the retirement account.

There were 244 charters issued to national banking associations during the last fiscal year, with an aggregate capital of $31,185,000. Of this number 128 were conversions of State banks, 86 were primary organizations, and 30 were reorganizations of national, State and private banks. Of these 244 banks 116 were organized with a capital of less than $50,000 each, the average being about $26,336, and their total capital was $3,055,000; and 128 were organized with a capital of $50,000 or more each, the average being approximately $219,766, or a total of $28,130,000. None of these 244 banks took out circulation at the time of organization, but by the end of the year 45 had deposited bonds as security therefor and had either issued or ordered circulation.

One hundred and eighty national banks increased their capital stock during the year by $28,306,000. The increases of 36 of these banks were effected partially or wholly by the declaration from the undivided-profit accounts of the banks of stock dividends to the aggregate amount of $7,690,300.

Including the capital stock of the new banks chartered and the banks restored to solvency, as well as the increases in the capital stock of the 180 banks heretofore referred to, there was a gross increase of $59,866,000 in the authorized capital of the national banks for the year ending June 30, 1922. The net increase in capital for the year, however, was $38,756,000, as the reductions resulting from voluntary liquidations, consolidations, etc., aggregated $21,110,000.

Of the 153 national banks closed during the past fiscal year, 23 were consolidated with other national banks under the act of November 7, 1918; 33 failed and were placed in charge of receivers, and 97 closed by voluntary liquidation. Five of the 33 banks that failed were afterwards restored to solvency; and the charters of 5 of the 97 banks closed by voluntary liquidation were permitted to expire by limitation. There was, therefore, a net gain of 96 in the total number of national banking associations.

The capital of the 97 national banks closed by voluntary liquidation aggregated $17,385,000. Fifty-four of these banks, with a capital of $7,700,000, were acquired by existing State banks; 10 others, with a capital of $915,000, were reorganized as State banks; 21 with a capital of $6,785,000 were absorbed or purchased by other national banks or were absorbed under the provisions of section 5223, United States Revised Statutes; 8, with a capital of $1,810,000, were succeeded by new national banks; and 4, with an aggregate capital of $175,000, retired from business.

The capital of the 33 national banks (including the 5 restored to solvency) for which receivers were appointed during the last fiscal year aggregated $2,095,000, while the liabilities at the date of suspension amounted to $20,296,946.29. Of this sum $3,090,144.06 represented the liabilities of the 5 banks restored to solvency.

Since the approval of the act of Congress of November 7, 1918, providing for the consolidation of national banking associations, 156 national banks have been merged into 77 associations. Twenty-three of these consolidations involving 46 banks were effected during the past year. The combined capital of these banks prior to consolidation was $34,450,000; after consolidation it was $36,525,000, showing an increase of $2,075,000 in their aggregate capital. Their combined assets aggregated $760,127,859.

The act of March 14, 1900, authorized the incorporation of national banks with a minimum capital of $25,000, permitted the issue of circulation to the par value of bonds deposited, and reduced the tax on circulating notes secured by 2 per cent bonds. There were

3,617 national banks in operation at that time with a capital of $485,-420,300. From 1900 to July 1, 1922, 6,966 additional associations had been authorized to begin business. Of the 6,966 banks, 4,323, with a capital aggregating $112,717,500, were chartered under the act of March 14, 1900, with an average individual capital of $26,074. The great majority of these banks, however, were incorporated with the minimum capital of $25,000. The remainder of the banks organized during that period numbered 2,643, and were incorporated under the act of 1864, with an aggregate capital of $372,702,800, or an average of about $141,015 each.

Compared with conditions on March 14, 1900, June 30, 1922, shows a net increase of 4,657 in the number of active national banks, and an increase in authorized capital of $699,168,470. During that period the outstanding circulation increased from $254,402,730 to $758,202,027, a net gain of $503,799,297. The net increase for the past year was $14,911,653.

The following table shows the number of national banks organized, consolidated under the act of November 7, 1918, insolvent, in voluntary liquidation, and in active operation on June 30, 1922, by States and geographical divisions:

*Number of national banks organized, consolidated under act of November 7, 1918, insolvent, in voluntary liquidation, and in operation on June 30, 1922.*

| State. | Organized. | Consolidated under act Nov. 7, 1918. | Insolvent. | In liquidation. | In operation. |
|---|---|---|---|---|---|
| Maine | 113 | | | 53 | 60 |
| New Hampshire | 72 | | 4 | 12 | 56 |
| Vermont | 76 | | 7 | 20 | 49 |
| Massachusetts | 333 | 1 | 15 | 157 | 160 |
| Rhode Island | 65 | | 1 | 47 | 17 |
| Connecticut | 111 | 2 | 5 | 40 | 64 |
| Total New England States | 770 | 3 | 32 | 329 | 406 |
| New York | 804 | 11 | 50 | 234 | 509 |
| New Jersey | 280 | 4 | 10 | 38 | 228 |
| Pennsylvania | 1,076 | 3 | 45 | 160 | 868 |
| Delaware | 28 | | | 10 | 18 |
| Maryland | 125 | | 2 | 35 | 88 |
| District of Columbia | 29 | 1 | 3 | 10 | 15 |
| Total Eastern States | 2,342 | 19 | 110 | 487 | 1,726 |
| Virginia | 224 | 3 | 7 | 35 | 179 |
| West Virginia | 156 | | 5 | 28 | 123 |
| North Carolina | 119 | 2 | 6 | 25 | 86 |
| South Carolina | 104 | 1 | 1 | 19 | 83 |
| Georgia | 158 | 1 | 10 | 50 | 97 |
| Florida | 91 | | 13 | 16 | 62 |
| Alabama | 153 | | 9 | 37 | 107 |
| Mississippi | 61 | | 2 | 27 | 32 |
| Louisiana | 80 | 2 | 8 | 36 | 34 |
| Texas | 880 | 6 | 44 | 273 | 557 |
| Arkansas | 111 | 1 | 8 | 18 | 84 |
| Kentucky | 222 | 5 | 6 | 75 | 136 |
| Tennessee | 178 | 1 | 8 | 68 | 101 |
| Total Southern States | 2,537 | 22 | 127 | 707 | 1,681 |

*Number of national banks organized, consolidated under act of November 7, 1918, insolvent, in voluntary liquidation, and in operation on June 30, 1922—Continued.*

| State. | Organized. | Consolidated under act Nov. 7, 1918. | Insolvent. | In liquidation. | In operation. |
|---|---|---|---|---|---|
| Ohio | 624 | 4 | 32 | 215 | 373 |
| Indiana | 390 | 5 | 17 | 117 | 251 |
| Illinois | 675 | 1 | 22 | 150 | 502 |
| Michigan | 245 | 1 | 16 | 109 | 119 |
| Wisconsin | 226 | 2 | 6 | 63 | 155 |
| Minnesota | 419 | 2 | 10 | 63 | 344 |
| Iowa | 482 | 2 | 18 | 112 | 350 |
| Missouri | 249 | 4 | 12 | 98 | 135 |
| Total Middle Western States | 3,310 | 21 | 133 | 927 | 2,229 |
| North Dakota | 230 | .......... | 18 | 30 | 182 |
| South Dakota | 183 | .......... | 14 | 35 | 134 |
| Nebraska | 338 | .......... | 26 | 129 | 183 |
| Kansas | 419 | 2 | 37 | 111 | 269 |
| Montana | 182 | 2 | 18 | 28 | 134 |
| Wyoming | 55 | .......... | 2 | 6 | 47 |
| Colorado | 198 | .......... | 13 | 42 | 143 |
| New Mexico | 71 | .......... | 5 | 19 | 47 |
| Oklahoma | 674 | 1 | 12 | 214 | 447 |
| Total Western States | 2,350 | 5 | 145 | 614 | 1,586 |
| Washington | 186 | 1 | 24 | 53 | 108 |
| Oregon | 128 | .......... | 9 | 22 | 97 |
| California | 411 | 8 | 13 | 90 | 300 |
| Idaho | 103 | .......... | 9 | 15 | 79 |
| Utah | 38 | .......... | 3 | 11 | 24 |
| Nevada | 16 | .......... | 2 | 3 | 11 |
| Arizona | 28 | .......... | 1 | 5 | 22 |
| Total Pacific States | 910 | 9 | 61 | 199 | 641 |
| Alaska | 4 | .......... | .......... | 1 | 3 |
| Hawaii | 6 | .......... | .......... | 4 | 2 |
| Porto Rico | 1 | .......... | .......... | 1 | .......... |
| Total foreign possessions | 11 | .......... | .......... | 6 | 5 |
| Total United States | 12,230 | 79 | 608 | 3,269 | 8,274 |

The following comparative statement of the principal items of resources and liabilities of all reporting national banks in the United States on June 30, 1921, and on June 30, 1922, shows that while the total resources of these banks increased during the year $188,148,000, loans and discounts (including rediscounts) decreased $756,301,000 and customers' liability on account of acceptances decreased $62,049,000; and while lawful reserve with the Federal reserve banks increased $111,400,000, cash in vault decreased $48,168,000. These differences were offset mainly by increased investments in United States and other bonds, securities, etc., and by increased balances due from other banks, exchanges for clearing houses, and other cash items.

The increase of 95 reporting national banks between the two dates, together with the number of banks increasing their capital stock above the limit fixed in the original articles of association, account for the increase of $33,336,000 in the amount of capital stock. The surplus fund increased $22,550,000, while undivided profits show a slight reduction.

The liability of national banks on account of circulating notes outstanding June 30, 1922, was $725,748,000, which is the greatest on record, with the exception of the period when emergency currency was issued in 1914 and 1915, and is $21,601,000 greater than in 1921.

Time deposits, including postal-savings deposits, amounted to $4,111,951,000 on June 30, 1922, which is a record mark for this class of deposits held by national banks and exceeds the amount reported June 30, 1921, by $416,145,000. All other classes of deposits, with the exception of United States deposits, which showed a reduction of $145,665,000, increased materially during the year. The increase in all classes of deposits was $1,178,233,000.

Acceptance liability of national banks decreased $61,544,000; bills payable, $364,082,000; and rediscounts, $599,145,000.

*Statement of the principal items of resources and liabilities of national banks June 30, 1922, compared with June 30, 1921.*

[In thousands of dollars.]

| | June 30, 1922—8,249 banks.[1] | June 30, 1921—8,154 banks. | Increase— 95 banks. | Decrease. |
|---|---|---|---|---|
| RESOURCES. | | | | |
| Loans and discounts (including rediscounts) | 11,248,214 | 12,004,515 | | 756,301 |
| Overdrafts | 9,198 | 9,970 | | 772 |
| Customers' liability account of acceptances | 176,238 | 238,287 | | 62,049 |
| United States Government securities owned | 2,285,459 | 2,019,497 | 265,962 | |
| Other bonds, stocks, securities, etc | 2,277,866 | 2,005,584 | 272,282 | |
| Banking house, furniture and fixtures, and other real estate owned | 516,817 | 462,134 | 54,683 | |
| Lawful reserve with Federal reserve bank | 1,151,605 | 1,040,205 | 111,400 | |
| Items with Federal reserve bank in process of collection | 355,666 | 328,002 | 27,664 | |
| Amount due from all other banks | 1,242,025 | 1,016,517 | 225,508 | |
| Exchanges for clearing house, checks and other cash items | 895,418 | 777,809 | 117,609 | |
| Cash in vault | 326,181 | 374,349 | | 48,168 |
| Other assets | 221,323 | 240,993 | | 19,670 |
| Total resources | 20,706,010 | 20,517,862 | 188,148 | |
| LIABILITIES. | | | | |
| Capital stock paid in | 1,307,216 | 1,273,880 | 33,336 | |
| Surplus fund | 1,048,806 | 1,026,256 | 22,550 | |
| Undivided profits, less expenses and taxes paid | 492,434 | 496,155 | | 3,721 |
| National bank notes outstanding | 725,748 | 704,147 | 21,601 | |
| Due to Federal reserve banks | 19,852 | 18,678 | 1,174 | |
| Amount due to all other banks | 2,482,199 | 2,132,333 | 349,866 | |
| Certified checks and cashiers' checks | 450,773 | 336,650 | 114,123 | |
| Demand deposits | 9,152,415 | 8,709,825 | 442,590 | |
| Time deposits (including postal savings) | 4,111,951 | 3,695,806 | 416,145 | |
| United States deposits | 103,374 | 249,039 | | 145,665 |
| Total deposits | 16,320,664 | 15,142,331 | 1,178,233 | |
| United States Government and other securities borrowed | 45,372 | 103,154 | | 57,782 |
| Bills payable (including all obligations representing borrowed money other than rediscounts) | 228,481 | 592,563 | | 364,082 |
| Notes and bills rediscounted (including acceptances of other banks and foreign bills of exchange or drafts sold with indorsement) | 280,271 | 879,416 | | 599,145 |
| Letters of credit and travelers' checks outstanding | 8,256 | 6,188 | 2,068 | |
| Acceptances | 189,381 | 250,925 | | 61,544 |
| Other liabilities | 59,481 | 42,847 | 16,634 | |
| Total liabilities | 20,706,010 | 20,517,862 | 188,148 | |

[1] Does not include 13 new banks not open for business. 6 banks temporarily suspended; and 6 banks liquidating or consolidating which had sold or transferred their assets, but not formally closed.

## Banks other than national.

The following table gives the principal resources and liabilities of banks other than national on June 30, 1922, as compared with June 30, 1921. During the year there was a decrease of 518 in the number of reporting State (commercial), savings, and private banks and loan and trust companies. Aggregate resources of these banks, however, increased $565,829,000 or 1.94 per cent.

*Principal resources and liabilities of banks other than national, June 30, 1922, compared with June 30, 1921.*

[In thousands of dollars.]

| | June 30, 1922, 22,140 banks. | June 30, 1921, 22,658 banks. | Increase. | Decrease 518 banks. |
|---|---|---|---|---|
| **RESOURCES.** | | | | |
| Loans and discounts (including rediscounts) | 16,435,991 | 16,689,209 | ............ | 253,218 |
| Overdrafts | 65,402 | 71,879 | ............ | 6,477 |
| Investments (including premiums on bonds) | 7,984,242 | 7,356,842 | 627,400 | ............ |
| Banking house (including furniture and fixtures) | 625,740 | 583,506 | 42,234 | ............ |
| Other real estate owned | 134,074 | 101,881 | 32,193 | ............ |
| Due from banks | 1,475,753 | 1,388,819 | 86,934 | ............ |
| Lawful reserve with Federal reserve bank or other reserve agents | 1,189,192 | 1,020,662 | 168,530 | ............ |
| Checks and other cash items | 515,692 | 119,444 | 396,248 | ............ |
| Exchanges for clearing house | 163,498 | 393,414 | ............ | 229,916 |
| Cash on hand | 503,711 | 572,218 | ............ | 68,507 |
| Other resources | 626,062 | 855,654 | ............ | 229,592 |
| Total resources | 29,719,357 | 29,153,528 | 565,829 | ............ |
| **LIABILITIES.** | | | | |
| Capital stock paid in | 1,636,734 | 1,630,081 | 6,653 | ............ |
| Surplus | 1,648,603 | 1,515,776 | 132,827 | ............ |
| Undivided profits (less expenses and taxes paid) | 441,409 | 414,588 | 26,821 | ............ |
| Due to all banks | 742,335 | 658,403 | 83,932 | ............ |
| Certified checks and cashiers' checks | 101,732 | 277,933 | ............ | 176,201 |
| Individual deposits (including dividends unpaid and postal savings) | 23,929,952 | 22,438,941 | 1,491,011 | ............ |
| United States deposits (exclusive of postal savings) | 25,513 | 141,191 | ............ | 115,678 |
| Notes and bills rediscounted | 155,440 | 392,268 | ............ | 236,828 |
| Bills payable | 407,083 | 783,028 | ............ | 375,945 |
| Other liabilities | 630,556 | 901,319 | ............ | 270,763 |
| Total liabilities | 29,719,357 | 29,153,528 | 565,829 | ............ |

## All reporting banks.

[National, State (commercial), savings, and private banks and loan and trust companies.]

The changes in the principal resources and liabilities of all reporting banks as of June 30, 1922, compared with June 30, 1921, are shown in the following statement. Investments increased 10.24 per cent, while loans decreased 3.70 per cent, and cash decreased 12.33 per cent. The net increase in total assets was 1.52 per cent. Individual deposits increased 6.74 per cent; rediscounts decreased 65.74 per cent, and bills payable decreased 53.80 per cent.

*Principal resources and liabilities of all reporting banks in the United States and island possessions June 30, 1922, compared with June 30, 1921.*

[In thousands of dollars.]

| | June 30, 1922, 30,389 banks. | June 30, 1921, 30,812 banks. | Increase. | Decrease, 423 banks. |
|---|---|---|---|---|
| **RESOURCES.** | | | | |
| Loans and discounts (including rediscounts)........... | 27,860,443 | 28,932,011 | ........... | 1,071,568 |
| Overdrafts........................................... | 74,600 | 81,849 | ........... | 7,249 |
| Investments (including premiums on bonds)........... | 12,547,567 | 11,381,923 | 1,165,644 | ........... |
| Banking house (including furniture and fixtures)....... | 1,078,174 | 993,898 | 84,377 | ........... |
| Other real estate owned............................. | 198,457 | 153,623 | 44,834 | ........... |
| Due from banks..................................... | 3,073,444 | 2,733,338 | 340,106 | ........... |
| Lawful reserve with Federal reserve bank or other reserve agents....................................... | 2,340,797 | 2,060,867 | 279,930 | ........... |
| Checks and other cash items.......................... | 644,014 | 241,160 | 402,854 | ........... |
| Exchanges for clearing house......................... | 930,594 | 1,049,507 | ........... | 118,913 |
| Cash on hand........................................ | 829,892 | 946,567 | ........... | 116,675 |
| Other resources...................................... | 847,385 | 1,096,647 | ........... | 249,262 |
| Total resources................................ | 50,425,367 | 49,671,390 | 753,977 | ........... |
| **LIABILITIES.** | | | | |
| Capital stock paid in................................ | 2,943,950 | 2,903,961 | 39,989 | ........... |
| Surplus............................................. | 2,697,409 | 2,542,032 | 155,377 | ........... |
| Undivided profits (less expenses and taxes paid)........ | 933,843 | 910,743 | 23,100 | ........... |
| National bank circulation............................ | 725,748 | 704,147 | 21,601 | ........... |
| Due to all banks.................................... | 3,244,386 | 2,809,414 | 434,972 | ........... |
| Certified checks and cashiers' checks.................. | 552,505 | 614,583 | ........... | 62,078 |
| Individual deposits (including dividends unpaid and postal savings)..................................... | 37,194,318 | 34,844,572 | 2,349,746 | ........... |
| United States deposits (exclusive of postal savings)..... | 128,887 | 390,230 | ........... | 261,343 |
| Notes and bills rediscounted.......................... | 435,711 | 1,271,684 | ........... | 835,973 |
| Bills payable........................................ | 635,564 | 1,375,591 | ........... | 740,027 |
| Other liabilities..................................... | 933,046 | 1,304,433 | ........... | 371,387 |
| Total liabilities............................... | 50,425,367 | 49,671,390 | 753,977 | ........... |

The following statement shows the number, capital, and aggregate assets of reporting national banks and of all reporting national, State, savings, and private banks and loan and trust companies in each State as of June 30, 1922.

*Number, capital, and assets of national banks and all reporting banks on June 30, 1922.*

| State. | National banks.[1] | | | All banks, including national banks. | | |
|---|---|---|---|---|---|---|
| | Number of banks. | Capital (000 omitted). | Aggregate assets (000 omitted). | Number of banks. | Capital (000 omitted). | Aggregate assets (000 omitted). |
| Maine................................. | 60 | $7,045 | $113,386 | 158 | $12,210 | $372,640 |
| New Hampshire........................ | 56 | 5,365 | 62,229 | 126 | 7,473 | 231,388 |
| Vermont.............................. | 49 | 5,410 | 54,983 | 108 | 7,926 | 198,321 |
| Massachusetts......................... | 159 | 63,517 | 1,025,910 | 459 | 105,185 | 3,224,654 |
| Rhode Island......................... | 17 | 5,570 | 66,753 | 46 | 15,180 | 416,858 |
| Connecticut........................... | 64 | 21,607 | 225,500 | 221 | 35,242 | 879,896 |
| Total New England States............ | 405 | 108,514 | 1,548,761 | 1,118 | 183,216 | 5,323,757 |
| New York............................. | 507 | 233,477 | 5,170,198 | 1,084 | 453,491 | 13,254,296 |
| New Jersey........................... | 228 | 29,449 | 593,968 | 434 | 66,349 | 1,546,811 |
| Pennsylvania.......................... | 866 | 134,749 | 2,426,341 | 1,620 | 281,798 | 4,658,719 |
| Delaware............................. | 18 | 1,660 | 21,067 | 57 | 7,104 | 102,107 |
| Maryland............................. | 87 | 18,429 | 264,712 | 247 | 37,993 | 717,675 |
| District of Columbia.................. | 15 | 7,677 | 118,249 | 50 | 21,614 | 233,283 |
| Total Eastern States................ | 1,721 | 425,441 | 8,594,535 | 3,492 | 868,349 | 20,512,881 |

*Number, capital, and assets of national banks and all reporting banks on June 30, 1922—*
Continued.

| State. | National banks.[1] | | | All banks, including national banks. | | |
|---|---|---|---|---|---|---|
| | Number of banks. | Capital (000 omitted). | Aggregate assets (000 omitted). | Number of banks. | Capital (000 omitted). | Aggregate assets (000 omitted). |
| Virginia | 179 | $28,643 | $368,275 | 509 | $52,563 | $553,502 |
| West Virginia | 122 | 12,002 | 179,884 | 347 | 29,932 | 391,822 |
| North Carolina | 86 | 13,290 | 163,561 | 582 | 36,862 | 407,127 |
| South Carolina | 82 | 12,140 | 120,681 | 454 | 29,440 | 269,730 |
| Georgia | 97 | 14,798 | 167,740 | 686 | 47,785 | 420,582 |
| Florida | 62 | 7,795 | 130,566 | 280 | 18,045 | 242,460 |
| Alabama | 107 | 12,840 | 132,427 | 356 | 24,329 | 244,156 |
| Mississippi | 32 | 4,535 | 54,270 | 351 | 17,000 | 201,197 |
| Louisiana | 34 | 8,700 | 115,037 | 264 | 31,687 | 428,016 |
| Texas | 555 | 68,192 | 730,617 | 1,563 | 113,914 | 1,046,966 |
| Arkansas | 84 | 7,548 | 74,726 | 486 | 23,825 | 220,424 |
| Kentucky | 136 | 17,858 | 233,807 | 601 | 39,446 | 460,502 |
| Tennessee | 101 | 15,409 | 192,183 | 571 | 38,188 | 420,284 |
| Total Southern States | 1,677 | 223,840 | 2,663,774 | 7,050 | 503,016 | 5,306,768 |
| Ohio | 373 | 63,150 | 857,476 | 1,123 | 160,363 | 2,339,181 |
| Indiana | 251 | 30,713 | 379,251 | 1,094 | 75,362 | 922,486 |
| Illinois | 500 | 90,615 | 1,448,300 | 1,906 | 233,027 | 3,491,527 |
| Michigan | 119 | 23,075 | 404,301 | 745 | 86,559 | 1,416,774 |
| Wisconsin | 155 | 24,885 | 346,906 | 1,002 | 59,613 | 833,076 |
| Minnesota | 343 | 37,901 | 565,089 | 1,517 | 73,506 | 1,080,641 |
| Iowa | 349 | 26,025 | 363,828 | 1,772 | 83,704 | 1,126,086 |
| Missouri | 135 | 42,800 | 528,797 | 1,651 | 115,351 | 1,380,562 |
| Total Middle Western States | 2,225 | 339,164 | 4,893,948 | 10,810 | 887,485 | 12,590,333 |
| North Dakota | 182 | 7,220 | 93,865 | 846 | 18,527 | 222,773 |
| South Dakota | 133 | 6,215 | 95,538 | 695 | 19,195 | 285,673 |
| Nebraska | 183 | 17,345 | 246,127 | 1,153 | 42,600 | 534,648 |
| Kansas | 267 | 17,847 | 226,201 | 1,364 | 46,388 | 533,386 |
| Montana | 132 | 8,115 | 92,682 | 400 | 19,710 | 197,631 |
| Wyoming | 47 | 3,195 | 56,022 | 146 | 6,148 | 82,765 |
| Colorado | 143 | 12,275 | 226,847 | 381 | 21,842 | 335,207 |
| New Mexico | 47 | 3,285 | 42,579 | 110 | 6,135 | 65,231 |
| Oklahoma | 447 | 28,810 | 377,713 | 933 | 38,610 | 479,073 |
| Total Western States | 1,581 | 104,307 | 1,457,574 | 6,028 | 219,155 | 2,736,387 |
| Washington | 108 | 16,030 | 255,421 | 392 | 29,477 | 412,336 |
| Oregon | 96 | 11,315 | 165,029 | 277 | 20,844 | 281,085 |
| California | 295 | 65,125 | 956,900 | 724 | 165,190 | 2,614,840 |
| Idaho | 79 | 5,240 | 65,704 | 198 | 9,425 | 106,610 |
| Utah | 24 | 4,130 | 49,045 | 121 | 11,998 | 138,765 |
| Nevada | 11 | 1,460 | 16,389 | 35 | 3,221 | 38,031 |
| Arizona | 22 | 1,900 | 30,788 | 80 | 6,460 | 85,720 |
| Total Pacific States | 635 | 105,200 | 1,539,276 | 1,827 | 246,615 | 3,677,387 |
| Alaska | 3 | 150 | 2,169 | 18 | 805 | 8,833 |
| Hawaii | 2 | 600 | 5,973 | 18 | 5,221 | 62,209 |
| Porto Rico | | | | 17 | 5,750 | 38,118 |
| Philippine Islands | | | | 11 | 24,338 | 168,694 |
| Total foreign possessions | 5 | 750 | 8,142 | 64 | 36,114 | 277,854 |
| Total United States | 8,249 | 1,307,216 | 20,706,010 | 30,389 | 2,943,950 | 50,425,367 |

[1] Exclusive of 25 nonreporting national banks.

*Comparative statement showing the number of banks, loans, lawful reserve, total deposits, and aggregate resources of all reporting banks in the United States on dates nearest to June 30 for the years 1921 and 1922.*

### STATE, SAVINGS, AND PRIVATE BANKS, AND LOAN AND TRUST COMPANIES.

[In thousands of dollars.]

| Year. | Number of banks. | Loans.[1] | Reserve held.[2] | Total deposits.[3] | Aggregate resources.[1] |
|---|---|---|---|---|---|
| 1922........................................ | 22,140 | 16,435,991 | 1,692,903 | 24,799,532 | 29,719,357 |
| 1921........................................ | 22,658 | 16,689,209 | 1,592,880 | 23,516,468 | 29,153,528 |
| Decrease............................... | 518 | 253,218 | ............ | ............ | ............ |
| Increase............................... | ............ | ............ | 100,023 | 1,283,064 | 565,829 |
| Per cent of increase..................... | ............ | ............ | 6.28 | 5.46 | 1.94 |
| Per cent of decrease..................... | 2.29 | 1.52 | ............ | ............ | ............ |

Per cent of lawful reserve [2] to total deposits: [3]

1922.............................................................................................................................. 6.82
1921.............................................................................................................................. 6.77

### NATIONAL BANKS.

| | | | | | |
|---|---|---|---|---|---|
| 1922........................................ | 8,249 | 11,424,452 | 1,151,605 | 16,320,564 | 20,706,010 |
| 1921........................................ | 8,154 | 12,242,802 | 1,040,205 | 15,142,331 | 20,517,862 |
| Decrease............................... | ............ | 818,350 | ............ | ............ | ............ |
| Increase............................... | 95 | ............ | 111,400 | 1,178,233 | 188,148 |
| Per cent of increase..................... | 1.17 | ............ | 10.71 | 7.78 | 0.92 |
| Per cent of decrease..................... | ............ | 6.68 | ............ | ............ | ............ |

Per cent of lawful reserve [2] to total deposits: [3]

1922.............................................................................................................................. 7.06
1921.............................................................................................................................. 6.87

### TOTAL NATIONAL, STATE, SAVINGS, AND PRIVATE BANKS AND LOAN AND TRUST COMPANIES.

| | | | | | |
|---|---|---|---|---|---|
| 1922........................................ | 30,389 | 27,860,443 | 2,844,508 | 41,120,096 | 50,425,367 |
| 1921........................................ | 30,812 | 28,932,011 | 2,633,085 | 38,658,799 | 49,671,390 |
| Decrease............................... | 423 | 1,071,568 | ............ | ............ | ............ |
| Increase............................... | ............ | ............ | 211,423 | 2,461,297 | 753,977 |
| Per cent of increase..................... | ............ | ............ | 8.03 | 6.37 | 1.52 |
| Per cent of decrease..................... | 1.37 | 3.70 | ............ | ............ | ............ |

Per cent of lawful reserve [2] to total deposits: [3]

1922.............................................................................................................................. 6.92
1921.............................................................................................................................. 6.81

[1] Includes rediscounts and customers' liability account of acceptances of national banks.
[2] For national banks this includes only the amount of reserve with Federal reserve banks, but for banks other than national, includes cash in vault, balances due from Federal reserve banks to State banks and trust companies, members of Federal reserve system, and other reserve banks or reserve agents.
[3] Includes amounts due to all banks, cashiers' checks and certified checks outstanding, individual demand and time, postal savings, and United States deposits.

*Comparative statement of growth in resources of national and State banking institutions for 5-year period.*

Resources national banks:

| | |
|---|---:|
| June 30, 1922 | $20,706,010,000 |
| June 30, 1917 | 16,290,406,000 |
| Increase (27.11 per cent) | 4,415,604,000 |

Resources State banking institutions:

| | |
|---|---:|
| June 30, 1922 | 29,719,357,000 |
| June 30, 1917 | 20,836,357,000 |
| Increase (42.63 per cent) | 8,883,000,000 |

## MINT SERVICE.

### Institutions of the Mint Service.

The following institutions of the Mint Service continued operations during the fiscal year ended June 30, 1922: Coinage mints at Philadelphia, San Francisco, and Denver; assay office at New York; mints at New Orleans and Carson City conducted as assay offices; and assay offices at Seattle, Boise, Helena, Salt Lake City, and Deadwood. The seven last-named institutions are, in effect, bullion purchasing agencies for the large institutions, and also serve the public by making, at nominal charge, assays of ores and bullion. Electrolytic refineries are operated at the New York and San Francisco institutions.

### Coin demand.

The coinage of gold was resumed during the past fiscal year, and nearly $53,000,000 in value was executed. Over 92,000,000 standard silver dollars were coined during the year from bullion purchased under the terms of the Pittman Act, practically all of these dollars going into storage and being represented in circulation by silver certificates issued against them, in place of Federal reserve bank notes retired. Of coins below the dollar but few were executed during the past year, those struck being confined to memorial half dollars and a small number of nickel and bronze coins for cleaning up partially completed lots. Approximately 12,000,000 pieces of coin were executed for foreign Governments, making the year's aggregate number of pieces executed by the three mints 117,912,205. Working periods of 16 hours and 24 hours per day were again a feature of the year's operations, incident to the effort to reduce the "dead" stock of Pittman silver bullion to an active asset in the form of silver dollars, against which silver certificates could be issued. Silver bullion can not be circulated as cash, nor is it available as a reserve against paper currency or other liabilities. While operating on a 24-hour basis the aggregate output reached 1,000,000 silver dollars per day—500,000 at the Philadelphia Mint, 280,000 at San Francisco, and 220,000 at Denver.

### Gold operations.

Gold receipts at the New York assay office, principally of imported refined bars, totaled some $480,000,000 during the fiscal year under review, as compared with $562,000,000 during the preceding year. The value of all gold acquired by the Government at the mints and assay offices during the fiscal year 1922, including the $480,000,000 mentioned above, was $540,629,997.69; United States coin received for recoinage amounted to $2,491,089.03; and transfers of gold between mint offices totaled $3,574,397.44; giving an aggregate of gold handled by the mint service during the fiscal year 1922 of $546,695,484.16.

### Silver operations.

Receipts of purchased silver were again very large; the total reached 54,566,332.02 ounces, including 52,671,710.05 ounces of Pittman Act silver costing $1 per ounce. The average cost of other purchased silver was $0.658 — per fine ounce, its total cost being $1,248,555.24. Silver received in exchange for bars bearing the Government stamp totaled 6,249,499.19 fine ounces; United States silver coin received for recoinage totaled 1,734,695.72 fine ounces, with a recoinage value of $2,398,058.70; silver deposited in trust by other Governments totaled 5,760,742.21 fine ounces; and transfers of silver between mint service offices totaled 652,533.92 fine ounces, making an aggregate quantity of silver handled by the mint service during the fiscal year 1922 of 68,963,803.06 fine ounces.

Silver purchased under the terms of the Pittman Act and delivered to mint institutions amounted to 117,512,000 ounces on June 30, 1922. Of the amount purchased 86,196,979 ounces have been coined into 111,431,473 standard silver dollars, of which 86,730,000 are of the old design. Purchases under the Pittman Act during the two years since they were begun in May, 1920, have totaled somewhat more than the quantity of silver produced from domestic mines during the same period. This is due to the working up of considerable stocks of crude domestic material, shown by sworn reports of reduction concerns to have been on hand at the time purchases were commenced. The New York price of silver which does not meet Pittman Act requirements averaged during the fiscal year ended June 30, 1922, $0.66821; the lowest New York price was at the opening of the fiscal year, 59½ cents; the highest, on May 22, 1922, 74$\frac{3}{16}$ cents.

### Refineries.

Considerably increased production of electrolytically refined gold, and reduction in silver, featured the refinery work of the past year.

*New coin designs.*

Four new coins were issued during the past year.

The "peace dollar" commemorates the declaration of peace between the United States and Germany and Austria, and takes the place of the old design of the standard silver dollar which was first issued in 1878. Exchanges of peace treaty ratifications had been made in Berlin on November 11, 1921, and in Vienna on November 8, 1921, and peace was proclaimed by the President of the United States on November 14 and 17, 1921, respectively. No special congressional authority was required for this change in design of the silver dollar, since the law permits changing the design of any of our coins once in 25 years, but not oftener. The design of the "peace dollar" was selected by the Fine Arts Commission from models submitted by a number of prominent sculptors, and is the work of Anthony de Francisci. On the obverse is a female head emblematic of Liberty, wearing a tiara of light rays, and the word "liberty"; on the reverse is an eagle perched on a mountain top, holding in its talons an olive branch, witnessing the dawn of a new day; the word "peace" also appears. Other mottoes and inscriptions are as required by the coinage laws. The design for the silver "peace dollar" was approved in December, 1921, and 1,006,473 pieces were executed by the close of the calendar year. Subsequent coins of this design will bear the year in which made. At the close of the fiscal year, 24,701,473 of the new coins had been struck.

The Alabama centennial half dollar bears on one side portraits of the first governor of Alabama and of the present governor of the State, also 22 stars indicative of the twenty-second State of the Union; the reverse is an adaptation of the seal of the State, an eagle standing on the shield, holding arrows in its talons, with the motto "Here We Rest," and the dates "1819–1919."

The Ulysses S. Grant memorial half dollar bears on one side a strong profile portrait of General Grant and on the other side a sketch of the historical log cabin in which he was born. The same design appears on the Ulysses S. Grant memorial gold dollar.

*Coinage.*

The amount of domestic coinage during the fiscal year 1922 was $145,712,742, classified as follows:

Gold:
    Double eagles.................................................... $52, 990, 000. 00
    Grant memorial dollars........................................ 10, 016. 00
Silver:
    Dollars—old design............................................. 67, 687, 000. 00
    Dollars—"peace" design ...................................... 24, 701, 473. 00

Silver—Continued.

Half dollars:

| | |
|---|---|
| Pilgrim tercentennial | $50,026.50 |
| Missouri centennial | 25,014.00 |
| Alabama centennial | 35,022.00 |
| Grant memorial | 50,030.50 |

Minor:

| | |
|---|---|
| Nickel 5 cent | 72,350.00 |
| Bronze 1 cent | 91,810.00 |
| Total | 145,712,742.00 |

The coinage other than domestic, totaling 11,916,030 pieces, included, at the Philadelphia Mint, 16,030 gold pieces for Costa Rica, 3,900,000 silver pieces for Venezuela, and 3,000,000 silver pieces for Colombia; at the San Francisco Mint, 5,000,000 silver pieces for Indo-China.

### Stock of coin and bullion in the United States.

On June 30, 1922, the estimated stock of domestic coin in the United States was $1,515,774,608, of which $863,389,318 was gold, $381,174,404 silver dollars, and $271,210,886 subsidiary silver coin.

The stock of gold bullion in the mints and assay offices on the same date was valued at $2,850,230,389.14, a gain over last year of $441,548,342.54, and the stock of silver bullion was 44,334,061.59 fine ounces, a decrease, as compared with last year, of 15,412,137.20 ounces.

### Production of gold and silver.

The production of gold and silver in the United States during the calendar year 1921 was as follows: Gold, $50,067,300, a reduction from last year of $1,119,600, and silver, 53,052,441 fine ounces, a reduction from last year of 2,309,132 ounces.

### Industrial arts.

The amount of gold consumed in the industrial arts during the calendar year 1921 was $50,674,270, of which $23,050,332 was new material. Silver consumed amounted to 35,867,946 fine ounces, of which 28,843,628 fine ounces were new material.

### Imports of gold coin.

Net imports of United States gold coin for the fiscal year ended June 30, 1922, were $1,774,498.

### Appropriations, expenses, and income.

Appropriations available for Mint Service use during the fiscal year 1922 totaled $1,791,527.65, and reimbursements to appropriations for services rendered were $548,407.20, making an available total of $2,339,934.85.

Total expenses during the year were $2,074,606.10, of which $2,070,-485.21 was chargeable to appropriations and $4,120.89 to income. The income realized by the Treasury from the Mint Service totaled $22,189,212.69, of which $21,088,524.79 was seigniorage. It should be noted, however, that the seigniorage on the coinage of silver dollars, which amounted to $20,919,928.83 for the fiscal year 1922, merely offsets an equal loss which was incurred when silver dollars were melted and sold under the terms of the Pittman Act.

Detailed figures for income and expenditures during the fiscal year 1922 are shown in the following tables:

INCOME.

Earnings
Credited to appropriations—

| | | |
|---|---|---|
| Charges on foreign coinage executed | $119,728.75 | |
| Silver dollar coinage costs, from special fund | 392,238.15 | |
| Charges for manufacture of special medals | 13,787.37 | |
| Charges for work done for other institutions, etc | 22,652.93 | |
| Total earnings credited to appropriations | | $548,407.20 |

Credited to revenues—

| | | |
|---|---|---|
| Mint charges on bullion | 404,652.33 | |
| Proceeds of medals sold | 3,926.52 | |
| Receipts from special assays of bullion and ores | 3,528.80 | |
| Total earnings credited to revenues | | 412,107.65 |
| Total earnings | | $960,514.85 |

Profits:

| | | |
|---|---|---|
| Gain on bullion shipments to refineries | $178.89 | |
| Less contra losses | .13 | |
| | 178.76 | |
| Surplus bullion recovered | 87,765.28 | |
| Proceeds of sale of by-products (platinum, etc.) | 49,993.68 | |
| Proceeds of sale of old materials | 2,067.02 | |
| Commission on telephone calls | 168.31 | |
| Total profits other than seigniorage | | 140,173.05 |
| Seigniorage on silver dollar coinage | 20,919,928.83 | |
| Seigniorage on subsidiary silver coinage | 40,661.82 | |
| Seigniorage on minor coinage— | | |
| Nickel | 63,047.68 | |
| Bronze | 64,886.46 | |
| Total seigniorage | | 21,088,524.79 |
| Total profits | | 21,228,697.84 |
| Total income | | 22,189,212.69 |

14263—FI 1922——26

Chargeable to appropriations:
Compensation of employees—
Mint Bureau, salaries appropriation .........   $22,626.37
Mint Bureau, increase of compensation appropriation................................   2,640.00
Mints and assay offices, salaries appropriations.   226,296.83
Mints and assay offices, wages appropriations..   1,145,580.86
Mints and assay offices, increase of compensation appropriation..........................   190,753.98

Total compensation of employees....................... $1,587,898.04
Equipment, stores, and other expenses—
Mint Bureau, contingent appropriation........   6,155.17
Mints and assay offices, contingent and permanent appropriations (including $13,624.56 wastage of gold and silver in operative departments and $6,592.97 loss on assay value of sweeps sold) ...........................   474,167.24
Transportation of bullion and coin between mints and assay offices, freight appropriation.........   2,264.76

Total miscellaneous expenses chargeable to appropriations..   482,587.17

Total expenses chargeable to appropriations..............   2,070,485.21
Chargeable to revenue:
Seigniorage on minor coinage—
Expense of distributing minor coin to Treasury offices................................   3,998.54
Wastage of minor metals in operative departments...................................   122.35

Total chargeable to revenue...........................   4,120.89.

Total expenses.......................................   2,074,606.10
Net income of the Government from the Mint Service..............   20,114,606.59

Total.......................................................   22,189,212.69

*Deposits, income, expenses, and employees, by institutions, fiscal year 1922.*

The number and value of deposits, the income (including seigniorage), the expenses of the fiscal year 1922, and the number of employees on June 30, 1922, at each institution, are shown in the following table:

| Institution. | Deposits. | Mint Service transfers. | United States coining value of gold and silver receipts. | Income.[1] | Expenses from appropriations.[2] | Transportation of bullion and coin. | Employees June 30, 1922. |
|---|---|---|---|---|---|---|---|
| Philadelphia........... | 28,331 | 714 | $37,589,721.82 | $11,657,758.59 | $897,963.09 | $590.17 | 356 |
| San Francisco......... | 23,449 | 3,327 | 84,181,271.59 | 4,969,217.70 | 431,331.42 | 180.64 | 149 |
| Denver............... | 14,095 | 6 | 24,933,115.87 | 4,675,818.28 | 298,768.16 | 69.09 | 82 |
| New York............ | 18,748 | ........ | 481,286,684.30 | 331,321.46 | 345,875.25 | .......... | 125 |
| New Orleans.......... | 456 | ........ | 652,022.83 | 1,103.57 | 11,571.74 | .......... | 6 |
| Carson City.......... | 241 | ........ | 61,009.29 | 454.15 | 4,461.16 | 9.78 | 3 |
| Boise................ | 527 | ........ | 340,157.01 | 1,292.06 | 6,559.59 | 94.66 | 4 |
| Helena............... | 357 | ........ | 99,211.65 | 437.65 | 6,383.13 | 34.60 | 3 |
| Deadwood............ | 10 | ........ | 3,286.49 | 566.00 | 5,557.31 | 7.91 | 3 |
| Seattle............... | 1,302 | ........ | 3,052,812.74 | 2,448.27 | 26,461.54 | 1,256.00 | 11 |
| Salt Lake City........ | 106 | ........ | 18,819.97 | 387.89 | 4,131.28 | 21.91 | 2 |
| Total............ | 87,622 | 4,047 | 632,218,113.56 | 21,640,805.62 | 2,039,063.67 | 2,264.76 | 744 |

[1] Does not include $548,407.20 received by the Mint Service for work performed.

[2] Includes transportation of bullion and coin between mints and assay offices. Does not include $31,421.54 Mint Bureau expenses charged against appropriations, or $4,121.02 Mint Service expenses paid from revenues.

## BUREAU OF INTERNAL REVENUE.[1]

The receipts from internal-revenue taxes for the fiscal year 1922 were as follows:

Income and profits tax..................... $2,086,918,464.85
Miscellaneous taxes......................... 1,110,532,618.15

$3,197,451,083.00

Fiscal year 1921:
    Income and profits tax.................. 3,228,137,673.75
    Miscellaneous taxes..................... 1,367,219,388.20

4,595,357,061.95

Net decrease in 1922..................................... 1,397,905,978.95

No deductions have been made in the foregoing statements of receipts on account of refunds during the fiscal year 1922, which were as follows:

Refunding taxes illegally collected, claims accrued prior to July 1, 1920................................................................. $34,539,563.19
Refunding taxes illegally collected, 1921........................... 10,768,893.50
Refunding taxes illegally collected, 1922........................... 2,825,671.14

Total....................................................... 48,134,127.83

[1] The figures concerning internal-revenue receipts as given in this statement differ from the figures carried in other Treasury statements showing the financial condition of the Government, because the former represent collections by internal-revenue officers throughout the country, including deposits by postmasters of amounts received from sale of internal-revenue stamps and deposits of internal revenue collected through customs offices, while the latter represent the deposits of these collections in the Treasury or depositaries during the fiscal year concerned, the differences being due to the fact that some of the collections in the latter part of the fiscal year can not be deposited, or are not reported to the Treasury as deposited until after June 30, thus carrying them into the following fiscal year as recorded in the statements showing the condition of the Treasury.

The following comparative statement shows in greater detail the internal-revenue receipts for the fiscal years 1921 and 1922:

| Sources. | 1921 | 1922 | Increase (+) or decrease (−). |
|---|---|---|---|
| Income and profits............................ | $3,228,137,673.75 | $2,086,918,464.85 | −$1,141,219,208.90 |
| Estates of decedents............................ | 154,043,260.39 | 139,418,846.04 | −14,624,414.35 |
| Distilled spirits and alcoholic beverages.......... | 82,623,428.83 | 45,609,436.47 | −37,013,992.36 |
| Receipts under provisions of the national prohibition act.................................... | 2,152,387.45 | 1,979,586.94 | −172,800.51 |
| Tobacco and tobacco manufactures............... | 255,219,385.49 | 270,759,384.44 | +15,539,998.95 |
| Oleomargarine, adulterated, and process or renovated butter and mixed flour................. | 3,037,442.72 | 2,154,535.24 | −882,907.48 |
| Bonds, capital stock issues, conveyances, capital stock transfers, sales of produce for future delivery, etc.... | 72,468,013.53 | [1] 58,799,485.45 | −13,668,528.08 |
| Transportation of freight, express, persons, etc., including telegraph and telephone, and oil by pipe lines.................... | 301,512,413.74 | 198,697,728.16 | −102,814,685.58 |
| Insurance (life, marine, inland, and casualty).... | 18,992,094.45 | 10,855,403.81 | −8,136,690.64 |
| Excise taxes (manufacturers'), including automobiles, motor cycles, pianos, organs, sporting goods, chewing gum, candy, articles made of fur, etc...... | 177,751,214.00 | 143,908,856.09 | −33,842,357.91 |
| Excise taxes (consumers or dealers), including sculpture and paintings; carpets, picture frames, and wearing apparel: jewelry, watches, clocks, etc.: perfumes, cosmetics, and medicinal articles; soft drinks, ice cream; etc............. | 110,271,619.59 | 63,938,485.53 | −46,333,134.06 |
| Corporations, on capital stock................... | 81,525,652.88 | 80,612,239.80 | −913,413.08 |
| Brokers, theaters, museums, bowling alleys, billiard and pool tables, shooting galleries, riding academies, passenger automobiles for hire, and use of pleasure boats, etc...................... | 8,585,540.11 | 8,662,759.89 | +77,219.78 |
| Admissions to places of amusement and entertainment, and club dues...................... | 95,890,650.63 | 80,000,589.53 | −15,890,061.10 |
| Narcotics: Opium, coca leaves, etc., including special taxes of importers, manufacturers, and dealers........................... | 1,170,291.32 | 1,269,039.90 | +98,748.58 |
| Internal revenue collected through customs offices [2]............. | 356,296.21 | 495,559.43 | +139,263.22 |
| Other miscellaneous receipts, including unidentified collections......................... | 1,619,696.86 | 3,370,681.43 | +1,750,984.57 |
| Total miscellaneous taxes.................. | 1,367,219,388.20 | 1,110,532,618.15 | −256,686,770.05 |
| Total receipts from all sources............. | 4,595,357,061.95 | 3,197,451,083.00 | −1,397,905,978.95 |

[1] Includes $14,616,958.05 from internal-revenue stamp sales by postmasters and $2,880,441.65 from playing cards.

[2] These receipts were not previously shown in the annual reports of the Internal Revenue Bureau.

### Cost of administration.

The cost of administering the internal-revenue laws for the fiscal year 1922 was $41,577,374.49. This does not include expenditures from the appropriations for refunding internal-revenue collections and for refunding taxes illegally collected which are in no sense administrative expenses but are properly deductions from the gross receipts. The cost of operation for the year on this basis was $1.30 for each $100 collected, compared with 87 cents for the preceding year. Included in these expenditures, however, was $7,202,723.07 for the administration of the prohibition and narcotic laws (of which amount $658,728.77 was for the enforcement of the narcotic law) and $88,000 for the enforcement of the child-labor section of the revenue act of 1918. Deducting these amounts from the total leaves $34,286,651.42 as the expenditure for collecting internal-revenue taxes for the fiscal year 1922, which is equivalent to a cost of $1.07 for each $100 collected. The cost of collection on a similar basis for the fiscal year 1921 was 72 cents for each $100 collected.

The difference in the relative cost of collection for the fiscal years 1921 and 1922 was due mainly to the large reduction in the revenues for 1922 incident to the shrinkage in business and incomes, the repeal of certain miscellaneous war taxes and various provisions of law such as the amortization of war time facilities and the increase in individual exemptions contained in the revenue act of 1921, with the consequent reduction in the income tax liability of corporations and individuals.

### Income and profits taxes.

During the fiscal year 954,731 income and excess profits returns were audited, of which 717,879 were individual and partnership returns and 236,852 were corporation returns. On office audits (those made without field examination) $22,736,236.26 additional tax was assessed on individual and partnership returns and $56,943,-624.71 on corporation returns, a total of $79,679,860.97.

The number of revenue agents' reports on individual and partnership returns reviewed in Washington was 24,868, and as a result $28,885,736.49 in additional tax was assessed. Corporation reports reviewed numbered 14,088, resulting in an additional assessment of $78,717,066.69, making the total additional tax assessed as the result of the audit of revenue agents' reports $107,602,803.18.

The number of claims adjusted during the year was 167,405, involving $332,479,050.60. Of these 139,631, involving $182,371,597.88 were allowed, and 27,744, involving $150,107,452.72, were rejected. During the year 135,637 claims, involving $467,829,361.91, were received.

### Committee on Appeals and Review.

' On account of the increasing volume of work, the personnel of the Committee on Appeals and Review was increased during the year from 5 to 10 members. The members of the committee give their entire time and attention to the hearing and consideration of cases that have been appealed by taxpayers and to questions upon which the advice of the committee has been requested by the commissioner or the Income Tax Unit. During the year the committee received 1,148 appeals from taxpayers and 70 requests for advice from the Income Tax Unit.

### Sales taxes.

These taxes include the taxes on telegraph, telephone, and radio messages, beverages and the constituent parts thereof, admissions and dues, automobiles, and other excise taxes. The tax collected on telegraph, telephone, and radio messages for the fiscal year 1922 was

$29,271,521.79, as compared with $28,442,412.46 for the fiscal year 1921. The tax collected on nonalcoholic beverages and the constituent parts thereof was $33,504,284.01, compared with $58,675,972.86 for the preceding fiscal year. Admission taxes amounted to $73,384,-955.61, compared with $89,730,832.94 for the fiscal year 1921. The tax on club dues was $6,615,633.92, compared with $6,159,817.69 for the fiscal year 1921. Excise taxes on sales of automobiles, pianos, sporting goods, yachts, motion picture films, candy, firearms, sculpture, jewelry, perfumes, cosmetics, and medicinal articles, etc., yielded $174,327,832.62 compared with $229,322,637.06 for the fiscal year 1921.

During the first six months of the fiscal year 1922, when the taxes imposed by the revenue act of 1918 were still in effect, an average of 366,000 returns were received monthly by the Sales Tax Unit. Since January 1, 1922, when the sections of the revenue act of 1921 administered by the Sales Tax Unit became effective, the average number of returns received monthly has been 240,000.

### Capital stock tax.

The amount of capital stock tax collected was $80,612,239.80, compared with $81,525,652.88 for the fiscal year 1921. The additional capital stock tax assessed and collected as a result of the audit for the fiscal year was $9,258,697.72, compared with $7,761,988.85 for the fiscal year 1921.

### Estate tax.

The amount of estate tax collections was $139,418,846.04, compared with $154,043,260.39 for the fiscal year 1921. The total number of estate-tax returns filed in 1922 was 13,192, showing a tax liability of $114,614,189.56. As the result of field examinations and division audits, additional taxes to the amount of $13,645,598.29 were disclosed.

On May 15, 1922, the child labor tax section of the revenue act of 1918 was declared unconstitutional by the Supreme Court of the United States⟩ The child labor tax division, formerly a part of the Estate Tax and Capital Stock Tax Unit, was thereupon abolished.

### Tobacco.

Receipts from all tobacco taxes during the fiscal year were $270,759,384.44, an increase of $15,539,998.95, or 6.09 per cent, compared with the preceding year. These receipts represent 8.46 per cent of the total internal-revenue receipts. The following seven States furnished 83.6 per cent of the total receipts from tobacco manufactures: North Carolina, $93,189,086.02; New York, $45,314,839.78; New Jersey, $23,257,628.83; Pennsylvania, $21,993,634.54; Virginia, $19,697,056.40; Ohio, $12,542,432.37; Missouri, $10,725,986.79; total, $226,720,664.73.

## Oleomargarine.

Receipts from the stamp tax on oleomargarine and the special tax imposed upon those engaged in the manufacture and sale of this product amounted to $2,121,079.68, compared with $2,986,465.35 for the preceding fiscal year, a decrease of $865,385.67. Receipts from special and stamp taxes on adulterated butter amounted to $17,871.84, compared with $34,239.96 for the fiscal year 1921, a decrease of $16,368.12, and on renovated butter to $14,416.27, compared with $15,511.56 for the preceding fiscal year, a decrease of $1,095.29.

## Mixed flour.

Receipts from the special and stamp taxes on mixed flour amounted to $1,167.45, compared with $1,225.85 for 1921, a decrease of $58.40.

## Accounts and Collections Unit.

On recommendation of the Tax Simplification Board, with the approval of the Secretary of the Treasury, the Accounts Unit and the office of the supervisor of collectors' offices were abolished, effective May 23, 1922, and the duties formerly performed in those units are now administered in a new unit known as the Accounts and Collections Unit. For purposes of effective administration the unit is divided into five divisions, the Collection Service Division, the Disbursement Division, the Office Accounts and Procedure Division, the Stamp Division, and the Field Procedure Division. Constant endeavor is being made to afford taxpayers the best possible service in the transaction of their business with the Internal Revenue Service. On June 30, 1922, there were open 183 division headquarters offices, 27 subdivision offices, and 18 offices at which stamps only were sold, in addition to 64 collectors' offices, a total of 292 offices and branch offices.

Collectors were instructed to give special attention to the serving of warrants of distraint, the verifying of returns showing additional tax due, and the conduct of delinquent drives. During the fiscal year a total of 211,635 warrants for distraint were served, which involved the collection of $9,902,306, compared with 169,409 warrants served during the fiscal year 1921; involving the collection of $7,034,335. A total of 789,384 revenue-producing investigations were made by collectors' field forces, compared with 769,065 during the previous fiscal year. The total amount collected and reported for assessment as the result of such investigations aggregated $56,791,914 in 1922, compared with $39,976,126 for the fiscal year 1921.

*Solicitor's office.*

During the fiscal year 1922, 2,000 new cases were received in the Civil Division and 841 pending cases closed. On June 30, 1922, there was a total of 2,400 pending cases, as follows: Civil cases, 1,014; bankruptcy, 1,249; receiverships, 137.

On July 1, 1922, there were pending before the Penal Division 383 cases involving alleged fraud in connection with the internal-revenue laws. Of this number criminal proceedings have been instituted in 255. Two hundred and seventy-three cases of this nature were disposed of during the year, in 126 of which criminal action had been brought.

Interpretative Division I assisted in drafting the technical provisions of the revenue act of 1921 and the income-tax provisions of the China Trade Act of 1922 and the proposed merchant marine act of 1922. It also prepared Regulations 62 and 63 under the revenue act of 1921.

Interpretative Division II assisted in the preparation and revision of Regulations 8, 40, 43, 47, 48, 52, 57, 59, 64. It also passed on over 100,000 cases.

*National prohibition.*

Collections under the penalty provisions of the national prohibition act aggregated $1,979,586.94 for the fiscal year 1922, compared with $2,152,387.45 for the fiscal year 1921. In addition to these receipts there are certain collections, such as fines, forfeitures, etc., made by the Department of Justice, which assists in enforcing the provisions of said act, amounting in 1922 to approximately $2,750,000.

The position of supervising Federal prohibition agent has been abolished, and permissive and enforcement work has been combined in the office of State prohibition directors. The supervising Federal prohibition agents formerly had charge of enforcement work, leaving the permissive features to be supervised by the State prohibition directors. The consolidation has eliminated duplication and simplified greatly the work of the Prohibition Unit in the enforcement of the national prohibition act.

The law forces of the Prohibition Unit were combined in the office of counsel for the Prohibition Unit. A mobile force of general prohibition agents, working under the direction of 18 divisional chiefs and directed from Washington by the chief general prohibition agent, has been established. This force works independently of State prohibition directors. A prohibition patrol service, consisting of six boats of the subchaser type, has been organized and assigned to various points along the Atlantic coast, and has proved very effective in the enforcement of the national prohibition act, especially with regard to the suppression of smuggling. In addition, there were placed on the Great Lakes five motor patrol boats which have rendered effective service in the prevention of smuggling from Canada.

Other changes are the reorganization of the Audit and Statistics Division, now known as the Audit Division, and the establishment of a Narcotic Division to handle all phases of the enforcement of the Harrison Narcotic Act.

### *Bureau and field personnel.*

The total personnel of the Bureau of Internal Revenue, including the prohibition enforcement service, increased during the year from 19,593 to 21,388. The number of employees in Washington increased from 7,052 to 7,275. Increases in the field service were as follows: Collectors' offices, 327; internal-revenue agents' force, 514; prohibition field service (including narcotic officers), 906; assistant supervisor of collectors, 3; special agents, Special Intelligence Unit, 16. There was a decrease from 769 to 575 in the number of storekeeper-gaugers.

### BUREAU OF ENGRAVING AND PRINTING.

The output of the Bureau of Engraving and Printing during the fiscal year ended June 30, 1922, by classes, as compared with the fiscal year 1921, is shown in the following table:

| Classes. | Sheets, 1922. | Increase over 1921. | Decrease from 1921. |
|---|---|---|---|
| Gold certificates | 1,146,000 | 1,146,000 | |
| Silver certificates | 81,921,000 | 67,680,000 | |
| United States notes | 37,901,000 | | 25,688,000 |
| Liberty bonds and Victory notes | 1,313,850 | | 21,407,708 |
| Certificates of indebtedness and Treasury notes | 511,950 | 98,719 | |
| National bank currency | 19,382,827 | 6,378,017 | |
| Federal reserve bank notes | 6,453,000 | | 38,577,000 |
| Federal reserve notes | 46,585,300 | | 26,075,600 |
| Internal-revenue stamps (6,271,283,002 stamps) | 80,022,596 | 12,031,630 | |
| Customs stamps | 66,750 | | 264,750 |
| Postage stamps, United States | 129,909,561 | 1,432,906 | |
| Checks, drafts, and similar work | 8,031,316 | 885,775 | |
| Other stamps, certificates, and documents | 3,574,963 | 485,300 | |
| Total | 416,820,113 | | 21,874,711 |

In addition to the output shown above, miscellaneous work to the amount of $175,344.44 was executed, of which amount $134,903.75 was reimbursed to the appropriations, $122.19 charged to the appropriations, and $40,318.50 deposited in the United States Treasury on account of miscellaneous receipts.

The face value of all perfect sheets delivered amounted to $14,915,115,872.08.

The following table shows appropriations, repayments, expenditures, and unexpended balance for the fiscal year 1922, compared with 1921:

| | 1922 | Increase over 1921. | Decrease from 1921. |
|---|---|---|---|
| Appropriations by Congress | $6,854,140.00 | $373,305.00 | |
| Reimbursed to bureau appropriations | 3,770,520.20 | | $3,121,539.18 |
| Increase of compensation | 1,246,543.34 | | 223,708.27 |
| Total | 11,871,203.54 | | 2,971,942.45 |
| Expenditures | 10,812,756.38 | | 3,152,477.19 |
| Unexpended balance | 1,058,447.16 | 180,534.74 | |

The expenditures include $12,611.60 for employees detailed to other offices of the department, of which $7,911.60 was repaid. The sum of $103,576.63 was expended for new machinery and equipment.

## CUSTOMS.[1]

The volume of customs business transacted during the fiscal year 1922 exceeded that of the preceding year both as to the amount of duties collected and as to the other activities of customs officers, such as the licensing of importations of dyes and chemicals and the enforcement of the antidumping provisions of the act of May 27, 1921; control of importation and exportation of narcotics under the act of May 26, 1922; collection of fines for violation of the pure food and drug laws; enforcement of the navigation laws; collection of internal revenue on importations; preparation of import and export statistics for the Bureau of Foreign and Domestic Commerce; cooperation with the State Department and the Department of Labor in enforcing consular and immigration laws; and cooperation in the enforcement of the prohibition laws.

While the collections on account of duties and tonnage for the fiscal year 1922 amounted to $357,544,712, an increase of $49,519,610 over the preceding year, the cost of collection was reduced by $53,536 through the strictest economy. Operating and maintenance expenses of the service (exclusive of the so-called increase of compensation) were $11,174,369. No deduction from receipts is made for drawbacks and other refunds, which amounted to $37,132,197.80 in the fiscal year 1922, as compared with $23,261,042.78 in the fiscal year 1921.

The increase in the customs receipts is accounted for by the larger number of articles of importation on the dutiable list in the emergency tariff act of May 27, 1921, rather than by an increase in importations. Foreign trade for the fiscal year just closed, as reflected by the values of imports and exports, was considerably

[1] See footnote 1, p. 31.

less than for the preceding fiscal year; imports amounted to $2,608,-009,008, a decrease of $1,046,440,422, and exports to $3,771,181,597, a decrease of $2,745,133,749. Due to changes in the price level, however, value is not an accurate index of the change in the volume of foreign trade. During the fiscal year 1922 there were 1,790,539 entries filed for imports, as compared with 1,702,969 in 1921, an increase of 87,570. Entries filed for exports during the fiscal years 1922 and 1921 were 3,191,369 and 3,918,646, respectively, a decrease of 727,277 in 1922.

The increase in popularity of the Postal Service as a channel for importing merchandise of all kinds, and especially merchandise of small bulk but great value, has created a situation which makes inadequate the joint regulations of the Post Office and Treasury Departments promulgated in February, 1907, for the control of such importations. At the time the regulations were issued customs receipts from mail importations at the port of Chicago, for instance, amounted to only $15,000 for the year, as compared with $1,000,000 for the fiscal year just closed. Investigations are now being conducted by representatives of both departments with a view to revising the regulations covering mail importations so as to afford better facilities for collecting the revenue from this important source

Owing to new legislation and changing conditions of business, the Customs Regulations of 1915 no longer fully cover the methods and practices of conducting the customs business. These regulations have been amended in many respects by Treasury decisions, and a committee of customs officers was appointed during the latter part of the year to revise them. The committee has already been able to do considerable preliminary work in this connection.

Under the provisions of the acts of August 24, 1921, and November 16, 1921, extending the life of Title V, section 501, of the act of May 27, 1921, the control of importations of dyes and chemicals was continued throughout the fiscal year 1922. The labor and time required to make the analyses of dyes and other coal-tar products which are necessary in carrying out the provisions cited above have greatly increased the work of the customs laboratories. At the port of New York during the fiscal year 1922 analyses were made of 20,144 samples of all kinds, as compared with 13,579 the previous year.

The completion by the American Sugar Refining Co. of its refinery at Baltimore, Md., made necessary the remodeling of the customs laboratory at that port and the installation of additional equipment for the testing of sugar samples. This work has been practically completed and several cargoes of sugar have been entered through Baltimore. Automatic electric scales for weighing the cargoes of sugar have also been installed at this port.

## CUSTOMS SPECIAL AGENCY SERVICE.

The Special Agency Service of the Customs was reestablished February 1, 1922, as a separate division of the Secretary's office in accordance with the provisions of sections 2649 and 2651, Revised Statutes, and a reorganization of the field forces has now been effected, with highly satisfactory results. A Washington office was established and methods were adopted which insured complete coordination with other customs activities and proper supervision of the field work of this service on an effective basis.

The foreign investigative corps, comprising Treasury attachés, confidential agents, and special experts, stationed in the principal European countries and the Orient, has been strengthened by augmenting the personnel, especially in Germany and other countries where depreciated currency renders the ascertainment of market values extremely difficult.

The Comparative Value Reports Bureau, formerly maintained as a part of the local special agency office in New York City, was discontinued and replaced by a Customs Information Exchange (at a saving of $16,000 per annum in salaries), operating directly under the supervision of the department. This exchange functions in accordance with law and by the adoption of sound methods renders notable assistance to appraising officers by gathering and disseminating information as to market values of imported merchandise.

An antidumping unit has been established to investigate problems arising under the antidumping law.

A border patrol along the international boundary line between New York State and Canada was instituted and continued for 50 days as an experimental measure to ascertain the value of such patrol in checking smuggling of narcotics, jewelry, live stock, and prohibited merchandise. The cost of this patrol was approximately $7,500, and the fines, forfeitures, and seizures collected aggregated $60,000 in value. Twenty-nine smugglers were punished by jail sentences. The value of this patrol as a deterrent against smuggling can not be reduced to figures.

Arrangements have been made for the resumption by special agents of their statutory duties of examination of books, records, and accounts of collectors of customs.

The operation of the special agency force as a separate unit of the customs has already proved to be of great service in the prevention and detection of fraud by undervaluation, fraudulent entry, and smuggling, or through the introduction into the United States of narcotics, liquor, and other prohibited merchandise.

## OFFICE OF SUPERVISING ARCHITECT.

The following statement shows in general the building operations of the Office of the Supervising Architect up to the close of the fiscal year ended June 30, 1922:

Number of buildings completed (occupied or ready for occupancy) at the end of the fiscal year 1921, exclusive of marine hospitals and quarantine stations.................................... 1,235

New buildings completed during the fiscal year ended June 30, 1922, exclusive of marine hospitals and quarantine stations.... 6

    Total buildings (completed) under control of the Treasury Department June 30, 1922.................................... 1,241

Buildings placed under contract during the fiscal year ended June 30, 1922, exclusive of hospitals.............................. 4

Buildings placed under contract prior to July 1, 1921, and not completed June 30, 1922....................................... 1

    Construction of new projects in force July 1, 1922............... 5

    Total buildings completed and in course of erection June 30, 1922, exclusive of marine hospitals and quarantine stations...... 1,246

Buildings authorized prior to act of Mar. 4, 1913, not under contract June 30, 1922....................................... 14

Buildings, miscellaneous projects, etc., authorized in acts of Mar. 4, 1913, and subsequent, not under contract June 30, 1922........ 141

                155

    Total buildings, etc., completed, in course or erection, or authorized (not including extensions)............................. 1,401

In addition to the above buildings and projects, there are 57 marine hospitals and quarantine stations under the control of the Treasury Department. Each of these hospitals and stations, moreover, includes several buildings.

During the fiscal year 1922 six Federal buildings were completed. Contracts for those completed at Birmingham, Ala., Columbia, S. C., Honolulu, Hawaii, and Lockhaven, Pa., had been placed prior to July 1, 1920, and for those at Park City, Utah, and Santa Fe, N. Mex., during the fiscal year 1921. Out of the 12 projects on which bids were invited during the fiscal year 1922, contracts could be let for only 4—Front Royal, and Salem, Va., Oconto, Wis., and Washington, Mo. These four projects, together with one at Franklin, N. H., the contracts for which were let during the fiscal year 1921, were all in the course of construction on June 30, 1922.

Extensions to buildings at Kansas City, Mo., and Chattanooga, Tenn., have been completed, and the extension to the post-office building at Hagerstown, Md., is still in the course of construction.

Nine miscellaneous major contracts, entailing a total expenditure of $212,286, were completed, as follows: A leprosarium at Carville, La.; a hygienic laboratory at Washington, D. C.; marine hospitals at

Cairo, Ill., Louisville, Ky., Memphis, Tenn., and Portland, Me.; and quarantine stations at Cape Fear, N. C., Port Townsend, Wash., and Baltimore, Md.

Five similar projects, the combined estimated cost of which is $839,258, are in the course of construction. These consist of the installation of a new boiler and remodeling the south wing of the marine hospital at Boston; rehabilitation and repair of the marine hospital at Mobile, Ala.; construction of a casement passage in the hygienic laboratory at Washington, D. C.; extension work on the quarantine station, New York City; and remodeling the fourth floor and constructing a new roof on the Treasury Building, Washington,. D. C.

Under the appropriation, "Remodeling and enlarging public buildings," which amounted to $380,000, a total of 98 buildings received attention. The contracts covering 48 of these ranged from $1,178 to $21,200 and aggregated $352,276. This work resulted in an increase of 69,642 square feet of floor space, at an average cost of $5.05 per square foot.

Fourteen large hospital projects with a total bed capacity of 4,783 were completed, at an aggregate cost of $14,188,437.13, and seven large hospital projects with a total bed capacity of 2,085 are under construction. The estimated cost of the latter is $6,760,018.16. The following tables show this work in detail:

*Hospital projects completed under the appropriation for "Hospital construction, Public Health Service," act March 3, 1919, and subsequent legislation.*

| Location. | Description of work. | Bed capacity. | Cost. |
|---|---|---|---|
| Chicago, Ill................ | Edward Hines, Jr., Hospital (formerly Broadview).[1] Acquisition of site, completion of main hospital buildings, and construction of five auxiliary buildings. | 1,000 | $3,400,000 |
| Dawson Springs, Ky...... | Sanatorium:[2] Construction of infirmary, one ambulant ward, 6 semiambulant wards, administration, and 13 other buildings for personnel, 3-mile road, and water supply. | 500 | 2,250,000 |
| Norfolk, Va............... | Purchase of site and construction of main hospital building, quarters for personnel, roads, utilities, etc.[3] | 100 | 900,000 |
| Stapleton, N. Y.......... | Marine Hospital: Construction and mechanical equipment junior officers' quarters, painting, remodeling, and repairs to certain buildings. (Other work, authorized, completed in previous years.) | ........ | 27,955 |
| Washington, D. C......... | Mount Alto Sanatorium:[4] Purchase of property and construction of two hospital units, mess hall, and kitchen, power house, garage, and roads. | 250 | 960,000 |
| | | 1,850 | 7,537,955 |

[1] Acts of March 3, 1919, and March 6, 1920.
[2] Acts of March 3, 1919, and June 6, 1921.
[3] Act of March 3, 1919.
[4] Acts of March 3, 1919, and June 5, 1920.

*Hospital projects under the appropriation "Hospital facilities, etc., for war patients."*

| Location. | Description of work. | Bed capacity. | Cost. |
|---|---|---|---|
| | COMPLETED. | | |
| Alexandria, La............... | Mess hall and kitchen; rehabilitation of water supply. | ........ | $58, 016. 17 |
| The Bronx, New York City. | Remodeling of two large 4-story buildings and two smaller buildings. | 1, 011 | ¹ 3, 462, 950. 00 |
| Fort Bayard, N. Mex........ | Construction of infirmary, three ambulant wards, two semiambulant wards, neuropsychiatric ward, boiler house, laundry, extension of mess hall, quarters for doctors, nurses, and attendants. Additional work contemplated. | 422 | 962, 725. 00 |
| Fort Logan H. Roots, Ark.. | Remodeling of 22 buildings for patients, doctors, nurses, and attendants, and construction of two new buildings. | 270 | 242, 500. 00 |
| Fort McKenzie, Wyo....... | Remodeling of four buildings, rehabilitation of water supply, including reservoir. Additional work under construction. | 245 | 175, 510. 96 |
| Fort Walla Walla, Wash.... | Remodeling of 20 buildings, construction of two ward buildings, boiler house, laundry, and additional water supply. | 163 | 447, 780. 00 |
| Lake City, Fla............... | Construction of two ward buildings, nurses' quarters, laundry, and remodeling four buildings. | 100 | 269, 000. 00 |
| Perryville, Md............... | New neuropsychiatric hospital unit, consisting of five reeducational buildings, mess hall and kitchen, administration building, service lines, roads, etc., incidental thereto. | 300 | 470, 000. 00 |
| Whipple Barracks, Ariz..... | Construction of three ambulant wards, two semiambulant wards, remodeling and extending nine buildings, water supply, refrigeration, etc. | 422 | 562, 000. 00 |
| Total............... | | 2, 933 | 6, 650, 482. 13 |
| | UNDER CONSTRUCTION. | | |
| Augusta, Ga................ | Construction of five ward buildings, mess hall and kitchen, power house, service lines, roads, etc., incidental thereto. | 265 | ² 844, 788. 51 |
| Jefferson Barracks, Mo...... | General hospital building; apartment houses for 11 officers, 34 nurses, and 58 attendants; laundry, garage, boiler house, and all necessary service lines. | 289 | 970, 000. 00 |
| Oteen, N. C................ | Construction of infirmary, service lines, and roads incidental thereto. | 200 | 450, 560. 00 |
| Rutland, Mass.............. | Construction of hospital, administration building, semiambulant ward, attendants' and nurses' quarters, laundry, garage, service lines incidental thereto. | 220 | ³ 790, 550. 00 |
| Palo Alto, Calif............ | Construction of nine ward buildings, quarters for officers and nurses, mess hall, kitchen, boiler house, service lines, roads, etc., incidental thereto. | 515 | 1, 261, 619. 65 |
| Tuskegee, Ala.............. | Construction of eight ward buildings, kitchen , mess hall, administration building, boiler house, freight house, and shop, officers' quarters, nurses' and attendants' quarters, also 4-mile road to towns of Chehaw and Tuskegee. | 596 | ⁴ 1, 942, 500. 00 |
| Total............... | | 2, 085 | 6, 260, 018. 16 |

¹ Includes $2,750,000 for purchase of property.
² Includes $368,300 for purchase of property.
³ Includes $240,000 for purchase of property.
⁴ Includes $7,000 for purchase of property.

*Hospital project in course of construction under the act of June 16, 1921.*

| Location. | Description of work. | Cost. |
|---|---|---|
| Chicago, Ill................ | Edward Hines, Jr., Hospital: Construction of recreation building, reservoir, water supply, pumping plant, roads, walks, and extensive improvements to grounds. | $500, 000 |

*Hospital projects under the appropriation, " Medical and hospital services."*

| Location. | Description of work. | Cost. |
|---|---|---|
| | COMPLETED. | |
| Algiers, La............... | Construction of several frame ward buildings...................... | $20,000 |
| Augusta, Ga.............. | Moving four buildings and salvaging materials from Camp Hancock. | 19,000 |
| Excelsior Springs, Mo...... | Remodeling a building and construction of annex thereto; construction of power house. | 200,000 |
| Gulfport, Miss............. | Construction of several buildings and remodeling of others.......... | 203,400 |
| Total............. | | 442,400 |
| | UNDER CONSTRUCTION. | |
| West Roxbury, Mass....... | Recreation building................................................ | 25,000 |

*Hospital projects under the $300,000 appropriation, "Hospital construction, Public Health Service."*

| Location. | Description of work. | Cost. |
|---|---|---|
| | COMPLETED. | |
| Alexandria, La............ | Refrigeration and improving ventilation......................... | $12,528.00 |
| Augusta, Ga.............. | Foundations and service connections for four buildings moved from Camp Hancock. | 1 7,000.00 |
| Camp Kearny, Calif....... | Laundry, garage, remodeling some buildings, improvements to roads, and ventilating system. | 27,575.00 |
| Fort Bayard, N. Mex..... | Reroofing old buildings, screened porches, remodeling officers' quarters, salvaging materials from Deming. | 39,466.62 |
| Fox Hills, N. Y.......... | Transferred to Public Health Service for improvements......... | 27,000.00 |
| Greenville, S. C.......... | Fire protection system and remodeling a number of buildings... | 49,657.00 |
| New Haven, Conn........ | Improvements to steam lines.................................... | 1,436.92 |
| Norfolk, Va.............. | Toilet facilities, reroofing, and screening porches................ | 5,800.00 |
| Oteen, N. C............. | Fire-alarm system............................................. | 15,000.00 |
| Palo Alto, Calif.......... | Service pipes.................................................. | 999.89 |
| Perryville, Md............ | Addition to kitchen............................................ | 1,500.00 |
| West Roxbury, Mass...... | Transferred to Public Health Service July 11, 1921, for improvements. | 20,000.00 |
| Whipple Barracks, Ariz... | Garbage can washing apparatus, incinerator, and additional refrigeration. | 13,500.00 |
| Total............. | | 221,463.43 |
| | UNDER CONSTRUCTION. | |
| Boise, Idaho.............. | Remodeling laundry building and construction of one semi-ambulant ward. | 50,000.00 |
| Houston, Tex............. | Garbage can washing apparatus, ground lighting, and remodeling officers' quarters. | 23,373.79 |
| Total............. | | 73,373.79 |

¹ Includes $1,000 for garage not yet completed.

A total of 339 claims, amounting to $3,167,716.78, have been filed under the act of August 25, 1919, as amended March 6, 1920, entitled "An act for the relief of contractors and subcontractors for the post offices and other buildings and work under supervision of the Treasury Department, and for other purposes." The status of these claims at the close of the fiscal year 1922 is given below:

*Status of claims filed under act of Congress approved August 25, 1919.*

| | Prior to July, 1921. | | Fiscal year 1922. | | Total. | |
|---|---|---|---|---|---|---|
| | Number. | Amount. | Number. | Amount. | Number. | Amount. |
| Claims allowed and paid.................. | 100 | $1,497,113.51 | 64 | $820,022.81 | 164 | $2,317,136.32 |
| Claims disallowed or withdrawn by claimants..................................... | 61 | 114,274.89 | 5 | 147,797.19 | 66 | 362,072.08 |
| Total adjudicated.................. | 161 | 1,611,388.40 | 69 | 967,820.00 | 230 | 2,579,208.40 |

The number of claims pending on June 30, 1922, was 109, as against 171 on June 30, 1921.

*Expenditures from July 1, 1921, to June 30, 1922, contract liabilities charged against appropriations, and unencumbered balances.*

| | Expenditures. | Contract liabilities charged against previous appropriations. | Unencumbered balances, June 30, 1922. |
|---|---|---|---|
| Statutory roll................................... | $205,644.90 | .................. | * $21,802.02 |
| Sites and additional land.......................... | 74,868.35 | $1,437,519.00 | 1,849,900.00 |
| Construction of new buildings...................... | 1,258,668.06 | 755,296.34 | 12,424,071.14 |
| Extensions to buildings............................ | 603,517.04 | 814,869.45 | 1,660,846.37 |
| Miscellaneous and special items..................... | 210,737.99 | 101,341.68 | 926,094.27 |
| Rent of buildings................................. | 3,960.00 | .................. | 52,325.00 |
| Veterans' hospitals................................ | 382,258.51 | 253,800.90 | 248,940.59 |
| Architectural competitions......................... | 4,563.77 | 8,738.18 | .................. |
| Remodeling and enlarging public buildings.......... | 352,886.56 | 73,508.60 | 620.82 |
| Relief of contractors, etc., for public buildings under Treasury Department........................... | 820,022.81 | 16,999.13 | 115,864.55 |
| Hospital construction, Public Health Service.......... | 2,693,030.03 | 229,079.58 | 162,583.43 |
| Hospital facilities, etc., for war patients............ | 7,478,692.44 | 8,434,433.00 | 379,921.78 |
| Lands and other property of the United States........ | .................. | .................. | .................. |
| Repairs and preservation......................... | 855,607.09 | 197,032.68 | 1 113,115.26 |
| Mechanical equipment............................. | 569,105.40 | 186,098.41 | 15,534.34 |
| Vaults and safes.................................. | 73,550.20 | 32,382.69 | 2 18,694.07 |
| Operating supplies................................ | 3,048,649.96 | 841,482.50 | 35,663.60 |
| General expenses.................................. | 384,766.33 | 27,619.95 | 103,506.59 |
| Furniture and repairs of same...................... | 521,558.66 | 196,571.94 | 3 32,112.45 |
| Operating force................................... | 3,880,115.38 | 3,785.81 | 11,831.53 |
| Total............................................ | 23,422,203.48 | 13,610,559.84 | 18,173,727.81 |

¹ Includes reserve of $100,000.   ² Includes reserve of $5,000.   ³ Includes reserve of $25,000.

*Statement of classification of public buildings under control of the Treasury Department, by titles, showing expenditures in each class, prepared pursuant to act approved June 6, 1900 (31 Stat., p. 592).*

| | Construction. | Extensions, alterations, and special items. | Annual repairs.¹ | Total expenditures to June 30, 1922. |
|---|---|---|---|---|
| Post office, courthouse, customhouse buildings, etc...................... | $102,085,716.39 | $15,200,001.74 | $14,167,571.43 | $131,453,289.56 |
| Courthouse buildings................. | 350,441.60 | 40,348.49 | 134,866.21 | 525,656.30 |
| Customhouse buildings............... | 23,112,241.60 | 3,257,630.00 | 1,959,857.67 | 28,329,729.27 |
| Marine hospital buildings............ | 4,165,882.80 | 1,649,775.35 | 2,331,971.18 | 8,147,629.33 |
| Post-office buildings................. | 79,385,265.12 | 3,721,598.51 | 6,260,469.53 | 89,367,333.16 |
| Quarantine-station buildings......... | 2,749,415.62 | 1,406,393.96 | 1,064,448.16 | 5,220,257.74 |
| Veterans' hospital buildings......... | 379,775.13 | 2,483.38 | 98,535.98 | 480,794.49 |
| Miscellaneous buildings.............. | 35,398,549.84 | 3,604,323.78 | 4,453,154.60 | 43,456,028.22 |
| Total.......................... | 247,627,288.10 | 28,882,555.21 | 30,470,874.76 | 306,980,718.07 |

¹ Includes purchase and repairs of vaults, safes, and certain permanent mechanical equipment.

14263—FI 1922——27

*Statement of classification of public buildings under control of the Treasury Department, by titles, showing expenditures in each class, prepared pursuant to act approved June 6, 1900 (31 Stat., p. 592).*

| | Cost of sites. | Outstanding liabilities chargeable against appropriations. | | Unencumbered balances of appropriations. |
| --- | --- | --- | --- | --- |
| | | Sites. | Buildings. | |
| Post office, courthouse, customhouse buildings, etc. | $19,858,393.07 | $363,448.00 | $165,680.11 | $2,732,922.38 |
| Courthouse buildings | 173,334.69 | ............. | 3,835.50 | 169,137.64 |
| Customhouse buildings | 3,783,322.33 | ............. | 12,121.75 | 65,011.95 |
| Marine hospital buildings | 573,736.96 | ............. | 162,803.78 | 573,983.82 |
| Post-office buildings | 22,931,284.85 | 984,000.00 | 408,973.01 | 12,023,655.08 |
| Quarantine-station buildings | 200,271.60 | 90,071.00 | 628,062.96 | 116,344.91 |
| Veterans' hospital buildings | ............. | ............. | 253,800.90 | 248,940.59 |
| Miscellaneous buildings | 8,740,812.44 | ............. | 290,030.36 | 1,232,181.00 |
| Total | 56,261,155.94 | 1,437,519.00 | 1,925,308.37 | 17,162,177.37 |

## PUBLIC HEALTH SERVICE.

The activities of the Public Health Service during the fiscal year 1922 are summarized by the Surgeon General as follows:

### Scientific research.

The Division of Scientific Research continued its studies of diseases of man, and matters relating to public health both in the field and at the Hygienic Laboratory. Among the diseases studied were: Amœbiasis, botulism, clonorchiasis, pellagra, Rocky Mountain spotted fever, tularaemia, leprosy, malaria, meningitis, pneumonia, smallpox, plague, venereal diseases, tuberculosis, and typhoid fever. In addition, studies of cancer are being undertaken.

The cooperative work with State and local health authorities for the control of trachoma was continued and an additional hospital opened in Arkansas. The investigations of botulism were extended to include food poisoning from other causes. Among the problems of industrial hygiene special attention was devoted to standards of illumination, dust hazards, cutting oil dermatoses, zinc and brass founders' ague, and temperature and humidity in the production of undue fatigue.

Studies of child hygiene were conducted with the view to establishing permanent child hygiene organizations supported by State or local funds. Child hygiene surveys were carried on in 10 States. Intensive studies were inaugurated bearing on the nutrition, growth, and development of children of different age groups.

Studies of stream pollution were continued with special reference to processes of natural purification and proper disposal of wastes.

Cooperative rural health work included projects in 56 counties in 16 States. During the calendar year cooperative demonstrations effected an increase of 42 in the number of county or equivalent divisions provided with local health service under the direction of whole-time health officers.

The control of the propagation and sale in interstate traffic of viruses, serums, toxins, and analogous products, including arsphenamine, was continued. Important studies of chemotherapy were conducted at the Hygienic Laboratory.

*Domestic quarantine (interstate sanitation).*

Plague suppressive measures have been taken in New Orleans, Galveston, Beaumont, and San Francisco with satisfactory results. Since plague infection has apparently disappeared, the station at Beaumont was discontinued. The forces on duty at Galveston and New Orleans have been greatly reduced, and, unless new infection is found, it will be practicable to discontinue these stations within a few months. Rodent surveys of New England and Middle Atlantic seaport cities have been undertaken for the purpose of determining whether or not there is any evidence of rodent plague.

Through cooperative efforts sanitary engineering divisions have been established by two States and existing divisions in 19 other States were aided. Divisions of communicable diseases of two State health departments have also been assisted. Supervision over 3,500 water supplies used for drinking and culinary purposes, more than 900 railroads, and thousands of vessels in interstate traffic has been actively continued.

*Foreign and insular quarantine and immigration.*

At the continental maritime quarantine stations, 18,985 vessels and 2,081,236 passengers and crews were inspected. At foreign and insular stations there were inspected 10,322 vessels and 1,010,496 passengers and crews. A total of 8,889 vessels were fumigated or disinfected and 7,823 were detained, either because of diseases aboard or because the vessels came from infected ports.

The Public Health Service maintains 64 quarantine stations in the United States and Alaska and 29 in the insular possessions.

By detailing medical officers to American consulates in foreign ports, as authorized by the quarantine act of July 1, 1902, measures of great value have been taken to prevent the occurrence of quarantinable diseases on vessels destined for the United States and its possessions. Although plague was reported in many foreign ports, and typhus fever and cholera prevail in eastern Europe, from which section large numbers of passengers come, no such infections occurred on vessels from those areas. There were 39 medical officers on duty at American consulates at ports in Europe, Mexico, South America, and the Orient.

At the immigration stations 551,454 aliens were examined for physical or mental defects or diseases contemplated in the immigration law. Of 28,815 aliens certified as having some defect or disease, 541 were found to be suffering from mental defects or tuberculosis, 1,243 afflicted with "loathsome contagious diseases" or "dangerous contagious diseases," and 17,172 having physical disabilities that would interfere with their ability to earn a living.

### Sanitary reports and statistics.

Through the weekly Public Health Reports, variations in the geographical distribution of diseases dangerous to the public health were made known to the health authorities and to the public generally.

Laws, ordinances, and regulations pertaining to public health work were published and abstracts made of court decisions for the information of health authorities. Statistical studies were made of morbidity, including industrial morbidity and the development of standardized sickness reports in industrial establishments, mortality from pulmonary tuberculosis, and the application of statistical methods to health problems. In cooperation with other divisions, statistical studies were also carried on in child hygiene, influenza, pellagra, and venereal diseases.

### Hospitals and relief.

In conformity with department order of April 19, 1921, and the act creating the United States Veterans' Bureau approved August 9, 1921, the operations of the Public Health Service district offices for the medical examination and treatment of veterans of the World War were discontinued on July 1, 1921, the dispensaries on February 1, 1922, and the veterans' hospitals on May 1, 1922, pursuant to Executive order. These activities were taken over by the United States Veterans' Bureau. The transfers included 14 district offices, 27 dispensaries, and 47 veterans' hospitals. That part of the Hospital Division having to do with these activities, was likewise transferred.

At the time of the transfer the total bed capacity of the above-mentioned hospitals was about 17,500, with approximately 13,000 patients. Special care was taken not to interfere with the efficiency of these agencies during the transfer.

Hospital care and relief by the Public Health Service accordingly reverts to the status which existed prior to the Armistice, November 11, 1918. There remain 24 Public Health hospitals and 116 relief stations devoted to the care and treatment of service beneficiaries under law. Most of these hospitals are well equipped and maintain high standards of professional care and treatment. Many of them, however, are in bad physical condition and several should be rebuilt.

During the year there were cared for in Public Health hospitals approximately 72,000 veterans and 35,250 other beneficiaries, making a total of 107,250 hospital patients, to whom were rendered 5,475,600 hospital relief days. The magnitude of the medical relief activities during the past three years is evidenced by the fact that within that period there were treated over 275,000 veterans, to whom were given more than 14,500,000 relief days. Approximately 2,000,000 out-patient treatments were given and 1,500,000 physical examinations made. For a considerable period the Public Health Service carried more than 80 per cent of the total volume of the work connected with the medical care and treatment of veterans, and, under what constituted a real national emergency, met these responsibilities in a highly commendable manner.

*Venereal disease control.*

No Federal appropriation to States for venereal disease control was made for the fiscal year 1922, but the unexpended balance of the $546,345.30 allotted in 1921 was made available to the States in 1922. Venereal disease clinics under joint State and Federal control numbered 542, an increase of 59 over the previous year. New admissions to these clinics totaled 141,279. Of these patients 60,169 were discharged after treatment as noninfectious. More than 2,000,000 treatments were given and 491,231 laboratory examinations made. The total number of cases of venereal diseases reported by State and local health authorities was 324,131. There were 32,493 requests for pamphlets received and 1,047 inquiries for medical information. Six new educational pamphlets were issued and one card exhibit revised and published. Reports were received of 6,902 lectures, 26 conferences, 3,251 exhibit and lantern slide demonstrations, and 1,206 motion-picture exhibits. Approximately $700,000 was appropriated or otherwise set aside by the States for continuing anti-venereal disease work.

Sixteen institutes, attended by more than 6,000 persons, were convened in different parts of the United States. At these institutes instructions were given by 35 service officers and many other authorities engaged in the work. Ten social hygiene conferences for non-professional women with a total attendance of 2,725 were held, largely in conjunction with the institutes.

Representatives from all the leading medical colleges and schools of public health were assembled to consider problems connected with the education of health officers. Two conferences of representatives of women's organizations throughout the country were convened to consider national health problems.

### General inspections.

A system of general inspection of service stations and activities was maintained.  The activities included 422 special investigations, 455 inspections of hospitals, and 84 inspections of relief stations.  With the transfer of the activities relating to the veterans of the World War, inspection activities have greatly decreased and the personnel conducting them has accordingly been reduced.

### Public Health library.

The library now contains 9,241 volumes and approximately 3,500 other publications.  These include medical and scientific books and journals; Federal, State, and municipal health records and documents; and health reports of foreign governments.  Through an index catalogue the usefulness of the library has been greatly increased.

### Purveying depots.

The total value of supplies distributed through the Purveying Service was $8,771,419.89, of which $2,522,584.39 was Army surplus stock received through the several coordinating agencies of the Government.  In addition to the distribution of these supplies two motor vehicle repair shops were maintained and steps were taken to restore to serviceable condition large quantities of hospital equipment.  With the transfer of the veterans' hospitals and the establishment of a Bureau of Supply in the department, this agency was discontinued.

### Personnel and accounts.

With the transfer to the Veterans' Bureau of the activities relating to the care of World War veterans there resulted a large decrease of personnel.  This decrease is shown in the following table, which shows the total personnel on duty June 30, 1922, as compared with June 30, 1921.  The 202 medical officers in the Regular commissioned corps include the Surgeon General, 3 assistant surgeons general at large, 11 senior surgeons, 99 surgeons, 51 passed assistant surgeons, and 20 assistant surgeons.  Seventeen additional officers in various grades are on waiting orders.  One senior surgeon and 6 surgeons were detailed as assistant surgeons general in charge of bureau divisions in conformity with acts of July 1, 1902, and July 1, 1918.  The table above referred to follows:

Number and distribution of personnel of the United States Public Health Service June 30, 1922, in comparison with June 30, 1921.

| Activity. | Regular corps. | | Reserve corps. | | Acting assistant surgeons. | | Attending specialists. | | Internes. | | Administrative assistants. | | Pharmacists. | | Scientific personnel. | | All other employees. | | Collaborating epidemiologists. | | Total. | |
|---|---|---|---|---|---|---|---|---|---|---|---|---|---|---|---|---|---|---|---|---|---|---|---|
| | 1921 | 1922 | 1921 | 1922 | 1921 | 1922 | 1921 | 1922 | 1921 | 1922 | 1921 | 1922 | 1921 | 1922 | 1921 | 1922 | 1921 | 1922 | 1921 | 1922 | 1921 | 1922 |
| Divisions of the bureau [1] | 19 | 12 | 48 | 2 | | | | | | | | | 2 | 2 | | | 634 | 232 | | | 703 | 248 |
| Hospitals and relief | 66 | 46 | 671 | 94 | 453 | 176 | 322 | 73 | 65 | 20 | 123 | 18 | 25 | 23 | | | 14,180 | 1,945 | | | 15,905 | 2,395 |
| Quarantine and immigration | 56 | 50 | | | 131 | 145 | | | | | 4 | 6 | 5 | 4 | | | 711 | 648 | | | 907 | 853 |
| Venereal disease control | 7 | 6 | | 3 | 60 | 48 | | 3 | | | | | | | | | 29 | 29 | | | 89 | 80 |
| Prevention of epidemics | 35 | 41 | | | 2 | 43 | | | | | | | | | | | 440 | 131 | 3,898 | 4,166 | 4,361 | 4,360 |
| Field investigations of public health | 1 | 1 | 4 | | 33 | 21 | | | | | | | 6 | | 20 | 11 | 308 | 304 | | | 424 | 353 |
| Purveying service | | | | | | | | | | | 3 | 2 | | 2 | 42 | 20 | 415 | 90 | | | 423 | 95 |
| Veterans' Bureau | | 19 | 243 | 884 | | | | | | | | | | 7 | | | | | | | 243 | 903 |
| Waiting orders | 17 | 17 | | 4 | | | | | | | | | | | | | | | | | 17 | 17 |
| Miscellaneous | | 10 | | | | | | | | | | | | | | | | | | | | 14 |
| Total | 201 | 202 | 966 | 987 | 679 | 433 | 322 | 76 | 65 | 20 | 130 | 26 | 38 | 38 | 62 | 31 | 16,717 | 3,379 | 3,898 | 4,166 | 23,078 | 9,358 |

[1] This constitutes the personnel of the central office, Washington, D. C.

During the year a system of allotments and encumbrance reports was inaugurated to provide a more accurate control of expenditures from the several appropriations. These expenditures during the fiscal year 1922 as compared with 1921 are set forth in the following table:

*Comparative statement of expenditures from appropriations of the Public Health Service, fiscal years 1921 and 1922.*

|  | Fiscal year 1921. | Fiscal year 1922. |
|---|---|---|
| Pay of commissioned officers and pharmacists | $962,195.77 | $1,017,738.20 |
| Pay of acting assistant surgeons | 333,387.64 | 300,000.00 |
| Pay of other employees | 883,500.59 | 840,000.00 |
| Freight, transportation, etc | 51,135.44 | [1] 57,000.00 |
| Fuel, light, and water | 133,982.39 | 116,505.84 |
| Furniture, etc | 7,066.98 | 3,950.21 |
| Purveying depot supplies | 114,821.04 | 79,196.57 |
| Maintenance, Hygienic Laboratory | 44,893.93 | 44,970.42 |
| Maintenance, marine hospitals | 1,180,000.00 | [1] 1,065,293.17 |
| Care of seamen, etc | 223,019.74 | 186,140.80 |
| Books | 499.12 | 499.84 |
| Quarantine service | 500,112.13 | [1] 594,307.35 |
| Prevention of epidemic diseases | 1,131,443.25 | 470,000.00 |
| Field investigation of public health | 295,777.48 | 296,272.61 |
| Interstate quarantine service | 24,204.38 | 24,359.66 |
| Studies of rural sanitation | 49,238.32 | 50,000.00 |
| Control of biologic products | 46,136.60 | 44,813.84 |
| Salaries, office of Surgeon General | 89,322.12 | 89,168.94 |
| Preparation and transportation of remains of officers, Public Health Service | 397.98 | 1,147.26 |
| Medical and hospital services, Public Health Service | 39,579,209.56 | 26,615,352.52 |
| Pay of personnel and maintenance of hospitals, Public Health Service | 6,534,368.05 | [1] 4,611,190.65 |
| Expenses, Division of Venereal Diseases | 197,331.11 | 181,343.44 |
| Hospital construction, Public Health Service | 2,159,373.09 | 523,597.45 |
| Hospital furniture, Public Health Service | 75,539.79 | 114,175.96 |
| Increase of compensation, Treasury Department | 3,003,638.92 | 2,526,512.16 |
| Equipment, Hygienic Laboratory | 14,254.66 | [2] |
| Special studies of pellagra | 8,277.21 | [2] |
| Total | 57,643,127.29 | 39,853,536.89 |

[1] Expenditures in excess of amount appropriated covered by repayments.
[2] No appropriation.

## COAST GUARD.

The following is a summary of the principal operations of the Coast Guard during the fiscal year ended June 30, 1922:

| | |
|---|---|
| Lives saved or persons rescued from peril | 2,954 |
| Persons on board vessels assisted | 14,531 |
| Persons in distress cared for | 702 |
| Vessels boarded and papers examined | 21,586 |
| Vessels seized or reported for violations of law | 596 |
| Regattas and marine parades patrolled in accordance with law | 13 |
| Instances of lives saved and vessels assisted | 2,224 |
| Instances of miscellaneous assistance | 1,535 |
| Derelicts and other obstructions to navigation removed or destroyed | 48 |
| Value of derelicts recovered and delivered to owners | $384,550 |
| Persons examined for certificates as lifeboat men | 14,569 |
| Value of vessels assisted (including cargoes) | $35,346,765 |
| Fines and penalties incurred by vessels reported | $135,990 |
| Appropriation for 1922, repairs to cutters | $360,000.00 |
| Net expenditure | $356,313.22 |
| Unexpended balance | $3,686.78 |

Appropriation, construction of new cutters:

Balance on hand July 1, 1921 ........................................ $36,341.96
Net expenditure ..................................................... 32,998.99
Unexpended balance ................................................. 3,342.97
Appropriation for 1922 for maintenance of Coast Guard .............. 9,811,857.50
Net expenditure ..................................................... 9,422,251.09
Unexpended balance ................................................. 389,606.41

### Ice patrol to promote safety at sea.

The international service of ice observation and ice patrol was carried on during the season of 1922 by the Coast Guard cutters *Seneca*, *Tampa*, and *Modoc*, based on Halifax, Nova Scotia. The *Seneca* left her station at New York on February 8, 1922, for the purpose of conducting the ice observations, making two cruises prior to March 31 in the vicinity of the Grand Banks off Newfoundland. On April 1, 1922, the *Tampa* began the ice patrol, which was maintained by that vessel and the *Seneca* until May 15, 1922, on which date the *Modoc* relieved the *Seneca*, the latter vessel returning to her regular duty at New York. The *Tampa* and *Modoc* then maintained a continuous patrol in the vicinity of the Grand Banks, along the trans-Atlantic steamship lanes, where, during the spring and early summer, icebergs appear and constitute a serious menace to navigation. The patrol was still in progress at the close of the year.

### Winter cruising.

The President annually designates certain Coast Guard vessels to perform special cruising upon the coast in the season of severe weather, usually from December 1 to March 31, to afford such aid to distressed navigators as their circumstances may require. On November 5, 1921, the President, upon the recommendation of the Secretary of the Treasury, designated the Coast Guard cutters *Ossipee*, *Tampa*, *Acushnet*, *Seneca*, *Gresham*, *Manning*, *Seminole*, and *Yamacraw* to perform this duty.

### Cruises in northern waters.

The annual visitation to and patrol of the waters of the North Pacific Ocean, Bering Sea, and southeastern Alaska were performed for the season of 1921 by the Coast Guard cutters *Bear*, *Unalga*, *Algonquin*, *Snohomish*, and *Bothwell*. The *Snohomish* and *Bothwell* conducted the seal patrol from the southerly boundary of Washington to Dixon Entrance, and the latter vessel later entered on a patrol of the fisheries in southeastern Alaska. The *Bear* made her regular annual Arctic cruise. The vessels returned to the west coast in the fall and early winter of 1921. For the present season of 1922 the *Haida* and *Algonquin* are assigned to the patrol of the Bering Sea, and the *Snohomish* and *Unalga* to the patrol of the waters of southeastern Alaska. The *Bear* departed in the early spring oñ her annual cruise to the Arctic.

### *Anchorage and movements of vessels.*

The scope of the activity of the Coast Guard having to do with the enforcement of the rules and regulations governing the anchorage and movements of vessels in the navigable waters of the United States has been extended during the year to include the ports of San Francisco, Calif., and Galveston, Tex., at which places Coast Guard officers were designated as captains of the port on August 27, 1921, and October 27, 1921, respectively. On January 19, 1922, a Coast Guard officer was detailed as captain of the port at Charleston, S. C., to look after the enforcement of the regulations previously issued for that port. The services of Coast Guard officers have been utilized during the year at the ports of Portland, Me.; Portsmouth, N. H.; Charleston, S. C., and Jacksonville, Fla., in assisting the United States Hydrographic Office in the distribution and dissemination of hydrographic information.

### *Removal of derelicts.*

The vessels and stations of the service removed from the paths of marine commerce during the year 48 derelicts and other floating dangers and obstructions to navigation. The value of the property involved, so far as ascertainable, amounted to $384,550.

### *Coastal communication.*

In the course of the year telephone lines and cables were overhauled, rebuilt, repaired, and improved at various localities on the sea and lake coasts, where such work was needed. Two and one-half miles of submarine cable were laid between Plum Island, Wis., and Pilot Island Lighthouse, thereby affording telephone service for that light station through the Coast Guard line on Plum Island. About 1½ miles of line were constructed on Ediz Hook, Wash., thus giving telephone service to the Ediz Hook Light Station and the Coast Guard cutter *Snohomish*, when she is lying at that point.

The system of coastal communication of the Coast Guard now comprises more than 2,200 miles of telephone circuits, including approximately 440 miles of submarine telephone cable. All Coast Guard stations except two are furnished telephone service. In addition to this, the most important light stations on the Atlantic, Pacific, and Gulf coasts, numbering about 150, are provided with service by the Coast Guard. Telephone service is also furnished to about 30 Navy radio and radio compass stations via the Coast Guard lines.

### Coast Guard Academy.

There were under instruction at the Coast Guard Academy, at New London, Conn., at the end of the fiscal year, 13 line cadets and 4 cadet engineers. During the year, 9 line cadets and 7 cadet engineers were appointed. The resignations of 3 line cadets and 1 cadet engineer were accepted, and 7 line cadets and 2 cadet engineers were graduated. A competitive examination to secure additional cadets, both line and engineer, was held on June 26, 1922. There were 101 candidates, of whom approximately one-half were designated for examination. Of this number, 32 candidates were successful for appointment as line cadets and 4 were successful for appointment as engineer cadets. They are now receiving instruction at the Coast Guard Academy.

The practice cruise for cadets on the Coast Guard cutter *Vicksburg* renamed the *Alexander Hamilton*, began the latter part of June.

### Coast Guard repair depot.

The Coast Guard repair depot at Arundel Cove, South Baltimore, Md., continued its operations during the year. The boat building plant at the depot constructed 41 standard small boats, among them 7 motor lifeboats and 17 motor self-bailing surfboats, all of which were issued to cutters and stations as needed.

### New vessels.

The five new vessels (*Tampa, Haida, Mojave, Modoc,* and *Shawnee*), which were noted in the previous year's report to be approaching completion, were completed during this fiscal year and placed in commission. It is gratifying to state that they embody characteristics of design found to be highly necessary for the rugged service which Coast Guard vessels are called upon to perform, and that they are proving to be an effective addition to the fleet. Five seagoing steel tugs were transferred to the Coast Guard from the United States Shipping Board and have been transformed into useful cutters, within certain limitations, at moderate expense. While the fleet has been augmented as indicated, there is still necessity for replacing the *Bear,* now 48 years old, and the *Androscoggin* and *Itasca,* which have been condemned and sold, as no longer serviceable for Coast Guard duty. A cruising cutter to be based on Key West is also much needed, in order that the Coast Guard may be prepared properly to render any assistance required of it in that locality.

*Stations.*

The statements and recommendations made in the reports for 1920 and 1921, with regard to rebuilding and repairing shore stations which have long ago, through age, usage, and the hardest kind of exposure, become unfit for further occupancy, are renewed at this time. The matter is one of serious concern, and it is respectfully urged that the Congress come to the relief of the service in this regard by granting sufficient appropriations so that this work of rehabilitation, so badly needed, may be instituted. Again, it is felt that attention should be invited to the fact that a number of stations have been specifically authorized by law to be established, and that no funds have been appropriated for their construction.

*Enforcement of customs and other laws.*

The duties of the Coast Guard in assisting in the enforcement of the customs laws, and the laws relating to navigation and motor boats, have been vigorously prosecuted by the service, both by cutters and stations, during the year. Assistance has been rendered, as needed, to other branches of the public service.

*Repairs and improvements to vessels and stations.*

In addition to the usual routine docking and minor repair and upkeep of vessels, five cutters (*Cahokia, Kickapoo, Mascoutin, Tamaroa,* and *Vicksburg*) have been reconditioned. No extensive major repairs were undertaken during the year on account of the limited appropriations.

Rebuilding, repairs, and improvements, changes and additions, of more or less magnitude, were made during the year at 22 shore stations, including some protective bulkheading and other improvements at the Coast Guard depot. Contracts were awarded, or work was begun, in connection with projects involving repairs, improvements, and additions, and other construction work at 12 shore stations.

*Discipline.*

During the year final action was taken on 528 court cases, 134 of which were general court cases, 69 were minor court cases, and 325 were deck court cases.

*Flood work.*

For many years the crews of a number of the shore stations of the Coast Guard have taken an active part in rendering assistance and giving aid and succor upon the periodic visitations of floods on the Ohio, Mississippi, and other middle western rivers. Their work upon these occasions has always been of the highest order. They have gone with their small boats into the extensively flooded areas and removed the imprisoned dwellers to places of safety, rescued victims from extremely dangerous situations, furnished food and water to those threatened with famine, and rendered countless other services. The latest notable flood of the kind, except the recent one of 1922, was in 1913, when the middle western and Mississippi country was transformed into an immense inland sea. The damage, the loss of life and of property, the misery and human suffering of the inhabitants of these regions caused by this calamity came as a shock to the civilized world. It was just such calamitous visitations as these that suggested to the Coast Guard authorities the necessity of providing cutters which might be stationed on the Ohio and Mississippi Rivers to meet especially these grave emergencies as well as to perform other duties with which the Coast Guard is charged. The matter was brought to the attention of the Congress with the result that two river cutters were provided, one (*Kankakee*) being stationed at Evansville, Ind., and the other (*Yocona*) being stationed at Vicksburg, Miss. In the early spring of this year another of these devastating floods swept the Ohio and Mississippi Rivers and tributaries, inundating trackless areas of the lowlands and spreading destruction, havoc, and suffering in every direction. As soon as the situation became known the department ordered the *Kankakee* and *Yocona*, and members of four Coast Guard stations at and in the vicinity of Chicago, to proceed into the stricken regions and render all aid possible. Hundreds of persons were taken from positions of peril to places of safety; immense quantities of food were transported and distributed; household goods, live stock, and other property were saved from destruction; refugees were picked up and returned to their homes after the floods had subsided. Large numbers of live stock were recovered and returned to their owners, and other needful services were extended to the unfortunate population of the flooded districts. This was the first real trial for the river cutters in the work for which they were primarily designed. It is a pleasure to say that on this occasion they abundantly fulfilled their mission in the Coast Guard.

### Award of life-saving medals.

During the year 30 awards of life-saving medals of honor of the second class were made by the Secretary of the Treasury, under authority of law. Seven awards were made to civilians; 3 to persons serving in the United States Army; 16 to persons serving in the United States Navy; 1 to a person in the Coast Guard; and 3 to police officers. Twenty of the rescues were performed in waters of the United States, 2 at sea, 2 in Hawaii, 1 in the Philippines, 1 in Portugal, and 1 in Santo Domingo, making in all 27 instances.

### *Personnel.*

At the close of the year there were in the service on the active list 206 commissioned officers, 13 cadets, 4 cadet engineers, 389 warrant officers, 3,548 enlisted men, and 421 temporary surfmen and substitutes, together with 44 civilian employees in the field.

### *Units.*

There were in the service at the close of the year 103 vessels of all classes, of which 77 were in commission. The active shore stations numbered 235.

#### LOANS AND CURRENCY.

The Division of Loans and Currency is the issue branch of the public debt service. It receives public debt securities from the Bureau of Engraving and Printing, and issues them from time to time as required. This division is specifically charged with the maintenance of the accounts of registered holders of United States bonds and notes and with the preparation and dispatch of checks issued in payment of interest thereon. Transactions in the interest-bearing debt of the United States as conducted by the Division of Loans and Currency are reflected in the general statements relating to the public debt service presented elsewhere in this report. Other transactions conducted by the division not included in such statements are summarized in the table following.

*Claims on account of lost, stolen, mutilated, or destroyed interest-bearing securities received and disposed of during the fiscal year 1922.*

| | Received during the year. | Settled. |
|---|---|---|
| **Registered:** | | |
| Liberty issues— | | |
| Number of claimants | 3,380 | 4,132 |
| Number of bonds and notes involved | 7,394 | 10,014 |
| Amount thereof | $4,324,950 | $3,815,550 |
| Other issues— | | |
| Number of claimants | 17 | 7 |
| Number of bonds involved | 44 | 34 |
| Amount thereof | $20,040 | $32,640 |
| **Coupon:** | | |
| Liberty issues— | | |
| Number of claimants | 830 | 954 |
| Number of bonds and notes involved | 3,703 | 4,784 |
| Amount thereof | $1,565,813 | $1,835,900 |
| Other issues— | | |
| Number of claimants | | 3 |
| Number of bonds involved | | 4 |
| Amount thereof | | $11,200 |
| **Certificates of indebtedness:** | | |
| Number of claimants | 50 | 18 |
| Number of certificates involved | 126 | 57 |
| Amount thereof | $277,500 | $276,000 |
| **Interim certificates:** | | |
| Number of claimants | 5 | 12 |
| Number of certificates involved | 9 | 21 |
| Amount thereof | $2,150 | $2,050 |
| **Treasury savings certificates:** | | |
| Number of claimants | 235 | 189 |
| Number of certificates and stamps involved | 938 | 877 |
| Amount thereof | $101,952 | $87,433.30 |
| **War savings certificates and thrift stamps:** | | |
| Number of claimants | 10,174 | 10,769 |
| Amount involved (maturity value) (exclusive of deceased owner claims) | $452,391.75 | (¹) |
| Number of claims on account of deceased owners ² | 6,233 | 6,422 |

¹ Not practicable to state maturity value. Claims are settled by issuance of check at various redemption values, issuance of duplicate stamps, and authorization of payment by Post Office Department.
² In this class of claims the money value is not stated. Authority for payment of the claim is transmitted to the Post Office Department.

*Insular and District of Columbia loans—changes during fiscal year ended June 30, 1922.*

| Title of loan. | Rate. | Outstanding June 30, 1921. | Issues. | Retirements. | Outstanding June 30, 1922. |
|---|---|---|---|---|---|
| **PHILIPPINE ISLANDS.** | *Per cent.* | | | | |
| Land purchase, 1914–1934 | 4 | $7,000,000 | .............. | .............. | $7,000,000 |
| Public improvement: | | | | | |
| 1915–1935 | 4 | 2,500,000 | .............. | .............. | 2,500,000 |
| 1916–1936 | 4 | 1,000,000 | .............. | .............. | 1,000,000 |
| 1919–1939 | 4 | 1,500,000 | .............. | .............. | 1,500,000 |
| Loan of 1916, 1926–1946 | 4 | 4,000,000 | .............. | .............. | 4,000,000 |
| City of Manila, sewer and water: | | | | | |
| First series, 1915–1935 | 4 | 1,000,000 | .............. | .............. | 1,000,000 |
| Second series, 1917–1937 | 4 | 2,000,000 | .............. | .............. | 2,000,000 |
| Third series, 1918–1938 | 4 | 1,000,000 | .............. | .............. | 1,000,000 |
| Certificates of indebtedness: | | | | | |
| Coupon, Aug. 2, 1920 | 4 | 10,000,000 | .............. | $10,000,000 | .............. |
| Coupon, Aug. 1, 1921 | 4 | .............. | $10,000,000 | .............. | 10,000,000 |
| City of Cebu, 1921–1941 | 4 | 125,000 | .............. | .............. | 125,000 |
| Manila port works and improvements, 1920–1930–1950 | 5½ | 6,000,000 | .............. | .............. | 6,000,000 |
| City of Manila, 1920–1930–1950 | 5½ | 2,750,000 | .............. | .............. | 2,750,000 |
| Public improvement, 1921–1941 | 5½ | .............. | [1] 10,000,000 | .............. | 10,000,000 |
| Loan of 1922–1952 | 5 | .............. | [1] 5,000,000 | .............. | 5,000,000 |
| Collateral loan of 1922–1950 | 4½ | .............. | [1] 2,750,000 | .............. | 2,750,000 |
| Total | .......... | 38,875,000 | 27,750,000 | 10,000,000 | 56,625,000 |
| **PORTO RICO.** | | | | | |
| Road loan of 1910 | 4 | 425,000 | .............. | .............. | 425,000 |
| San Juan Harbor: | | | | | |
| Series 1912 | 4 | 100,000 | .............. | .............. | 100,000 |
| Series 1914 | 4 | [1] 200,000 | .............. | .............. | 200,000 |
| Series 1915 | 4 | [1] 200,000 | .............. | .............. | 200,000 |
| Series 1917 | 4 | [1] 100,000 | .............. | .............. | 100,000 |
| Irrigation loans: | | | | | |
| Series 1913–1933–1943 | 4 | 1,000,000 | .............. | .............. | 1,000,000 |
| Series 1913–1944–1950 | 4 | 700,000 | .............. | .............. | 700,000 |
| Series 1914–1951–1954 | 4 | 400,000 | .............. | .............. | 400,000 |
| Series 1915–1955–1958 | 4 | 400,000 | .............. | .............. | 400,000 |
| Series 1916–1959–1960 | 4 | 200,000 | .............. | .............. | 200,000 |
| Series 1918–1958–1959 | 4 | 200,000 | .............. | .............. | 200,000 |
| Public improvements: | | | | | |
| Series 1914–1925–1939 | 4 | 1,000,000 | .............. | .............. | 1,000,000 |
| Series 1916–1927–1930 | 4 | 500,000 | .............. | .............. | 500,000 |
| Series 1918–1927–1930 | 4 | 500,000 | .............. | .............. | 500,000 |
| Series 1919–1931–1934 | 4½ | [1] 1,000,000 | .............. | .............. | 1,000,000 |
| Series 1920–1937–1940 | 4½ | .............. | 1,000,000 | .............. | 1,000,000 |
| Refunding loans, series 1914–1923–1953 | 4 | 655,000 | .............. | .............. | 655,000 |
| Refunding municipal loans: | | | | | |
| Series 1915–1922–1935 | 4 | 257,000 | .............. | 21,000 | 236,000 |
| Series 1916–1922–1927 | 4 | 210,000 | .............. | 30,000 | 180,000 |
| High-school building loan, 1920–1945 | 4½ | [1] 300,000 | .............. | .............. | 300,000 |
| House construction loan, series A, 1920–1945 | 4½ | 250,000 | .............. | .............. | 250,000 |
| Workingmen's house construction, 1920: | | | | | |
| Series A, 1941 | 4½ | [1] 250,000 | .............. | .............. | [1,2] 250,000 |
| Series B, 1942 | 4½ | [1] 250,000 | .............. | .............. | [1,2] 250,000 |
| Total | .......... | 9,097,000 | 1,000,000 | 51,000 | 10,046,000 |
| **DISTRICT OF COLUMBIA.** | | | | | |
| 50-year funded loan of 1924 | 3.65 | [1,2] 4,915,750 | .............. | 196,050 | [1,2] 4,719,700 |

[1] Coupon issues.      [2] Registered issues.

## Circulation.

The form of the circulation statement has been revised beginning with the issue for July 1, 1922, in order to show more accurately the distribution of the stock of money in the United States. On the new form of statement only money outside of the Treasury and the Federal reserve banks is included in circulation. In previous circulation statements, money held by the Federal reserve banks (other than money held by or for Federal reserve agents, and Federal reserve notes held by the issuing banks in their own vaults) was included in the amount in circulation. Under that method of computing money in circulation, transfers of gold between a Federal reserve bank and a Federal reserve agent resulted in an apparent change in the amount of money in circulation, and there are instances where the circulation statement owing to such transfers showed a decline in money in circulation when, as a matter of fact, there had been an actual increase, and an increase when in fact there had been a decrease. The new form shows a per capita circulation on July 1, 1922, of $39.87, whereas under the form of statement heretofore used it would have been $49.17. This revision, however, does not necessitate any adjustment in figures of per capita circulation prior to the establishment of the Federal reserve system.

The revised form of statement shows more clearly the distribution of the money held in the Treasury and the amount of money held by or for Federal reserve banks and agents. Certain changes have also been made in the column showing stock of money in the United States. The amounts of outstanding gold certificates and silver certificates have been inserted in this column, but have not been included in the total since the gold and silver held in trust against the certificates is included under gold coin and bullion and standard silver dollars, respectively. Treasury notes of 1890 are still shown separately, but have not been included in the total, since standard silver dollars are held against them equal to 100 per cent of the amount of notes outstanding.

There have been added to the new form of statement comparative totals for July 1, 1914, just before the organization of the Federal Reserve System, and April 1, 1917, just before the entry of the United States into the World War.

For the sake of comparability, revised figures on the new basis for each month of the last fiscal year have been added to the following circulation statement for July 1, 1922. Revised figures on the new basis for the end of each fiscal year since 1914 will be found in Table T, page 526.

14263—FI 1922——28

Circulation statement, July 1, 1922 (revised figures).

| Kind of money. | Stock of money in the United States. | Money held in the Treasury — Total. | Amount held in trust against gold and silver certificates (and Treasury notes of 1890). | Reserve against United States notes (and Treasury notes of 1890). | Held for Federal reserve banks and agents. | All other money. | Money outside of the Treasury — Total. | Held by Federal reserve banks and agents. | In circulation — Amount. | Per capita. | Population of continental United States (estimated). |
|---|---|---|---|---|---|---|---|---|---|---|---|
| Gold coin and bullion | $3,784,651,712 | $3,157,202,556 | $695,000,469 | $152,979,026 | $2,108,886,911 | $200,336,150 | $627,449,156 | $211,611,603 | $415,937,553 | $3.79 | 109,743,000 |
| Gold | ²(695,000,469) | | | | | | 695,000,469 | 521,658,270 | 173,342,199 | 1.58 | |
| Standard silver dollars | 381,174,404 | 313,504,308 | 305,577,136 | | | 7,927,172 | 67,670,096 | 9,697,027 | 87,973,069 | .53 | |
| Silver certificates | ²(304,066,593) | | | | | | 304,066,593 | 35,731,219 | 265,335,374 | 2.42 | |
| Treasury notes of 1890 | 271,210,886 | | | | | | 1,510,543 | 1,000 | 1,509,543 | | |
| Subsidiary silver | (1,510,543) | 17,747,502 | | | | 17,747,502 | 233,463,394 | 24,153,011 | 229,310,373 | 2.01 | |
| United States notes | 346,631,016 | 4,145,964 | | | | 4,145,964 | 342,535,052 | 50,192,056 | 292,342,996 | 2.66 | |
| Federal reserve notes | 2,555,061,660 | 2,557,722 | | | | 2,557,722 | 2,652,506,938 | 413,785,985 | 2,138,714,953 | 10.49 | |
| Federal reserve bank notes | 80,495,400 | 1,030,273 | | | | 1,030,273 | 79,465,127 | 7,597,198 | 71,867,941 | .66 | |
| National bank notes | 758,202,027 | 15,774,366 | | | | 15,774,366 | 742,427,661 | 14,746,625 | 727,681,036 | 6.63 | |
| Total, July 1, 1922 | 8,177,477,105 | 3,511,962,691 | 1,000,577,605 | 152,979,026 | 2,108,886,911 | 249,519,149 | 5,666,092,019 | 1,292,076,982 | 4,374,015,037 | 39.86 | 109,743,000 |
| **Totals:** | | | | | | | | | | | |
| June 1, 1922 | 8,126,500,982 | 3,495,160,978 | 994,959,698 | 152,979,026 | 2,082,738,419 | 264,453,835 | 5,028,299,702 | 1,255,829,710 | 4,370,469,992 | 39.87 | 109,605,000 |
| May 1, 1922 | 8,147,006,394 | 3,482,460,013 | 983,510,981 | 152,979,026 | 2,078,081,822 | 257,888,184 | 5,635,437,362 | 1,273,208,855 | 4,384,545,507 | 40.06 | 109,468,000 |
| Apr. 1, 1922 | 8,108,976,196 | 3,462,797,007 | 991,024,975 | 152,979,026 | 2,038,470,368 | 280,322,638 | 5,637,204,164 | 1,224,073,450 | 4,413,130,714 | 40.37 | 109,330,000 |
| Mar. 1, 1922 | 8,076,223,365 | 3,421,492,051 | 978,833,951 | 152,979,026 | 2,028,262,966 | 264,416,108 | 5,630,565,265 | 1,228,580,723 | 4,401,984,542 | 40.31 | 09,192,000 |
| Feb. 1, 1922 | 8,079,226,057 | 3,384,013,215 | 980,393,276 | 152,979,026 | 1,979,828,505 | 270,812,408 | 5,675,606,118 | 1,323,067,678 | 4,352,538,440 | 39.91 | 109,055,000 |
| Jan. 1, 1922 | 8,282,070,452 | 3,351,639,545 | 990,471,711 | 152,979,026 | 1,933,539,265 | 274,649,543 | 5,920,902,618 | 1,399,336,048 | 4,521,566,570 | 41.51 | 108,917,000 |
| Dec. 1, 1921 | 8,156,446,983 | 3,310,194,362 | 1,182,278,656 | 152,979,026 | 1,677,305,562 | 297,631,118 | 6,028,531,277 | 1,467,312,375 | 4,561,218,902 | 41.93 | 108,779,000 |
| Nov. 1, 1921 | 8,117,812,092 | 3,245,838,774 | 1,130,530,646 | 152,979,026 | 1,657,020,126 | 305,008,976 | 6,002,803,964 | 1,391,815,300 | 4,610,988,664 | 42.44 | 108,641,000 |
| Oct. 1, 1921 | 8,150,732,649 | 3,168,037,640 | 1,115,177,696 | 152,979,026 | 1,622,279,940 | 277,600,988 | 6,097,892,735 | 1,433,194,831 | 4,664,697,904 | 42.99 | 108,503,000 |
| Sept. 1, 1921 | 8,082,456,974 | 3,086,054,358 | 1,045,907,596 | 152,979,026 | 1,608,522,856 | 278,644,880 | 6,042,310,212 | 1,383,432,714 | 4,658,877,498 | 42.99 | 108,365,000 |
| Aug. 1, 1921 | 8,059,103,327 | 2,990,444,729 | 977,318,557 | 152,979,026 | 1,580,655,064 | 279,492,082 | 6,045,977,674 | 1,322,571,674 | 4,723,405,431 | 43.64 | 108,226,000 |
| July 1, 1921 | 8,099,006,237 | 2,918,696,736 | 919,643,386 | 152,979,026 | 1,537,856,895 | 308,217,429 | 6,099,952,887 | 1,257,368,483 | 4,842,584,404 | 44.80 | 108,087,000 |
| Apr. 1, 1917 | 5,312,109,272 | ²2,942,998,527 | 2,684,800,085 | 152,979,026 | | 105,219,416 | 5,033,910,830 | 953,320,126 | 4,080,590,704 | 39.54 | 103,716,000 |
| July 1, 1914 | 3,738,288,571 | ²1,843,452,323 | 1,507,175,879 | 150,000,000 | | 186,273,444 | 3,402,015,427 | | 3,402,015,427 | 34.35 | 99,027,000 |
| Jan. 1, 1879 | 1,007,084,483 | ²1,212,420,402 | 21,602,640 | 100,000,000 | | 90,817,762 | 816,296,721 | | 816,296,721 | 16.92 | 48,231,000 |

¹ Does not include gold bullion or foreign coin outside of vaults of the Treasury, Federal reserve banks, and       reserve agents.
² These amounts are not included in the   that since the money held in trust against gold and       notes and       ry notes of 1890 is included under gold coin and bullion and standard silver    s,     .
³ The       nt of money held in trust against gold and       fer certificates and        notes of 1890 should be       ted from this    tal    ore    thing it       l       ny      of the Treasury to arrive at the stock of money in the United States.
⁴ This total includes $17,249,719 of    notes in process of redemption, $178,459,108 of gold       ed for 1   1   tion of            reserve    ries, $6,415,374 of lawful     ney deposited for        ion of Federal       rve bank notes, $14,251,012 deposited for      on of national    bsk    ries, $31,060 deposited for      tion (act of May 30, 1908), and $7,047,173 deposited as a       rve against postal-saving deposits.
   NOTE.—Gold       tes are secured dollar for dollar by gold held in the       ury for their       tion; silver certificates are   red dollar for dollar by standard silver dollars held in the Treasury for their       tion; United       tes notes are       red by a gold      rve of $152,979,025.63 held in the Treasury.   This       nd fund may also be used for the redemption of Treasury       tes of 1890, which are also secured dollar for dollar by       dard silver    as, held in the       ury.   Federal reserve notes are obligations of the United       tes and a first lien on all the       sets of the issuing Federal    rve bank.   Federal reserve notes are       sed by the       nt with Federal reserve agents of a   ike   nt of gold or of gold and such discounted or purchased paper as is       ible       er the       ms of the         ral       ve act.        se    nks    nst maintain a gold       rve of at least 40 per    nt, including the gold       tion fund       hich must be deposited with the United States       sury, against Federal reserve notes in    tual.   Federal reserve bank       tes and       onal bank       tes are secured by United States Government obligations, and a 5 per cent fund for their redemption is required to be maintained with the       ser of the United States in gold or lawful money.

### DIVISION OF PAPER CUSTODY.

This division, formerly known as the Section of Paper Custody in the Division of Loans and Currency, was established as the Division of Paper Custody in the office of the Secretary, under the Commissioner of Public Debt, on August 24, 1921. It receives from contractors the distinctive papers used by the Bureau of Engraving and Printing in printing public debt obligations, paper currency, internal revenue and postage stamps, etc. The division maintains records showing the amount of paper issued to the bureau on requisitions; the perfect and imperfect work delivered in sheets and value, and balances in the bureau. The transactions during the fiscal year 1922 are shown in the following table:

*Paper custody.*

| Kind. | On hand July 1, 1921. | Received from contractors. | Issued to bureau. | On hand June 30, 1922. |
|---|---|---|---|---|
| | *Sheets.* | *Sheets.* | *Sheets.* | *Sheets.* |
| Distinctive paper for United States currency, Federal reserve notes, Federal reserve, and national-bank currency | 3,320,661 | 224,270,173 | 195,163,194 | 32,427,640 |
| Internal-revenue paper | 6,731,820 | 87,984,347 | 75,957,672 | 18,758,495 |
| Postage-stamp paper | 7,841,186 | 21,289,827 | 23,793,997 | 5,337,016 |
| Check paper | 449,718 | 1,326,863 | 1,743,528 | 33,053 |
| United States bond paper | 4,306,521 | 4,830,652 | 3,076,002½ | 6,061,170½ |
| Parchment, artificial parchment, and parchment deed paper | 184,976 | 155,222 | 183,496 | 156,702 |
| Postal savings cards | 156,126 | | | 156,126 |
| Customs-stamp paper | 851 | 50,000 | 39,386 | 11,465 |
| Miscellaneous paper | 725,928 | 2,668,676 | 2,204,714 | 1,189,890 |
| Philippine Islands paper: | | | | |
| Distinctive paper for silver certificates, national-bank and Treasury notes | 1,138,525 | | 161,800 | 976,725 |
| Postage-stamp paper | 22,384 | 86 | 12,761 | 9,709 |
| Internal revenue and check paper | 52,116 | 160,067 | 110,295 | 101,888 |
| Porto Rican internal-revenue paper | 64,305 | 288,000 | 311,851 | 40,454 |
| Total | 24,995,117 | 343,023,913 | 302,758,696½ | 65,260,333½ |
| Rolls postage-stamp paper | 367 | 2,583 | 2,565 | 385 |
| Rolls internal-revenue paper | 120 | 399 | 410 | 109 |
| Rolls United States security paper | 3 | | | 3 |

The chief of the division of paper custody is also the custodian, representing the Secretary of the Treasury, of the reserve stock of Federal reserve notes, Series 1914 and 1918, prepared for issue as authorized in the Federal reserve act, the other custodians being representatives of the Director of the Bureau of Engraving and Printing and the Federal Reserve Board  The table following shows the transactions in such notes during the year.

*Custody of Federal reserve notes, series of 1914 and 1918.*

| Federal reserve bank. | On hand July 1, 1921. | Received. | Issued. | On hand June 30, 1922. |
|---|---|---|---|---|
| Boston | $175,020,000 | $100,940,000 | $85,400,000 | $190,560,000 |
| New York | 564,060,000 | 571,160,000 | 637,160,000 | 498,060,000 |
| Philadelphia | 170,520,000 | 172,320,000 | 148,180,000 | 194,660,000 |
| Cleveland | 147,040,000 | 116,320,000 | 126,640,000 | 136,720,000 |
| Richmond | 171,920,000 | 101,420,000 | 84,700,000 | 188,640,000 |
| Atlanta | 146,240,000 | 58,560,000 | 50,000,000 | 154,800,000 |
| Chicago | 384,600,000 | 247,660,000 | 186,300,000 | 445,960,000 |
| St. Louis | 146,100,000 | 48,360,000 | 45,700,000 | 148,760,000 |
| Minneapolis | 81,700,000 | 46,320,000 | 33,800,000 | 94,220,000 |
| Kansas City | 105,580,000 | 43,740,000 | 51,760,000 | 97,560,000 |
| Dallas | 104,400,000 | 2,820,000 | 9,920,000 | 97,300,000 |
| San Francisco | 75,000,000 | 302,760,000 | 208,560,000 | 169,200,000 |
| Total | 2,272,180,000 | 1,812,380,000 | 1,668,120,000 | 2,416,440,000 |

## REGISTER OF THE TREASURY.

During the fiscal year 1922 the total amount of securities received by the Register of the Treasury was $14,170,831,888.36¼ as compared with $24,834,653,220.74½ during 1921. The number of pieces handled, however, increased from 227,850,967 in 1921 to 239,931,556 in 1922. As usual, the greater part of the securities handled were in bearer form, there being 232,126,681 pieces of bearer securities with an aggregate face value of $10,761,404,931.00½ as compared with 7,804,877 pieces with an aggregate face value of $3,409,426,957.36 in registered form.

Inasmuch as the volume of work in the register's office depends on the number of pieces handled rather than on their aggregate face value, personnel requirements continue to be large. The great amount of work connected with handling interest coupons is chiefly responsible for the maintenance of a large personnel. The present organization embraces 10 units, namely, office of the chief clerk, section of inquiries, and divisions of accounts, canceled securities, destruction, interest coupons, numerical records, paid securities, registered files, and vaults and files. These divisions have been coordinated in such a way that the maximum efficiency is being attained.

Securities received are audited currently for the purpose of closing accounts with fiscal agents and other departments connected with the public-debt service, and are reaudited prior to delivery to the destruction committee for maceration. This procedure entails a great deal of clerical work, but is absolutely necessary in connection with the retirement of securities. In addition to the audit, each bearer security, with the exception of Treasury (war) savings securities, is entered on what is known as a numerical register. Each security bears a serial number, and when it is retired this fact is recorded opposite the corresponding number in the register, together with a code giving all other necessary information. During the fiscal year 1922 more than 19,000,000 such entries were made.

As stated, most of the administrative expense of the register's office is due to the great number of interest coupons received and in process of assortment and recordation. On June 30, 1922, out of a personnel of 1,140—760 clerks, including 169 released from the division of destruction on April 22, 1922, together with 140 clerks detailed from the Division of Loans and Currency on May 1, 1922, were engaged in auditing, arranging in numerical sequence, filing, and entering data in the numerical records. At present this is the main problem of the register's office, and every method has been used to promote greater speed and economy. In April, 1922, an improved method of recording interest coupons was introduced, and special attention has since been devoted to working off the accumulation of coupons. With the present office force of 1,140, as now functioning, it is estimated that the work will become current about June 30, 1923.

The following statement gives comparative figures for the classes, pieces, and amounts of retired securities received, examined, and filed in the register's office during the fiscal years 1921 and 1922:

*Retired securities received, examined, and filed in the register's office during the fiscal years 1921 and 1922.*

| Class of securities. | 1921 | | 1922 | |
|---|---|---|---|---|
| | Pieces. | Amount. | Pieces. | Amount. |
| **Redeemed:** | | | | |
| Bearer— | | | | |
| Pre-war loans.............. | 466 | $89,060.00 | 220 | $28,610.00 |
| Liberty loans.............. | 305,517 | 413,073,700.00 | 1,206,457 | 1,884,018,300.00 |
| Certificates of indebtedness. | 637,874 | 3,470,216,500.00 | 669,511 | 2,809,044,500.00 |
| Treasury (War) savings securities............... | 23,138,658 | 102,750,604.05 | 13,679,887 | 51,473,405.17 |
| Interest coupons.......... | 112,924,776 | 777,544,734.98 | 91,776,882 | 776,338,623.33 |
| District of Columbia loans.. | 81 | 38,700.00 | 63 | 22,050.00 |
| District of Columbia interest coupons.............. | 1,892 | 10,431.68½ | 1,738 | 8,106.64½ |
| Total................ | 137,009,264 | 4,763,723,730.71½ | 107,334,758 | 5,520,933,595.14½ |
| **Registered—** | | | | |
| Pre-war loans.............. | 250 | 62,520.00 | 108 | 28,530.00 |
| Liberty loans.............. | 1,059 | 19,138,950.00 | 45,893 | 177,571,400.00 |
| Certificates of indebtedness. | 505 | 5,082,000,000.00 | 397 | 1,966,829,450.00 |
| Treasury (War) savings securities............... | 11,789,520 | 56,983,841.98 | 6,285,838 | 33,952,907.35 |
| Interest checks (Liberty loans).................... | 6,929 | 602,667.83 | 4,711 | 153,549.76 |
| District of Columbia loans.. | 123 | 527,000.00 | 1,530 | 6,138,000.00 |
| District of Columbia interest checks................ | 329 | 168,429.25 | 337 | 171,130.25 |
| Total................ | 11,798,715 | 5,159,483,409.06 | 6,338,814 | 2,184,844,967.36 |
| **Retired on account of exchanges for other securities, etc.:** | | | | |
| Bearer— | | | | |
| Pre-war loans.............. | 4,092 | 3,230,780.00 | 3,628 | 2,877,730.00 |
| Liberty loans.............. | 49,518,628 | 11,724,172,350.00 | 13,154,929 | 2,873,611,800.00 |
| Treasury notes............ | 1,141 | 2,384,500.00 | 39,042 | 72,180,900.00 |
| Certificates of indebtedness. | 453,277 | 2,120,351,500.00 | 427,644 | 1,971,651,000.00 |
| Interim certificates (Liberty loans)............... | 3,307 | 4,560,700.00 | 1,031 | 105,640.00 |
| Treasury (War) savings securities............... | 21,262,258 | 143,311,260.00 | 99,639,249 | 40,827,056.75 |
| Insular possessions loans... | 2,166 | 11,076,000.00 | 22,926 | 32,016,000.00 |
| Interest coupons.......... | 7,002,906 | 119,048,050.97 | 11,503,474 | 247,201,209.11 |
| Total................ | 78,247,775 | 14,128,135,140.97 | 124,791,923 | 5,240,471,335.86 |

*Retired securities received, examined, and filed in the register's office during the fiscal years 1921 and 1922—Continued.*

| Class of securities. | 1921 | | 1922 | |
|---|---|---|---|---|
| | Pieces. | Amount. | Pieces. | Amount. |
| Retired on account of exchanges for other securities, etc.—Continued. Registered— | | | | |
| Pre-war loans | 18,665 | $62,649,390.00 | 85,429 | $170,448,090.00 |
| Liberty loans | 751,150 | 512,535,800.00 | 1,043,791 | 993,778,600.00 |
| Certificates of indebtedness | 154 | 187,338,000.00 | | |
| Treasury (War) savings securities | 13,750 | 68,750.00 | 323,146 | 26,646,300.00 |
| Insular possessions loans | 11,348 | 20,245,000.00 | 12,797 | 29,867,000.00 |
| District of Columbia loans | 146 | 474,000.00 | 898 | 3,842,000.00 |
| Total | 795,213 | 783,310,940.00 | 1,466,063 | 1,224,581,990.00 |
| Recapitulation: Bearer— | | | | |
| Pre-war loans | 4,558 | 3,319,840.00 | 3,848 | 2,906,340.00 |
| Liberty loans | 49,824,145 | 12,137,246,050.00 | 14,361,386 | 4,757,630,100.00 |
| Treasury notes | 1,141 | 2,384,500.00 | 39,042 | 72,180,900.00 |
| Certificates of indebtedness | 1,091,151 | 5,590,568,000.00 | 1,097,155 | 4,780,695,500.00 |
| Interim certificates (Liberty loans) | 3,307 | 4,560,700.00 | 1,031 | 105,640.00 |
| Treasury (War) savings securities | 44,400,916 | 246,061,864.05 | 113,319,136 | 92,300,461.92 |
| Interest coupons (Liberty loans) | 119,927,682 | 896,592,785.95 | 103,280,356 | 1,023,539,832.44 |
| District of Columbia loans | 81 | 38,700.00 | 63 | 22,050.00 |
| District of Columbia interest coupons | 1,892 | 10,431.68½ | 1,738 | 8,106.64½ |
| Insular possessions loans | 2,166 | 11,076,000.00 | 22,926 | 32,016,000.00 |
| Total | 215,257,039 | 18,891,858,871.68½ | 232,126,681 | 10,761,404,931.00½ |
| Registered— | | | | |
| Pre-war loans | 18,915 | 62,711,910.00 | 85,537 | 170,476,620.00 |
| Liberty loans | 752,209 | 531,674,750.00 | 1,089,684 | 1,171,350,000.00 |
| Certificates of indebtedness | 659 | 5,269,338,000.00 | 397 | 1,966,829,450.00 |
| Treasury (War) savings securities | 11,803,270 | 57,052,591.98 | 6,608,984 | 60,599,207.35 |
| Interest checks (Liberty loans) | 6,929 | 602,667.83 | 4,711 | 153,549.76 |
| District of Columbia loans | 269 | 1,001,000.00 | 2,428 | 9,980,000.00 |
| District of Columbia interest checks | 329 | 168,429.25 | 337 | 171,130.25 |
| Insular possessions loans | 11,348 | 20,245,000.00 | 12,797 | 29,867,000.00 |
| Total | 12,593,928 | 5,942,794,349.06 | 7,804,877 | 3,409,426,957.36 |
| Grand total | 227,850,967 | 24,834,653,220.74½ | 239,931,556 | 14,170,831,888.36½ |

## DIVISION OF DEPOSITS.

The following statements indicate the number of depositaries maintained by the Treasury, other than the Treasurer of the United States, and the amounts of public moneys held by such depositaries, on the basis of revised Treasury statements, at the end of the fiscal years 1921 and 1922:

*Number of depositaries.*

| | June 30, 1921. | June 30, 1922. |
|---|---|---|
| Federal land banks | 12 | 12 |
| Federal reserve banks (including branches) | 12 | 12 |
| Special depositaries | 9,412 | 8,439 |
| Foreign depositaries | 16 | 12 |
| General national-bank depositaries | 533 | 335 |
| Limited national-bank depositaries | 187 | 845 |
| Insular depositaries (including Philippine treasury) | 5 | 5 |
| Total | 10,177 | 9,660 |

*Amount of deposits.*

| | June 30, 1921. | June 30, 1922. |
|---|---|---|
| Deposits in Federal reserve banks and branches......................... | $43,475,862.73 | $33,091,888.68 |
| Deposits in special depositaries............................................ | 395,738,063.16 | 146,476,840.69 |
| Deposits in foreign depositaries:[1] | | |
| To credit of Treasurer of the United States........................... | 710,262.94 | 701,760.43 |
| To credit of other Government officers............................... | 51,548,267.84 | 521,190.60 |
| Deposits in national banks: | | |
| To credit of Treasurer of the United States........................... | 8,207,647.02 | 7,832,260.63 |
| To credit of other Government officers................................ | 16,036,064.70 | 16,169,825.24 |
| Deposits in the Philippine treasury to credit of Treasurer of the United States[1]........................................................................... | 7,917,707.88 | 4,418,311.48 |
| Total................................................. | 523,633,876.27 | 209,212,077.75 |

[1] Includes items in transit.

*General and limited national-bank depositaries of public moneys.*

Two complete analyses of the depositary accounts of all general national-bank depositaries of public moneys were made during the fiscal year ended June 30, 1922, resulting in the discontinuance of 221 general depositaries which were transacting no essential Government business, and reductions in the fixed balances held to the credit of the Treasurer's general account in 67 other such depositaries which were holding balances out of proportion to the essential Government business transacted. During the same period the Treasury designated 23 additional general national-bank depositaries of public moneys and increased the fixed balances to be held to the credit of the Treasurer's general account in 44 general depositaries. The net reduction in the total fixed balances carried with all general national-bank depositaries to the credit of the Treasurer's general account during the fiscal year ended June 30, 1922, amounted to $1,186,000. Limited national-bank depositaries of public moneys to the number of 704 were designated and 46 limited depositaries were discontinued.

*Special depositaries of public moneys.*

During the fiscal year 83 banks were designated and 1,056 banks were discontinued as special depositaries of public moneys. Special depositaries of public moneys are designated under the provisions of the act approved September 24, 1917, as amended and supplemented, and are authorized to participate in deposits of public moneys arising from such sales of bonds, notes, or Treasury certificates of indebtedness of the United States offered from time to time, as, under the terms of the official offering, may be paid for by credit. National and State banks and trust companies are eligible for designation as special depositaries of public moneys, and of the 8,439 special depositaries of public moneys carried on the books of the Treasury at the close of the fiscal year 4,092 were national banks and 4,347 State banks and trust companies.

*Foreign depositaries of public moneys.*

At the close of the fiscal year ended June 30, 1921, there were 16 foreign depositaries of public moneys maintained by the Treasury. During the fiscal year 1922, however, 5 of these depositaries were discontinued—2 in Canada, 2 in Paris, and 1 in Haiti. During the same period 1 new depositary of public moneys was designated in Paris, making a total of 12 foreign depositaries of public moneys maintained by the Treasury at the close of the fiscal year ended June 30, 1922, located as follows: 2 in Belgium, 4 in England, 3 in France, 1 in Haiti, and 2 in Italy.

*Deposits in Federal land banks.*

Temporary deposits aggregating $11,250,000 were made by the Treasury with Federal land banks during the fiscal year ended June 30, 1922, under the provisions of section 32 of the act approved July 17, 1916, as amended July 1, 1921. All of these deposits were repaid to the Treasury prior to June 30, 1922.

### DIVISION OF BOOKKEEPING AND WARRANTS.

A summary of the receipts and expenditures during the fiscal year ended June 30, 1922, adjusted to the basis of daily Treasury statements revised, is set forth in the following table:

| | |
|---|---:|
| Ordinary receipts | $4,103,596,531.04 |
| Ordinary expenditures, including decrease in credits of disbursing officers, etc., with the Treasurer of the United States | 3,360,196,364.64 |
| Excess of ordinary receipts over ordinary expenditures | 743,400,166.40 |
| Public debt redemptions chargeable against ordinary receipts | 422,352,950.00 |
| Excess of ordinary receipts over total ordinary cash expenditures, including public debt redemptions chargeable against ordinary receipts | 321,047,216.40 |
| Public debt receipts | 6,018,017,902.60 |
| Public debt expenditures | 7,030,189,462.92 |
| Excess of public debt expenditures over public debt receipts | 1,012,171,560.32 |
| Public debt redemptions chargeable against ordinary receipts | 422,352,950.00 |
| Excess of public debt expenditures over public debt receipts, exclusive of redemptions chargeable against ordinary receipts | 589,818,610.32 |
| Total ordinary and public debt receipts | 10,121,614,433.64 |
| Total ordinary and public debt expenditures | 10,390,385,827.56 |
| Excess of all expenditures over all receipts | 268,771,393.92 |

This shows an excess of ordinary receipts over total ordinary cash expenditures of $743,400,166.40; an excess of ordinary receipts over total ordinary cash expenditures (including public debt redemptions chargeable against ordinary receipts) of $321,047,216.40; an excess of public debt redemptions over public debt issues of $1,012,171,560.32; an excess of public debt expenditures over public debt receipts (excluding redemptions chargeable against ordinary receipts) of $589,818,-610.32; an excess of all expenditures over all receipts of $268,771,-393.92, taking into account public debt transactions, special accounts, and payments by warrants from the general fund of the Treasury during the year of $2,791,035.40 for the Panama Canal, offset by receipts from Panama Canal tolls of $12,049,660.65.

*The general fund.*

| | |
|---|---:|
| Balance, according to daily Treasury statement June 30, 1921...... | $549,678,105.76 |
| Deduct: Net excess of expenditures over receipts in June reports subsequently received........................................ | 16,779,775.99 |
| | 532,898,329.77 |
| Pay warrants issued in excess of receipts, fiscal year 1922........................................... $104,259,876.69 | |
| Add: | |
| Decrease in unpaid warrants June 30, 1922, under such amount on June 30, 1921.......... 19,618,905.14 | |
| Decrease in book credits of disbursing officers and agencies with the Treasurer, June 30, 1922, under such amount June 30, 1921..... 144,892,612.09 | |
| | 268,771,393.92 |
| Balance held by the Treasurer of the United States June 30, 1922..................................................... | 264,126,935.85 |
| Balance held by the Treasurer, according to daily Treasury statement June 30, 1922............................................ | 272,105,512.63 |
| Deduct: Net excess of expenditures over receipts in June reports subsequently received............................................ | -7,978,576.78 |
| | 264,126,935.85 |

The following table shows the total number of warrants issued, together with the gross amounts involved, on account of the receipts and disbursements recorded during the fiscal year:

*Warrants issued during the fiscal year 1922.*

| General classes. | Number of warrants issued. | Gross amount involved. |
|---|---:|---:|
| Receipt warrants, ordinary........... | 561 | $4,103,741,926.79 |
| Receipt warrants, public debt........... | 15 | 6,018,017,902.60 |
| Total receipt warrants............... | 576 | 10,121,759,829.39 |
| Repay and counter warrants, ordinary..................... | 1,097 | 2,332,654,862.19 |
| Repay and counter warrants, public debt................. | 25 | 2,571.70 |
| Total repay and counter warrants................... | 1,122 | 2,332,657,433.89 |
| Pay and transfer warrants, ordinary..................... | 186,535 | 5,528,277,592.15 |
| Pay and transfer warrants, public debt.................... | 87 | 7,030,192,034.62 |
| Total pay and transfer warrants..................... | 186,622 | 12,558,469,626.77 |
| Total............... | 188,320 | 25,012,886,890.05 |

Receipt accounts to the number of 1,081, representing receipts from customs, internal revenue, public lands, miscellaneous, Panama Canal tolls, etc., and public debt in the amount of $10,121,759,829.39, and appropriation accounts to the number of 7,350 covering net disbursements for all executive departments, other Government establishments, the District of Columbia, and the public debt, in the sum of $10,225,812,192.88, have been credited and charged, respectively, to the general fund of the Treasury, details of which are exhibited in the annual report of the department. Of the total receipts deposited during the year, only $2,875.81 represented unadjusted items awaiting further information and remained uncovered by warrants as of June 30, 1922.

Transfer and counter warrants amounting to $2,364,681,634.68 were issued for adjustment of appropriation accounts, largely for the service of the Army and Navy, without affecting the general fund.

Appropriation warrants have been issued to the number of 461, crediting detailed appropriation accounts with amounts provided by law for disbursement, and transfer-appropriation and surplus-fund warrants, charging and crediting detailed appropriation accounts to the number of 431, a total of 892.

### Alien Property Custodian account.

Under the provisions of the act of Congress, approved October 6, 1917, and the proclamations and Executive orders issued thereunder by the President, the Secretary of the Treasury purchased during the year for account of the Alien Property Custodian United States securities of a par value of $279,750,000. There were on hand on July 1, 1921, similar securities of a par value of $158,031,000. Securities amounting to $273,836,000 matured and were redeemed during the year, the proceeds being reinvested as available. The total face amount of such securities carried by the Secretary of the Treasury in trust for the Alien Property Custodian on June 30, 1922, was $163,945,000.

Refunds and payments of alien property funds during the fiscal year 1922 were made to approximately 3,000 individuals, firms, or corporations, aggregating $19,940,834.05.

### Purchase of farm loan bonds.

On July 1, 1921, there were held by the Secretary of the Treasury $183,035,000 Federal farm loan bonds, purchased under the provisions of the act of January 18, 1918, as amended by the joint resolution dated May 26, 1920. During the fiscal year 1922 the Secretary made no further purchases of Federal farm loan bonds, but farm loan bonds amounting to $44,400,000 were repurchased by the Federal land banks, thus leaving the total amount of such bonds on hand at the close of the fiscal year 1922, $138,635,000.

*Civil Service Retirement and Disability Fund.*

The unexpended balance in the Civil Service Retirement and Disability Fund on June 30, 1921, amounted to $1,486,389.37. Under the provisions of section 8 of the act of May 22, 1920, for the retirement of employees in the classified civil service of the United States deductions to the amount of $14,071,553.97, representing 2½ per cent of the basic compensation payable to employees to whom the act applies from July 1, 1921, to June 30, 1922, were made for transfer to the credit of the Civil Service Retirement and Disability Fund. Receipts amounting to $610,940.73, which sum includes $587,254.64 interest and profits on investments, were also appropriated to the credit of the retirement fund during the fiscal year. Net disbursements from the fund, including $9,283,138.54 for investment in United States securities plus accrued interest, were made to the amount of $15,462,756.93, leaving an unexpended balance on June 30, 1922, of $706,127.14. Total deductions to the amount of $26,585,190.66, representing 2½ per cent of the basic compensation payable to employees to whom the act applies, were made from August 1, 1920, to June 30, 1922. The total net investments for account of the fund from August 1, 1920, to June 30, 1922, amounted to $17,984,250, face amount, of which $8,120,000, face amount, is in Second Liberty Loan Converted 4¼ per cent bonds, and $9,864,250 is in Fourth Liberty Loan 4¼ per cent bonds. These bonds, which are all registered in the name of the Secretary of the Treasury for account of the Civil Service Retirement and Disability Fund and held in safekeeping by the Division of Loans and Currency of the Secretary's office, have been purchased at a principal cost plus accrued interest of $17,283,138.54.

### SECRET SERVICE DIVISION.

During the fiscal year ended June 30, 1922, 1,195 persons were arrested by Secret Service agents or under their direction for violations of the currency laws and other statutes relating to the Treasury Department. Two of this number died while their cases were pending in court, 609 were convicted, 180 acquitted, and 404 are awaiting trial. Forty-five new counterfeit note issues were discovered in circulation. This was an unusually large number, but most of the notes were so crude as to have had practically no circulation, and they were quickly suppressed. In fact, only five of the issues had extensive circulation. In some instances agents of the service succeeded in suppressing extensive preparations for note counterfeiting before any of the bills were placed in circulation. One particularly ambitious band of criminals was captured and a most elaborate and expensive plant seized, including about 30 copper plates in various stages of completion. During the year $249,326.73 in counterfeit.

notes, $14,644.13 in counterfeit coins, 59 note plates, 11 coin dies, and 57½ molds were captured or seized. Several of the seizures were exceptionally large, a notable case being the arrest of a group of New York Italians in whose possession $63,660 in counterfeit $20 Federal reserve notes was found. Included in the seizures were several hundred thousand counterfeit internal-revenue strip stamps, machines for making bogus money, outfits used in note-raising operations, fake Secret Service badges, and a large quantity of miscellaneous materials, tools, and apparatus intended for counterfeiting. Bill raisers continue very active. Three hundred and eighty-one persons were arrested either for raising currency or for passing raised currency.

Investigation was made of 3,139 cases of forged checks, 719 bond forgeries or thefts, and 259 war-savings stamp cases. One of the bond cases resulted in the recovery of $175,000 in large-denomination coupon bonds stolen from a Treasury bureau. Most of the forgeries of Government checks were for small amounts, but agents succeeded in recovering an aggregate of $8,497.71 to reimburse the Treasury, in addition to the successful prosecution of more than 300 criminal charges in the courts.

This unprecedented record was accomplished only through the loyalty and efficiency of our field agents and the cordial cooperation accorded this division by State and municipal peace officers throughout the country.

### DIVISION OF PRINTING AND STATIONERY.

#### Printing and binding.

The total allotment for printing and binding for the Treasury service for the fiscal year 1922 was $750,000. Of this amount, $49,445.36 was transferred to the credit of the Office of the Comptroller General, created by the act of July 10, 1921, leaving a working balance of $700,554.64.

Total expenditures for printing and binding for 1922, including repayments, were $1,151,448.56, a decrease of $971,297.44 from the previous fiscal year. At the close of the year there was a balance of $323,208.12, attributable in part to rigid economy and in part to the decline in prices of materials. A detailed statement of expenditures and reimbursed expenditures will be found on page 447.

#### Stationery.

The appropriation for stationery for the entire Treasury service for the fiscal year 1922 amounted to $446,500. Owing to a fire on August 23, 1921, which destroyed a large quantity of stationery supplies, Congress granted an additional appropriation of $40,000 to cover this loss, making total appropriations of $486,500.

Total issues of stationery articles amounted to $721,692.57, of which $311,909.77 was reimbursed from other appropriations. Stock in the warehouse was reduced during the fiscal year by approximately $180,000. Transactions in stationery for the year are shown in the statement on page 447.

On July 1, 1922, all stationery and other supplies in the Division of Printing and Stationery, and the personnel handling such stationery and other supplies, were transferred to the Bureau of Supply, which had been created in and for the Treasury Department by order of the Secretary, dated March 28, 1922.

### Postage and materials for bookbinder.

Appropriations, expenditures, and unexpended balances on account of postage and materials for bookbinding for the fiscal years 1921 and 1922 are shown in the following tables:

| Fiscal year. | Appropriation. | Expended. | Unexpended balance. |
|---|---|---|---|
| POSTAGE. | | | |
| 1921 | $1,500.00 | $1,360.79 | $139.21 |
| 1922 | 1,500.00 | 1,277.54 | 222.46 |
| MATERIALS FOR BOOKBINDER. | | | |
| 1921 | 250.00 | 249.80 | .20 |
| 1922 | 250.00 | 249.67 | .33 |

### Department advertising.

| | Fiscal year. | | Increase. |
|---|---|---|---|
| | 1921 | 1922 | |
| Number of authorizations | 2,244 | 2,392 | 148 |
| Amount expended | $14,796.44 | $17,724.44 | $2,928.00 |

Appropriations, expenditures, and reimbursements for printing and binding and stationery.

| | Printing and binding. | | | | Stationery. | | | |
|---|---|---|---|---|---|---|---|---|
| | Fiscal year 1921. | Fiscal year 1922. | Increase. | Decrease. | Fiscal year 1921. | Fiscal year 1922. | Increase. | Decrease. |
| Appropriation | $665,000.00 | $750,000.00 | $85,000.00 | | $676,250.00 | $486,500.00 | | $189,750.00 |
| Reimbursements | 1,497,079.03 | 774,102.04 | | $722,976.99 | 1,166,726.88 | 311,909.77 | | 854,817.11 |
| Total credits | 2,162,079.03 | 1,524,102.04 | 85,000.00 | 722,976.99 | 1,842,976.88 | 798,409.77 | | 1,044,567.11 |
| Transferred to the General Accounting Office under the provisions of the Budget and accounting act, approved June 10, 1921. | | 49,445.36 | 49,445.36 | | | 36,554.37 | $36,554.37 | |
| Available credits | 2,162,079.03 | 1,474,656.68 | 35,554.64 | 722,976.99 | 1,842,976.88 | 761,855.40 | −36,554.37 | 1,044,567.11 |
| Total expenditures | 2,122,746.00 | 1,151,448.56 | | 687,422.33 | 1,793,447.33 | 566,124.92 | | 1,081,121.45 |
| | | | | 971,297.44 | | | | 1,227,322.46 |
| Balance | 39,333.03 | 323,208.12 | 283,875.09 | | 49,529.50 | 195,730.48 | 146,200.98 | |

EXPENDITURES BY BUREAUS, OFFICES, AND DIVISIONS.

| | Fiscal year 1921. | Fiscal year 1922. | Increase. | Decrease. | Fiscal year 1921. | Fiscal year 1922. | Increase. | Decrease. |
|---|---|---|---|---|---|---|---|---|
| Secretary, Undersecretary, and Assistant Secretaries | $16,620.09 | $9,527.44 | | $7,092.65 | $2,223.53 | $2,586.80 | $363.22 | |
| Appointment Division | 1,713.74 | 1,602.06 | | 111.68 | 2,124.91 | 1,330.80 | | $794.11 |
| Bookkeeping and Warrants Division | 29,413.24 | 9,622.06 | | 19,791.18 | 893.85 | 994.88 | 101.03 | |
| Bureau of Engraving and Printing | 9,169.98 | 6,573.91 | | 2,596.07 | 12,735.50 | 6,676.85 | | 6,058.65 |
| Division of Supply | 1,533.68 | 2,914.43 | 1,380.75 | | | 112.89 | 112.89 | |
| Chief clerk and superintendent | 174.07 | 439.24 | 265.17 | | 2,098.48 | 1,512.70 | | 585.78 |
| Commissioner of accounts and deposits | 41,768.54 | 21,247.22 | | 20,521.32 | | 98.28 | 98.28 | |
| Comptroller of the Currency | 49,445.36 | | | 49,445.36 | 27,744.61 | 15,723.77 | | 12,020.84 |
| Comptroller of the Treasury and 6 auditors | 2,113.23 | 2,073.70 | | | 36,554.37 | | | 36,554.37 |
| Custodians of public buildings | 68,801.58 | 31,473.72 | | 37,327.86 | 3,281.11 | 1,326.46 | | 1,954.65 |
| Customs Division | 1,091.05 | 737.08 | | 353.07 | 81,860.07 | 48,847.53 | | 32,952.54 |
| Disbursing clerk | 871.67 | 339.41 | | 532.26 | 1,917.82 | 499.47 | | 1,418.35 |
| Division of Deposits | 2,342.13 | 3,238.44 | 896.31 | | 807.98 | 257.37 | | 550.61 |
| Federal Farm Loan Bureau | 29,030.26 | 24,665.13 | | 4,365.13 | 1,317.68 | 1,379.09 | 61.41 | |
| General Supply Committee | 795.53 | 939.19 | 143.66 | | 1,611.62 | 2,842.35 | 1,230.73 | |
| Government actuary | 978.64 | | | 978.64 | 7.17 | 23.16 | 15.99 | |
| Independent Treasury Service | 151,110.03 | 100,998.98 | | 50,111.05 | 1,441.18 | | 1,441.18 | |
| Internal Revenue Bureau | [1] 1,994.47 | 2,112.71 | 118.24 | | 1,232,878.74 | [2] 1,267,738.80 | 34,860.06 | |
| Loans and Currency Division | 6,952.40 | 5,841.48 | | 1,110.92 | | | | |
| Mail and Files Division | 8,439.05 | 3,306.00 | | 5,133.05 | | | | |
| Mint Bureau | 684.14 | 526.11 | | 158.03 | 127.72 | 94.80 | | 32.92 |
| National bank depositaries | | 30.26 | 30.26 | | 3,599.27 | 1,812.45 | | 1,786.82 |
| Printing and Stationery Division | | 10.70 | 10.70 | | 20,534.98 | 15,470.98 | | 5,064.00 |

[1] In addition to this amount the Internal Revenue Bureau paid direct $284,772.30.

[2] In addition to this amount the Internal Revenue Bureau paid direct $22,850.02.

Appropriations, expenditures, and reimbursements for printing and binding and stationery—Continued.

EXPENDITURES BY BUREAUS, OFFICES, AND DIVISIONS—Continued.

| | Printing and binding. | | | | Stationery. | | | |
|---|---|---|---|---|---|---|---|---|
| | Fiscal year 1921. | Fiscal year 1922. | Increase. | Decrease. | Fiscal year 1921. | Fiscal year 1922. | Increase. | Decrease. |
| Public Health Service | $111,828.82 | $76,569.26 | | $35,259.56 | $27,791.14 | $10,953.76 | | $16,837.38 |
| Register of the Treasury | 1,198.80 | 860.49 | | 338.31 | 1,753.84 | 988.55 | | 765.29 |
| Secret Service | 781.29 | 557.86 | | 223.43 | 516.45 | 777.52 | $261.07 | |
| Superintendents of construction | 11,365.32 | 3,288.82 | | 8,076.50 | 7,066.65 | 3,944.94 | | 3,121.71 |
| Supervising Architect | | 43.28 | $43.28 | | | | | |
| Tax Simplification Board | 11,122.91 | 12,768.60 | 1,645.69 | | 28,330.21 | 11,849.37 | | 16,480.84 |
| Treasurer of the United States | 20,574.56 | 19,312.85 | | 1,261.71 | 17,669.93 | 11,939.23 | | 5,730.70 |
| United States Coast Guard | 43,752.39 | 35,720.19 | | 8,032.20 | | | | |
| Miscellaneous | | | | | | | | |
| Total | 625,666.97 | 377,346.52 | 4,534.06 | 252,854.51 | 516,823.86 | 409,782.80 | 37,104.68 | 144,145.74 |
| Net decrease | | | | 248,320.45 | | | | 107,041.06 |
| **REIMBURSED EXPENDITURES.** | | | | | | | | |
| Bureau of Engraving and Printing | $336.91 | $582.61 | | $254.30 | | $1,433.08 | $1,433.08 | |
| Bureau of the Budget | | 27,485.63 | $27,485.63 | | | | | |
| Chief coordinator | | 524.38 | 524.38 | | $658.52 | 183.80 | | $474.72 |
| [illegible], San Juan, P. R. | | | | | 4,332.57 | 842.30 | | 3,490.27 |
| Contingent expenses, national currency | 2,269.50 | 1,252.17 | | 1,017.33 | | | | |
| Customs service blank | 27,382.50 | 22,972.41 | | 4,410.09 | | | | |
| Federal farm loan banks | 5,819.74 | 1,845.28 | | 3,974.46 | 12,401.19 | 5,118.06 | | 7,283.13 |
| Federal Reserve Board | | 9,882.88 | 9,882.88 | | | 3,696.37 | 3,696.37 | |
| General Accounting Office | 245.85 | 66.53 | | 179.32 | | 140.88 | 140.88 | |
| Insolvent national-bank fund | 824,970.59 | 525,246.37 | | 299,724.22 | 300,180.24 | 60,724.02 | | 239,456.22 |
| National-bank examiners | 10,301.81 | 12,722.35 | 2,420.54 | | 3,537.73 | 3,694.72 | 156.99 | |
| National Bank Redemption Agency | 15,057.38 | 12,622.42 | | 2,434.94 | 7,874.30 | 4,944.31 | | 2,929.99 |
| Public debt | 160,836.53 | 99,505.68 | | 61,330.90 | 155,927.07 | 61,326.06 | | 94,601.01 |
| Public Health Service | 162,277.12 | 28,604.28 | | 133,672.94 | 537,305.35 | 130,937.49 | | 406,367.88 |
| Second Pan [illegible] | | | | | 6.51 | 35.95 | 29.44 | |
| Veterans' Bureau | 287,081.07 | 30,761.56 | | 256,313.51 | 143,919.92 | 35,172.82 | | 108,747.10 |
| War Finance Corporation | | 21.49 | 21.49 | | | | | |
| World War Foreign Debt Commission | | | | | 583.48 | 3,659.91 | 3,076.43 | |
| Total | 1,497,079.03 | 774,102.04 | 40,334.92 | 763,311.91 | 1,166,726.88 | 311,909.77 | 8,533.19 | 863,350.30 |
| Net decrease | | | | 722,976.99 | | | | 854,817.11 |

STOCK.

| | | | | |
|---|---|---|---|---|
| On hand at beginning of fiscal year | $337,657.51 | $374,495.96 | $36,769.45 | $1,227,322.46 |
| Purchase orders | 1,793,447.38 | 566,124.92 | | |
| Total | 2,131,104.89 | 940,551.88 | | 1,190,553.01 |
| Issues for the year | 1,653,550.74 | 721,692.57 | | 961,858.17 |
| Loss by fire, Aug. 23, 1921 | | 218,859.31 | 25,377.33 | |
| | | 25,377.33 | | |
| Inventory as of July 1 (taking inventory values on contract prices as of July 1): | | | | |
| Value at end of fiscal year | 447,554.15 | 193,481.98 | | 254,072.17 |
| Value in next fiscal year | 374,426.96 | 173,477.27 | | 200,949.69 |

## DISBURSING CLERK.

The following is a summary of the work performed by the office of the disbursing clerk during the fiscal year ended June 30, 1922:

|  | Number. | Amount. |
|---|---|---|
| Disbursements: | | |
| Checks | 569,606 | $90,483,749.83 |
| Cash (salaries) | 150,264 | 8,546,138.66 |
| Total | 719,870 | 99,029,888.49 |
| Collections on account of rents, sales, etc | 3,180 | 341,785.00 |
| Vouchers paid | 261,269 | |
| Appropriations under which disbursements were made | 332 | |

As required by law, the office has continued to make disbursements for all salaries and expenses of the Treasury Department in the District of Columbia (except the Bureau of Engraving and Printing), and for a large proportion of the salaries and expenses outside the District of Columbia under the Public Health Service, the Supervising Architect's Office, the Bureau of Internal Revenue, the Federal Farm Loan Board, the Comptroller of the Currency, the Coast Guard, the Secret Service, the Customs Division, and the Division of Loans and Currency.

In addition to making disbursements, an important function of the office is receiving and accounting for moneys due the United States on account of rents for buildings and real estate owned by the Government, sales of public property, etc., under the various bureaus and offices, notably those of the chief clerk, the Supervising Architect, the Public Health Service, the Coast Guard, the Secret Service, the Bureau of Internal Revenue, and the Public Debt Service.

An important change in the procedure of this office was brought about by the Secretary's order dated December 8, 1921, which provided, among other things, that all claims for refund of internal revenue taxes illegally collected should be paid by the disbursing clerk by check instead of being forwarded to the accounting officers for direct settlement by certificate and warrant as had previously been the practice. Under this order the schedules of claims for refund, upon approval by the commissioner, are forwarded directly to the disbursing clerk, and checks in payment thereof are issued immediately and mailed to the taxpayers. The plan is working satisfactorily, and there has been no delay in the payment of claims after their approval. The claims which come from the various units of the Bureau of Internal Revenue, principally the Income Tax, Estate Tax, Capital Stock Tax, and Sales Tax Units, are being paid at the rate of more than 25,000 per month. Under the new method of paying claims there is thus a considerable saving of time and labor to the offices which heretofore prepared and issued the necessary certificates and warrants, namely, the General Accounting Office, the Division of Bookkeeping and Warrants, and the Office of the Treasurer of the United States.

## GENERAL SUPPLY COMMITTEE.

The accompanying tables and statements present briefly the operations of the General Supply Committee during the fiscal year 1922.

Purchases under General Supply Committee contracts were $6,777,022 during the fiscal year 1922 as compared with $8,313,379 during 1921, a decrease of about 18 per cent, which may be accounted for in part by lower prices, but in large measure by the cooperation effected between the Bureau of the Budget and the heads of the various bureaus and divisions in carrying out the Government's program of economy. The reduction in purchases since the peak in 1919 was $3,544,416 or about 34 per cent.

The statement of surplus property on hand on June 30, 1922, shows an increase of approximately $341,000 as compared with June 30, 1921, which is due to a reduction in purchases of surplus property as well as to further declarations of surplus property by the various departments in connection with the curtailment of their activities.

Comparative statement showing total purchases as reported under contracts negotiated by the Secretary of the Treasury through the General Supply Committee.

| Class | Name of class | 1914 | 1915 | 1916 | 1917 | 1918 | 1919 | 1920 | 1921 | 1922 |
|---|---|---|---|---|---|---|---|---|---|---|
| 1 | Stationery, paper and paper ..., and drafting supplies. | $597,511.37 | $446,767.89 | $473,358.73 | $555,922.62 | $2,096,321.53 | $2,103,974.31 | $1,641,112.03 | $2,149,091.04 | $1,371,881.92 |
| 2 | Hardware, ..., and leather and ... | 95,765.64 | 96,529.62 | 61,632.32 | 72,929.44 | 113,616.94 | 138,763.59 | 97,032.92 | 181,574.90 | 87,847.50 |
| 3 | Dry goods, clothing, boots and ..., cloth bags, flags, wearing apparel, ... | 100,669.72 | 84,716.82 | 101,775.84 | 106,340.26 | 196,087.94 | 78,288.54 | 282,145.21 | 206,681.43 | 190,714.63 |
| 4 | Drugs and ... | 52,997.71 | 63,942.06 | 59,638.34 | 47,868.96 | 77,760.43 | 102,438.75 | 163,939.37 | 96,785.48 | 179,357.34 |
| 5 | ...tory apparatus, and ... appliances and ... instruments. | 36,183.24 | 44,385.31 | 40,400.14 | 47,604.65 | 60,625.93 | 54,671.79 | 63,631.37 | 83,308.28 | 64,064.59 |
| 6 | ..., engineering, ... and plumbing supplies. | 86,546.75 | 98,856.25 | 81,905.16 | 115,387.46 | 220,721.80 | 174,502.43 | 138,241.44 | 183,773.30 | 112,954.79 |
| 7 | ..., millwork and sawdust, packing (...), and building materials. | 95,587.75 | 96,588.39 | 81,594.30 | 85,844.02 | 97,432.97 | 31,253.09 | 142,954.84 | 48,125.03 | 124,815.24 |
| 8 | Brushes, glass, ... and paints. | 59,386.76 | 66,163.87 | 84,700.24 | 60,097.31 | 85,216.89 | 100,930.01 | 116,397.28 | 149,400.10 | 204,822.37 |
| 9 | Furniture and floor coverings. | 162,476.11 | 240,660.95 | 313,654.83 | 520,332.64 | 1,423,139.12 | 1,429,884.64 | 999,664.35 | 809,858.98 | 615,965.55 |
| 10 | ..., soap, meat and meat products. | 247,971.94 | 218,687.27 | 248,013.80 | 279,391.78 | 242,403.59 | 171,593.89 | 458,324.05 | 407,640.98 | 345,089.87 |
| 11 | ..., fish, and household supplies. | 97,050.53 | 104,053.15 | 95,585.12 | 122,937.42 | 41,360.20 | 188,363.21 | 207,816.93 | 128,895.55 | 99,030.86 |
| 12 | Forage, flour, and seed. | | | | | | | | | |
| 13 | ...ic sup... ... instruments, ..., etc., and meat-inspection supplies. | 72,481.55 | 63,490.42 | 77,626.88 | 72,501.30 | 101,381.81 | 121,814.71 | 161,280.90 | 148,757.20 | 237,055.15 |
| 14 | Engraving, ..., and lithographic supplies (excluding supplies for the Government Printing Office and the Bureau of Engraving and Printing). | 4,384.99 | 5,514.96 | 4,476.20 | 4,928.88 | 12,831.02 | 5,262.73 | 21,289.55 | 20,692.25 | 11,289.56 |
| 15 | Ice. | 298,014.08 | 357,411.93 | 324,698.80 | 342,123.46 | 175,893.06 | 3,234.22 | 38,297.73 | 45,583.09 | 32,451.41 |
| 16 | Incandescent electric lamps. | 184,907.33 | 287,411.07 | 405,377.84 | 630,647.68 | 630,121.80 | 2,530,664.35 | 1,326,218.87 | 1,314,772.50 | 1,167,779.99 |
| 17 | Incandescent gas-lamp supplies. | 236.88 | 41.35 | 3,375.75 | 2,950.90 | 1,955.99 | 3,121.64 | 3,252.69 | 4,444.08 | 1,504.57 |
| 18 | Motor trucks, tires, tubes, and accessories. | 3,768.00 | 5,620.00 | 6,605.00 | 18,372.40 | 26,615.00 | (1) | 7,579.38 | (2) | 50,473.15 |
| 19 | Machines: Computing, dictating and transcribing, duplicating, folding, sealing, and typewriting. | 30,380.39 | 74,861.57 | 63,126.51 | 421,869.49 | 1,592,225.85 | 1,088,558.88 | 475,496.85 | 223,516.45 | 189,413.01 |
| 20 | Electric service. | 91,753.94 | 105,688.00 | 104,923.86 | 131,736.25 | 290,811.04 | 509,022.58 | 489,719.30 | 496,263.77 | 464,000.10 |
|  | Telephone service. | 94,028.84 | 96,103.66 | 82,413.51 | 95,116.93 | 456,496.38 | 1,485,154.81 | 795,059.76 | 634,976.99 | 541,383.94 |
|  | Cost of supplies purchased from the General Supply Committee under the Executive order of Dec. 3, 1918. | | | | | | | 760,355.74 | 989,234.25 | 685,097.35 |
|  | Total. | 2,382,203.52 | 2,557,497.54 | 2,714,883.17 | 3,734,923.85 | 10,180,021.31 | 10,321,438.18 | 8,387,420.56 | 8,313,379.65 | 6,777,022.89 |

1 No purchases.          2 Not advertised.

NOTE.—The total purchases on class 1 to 20, inclusive, for the fiscal year 1913 were $2,728,767.64.

*Statement showing specifications issued, bids received, contracts entered into, items on which awards were made, no-award items, samples received and retained by the General Supply Committee for the fiscal year 1922.*

| Class No. | Sets of specifications issued. | Bids received. | Samples received. | Contracts. | | | Number of no-award items. |
|---|---|---|---|---|---|---|---|
| | | | | Number of contracts by classes. | Number of items covered by contracts. | Samples retained on contracts. | |
| 1 | 2,453 | 304 | 5,057 | 137 | 2,241 | 1,139 | 162 |
| 2 | 2,644 | 115 | 1,159 | 75 | 1,951 | 367 | 541 |
| 3 | 817 | 65 | 583 | 43 | 500 | 195 | 194 |
| 4 | 1,174 | 90 | 44 | 48 | 1,033 | 6 | 100 |
| 5 | 549 | 67 | 962 | 41 | 865 | 231 | 325 |
| 6 | 1,954 | 145 | 1,507 | 64 | 949 | 20 | 420 |
| 7 | 1,330 | 39 | 82 | 26 | 589 | 28 | 30 |
| 8 | 1,084 | 121 | 1,162 | 68 | 487 | 230 | 70 |
| 9 | 1,436 | 94 | 421 | 40 | 1,265 | 181 | 180 |
| 10 | 2,938 | 287 | 1,274 | 121 | 399 | 449 | 196 |
| 11 | 489 | 45 | 16 | 22 | 77 | 7 | 3 |
| 12 | 273 | 52 | 76 | 38 | 733 | 58 | 172 |
| 13 | 216 | 15 | 62 | 11 | 57 | 56 | 19 |
| 14 | 56 | 3 | ......... | 3 | 23 | ......... | ......... |
| 15 | 82 | 7 | ......... | 5 | 105 | ......... | ......... |
| 16 | 35 | 1 | ......... | 1 | 97 | ......... | ......... |
| 17 | 504 | 108 | 354 | 41 | 751 | 115 | 90 |
| 18 | 220 | 39 | 59 | 25 | 553 | 9 | 43 |
| 19 | 1 | 1 | ......... | 1 | 33 | ......... | ......... |
| 20 | 1 | 1 | ......... | 1 | 84 | ......... | ......... |
| Total | 18,237 | 1,597 | 12,818 | 811 | 12,792 | 3,091 | 2,545 |

*Statement of surplus property received from and issued to the various Government services by the General Supply Committee July 1, 1921, to June 30, 1922.*

| | Receipts, invoice price. | Issues. | |
|---|---|---|---|
| | | Cost.[1] | Charge.[2] |
| Agriculture, Department of | $2,975.93 | $53,359.80 | $45,609.53 |
| Alien Property Custodian | 3,621.00 | 407.06 | 353.01 |
| Botanic Garden | | 193.84 | 172.01 |
| Bureau of Efficiency | | 809.30 | 718.17 |
| Commerce, Department of | 19,443.73 | 19,245.37 | 16,402.43 |
| Commission to appraise Washington Market Co. property | 613.04 | 636.62 | 534.25 |
| Council of National Defense | 6,929.60 | | |
| District of Columbia | 89.36 | 20,861.55 | 17,999.78 |
| Employees Compensation Commission | | 447.53 | 374.06 |
| Federal Board for Vocational Education | 3,107.70 | 70,222.09 | 59,432.53 |
| Federal Power Commission | | 2,235.57 | 1,806.60 |
| Federal Trade Commission | 2,416.03 | 1,747.10 | 1,473.71 |
| Food Administration | 215.15 | | |
| Government Printing Office | 1,590.00 | 8,893.19 | 7,348.52 |
| House of Representatives | | 1,207.93 | 954.10 |
| Interior Department | 8,816.78 | 37,328.38 | 30,220.59 |
| Interdepartmental Social Hygiene Board | 2,837.26 | 11.54 | 10.84 |
| Interstate Commerce Commission | 674.15 | 16,275.11 | 13,889.48 |
| Justice, Department of | 625.53 | 23,235.07 | 18,623.29 |
| Labor, Department of | 15,786.01 | 4,126.13 | 3,406.73 |
| Library of Congress | 413.05 | 709.32 | 547.16 |
| Marine Corps | | 9,167.99 | 5,499.47 |
| National Advisory Committee for Aeronautics | | 728.11 | 568.01 |
| National Museum | 2,034.31 | 1,833.49 | 1,548.56 |
| National Training School for Boys | | 330.87 | 317.13 |
| Navy Department | 24,743.70 | 3,558.86 | 2,752.89 |
| Pan American Union | | 120.84 | 106.14 |
| Panama Canal | 415.15 | 189.18 | 182.08 |
| Post Office Department | 119.60 | 50,063.36 | 42,283.63 |
| Railroad Administration | 20,630.00 | 1,527.98 | 1,399.70 |
| Railroad Labor Board | | 567.30 | 512.65 |
| Reclaimed by salvage | 6,045.94 | | |
| Recorder of Deeds | | 928.69 | 809.40 |
| Senate | | 742.50 | 614.61 |
| Shipping Board | 120,874.42 | 23,695.53 | 20,396.94 |

[1] Original cost as shown by transfer invoices.     [2] Net amount of vouchers.

*Statement of surplus property received from and issued to the various Government services by General Supply Committee July 1, 1921, to June 30, 1922—Continued.*

|  | Receipts, invoice price. | Issues. | |
|---|---|---|---|
|  |  | Cost.[1] | Charge.[2] |
| Soldiers' Home | | $53.00 | $47.70 |
| State Department | $2,951.92 | 7,278.67 | 6,915.88 |
| State, War, and Navy Buildings | 25,527.18 | 1,039.13 | 822.72 |
| Tariff Commission | | 546.31 | 479.32 |
| Treasury Department | 27,912.05 | 276,403.56 | 229,634.05 |
| War Department | 833,416.76 | 10,880.67 | 9,017.59 |
| War Finance Corporation | | 32,776.46 | 27,731.83 |
| War Trade Board | 3,844.91 | | |
| White House | | 212.35 | 119.60 |
|  | 1,138,700.35 | 685,097.35 | 571,636.69 |
| Proceeds of auction sales | | | 79,595.35 |
|  | 1,138,700.35 | 685,097.35 | 651,232.04 |

[1] Original cost as shown by transfer invoices.      [2] Net amount of vouchers.

*Recapitulation of surplus property stores account July 1, 1921, to June 30, 1922.*

| | | | |
|---|---|---|---|
| Balance of stores as of June 30, 1921... | $1,602,570.10 | June 30: | |
| June 30, transferred to General Supply Committee as per detailed monthly statements | 1,138,700.35 | Net sales as per detailed monthly statements | $571,636.69 |
| | | Discount allowed on gross sales.. | 113,460.66 |
| | | Net proceeds from auction sales.. | 79,595.35 |
| | | Difference between invoiced value and proceeds from auction sales | 32,611.94 |
| | | Balance July 1, 1922 | 1,943,965.81 |
| June 30 | 2,741,270.45 | June 30 | 2,741,270.45 |

Net increase in stores during fiscal year 1922 ................................................... 341,395.71

*Receipts and issues of supplies during the fiscal year 1922.*

| Article | Balance June 30, 1921. | Received. | Issued. | Balance June 30, 1922. |
|---|---|---|---|---|
| Furniture: | | | | |
| Bases— | | | | |
| Filing, bookcase and storage sections | 975 | 1,155 | 440 | 1,690 |
| Leg, pairs [1] | 1,471 | 217 | 282 | 1,406 |
| Boards— | | | | |
| Drafting | 315 | 90 | 18 | 387 |
| Trestles for | 253 | 30 | 11 | 272 |
| Cabinets, all kinds | 1,967 | 2,244 | 2,623 | 1,588 |
| Chairs, all kinds | 16,790 | 10,282 | 10,780 | 16,292 |
| Costumers | 925 | 1,169 | 1,242 | 852 |
| Cots (includes all beds) | 1,238 | 7 | 259 | 986 |
| Desks, all kinds | 6,365 | 5,511 | 3,730 | 8,146 |
| Ends, for upright sections, pairs [1] | 352 | 301 | 23 | 630 |
| Files— | | | | |
| Visible index (all makes) | 588 | 7 | 29 | 566 |
| Leaves for | 3,987 | 2,897 | 316 | 6,568 |
| Lockers, steel | 316 | 314 | 174 | 456 |
| Safes, steel | 59 | 54 | 25 | 88 |
| Sections— | | | | |
| Bookcase, all kinds | 300 | 368 | 309 | 359 |
| Filing, all kinds | 6,456 | 4,681 | 5,302 | 5,835 |
| Stands, all kinds | 3,038 | 962 | 805 | 3,195 |
| Stools | 1,084 | 304 | 687 | 701 |
| Tables, all kinds | 6,292 | 1,948 | 880 | 7,360 |
| Tops for filing and bookcase sections | 787 | 480 | 366 | 901 |
| Trays, all kinds | 13,308 | 9,995 | 4,778 | 18,525 |
| Stationery, paper, and drafting supplies. | | | | |
| Baskets— | | | | |
| Desk, all kinds | 5,704 | 10,264 | 3,575 | 12,393 |
| Waste, all kinds | 4,881 | 1,441 | 3,646 | 2,676 |
| Binders, all kinds | 9,061 | 42,874 | 2,249 | 49,686 |
| Indexes for, sets | 2,529 | 712 | 385 | 2,856 |
| Filler sheets for | 175,650 | 695,700 | 96,800 | 774,550 |
| Calendar stands | 2,830 | 2,165 | 926 | 4,069 |

[1] Fractions omitted.

*Receipts and issues of supplies during the fiscal year 1922—Continued.*

| Article. | Balance June 30, 1921. | Received. | Issued. | Balance June 30, 1922. |
|---|---|---|---|---|
| Stationery, paper, and drafting supplies—Continued. | | | | |
| Cards— | | | | |
| Guide, blank, all kinds.......................... | 1,372,201 | 1,405,392 | 595,548 | 2,182,045 |
| Guide, in sets, all kinds....................... | 6,434 | 24,005 | 7,680 | 22,759 |
| Index, all kinds.................................. | 1,759,310 | 4,546,364 | 2,251,594 | 4,054,080 |
| Copyholders...................................... | 386 | 436 | 439 | 383 |
| Desk pads........................................ | 1,618 | 997 | 1,392 | 1,223 |
| Files, Phoenix, transfer, etc.................... | 2,706 | 1,871 | 2,047 | 2,530 |
| Fixtures, paper towel............................ | 335 | 63 | | 398 |
| Folders, all kinds............................... | 612,412 | 130,794 | 433,496 | 309,710 |
| Inkstands, sets.................................. | 543 | 73 | 112 | 504 |
| Bases for.................................... | 166 | 141 | 187 | 120 |
| Inkwells, all kinds.............................. | 8,952 | 7,889 | 3,350 | 13,491 |
| Paper, carbon— | | | | |
| Boxes........................................ | 1,140 | 1,089 | 153 | 2,076 |
| Sheets....................................... | 51,850 | 2,275 | 105 | 54,020 |
| Paper— | | | | |
| Computing machine, rolls.................... | 483 | 731 | 56 | 1,158 |
| Press copy— | | | | |
| Rolls.................................... | 10 | | | 10 |
| Reams................................... | 399 | 200 | | 599 |
| Stencil, quires.............................. | 1,476 | 50 | 1,444 | 82 |
| Toilet— | | | | |
| Rolls.................................... | 57,755 | 351,445 | 404,627 | 4,573 |
| Packages................................ | 54 | 6,900 | | 6,954 |
| Towels, rolls................................ | 2 | | | 2 |
| Drinking cups............................... | | 420,825 | 500 | 420,325 |
| Typewriter— | | | | |
| Mimeograph, reams....................... | 2,091 | | 1,060 | 1,031 |
| Manifolding, reams....................... | 4,445 | 2,272 | 1,358 | 5,359 |
| Writing bond, reams..................... | 4,140 | 1,315 | 1,627 | 3,828 |
| Wrapping— | | | | |
| Reams....................................... | 3 | 141 | 20 | 124 |
| Rolls....................................... | 40 | | 2 | 38 |
| Paper-fastening machines........................ | 1,397 | 1,194 | 1,117 | 1,474 |
| Staples for, boxes [1]........................... | 4,920 | 1,187 | 3,198 | 2,909 |
| Paper clips— | | | | |
| Boxes........................................ | 9,962 | 2,501 | 3,835 | 8,628 |
| Dozen [1].................................... | 876 | 800 | 44 | 1,632 |
| Pencils, all kinds, dozen........................ | 3,416 | 615 | 1,864 | 2,167 |
| Pencil-sharpening machines...................... | 415 | 502 | 573 | 344 |
| Pens, steel, gross............................... | 853 | 2,114 | 394 | 2,573 |
| Penholders, all kinds, dozen..................... | 134 | 1,737 | 1,013 | 858 |
| Penracks and trays, all kinds, dozen ............ | 132 | 209 | 60 | 281 |
| Perforating machines............................ | 965 | 746 | 921 | 790 |
| Pins— | | | | |
| Pounds...................................... | 167 | 150 | 57 | 260 |
| Pyramids, dozen............................. | 30 | 104 | 39 | 95 |
| Ribbons, typewriter, dozen [1].................. | 1,480 | 1,058 | 734 | 1,804 |
| Rubber bands, pounds........................... | 4,148 | 242 | 2,443 | 1,947 |
| Rulers, dozen [1]................................ | 224 | 497 | 206 | 515 |
| Shears, office, pairs............................ | 298 | 62 | 54 | 306 |
| Sponge cups, dozen [1].......................... | 117 | 277 | 284 | 110 |
| Stamps, dater................................... | 385 | 169 | 73 | 481 |
| Stamps, self-inking and time.................... | 382 | 132 | 4 | 510 |
| Stamp pads...................................... | 4,964 | 9,099 | 5,202 | 8,861 |
| Weights, paper, dozen [1]....................... | 182 | 365 | 341 | 206 |
| Stenographers' note books, dozen ............... | 124 | 311 | 118 | 317 |
| Straight edges................................... | 315 | 114 | | 429 |
| T squares........................................ | 344 | 421 | 78 | 687 |
| Tags, shipping................................... | 28,500 | 100,000 | 16,500 | 112,000 |
| Tracing cloth, rolls.............................. | 3 | 1 | | 4 |
| Tracing paper, rolls............................. | 365 | 84 | 109 | 340 |
| Triangles........................................ | 37 | 6 | 28 | 15 |
| Miscellaneous: | | | | |
| Bottles, water cooler............................ | 148 | 458 | 228 | 378 |
| Brooms.......................................... | 312 | | 6 | 306 |
| Brushes, scrub................................... | 14,335 | 72 | 6,769 | 7,638 |
| Buckets.......................................... | 211 | 87 | 39 | 259 |
| Blankets, all kinds.............................. | 153 | 4 | 39 | 118 |
| Cafeteria equipment: | | | | |
| Cream or sirup jugs............................. | 363 | | 8 | 355 |
| Knives, all kinds................................ | 6 | 43 | 42 | 7 |
| Spoons, all kinds................................ | 67 | 149 | 38 | 178 |
| Forks, all kinds................................. | 35 | 9 | 7 | 37 |
| Cups, all kinds.................................. | 4,423 | 1,261 | 1,217 | 4,467 |
| Saucers, all kinds............................... | 148 | 39 | 29 | 158 |
| Glasses, all kinds............................... | 1,152 | 4,883 | 5,116 | 919 |
| Plates, all kinds................................ | 3,385 | 3,350 | 2,076 | 4,659 |
| Trays, serving................................... | 2,936 | | 13 | 2,923 |
| Bowls........................................... | 4,135 | 36 | 151 | 4,020 |

[1] Fractions omitted.

*Receipts and issues of supplies during the fiscal year 1922*—Continued.

| Article. | Balance June 30, 1921. | Received. | Issued. | Balance June 30, 1922. |
|---|---|---|---|---|
| Cafeteria equipment—Continued. | | | | |
| Cans, ash, garbage, and oil........................ | 138 | 18 | 52 | 104 |
| Clocks, time recording........................... | 207 | 2 | 8 | 201 |
| Stations for..... ............................ | 304 | 15 | 20 | 299 |
| Dials for, boxes.............................. | 16 | ............. | 3 | 13 |
| Racks for.................................. | 474 | 14 | 1 | 487 |
| Cards for.................................. | 89,000 | ............. | 5,000 | 84,000 |
| Coolers, water................................. | 449 | 209 | 289 | 369 |
| Ice containers for............................ | 262 | 580 | 34 | 808 |
| Stands for.................................. | 281 | 522 | 35 | 768 |
| Cuspidors..................................... | 1,604 | 930 | 869 | 1,665 |
| Fans, electric.................................. | 1,340 | 823 | 918 | 1,245 |
| Fire extinguishers.............................. | 885 | 60 | 574 | 371 |
| Hatchets...................................... | 896 | ............. | 9 | 887 |
| Lamps, desk, portable.......................... | 82 | 14 | 63 | 33 |
| Mailing tubes.................................. | 13,214 | 18,300 | 300 | 31,214 |
| Mattresses.................................... | 256 | 4 | 103 | 157 |
| Mop handles.................................... | 167 | 321 | 144 | 344 |
| Pillows, feather............................... | 614 | 7 | 166 | 455 |
| Pillowcases.................................... | 112 | ............. | 58 | 54 |
| Screw drivers................................. | 2,306 | 8 | 195 | 2,119 |
| Sheets, bed................................... | 408 | 141 | 532 | 17 |
| Window shades and awnings..................... | 1,071 | 108 | ............. | 1,179 |
| Wrenches..................................... | 524 | 26 | 38 | 512 |
| Machines: | | | | |
| Computing.................................. | 120 | 177 | 156 | 141 |
| Bookkeeping................................ | 18 | 38 | 35 | 21 |
| Adding and subtracting typewriters............... | 14 | 4 | 6 | 12 |
| Duplicating, all kinds......................... | ............. | 377 | 104 | 273 |
| Numbering................................. | ............. | 460 | 226 | 234 |
| Typewriters................................ | 6,944 | 17,081 | 4,333 | 19,692 |

# TABLES ACCOMPANYING THE REPORT ON THE FINANCES.

TABLE A.—*Public debt of the United States outstanding June 30, 1922.*

| Title and authorizing act. | Date of loan. | When redeemable or payable. | Rate of interest. | Interest payable. | Average price received. | Amount authorized. | Amount issued. | Amount outstanding. |
|---|---|---|---|---|---|---|---|---|
| INTEREST-BEARING DEBT. | | | *Per cent* | | | | | |
| LOAN OF 1925. | | | | | | | | |
| Acts of July 14, 1870 (16 Stats. 272), as amended; Jan. 14, 1875 (18 Stats. 296). | Feb. 1, 1895.. | After Feb. 1, 1925.. | 4 | Feb., May, Aug., and Nov. 1. | {104.4946... / 111.166...} | Unlimited...... | $162,315,400.00 | $118,489,900.00 |
| CONSOLS OF 1930. | | | | | | | | |
| Act of Mar. 14, 1900 (31 Stats. 45)...... | Apr. 1, 1900.. | After Apr. 1, 1930. | 2 | Jan., Apr., July, and Oct. 1. | 100.5116... | $839,146,340.00 | 646,250,150.00 | 599,724,050.00 |
| PANAMA CANAL LOAN. | | | | | | | | |
| Acts of June 28, 1902 (32 Stats. 484) and Dec. 21, 1905 (34 Stats. 5)...... | {Aug. 1, 1906.. / Nov. 1, 1908..} | {After Aug. 1, 1916; on Aug. 1, 1936. / After Nov. 1, 1918; on Nov. 1, 1938.} | 2 / 2 | Feb., May, Aug., and Nov. 1. / ...do...... | 103.513... / 102.436... | 130,000,000.00 | 54,631,980.00 / 30,000,000.00 | 48,954,180.00 / 25,947,400.00 |
| Acts of Aug. 5, 1909 (36 Stats. 117); Feb. 4, 1910 (36 Stats. 192); and Mar. 2, 1911 (36 Stats. 1013). | June 1, 1911... | On June 1, 1961... | 3 | Mar., June, Sept., and Dec. 1. | 102.582... | 290,569,000.00 | 50,000,000.00 | 50,000,000.00 |
| POSTAL SAVINGS BONDS. | | | | | | | | |
| Act of June 25, 1910 (36 Stats. 817)...... | Jan. 1, July 1, 1911–1922. | On and after one year; 20 years from issue. | 2½ | Jan. and July 1.... | Par....... | Indefinite...... | 11,830,440.00 | 11,830,440.00 |
| CONVERSION BONDS. | | | | | | | | |
| Act of Dec. 23, 1913 (38 Stats. 269)...... | Jan. 1, 1916 and 1917. | 30 years from issue. | 3 | Jan., Apr., July, and Oct. 1. | Exchange. | | 28,894,500.00 | 28,894,500.00 |
| FIRST LIBERTY LOAN. | | | | | | | | |
| First 3½'s, act of Apr. 24, 1917 (40 Stats. 35)..... | June 15, 1917. | On and after June 15, 1932; on June 15, 1947. | 3½ | | Par....... | 5,538,945,460.00 | 1,989,455,550.00 | 1,410,002,050.00 |
| First 4's, acts of Apr. 24, 1917 (40 Stats. 35), Sept. 24, 1917 (40 Stats. 292), as amended. | Nov. 15, 1917. | ...do...... | 4 | June and Dec. 15. | Exchange. | 1,989,455,550.00 | 568,318,450.00 | 12,523,500.00 |
| First 4¼'s, acts of Apr. 24, 1917 (40 Stats. 35), Sept. 24, 1917 (40 Stats. 292), as amended. | May 9, 1918.. | ...do...... | 4¼ | | ...do...... | 1,989,455,550.00 | | 525,826,050.00 |
| First Second 4¼'s, acts of Apr. 24, 1917 (40 Stats. 35); Sept. 24, 1917 (40 Stats. 292), as amended. | Oct. 24, 1918.. | ...do...... | 4¼ | | ...do...... | 1,413,566,550.00 | 3,492,150.00 | 3,492,150.00 |
| SECOND LIBERTY LOAN. | | | | | | | | |
| Second 4's, act of Sept. 24, 1917 (40 Stats. 288), as amended. | Nov. 15, 1917. | On and after Nov. 15, 1927; on Nov 15, 1942. | 4 | May and Nov. 15. | Par....... | 7,538,945,460.00 | 3,807,865,000.00 | 54,420,900.00 |
| Second 4¼'s, act of Sept. 24, 1917 (40 Stats. 288), as amended. | May 9, 1918.. | ...do...... | 4¼ | ...do...... | Exchange. | 3,807,865,000.00 | | 3,256,176,250.00 |

| | | | | | | | | |
|---|---|---|---|---|---|---|---|---|
| THIRD LIBERTY LOAN. | | | | | | | | |
| Act of Sept. 24, 1917 (40 Stats. 288), as amended. | May 9, 1918 | On Sept. 15, 1928 | 4¼ | Mar. and Sept. 15 | Par | 8,192,135,000.00 | 4,175,650,050.00 | 3,473,788,000.00 |
| FOURTH LIBERTY LOAN. | | | | | | | | |
| Act of Sept. 24, 1917 (40 Stats. 288), as amended. | Oct. 24, 1918 | On and after Oct. 15, 1933; on Oct. 15, 1938. | 4¼ | Apr. and Oct. 15 | Par | 12,016,484,950.00 | 6,964,581,100.00 | 6,345,383,750.00 |
| VICTORY LIBERTY LOAN. | | | | | | | | |
| Act of Sept. 24, 1917 (40 Stats. 288), as amended | May 20, 1919 | On June 15 and December 15, 1922, on May 20, 1923. | 3¾<br>4¾ | June and Dec. 15 | Par | | 4,495,373,000.00 | (1)<br>1,991,183,400.00 |
| TREASURY NOTES. | | | | | | | | |
| Act of Sept. 24, 1917 (40 Stats. 288), as amended: | | | | | | Not exceeding $7,500,000,000 outstanding at any one time | | |
| Series A-1924 | June 15, 1921 | On June 15, 1924 | 5¾ | do | do | | 311,191,600.00 | 311,191,600.00 |
| Series B-1924 | Sept. 15, 1921 | On Sept. 15, 1924 | 5½ | Mar. and Sept. 15 | do | | 390,706,100.00 | 390,706,100.00 |
| Series A-1925 | Feb. 1, 1922 | On Mar. 15, 1925 | 4¾ | May 1 and Sept. 15 | Par and exchange. | | 601,599,500.00 | 601,599,500.00 |
| Series 1926 | Mar. 15, 1922 | On Mar. 15, 1926 | 4¾ | do | Exchange. | | 617,769,700.00 | 617,769,700.00 |
| Series B-1925 | June 15, 1922 | On Dec. 15, 1925 | 4⅜ | June and Dec. 15 | do | | 325,329,450.00 | 325,329,450.00 |
| CERTIFICATES OF INDEBTEDNESS. | | | | | | | | |
| Act of Sept. 24, 1917 (40 Stats. 288), as amended, and Apr. 23, 1918: | | | | | | Not exceeding $10,000,000,000 outstanding at any one time. | | |
| Tax— | | | | | | | | |
| Series TS-1922 | Sept. 15, 1921 | On Sept. 15, 1922 | 5¼ | Mar. and Sept. 15 | Par | | 182,871,000.00 | 182,871,000.00 |
| Series TS2-1922 | Nov. 1, 1921 | do | 4½ | do | do | | 179,691,500.00 | 179,691,500.00 |
| Series TD-1922 | Dec. 15, 1921 | On Dec. 15, 1922 | 4½ | June and Dec. 15 | do | | 243,544,000.00 | 243,544,000.00 |
| Series M-1923 | Mar. 15, 1922 | On Mar. 15, 1923 | 4¼ | Mar. and Sept. 15 | do | | 266,250,000.00 | 266,250,000.00 |
| Series TD2-1922 | June 1, 1922 | On Dec. 15 1922 | 3½ | Dec. 15 | do | | 200,000,000.00 | 200,000,000.00 |
| Series TJ-1923 | June 15, 1922 | On June 15, 1923 | 3¾ | June and Dec. 15 | do | | 273,000,000.00 | 273,000,000.00 |
| ab— | | | | | | | | |
| Series B-1922 | Aug. 1, 1921 | On Aug. 1, 1922 | 5½ | Feb. and Aug. 1 | do | | 259,471,500.00 | 259,431,000.00 |
| Series D-1922 | Apr. 15, 1922 | On Oct. 16, 1922 | 3½ | Maturity | do | | 150,000,000.00 | 150,000,000.00 |
| Pittman Act 40 Stats. 535) | 1918-1919 | After one year | 2 | Jan. and July 1 | do | | [2] 259,375,000.00 | 74,000,000.00 |
| TREASURY (WAR) SAVINGS SECURITIES.[3] | | | | | | | | |
| Act of Sept. 24, 1917 (40 Stats. 288), as amended: | | | | | | Not exceeding $4,000,000,000 outstanding at any one time. | | |
| Series 1918 | Jan. 2, 1918 | On Jan. 1, 1923 | 3-4 | Sold at a discount. Payable at par on maturity. | | | 1,022,105,582.16 | 515,871,847.03 |
| Series 1919 | Jan. 2, 1919 | On Jan. 1, 1924 | 3-4 | | | | 102,642,803.39 | 54,397,934.19 |
| Series 1920 | Jan. 2, 1920 | On Jan. 1, 1925 | 3-4 | | | | 43,668,495.58 | 25,039,234.21 |
| Series 1921 | Jan. 2, 1921 | On Jan. 1, 1926 | 3-4 | | | | 22,079,899.23 | 15,283,549.61 |
| Series 1921, New Issue | Various dates from Dec. 15, 1921. | Five years from date of issue. | 3½-4½ | | | | 1,942,809.33 | 1,801,469.33 |
| Series 1922, New Issue | do | do | 3½-4½ | | | | 59,542,732.58 | 58,226,872.58 |
| Thrift stamps, Treasury Savings Stamps, etc. | Various | Various | None | None | Par | | 9,019,270.75 | 8,394,410.50 |
| Total interest-bearing debt | | | | | | | | 22,711,035,587.45 |

[1] See matured debt. [2] Greatest amount outstanding at any one time.

[3] Amounts of the series of 1918, 1919, 1920, and 1921 (except new issue) are on the basis of reports of sales or of cash receipts less amounts redeemed. Amounts of the series of 1921 and 1922, new issue, are on the basis of cash receipts plus accrued discount, the amount outstanding being the net redemption value. Includes net receipts from sales of thrift stamps and Treasury savings stamps.

TABLE A.—*Public debt of the United States outstanding June 30, 1922*—Continued.

| Title and authorizing act. | Date of loan. | When payable. | Rate of interest. | Interest payable. | Average price received. | Amount authorized. | Amount issued. | Amount outstanding. |
|---|---|---|---|---|---|---|---|---|
| MATURED DEBT ON WHICH INTEREST HAS CEASED. | | | | | | | | |
| OLD DEBT. | | | | | | | | |
| For detailed information in regard to the earlier loans embraced under this head, see Finance Report for 1876. | | On demand | *Per cent* Various. | | | | | $151,610.26 |
| LOAN OF 1847. | | | | | | | | |
| Act of Jan. 28, 1847 (9 Stats. 118) | 1847-1850 | Jan. 1, 1868 | 6 | | | | $28,230,350.00 | 950.00 |
| TEXAS INDEMNITY STOCK. | | | | | | | | |
| Act of Sept. 9, 1850 (9 Stats. 447) | 1851 | Jan. 1, 1865 | 5 | | | | 5,000,000.00 | 19,000.00 |
| LOAN OF 1858. | | | | | | | | |
| Act of June 14, 1858 (11 Stats. 365) | 1858-1860 | Jan. 1, 1874 | 5 | | | | 20,000,000.00 | 2,000.00 |
| LOAN OF FEBRUARY, 1861 (1881s). | | | | | | | | |
| Act of Feb. 8, 1861 (12 Stats. 129) | 1861 | Dec. 31, 1880 | 6 | | | | 18,415,000.00 | 5,000.00 |
| TREASURY NOTES OF 1861. | | | | | | | | |
| Act of Mar. 2, 1861 (12 Stats. 178) | 1861-1863 | 60 days or 2 years after date. | 6 | | | | 35,364,450.00 | 2,300.00 |
| OREGON WAR DEBT. | | | | | | | | |
| Act of Mar. 2, 1861 (12 Stats. 198) | 1861-1862 | July 1, 1881 | 6 | | | | 1,090,850.00 | 2,250.00 |
| LOAN OF JULY AND AUGUST, 1861. | | | | | | | | |
| Acts of July 17, 1861 (12 Stats. 259); Aug. 5, 1861 (12 Stats. 316). | 1861-1872 | After June 30, 1881 | 6 | | | | 189,321,350.00 | 15,050.00 |
| Bonds of this loan continued at 3½ per cent interest and redeemable at the pleasure of the Government. | 1881 | Various | 3½ | | | | | 600.00 |
| SEVEN-THIRTIES OF 1861. | | | | | | | | |
| Act of July 17, 1861 (12 Stats. 259) | 1861-1862 | Aug. 19 and Oct. 1, 1864. | 7 3/10 | | | | 139,999,750.00 | 9,300.00 |

| Title and Acts | Year | Maturity | Rate | Amount | Amount |
|---|---|---|---|---|---|
| **FIVE-TWENTIES OF 1862.**<br>Acts of Feb. 25, 1862 (12 Stats. 345); Mar. 3, 1864 (13 Stats. 13); Jan. 28, 1865 (13 Stats. 425). | 1862-1865 | May 1, 1867 | 6 | 514,771,600.30 | 105,250.00 |
| **TEMPORARY LOAN.**<br>Acts of Feb. 25, 1862 (12 Stats. 346); Mar. 17, 1862 (12 Stats. 370); July 11, 1862 (12 Stats. 532); June 30, 1864 (13 Stats. 218). | 1862-1866 | After 10 days' notice | 4, 5, 6 | 716,099,247.16 | 2,850.00 |
| **CERTIFICATES OF INDEBTEDNESS.**<br>Acts of Mar. 1, 1862 (12 Stats 37, May 17, 1862 (12 Stats. 37, Mar. 3, 1863 (12 Stats. 710). | 1862-1866 | 1 year after date | 6 | 561,753,241.65 | 3,000.00 |
| **IN OF 1863.**<br>Acts of Mar. 3, 1863 (12 Stats. 709); June 30, 1864 (13 Stats. 219). | 1864-1865 | July 1, 1881 | 6 | 75,000,000.00 | 3,100.00 |
| Bonds of this loan continued at 3½ per cent interest and redeemable at the pleasure of the Government. |  | Various | 3½ |  | 100.00 |
| **ONE-YEAR NOTES OF 1863.**<br>Act of Mar. 3, 1863 (12 Stats. 710). | 1864 | 1 year after date | 5 | 44,520,000.00 | 30,120.00 |
| **TWO-YEAR NOTES OF 1863.**<br>Act of Mar. 3, 1863 (12 Stats. 710). | 1863-1864 | 2 years after date | 5 | 166,480,000.00 | 26,700.00 |
| **COMPOUND-INTEREST NOTES.**<br>Acts of Mar. 3, 1863 (12 Stats. 710); June 30, 1864 (13 Stats. 218). | 1864-1866 | 3 years from date | b 6 | 266,595,440.00 | 157,840.00 |
| **TEN-FORTIES OF 1864.**<br>Act of Mar. 3, 1864 (13 Stats. 13). | 1864-1868 | Mar. 1, 1874 | 5 | 196,118,300.00 | 18,550.00 |
| **FIVE-TWENTIES OF 1864.**<br>Act of June 30, 1864 (13 Stats. 218). | 1864-1867 | Nov. 1, 1869 | 6 | 125,561,300.00 | 13,950.00 |
| **SEVEN-THIRTIES OF 1864 AND 1865.**<br>Acts of June 30, 1864 (13 Stats. 218); Jan. 28 1865 (13 Stats. 425); Mar. 3, 1865 (13 Stats. 468). | 1864-1868 | Aug. 15, 1867<br>June 15, 1868<br>July 15, 1868 | 7 3/10 | a 829,992,500.00 | 119,500.00 |

a Including conversion of Treasury notes.   b Interest compounded.   c Including reissues.

TABLE A.—*Public debt of the United States outstanding June 30, 1922*—Continued.

| Title and authorizing act. | Date of loan. | When payable. | Rate of interest. | Interest payable. | Average price received. | Amount authorized. | Amount issued. | Amount outstanding. |
|---|---|---|---|---|---|---|---|---|
| MATURED DEBT ON WHICH INTEREST HAS CEASED—Continued. | | | *Per cent* | | | | | |
| FIVE-TWENTIES OF 1865. | | | | | | | | |
| Acts of Mar. 3, 1865 (13 Stats., 468); Apr. 12, 1866 (14 Stats., 31). | 1865–1868 | Nov. 1, 1870 | 6 | | | | $203,327,250.00 | $19,850.00 |
| CONSOLS OF 1865. | | | | | | | | |
| Acts of Mar. 3, 1865 (13 Stats., 468); Apr. 12, 1866 (14 Stats., 31). | 1865–1868 | July 1, 1870 | 6 | | | | 332,998,950.00 | 55,350.00 |
| CONSOLS OF 1867. | | | | | | | | |
| Acts of Mar. 3, 1865 (13 Stats., 468); Apr. 12, 1866 (14 Stats., 31). | 1867–1877 | July 1, 1872 | 6 | | | | 379,618,000.00 | 92,050.00 |
| CONSOLS OF 1868. | | | | | | | | |
| Acts of Mar. 3, 1865 (13 Stats., 468); Apr. 12, 1866 (14 Stats., 31). | 1868–1869 | July 1, 1873 | 6 | | | | 42,539,930.00 | 9,800.00 |
| THREE PER CENT CERTIFICATES. | | | | | | | | |
| Acts of Mar. 2, 1867 (14 Stats., 558); July 25, 1868 (15 Stats., 183). | 1867–1872 | Called | 3 | | | | $85,155,000.00 | 5,000.00 |
| FUNDED LOAN OF 1881. | | | | | | | | |
| Acts of Jan. 14, 1875 (18 Stats., 296); Mar. 3, 1875 (18 Stats., 466); July 14, 1870 (16 Stats., 272); Jan. 20, 1871 (16 Stats., 399); Dec. 17, 1873 (18 Stats., 1). | 1871–1877 | May 1, 1881 | 5 | | | | 517,994,150.00 | 22,400.00 |
| FUNDED LOAN OF 1891 (REFUNDING). | | | | | | | | |
| Act of July 14, 1870 (16 Stats., 272). | 1876–1878 | Sept. 1, 1891 | 4½ | | | | 185,000,000.00 | 19,800.00 |
| FUNDED LOAN OF 1891 (RESUMPTION). | | | | | | | | |
| Act of Jan. 14, 1875 (18 Stats. 296). | 1876–1878 | do | 4½ | | | | 65,000,000.00 | |

| | | | | | |
|---|---|---|---|---|---|
| FUNDED LOAN OF 1907 (REFUNDING). | | | | | |
| Act of July 14, 1870 (16 Stats., 272)............ | 1877-1880.... | July 1, 1907.... | 4 | 710,398,200.00 | 374,600.00 |
| FUNDED LOAN OF 1907 (RESUMPTION). | | | | | |
| Act of Jan. 14, 1875 (18 Stats., 296)...... | 1877-1880.... | ......do.... | 4 | 30,500,000.00 | |
| REFUNDING CERTIFICATES. | | | | | |
| Act of Feb. 26, 1879 (20 Stats., 321)............ | 1879.... | Called.... | 4 | 40,012,750.00 | 10,270.00 |
| FUNDED LOAN OF 1881 (CONTINUED). | | | | | |
| These bonds were issued in exchange for 5 per cent bonds of the funded loan of 1881, by mutual agreement between the Secretary of the Treasury and the holders, and were made redeemable at the pleasure of the Government. | 1881.... | Various.... | 3½ | | 50.00 |
| FUNDED LOAN OF 1891 (CONTINUED). | | | | | |
| These bonds were issued in exchange for the 4½ per cent funded loan of 1891, by mutual agreement between the Secretary of the Treasury and the holders, and were made redeemable at the pleasure of the Government. | 1891.... | ......do.... | 2 | 25,364,500.00 | 1,000.00 |
| LOAN OF JULY 12, 1882. | | | | | |
| Act of July 12, 1882............. | 1882-1883.... | ......do.... | 3 | | 90 . 00 |
| LOAN OF 1904. | | | | | |
| Act of Jan. 14, 1875 (18 Stats., 296)............ | 1894.... | On Feb. 1, 1904.. | 5 | 100,000,000.00 | 13,0.  00 |
| LOAN OF 1908-1918. | | | | | |
| Act of June 13, 1898 (30 Stats., 467)............ | 1898.... | On Aug. 1, 1918.. | 3 | 198,792,660.00 | 326,90 . 00 |
| VICTORY NOTES. | | | | | |
| Victory notes, 3¾................. | 1919.... | Called.... | 3¾ | | 14,609,400.00 |
| CERTIFICATES OF INDEBTEDNESS. | | | | | |
| Certificates of indebtedness.............. | Various.... | Various.... | Various | | 9,003,000.00 |
| Total matured debt on which interest has ceased. | | | | | 25,250,880.26 |

a Including reissues.

TABLE A.—*Public debt of the United States outstanding June 30, 1922*—Continued.

| | Authorized to be outstanding at one time. | Issues or deposits, including reissues. | Authorized to be outstanding at present time. | Outstanding. |
|---|---|---|---|---|
| **NONINTEREST-BEARING DEBT.** | | | | |
| OLD DEMAND NOTES. | | | | |
| Acts of July 17, 1861 (12 Stats., 259); Aug. 5, 1861 (12 Stats., 313); Feb. 12, 1862 (12 Stats., 338) | $60,000,000 | [6] $60,030,000 | | $53,012.50 |
| FRACTIONAL CURRENCY. | | | | |
| Acts of July 17, 1862 (12 Stats., 592); Mar. 3, 1863 (12 S.ats., 711); June 30, 1864 (13 Stats., 220) | 50,000,000 | [6] 368,720,080 | | [7] 1,998,368.50 |
| LEGAL-TENDER NOTES. | | | | |
| Acts of Feb. 25, 1862 (12 Stats., 345); July 11, 1862 (12 Stats., 532); Mar. 3, 1863 (12 Stats., 710); May 31, 1878 (20 Stats., 87); Mar. 4, 1900 (31 Stats., 45) | 450,000,000 | | $346,681,016 | 346,681,016.00 |
| NATIONAL-BANK NOTES (REDEMPTION ACCOUNT). | | | | |
| The act of July 14, 1890 (26 Stats., 289), provides that balances standing with the Treasurer of the United States to the respective credits of national banks for deposits made to redeem the circulating notes of such banks, and all deposits thereafter received for like purpose, shall be covered into the Treasury as a miscellaneous receipt, and the Treasurer of the United States shall redeem from the general cash in the Treasury the circulating notes of said banks which may come into his possession subject to redemption, * * * and the balance remaining of the deposits so covered shall, at the close of each month, be reported on the monthly public debt statement as debts of the United States bearing no interest. | Indefinite | | | 32,039,351.50 |
| Total noninterest-bearing debt. | | | | 380,771,748.50 |
| Total debt. | | | | 23,117,058,216.21 |
| Less gold reserve. | | | | 152,979,025.63 |
| Gross debt as shown on statement of the public debt June 30, 1922. | | | | 22,964,079,190.58 |

[6] Including reissues.    [7] After deducting amounts officially estimated to have been lost or irrevocably destroyed.

TABLE B.—*Principal of the public debt at the end of each fiscal year, from 1853 to 1922,*[1] *exclusive of gold certificates, silver certificates, currency certificates, and Treasury notes of 1890.*

| June 30— | Interest bearing.[2] | Matured. | Non-interest bearing.[3] | Total gross debt. |
|---|---|---|---|---|
| 1853 | $59,642,412 | $162,249 | | $59,804,661 |
| 1854 | 42,044,517 | 199,248 | | 42,243,765 |
| 1855 | 35,418,001 | 170,498 | | 35,588,499 |
| 1856 | 31,805,180 | 168,901 | | 31,974,081 |
| 1857 | 28,503,377 | 197,998 | | 28,701,375 |
| 1858 | 44,743,256 | 170,163 | | 44,913,424 |
| 1859 | 58,333,156 | 165,225 | | 58,498,381 |
| 1860 | 64,683,256 | 160,575 | | 64,843,831 |
| 1861 | 90,423,292 | 159,125 | | 90,582,417 |
| 1862 | 365,356,045 | 230,520 | $158,591,390 | 524,177,955 |
| 1863 | 707,834,255 | 171,970 | 411,767,456 | 1,119,773,681 |
| 1864 | 1,360,026,914 | 366,629 | 455,437,271 | 1,815,830,814 |
| 1865 | 2,217,709,407 | 2,129,425 | 458,090,180 | 2,677,929,012 |
| 1866 | 2,322,116,330 | 4,435,865 | 429,211,734 | 2,755,763,929 |
| 1867 | 2,238,954,794 | 1,739,108 | 409,474,321 | 2,650,168,223 |
| 1868 | 2,191,326,130 | 1,246,334 | 390,873,992 | 2,583,446,456 |
| 1869 | 2,151,495,065 | 5,112,031 | 388,503,491 | 2,545,110,590 |
| 1870 | 2,035,881,095 | 3,539,654 | 397,002,510 | 2,436,453,269 |
| 1871 | 1,920,696,750 | 1,948,902 | 399,406,489 | 2,322,052,141 |
| 1872 | 1,800,794,100 | 7,926,547 | 401,270,191 | 2,209,990,838 |
| 1873 | 1,696,483,950 | 51,929,463 | 402,796,935 | 2,151,210,348 |
| 1874 | 1,724,930,750 | 3,216,340 | 431,785,640 | 2,159,932,730 |
| 1875 | 1,708,676,300 | 11,425,570 | 436,174,779 | 2,156,276,649 |
| 1876 | 1,696,685,450 | 3,902,170 | 430,258,158 | 2,130,845,778 |
| 1877 | 1,697,888,500 | 16,648,610 | 393,222,793 | 2,107,759,903 |
| 1878 | 1,780,735,650 | 5,594,070 | 373,088,595 | 2,159,418,315 |
| 1879 | 1,887,716,110 | 37,015,380 | 374,181,153 | 2,298,912,643 |
| 1880 | 1,709,993,100 | 7,621,205 | 373,294,567 | 2,090,908,872 |
| 1881 | 1,625,567,750 | 6,723,615 | 386,994,363 | 2,019,285,728 |
| 1882 | 1,449,810,400 | 16,260,555 | 390,844,689 | 1,856,915,644 |
| 1883 | 1,324,229,150 | 7,831,165 | 389,898,603 | 1,721,958,918 |
| 1884 | 1,212,563,850 | 19,655,955 | 393,087,639 | 1,625,307,444 |
| 1885 | 1,182,150,950 | 4,100,745 | 392,299,474 | 1,578,551,169 |
| 1886 | 1,132,014,100 | 9,704,195 | 413,941,255 | 1,555,659,550 |
| 1887 | 1,007,692,350 | 6,114,915 | 451,678,029 | 1,465,485,294 |
| 1888 | 936,522,500 | 2,495,845 | 445,613,311 | 1,384,631,656 |
| 1889 | 815,853,990 | 1,911,235 | 431,705,286 | 1,249,470,511 |
| 1890 | 711,313,110 | 1,815,555 | 409,267,919 | 1,122,396,584 |
| 1891 | 610,529,120 | 1,614,705 | 393,662,736 | 1,005,805,561 |
| 1892 | 585,029,330 | 2,785,875 | 380,403,636 | 968,218,841 |
| 1893 | 585,037,100 | 2,094,060 | 374,300,606 | 961,431,766 |
| 1894 | 635,041,890 | 1,851,240 | 380,004,687 | 1,016,897,817 |
| 1895 | 716,202,060 | 1,721,590 | 378,989,470 | 1,096,913,120 |
| 1896 | 847,363,890 | 1,636,890 | 373,728,570 | 1,222,729,350 |
| 1897 | 847,365,130 | 1,346,880 | 378,081,703 | 1,226,793,713 |
| 1898 | 847,367,470 | 1,262,680 | 384,112,913 | 1,232,743,063 |
| 1899 | 1,046,048,750 | 1,218,300 | 389,433,654 | 1,436,700,704 |
| 1900 | 1,023,478,890 | 1,176,320 | 238,761,733 | 1,263,416,913 |
| 1901 | 987,141,040 | 1,415,620 | 233,015,585 | 1,221,572,245 |
| 1902 | 931,070,340 | 1,280,880 | 245,680,157 | 1,178,031,357 |
| 1903 | 914,541,410 | 1,205,090 | 243,659,413 | 1,159,405,913 |
| 1904 | 895,157,440 | 1,970,920 | 239,130,656 | 1,136,259,016 |
| 1905 | 895,158,340 | 1,370,245 | 235,828,510 | 1,132,357,095 |
| 1906 | 895,159,140 | 1,128,135 | 246,235,695 | 1,142,522,970 |
| 1907 | 894,834,280 | 1,086,815 | 251,257,098 | 1,147,178,193 |
| 1908 | 897,503,990 | 4,130,015 | 276,056,398 | 1,177,690,403 |
| 1909 | 913,317,490 | 2,883,855 | 232,114,027 | 1,148,315,372 |
| 1910 | 913,317,490 | 2,124,895 | 231,497,584 | 1,148,939,969 |

[1] Figures for 1853 to 1885, inclusive, are taken from "Statement of Receipts and Expenditures of the Government from 1855 to 1885 and Principal of Public Debt from 1791 to 1885," compiled from the official records of the Register's office. Later figures are taken from the monthly debt statements and revised figures published in the annual reports of the Secretary of the Treasury

[2] Exclusive of bonds issued to the Pacific railways (provision having been made by law to secure the Treasury against both principal and interest) and the Navy pension fund (which was in no sense a debt, the principal being the property of the United States).

[3] Includes old demand notes; United States notes, less the amount of the gold reserve since 1900; postal currency and fractional currency less the amounts officially estimated to have been destroyed; and also the redemption fund held by the Treasury to retire national bank notes of national banks failed, in liquidation, and reducing circulation, which prior to 1890 was not included in the published debt statements. Does not include gold, silver, or currency certificates or Treasury notes of 1890 for redemption of which an exact equivalent of the respective kinds of money or bullion was held in the Treasury.

TABLE B.—*Principal of the public debt at the end of each fiscal year, from 1853 to 1922, exclusive of gold certificates, silver certificates, currency certificates, and Treasury notes of 1890*—Continued.

| June 30— | Interest bearing. | Matured. | Non-interest bearing. | Total gross debt. |
|---|---|---|---|---|
| 1911 | $915,353,190 | $1,879,830 | $236,751,917 | $1,153,984,937 |
| 1912 | 963,776,770 | 1,760,450 | 228,301,285 | 1,193,838,505 |
| 1913 | 965,706,610 | 1,659,550 | 225,681,585 | 1,193,047,745 |
| 1914 | 967,953,310 | 1,552,560 | 218,729,530 | 1,188,235,400 |
| 1915 | 969,759,090 | 1,507,260 | 219,997,718 | 1,191,264,068 |
| 1916 | 971,562,590 | 1,473,100 | 252,109,878 | 1,225,145,568 |
| 1917 | 2,712,549,477 | 14,232,230 | 248,836,878 | 2,975,618,585 |
| 1918 | 11,985,882,436 | 20,242,550 | 237,503,733 | 12,243,628,719 |
| 1919 | 25,234,496,274 | 11,109,370 | 236,428,775 | 25,482,034,419 |
| 1920 | 24,061,095,362 | 6,747,700 | 230,075,350 | 24,297,918,412 |
| 1921 | 23,737,352,080 | 10,939,620 | 227,958,908 | 23,976,250,608 |
| 1922 | 22,711,035,587 | 25,250,880 | 227,792,723 | 22,964,079,190 |

[000 omitted.]

| | $50 | $100 | $500 | $1,000 | $5,000 | $10,000 | $50,000 | $100,000 | Denominations unavailable. | Total. | Registered. | Coupon. |
|---|---|---|---|---|---|---|---|---|---|---|---|---|
| **1919.** | | | | | | | | | | | | |
| June 30 | $1,995,251 | $2,672,569 | $1,800,678 | $7,938,079 | $1,271,070 | $2,653,470 | $192,150 | $601,500 | $1,750 | $19,126,517 | $2,508,571 | $16,617,946 |
| Dec. 31 | 1,814,120 | 2,576,529 | 1,870,411 | 8,668,804 | 1,404,955 | 3,022,920 | 231,150 | 766,100 | ¹15,419 | 20,239,570 | 3,106,936 | 17,132,634 |
| **1920.** | | | | | | | | | | | | |
| Mar. 31 | 1,682,963 | 2,445,204 | 1,833,454 | 8,428,670 | 1,400,240 | 3,045,430 | 247,950 | 857,000 | 98,606 | 20,039,517 | 3,327,868 | 16,711,649 |
| Apr. 30 | 1,633,767 | 2,409,268 | 1,826,731 | 8,383,972 | 1,408,500 | 3,058,760 | 250,250 | 879,000 | 123,580 | 19,975,828 | 3,415,372 | 16,560,456 |
| May 31 | 1,563,067 | 2,369,699 | 1,813,580 | 8,042,104 | 1,385,590 | 3,101,500 | 252,850 | 876,700 | 242,741 | 19,647,741 | 3,462,342 | 16,185,399 |
| June 30 | 1,526,353 | 2,348,025 | 1,808,337 | 8,033,514 | 1,400,675 | 3,115,740 | 255,850 | 879,300 | 213,407 | 19,581,201 | 3,515,714 | 16,065,487 |
| July 31 | 1,497,104 | 2,336,920 | 1,815,944 | 8,026,896 | 1,414,395 | 3,184,620 | 259,250 | 919,600 | 118,399 | 19,573,118 | 3,592,862 | 15,980,256 |
| Aug. 31 | 1,472,302 | 2,324,345 | 1,824,945 | 8,082,997 | 1,433,075 | 3,240,450 | 256,500 | 889,700 | 46,781 | 19,571,095 | 3,636,680 | 15,934,415 |
| Sept. 30 | 1,447,235 | 2,307,421 | 1,822,585 | 8,033,153 | 1,442,365 | 3,250,700 | 263,550 | 941,900 | 22,891 | 19,533,800 | 3,671,588 | 15,862,212 |
| Oct. 31 | 1,420,389 | 2,283,581 | 1,819,598 | 8,004,247 | 1,453,235 | 3,319,430 | 266,050 | 950,400 | 11,608 | 19,528,298 | 3,712,603 | 15,815,695 |
| Nov. 30 | 1,395,972 | 2,260,585 | 1,812,118 | 8,005,902 | 1,461,415 | 3,320,950 | 269,950 | 982,300 | 6,469 | 19,515,601 | 3,776,247 | 15,739,354 |
| Dec. 31 | 1,369,187 | 2,234,009 | 1,809,547 | 8,015,654 | 1,468,750 | 3,331,420 | 275,200 | 1,005,200 | 2,794 | 19,511,761 | 3,827,438 | 15,684,323 |
| **1921.** | | | | | | | | | | | | |
| Jan. 31 | 1,291,859 | 2,163,906 | 1,781,033 | 7,727,427 | 1,485,965 | 3,571,070 | 277,450 | 1,048,300 | 138,116 | 19,485,126 | 3,901,717 | 15,583,409 |
| Feb. 28 | 1,251,379 | 2,139,453 | 1,784,903 | 7,629,469 | 1,522,210 | 3,654,030 | 281,500 | 1,113,200 | 55,447 | 19,431,591 | 4,006,678 | 15,424,913 |
| Mar. 31 | 1,208,132 | 2,105,678 | 1,778,141 | 7,529,121 | 1,557,360 | 3,763,020 | 285,100 | 1,139,200 | 14,123 | 19,379,875 | 4,071,698 | 15,308,177 |
| Apr. 30 | 1,174,422 | 2,072,618 | 1,761,518 | 7,418,464 | 1,573,430 | 3,834,130 | 287,800 | 1,145,400 | 9,675 | 19,343,465 | 4,099,966 | 15,243,499 |
| May 31 | 1,153,422 | 2,045,904 | 1,759,448 | 7,348,075 | 1,578,320 | 3,867,020 | 288,300 | 1,147,800 | 3,540 | 19,291,360 | 4,111,413 | 15,179,947 |
| June 30 | 1,122,543 | 2,019,466 | 1,747,448 | 7,387,231 | 1,572,490 | 3,855,080 | 289,300 | 1,149,000 | 1,390 | 19,145,948 | 4,117,754 | 15,031,194 |
| July 31 | 1,110,948 | 2,009,353 | 1,741,529 | 7,369,217 | 1,571,560 | 3,885,460 | 287,900 | 1,139,800 | 2,067 | 19,088,834 | 4,111,335 | 14,977,499 |
| Aug. 31 | 1,095,091 | 1,980,432 | 1,733,593 | 7,353,884 | 1,571,345 | 3,878,130 | 285,550 | 1,137,800 | 1,225 | 19,036,960 | 4,111,192 | 14,925,768 |
| Sept. 30 | 1,077,966 | 1,957,697 | 1,722,991 | 7,311,084 | 1,569,305 | 3,871,940 | 285,750 | 1,137,600 | 1,904 | 18,958,147 | 4,127,203 | 14,824,562 |
| Oct. 31 | 1,068,678 | 1,930,177 | 1,709,974 | 7,255,791 | 1,571,820 | 3,911,380 | 288,300 | 1,145,600 | 66 | 18,871,011 | 4,113,585 | 14,743,808 |
| Nov. 30 | 1,037,854 | 1,897,978 | 1,692,261 | 7,203,185 | 1,571,955 | 3,928,120 | 284,350 | 1,167,100 | 297 | 18,833,000 | 4,119,888 | 14,713,162 |
| Dec. 31 | 1,011,947 | 1,856,281 | 1,667,707 | 7,135,799 | 1,581,095 | 4,064,260 | 284,800 | 1,153,300 | 197 | 18,755,446 | 4,091,308 | 14,664,078 |
| **1922.** | | | | | | | | | | | | |
| Jan. 31 | 987,820 | 1,818,517 | 1,645,846 | 7,069,631 | 1,627,780 | 4,148,580 | 284,100 | 1,146,100 | | 18,718,624 | 4,061,477 | 14,657,147 |
| Feb. 28 | 969,186 | 1,789,175 | 1,624,324 | 6,948,032 | 1,595,075 | 4,117,680 | 279,350 | 1,150,000 | | 18,472,822 | 4,040,850 | 14,431,972 |
| Mar. 31 | 941,098 | 1,741,083 | 1,581,193 | 6,661,321 | 1,520,980 | 3,908,370 | 273,250 | 1,121,400 | | 17,798,695 | 3,961,722 | 13,836,973 |
| Apr. 30 | 913,058 | 1,693,561 | 1,552,934 | 6,566,023 | 1,520,890 | 4,102,230 | 272,250 | 1,119,600 | | 17,740,133 | 3,929,029 | 13,811,104 |
| May 31 | 885,688 | 1,646,315 | 1,522,934 | 6,473,443 | 1,526,090 | 4,232,410 | 273,700 | 1,126,500 | | 17,687,080 | 3,907,653 | 13,779,427 |
| June 30 | 855,803 | 1,593,483 | 1,479,784 | 6,202,469 | 1,459,005 | 4,112,270 | 270,300 | 1,114,300 | | ²17,087,405 | 3,843,995 | 13,243,410 |
| July 31 | 835,501 | 1,555,696 | 1,457,452 | 6,163,276 | 1,463,050 | 4,241,300 | 266,050 | 1,089,700 | | ²17,070,925 | 3,812,923 | 13,258,002 |
| Aug. 31 | 812,446 | 1,519,046 | 1,430,362 | 6,053,709 | 1,452,035 | 4,278,870 | 271,600 | 1,107,600 | | ²16,926,268 | 3,787,411 | 13,138,857 |

¹ This amount should be deducted from the aggregate denominational totals to equal the grand total of $20,239,570.  ² Includes matured 3½ per cent Victory notes.

TABLE D.—*Liberty bonds and Victory notes—Ratio of amount of each denomination to total outstanding, from June 30, 1919, to August 31, 1922.*

| | $50 | $100 | $500 | $1,000 | $5,000 | $10,000 | $50,000 | $100,000 | Denominations unavailable. | Total. | Registered. | Coupon. |
|---|---|---|---|---|---|---|---|---|---|---|---|---|
| **1919.** | Per cent. | Per cent. | Per cent. | Per cent. | Per cent. | Per cent. | Per cent. | Per cent. | Per cent. | Per cent. | Per cent. | Per cent. |
| June 30 | 10.43 | 13.97 | 9.41 | 41.50 | 6.65 | 13.87 | 1.01 | 3.15 | 0.01 | 100.00 | 13.12 | 85.88 |
| Dec. 31 | 8.96 | 12.73 | 9.24 | 42.34 | 6.94 | 14.94 | 1.14 | 3.78 | 1.07 | 100.00 | 15.35 | 81.65 |
| **1920.** | | | | | | | | | | | | |
| Mar. 31 | 8.40 | 12.20 | 9.15 | 42.06 | 6.99 | 15.20 | 1.24 | 4.27 | .49 | 100.00 | 16.61 | 83.39 |
| Apr. 30 | 8.18 | 12.06 | 9.15 | 41.98 | 7.05 | 15.31 | 1.25 | 4.40 | .62 | 100.00 | 17.10 | 82.90 |
| May 31 | 7.96 | 12.06 | 9.23 | 40.93 | 7.06 | 15.79 | 1.29 | 4.46 | .23 | 100.00 | 17.62 | 82.38 |
| June 30 | 7.79 | 11.94 | 9.24 | 41.03 | 7.15 | 15.91 | 1.31 | 4.49 | 1.09 | 100.00 | 17.95 | 82.05 |
| July 31 | 7.62 | 11.88 | 9.28 | 41.01 | 7.23 | 16.27 | 1.32 | 4.70 | .60 | 100.00 | 18.36 | 81.64 |
| Aug. 31 | 7.52 | 11.81 | 9.33 | 41.30 | 7.32 | 16.56 | 1.31 | 4.55 | .24 | 100.00 | 18.58 | 81.42 |
| Sept. 30 | 7.41 | 11.81 | 9.33 | 41.14 | 7.38 | 16.64 | 1.35 | 4.82 | .12 | 100.00 | 18.80 | 81.20 |
| Oct. 31 | 7.27 | 11.69 | 9.32 | 40.29 | 7.44 | 17.00 | 1.36 | 4.87 | .06 | 100.00 | 19.01 | 80.99 |
| Nov. 30 | 7.16 | 11.58 | 9.29 | 41.02 | 7.49 | 17.02 | 1.38 | 5.03 | .03 | 100.00 | 19.35 | 80.65 |
| Dec. 31 | 7.02 | 11.45 | 9.27 | 41.08 | 7.33 | 17.07 | 1.41 | 5.15 | .02 | 100.00 | 19.62 | 80.38 |
| **1921.** | | | | | | | | | | | | |
| Jan. 31 | 6.63 | 11.10 | 9.14 | 38.66 | 7.63 | 18.33 | 1.42 | 5.38 | .71 | 100.00 | 20.02 | 79.98 |
| Feb. 28 | 6.44 | 11.04 | 9.19 | 39.36 | 7.83 | 18.80 | 1.45 | 5.73 | .29 | 100.00 | 20.62 | 79.38 |
| Mar. 31 | 6.23 | 10.87 | 9.17 | 38.85 | 8.04 | 19.42 | 1.47 | 5.88 | .07 | 100.00 | 21.01 | 78.99 |
| Apr. 30 | 6.07 | 10.72 | 9.14 | 38.66 | 8.13 | 19.82 | 1.49 | 5.92 | .05 | 100.00 | 21.20 | 78.80 |
| May 31 | 5.98 | 10.66 | 9.12 | 38.61 | 8.18 | 20.05 | 1.51 | 5.95 | .02 | 100.00 | 21.31 | 78.69 |
| June 30 | 5.89 | 10.55 | 9.13 | 38.58 | 8.21 | 20.13 | 1.51 | 6.00 | | 10.00 | 21.50 | 78.50 |
| July 31 | 5.82 | 10.48 | 9.12 | 38.61 | 8.23 | 20.25 | 1.51 | 5.97 | .01 | 100.00 | 21.54 | 78.46 |
| Aug. 31 | 5.75 | 10.40 | 9.11 | 38.63 | 8.25 | 20.37 | 1.50 | 5.98 | .01 | 100.00 | 21.60 | 78.40 |
| Sept. 30 | 5.69 | 10.34 | 9.10 | 38.60 | 8.29 | 20.44 | 1.52 | 6.01 | .01 | 100.00 | 21.72 | 78.28 |
| Oct. 31 | 5.61 | 10.23 | 9.06 | 38.45 | 8.33 | 20.72 | 1.53 | 6.07 | | 100.00 | 21.87 | 78.13 |
| Nov. 30 | 5.51 | 10.08 | 8.98 | 38.25 | 8.25 | 21.12 | 1.53 | 6.20 | | 100.00 | 21.88 | 78.12 |
| Dec. 31 | 5.39 | 9.90 | 8.89 | 38.65 | 8.43 | 21.67 | 1.52 | 6.15 | .01 | 100.00 | 21.81 | 78.19 |
| **1922.** | | | | | | | | | | | | |
| Jan. 31 | 5.28 | 9.72 | 8.79 | 37.71 | 8.70 | 22.16 | 1.52 | 6.12 | | 100.00 | 21.70 | 78.30 |
| Feb. 28 | 5.25 | 9.69 | 8.79 | 37.61 | 8.63 | 22.29 | 1.51 | 6.23 | | 100.00 | 21.87 | 78.13 |
| Mar. 31 | 5.29 | 9.78 | 8.88 | 37.37 | 8.55 | 22.30 | 1.53 | 6.30 | | 100.00 | 22.25 | 77.74 |
| Apr. 30 | 5.15 | 9.55 | 8.75 | 37.04 | 8.57 | 23.12 | 1.54 | 6.31 | | 100.00 | 22.15 | 77.85 |
| May 31 | 5.01 | 9.31 | 8.61 | 36.60 | 8.63 | 23.93 | 1.54 | 6.37 | | 100.00 | 22.09 | 77.91 |
| June 30 | 5.01 | 9.32 | 8.65 | 36.30 | 8.54 | 24.07 | 1.58 | 6.52 | | ²100.00 | 22.50 | 77.50 |
| July 31 | 4.88 | 9.11 | 8.54 | 36.11 | 8.57 | 24.85 | 1.56 | 6.34 | | ²100.00 | 22.34 | 77.66 |
| Aug. 31 | 4.80 | 8.98 | 8.45 | 35.77 | 8.58 | 25.2² | 1.60 | 6.54 | | ²100.00 | 22.38 | 77.62 |

¹ Deduct.    See note (1) on Table C.      ² Includes matured 3¾ per cent Victory notes.

TABLE E.—*United States interest-bearing debt outstanding at end of each month, from February 28, 1917, to August 31, 1922.*

[000,000 omitted.]

| Date. | Pre-war loans. | First 3½'s. | First 4's. | First 4¼'s. | First second 4¼'s. | Second 4's. | Second 4¼'s. | Third 4¼'s. | Fourth 4¼'s. | Total Liberty bonds. | Victory 4¾'s. | Victory 3¾'s. | Treasury notes. | Loan and tax certificates of indebtedness. | Pittman Act certificates. | Special certificates of indebtedness. | Treasury (war) savings securities.[1] | Total short-term debt. | Total interest-bearing debt. |
|---|---|---|---|---|---|---|---|---|---|---|---|---|---|---|---|---|---|---|---|
| **1917.** | | | | | | | | | | | | | | | | | | | |
| Feb. 28 | $973 | | | | | | | | | | | | | | | | | | $973 |
| Mar. 31 | 1,023 | | | | | | | | | | | | | | | | | | 1,023 |
| Apr. 30 | 1,023 | | | | | | | | | | | | | $265 | | | | $265 | 1,288 |
| May 31 | 1,024 | | | | | | | | | | | | | 668 | | | | 668 | 1,692 |
| June 30 | 974 | $1,466 | | | | | | | | $1,466 | | | | 273 | | | | 273 | 2,713 |
| July 31 | 974 | 1,529 | | | | | | | | 1,529 | | | | | | | | | 2,503 |
| Aug. 31 | 974 | 1,923 | | | | | | | | 1,923 | | | | 550 | | | | 550 | 3,447 |
| Sept. 30 | 974 | 1,976 | | | | | | | | 1,976 | | | | 1,076 | | | | 1,076 | 4,026 |
| Oct. 31 | 974 | 1,977 | | | | $267 | | | | 2,244 | | | | 2,315 | | | | 2,315 | 5,533 |
| Nov. 30 | 974 | 1,977 | | | | 2,813 | | | | 4,790 | | | | 1,879 | | | | 1,879 | 7,643 |
| Dec. 31 | 974 | 1,987 | | | | 3,450 | | | | 5,437 | | | | 691 | | | $14 | 705 | 7,116 |
| **1918.** | | | | | | | | | | | | | | | | | | | |
| Jan. 31 | 974 | 1,987 | | | | 3,806 | | | | 5,793 | | | | 1,384 | | | 45 | 1,429 | 8,196 |
| Feb. 28 | 974 | 1,987 | | | | 3,807 | | | | 5,794 | | | | 2,469 | | | 87 | 2,556 | 9,324 |
| Mar. 31 | 974 | 1,987 | | | | 3,808 | | | | 5,795 | | | | 3,251 | | | 144 | 3,395 | 10,164 |
| Apr. 30 | 966 | 1,987 | | | | 3,774 | | $246 | | 6,007 | | | | 3,936 | | | 203 | 4,139 | 11,112 |
| May 31 | 966 | 1,986 | | | | 3,747 | | 3,044 | | 8,777 | | | | 2,516 | | $60 | 260 | 2,836 | 12,579 |
| June 30 | 956 | [2] 1,989 | | | | [3] 3,747 | | 3,228 | | 8,964 | | | | 1,516 | | 190 | 350 | 2,056 | 11,986 |
| July 31 | 962 | [2] 1,989 | | | | [3] 3,747 | | 3,778 | | 9,514 | | | | 2,145 | | | 558 | 2,703 | 13,179 |
| Aug. 31 | 898 | [2] 1,989 | | | | [3] 3,747 | | 4,153 | | 9,889 | | | | 2,820 | | 79 | 670 | 3,569 | 11,355 |
| Sept. 30 | 898 | [2] 1,989 | | | | [3] 3,697 | | 4,146 | $19 | 9,851 | | | | 4,098 | $26 | | 760 | 4,884 | 15,633 |
| Oct. 31 | 893 | [2] 1,989 | | | | [3] 3,635 | | 4,100 | 3,524 | 13,248 | | | | 3,286 | 61 | | 847 | 4,194 | 18,335 |
| Nov. 30 | 893 | 1,414 | $191 | $384 | | 822 | $2,790 | 4,054 | 5,423 | 15,078 | | | | 2,183 | 74 | 15 | 908 | 3,180 | 19,151 |
| Dec. 31 | 893 | 1,414 | 190 | 385 | | 821 | 2,791 | 4,054 | 6,042 | 15,697 | | | | 2,966 | 105 | 185 | 975 | 4,231 | 20,821 |
| **1919.** | | | | | | | | | | | | | | | | | | | |
| Jan. 31 | 883 | 1,414 | 190 | 385 | | 821 | 2,792 | 4,056 | 6,745 | 16,403 | | | | 4,230 | 123 | 302 | 1,013 | 5,668 | 22,954 |
| Feb. 28 | 883 | 1,414 | 190 | 385 | | 821 | 2,792 | 4,007 | 6,913 | 16,522 | | | | 5,504 | 130 | 175 | 1,005 | 6,814 | 24,219 |
| Mar. 31 | 883 | 1,414 | 188 | 383 | | 810 | 2,772 | 3,973 | 6,809 | 16,349 | | | | 5,414 | 143 | 177 | 993 | 6,727 | 23,959 |
| Apr. 30 | 883 | 1,410 | 183 | 388 | $3 | 785 | 2,782 | 3,973 | 6,810 | 16,334 | [4] $123 | | | 5,988 | 157 | 111 | 981 | 7,360 | 24,577 |

[1] Amounts of the series of 1918, 1919, 1920, and 1921 (except new issue) are on the basis of reports of sales or of cash receipts less amounts redeemed. Amounts of the series of 1921 and 1922, new issue, are on the basis of cash receipts plus accrued discount, the amount outstanding being the net redemption value. Includes net receipts from sales of thrift stamps and Treasury savings stamps.

[2] Separate figures for first 3½'s and first 4's not available.

[3] Separate figures for second 4's and second 4¼'s not available.

[4] Separate figures for Victory 4¾'s and Victory 3¾'s not available.

TABLE E.—*United States interest-bearing debt outstanding at end of each month, from February 28, 1917, to August 31, 1922*—Continued.

[000,000 omitted.]

| Date | Pre-war loans. | First 3½'s. | First 4's. | First 4¼'s. | First second 4¼'s. | Second 4's. | Second 4¼'s. | Third 4¼'s. | Fourth 4¼'s. | Total Liberty bonds. | Victory 4¾'s. | Victory 3¾'s. | Treasury notes. | Loan and tax certificates of indebtedness. | Pittman Act certificates. | Special certificates of indebtedness. | Treasury (war) savings securities. | Total short-term debt. | Total interest-bearing debt. |
|---|---|---|---|---|---|---|---|---|---|---|---|---|---|---|---|---|---|---|---|
| **1919.** | | | | | | | | | | | | | | | | | | | |
| May 31 | $883 | $1,410 | $179 | $392 | $3 | $718 | $2,849 | $3,959 | $6,809 | $16,319 | $2,279 | | | $4,944 | $167 | $111 | $966 | $8,467 | $25,669 |
| June 30 | 883 | 1,410 | 168 | 403 | 3 | 704 | 2,862 | 3,959 | 6,795 | 16,304 | 3,468 | | | 3,264 | 179 | 182 | 954 | 8,047 | 25,234 |
| July 31 | 883 | 1,410 | 166 | 405 | 3 | 695 | 2,871 | 3,959 | 6,785 | 16,224 | 3,892 | | | 3,314 | 196 | 35 | 942 | 8,379 | 25,556 |
| Aug. 31 | 883 | 1,410 | 165 | 406 | 3 | 698 | 2,879 | 3,954 | 6,714 | 16,219 | 4,114 | | | 3,933 | 220 | 43 | 932 | 9,247 | 26,349 |
| Sept. 30 | 883 | 1,410 | 164 | 408 | 3 | 680 | 2,846 | 3,931 | 6,680 | 16,122 | 4,278 | | | 3,462 | 241 | 34 | 919 | 8,934 | 25,939 |
| Oct. 31 | 883 | 1,410 | 160 | 411 | 3 | 658 | 2,869 | 3,904 | 6,614 | 16,029 | 4,414 | | | 3,462 | 256 | 16 | 910 | 9,058 | 25,970 |
| Nov. 30 | 883 | 1,410 | 147 | 404 | 3 | 577 | 2,860 | 3,826 | 6,594 | 15,821 | 4,493 | | | 3,462 | 258 | 57 | 903 | 9,173 | 25,877 |
| Dec. 31 | 883 | 1,410 | 140 | 411 | 3 | 573 | 2,854 | 3,781 | 6,574 | 15,746 | 4,494 | | | 3,260 | 259 | 57 | 896 | 8,966 | 25,565 |
| **1920.** | | | | | | | | | | | | | | | | | | | |
| Jan. 31 | 884 | 1,410 | 139 | 410 | 3 | 570 | 2,849 | 3,747 | 6,559 | 15,687 | 4,495 | | | 3,125 | 259 | 88 | 886 | 8,853 | 25,424 |
| Feb. 29 | 884 | 1,410 | 139 | 409 | 3 | 569 | 2,837 | 3,739 | 6,535 | 15,641 | 4,459 | | | 2,936 | 259 | 107 | 876 | 8,637 | 25,162 |
| Mar. 31 | 884 | 1,410 | 132 | 415 | 3 | 541 | 2,863 | 3,720 | 6,533 | 15,617 | 4,423 | | | 2,278 | 259 | 130 | 864 | 7,954 | 24,455 |
| Apr. 30 | 884 | 1,410 | 115 | 425 | 3 | 463 | 2,710 | 3,710 | 6,515 | 15,571 | 4,405 | | | 2,734 | 259 | 1 | 853 | 8,252 | 24,707 |
| May 31 | 884 | 1,410 | 97 | 442 | 3 | 294 | 3,066 | 3,678 | 6,414 | 15,384 | 4,263 | | | 2,837 | 259 | 269 | 840 | 8,468 | 24,736 |
| June 30 | 884 | 1,410 | 66 | 473 | 3 | 240 | 3,085 | 3,663 | 6,395 | 15,335 | 3,428 | $818 | | 2,496 | 259 | 24 | 827 | 7,842 | 24,985 |
| July 31 | 884 | 1,410 | 55 | 484 | 3 | 209 | 3,116 | 3,661 | 6,394 | 15,332 | 3,438 | 803 | | 2,433 | 259 | 20 | 816 | 7,769 | 24,061 |
| Aug. 31 | 884 | 1,410 | 48 | 491 | 3 | 189 | 3,136 | 3,659 | 6,394 | 15,330 | 3,445 | 796 | | 2,571 | 259 | | 806 | 7,877 | 24,091 |
| Sept. 30 | 884 | 1,410 | 43 | 497 | 3 | 170 | 3,154 | 3,650 | 6,366 | 15,293 | 3,450 | 791 | | 2,348 | 259 | | 795 | 7,676 | 23,853 |
| Oct. 31 | 884 | 1,410 | 37 | 502 | 3 | 153 | 3,171 | 3,649 | 6,365 | 15,290 | 3,453 | 785 | | 2,357 | 259 | 33 | 784 | 7,651 | 23,825 |
| Nov. 30 | 884 | 1,410 | 33 | 506 | 3 | 137 | 3,187 | 3,649 | 6,364 | 15,289 | 3,453 | 774 | | 2,475 | 259 | 33 | 772 | 7,766 | 23,939 |
| Dec. 31 | 884 | 1,410 | 30 | 509 | 3 | 125 | 3,198 | 3,647 | 6,364 | 15,236 | 3,482 | 744 | | 2,300 | 259 | 33 | 757 | 7,675 | 23,745 |
| **1921.** | | | | | | | | | | | | | | | | | | | |
| Jan. 31 | 884 | 1,410 | 28 | 511 | 3 | 116 | 3,207 | 3,646 | 6,363 | 15,294 | 3,190 | 711 | | 2,351 | 259 | 33 | 744 | 7,598 | 23,756 |
| Feb. 28 | 884 | 1,410 | 26 | 513 | 3 | 109 | 3,213 | 3,646 | 6,362 | 15,282 | 3,164 | 686 | | 2,484 | 254 | 33 | 733 | 7,654 | 23,820 |
| Mar. 31 | 884 | 1,410 | 25 | 514 | 3 | 102 | 3,220 | 3,645 | 6,360 | 15,279 | 3,423 | 678 | | 2,475 | 247 | 33 | 722 | 7,578 | 23,741 |
| Apr. 30 | 884 | 1,410 | 23 | 516 | 3 | 97 | 3,222 | 3,644 | 6,359 | 15,274 | 3,396 | 673 | | 2,548 | 239 | 33 | 713 | 7,602 | 23,760 |
| May 31 | 884 | 1,410 | 20 | 519 | 3 | 87 | 3,239 | 3,643 | 6,357 | 15,269 | 3,361 | 661 | | 2,572 | 227 | 33 | 703 | 7,557 | 23,710 |
| June 30 | 884 | 1,410 | 18 | 521 | 3 | 78 | 3,241 | 3,611 | 6,355 | 15,233 | 3,273 | 641 | | 2,450 | 216 | 33 | 694 | 7,618 | 23,737 |
| July 31 | 884 | 1,410 | 17 | 522 | 3 | 75 | 3,243 | 3,610 | 6,354 | 15,233 | 3,241 | 615 | $311 | 2,322 | 209 | 33 | 687 | 7,418 | 23,535 |
| Aug. 31 | 884 | 1,410 | 16 | 522 | 3 | 70 | 3,244 | 3,610 | 6,353 | 15,231 | 3,204 | 602 | 311 | 2,542 | 194 | | 679 | 7,565 | 23,680 |
| Sept. 30 | 884 | 1,410 | 16 | 523 | 3 | 68 | 3,246 | 3,609 | 6,353 | 15,229 | 3,152 | 557 | 311 | 2,307 | 172 | | 672 | 7,562 | 23,675 |
| Oct. 31 | 884 | 1,410 | 15 | 523 | 3 | 66 | 3,248 | 3,609 | 6,351 | 15,226 | 3,108 | 537 | 702 | 1,932 | 146 | | 664 | 7,089 | 23,199 |
| Nov. 30 | 884 | 1,410 | 15 | 524 | 3 | 64 | 3,249 | 3,593 | 6,350 | 15,208 | 3,110 | 498 | 702 | 2,162 | 126 | | 657 | 7,255 | 23,364 |
| Dec. 31 | 884 | 1,410 | 15 | 524 | 3 | | | | 6,349 | 15,207 | 3,093 | 455 | 702 | 2,083 | 113 | | 651 | 7,097 | 23,188 |

| 1922. | | | | | | | | | | | | | | | | | | |
|---|---|---|---|---|---|---|---|---|---|---|---|---|---|---|---|---|---|---|
| Jan. 31 | 884 | 1,410 | 14 | 524 | 3 | 62 | 3,251 | 3,592 | 6,349 | 15,205 | 3,124 | 389 | 702 | 2,081 | 113 | 654 | 7,063 | 23,152 |
| Feb. 28 | 884 | 1,410 | 14 | 525 | 3 | 61 | 3,251 | 3,591 | 6,348 | 15,203 | 2,937 | 333 | 1,304 | 1,825 | 97 | 656 | 7,152 | 23,239 |
| Mar. 31 | 884 | 1,410 | 13 | 525 | 3 | 59 | 3,253 | 3,567 | 6,347 | 15,177 | 2,326 | 296 | 1,913 | 1,559 | 89 | 660 | 6,943 | 22,904 |
| Apr. 30 | 884 | 1,410 | 13 | 525 | 3 | 58 | 3,254 | 3,532 | 6,347 | 15,142 | 2,317 | 281 | 1,921 | 1,661 | 83 | 666 | 6,929 | 22,955 |
| May 31 | 884 | 1,410 | 13 | 526 | 3 | 56 | 3,255 | 3,507 | 6,346 | 15,116 | 2,317 | 254 | 1,921 | 1,660 | 77 | 671 | 6,900 | 22,900 |
| June 30 | 884 | 1,410 | 13 | 526 | 3 | 55 | 3,256 | 3,474 | 6,345 | 15,082 | 1,991 | (²) | 2,217 | 1,754 | 74 | 679 | 6,745 | 22,711 |
| July 31 | 884 | 1,410 | 12 | 526 | 3 | 54 | 3,257 | 3,474 | 6,345 | 15,081 | 1,991 |  | 2,256 | 1,754 | 71 | 690 | 6,752 | 22,717 |
| Aug. 31 | 884 | 1,410 | 12 | 527 | 3 | 52 | 3,258 | 3,474 | 6,345 | 15,081 | 1,839 |  | 2,743 | 1,493 | 58 | 698 | 6,831 | 22,796 |

² Separate figures for Victory 4¾'s and Victory 3¾'s not available.
³ Matured June 15, 1922.

TABLE F.—*Public debt transactions from July 1, 1921, to June 30, 1922, inclusive.*

| Debt. | Received for conversion, transfer, and exchange.[1] | Received for redemption. | Total received. | Issued on conversion, transfer, and exchange.[2] | Issued for cash, or in exchange for other securities. | Total issued. |
|---|---|---|---|---|---|---|
| INTEREST-BEARING DEBT: | | | | | | |
| Consols of 1930 | $27,078,900.00 | | $27,078,900.00 | $27,078,900.00 | | $27,078,900.00 |
| Loan of 1925 | 14,469,700.00 | | 14,469,700.00 | 14,469,700.00 | | 14,469,700.00 |
| Panama Canal loan 1916-1936 | 1,538,460.00 | | 1,538,460.00 | 1,538,460.00 | | 1,538,460.00 |
| Panama Canal loan 1918-1938 | 1,082,140.00 | | 1,082,140.00 | 1,082,140.00 | | 1,082,140.00 |
| Panama Canal loan 1961 | 5,435,300.00 | | 5,435,300.00 | 5,435,300.00 | | 5,435,300.00 |
| Conversion bonds | 2,648,200.00 | | 2,648,200.00 | 2,648,200.00 | | 2,648,200.00 |
| Postal savings bonds 1st-20th series | 837,920.00 | | 837,920.00 | 837,920.00 | | 837,920.00 |
| Postal savings bonds 21st series | 6,960.00 | | 6,960.00 | 6,960.00 | $55,780.00 | 62,740.00 |
| Postal savings bonds 22d series | 4,800.00 | | 4,800.00 | 4,800.00 | 56,420.00 | 61,220.00 |
| First Liberty loan— | | | | | | |
| Interim certificates | 104,100.00 | | 104,100.00 | | | |
| First 3½'s | 147,714,550.00 | $72,200.00 | 147,786,750.00 | 147,818,650.00 | | 147,818,650.00 |
| First 4's | 8,696,050.00 | 300.00 | 8,696,350.00 | 2,638,700.00 | | 2,638,700.00 |
| First 4¼'s | 89,667,400.00 | 341,050.00 | 90,908,450.00 | 94,817,650.00 | | 94,817,650.00 |
| First second 4¼'s | 704,130.00 | | 704,130.00 | 706,250.00 | | 706,250.00 |
| Second Liberty loan— | | | | | | |
| Second 4's | 36,219,150.00 | 650.00 | 36,219,800.00 | 12,773,100.00 | | 12,773,100.00 |
| Second 4¼'s | 488,884,300.00 | 5,922,330.00 | 494,806,650.00 | 512,281,650.00 | | 512,281,650.00 |
| Third Liberty loan— | | | | | | |
| Third 4¼'s | 627,852,200.00 | 137,767,250.00 | 765,619,450.00 | 627,784,950.00 | | 627,784,950.00 |
| Fourth Liberty loan— | | | | | | |
| Fourth 4¼'s | 1,079,130,350.00 | 9,461,750.00 | 1,088,592,100.00 | 1,080,498,150.00 | | 1,080,498,150.00 |
| Victory Liberty loan— | | | | | | |
| Victory 4¾'s | 720,955,100.00 | 1,474,616,700.00 | 2,195,571,800.00 | 913,985,350.00 | $1,300.00 | 913,994,650.00 |
| Victory 3¾'s | 253,024,600.00 | 433,359,550.00 | 686,384,150.00 | 60,065,550.00 | | 60,065,550.00 |
| Treasury notes— | | | | | | |
| Series TM, 5¼ per cent | 59,664,400.00 | | 59,664,400.00 | 59,664,400.00 | 390,706,100.00 | 59,664,400.00 |
| Series B-1924, 5¼ per cent | 95,402,900.00 | | 95,402,900.00 | 95,402,900.00 | 601,599,500.00 | 496,109,000.00 |
| Series A-1925, 4¾ per cent | 131,829,900.00 | | 131,829,900.00 | 131,829,900.00 | 601,599,500.00 | 733,429,400.00 |
| Series AB2, 4¾ per cent | 46,270,300.00 | | 46,270,300.00 | 46,270,300.00 | 617,769,700.00 | 664,040,000.00 |
| Series B 1924, 4¾ per cent | 7,566,500.00 | | 7,566,500.00 | 7,566,500.00 | 325,329,450.00 | 332,895,930.00 |
| Certificates of indebtedness— | | | | | | |
| Series TM2, 6 per cent | | 341,870,070.03 | 341,870,000.00 | 17,470,500.00 | | 17,470,500.00 |
| Series TD-1921, 6 per cent | | 389,242,510.03 | 389,242,500.00 | 48,404,000.00 | | 48,404,000.00 |
| Series TM, 5½ per cent | 17,470,500.00 | 193,294,001.00 | 193,294,000.00 | 22,635,500.00 | 116,891,000.00 | 139,526,500.00 |
| Series TJ-1922, 5½ per cent | 48,404,000.00 | 287,739,000.00 | 305,229,500.00 | 22,635,500.00 | 182,871,000.00 | 219,014,900.00 |
| Series MD-1922, 5¼ per cent | 22,635,500.00 | 309,482,000.00 | 357,886,000.00 | 36,143,500.00 | 124,572,000.00 | 141,343,590.00 |
| Series TS-1922, 5¼ per cent | 36,143,500.00 | 116,801,500.03 | 139,437,000.00 | 36,143,500.00 | 179,691,500.00 | 253,740,500.00 |
| Series TM3-1922, 5 per cent | 16,771,500.00 | | 141,034,000.00 | 74,049,000.00 | | |
| Series TM2, 4½ per cent | 74,049,000.00 | 124,2 2,500.00 | 74,049,000.00 | 74,049,000.00 | | |

| | | | | | | |
|---|---|---|---|---|---|---|
| Series TJ2-1922, 4¼ per cent | 23,075,000.00 | 63,550,500.00 | 86,625,500.00 | 23,075,000.00 | 64,903,000.00 | 87,978,000.00 |
| Series [illegible]-1922, 4½ per cent | 75,612,500.00 | | 75,612,500.00 | 75,612,500.00 | 243,544,000.00 | 319,156,500.00 |
| Series TM-1923, 4¼ per cent | 77,902,000.00 | | 77,902,000.00 | 77,902,000.00 | 266,250,000.00 | 344,152,000.00 |
| Series TD2-1922, 3½ per cent | 57,163,500.00 | | 57,163,500.00 | 57,163,500.00 | 200,000,000.00 | 257,163,500.00 |
| Series TJ-1923, 3¾ per cent | 47,456,500.00 | | 47,456,500.00 | 47,456,500.00 | 273,000,000.00 | 320,456,500.00 |
| Series C-1921, 6 per cent | | 155,416,000.00 | 155,416,000.00 | | | |
| Series F-1921, 5¾ per cent | | 191,619,000.00 | 191,619,000.00 | | | |
| Series G-1921, 5½ per cent | | 128,869,000.00 | 128,869,000.00 | | | |
| Series H-1921, 5½ per cent | | 190,472,500.00 | 190,472,500.00 | | | |
| Series A-1922, 5½ per cent | 20,269,500.00 | 255,699,000.00 | 275,968,500.00 | 20,269,500.00 | | 20,269,500.00 |
| Series B-1922, 5½ per cent | 88,772,500.00 | 40,500.00 | 88,813,000.00 | 88,772,500.00 | 259,471,500.00 | 348,244,000.00 |
| Series C-1922, 4¾ per cent | 13,030,500.00 | 51,647,500.00 | 64,678,000.00 | 13,030,500.00 | 51,796,000.00 | 64,826,500.00 |
| Series [illegible]-1922, 3½ per cent | 72,195,500.00 | | 72,195,500.00 | 72,195,500.00 | 150,000,000.00 | 222,195,500.00 |
| Pittman Act certificates, 2 per cent | | 141,875,000.00 | 141,875,000.00 | | | |
| Specials, various | | 1,824,954,450.00 | 1,824,954,450.00 | | 1,792,100,000.00 | 1,792,100,000.00 |
| Treasury (war) savings securities: | | | | | | |
| Series 1918 | 83,500.00 | 64,300,602.17 | 64,384,102.17 | 80,365.18 | | 80,365.18 |
| Series 1919 | 16,100.00 | 8,088,941.89 | 8,105,041.89 | [3] 15,152.77 | 27,187.47 | 12,034.70 |
| Series 1920 | 91,067.20 | 5,574,275.14 | 5,665,342.34 | 37,087,075.00 | 22,432.95 | 37,109,507.95 |
| Series 1921 | 2,845.55 | 5,642,070.96 | 5,644,916.51 | [3] 8,339,511.10 | 9,119,307.41 | 779,796.31 |
| Series 1921, new issue | | 141,340.00 | 141,340.00 | 200,910.67 | 1,942,809.33 | 2,143,720.00 |
| Series 1922, new issue | | 1,315,860.00 | 1,315,860.00 | 1,430,327.42 | 59,542,732.58 | 60,973,060.00 |
| Thrift stamps and Treasury savings stamps, unclassified sales, etc | 5,187,599.00 | 681,472.50 | 5,869,071.50 | | 4,885,220.00 | 4,885,220.00 |
| Total | 4,542,520,941.75 | 6,914,141,312.66 | 11,456,662,254.41 | 4,568,601,894.40 | 5,916,145,339.74 | 10,484,747,234.14 |
| MATURED DEBT ON WHICH INTEREST HAS CEASED: | | | | | | |
| Funded loan of 1907 | | 6,200.00 | 6,200.00 | | | |
| Refunding certificates | | 80.00 | 80.00 | | | |
| Old debt—five-twenties of 1862— | | | | | | |
| Fifth series | | 100.00 | 100.00 | | | |
| One-year Treasury notes | | 20.00 | 20.00 | | | |
| Compound interest notes | | 70.00 | 70.00 | | | |
| Seven-thirties of 1861 | | 50.00 | 50.00 | | | |
| Loan of [illegible] | | 50,620.00 | 50,620.00 | | | |
| Certificates of indebtedness— | | | | | | |
| 4 per cent | | 5,000.00 | 5,000.00 | | | |
| 4¼ per cent | | 3,000.00 | 3,000.00 | | | |
| 4½ per cent | | 107,000.00 | 107,000.00 | | | |
| 4¾ per cent | | 319,500.00 | 319,500.00 | | | |
| 5 per cent | | 500.00 | 500.00 | | | |
| 5¼ per cent | | 25,000.00 | 25,000.00 | | | |
| 5½ per cent | | 84,000.00 | 84,000.00 | | | |
| 5¾ per cent | | 3,114,000.00 | 3,114,000.00 | | | |
| 6 per cent | | 5,361,000.00 | 5,361,000.00 | | | |
| Total matured debt on which interest has ceased | | 9,076,140.00 | 9,076,140.00 | | | |

[1] Includes securities received during the fiscal year 1922 for exchanges which will be completed in the fiscal year 1923.
[2] Includes securities issued in the fiscal year 1922 in exchange for securities received in the fiscal year 1921.
[3] Counter entry; deduct.

TABLE F.—*Public debt transactions from July 1, 1921, to June 30, 1922, inclusive*—Continued.

| Debt. | Received for conversion, transfer, and exchange. | Received for redemption. | Total received. | Issued on conversion, transfer, and exchange. | Issued for cash, or in exchange for other securities. | Total issued. |
|---|---|---|---|---|---|---|
| DEBT BEARING NO INTEREST: | | | | | | |
| United States notes | $339,348,000.00 | | $339,348,000.00 | $339,348,000.00 | | $339,348,000.00 |
| National bank notes and Federal reserve bank notes | | $107,251,870.00 | 107,251,870.00 | | $107,086,627.50 | 107,086,627.50 |
| Fractional currency | | 942.40 | 942.40 | | | |
| Total debt bearing no interest | 339,348,000.00 | 107,252,812.40 | 446,600,812.40 | 339,348,000.00 | 107,086,627.50 | 446,434,627.50 |
| Total gross debt | 4,881,888,941.75 | 7,030,470,265.06 | 11,912,339,206.81 | 4,907,949,894.40 | 6,023,231,967.24 | 10,931,181,861.64 |
| Soldiers' and sailors' civil relief insurance bonds, 3½ per cent, not included in the public debt | | 2,900.00 | 2,900.00 | | | |

TABLE F.—*Public debt transactions from July 1, 1921, to June 30, 1922, inclusive*— Continued.

RECONCILIATION OF TABLE "F" WITH THE STATEMENTS OF THE PUBLIC DEBT FOR JUNE 30, 1921, AND JUNE 30, 1922.

| | | | |
|---|---|---|---|
| Interest-bearing debt outstanding June 30, 1921.... | $23,737,352,080.37 | | |
| Issued for cash or on exchange for other securities during fiscal year 1922, above.................. | 5,916,145,339.74 | | |
| Total............................................ | | $29,653,497,420.11 | |
| Interest-bearing debt received for redemption...... | 6,914,141,312.66 | | |
| In transit on June 30, 1921, not included above..... | 47,900.00 | | |
| Adjustment on account of Treasury (war) savings securities................................ | 4,885,220.00 | | |
| Outstanding certificates of indebtedness which matured prior to June 30, 1922..................... | 8,778,000.00 | | |
| Outstanding Victory notes, 3¾ per cent, which matured prior to June 30, 1922..................... | 14,609,400.00 | | |
| Total.......................................... | | 6,942,461,832.66 | |
| Interest-bearing debt outstanding June 30, 1922............................................ | | | $22,711,035,587.45 |
| Matured debt outstanding June 30, 1921............ | 10,939,620.26 | | |
| Add interest-bearing debt which matured prior to June 30, 1922................................... | 23,387,400.00 | | |
| Total....................................... | | 34,327,020.26 | |
| Matured debt received for redemption................................ | | 9,076,140.00 | |
| Matured debt outstanding June 30, 1922................................ | | | 25,250,880.26 |
| Debt bearing no interest outstanding June 30, 1921. | 227,958,907.77 | | |
| Deposits for retirement of national and Federal reserve bank notes................................ | 107,086,627.50 | | |
| Total......................................... | | 335,045,535.27 | |
| Debt bearing no interest received for redemption...................... | | 107,252,812.40 | |
| Debt bearing no interest outstanding June 30, 1922...................................... | | | 227,792,722.87 |
| Gross debt June 30, 1922......................................... | | | 22,964,079,190.58 |
| Gross debt June 30, 1921......................................... | | | [1] 23,976,250,608.40 |
| Decrease during the fiscal year 1922................................ | | | [1] 1,012,171,417.82 |

RECONCILIATION OF THE STATEMENT OF THE PUBLIC DEBT FOR JUNE 30, 1922, WITH CASH RECEIPTS AND REDEMPTIONS ON ACCOUNT OF THE PUBLIC DEBT, ON THE BASIS OF DAILY TREASURY STATEMENTS.

| | | |
|---|---|---|
| Gross debt as shown by the statement of the public debt June 30, 1921.................. | | $23,976,250,608.40 |
| Net excess of public debt receipts over redemptions in transit on June 30, 1921...................... | $1,199,944.14 | |
| Public debt receipts during fiscal year 1922 on the basis of daily Treasury statements................ | 6,017,157,652.70 | |
| Receipts...................................... | | $6,018,357,596.84 |
| Public debt redemptions during fiscal year 1922 on the basis of daily Treasury statements........... | 7,031,226,496.93 | |
| Deduct receipts in transit on June 30, 1922.......... | 697,482.27 | |
| Redemptions ............................................... | | 7,030,529,014.66 |
| Excess of redemptions............................................ | | 1,012,171,417.82 |
| Gross debt as shown by the statement of the public debt June 30, 1922 ..................................... | | 22,964,079,190.58 |

[1] According to warrants issued the excess of public debt expenditures over public debt receipts was $1,012,171,560.32. The difference between this amount and the decrease shown above is due to the inclusion in covering warrants of an item of $142.50 on account of reimbursement for Treasury (war) savings securities returned by a cash agent. This item was not included in the statement of the public debt until July.

TABLE G.—*Issues of certificates of indebtedness, from April 6. 1917, to October 31, 1922.*

| Authorizing act. | Date of issue. | Date of maturity. | Rate (per cent). | Amount subscribed. | Amount issued. |
|---|---|---|---|---|---|
| Issued in anticipation of the first Liberty loan: | | | | | |
| Apr. 24, 1917...................... | Apr. 25, 1917 | June 30, 1917 | 3 | $268,205,000 | $268,205,000 |
| Do.......................... | May 10, 1917 | July 17, 1917 | 3 | 200,000,000 | 200,000,000 |
| Do.......................... | May 25, 1917 | July 30, 1917 | 3½ | 200,000,000 | 200,000,000 |
| Do.......................... | June 8, 1917 | ....do........ | 3½ | 230,524,000 | 200,000,000 |
| Total...................... | | | | 898,729,000 | 868,205,000 |
| Issued in anticipation of the second Liberty loan: | | | | | |
| Apr. 24, 1917...................... | Aug. 9, 1917 | Nov. 15, 1917 | 3½ | 361,525,000 | 300,000,000 |
| Do.......................... | Aug. 28, 1917 | Nov. 30, 1917 | 3½ | 308,246,000 | 250,000,000 |
| Do.......................... | Sept. 17, 1917 | Dec. 15, 1917 | 3½ | 300,000,000 | 300,000,000 |
| Sept. 24, 1917...................... | Sept. 26, 1917 | ....do........ | 4 | 400,000,000 | 400,000,000 |
| Do.......................... | Oct. 18, 1917 | Nov. 22, 1917 | 4 | 385,197,000 | 385,197,000 |
| Do.......................... | Oct. 24, 1917 | Dec. 15, 1917 | 4 | 685,296,000 | 685,296,000 |
| Total...................... | | | | 2,440,264,000 | 2,320,493,000 |
| Issued in anticipation of the third Liberty loan: | | | | | |
| Sept. 24, 1917...................... | Jan. 22, 1918 | Apr. 22, 1918 | 4 | 400,000,000 | 400,000,000 |
| Do.......................... | Feb. 8, 1918 | May 9, 1918 | 4 | 500,000,000 | 500,000,000 |
| Do.......................... | Feb. 27, 1918 | May 28, 1918 | 4½ | 524,929,000 | 500,000,000 |
| Do.......................... | Mar. 20, 1918 | June 18, 1918 | 4½ | 543,032,500 | 543,032,500 |
| Do.......................... | Apr. 10, 1918 | July 9, 1918 | 4½ | 551,226,500 | 551,226,500 |
| Sept. 24, 1917, as amended Apr. 4, 1918.......................... | Apr. 22, 1918 | July 18, 1918 | 4½ | 517,826,500 | 517,826,500 |
| Total...................... | | | | 3,037,014,500 | 3,012,085,500 |
| Issued in anticipation of the fourth Liberty loan: | | | | | |
| Sept. 24, 1917, as amended Apr. 4, 1918— | | | | | |
| Series IV, A................... | June 25, 1918 | Oct. 24, 1918 | 4½ | 839,646,500 | 839,646,500 |
| Series IV, B................... | July 9, 1918 | Nov. 7, 1918 | 4½ | 759,438,000 | 753,938,000 |
| Series IV, C................... | July 23, 1918 | Nov. 21, 1918 | 4½ | 584,750,500 | 584,750,500 |
| Series IV, D................... | Aug. 6, 1918 | Dec. 5, 1918 | 4½ | 575,706,500 | 575,706,500 |
| Series IV, E................... | Sept. 3, 1918 | Jan. 2, 1919 | 4½ | 639,493,000 | 639,493,000 |
| Series IV, F................... | Sept. 17, 1918 | Jan. 16, 1919 | 4½ | 625,216,500 | 625,216,500 |
| Series IV, G................... | Oct. 1, 1918 | Jan. 30, 1919 | 4½ | 641,069,000 | 641,069,000 |
| Total...................... | | | | 4,665,320,000 | 4,659,820,000 |
| Issued in anticipation of the Victory Liberty loan: | | | | | |
| Sept. 24, 1917, as amended Apr. 4, 1918— | | | | | |
| Series V, A................... | Dec. 5, 1918 | May 6, 1919 | 4½ | 613,438,000 | 613,438,000 |
| Series V, B................... | Dec. 19, 1918 | May 20, 1919 | 4½ | 572,494,000 | 572,494,000 |
| Series V, C................... | Jan. 2, 1919 | June 3, 1919 | 4½ | 751,681,500 | 751,684,500 |
| Series V, D................... | Jan. 16, 1919 | June 17, 1919 | 4½ | 600,101,500 | 600,101,500 |
| Series V, E................... | Jan. 30, 1919 | July 1, 1919 | 4½ | 687,381,500 | 687,381,500 |
| Series V, F................... | Feb. 13, 1919 | July 15, 1919 | 4½ | 620,578,500 | 620,578,500 |
| Series V, G................... | Feb. 27, 1919 | July 29, 1919 | 4½ | 532,381,500 | 532,381,500 |
| Sept. 24, 1917, as amended Apr. 4, 1918 and Mar. 3, 1919— | | | | | |
| Series V, H................... | Mar. 13, 1919 | Aug. 12, 1919 | 4½ | 542,197,000 | 542,197,000 |
| Series V, J................... | Apr. 10, 1919 | Sept. 9, 1919 | 4½ | 646,025,000 | 646,025,000 |
| Series V, K................... | May 1, 1919 | Oct. 7, 1919 | 4½ | 591,308,000 | 591,308,000 |
| Total...................... | | | | 6,157,589,500 | 6,157,589,500 |
| Loan certificates of 1920: | | | | | |
| Sept. 24, 1917, as amended Apr 4, 1918, and Mar. 3, 1919— | | | | | |
| Series A, 1920................. | Aug 1, 1919 | Jan. 2, 1920 | 4½ | 533,801,500 | 533,801,500 |
| Series B, 1920................. | Aug. 15, 1919 | Jan. 15, 1920 | 4½ | 532,152,000 | 532,152,000 |
| Series C, 1920................. | Sept. 2, 1919 | Feb. 2, 1920 | 4½ | 573,841,500 | 573,841,500 |
| Series D, 1920................. | Dec. 1, 1919 | Feb. 16, 1920 | 4½ | 162,178,500 | 162,178,500 |
| Series ', 1920................. | Apr. 1, 1920 | July 1, 1920 | 4¾ | 200,669,500 | 200,669,500 |
| Series F, 1920................. | Apr 15, 1920 | July 15, 1920 | 5 | 83,903,000 | 83,903,000 |
| Series G, 1920................. | ....do........ | Oct. 15, 1920 | 5½ | 170,633,500 | 170,633,500 |
| Series H, 1920................. | May 17, 1920 | Nov 15, 1920 | 5½ | 129,749,500 | 102,865,000 |
| Total...................... | | | | 2,386,929,000 | 2,360,044,500 |

TABLE G.—*Issues of certificates of indebtedness, from April 6, 1917, to October 31, 1922*—Continued.

| Authorizing act. | Date of issue. | Date of maturity. | Rate (per cent). | Amount subscribed. | Amount issued. |
|---|---|---|---|---|---|
| Loan certificates of 1921: | | | | | |
| Sept. 24, 1917, as amended Apr. 4, 1918, and Mar. 3, 1919— | | | | | |
| Series A, 1921 | June 15, 1920 | Jan. 3, 1921 | 5¾ | $176,604,000 | $176,604,000 |
| Series B, 1921 | July 15, 1920 | Jan. 15, 1921 | 5¾ | 126,783,500 | 126,783,500 |
| Series C, 1921 | Aug. 16, 1920 | Aug. 16, 1921 | 6 | 208,347,500 | 157,654,500 |
| Series D, 1921 | Nov. 15, 1920 | May 16, 1921 | 5¾ | 292,696,500 | 232,124,000 |
| Series E, 1921 | Jan. 15, 1921 | Apr. 15, 1921 | 5½ | 182,187,500 | 118,660,000 |
| Series F, 1921 | .....do........ | Oct. 15, 1921 | 5¾ | 406,409,000 | 192,026,500 |
| Series G, 1921 | Feb. 15, 1921 | July 15, 1921 | 5½ | 218,924,500 | 132,886,500 |
| Series H, 1921 | Apr. 15, 1921 | Oct. 15, 1921 | 5½ | 320,036,000 | 190,511,500 |
| Total | | | | 1,931,988,500 | 1,327,250,500 |
| Loan certificates of 1922: | | | | | |
| Sept. 24, 1917, as amended Apr. 4, 1918, and Mar. 3, 1919— | | | | | |
| Series A, 1922 | May 16, 1921 | Feb. 16, 1922 | 5½ | 532,100,000 | 256,170,000 |
| Series B, 1922 | Aug. 1, 1921 | Aug. 1, 1922 | 5½ | 709,919,500 | 259,471,500 |
| Series C, 1922 | Nov. 1, 1921 | Apr. 1, 1922 | 4¼ | 189,255,000 | 51,796,000 |
| Series D, 1922 | Apr. 15, 1922 | Oct. 16, 1922 | 3½ | 309,212,000 | 150,000,000 |
| Total | | | | 1,740,486,500 | 717,437,500 |
| Issued in anticipation of income and profits taxes, 1918: | | | | | |
| Sept. 24, 1917 | Nov. 30, 1917 | June 25, 1918 | 4 | 691,872,000 | 691,872,000 |
| Do | Jan. 2, 1918 | .....do........ | 4 | 491,822,500 | 491,822,500 |
| Do | Feb. 15, 1918 | .....do........ | 4 | 74,100,000 | 74,100,000 |
| Do | Mar. 15, 1918 | .....do........ | 4 | 110,962,000 | 110,962,000 |
| Sept. 24, 1917, as amended Apr. 4, 1918 | Apr. 15, 1918 | .....do........ | 4 | 71,880,000 | 71,880,000 |
| Do | May 15, 1918 | .....do........ | 4 | 183,767,000 | 183,767,000 |
| Total | | | | 1,624,403,500 | 1,624,403,500 |
| Issued in anticipation of income and profits taxes, 1919: | | | | | |
| Sept. 24, 1917, as amended Apr. 4, 1918— | | | | | |
| Tax series of 1919 | Aug. 20, 1918 | July 15, 1919 | 4 | 157,552,500 | 157,552,500 |
| Series T | Nov. 7, 1918 | Mar. 15, 1919 | 4½ | 794,172,500 | 794,172,500 |
| Series T-2 | Jan. 16, 1919 | June 17, 1919 | 4½ | 392,381,000 | 392,381,000 |
| Sept. 24, 1917, as amended Apr. 4, 1918, and Mar. 3, 1919— | | | | | |
| Series T-3 | Mar. 15, 1919 | June 16, 1919 | 4½ | 407,918,500 | 407,918,500 |
| Series T-4 | June 3, 1919 | Sept. 15, 1919 | 4½ | 526,139,500 | 526,139,500 |
| Series T-5 | .....do........ | Dec. 15, 1919 | 4½ | 238,711,500 | 238,711,500 |
| Series T-6 | July 1, 1919 | Sept. 15, 1919 | 4½ | 326,468,000 | 326,468,000 |
| Series T-7 | .....do........ | Dec. 15, 1919 | 4½ | 511,444,000 | 511,444,000 |
| Total | | | | 3,354,787,500 | 3,354,787,500 |
| Issued in anticipation of income and profits taxes, 1920. | | | | | |
| Sept. 24, 1917, as amended— | | | | | |
| Series T-8 | July 15, 1919 | Mar. 15, 1920 | 4½ | 323,074,500 | 323,074,500 |
| Series T-9 | Sept. 15, 1919 | .....do........ | 4½ | 101,131,500 | 101,131,500 |
| Series T-10 | .....do........ | Sept. 15, 1920 | 4½ | 657,469,000 | 657,469,000 |
| Series T M3-1920 | Dec. 1, 1919 | Mar. 15, 1920 | 4¼ | 260,322,000 | 260,322,000 |
| Series T J-1920 | Dec. 15, 1919 | June 15, 1920 | 4½ | 728,130,000 | 728,130,000 |
| Series T D-1920 | Jan. 2, 1920 | Dec. 15, 1920 | 4¾ | 703,026,000 | 703,026,000 |
| Series T M4-1920 | Feb. 2, 1920 | Mar. 15, 1920 | 4½ | 304,877,000 | 304,877,000 |
| Total | | | | 3,078,030,000 | 3,078,030,000 |
| Issued in anticipation of income and profits taxes, 1921: | | | | | |
| Sept. 24, 1917, as amended— | | | | | |
| Series T M-1921 | Mar. 15, 1920 | Mar. 15, 1921 | 4¾ | 201,370,500 | 201,370,500 |
| Series T J-1921 | June 15, 1920 | June 15, 1921 | 6 | 242,517,000 | 242,517,000 |
| Series T M2-1921 | July 15, 1920 | Mar. 15, 1921 | 5¾ | 74,278,000 | 74,278,000 |
| Series T M3-1921 | Sept. 15, 1920 | .....do........ | 5¼ | 116,732,000 | 106,626,500 |
| Series T S-1921 | .....do........ | Sept. 15, 1921 | 6 | 375,530,000 | 341,969,500 |
| Series T M4-1921 | Oct. 15, 1920 | Mar. 15, 1921 | 5¾ | 185,076,500 | 124,252,500 |
| Series T J2-1921 | Dec. 15, 1920 | June 15, 1921 | 5¾ | 275,649,000 | 188,123,000 |
| Series T D-1921 | .....do........ | Dec. 15, 1921 | 6 | 514,800,500 | 401,557,500 |
| Series T S2-1921 | Mar. 15, 1921 | Sept. 15, 1921 | 5½ | 198,086,500 | 193,302,000 |
| Total | | | | 2,184,040,000 | 1,873,996,500 |

TABLE G.—*Issues of certificates of indebtedness, from April 6, 1917, to October 31, 1922*—
Continued.

| Authorizing act. | Date of issue. | Date of maturity. | Rate (per cent). | Amount subscribed. | Amount issued. |
|---|---|---|---|---|---|
| Issued in anticipation of income and profits taxes, 1922: Sept. 24, 1917, as amended— | | | | | |
| Series T M–1922 | Mar. 15, 1921 | Mar. 15, 1922 | 5¾ | $305,350,000 | $288,501,000 |
| Series T J–1922 | June 15, 1921 | June 15, 1922 | 5½ | 432,599,500 | 314,134,000 |
| Series T M2–1922 | Aug. 1, 1921 | Mar. 15, 1922 | 5¼ | 320,087,000 | 116,891,000 |
| Series T S–1922 | Sept. 15, 1921 | Sept. 15, 1922 | 5¼ | 462,818,000 | 182,871,000 |
| Series T M3–1922 | ....do | Mar. 15, 1922 | 5 | 339,938,000 | 124,572,000 |
| Series T S2–1922 | Nov. 1, 1921 | Sept. 15, 1922 | 4½ | 621,809,000 | 179,691,500 |
| Series T J2–1922 | Dec. 15, 1921 | June 15, 1922 | 4½ | 255,653,000 | 64,903,000 |
| Series T–D–1922 | ....do | Dec. 15, 1922 | 4½ | 927,449,000 | 243,544,000 |
| Series T D2–1922 | June 1, 1922 | ....do | 3½ | 383,541,500 | 200,000,000 |
| Total | | | | 4,049,245,000 | 1,715,157,500 |
| Issued in anticipation of income and profits taxes, 1923: Sept. 24, 1917, as amended— | | | | | |
| Series T M–1923 | Mar. 15, 1922 | Mar. 15, 1923 | 4½ | 674,830,500 | 266,250,000 |
| Series T J–1923 | June 15, 1922 | June 15, 1923 | 3¾ | 469,797,000 | 273,000,000 |
| Series T S–1923 | Sept. 15, 1922 | Sept. 15, 1923 | 3¾ | 570,476,500 | 227,000,000 |
| Total | | | | 1,715,104,000 | 766,250,000 |

RECAPITULATION.

| Issues. | Amount subscribed. | Amount issued. |
|---|---|---|
| Loan certificates: | | |
| In anticipation of the first Liberty loan | $898,729,000 | $868,205,000 |
| In anticipation of the second Liberty loan | 2,440,264,000 | 2,320,493,030 |
| In anticipation of the third Liberty loan | 3,037,014,500 | 3,012,085,500 |
| In anticipation of the fourth Liberty loan | 4,665,320,000 | 4,659,820,000 |
| In anticipation of the Victory Liberty loan | 6,157,589,500 | 6,157,589,500 |
| Series 1920 | 2,386,929,000 | 2,360,044,500 |
| Series 1921 | 1,931,988,500 | 1,327,250,500 |
| Series 1922 | 1,740,486,500 | 717,437,500 |
| Total loan certificates | 23,258,321,000 | 21,422,925,500 |
| Tax certificates: | | |
| In anticipation of income and profits taxes, 1918 | 1,624,403,500 | 1,624,403,500 |
| In anticipation of income and profits taxes, 1919 | 3,354,787,500 | 3,354,787,500 |
| In anticipation of income and profits taxes, 1920 | 3,078,030,000 | 3,078,030,000 |
| In anticipation of income and profits taxes, 1921 | 2,184,040,000 | 1,873,996,500 |
| In anticipation of income and profits taxes, 1922 | 4,049,245,000 | 1,715,157,500 |
| In anticipation of income and profits taxes, 1923 | 1,715,104,000 | 766,250,000 |
| Total tax certificates | 16,005,610,000 | 12,412,625,000 |
| Special issues (Pittman) to secure Federal reserve bank notes: | | |
| Fiscal year 1919 | | 178,723,000 |
| Fiscal year 1920 | | 80,652,000 |
| Total | | 259,375,000 |
| Special issues payable in foreign currency: | | |
| Fiscal year 1919 | | 79,540,000 |
| Fiscal year 1920 | | 32,551,700 |
| Total | | 112,091,700 |
| Special (short term) issues: | | |
| Fiscal year 1918 | | 1,325,000,000 |
| Fiscal year 1919 | | 4,105,278,390 |
| Fiscal year 1920 | | 7,712,212,269 |
| Fiscal year 1921 | | 5,014,500,000 |
| Fiscal year 1922 | | 1,792,100,000 |
| Fiscal year 1923 (to Oct. 31, 1922) | | 482,500,000 |
| Total | | 20,431,590,659 |
| Special issue (War Finance Corporation): | | |
| Fiscal year 1921 | | 32,854,450 |
| Total special issues | | 20,835,911,809 |
| Grand total, all issues | | 54,671,462,309 |

TABLE **H.**—*Condition of the United States Treasury at the close of the fiscal years 1920, 1921, and 1922.*

[Revised figures.]

| | 1922 | 1921 | 1920 |
|---|---|---|---|
| **Assets:** GOLD. | | | |
| Gold coin......................... | $306,957,667.39 | $258,881,883.67 | $376,051,010.45 |
| Gold bullion........................ | 2,850,244,888.57 | 2,411,502,196.43 | 1,795,908,912.41 |
| Total........................... | 3,157,202,555.96 | 2,670,384,080.10 | 2,171,959,922.86 |
| **Liabilities:** | | | |
| Gold certificates................... | 695,000,469.00 | 716,532,989.00 | 584,723,645.00 |
| Gold fund, Federal Reserve Board.......... | 2,108,886,911.43 | 1,537,856,895.45 | 1,184,275,551.87 |
| Gold reserve...................... | 152,979,025.63 | 152,979,025.63 | 152,979,025.63 |
| Gold in general fund.................. | 200,336,149.90 | 263,015,170.02 | 249,981,700.36 |
| Total........................... | 3,157,202,555.96 | 2,670,384,080.10 | 2,171,959,922.86 |
| **Assets:** SILVER. | | | |
| Silver dollars....................... | 313,504,308.00 | 213,735,045.00 | 134,849,784.00 |
| **Liabilities:** | | | |
| Silver certificates................... | 304,066,593.00 | 201,534,213.00 | 118,257,883.00 |
| Treasury notes of 1890................ | 1,510,543.00 | 1,576,184.00 | 1,656,227.00 |
| Silver in general fund................ | 7,927,172.00 | 10,624,648.00 | 14,935,674.00 |
| Total........................... | 313,504,308.00 | 213,735,045.00 | 134,849,784.00 |
| **Assets:** GENERAL FUND. | | | |
| Gold............................ | 200,336,149.90 | 263,015,170.02 | 249,981,700.36 |
| Silver dollars....................... | 7,927,172.00 | 10,624,648.00 | 14,935,674.00 |
| United States notes.................. | 4,145,964.00 | 4,031,479.00 | 9,567,164.00 |
| Federal reserve notes................ | 2,557,721.50 | 4,719,921.00 | 30,096,579.00 |
| Federal reserve bank notes............. | 1,030,273.00 | 2,422,847.50 | 2,545,783.00 |
| National bank notes.................. | 15,774,366.63 | 13,739,860.98 | 22,962,455.92 |
| Subsidiary silver.................... | 17,747,501.85 | 9,663,502.04 | 6,605,093.65 |
| Minor coin........................ | 3,620,013.33 | 2,392,673.78 | 1,076,790.26 |
| Silver bullion at cost................. | 44,284,867.40 | 56,720,406.41 | 19,516,565.10 |
| Unclassified....................... | 3,283,342.53 | 3,141,005.13 | 6,309,473.65 |
| Public debt paid awaiting reimbursement.... | 503,020.03 | 727,446.76 | 1,242,633.03 |
| Total in Treasury offices............... | 301,210,392.17 | 371,198,960.62 | 364,839,911.97 |
| In Federal land banks.................. | .................. | .................. | 5,950,000.00 |
| In Federal reserve banks— | | | |
| To credit of Treasurer of the United States. | 33,091,888.68 | 43,475,862.73 | 30,483,519.22 |
| In transit......................... | 21,991,600.88 | 30,083,061.41 | 14,843,266.02 |
| Total in Federal reserve banks......... | 55,083,489.56 | 73,558,924.14 | 45,326,785.24 |
| In special depositaries account of sales of Treasury notes and certificates............... | 146,476,840.69 | 395,738,063.16 | 273,428,577.33 |
| In national bank depositaries— | | | |
| To credit of Treasurer of the United States. | 7,832,260.63 | 8,207,647.02 | 11,863,207.11 |
| To credit other Government officers...... | 16,169,825.24 | 16,036,064.70 | 15,138,161.88 |
| In transit......................... | 2,129,381.31 | 2,440,380.72 | 5,300,185.33 |
| Total in national bank depositaries..... | 26,131,467.18 | 26,684,092.44 | 32,301,554.32 |
| In treasury Philippine Islands[1]............... | 4,418,311.48 | 7,917,707.88 | 798,910.54 |
| In foreign depositaries[1]— | | | |
| To credit of Treasurer of the United States. | 701,760.43 | 710,262.94 | 8,301,507.40 |
| To credit other Government officers...... | 521,190.60 | 51,548,267.84 | .................. |
| Total in foreign depositaries........... | 1,222,951.03 | 52,258,530.78 | 8,301,507.40 |
| Total assets in general fund............. | 534,543,452.11 | 927,356,279.02 | 730,947,246.80 |

[1] Includes transit items.

TABLE H.—*Condition of the United States Treasury at the close of the fiscal years 1920, 1921, and 1922*—Continued.

|  | 1922 | 1921 | 1920 |
|---|---|---|---|
| GENERAL FUND—continued. |  |  |  |
| Liabilities: |  |  |  |
| Deposits— |  |  |  |
| Redemption of Federal reserve notes (5 per cent fund, gold)................... | $179,138,539.55 | $259,178,087.04 | $239,669,857.39 |
| Redemption of Federal reserve bank notes (5 per cent fund, lawful money.... | 7,445,646.55 | 9,442,096.55 | 11,642,140.00 |
| Redemption of national-bank notes (5 per cent fund, lawful money).......... | 29,791,025.87 | 18,495,044.98 | 21,332,789.12 |
| Retirement of additional circulating notes act of May 30, 1908..................... | 31,080.00 | 67,560.00 | 138,860.00 |
| Board of trustees, Postal Savings System (5 per cent reserve, lawful money)...... | 7,047,173.05 | 3,982,976.76 | 7,698,473.64 |
| Undistributed assets of insolvent national banks................................... | 1,931,759.56 | 1,630,871.72 | 1,168,284.92 |
| Total redemption and trust funds in the general fund...................... | 225,385,224.58 | 292,796,637.05 | 281,650,405.07 |
| Exchanges of currency, coin, etc.............. | 3,197,276.59 | 4,795,176.84 | 18,978,238.06 |
| Treasurer's checks outstanding.............. | 447,858.57 | 298,047.10 | 466,273.36 |
| Post Office Department balance.............. | 12,427,459.46 | 18,769,940.53 | 35,838,627.79 |
| Board of trustees Postal Savings System current account............................ | 56,561.64 | 138,567.25 | 92,581.00 |
| Balance to credit of postmasters, clerks of courts, etc............................... | 28,902,135.42 | 77,659,580.48 | 33,974,101.19 |
| Total liabilities, general fund........... | 270,416,516.26 | 394,457,949.25 | 371,000,226.47 |
| Balance in general fund.................. | 264,126,935.85 | 532,898,329.77 | 359,947,020.33 |
| Total................................... | 534,543,452.11 | 927,356,279.02 | 730,947,246.80 |

TABLE I.—*Balance in the general fund of the Treasury, by calendar years from 1791 to 1842, and by fiscal years from 1843 to 1922.*[1]

| Year ended— | Balance in general fund. | Year ended— | Balance in general fund. |
|---|---|---|---|
| Dec. 31: | | June 30—Continued. | |
| 1791 | $973,905.75 | 1857 | $18,218,770.40 |
| 1792 | 783,444.51 | 1858 | 6,698,157.91 |
| 1793 | 753,661.69 | 1859 | 4,685,625.04 |
| 1794 | 1,151,924.17 | 1860 | 3,931,287.72 |
| 1795 | 516,442.61 | | |
| 1796 | 888,995.42 | 1861 | 2,005,285.24 |
| 1797 | 1,021,899.04 | 1862 | 18,265,984.84 |
| 1798 | 617,451.43 | 1863 | 8,395,443.73 |
| 1799 | 2,161,867.77 | 1864 | 112,002,776.10 |
| 1800 | 2,623,311.99 | 1865 | 26,440,930.29 |
| | | 1866 | 112,476,770.66 |
| 1801 | 3,295,391.00 | 1867 | 161,175,174.31 |
| 1802 | 5,020,697.64 | 1868 | 115,133,529.82 |
| 1803 | 4,825,811.60 | 1869 | 126,542,842.77 |
| 1804 | 4,037,005.26 | 1870 | 113,485,981.01 |
| 1805 | 3,999,388.99 | | |
| 1806 | 4,538,123.80 | 1871 | 91,739,739.00 |
| 1807 | 9,643,850.07 | 1872 | 74,437,358.54 |
| 1808 | 9,941,809.96 | 1873 | 59,762,346.64 |
| 1809 | 3,848,056.78 | 1874 | 72,159,597.17 |
| 1810 | 2,672,276.57 | 1875 | [4]63,274,721.71 |
| | | 1876 | 58,947,608.99 |
| 1811 | 3,502,305.80 | 1877 | 91,694,006.29 |
| 1812 | 3,862,217.41 | 1878 | 177,498,846.71 |
| 1813 | 5,196,542.00 | 1879 | 367,054,575.14 |
| 1814 | 1,727,848.63 | 1880 | 168,299,404.40 |
| 1815 | 13,106,592.88 | | |
| 1816 | 22,033,519.19 | 1881 | 182,678,977.44 |
| 1817 | 14,989,465.48 | 1882 | 162,323,331.14 |
| 1818 | 1,478,526.74 | 1883 | 161,382,637.70 |
| 1819 | 2,079,992.38 | 1884 | 165,046,380.59 |
| 1820 | 1,198,461.21 | 1885 | 182,622,360.17 |
| | | 1886 | 232,099,178.05 |
| 1821 | 1,681,592.24 | 1887 | 207,600,698.44 |
| 1822 | 4,193,690.68 | 1888 | 244,094,169.01 |
| 1823 | 9,431,353.20 | 1889 | 210,737,083.76 |
| 1824 | 1,887,799.80 | 1890 | 190,841,184.72 |
| 1825 | 5,296,306.74 | | |
| 1826 | 6,342,289.48 | 1891 | 156,847,826.49 |
| 1827 | 6,649,604.31 | 1892 | 129,182,494.70 |
| 1828 | 5,965,974.27 | 1893 | 124,824,804.94 |
| 1829 | [2]4,362,770.76 | 1894 | 118,885,988.16 |
| 1830 | 4,761,409.34 | 1895 | 196,348,193.17 |
| | | 1896 | 269,637,307.07 |
| 1831 | 3,053,513.24 | 1897 | 244,466,201.59 |
| 1832 | 911,863.16 | 1898 | 209,282,643.13 |
| 1833 | 10,658,283.61 | 1899 | 284,488,516.20 |
| 1834 | 7,861,093.60 | 1900 | 156,827,608.37 |
| 1835 | 25,729,315.72 | | |
| 1836 | 45,756,833.54 | 1901 | 178,406,795.13 |
| 1837 | [3]6,804,953.64 | 1902 | 212,187,361.16 |
| 1838 | 6,633,715.23 | 1903 | 238,686,114.23 |
| 1839 | 4,683,416.48 | 1904 | 172,051,568.02 |
| 1840 | 1,704,561.80 | 1905 | 145,477,491.89 |
| | | 1906 | 180,689,354.82 |
| 1841 | 375,692.47 | 1907 | 272,061,445.47 |
| 1842 | 2,079,908.13 | 1908 | 245,171,347.73 |
| June 30: | | 1909 | 126,375,428.10 |
| 1843 | 11,195,156.21 | 1910 | 106,894,675.67 |
| 1844 | 8,612,850.23 | | |
| 1845 | 8,110,649.86 | 1911 | 140,176,926.13 |
| 1846 | 9,683,869.83 | 1912 | 167,152,478.99 |
| 1847 | 5,446,382.16 | 1913 | 165,960,984.79 |
| 1848 | 758,332.15 | 1914 | 161,612,615.53 |
| 1849 | 3,208,822.43 | 1915 | 104,170,105.78 |
| 1850 | 7,431,022.72 | 1916 | 235,925,945.68 |
| | | 1917 | 1,119,764,531.68 |
| 1851 | 12,142,193.97 | 1918 | 1,684,929,580.21 |
| 1852 | 15,097,880.36 | 1919 | 1,226,164,935.26 |
| 1853 | 22,286,462.49 | 1920 | 359,947,020.33 |
| 1854 | 20,300,636.61 | | |
| 1855 | 19,529,841.06 | 1921 | 532,898,329.77 |
| 1856 | 20,304,844.78 | 1922 | 264,126,935.85 |

[1] This statement is made from warrants paid by the Treasurer of the United States to Dec. 31, 1821, and by warrants issued after that date, and up to and including 1915 is exclusive of disbursing officers' credits and outstanding warrants.
[2] The unavailable funds are not included on and after 1829.
[3] The amount deposited with the States under act of June 23, 1836, having been taken out of the control of the Treasury Department by the act of Oct. 2, 1837, is not included on and after that date.
[4] Includes gold reserve from this date to 1900.

TABLE J.—*Appropriations, expenditures, amounts carried to surplus fund, and unexpended balances for fiscal years 1885 to 1922.*

| Fiscal year. | Unexpended balances brought forward.[1] | Appropriations by Congress exclusive of appropriations for Postal Service from postal revenues, and redemptions of the principal of the public debt. | | Total available appropriations. | Expenditures exclusive of expenditures for the Postal Service payable from postal revenues, and principal of the public debt redeemed.[3] | Carried to surplus funds.[2] | Unexpended balances carried forward.[1] | Principal of public debt redeemed not included in foregoing statement. | Postal expenditures from postal revenues not included in foregoing statement. |
|---|---|---|---|---|---|---|---|---|---|
| | | Appropriations for fiscal years as entered on the books during the respective fiscal years. | Permanent annual appropriations. | | | | | | |
| 1885 | $101,889,060.40 | $160,000,940.16 | $77,514,965.61 | $339,404,866.17 | $290,226,935.11 | $5,539,431.95 | $73,338,499.11 | $74,504,860.43 | $42,560,843.83 |
| 1886 | 73,338,499.11 | 172,914,330.08 | 72,293,586.66 | 318,546,415.85 | 242,483,138.50 | 2,643,213.08 | 73,420,064.27 | 74,141,431.36 | 43,948,422.95 |
| 1887 | 73,420,064.27 | 232,699,301.37 | 75,513,215.59 | 381,632,781.23 | 267,898,188.87 | 29,271,191.23 | 84,363,401.13 | 165,327,657.15 | 48,837,609.39 |
| 1888 | 84,363,401.13 | 193,345,626.56 | 66,606,102.68 | 349,315,130.37 | 267,924,801.13 | 6,076,268.18 | 75,314,061.06 | 125,026,170.50 | 52,695,176.79 |
| 1889 | 75,314,061.06 | 282,554,789.62 | 62,572,339.39 | 420,441,160.07 | 299,288,978.25 | 4,817,370.54 | 116,334,811.28 | 167,674,910.25 | 56,175,611.18 |
| 1890 | 116,334,811.28 | 241,231,209.33 | 59,028,067.79 | 416,694,088.40 | 318,040,710.66 | 10,081,406.86 | 88,471,970.88 | 138,297,688.50 | 60,882,097.92 |
| 1891 | 88,471,970.88 | 337,895,329.58 | 80,038,878.20 | 506,406,178.66 | 365,774,681.61 | 4,706,145.02 | 135,925,352.03 | 126,332,063.87 | 65,931,785.72 |
| 1892 | 135,925,352.03 | 275,031,685.27 | 58,085,253.96 | 469,042,291.26 | 345,023,275.83 | 4,060,726.14 | 119,958,239.29 | 40,580,807.98 | 70,930,475.98 |
| 1893 | 119,958,239.29 | 347,190,061.44 | 62,201,680.49 | 529,349,981.22 | 383,477,954.49 | 14,320,826.03 | 131,551,200.70 | 9,747,554.59 | 75,896,993.16 |
| 1894 | 131,551,200.51 | 293,642,449.44 | 64,745,458.84 | 489,939,108.98 | 387,525,279.83 | 5,757,208.64 | 116,656,620.51 | 11,185,962.95 | 75,080,479.04 |
| 1895 | 116,656,620.51 | 341,504,421.98 | 54,564,438.16 | 512,725,480.65 | 356,195,298.29 | 8,654,642.71 | 147,875,539.65 | 15,562,918.93 | 76,983,128.19 |
| 1896 | 147,875,539.65 | 294,200,426.21 | 56,597,280.53 | 498,673,246.39 | 352,179,446.08 | 30,313,317.49 | 116,180,482.82 | 18,317,253.35 | 82,499,208.40 |
| 1897 | 116,180,482.82 | 338,746,047.56 | 61,358,528.34 | 516,285,058.72 | 365,774,159.57 | 14,868,817.48 | 135,642,081.67 | 22,470,657.50 | 82,665,462.73 |
| 1898 | 135,642,081.67 | 443,832,514.59 | 60,314,975.42 | 639,789,571.68 | 443,368,582.80 | 6,968,244.48 | 189,452,744.40 | 45,932,522.00 | 89,012,618.55 |
| 1899 | 189,452,744.40 | 623,585,762.99 | 71,447,806.13 | 884,486,313.52 | 605,072,179.85 | 4,126,647.22 | 275,287,486.45 | 31,271,638.98 | 95,021,384.17 |
| 1900 | 275,287,486.45 | 394,601,309.30 | 103,057,092.00 | 772,945,887.75 | 520,860,846.52 | 27,273,090.02 | 224,811,951.21 | 40,609,851.25 | 102,354,579.29 |
| 1901 | 224,811,951.21 | 486,014,663.01 | 81,378,628.73 | 792,205,242.95 | 524,616,926.10 | 26,553,269.06 | 241,005,047.79 | 54,739,236.28 | 111,631,193.39 |
| 1902 | 241,005,047.79 | 462,681,026.18 | 75,335,556.23 | 779,021,630.20 | 485,234,248.78 | 35,945,270.39 | 257,842,110.83 | 76,309,192.50 | 121,848,047.26 |
| 1903 | 257,842,110.63 | 545,981,442.88 | 75,054,298.24 | 878,877,851.95 | 517,006,136.88 | 45,663,839.98 | 316,267,885.23 | 42,580,919.00 | 133,224,443.24 |
| 1904 | 316,267,885.23 | 522,601,322.39 | 62,027,358.99 | 900,896,566.61 | 583,639,999.32 | 56,154,488.07 | 261,082,228.52 | 24,580,701.75 | 143,582,624.34 |
| 1905 | 261,082,228.52 | 510,015,853.17 | 62,831,521.38 | 833,929,603.05 | 567,278,913.45 | 26,480,228.52 | 240,488,800.67 | 26,462,598.80 | 152,826,585.10 |
| 1906 | 240,488,800.67 | 457,156,765.19 | 67,247,048.30 | 764,892,614.16 | 570,202,278.59 | 10,546,354.53 | 183,733,951.04 | 24,968,846.80 | 167,932,782.95 |
| 1907 | 183,733,951.04 | 615,679,778.74 | 75,798,831.74 | 875,172,694.52 | 579,129,843.72 | 9,045,251.73 | 296,948,599.02 | 55,827,297.50 | 183,585,005.57 |
| 1908 | 296,948,599.02 | 539,572,505.46 | 73,572,748.77 | 920,293,853.25 | 639,196,319.68 | 11,007,455.48 | 250,090,078.09 | 73,891,906.50 | 191,478,663.41 |
| 1909 | 250,090,078.09 | 660,936,700.48 | 72,677,728.66 | 983,704,567.73 | 693,743,897.18 | 16,274,203.09 | 273,686,476.98 | 104,996,770.00 | 203,562,383.07 |
| 1910 | 273,686,476.98 | 603,617,145.69 | 69,999,395.12 | 952,303,217.77 | 693,617,061.45 | 23,068,345.79 | 235,617,807.53 | 33,049,695.50 | 224,128,657.62 |
| 1911 | 235,223,807.53 | 661,119,312.30 | 79,529,394.05 | 976,266,513.88 | 691,201,513.22 | 22,890,702.12 | 262,174,298.54 | 35,223,336.35 | 237,660,705.48 |
| 1912 | 262,174,298.54 | 616,054,909.78 | 81,703,426.70 | 959,932,635.02 | 639,881,334.13 | 18,393,716.80 | 251,657,534.09 | 28,648,327.53 | 246,744,015.88 |
| 1913 | 251,657,584.00 | 690,778,086.41 | 80,814,477.27 | 1,023,250,147.77 | 724,511,963.54 | 15,523,748.99 | 283,214,435.24 | 24,191,610.50 | 262,108,874.74 |

| | | | | | | | | | |
|---|---|---|---|---|---|---|---|---|---|
| 1914 | 283,214,435.24 | 636,835,844.03 | 73,292,480.02 | 993,332,759.29 | 735,081,431.47 | 12,434,558.71 | 245,816,769.11 | 26,961,327.00 | 283,558,102.62 |
| 1915 | 245,816,769.11 | 707,231,005.83 | 95,251,877.48 | 1,048,299,652.42 | 760,586,801.33 | 17,229,236.31 | 270,483,674.78 | 17,253,491.00 | 287,248,165.27 |
| 1916 | 270,483,614.78 | 643,037,750.30 | 77,227,262.33 | 990,748,567.41 | 740,980,416.47 | 20,400,442.40 | 229,367,708.54 | 21,668,913.50 | 306,228,452.76 |
| 1917 | 229,367,708.54 | 8,267,364,375.04 | 95,065,791.26 | 8,591,795,874.84 | 2,085,894,308.58 | 23,217,384.12 | 6,482,684,182.14 | 677,544,782.25 | 319,889,994.41 |
| 1918 | 6,482,684,182.14 | 14,469,457,762.24 | 309,441,481.56 | 21,261,583,425.94 | 13,705,287,290.39 | 18,671,000.15 | 7,447,625,126.40 | 7,706,879,075.13 | 324,849,188.16 |
| 1919 | 7,447,625,126.40 | 23,747,189,792.25 | 783,391,870.92 | 31,978,206,789.57 | 18,952,075,835.61 | 7,234,325,874.78 | 5,791,805,079.18 | 15,837,566,009.13 | 362,504,271.24 |
| 1920 | 5,791,805,079.18 | 4,300,395,182.99 | 1,266,212,148.73 | 11,368,412,410.90 | 6,139,748,221.24 | 1,011,050,482.23 | 4,207,613,707.43 | 17,036,444,271.25 | 418,722,295.05 |
| 1921 | 4,207,613,707.43 | 1,957,013,156.37 | ⁴2,554,248,639.10 | 8,748,875,592.90 | ³⁴,880,049,960.36 | 1,839,406,923.53 | 2,029,418,619.01 | 8,769,056,632.49 | 463,491,274.70 |
| 1922 | 2,029,418,619.01 | 1,843,864,000.60 | ⁴1,940,743,388.66 | 5,814,026,068.27 | ³³,615,733,139.08 | 778,030,215.62 | 1,420,262,713.57 | 6,610,079,033.80 | 484,653,540.71 |

1 Balances of annual appropriations are available for use only in accordance with the provision of section 3690, R. S.
2 Net expenditures by warrants.
3 Exclusive of appropriations repealed before being entered on the books but inclusive of all other repealed appropriations.
4 Includes appropriations for retirement of public debt chargeable against ordinary receipts.
5 Includes public debt redemptions chargeable against ordinary receipts.

TABLE K.—*Receipts and expenditures of the United States Government by fiscal years from 1791 to 1922.*

[The term "expenditures" as used in this table is on the basis of warrants issued (net) and includes unexpended balances to the credit of disbursing officers at the end of the year but not expenditures under unexpended balances at the beginning of the year]

| Fiscal year | Ordinary receipts. | | | | | | | | Surplus (+) or deficit (−) ordinary receipts compared with expenditures chargeable against ordinary receipts. |
|---|---|---|---|---|---|---|---|---|---|
| | Customs. | Internal revenue. | | Sales of public lands. | Surplus postal receipts covered into the Treasury. | Miscellaneous receipts. | Total ordinary receipts. | | |
| | | Income and profits tax. | Miscellaneous. | | | | | | |
| 1791 | $4,399,473 | | | | | $19,440 | $4,418,913 | | +9,456 |
| 1792 | 3,443,071 | | $208,943 | | | 17,946 | 3,669,960 | | −1,409,572 |
| 1793 | 4,255,307 | | 337,706 | | $11,021 | 48,889 | 4,652,923 | | +170,610 |
| 1794 | 4,801,065 | | 274,060 | | 29,478 | 327,272 | 5,431,905 | | −1,558,934 |
| 1795 | 5,588,461 | | 337,755 | | 22,400 | 165,918 | 6,114,534 | | −1,425,275 |
| 1796 | 6,567,988 | | 475,290 | $4,836 | 72,910 | 1,256,506 | 8,377,530 | | +2,650,544 |
| 1797 | 7,549,650 | | 575,491 | 83,541 | 64,500 | 415,399 | 8,688,781 | | +2,555,147 |
| 1798 | 7,106,062 | | 644,358 | 11,963 | 39,500 | 98,613 | 7,900,496 | | +223,992 |
| 1799 | 6,610,449 | | 779,136 | | 41,000 | 116,228 | 7,546,813 | | −2,119,642 |
| 1800 | 9,080,933 | | 809,396 | 444 | 78,000 | 879,976 | 10,848,749 | | +62,674 |
| 1801 | 10,750,779 | | 1,048,033 | 167,726 | 79,500 | 889,293 | 12,935,331 | | +3,540,749 |
| 1802 | 12,438,236 | | 621,899 | 188,628 | 35,000 | 1,712,031 | 14,995,794 | | +7,133,676 |
| 1803 | 10,479,418 | | 215,180 | 165,676 | 16,427 | 187,397 | 11,064,098 | | +3,212,445 |
| 1804 | 11,098,565 | | 50,941 | 487,527 | 26,500 | 162,774 | 11,826,307 | | +4,306,865 |
| 1805 | 12,936,487 | | 21,747 | 540,194 | 21,343 | 40,922 | 13,560,693 | | +3,054,459 |
| 1806 | 14,667,698 | | 20,101 | 765,246 | 41,118 | 65,768 | 15,559,931 | | +5,756,314 |
| 1807 | 15,845,522 | | 13,051 | 466,163 | 3,615 | 69,668 | 16,398,019 | | +843,888 |
| 1808 | 16,363,551 | | 8,211 | 647,939 | | 40,961 | 17,060,662 | | +7,128,170 |
| 1809 | 7,296,021 | | 4,044 | 442,252 | | 31,156 | 7,773,473 | | −2,507,275 |
| 1810 | 8,583,309 | | 7,431 | 696,549 | | 96,926 | 9,384,215 | | +1,227,705 |
| 1811 | 13,313,223 | | 2,290 | 1,040,238 | 33 | 67,734 | 14,423,529 | | +6,365,192 |
| 1812 | 8,958,778 | | 4,903 | 710,428 | 85,040 | 41,984 | 9,801,133 | | −10,479,638 |
| 1813 | 13,224,623 | | 4,755 | 835,655 | 35,000 | 240,377 | 14,340,410 | | −17,341,442 |
| 1814 | 5,998,772 | | 1,662,985 | 1,135,971 | 45,000 | 2,338,897 | 11,181,625 | | −23,539,301 |
| 1815 | 7,282,942 | | 4,678,059 | 1,287,959 | 135,000 | 2,345,064 | 15,729,024 | | −16,979,115 |
| 1816 | 36,306,875 | | 5,124,708 | 1,717,985 | 149,788 | 4,378,315 | 47,677,671 | | +990,980 |
| 1817 | 26,283,348 | | 2,678,101 | 1,991,226 | 29,372 | 2,117,003 | 33,099,050 | | +11,255,230 |
| 1818 | 17,176,385 | | 955,270 | 2,606,565 | 20,070 | 826,881 | 21,585,171 | | +1,760,050 |
| 1819 | 20,283,609 | | 229,594 | 3,274,423 | 71 | 815,678 | 24,603,375 | | +3,139,565 |
| 1820 | 15,005,612 | | 106,261 | 1,635,872 | 6,466 | 1,126,459 | 17,880,670 | | −379,957 |

| Year | (1) | (2) | (3) | (4) | (5) | (6) | (7) | (8) |
|---|---|---|---|---|---|---|---|---|
| 1821 | −1,237,373 | 14,573,380 | 296,422 | 517 | 1,212,066 | 69,028 | | 13,004,447 |
| 1822 | +5,232,208 | 20,232,428 | 770,816 | 602 | 1,803,582 | 67,666 | | 17,589,762 |
| 1823 | +5,833,826 | 20,540,666 | 501,357 | 111 | 916,523 | 34,242 | | 19,088,433 |
| 1824 | −945,495 | 19,381,213 | 453,806 | | 984,418 | 34,663 | | 17,878,325 |
| 1825 | +5,983,629 | 21,840,858 | 499,813 | 470 | 1,216,091 | 25,771 | | 20,098,713 |
| 1826 | +8,224,637 | 25,260,434 | 503,427 | 300 | 1,393,785 | 21,590 | | 23,341,332 |
| 1827 | +6,827,196 | 22,966,364 | 1,738,249 | 101 | 1,495,845 | 19,886 | | 19,712,283 |
| 1828 | +8,368,787 | 24,763,630 | 522,325 | 20 | 1,018,309 | 17,452 | | 23,205,524 |
| 1829 | +9,624,294 | 24,827,627 | 613,896 | 87 | 1,517,175 | 14,503 | | 22,681,966 |
| 1830 | +9,701,650 | 24,844,116 | 580,153 | 55 | 2,329,356 | 12,161 | | 21,922,391 |
| 1831 | +13,279,170 | 28,526,821 | 1,084,009 | 561 | 3,210,815 | 6,934 | | 24,224,442 |
| 1832 | +14,576,611 | 31,865,561 | 765,067 | 245 | 2,623,381 | 11,631 | | 28,465,237 |
| 1833 | +10,930,875 | 33,948,427 | 945,576 | | 3,967,683 | 2,759 | | 29,032,509 |
| 1834 | −3,164,367 | 21,791,936 | 715,082 | 100 | 4,857,601 | 4,196 | | 16,214,957 |
| 1835 | +17,857,274 | 35,430,087 | 1,269,823 | 893 | 14,757,601 | 10,459 | | 19,391,311 |
| 1836 | +19,955,632 | 50,826,796 | 2,539,294 | 11 | 24,877,180 | 370 | | 11,169,290 |
| 1837 | −12,298,343 | 24,954,153 | 7,003,132 | | 3,081,940 | 5,494 | | 16,158,800 |
| 1838 | −7,562,497 | 26,302,562 | 7,059,355 | | 7,075,447 | 2,467 | | 23,137,925 |
| 1839 | +4,583,621 | 31,482,749 | 1,265,824 | | 3,392,653 | 2,553 | | 13,499,502 |
| 1840 | −4,837,464 | 19,480,115 | 2,886,248 | | | 1,682 | | 14,487,217 |
| 1841 | −9,705,713 | 16,860,160 | 1,004,055 | | 1,365,627 | 3,261 | | 18,187,909 |
| 1842 | −5,229,563 | 19,976,198 | 451,996 | | 1,235,798 | 495 | | 7,046,844 |
| 1843 | −5,983,803 | 8,302,702 | 357,937 | | 897,818 | 103 | | 26,183,571 |
| 1844 | +6,032,698 | 29,321,374 | 1,076,086 | | 2,059,940 | 1,777 | | 27,528,113 |
| 1845 | +7,032,698 | 29,970,106 | 361,454 | | 2,077,022 | 3,517 | | 26,712,668 |
| 1846 | +1,933,042 | 29,699,967 | 289,950 | | 2,694,452 | 2,897 | | 23,747,865 |
| 1847 | −30,785,643 | 26,495,769 | 249,174 | | 2,498,355 | 375 | | 31,757,071 |
| 1848 | −9,641,447 | 35,735,779 | 649,690 | | 3,325,643 | 375 | | 28,346,739 |
| 1849 | −13,843,514 | 31,208,143 | 1,172,444 | | 1,688,960 | | | 39,668,698 |
| 1850 | −4,059,947 | 43,603,439 | 2,074,359 | | 1,859,894 | | | 49,017,568 |
| 1851 | +4,850,287 | 52,559,304 | 1,189,431 | | 2,352,305 | | | 47,339,327 |
| 1852 | +5,651,897 | 49,846,816 | 464,249 | | 2,043,240 | | | 58,931,986 |
| 1853 | +13,402,943 | 61,587,054 | 988,103 | | 1,667,085 | | | 64,224,190 |
| 1854 | +15,755,479 | 73,800,341 | 1,105,353 | | 8,470,798 | | | 53,025,794 |
| 1855 | +5,607,907 | 65,350,575 | 827,732 | | 8,917,645 | | | 64,022,863 |
| 1856 | +4,485,673 | 74,056,699 | 1,116,191 | | 3,829,457 | | | 63,875,905 |
| 1857 | −1,169,605 | 68,965,313 | 1,259,921 | | 3,513,716 | | | 41,789,621 |
| 1858 | −27,529,904 | 46,655,365 | 1,332,029 | | 1,756,687 | | | 49,565,824 |
| 1859 | −15,584,512 | 53,486,465 | 2,163,964 | | 1,778,558 | | | 53,187,512 |
| 1860 | −7,065,990 | 56,064,608 | 1,058,533 | | 870,659 | | | |
| 1861 | −25,036,714 | 41,509,931 | 1,057,146 | | 132,204 | | | 39,582,126 |
| 1862 | −422,774,363 | 51,987,456 | 2,778,854 | | 167,617 | | | 49,056,398 |
| 1863 | −602,043,434 | 112,697,291 | 5,829,244 | | 588,333 | 34,898,930 | $2,741,858 | 69,059,642 |
| 1864 | −600,695,871 | 264,626,771 | 51,981,151 | | 995,553 | 89,446,402 | 20,294,732 | 102,316,153 |
| 1865 | −963,840,619 | 333,714,605 | 38,325,576 | | 665,031 | 143,484,886 | 60,979,329 | 84,928,261 |
| 1866 | +37,223,203 | 558,032,620 | 69,094,124 | | 1,163,576 | 235,244,654 | 72,982,159 | 179,046,652 |
| 1867 | +133,091,335 | 490,634,010 | 47,025,086 | | 1,348,715 | 200,013,108 | 66,014,423 | 176,417,811 |
| 1868 | +28,297,798 | 405,638,083 | 48,737,179 | | | 149,631,991 | 41,435,598 | 164,464,600 |
| 1869 | +48,078,469 | 370,943,747 | 22,518,516 | | 4,020,344 | 123,544,665 | 34,791,836 | 180,048,427 |
| 1870 | +101,601,916 | 411,255,477 | 28,465,865 | | 3,350,482 | 147,123,252 | 37,775,874 | 194,538,374 |

TABLE K.—Receipts and expenditures of the United States Government by fiscal years from 1791 to 1922—Continued.

| Fiscal year. | Customs. | Internal revenue. Income and profits tax. | Internal revenue. Miscellaneous. | Sales of public lands. | Surplus postal receipts covered into the Treasury. | Miscellaneous receipts. | Total ordinary receipts. | Surplus (+) or deficit (−) of ordinary receipts compared with expenditures chargeable against ordinary receipts. |
|---|---|---|---|---|---|---|---|---|
| 1871 | $206,270,408 | $19,162,651 | $123,935,503 | $2,388,647 | | $31,566,736 | $383,323,945 | +$91,146,757 |
| 1872 | 216,370,287 | 14,436,862 | 116,205,316 | 2,575,714 | | 24,518,639 | 374,106,868 | +96,588,905 |
| 1873 | 188,089,523 | 5,062,312 | 108,647,002 | 2,882,312 | | 29,037,056 | 333,738,205 | +43,392,960 |
| 1874 | 163,103,834 | 139,472 | 102,270,313 | 1,852,429 | | 37,612,708 | 304,978,756 | +2,344,883 |
| 1875 | 157,167,722 | 233 | 110,007,261 | 1,413,640 | | 19,411,195 | 288,000,051 | +13,376,658 |
| 1876 | 148,071,985 | 588 | 116,700,144 | 1,129,467 | | 28,193,681 | 294,095,865 | +28,994,780 |
| 1877 | 130,956,493 | 98 | 118,630,310 | 976,254 | | 30,943,264 | 281,406,419 | +40,071,944 |
| 1878 | 130,170,680 | | 110,581,625 | 1,079,743 | | 15,931,831 | 257,763,879 | +20,799,552 |
| 1879.1 | 137,250,048 | | 113,561,611 | 924,781 | | 22,090,745 | 273,827,185 | +6,879,301 |
| 1880 | 186,522,064 | | 124,009,374 | 1,016,507 | | 21,978,666 | 333,526,611 | +65,883,653 |
| 1881 | 198,159,676 | 3,022 | 135,261,364 | 2,201,863 | | 25,158,388 | 360,782,293 | +100,069,405 |
| 1882 | 220,410,730 | | 146,497,596 | 4,753,140 | | 31,863,784 | 403,525,250 | +145,543,810 |
| 1883 | 214,706,497 | | 144,720,369 | 7,955,864 | | 30,904,882 | 398,287,582 | +132,879,444 |
| 1884 | 195,067,490 | 55,628 | 121,530,445 | 9,810,705 | | 22,655,602 | 348,519,870 | +104,393,626 |
| 1885 | 181,471,939 | | 112,498,726 | 5,705,986 | | 23,014,465 | 323,690,706 | +63,463,771 |
| 1886 | 192,905,023 | | 116,805,936 | 5,630,999 | | 21,097,708 | 336,439,726 | +93,956,587 |
| 1887 | 217,286,893 | | 118,823,391 | 9,254,286 | | 26,483,707 | 371,403,277 | +103,471,098 |
| 1888 | 219,091,174 | | 124,296,872 | 11,202,017 | | 24,676,012 | 379,266,075 | +111,341,274 |
| 1889 | 223,832,742 | | 130,881,514 | 8,038,652 | | 24,297,151 | 387,050,059 | +87,761,081 |
| 1890 | 229,668,585 | | 142,606,706 | 6,358,273 | | 24,447,420 | 403,080,984 | +85,040,273 |
| 1891 | 219,522,205 | | 145,686,250 | 4,029,535 | | 23,374,457 | 392,612,447 | +26,838,543 |
| 1892 | 177,452,964 | | 153,971,072 | 3,261,876 | | 20,251,872 | 354,937,784 | +9,914,453 |
| 1893 | 203,355,017 | | 161,027,624 | 3,182,090 | | 18,254,898 | 385,819,629 | +2,341,676 |
| 1894 | 131,818,531 | 77,131 | 147,111,233 | 1,103,347 | | 25,751,915 | 306,355,316 | −61,169,965 |
| 1895 | 152,158,617 | | 143,344,541 | 1,005,523 | | 28,045,783 | 324,729,419 | −31,465,879 |
| 1896 | 160,021,752 | | 146,762,865 | 864,581 | | 30,332,307 | 338,142,447 | −14,036,999 |
| 1897 | 176,554,127 | | 146,688,574 | 1,243,129 | | 23,614,423 | 347,721,705 | −18,052,464 |
| 1898 | 149,575,062 | | 170,900,642 | 1,678,247 | | 34,902,902 | 405,321,335 | −38,047,248 |
| 1899 | 206,128,482 | | 273,437,162 | 1,678,247 | | 34,716,730 | 515,960,621 | −89,111,558 |
| 1900 | 233,164,871 | | 295,327,927 | 2,836,883 | | 35,911,171 | 567,240,852 | +46,380,005 |
| 1901 | 238,585,456 | | 307,180,664 | 2,965,120 | | 38,954,098 | 587,685,338 | +63,088,413 |
| 1902 | 254,444,708 | | 271,880,122 | 4,144,123 | | 32,009,290 | 562,478,233 | +77,243,984 |
| 1903 | 284,479,582 | | 230,810,124 | 8,925,311 | | 37,664,705 | 561,880,722 | +44,874,595 |
| 1904 | 261,274,565 | | 232,904,119 | 7,453,480 | | 39,454,921 | 541,087,066 | −42,572,815 |

| | | | | | | | | |
|---|---|---|---|---|---|---|---|---|
| 1905 | 261,798,857 | | 224,095,741 | 4,859,250 | | 43,520,837 | 544,274,085 | −23,004,229 |
| 1906 | 300,251,878 | | 249,150,213 | 4,879,834 | | 40,702,521 | 594,984,446 | +24,782,168 |
| 1907 | 332,233,363 | | 269,666,773 | 7,878,811 | | 56,061,439 | 665,860,386 | +86,731,544 |
| 1908 | 286,113,130 | | 294,711,127 | 9,731,560 | | 54,06,690 | 601,861,907 | −57,334,413 |
| 1909 | 300,711,934 | | 246,212,644 | 7,700,568 | | 49,695,352 | 604,320,498 | −89,423,387 |
| 1910 | 333,683,445 | 20,951,781 | 268,981,738 | 6,355,797 | | 45,538,954 | 675,511,715 | −18,105,350 |
| 1911 | 314,497,071 | 33,516,977 | 289,012,224 | 5,731,637 | | 59,075,002 | 701,832,911 | +10,631,399 |
| 1912 | 311,321,672 | 28,583,304 | 293,028,896 | 5,392,797 | | 54,282,535 | 692,609,204 | +2,727,870 |
| 1913 | 318,891,396 | 35,006,300 | 309,410,666 | 2,910,205 | | 57,892,663 | 724,111,230 | −400,733 |
| 1914 | 292,320,014 | 71,381,275 | 308,659,733 | 2,571,775 | $3,800,000 | 55,940,370 | 734,673,167 | −408,264 |
| 1915 | 209,786,672 | 80,201,759 | 335,467,887 | 2,167,136 | 3,500,000 | 66,787,373 | 697,910,827 | −62,675,975 |
| 1916 | 213,185,846 | 124,937,253 | 387,764,776 | 1,887,662 | | 54,759,011 | 782,534,548 | +40,537,821 |
| 1917 | 225,962,393 | 359,681,228 | 449,684,980 | 1,892,893 | 5,200,000 | 81,903,301 | 1,124,324,795 | −961,717,309 |
| 1918 | 182,758,989 | 2,838,999,894 | 857,043,591 | 1,949,455 | 9,557,701 | 290,095,526 | 4,180,425,156 | −9,641,482,739 |
| 1919 | 183,428,625 | 2,600,762,735 | 1,239,468,260 | 1,404,705 | 18,000,000 | 611,316,574 | 4,654,380,899 | −14,297,760,281 |
| 1920 | 323,536,559 | 3,956,936,004 | 1,442,213,241 | 1,910,140 | 300,000 | 979,518,493 | 6,704,414,437 | +562,609,197 |
| 1921 | 308,025,102 | 3,228,137,674 | 1,351,835,935 | 1,530,439 | | 694,987,895 | 5,584,517,045 | +693,410,228 |
| 1922 | 357,544,713 | 2,086,918,465 | 1,121,239,843 | 895,391 | 81,494 | 536,916,625 | 4,103,596,531 | +485,558,734 |

NOTE.—Beginning with 1921, figures for surplus or deficit are after taking into account public debt expenditures chargeable against ordinary receipts.

TABLE K.—*Receipts and expenditures of the United States Government by fiscal years from 1791 to 1922*—Continued.

Expenditures chargeable against ordinary receipts.

| Fiscal year. | Civil and miscellaneous.[1] | War Department (including rivers and harbors and Panama Canal)[2] | Navy Department.[3] | Indians. | Pensions. | Postal deficiencies. | Interest on the public debt. | Total ordinary expenditures. | Public debt retirements chargeable against ordinary receipts. | Total expenditures chargeable against ordinary receipts. |
|---|---|---|---|---|---|---|---|---|---|---|
| 1791 | $1,083,402 | $632,804 | $570 | $27,000 | $175,814 | | $2,349,437 | $4,269,027 | | $4,269,027 |
| 1792 | 654,257 | 1,100,702 | 53 | 13,649 | 109,243 | | 3,201,628 | 5,079,532 | | 5,079,532 |
| 1793 | 472,451 | 1,130,249 | | 27,283 | 80,088 | | 2,772,242 | 4,482,313 | | 4,482,313 |
| 1794 | 705,598 | 2,639,098 | 61,409 | 13,042 | 81,399 | | 3,490,293 | 6,990,839 | | 6,990,839 |
| 1795 | 1,367,037 | 2,480,910 | 410,562 | 23,476 | 68,673 | | 3,189,151 | 7,539,809 | | 7,539,809 |
| 1796 | 782,475 | 1,260,264 | 274,784 | 113,564 | 100,844 | | 3,195,055 | 5,726,996 | | 5,726,996 |
| 1797 | 1,256,903 | 1,039,403 | 382,632 | 62,396 | 92,257 | | 3,303,043 | 6,133,634 | | 6,133,634 |
| 1798 | 1,111,033 | 2,009,522 | 1,381,348 | 16,470 | 104,845 | | 3,053,281 | 7,676,504 | | 7,676,504 |
| 1799 | 1,039,392 | 2,466,947 | 2,858,082 | 20,302 | 95,444 | | 3,186,298 | 9,666,455 | | 9,666,455 |
| 1800 | 1,337,613 | 2,560,879 | 3,448,716 | 31 | 64,131 | | 3,374,705 | 10,786,075 | | 10,786,075 |
| 1801 | 1,114,768 | 1,672,944 | 2,111,424 | 9,000 | 73,533 | | 4,412,913 | 9,394,582 | | 9,394,582 |
| 1802 | 1,462,929 | 1,179,148 | 915,562 | 94,000 | 85,440 | | 4,125,039 | 7,862,118 | | 7,862,118 |
| 1803 | 1,842,636 | 822,056 | 1,215,231 | 60,000 | 62,902 | | 3,848,828 | 7,851,653 | | 7,851,653 |
| 1804 | 2,191,009 | 875,424 | 1,189,833 | 116,500 | 80,093 | | 4,266,583 | 8,719,442 | | 8,719,442 |
| 1805 | 3,768,599 | 712,781 | 1,597,500 | 196,500 | 81,855 | | 4,149,999 | 10,506,234 | | 10,506,234 |
| 1806 | 2,890,137 | 1,224,355 | 1,649,641 | 234,200 | 81,876 | | 3,723,408 | 9,803,617 | | 9,803,617 |
| 1807 | 1,697,898 | 1,288,686 | 1,722,064 | 205,425 | 70,500 | | 3,359,578 | 8,354,151 | | 8,354,151 |
| 1808 | 1,423,286 | 2,900,834 | 1,884,068 | 213,575 | 82,576 | | 3,428,153 | 9,932,492 | | 9,932,492 |
| 1809 | 1,215,804 | 3,345,772 | 2,427,759 | 337,504 | 87,834 | | 2,866,075 | 10,280,748 | | 10,280,748 |
| 1810 | 1,101,145 | 2,294,324 | 1,654,244 | 177,625 | 83,744 | | 2,845,428 | 8,156,510 | | 8,156,510 |
| 1811 | 1,367,291 | 2,032,828 | 1,965,566 | 151,875 | 75,044 | | 2,465,733 | 8,058,337 | | 8,058,337 |
| 1812 | 1,683,088 | 11,817,798 | 3,959,365 | 277,845 | 91,402 | | 2,451,273 | 20,280,771 | | 20,280,771 |
| 1813 | 1,729,436 | 19,652,013 | 6,446,600 | 167,358 | 86,990 | | 3,599,455 | 31,681,852 | | 31,681,852 |
| 1814 | 2,208,030 | 20,350,807 | 7,311,291 | 167,395 | 90,164 | | 4,593,239 | 34,720,926 | | 34,720,926 |
| 1815 | 2,898,870 | 14,794,294 | 8,660,000 | 530,750 | 69,656 | | 5,754,569 | 32,708,139 | | 32,708,139 |
| 1816 | 2,989,741 | 16,012,097 | 3,908,578 | 274,512 | 188,804 | | 7,213,259 | 30,586,691 | | 30,586,691 |
| 1817 | 3,518,937 | 8,004,237 | 3,314,598 | 319,464 | 297,374 | | 6,389,210 | 21,843,820 | | 21,843,820 |
| 1818 | 3,825,840 | 5,622,715 | 2,953,695 | 505,704 | 890,720 | | 5,016,447 | 19,825,121 | | 19,825,121 |
| 1819 | 3,067,211 | 6,506,300 | 3,847,640 | 463,181 | 2,415,940 | | 5,163,538 | 21,463,810 | | 21,463,810 |
| 1820 | 2,592,022 | 2,630,392 | 4,387,990 | 315,750 | 3,208,376 | | 5,126,097 | 18,260,627 | | 18,260,627 |
| 1821 | 2,223,122 | 4,461,292 | 3,319,243 | 477,005 | 242,817 | | 5,087,274 | 15,810,753 | | 15,810,753 |
| 1822 | 1,967,996 | 3,111,981 | 2,224,459 | 575,007 | 948,199 | | 5,172,578 | 15,000,220 | | 15,000,220 |
| 1823 | 1,022,094 | 3,096,924 | 2,503,766 | 380,782 | 1,780,589 | | 4,922,645 | 14,706,840 | | 14,706,840 |
| 1824 | 7,155,309 | 3,340,940 | 2,904,582 | 429,988 | 1,499,327 | | 4,996,562 | 20,326,708 | | 20,326,708 |
| 1825 | 2,748,545 | 3,659,914 | 3,049,084 | 724,106 | 1,308,811 | | 4,366,769 | 15,857,229 | | 15,857,229 |

| Year | | | | | | | | | |
|---|---|---|---|---|---|---|---|---|---|
| 1826 | 2,600,178 | 3,943,194 | 4,218,902 | 743,448 | 1,556,894 | .... | 3,973,481 | 17,035,797 | 17,035,797 |
| 27 | 2,713,477 | 3,938,978 | 4,263,877 | 760,625 | 976,139 | .... | 3,486,072 | 16,139,163 | 16,139,163 |
| 28 | 3,676,053 | 4,145,545 | 3,918,786 | 705,084 | 850,594 | .... | 3,098,801 | 16,394,843 | 16,394,843 |
| 29 | 3,101,515 | 4,724,291 | 3,308,745 | 576,345 | 949,594 | .... | 2,542,843 | 15,203,333 | 15,203,333 |
| 30 | 3,237,416 | 4,767,129 | 3,239,429 | 622,262 | 1,363,297 | .... | 1,913,533 | 15,143,066 | 15,143,066 |
| 1831 | 3,064,646 | 4,841,836 | 3,856,153 | 930,738 | 1,170,665 | .... | 1,383,583 | 15,247,651 | 15,247,651 |
| 32 | 4,577,141 | 5,446,035 | 3,956,370 | 1,352,420 | 1,184,422 | .... | 772,592 | 17,288,950 | 17,288,950 |
| 33 | 5,716,246 | 6,704,019 | 3,901,357 | 1,802,981 | 4,589,152 | .... | 303,797 | 23,017,552 | 23,017,552 |
| 34 | 4,404,729 | 5,696,189 | 3,936,260 | 1,003,953 | 3,364,285 | .... | 202,153 | 18,627,569 | 18,627,569 |
| 35 | 4,229,699 | 5,739,157 | 3,864,939 | 1,706,444 | 954,711 | .... | 57,863 | 17,572,813 | 17,572,813 |
| 36 | 9,893,609 | 12,169,227 | 5,807,718 | 4,613,141 | 2,882,798 | .... | .... | 30,988,164 | 30,988,164 |
| 37 | .... | 13,682,734 | 6,646,915 | 4,348,076 | 672,162 | $407,657 | 14,997 | 37,243,496 | 37,243,496 |
| 38 | .... | 12,897,224 | 6,131,596 | 5,504,191 | 2,156,098 | 53,697 | 399,834 | 33,985,059 | 33,985,059 |
| 39 | 9,160,965 | 8,916,996 | 6,182,294 | 2,528,917 | 3,142,884 | 21,303 | 174,598 | 26,899,128 | 26,899,128 |
| 40 | 5,728,203 | 7,097,070 | 6,113,897 | 2,331,795 | 2,603,950 | .... | .... | 24,317,579 | 24,317,579 |
| 1841 | 5,996,269 | 6,805,545 | 6,001,077 | 2,594,063 | 2,388,496 | .... | 284,978 | 26,565,873 | 26,565,873 |
| 42 | 6,084,037 | 6,611,857 | 8,397,243 | 1,201,062 | 1,379,469 | .... | 773,550 | 25,205,761 | 25,205,761 |
| 43 | 6,788,853 | 2,957,300 | 3,727,711 | 581,680 | 843,323 | 810,232 | 523,595 | 11,858,075 | 11,858,075 |
| 44 | 3,203,163 | 5,310,220 | 6,498,199 | 1,179,279 | 2,030,598 | 536,299 | 1,833,867 | 22,337,571 | 22,337,571 |
| 45 | 5,616,408 | 5,752,644 | 6,297,245 | 1,540,817 | 2,306,642 | 22,222 | 1,030,032 | 22,937,408 | 22,937,408 |
| 46 | 5,034,524 | 10,793,867 | 6,454,947 | 1,021,461 | 1,810,371 | .... | 842,723 | 27,766,925 | 27,766,925 |
| 47 | 6,201,519 | 38,305,920 | 7,900,636 | 1,470,306 | 1,747,917 | .... | 1,119,215 | 57,281,412 | 57,281,412 |
| 48 | 5,623,678 | 25,501,963 | 9,408,476 | 1,221,792 | 1,211,270 | .... | 2,390,825 | 43,377,226 | 43,377,226 |
| 49 | 14,143,278 | 14,832,966 | 9,786,706 | 1,373,119 | 1,330,010 | .... | 3,565,578 | 45,051,657 | 45,051,657 |
| 50 | 14,920,119 | 9,400,239 | 7,904,709 | 1,665,802 | 1,570,292 | .... | 3,782,331 | 39,543,492 | 39,543,492 |
| 1851 | 18,008,594 | 11,811,703 | 9,005,931 | 2,895,700 | 2,290,278 | 1,041,444 | 3,696,721 | 47,709,017 | 47,709,017 |
| 52 | 16,597,773 | 9,952,801 | 8,952,801 | 2,980,403 | 2,403,953 | 2,153,750 | 4,000,298 | 44,194,919 | 44,194,919 |
| 53 | 15,814,840 | 9,947,291 | 10,918,781 | 1,905,745 | 1,777,871 | 3,207,346 | 3,665,833 | 48,184,111 | 48,184,111 |
| 54 | 26,443,374 | 11,733,629 | 10,798,586 | 1,553,031 | 1,231,873 | 3,078,814 | 3,071,017 | 58,044,862 | 58,044,862 |
| 55 | 22,020,924 | 14,773,826 | 13,312,024 | 2,792,552 | 1,450,152 | 3,199,118 | 2,314,375 | 59,742,668 | 59,742,668 |
| 56 | 24,911,223 | 16,948,197 | 14,091,781 | 2,769,430 | 1,298,209 | 616,883 | 1,953,822 | 69,571,026 | 69,571,026 |
| 57 | 24,256,130 | 19,261,774 | 12,747,977 | 4,267,543 | 1,312,043 | 4,748,923 | 1,678,265 | 67,795,708 | 67,795,708 |
| 58 | 18,891,737 | 25,485,383 | 13,984,551 | 4,925,739 | 1,217,488 | 4,808,558 | 1,567,056 | 74,185,270 | 74,185,270 |
| 59 | 18,086,888 | 23,243,823 | 14,642,990 | 3,625,027 | 1,220,378 | 9,839,546 | 2,638,464 | 69,070,977 | 69,070,977 |
| 60 | .... | 16,409,767 | 11,514,965 | 2,949,191 | 1,102,926 | .... | 3,177,315 | 63,130,598 | 63,130,598 |
| 1861 | 18,096,116 | 22,981,150 | 12,420,888 | 2,841,358 | 1,036,064 | 5,170,895 | 4,000,174 | 66,546,645 | 66,546,645 |
| 62 | 17,846,762 | 394,368,407 | 42,668,277 | 2,273,224 | 853,095 | 3,561,729 | 13,190,225 | 474,761,819 | 474,761,819 |
| 63 | 22,507,651 | 599,298,601 | 63,221,964 | 3,154,357 | 1,078,991 | 749,314 | 24,729,847 | 714,740,725 | 714,740,725 |
| 64 | 26,505,619 | 690,791,843 | 85,725,995 | 2,629,859 | 4,983,924 | 999,980 | 53,685,422 | 985,322,642 | 985,322,642 |
| 65 | 44,515,558 | 1,031,323,361 | 122,612,945 | 5,116,537 | 15,605,352 | 250,000 | 77,397,712 | 1,297,555,224 | 1,297,555,224 |
| 66 | 58,406,906 | 284,449,702 | 43,324,118 | 3,247,065 | 2036,552 | .... | 133,067,742 | 520,809,417 | 520,809,417 |
| 67 | 55,957,827 | 95,224,415 | 31,034,011 | 4,642,532 | 23,782,387 | 3,516,667 | 143,781,592 | 357,542,675 | 357,542,675 |
| 68 | .... | 123,246,048 | 25,775,503 | 4,100,682 | 28,476,622 | 4,053,192 | 140,424,046 | 377,340,285 | 377,340,285 |
| 69 | 52,733,231 | 78,501,991 | 20,000,758 | 7,042,923 | 28,340,202 | 5,395,510 | 130,694,243 | 322,865,278 | 322,865,278 |
| 1870 | 64,389,438 | 57,655,676 | 21,780,230 | 3,407,538 | .... | 4,844,579 | 129,235,498 | 309,653,561 | 309,653,561 |

TABLE K.—*Receipts and expenditures of the United States Government by fiscal years from 1791 to 1922*—Continued.

| Fiscal year. | Civil and miscellaneous. | War Department (including rivers and harbors and Panama Canal). | Navy Department. | Indians. | Pensions. | Postal deficiencies. | Interest on the public debt. | Total ordinary expenditures. | Public debt retirements chargeable against ordinary receipts. | Total expenditures chargeable against ordinary receipts. |
|---|---|---|---|---|---|---|---|---|---|---|
| | | | | | Expenditures chargeable against ordinary receipts. | | | | | |
| 1871 | $64,367,461 | $35,799,992 | $19,431,027 | $7,426,997 | $34,443,895 | $5,131,250 | $125,576,566 | $292,177,188 | | $292,177,188 |
| 1872 | 62,768,024 | 35,372,157 | 21,249,810 | 7,061,729 | 28,533,403 | 5,175,000 | 117,357,840 | 277,517,963 | | 277,517,963 |
| 1873 | 72,943,555 | 46,323,138 | 23,526,257 | 7,951,705 | 29,359,427 | 5,490,475 | 104,750,688 | 290,345,246 | | 290,345,246 |
| 1874 | 81,822,622 | 42,313,927 | 30,932,587 | 6,692,462 | 29,038,415 | 4,714,045 | 107,119,815 | 302,633,873 | | 302,633,873 |
| 1875 | 63,859,657 | 41,120,646 | 21,497,626 | 8,384,657 | 29,456,216 | 7,211,646 | 103,093,545 | 274,623,393 | | 274,623,393 |
| 1876 | 68,507,121 | 38,070,889 | 18,963,310 | 5,966,558 | 28,257,396 | 5,092,540 | 100,243,271 | 265,101,085 | | 265,101,085 |
| 1877 | 52,756,194 | 37,082,736 | 14,939,935 | 5,277,007 | 27,963,752 | 6,170,339 | 97,124,512 | 241,334,475 | | 241,334,475 |
| 1878 | 47,424,310 | 32,154,118 | 17,365,301 | 4,629,280 | 27,137,019 | 5,733,394 | 102,500,875 | 236,964,327 | | 236,964,327 |
| 1879 | 60,968,032 | 40,425,661 | 15,125,127 | 5,206,109 | 35,121,482 | 4,773,524 | 105,327,949 | 266,947,884 | | 266,947,884 |
| 1880 | 54,437,850 | 38,116,916 | 13,536,985 | 5,945,457 | 56,777,175 | 3,071,000 | 95,757,575 | 267,642,958 | | 267,642,958 |
| 1881 | 61,581,934 | 40,466,461 | 15,686,672 | 6,514,161 | 50,059,280 | 3,895,639 | 82,508,741 | 260,712,888 | | 260,712,888 |
| 1882 | 57,219,751 | 43,570,494 | 15,032,046 | 9,736,748 | 61,345,194 | | 71,077,207 | 257,981,440 | | 257,981,440 |
| 1883 | 68,603,519 | 48,911,383 | 15,283,437 | 7,362,591 | 66,012,574 | 74,563 | 59,160,131 | 265,408,138 | | 265,408,138 |
| 1884 | 70,920,434 | 39,429,603 | 17,292,601 | 6,475,999 | 55,429,228 | | 54,578,379 | 244,126,244 | | 244,126,244 |
| 1885 | 82,952,647 | 42,670,578 | 16,021,080 | 6,552,495 | 56,102,268 | 4,541,611 | 51,386,256 | 260,226,935 | | 260,226,935 |
| 1886 | 65,973,278 | 34,324,153 | 13,907,888 | 6,099,158 | 63,404,864 | 8,193,652 | 50,580,146 | 242,483,139 | | 242,483,139 |
| 1887 | 78,763,579 | 34,561,026 | 15,141,127 | 6,194,523 | 75,029,102 | 6,601,247 | 47,741,577 | 267,932,181 | | 267,932,181 |
| 1888 | 78,167,066 | 38,522,436 | 16,926,438 | 6,249,308 | 80,288,509 | 6,056,037 | 44,715,007 | 267,924,801 | | 267,924,801 |
| 1889 | 94,087,507 | 44,435,271 | 21,378,809 | 6,892,208 | 87,624,779 | 3,585,920 | 41,001,484 | 299,288,978 | | 299,288,978 |
| 1890 | 94,832,444 | 44,582,838 | 22,006,206 | 6,708,047 | 106,936,855 | 6,875,237 | 36,099,284 | 318,040,711 | | 318,040,711 |
| 1891 | 115,707,616 | 48,720,065 | 26,113,896 | 8,527,469 | 124,415,951 | 4,741,772 | 37,547,135 | 365,773,904 | | 365,773,904 |
| 1892 | 95,790,499 | 46,895,456 | 29,174,139 | 11,150,547 | 134,583,053 | 4,051,499 | 23,378,116 | 345,023,331 | | 345,023,331 |
| 1893 | 97,736,004 | 49,641,773 | 30,136,084 | 13,345,347 | 159,357,558 | 5,946,795 | 27,264,392 | 383,477,953 | | 383,477,953 |
| 1894 | 93,693,884 | 54,567,930 | 31,701,294 | 10,293,482 | 141,177,285 | 8,250,000 | 27,841,406 | 367,525,281 | | 367,525,281 |
| 1895 | 82,263,188 | 51,804,759 | 28,797,796 | 9,939,754 | 141,395,229 | 11,016,542 | 30,978,030 | 356,195,298 | | 356,195,298 |
| 1896 | 77,916,235 | 50,830,921 | 27,147,732 | 12,165,528 | 139,434,001 | 9,300,000 | 35,385,029 | 352,179,446 | | 352,179,446 |
| 1897 | 79,232,462 | 48,950,268 | 34,561,546 | 13,016,802 | 141,053,165 | 11,149,206 | 37,791,110 | 365,774,159 | | 365,774,159 |
| 1898 | 88,016,465 | 91,992,000 | 58,823,985 | 10,994,663 | 147,452,369 | 10,504,040 | 37,585,056 | 443,368,583 | | 443,368,583 |
| 1899 | 110,979,636 | 229,841,254 | 63,942,104 | 12,805,711 | 139,394,929 | 8,211,570 | 39,896,925 | 605,072,179 | | 605,072,179 |
| 1900 | 131,689,466 | 134,774,768 | 55,953,078 | 10,175,107 | 140,877,316 | 7,230,779 | 40,160,333 | 520,860,847 | | 520,860,847 |
| 1901 | 131,976,814 | 144,615,697 | 60,506,978 | 10,895,073 | 139,323,622 | 4,954,762 | 32,342,979 | 524,616,925 | | 524,616,925 |
| 1902 | 125,110,562 | 112,272,216 | 67,803,128 | 10,049,585 | 138,488,560 | 2,402,153 | 29,108,045 | 485,234,249 | | 485,234,249 |
| 1903 | 132,072,506 | 118,629,505 | 82,618,034 | 12,935,168 | 138,425,646 | 2,768,919 | 28,556,349 | 517,006,127 | | 517,006,127 |
| 1904 | 131,337,250 | 165,199,911 | 102,956,102 | 10,438,350 | 142,559,266 | 6,502,531 | 24,646,490 | 583,659,900 | | 583,659,900 |
| 1905 | 127,968,472 | 126,093,894 | 117,550,308 | 14,236,074 | 141,773,965 | 15,065,257 | 24,590,944 | 567,278,914 | | 567,278,914 |

| | | | | | | | | | |
|---|---|---|---|---|---|---|---|---|---|
| 1906 | 131,638,657 | 137,326,066 | 110,474,264 | 12,746,839 | 141,034,562 | 12,673,294 | 24,308,576 | 570,202,278 | ............ | 570,202,278 |
| 1907 | 145,611,628 | 149,775,084 | 97,128,469 | 15,163,608 | 139,309,514 | 7,629,383 | 24,481,158 | 579,128,842 | ............ | 579,128,842 |
| 1908 | 162,532,368 | 175,840,453 | 118,037,097 | 14,579,756 | 153,892,467 | 12,888,041 | 21,426,138 | 659,196,320 | ............ | 659,196,320 |
| 1909 | 167,001,087 | 192,486,904 | 115,546,041 | 15,694,618 | 161,710,367 | 19,501,062 | 21,804,836 | 693,743,885 | ............ | 693,743,885 |
| 1910 | 191,580,530 | 189,823,379 | 123,173,777 | 18,504,132 | 160,696,416 | 8,495,612 | 21,342,979 | 693,617,065 | ............ | 693,617,065 |
| 1911 | 173,328,599 | 197,199,491 | 119,937,644 | 20,933,869 | 157,990,575 | ............ | 21,311,334 | 691,201,512 | ............ | 691,201,512 |
| 1912 | 172,256,794 | 184,122,793 | 135,591,956 | 20,134,840 | 153,590,456 | 1,568,196 | 22,616,300 | 689,881,334 | ............ | 689,881,334 |
| 1913 | 169,802,304 | 202,128,711 | 133,262,862 | 20,306,159 | 175,085,450 | 1,027,369 | 22,899,108 | 724,511,963 | ............ | 724,511,963 |
| 1914 | 170,530,235 | 208,349,746 | 139,682,186 | 20,215,076 | 173,440,231 | ............ | 22,863,957 | 735,081,431 | ............ | 735,081,431 |
| 1915 | 200,533,231 | 202,160,134 | 141,835,654 | 22,130,351 | 164,387,942 | 6,636,593 | 22,902,897 | 760,586,802 | ............ | 760,586,802 |
| 1916 | 199,555,048 | 182,139,305 | 155,029,426 | 17,570,284 | 159,302,351 | 5,500,000 | 22,900,313 | 741,996,727 | ............ | 741,996,727 |
| 1917 | 1,133,677,360 | 459,539,678 | 257,166,437 | 30,599,094 | 160,318,406 | ............ | 24,742,129 | 2,086,042,104 | ............ | 2,086,042,104 |
| 1918 | 6,306,334,995 | 5,705,136,249 | 1,365,642,794 | 30,888,400 | 181,137,754 | 2,221,035 | 197,526,608 | 13,791,907,895 | ............ | 13,791,907,895 |
| 1919 | 6,805,124,746 | 9,265,325,159 | 2,009,272,389 | 34,593,257 | 221,614,781 | 343,511 | 615,867,337 | 18,952,141,180 | ............ | 18,952,141,180 |
| 1920 | 3,133,100,982 | 1,100,865,666 | 629,893,116 | 40,516,832 | 213,344,204 | ............ | 1,024,024,440 | 6,141,745,240 | ............ | 6,141,745,240 |
| 1921 | 1,822,003,586 | 573,399,201 | 644,278,809 | 41,470,808 | 260,611,416 | 130,272,845 | 996,676,904 | 4,468,713,469 | $422,393,350 | 4,891,106,819 |
| 1922 | 998,256,379 | 396,180,775 | 456,338,787 | 38,500,413 | 252,576,848 | 64,346,235 | 989,485,410 | 3,195,684,847 | 422,352,950 | 3,618,037,797 |

1 Includes civil expenditures under War and Navy Departments at Washington.
2 Exclusive of civil expenditures under War Department at Washington.
3 Exclusive of civil expenditures under Navy Department at Washington.

NOTE.—The term "expenditures" as used in this table is on the basis of warrants issued (net) and includes unexpended balances to the credit of disbursing officers at the end of the year but not expenditures under unexpended balances at the beginning of the year.

TABLE K.—Receipts and expenditures of the United States Government by fiscal years from 1791 to 1922—Continued.

| Fiscal year. | Public debt expenditures chargeable against public debt receipts. | | | Public debt receipts. | | | Surplus (+) or deficit (−) public debt receipts compared with public debt expenditures (exclusive of public debt expenditures chargeable against ordinary receipts). | Recapitulation of total receipts and expenditures. | | |
|---|---|---|---|---|---|---|---|---|---|---|
| | Public debt retirements, exclusive of retirements chargeable against ordinary receipts. | Redemption of national bank and Federal reserve bank notes. | Total public debt retirements chargeable against public debt receipts. | Public debt receipts, proceeds of bonds, and other securities. | Deposits to retire national bank and Federal reserve bank notes. | Total public debt receipts. | | Total ordinary and public debt receipts. | Total ordinary and public debt expenditures. | Surplus (+) or deficit (−) of all receipts. |
| 1791 | $2,928,512 | | $2,928,512 | $5,791,113 | | $5,791,113 | +$2,852,601 | $10,210,026 | $7,207,539 | +$3,002,487 |
| 1792 | 4,062,038 | | 4,062,038 | 5,070,806 | | 5,070,806 | +1,008,768 | 8,740,766 | 9,141,570 | −400,804 |
| 1793 | 3,047,263 | | 3,047,263 | 1,067,701 | | 1,067,701 | −1,979,562 | 5,720,624 | 7,529,576 | −1,808,952 |
| 1794 | 2,311,296 | | 2,311,296 | 4,609,197 | | 4,609,197 | +2,297,911 | 10,041,102 | 9,302,125 | +738,977 |
| 1795 | 2,895,260 | | 2,895,260 | 3,305,268 | | 3,305,268 | +410,008 | 9,419,802 | 10,435,069 | −1,015,267 |
| 1796 | 2,640,792 | | 2,640,792 | 362,800 | | 362,800 | −2,277,992 | 8,740,330 | 8,367,778 | +372,552 |
| 1797 | 2,492,379 | | 2,492,379 | 70,135 | | 70,135 | −2,422,244 | 8,758,916 | 8,626,013 | +132,903 |
| 1798 | 937,013 | | 937,013 | 308,574 | | 308,574 | −628,439 | 8,209,070 | 8,613,517 | −404,447 |
| 1799 | 1,410,589 | | 1,410,589 | 5,074,647 | | 5,074,647 | +3,664,058 | 12,621,460 | 11,077,044 | +1,544,416 |
| 1800 | 1,203,665 | | 1,203,665 | 1,602,435 | | 1,602,435 | +398,770 | 12,451,184 | 11,989,740 | +461,444 |
| 1801 | 2,878,794 | | 2,878,794 | 10,125 | | 10,125 | −2,868,669 | 12,945,456 | 12,273,376 | +672,080 |
| 1802 | 5,413,966 | | 5,413,966 | 5,597 | | 5,597 | −5,408,369 | 15,001,391 | 13,276,084 | +1,725,307 |
| 1803 | 3,407,331 | | 3,407,331 | | | | −3,407,331 | 11,064,098 | 11,258,984 | −194,886 |
| 1804 | 3,905,205 | | 3,905,205 | 9,533 | | 9,533 | −3,895,672 | 11,835,840 | 12,624,647 | −788,807 |
| 1805 | 3,220,891 | | 3,220,891 | 128,815 | | 128,815 | −3,092,076 | 13,689,508 | 13,727,125 | −37,617 |
| 1806 | 5,266,477 | | 5,266,477 | 48,898 | | 48,898 | −5,217,579 | 15,608,829 | 15,070,094 | +538,735 |
| 1807 | 2,938,142 | | 2,938,142 | | | | −2,938,142 | 16,398,019 | 11,292,293 | +5,105,726 |
| 1808 | 6,832,092 | | 6,832,092 | 1,882 | | 1,882 | −6,830,210 | 17,062,544 | 16,764,584 | +297,960 |
| 1809 | 3,586,479 | | 3,586,479 | | | | −3,586,479 | 7,773,473 | 7,867,227 | −93,754 |
| 1810 | 5,163,477 | | 5,163,477 | 2,759,992 | | 2,759,992 | −2,403,485 | 12,144,207 | 13,319,987 | −1,175,780 |
| 1811 | 5,543,471 | | 5,543,471 | 8,309 | | 8,309 | −5,535,162 | 14,431,838 | 13,601,908 | +830,030 |
| 1812 | 1,998,350 | | 1,998,350 | 12,837,900 | | 12,837,900 | +10,839,550 | 22,639,033 | 22,279,121 | +359,912 |
| 1813 | 7,505,668 | | 7,505,668 | 26,184,435 | | 26,184,435 | +18,678,767 | 40,524,845 | 39,187,520 | +1,337,325 |
| 1814 | 3,307,305 | | 3,307,305 | 23,377,912 | | 23,377,912 | +20,070,607 | 34,559,537 | 38,028,231 | −3,468,694 |
| 1815 | 6,874,354 | | 6,874,354 | 35,264,321 | | 35,264,321 | +28,389,967 | 50,993,345 | 39,582,493 | +11,410,852 |
| 1816 | 17,657,804 | | 17,657,804 | 9,494,436 | | 9,494,436 | −8,163,368 | 57,172,107 | 48,244,495 | +8,927,612 |
| 1817 | 19,041,826 | | 19,041,826 | 734,543 | | 734,543 | −18,307,283 | 33,833,593 | 40,885,646 | −7,052,053 |
| 1818 | 15,279,755 | | 15,279,755 | 8,766 | | 8,766 | −15,270,989 | 21,593,937 | 35,104,876 | −13,510,939 |
| 1819 | 2,540,388 | | 2,540,388 | 2,291 | | 2,291 | −2,538,097 | 24,605,666 | 24,004,198 | +601,468 |
| 1820 | 3,502,397 | | 3,502,397 | 3,040,824 | | 3,040,824 | −461,573 | 20,921,494 | 21,763,024 | −841,530 |

| Year | (1) | (2) | (3) | (4) | (5) | (6) | (7) | (8) | (9) | (10) | (11) | (12) |
|---|---|---|---|---|---|---|---|---|---|---|---|---|
| 1821 | +483,129 | 19,090,575 | 19,573,704 | +1,720,502 | 5,000,324 | | | 5,000,324 | | 3,279,822 | | 3,279,822 |
| 1822 | +2,555,537 | 17,676,591 | 20,232,428 | −2,676,371 | 5,000,000 | | | 5,000,000 | | 2,676,371 | | 2,676,371 |
| 1823 | +5,225,494 | 15,314,172 | 20,540,666 | −607,332 | 5,000,000 | | | 5,000,000 | | 607,332 | | 607,332 |
| 1824 | +7,517,327 | 31,898,510 | 24,381,213 | −6,571,832 | | | | | | 11,571,832 | | 11,571,832 |
| 1825 | +3,255,063 | 23,585,805 | 26,840,858 | −6,728,576 | | | | | | 7,728,576 | | 7,728,576 |
| 1826 | +1,157,035 | 24,103,399 | 25,260,434 | −7,067,602 | | | | | | 7,067,602 | | 7,067,602 |
| 1827 | +309,599 | 22,656,765 | 22,763,630 | −6,517,597 | | | | | | 6,517,597 | | 6,517,597 |
| 1828 | −695,850 | 25,459,480 | 24,827,627 | −9,064,637 | | | | | | 9,064,637 | | 9,064,637 |
| 1829 | −216,731 | 25,044,358 | 24,844,116 | −9,841,025 | | | | | | 9,841,025 | | 9,841,025 |
| 1830 | +258,835 | 24,585,281 | | −9,442,215 | | | | | | 9,442,215 | | 9,442,215 |
| 1831 | −1,511,625 | 30,038,446 | 28,526,821 | −14,790,795 | | | | | | 14,790,795 | | 14,790,795 |
| 1832 | −2,491,137 | 34,356,698 | 31,865,561 | −17,067,748 | | | | | | 17,067,748 | | 17,067,748 |
| 1833 | +9,691,128 | 24,257,299 | 33,948,427 | −1,239,747 | | | | | | 1,239,747 | | 1,239,747 |
| 1834 | −2,810,045 | 24,601,981 | 21,791,935 | −5,974,412 | | | | | | 5,974,412 | | 5,974,412 |
| 1835 | +17,856,946 | 17,573,141 | 35,430,087 | 328 | | | | | | 328 | | 328 |
| 1836 | +19,938,632 | 30,986,164 | 50,825,796 | +2,971,166 | | | | | | | | |
| 1837 | −9,313,177 | 37,265,319 | 27,947,142 | +7,126,097 | 2,992,989 | | | 2,992,989 | 2,992,989 | 21,823 | | 21,823 |
| 1838 | +1,557,942 | 39,455,783 | 39,019,383 | +80,878 | 12,716,821 | | | 12,716,821 | 12,716,821 | 5,590,724 | | 5,590,724 |
| 1839 | −1,423,120 | 37,617,282 | 39,341,025 | +1,677,532 | 3,857,276 | | | 3,857,276 | 3,857,276 | 10,718,154 | | 10,718,154 |
| 1840 | +4,450,862 | 28,229,595 | 25,069,663 | +1,677,532 | 5,589,548 | | | 5,589,548 | 5,589,548 | 3,912,016 | | 3,912,016 |
| 1841 | +1,362,108 | 31,881,585 | 30,519,477 | +8,343,605 | 13,659,317 | | | 13,659,317 | 13,659,317 | 5,315,712 | | 5,315,712 |
| 1842 | +1,777,183 | 33,007,751 | 34,784,934 | +7,006,746 | 14,808,736 | | | 14,808,736 | 14,808,736 | 7,801,990 | | 7,801,990 |
| 1843 | +2,586,322 | 12,196,088 | 20,782,410 | +12,141,695 | 12,479,708 | | | 12,479,708 | 12,479,708 | 338,013 | | 338,013 |
| 1844 | −2,297,467 | 54,595,085 | 31,198,555 | −9,281,270 | 1,877,181 | | | 1,877,181 | 1,877,181 | 11,158,451 | | 11,158,451 |
| 1845 | −503,651 | 75,619,007 | 29,970,106 | −7,536,349 | | | | | | 7,536,349 | | 7,536,349 |
| 1846 | +1,557,942 | 66,395,734 | 29,699,967 | +375,100 | | | | | | 375,100 | | 375,100 |
| 1847 | −1,509,312 | 73,155,645 | 55,968,168 | +23,276,331 | 28,872,399 | | | 28,872,399 | 28,872,399 | 5,596,068 | | 5,596,068 |
| 1848 | −1,423,120 | 71,072,311 | 58,415,599 | +8,218,327 | 21,256,700 | | | 21,256,700 | 21,256,700 | 13,038,373 | | 13,038,373 |
| 1849 | +1,940,407 | 81,690,521 | 59,796,883 | +15,783,921 | 28,588,750 | | | 28,588,750 | 28,588,750 | 12,804,829 | | 12,804,829 |
| 1850 | +4,450,862 | 83,773,520 | 47,649,399 | +390,915 | 4,045,950 | | | 4,46,950 | 4,045,950 | 3,655,035 | | 3,655,035 |
| 1851 | +4,398,736 | 48,363,968 | 52,762,704 | −451,531 | 203,400 | | | 203,400 | 203,400 | 654,951 | | 654,951 |
| 1852 | +3,546,443 | 46,346,673 | 49,893,116 | −2,105,224 | 46,300 | | | 46,300 | 46,300 | 2,151,754 | | 2,151,754 |
| 1853 | +7,006,719 | 54,595,685 | 61,603,404 | −2,370,847 | 16,350 | | | 16,350 | 16,350 | 6,412,574 | | 6,412,574 |
| 1854 | −1,815,358 | 75,619,007 | 73,808,639 | +6,655,266 | 3,298 | | | 3,298 | 3,298 | 17,574,145 | | 17,574,145 |
| 1855 | +1,247,359 | 66,395,734 | 65,351,375 | −3,614,419 | 800 | | | 800 | 800 | 6,636,066 | | 6,636,066 |
| 1856 | −871,254 | 73,155,645 | 74,056,889 | −3,272,706 | 3,900 | | | 200 | 200 | 3,614,619 | | 3,614,619 |
| 1857 | −2,103,101 | 71,072,311 | 70,969,213 | +16,212,706 | | | | 3,900 | 3,900 | 3,276,606 | | 3,276,606 |
| 1858 | −2,313,855 | 81,690,521 | 70,372,666 | +13,584,957 | 23,717,300 | | | 23,717,300 | 23,717,300 | 7,505,251 | | 7,505,251 |
| 1859 | −1,999,555 | 83,773,520 | 81,773,985 | +6,345,450 | 28,287,500 | | | 28,287,500 | 28,287,500 | 14,702,543 | | 14,702,543 |
| 1860 | −720,540 | 77,501,948 | 76,841,408 | | 20,776,800 | | | 20,776,800 | 20,776,800 | 14,431,350 | | 14,431,350 |
| 1861 | −1,317,904 | 84,689,545 | 83,371,641 | +23,718,810 | 41,861,710 | | | 41,861,710 | 41,861,710 | 18,142,900 | | 18,142,900 |
| 1862 | +10,821,176 | 570,858,741 | 581,679,917 | +433,595,539 | 529,692,451 | | | 529,692,461 | 529,692,461 | 96,096,922 | | 96,096,922 |
| 1863 | −8,546,707 | 895,827,360 | 887,280,653 | +593,496,727 | 774,583,362 | | | 774,583,362 | 774,583,362 | 181,086,635 | | 181,086,635 |
| 1864 | +95,316,361 | 1,250,116,307 | 1,345,432,668 | +696,012,232 | 1,080,805,897 | | | 1,080,805,897 | 1,080,805,897 | 384,793,663 | | 384,793,663 |
| 1865 | −98,977,120 | 1,889,340,884 | 1,790,363,764 | +864,863,499 | 1,456,649,159 | | | 1,456,649,159 | 1,456,649,159 | 591,785,660 | | 591,785,660 |
| 1866 | +119,029,367 | 1,034,903,797 | 1,153,933,154 | +81,806,164 | 593,900,534 | $83,490 | | 593,900,534 | 593,900,534 | 514,094,370 | $802,180 | 514,094,370 |
| 1867 | +29,984,285 | 915,821,648 | 945,805,971 | −103,107,050 | 455,090,471 | 740,370 | | 455,090,471 | 455,090,471 | 553,186,181 | 602,180 | 553,186,181 |
| 1868 | −37,913,125 | 961,123,724 | 923,210,599 | −66,210,923 | 517,572,516 | 765,720 | | 516,832,146 | 516,832,146 | 583,783,439 | 458,409 | 583,092,117 |
| 1869 | +9,743,602 | 438,325,804 | 443,069,406 | −38,334,867 | 77,125,639 | 788,160 | | 76,359,899 | 76,359,899 | 115,460,526 | 202,755 | 115,092,117 |
| 1870 | −7,035,405 | 427,428,869 | 420,373,454 | −108,657,321 | 9,117,957 | | | 8,331,827 | 8,331,827 | 117,775,308 | | 117,572,653 |

TABLE K.—*Receipts and expenditures of the United States Government by fiscal years from 1791 to 1922*—Continued.

| Fiscal year. | Public debt retirements, exclusive of retirements chargeable against ordinary receipts. | Redemption of national bank and Federal reserve bank notes. | Total public debt retirements chargeable against public debt receipts. | Public debt receipts, proceeds of bonds, and other securities. | Deposits to retire national bank and Federal reserve bank notes. | Total public debt receipts. | Surplus (+) or deficit (−) public debt receipts compared with public debt expenditures (exclusive of public debt expenditures chargeable against ordinary receipts). | Total ordinary and public debt receipts. | Total ordinary and public debt expenditures. | Surplus (+) or deficit (−) of all receipts. |
|---|---|---|---|---|---|---|---|---|---|---|
| 1871 | $177,323,434 | $1,307,527 | $178,630,961 | $61,249,107 | $3,017,071 | $64,266,178 | −$114,364,783 | $447,590,123 | $470,808,149 | −$23,218,026 |
| 1872 | 254,334,064 | 3,374,154 | 257,708,218 | 142,173,811 | 3,473,104 | 145,646,915 | −112,061,303 | 519,753,783 | 535,226,181 | −15,472,398 |
| 1873 | 61,822,216 | 3,241,778 | 65,063,994 | 3,950,180 | 2,333,321 | 6,283,501 | −58,780,493 | 340,021,706 | 355,409,239 | −15,387,533 |
| 1874 | 136,070,505 | 1,374,500 | 137,445,005 | 142,882,880 | 3,284,510 | 146,167,390 | +8,722,385 | 451,147,046 | 440,079,778 | +11,067,268 |
| 1875 | 20,541,836 | 104,912,666 | 125,454,502 | 96,505,700 | 25,288,721 | 121,794,421 | −3,666,081 | 410,421,392 | 400,700,815 | +9,720,577 |
| 1876 | 137,752,615 | 24,324,687 | 162,077,302 | 104,553,060 | 32,093,381 | 136,646,431 | −25,430,871 | 431,143,562 | 427,579,653 | +3,563,909 |
| 1877 | 151,239,535 | 25,050,755 | 176,290,290 | 141,134,650 | 12,099,755 | 153,204,405 | −23,085,875 | 433,260,138 | 418,274,099 | +14,986,039 |
| 1878 | 143,997,994 | 12,009,876 | 156,007,870 | 198,850,250 | 8,816,027 | 207,666,277 | +51,658,408 | 455,853,923 | 383,395,963 | +72,457,960 |
| 1879 | 479,882,226 | 8,056,701 | 487,938,927 | 617,578,010 | 9,855,249 | 627,433,259 | +139,494,332 | 902,012,098 | 755,638,465 | +146,373,633 |
| 1880 | 280,434,937 | 6,401,916 | 286,836,853 | 73,065,540 | 14,143,476 | 87,209,016 | −199,627,837 | 420,908,238 | 554,652,422 | −133,744,184 |
| 1881 | 86,110,581 | 12,344,799 | 98,455,380 | 678,200 | 26,154,037 | 26,832,237 | −71,623,143 | 389,131,976 | 360,685,714 | +28,446,262 |
| 1882 | 166,505,256 | 16,808,607 | 183,313,863 | 225,300 | 20,718,477 | 20,943,777 | −162,370,098 | 428,206,396 | 445,032,672 | −16,826,276 |
| 1883 | 438,430,757 | 23,552,280 | 461,983,037 | 304,372,850 | 22,653,461 | 327,026,311 | −134,956,726 | 726,598,598 | 728,675,880 | −2,077,282 |
| 1884 | 101,266,335 | 26,857,690 | 128,124,025 | 1,404,650 | 30,971,900 | 31,472,550 | −96,651,474 | 389,964,721 | 373,222,569 | +16,742,152 |
| 1885 | 46,042,635 | 28,462,225 | 74,504,860 | 58,150 | 27,690,436 | 27,748,586 | −46,756,274 | 355,198,403 | 338,490,911 | +16,707,497 |
| 1886 | 44,583,843 | 29,557,588 | 74,141,431 | 39,850 | 51,209,962 | 51,249,812 | −22,891,619 | 389,081,844 | 318,016,876 | +71,064,968 |
| 1887 | 127,959,368 | 37,368,289 | 165,327,657 | 40,900 | 75,112,501 | 75,153,401 | −90,174,256 | 447,574,075 | 434,277,235 | +13,296,840 |
| 1888 | 74,862,213 | 50,163,957 | 125,026,170 | 48,650 | 44,123,883 | 44,172,533 | −80,853,638 | 425,835,411 | 395,347,775 | +30,487,636 |
| 1889 | 121,288,788 | 46,386,122 | 167,674,910 | 24,350 | 32,494,415 | 32,508,765 | −135,166,145 | 420,257,545 | 467,662,609 | −47,405,064 |
| 1890 | 104,663,800 | 33,633,889 | 138,297,689 | 21,650 | 11,202,112 | 11,223,762 | −127,073,927 | 414,752,744 | 456,786,398 | −42,033,654 |
| 1891 | 101,003,056 | 25,329,023 | 126,332,064 | 113,750 | 9,628,060 | 9,741,810 | −116,590,274 | 402,768,512 | 492,520,243 | −89,751,731 |
| 1892 | 24,345,087 | 16,232,721 | 40,580,808 | 15,550 | 2,977,538 | 2,993,088 | −37,587,720 | 357,930,872 | 385,604,139 | −27,673,267 |
| 1893 | 709,903 | 9,037,662 | 9,747,565 | 22,900 | 2,937,589 | 2,960,480 | −6,787,075 | 388,780,109 | 393,225,508 | −4,445,399 |
| 1894 | 296,447 | 10,889,536 | 11,185,983 | 50,014,050 | 16,637,784 | 66,652,634 | +55,496,051 | 373,007,350 | 378,711,264 | −5,703,914 |
| 1895 | 2,534,550 | 13,028,369 | 15,562,919 | 81,165,050 | 12,056,173 | 93,221,223 | +77,658,304 | 417,950,642 | 371,758,217 | +46,192,425 |
| 1896 | 7,291,884 | 11,225,369 | 18,517,253 | 131,168,800 | 5,965,684 | 137,134,484 | +118,617,231 | 475,276,931 | 370,696,699 | +104,580,232 |
| 1897 | 11,468,502 | 11,002,356 | 22,470,858 | 3,250 | 15,448,970 | 15,452,220 | −7,018,633 | 385,173,925 | 398,245,017 | −13,071,092 |
| 1898 | 29,942,062 | 15,990,460 | 45,932,522 | 5,950 | 22,024,970 | 22,030,920 | −23,901,602 | 427,335,341 | 489,284,191 | −61,948,850 |
| 1899 | 14,622,363 | 16,649,276 | 31,271,639 | 199,201,210 | 21,973,510 | 221,174,720 | +189,903,081 | 636,343,818 | 535,552,295 | +100,791,523 |
| 1900 | 22,790,058 | 17,909,793 | 40,699,851 | 117,770 | 17,240,290 | 17,358,060 | −23,341,791 | 584,598,912 | 561,560,698 | +23,038,214 |

| Year | | | | | | | | | | |
|---|---|---|---|---|---|---|---|---|---|---|
| 1901 | 36,112,799 | 18,626,438 | 54,739,237 | 3,700 | 12,882,869 | 12,886,569 | −41,852,668 | 600,571,907 | 579,356,162 | +21,215,745 |
| 1902 | 56,223,918 | 20,085,275 | 76,309,193 | 2,370 | 32,725,435 | 32,737,805 | −43,571,388 | 595,216,038 | 561,543,442 | +33,672,596 |
| 1903 | 16,608,833 | 26,272,086 | 42,880,919 | 2,050 | 24,270,925 | 24,272,975 | −18,607,944 | 586,153,697 | 559,887,046 | +26,296,651 |
| 1904 | 18,622,731 | 30,936,971 | 49,559,702 | 2,600 | 26,410,205 | 26,412,805 | −23,146,897 | 567,499,890 | 633,219,602 | −65,719,712 |
| 1905 | 605,231 | 25,857,368 | 26,462,599 | 2,750 | 22,557,928 | 22,560,678 | −3,901,921 | 566,635,363 | 593,741,513 | −26,906,150 |
| 1906 | 244,712 | 24,724,135 | 24,968,847 | 2,050 | 35,132,672 | 35,134,722 | +10,165,875 | 630,119,168 | 595,171,125 | +34,948,043 |
| 1907 | 30,373,043 | 25,454,255 | 55,827,298 | 30,005,100 | 30,477,420 | 60,482,520 | +4,653,222 | 726,342,906 | 634,956,140 | +91,336,766 |
| 1908 | 34,356,750 | 39,535,157 | 73,891,907 | 40,068,480 | 64,333,137 | 104,401,617 | +30,509,710 | 706,263,524 | 733,088,227 | −2,024,703 |
| 1909 | 15,434,687 | 89,562,083 | 104,996,770 | 30,000,000 | 45,624,240 | 75,624,240 | −29,372,530 | 679,944,738 | 798,740,655 | −118,795,917 |
| 1910 | 760,925 | 32,288,771 | 33,049,696 | .......... | 31,674,293 | 31,674,293 | −1,375,403 | 707,186,008 | 726,666,761 | −19,490,753 |
| 1911 | 246,496 | 34,976,840 | 35,223,336 | 17,641,634 | 40,232,555 | 57,874,199 | +22,650,853 | 759,707,100 | 726,424,848 | +33,282,252 |
| 1912 | 120,616 | 28,527,712 | 28,648,328 | 32,817,646 | 20,078,365 | 52,596,011 | +24,247,653 | 745,505,215 | 718,529,662 | +26,975,553 |
| 1913 | 102,575 | 24,089,036 | 24,191,611 | 1,929,940 | 21,471,010 | 23,400,850 | −790,761 | 747,512,080 | 748,703,574 | −1,191,494 |
| 1914 | 109,127 | 26,852,200 | 26,961,327 | 3,118,940 | 19,902,283 | 23,021,223 | −3,940,104 | 757,694,390 | 762,042,758 | −4,345,368 |
| 1915 | 47,533 | 17,205,958 | 17,253,491 | 933,340 | 21,553,415 | 22,486,955 | +5,233,464 | 720,397,782 | 777,840,283 | −57,442,511 |
| 1916 | 35,903 | 24,633,011 | 24,668,914 | 1,803,500 | 56,648,903 | 58,452,403 | +33,783,489 | 840,986,951 | 766,665,641 | +74,321,310 |
| 1917 | 636,980,667 | 40,564,116 | 677,544,783 | 2,390,724,755 | 37,293,045 | 2,428,017,800 | +1,750,473,017 | 3,552,342,595 | 2,763,596,887 | +788,755,708 |
| 1918 | 7,685,207,850 | 21,611,225 | 7,706,879,075 | 16,964,609,560 | 10,279,050 | 16,974,889,210 | +9,268,010,135 | 21,155,314,366 | 21,498,786,970 | −343,472,604 |
| 1919 | 15,813,845,117 | 23,617,883 | 15,837,566,010 | 29,053,331,758 | 22,644,738 | 29,075,976,316 | +13,238,410,506 | 33,730,357,415 | 34,789,707,190 | −1,069,349,775 |
| 1920 | 17,013,020,107 | 23,424,165 | 17,036,444,272 | 15,835,273,962 | 17,071,988 | 15,852,345,950 | −1,184,098,322 | 22,355,760,387 | 23,178,189,512 | −621,429,125 |
| 1921 | 8,721,920,033 | 37,490,631 | 8,759,380,664 | 8,824,738,539 | 40,186,945 | 8,864,925,784 | +105,545,120 | 14,449,442,829 | 13,650,487,483 | +706,955,346 |
| 1922 | 6,500,584,643 | 107,251,870 | 6,607,836,513 | 5,910,931,276 | 107,086,627 | 6,018,017,903 | −589,818,610 | 10,121,614,434 | 10,225,874,310 | −104,239,876 |

TABLE L.—*Postal receipts and expenditures for the fiscal years 1791 to 1922.*

| Fiscal year. | Receipts. | Ex-penditures.[1] | Excess of receipts. | Excess of ex-penditures. |
|---|---|---|---|---|
| 1791 | $71,296 | $67,114 | $4,182 | |
| 1792 | 92,988 | 76,586 | 16,402 | |
| 1793 | 103,883 | 74,161 | 29,722 | |
| 1794 | 129,196 | 95,398 | 33,788 | |
| 1795 | 163,795 | 125,039 | 38,756 | |
| 1796 | 195,043 | 136,639 | 58,404 | |
| 1797 | 213,993 | 156,588 | 57,405 | |
| 1798 | 233,145 | 185,308 | 47,837 | |
| 1799 | 264,850 | 184,835 | 80,015 | |
| 1800 | 280,806 | 207,136 | 73,670 | |
| 1801 | 320,445 | 248,142 | 72,303 | |
| 1802 | 326,832 | 275,857 | 50,975 | |
| 1803 | 359,952 | 316,312 | 43,640 | |
| 1804 | 389,711 | 333,977 | 55,734 | |
| 1805 | 422,129 | 386,115 | 36,014 | |
| 1806 | 446,520 | 413,814 | 32,706 | |
| 1807 | 484,134 | 418,916 | 65,218 | |
| 1808 | 460,718 | 446,915 | 13,803 | |
| 1809 | 506,634 | 505,116 | 1,518 | |
| 1810 | 551,755 | 550,991 | 764 | |
| 1811 | 587,267 | 517,921 | 69,346 | |
| 1812 | 649,151 | 552,472 | 96,679 | |
| 1813 | 703,221 | 635,412 | 67,809 | |
| 1814 | 730,953 | 726,375 | 4,578 | |
| 1815 | 1,043,022 | 743,756 | 299,266 | |
| 1816 | 961,718 | 807,875 | 153,843 | |
| 1817 | 1,022,973 | 917,129 | 85,844 | |
| 1818 | 1,130,203 | 1,031,799 | 98,404 | |
| 1819 | 1,204,737 | 1,114,032 | 90,705 | |
| 1820 | 1,111,760 | 1,163,191 | | $51,431 |
| 1821 | 1,058,302 | 1,177,526 | | 119,224 |
| 1822 | 1,117,555 | 1,167,359 | | 49,804 |
| 1823 | 1,130,214 | 1,158,777 | | 28,563 |
| 1824 | 1,197,299 | 1,190,478 | 6,821 | |
| 1825 | 1,306,253 | 1,238,912 | 67,341 | |
| 1826 | 1,447,660 | 1,395,799 | 51,861 | |
| 1827 | 1,524,602 | 1,481,620 | 42,982 | |
| 1828 | 1,660,276 | 1,679,316 | | 19,040 |
| 1829 | 1,778,472 | 1,872,705 | | 94,233 |
| 1830 | 1,919,314 | 1,950,116 | | 30,802 |
| 1831 | 2,105,722 | 2,006,743 | 98,979 | |
| 1832 | 2,258,570 | 2,266,171 | | 7,601 |
| 1833 | 2,617,012 | 2,930,415 | | 313,403 |
| 1834 | 2,823,749 | 2,910,605 | | 86,856 |
| 1835 | 2,993,557 | 2,757,350 | 236,207 | |
| 1836 | 3,408,323 | 2,841,766 | 566,557 | |
| 1837 | 4,945,668 | 3,288,319 | 1,657,349 | |
| 1838 | 4,238,733 | 4,430,662 | | 191,929 |
| 1839 | 4,484,656 | 4,636,536 | | 151,880 |
| 1840 | 4,543,522 | 4,718,236 | | 174,714 |
| 1841 | 4,407,726 | 4,907,184 | | 499,458 |
| 1842 | 4,546,850 | 5,728,449 | | 1,181,599 |
| 1843 | 4,296,225 | 4,396,056 | | 99,831 |
| 1844 | 4,237,288 | 4,296,513 | | 59,225 |
| 1845 | 4,289,842 | 4,320,732 | | 30,890 |
| 1846 | 3,487,199 | 4,886,268 | | 1,399,069 |
| 1847 | 3,880,309 | 4,515,841 | | 635,532 |
| 1848 | 4,555,211 | 4,349,072 | 206,139 | |
| 1849 | 4,705,176 | 4,479,049 | 226,127 | |
| 1850 | 5,499,984 | 5,212,953 | 287,031 | |
| 1851 | 6,410,604 | 6,278,401 | 132,203 | |
| 1852 | 5,184,526 | 8,149,894 | | 2,965,368 |
| 1853 | 5,240,725 | 7,394,475 | | 2,153,750 |
| 1854 | 6,255,586 | 9,462,932 | | 3,207,346 |
| 1855 | 6,642,136 | 9,720,950 | | 3,078,814 |
| 1856 | 6,920,822 | 10,119,940 | | 3,199,118 |
| 1857 | 7,353,952 | 10,970,835 | | 3,616,883 |
| 1858 | 7,486,793 | 12,235,716 | | 4,748,923 |
| 1859 | 7,968,484 | 12,777,042 | | 4,808,558 |
| 1860 | 8,518,067 | 18,407,613 | | 9,889,546 |

[1] Exclusive of departmental expenditures in Washington by the office of the Postmaster General.

TABLE L.—*Postal receipts and expenditures for the fiscal years 1791 to 1922*—Contd.

| Fiscal year. | Receipts. | Expenditures. | Excess of receipts. | Excess of expenditures. |
|---|---|---|---|---|
| 1861 | $8,349,296 | $13,520,191 | | $5,170,895 |
| 1862 | 8,299,820 | 11,861,549 | | 3,561,729 |
| 1863 | 11,163,790 | 11,913,104 | | 749,314 |
| 1864 | 12,438,254 | 13,438,234 | | 999,980 |
| 1865 | 14,556,159 | 14,806,159 | | 250,000 |
| 1866 | 14,436,986 | 14,436,986 | | |
| 1867 | 15,297,027 | 18,813,694 | | 3,516,667 |
| 1868 | 16,292,600 | 20,345,792 | | 4,053,192 |
| 1869 | 18,344,511 | 23,740,021 | | 5,395,510 |
| 1870 | 19,772,221 | 24,616,800 | | 4,844,579 |
| 1871 | 20,037,045 | 25,168,295 | | 5,131,250 |
| 1872 | 21,915,426 | 27,090,426 | | 5,175,000 |
| 1873 | 22,996,742 | 28,487,217 | | 5,490,475 |
| 1874 | 26,471,072 | 31,185,117 | | 4,714,045 |
| 1875 | 26,791,361 | 34,003,007 | | 7,211,646 |
| 1876 | 28,644,198 | 33,736,738 | | 5,092,540 |
| 1877 | 27,531,585 | 33,701,924 | | 6,170,339 |
| 1878 | 29,277,517 | 35,030,911 | | 5,753,394 |
| 1879 | 30,041,983 | 34,815,507 | | 4,773,524 |
| 1880 | 33,315,479 | 36,386,479 | | 3,071,000 |
| 1881 | 36,785,398 | 40,681,037 | | 3,895,639 |
| 1882 | 41,876,410 | 41,876,410 | | |
| 1883 | 45,508,693 | 45,583,196 | | 74,503 |
| 1884 | 43,325,959 | 43,325,959 | | |
| 1885 | 42,560,843 | 47,102,454 | | 4,541,611 |
| 1886 | 43,948,423 | 52,142,075 | | 8,193,652 |
| 1887 | 48,837,609 | 55,338,856 | | 6,501,247 |
| 1888 | 52,695,177 | 55,751,214 | | 3,056,037 |
| 1889 | 56,175,611 | 60,044,531 | | 3,868,920 |
| 1890 | 60,882,098 | 67,757,135 | | 6,875,037 |
| 1891 | 65,931,786 | 70,673,558 | | 4,741,772 |
| 1892 | 70,930,476 | 74,981,966 | | 4,051,490 |
| 1893 | 73,896,993 | 81,843,788 | | 5,946,795 |
| 1894 | 75,080,479 | 83,330,479 | | 8,250,000 |
| 1895 | 76,983,128 | 87,999,670 | | 11,016,542 |
| 1896 | 82,499,208 | 91,799,208 | | 9,300,000 |
| 1897 | 82,665,463 | 93,814,669 | | 11,149,206 |
| 1898 | 89,012,619 | 99,516,659 | | 10,504,040 |
| 1899 | 95,021,384 | 103,232,954 | | 8,211,570 |
| 1900 | 102,354,579 | 109,585,358 | | 7,230,779 |
| 1901 | 111,631,193 | 116,585,955 | | 4,954,762 |
| 1902 | 121,848,047 | 124,250,200 | | 2,402,153 |
| 1903 | 134,224,443 | 136,993,362 | | 2,768,919 |
| 1904 | 143,582,624 | 150,085,155 | | 6,502,531 |
| 1905 | 152,826,585 | 167,891,842 | | 15,065,257 |
| 1906 | 167,932,783 | 180,606,077 | | 12,673,294 |
| 1907 | 183,585,005 | 191,214,388 | | 7,629,383 |
| 1908 | 191,478,663 | 204,366,704 | | 12,888,041 |
| 1909 | 203,562,383 | 223,063,445 | | 19,501,062 |
| 1910 | 224,128,658 | 232,624,270 | | 8,495,612 |
| 1911 | 237,879,823 | 237,660,705 | $219,118 | |
| 1912 | 246,744,016 | 248,312,211 | | 1,568,195 |
| 1913 | 266,619,526 | 263,136,244 | 3,483,282 | |
| 1914 | 287,934,566 | 283,558,103 | 4,376,463 | |
| 1915 | 287,248,165 | 293,884,758 | | 6,636,593 |
| 1916 | 312,057,689 | 311,728,453 | 329,236 | |
| 1917 | 329,726,116 | 319,889,904 | 9,836,212 | |
| 1918 | 344,475,962 | 327,070,282 | 17,405,680 | |
| 1919 | 364,847,128 | 362,847,785 | 1,999,341 | |
| 1920 | 437,150,212 | 418,722,295 | 18,427,917 | |
| 1921 | 463,491,275 | 593,764,120 | | 130,272,845 |
| 1922 | 484,853,541 | 545,668,941 | | 60,815,400 |

TABLE M.—*Sources of internal revenue, 1863 to 1922.*

[On basis of reports of collections.]

| Fiscal year. | Spirits.[1] | Fermented liquors.[1] | Tobacco.[1] | Income and profits.[2] | Legacies, successions, inheritances. | Estates. | Manufactures and products.[1,2] | Banks and bankers. | Gross receipts. |
|---|---|---|---|---|---|---|---|---|---|
| 1863 | $5,176,530.50 | $1,628,933.82 | $3,097,620.47 | $2,741,858.25 | $56,592.61 | | $15,524,989.24 | $2,837,719.82 | $1,661,273.51 |
| 1864 | 30,329,149.53 | 2,290,009.14 | 8,592,098.98 | 20,294,731.74 | 311,161.02 | | 36,222,716.67 | 4,940,870.90 | 3,428,446.33 |
| 1865 | 18,731,422.45 | 3,734,928.06 | 11,401,373.10 | 60,979,329.46 | 545,703.17 | | 73,318,450.37 | 3,463,988.05 | 9,853,377.12 |
| 1866 | 33,268,171.52 | 5,220,552.72 | 16,531,007.83 | 72,982,159.03 | 1,170,978.85 | | 127,230,608.66 | 2,046,562.46 | 11,262,429.82 |
| 1867 | 33,542,951.72 | 6,067,500.63 | 19,765,148.41 | 66,014,429.34 | 1,865,315.15 | | 91,531,331.31 | 1,866,745.55 | 7,444,719.00 |
| 1868 | 18,655,630.90 | 5,955,868.92 | 18,730,095.32 | 41,455,598.36 | 1,823,411.29 | | 61,649,902.56 | 2,196,054.17 | 6,280,099.34 |
| 1869 | 45,071,230.86 | 6,099,879.54 | 23,430,707.57 | 34,791,855.84 | 2,434,583.23 | | 3,345,362.95 | 3,020,083.61 | 6,300,998.82 |
| 1870 | 55,606,094.15 | 6,319,126.90 | 31,350,707.88 | 37,775,873.62 | 3,091,825.50 | | 3,017,027.70 | | 6,894,799.99 |
| 1871 | 46,281,848.10 | 7,389,501.82 | 33,578,907.18 | 19,162,650.75 | 2,505,067.13 | | 3,631,516.10 | 3,644,241.53 | 2,800,563.44 |
| 1872 | 49,475,516.36 | 8,258,498.46 | 33,736,170.52 | 14,436,861.78 | | | 4,616,144.75 | 3,628,229.14 | |
| 1873 | 52,099,371.78 | 9,324,937.84 | 34,386,303.09 | 5,062,311.62 | | | 1,267,470.38 | 3,771,031.46 | |
| 1874 | 49,444,089.85 | 9,304,679.72 | 33,242,875.62 | 139,472.09 | | | 625,408.05 | 3,357,160.67 | |
| 1875 | 52,081,991.12 | 9,144,004.41 | 37,303,461.88 | 232.64 | | | 863,851.46 | 4,097,248.12 | |
| 1876 | 56,426,365.13 | 9,571,280.66 | 39,795,339.91 | 588.27 | | | 509,042.82 | 4,006,698.03 | |
| 1877 | 57,469,429.72 | 9,480,789.17 | 41,106,546.92 | 97.79 | | | 238,162.76 | 3,829,729.33 | |
| 1878 | 50,420,815.80 | 9,937,051.78 | 40,091,754.67 | | | | 429,658.71 | 3,492,031.85 | |
| 1879 | 52,570,284.69 | 10,729,320.08 | 40,135,002.65 | | | | 299,094.00 | 3,198,883.59 | |
| 1880 | 61,185,508.79 | 12,829,802.84 | 38,870,140.08 | | | | 228,027.73 | 3,350,985.28 | |
| 1881 | 67,153,974.88 | 13,700,241.21 | 42,854,991.31 | | | | 149,140.98 | 3,762,208.07 | |
| 1882 | 69,873,408.18 | 16,153,920.42 | 47,391,988.91 | 3,021.92 | | | 81,559.00 | 5,253,458.47 | |
| 1883 | 74,368,775.20 | 16,900,615.81 | 42,104,249.79 | | | | 71,862.43 | 3,748,944.60 | |
| 1884 | 76,905,385.26 | 18,084,954.11 | 26,062,399.98 | 55,627.64 | | | 24,345.01 | 2,391.57 | |
| 1885 | 67,511,208.63 | 18,230,762.03 | 26,407,088.48 | | | | 22,730.25 | 25,000.00 | |
| 1886 | 69,092,266.00 | 19,676,731.29 | 27,907,362.53 | | | | 24,199.94 | | |
| 1887 | 65,829,321.71 | 21,922,187.49 | 30,108,067.53 | | | | 21,506.41 | 4,288.57 | |
| 1888 | 69,306,166.41 | 23,324,218.48 | 30,662,431.52 | | | | 6,745.05 | 6,202.55 | |
| 1889 | 74,312,206.33 | 23,723,835.26 | 31,866,860.42 | | | | 6,063.08 | 6,213.91 | |
| 1890 | 81,687,375.09 | 26,008,534.74 | 33,958,991.06 | | | | 9,204.66 | 69.90 | |
| 1891 | 83,335,963.64 | 28,565,129.92 | 32,796,270.97 | | | | 3,680.95 | | |
| 1892 | 91,309,983.65 | 30,037,432.77 | 31,000,493.17 | | | | 6,198.15 | | |
| 1893 | 94,720,260.55 | 32,548,983.07 | 31,889,711.74 | | | | 6,908.24 | | |
| 1894 | 85,259,252.25 | 31,414,788.04 | 28,617,898.62 | 77,130.90 | | | 1,572.84 | 2.26 | |
| 1895 | 79,862,627.41 | 31,640,617.54 | 29,704,907.63 | | | | 376.04 | | |
| 1896 | 80,670,070.77 | 32,784,235.26 | 30,711,629.11 | | | | 526.38 | | |
| 1897 | 82,008,542.92 | 32,472,162.07 | 30,710,297.42 | | | | 9,119.01 | 134.85 | |
| 1898 | 92,546,999.77 | 39,515,421.14 | 36,230,522.37 | | | | 1,060.76 | 85.38 | |
| 1899 | 99,283,534.16 | 39,644,558.45 | 52,493,207.64 | | 1,235,435.25 | | 4,716.97 | 1,180.00 | 643,446.41 |
| 1900 | 109,868,817.18 | 73,550,754.49 | 59,355,084.27 | | 2,894,491.55 | | 2,921.80 | 1,460.50 | 1,079,405.14 |

| | | | | | | | | |
|---|---|---|---|---|---|---|---|---|
| 1901 | 116,022,976.56 | 75,669,907.65 | 62,491,907.13 | | 5,211,898.68 | | 1,493.94 | 1,918.00 | 1,027,294.99 |
| 1902 | 124,135,013.13 | 71,988,902.39 | 51,937,925.19 | | 4,842,966.52 | | | 227.50 | 730,376.50 |
| 1903 | 131,965,472.39 | 47,547,836.08 | 43,514,810.24 | | 5,356,774.90 | | | 899.50 | |
| 1904 | 135,810,015.42 | 49,083,458.77 | 44,655,808.75 | | 2,072,132.12 | | | | |
| 1905 | 135,953,513.12 | 50,360,553.18 | 45,659,910.50 | | 774,354.59 | | | 50.10 | |
| 1906 | 143,394,053.12 | 55,644,858.56 | 48,422,997.38 | | 142,148.22 | | | 100.00 | |
| 1907 | 156,336,901.89 | 59,567,818.18 | 51,814,069.69 | | 49,515.29 | | | | |
| 1908 | 140,158,807.15 | 59,807,616.81 | 49,862,754.26 | | | | | 174.85 | |
| 1909 | 234,868,034.12 | 57,456,411.42 | 53,887,178.04 | | | | | | |
| 1910 | 148,029,311.54 | 60,572,288.54 | 58,118,457.03 | 20,959,783.74 | | | | | |
| 1911 | 155,279,858.25 | 64,367,777.65 | 67,005,950.56 | 33,511,525.00 | | | | | |
| 1912 | 156,391,487.77 | 63,268,770.51 | 70,590,151.60 | 28,583,259.81 | | | | | |
| 1913 | 163,879,342.54 | 66,266,8.60 | 76,789,424.75 | 35,006,299.84 | | | | | |
| 1914 | 159,098,177.31 | 67,081,512.45 | 79,986,639.68 | 71,381,274.74 | | | | | |
| 1915 | 144,619,699.37 | 79,328,946.72 | 79,957,373.54 | 80,201,758.86 | | | | | |
| 1916 | 158,682,439.53 | 88,771,103.99 | 88,063,947.51 | 124,937,252.61 | | $6,076,575.26 | | | |
| 1917 | 192,111,318.81 | 91,697,193.81 | 103,201,592.16 | 387,382,343.96 | | 47,452,879.73 | 36,570,478.37 | | |
| 1918 | 377,553,687.33 | 126,285,857.65 | 156,188,659.90 | 2,852,324,865.89 | | 82,029,983.13 | 75,463,674.04 | | |
| 1919 | 365,211,252.26 | 117,839,602.21 | 206,003,091.84 | 2,600,783,902.70 | | 103,635,563.24 | 216,146,750.07 | | |
| 1920 | 97,905,275.71 | 41,905,874.09 | 295,809,355.44 | 3,966,936,003.60 | | | | | |
| 1921 | 82,598,065.01 | 25,363.82 | 255,219,385.49 | 3,228,137,673.75 | | 154,043,260.39 | 177,751,214.00 | | |
| 1922 | 45,563,350.47 | 46,086.00 | 270,759,384.44 | 2,086,918,464.85 | | 139,418,846.04 | 143,908,856.00 | | |

1 Including special taxes relating to manufacture and sale.

2 Including receipts from excise tax on corporations as follows: Fiscal year 1910, $20,959,783.74; 1911, $33,511,525.00; 1912, $28,583,259.81; 1913, $35,006,299.84; and 1914, $10,671,077.22; also munition manufacturers' tax for 1917, $27,663,839.63; and 1918, $13,286,927.32.

3 Including receipts from the tax on raw cotton as follows: Fiscal year 1863, $351,311.48; 1864, $1,268,412.56; 1865, $1,772,983.48; 1866, $18,409,654.90; 1867, $23,769,078.80; and 1868, $22,500,947.77.

4 Includes tax on distilled spirits (nonbeverage) amounting to $42,259,347.44.

TABLE M.—*Sources of internal revenue, 1863 to 1922*—Continued.

| Fiscal year. | Sales (consumers' or dealers'[1]). | Stamps.[5] | Playing cards. | Freight transportation. | Express transportation. | Passenger transportation. | Transportation of oil by pipe lines. | Telegraph and telephone. | Insurance. | Beverages (non-alcoholic), soft drinks, etc. |
|---|---|---|---|---|---|---|---|---|---|---|
| 1863 | $64,003.87 | $4,140,175.29 | | | | | | | | |
| 1864 | 141,231.58 | 5,714,774.88 | | | | | | | | |
| 1865 | 4,062,243.54 | 10,888,727.50 | | | | | | | | |
| 1866 | 4,002,282.91 | 14,257,837.14 | | | | | | | | |
| 1867 | 3,999,380.31 | 15,239,181.78 | | | | | | | | |
| 1868 | 4,595,909.04 | 14,046,613.33 | | | | | | | | |
| 1869 | 8,206,839.03 | 15,505,492.58 | | | | | | | | |
| 1870 | 8,837,394.97 | 15,611,003.43 | | | | | | | | |
| 1871 | 3,649,642.08 | 14,529,885.32 | | | | | | | | |
| 1872 | | 15,296,470.77 | | | | | | | | |
| 1873 | | 7,130,933.57 | | | | | | | | |
| 1874 | | 5,683,114.64 | | | | | | | | |
| 1875 | | 6,083,580.42 | | | | | | | | |
| 1876 | | 6,049,496.92 | | | | | | | | |
| 1877 | | 6,004,475.15 | | | | | | | | |
| 1878 | | 5,936,843.01 | | | | | | | | |
| 1879 | | 6,237,538.57 | | | | | | | | |
| 1880 | | 7,133,696.30 | | | | | | | | |
| 1881 | | 7,375,255.72 | | | | | | | | |
| 1882 | | 7,569,108.70 | | | | | | | | |
| 1883 | | 7,053,053.46 | | | | | | | | |
| 1884 | | 165,792.14 | | | | | | | | |
| 1885 | | 1,630.49 | | | | | | | | |
| 1886 | | 7,887.23 | | | | | | | | |
| 1887 | | 7,777.08 | | | | | | | | |
| 1888 | | 23.82 | | | | | | | | |
| 1889 | | 14.50 | | | | | | | | |
| 1890 | | 7,508.50 | | | | | | | | |
| 1891 | | 231.96 | | | | | | | | |
| 1892 | | 658.50 | | | | | | | | |
| 1893 | | | | | | | | | | |
| 1894 | | | | | | | | | | |
| 1895 | | | $382,402.50 | | | | | | | |
| 1896 | | | 299,853.76 | | | | | | | |
| 1897 | | 794,417.60 | 251,306.52 | | | | | | | |
| 1898 | | 43,837,818.66 | 261,080.66 | | | | | | | |
| 1899 | | 40,964,365.30 | 271,128.84 | | | | | | | |
| 1900 | | | 331,010.66 | | | | | | | |

| Year | | | | | | | | | |
|---|---|---|---|---|---|---|---|---|---|
| 1901 | 39,241,036.32 | 317,2__.84 | | | | | | | |
| 1902 | 13,442,792.69 | 364,677.72 | | | | | | | |
| 1903 | | 422,580.32 | | | | | | | |
| 1904 | | 376,408.34 | | | | | | | |
| 1905 | | 435,575.44 | | | | | | | |
| 1906 | | 489,347.26 | | | | | | | |
| 190? | | 572,714.48 | | | | | | | |
| 1908 | | 459,860.12 | | | | | | | |
| 1909 | | 502,252.58 | | | | | | | |
| 1910 | | 565,524.34 | | | | | | | |
| 1911 | | 581,640.78 | | | | | | | |
| 19?2 | | 616,283.60 | | | | | | | |
| 1913 | | 635,283.10 | | | | | | | |
| 1914 | 23,435,965.34 | 714,307.26 | | | | | | | |
| 1915 | 42,196,443.49 | 673,847.54 | | | | | | | |
| 1916 | 8,926,310.30 | 819,654.20 | | | | | | | |
| 191? | 21,874,734.47 | 820,897.26 | | | | | | | |
| 1918 | 45,251,358.97 | 1,276,505.42 | $30,002,163.38 | $6,458,994.82 | $26,343,050.02 | $1,433,324.61 | $6,299,017.18 | $6,492,025.48 | $2,215,181.03 |
| 19?9 | 2,301,989.95 | 2,091,790.62 | 1,115,345,976.85 | 14,301,901.49 | 83,687,611.52 | 5,601,693.60 | 17,902,388.84 | 14,508,881.31 | 7,182,219.25 |
| 1920 | 45,310,351.30 | 3,088,462.02 | 130,785,810.57 | 17,397,637.69 | 104,861,192.22 | 8,426,405.08 | 27,677,041.19 | 18,421,754.01 | 57,460,956.04 |
| 1921 | 75,664,840.52 | 2,603,_11.82 | 140,019,200.14 | 17,083,935.58 | 105,966,991.94 | 9,089,873.62 | 28,442,412.46 | 18,992,094.45 | 58,675,_72.86 |
| 1922 | 58,224,526.05 | 2,880,440.65 | 85,292,665.34 | 12,475,870.18 | 64,033,854.34 | 7,023,816.51 | 29,271,521.79 | 10,855,403.81 | 33,504,284.01 |

Including sales by postmasters of documentary s[t]amps as follows' Fiscal year 1918, $4,336,182.21; 1919, $10,199,466.51; 1920, $24,437,893.75; 1921, $20,880,868.86; and 1922, $14,616,958.05.

Includes consumers' or dealers' excise tax on perfumes, cosmetics, and medicinal articles amounting to $2,305,482.25

TABLE M.—Sources of internal revenue, 1863 to 1922—Continued.

| Fiscal year. | Oleomargarine.[7] | Opium and narcotics.[7] | Corporation capital stock. | Occupational (special taxes). | Admissions. | Dues. | Receipts under the national prohibition act. | Penalties, etc.[2] | Miscellaneous.[2] | Total. |
|---|---|---|---|---|---|---|---|---|---|---|
| 1863 | | | | $4,799,195.73 | | | | $27,170.14 | $1,084,849.50 | $41,003,192.93 |
| 1864 | | | | 5,205,598.94 | | | | 193,600.48 | 1,406,429.16 | 116,965,578.26 |
| 1865 | | | | 9,806,914.25 | | | | 520,362.70 | 2,071,161.91 | 210,855,864.53 |
| 1866 | | | | 14,144,413.05 | | | | 1,142,853.26 | 5,443,160.05 | 310,120,448.13 |
| 1867 | | | | 13,627,903.25 | | | | 1,459,170.80 | 2,471,364.27 | 265,064,933.43 |
| 1868 | | | | 11,839,540.09 | | | | 1,256,881.59 | 1,168,650.35 | 190,374,925.59 |
| 1869 | | | | 9,949,917.02 | | | | 877,088.79 | 923,106.46 | 159,124,126.86 |
| 1870 | | | | 11,020,787.78 | | | | 827,904.72 | 930,198.09 | 184,302,528.34 |
| 1871 | | | | 5,002,452.85 | | | | 636,980.35 | 385,065.45 | 143,198,322.10 |
| 1872 | | | | | | | | 442,205.12 | | 130,890,096.90 |
| 1873 | | | | | | | | 461,633.06 | | 113,504,012.80 |
| 1874 | | | | | | | | 364,246.34 | | 102,191,016.98 |
| 1875 | | | | | | | | 281,107.61 | 216,027.34 | 110,071,515.00 |
| 1876 | | | | | | | | 409,284.48 | | 116,788,604.22 |
| 1877 | | | | | | | | 419,999.41 | | 118,549,230.25 |
| 1878 | | | | | | | | 346,007.55 | | 110,654,163.37 |
| 1879 | | | | | | | | 279,497.80 | | 113,449,621.38 |
| 1880 | | | | | | | | 383,755.08 | | 123,981,916.10 |
| 1881 | | | | | | | | 231,078.21 | | 135,229,912.30 |
| 1882 | | | | | | | | 199,820.04 | | 146,523,273.72 |
| 1883 | | | | | | | | 305,803.57 | | 114,553,344.86 |
| 1884 | | | | | | | | 289,144.12 | | 121,590,039.83 |
| 1885 | | | | | | | | 222,681.19 | | 112,421,121.07 |
| 1886 | | | | | | | | 194,422.45 | | 116,902,869.44 |
| 1887 | $723,948.04 | | | | | | | 220,204.83 | | 118,837,301.06 |
| 1888 | 864,139.88 | | | | | | | 155,547.61 | | 124,326,475.32 |
| 1889 | 894,247.91 | | | | | | | 84,991.89 | | 130,894,434.20 |
| 1890 | 786,291.72 | | | | | | | 136,720.90 | | 142,594,696.57 |
| 1891 | 1,077,924.14 | | | | | | | 256,214.39 | | 146,035,415.97 |
| 1892 | 1,266,326.00 | $700.00 | | | | | | 239,732.21 | | 153,857,544.35 |
| 1893 | 1,670,643.50 | 125.00 | | | | | | 163,357.57 | | 161,004,989.67 |
| 1894 | 1,723,479.90 | 410.00 | | | | | | 151,045.79 | | 147,168,449.70 |
| 1895 | 1,409,211.18 | | | | | | | 166,804.55 | | 143,246,077.75 |
| 1896 | 1,219,432.46 | 22.50 | | | | | | 134,710.57 | | 146,830,615.66 |
| 1897 | 1,034,129.60 | | | | | | | 114,958.17 | 18,992.38 | 146,619,593.47 |
| 1898 | 1,315,780.54 | 114.90 | | 46,973.00 | | | | 135,750.07 | 16,515.55 | 170,866,819.36 |
| 1899 | 1,956,618.56 | | | 4,921,593.21 | | | | 166,576.25 | 25,489.04 | 273,484,573.44 |
| 1900 | 2,543,785.18 | 145.25 | | 4,515,640.85 | | | | 183,721.46 | 24,303.94 | 295,316,107.57 |

| Year | | | | | | | | | | | |
|---|---|---|---|---|---|---|---|---|---|---|---|
| 1901 | 2,518,101.44 | | | | | | | 4,165,735.14 | 185,867.83 | 21,259.00 | 306,871,669.42 |
| 1902 | 2,944,492.46 | | | | | | | 4,262,902.32 | 208,209.05 | 6,504.78 | 271,867,990.25 |
| 1903 | 736,783.31 | | | | | | | | 148,411.07 | 148,411.07 | 230,740,925.22 |
| 1904 | 484,097.45 | | | | | | | | 206,988.55 | 1,059,334.41 | 232,903,781.06 |
| 1905 | 605,478.81 | | | | | | | | 228,594.73 | 214,901.66 | 234,187,976.37 |
| 1906 | 570,037.93 | | | | | | | | 283,991.62 | 178,996.00 | 291,102,738.00 |
| 1907 | 887,641.31 | | | | | | | | 253,652.48 | 158,251.81 | 289,684,022.85 |
| 1908 | 954,304.96 | | | | | | | | 241,680.16 | 184,709.58 | 251,665,960.04 |
| 1909 | 902,197.31 | | | | | | | | 411,987.53 | 180,826.38 | 246,212,719.22 |
| 1910 | 1,099,502.84 | | | | | | | | 434,705.95 | 177,471.33 | 289,957,220.16 |
| 1911 | 1,000,214.79 | 847.00 | | | | | | | 597,416.58 | 181,069.12 | 322,526,299.73 |
| 1912 | 1,128,707.25 | | | | | | | | 856,407.83 | 180,876.32 | 321,615,894.69 |
| 1913 | 1,259,887.67 | | | | | | | | 401,910.26 | 165,216.09 | 344,424,453.85 |
| 1914 | 1,325,219.13 | 738.00 | | | | | | | 284,501.61 | 136,523.78 | 380,008,893.96 |
| 1915 | 1,685,256.95 | 250,474.74 | | | | | | | 379,288.93 | 151,232.64 | 415,681,023.86 |
| 1916 | 1,485,970.72 | 245,072.07 | | 4,967,179.18 | | | | | 458,772.77 | 154,522.68 | 512,723,287.77 |
| 1917 | 1,496,720.02 | 277,165.03 | $10,471,688.90 | 6,908,108.21 | | | | | 871,606.22 | 124,184.74 | 809,393,640.44 |
| 1918 | 2,336,907.00 | 185,358.93 | 24,996,204.54 | 5,237,043.97 | $26,357,338.80 | $2,259,036.57 | | | 985,219.86 | 172,723.03 | 3,698,935,830.93 |
| 1919 | 2,791,831.08 | 726,136.79 | 28,775,749.66 | 2,691,866.87 | 50,919,668.42 | 4,072,548.59 | | | | 1,635,587.28 | 3,850,150,078.56 |
| 1920 | 3,728,276.05 | 1,514,229.50 | 93,020,420.50 | 9,913,280.85 | 76,720,555.43 | 5,196,001.31 | $641,029.34 | | | 3,128,779.41 | 5,407,580,231.81 |
| 1921 | 2,986,465.35 | 1,170,316.32 | 81,525,652.88 | 8,585,540.11 | 89,730,832.94 | 6,159,817.69 | 2,152,357.45 | | | 1,670,649.23 | 4,595,000,765.74 |
| 1922 | 2,121,079.68 | 1,269,089.90 | 80,612,239.80 | 8,662,759.89 | 73,384,955.61 | 6,615,633.92 | 1,979,585.94 | | | [10]3,899,646.42 | [10]3,197,451,083.00 |

[7] Including special taxes relating to manufacture and sale.

[8] After the fiscal year 1918, all penalties are included with other receipts from the respective taxes to which they relate.

[9] Including for fiscal year 1903 receipts from sundry taxes repealed by the act of Apr. 12, 1902 (war-revenue repeal act), and for 1919, 1920, 1921, and 1922 receipts from tax on adulterated and process or renovated butter, and mixed flour, and receipts which remained unclassified at the time the statistical tables were compiled.

[10] Includes internal revenue collected through customs offices amounting to $495,559.43.

TABLE N.—Internal revenue receipts, by States and Territories, for the fiscal years 1921 and 1922.

| States and Territories. | Income and profits taxes. 1921 | Income and profits taxes. 1922 | Miscellaneous internal revenue. 1921 [1] | Miscellaneous internal revenue. 1922 [2] | Total. 1921 | Total. 1922 | Per cent decrease. |
|---|---|---|---|---|---|---|---|
| Alabama | $14,222,196.12 | $9,009,980.66 | $4,207,335.29 | $2,454,200.10 | $18,429,531.41 | $11,464,180.76 | 37.8 |
| Alaska | 279,821.67 | 173,787.12 | 113,115.46 | 90,444.90 | 392,937.13 | 264,232.02 | 32.8 |
| Arizona | 2,784,941.73 | 1,427,375.40 | 1,417,721.69 | 713,859.52 | 4,202,663.42 | 2,141,234.92 | 59.1 |
| Arkansas | 8,228,325.73 | 5,334,259.50 | 2,335,942.26 | 1,642,785.56 | 10,564,467.99 | 6,979,045.06 | 33.9 |
| California | 129,170,961.21 | 92,251,113.85 | 53,078,378.13 | 39,401,742.04 | 182,249,339.34 | 131,652,855.89 | 27.8 |
| Colorado | 25,085,242.95 | 14,545,632.75 | 9,129,720.31 | 5,411,017.93 | 34,214,963.26 | 19,956,650.68 | 41.7 |
| Connecticut | 49,208,464.34 | 27,245,125.42 | 22,394,497.21 | 22,979,517.53 | 71,603,071.55 | 50,224,645.95 | 29.9 |
| Delaware | 9,848,404.28 | 3,384,808.83 | 1,999,793.86 | 1,902,457.34 | 11,848,203.14 | 5,889,266.17 | 50.3 |
| District of Columbia | 8,654,914.26 | 10,521,286.04 | 10,880,655.64 | 7,333,400.12 | 18,934,969.90 | 17,854,686.16 | 5.7 |
| Florida | 10,108,633.94 | 8,433,602.21 | 6,368,900.15 | 5,886,255.07 | 16,476,054.09 | 14,319,857.23 | 13.1 |
| Georgia | 28,792,002.73 | 14,270,049.82 | 8,442,768.12 | 6,718,656.78 | 37,234,770.85 | 20,988,706.60 | 43.6 |
| Hawaii | 13,859,082.76 | 14,632,590.97 | 1,821,029.47 | 882,472.06 | 20,680,103.23 | 15,515,063.03 | 25.0 |
| Idaho | 3,493,317.45 | 1,372,636.22 | 1,122,441.47 | 739,232.79 | 4,617,761.92 | 2,111,881.01 | 54.3 |
| Illinois | 290,944,632.48 | 179,633,973.81 | 127,980,332.27 | 90,698,593.92 | 388,924,964.75 | 270,332,567.73 | 30.5 |
| Indiana | 49,809,541.01 | 30,715,323.47 | 28,348,905.39 | 22,317,076.08 | 78,158,446.40 | 53,032,399.55 | 32.1 |
| Iowa | 28,893,632.48 | 17,046,702.88 | 8,852,113.51 | 6,612,026.31 | 37,745,745.99 | 23,658,789.19 | 37.3 |
| Kansas | 26,873,519.31 | 22,242,152.01 | 11,813,002.37 | 8,137,460.68 | 38,689,551.68 | 30,379,621.69 | 21.5 |
| Kentucky | 25,091,391.05 | 16,285,993.78 | 25,694,878.78 | 16,836,292.43 | 50,690,269.84 | 33,122,196.21 | 34.7 |
| Louisiana | 29,242,438.18 | 15,477,826.58 | 10,878,658.40 | 7,276,131.32 | 40,121,096.58 | 22,733,957.90 | 43.3 |
| Maine | 14,459,568.04 | 10,989,939.85 | 3,579,296.05 | 3,814,388.22 | 18,038,864.09 | 14,804,208.07 | 17.9 |
| Maryland | 44,948,063.92 | 29,070,268.90 | 27,323,480.01 | 16,901,667.66 | 72,271,543.93 | 45,971,936.56 | 36.4 |
| Massachusetts | 214,058,413.88 | 130,189,292.05 | 45,806,799.97 | 39,633,001.46 | 259,865,213.95 | 169,813,493.51 | 34.7 |
| Michigan | 184,494,529.82 | 112,258,181.64 | 87,889,763.89 | 89,616,002.86 | 272,384,284.71 | 201,874,184.50 | 25.9 |
| Minnesota | 53,886,224.54 | 30,297,528.71 | 23,835,933.26 | 15,565,114.17 | 77,722,157.80 | 46,253,942.88 | 40.5 |
| Mississippi | 7,244,977.45 | 3,405,262.01 | 1,751,594.50 | 1,555,235.49 | 8,995,571.95 | 4,640,497.50 | 48.4 |
| Missouri | 86,121,595.25 | 55,035,012.61 | 40,012,071.35 | 32,421,475.49 | 125,133,666.60 | 87,456,488.10 | 30.7 |
| Montana | 3,925,062.65 | 9,215,553.66 | 1,521,502.87 | 1,129,830.32 | 5,446,565.52 | 3,432,162.06 | 37.0 |
| Nebraska | 15,828,609.66 | 9,215,053.66 | 7,854,399.06 | 6,045,837.69 | 23,683,008.72 | 15,261,390.75 | 35.6 |
| Nevada | 718,136.11 | 564,023.45 | 489,696.80 | 273,522.94 | 1,207,832.91 | 837,546.39 | 30.7 |
| New Hampshire | 8,304,563.93 | 4,311,758.90 | 2,016,702.04 | 1,598,240.32 | 10,321,265.97 | 5,909,999.22 | 42.7 |
| New Jersey | 97,301,062.92 | 67,766,027.83 | 46,029,573.83 | 39,383,311.18 | 143,411,636.75 | 107,149,339.01 | 25.3 |
| New Mexico | 1,306,243.22 | 811,595.86 | 467,928.64 | 419,114.68 | 1,774,171.86 | 1,230,700.50 | 30.6 |
| New York | 814,734,708.37 | 527,695,268.75 | 310,736,065.77 | 252,077,508.69 | 1,125,472,774.14 | 779,772,777.44 | 30.7 |
| North Carolina | 38,664,722.96 | 23,179,559.81 | 86,225,776.10 | 99,233,769.53 | 124,890,499.06 | 122,413,329.34 | 2.0 |
| North Dakota | 2,072,432.20 | 1,163,686.83 | 971,473.53 | 748,052.55 | 3,043,905.73 | 1,911,739.38 | 37.2 |
| Ohio | 203,847,472.40 | 128,898,272.31 | 81,821,061.05 | 63,403,407.65 | 285,668,533.45 | 192,301,679.96 | 32.6 |
| Oklahoma | 21,637,304.77 | 14,276,549.14 | 5,932,338.35 | 4,125,903.43 | 27,569,643.12 | 18,402,452.57 | 33.3 |
| Oregon | 21,973,313.00 | 14,934,997.18 | 6,152,662.16 | 3,857,192.08 | 28,135,975.16 | 18,792,189.26 | 33.2 |

| | | | | | | |
|---|---|---|---|---|---|---|
| Pennsylvania | 351,737,751.22 | 245,798,087.82 | 137,320,349.21 | 90,909,954.76 | 489,055,100.43 | 336,708,042.58 | 31.2 |
| Rhode Island | 36,086,774.07 | 19,992,123.36 | 6,173,120.74 | 15,751,583.62 | 42,259,894.81 | 35,743,706.98 | 15.4 |
| South Carolina | 26,032,367.96 | 9,699,041.79 | 2,578,255.41 | 1,748,343.48 | 28,610,623.37 | 11,447,385.27 | 60.0 |
| South Dakota | 3,646,484.22 | 1,613,613.83 | 1,400,617.49 | 921,880.22 | 5,049,101.71 | 2,565,444.05 | 49.2 |
| Tennessee | 25,606,805.43 | 14,174,092.51 | 8,762,315.28 | 7,620,584.42 | 34,369,120.71 | 21,794,676.93 | 36.6 |
| Texas | 52,190,451.75 | 34,975,009.92 | 26,035,822.38 | 17,369,665.81 | 78,226,274.13 | 52,347,675.73 | 33.1 |
| Utah | 7,116,197.70 | 2,971,391.01 | 3,458,651.43 | 2,159,096.25 | 10,574,849.13 | 5,130,487.26 | 51.5 |
| Vermont | 4,803,370.92 | 2,957,106.08 | 1,554,825.12 | 1,160,190.15 | 6,358,196.04 | 4,157,296.23 | 34.6 |
| Virginia | 31,394,403.02 | 18,577,380.51 | 30,239,938.09 | 28,018,263.18 | 61,854,341.11 | 46,305,648.69 | 24.7 |
| Washington | 29,221,005.72 | 18,733,630.39 | 7,201,197.86 | 4,877,151.88 | 36,422,203.58 | 23,610,782.27 | 35.2 |
| West Virginia | 35,819,848.89 | 27,961,834.15 | 6,039,021.07 | 5,490,603.44 | 41,878,872.96 | 33,432,437.59 | 20.1 |
| Wisconsin | 57,131,042.40 | 36,879,538.91 | 17,178,896.80 | 13,509,067.25 | 74,309,939.20 | 50,488,606.16 | 32.1 |
| Wyoming | 2,537,052.67 | 1,547,897.02 | 713,298.44 | 531,661.15 | 3,250,361.11 | 2,079,558.17 | 36.0 |
| Philippine Islands | | | 945,859.66 | 457,430.29 | 945,859.66 | 457,430.29 | 51.6 |
| Total | 3,228,137,673.75 | 2,086,918,464.85 | 1,366,863,091.99 | 1,110,532,618.15 | 4,595,000,765.74 | 3,197,451,083.00 | 30.4 |

1 Does not include $356,296.21 internal revenue collected through customs offices.
2 Includes $495,559.43 internal revenue collected through customs offices.

NOTE.—Internal revenue stamp sales by postmasters for Alaska are included in amount reported for the State of Washington and for District of Columbia in amount reported for the State of Maryland.

TABLE O.—*Merchandise imported and customs duties collected from 1890 to 1921, and recapitulation from 1867 to 1921.*

[By schedules of the respective tariffs in force from 1890 to 1921.]

| Year ended— | SCHEDULE A.—Chemicals, oils, and paints. | | | SCHEDULE B.—Earths, earthenware, and glassware. | | | SCHEDULE C.—Metals, and manufactures of. | | | SCHEDULE D.—Wood, and manufactures of. | | |
|---|---|---|---|---|---|---|---|---|---|---|---|---|
| | Values. | Duties collected. | Average ad valorem rates. | Values. | Duties collected. | Average ad valorem rates. | Values. | Duties collected. | Average ad valorem rates. | Values. | Duties collected. | Average ad valorem rates. |
| | | | *Per cent.* | | | *Per cent.* | | | *Per cent.* | | | *Per cent.* |
| June 30: | | | | | | | | | | | | |
| 1890 | $21,865,347 | $7,006,211 | 32.04 | $14,362,557 | $8,221,583 | 57.24 | $48,460,028 | $17,131,406 | 35.35 | $9,873,687 | $1,856,577 | 16.07 |
| 1891 | 20,052,010 | 6,086,113 | 30.35 | 22,716,823 | 10,946,381 | 48.19 | 68,788,174 | 23,109,252 | 33.59 | 12,074,128 | 2,052,392 | 17.00 |
| 1892 | 18,980,722 | 5,963,770 | 31.40 | 23,734,881 | 12,131,725 | 51.11 | 42,449,094 | 21,507,930 | 50.67 | 11,753,621 | 1,942,175 | 16.52 |
| 1893 | 20,973,252 | 6,429,758 | 30.36 | 23,836,492 | 12,438,327 | 52.18 | 47,556,663 | 27,248,271 | 57.30 | 12,245,089 | 1,759,944 | 14.37 |
| 1894 | 13,951,923 | 4,649,309 | 33.32 | 10,877,496 | 5,933,326 | 52.93 | 30,271,453 | 17,791,784 | 58.77 | 9,393,008 | 1,289,544 | 13.73 |
| 1895 | 18,623,919 | 5,575,075 | 29.94 | 22,285,374 | 8,324,735 | 37.36 | 33,168,037 | 14,929,358 | 45.01 | 3,218,450 | 679,907 | 21.13 |
| 1896 | 18,697,067 | 5,619,239 | 28.53 | 22,871,366 | 8,065,292 | 35.26 | 34,853,090 | 13,232,162 | 37.97 | 1,794,888 | 412,644 | 22.99 |
| 1897 | 19,003,638 | 5,440,024 | 28.63 | 21,166,515 | 7,605,169 | 35.93 | 23,603,665 | 8,955,132 | 37.94 | 1,485,479 | 339,974 | 22.88 |
| 1898 | 19,513,037 | 6,146,884 | 31.50 | 15,192,178 | 7,387,433 | 48.63 | 18,847,123 | 8,454,288 | 44.86 | 5,341,083 | 1,205,278 | 22.57 |
| 1899 | 21,570,616 | 7,009,695 | 32.50 | 17,244,220 | 8,863,349 | 51.40 | 18,152,727 | 7,809,281 | 43.02 | 7,508,420 | 1,671,048 | 22.08 |
| 1900 | 26,955,991 | 8,184,044 | 30.36 | 20,090,172 | 10,106,541 | 50.31 | 29,089,333 | 11,280,853 | 38.78 | 11,711,446 | 2,351,940 | 20.08 |
| 1901 | 26,414,360 | 7,415,496 | 28.07 | 20,166,399 | 10,301,486 | 51.08 | 28,631,743 | 10,922,077 | 38.15 | 10,635,183 | 2,049,457 | 19.27 |
| 19 Ǫ | 29,991,974 | 8,499,709 | 28.34 | 21,424,011 | 11,365,381 | 53.05 | 38,870,207 | 14,973,244 | 38.52 | 14,556,267 | 2,572,527 | 17.67 |
| 1903 | 31,249,644 | 8,989,673 | 28.74 | 25,735,463 | 13,321,181 | 51.76 | 65,164,750 | 22,368,210 | 34.33 | 16,659,208 | 2,814,734 | 16.90 |
| 1904 | 30,808,543 | 8,813,962 | 28.61 | 24,704,368 | 13,163,258 | 53.28 | 40,011,304 | 15,682,484 | 39.20 | 14,449,585 | 2,463,948 | 17.05 |
| 1905 | 31,010,996 | 8,845,176 | 28.52 | 23,126,296 | 12,193,546 | 52.73 | 36,327,218 | 14,448,673 | 39.77 | 16,707,735 | 2,750,017 | 16.46 |
| 1906 | 33,481,921 | 9,664,910 | 28.87 | 26,589,979 | 13,749,020 | 51.71 | 50,917,147 | 18,763,616 | 36.86 | 22,760,988 | 3,650,271 | 16.04 |
| 19 Ǫ | 40,246,137 | 11,124,083 | 27.64 | 31,306,009 | 15,350,019 | 49.03 | 67,148,963 | 21,682,145 | 32.59 | 16,472,483 | 3,701,201 | 15.12 |
| 1908 | 39,127,306 | 10,530,174 | 26.91 | 26,229,241 | 15,250,558 | 50.53 | 45,279,789 | 16,903,780 | 35.31 | 23,349,683 | 3,301,256 | 14.14 |
| 19 Ọ | 42,936,600 | 11,217,784 | 26.13 | 21,148,142 | 10,641,572 | 50.33 | 41,103,417 | 15,655,102 | 38.09 | 23,285,336 | 3,140,844 | 13.49 |
| 1910 | 42,021,558 | 11,072,239 | 26.41 | 24,774,351 | 12,467,509 | 50.33 | 66,960,781 | 22,333,344 | 33.35 | 27,489,155 | 3,184,697 | 11.59 |
| 1911 | 45,989,382 | 11,563,788 | 25.71 | 24,486,258 | 12,669,182 | 51.72 | 53,757,341 | 18,969,321 | 32.11 | 24,700,532 | 2,959,669 | 11.98 |
| 1912 | 47,235,641 | 12,233,742 | 25.36 | 21,994,265 | 11,156,221 | 50.72 | 50,491,870 | 17,346,221 | 31.90 | 23,414,943 | 3,042,834 | 12.46 |
| 1913 | 49,386,692 | 13,017,094 | 26.36 | 23,601,873 | 11,385,195 | 49.50 | 64,299,772 | 20,513,674 | 24.02 | 27,851,245 | 3,408,227 | 12.24 |
| 1914 | 60,314,179 | 13,099,963 | 21.72 | 25,222,093 | 10,187,128 | 40.39 | 50,742,814 | 12,190,222 | 21.96 | 12,181,772 | 1,618,723 | 13.29 |
| 1915 | 54,098,081 | 11,221,795 | 20.74 | 14,656,909 | 6,804,909 | 37.51 | 31,835,773 | 6,990,064 | 18.98 | 4,456,846 | 1,708,531 | 15.90 |
| 1916 | 52,806,178 | 9,309,151 | 17.63 | 13,023,527 | 4,676,615 | 35.91 | 33,244,863 | 6,908,568 | 20.75 | 4,583,269 | 659,795 | 14.40 |
| 1917 | 65,613,701 | 12,056,119 | 18.37 | 13,530,965 | 4,613,852 | 34.10 | 33,913,977 | 7,038,419 | 20.51 | 5,207,265 | 756,236 | 14.52 |
| 1918 | 65,762,304 | 10,507,121 | 15.98 | 13,444,272 | 4,706,906 | 35.01 | 33,227,040 | 6,813,460 | | 4,411,540 | 635,840 | 14.41 |
| Dec. 31: | | | | | | | | | | | | |
| 1918 (6 months) | 27,215,615 | 4,307,849 | 15.83 | 5,783,586 | 2,064,736 | 35.71 | 16,621,637 | 3,450,648 | 20.76 | 1,674,678 | 217,514 | 12.99 |
| 1919 | 108,150,726 | 13,922,389 | 12.87 | 14,032,336 | 5,009,456 | 33.55 | 43,185,823 | 8,671,888 | 20.08 | 6,090,259 | 851,797 | 13.99 |
| 1920 | 120,319,609 | 15,335,010 | 12.75 | 30,256,646 | 9,240,533 | 30.54 | 83,337,492 | 16,676,983 | 20.01 | 13,366,877 | 1,978,931 | 14.80 |
| 1921 | 64,753,030 | 14,143,735 | 21.84 | 28,591,086 | 9,894,043 | 34.50 | 62,792,649 | 13,671,791 | 21.77 | 9,894,212 | 1,546,231 | 15.63 |

| Year ended— | SCHEDULE E.—Sugar, molasses, and manufactures of. | | | SCHEDULE F.—Tobacco, and manufactures of. | | | SCHEDULE G.—Agricultural products and provisions. | | | SCHEDULE H.—Spirits, wines, and other beverages. | | |
|---|---|---|---|---|---|---|---|---|---|---|---|---|
| | Values. | Duties collected. | Average ad valorem rates. | Values. | Duties collected. | Average ad valorem rates. | Values. | Duties collected. | Average ad valorem rates. | Values. | Duties collected. | Average ad valorem rates. |
| June 30: | | | *Per cent.* | | | *Per cent.* | | | *Per cent.* | | | *Per cent.* |
| 1890 | $87,613,335 | $55,168,658 | 62.97 | $16,626,045 | $13,317,367 | 80.10 | $37,298,471 | $10,647,676 | 28.55 | $12,499,327 | $8,506,503 | 68.54 |
| 1891 | 43,057,639 | 32,511,296 | 75.51 | 21,065,983 | 16,172,277 | 76.77 | 46,560,858 | 14,275,401 | 30.66 | 13,572,368 | 9,547,548 | 70.33 |
| 1892 | 659,153 | 128,900 | 19.56 | 10,150,633 | 10,285,067 | 101.13 | 34,579,463 | 11,063,116 | 31.99 | 12,717,443 | 8,828,333 | 69.50 |
| 1893 | 1,328,999 | 193,294 | 14.54 | 12,589,004 | 14,831,989 | 117.82 | 38,427,051 | 12,735,144 | 33.14 | 13,921,436 | 9,435,263 | 67.77 |
| 1894 | 1,955,360 | 273,764 | 14.00 | 11,289,510 | 13,668,906 | 121.06 | 28,422,078 | 9,562,098 | 33.64 | 10,160,219 | 7,063,170 | 69.12 |
| 1895 | 39,228,916 | 15,600,529 | 39.77 | 10,725,299 | 14,916,305 | 109.10 | 37,733,091 | 9,925,557 | 26.30 | 11,285,766 | 7,068,176 | 62.63 |
| 1896 | 73,094,318 | 29,910,006 | 40.94 | 13,025,272 | 14,839,117 | 109.03 | 34,175,778 | 7,721,677 | 22.59 | 11,287,894 | 6,859,390 | 60.77 |
| 1897 | 98,283,469 | 41,346,400 | 42.07 | 18,782,759 | 20,971,882 | 111.66 | 33,716,953 | 8,613,987 | 25.55 | 11,890,430 | 8,136,011 | 68.48 |
| 1898 | 38,330,580 | 29,695,301 | 77.47 | 8,225,482 | 9,916,183 | 120.55 | 29,853,286 | 11,608,121 | 38.88 | 9,319,646 | 6,026,697 | 64.66 |
| 1899 | 81,227,498 | 61,660,942 | 75.91 | 9,371,597 | 10,627,399 | 113.40 | 32,505,236 | 12,743,785 | 39.21 | 11,072,774 | 7,490,074 | 67.64 |
| 1900 | 80,890,937 | 57,823,285 | 71.48 | 13,597,162 | 14,382,305 | 105.77 | 35,762,588 | 13,183,635 | 36.80 | 12,897,506 | 8,329,650 | 63.45 |
| 1901 | 87,079,079 | 63,089,412 | 72.45 | 15,065,501 | 16,655,744 | 110.63 | 38,566,704 | 13,043,820 | 33.82 | 14,099,924 | 9,533,524 | 67.61 |
| 1902 | 61,116,367 | 53,040,877 | 86.79 | 16,331,536 | 18,756,035 | 114.85 | 43,632,461 | 16,012,639 | 36.66 | 15,367,757 | 10,562,022 | 68.73 |
| 1903 | 65,959,060 | 63,625,731 | 96.46 | 18,298,780 | 21,891,687 | 119.63 | 46,221,428 | 16,282,144 | 35.23 | 16,734,608 | 11,646,532 | 69.39 |
| 1904 | 77,898,029 | 58,132,347 | 74.65 | 17,875,683 | 21,176,293 | 118.46 | 49,013,792 | 16,880,988 | 34.46 | 17,120,014 | 12,105,795 | 70.71 |
| 1905 | 91,577,274 | 51,442,112 | 56.17 | 20,725,297 | 22,689,611 | 109.48 | 47,570,416 | 15,415,334 | 32.41 | 17,912,332 | 12,347,930 | 70.05 |
| 1906 | 86,733,491 | 52,648,986 | 61.12 | 22,917,352 | 23,927,700 | 104.41 | 53,868,946 | 18,126,575 | 33.65 | 19,669,398 | 14,009,516 | 71.22 |
| 1907 | 92,784,081 | 60,333,323 | 65.03 | 29,959,081 | 26,125,037 | 87.20 | 63,720,855 | 19,203,886 | 30.14 | 23,063,420 | 16,318,120 | 70.69 |
| 1908 | 93,626,684 | 50,168,155 | 59.99 | 26,495,243 | 22,160,089 | 83.64 | 69,609,535 | 21,618,559 | 31.06 | 21,419,770 | 15,213,045 | 71.02 |
| 1909 | 93,478,607 | 56,414,434 | 60.35 | 27,332,038 | 23,289,458 | 85.11 | 71,719,009 | 23,633,333 | 32.95 | 23,381,943 | 16,144,031 | 69.05 |
| 1910 | 101,586,708 | 53,105,357 | 52.28 | 29,581,409 | 24,124,239 | 81.55 | 84,872,747 | 25,160,516 | 29.64 | 25,315,878 | 18,113,512 | 71.55 |
| 1911 | 97,877,463 | 52,909,371 | 53.05 | 29,788,180 | 26,159,615 | 87.82 | 105,974,044 | 28,744,265 | 27.12 | 20,334,301 | 17,298,838 | 84.99 |
| 1912 | 105,744,519 | 50,951,199 | 48.18 | 31,116,052 | 25,571,508 | 82.18 | 117,711,156 | 34,146,071 | 29.01 | 20,731,253 | 17,409,815 | 83.98 |
| 1913 | 91,447,551 | 53,431,801 | 58.48 | 32,437,743 | 26,748,124 | 82.46 | 99,798,484 | 27,454,576 | 27.51 | 21,372,476 | 19,475,362 | 87.05 |
| 1914 | 108,255,115 | 61,870,457 | 57.15 | 32,332,229 | 26,892,273 | 83.17 | 122,304,972 | 24,874,322 | 20.29 | 21,765,994 | 19,674,992 | 90.40 |
| 1915 | 157,570,801 | 49,607,651 | 31.48 | 29,499,102 | 24,875,246 | 84.33 | 87,672,955 | 18,035,830 | 20.57 | 14,392,643 | 13,404,931 | 93.14 |
| 1916 | 205,512,242 | 55,875,639 | 27.19 | 30,195,472 | 27,580,585 | 91.34 | 94,673,995 | 16,164,123 | 17.08 | 14,330,417 | 13,550,582 | 89.73 |
| 1917 | 243,354,335 | 55,471,364 | 22.79 | 37,289,651 | 29,837,013 | 79.99 | 132,717,946 | 17,916,075 | 13.50 | 18,611,977 | 13,586,271 | 73.00 |
| 1918 | 240,380,144 | 49,092,779 | 20.42 | 31,963,105 | 21,960,646 | 68.76 | 125,359,740 | 14,594,871 | 11.64 | 10,563,410 | 7,038,123 | 66.63 |
| Dec. 31: | | | | | | | | | | | | |
| 1918 (6 months) | 87,179,747 | 18,249,994 | 20.93 | 20,308,623 | 12,269,984 | 60.42 | 49,322,271 | 5,546,942 | 11.25 | 3,109,079 | 1,628,191 | 52.37 |
| 1919 | 337,282,529 | 68,608,819 | 17.72 | 51,609,315 | 27,562,571 | 53.41 | 161,165,393 | 15,802,553 | 9.80 | 2,338,327 | 1,194,499 | 51.08 |
| 1920 | 926,467,270 | 79,536,137 | 8.58 | 63,315,739 | 33,695,003 | 52.80 | 253,569,428 | 24,521,305 | 9.67 | 2,542,570 | 1,157,483 | 45.52 |
| 1921 | 233,451,028 | 71,325,054 | 30.51 | 66,614,395 | 35,949,905 | 53.81 | 156,495,923 | 26,206,159 | 16.11 | 3,197,179 | 1,514,604 | 47.37 |

Table O.—*Merchandise imported and customs duties collected from 1890 to 1921, etc.*—Continued.

| Year ended— | Schedule I.—Cotton manufactures. | | | Schedule J.—Flax, hemp, and jute, and manufactures of. | | | Schedule K.—Wool, and manufactures of. | | | Schedule L.—Silk, and silk goods. | | |
|---|---|---|---|---|---|---|---|---|---|---|---|---|
| | Values. | Duties collected. | Average ad valorem rates. | Values. | Duties collected. | Average ad valorem rates. | Values. | Duties collected. | Average ad valorem rates. | Values. | Duties collected. | Average ad valorem rates. |
| | | | *Per cent.* | | | *Per cent.* | | | *Per cent.* | | | *cent.* |
| **June 30:** | | | | | | | | | | | | |
| 1890 | $29,312,025 | $11,691,611 | 39.89 | $48,325,898 | $12,219,836 | 25.29 | $70,375,615 | $42,918,996 | 60.99 | $33,246,787 | $18,945,959 | 49.54 |
| 1891 | 20,197,123 | 9,892,223 | 48.98 | 38,784,230 | 15,034,834 | 38.77 | 60,305,714 | 41,410,169 | 68.67 | 37,300,387 | 19,388,764 | 51.93 |
| 1892 | 17,162,325 | 9,468,347 | 55.52 | 40,025,471 | 17,360,296 | 43.37 | 53,498,633 | 42,096,021 | 78.69 | 31,442,180 | 16,965,637 | 53.96 |
| 1893 | 20,510,438 | 11,333,605 | 55.25 | 43,493,657 | 18,983,344 | 43.66 | 53,410,291 | 44,608,120 | 80.51 | 37,919,948 | 20,310,258 | 53.56 |
| 1894 | 13,724,012 | 7,446,758 | 54.26 | 28,060,445 | 12,174,473 | 43.39 | 24,798,231 | 21,200,283 | 85.49 | 24,160,529 | 12,824,094 | 53.08 |
| 1895 | 19,626,096 | 8,906,189 | 45.37 | 34,874,867 | 14,060,096 | 40.32 | 37,014,061 | 20,922,958 | 56.53 | 31,023,148 | 14,739,550 | 47.51 |
| 1896 | 21,275,403 | 9,311,340 | 43.76 | 29,736,618 | 12,018,082 | 40.39 | 48,352,585 | 23,127,569 | 47.83 | 26,627,731 | 12,504,005 | 46.96 |
| 1897 | 22,650,231 | 9,903,895 | 43.73 | 34,852,418 | 14,110,685 | 40.49 | 48,902,866 | 23,702,726 | 48.42 | 26,517,092 | 12,421,970 | 46.85 |
| 1898 | 14,663,418 | 7,500,252 | 51.15 | 33,704,889 | 15,712,121 | 46.62 | 18,360,631 | 13,057,164 | 71.12 | 22,639,597 | 12,231,681 | 54.03 |
| 1899 | 17,002,769 | 8,934,913 | 52.55 | 44,412,434 | 20,892,285 | 47.04 | 22,342,090 | 17,230,152 | 77.12 | 25,026,504 | 13,506,312 | 53.97 |
| 1900 | 20,654,578 | 10,565,562 | 51.08 | 54,732,531 | 25,701,451 | 46.96 | 30,656,717 | 21,637,428 | 70.58 | 30,358,771 | 15,771,795 | 51.95 |
| 1901 | 19,568,242 | 9,715,747 | 49.65 | 57,669,270 | 26,218,962 | 45.46 | 30,727,663 | 21,575,104 | 70.21 | 26,836,267 | 14,245,693 | 53.12 |
| 1902 | 21,129,139 | 10,422,930 | 49.33 | 68,133,003 | 30,694,894 | 45.05 | 35,363,788 | 26,396,923 | 74.64 | 32,242,228 | 17,293,290 | 53.64 |
| 1903 | 25,332,216 | 11,944,300 | 47.15 | 71,297,682 | 33,190,646 | 46.55 | 40,560,037 | 29,195,736 | 71.98 | 36,047,873 | 19,276,546 | 53.47 |
| 1904 | 23,442,254 | 11,035,018 | 47.07 | 71,460,146 | 32,898,495 | 46.04 | 39,962,848 | 27,252,492 | 68.19 | 31,483,007 | 16,610,210 | 52.78 |
| 1905 | 22,027,367 | 10,409,188 | 47.26 | 73,284,154 | 33,768,719 | 46.08 | 53,465,490 | 33,077,578 | 61.87 | 31,822,655 | 17,010,130 | 53.45 |
| 1906 | 26,656,366 | 12,292,890 | 46.12 | 92,055,269 | 41,777,068 | 45.38 | 63,265,115 | 37,968,695 | 60.02 | 32,591,910 | 17,351,095 | 53.24 |
| 1907 | 31,857,017 | 14,294,628 | 44.84 | 114,124,372 | 49,890,953 | 43.72 | 62,831,601 | 36,561,217 | 58.19 | 35,816,839 | 20,313,706 | 52.33 |
| 1908 | 31,577,132 | 13,878,022 | 43.95 | 91,209,596 | 41,921,732 | 43.59 | 45,822,498 | 28,845,245 | 62.95 | 31,755,212 | 16,493,078 | 51.94 |
| 1909 | 26,225,434 | 11,666,308 | 44.48 | 91,209,596 | 42,144,980 | 46.21 | 52,814,238 | 33,365,316 | 63.17 | 31,001,307 | 16,284,117 | 52.53 |
| 1910 | 28,310,523 | 13,619,191 | 48.11 | 105,374,854 | 49,735,027 | 46.15 | 70,745,252 | 41,904,850 | 59.23 | 32,295,926 | 17,023,622 | 52.71 |
| 1911 | 26,204,150 | 12,325,594 | 47.04 | 99,401,935 | 47,053,000 | 47.34 | 48,395,406 | 28,982,553 | 59.39 | 30,993,562 | 16,053,261 | 51.80 |
| 1912 | 24,355,360 | 11,085,150 | 45.51 | 106,698,102 | 49,662,348 | 44.14 | 45,361,374 | 27,072,116 | 55.98 | 29,571,610 | 13,695,229 | 51.54 |
| 1913 | 25,657,288 | 11,291,514 | 44.14 | 116,587,296 | 48,911,742 | 41.95 | 45,315,633 | 25,833,028 | 55.08 | 34,224,018 | 14,811,561 | 50.68 |
| 1914 | 32,529,134 | 9,290,408 | 28.47 | 56,470,796 | 19,913,016 | 35.26 | 39,434,523 | 16,917,341 | 43.10 | 34,089,755 | 15,376,702 | 45.17 |
| 1915 | 24,665,209 | 6,442,467 | 26.11 | 35,670,243 | 8,794,568 | 24.65 | 39,437,555 | 9,881,637 | 32.56 | 32,098,167 | 9,810,495 | 42.47 |
| 1916 | 24,244,523 | 5,988,827 | 24.62 | 30,943,574 | 8,619,140 | 27.85 | 18,332,968 | 6,128,567 | 33.43 | 32,304,619 | 11,927,952 | 42.14 |
| 1917 | 36,417,492 | 9,259,958 | 22.68 | 29,130,379 | 8,206,910 | 28.19 | 21,184,027 | 7,080,906 | 33.43 | 35,123,949 | 14,654,690 | 41.72 |
| 1918 | 30,946,531 | 6,871,746 | 22.21 | 29,587,130 | 7,199,925 | 27.08 | 27,047,896 | 8,956,449 | 33.11 | 24,473,609 | 10,066,714 | 41.13 |
| **Dec. 31:** | | | | | | | | | | | | |
| 1918 (6 months) | 13,622,237 | 3,105,547 | 22.80 | 10,873,228 | 2,682,414 | 24.67 | 9,826,501 | 2,962,190 | 30.14 | 10,748,947 | 4,307,698 | 40.08 |
| 1919 | 33,219,052 | 7,715,796 | 23.23 | 27,187,093 | 6,552,591 | 24.10 | 18,127,853 | 5,695,227 | 31.42 | 49,684,244 | 20,276,171 | 40.81 |
| 1920 | 89,274,578 | 21,185,002 | 23.73 | 52,925,870 | 13,362,335 | 25.25 | 49,800,160 | 16,720,378 | 33.57 | 55,793,487 | 21,772,950 | 39.02 |
| 1921 | 58,413,927 | 15,242,215 | 26.09 | 36,827,735 | 10,118,185 | 27.47 | 52,410,182 | 18,307,296 | 34.93 | 45,054,936 | 18,575,772 | 41.23 |

| Year ended— | SCHEDULE M.—Pulp, paper, and books. | | | SCHEDULE N.—Sundries. | | | Tea. | | |
|---|---|---|---|---|---|---|---|---|---|
| | Values. | Duties collected. | Average ad valorem rates. | Values. | Duties collected. | Average ad valorem rates. | Values. | Duties collected. | Average ad valorem rates. |
| | | | Per cent. | | | Per cent. | | | Per cent. |
| **June 30:** | | | | | | | | | |
| 1890 | $7,480,109 | $1,445,025 | 19.33 | $65,232,530 | $16,179,068 | 24.65 | | | |
| 1891 | 7,398,716 | 1,690,669 | 22.85 | 54,580,110 | 13,693,067 | 25.09 | | | |
| 1892 | 7,191,116 | 1,599,161 | 25.16 | 51,290,806 | 13,561,172 | 26.44 | | | |
| 1893 | 8,680,133 | 2,070,034 | 23.85 | 63,390,176 | 15,990,103 | 25.22 | | | |
| 1894 | 5,761,472 | 1,402,193 | 24.34 | 38,819,967 | 10,602,196 | 27.31 | | | |
| 1895 | 5,443,425 | 1,257,348 | 23.10 | 47,072,376 | 10,995,435 | 23.36 | | | |
| 1896 | 5,664,593 | 1,260,864 | 22.28 | 47,748,386 | 11,203,210 | 23.46 | | | |
| 1897 | 5,319,055 | 1,200,043 | 22.56 | 41,184,008 | 10,031,293 | 25.04 | | | |
| 1898 | 4,684,291 | 1,202,328 | 25.67 | 56,808,214 | 14,073,599 | 21.75 | $76,240 | $11,322 | 54.20 |
| 1899 | 5,223,698 | 1,349,575 | 25.84 | 66,420,324 | 16,272,012 | 24.50 | 6,631,988 | 4,812,607 | 72.57 |
| 1900 | 7,695,417 | 1,761,834 | 22.93 | 77,891,134 | 18,773,587 | 24.13 | 10,835,047 | 8,008,636 | 73.91 |
| 1901 | 7,021,206 | 1,702,776 | 24.25 | 76,193,074 | 17,912,848 | 23.51 | 10,005,430 | 8,259,353 | 82.55 |
| 1902 | 8,047,824 | 1,898,456 | 23.56 | 86,667,841 | 20,180,981 | 23.29 | 10,327,118 | 7,882,607 | 76.33 |
| 1903 | 9,907,819 | 2,220,756 | 22.28 | 98,422,646 | 20,843,433 | 21.18 | 3,028,168 | 2,178,278 | 71.93 |
| 1904 | 10,771,269 | 2,379,351 | 22.09 | 78,680,617 | 18,777,250 | 23.85 | | | |
| 1905 | 11,971,859 | 2,525,896 | 21.31 | 92,512,767 | 20,771,250 | 22.45 | | | |
| 1906 | 14,173,917 | 3,020,980 | 21.31 | 119,640,146 | 26,600,776 | 22.23 | | | |
| 1907 | 20,095,025 | 4,136,029 | 20.67 | 133,092,951 | 29,892,107 | 22.45 | | | |
| 1908 | 22,335,007 | 4,414,633 | 20.75 | 94,616,374 | 24,475,666 | 25.87 | | | |
| 1909 | 22,761,740 | 4,412,020 | 19.39 | 113,862,410 | 25,387,061 | 23.17 | | | |
| 1910 | 24,852,627 | 5,285,103 | 21.23 | 120,594,291 | 29,133,889 | 24.16 | | | |
| 1911 | 26,110,975 | 5,645,302 | 21.62 | 109,049,968 | 27,483,145 | 25.17 | | | |
| 1912 | 22,828,121 | 4,886,671 | 21.11 | 108,952,789 | 26,031,900 | 24.72 | | | |
| 1913 | 24,599,335 | 5,091,232 | 20.45 | 128,017,638 | 30,758,685 | 24.03 | | | |
| 1914 | 13,999,054 | 3,114,380 | 22.25 | 114,587,674 | 48,538,937 | 33.57 | | | |
| 1915 | 9,385,676 | 1,988,769 | 21.19 | 100,816,766 | 37,158,600 | 36.86 | | | |
| 1916 | 6,491,285 | 1,257,726 | 19.38 | 123,485,312 | 39,495,871 | 31.98 | | | |
| 1917 | 8,036,259 | 1,681,547 | 20.92 | 134,557,532 | 40,286,383 | 29.94 | | | |
| 1918 | 6,363,356 | 1,184,752 | 18.60 | 106,803,244 | 30,567,547 | 28.62 | | | |
| **Dec. 31:** | | | | | | | | | |
| 1918 (6 months) | 2,759,314 | 460,009 | 16.67 | 44,034,747 | 12,653,317 | 28.73 | | | |
| 1919 | 6,797,212 | 1,105,951 | 16.27 | 206,447,070 | 54,433,012 | 26.37 | | | |
| 1920 | 10,487,811 | 1,749,499 | 16.68 | 283,907,615 | 68,703,615 | 29.37 | | | |
| 1921 | 8,901,536 | 1,671,817 | 18.78 | 165,192,437 | 54,222,384 | 32.82 | | | |

TABLE O.—*Merchandise imported and customs duties collected from 1890 to 1921, etc.—Continued.*

[Recapitulation of merchandise imported and duties collected from 1867 to 1921.]

| Year ended— | Values. | | | | Amount of duties collected. | | | Average ad valorem rate of duty on— | |
|---|---|---|---|---|---|---|---|---|---|
| | Free. | Dutiable. | Total. | Free. | Ordinary. | Additional. | Total. | Dutiable. | Free and dutiable. |
| | | | | *Per cent.* | | | | *Per cent.* | *Per cent.* |
| **June 30:** | | | | | | | | | |
| 1867 | $17,033,130 | $361,125,553 | $378,158,683 | 4.50 | $168,503,750 | | $168,503,750 | 46.66 | 44.56 |
| 1868 | 15,147,618 | 329,661,302 | 344,808,920 | 4.39 | 160,309,941 | $222,833 | 160,532,779 | 48.63 | 46.56 |
| 1869 | 21,692,532 | 372,756,642 | 394,449,174 | 5.50 | 176,114,904 | 442,680 | 176,557,584 | 47.25 | 44.76 |
| 1870 | 20,214,105 | 426,131,905 | 426,346,010 | 4.74 | 191,221,709 | 292,205 | 191,513,974 | 47.08 | 44.92 |
| 1871 | 40,619,064 | 459,597,058 | 500,216,122 | 8.12 | 201,985,575 | 461,098 | 202,446,673 | 43.95 | 40.47 |
| 1872 | 47,683,747 | 512,735,287 | 560,419,034 | 8.51 | 212,030,727 | 588,378 | 212,619,105 | 41.35 | 37.94 |
| 1873 | 178,399,796 | 484,748,861 | 663,146,657 | 26.90 | 184,556,045 | 372,997 | 184,929,042 | 38.07 | 27.89 |
| 1874 | 151,694,834 | 415,748,693 | 567,443,527 | 26.73 | 160,185,383 | 336,902 | 160,522,285 | 38.53 | 28.29 |
| 1875 | 146,465,463 | 379,795,113 | 526,290,576 | 27.83 | 154,271,806 | 283,177 | 154,554,983 | 40.62 | 28.37 |
| 1876 | 140,561,381 | 324,024,926 | 464,586,307 | 30.26 | 144,982,442 | 206,161 | 145,178,603 | 44.74 | 31.25 |
| 1877 | 140,840,149 | 298,989,240 | 439,829,389 | 32.02 | 128,223,207 | 205,136 | 128,428,343 | 42.89 | 29.20 |
| 1878 | 141,339,059 | 297,083,409 | 438,422,468 | 32.24 | 127,015,183 | 179,974 | 127,195,159 | 42.75 | 29.01 |
| 1879 | 142,550,159 | 296,742,215 | 439,292,374 | 32.45 | 133,139,025 | 226,411 | 133,365,436 | 44.87 | 30.37 |
| 1880 | 208,049,180 | 419,506,091 | 627,555,271 | 33.15 | 182,415,162 | 332,492 | 182,747,654 | 43.48 | 29.12 |
| 1881 | 202,557,412 | 448,061,587 | 650,618,999 | 31.13 | 193,561,011 | 239,869 | 193,800,880 | 43.20 | 29.79 |
| 1882 | 210,721,981 | 505,491,937 | 716,213,918 | 29.42 | 215,617,669 | 521,247 | 216,138,916 | 42.66 | 30.18 |
| 1883 | 206,913,289 | 493,916,384 | 700,829,673 | 29.52 | 209,659,699 | 977,594 | 210,637,293 | 42.45 | 30.06 |
| 1884 | 211,280,265 | 456,295,124 | 667,575,389 | 31.65 | 189,944,995 | 437,841 | 190,282,836 | 41.61 | 28.50 |
| 1885 | 192,912,234 | 386,667,820 | 579,580,054 | 33.28 | 177,319,550 | 832,051 | 178,151,601 | 45.86 | 30.74 |
| 1886 | 211,530,759 | 413,775,055 | 625,305,814 | 33.83 | 188,379,397 | 1,031,051 | 189,410,448 | 45.53 | 30.29 |
| 1887 | 233,093,639 | 450,325,322 | 683,418,981 | 34.11 | 212,032,424 | 2,189,886 | 214,222,310 | 47.08 | 31.35 |
| 1888 | 244,104,852 | 468,143,774 | 712,248,626 | 34.27 | 213,509,802 | 2,532,454 | 216,042,256 | 45.61 | 30.33 |
| 1889 | 256,574,630 | 484,856,768 | 741,431,398 | 34.61 | 218,701,774 | 1,875,215 | 229,576,989 | 45.11 | 29.75 |
| 1890 | 266,103,048 | 507,571,764 | 773,674,812 | 34.39 | 225,317,076 | 1,222,961 | 226,540,037 | 44.39 | 29.28 |
| 1891 | 388,064,404 | 466,455,173 | 854,519,577 | 45.41 | 215,790,686 | 1,095,015 | 216,885,701 | 46.26 | 25.38 |
| 1892 | 458,074,604 | 355,526,741 | 813,601,345 | 56.30 | 173,097,670 | 1,026,600 | 174,124,270 | 48.69 | 21.40 |
| 1893 | 444,172,064 | 400,282,519 | 844,454,583 | 52.60 | 198,373,452 | 770,226 | 199,143,678 | 49.56 | 23.58 |
| 1894 | 378,968,717 | 257,645,703 | 636,614,420 | 59.53 | 128,881,868 | 677,021 | 129,558,892 | 50.03 | 20.35 |
| 1895 | 376,890,100 | 354,271,990 | 731,162,090 | 51.55 | 147,901,218 | 1,549,390 | 149,450,608 | 41.75 | 20.44 |
| 1896 | 368,897,523 | 390,796,561 | 759,694,084 | 48.56 | 156,104,598 | 908,908 | 157,013,506 | 39.95 | 20.67 |
| 1897 | 381,902,414 | 407,348,616 | 789,251,030 | 48.39 | 171,779,191 | 981,167 | 172,760,361 | 42.17 | 21.59 |
| 1898 | 291,534,005 | 295,619,695 | 587,153,700 | 49.65 | 144,268,963 | 1,179,822 | 145,433,353 | 48.80 | 24.77 |
| 1899 | 299,668,977 | 385,772,915 | 685,441,892 | 43.72 | 200,873,429 | 1,198,621 | 202,072,050 | 52.07 | 29.48 |
| 1900 | 366,759,922 | 463,759,330 | 830,519,252 | 44.16 | 228,364,556 | 996,215 | 229,360,771 | 49.24 | 27.62 |

| | | | | | | | | | |
|---|---|---|---|---|---|---|---|---|---|
| 1901 | 339,093,256 | 468,670,045 | 807,763,301 | 41.98 | 232,641,499 | 914,610 | 233,556,109 | 49.64 | 28.91 |
| 1902 | 396,542,233 | 503,251,521 | 899,793,754 | 44.07 | 250,550,428 | 902,727 | 251,453,155 | 49.79 | 27.95 |
| 1903 | 437,290,728 | 570,669,382 | 1,007,960,110 | 43.38 | 279,779,587 | 972,828 | 290,752,415 | 49.03 | 27.85 |
| 1904 | 454,153,100 | 527,681,459 | 981,834,559 | 46.36 | 257,392,055 | 830,188 | 238,222,243 | 48.78 | 26.30 |
| 1905 | 517,073,277 | 570,044,856 | 1,087,118,133 | 47.56 | 257,898,130 | 525,165 | 238,426,295 | 45.24 | 23.77 |
| 1906 | 548,695,764 | 664,721,885 | 1,213,417,619 | 45.22 | 283,557,983 | 352,412 | 283,910,396 | 44.16 | 24.22 |
| 1907 | 641,953,451 | 773,448,834 | 1,415,402,285 | 45.33 | 329,121,659 | 353,339 | 329,480,048 | 42.55 | 23.28 |
| 1908 | 525,704,745 | 657,415,920 | 1,183,120,665 | 44.43 | 282,273,432 | 309,462 | 282,382,894 | 42.94 | 23.88 |
| 1909 | 599,375,868 | 682,286,867 | 1,281,641,735 | 46.77 | 294,377,360 | 289,604 | 284,667,054 | 43.15 | 22.99 |
| 1910 | 761,353,117 | 785,756,020 | 1,517,409,137 | 49.21 | 325,263,095 | 295,588 | 325,561,683 | 41.52 | 21.11 |
| 911 | 776,963,955 | 750,981,697 | 1,527,945,652 | 50.85 | 309,581,944 | 383,748 | 309,965,692 | 41.22 | 20.29 |
| 1912 | 881,512,987 | 759,209,915 | 1,640,722,902 | 53.73 | 304,597,033 | 302,331 | 301,899,366 | 40.12 | 18.58 |
| 1913 | 986,972,333 | 779,717,079 | 1,766,689,412 | 55.57 | 312,252,215 | 257,731 | 312,509,946 | 40.05 | 17.69 |
| 1914 | 1,152,392,059 | 754,008,335 | 1,906,400,394 | 60.45 | 283,511,564 | 207,517 | 283,719,081 | 37.60 | 14.88 |
| 1915 | 1,032,863,558 | 615,522,722 | 1,618,386,280 | 62.66 | 205,755,073 | 191,769 | 205,946,842 | 33.43 | 12.49 |
| 1916 | 1,495,881,357 | 683,152,244 | 2,179,034,601 | 63.6 | 209,523,151 | 202,630 | 209,725,801 | 30.67 | 9.62 |
| 1917 | 1,852,530,538 | 814,689,485 | 2,607,220,021 | 69.46 | 221,447,743 | 211,323 | 209,659,066 | 27.18 | 8.31 |
| 1918 | 2,117,553,366 | 747,338,621 | 2,864,893,987 | 73.91 | 180,196,879 | 392,955 | 180,589,834 | 24.11 | 6.30 |
| Dec. 31: | | | | | | | | | |
| 1918 (6 months) | 1,149,881,796 | 303,079,210 | 1,432,961,006 | 79.14 | 73,907,033 | 21,037 | 73,928,070 | 21.39 | 5.09 |
| 1919 | 2,711,462,069 | 1,116,221,362 | 3,827,683,431 | 70.84 | 237,402,680 | 54,000 | 237,456,680 | 21.27 | 6.20 |
| 1920 | 3,115,953,238 | 1,985,865,155 | 5,101,823,393 | 61.08 | 325,635,175 | 10,390 | 325,645,565 | 16.40 | -6.38 |
| 1921 | 1,564,278,455 | 992,591,256 | 2,556,889,711 | 61.18 | 292,359,221 | 37,531 | 292,396,752 | 29.45 | 11.43 |

TABLE P.—Receipts from customs, internal revenue, and sales of public lands, collected in each State and Territory, by fiscal years, from 1879 to 1922.

| | 1879 | 1880 | 1881 | 1882 | 1883 | 1884 | 1885 | 1886 | 1887 |
|---|---|---|---|---|---|---|---|---|---|
| Alabama | $167,889.38 | $239,095.56 | $525,517.52 | $364,040.97 | $441,716.82 | $322,863.01 | $129,113.78 | $150,919.09 | $448,653.54 |
| Alaska | 1,437.18 | 11,950.50 | 12,188.63 | 11,046.66 | 12,856.52 | 1,645.40 | 1,298.09 | 1,276.42 | 3,637.56 |
| Arizona | 35,513.65 | 43,177.31 | 49,378.53 | 64,119.88 | 68,247.92 | 26,778.87 | 45,100.06 | 56,351.45 | 58,477.66 |
| Arkansas | 125,769.23 | 156,467.82 | 170,339.22 | 189,813.94 | 236,630.97 | 154,670.05 | 124,047.25 | 129,771.97 | 381,000.23 |
| California | 8,701,065.51 | 8,665,218.52 | 10,182,136.44 | 13,310,394.50 | 15,158,419.73 | 11,290,987.88 | 9,933,087.60 | 8,570,393.23 | 9,652,590.49 |
| Colorado | 161,295.21 | 234,381.54 | 341,736.22 | 384,978.90 | 576,713.87 | 550,890.08 | 521,462.10 | 648,083.49 | 824,689.96 |
| Connecticut | 837,327.63 | 1,020,624.69 | 934,653.14 | 985,299.21 | 930,751.23 | 749,818.70 | 814,020.39 | 1,026,898.53 | 979,848.80 |
| Delaware | 396,178.68 | 325,544.15 | 329,734.77 | 327,082.56 | 319,827.70 | 237,903.88 | 264,527.16 | 258,927.22 | 279,084.31 |
| District of Columbia | 8,073.34 | 9,496.37 | 15,038.47 | 19,117.71 | 20,199.12 | 22,610.43 | 20,209.33 | 20,182.07 | 25,750.29 |
| Florida | 514,737.99 | 431,987.22 | 680,861.35 | 910,710.67 | 928,635.54 | 1,059,558.65 | 865,608.61 | 911,381.81 | 1,121,863.47 |
| Georgia | 403,550.84 | 391,656.28 | 708,182.93 | 529,157.87 | 493,946.45 | 483,762.75 | 368,393.54 | 362,516.66 | 383,252.77 |
| Hawaii | | | | | | | | | |
| Idaho | 50,077.05 | 61,057.80 | 73,293.24 | 70,171.46 | 118,135.97 | 105,906.56 | 192,999.96 | 185,361.83 | 92,535.39 |
| Illinois | 20,987,306.27 | 25,255,416.51 | 28,392,529.02 | 31,612,815.78 | 30,116,920.23 | 27,423,313.79 | 27,245,398.54 | 27,876,503.49 | 29,419,788.86 |
| Indiana | 5,857,240.79 | 6,214,206.75 | 7,287,679.37 | 6,557,191.85 | 5,640,611.73 | 5,756,115.90 | 4,107,312.87 | 4,946,184.44 | 4,346,321.15 |
| Iowa | 849,810.54 | 851,598.86 | 926,988.11 | 1,842,642.05 | 4,073,267.66 | 2,738,063.13 | 2,227,623.98 | 2,551,472.20 | 1,953,888.89 |
| Kansas | 266,593.06 | 300,873.11 | 288,952.83 | 359,780.58 | 4,323,956.16 | 337,521.49 | 532,986.39 | 1,092,428.49 | 2,313,640.32 |
| Kentucky | 7,676,098.37 | 8,947,268.53 | 8,789,867.38 | 10,601,981.53 | 15,476,973.96 | 18,689,361.73 | 14,975,226.36 | 15,857,294.68 | 12,749,216.77 |
| Louisiana | 1,963,851.22 | 2,909,757.74 | 3,453,741.15 | 4,455,873.83 | 3,295,334.31 | 3,064,850.70 | 2,122,865.96 | 1,954,320.90 | 3,199,255.90 |
| Maine | 434,111.98 | 513,024.53 | 747,374.72 | 1,141,751.62 | 1,151,447.07 | 803,403.09 | 851,413.73 | 1,102,019.14 | 1,236,307.79 |
| Maryland | 4,289,289.07 | 5,452,618.00 | 5,501,323.86 | 5,861,639.65 | 6,511,788.14 | 5,453,007.65 | 4,798,491.45 | 5,021,756.03 | 5,907,860.08 |
| Massachusetts | 16,089,611.37 | 23,367,825.57 | 24,161,410.64 | 26,883,586.65 | 26,327,609.74 | 24,451,810.30 | 21,999,384.49 | 23,403,101.24 | 25,671,278.70 |
| Michigan | 1,932,615.84 | 2,178,280.21 | 2,581,095.16 | 3,478,285.30 | 2,745,281.34 | 2,059,207.81 | 1,932,526.34 | 2,148,961.70 | 2,465,565.64 |
| Minnesota | 423,928.48 | 460,022.69 | 705,131.12 | 1,003,022.36 | 1,826,871.72 | 1,522,030.07 | 821,098.11 | 873,211.38 | 1,251,299.87 |
| Mississippi | 94,744.79 | 105,250.73 | 135,669.30 | 376,495.42 | 521,736.61 | 181,319.22 | 71,179.19 | 92,506.01 | 211,652.35 |
| Missouri | 6,143,819.61 | 6,645,779.91 | 7,564,750.26 | 9,358,490.35 | 9,100,518.23 | 8,176,920.56 | 7,428,993.30 | 8,400,065.17 | 9,742,719.08 |
| Montana | 53,890.46 | 74,041.00 | 96,360.08 | 153,430.47 | 212,482.08 | 318,338.39 | 241,252.81 | 278,369.80 | 276,408.86 |
| Nebraska | 907,279.74 | 937,079.01 | 1,019,541.29 | 1,246,958.53 | 1,562,670.87 | 1,972,688.04 | 2,561,188.95 | 2,597,865.25 | 3,453,422.72 |
| Nevada | 79,214.66 | 90,395.47 | 77,079.30 | 64,991.85 | 48,237.70 | 9,745.50 | 58,861.53 | 65,591.81 | 74,499.01 |
| New Hampshire | 233,165.38 | 282,460.55 | 348,590.10 | 387,446.47 | 413,035.57 | 440,716.06 | 383,551.74 | 387,862.77 | 378,819.56 |
| New Jersey | 4,683,141.40 | 4,723,702.22 | 4,926,296.36 | 5,541,651.80 | 5,521,765.56 | 3,512,188.81 | 3,717,540.44 | 3,980,024.36 | 4,747,613.10 |
| New Mexico | 31,053.43 | 45,928.36 | 53,028.47 | 70,229.83 | 99,929.09 | 129,342.57 | 124,972.58 | 197,032.63 | 132,985.25 |
| New York | 114,622,587.92 | 150,013,869.49 | 159,192,279.65 | 175,029,428.41 | 168,375,869.68 | 150,703,978.52 | 142,092,275.56 | 149,904,950.01 | 164,463,276.07 |
| North Carolina | 2,469,947.91 | 2,410,043.59 | 2,549,328.27 | 3,020,667.52 | 2,500,879.75 | 1,828,064.32 | 1,716,222.34 | 1,769,461.09 | 1,974,538.69 |
| North Dakota | 151,000.23 | 124,368.75 | 2,334,217.98 | 99,707.71 | 1,882,659.31 | 3,706,292.30 | 1,981,558.59 | 1,167,573.25 | 1,650,455.60 |
| Ohio | 16,403,742.13 | 18,692,463.74 | 20,117,631.94 | 19,421,232.70 | 16,824,710.76 | 14,543,493.36 | 13,602,139.41 | 14,056,171.59 | 15,465,020.72 |
| Oklahoma | | | | | | | | | |
| Oregon | 232,644.27 | 214,708.48 | 554,903.79 | 560,171.93 | 680,990.14 | 844,091.79 | 541,998.45 | 542,190.66 | 636,376.91 |
| Pennsylvania | 14,956,468.10 | 19,852,577.66 | 19,149,278.23 | 21,231,716.87 | 21,396,516.43 | 21,283,794.15 | 20,066,996.48 | 22,663,533.42 | 26,539,038.79 |

|  |  |  |  |  |  |  |  |  |  |
|---|---|---|---|---|---|---|---|---|---|
| Porto Rico | 370,423.89 | 607,641.73 | 405,234.93 | 443,034.82 | 676,138.38 | 328,166.81 | 328,076.47 | 310,809.66 | 449,063.87 |
| Rhode Island [4] | 175,880.41 | 186,286.95 | 380,164.49 | 249,670.08 | 197,934.60 | 151,236.89 | 140,292.85 | 151,525.77 | 136,063.07 |
| South Dakota [6] |  |  |  |  |  |  |  |  |  |
| Tennessee [6] | 923,816.32 | 1,020,641.61 | 1,163,415.13 | 1,040,593.95 | 1,194,171.82 | 1,257,806.63 | 1,064,282.02 | 1,038,597.66 | 1,043,843.27 |
| Texas [11] | 389,734.71 | 671,718.49 | 1,923,649.63 | 1,802,576.73 | 966,142.44 | 508,525.64 | 463,204.67 | 531,580.22 | 545,518.06 |
| Utah [4] | [2] 177,050.63 | [5] 104,504.35 | [3] 94,798.56 | [3] 98,388.25 | [3] 119,617.42 | [3] 34,137.88 | [4] 35,304.54 | [4] 48,460.63 | [4] 66,308.66 |
| Vermont [5] | 616,588.78 | 804,575.13 | 1,126,234.57 | 1,144,614.15 | 884,472.24 | 763,318.09 | 695,276.22 | 760,303.48 | 716,379.31 |
| Virginia [6] | 6,536,640.04 | 5,848,786.44 | 6,112,139.49 | 6,286,704.64 | 5,157,108.55 | 3,296,754.42 | 3,091,700.21 | 3,021,135.25 | 3,062,292.76 |
| Washington | 116,642.41 | 97,515.98 | 136,885.98 | 300,638.01 | 621,204.35 | 764,864.16 | [2] 263,810.70 | [2] 210,474.79 | [2] 316,839.58 |
| West Virginia [6] | 311,414.64 | 374,882.61 | 451,930.15 | 499,714.18 | 561,562.06 | 560,913.24 | 547,736.16 | 494,533.91 | 543,859.97 |
| Wisconsin | 2,734,573.97 | 2,909,846.40 | 3,326,029.81 | 3,944,075.75 | 3,895,427.73 | 3,395,356.89 | 3,301,711.64 | 3,495,919.10 | 3,738,720.34 |
| Wyoming [3] | 25,346.15 | 27,361.38 | 32,364.07 | 72,366.53 | 89,197.62 | 108,951.52 | [2] 334,516.76 | [2] 184,597.21 | [2] 224,288.49 |
| Philippine Islands |  |  |  |  |  |  |  |  |  |
| Miscellaneous | 6,217,153.68 | 7,132,369.83 | 7,428,006.05 | 7,561,963.06 | 7,061,670.89 | 166,159.60 | 791.62 | 8,506.29 | 8,788.15 |
| Total | 251,736,439.34 | 311,547,945.12 | 335,625,924.70 | 371,661,466.07 | 367,382,730.33 | 326,464,267.28 | 299,676,651.32 | 315,341,959.26 | 345,364,570.77 |

[1] Exclusive of internal revenue; no sales of public lands.
[2] Exclusive of internal revenue.
[3] Exclusive of ...pts from customs.
[4] Exclusive of ... and ... from customs.
[5] No sales of public lands.
[6] Includes ...pts from customs ... ted in Montana.
[7] ...pts from ... ...ins collected in Oklahoma, Kansas, and Arkansas.
[8] Includes ...pts from ... ...ins ...ted in Wyoming.
[9] ..., exclusive of receipts from customs.
[10] No sales of public lands; includes ...pts from customs collected in West Virginia.
[11] No sales of public ...nds; ...les ...pts from customs ...ted in New Mexico.

14263—FI 1922——33

TABLE P.—Receipts from customs, internal revenue, and sales of public lands, collected in each State and Territory, by fiscal years, from 1879 to 1922—Continued.

| | 1888 | 1889 | 1890 | 1891 | 1892 | 1893 | 1894 | 1895 | 1896 |
|---|---|---|---|---|---|---|---|---|---|
| Alabama | $361,214.68 | $147,083.41 | $163,663.48 | $135,496.67 | $133,240.38 | $150,967.68 | $139,374.49 | $123,516.72 | $174,267.07 |
| Alaska [1] | [a]2,338.44 | 5,647.36 | 7,676.83 | 5,917.17 | 6,251.03 | 7,238.33 | 19,052.47 | 13,465.08 | 9,085.58 |
| Arizona [1] | [a]129,816.64 | [a]77,820.32 | [a]84,042.47 | 89,293.08 | 89,291.62 | 135,661.94 | 72,030.10 | 65,657.96 | 115,521.27 |
| Arkansas [1] | 219,690.28 | 137,604.16 | 126,635.91 | 104,428.02 | 105,068.57 | 110,686.20 | 108,952.62 | 89,454.84 | 99,495.85 |
| California | 13,120,636.69 | 13,169,175.27 | 11,397,598.86 | 10,781,777.17 | 10,944,285.53 | 10,317,380.03 | 8,219,041.60 | 7,957,701.45 | 8,324,591.73 |
| Colorado | 1,479,052.77 | 1,923,633.89 | 1,217,640.43 | 720,765.05 | 655,035.81 | 741,728.97 | 446,204.69 | 428,724.46 | 505,417.34 |
| Conn [5] | 1,231,721.27 | 1,153,730.34 | 1,188,162.89 | 1,431,112.15 | 1,416,565.19 | 1,477,403.64 | 1,283,917.72 | 1,339,911.83 | 1,397,997.21 |
| Delaware [1] | 6,155.30 | 11,167.95 | 6,536.10 | 16,268.61 | 10,533.75 | 14,161.58 | 12,438.67 | 7,911.04 | 10,189.54 |
| District of Columbia [1] | 30,088.53 | 62,719.66 | 78,382.19 | 80,766.39 | 75,021.69 | 81,150.09 | 36,802.40 | 41,806.01 | 37,209.09 |
| Florida | 1,335,464.44 | 1,442,416.97 | 1,590,788.78 | 1,726,240.46 | 1,687,006.31 | 1,699,569.94 | 1,408,180.59 | 1,631,105.95 | 1,752,120.49 |
| Georgia [5] | 528,203.08 | 514,522.36 | 635,817.90 | 650,513.11 | 549,515.95 | 511,349.41 | 475,681.25 | 463,019.32 | 552,841.33 |
| Hawaii / Idaho [1,6] | 96,157.83 | 106,931.57 | 135,816.01 | 179,417.39 | 147,529.37 | 173,351.15 | 97,631.54 | 70,969.13 | 86,163.74 |
| Illinois [1] | 34,995,568.95 | [a]35,941,501.32 | [a]39,942,319.02 | [a]44,132,384.57 | [a]43,372,195.08 | [a]42,873,672.50 | [a]37,023,542.45 | [a]36,427,849.85 | [a]37,435,707.17 |
| Indiana [1] | 4,267,125.63 | 5,896,285.66 | 6,427,671.53 | 6,630,319.91 | 6,671,438.40 | 6,718,318.48 | 5,104,991.64 | 7,024,677.57 | 7,799,352.31 |
| Iowa | 529,600.86 | 402,883.31 | 440,112.53 | 446,321.01 | 492,027.76 | 570,939.56 | 512,518.16 | 495,524.56 | 185,969.47 |
| Kansas [6] | 3,026,316.71 | 1,639,566.00 | 623,699.61 | 288,267.44 | 413,694.32 | 479,608.33 | 386,794.55 | 293,824.10 | 252,968.83 |
| Kentucky [1] | 14,625,883.06 | 17,392,188.28 | 17,397,963.58 | 16,105,521.09 | 22,094,518.97 | 26,984,718.87 | 24,483,092.87 | 20,568,523.60 | 15,146,631.83 |
| Louisiana [11] | 4,035,717.99 | 3,516,654.97 | 3,401,544.72 | 2,749,058.22 | 2,314,234.49 | 2,255,306.58 | 2,105,744.00 | 2,202,318.31 | 3,171,038.15 |
| Maine [1] | 843,088.16 | 460,345.13 | 452,197.98 | 607,025.73 | 634,906.80 | 255,875.55 | 469,458.96 | 274,367.99 | 226,374.86 |
| Maryland [1] | 6,338,200.93 | 6,867,963.12 | 6,208,773.47 | 6,772,331.18 | 6,105,615.97 | 8,210,582.98 | 6,828,649.15 | 6,675,243.98 | 8,756,253.27 |
| Massachusetts [1] | 24,113,208.03 | 23,613,184.20 | 21,849,513.63 | 20,574,627.63 | 17,147,661.13 | 18,813,047.66 | 11,706,853.90 | 12,191,826.34 | 15,770,539.66 |
| Michigan [1] | 2,375,560.18 | 2,566,319.20 | 2,869,513.63 | 3,129,174.26 | 3,704,330.62 | 3,572,418.02 | 3,163,595.58 | 3,164,611.00 | 3,020,830.73 |
| Minn [1] | 1,624,556.17 | 1,783,244.12 | 3,458,854.16 | 3,162,802.27 | 2,764,757.81 | 3,282,172.50 | 2,747,672.21 | 2,562,395.16 | 2,513,589.75 |
| Mississippi [1] | 548,017.31 | [a]8,942.92 | 13,114.29 | 14,692.45 | 19,229.12 | 19,930.35 | 8,967.02 | 9,486.08 | 13,564.98 |
| Missouri [1] | 9,773,118.35 | 9,178,793.47 | 9,584,671.32 | 9,387,898.56 | 10,073,906.20 | 10,754,293.57 | 8,744,823.69 | 9,471,121.07 | 8,497,198.93 |
| Montana [1] | 309,597.12 | 430,069.08 | 446,619.58 | 379,567.07 | 449,548.59 | 457,142.85 | 283,888.63 | 299,482.49 | 338,059.80 |
| Nebraska [8] | 4,192,945.64 | 3,361,210.73 | 3,775,138.29 | 3,531,720.90 | 5,237,974.92 | 4,170,625.08 | 2,422,554.05 | 1,304,542.18 | 739,634.32 |
| Nevada [1] | | [a]5,755.00 | [a]3,446.00 | [a]5,308.32 | [a]4,271.97 | [a]2,886.56 | [a]11,295.00 | [a]2,050.75 | [a]2,703.10 |
| New Hampshire [5] | 467,903.38 | 482,438.87 | 594,275.43 | 524,252.65 | 619,755.37 | 644,851.23 | 612,282.95 | 551,203.89 | 545,435.99 |
| New Jersey [5] | 4,137,579.58 | 4,378,998.10 | 4,247,478.22 | 4,116,787.24 | 4,416,786.24 | 4,489,501.46 | 4,287,495.74 | 4,473,587.40 | 4,337,567.37 |
| New Mexico [1] | 110,495.51 | 122,310.62 | 121,846.91 | 111,294.97 | 123,596.95 | 137,492.67 | 77,868.59 | 60,569.30 | 52,054.43 |
| New York [6] | 162,931,014.19 | 165,678,202.68 | 173,142,867.31 | 166,416,219.34 | 140,355,008.77 | 159,593,633.98 | 108,033,565.75 | 124,130,955.59 | 131,496,033.90 |
| North Carolina [5] | 2,234,391.18 | 2,491,458.59 | 2,784,374.34 | 2,499,811.34 | 2,399,221.77 | 2,443,547.62 | 2,371,791.52 | 2,640,637.52 | 2,746,286.62 |
| North Dakota [13] | [a]882,774.10 | [a]619,563.41 | [a]237,041.45 | [a]130,726.02 | [a]130,540.83 | [a]147,994.11 | [a]146,171.49 | [a]149,590.19 | [a]134,107.11 |
| Ohio [5] | 14,124,685.69 | 13,076,118.40 | 14,890,085.97 | 15,843,227.59 | 14,515,945.83 | 15,289,905.51 | 13,664,011.98 | 13,933,321.72 | 13,391,499.90 |
| Oklahoma [4] | | [a]1,736.16 | 2,810.94 | 74,095.83 | 63,297.67 | 87,009.10 | 111,666.93 | 183,889.87 | 155,257.42 |
| Oregon [1] | 1,016,430.57 | 1,319,640.99 | 1,589,725.57 | 1,528,239.72 | 1,453,837.28 | 1,236,921.48 | 778,517.71 | 698,288.91 | 691,477.98 |
| Pennsylvania [10] | 27,343,335.09 | 31,186,030.84 | 34,372,209.03 | 31,360,850.80 | 20,856,680.03 | 24,273,025.78 | 20,209,265.88 | 23,024,409.74 | 24,582,583.17 |

| | 1 | 2 | 3 | 4 | 5 | 6 | 7 | 8 | 9 |
|---|---|---|---|---|---|---|---|---|---|
| Porto Rico [1] | 242,165.36 | 291,246.72 | 270,411.02 | 329,115.09 | 365,694.60 | 370,823.87 | 227,396.94 | 254,340.29 | 229,210.35 |
| Rhode Island [1] | 182,760.51 | 117,746.76 | 120,427.39 | 103,629.48 | 96,435.74 | 76,737.33 | 95,146.75 | 131,560.17 | 140,539.95 |
| South Carolina [2] | | | 305,187.80 | | 131,774.60 | 159,910.78 | 73,629.17 | 71,729.37 | 32,073.27 |
| South Dakota [3] | 1,081,766.17 | 1,150,559.13 | 1,233,017.75 | 149,414.87 | | | | | |
| Tennessee [4] | 571,617.28 | 601,354.25 | 573,710.23 | 1,334,075.72 | 1,351,948.74 | 1,397,495.86 | 1,069,574.05 | 972,660.68 | 1,021,553.39 |
| Texas [5] | 61,971.18 | 64,261.21 | 95,806.64 | 903,464.57 | 1,267,124.70 | 1,315,141.68 | 1,030,656.29 | 692,396.05 | 997,178.13 |
| Utah [4] | 882,309.90 | 811,607.77 | 856,526.08 | 101,609.11 | 92,454.27 | 79,976.19 | 51,555.78 | 31,023.48 | 42,780.57 |
| Vermont [1] | 3,461,922.90 | 3,358,232.98 | 3,566,372.04 | 767,748.26 | 809,357.23 | 982,582.12 | 653,761.58 | 498,952.50 | 483,351.95 |
| Virginia [6] | 513,770.53 | 647,691.89 | 1,110,005.41 | 3,229,677.41 | 2,994,707.66 | 2,953,219.64 | 2,676,758.99 | 2,883,921.89 | 3,138,128.30 |
| Washington [2] | | | | 900,817.89 | 567,899.61 | 567,357.30 | 422,469.14 | 2,283,227.88 | 337,372.69 |
| West Virginia [14] | 567,844.53 | 789,354.84 | 908,901.58 | 835,079.03 | 812,842.28 | 864,760.34 | 868,904.88 | 689,301.62 | 649,992.15 |
| Wisconsin | 3,358,516.79 | 3,518,450.21 | 3,719,787.58 | 4,070,799.49 | 4,211,305.77 | 4,882,509.53 | 4,900,749.32 | 5,132,739.52 | 5,422,814.80 |
| Wyoming [4] | 272,132.05 | 253,516.93 | 253,641.32 | 154,002.70 | 101,019.89 | 71,001.96 | 43,812.75 | 35,802.78 | 39,307.00 |
| Philippine Islands | | | | | | | | | |
| Miscellaneous | 1,888.12 | 33.26 | 8,457.00 | 529.33 | 2,137.12 | 942.50 | 593.59 | 827.85 | 996.00 |
| Total | 354,590,062.84 | 362,752,907.40 | 378,633,562.89 | 369,237,990.08 | 334,685,912.30 | 367,564,730.44 | 280,603,400.73 | 296,683,636.63 | 307,790,139.84 |

[1] Exclusive of internal revenue; no sales of public lands.
[2] Exclusive of internal revenue.
[3] Exclusive of receipts from customs.
[4] Exclusive of internal revenue, and receipts from customs
[5] No sales of public lands.
[6] Includes receipts from customs collected in Montana.
[7] Includes receipts from customs collected in Idaho, Kansas, and Arkansas.
[8] Includes receipts from customs collected in Wyoming.
[9] Exclusive of receipts from internal revenue.
[10] Dakota, Exclusive of receipts from internal revenue.
[11] No sales of public lands; includes receipts from customs collected in West Virginia.
[12] No sales of public lands; includes receipts from internal revenue.
[13] Includes internal revenue collected in New Mexico.
[14] Exclusive of receipts from customs; no sales of public lands.

TABLE P.—*Receipts from customs, internal revenue, and sales of public lands, collected in each State and Territory, by fiscal years, from 1879 to 1922*—Continued.

| | 1897 | 1898 | 1899 | 1900 | 1901 | 1902 | 1903 | 1904 | 1905 |
|---|---|---|---|---|---|---|---|---|---|
| Alabama | $202,325.39 | $228,156.28 | $542,004.55 | $579,698.68 | $634,674.72 | $443,895.61 | $404,225.18 | $408,195.82 | $390,268.65 |
| Alaska | 11,203.80 | 35,721.60 | 48,570.86 | 59,999.94 | 88,482.81 | 68,502.43 | 73,225.22 | 90,736.34 | 143,664.02 |
| Arizona | 142,938.94 | 166,566.73 | 155,718.32 | 195,685.47 | 257,019.39 | 181,062.82 | 167,666.83 | 119,064.83 | 128,141.30 |
| Arkansas | 101,670.38 | 122,241.98 | 279,830.62 | 319,771.47 | 313,734.15 | 242,796.78 | 220,665.85 | 216,394.01 | 171,110.58 |
| California | 8,547,731.81 | 8,030,033.22 | 11,280,235.11 | 12,050,967.70 | 12,624,453.76 | 12,014,483.08 | 12,057,953.13 | 11,940,929.90 | 12,104,619.49 |
| Colorado | 576,240.50 | 585,813.77 | 1,403,894.00 | 1,565,769.03 | 1,561,491.43 | 1,447,501.99 | 1,239,463.40 | 1,143,253.35 | 984,020.18 |
| Connecticut | 1,345,887.82 | 1,404,961.97 | 3,191,881.36 | 3,522,266.41 | 3,529,691.74 | 3,552,227.40 | 2,504,163.66 | 2,188,569.85 | 2,006,393.78 |
| Dist. of Columbia | 10,213.60 | 23,446.23 | 27,283.33 | 23,031.66 | 17,446.23 | 15,318.22 | 11,210.37 | 16,208.88 | 13,172.15 |
| Florida | 32,999.35 | 61,031.79 | 60,254.95 | 96,620.98 | 93,516.51 | 113,074.37 | 136,791.96 | 129,156.35 | 113,851.90 |
| | 1,837,175.34 | 1,080,377.36 | 1,405,260.46 | 1,751,245.88 | 2,266,859.34 | 2,130,397.55 | 2,764,545.45 | 2,636,260.55 | 3,211,665.78 |
| Georgia | 507,060.47 | 526,067.04 | 1,015,784.14 | 1,010,190.50 | 1,022,093.71 | 661,666.76 | 552,519.91 | 567,272.85 | 579,133.02 |
| Hawaii | | | | 150,141.04 | 1,188,244.14 | 1,528,426.39 | 1,195,365.20 | 1,229,762.92 | 1,040,068.29 |
| Idaho | 73,373.67 | 94,602.95 | 113,096.91 | 60,227,587.79 | 235,817.94 | 399,236.81 | 696,189.79 | 556,007.98 | 616,438.09 |
| Illinois | 37,174,784.16 | 43,819,143.63 | 53,791,341.71 | 23,441,971.71 | 63,743,130.34 | 63,384,472.64 | 60,325,611.16 | 60,595,617.04 | 59,891,585.89 |
| Indiana | 8,742,443.95 | 10,166,921.81 | 17,374,354.14 | 1,975,019.10 | 23,708,780.26 | 25,376,679.76 | 28,389,396.69 | 24,322,777.13 | 24,765,689.92 |
| Iowa | 466,963.89 | 519,121.04 | 2,046,249.17 | 1,014,207.43 | 1,942,188.91 | 1,344,769.11 | 912,654.01 | 931,414.97 | 921,877.41 |
| Kansas | 253,106.01 | 433,261.07 | 949,446.59 | 24,745,357.84 | 1,014,673.39 | 738,239.37 | 326,130.76 | 313,218.27 | 323,580.83 |
| Kentucky | 16,093,443.31 | 18,477,377.80 | 22,470,390.92 | 9,292,023.57 | 25,490,851.35 | 22,314,653.54 | 21,459,538.47 | 22,087,810.67 | 22,125,013.64 |
| Louisiana | 4,205,000.50 | 2,976,335.70 | 6,091,621.33 | | 9,195,219.50 | 8,306,450.89 | 11,652,301.49 | 13,523,135.62 | 11,409,697.85 |
| Maine | 205,368.12 | 311,575.66 | 320,223.89 | 472,871.96 | 456,771.99 | 506,775.22 | 660,024.72 | 678,970.42 | 562,749.75 |
| Maryland | 7,783,648.83 | 6,742,889.06 | 10,204,476.28 | 11,786,588.38 | 12,607,187.19 | 10,861,073.83 | 10,598,409.31 | 9,304,504.28 | 9,161,892.65 |
| Mass. | 16,472,229.93 | 13,725,145.03 | 23,836,102.21 | 26,880,566.19 | 27,613,090.38 | 27,704,047.11 | 27,704,047.11 | 25,581,682.48 | 27,988,158.17 |
| Minn. | 3,288,223.15 | 3,108,493.55 | 5,624,110.14 | 6,250,993.26 | 5,795,442.88 | 6,446,944.06 | 5,936,507.42 | 5,703,823.07 | 5,642,406.65 |
| Minnesota | 2,480,027.51 | 1,499,651.55 | 3,109,439.50 | 3,680,646.19 | 3,548,271.66 | 3,268,427.28 | 2,694,585.85 | 2,694,585.85 | 2,750,653.43 |
| Mississippi | 23,217.60 | 20,376.73 | 22,695.85 | 29,235.04 | 36,012.72 | 34,232.82 | 31,092.02 | 31,092.02 | 35,016.47 |
| Missouri | 8,703,075.00 | 10,177,475.31 | 17,635,593.88 | 18,684,669.51 | 19,649,059.51 | 16,453,754.86 | 11,352,467.94 | 11,689,627.74 | 11,201,096.52 |
| Montana | 325,689.04 | 440,621.43 | 807,246.90 | 1,075,311.30 | 1,104,078.09 | 1,178,205.26 | 990,307.98 | 998,260.15 | 822,033.88 |
| Neb. | 1,432,393.83 | 2,568,861.82 | 3,551,999.57 | 3,530,665.43 | 3,561,798.10 | 3,067,707.79 | 2,350,882.38 | 2,858,511.23 | 2,389,672.30 |
| Nevada | 2,150.00 | 3,385.00 | 1,340.00 | 7,837.50 | 9,891.90 | 14,374.19 | 14,230.09 | 15,250.83 | 10,706.94 |
| New Hampshire | 431,107.84 | 473,770.79 | 1,341,207.23 | 1,333,419.80 | 1,205,088.94 | 967,780.75 | 598,984.60 | 562,032.50 | 513,297.44 |
| New Jersey | 4,220,579.80 | 4,864,224.19 | 8,179,343.44 | 9,167,004.49 | 10,069,050.91 | 8,189,710.94 | 6,186,919.41 | 6,253,431.95 | 6,401,633.63 |
| New Mexico | 73,220.23 | 74,787.69 | 154,606.30 | 161,347.35 | 205,452,020.43 | 125,469.02 | 195,628.82 | 138,728.55 | 198,025.31 |
| New York | 140,534,533.49 | 125,841,709.42 | 185,330,527.91 | 201,478,399.23 | 7,147,229.05 | 207,105,905.59 | 211,176,005.90 | 199,736,461.31 | 202,746,328.44 |
| North Carolina | 2,763,713.03 | 3,262,697.38 | 4,914,527.91 | 6,344,796.28 | 7,400,523.93 | 5,625,475.27 | 4,251,926.77 | 4,251,928.84 | 4,998,509.80 |
| North Dakota | 4,333,128.38 | 3,167,764.44 | 4,156,773.13 | 22,922,405.82 | 24,135,420.24 | 5,831,207.67 | 1,237,143.01 | 1,275,914.94 | 4,924,835.61 |
| Ohio | 14,346,824.09 | 17,392,782.62 | 22,705,773.28 | | 189,448.24 | 24,362,446.71 | 23,386,090.11 | 23,129,110.65 | 21,845,833.76 |
| Oklahoma | 89,337.78 | 292,999.06 | 533,105.89 | 550,850.41 | 2,097,471.60 | 224,446.71 | 722,383.12 | 805,783.37 | 422,827.90 |
| Oregon | 746,838.38 | 957,844.01 | 1,597,755.97 | 2,089,584.36 | 47,334,017.42 | 2,335,645.86 | 3,071,603.54 | 2,242,922.74 | 1,473,432.78 |
| Pennsylvania | 28,191,557.16 | 26,649,928.81 | 45,990,255.93 | 46,552,423.15 | | 42,807,704.38 | 42,458,617.23 | 38,235,154.39 | 38,815,750.61 |

| | | | | | | | | |
|---|---|---|---|---|---|---|---|---|
| Porto Rico [1] | | 207,268.64 | 256,824.08 | 352,774.07 | 371,234.76 | 333,824.64 | 36,492.44 | 12,953.22 | 11,363.97 |
| Rhode Island | 190,975.89 | 254,143.35 | 392,670.89 | 392,290.06 | 333,226.66 | 491,536.10 | 379,877.48 | 304,092.19 | 438,808.25 |
| South Carolina [2] | 162,529.30 | 63,318.39 | 110,794.22 | 137,704.87 | 80,751.69 | 153,180.27 | 669,311.37 | 819,187.62 | 834,107.29 |
| South Dakota [3] | 38,530.64 | 1,331,368.31 | 2,210,743.47 | 2,337,383.75 | 2,474,534.76 | 2,017,265.88 | 202,989.13 | 200,613.77 | 146,366.54 |
| Tennessee [4] | 1,130,123.56 | 1,474,551.14 | 2,271,282.69 | 2,276,431.47 | 2,299,681.63 | 1,798,282.47 | 1,715,108.94 | 1,764,237.54 | 1,849,141.61 |
| Utah | 1,003,513.56 | [4] 150,903.03 | [4] 44,323.94 | [4] 60,257.78 | [4] 94,428.88 | [4] 43,368.42 | 1,470,469.57 | 1,289,891.20 | 1,288,823.30 |
| Vermont [5] | [4] 135,778.65 | 434,950.85 | 555,560.86 | 1,125,511.46 | 889,271.58 | 829,645.29 | [4] 85,780.61 | [4] 47,703.61 | [4] 62,003.72 |
| Virginia [6] | 295,657.86 | 3,739,333.82 | 5,204,996.16 | 6,260,567.36 | 6,766,564.16 | 5,555,091.53 | 1,385,952.00 | 1,113,094.88 | 978,175.00 |
| Washington | 2,896,669.04 | [3] 439,517.12 | [3] 388,261.09 | [3] 540,293.42 | [3] 705,258.23 | [3] 1,315,274.82 | 5,023,167.67 | 4,185,303.26 | 4,088,561.51 |
| West Virginia [7] | 702,319.75 | 818,745.20 | 1,433,008.66 | 1,553,744.98 | 1,634,597.88 | 1,404,901.61 | 1,115,103.93 | [14] 1,200,581.24 | [14] 1,152,704.83 |
| Wisconsin | 4,931,818.07 | 5,592,650.97 | 9,780,840.13 | 10,957,989.96 | 11,284,259.86 | 10,565,793.98 | 8,006,764.29 | 8,138,130.49 | 7,976,447.20 |
| Wyoming [8] | 35,578.20 | 70,916.28 | 69,801.49 | 158,962.70 | 191,067.48 | 153,247.59 | 256,640.06 | 335,918.19 | 191,510.65 |
| Philippine Islands | | | | | | | | | |
| Miscellaneous | .60 | .60 | 69.40 | 1.04 | 24,176.87 | 7,041.54 | 61.42 | 56.12 | 1,200.00 |
| Total | 324,107,282.35 | 321,718,833.26 | 481,243,890.07 | 531,329,680.90 | 548,731,239.41 | 530,408,953.07 | 524,216,017.20 | 501,632,163.98 | 500,753,847.56 |

[7] ... Md in West Virginia.
[10] No ... Md in New Mexico.
... Kansas, and ...
Md in South Dakota.
Md in South Dakota.

TABLE P.—*Receipts from customs, internal revenue, and sales of public lands, collected in each State and Territory, by fiscal years, from 1819 to 1922—*
Continued.

| | 1906 | 1907 | 1908 | 1909 | 1910 | 1911 | 1912 | 1913 | 1914 |
|---|---|---|---|---|---|---|---|---|---|
| Ala. | $508,162.04 | $542,811.31 | $110,475.93 | [12]$245,968.22 | [12]$301,364.67 | [12]$424,699.29 | [12]$158,664.69 | [12]$561,413.37 | [12]$0,595.62 |
| | [2]91,066.77 | [2]152,644.67 | [2]87,622.56 | [2]146,142.05 | [2]187,612.28 | [2]181,595.13 | [2]60,413.96 | [2]57,393.94 | 65,310.82 |
| | [2]114,342.86 | [2]133,285.17 | [2]160,309.26 | [2]233,046.94 | [2]375,595.31 | [2]337,385.08 | [2]480,350.11 | [2]503,892.84 | 353,377.00 |
| | 265,753.48 | 312,903.88 | 405,544.56 | 171,701.37 | 188,050.96 | 206,744.35 | 192,363.18 | 213,692.94 | 262,776.79 |
| | 12,931,527.77 | 16,417,550.51 | 15,104,043.96 | 14,295,913.27 | 15,894,255.04 | 17,404,942.00 | 17,302,901.94 | 17,480,002.98 | 18,416,929.61 |
| | 2,203,731.72 | 1,209,089.86 | 1,499,508.60 | 1,488,804.73 | 1,607,302.76 | 1,816,670.71 | 1,709,320.81 | 1,443,443.31 | 1,483,651.89 |
| | 2,320,553.93 | 2,324,772.62 | 2,274,011.07 | 3,512,916.87 | 4,175,857.96 | 4,031,744.91 | 4,126,355.27 | 3,382,341.88 |
| Dist. of Col. | 1,149,969.60 | 1,8,872.99 | 1,21,026.52 | 1,12,490.56 | 1,111,837.04 | 1,48,550.65 | 1,48,995.04 | 1,170,304.20 | 654,311.61 |
| Florida | 3,459,551.51 | 176,649.36 | 1,170,091.09 | 1,162,209.85 | 1,188,425.43 | 1,235,995.53 | 1,201,160.04 | 1,307,718.59 | [5]1,482,745.39 |
| | 3,614,549.18 | 3,254,319.42 | 3,429,817.94 | 4,051,564.94 | 4,002,670.89 | 3,931,042.26 | 3,947,723.83 | 3,871,291.78 |
| Hawaii [5] | 698,946.54 | 788,251.27 | 38,651.10 | 42,967.30 | 83,969.57 | 61,384.37 | 718,861.64 | 713,185.97 | 923,722.85 |
| Idaho [5] | 1,222,952.30 | 1,438,623.08 | 1,594,466.87 | 1,465,864.26 | 1,772,869.56 | 1,863,447.10 | 1,896,805.76 | 2,094,060.67 | 1,49,541.38 |
| Illinois [5] | 1,540,280.87 | 1,913,150.70 | 1,813,764.81 | 1,588,348.68 | [2]12.90 | 1,651,833.97 | 1,411,831.06 | 1,547,963.13 | 354,405.56 |
| | 62,488,279.47 | 65,032,411.99 | 55,841,454.20 | 52,631,145.56 | 59,685,925.41 | 64,382,103.96 | 62,662,971.21 | 69,149,691.48 | 72,017,976.08 |
| | 25,616,912.48 | 29,933,014.65 | 26,884,292.63 | 25,508,772.37 | 29,237,507.72 | 31,571,765.86 | 30,706,138.22 | 32,003,911.96 | 30,04,184.11 |
| Kas [5] | 953,663.44 | 1,068,007.83 | 1,043,685.16 | 1,064,141.81 | 1,225,967.83 | [6]1,361,803.06 | 595,097.10 | [5]1,281,156.15 | [6]1,561,985.52 |
| | 338,434.57 | 381,097.71 | 450,921.35 | 61,243.85 | 445.02 | 689,518.36 | 32,350,532.10 | 759,132.73 | 548,923.74 |
| | 24,901,252.40 | 28,818,783.12 | 27,171,641.05 | 28,374,699.69 | [5]5.43 | 33,509,941.00 | 13,906,706.60 | 35,422,458.17 | 35,593,207.41 |
| | [12]12,280,423.55 | [12]13,218,453.53 | [12]12,332,355.60 | 12,144,991.14 | 0, 6, 9.50 | 13,628,302.30 | | 16,154,493.73 | 16,959,880.15 |
| Me. | 1,707,476.03 | 1,731,097.18 | 67,306.79 | 67,511.17 | 62,039.92 | 85,626.40 | 780,278.50 | 888,654.91 | 306,305.97 |
| Md. | 11,419,777.63 | 12,393,712.25 | 11,762,042.10 | 10,749,963.37 | 12,722,760.96 | 14,188,765.38 | 13,579,725.37 | 13,525,813.21 | 11,409,957.28 |
| | 31,363,773.84 | 32,713,708.46 | 27,247,088.11 | 31,413,062.38 | 36,741,357.08 | 14,402,429.30 | 31,904,071.46 | 32,003,433.30 | 24,349,263.79 |
| Miss. | 2,701,809.01 | 7,948,892.07 | 9,004,593.77 | 9,375,289.38 | 9,638,755.80 | 9,992,380.77 | 10,632,429.36 | 11,271,370.34 | 24,950,913.78 |
| | 7,38,654.92 | 3,440,244.65 | 832,907.64 | 3,375,298.21 | 4,424,765.89 | 4,550,309.71 | 4,641,984.20 | 4,825,003.61 | 155,620.95 |
| | 11,324,519.63 | 12,446,879.70 | 12,787,917.75 | 12,663,473.95 | [5]20,284.32 | 22,334.13 | 21,577.99 | 22,936.34 | 890,842.80 |
| Dak [5] | 1,001,597.75 | 1,339,116.11 | 1,227,008.01 | 1,185,147.36 | 14,243,635.96 | 15,574,621.05 | 14,8,6,343.74 | 15,513,767.36 | 1,054,452.17 |
| N bas [5] | 2,729,589.20 | 1,879,574.68 | 2,359,011.69 | 2,707,981.81 | 1,516,955.86 | 1,542,322.11 | 1,561,798.03 | 1,442,310.21 | 48,800.15 |
| Nevada | 1,33,395.42 | 1,45,341.52 | 1,57,265.32 | 1,74,691.99 | 2,972,676.25 | 3,044,221.69 | 3,337,423.33 | 2,807,455.62 | [9]157,426.96 |
| | | | | | [5]57,023.28 | [5]77,010.39 | [5]59,614.67 | [5]52,277.03 | |
| New Hampshire [5] | 479,574.19 | 495,949.77 | 483,281.70 | [4]694.69 | 65,156.09 | 85,626.40 | 780,278.50 | 888,654.91 | 579,120.39 |
| New [5] | 6,965,231.07 | 7,158,037.73 | [5]724.91 | 7, 8, 4.74 | 9,366,354.04 | 10,515,286.60 | 11,354,883.39 | 13,349,920.95 | 14,32,129.85 |
| New Mo [5] | 216,016.79 | 251,892.48 | 429,161.02 | 640,921.74 | 633,042.12 | 519,229.35 | 406,835.36 | 375,543.73 | 203,918.03 |
| New York [5] | 230,871,017.30 | 255,480,363.07 | 20,571,760.88 | 21,608,583.13 | 250,638,586.44 | 33,789,536.36 | 250,438,567.79 | 255,602,000.62 | 83,691,341.72 |
| North [5] | 4,962,403.79 | 4,901,250.80 | 82,956.69 | 5,183,162.82 | 5,945,918.65 | 7,317,285.03 | 8,990,474.07 | 10,797,041.77 | 11,971,581.29 |
| North Ga [5] | 16,958,944.82 | 15,1,175,848.92 | [5]2, 28,352.29 | 1,450,594.60 | [5]1,157,151.78 | [5]1,002,386.90 | [5]888,086.88 | [5]406,381.39 | 90,163.03 |
| Ohio [5] | 23,023,918.02 | 24,485,473.52 | 83.79 | 21,780,894.47 | 23,937,305.20 | 24,688,325.37 | 26,496,479.97 | 27,988,341.84 | 27,203,793.82 |
| | 4,388,773.85 | 4,415,891.46 | [4]2,538,299.85 | [4]494,738.29 | [4]240,825.39 | 1,207,088.36 | 1,222,029.89 | 1,265,501.04 | 1,395,438.07 |
| Oregon | 1,578,294.87 | 3,140,328.99 | 2,921,602.24 | 2,189,399.83 | 0, 6.68 | 2,065,297.54 | 1,915,877.17 | 1,731,771.82 | 1,684,267.71 |
| Ia [10] | [12]42,247,292.28 | 44,538,831.91 | 40, 0, 1.98 | 40,100,906.40 | 48,994,934.52 | 49,102,129.94 | 46,559,914.43 | 50,295,562.38 | 51,771,444.03 |

| | | | | | | | | |
|---|---|---|---|---|---|---|---|---|
| Porto Rico | 12,591.08 | 15,406.92 | 13,586.63 | 12,057.42 | 15,071.33 | 17,774.27 | 14,504.63 | 15,124.01 |
| Rhode Island | 447,720.41 | 1,555,142.95 | 1,548,232.25 | 1,538,194.73 | 674,585.34 | 836,272.94 | 772,829.21 | 797,056.50 |
| South Carolina | 592,490.15 | 297,045.54 | 284,653.24 | 203,324.54 | 223,490.55 | 227,783.68 | 212,845.81 | 72,031.76 |
| South Dakota | 152,043.50 | 397,147.25 | 613,366.46 | 845,374.89 | 743,030.30 | 1,006,423.05 | 935,700.83 | 255,213.55 |
| Tennessee | 2,238,653.23 | 2,335,812.62 | 2,509,498.42 | 2,529,247.69 | 2,506,334.51 | 2,584,486.93 | 2,488,233.08 | 2,511,167.56 |
| Texas | 1,999,237.81 | 1,806,634.83 | 1,840,803.18 | 2,004,364.12 | 2,595,939.46 | 2,910,906.41 | 3,787,615.61 | 4,456,755.02 |
| Utah | 118,167.56 | 157,986.02 | 174,361.16 | 1,239,687.85 | 1,377,482.48 | 116,562.50 | 140,880.54 | 196,615.28 |
| Vermont | 1,115,721.73 | 1,072,920.16 | 1,072,908.13 | 887,391.45 | 1,073,457.24 | 1,545,933.84 | 1,770,827.94 | 1,162,817.64 |
| Virginia | 5,034,649.29 | 5,880,115.24 | 5,880,115.24 | 5,448,983.53 | 6,731,411.03 | 9,109,235.20 | 9,659,348.83 | 9,653,111.45 |
| Washington | 2,381,513.15 | 3,368,988.33 | 3,554,310.11 | 2,870,829.04 | 3,242,516.38 | 3,352,833.90 | 3,416,221.00 | 3,638,438.66 |
| West Virginia | 1,233,975.84 | 1,396,043.79 | 1,456,021.05 | 1,417,070.20 | 1,593,868.92 | 1,783,861.81 | 1,799,445.62 | 1,911,650.59 |
| Wisconsin | 8,681,308.51 | 9,302,122.23 | 9,036,349.27 | 8,633,607.51 | 9,451,759.71 | 10,469,979.23 | 10,131,771.37 | 10,308,920.60 |
| Wyoming | 329,374.09 | 306,900.14 | 602,093.89 | 390,593.45 | 316,931.52 | 323,345.25 | 511,529.01 | 194,409.45 |
| Philippine Islands | | | | | 218,953.11 | 94,401.03 | 210,590.62 | 311,852.85 |
| Miscellaneous | 35,259.26 | 5,437.05 | 50.00 | 85.19 | 200.00 | 40,279.10 | 2,090.00 | 9,578.38 |
| Total | 551,281,924.33 | 609,778,946.68 | 547,555,817.22 | 554,025,145.32 | 629,972,761.97 | 642,757,908.91 | 638,326,668.63 | 666,218,506.20 |

TABLE P.—Receipts from customs, internal revenue, and sales of public lands, collected in each State and Territory, by fiscal years, from 1879 to 1922—Continued.

| | 1915 | 1916 | 1917 | 1918 | 1919 | 1920 | 1921 | 1922 |
|---|---|---|---|---|---|---|---|---|
| Ala. | $755,246.42 | $757,185.74 | $1,489,418.14 | $19,273,002.98 | $3, 01, 0.89 | $8, 36, 0.96 | $18,412,506.55 | $1, 60,682.20 |
| Alaska | 66,743.14 | 99,275.33 | 128,040.40 | 393,058.25 | 83, 0.56 | 518, 0.62 | 407,232.70 | 284,355.28 |
| Ariz. | 293,550.73 | 441,646.30 | 1,002,764.88 | 6,810,578.27 | 5, 80, 0.03 | 3, 81, 0.80 | 4,515,746.64 | 2,399,580.17 |
| Ark. | 409,281.53 | 471,649.87 | 635,726.50 | 6,379,873.69 | 7, 60,414.50 | 12, 64, 0.80 | 10,653,144.35 | 6,993,897.80 |
| Cal. | 18,798,578.21 | 20,428,495.88 | 29,279,702.54 | 114,419,709.63 | 125,882,764.43 | 35, 83, 0.85 | 189,745,834.11 | 142,481,119.46 |
| Colorado | 1,846,684.39 | 1,890,539.81 | 3,499,002.33 | 25,217,494.47 | 21,817,014.87 | 35, 99, 0.85 | 34,537,392.37 | 20,169,688.25 |
| Conn. | 3,794,939.93 | 5,808,228.58 | 14,195,830.88 | 75,287,555.19 | 80, 61, 0.88 | 08, 87,366.52 | 73,365,855.48 | 50, 00, 0.39 |
| District of Col. | 738,015.20 | 3,089,945.57 | 18,235,635.81 | 32,950,653.10 | 22, 43, 0.92 | 21,149,689.35 | 11,819,480.31 | 6, 62,784.17 |
| Florida | 1,582,015.00 | 1,505,686.20 | 2,604,722.47 | 12,918,562.22 | 15, 60, 2.89 | 18,767,021.18 | 19,109,851.06 | 19, 89,853.02 |
| | 3,603,440.31 | 4,061,739.15 | 4,914,775.41 | 10,201,539.38 | 11,606,015.62 | 18,078,272.47 | 13,267,298.70 | 16, 62, 0.49 |
| Hawaii | 1,153,665.46 | 1,435,562.86 | 2,209,110.54 | 20,567,194.59 | 33,408,300.16 | 45,697,815.17 | 39,419,615.12 | 25, 21, 20.75 |
| Idaho | 1,442,851.62 | 1,840,074.07 | 2,675,972.47 | 10,642,284.36 | 6,639,043.85 | 12,655,084.67 | 22,458,094.66 | 16,527,354.09 |
| Illinois | 385,840.20 | 506,053.49 | 695,625.26 | 2,486,128.64 | 3,711, 2.91 | 5,180,974.33 | 4,788,886.48 | 2,373,275.82 |
| | 63,710,929.94 | 71,365,478.31 | 94,672,171.05 | 367,387,628.45 | 327,818,601.00 | 451,591,078.89 | 307,632,250.59 | 281,000,886.85 |
| Ind. | 8,029,502.31 | 31,131,562.59 | 36,940,225.97 | 58,131,017.09 | 60,906,391.67 | 74,952,735.63 | 78,392,412.57 | 53, 82,120.17 |
| Iowa | 2,664,825.51 | 2,587,887.28 | 3,461,411.00 | 17,785,728.55 | 27,961,457.56 | 40,369,042.61 | 37,791,865.31 | 23,790,258.71 |
| Kansas | 1,113,340.70 | 1,220,045.86 | 3,461,411.00 | 29,047,835.61 | 27, 67,018.77 | 40,747,553.53 | 39,117,175.24 | 30,401,381.38 |
| Ky. | 3,793,203.43 | 37,332,526.91 | 47,207,139.22 | 98,979,306.11 | 179,189,029.92 | 49,742,316.58 | 50,883,375.33 | 3, 0, 0.77 |
| Louisiana | 5,777,924.67 | 16,746,846.62 | 23,045,542.37 | 44,934,892.19 | 39,775,586.51 | 63,710,343.13 | 49,890,975.06 | 38,836,157.66 |
| Me. | 856,618.01 | 1,045,652.84 | 1,744,961.61 | 13,594,067.48 | 12,625,728.63 | 20, 88, 8.05 | 18,104,841.60 | 15,055,917.60 |
| Md. | 9,593,218.45 | 10,455,380.17 | 15,220,904.14 | 62,579,505.60 | 68,975, 1.44 | 82,859,300.80 | 73,404,542.21 | 18, 87, 8.97 |
| | 22,333,270.19 | 23,774,768.50 | 38,538,655.04 | 199,245,180.75 | 254,445, 0.59 | 363,999,323.78 | 272,312,945.07 | 90, 81, 8.62 |
| Michigan | 5,969,679.85 | 14,052,744.77 | 21,039,005.49 | 105,556,171.96 | 51, 85, 0.50 | 85,962,218.26 | 273,514,665.50 | 201, 60, 8.62 |
| Minn. | 5,224,723.92 | 7,521,574.77 | 11,569,964.88 | 71,583,078.68 | 51, 85, 9.31 | 78,396, 8.31 | 47,671,045.40 | 47,671,045.40 |
| Mississippi | 16,598,445.22 | 18,036,170.95 | 558,204.18 | 5,404,503.08 | 0, 62, 25.12 | 11, 85, 6.70 | 9,050,065.12 | 4, 64,236.01 |
| Missouri | 1,271,069.95 | 1,389,475.56 | 23,309,797.04 | 89,546,427.72 | 7, 89, 3.95 | 30, 86, 6.93 | 128,165,741.11 | 89,945,561.93 |
| N. Dak. | 3,022,461.83 | 4,795,553.43 | 4,936,886.57 | 4,466,210.60 | 18,601,240.05 | 6, 76, 0.47 | 5,631,873.32 | 3, 99, 0.16 |
| Nevada | 221,559.82 | 185,840.16 | 204,749.70 | 14,114,726.95 | 6,432,175.49 | 25,185,344.76 | 24,522,793.79 | 15, 95,541.98 |
| | | | | 926,930.30 | | 1,329,502.73 | 1,236,383.57 | 82, 6.67 |
| New Hampshire | 783,954.86 | 923,782.65 | 1,235,602.92 | 7,766,098.66 | 9, 86,210.40 | 14, 87,657.24 | 10,473,277.53 | 6,338,369.78 |
| New Jersey | 5,494,398.04 | 18,957,359.56 | 25,579,453.22 | 104,084,466.67 | 102,199,290.11 | 155,199,609.64 | 142,573,099.31 | 108,022,388.59 |
| New Mex. | 223,584.16 | 352,400.33 | 562,370.37 | 2,572,236.89 | 1,383,717.12 | 4,899,258.45 | 1,817,915.05 | 1,257,653.58 |
| New York | 25,014,901.24 | 258,015,515.36 | 347,072,419.57 | 955,511,021.52 | 1,043,317,136.29 | 1,646,681,650.35 | 1,329,972,637.81 | 1,010,138,613.29 |
| North | 3,666,884.87 | 19,562,458.68 | 32,598,704.66 | 71,328,399.69 | 64, 33, 0.39 | 165,486,807.59 | 127,981,778.75 | 26, 69, 8.52 |
| Dak. | 358,029.09 | 506,280.39 | 608,961.73 | 2,162,335.08 | 3,013, 0.33 | 3,454, 8.50 | 3,162,000.04 | 2, 69, 8.00 |
| Ohio | 28,877,610.56 | 35,095,892.18 | 52,476,876.94 | 301,851,403.08 | 260,359, 8.82 | 24, 87, 8.10 | 287,945,088.87 | 85,618,053.52 |
| | 746,836.50 | 1,330,220.08 | 6,897,514.60 | 19,670,805.18 | 17, 85, 8.82 | 27, 44, 0.32 | 257,945,088.87 | 18,400,402.70 |
| | 1,666,683.96 | 1,382,835.97 | 1,453,755.76 | 11,758,045.65 | 16,985,016.05 | 27, 88, 0.32 | 28,794,219.59 | 19,621,898.30 |
| Pennsylvania | 5,056,695.52 | 60,421,612.58 | 99,541,518.21 | 604,696,714.53 | 456,204, 0.11 | 99, 85, 0.80 | 509,949,353.76 | 375,881,768.10 |

|  | | | | | | | |
|---|---|---|---|---|---|---|---|
| Porto Rico [5] | 636,565.02 | 601,202.44 | 774,370.10 | 1,032,991.88 | 1,584,306.38 | 1,892,744.98 | 359,990.41 | 33,539.53 |
| Rhode Island [6] | 2,102,827.51 | 2,651,027.38 | 5,239,964.10 | 20,497,283.73 | 21,076,507.12 | 44,953,852.65 | 41,663,083.67 | 37,234,866.07 |
| South Carolina [6] | 468,666.22 | 608,144.73 | 807,649.71 | 8,444,456.20 | 18,831,542.22 | 27,085,289.60 | 28,570,912.11 | 11,505,228.24 |
| South Dakota [6] | 474,568.48 | 549,614.01 | 474,225.31 | 3,026,158.15 | 5,909,270.97 | 6,617,329.14 | 5,085,727.75 | 2,594,719.47 |
| Tennessee [9] | 2,415,281.19 | 2,906,160.07 | 3,475,678.75 | 18,096,608.02 | 23,651,807.53 | 36,411,851.06 | 34,439,919.59 | 21,83 174.60 |
| Texas [14] | 4,247,774.77 | 5,246,021.37 | 8,589,891.33 | 41,558,839.78 | 64,219,188.13 | 106,102,200.68 | 80,740,029.82 | 57 [98 882.61 |
| Utah [16] | 639,658.21 | 1,058,689.60 | 1,887,228.94 | 6,975,977.25 | 12,584,041.09 | 10,023,827.07 | 10,846,039.80 | 5, 38,948.16 |
| Vermont [6] | 439,002.23 | 754,696.31 | 1,006,614.97 | 4,638,160.21 | 4,672,679.90 | 7,488,760.87 | 6,973,007.29 | 4,781,718.51 |
| Virginia [6] | 9,886,867.07 | 10,738,623.66 | 12,195,977.83 | 37,206,171.09 | 46,353,448.88 | 71,041,954.12 | 63,746,750.58 | 47, 60, 3.94 |
| Washington | 3,796,766.51 | 3,750,344.04 | 4,921,149.74 | 25,080,047.29 | 32,916,066.01 | 46,287,407.43 | 40,562,012.72 | 26,345,194.42 |
| West Virginia [14] | 1,969,463.72 | 2,099,127.46 | 3,466,370.38 | 48,050,772.13 | 25,844,985.52 | 33,455,945.23 | 41,936,457.86 | 33, 83,933.87 |
| Wisconsin | 11,812,415.13 | 13,331,222.28 | 16,652,220.39 | 59,086,628.16 | 68,279,678.08 | 93,485,973.87 | 74,168,791.42 | 51,406,670.28 |
| Wyoming [6] | 356,394.04 | 349,079.66 | 525,102.23 | 4,108,174.88 | 3,601,572.41 | 4,524,436.06 | 3,475,685.13 | 2,215,555.99 |
| Philippine Islands [14] | 131,564.03 | 236,825.30 | 479,794.28 | 746,053.77 | 1,178,118.49 | 1,191,940.50 | 1,151,349.04 | 434,729.35 |
| Miscellaneous | 100.00 | 148.40 | 23,161.99 | 243.17 | 967.00 | 324.35 | 18 18,195.22 | 18 16,029.64 |
| Total | 627,623,454.68 | 727,775,536.21 | 1,037,221,494.34 | 3,880,771,928.83 | 4,025,064,324.75 | 5,724,595,944.51 | 4,889,529,150.65 | 3,566,598,411.92 |

[5] ... tes.

[6] No ... of ... tes ... ... in Me. ... . at Arkansas.

[7] ... tes from ... det in ... tes. ... ... cat b ... Wt. Virginia

[10] No ... tes ... cat in Nbg., ... tes ... det in Nw Mexico.

[11] No ... tes ... det in ... tes

[14] Exclusive of ... tes; no ... tes of ... Hic ... tes ... collected in ... Mn.

[16] ... tes from ... det in ... Nw Hampshire.

[17] ... er ... ts from ... det in ... di.

[18] ... at ... a ... on ... sle of ... tp ... det.

TABLE Q.—*Customs statistics, by districts, for the fiscal year 1922.*

| District. | Value of imports. | Value of exports. | Receipts. | | | | Payments. | | | | Cost to collect one dollar. | Vessels cleared from ports. | | | |
|---|---|---|---|---|---|---|---|---|---|---|---|---|---|---|---|
| | | | Duties. | Tonnage tax. | Head tax. | All other. | Total. | Excess deposits refunded. | Drawback paid. | Expenses. | | Foreign for foreign ports. | Domestic for foreign ports. | Domestic to for domestic ports. | Domestic to or domestic ports. |
| Alaska (No. 31) | $1,202,525 | $1,441,310 | $7,572.37 | $2,021.92 | $240 | $10,133.20 | $20,567.49 | $8.65 | $85.46 | $40,619.06 | $1.97 | 516 | 788 | 1,287 | |
| Ills (No. 26) | 1,999,440 | 8,352,207 | 171,325.59 | | 14,088 | 18,781.50 | 204,195.09 | 36,496.33 | 21,801.94 | 58,228.96 | .285 | 1,114 | 1,896 | 2,202 | |
| Buffalo (No. 9) | 58,123,625 | 139,972,233 | 4,538,645.68 | 1,649.62 | | 23,669.49 | 4,563,964.79 | 279,860.14 | 47,800.45 | 178,265.23 | .039 | 1,308 | 3,931 | 3,718 | |
| Chicago (No. 39) | 46,098,026 | 43,856,948 | 9,852,676.63 | | | 21,659.70 | 9,874,336.33 | 1,646.26 | | 289,733.56 | .02934 | | 9 | | |
| Colorado (No. 47) | 435,682 | | 113,398.74 | 364.80 | 8 | 3,890.84 | 117,299.58 | 19,144.28 | 10,327.17 | 11,515.03 | .098 | 28 | | 33 | |
| Connecticut (No. 6) | 5,020,239 | .426 | 440,868.63 | | | 9,104.98 | 450,224.41 | 4,398.20 | 9,718.98 | 35,479.29 | .079 | | | | |
| Dakota (No. 34) | 15,256,462 | 35,365,373 | 835,746.12 | | | 8,070.28 | 843,816.40 | | | 44,151.62 | .052 | | | | |
| Duluth and Superior No. 63 | 11,706,723 | 24,853,152 | 7 56.82 | | 87,648 | 25,973.47 | 503,490.29 | 1 .99 | 250.87 | 45,240.90 | .089 | 493 | 2,752 | 2,818 | |
| El Paso (No. 24) | 3,761,491 | 12,333,232 | 2.75 | | 81,798.11 | | 242,018.86 | 3,603.23 | | 98,477.15 | .406 | | | | |
| Ills (No. 18) | 14,282,774 | 45,318,801 | 2,045,747.67 | 46,402.44 | 48,824 | 82,692.50 | 2,223,666.61 | | 9,337.53 | 119,852.17 | .0539 | 2,096 | 678 | 702 | |
| Ills (No. 22) | 18,943,620 | 402,337,575 | 3,710,672.73 | 91,996.47 | 608 | 56,770.60 | 3,860,012.80 | 8,880.51 | 213,155.22 | 88,271.05 | .022 | 1,165 | 859 | 648 | |
| Ills (No. 17) | 9,960,968 | 74,300,519 | 4,607,522.66 | 10,658.94 | 96 | 14,801.44 | 4,633,079.04 | 15,557.99 | 608,081.09 | 97,166.92 | .0092 | 238 | 671 | 565 | |
| Hawaii (No. 32) | 6,610,946 | 977,257 | 978,529.64 | 36,874.20 | 34,392 | 26,366.18 | 1,076,162.04 | 19,829.69 | 2,020.95 | 14,568.72 | .0092 | 133 | 330 | 323 | |
| Ills (No. 40) | 1,398,482 | | 312,748.47 | | | 1,125.53 | 313,874.00 | 3,429.20 | | 8,802.75 | .046 | | | | |
| Iowa (b. 44) | 176,201 | | 71,342.20 | | | 7,185.65 | 78,527.85 | 2,340.14 | | 13,250.00 | .112 | | | | |
| Ills (No. 42) | 306,039 | | 72,833.76 | | | 3,300.89 | 76,134.65 | 964.25 | 2,607.42 | 13,250.00 | .174 | | | | |
| Ills (No. 27) | 14,639,748 | 15,422,276 | 1,509,974.97 | 36,033.62 | 1,464 | 25,025.63 | 1,572,498.22 | 9.61 | | 62,012.94 | .0394 | 546 | 1,355 | 1,201 | |
| Maine and New Hampshire (No. 1) | 20,558,494 | 14,87,477 | 625,529.09 | 19,8.94 | 728 | 37,225.62 | 682,789.65 | 2,677.61 | 378.64 | 163,780.42 | .239 | 1,937 | 138 | 92 | |
| Maryland (No. 13) | 41,346,335 | 123,243,840 | 2,483,474.47 | 73,979.98 | 1,200 | 70,669.72 | 2,629,224.17 | 33,8.64 | 130,462.40 | 296,185.06 | .1088 | 721 | 1,666 | 61 | |
| Ills (No. 4) | 163,075,778 | 50,89,797 | 19,140,831.57 | 98,475.10 | 53,744 | 101,046.21 | 19,394,116.88 | 204,525.96 | 1,483,487.93 | 914,967.60 | .047 | 1,037 | 1,142 | 1,435 | |
| Michigan (No. 38) | 59,383,185 | 177,461,773 | 1,333,273.06 | 1.36 | | 28,881.06 | 1,362,329.50 | 103,046.08 | 11,161.16 | 224,294.96 | .164 | 4,098 | 5,277 | 5,344 | |
| Ills (No. 35) | 3,138,521 | | 46,9.18 | | 320 | 7,1.02 | 554,073.21 | 8,991.88 | | 43,008.86 | .0876 | | | | |
| Ills and Idaho (No. 23) | 2,466,478 | 34,215,655 | 39,208.93 | 17,844.74 | | 29,262.79 | 86,636.46 | 1.90 | 3,351.08 | 27,779.11 | .32 | 503 | 382 | 324 | |
| Ills and Idaho (No. 33) | 4,558,078 | 4,00,240 | 155,060.53 | 167,969.91 | | 2,344.98 | 157,405.51 | 1.50 | | 37,568.82 | .233 | | | | |
| New Orleans (No. 20) | 104,056,671 | 365,116,311 | 80,1.96 | 690,699.46 | 12,232 | 12,104.26 | 16,183,184.13 | 0.95 | 1,898,721.69 | 350,272.31 | .0216 | 2,340 | 815 | 742 | |
| Ills (No. 10) | 1,365,434,094 | 1,317,440,816 | 226,761,838.99 | 1,649,248 | | 1,735,122.99 | 230,806,909.44 | 11,151,644.20 | 21,065,217.46 | 4,640,013.42 | .022 | 5,503 | 2,945 | 2,523 | |
| North (No. 15) | 3,981,985 | 9,200,071 | 4,697,064.81 | 2,387.20 | 8 | 22,819.09 | 4,722,279.10 | 7, 0.79 | | 16,630.39 | .0035 | 16 | 91 | 92 | |
| Ills (No. 41) | 10,784,941 | 22, 86,580 | 4,85,8.61 | 1,771.34 | | 23 592.71 | 1,580,726.06 | 37,428.42 | 567.67 | 104,249.40 | .055 | 3,462 | 3,939 | 3,997 | |
| Ills (No. 46) | 550,332 | | 149,254.37 | | | 2 2.96 | 149,382.83 | 1,504.77 | | 9,139.36 | .0611 | | | | |
| Oregon (b. 29) | 6,530,395 | 66,400,894 | 606,759.19 | 41,541.20 | 480 | 22, 1.89 | 671,295.28 | 5,503.27 | 1,012.43 | 73,983.19 | .1102 | 278 | 1, 20 | 1,072 | |

¹ Porto Rico figures not included in totals, except those relating to values of imports and exports.

NOTE.—The duties and tonnage covered into the Treasury by warrants during the fiscal year 1922 amounted to $357,344,712.40. This sum represents the official "customs receipts" for 1922. The figures in the above statement are based on reports by collectors of receipts from all sources, and include estimated duties, duties and fines on mail importations, increased and additional duties, fines, penalties and forfeitures, and sundry miscellaneous receipts, as well as collections for the Departments of Commerce and Labor.

## SUMMARY.

Total expenses paid from customs appropriation during the fiscal year 1922, as reported by collectors ..................... $10,357,043.55

*Items not included in above table.*

| | |
|---|---|
| Salaries and expenses of the Board of United States General Appraisers ..................... | 45,239.62 |
| Salaries and expenses on account of detection and prevention of frauds ..................... | 174,709.61 |
| Salaries and expenses of the special agents' force ..................... | 218,486.12 |
| Travel, transportation, and miscellaneous expenses not reported by collectors ..................... | 32,569.06 |
| Amount transferred from customs appropriation for stationery for the customs service ..................... | 75,000.00 |
| Salaries and expenses of the Bureau of Customs Statistics at New York ..................... | 151,321.86 |

Total expenses paid from the customs appropriations, including expenses incurred on account of enforcement of navigation laws and compilation of statistics. 11, 74,369.82
Payments on account of the $240 bonus from the appropriation "Increase of compensation, Treasury Department" ..................... 1,493,396.48

Total ..................... 12, 67,766.30

Cost to collect one dollar (based on total receipts from all sources and total expenditures, including increased compensation) ..................... 04

TABLE R.—Stock of money in the United States, classified by kind, at the end of each fiscal year from 1860 to 1889.[1]

| Fiscal year. | Gold coin and bullion.[2] | Silver dollars. | Subsidiary silver. | United States notes. | Fractional currency.[3] | Other United States currency. | State-bank notes. | National-bank notes. | Total. | Percentage of gold to total money. |
|---|---|---|---|---|---|---|---|---|---|---|
| 1860 | $214,000,000 | | $21,000,000 | | | | $207,102,477 | | $442,102,477 | 48.41 |
| 1861 | 270,000,000 | | 16,000,000 | | | | 202,005,767 | | 488,005,767 | 55.33 |
| 1862 | 283,000,000 | | 16,000,000 | $96,620,000 | | $53,040,000 | 183,792,079 | | 629,452,079 | 44.9 |
| 1863 | 290,000,000 | | 14,000,000 | 387,646,589 | $20,192,456 | 93,230,495 | 238,677,218 | | 1,010,746,758 | 25.72 |
| 1864 | 203,000,000 | | 11,000,000 | 447,300,203 | 22,894,877 | 169,252,449 | 179,157,717 | | 1,062,840,516 | 19.10 |
| 1865 | 189,000,000 | | 10,000,000 | 431,066,428 | 25,005,829 | 236,567,393 | 142,919,638 | $31,235,270 | 1,180,197,148 | 16.01 |
| 1866 | 157,000,000 | | 9,500,000 | 400,780,306 | 27,070,877 | 162,738,532 | 19,995,163 | 281,479,908 | 1,068,065,786 | 15.64 |
| 1867 | 198,000,000 | | 9,000,000 | 371,783,597 | 28,307,524 | 123,726,542 | 4,484,112 | 296,625,379 | 1,020,927,154 | 18.22 |
| 1868 | 160,000,000 | | 8,000,000 | 356,000,000 | 32,626,952 | 28,859,025 | 3,163,771 | 299,762,855 | 888,412,603 | 18.01 |
| 1869 | 173,000,000 | | 7,000,000 | 355,935,194 | 32,114,637 | 3,342,921 | 2,558,874 | 299,742,475 | 873,694,101 | 19.80 |
| 1870 | 189,500,000 | | 10,000,000 | 356,000,000 | 39,878,684 | 2,507,433 | 2,222,793 | 299,766,984 | 899,875,899 | 21.06 |
| 1871 | 163,500,000 | | 13,000,000 | 357,500,000 | 40,582,875 | 1,063,578 | 1,968,658 | 315,261,241 | 894,375,752 | 18.28 |
| 1872 | 148,000,000 | | 14,000,000 | 357,500,000 | 40,855,835 | 849,333 | 1,700,935 | 337,664,796 | 900,570,903 | 16.43 |
| 1873 | 135,000,000 | | 17,000,000 | 358,000,000 | 44,799,365 | 701,473 | 1,294,470 | 347,267,061 | 903,211,674 | 14.95 |
| 1874 | 147,379,493 | $2,742,548 | 19,500,000 | 382,000,000 | 45,581,296 | 619,568 | 1,099,621 | 351,861,032 | 949,962,671 | 15.51 |
| 1875 | 121,134,906 | 97,438 | 28,000,000 | 375,771,580 | 42,129,424 | 590,873 | 788,844 | 354,408,008 | 925,524,183 | 13.09 |
| 1876 | 130,056,907 | 4,626,921 | 32,418,734 | 369,772,284 | 34,446,595 | 500,383 | 658,983 | 332,998,336 | 904,849,435 | 14.37 |
| 1877 | 167,501,472 | 16,369,079 | 45,837,506 | 359,764,332 | 20,403,137 | 486,318 | 521,611 | 317,048,872 | 916,160,169 | 18.28 |
| 1878 | 213,109,977 | 41,276,356 | 63,778,823 | 346,681,016 | 16,547,769 | 427,703 | 426,504 | 324,514,284 | 983,845,160 | 21.67 |
| 1879 | 245,741,837 | 72,480,646 | 70,249,985 | 346,681,016 | | | | 329,691,697 | 1,033,640,891 | 23.77 |
| 1880 | 351,841,206 | 95,297,083 | 72,882,270 | 346,681,016 | | | | 344,505,427 | 1,185,559,327 | 29.68 |
| 1881 | 478,484,538 | 122,788,544 | 74,087,061 | 346,681,016 | | | | 355,042,675 | 1,349,592,373 | 35.45 |
| 1882 | 506,757,715 | 152,047,685 | 74,428,580 | 346,681,016 | | | | 358,742,034 | 1,409,397,889 | 35.96 |
| 1883 | 542,732,063 | 180,306,797 | 74,960,300 | 346,681,016 | | | | 356,815,510 | 1,473,235,574 | 36.84 |
| 1884 | 545,500,797 | 203,882,554 | 75,261,528 | 346,681,016 | | | | 339,499,883 | 1,487,249,838 | 36.68 |
| 1885 | 588,697,036 | 237,191,906 | 74,939,820 | 346,681,016 | | | | 319,069,933 | 1,537,925,771 | 38.28 |
| 1886 | 590,774,461 | 277,445,767 | 75,090,937 | 346,681,016 | | | | 309,010,460 | 1,558,718,780 | 37.90 |
| 1887 | 654,520,335 | 310,166,459 | 75,547,799 | 346,681,016 | | | | 279,217,788 | 1,633,412,705 | 40.07 |
| 1888 | 705,818,855 | 343,947,093 | 76,406,376 | 346,681,016 | | | | 252,382,321 | 1,691,435,027 | 41.73 |
| 1889 | 680,063,505 | | 76,601,836 | 346,681,016 | | | | 211,378,963 | 1,658,672,413 | |

[1] Figures for the stock of money in the country from 1861 to 1878, inclusive, have been revised to include all gold in the Treasury; gold coin in the vaults of banks and in circulation; the monetary stock of silver; and all United States currency, including one and two year notes and compound interest notes, as published in previous annual reports of the Secretary of the Treasury. This table has been compiled on the basis of revised figures for June 30 of each year and therefore differs slightly from the monthly circulation statements.

[2] Does not include gold bullion and foreign coin outside of the vaults of the Treasury.

[3] There has been no fractional currency in circulation since 1878.

TABLE S.—Stock of money in the United States, classified by kind, at the end of each fiscal year from 1890 to 1922.[1]

| Fiscal year. | Gold coin and bullion.[2] | Silver dollars. | Subsidiary silver. | United States notes. | Fractional currency.[3] | Federal reserve notes. | Federal reserve bank notes. | National-bank notes. | Total. | Percentage of gold to total money. |
|---|---|---|---|---|---|---|---|---|---|---|
| 1890 | $695,563,029 | $380,083,304 | $76,825,305 | $346,681,016 | | | | $185,970,775 | $1,685,123,429 | $41.28 |
| 1891 | 646,582,852 | 438,753,502 | 77,848,700 | 346,681,016 | | | | 167,927,574 | 1,677,793,644 | 38.54 |
| 1892 | 664,275,335 | 491,067,518 | 77,521,478 | 346,681,016 | | | | 172,683,850 | 1,752,229,197 | 37.91 |
| 1893 | 597,697,685 | 538,300,776 | 77,415,123 | 346,681,016 | | | | 178,713,692 | 1,738,808,292 | 34.37 |
| 1894 | 627,293,201 | 548,000,032 | 76,249,925 | 346,681,016 | | | | 207,353,244 | 1,885,577,418 | 34.74 |
| 1895 | 636,256,023 | 547,777,049 | 76,954,434 | 346,681,016 | | | | 211,691,035 | 1,819,359,557 | 34.97 |
| 1896 | 599,597,964 | 551,723,999 | 75,971,507 | 346,681,016 | | | | 226,000,547 | 1,799,975,033 | 33.31 |
| 1897 | 696,239,016 | 556,590,184 | 75,818,369 | 346,681,016 | | | | 231,441,686 | 1,906,770,271 | 36.51 |
| 1898 | 861,514,780 | 561,330,850 | 76,127,610 | 346,681,016 | | | | 227,900,177 | 2,073,574,442 | 41.55 |
| 1899 | 963,498,384 | 563,697,082 | | 346,681,016 | | | | 241,330,871 | 2,190,093,903 | 43.99 |
| 1900 | 1,034,384,444 | 566,131,027 | 82,363,742 | 346,681,016 | | | | 309,640,444 | 2,339,700,673 | 44.21 |
| 1901 | 1,124,639,062 | 568,182,941 | 89,822,771 | 346,681,016 | | | | 353,742,187 | 2,483,067,097 | 45.29 |
| 1902 | 1,192,594,589 | 570,135,200 | 97,183,762 | 346,681,016 | | | | 356,672,091 | 2,563,286,658 | 46.53 |
| 1903 | 1,248,681,528 | 573,643,226 | 102,034,567 | 346,681,016 | | | | 413,670,650 | 2,664,710,987 | 46.51 |
| 1904 | 1,327,656,398 | 572,869,605 | 107,062,021 | 346,681,016 | | | | 449,235,095 | 2,833,504,135 | 47.35 |
| 1905 | 1,357,655,988 | 568,228,865 | 114,824,189 | 346,681,016 | | | | 495,719,806 | 2,883,109,864 | 47.09 |
| 1906 | 1,475,706,765 | 568,251,530 | 118,224,920 | 346,681,016 | | | | 561,112,300 | 3,069,976,591 | 48.07 |
| 1907 | 1,466,389,101 | 568,249,982 | 130,452,218 | 346,681,016 | | | | 603,788,690 | 3,115,561,007 | 47.06 |
| 1908 | 1,618,133,492 | 568,239,812 | 147,355,783 | 346,681,016 | | | | 698,333,917 | 3,288,764,020 | 47.89 |
| 1909 | 1,642,041,999 | 568,276,719 | 159,408,546 | 346,681,016 | | | | 689,920,074 | 3,366,328,354 | 48.21 |
| 1910 | 1,636,043,478 | 568,277,508 | 155,158,748 | 346,681,016 | | | | 713,430,733 | 3,449,091,083 | 47.84 |
| 1911 | 1,753,196,722 | 568,279,367 | 159,607,364 | 346,681,016 | | | | 728,194,508 | 3,555,938,977 | 49.30 |
| 1912 | 1,818,188,417 | 568,278,020 | 170,588,205 | 346,681,016 | | | | 745,134,992 | 3,658,870,650 | 49.83 |
| 1913 | 1,870,761,835 | 568,273,263 | 175,195,996 | 346,681,016 | | | | 759,157,906 | 3,720,070,016 | 50.28 |
| 1914 | 1,880,656,791 | 568,272,478 | 182,006,687 | 346,681,016 | | | | 750,671,899 | 3,726,288,871 | 50.38 |
| 1915 | 1,985,539,172 | 568,271,655 | 185,430,250 | 346,681,016 | | $84,290,500 | | 819,273,593 | 3,999,485,186 | 49.77 |
| 1916 | 2,449,739,010 | 568,270,319 | 188,858,483 | 346,681,016 | | 176,168,450 | $9,000,000 | 744,174,660 | 4,282,891,938 | 54.65 |
| 1917 | 3,019,146,563 | 568,269,513 | 198,274,179 | 346,681,016 | | 547,407,960 | 12,790,245 | 715,420,010 | 5,187,990,026 | 55.63 |
| 1918 | 3,075,788,838 | 499,515,930 | 231,896,580 | 346,681,016 | | 1,847,580,445 | 15,444,000 | 724,205,485 | 6,531,072,294 | 45.63 |
| 1919 | 3,113,168,661 | 305,145,759 | 242,870,438 | 346,681,016 | | 2,687,556,985 | 187,666,980 | 719,276,732 | 7,305,366,571 | 40.93 |
| 1920 | 2,709,463,700 | 258,857,494 | 258,855,239 | 346,681,016 | | 3,405,877,120 | 201,225,830 | 719,037,730 | 7,699,098,099 | 34.25 |
| 1921 | 3,297,729,834 | 288,788,378 | 271,314,375 | 346,681,016 | | 3,000,429,860 | 130,772,400 | 743,290,374 | 7,869,006,237 | 40.72 |
| 1922 | 3,784,651,712 | 381,174,404 | 271,210,886 | 346,681,016 | | 2,535,061,660 | 80,495,400 | 738,202,027 | 7,777,477,105 | 46.28 |

[1] The stock of money in the country from 1919 to 1921, inclusive, has been revised to include gold bullion and foreign gold coin held by the Federal reserve banks. This table has been compiled on the basis of revised figures for June 30 of each year and therefore differs slightly from the monthly circulation statements.

[2] Does not include gold bullion and foreign coin outside of the vaults of the Treasury, Federal reserve banks, and Federal reserve agents.

[3] There has been no fractional currency in circulation since 1878.

TABLE T.—*Stock of money, money in circulation and amount of circulation per capita, in the United States from 1860 to 1922, inclusive.*

| Date | Stock of money in the United States.[1] | Money held in the Treasury. | | | | | Money outside of the Treasury. | | | | Population of continental United States (estimated). |
|---|---|---|---|---|---|---|---|---|---|---|---|
| | | Total.[2] | Amount held in trust against gold and silver certificates (and Treasury notes of 1890). | Reserve against United States notes (and Treasury notes of 1890). | Held for Federal reserve banks and agents. | All other money. | Total.[2] | Held by Federal reserve banks and agents. | In circulation. | | |
| | | | | | | | | | Amount. | Per capita. | |
| July 1— | | | | | | | | | | | |
| 1860. | $442,102,477 | $6,695,225 | | | | $6,695,225 | $435,407,252 | | $435,407,252 | $13.85 | 31,443,321 |
| 1861[3] | 488,005,767 | 3,600,000 | | | | 3,600,000 | 484,405,767 | | 484,405,767 | 15.11 | 32,064,000 |
| 1862[3] | 629,452,079 | 23,754,335 | | | | 23,754,335 | 605,697,744 | | 605,697,744 | 18.52 | 32,704,000 |
| 1863[3] | 1,010,746,758 | 83,735,922 | | | | 83,735,922 | 927,010,836 | | 927,010,836 | 27.78 | 33,365,000 |
| 1864[3] | 1,092,840,516 | 55,225,536 | | | | 55,225,536 | 1,007,614,980 | | 1,007,614,980 | 28.60 | 33,946,000 |
| 1865[3] | 1,180,197,148 | 96,656,634 | | | | 96,656,634 | 1,083,540,514 | | 1,083,540,514 | 31.18 | 34,748,000 |
| 1866[3] | 1,685,085,786 | 138,892,893 | $10,505,220 | | | 128,387,673 | 939,673,113 | | 939,673,113 | 26.49 | 35,469,000 |
| 1867[3] | 1,020,927,154 | 180,244,975 | 18,678,110 | | | 161,566,865 | 859,360,259 | | 859,360,259 | 25.73 | 36,211,000 |
| 1868[3] | 888,412,603 | 134,171,600 | 17,643,380 | | | 116,528,220 | 771,884,383 | | 771,884,383 | 20.88 | 36,973,000 |
| 1869[3] | 873,694,101 | 163,073,946 | 29,955,960 | | | 133,117,986 | 740,576,215 | | 740,576,215 | 19.61 | 37,756,000 |
| 1870[3] | 899,875,899 | 156,994,322 | 32,084,800 | | | 124,909,522 | 774,966,377 | | 774,966,377 | 20.10 | 38,558,371 |
| 1871[3] | 894,375,752 | 118,009,599 | 17,789,680 | | | 100,210,919 | 794,155,833 | | 794,155,833 | 20.08 | 39,555,000 |
| 1872. | 900,570,903 | 97,773,426 | 26,411,660 | | | 71,361,766 | 829,209,137 | | 829,209,137 | 20.43 | 40,596,000 |
| 1873[3] | 903,211,674 | 130,830,643 | 34,251,320 | | | 96,579,323 | 806,632,351 | | 806,632,351 | 19.35 | 41,677,000 |
| 1874. | 949,962,671 | 162,525,145 | 18,015,380 | | | 144,509,765 | 805,452,906 | | 805,452,906 | 18.82 | 42,796,000 |
| 1875[3] | 925,524,183 | 67,141,382 | 17,548,800 | | | 149,882,382 | 775,641,801 | | 775,641,801 | 17.65 | 43,951,000 |
| 1876[3] | 904,849,435 | 133,853,758 | 24,174,980 | | | 129,673,778 | 775,170,657 | | 775,170,657 | 17.17 | 45,137,000 |
| 1877[3] | 916,160,169 | 188,581,357 | 32,298,040 | | | 156,283,317 | 759,876,852 | | 759,876,852 | 16.39 | 46,353,000 |
| 1878[3] | 983,845,160 | 235,808,65 | 24,804,600 | | | 210,465,85 | 773,379,295 | | 773,379,295 | 16.25 | 47,598,000 |
| 1879.. | 1,033,640,891 | 230,703,398 | 25,694,300 | $100,000,000 | | 215,009,098 | 818,631,793 | | 818,631,793 | 16.75 | 48,866,000 |
| 1880. | 1,185,550,327 | 225,921,568 | 13,753,469 | 100,000,000 | | 112,168,69 | 973,382,228 | | 973,382,228 | 19.41 | 50,155,783 |
| 1881. | 1,349,592,373 | 294,642,63 | 4,688,19 | 100,000,000 | | 135,354,254 | 1,114,238,119 | | 1,114,238,119 | 21.71 | 51,316,000 |
| 1882. | 1,409,397,839 | 294,642,580 | 59,535,110 | 100,000,000 | | 135,107,470 | 1,174,290,419 | | 1,174,290,419 | 22.37 | 52,495,000 |
| 1883.. | 1,473,226,574 | 375,358,934 | 132,428,056 | 100,000,000 | | 142,930,878 | 1,230,305,696 | | 1,230,305,696 | 22.91 | 53,693,000 |
| 1884.. | 1,487,249,838 | 374,358,969 | 167,573,651 | 100,000,000 | | 106,785,69 | 1,243,925,999 | | 1,243,925,999 | 22.65 | 54,911,000 |
| 1885.. | 1,537,926,771 | 473,618,832 | 228,290,66 | 100,000,000 | | 145,358,156 | 1,292,568,615 | | 1,292,568,615 | 23.02 | 56,148,000 |
| 1886.. | 1,558,718,780 | 470,178,855 | 164,160,600 | 100,000,000 | | 206,018,255 | 1,252,700,525 | | 1,252,700,525 | 21.82 | 57,404,000 |
| 1887.. | 1,633,412,705 | 549,217,016 | 233,343,454 | 100,000,000 | | 25,873,862 | 1,317,539,143 | | 1,317,539,143 | 22.45 | 58,680,000 |
| 1888.. | 1,691,435,027 | 641,118,464 | 321,854,307 | 100,000,000 | | 219,264,57 | 1,372,170,870 | | 1,372,170,870 | 22.88 | 59,974,000 |
| 1889.. | 1,658,672,413 | 652,596,558 | 374,285,794 | 100,000,000 | | 178,364,64 | 1,380,361,649 | | 1,380,361,649 | 22.52 | 61,289,000 |

1 The form of circulation statement was revised as of July 1, 1922, so as to exclude from money in circulation all forms of money held by the Federal reserve agents and Federal reserve banks whether as reserve against Federal reserve notes or otherwise. This change did not affect figures for money in circulation prior to the establishment of the Federal reserve system. For the sake of comparability the figures for 1915 to 1922, inclusive, have been compiled on this statement in the same manner as those of July 1, 1922.

2 The amount of money held in trust against gold and silver certificates and Treasury notes of 1890 should be deducted from these totals before combining them with total money outside of the Treasury to arrive at the stock of money in the United States.

3 Revised figures: See footnote (3) on p. 524.

4 Revised figures: See footnote (4) on p. 525.

TREASURY D

# APPENDIX TO REPORT ON THE FINANCES.

# APPENDIX.

## REPORTS OF HEADS OF BUREAUS.

### REPORT OF THE TREASURER.

TREASURY DEPARTMENT,
OFFICE OF THE TREASURER,
*Washington, October 14, 1922.*

SIR: The transactions of the Treasury of the United States for the fiscal year ended June 30, 1922, and its condition at the close of the year are presented in the following report.

The ordinary receipts and expenditures, by warrants drawn, classified for the past two years and adjusted to the basis of the daily Treasury statements, revised, are compared in the following table:

*Ordinary receipts and expenditures for the fiscal years 1921 and 1922 (on basis of warrants drawn, adjusted to basis of daily Treasury statements, revised).*

| Account. | 1921 | 1922 | Increase. | Decrease. |
|---|---|---|---|---|
| **RECEIPTS.** | | | | |
| Customs | $308,025,102.17 | $357,544,712.40 | $49,519,610.23 | |
| Internal revenue: | | | | |
| Income and excess profits taxes | 3,228,137,673.75 | 2,086,918,464.85 | | $1,141,219,208.90 |
| Miscellaneous | 1,351,835,935.31 | 1,121,239,843.45 | | 230,596,091.86 |
| Sale of public lands | 1,530,439.42 | 895,391.22 | | 635,048.20 |
| Miscellaneous | 667,675,758.56 | 508,281,071.05 | | 159,394,687.51 |
| Receipts of the District of Columbia | 16,356,423.32 | 16,812,783.17 | 456,359.85 | |
| Panama Canal tolls, etc | 11,914,361.32 | 12,049,660.65 | 135,299.33 | |
| Total | 5,585,475,693.85 | 4,103,741,926.79 | 50,111,269.41 | 1,531,845,036.47 |
| Deduct moneys covered by warrant in the year subsequent to the deposit thereof | 1,105,240.83 | 146,592.21 | 958,648.62 | |
| Total | 5,584,370,453.02 | 4,103,595,334.58 | 51,069,918.03 | 1,531,845,036.47 |
| Add moneys received in fiscal year but not covered by warrant | 146,592.21 | 1,196.46 | | 145,395.75 |
| Total ordinary receipts | 5,584,517,045.23 | 4,103,596,531.04 | | 1,480,920,514.19 |
| **EXPENDITURES.** | | | | |
| 1. Pay warrants drawn (net): | | | | |
| Legislative | 18,480,866.22 | 16,725,922.69 | | 1,754,943.53 |
| Executive proper | 1,134,796.95 | 216,534.74 | | 918,262.12 |
| European food relief | 1,658,829.74 | 107,746.17 | | 1,551,083.57 |
| State Department | 8,523,891.27 | 10,359,591.47 | 1,835,700.20 | |
| Treasury Department proper | 206,601,260.51 | 219,553,617.78 | 12,952,357.27 | |
| Public buildings | 15,865,265.57 | 21,077,036.02 | 5,211,770.45 | |
| War-risk insurance | 255,752,739.49 | [1] 19,986,067.36 | | 235,766,672.13 |
| War Department proper | 7,395,690.32 | 5,877,674.96 | | 1,518,015.36 |
| Navy Department proper | 3,591,836.57 | 2,456,025.26 | | 1,135,811.31 |
| Interior Department, civil | 48,804,923.39 | 47,578,768.08 | | 1,226,155.31 |
| Post Office Department proper | 2,397,129.12 | 3,471,135.56 | 1,074,006.44 | |
| Postal deficiencies | 130,272,845.36 | 64,346,234.52 | | 65,926,610.84 |
| Additional compensation, Postal Service | 1,374,014.56 | 6,700.53 | | 1,367,314.03 |
| Federal control of telegraph and telephone systems | 1,195,708.79 | 613.20 | | 1,195,095.59 |

[1] To Aug. 9, 1921, only.

531

*Ordinary receipts and expenditures for the fiscal years 1921 and 1922 (on basis of warrants drawn, adjusted to basis of daily Treasury statements, revised)—Continued.*

| Account. | 1921 | 1922 | Increase. | Decrease. |
|---|---|---|---|---|
| EXPENDITURES—continued. | | | | |
| 1. Pay warrants drawn (net)—Continued. | | | | |
| Department of Agriculture... | $120,599,697 08 | $143,984,462.69 | $23,384,765.61 | .............. |
| Department of Commerce.... | 25,892,589.05 | 21,170,146.99 | .............. | $4,722,442.06 |
| Department of Labor........ | 7,040,856.88 | 6,229,602.39 | .............. | 811,254.49 |
| Department of Justice........ | 17,647,450.53 | 17,850,283.55 | 202,833.02 | .............. |
| Federal control and transportation act, 1920......... | 739,019,362.64 | ² 125,232,444.02 | .............. | 864,251,806.66 |
| United States Shipping Board................ | 92,886,783.88 | 86,145,816.32 | .............. | 6,740,967.56 |
| Other independent bureaus and offices............... | 124,985,315.34 | 42,450,974.51 | .............. | 82,534,340.83 |
| Expenses of loans............ | 14,034,731.52 | 2,933,195.81 | .............. | 11,101,535.71 |
| Purchase of obligations of foreign governments....... | 73,896,697.44 | 717,834 36 | .............. | 73,178,863.08 |
| Purchase of farm-loan bonds.. | 8,600,000.00 | ² 175,133.04 | .............. | 8,775,133.04 |
| District of Columbia......... | 23,242,259.54 | 23,989,185.60 | 746,926.06 | .............. |
| Veterans' Bureau............ | .............. | 430,712,903.73 | 430,712,903.73 | .............. |
| Total Civil Establishment.. | 1,950,895,541.76 | 1,062,540,497.23 | 476,121,262.78 | 1,364,476,307.31 |
| Military Establishment proper...................... | 472,064,272.77 | 329,050,896.45 | .............. | · 143,013,376.32 |
| Rivers and harbors........ | 58,820,322.30 | 43,262,427.26 | .............. | 15,557,895.04 |
| War, miscellaneous, civil. | 26,284,215.24 | 21,076,415.55 | .............. | 5,207,799.69 |
| Naval Establishment proper. | 644,278,808.64 | 456,338,787.36 | .............. | 187,940,021.28 |
| Indian Service.............. | 41,470,807.60 | 38,500,413.08 | .............. | 2,970,394.52 |
| Pensions................... | 260,611,416.13 | 252,576,847.70 | .............. | 8,034,568.43 |
| Panama Canal.............. | 16,230,390.79 | 2,791,035.40 | .............. | 13,439,355.39 |
| Interest on the public debt... | 996,676,803.75 | 989,485,409.93 | .............. | 7,191,393.82 |
| Total................... | 4,467,332,578.98 | 3,195,622,729.96 | 476,121,262.78 | 1,747,831,111.80 |
| Deduct repayments received in year but not covered by warrant.................... | 68,202.86 | 6,085.41 | 62,117.45 | .............. |
| Total................... | 4,467,264,376.12 | 3,195,616,644.55 | 476,183,380.23 | 1,747,831,111.80 |
| Add repayments covered by warrant in year subsequent to the deposit thereof....... | 1,449,091.98 | 68,202.86 | .............. | 1,380,889.12 |
| Total (net)............. | 4,468,713,468.10 | 3,195,684,847.41 | .............. | 1,273,028,620.69 |
| Add decrease in amount of unpaid warrants at close of fiscal year under previous fiscal year................. | ³ 4,827,582 56 | 19,618,905.14 | 24,446,487.70 | .............. |
| | 4,463,885,885.54 | 3,215,303,752.55 | 24,446,487.70 | 1,273,028;620.69 |
| 2. Decrease in book credits of disbursing officers and agencies with Treasurer United States during fiscal year............. | 630,831,620.57 | 144,892,612.09 | .............. | 485,939,008.48 |
| Total ordinary expenditures............... | 5,094,717,506.11 | 3,360,196,364.64 | .............. | 1,734,521,141.47 |
| Public debt retirements chargeable against ordinary receipts— | | | | |
| Sinking fund............ | 261,250,250.00 | 275,896,000.00 | .............. | .............. |
| Purchases from foreign repayments............ | 73,939,300 00 | 64,837,900 00 | .............. | .............. |
| Receipts from estate taxes .................. | 26,479,300.00 | 20,893,200.00 | .............. | .............. |
| Purchases from franchise tax receipts (Federal reserve banks)......... | 60,724,500.00 | 60,333,000.00 | .............. | .............. |
| Forfeitures, gifts, etc...... | 168,500.00 | 392,850.00 | .............. | .............. |
| Total................. | 422,561,850.00 | 422,352,950.00 | .............. | 208,900.00 |
| Total expenditures chargeable against ordinary receipts..... | 5,517,279,356 11 | 3,782,549,314.64 | .............. | 1,734,730;041.47 |
| Excess of receipts over expenditures......... | 67,237,689.12 | 321,047,216.40 | ...[.... | .............. |

¹ Deduct excess of repayments.
² Deduct excess of unpaid warrants over previous fiscal year.

## PANAMA CANAL.

The total amount expended on account of the canal proper, the receipts from tolls, etc., and the proceeds from sales of bonds to the close of the fiscal year 1922 appear from the following statement:

*Receipts and disbursements on account of the Panama Canal.*

| | Total amount expended. | Receipts from tolls, etc. | Net amount expended. |
|---|---|---|---|
| To June 30, 1914 | $346,356,413.91 | ................ | $346,356,413.91 |
| Fiscal year— | | | |
| 1915 | 24,427,107.29 | $4,130,215.15 | 20,296,892.14 |
| 1916 | 14,638,194.78 | 2,869,995.28 | 11,768,199.50 |
| 1917 | 15,949,262.47 | 6,150,668.59 | 9,798,593.88 |
| 1918 | 17,299,762.56 | 6,414,570.25 | 10,885,192.31 |
| 1919 | 10,704,409.74 | 6,777,046.55 | 3,927,363.19 |
| 1920 | 6,031,463.72 | 9,039,670.95 | ¹3,008,207.23 |
| 1921 | 16,230,390.79 | 11,914,361.32 | 4,316,029.47 |
| 1922 | 2,791,035.40 | 12,049,660.65 | ¹9,258,625.25 |
| Total | 454,428,040.66 | 59,346,188.74 | 395,081,851.92 |
| Deduct proceeds of bonds sold | ................ | ................ | 138,600,869.02 |
| Net balance expended out of the general fund of the Treasury | ................ | ................ | 256,480,982.90 |

¹ Net receipts in excess of disbursements.

## RECEIPTS AND DISBURSEMENTS ON ACCOUNT OF THE POST OFFICE DEPARTMENT.

The postal receipts deposited in the Treasury and credited to the Post Office Department during the fiscal year 1922 were $175,-674,541.19; other receipts to the amount of $415,341,351.43 were received and disbursed directly by postmasters without being deposited in the Treasury. Such disbursements are authorized by existing law and are accounted for under the provisions of section 406 of the Revised Statutes of the United States. The Postmaster General has exclusive control of the receipts and disbursements of the Post Office Department. All Post Office Department warrants are issued by the Postmaster General on the Treasurer of the United States, and under Treasury Department regulations may be cashed by any Federal reserve bank or regular national bank depositary of the United States.

The transactions relating to the account with the Treasury during the fiscal year 1922 appear from the following statement:

| | Balance June 30, 1921. | Fiscal year 1922. | | Balance June 30, 1922. |
|---|---|---|---|---|
| | | Receipts. | Disbursements. | |
| Washington | $18,769,940.53 | $175,674,541.19 | $182,017,022.26 | $12,427,459.46 |
| Receipts and disbursements by postmasters during quarter ended— | | | | |
| Sept. 30, 1921 | ................ | 104,002,793.26 | 104,002,793.26 | ................ |
| Dec. 31, 1921 | ................ | 105,628,146.28 | 105,628,146.28 | ................ |
| Mar. 31, 1922 | ................ | 103,033,709.55 | 103,033,709.55 | ................ |
| June 30, 1922 | ................ | 102,676,702.34 | 102,676,702.34 | ................ |
| Total | ................ | 591,015,892.62 | 597,358,373.69 | ................ |

## TRANSACTIONS IN THE PUBLIC DEBT.

The receipts and expenditures on account of the principal of the public debt for the fiscal years 1921 and 1922 are compared in the following statement:

| Account. | 1921 | 1922 | Increase. | Decrease. |
|---|---|---|---|---|
| **RECEIPTS.** | | | | |
| Postal savings bonds | $178,880.00 | $112,200.00 | | $66,680.00 |
| Lawful money to retire national bank notes and Federal reserve bank notes | 40,186,945.00 | 107,086,627.50 | $66,899,682.50 | |
| Certificates of indebtedness | 8,486,964,950.00 | 3,905,090,000.00 | | 4,581,874,950.00 |
| United States bonds and notes: | | | | |
| Fourth Liberty loan | [1] 2,213.00 | | 2,213.00 | |
| Victory Liberty loan | [1] 12,730.00 | [1] 1,300.00 | 11,430.00 | |
| Treasury notes | 311,191,600.00 | 1,935,404,750.00 | 1,624,213,150.00 | |
| War savings securities | 26,418,352.19 | 70,325,625.10 | 43,907,272.91 | |
| Total | 8,864,925,784.19 | 6,018,017,902.60 | | 2,846,907,881.59 |
| **EXPENDITURES.** | | | | |
| United States bonds matured and retired | 151,580.00 | 57,140.00 | | 94,440.00 |
| Fractional currency retired | 689.69 | 942.40 | 252.71 | |
| Certificates of indebtedness retired | 8,552,216,500.00 | 4,775,873,950.00 | | 3,776,342,550.00 |
| National bank notes and Federal reserve bank notes retired | 37,460,631.00 | 107,251,870.00 | 69,791,239.00 | |
| War savings securities redeemed | 159,731,963.18 | 85,415,860.52 | | 74,316,102.66 |
| United States bonds and notes purchased and retired: | | | | |
| First Liberty bonds | 200,000.00 | 415,050.00 | 215,050.00 | |
| Second Liberty bonds | 8,770,450.00 | 5,939,500.00 | | 2,830,950.00 |
| Third Liberty bonds | 51,155,500.00 | 137,772,300.00 | 86,616,800.00 | |
| Fourth Liberty bonds | 39,499,250.00 | 9,476,600.00 | | 30,022,650.00 |
| Victory notes | 332,587,450.00 | 1,907,986,250.00 | 1,575,398,800.00 | |
| Total | 9,181,774,013.87 | 7,030,189,462.92 | | 2,151,584,550.95 |
| Excess of expenditures | 316,848,229.68 | 1,012,171,560.32 | | |

[1] Counter entry, deduct.

## APPROPRIATION OF THE NET EARNINGS DERIVED BY THE UNITED STATES FROM FEDERAL RESERVE BANKS.

Section 7 of the Federal reserve act, as amended, provides—

That the net earnings derived by the United States from Federal reserve banks shall, in the discretion of the Secretary, be used to supplement the gold reserve held against outstanding United States notes, or shall be applied to the reduction of the outstanding indebtedness of the United States under regulations to be prescribed by the Secretary of the Treasury.  *  *  *

The net earnings derived by the United States from the Federal reserve banks during the fiscal year 1922 amounted to $59,974,459.74, which was applied by the Secretary of the Treasury to the retirement of interest-bearing obligations of the United States as shown in the statement following:

| Loan. | Principal. | Interest. | Premium. | Total paid. |
|---|---|---|---|---|
| Victory Liberty loan: | | | | |
| 3¾ per cent notes of 1922–23 | $741,000 | $3,199.80 | | $742,865.89 |
| 4¾ per cent notes of 1922–23 | 8,707,000 | 45,770.81 | $22,102.61 | 8,727,236.72 |
| Third Liberty loan | 50,885,000 | 141,244.09 | 2,949.53 | 50,504,357.13 |
| Total | 60,333,000 | 190,214.70 | 25,052.14 | 59,974,459.74 |

## PAYMENT OF OBLIGATIONS OF FOREIGN GOVERNMENTS PURCHASED ON BEHALF OF THE UNITED STATES.

Section 3 of the act approved September 24, 1917, as amended, provides in part—

That the Secretary of the Treasury is hereby authorized, under such terms and conditions as he may from time to time prescribe, to receive payment, on or before maturity, of any obligations of such foreign Governments acquired on behalf of the United States under authority of this act or of said act approved April twenty-fourth, nineteen hundred and seventeen, and, with the approval of the President, to sell any of such obligations (but not at less than the purchase price with accrued interest unless otherwise hereafter provided by law), and to apply the proceeds thereof, and any payments so received from foreign Governments on account of the principal of their said obligations, to the redemption or purchase, at not more than par and accrued interest, of any bonds of the United States issued under authority of this act or of said act approved April twenty-fourth, nineteen hundred and seventeen; and if such bonds can not be so redeemed or purchased the Secretary of the Treasury shall redeem or purchase any other outstanding interest-bearing obligations of the United States which may at such time be subject to redemption or which can be purchased at not more than par and accrued interest.

During the fiscal year 1922 there were received payments to the amount of $64,941,778.95 from foreign Governments on account of the principal of their obligations, and purchases of interest-bearing bonds of the United States were made under the foregoing provisions, as follows:

| Loan. | Principal. | Interest. | Total. |
|---|---|---|---|
| Third Liberty loan | $64,837,900 | $527,569.66 | $65,365,469.66 |

### CUMULATIVE SINKING FUND.

During the fiscal year 1922 purchases of interest-bearing obligations of the United States were made for account of the cumulative sinking fund established by section 6 of the Victory Liberty loan act, approved March 3, 1919, as follows:

| Loan. | Amount paid. | Par amount purchased. | Accrued interest paid. |
|---|---|---|---|
| Victory Liberty loan: | | | |
| 3¾ per cent notes of 1922–23 | $46,922,491.16 | $47,293,000 | $314,923.98 |
| 4¾ per cent notes of 1922–23 | 209,973,819.00 | 211,017,000 | 2,294,915.53 |
| First Liberty loan | 27,850.00 | 27,850 | ................ |
| Second Liberty loan | 109,000.00 | 109,000 | ................ |
| Third Liberty loan | 17,393,720.38 | 17,208,500 | 185,220.38 |
| Fourth Liberty loan | 240,650.00 | 240,650 | ................ |
| Total | 274,667,530.54 | 275,896,000 | 2,795,059.89 |

### FIVE PER CENT BOND PURCHASE FUND.

Purchases of interest-bearing obligations of the United States were made during the fiscal year 1922 under authority of section 15 of the second Liberty bond act, as amended, for account of the bond purchase fund, as follows:

| Loan. | Principal. | Interest. | Purchase price. |
|---|---|---|---|
| Victory Liberty loan: | | | |
| 3¾ per cent notes of 1922–23 | $17,859,000 | $172,264.58 | $17,727,631.41 |
| 4¾ per cent notes of 1922–23 | 112,661,000 | 1,313,244.04 | 111,741,075.07 |
| Total | 130,520,000 | 1,485,508.62 | 129,468,706.48 |

## INTEREST-BEARING BONDS AND NOTES RETIRED ON MISCELLANEOUS ACCOUNTS.

The retirements of Liberty bonds and Victory notes on account of presentation for estate and inheritance taxes, forfeitures to the United States, and gifts during the fiscal year 1922 are shown in the statement following:

| Loan. | Principal retired on account of— | | | Total. |
|---|---|---|---|---|
| | Estate and inheritance taxes. | Forfeitures to the United States. | Gifts to the United States. | |
| First Liberty loan | $323,500 | $62,950 | $750 | $387,200 |
| Second Liberty loan | 5,693,750 | 136,700 | 50 | 5,830,500 |
| Third Liberty loan | 4,834,150 | 6,700 | 50 | 4,840,900 |
| Fourth Liberty loan | 9,217,000 | 18,450 | 500 | 9,235,950 |
| Victory Liberty loan, 4¾ per cent notes of 1922–23 | 824,800 | 166,150 | 550 | 991,500 |
| Total | 20,893,200 | 390,950 | 1,900 | 21,286,050 |

## PAYMENT OF INTEREST ON THE REGISTERED BONDS AND NOTES OF THE UNITED STATES.

Checks are prepared and mailed from the office of the Secretary of the Treasury in payment of the interest on registered bonds and notes of the United States. Such checks indicate the title of the loan for which they are drawn and the rate of interest it bears per annum; the name of the Secretary of the Treasury is printed on the checks, and they are countersigned by a clerk in his office. These checks are drawn on the Treasurer of the United States, but may be cashed by any Federal reserve bank or regular national-bank depositary of the United States. The amount so disbursed is included in the requisition for reimbursement made by the Treasurer at the end of each month. The paid checks are sent to the General Accounting Office, Treasury Department Division. There were 6,531,021 checks drawn during the fiscal year 1922, amounting to $192,945,758.12, while the paid checks numbered 6,676,854, of the total value of $193,282,095.31. See Table No. 23 for details of loans, page 566.

## THE RESERVE FUND.

There were no redemptions of United States notes from the reserve fund during the fiscal year 1922.

## STATEMENT OF THE TREASURY OF THE UNITED STATES.

The Treasury holdings of moneys at the close of the fiscal year 1922 amounted to $4,088,736,224.17, and from the revised figures of the several funds it was set apart as follows:

### RESERVE FUND.

Gold coin and bullion.................................................................................... $152,979,025.63

### TRUST FUNDS.

[Held for redemption of the notes and certificates for which they are respectively pledged.]

| | | | | |
|---|---|---|---|---|
| Gold coin and bullion.......... | $695,000,469.00 | Gold certificates outstanding.... | $985,163,129.00 | |
| Silver dollars..................... | 304,066,593.00 | Less amount in the Treasury.... | 290,162,660.00 | |
| Silver dollars of 1890............. | 1,510,543.00 | | | |
| | | Net......................... | | 695,000,469.00 |
| | | Silver certificates outstanding... | 305,653,163.00 | |
| | | Less amount in the Treasury.... | 1,586,570.00 | |
| | | Net......................... | | 304,066,593.00 |
| | | Treasury notes (1890) outstanding............................... | 1,510,543.00 | |
| | | Less amount in the Treasury................... | | |
| | | Net......................... | | 1,510,543.00 |
| Total..................... | 1,000,577,605.00 | Total..................... | | 1,000,577,605.00 |

### GOLD FUND, FEDERAL RESERVE BOARD.

Gold coin and bullion.................................................................................... $2,108,886,911.43

### GENERAL FUND.

The items composing the general fund are subdivided; the first part shows the amount of each kind of available cash actually held in the vaults of Treasury offices, after setting out from the assets the appropriate kinds of money to meet the requirements of the reserve fund, trust funds, and gold fund, followed by the amounts of public moneys in Federal reserve banks, national banks, and other depositaries to the credit of the Treasurer of the United States and of disbursing officers; the second part shows the current demands against the same, and finally the net balance in the general fund.

| | | |
|---|---|---|
| In Treasury offices: | | |
| Gold coin.................................................................. | $200,336,149.90 | |
| Standard silver dollars................................................... | 7,927,172.00 | |
| United States notes....................................................... | 4,145,964.00 | |
| Federal reserve notes.................................................... | 1,878,289.00 | |
| Federal reserve bank notes............................................. | | |
| National-bank notes...................................................... | 234,352.00 | |
| Subsidiary silver coin.................................................... | 17,747,501.85 | |
| Minor coin................................................................ | 3,620,013.33 | |
| Silver bullion (at cost)................................................... | 44,284,867.40 | |
| Unclassified (unassorted currency, etc.)................................ | 3,283,342.53 | |
| Public debt obligations paid, awaiting reimbursement................. | 503,020.03 | $283,960,672.04 |
| In Federal reserve banks.................................................... | 33,091,888.68 | |
| In transit (including collection account)................................... | 21,991,600.88 | |
| | | 55,083,489.56 |
| In special depositaries: | | |
| Account of sales of certificate of indebtedness, etc..................... | | 146,476,840.69 |
| In national-bank depositaries: | | |
| To credit of Treasurer of United States................................. | 7,832,260.63 | |
| To credit of other Government officers.................................. | 16,169,825.24 | |
| In transit................................................................. | 2,129,381.31 | |
| | | 26,131,467.18 |
| In foreign depositaries: | | |
| To credit of Treasurer of the United States............................. | 700,619.43 | |
| To credit of other Government officers.................................. | 521,190.60 | |
| In transit................................................................. | 1,141.00 | |
| | | 1,222,951.03 |
| In treasury of Philippine Islands: | | |
| To credit of Treasurer of United States................................. | 4,417,757.43 | |
| In transit................................................................. | 554.05 | |
| | | 4,418,311.48 |
| | | 517,293,731.98 |

Deduct current liabilities:

| | | |
|---|---:|---:|
| Federal reserve note 5 per cent fund | $179,138,539.55 | |
| Less notes in process of redemption | 679,432.50 | $178,459,107.05 |
| Federal reserve bank note 5 per cent fund | 7,445,646.55 | |
| Less notes in process of redemption | 1,030,273.00 | 6,415,373.55 |
| National-bank note 5 per cent fund | 29,791,025.87 | |
| Less notes in process of redemption | 15,540,014.63 | 14,251,011.24 |
| Treasurer's checks outstanding | | 447,858.57 |
| Post Office Department balances | | 12,427,459.46 |
| Board of trustees, Postal Savings System, balance | | 7,103,734.69 |
| Balance to credit of postmasters, etc | | 28,902,135.42 |
| Undistributed assets of insolvent national banks | | 1,931,750.56 |
| Retirement of additional circulating notes (act of May 30, 1908) | | 31,080.00 |
| Miscellaneous redemption accounts | | 3,197,276.59 |
| | | $253,166,796.13 |

Balance in Treasury June 30, 1922 ............................... 264,126,935.85

The net excess of all disbursements over all receipts was $268,771,-393.92. This sum deducted from $532,898,329.77, the balance in the Treasury June 30, 1921, leaves $264,126,935.85, the balance in the Treasury June 30, 1922.

The balance in the Treasury at the end of each month from January, 1920, is stated in Table 6, page 558, and for July 1 in each year since 1914 in the statement following:

*Available cash balance (exclusive of the reserve fund) on the dates named.*

| Date. | Available cash balance, general fund. |
|---|---:|
| July 1, 1914 | $161,612,613.53 |
| 1915 | 104,170,105.78 |
| 1916 | 178,491,415.58 |
| 1917 | 967,247,123.48 |
| 1918 | [1] 1,684,929,580.21 |
| 1919 | [1] 1,226,164,935.26 |
| 1920 | [1] 359,947,020.33 |
| 1921 | [1] 532,898,329.77 |
| 1922 | [1] 264,126,935.85 |

[1] Including credits to disbursing officers.

## GOLD IN THE TREASURY.

The gold holdings of the Treasury increased steadily during the entire fiscal year and on June 30, 1922, amounted to $3,157,202,555.96. This increase was primarily due to imports of gold, which were $468,310,273, as against exports of only $27,345,282, leaving a net excess of imports of $440,964,991.

The total amount of gold in the Treasury on July 1 in each year from 1914, set apart for the respective uses, is shown in the statement following:

*Gold in the Treasury.*

| Date. | Reserve. | For certificates in circulation. | Gold fund, Federal Reserve Board. | General fund. | Total. |
|---|---:|---:|---:|---:|---:|
| July 1, 1914 | $150,000,000.00 | $1,026,149,139.00 | | $102,962,970.70 | $1,279,112,109.70 |
| 1915 | 152,977,036.63 | 1,135,213,619.00 | | 94,769,333.55 | 1,382,959,989.18 |
| 1916 | 152,979,025.63 | 1,565,400,289.00 | | 85,114,618.20 | 1,803,493,932.83 |
| 1917 | 152,979,025.63 | 1,584,235,909.00 | $526,295,000.00 | 61,962,101.24 | 2,325,472,035.87 |
| 1918 | 152,979,025.63 | 1,026,631,669.00 | 1,205,082,010.00 | 95,262,262.46 | 2,479,954,967.09 |
| 1919 | 152,979,025.63 | 735,779,491.00 | 1,416,086,099.10 | 211,596,388.87 | 2,516,441,004.60 |
| 1920 | 152,079,025.63 | 584,723,645.00 | 1,184,275,551.87 | 249,981,700.36 | 2,171,959,922.86 |
| 1921 | 152,979,025.63 | 716,532,989.00 | 1,537,856,895.45 | 263,015,170.02 | 2,670,384,080.10 |
| 1922 | 152,979,025.63 | 695,000,469.00 | 2,108,886,911.43 | 200,336,149.90 | 3,157,202,555.96 |

## SECURITIES HELD IN TRUST.

The Treasurer is custodian of the United States bonds pledged as security for the circulating notes of banks, of the securities pledged for the safe-keeping of public deposits in the depositary banks, and of the obligations held as security for postal savings funds deposited in designated depositaries.

The kinds of securities held and the changes therein during the fiscal year 1922 are recorded in the tables following:

*Securities held for national banks June 30, 1921, and June 30, 1922, and changes during 1922.*

| Kind of securities. | Rate. | Held June 30, 1921. | Transactions during 1922. | | Held June 30, 1922. |
|---|---|---|---|---|---|
| | | | Deposited. | Withdrawn. | |
| **TO SECURE CIRCULATION.** | *Per cent.* | | | | |
| United States loan of 1925.................. | 4 | $75,053,500 | $12,388,900 | $5,994,000 | $81,448,400 |
| United States consols of 1930............... | 2 | 574,657,700 | 24,591,350 | 19,776,850 | 579,472,200 |
| United States Panama Canal 1916–36......... | 2 | 47,826,980 | 1,271,520 | 1,007,400 | 48,091,100 |
| United States Panama Canal 1918–38......... | 2 | 25,360,260 | 828,840 | 654,500 | 25,534,600 |
| Total............................... | | 722,898,440 | 39,080,610 | 27,432,750 | 734,546,300 |
| **TO SECURE PUBLIC DEPOSITS.** | | | | | |
| Held by the Treasurer of the United States: | | | | | |
| First Liberty loan of 1932–47.............. | 3½ | 1,367,150 | 748,400 | 1,146,500 | 969,050 |
| Second Liberty loan of 1927–42........... | 4 | 21,400 | 2,200 | 23,600 | ........... |
| Third Liberty loan of 1928................ | 4¼ | 3,921,050 | 1,784,150 | 930,650 | 4,774,550 |
| Fourth Liberty loan of 1933–38........... | 4¼ | 7,058,050 | 3,764,000 | 2,426,750 | 8,395,300 |
| Victory Liberty loan 4¾ per cent notes.... | 4¾ | 2,945,500 | 830,650 | 2,992,150 | 784,000 |
| Victory Liberty loan 3¾ per cent notes.... | 3¾ | 196,000 | 25,000 | 221,000 | ........... |
| First Liberty loan, converted.............. | 4 | 4,250 | 150 | 4,400 | ........... |
| Do.............................. | 4¼ | 1,085,450 | 642,800 | 393,900 | 1,334,350 |
| First Liberty loan, second converted....... | 4¼ | 500 | ........... | ........... | 500 |
| Second Liberty loan, converted........... | 4¼ | 10,046,550 | 4,153,600 | 3,470,950 | 10,729,200 |
| Treasury notes......................... | 4¾ | ........... | 75,600 | ........... | 75,600 |
| Do.............................. | 4¾ | ........... | 1,563,800 | ........... | 1,563,800 |
| Do.............................. | 5¼ | ........... | 248,000 | 125,000 | 123,000 |
| Do.............................. | 5¾ | 180,000 | 60,000 | 180,000 | 60,000 |
| Certificates of indebtedness............... | (1) | 578,000 | 566,000 | 1,059,000 | 85,000 |
| United States loan of 1925................ | 4 | 266,400 | ........... | 94,900 | 171,500 |
| United States consols of 1930.............. | 2 | 1,496,300 | 16,500 | 263,800 | 1,249,000 |
| United States loan of 1908–18............. | 3 | 1,000 | ........... | 1,000 | ........... |
| United States Panama Canal 1916–36..... | 2 | 251,000 | 3,000 | 102,000 | 152,000 |
| United States Panama Canal 1918–38..... | 2 | 44,000 | 1,000 | 1,000 | 44,000 |
| United States Panama Canal of 1961...... | 3 | 4,158,000 | 292,500 | 416,500 | 4,034,000 |
| United States conversions................. | 3 | 566,000 | ........... | 5,000 | 561,000 |
| Federal land bank farm loan.............. | (1) | 95,000 | 239,000 | ........... | 334,000 |
| Philippine loans..........................\ | (1) | 5,009,000 | 443,000 | 485,000 | 4,967,000 |
| Porto Rico loans......................... | 4 | 343,000 | 96,000 | 92,000 | 347,000 |
| District of Columbia...................... | 3.65 | 43,000 | ........... | ........... | 43,000 |
| Hawaii loans............................. | (1) | 662,000 | 116,300 | 10,000 | 768,300 |
| Miscellaneous............................ | (1) | 14,000 | 5,839 | 15,000 | 4,839 |
| Total............................... | | 40,352,600 | 15,677,489 | 14,460,100 | 41,569,989 |

[1] Various.

## SECURITIES HELD TO SECURE CIRCULATION ISSUED BY FEDERAL RESERVE BANKS.

*Securities held for Federal reserve banks June 30, 1921, and June 30, 1922, and changes during 1922.*

| Kind of securities. | Rate. | Held June 30, 1921. | Transactions during 1922. | | Held June 30, 1922. |
|---|---|---|---|---|---|
| | | | Deposited. | Withdrawn. | |
| | *Per cent.* | | | | |
| United States loan of 1925 | 4 | $2,593,000 | ............ | $825,000 | $1,768,000 |
| United States consols of 1930 | 2 | 11,468,400 | ............ | 3,405,000 | 8,063,400 |
| United States Panama Canal 1916–36 | 2 | 383,500 | ............ | 126,500 | 257,000 |
| United States Panama Canal 1918–38 | 2 | 285,300 | ............ | 155,000 | 130,300 |
| United States 1-year special certificates of indebtedness | 2 | 215,875,000 | ............ | 141,875,000 | 74,000,000 |
| Total | ........ | 230,605,200 | ............ | 146,386,500 | 84,218,700 |

*Securities held to secure postal savings funds June 30, 1921, and June 30, 1922, and changes during 1922.*

| Kind of securities. | Rate. | Held June 30, 1921. | Transactions during 1922. | | Held June 30, 1922. |
|---|---|---|---|---|---|
| | | | Deposited. | Withdrawn. | |
| | *Per cent.* | | | | |
| United States first Liberty loan | 3½ | $4,700,150.00 | $292,050 | $3,665,000.00 | $1,327,200.00 |
| United States second Liberty loan | 4 | 74,650.00 | 750 | 38,300.00 | 37,100.00 |
| United States third Liberty loan | 4¼ | 9,176,300.00 | 6,235,800 | 6,325,500.00 | 9,086,600.00 |
| United States fourth Liberty loan | 4¼ | 12,110,550.00 | 4,967,050 | 7,572,050.00 | 9,505,550.00 |
| United States Victory Liberty loan | 3¾ | 4,415,800.00 | 350,250 | 4,766,050.00 | ............ |
| Do | 4¾ | 2,315,650.00 | 1,680,350 | 3,135,950.00 | 860,050.00 |
| United States 4¼ per cent first Liberty loan, converted | 4¼ | 2,767,950.00 | 409,900 | 948,000.00 | 2,229,850.00 |
| United States 4¼ per cent second Liberty loan, converted | 4¼ | 11,951,500.00 | 5,908,650 | 5,560,250.00 | 12,299,900.00 |
| United States 4 per cent first Liberty loan, converted | 4 | 61,850.00 | ............ | 30,000.00 | 31,850.00 |
| United States 4¼ per cent first Liberty loan, second converted | 4¼ | 6,100.00 | 1,000 | ............ | 7,100.00 |
| Treasury notes | 4¾ | ............ | 3,057,000 | 55,000.00 | 3,002,000.00 |
| Do | 5½ | ............ | 3,676,000 | ............ | 3,676,000.00 |
| Do | 5¾ | 475,000.00 | 62,000 | 15,000.00 | 522,000.00 |
| United States certificates of indebtedness | (1) | 488,000.00 | 1,002,000 | 1,145,000.00 | 345,000.00 |
| United States loan of 1925 | 4 | 154,400.00 | 2,000 | 63,000.00 | 93,400.00 |
| United States consols of 1930 | 2 | 591,700.00 | 149,000 | 508,000.00 | 232,700.00 |
| United States Canal loan of 1961 | 3 | 2,246,600.00 | 262,000 | 531,600.00 | 1,977,000.00 |
| United States Canal loan of 1916–36 | 2 | 63,000.00 | ............ | 28,000.00 | 35,000.00 |
| United States Canal loan of 1918–38 | 2 | 24,500.00 | ............ | 14,000.00 | 10,500.00 |
| United States conversions | 3 | 240,000.00 | ............ | 175,000.00 | 65,000.00 |
| Philippine loans | 4 | 3,376,000.00 | 205,000 | 1,044,000.00 | 2,537,000.00 |
| Porto Rico loans | 4 | 998,000.00 | 15,000 | 346,000.00 | 667,000.00 |
| District of Columbia | 3.65 | 70,500.00 | ............ | 25,000.00 | 45,500.00 |
| Territory of Hawaii | (1) | 767,000.00 | 25,000 | 298,500.00 | 493,500.00 |
| State loans | (1) | 16,779,600.00 | 949,250 | 6,630,500.00 | 11,098,350.00 |
| Municipal loans | (1) | 47,021,715.44 | 1,678,525 | 19,463,862.94 | 29,236,377.50 |
| County loans | (1) | 11,766,200.00 | 689,000 | 4,940,900.00 | 7,514,300.00 |
| Miscellaneous | (1) | 9,919,889.00 | 468,600 | 4,521,089.00 | 5,867,400.00 |
| Federal land bank farm loan | (1) | 294,000.00 | 689,000 | 552,000.00 | 431,000.00 |
| Federal land bank farm loan, joint stock | 5 | 86,000.00 | 91,000 | 59,000.00 | 118,000.00 |
| Total | ........ | 142,942,604.44 | 32,866,175 | 72,456,551.94 | 103,352,227.50 |

[1] Various.

## SPECIAL TRUST FUNDS.

Under provisions of law or by direction of the Secretary of the Treasury, the Treasurer of the United States is custodian of several special trusts, consisting of bonds and other obligations.

The kinds of bonds or obligations held on each account and transactions therein during the fiscal year 1922 are set out in the statement following:

| Account and kinds. | Held June 30, 1921. | Fiscal year 1922. | | Held June 30, 1922. |
|---|---|---|---|---|
| | | Deposited. | Withdrawn. | |
| State bonds belonging to the United States: | | | | |
| Louisiana State bonds.......... | $37,000.00 | ................ | ................ | $37,000.00 |
| North Carolina State bonds.... | 58,000.00 | ................ | ................ | 58,000.00 |
| Tennessee State bonds......... | 335,666.66⅔ | ................ | ................ | 335,666.66⅔ |
| Held for the District of Columbia: United States securities for account District of Columbia sinking fund................. | 3,747,500.00 | $870,000.00 | $100,000.00 | 4,517,500.00 |
| Chesapeake & Ohio Canal bonds | 84,285.00 | ................ | ................ | 84,285.00 |
| Board of audit certificates..... | 20,134.72 | ................ | ................ | 20,134.72 |
| Held for the board of trustees, Postal Savings System: United States bonds..................... | 118,758,330.00 | 809,220.00 | 14,000,000.00 | 105,567,550.00 |
| Held for the Secretary of War: Captured bonds of the State of Louisiana..................... | 545,480.00 | ................ | ................ | 545,480.00 |
| Obligations belonging to the Lincoln Farm Association.... | 46,000.00 | ................ | ................ | 46,000.00 |
| Held for the Secretary of the Treasury: | | | | |
| Panama R. R. notes.;......... | 3,247,332.11 | ................ | ................ | 3,247,332.11 |
| Certificates of indebtedness representing loans to foreign Governments approved Apr. 24, 1917, Sept. 24, 1917, as amended..................... | 9,496,941,248.70 | 10,104,321.86 | 51,930,635.22 | 9,455,114,935.34 |
| Donations to the Government.. | 625.00 | ................ | ................ | 625.00 |
| Bonds held to secure Government funds in Federal land banks— | | | | |
| Notes...................... | ................ | 11,250,000.00 | 11,250,000.00 | ................ |
| Collateral................. | ................ | 11,250,000.00 | 11,250,000.00 | ................ |
| Farm loan bonds held under act of Congress approved Jan. 18, 1918......................... | 136,885,000.00 | ................ | ................ | 136,885,000.00 |
| Farm loan bonds held under act of Congress approved May 26, 1920......................... | 46,150,000.00 | ................ | 44,400,000.00 | 1,750,000.00 |
| Bonds and certificates held in trust for the Alien Property Custodian— | | | | |
| Trust account.............. | 18,557,256.74 | 3,137,009.80 | 1,974,455.00 | 19,719,811.54 |
| Investment account........ | 59,191,000.00 | 4,673,000.00 | 63,864,000.00 | ................ |
| Bonds received from the Secretary of War on account of sales of surplus War Department property sold by United States Liquidation Commission................. | 562,781,704.14 | 9,795,881.76 | 9,694.43 | 572,567,891.47 |
| Obligations received from Secretary of Navy on account of sales of surplus Navy Department property........... | 2,266,709.66 | ................ | ................ | 2,266,709.66 |
| Obligations received from American Relief Administration, United States Grain Corporation................. | 84,093,963.55 | ................ | ................ | 84,093,963.55 |
| Capital stock of Federal land banks....................... | 6,700,675.00 | ................ | 1,057,830.00 | 5,642,845.00 |
| Coos Bay wagon-road grant fund....................... | 20,000.00 | ................ | ................ | 20,000.00 |
| Obligations held in custody for Secretary of the Navy— | | | | |
| Notes...................... | 5,206,496.01 | 1,445,860.98 | 786,518.03 | 5,865,838.96 |
| Collateral................. | 730,229.67 | 50,000.00 | 140,820.69 | 639,408.98 |

| Account and kinds. | Held June 30, 1921. | Fiscal year 1922. | | Held June 30, 1922. |
| --- | --- | --- | --- | --- |
| | | Deposited. | Withdrawn. | |
| **Held for the Secretary of the Treasury—Continued.** | | | | |
| Transportation act of 1920— | | | | |
| Notes.................... | $347,749,652.67 | $99,705,839.33 | $95,618,210.00 | $351,837,282.00 |
| Collateral................ | 73,913,850.00 | 25,319,865.80 | 5,906,002.08 | 93,327,713.72 |
| Account Director General of Railroads— | | | | |
| Notes.................... | 37,152,250.00 | 64,620,000.00 | 7,450,250.00 | 94,322,000.00 |
| Collateral................ | 19,945,350.00 | 1,012,000.00 | .............. | 20,957,350.00 |
| Liberty bonds held for account of civil-service retirement and disability fund......... | .............. | 8,120,000.00 | 8,120,000.00 | .............. |
| **Held for account of Secretary of Interior:** | | | | |
| Indian trust funds............. | 9,334,900.00 | 14,500.00 | 197,450.00 | 9,151,950.00 |
| District of Columbia teachers' retirement fund.............. | 227,450.00 | 236,300.00 | .............. | 463,750.00 |
| **Held for account of Employees' Compensation Commission.......** | 10,000.00 | .............. | .............. | 10,000.00 |
| **Securities held for account War Finance Corporation.............** | 33,904,450.00 | .............. | 32,854,450.00 | 1,050,000.00 |
| **Securities held for account receivers of insolvent banks...............** | 350,000.00 | 379,450.00 | .............. | 729,450.00 |
| **Securities held for account John Ericsson Memorial Commission...** | 25,000.00 | .............. | .............. | 25,000.00 |
| **Notes received from Secret Service Division.....................** | 900.00 | .............. | .............. | 900.00 |
| **Liberty bonds held account war relief notes.....................** | 400.00 | .............. | .............. | 400.00 |
| **Liberty bonds held in lieu of surety bonds, under provisions of Treasury Department Circular No. 154:** | | | | |
| For contracts performed under internal-revenue act, 1918..... | 1,047,450.00 | 531,130.00 | 463,120.00 | 1,115,460.00 |
| For use of alcohol for nonbeverage purposes............... | 160,450.00 | 18,000.00 | 116,850.00 | 61,600.00 |
| For internal-revenue taxes..... | 157,150.00 | 147,950.00 | 39,800.00 | 265,300.00 |
| For contracts with General Supply Committee........... | 41,150.00 | 30,550.00 | 46,950.00 | 24,750.00 |
| For Secretary of Labor Department................... | 50,550.00 | .............. | 23,550.00 | 27,000.00 |
| For United States Air Service.. | 250,000.00 | .............. | 250,000.00 | .............. |
| For Chemical Warfare Service.. | 285,000.00 | .............. | 28,500.00 | 256,500.00 |
| For Commissioner of Indian Affairs..................... | 542,500.00 | 452,600.00 | 197,200.00 | 797,900.00 |
| Total..................... | 11,071,553,089.63⅜ | 253,973,479.53 | 352,076,285.45 | 10,973,450,283.71⅞ |

The State of North Carolina has authorized and appointed commissioners to take under consideration a plan for settling the indebtedness of that State to the United States, but Congress postponed action on a measure providing for representatives on the part of the Government.

Commissioners representing the Government and the State of Tennessee, under provisions of law, have had under consideration a plan for settling with that State. It is apparent that some progress has been made toward a settlement with the two States named in the foregoing for the unpaid matured bonds of those States belonging to the United States.

The special trust held for the District of Columbia represents, first, investments on account of the sinking fund; and, second, obligations that belong to the District of Columbia.

The special trust held for the board of trustees, Postal Savings System, consists of postal savings bonds and Liberty loan bonds, representing investments made by said board.

Recommendation has been made to Congress for authority to return to the State of Louisiana the bonds of that State captured at Shreveport by the Union forces during the War of the Rebellion, now held as a special deposit by the Secretary of War.

The special trusts held for the Secretary of the Treasury are composed of notes of the Panama Railroad Co., drawing 4 per cent interest, payable to the United States, and is security for money advanced for the equipment and construction of said railroad; and interest-bearing obligations of foreign Governments payable to the United States, purchased at par from such Governments engaged in war with the enemies of the United States, act of April 24, 1917.

### POSTAL SAVINGS BONDS AND INVESTMENTS THEREIN.

Under a general authority in the postal savings law (act of June 25, 1910), the trustees of the Postal Savings System have arranged to take over at par any of the postal savings bonds that depositors may wish to turn back.

Under the arrangement made by the trustees they have taken over at par all of the bonds offered by the depositors, and at the close of the fiscal year 1922 the Treasurer of the United States held $8,278,800 of such bonds, which are registered in the name of the board of trustees.

### WITHDRAWAL OF BONDS TO SECURE CIRCULATION.

National banks did not file with the Treasurer of the United States any applications to sell for their account United States bonds securing circulation during the fiscal year 1922.

### LAWFUL MONEY DEPOSITED IN THE TREASURY DURING THE FISCAL YEAR 1922 FOR THE REDEMPTION OF NATIONAL-BANK NOTES.

The lawful money deposited in the Treasury each month of the fiscal year 1922 for the redemption of notes of banks insolvent, in liquidation, and reducing their circulation is shown in Table 24, page 567.

### DEPOSITARIES OF THE UNITED STATES.

The Secretary of the Treasury determines the number of such depositaries and the amount of public money required in each for the transaction of the public business, fixes the amount of balances they may hold, and requires the banks thus designated to give satisfactory security, by the deposit of United States bonds and otherwise, for the safe-keeping and prompt payment of the public money deposited with them and for the faithful performance of their duties as financial agents of the Government. All of the national-bank depositaries are required to pay interest at the rate of 2 per cent per annum on the average monthly amount of public deposits held.

The number of depositary banks (excluding special depositaries appointed under the Liberty loan acts) at the close of the fiscal years 1921 and 1922 are here stated:

|  | Federal reserve banks. | National banks. | Special. | Total. |
|---|---|---|---|---|
| June 30, 1921 | 12 | 718 | 13 | 743 |
| June 30, 1922 | 12 | 1,185 | 13 | 1,210 |

## PUBLIC MONEYS IN DEPOSITARY BANKS.

The depositary banks held public moneys at the close of the fiscal years 1921 and 1922, as follows:

| Depositaries. | June 30, 1921. | June 30, 1922. |
|---|---|---|
| Federal reserve banks | $43,475,862.73 | $33,091,888.68 |
| Special depositaries | 395,738,063.16 | 146,476,840.69 |
| National banks | 24,243,711.72 | 24,002,085.87 |
| Foreign depositaries | 52,258,530.78 | 1,221,810.03 |
| Treasury of Philippine Islands | 7,917,707.88 | 4,417,757.43 |
| Total | 523,633,876.27 | 209,210,382.70 |

### INTEREST ON PUBLIC MONEYS HELD BY DEPOSITARY BANKS.

Interest is collected semiannually from depositaries of public moneys (except Federal reserve banks) at the rate of 2 per cent per annum on the basis of 181 days to the half year from January 1 to June 30 and 184 days from July 1 to December 31. Each depositary is required to render to the Treasurer semiannually (January 1 and July 1) an interest report showing daily balances held by such bank for the prior six months and the amount of interest due and paid thereon. These reports are checked by the ledgers of this office.

Interest was first collected by the department under the provisions of the act of May 30, 1908, on all special and additional deposits in general depositaries and on all deposits in special depositaries at the rate of 1 per cent per annum. In accordance with instructions contained in letter of the Secretary of the Treasury, dated April 22, 1912, the rate of interest was increased from 1 per cent to 2 per cent per annum, beginning July 1, 1912.

During the fiscal year 1922 the interest accrued on ordinary balances held was $796,871.71, and on balances arising from sales of bonds, certificates of indebtedness, etc., $5,957,918.35, making a total of $6,754,790.06. The total amount of interest collected on depositary balances since May 30, 1908, may be studied from the revised statement following:

| Fiscal year. | Interest on balances arising from— | | |
|---|---|---|---|
| | Ordinary accounts. | Sales of bonds, notes, and certificates. | Total. |
| Total to June 30, 1913 | $810,626.15 | | $810,626.15 |
| 1914 | 1,409,426.07 | | 1,409,426.07 |
| 1915 | 1,222,706.93 | | 1,222,706.93 |
| 1916 | 791,671.45 | | 791,671.45 |
| 1917 | 703,771.76 | | 1,061,993.19 |
| 1918 | 1,134,569.09 | $358,221.43 | 11,701,227.12 |
| 1919 | 5,507,742.43 | 10,566,658.03 | 26,503,951.44 |
| 1920 | 1,865,975.76 | 20,996,209.01 | 13,324,952.65 |
| 1921 | 2,580,746.84 | 11,458,976.89 | 6,093,054.86 |
| 1922 | 796,871.71 | 3,512,308.02 | 6,754,790.06 |
| | | 5,957,918.35 | |
| Aggregate | 16,824,108.19 | 52,850,291.73 | 69,674,399.92 |

## GOLD FUND, FEDERAL RESERVE BOARD.

The balance to the credit of the gold fund of the Federal Reserve Board on June 30, 1921, was $1,537,856,895.45. During the fiscal year 1922 deposits amounted to $2,421,691,036.13 and withdrawals $1,850,661,020.15, leaving a balance to the credit of the fund on June 30, 1922, of $2,108,886,911.43.

## UNITED STATES PAPER CURRENCY ISSUED AND REDEEMED.

There was an increase of $386,768,000 in the volume of paper currency issued under the direct authority of the Government during the fiscal year 1922 as compared with that of 1921. This increase results from the extension of facilities for making redemptions and replacements of worn and unfit currency through Federal reserve banks and branches, the resumption of the issue of gold certificates, and the issue of silver certificates against silver dollars coined to replace those broken up and sold under provisions of the act of April 23, 1918.

The amount of each kind of paper currency issued and redeemed during the fiscal year 1922 is recorded in the following statement:

| | United States notes. | Trust-fund obligations. | | | Total. |
|---|---|---|---|---|---|
| | | Treasury notes of 1890. | Gold certificates. | Silver certificates. | |
| Outstanding June 30, 1921......... | $346,681,016 | $1,576,184 | $795,848,929 | $202,578,683 | $1,346,684,812 |
| Issued during fiscal year 1922...... | 339,348,000 | ............ | 226,420,000 | 378,276,000 | 944,044,000 |
| | 686,029,016 | 1,576,184 | 1,022,268,929 | 580,854,683 | 2,290,728,812 |
| Redeemed during fiscal year 1922.. | 339,348,000 | 65,641 | 37,105,800 | 275,201,520 | 651,720,961 |
| Outstanding June 30, 1922......... | 346,681,016 | 1,510,543 | 985,163,129 | 305,653,163 | 1,639,007,851 |
| Less amount held in Treasury..... | 4,145,964 | ............ | 290,162,660 | 1,586,570 | 295,895,194 |
| Net...................... | 342,535,052 | 1,510,543 | 695,000,469 | 304,066,593 | 1,343,112,657 |

In a study of the foregoing table it will be observed that the United States notes issued and credited in the general account as a receipt are offset by an equal amount of worn or unfit notes in kind withdrawn therefrom, canceled, and retired, which is in accordance with the provisions of the act of May 31, 1878. In explanation of the manner of issuing and redeeming gold certificates, silver certificates, and Treasury notes of 1890, it may be said that for certificates issued and credited in the general account an equal amount of the respective kinds of money held in the general account is transferred therefrom to, and retained in, the trust funds for their redemption; for gold certificates, silver certificates, and Treasury notes withdrawn from the general fund, canceled, and retired, a like amount of the respective coins is released from the trust funds and brought into the general fund in their stead.

UNITED STATES PAPER CURRENCY PREPARED FOR ISSUE AND AMOUNT
ISSUED.

The paper currency prepared for issue and the amount issued
during each fiscal year from 1917 appears from the following statement:

| Fiscal year. | Prepared for issue. | | | Paper currency issued. | | |
|---|---|---|---|---|---|---|
| | Number of notes and certificates. | Total value. | Average value. | Number of notes and certificates. | Total value. | Average value. |
| 1917 | 391,962,000 | $2,919,228,000 | $7.447 | 390,016,642 | $2,068,356,000 | $5.303 |
| 1918 | 352,523,000 | 1,028,488,000 | 2.917 | 354,519,271 | 753,124,000 | 2.125 |
| 1919 | 267,264,000 | 348,824,000 | 1.305 | 260,333,387 | 350,138,000 | 1.345 |
| 1920 | 280,448,000 | 371,112,000 | 1.323 | 284,853,221 | 398,018,000 | 1.397 |
| 1921 | 311,320,000 | 400,420,000 | 1.286 | 318,842,004 | 557,276,000 | 1.747 |
| 1922 | 483,872,000 | 1,236,048,000 | 2.554 | 463,884,578 | 944,044,000 | 2.035 |

The number of pieces and amount of paper currency issued directly
by the Government monthly for the fiscal years 1921 and 1922 are
recorded in the statement following:

*United States paper currency issued during the fiscal years 1921 and 1922.*

| Month. | Fiscal year 1921. | | | Fiscal year 1922. | | |
|---|---|---|---|---|---|---|
| | Number of notes and certificates. | Total value. | Average value of notes and certificates. | Number of notes and certificates. | Total value. | Average value of notes and certificates. |
| July | 20,292,000 | $27,268,000 | $1.343 | 35,086,000 | $96,064,000 | $2.737 |
| August | 15,788,100 | 26,204,000 | 1.659 | 42,537,000 | 104,676,000 | 2.460 |
| September | 23,604,000 | 30,684,000 | 1.299 | 40,001,000 | 107,868,000 | 2.696 |
| October | 31,148,000 | 65,252,000 | 2.094 | 38,473,000 | 122,924,000 | 3.195 |
| November | 20,920,000 | 29,144,000 | 1.393 | 32,188,000 | 67,868,000 | 2.108 |
| December | 20,348,000 | 21,724,000 | 1.067 | 38,280,000 | 67,444,000 | 1.761 |
| January | 24,500,000 | 30,752,000 | 1.255 | 27,692,000 | 57,700,000 | 2.083 |
| February | 23,868,000 | 47,948,000 | 2.008 | 33,200,075 | 58,914,000 | 1.774 |
| March | 28,576,004 | 35,480,000 | 1.241 | 43,382,003 | 77,478,000 | 1.785 |
| April | 31,052,000 | 36,836,000 | 1.186 | 40,505,200 | 60,312,000 | 1.488 |
| May | 41,100,900 | 101,524,000 | 2.470 | 43,876,000 | 63,916,000 | 1.456 |
| June | 37,645,000 | 104,460,000 | 2.774 | 48,657,100 | 58,880,000 | 1.210 |
| Total | 318,842,004 | 557,276,000 | 1.747 | 463,877,378 | 944,044,000 | 2.035 |
| Per cent of increase over preceding year | 11.9 | 40.0 | .......... | 45.4 | 69.4 | .......... |

REDEMPTIONS OF PAPER CURRENCY.

The pieces of United States notes, Treasury notes of 1890, and
gold and silver certificates redeemed during the fiscal year 1922
numbered 418,767,973, of the total value of $651,720,961. The
pieces redeemed were 45,109,405 less than those issued, and the
amount was $292,323,039 less than the amount issued during the
year.

A comparison, by months, for the fiscal years 1921 and 1922 may be observed in the annexed table:

*United States paper currency redeemed during the fiscal years 1921 and 1922.*

| Month. | Fiscal year 1921. | | Fiscal year 1922. | |
|---|---|---|---|---|
| | United States notes, Treasury notes of 1890, and gold and silver certificates. | Total value. | United States notes, Treasury notes of 1890, and gold and silver certificates. | Total value. |
| July | 19,588,805 | $70,131,000 | 28,911,102 | $42,971,660 |
| August | 19,256,692 | 119,701,500 | 31,086,687 | 53,246,410 |
| September | 24,019,453 | 86,109,000 | 32,829,715 | 50,659,810 |
| October | 26,038,751 | 355,606,400 | 38,066,505 | 55,015,730 |
| November | 20,851,226 | 66,014,900 | 32,019,856 | 48,324,220 |
| December | 18,556,492 | 72,864,100 | 38,467,652 | 58,445,960 |
| January | 27,933,654 | 57,906,891 | 40,377,231 | 63,620,870 |
| February | 21,641,262 | 78,604,723 | 35,162,152 | 55,831,075 |
| March | 27,889,772 | 38,892,665 | 40,467,267 | 62,453,006 |
| April | 23,184,215 | 32,078,044 | 34,538,915 | 53,573,250 |
| May | 28,496,941 | 40,927,030 | 34,450,619 | 55,030,070 |
| June | 27,327,912 | 39,994,920 | 32,390,272 | 52,548,900 |
| Total | 284,785,175 | 1,058,831,173 | 418,767,973 | 651,720,961 |
| Per cent of increase over preceding year | [1]10.9 | 62.2 | 47.0 | [1]39.3 |

[1] Decrease.

## PIECES OF UNITED STATES PAPER CURRENCY OUTSTANDING.

The number of pieces of United States notes, Treasury notes of 1890, and gold and silver certificates outstanding and their total value at the close of each month for the fiscal years 1921 and 1922 are shown in the following statement:

| Month. | Fiscal year 1921. | | Fiscal year 1922. | |
|---|---|---|---|---|
| | Number of pieces. | Total value. | Number of pieces. | Total value. |
| July | 300,260,072 | $1,806,376,985 | 340,459,505 | $1,400,777,152 |
| August | 297,425,980 | 1,712,879,485 | 351,909,818 | 1,452,206,742 |
| September | 297,010,528 | 1,657,454,485 | 359,081,103 | 1,509,414,932 |
| October | 302,119,777 | 1,367,100,085 | 359,487,598 | 1,577,323,202 |
| November | 302,188,951 | 1,330,229,185 | 359,655,740 | 1,596,866,982 |
| December | 303,980,458 | 1,279,089,085 | 359,468,090 | 1,605,865,022 |
| January | 300,622,804 | 1,251,934,194 | 346,782,860 | 1,599,944,152 |
| February | 302,809,543 | 1,221,277,471 | 344,820,783 | 1,603,027,077 |
| March | 303,495,974 | 1,217,864,806 | 347,735,518 | 1,618,052,071 |
| April | 311,363,559 | 1,222,622,762 | 353,701,803 | 1,624,790,821 |
| May | 323,967,518 | 1,283,219,732 | 363,127,185 | 1,633,676,751 |
| June | 334,284,603 | 1,347,684,812 | 379,394,013 | 1,640,007,851 |

### PAPER CURRENCY OUTSTANDING, BY DENOMINATIONS.

The total amount of paper currency of each kind and denomination outstanding on June 30, 1922, is shown by the following statement:

*Paper currency of each denomination outstanding June 30, 1922.*

| Denomination. | United States notes. | Treasury notes of 1890. | Federal reserve notes. | Federal reserve bank notes. |
|---|---|---|---|---|
| One dollar | $95,852,899 | $314,259 | .......... | $42,188,8? |
| Two dollars | 45,592,424 | 193,306 | .......... | 19,413,3? |
| Five dollars | 61,135,635 | 387,338 | $403,870,840 | 14,073,8? |
| Ten dollars | 103,524,871 | 351,000 | 650,094,620 | 2,713,8? |
| Twenty dollars | 31,749,562 | 142,090 | 869,758,600 | 2,087,4? |
| Fifty dollars | 1,378,225 | 7,050 | 224,362,200 | 86,1? |
| One hundred dollars | 1,319,400 | 64,500 | 239,377,400 | .......... |
| Five hundred dollars | 992,000 | .......... | 42,849,000 | .......... |
| One thousand dollars | 6,126,000 | 51,000 | 94,189,000 | .......... |
| Five thousand dollars | .......... | .......... | 13,770,000 | .......... |
| Ten thousand dollars | 10,000 | .......... | 16,790,000 | .......... |
| Fractional parts | .......... | | | |
| **Total** | 347,681,016 | 1,510,543 | 2,555,061,660 | 80,563,4? |
| Deduct: | | | | |
| Unknown, destroyed | 1,000,000 | | | |
| Held in Treasury | 4,145,964 | .......... | 2,559,644 | 1,030,2? |
| Held by Federal reserve banks and Federal reserve agents | 50,192,056 | 1,000 | 413,788,985 | 7,597,1? |
| Redeemed but not assorted by denominations | | | | 68,0? |
| Net | 292,342,996 | 1,509,543 | 2,138,713,031 | 71,867,9? |

| Denomination. | National bank notes. | Gold certificates. | Silver certificates. | Total. |
|---|---|---|---|---|
| One dollar | $341,844 | .......... | $201,664,667 | $340,362,? |
| Two dollars | 163,190 | .......... | 10,277,712 | 75,639,9 |
| Five dollars | 143,245,230 | .......... | 77,194,718 | 699,907,6 |
| Ten dollars | 320,148,100 | $74,277,975 | 5,621,511 | 1,156,731,? |
| Twenty dollars | 244,058,630 | 83,975,824 | 5,874,950 | 1,237,647,? |
| Fifty dollars | 26,610,700 | 28,192,730 | 4,794,085 | 285,431,? |
| One hundred dollars | 26,878,700 | 44,452,100 | 200,020 | 312,292,? |
| Five hundred dollars | 87,500 | 13,687,000 | 10,500 | 57,626,? |
| One thousand dollars | 21,000 | 63,162,500 | 15,000 | 163,564,? |
| Five thousand dollars | .......... | 79,935,000 | .......... | 93,705,? |
| Ten thousand dollars | .......... | 597,480,000 | .......... | 614,280,? |
| Fractional parts | 60,713 | .......... | .......... | 60,7? |
| **Total** | 761,615,607 | 985,163,129 | 305,653,163 | 5,037,248,? |
| Deduct: | | | | |
| Unknown, destroyed | | | | 1,000,? |
| Held in Treasury | 15,774,366 | 290,162,640 | 1,586,570 | 315,259,? |
| Held by Federal reserve banks and Federal reserve agents | 14,746,625 | 521,658,270 | 38,731,219 | 1,046,715,? |
| Redeemed but not assorted by denominations | 3,413,580 | .......... | .......... | 3,481,? |
| Net | 727,681,036 | 173,342,219 | 265,335,374 | 3,670,792,? |

## SUPPLY OF UNITED STATES PAPER CURRENCY HELD IN RESERVE.

The number of pieces and amount of each denomination of United States paper currency held in the reserve vault at the close of the fiscal years 1921 and 1922 may be studied in the statement following:

| Denomination. | Held June 30, 1921. | | Held June 30, 1922. | |
|---|---|---|---|---|
| | Number of pieces. | Total value. | Number of pieces. | Total value. |
| One dollar.......................... | 7,040,000 | $7,040,000 | 20,676,000 | $20,676,000 |
| Two dollars........................ | 5,868,000 | 11,736,000 | 2,592,000 | 5,184,000 |
| Five dollars........................ | 2,180,000 | 10,900,000 | 7,448,000 | 37,240,000 |
| Ten dollars........................ | 1,952,000 | 19,520,000 | 3,820,000 | 38,200,000 |
| Twenty dollars..................... | 1,576,000 | 31,520,000 | 4,160,000 | 83,200,000 |
| Fifty dollars....................... | 612,000 | 30,600,000 | 548,000 | 27,400,000 |
| One hundred dollars................ | 420,000 | 42,000,000 | 384,000 | 38,400,000 |
| Five hundred dollars............... | 48,500 | 24,250,000 | 46,500 | 23,250,000 |
| One thousand dollars............... | 36,400 | 36,400,000 | 34,200 | 34,200,000 |
| Five thousand dollars.............. | 21,300 | 106,500,000 | 19,300 | 96,500,000 |
| Ten thousand dollars............... | 35,200 | 352,000,000 | 56,100 | 561,000,000 |
| Order gold certificates............. | 70,913 | 709,130,000 | 70,835 | 708,350,000 |
| Total.......................... | 19,860,313 | 1,381,596,000 | 39,854,935 | 1,673,600,000 |

## REDEMPTION OF FEDERAL RESERVE AND NATIONAL CURRENCY.

The proceeds of currency counted into its cash by the National Bank Redemption Agency during the fiscal year amounted to $853,026,354.15. Of this sum $624,309,160.65 was in national-bank notes, $157,600,425.50 in Federal reserve bank notes, $68,455,037.50 in Federal reserve notes, and $2,661,730.50 in United States currency. Comparative figures as to total redemptions in this and previous years are contained in Table No. 25, page 568.

Payments for currency redeemed were made as follows: In Treasurer's checks, $503,190; in United States currency, $445,282.01; by credits to Treasury offices as transfers of funds, $52,097,364.50; by credits to Government depositary banks (Federal reserve and national banks) as transfers of funds, $709,952,265.63; by credits to Federal reserve banks and branches as transfers of funds covering remittances by member banks, $89,432,176.16; by other credits, $596,075.85.

The notes of all issues counted and assorted amounted to $2,977,338,282.50, and were disposed of as follows:

| | Amount. | Per cent. |
|---|---|---|
| National-bank notes: | | |
| Fit for use returned to banks of issue.............................. | $8,006,740.00 | 1.29 |
| Unfit for use delivered to the Comptroller of the Currency for— | | |
| Destruction and reissue................................... | 597,684,942.50 | 96.05 |
| Destruction and retirement.............................. | 16,568,350.00 | 2.66 |
| | 622,260,032.50 | 100.00 |
| Federal reserve bank notes: | | |
| Fit for use returned to banks............................ | | |
| Unfit for use delivered to the Comptroller of the Currency for— | | |
| Destruction and reissue................................... | 68,273,000.00 | 42.94 |
| Destruction and retirement.............................. | 90,720,000.00 | 57.06 |
| | 158,993,000.00 | 100.00 |
| Federal reserve notes: | | |
| Fit for use returned to banks............................ | | |
| Unfit for use delivered to the Comptroller of the Currency for destruction. | 68,679,100.00 | 100.00 |
| Federal reserve notes, canceled and uncanceled, forwarded by Federal reserve banks and branches: | | |
| Delivered to Comptroller of the Currency for credit of Federal reserve agents................................... | 2,127,406,150.00 | |

Canceled and uncanceled Federal reserve notes amounting to $2,127,406,150 were received from Federal reserve banks and branch Federal reserve banks for credit of Federal reserve agents. Such notes are settled for between the Federal reserve banks and Federal reserve agents either direct or by adjustments in their redemption funds, and are, therefore, not taken into the cash of the National Bank Redemption Agency.

The amount of expenses of the agency for the fiscal year, including salaries, transportation, and contingent expenses, is set forth in Table No. 30, page 570.

### SHIPMENTS OF CURRENCY FROM WASHINGTON.

The total currency distributed from the Treasury in Washington to Treasury offices and to Federal reserve banks and other banks during the fiscal year 1922 was largely in excess of such shipments in the preceding year, as shown by the comparative following statement:

|  | Fiscal year 1921. | | Fiscal year 1922. | |
|---|---|---|---|---|
|  | Number of packages. | Total amount. | Number of packages. | Total amount. |
| Total by express | 1,715 | $23,235,025 | 106 | $599,00 |
| Total by registered mail | 81,981 | 436,780,164 | 112,174 | 673,278,49 |
| Aggregate | 83,696 | 460,015,189 | 112,280 | 673,877,49 |

### DEPOSITS OF GOLD BULLION AT MINTS AND ASSAY OFFICES.

The deposits of gold bullion at the mints and assay offices during the fiscal years 1920, 1921, and 1922 may be observed in the following statement:

| Office. | 1920 | 1921 | 1922 |
|---|---|---|---|
| Philadelphia | $2,801,776.12 | $31,751,374.82 | $5,548,493.2 |
| San Francisco | 66,502,559.24 | 71,449,593.98 | 58,222,890.7 |
| Denver | 9,624,866.69 | 6,686,169.24 | 7,561,464.6 |
| New York | 140,609,635.79 | 560,174,686.93 | 480,618,593.0 |
| New Orleans | 625,304.57 | 461,883.20 | 528,193.3 |
| Carson | 114,171.87 | 70,650.63 | 58,970.9 |
| Helena | 680,744.06 | 168,343.35 | 96,265.6 |
| Boise | 609,750.78 | 341,410.31 | 333,631.7 |
| Deadwood | 429,153.83 | 102,971.27 | 2,333.6 |
| Seattle | 4,418,415.74 | 3,312,866.63 | 3,020,346.3 |
| Salt Lake City | 16,536.41 | 18,147.03 | 17,595.2 |
| Total | 226,432,915.10 | 674,538,097.39 | 556,008,777.6 |

### RECOINAGE IN THE FISCAL YEAR 1922.

¶ Gold coins of the United States presented for payment or deposit on any account at the Treasury offices and Federal reserve banks which have assumed subtreasury functions are weighed and if reduced in weight by natural abrasion not more than one-half of 1 per cent below the standard weight prescribed by law, after a circulation of

20 years, as shown by the date of coinage, and at a ratable proportion for any period less than 20 years, shall be received at their nominal value, under such regulations as the Secretary of the Treasury may prescribe for the protection 'of the Government against fraudulent abrasion or other practices. Gold coins that are below the limit prescribed in the foregoing are discounted at the rate of 4 cents per grain for each grain or fraction thereof below the standard weight of the coin. This regulation protects the Government from loss by unnatural abrasion or the "sweating process" practiced by dishonest persons. The subsidiary silver coins and minor coins received are assorted but are not discounted for natural abrasion; when worn so as to be unfit for circulation they are recoined. The loss resulting from recoinage is reimbursed from an appropriation made by Congress for the purpose.

The face value, by denominations and kinds, and the loss on the recoinage during the past two fiscal years is compared in the statement following:

| Denomination. | Fiscal year 1921. | | Fiscal year 1922. | |
|---|---|---|---|---|
| | Face value. | Loss reimbursed. | Face value. | Loss reimbursed. |
| Double eagles | $140,831.00 | | $269,660.00 | |
| Eagles | 196,443.00 | | 326,500.00 | |
| Half eagles | 187,845.00 | | 387,785.00 | |
| Three-dollar pieces | 18.00 | | 18.00 | |
| Quarter eagles | 1,405.00 | | 637.50 | |
| Dollars | 52.00 | | 35.00 | |
| Total gold | 526,594.00 | $374.81 | 984,635.50 | $1,201.15 |
| Half dollars | 245,776.00 | | 1,096,550.00 | |
| Quarter dollars | 233,819.25 | | 1,089,859.50 | |
| Twenty-cent pieces | 44.20 | | 31.00 | |
| Dimes | 149,656.60 | | 378,849.20 | |
| Half dimes | 435.80 | | 167.15 | |
| Three-cent pieces | 93.18 | | 37.14 | |
| Total silver | 629,825.03 | 46,677.64 | 2,565,493.99 | 173,252.75 |
| Minor coins | 112,114.08 | 5,533.94 | 92,413.57 | 4,999.62 |
| Aggregate | 1,268,533.11 | 53,086.39 | 3,642,543.06 | 179,453.52 |

## DISTRICT OF COLUMBIA.

The transactions of the Treasurer of the United States, ex officio commissioner of the sinking fund of the District of Columbia pertaining to the affairs of the District, are fully set forth in a separate report.

During the fiscal year 1922 the 3.65 per cent bonds of the funded debt retired amounted to $196,050, thus reducing the bonded debt of the District of Columbia to $4,719,700. A net purchase for the sinking fund of $770,000 in United States obligations was made during the year, making a total of $4,517,500 of such obligations held in trust as an offset against the outstanding debt of the District of Columbia.

The old securities of the District of Columbia held in the care and custody of the Treasurer are:

Chesapeake & Ohio Canal bonds........................... $84,285.00
Board of audit certificates................................... 20,134.72

There is also an unexpended balance of $132.51 in the District of Columbia contractor's guarantee fund.

### GENERAL ACCOUNT OF THE TREASURER OF THE UNITED STATES.

The Treasurer receives and keeps the moneys of the United States and disburses the same upon warrants drawn by the Secretary of the Treasury, countersigned by the Comptroller General, and not otherwise. He takes receipts for all moneys paid by him and gives receipts for all moneys received by him; and all receipts for moneys received by him are indorsed upon warrants signed by the Secretary of the Treasury, without which warrant, so signed, no acknowledgment for money received into the Public Treasury is valid. He renders his accounts quarterly, or oftener if required, and at all times submits to the Secretary of the Treasury and the Comptroller General, or either of them, the inspection of the moneys in his hands.

As a matter of information, it may be said that all public moneys paid into any treasury office, national-bank depositary, or other depositary are placed to the credit of the Treasurer of the United States and held subject to his draft. The public moneys in the hands of any depositary of public moneys may be transferred to the Treasury of the United States or may be transferred from one depositary to any other depositary, as the safety of the public moneys and the convenience of the public service shall require.

The Treasurer is redemption agent for Federal reserve and national bank notes; is trustee for bonds held to secure bank circulation, public deposits in depositary banks, and bonds held to secure postal savings in banks; is custodian of miscellaneous trust funds; is fiscal agent for the issue and redemption of the United States paper currency, for the payment of the interest on the public debt and the redemption of matured obligations of the Government, for collecting the interest on public deposits held by banks, and for the collection of semiannual duty on bank circulation; is fiscal agent for paying principal and interest of the land-purchase bonds of the Philippine Islands; is treasurer of the board of trustees of the Postal Savings System; and is ex officio commissioner of the sinking fund of the District of Columbia.

It will be seen from the foregoing recital that the immense financial transactions of the Government imposes on the Treasurer's office the keeping of many and varied accounts with vast responsibilities. In the performance of these duties, under the system of accounting inaugurated on February 1, 1913, the work is appropriately distributed to seven divisions, viz: Chief clerk, Cash Division, Division of Securities, Division of General Accounts, Accounting Division, Division of Redemption, and the National Bank Redemption Agency, the Division of Issue having been discontinued August 3, 1921. The duties of the several divisions are fully stated in the Treasurer's annual report for the fiscal year 1920, pages 47–51.

An act to permit the correction in the general account of John Burke, former Treasurer of the United States, was passed by Congress and approved June 3, 1922, thus relieving him from further accountability of the items of unavailable funds as set forth in House Document No. 756, Sixty-sixth Congress, second session.

The tasks and responsibilities of the office have been smoothed and lightened by the zeal, the diligence, the loyalty, and the ability exhibited in the hearty cooperation of the staff, the chiefs of divisions, the clerks, and of every person employed. They have met well every requirement, and it is a pleasure to record this acknowledgment due to each one of them.

Respectfully,

FRANK WHITE, *Treasurer.*

Hon. A. W. MELLON,
*Secretary of the Treasury.*

# TABLES.

No. 1.—*General distribution of the assets and liabilities of the Treasury, June 30, 1922.*

| | Treasury offices. | Mints and assay offices. | Designated depositaries of the United States. | In transit. | Total. |
|---|---|---|---|---|---|
| **ASSETS.** | | | | | |
| Gold coin | $4,338,422.04 | $302,619,245.35 | | | $306,957,667.39 |
| Gold bullion | | 2,850,244,888.57 | | | 2,850,244,888.57 |
| Standard silver dollars | 46,532,430.00 | 266,951,878.00 | | $20,000.00 | 313,504,308.00 |
| Subsidiary silver coin | 1,569,412.35 | 16,178,089.50 | | | 17,747,501.85 |
| Silver bullion | | 44,284,867.40 | | | 44,284,867.40 |
| United States notes | 3,991,851.00 | | | 154,113.00 | 4,145,964.00 |
| Treasury notes of 1890 | | | | | |
| Gold certificates (active) | 2,224,030.00 | 60,338,630.00 | | | 62,562,660.00 |
| Gold certificates (inactive) | 1,010,000.00 | 226,590,000.00 | | | 227,600,000.00 |
| Silver certificates | 1,586,570.00 | | | | 1,586,570.00 |
| Federal reserve notes | 1,765,682.50 | 792,039.00 | | | 2,557,721.50 |
| Federal reserve bank notes | 1,030,273.00 | | | | 1,030,273.00 |
| National-bank notes | 15,540,014.63 | | | 234,352.00 | 15,774,366.63 |
| Unclassified (unassorted currency, etc.) | 3,131,471.57 | 151,218.37 | | 652.59 | 3,283,342.53 |
| Minor coin | 299,013.50 | 3,320,999.83 | | | 3,620,013.33 |
| Public debt interest, etc., paid but not reimbursed by warrant | | | | 503,020.03 | 503,020.03 |
| Deposits in Federal reserve banks | | | $33,091,888.68 | | 33,091,888.68 |
| Deposits in special depositaries (act Apr. 24, 1917) | | | 146,476,840.69 | | 146,476,840.69 |
| Deposits in national banks, etc. | | | 29,641,653.33 | | 29,641,653.33 |
| Public moneys in transit to or from depositary banks | | | | 24,122,677.24 | 24,122,677.24 |
| Total available assets | 83,019,170.59 | 3,771,471,856.02 | 209,210,382.70 | 25,034,814.86 | 4,088,736,224.17 |
| Balance with Treasurer United States | | 96,232.67 | | | 96,232.67 |
| Warrants paid but not cleared | | | | 209,749.95 | 209,749.95 |
| Aggregate | 83,019,170.59 | 3,771,568,088.69 | 209,210,382.70 | 25,244,564.81 | 4,089,042,206.79 |
| **LIABILITIES.** | | | | | |
| Outstanding Treasurer's checks and warrants paid but not cleared | | | | | 657,608.52 |
| Disbursing officers' balances on books of Treasurer and depositary banks | | | | | 28,902,135.42 |
| Post Office Department account | | | | | 12,427,459.46 |
| Other deposit and redemption accounts | | | | | 3,197,276.59 |
| Board of trustees Postal Savings System | | | | | 7,103,734.69 |
| Redemption fund: | | | | | |
| Federal reserve notes | | | | | 179,138,539.55 |
| Federal reserve bank notes | | | | | 7,445,646.55 |
| National-bank notes | | | | | 29,791,025.87 |
| Retirement of additional cirlating notes (act May 30, 1908) | | | | | 31,080.00 |
| Assets of insolvent banks | | | | | 1,931,759.56 |
| Total agency accounts | | | | | 270,626,266.21 |
| Balance to credit of mints and assay offices | | | | | 96,232.67 |
| Balance to credit of gold fund, Federal Reserve Board | | | | | 2,108,886,911.43 |
| Balance to credit of trust funds (act Mar. 14, 1900) | | | | | 1,292,326,835.00 |
| Balance in general fund, including the gold reserve | | | | | [1] 417,105,961.48 |
| Aggregate | | | | | 4,089,042,206.79 |

[1] Including credits to disbursing offices.

No. 2.—*Available assets and net liabilities of the Treasury at the close of June, 1921 and 1922.*

| | June 30, 1921. | June 30, 1922. |
|---|---|---|
| **ASSETS.** | | |
| Gold: | | |
| Coin | $258,881,883.67 | $306,957,667.39 |
| Bullion | 2,411,502,196.43 | 2,850,244,888.57 |
| Total | 2,670,384,080.10 | 3,157,202,555.96 |
| Silver: | | |
| Dollars | 213,735,045.00 | 313,504,308.00 |
| Subsidiary coin | 9,663,502.04 | 17,747,501.85 |
| Bullion | 56,720,406.41 | 44,284,867.40 |
| Total | 280,118,953.45 | 375,536,677.25 |
| Paper: | | |
| United States notes | 4,031,479.00 | 4,145,964.00 |
| Treasury notes of 1890 | | |
| Federal reserve notes | 4,719,921.00 | 2,557,721.50 |
| Federal reserve bank notes | 2,422,847.50 | 1,030,273.00 |
| National-bank notes | 13,739,860.98 | 15,774,366.63 |
| Gold certificates | 79,315,940.00 | 290,162,660.00 |
| Silver certificates | 1,044,470.00 | 1,586,570.00 |
| Unclassified (unassorted currency, etc.) | 3,141,005.13 | 3,283,342.53 |
| Total | 108,415,523.61 | 318,540,897.66 |
| Other: | | |
| Minor coin | 2,392,673.78 | 3,620,013.33 |
| Deposits in Federal reserve banks | 43,475,862.73 | 33,091,888.68 |
| Deposits in Federal land banks | | |
| Deposits in national banks, special and foreign depositaries | 480,202,028.40 | 176,118,494.02 |
| Public moneys in transit between Federal reserve banks and to and from national banks | 32,479,427.27 | 24,122,677.24 |
| Public debt interest, etc., paid but not reimbursed by warrant | 727,446.76 | 503,020.03 |
| Total | 559,277,438.94 | 237,456,093.30 |
| Aggregate | 3,618,195,996.10 | 4,088,736,224.17 |
| **LIABILITIES.** | | |
| Outstanding Treasurer's checks and warrants paid but not cleared | 2,578,789.10 | 657,608.52 |
| Disbursing officers' balances on books of Treasurer and depositary banks | 77,659,580.48 | 28,902,135.42 |
| Post Office Department account | 18,769,940.53 | 12,427,459.46 |
| Other deposit and redemption accounts | 4,795,176.84 | 3,197,276.59 |
| Board of trustees, Postal Savings System | 4,121,544.01 | 7,103,734.69 |
| Redemption fund: | | |
| Federal reserve notes | 259,178,087.04 | 179,138,539.55 |
| Federal reserve bank notes | 9,442,096.55 | 7,445,646.55 |
| National-bank notes | 18,495,044.98 | 29,791,025.87 |
| Retirement of additional circulating notes, act of May 30, 1908 | 67,560.00 | 31,080.00 |
| Assets of insolvent national banks | 1,630,871.72 | 1,931,759.56 |
| Total agency accounts | 396,738,691.25 | 270,626,266.21 |
| Less warrants paid but not cleared | 2,280,742.00 | 209,749.95 |
| Total | 394,457,949.25 | 270,416,516.26 |
| General account: | | |
| Gold certificates | 795,848,929.00 | 985,163,129.00 |
| Silver certificates | 202,578,683.00 | 305,653,163.00 |
| Treasury notes of 1890 | 1,576,184.00 | 1,510,543.00 |
| Gold fund, Federal reserve board | 1,537,856,895.45 | 2,108,886,911.43 |
| Reserve fund | 152,979,025.63 | 152,979,025.63 |
| Balance | [1] 532,898,329.77 | [1] 264,126,935.85 |
| Total | 3,223,738,046.85 | 3,818,319,707.91 |
| Aggregate | 3,618,195,996.10 | 4,088,736,224.17 |

[1] Including credits to disbursing officers.

No. 3.—*Distribution of the General Treasury balance, June 30, 1922.*

| | |
|---|---:|
| Washington | $82,959,891.12 |
| Baltimore | 32,000.00 |
| New York | 5,429.68 |
| Boston | 15,956.00 |
| San Francisco | 514.95 |
| Mints and assay offices: | |
|   Boise | 12,326.58 |
|   Carson City | 4,726.66 |
|   Deadwood | 587.05 |
|   Helena | 16,266.62 |
|   Salt Lake City | 4,579.62 |
|   Seattle | 68,140.58 |
|   New York | 2,329,593,928.56 |
|   New Orleans | 6,455,300.63 |
|   Denver | 343,269,626.15 |
|   Philadelphia | 557,112,684.65 |
|   San Francisco | 535,029,921.59 |
| Federal reserve banks | 33,091,888.68 |
| Special depositaries | 146,476,840.69 |
| National banks | 7,832,260.63 |
| Foreign depositaries | 700,619.43 |
| Treasury of Philippine Islands | 4,417,757.43 |
| In transit | 25,244,564.81 |

| | |
|---|---:|
|     Total | 4,072,345,812.11 |

Deduct:

| | | |
|---|---:|---:|
| Agency accounts on books of Treasurer of the United States | $254,026,104.20 | |
| Gold fund, Federal Reserve Board | 2,108,886,911.43 | |
| | | 2,362,913,015.63 |

| | |
|---|---:|
|     General account | 1,709,432,796.48 |

Deduct:

| | |
|---|---:|
| Trust funds, act Mar. 14, 1900 | 1,292,326,835.00 |
| Balance, including gold reserve | 417,105,961.48 |

No. 4.—*Assets of the Treasury other than gold, silver, notes, and certificates at the end of each month, from July, 1920.*

| Month. | Minor coin. | Unassorted currency, etc. | Deposits in Federal reserve and national banks. | Deposits in treasury of Philippine Islands. | Bonds and interest paid. | Total. |
|---|---:|---:|---:|---:|---:|---:|
| 1920—July | $819,451 | $18,213,435 | $205,565,860 | $2,799,099 | | $227,397,845 |
| August | 933,400 | 15,044,480 | 253,725,967 | 2,152,773 | | 271,856,620 |
| September | 634,145 | 13,984,899 | 430,992,720 | 538,569 | | 446,150,333 |
| October | 939,547 | 9,916,596 | 190,131,986 | 2,522,449 | | 203,510,578 |
| November | 1,049,289 | 12,985,612 | 183,817,285 | 2,781,239 | | 200,633,425 |
| December | 841,269 | 24,603,282 | 503,403,495 | 2,348,651 | | 531,196,697 |
| 1921—January | 1,298,033 | 14,709,293 | 326,479,323 | 2,174,266 | | 344,660,915 |
| February | 1,435,886 | 11,381,450 | 311,695,385 | 2,215,097 | | 326,727,818 |
| March | 1,875,885 | 9,653,496 | 575,337,751 | 5,822,841 | | 592,689,973 |
| April | 2,157,212 | 5,753,131 | 398,123,066 | 8,600,061 | | 414,633,470 |
| May | 2,295,220 | 5,034,063 | 222,852,786 | 8,369,942 | | 238,552,011 |
| June | 2,392,674 | 3,141,005 | 548,239,611 | 7,917,708 | $727,447 | 562,418,445 |
| July | 2,433,262 | 4,411,798 | 177,575,575 | 7,598,341 | | 192,023,976 |
| August | 2,479,993 | 3,576,306 | 278,104,483 | 7,557,840 | | 291,718,622 |
| September | 2,537,793 | 4,970,811 | 716,877,414 | 7,333,706 | | 731,719,724 |
| October | 2,586,994 | 5,865,162 | 182,975,073 | 7,182,333 | | 198,609,562 |
| November | 2,561,109 | 7,209,438 | 229,191,758 | 6,795,980 | | 245,758,285 |
| December | 2,662,470 | 8,550,724 | 458,120,242 | 6,334,872 | | 475,668,308 |
| 1922—January | 2,958,726 | 7,367,038 | 344,498,173 | 6,147,669 | | 360,971,606 |
| February | 3,144,402 | 6,586,636 | 433,553,808 | 6,094,044 | | 449,378,890 |
| March | 3,477,032 | 4,153,925 | 332,166,653 | 5,851,407 | | 345,649,017 |
| April | 3,536,245 | 5,394,000 | 331,888,560 | 5,631,721 | | 346,450,526 |
| May | 3,536,238 | 6,896,188 | 241,166,380 | 5,351,622 | | 256,950,428 |
| June | 3,620,013 | 3,283,343 | 228,914,748 | 4,418,312 | 503,020 | 240,739,436 |

No. 5.—*Assets of the Treasury at the end of each month, from July, 1920.*

| Month. | Gold. | Silver. | Notes. | Certificates. | Other. | Total. |
|---|---|---|---|---|---|---|
| 1920—July | $2,171,488,538 | $160,995,752 | $59,638,811 | $751,375,911 | $227,397,845 | $3,370,896,857 |
| August | 2,159,298,081 | 166,079,587 | 53,568,986 | 655,143,501 | 271,856,620 | 3,305,946,775 |
| September | 2,169,254,520 | 168,036,233 | 48,343,935 | 588,926,475 | 446,150,333 | 3,420,711,496 |
| October | 2,199,237,709 | 189,210,754 | 50,938,808 | 322,561,710 | 203,510,578 | 2,965,459,559 |
| November | 2,209,414,282 | 212,138,026 | 42,394,136 | 273,058,923 | 200,633,425 | 2,937,638,792 |
| December | 2,220,876,282 | 214,338,641 | 38,167,990 | 244,683,024 | 531,196,697 | 3,249,262,634 |
| 1921—January | 2,300,548,525 | 222,078,936 | 41,656,556 | 294,743,721 | 344,660,915 | 3,203,688,653 |
| February | 2,371,327,562 | 244,650,696 | 31,687,048 | 198,295,119 | 326,727,818 | 3,172,688,243 |
| March | 2,454,828,938 | 255,757,501 | 34,191,591 | 131,772,710 | 592,689,973 | 3,469,240,713 |
| April | 2,541,372,072 | 262,337,135 | 28,888,705 | 66,715,452 | 414,633,470 | 3,313,946,834 |
| May | 2,623,783,394 | 271,054,296 | 38,323,379 | 70,326,460 | 238,552,011 | 3,242,039,540 |
| June | 2,670,384,080 | 280,118,953 | 24,914,108 | 80,360,410 | 562,418,445 | 3,618,195,996 |
| July | 2,733,309,183 | 285,183,592 | 30,244,315 | 75,777,579 | 192,023,976 | 3,316,538,645 |
| August | 2,820,696,501 | 292,527,629 | 25,323,211 | 58,618,130 | 291,718,622 | 3,488,884,093 |
| September | 2,888,781,529 | 300,920,294 | 25,165,986 | 46,556,220 | 731,719,724 | 3,993,143,753 |
| October | 2,936,260,827 | 313,868,734 | 28,725,920 | 98,811,540 | 198,609,562 | 3,576,276,583 |
| November | 2,982,139,779 | 324,423,239 | 31,022,363 | 66,907,310 | 245,758,285 | 3,650,250,976 |
| December | 3,023,192,261 | 338,085,333 | 26,934,399 | 267,712,295 | 475,668,308 | 4,056,406,682 |
| 1922—January | 3,049,525,465 | 345,121,630 | 28,918,121 | 271,869,860 | 360,971,606 | 4,191,366,197 |
| February | 3,090,057,297 | 350,965,948 | 24,448,952 | 276,512,110 | 449,378,890 | 4,127,844,959 |
| March | 3,113,322,875 | 356,844,305 | 27,682,682 | 279,346,080 | 345,649,017 | 4,153,587,659 |
| April | 3,134,198,348 | 362,957,146 | 26,382,815 | 283,598,824 | 346,450,526 | 4,083,459,464 |
| May | 3,141,842,818 | 368,297,182 | 25,332,999 | 291,036,037 | 256,950,428 | 4,083,459,464 |
| June | 3,157,202,556 | 375,536,677 | 23,508,325 | 291,749,230 | 240,739,436 | 4,088,736,224 |

No. 6.—*Liabilities of the Treasury at the end of each month, from July, 1920, to June, 1922.*

| Month. | Gold and silver certificates, and Treasury notes. | Gold fund, redemption funds, etc. | Gold reserve. | Net balance in general fund. | Total. |
|---|---|---|---|---|---|
| 1920—July | $1,458,695,969 | $1,554,059,947 | $152,979,026 | $205,161,915 | $3,370,896,857 |
| August | 1,365,198,469 | 1,530,022,652 | 152,979,026 | 257,746,628 | 3,305,946,775 |
| September | 1,309,773,469 | 1,522,997,951 | 152,979,026 | 434,961,050 | 3,420,711,496 |
| October | 1,019,419,069 | 1,589,409,437 | 152,979,026 | 203,652,027 | 2,965,459,559 |
| November | 982,548,169 | 1,636,484,500 | 152,979,026 | 165,627,097 | 2,937,638,792 |
| December | 931,408,069 | 1,659,924,145 | 152,979,026 | 504,951,394 | 3,249,262,634 |
| 1921—January | 904,253,178 | 1,801,345,364 | 152,979,026 | 345,111,085 | 3,203,688,653 |
| February | 873,596,455 | 1,845,090,247 | 152,979,026 | 301,022,515 | 3,172,688,243 |
| March | 870,183,790 | 1,831,484,471 | 152,979,026 | 614,593,426 | 3,469,240,713 |
| April | 874,941,746 | 1,853,892,780 | 152,979,026 | 432,133,282 | 3,313,946,834 |
| May | 935,538,716 | 1,908,955,847 | 152,979,026 | 244,565,951 | 3,242,039,540 |
| June | 1,000,003,796 | 1,932,314,845 | 152,979,026 | 532,898,329 | 3,618,195,996 |
| July | 1,053,096,136 | 1,879,749,036 | 152,979,026 | 230,714,447 | 3,316,538,645 |
| August | 1,104,525,726 | 1,898,286,897 | 152,979,026 | 333,092,444 | 3,488,884,093 |
| September | 1,161,733,916 | 1,920,755,581 | 152,979,026 | 757,675,230 | 3,993,143,753 |
| October | 1,229,642,186 | 1,967,250,214 | 152,979,026 | 226,405,157 | 3,576,276,583 |
| November | 1,249,185,966 | 1,990,744,131 | 152,979,026 | 257,341,853 | 3,650,250,976 |
| December | 1,258,184,006 | 2,232,662,035 | 152,979,026 | 487,767,529 | 4,131,592,596 |
| 1922—January | 1,252,263,136 | 2,254,083,248 | 152,979,026 | 397,081,272 | 4,056,406,682 |
| February | 1,255,346,061 | 2,302,390,771 | 152,979,026 | 480,650,339 | 4,191,366,197 |
| March | 1,270,371,055 | 2,333,093,090 | 152,979,026 | 371,401,788 | 4,127,844,959 |
| April | 1,277,109,805 | 2,351,153,499 | 152,979,026 | 372,345,329 | 4,153,587,659 |
| May | 1,285,995,735 | 2,355,087,840 | 152,979,026 | 289,396,863 | 4,083,459,464 |
| June | 1,292,326,835 | 2,379,303,428 | 152,979,026 | 264,126,935 | 4,088,736,224 |

No. 7.—*United States notes of each denomination issued, redeemed, and outstanding at the close of the fiscal years 1921 and 1922.*

| Denomination. | Issued during year. | Total issued. | Redeemed during year. | Total redeemed. | Outstanding. |
|---|---|---|---|---|---|
| **1921.** | | | | | |
| One dollar............ | $219,284,000 | $769,456,160 | $187,786,096 | $596,598,440.80 | $172,857,719.20 |
| Two dollars............ | 53,720,000 | 405,595,048 | 53,347,934 | 354,943,754.20 | 50,651,293.80 |
| Five dollars............ | 18,440,000 | 1,942,451,760 | 66,914,920 | 1,872,490,055.00 | 69,961,705.00 |
| Ten dollars............ | 17,680,000 | 1,700,551,240 | 6,894,020 | 1,668,693,719.00 | 31,857,521.00 |
| Twenty dollars.......... | 8,000,000 | 560,122,400 | 1,309,380 | 547,662,298.00 | 12,460,102.00 |
| Fifty dollars............ | 2,200,000 | 150,015,200 | 2,282,650 | 149,098,725.00 | 916,475.00 |
| One hundred dollars.... | ............ | 197,104,000 | 140,600 | 195,657,800.00 | 1,446,200.00 |
| Five hundred dollars.... | ............ | 226,276,000 | 75,000 | 225,205,000.00 | 1,071,000.00 |
| One thousand dollars... | ............ | 467,628,000 | 574,000 | 461,179,000.00 | 6,449,000 00 |
| Five thousand dollars... | ............ | 20,000,000 | ............ | 20,000,000.00 | ............ |
| Ten thousand dollars... | ............ | 40,000,000 | ............ | 39,990,000.00 | 10,000.00 |
| Total............ | 319,324,000 | 6,479,199,808 | 319,324,000 | 6,131,518,792.00 | 347,681,016.00 |
| Unknown, destroyed.... | ............ | ............ | ............ | 1,000,000.00 | 1,000,000.00 |
| Net............ | 319,324,000 | 6,479,199,808 | 319,324,000 | 6,132,518,792.00 | 346,681,016.00 |
| **1922.** | | | | | |
| One dollar............ | 113,236,000 | 882,692,160 | 190,240,820 | 786,839,260.80 | 95,852,899.20 |
| Two dollars............ | 50,792,000 | 456,387,048 | 55,850,870 | 410,794,624.20 | 45,592,423.80 |
| Five dollars............ | 37,920,000 | 1,980,371,760 | 46,746,070 | 1,919,236,125.00 | 61,135,635.00 |
| Ten dollars............ | 105,120,000 | 1,805,671,240 | 33,452,650 | 1,702,146,369.00 | 103,524,871.00 |
| Twenty dollars.......... | 31,680,000 | 591,802,400 | 12,390,540 | 560,052,838.00 | 31,749,562.00 |
| Fifty dollars............ | 600,000 | 150,615,200 | 138,250 | 149,236,975.00 | 1,378,225.00 |
| One hundred dollars.... | ............ | 197,104,000 | 126,800 | 195,784,600.00 | 1,319,400.00 |
| Five hundred dollars.... | ............ | 226,276,000 | 79,000 | 225,284,000.00 | 992,000.00 |
| One thousand dollars... | ............ | 467,628,000 | 323,000 | 461,502,000.00 | 6,126,000.00 |
| Five thousand dollars... | ............ | 20,000,000 | ............ | 20,000,000.00 | ............ |
| Ten thousand dollars... | ............ | 40,000,000 | ............ | 39,990,000.00 | 10,000.00 |
| Total............ | 339,348,000 | 6,818,547,808 | 339,348,000 | 6,470,866,792.00 | 347,681,016.00 |
| Unknown, destroyed.... | ............ | ............ | ............ | 1,000,000.00 | 1,000,000.00 |
| Net............ | 339,348,000 | 6,818,547,808 | 339,348,000 | 6,471,866,792.00 | 346,681,016.00 |

No. 8.—*Treasury notes of 1890 of each denomination redeemed and outstanding at the close of the fiscal years 1921 and 1922.*

| Denomination. | Total issued. | Redeemed during year. | Total redeemed. | Outstanding. |
|---|---|---|---|---|
| **1921.** | | | | |
| One dollar...................... | $64,704,000 | $4,526 | $64,386,749 | $317,251 |
| Two dollars...................... | 49,808,000 | 4,480 | 49,612,300 | 195,700 |
| Five dollars...................... | 120,740,000 | 18,330 | 120,341,527 | 398,473 |
| Ten dollars...................... | 104,680,000 | 29,450 | 104,305,000 | 375,000 |
| Twenty dollars.................... | 35,760,000 | 18,980 | 35,601,390 | 158,610 |
| Fifty dollars...................... | 1,175,000 | 650 | 1,167,350 | 7,650 |
| One hundred dollars.............. | 18,000,000 | 4,400 | 17,930,500 | 69,500 |
| One thousand dollars............. | 52,568,000 | 2,000 | 52,514,000 | 54,000 |
| Total...................... | 447,435,000 | 82,816 | 445,858,816 | 1,576,184 |
| **1922.** | | | | |
| One dollar...................... | 64,704,000 | 2,992 | 64,389,741 | 314,259 |
| Two dollars...................... | 49,808,000 | 2,394 | 49,614,694 | 193,306 |
| Five dollars...................... | 120,740,000 | 11,135 | 120,352,662 | 387,338 |
| Ten dollars...................... | 104,680,000 | 24,000 | 104,329,000 | 351,000 |
| Twenty dollars.................... | 35,760,000 | 16,520 | 35,617,910 | 142,090 |
| Fifty dollars...................... | 1,175,000 | 600 | 1,167,950 | 7,050 |
| One hundred dollars.............. | 18,000,000 | 5,000 | 17,935,500 | 64,500 |
| One thousand dollars............. | 52,568,000 | 3,000 | 52,517,000 | 51,000 |
| Total...................... | 447,435,000 | 65,641 | 445,924,457 | 1,510,543 |

No. 9.—*Gold certificates of each denomination issued, redeemed, and outstanding at the close of the fiscal years 1921 and 1922.*

| Denomination. | Issued during year. | Total issued. | Redeemed during year. | Total redeemed. | Outstanding. |
|---|---|---|---|---|---|
| **1921.** | | | | | |
| Ten dollars | | $1,317,268,000 | $112,778,630 | $1,233,415,255 | $83,852,745 |
| Twenty dollars | | 1,320,640,000 | 86,994,360 | 1,240,535,396 | 80,104,604 |
| Fifty dollars | | 292,200,000 | 28,298,950 | 264,409,520 | 27,790,480 |
| One hundred dollars | | 408,034,300 | 36,634,700 | 364,637,200 | 43,397,100 |
| Five hundred dollars | | 144,594,000 | 4,920,000 | 131,321,500 | 13,272,500 |
| One thousand dollars | $3,000,000 | 497,481,000 | 49,859,000 | 435,054,500 | 62,426,500 |
| Five thousand dollars | 12,000,000 | 890,040,000 | 82,935,000 | 819,015,000 | 71,025,000 |
| Ten thousand dollars | 90,040,000 | 4,110,770,000 | 282,430,000 | 3,696,790,000 | 413,980,000 |
| Total | 105,040,000 | 8,981,027,300 | 684,850,640 | 8,185,178,371 | 795,848,929 |
| **1922.** | | | | | |
| Ten dollars | 440,000 | 1,317,708,000 | 10,014,770 | 1,243,430,025 | 74,277,975 |
| Twenty dollars | 14,800,000 | 1,335,440,000 | 10,928,780 | 1,251,464,176 | 83,975,824 |
| Fifty dollars | 2,600,000 | 294,800,000 | 2,197,750 | 266,607,270 | 28,192,730 |
| One hundred dollars | 3,600,000 | 411,634,300 | 2,545,000 | 367,182,200 | 44,452,100 |
| Five hundred dollars | 1,000,000 | 145,594,000 | 585,500 | 131,907,000 | 13,687,000 |
| One thousand dollars | 2,200,000 | 499,681,000 | 1,464,000 | 436,518,500 | 63,162,500 |
| Five thousand dollars | 10,000,000 | 900,040,000 | 1,090,000 | 820,105,000 | 79,935,000 |
| Ten thousand dollars | 191,780,000 | 4,302,550,000 | 8,280,000 | 3,705,070,000 | 597,480,000 |
| Total | 226,420,000 | 9,207,447,300 | 37,105,800 | 8,222,284,171 | 985,163,129 |

No. 10.—*Silver certificates of each denomination issued, redeemed, and outstanding at the close of the fiscal years 1921 and 1922.*

| Denomination. | Issued during year. | Total issued. | Redeemed during year. | Total redeemed. | Outstanding. |
|---|---|---|---|---|---|
| **1921.** | | | | | |
| One dollar | $50,924,000 | $3,055,351,600 | $32,613,460 | $2,976,296,043.90 | $79,055,556.10 |
| Two dollars | 7,088,000 | 1,101,508,000 | 7,889,202 | 1,086,041,876.60 | 15,466,123.40 |
| Five dollars | 55,420,000 | 2,957,230,000 | 10,190,175 | 2,879,856,822.50 | 77,373,177.50 |
| Ten dollars | 9,000,000 | 676,554,000 | 1,261,260 | 663,574,289.00 | 12,979,711.00 |
| Twenty dollars | 5,280,000 | 335,106,000 | 1,725,620 | 325,768,290.00 | 9,337,710.00 |
| Fifty dollars | 5,200,000 | 128,250,000 | 871,600 | 120,125,915.00 | 8,124,085.00 |
| One hundred dollars | | 81,540,000 | 22,400 | 81,326,180.00 | 213,820.00 |
| Five hundred dollars | | 16,650,000 | | 16,636,500.00 | 13,500.00 |
| One thousand dollars | | 32,490,000 | | 32,475,000.00 | 15,000.00 |
| Total | 132,912,000 | 8,384,679,600 | 54,573,717 | 8,182,100,917.00 | 202,578,683.00 |
| **1922.** | | | | | |
| One dollar | 284,436,000 | 3,339,787,600 | 161,826,889 | 3,138,122,932.90 | 201,664,667.10 |
| Two dollars | 6,360,000 | 1,107,868,000 | 11,548,411 | 1,097,590,287.60 | 10,277,712.40 |
| Five dollars | 84,440,000 | 3,041,670,000 | 84,618,460 | 2,964,475,282.50 | 77,194,717.50 |
| Ten dollars | | 676,554,000 | 7,358,200 | 670,932,489.00 | 5,621,511.00 |
| Twenty dollars | 3,040,000 | 338,146,000 | 6,502,760 | 332,271,050.00 | 5,874,950.00 |
| Fifty dollars | | 128,250,000 | 3,330,000 | 123,455,915.00 | 4,794,085.00 |
| One hundred dollars | | 81,540,000 | 13,800 | 81,339,980.00 | 200,020.00 |
| Five hundred dollars | | 16,650,000 | 3,000 | 16,639,500.00 | 10,500.00 |
| One thousand dollars | | 32,490,000 | | 32,475,000.00 | 15,000.00 |
| Total | 378,276,000 | 8,762,955,600 | 275,201,520 | 8,457,302,437.00 | 305,653,163.00 |

No. 11.—*Amount of United States notes, Treasury notes, gold and silver certificates of each denomination issued, redeemed, and outstanding at the close of each fiscal year from 1919.*

| Denomination. | Issued during year. | Total issued. | Redeemed during year. | Total redeemed. | Outstanding. |
|---|---|---|---|---|---|
| **1919.** | | | | | |
| One dollar | $213,880 000 | $3,385,787,760 | $249,349,706 | $3,165,078,145.70 | $220,709,614.30 |
| Two dollars | 73,448 000 | 1,426,511,048 | 89,279,559 | 1,356,394,330.80 | 70,116,717.20 |
| Five dollars | 48,340,000 | 4,863,861,760 | 167,980,465 | 4,675,163,889.50 | 188,697,870.50 |
| Ten dollars | 600,000 | 3,772,373,240 | 123,092,450 | 3,498,108,033.00 | 274,265,207.00 |
| Twenty dollars | | 2,238,348,400 | 47,636,970 | 2,015,597,734.00 | 222,750,666.00 |
| Fifty dollars | | 564,240,200 | 15,333,150 | 497,869,710.00 | 66,370,490.00 |
| One hundred dollars | | 704,678,300 | 18,791,200 | 617,757,680.00 | 86,920,620.00 |
| Five hundred dollars | | 387,520,000 | 2,279,500 | 360,961,000.00 | 26,559,000.00 |
| One thousand dollars | | 1,047,167,000 | 7,092,000 | 913,259,500.00 | 133,907,500.00 |
| Five thousand dollars | | 893,040,000 | 450,000 | 755,840,000.00 | 142,200,000.00 |
| Ten thousand dollars | 13,870,000 | 4,048,520,000 | 68,450,000 | 3,377,380,000.00 | 671,140,000.00 |
| Total | 350,138,000 | 23,337,047,708 | 789,735,000 | 21,233,410,023.00 | 2,103,637,685.00 |
| Unknown, destroyed | | | | 1,000,000.00 | 1,000,000.00 |
| Net | 350,138,000 | 23,337,047,708 | 789,735,000 | 21,234,410,023.00 | 2,102,637,685.00 |
| **1920.** | | | | | |
| One dollar | 233,516,000 | 3,619,303,760 | 251,799,006 | 3,416,877,151.70 | 202,426,608.30 |
| Two dollars | 69,592,000 | 1,496,103,048 | 72,961,984 | 1,429,356,314.80 | 66,746,733.20 |
| Five dollars | 82,700,000 | 4,946,561,760 | 120,401,090 | 4,795,564,979.50 | 150,996,780.50 |
| Ten dollars | | 3,772,373,240 | 50,916,870 | 3,549,024,903.00 | 223,348,337.00 |
| Twenty dollars | | 2,238,348,400 | 43,921,300 | 2,059,519,034.00 | 178,829,366.00 |
| Fifty dollars | | 564,240,200 | 5,477,950 | 503,347,660.00 | 60,892,540.00 |
| One hundred dollars | | 704,678,300 | 4,992,500 | 622,750,180.00 | 81,928,120.00 |
| Five hundred dollars | | 387,520,000 | 7,207,000 | 368,168,000.00 | 19,352,000.00 |
| One thousand dollars | | 1,047,167,000 | 17,528,000 | 930,787,500.00 | 116,379,500.00 |
| Five thousand dollars | | 898,040,000 | 240,000 | 756,080,000.00 | 141,960,000.00 |
| Ten thousand dollars | 12,210,000 | 4,060,730,000 | 76,970,000 | 3,454,350,000.00 | 606,380,000.00 |
| Total | 398,018,000 | 23,735,065,708 | 652,415,700 | 21,885,825,723.00 | 1,849,239,985.00 |
| Unknown, destroyed | | | | 1,000,000.00 | 1,000,000.00 |
| Net | 398,018,000 | 23,735,065,708 | 652,415,700 | 21,886,825,723 00 | 1,848,239,985.00 |
| **1921.** | | | | | |
| One dollar | 270,208,000 | 3,889,511,760 | 220,404,082 | 3,637,281,233.70 | 252,230,526.30 |
| Two dollars | 60,808,000 | 1,556,911,048 | 61,241,616 | 1,490,597,930.80 | 66,313,117.20 |
| Five dollars | 73,860,000 | 5,020,421,760 | 77,123,425 | 4,872,688,404.50 | 147,733,355.50 |
| Ten dollars | 26,680,000 | 3,799,053,240 | 120,963,360 | 3,669,988,263.00 | 129,064,977.00 |
| Twenty dollars | 13,280,000 | 2,251,628,400 | 90,048,340 | 2,149,567,374.00 | 102,061,026.00 |
| Fifty dollars | 7,400,000 | 571,640,200 | 31,453,850 | 534,801,510.00 | 36,838,690.00 |
| One hundred dollars | | 704,678,300 | 4,995,000 | 659,551,680.00 | 45,126,620.00 |
| Five hundred dollars | | 387,520,000 | 4,995,000 | 373,163,000.00 | 14,357,000.00 |
| One thousand dollars | 3,000,000 | 1,050,167,000 | 50,435,000 | 981,222,500.00 | 68,944,500.00 |
| Five thousand dollars | 12,000,000 | 910,040,000 | 82,935,000 | 839,015,000.00 | 71,025,000.00 |
| Ten thousand dollars | 90,040,000 | 4,150,770,000 | 282,430,000 | 3,736,780,000.00 | 413,990,000.00 |
| Total | 557,276,000 | 24,292,341,708 | 1,058,831,173 | 22,944,656,896.00 | 1,347,684,812.00 |
| Unknown, destroyed | | | | 1,000,000.00 | 1,000,000.00 |
| Net | 557,276,000 | 24,292,341,708 | 1,058,831,173 | 22,945,656,896.00 | 1,346,684,812.00 |
| **1922.** | | | | | |
| One dollar | 397,672,000 | 4,287,183,760 | 352,070,701 | 3,989,351,934.70 | 297,831,825.30 |
| Two dollars | 57,152,000 | 1,614,063,048 | 67,401,675 | 1,557,999,605.80 | 56,063,442.20 |
| Five dollars | 122,360,000 | 5,142,781,760 | 131,375,665 | 5,004,064,069.50 | 138,717,690.50 |
| Ten dollars | 105,560,000 | 3,904,613,240 | 50,849,620 | 3,720,837,883.00 | 183,775,357.00 |
| Twenty dollars | 49,520,000 | 2,301,148,400 | 29,838,600 | 2,179,405,974.00 | 121,742,426.00 |
| Fifty dollars | 3,200,000 | 574,840,200 | 5,666,600 | 540,468,110.00 | 34,372,090.00 |
| One hundred dollars | 3,600,000 | 708,278,300 | 2,690,600 | 662,242,280.00 | 46,036,020.00 |
| Five hundred dollars | 1,000,000 | 388,520,000 | 667,500 | 373,830,500.00 | 14,689,500.00 |
| One thousand dollars | 2,200,000 | 1,052,367,000 | 1,790,000 | 983,012,500.00 | 69,354,500.00 |
| Five thousand dollars | 10,000,000 | 920,040,000 | 1,090,000 | 840,105,000.00 | 79,935,000.00 |
| Ten thousand dollars | 191,780,000 | 4,342,550,000 | 8,280,000 | 3,745,060,000.00 | 597,490,000.00 |
| Total | 944,044,000 | 25,236,385,708 | 651,720,961 | 23,596,377,857.00 | 1,640,007,851.00 |
| Unknown, destroyed | | | | 1,000,000.00 | 1,000,000.00 |
| Net | 944,044,000 | 25,236,385,708 | 651,720,961 | 23,597,377,857.00 | 1,639,007,851.00 |

No. 12.—*Old demand notes of each denomination issued, redeemed, and outstanding June 30, 1922.*

| Denomination. | Total issued. | Redeemed during year. | Total redeemed. | Outstanding. |
|---|---|---|---|---|
| Five dollars | $21,800,000.00 | ................ | $21,778,752.50 | $21,247.50 |
| Ten dollars | 20,030,000.00 | ................ | 20,010,355.00 | 19,645.00 |
| Twenty dollars | 18,200,000.00 | ................ | 18,187,880.00 | 12,120.00 |
| Total | 60,030,000.00 | ................ | 59,976,987.50 | 53,012.50 |

No. 13.—*Fractional currency of each denomination issued, redeemed, and outstandin., June 30, 1922.*

| Denomination. | Total issued. | Redeemed during year. | Total redeemed. | Outstanding. |
|---|---|---|---|---|
| Three cents | $601,923.90 | $2.22 | $511,747.96 | $90,175.94 |
| Five cents | 5,694,717.85 | 11.20 | 3,836,417.11 | 1,858,300.74 |
| Ten cents | 82,198,456.80 | 138.15 | 77,145,495.98 | 5,052,960.82 |
| Fifteen cents | 5,305,568.40 | 13.05 | 5,065,762.20 | 239,806.20 |
| Twenty-five cents | 139,031,482.00 | 362.28 | 134,770,775.30 | 4,260,706.70 |
| Fifty cents | 135,891,930.50 | 415.50 | 132,145,511.95 | 3,746,418.55 |
| Total | 368,724,079.45 | 942.40 | 353,475,710.50 | 15,248,368.95 |
| Unknown, destroyed | | | 32,000.00 | 32,000.00 |
| Net | 368,724,079.45 | 942.40 | 353,507,710.50 | 15,216,368.95 |
| Estimated amount lost or destroyed while in circulation | | | | 13,218,000.45 |
| Balance | | | | 1,998,368.50 |

No. 14.—*Compound-interest notes of each denomination issued, redeemed, and outstanding June 30, 1922.*

| Denomination. | Total issued. | Redeemed during year. | Total redeemed. | Outstanding. |
|---|---|---|---|---|
| Ten dollars | $23,285,200 | $10 | $23,266,270 | $18,930 |
| Twenty dollars | 30,125,840 | 60 | 30,094,750 | 31,090 |
| Fifty dollars | 60,824,000 | ................ | 60,762,950 | 61,050 |
| One hundred dollars | 45,094,400 | ................ | 45,062,600 | 31,800 |
| Five hundred dollars | 67,846,000 | ................ | 67,835,000 | 11,000 |
| One thousand dollars | 39,420,000 | ................ | 39,416,000 | 4,000 |
| Total | 266,595,440 | 70 | 266,437,570 | 157,870 |

No. 15.—*One and two year notes of each denomination issued, redeemed, and outstanding June 30, 1922.*

| Denomination. | Total issued. | Redeemed during year. | Total redeemed. | Outstanding. |
|---|---|---|---|---|
| Ten dollars | $6,200,000 | ................ | $6,194,120 | $5,880 |
| Twenty dollars | 16,440,000 | $20 | 16,427,920 | 12,080 |
| Fifty dollars | 20,945,600 | ................ | 20,932,350 | 13,250 |
| One hundred dollars | 37,804,400 | ................ | 37,788,700 | 15,700 |
| Five hundred dollars | 40,302,000 | ................ | 40,300,500 | 1,500 |
| One thousand dollars | 89,308,000 | ................ | 89,289,000 | 19,000 |
| Total | 211,000,000 | 20 | 210,932,590 | 67,410 |
| Unknown, destroyed | | | 10,590 | 10,590 |
| Net | 211,000,000 | 20 | 210,943,180 | 56,820 |

No. 16.—*Federal reserve banks (with branches) and national banks designated as depositaries of public moneys, with the balance held June 30, 1922.*

## FEDERAL RESERVE BANKS.

| Title of bank. | To the credit of the Treasurer of the United States, collected funds. |
|---|---|
| Federal reserve bank, Boston, Mass. | $981,502.42 |
| Federal reserve bank, New York, N. Y. | 8,613,134.61 |
| Federal reserve branch bank of New York, Buffalo, N. Y. | |
| Federal reserve bank, Philadelphia, Pa. | 2,140,713.86 |
| Federal reserve bank, Cleveland, Ohio. | 1,909,776.77 |
| Federal reserve branch bank of Cleveland, Pittsburgh, Pa. | 2.38 |
| Federal reserve branch bank of Cleveland, Cincinnati, Ohio. | |
| Federal reserve bank, Richmond, Va. | 1,769,424.25 |
| Federal reserve branch bank of Richmond, Baltimore, Md. | 1,166,830.78 |
| Federal reserve bank, Atlanta, Ga. | 1,459,389.69 |
| Federal reserve branch bank of Atlanta, New Orleans, La. | 1,152,279.81 |
| Federal reserve branch bank of Atlanta, Jacksonville, Fla. | |
| Federal reserve branch bank of Atlanta, Birmingham, Ala. | 49.98 |
| Federal reserve branch bank of Atlanta, Nashville, Tenn. | 4.53 |
| Federal reserve bank, Chicago, Ill. | 3,073,425.76 |
| Federal reserve branch bank of Chicago, Detroit, Mich. | 7.25 |
| Federal reserve bank, St. Louis, Mo. | 1,175,461.03 |
| Federal reserve branch bank of St. Louis, Louisville, Ky. | 300,002.14 |
| Federal reserve branch bank of St. Louis, Little Rock, Ark. | 200,000.00 |
| Federal reserve branch bank of St. Louis, Memphis, Tenn. | 100,000.00 |
| Federal reserve bank, Minneapolis, Minn. | 1,167,169.93 |
| Federal reserve branch bank of Minneapolis, Helena, Mont. | 169,649.31 |
| Federal reserve bank, Kansas City, Mo. | 1,852,688.30 |
| Federal reserve branch bank of Kansas City, Denver, Colo. | 304,660.60 |
| Federal reserve branch bank of Kansas City, Omaha, Nebr. | 180,246.71 |
| Federal reserve branch bank of Kansas City, Oklahoma City, Okla. | 40.00 |
| Federal reserve bank, Dallas, Tex. | 1,848,924.13 |
| Federal reserve branch bank of Dallas, El Paso, Tex. | 148,407.91 |
| Federal reserve branch bank of Dallas, Houston, Tex. | 353,710.03 |
| Federal reserve bank, San Francisco, Calif. | 1,605,160.53 |
| Federal reserve branch bank of San Francisco, Los Angeles, Calif. | 161,297.42 |
| Federal reserve branch bank of San Francisco, Seattle, Wash. | 196,952.22 |
| Federal reserve branch bank of San Francisco, Portland, Oreg. | 813,425.07 |
| Federal reserve branch bank of San Francisco, Spokane, Wash. | 143,866.72 |
| Federal reserve branch bank of San Francisco, Salt Lake City, Utah. | 103,684.44 |
| Total | 33,091,888.68 |

## SPECIAL DEPOSITARIES.

| Total balances in special depositaries in each Federal reserve district arising from sales of notes and certificates of indebtedness reported to fiscal agents of the United States. | To the credit of the Treasurer of the United States, collected funds. |
|---|---|
| **FISCAL AGENTS.** | |
| Federal reserve bank, Boston, Mass. | $14,154,975.00 |
| Federal reserve bank, New York, N. Y. | 45,831,650.00 |
| Federal reserve bank, Philadelphia, Pa. | 11,635,650.00 |
| Federal reserve bank, Cleveland, Ohio. | 13,967,101.43 |
| Federal reserve bank, Richmond, Va. | 5,676,250.00 |
| Federal reserve bank, Atlanta, Ga. | 2,697,950.00 |
| Federal reserve branch bank of Atlanta, New Orleans, La. | 2,019,937.00 |
| Federal reserve bank, Chicago, Ill. | 19,781,575.00 |
| Federal reserve bank, St. Louis, Mo. | 6,072,933.26 |
| Federal reserve bank, Minneapolis, Minn. | 5,183,062.00 |
| Federal reserve bank, Kansas City, Mo. | 5,535,200.00 |
| Federal reserve bank, Dallas, Tex. | 3,529,575.00 |
| Federal reserve bank, San Francisco, Calif. | 10,390,982.00 |
| Total | 146,476,840.69 |

No. 16.—*Federal reserve banks (with branches) and national banks designated as depositaries of public moneys, with the balance held June 30, 1922*—Continued.

## NATIONAL BANKS.

### GENERAL AND LIMITED.

| State. | Number of depositaries. | Amount of public moneys on deposit, collected funds. | State. | Number of depositaries. | Amount of public moneys on deposit, collected funds. |
|---|---|---|---|---|---|
| Alabama | 21 | $373,148.36 | New Mexico | 7 | $235,772.76 |
| Alaska | 2 | 234,543.86 | New York | 69 | 1,725,907.24 |
| Arizona | 9 | 187,055.06 | North Carolina | 23 | 393,456.18 |
| Arkansas | 11 | 229,890.71 | North Dakota | 14 | 146,880.95 |
| California | 41 | 727,103.46 | Ohio | 61 | 787,635.99 |
| Colorado | 22 | 309,584.98 | Oklahoma | 30 | 478,033.88 |
| Connecticut | 16 | 333,346.83 | Oregon | 15 | 196,842.04 |
| Delaware | 3 | 169,130.03 | Pennsylvania | 94 | 861,286.73 |
| District of Columbia | 5 | 82,457.97 | Rhode Island | 3 | 318,219.12 |
| Florida | 18 | 343,351.92 | South Carolina | 10 | 333,805.07 |
| Georgia | 19 | 443,170.82 | South Dakota | 18 | 214,945.50 |
| Idaho | 10 | 141,236.27 | Tennessee | 19 | 388,973.77 |
| Illinois | 61 | 660,284.73 | Texas | 49 | 628,458.81 |
| Indiana | 50 | 634,153.03 | Utah | 3 | 62,314.21 |
| Iowa | 40 | 893,330.08 | Vermont | 5 | 70,150.17 |
| Kansas | 28 | 643,105.98 | Virginia | 37 | 1,461,421.88 |
| Kentucky | 19 | 281,352.49 | Washington | 18 | 780,230.06 |
| Louisiana | 8 | 114,472.75 | West Virginia | 19 | 491,478.81 |
| Maine | 9 | 266,495.85 | Wisconsin | 44 | 517,575.61 |
| Maryland | 9 | 129,274.28 | Wyoming | 13 | 142,241.86 |
| Massachusetts | 33 | 394,173.31 | | | |
| Michigan | 34 | 790,362.08 | ADDITIONAL DEPOSITARIES. | | |
| Minnesota | 26 | 745,941.57 | | | |
| Mississippi | 12 | 278,803.34 | Canal Zone | 1 | 127,803.58 |
| Missouri | 20 | 398,385.95 | Hawaii | 2 | 1,153,936.01 |
| Montana | 12 | 130,675.30 | Panama | 1 | 1,041,523.13 |
| Nebraska | 29 | 281,139.04 | Porto Rico | 2 | 81,822.17 |
| Nevada | 1 | 87,188.55 | Philippine Islands | 1 | 4,417,757.43 |
| New Hampshire | 13 | 234,242.09 | | | |
| New Jersey | 46 | 843,969.65 | Total | 1,185 | 28,419,843.30 |

## FOREIGN DEPOSITARIES.

| Title of bank. | To the credit of the Treasurer of the United States and United States disbursing officers. | Title of bank. | To the credit of the Treasurer of the United States and United States disbursing officers. |
|---|---|---|---|
| Antwerp branch of the National City Bank of New York, Antwerp, Belgium | $13,469.42 | Paris branch of the Equitable Trust Co., of New York City, Paris, France | $5,972.73 |
| Brussels branch of the Guaranty Trust Co., of New York City, Brussels, Belgium | 6.16 | Paris branch of the Guaranty Trust Co., of New York City, Paris, France | 212,429.82 |
| London branch of the Farmers Loan & Trust Co., of New York City, London, England | 111,058.10 | Banque Nationale de la Republique, Port au Prince, Haiti | 38,781.00 |
| London branch of the Guaranty Trust Co., of New York City, London, England | 177,142.64 | Bank of Italy, Rome, Italy | 188.87 |
| London branch of the International Banking Corporation, of New York City, London, England | 52.98 | Genoa branch of the National City Bank of New York, Genoa, Italy | 662,708.31 |
| | | Total | 1,221,810.03 |

## RECAPITULATION.

| | |
|---|---|
| Federal reserve banks | $33,091,888.68 |
| Special depositaries: Federal reserve banks, fiscal agents | 146,476,840.69 |
| National banks, general and limited | 28,419,843.30 |
| Foreign depositaries | 1,221,810.03 |
| Total | 209,210,382.70 |

No. 17.—*Number of banks with semiannual duty levied, by fiscal years, and number of depositaries with bonds as security at close of each fiscal year from 1915.*

| Fiscal year. | Number of banks. | Bonds held to secure circulation. | Semiannual duty levied. | Number of depositaries. | Bonds held to secure deposits. | Total bonds held. |
|---|---|---|---|---|---|---|
| 1915 | [1] 7,503 | $736,024,190 | $3,901,541.18 | 1,491 | $54,854,619 | $790,878,809 |
| 1916 | 7,412 | 690,440,930 | 3,744,967.77 | 1,381 | 42,674,350 | 733,115,280 |
| 1917 | 7,363 | 671,333,060 | 3,533,631.28 | 1,368 | 43,054,350 | 714,397,410 |
| 1918 | 7,388 | 708,680,900 | 3,656,895.34 | 1,386 | 50,344,700 | 759,025,600 |
| 1919 | 7,416 | 888,387,750 | 4,090,246.76 | 1,399 | 53,720,400 | 942,108,150 |
| 1920 | 7,381 | 984,488,600 | 4,730,245.91 | 671 | 37,637,500 | 1,022,126,100 |
| 1921 | 7,422 | 953,503,640 | 4,753,995.02 | 718 | 40,352,600 | 993,856,240 |
| 1922 | 7,420 | 818,765,000 | 4,387,405.18 | 1,185 | 41,569,989 | 860,334,989 |

[1] Number of banks having bonds on deposit with Treasurer from and after this date.

No. 18.—*Seven-thirty notes redeemed and outstanding June 30, 1922.*

| Issue. | Total issued. | Redeemed to June 30, 1921. | Redeemed during year. | Total retired to June 30, 1922. | Outstanding. |
|---|---|---|---|---|---|
| July 17, 1861 | $140,094,750 | $140,085,400 | .............. | $140,085,400 | $9,350 |
| Aug. 15, 1864 | 299,992,500 | 299,947,200 | $50 | 299,947,250 | 45,250 |
| June 15, 1865 | 331,000,000 | 330,970,200 | .............. | 330,970,200 | 29,800 |
| July 15, 1865 | 199,000,000 | 198,955,600 | .............. | 198,955,600 | 44,400 |
| Total | 970,087,250 | 969,958,400 | 50 | 969,958,450 | 128,800 |

No. 19.—*Refunding certificates, act of February 26, 1879, redeemed and outstanding June 30, 1922.*

| How payable. | Total issued. | Redeemed during year. | Total retired to June 30, 1922. | Outstanding. |
|---|---|---|---|---|
| To order | $58,500 | .............. | $58,480 | $20 |
| To bearer | 39,954,250 | $80 | 39,944,000 | 10,250 |
| Total | 40,012,750 | 80 | 40,002,480 | 10,270 |

No. 20.—*Checks issued by the Treasurer for interest on registered bonds during the fiscal year 1922.*

| Title of loan. | Number. | Amount. | Title of loan. | Number. | Amount. |
|---|---|---|---|---|---|
| Philippine loan of— | | | Porto Rican gold loan of— | | |
| 1914–1934 (L. P.) | 2,559 | $280,000.00 | 1950 | 28 | $4,000.00 |
| 1915–1935 (P. I. B.) | 1,052 | 100,000.00 | 1951 | 22 | 4,000.00 |
| 1915–1935 (M. S. & W.) | 336 | 40,000.00 | 1952 | 23 | 4,000.00 |
| 1916–1936 (P. I. B.) | 307 | 40,000.00 | 1953 | 49 | 4,000.00 |
| 1917–1937 (M. S. & W.) | 494 | 80,000.00 | 1954 | 14 | 4,000.00 |
| 1918–1938 (M. S. & W.) | 355 | 40,000.00 | 1925–1939 | 224 | 40,000.00 |
| 1919–1939 (P. I. B.) | 707 | 60,000.00 | Refunding, 1914 | 215 | 26,200.00 |
| 1921–1941 (Cebu) | 88 | 5,000.00 | Refunding, municipal | 14 | 7,800.00 |
| 1926–1946 (loan 1916) | 974 | 160,000.00 | Irrigation, 1915 | 70 | 24,000.00 |
| 1930–1950 (M. P. & I.) | 1,146 | 330,000.00 | Insular, refunding | 99 | 9,860.00 |
| City of Manila (1920–1930–1950) | 4 | 151,250.00 | Public improvement, 1916 | 79 | 20,000.00 |
| Porto Rican gold loan of— | | | Public improvement, 1918 | 21 | 20,000.00 |
| 1920–1927 | 69 | 17,000.00 | Irrigation, 1918 | 36 | 8,000.00 |
| 1922–1937 | 18 | 4,000.00 | House construction, 1920 | 92 | 11,250.00 |
| 1933–1943 | 90 | 40,000.00 | Public improvement, 1937–1940 | 52 | 22,500.00 |
| 1944 | 30 | 4,000.00 | Workingmen's house construction, 1941–42 | 2 | 585.00 |
| 1945 | 26 | 4,000.00 | District of Columbia 3.65 | 333 | 170,382.00 |
| 1946 | 30 | 4,000.00 | Total | 9,732 | 1,751,827.00 |
| 1947 | 2 | 4,000.00 | | | |
| 1948 | 48 | 4,000.00 | | | |
| 1949 | 24 | 4,000.00 | | | |

No. 21.—*Interest paid by the Treasurer of the United States on District of Columbia 3.65 per cent bonds during the fiscal year 1922.*

| | |
|---|---|
| Coupons | $7,606.54 |
| Checks | 170,363.75 |
| Total | 177,970.29 |

No. 22.—*Coupons from United States bonds, certificates, and notes paid during the fiscal year 1922, classified by loans.*

| Title of loan. | Number. | Amount. |
|---|---|---|
| First Liberty loan 3½ per cent bonds, 1932–47 | 4,577,601 | $38,416,601.59 |
| First Liberty loan converted, 4 per cent, 1932–47 | 391,411 | 720,470.00 |
| First Liberty loan converted, 4¼ per cent, 1932–47 | 3,417,137 | 16,922,124.59 |
| First Liberty loan second converted, 4¼ per cent, 1932–47 | 15,426 | 108,764.95 |
| First Liberty loan 3½ per cent, 1932–47, converted account | ........ | 7,753.61 |
| Second Liberty loan 4 per cent, 1927–42 | 1,426,514 | 2,989,109.52 |
| Second Liberty loan converted, 4¼ per cent, 1927–42 | 12,950,811 | 109,740,663.81 |
| Third Liberty loan 4¼ per cent, 1928 | 21,505,102 | 121,512,745.54 |
| Fourth Liberty loan 4¼ per cent, 1933–38 | 27,085,563 | 209,837,354.46 |
| 4¾ per cent Victory notes, 1922–23 | 18,468,675 | 111,157,463.20 |
| 3¾ per cent Victory notes, 1922–23 | 376,638 | 12,580,667.15 |
| 4 per cent consols, 1907 | 193 | 144.50 |
| 4 per cent loan, 1925 | 42,672 | 346,648.50 |
| 3 per cent loan, 1908–18 | 5,024 | 3,595.05 |
| 2 per cent consols, 1930 | 7,199 | 23,441.50 |
| 2½ per cent postal savings loan, consolidated | 7,851 | 11,862.75 |
| 2½ per cent postal savings loan, second series | 15 | 8.75 |
| 2½ per cent postal savings loan, third series | 11 | 9.75 |
| 2½ per cent postal savings loan, fourth series | 18 | 28.50 |
| 2½ per cent postal savings loan, fifth series | 14 | 25.50 |
| 2½ per cent postal savings loan, sixth series | 5 | 4.25 |
| 3 per cent Panama Canal, 1961 | 26,176 | 172,027.25 |
| 2 per cent Panama Canal, 1916–36 | 156 | 321.00 |
| 2 per cent Panama Canal, 1918–38 | 332 | 1,431.60 |
| 3 per cent conversion bond | 80,275 | 589,168.00 |
| 5 per cent loan, 1904 | 1 | 1.25 |
| 5½ per cent Treasury notes | 98,816 | 10,520,999.37 |
| 5¾ per cent Treasury notes | 205,066 | 16,704,454.37 |
| 4 per cent certificates of indebtedness | 21 | 150.89 |
| 4¼ per cent certificates of indebtedness | 27,929 | 2,182,744.29 |
| 4½ per cent certificates of indebtedness | 62,231 | 8,608,612.76 |
| 4¾ per cent certificates of indebtedness | 255 | 9,333.14 |
| 5 per cent certificates of indebtedness | 23,934 | 3,083,081.25 |
| 5¼ per cent certificates of indebtedness | 56,659 | 8,310,749.67 |
| 5½ per cent certificates of indebtedness | 406,285 | 47,029,558.47 |
| 5¾ per cent certificates of indebtedness | 237,673 | 24,790,166.45 |
| 6 per cent certificates of indebtedness | 274,673 | 29,964,675.00 |
| Total | 91,778,362 | 776,346,962.23 |

No. 23.—*Checks drawn by the Secretary and paid by the Treasurer for interest on registered bonds and notes of the United States during the fiscal year 1922.*

| Title of loan. | Rate of interest. | Checks drawn by the Secretary of the Treasury. | | Checks paid by the Treasurer of the United States. | |
|---|---|---|---|---|---|
| | | Number. | Amount. | Number. | Amount. |
| | *Per ct.* | | | | |
| Funded loan of 1907 | 4 | ........ | ........ | 5 | $196.00 |
| Loan of 1925 | 4 | 12,158 | $4,377,458.00 | 12,361 | 4,393,320.25 |
| Loan of 1908–1918 | 3 | ........ | ........ | 217 | 715.89 |
| Consols of 1930 | 2 | 31,983 | 11,971,045.25 | 25,289 | 11,943,212.56 |
| Panama Canal loan of 1961 | 3 | 7,345 | 1,321,731.00 | 7,163 | 1,322,118.75 |
| Panama Canal loan of 1916–1936 | 2 | 3,912 | 978,936.10 | 3,953 | 975,584.80 |
| Panama Canal loan of 1918–1938 | 2 | 2,190 | 517,333.90 | 2,086 | 517,734.49 |
| Postal savings | 2½ | 10,821 | 281,968.25 | 10,892 | 283,030.50 |
| Soldiers and sailors' civil relief insurance | 3½ | 106 | 1,835.75 | 160 | 1,940.75 |
| Special certificates of indebtedness | 2 | 2 | 3,280,294.71 | 2 | 3,280,294.71 |
| Conversion | 3 | 409 | 278,547.00 | 577 | 279,816.25 |
| First Liberty loan | 3½ | 61,493 | 11,498,072.25 | 60,258 | 11,485,469.06 |
| First Liberty loan, converted | 4 | 49,291 | 370,682.00 | 57,221 | 409,796.00 |
| Do | 4¼ | 252,047 | 5,403,677.85 | 239,310 | 5,368,619.93 |
| First Liberty loan, second converted | 4¼ | 2,872 | 39,488.32 | 3,010 | 40,326.59 |
| Second Liberty loan | 4 | 209,920 | 1,545,167.00 | 230,307 | 1,580,776.00 |
| Second Liberty loan, converted | 4¼ | 761,111 | 28,651,112.07 | 759,195 | 28,553,021.76 |
| Third Liberty loan | 4¼ | 1,632,434 | 33,448,833.08 | 1,629,411 | 33,414,183.78 |
| Fourth Liberty loan | 4¼ | 2,332,146 | 62,644,846.96 | 2,330,476 | 62,619,978.39 |
| Victory loan | 3¾ | 1,387 | 1,200,070.62 | 1,616 | 1,266,458.84 |
| Do | 4¾ | 1,159,394 | 25,134,658.01 | 1,303,345 | 25,545,500.01 |
| Total | ........ | 6,531,021 | 192,945,758.12 | 6,676,854 | 193,282,095.31 |

No. 24.—*Money deposited in the Treasury each month of the fiscal year 1922 for the redemption of national-bank notes and Federal reserve bank notes.*

| Month. | 5 per cent account. | Retirement account. | | | Total. |
|---|---|---|---|---|---|
| | | By insolvent and liquidating banks. | By banks reducing their circulation. | | |
| | | | National banks. | Federal reserve banks. | |
| 1921—July | $45,799,658.50 | $778,997.50 | $236,700.00 | $1,500,000.00 | $48,315,356.00 |
| August | 59,669,559.90 | 204,992.50 | 224,500.00 | 10,500,000.00 | 70,599,052.40 |
| September | 51,436,885.45 | 603,300.00 | 385,200.00 | 16,500,000.00 | 68,925,385.45 |
| October | 52,538,777.87 | 553,697.50 | 472,400.00 | 21,000,000.00 | 74,564,875.37 |
| November | 51,692,136.90 | 262,015.00 | 255,000.00 | 15,375,000.00 | 67,584,151.90 |
| December | 48,156,121.95 | 378,250.00 | 895,347.50 | 3,000,000.00 | 52,429,719.45 |
| 1922—January | 62,899,860.26 | 346,550.00 | 88,900.00 | | 63,335,310.26 |
| February | 56,471,641.19 | 334,600.00 | 92,800.00 | 1,500,000.00 | 58,399,041.19 |
| March | 47,837,784.72 | 325,612.50 | 888,850.00 | 7,966,000.00 | 57,018,247.22 |
| April | 45,379,865.65 | 289,450.00 | 1,109,992.50 | 6,825,000.00 | 53,604,308.15 |
| May | 48,938,592.50 | 1,145,767.50 | 667,250.00 | 8,350,000.00 | 59,101,610.00 |
| June | 48,805,294.92 | 135,522.50 | 894,932.50 | 3,000,000.00 | 52,835,749.92 |
| Total | 619,626,179.81 | 5,358,755.00 | 6,211,872.50 | 95,516,000.00 | 726,712,807.31 |

No. 25.—*Amount of currency counted into the cash of the National Bank Redemption Agency and redeemed notes delivered, by fiscal years from 1916 to 1921, and by months during the fiscal year 1922.*

| Fiscal Year | Counted into cash | National-bank notes — For return to banks of issue | National-bank notes — For destruction and reissue | National-bank notes — For destruction and retirement — Bond secured | National-bank notes — For destruction and retirement — Emergency | Federal reserve notes — For return to banks of issue | Federal reserve notes — For destruction | Federal reserve bank notes — For return to banks of issue | Federal reserve bank notes — For destruction and reissue | Federal reserve bank notes — For destruction and retirement | Total | United States currency deposited in Treasury | Balance |
|---|---|---|---|---|---|---|---|---|---|---|---|---|---|
| | Dollars. | Dollars. | Dollars. | Dollars. | Dollars. | Dollars. | Dollars. | Dollars. | Dollars. | Dollars. | Dollars. | Dollars. | Dollars. |
| 1916 | 559,976,130.90 | 86,938,900 | 351,812,445.00 | 24,633,910.50 | 61,518,352.50 | 14,410,600 | 24,758,450.00 | | 54,900 | 1,154,775 | 564,071,758.00 | 867,242.00 | 23,978,217.10 |
| 1917 | 457,447,296.37 | 37,50,655,630 | 313,657,970.00 | 39,409,340.50 | 3,808,650.00 | 12,430,300 | 41,582,865.00 | 27,550 | 972,620 | 1,934,225 | 462,782,000.50 | 613,219.00 | 18,030,293.97 |
| 1918 | 393,429,111.16 | 462,100,256 | 256,911,175.00 | 39,677,000.00 | 1,465,990.00 | 15,893,550 | 46,810,780.00 | 80,550 | 32,967,000 | 882,529 | 389,207,790.00 | 681,351.50 | 21,570,263.63 |
| 1919 | 603,914,628.55 | 528,599,350 | 257,543,020.00 | 22,835,072.50 | 618,495.00 | 37,297,650 | 141,633,275.00 | 2,688,700 | 228,090,000 | 289,780 | 524,465,382.50 | 857,979.50 | 100,161,530.18 |
| 1920 | 911,414,508.74 | 743,373,500 | 229,862,502.50 | 23,862,134.50 | 136,240.00 | 30,780,650 | 242,582,997.50 | 390,750 | | 289,780 | 978,008,164.50 | 7,524,353.50 | 26,043,520.92 |
| 1921 | 1,015,557,593.50 | 16,246,000 | 488,931,357.50 | 18,302,631.00 | 71,370.00 | 30,719,100 | 229,810,500.00 | 232,250 | 229,483,400 | 19,158,000 | 1,012,954,608.50 | 11,829,277.00 | 16,817,228.98 |
| **1921.** | | | | | | | | | | | | | |
| July | 83,907,462.13 | | 50,858,830.00 | 1,785,655.00 | 4,380.00 | | 8,125,500.00 | | 15,857,000 | 2,755,000 | 79,386,365.00 | 126,583.00 | 21,211,743.11 |
| Aug | 80,749,927.32 | | 54,450,830.00 | 2,095,345.00 | 5,150.00 | | 7,069,300.00 | | 13,878,000 | 5,296,000 | 82,794,625.00 | 102,279.50 | 19,064,765.93 |
| Sept | 73,846,665.13 | | 50,488,300.00 | 1,694,930.00 | 4,450.00 | | 6,253,100.00 | | 3,553,000 | 13,128,000 | 75,121,210.00 | 125,818.50 | 17,664,402.56 |
| Oct | 75,263,550.15 | 587,970 | 50,891,977.50 | 1,495,930.00 | 4,600.00 | | 6,059,900.00 | | 2,644,000 | 12,358,000 | 74,042,377.50 | 361,685.50 | 18,523,889.71 |
| Nov | 71,046,695.95 | 587,970 | 47,149,090.00 | 1,213,880.00 | 4,030.00 | | 5,777,700.00 | | 2,742,000 | 10,636,000 | 68,286,070.00 | 419,385.00 | 20,865,130.66 |
| Dec | 73,222,878.99 | 743,370 | 52,295,432.50 | 1,423,950.00 | 3,170.00 | | 5,565,700.00 | | 3,966,000 | 8,865,000 | 72,119,252.50 | 258,438.50 | 21,710,318.65 |
| **1922.** | | | | | | | | | | | | | |
| Jan | 85,477,674.78 | | 64,089,022.50 | 1,431,900.00 | 2,550.00 | | 6,149,600.00 | | 5,762,000 | 7,044,000 | 84,478,072.50 | 560,021.50 | 22,149,999.43 |
| Feb | 62,475,678.57 | | 48,896,465.00 | 992,500.00 | 1,400.00 | | 4,416,000.00 | | 6,188,000 | 4,671,000 | 65,165,365.00 | 245,510.00 | 19,214,703.00 |
| Mar | 67,535,892.30 | 1,755,650 | 48,330,310.00 | 935,800.00 | 2,250.00 | | 4,862,100.00 | | 1,993,000 | 9,517,000 | 65,640,460.00 | 339,387.00 | 20,770,748.30 |
| Apr | 60,953,530.93 | 2,821,800 | 43,478,025.00 | 1,142,150.00 | 1,400.00 | | 4,372,400.00 | | 3,990,000 | 5,090,000 | 59,829,625.00 | 44,436.00 | 21,850,218.23 |
| May | 60,319,061.39 | 2,097,950 | 44,178,200.00 | 1,211,200.00 | 1,400.00 | | 4,646,700.00 | | 4,368,000 | 5,145,000 | 62,375,300.00 | 40,125.50 | 19,753,854.12 |
| June | 58,227,336.51 | | 42,579,460.00 | 1,109,200.00 | 1,700.00 | | 5,383,100.00 | | 3,332,000 | 6,192,000 | 60,683,410.00 | 38,060.50 | 17,249,720.13 |
| Total | 853,026,354.16 | 8,006,740 | 597,684,942.50 | 16,531,870.00 | 36,480.00 | | 68,679,100.00 | | 68,273,000 | 90,720,000 | 849,932,132.50 | 2,661,730.50 | ............ |

No. 26.—*Currency received for redemption by the National Bank Redemption Agency from the principal cities and other places, by fiscal years, from 1916, in thousands of dollars.*

| Fiscal year. | New York. | Boston. | Phila-delphia. | Balti-more. | Chicago. | Cincin-nati. | St. Louis. | New Orleans. | Other places. | Total. |
|---|---|---|---|---|---|---|---|---|---|---|
| 1916...... | $211,596 | $46,594 | $34,314 | $13,835 | $77,998 | $16,991 | $35,334 | $7,847 | $120,368 | $564,877 |
| 1917...... | 149,447 | 33,452 | 30,240 | 8,944 | 58,043 | 14,892 | 34,497 | 6,467 | 126,463 | 462,445 |
| 1918...... | 104,072 | 23,171 | 25,281 | 9,855 | 39,257 | 18,021 | 25,720 | 4,783 | 148,150 | 398,310 |
| 1919...... | 153,647 | 34,082 | 45,582 | 8,483 | 50,350 | 49,569 | 29,207 | 8,296 | 237,632 | 616,848 |
| 1920...... | 174,302 | 43,686 | 84,455 | 12,208 | 80,763 | 61,672 | 33,955 | 9,631 | 407,350 | 908,022 |
| 1921...... | 143,062 | 47,236 | 90,028 | 13,376 | 90,645 | 47,449 | 29,940 | 9,679 | 545,338 | 1,016,753 |
| 1922...... | 161,928 | 49,176 | 73,845 | 12,498 | 72,232 | 20,432 | 30,930 | 10,114 | 421,904 | 853,059 |

No. 27.—*Mode of payment for currency redeemed at the National Bank Redemption Agency, by fiscal years, from 1916.*

| Fiscal year. | Treasurer's checks. | United States currency. | Gold, silver, and minor coin. | Credit in general account. | Credit in redemption account. | Total. |
|---|---|---|---|---|---|---|
| 1916..... | $34,137,302.52 | $418,381,906.13 | $19,500.50 | $104,343,158.40 | $3,094,263.35 | $559,976,130.90 |
| 1917..... | 94,416,415.22 | 273,264,891.03 | 21,799.90 | 87,044,474.76 | 2,699,715.46 | 457,447,296.37 |
| 1918..... | 41,098,909.60 | 101,362,222.83 | .............. | 249,350,534.39 | 1,617,444.34 | 393,429,111.16 |
| 1919..... | 18,418,673.20 | 173,265,442.78 | .............. | 410,481,596.25 | 1,748,916.32 | 603,914,628.55 |
| 1920..... | 40,530,245.32 | 45,418,429.73 | .............. | 823,041,581.41 | 2,424,252.28 | 911,414,508.74 |
| 1921..... | 2,997,501.43 | 21,585,953.87 | .............. | 989,478,454.43 | 1,495,683.83 | 1,015,557,593.56 |
| 1922..... | 503,190.00 | 445,282.01 | .............. | 851,481,806.29 | 596,075.85 | 853,026,354.15 |

No. 28.—*Deposits, redemptions, assessments for expenses, and transfers and repayments on account of the 5 per cent redemption fund of national and Federal reserve banks, by fiscal years, from 1916.*

| Fiscal year. | Deposits. | Redemptions. | Assessments. | Transfers and repayments. | Balance. |
|---|---|---|---|---|---|
| 1916............... | $441,182,576.23 | $438,751,345.00 | $501,119.09 | $3,243,633.86 | $24,220,193.11 |
| 1917............... | 368,714,326.53 | 364,396,070.00 | 438,261.36 | 2,320,704.57 | 25,779,483.71 |
| 1918............... | 444,389,017.14 | 366,130,575.00 | 417,333.50 | 18,888,159.51 | 113,459,699.13 |
| 1919............... | 934,977,257.23 | 500,128,995.00 | 409,138.94 | 323,245,597.09 | 224,653,225.33 |
| 1920............... | 1,772,280,776.57 | 954,447,760.00 | 535,201.43 | 773,734,755.96 | 268,216,284.51 |
| 1921............... | 2,041,796,421.11 | 975,422,607.50 | 975,457.83 | 1,046,642,184.48 | 286,972,455.81 |
| 1922............... | 1,866,252,022.45 | 742,643,782.50 | 1,113,761.64 | 1,193,172,412.12 | 216,294,522.00 |

NOTE.—Federal reserve notes not included until fiscal year 1918. Federal reserve note balance June 30, 1917, was $28,727,266.29.

No. 29.—*Deposits and redemptions on account of the retirement of circulation, by fiscal years, from 1916.*

| Fiscal year. | National-bank notes. | | | | | Federal reserve bank notes. | | |
| --- | --- | --- | --- | --- | --- | --- | --- | --- |
| | Deposits. | | | Redemptions. | Balance. | Deposits. | Redemptions. | Balance. |
| | Insolvent and liquidating. | Reducing. | Total. | | | | | |
| 1916 [1] | $9,995,455.00 | $47,435,911.95 | $57,431,366.95 | $56,151,363.00 | $57,590,975.00 | .......... | .......... | .......... |
| 1917 | 6,270,262.50 | 27,106,280.00 | 33,376,542.50 | 43,217,990.50 | 47,749,527.00 | $4,000,000 | $1,154,775 | $2,845,225 |
| 1918 | 4,160,762.50 | 6,090,327.50 | 10,251,090.00 | 21,142,990.00 | 36,857,627.00 | .......... | 1,934,225 | 911,000 |
| 1919 | 2,397,900.00 | 20,275,417.50 | 22,673,317.50 | 23,453,567.50 | 36,077,377.00 | .......... | 882,820 | 28,180 |
| 1920 | 5,474,810.00 | 11,335,577.50 | 16,810,387.50 | 23,270,624.50 | 29,617,140.00 | 261,600 | 289,780 | .......... |
| 1921 | 10,948,735.00 | 8,318,280.00 | 19,267,015.00 | 18,374,001.00 | 30,510,154.00 | 20,920,000 | 19,158,000 | 1,762,000 |
| 1922 | 5,358,755.00 | 6,211,872.50 | 11,570,627.50 | 16,568,350.00 | 25,512,431.50 | 95,516,000 | 90,720,000 | 6,558,000 |

[1] Emergency currency included.

No. 30.—*Expenses incurred in the redemption of national and Federal reserve currency, by fiscal years, from 1916.*

| Fiscal year. | Office of Treasurer of the United States. | | | Office of Comptroller of the Currency. | | Total. | Rate of expense per $1,000. | | | | | | | | |
| --- | --- | --- | --- | --- | --- | --- | --- | --- | --- | --- | --- | --- | --- | --- | --- |
| | Charges for transportation. | Salaries. | Contingent expenses. | Salaries. | Contingent expenses. | | National-bank notes. | | | Federal reserve bank notes. | | | Federal reserve notes. | | |
| | | | | | | | Active. | | Retirement. | Active. | | Retirement. | From banks of issue. | From other sources. | |
| | | | | | | | Fit for use. | Unfit for use. | | Fit for use. | Unfit for use. | | | Fit for use. | Unfit for use. |
| 1916 | $177,243.42 | $216,476.96 | $13,332.13 | $42,658.70 | $439.01 | $450,150.22 | $0.81722 | .......... | $0.75066 | $0.98350 | $0.98350 | $0.75066 | $0.19523 | $0.41880 | $0.41880 |
| 1917 | 154,315.56 | 214,715.47 | 7,639.20 | 42,930.86 | 659.33 | 420,160.42 | .98350 | $1.11822 | .78946 | .72881 | .78946 | .78946 | .21470 | .26857 | .34754 |
| 1918 | 159,406.20 | 196,241.31 | 11,570.29 | 45,023.67 | 544.45 | 412,785.92 | .84676 | 1.18390 | .92882 | 1.10002 | .92882 | .92882 | .17295 | .67248 | .43992 |
| 1919 | 229,039.24 | 239,736.42 | 13,248.62 | 46,055.22 | 344.74 | 528,424.24 | .72976 | .94490 | .76984 | .95741 | 1.15854 | 1.15854 | .10314 | .56390 | .37080 |
| 1920 | 326,112.76 | 499,385.51 | 63,896.26 | 91,871.24 | 1,247.67 | 982,503.44 | .64823 | 1.04644 | .77429 | .81171 | .97963 | .97963 | .00437 | .54137 | .39637 |
| 1921 | 319,995.66 | 596,963.82 | 117,183.19 | 117,183.19 | 6,668.27 | 1,115,146.16 | .81738 | .96382 | .71244 | .......... | .91759 | .91759 | .12009 | .64583 | .47018 |
| 1922 | 265,809.00 | 567,518.28 | 31,687.36 | 117,129.58 | 3,111.61 | 985,255.83 | .78670 | .......... | .......... | .......... | .......... | .......... | .10062 | .......... | .45312 |

NOTE.—For 1916 the rate for national-bank notes was the same for both active and retirement, and fit and unfit for use, to adjust transportation charges. For 1917 only, a rate of $0.80183 was established for District of Columbia banks for active notes, both fit and unfit for use, to adjust transportation charges.

No. 31.—*General cash account of the National Bank Redemption Agency for the fiscal year 1922, and from July 1, 1874:*

| | For fiscal year. | From July 1, 1874. |
|---|---|---|
| **DR.** | | |
| Balance from previous year | $16,817,228.98 | |
| Currency received for redemption | 853,058,626.60 | $14,066,274,010.75 |
| "Overs" | 16,611.36 | 2,737,997.11 |
| Total | 869,892,466.94 | 14,069,012,007.86 |
| **CR.** | | |
| National-bank notes returned to banks of issue | 8,006,740.00 | 2,969,633,686 00 |
| National-bank notes delivered to Comptroller of the Currency | 614,253,292.50 | 9,240,101,321.60 |
| Federal reserve bank notes returned to banks of issue | | 3,419,600.00 |
| Federal reserve bank notes delivered to Comptroller of the Currency | 158,993,000.00 | 673,950,520.00 |
| Federal reserve notes returned to banks of issue | | 141,531,850.00 |
| Federal reserve notes delivered to Comptroller of the Currency | 68,679,100.00 | 775,257,967.50 |
| Money deposited in Treasury | 2,661,730.50 | 169,056,457.73 |
| Packages referred and moneys returned | 195.00 | 76,433,563.59 |
| Express charges deducted | 1,720.03 | 143,016.22 |
| Counterfeit notes returned | 646.25 | 110,666.35 |
| Uncurrent notes returned or discounted | 33,323.03 | 380,537.14 |
| "Shorts" | 12,999.50 | 1,713,101.60 |
| Cash balance June 30, 1922 | 17,249,720.13 | 17,249,720.13 |
| Total | 869,892,466.94 | 14,069,012.007.86 |

No. 32.—*Average amount of national bank notes outstanding and the redemptions, by fiscal years, from 1875 (the first year of the agency).*

| Year. | Average outstanding. | Redemptions. | | Year. | Average outstanding. | Redemptions. | |
|---|---|---|---|---|---|---|---|
| | | Amount. | Per cent. | | | Amount. | Per cent. |
| 1875 | $354,238,291 | $155,520,880 | 43.90 | 1899 | $239,287,673 | $90,838,301 | 37.96 |
| 1876 | 344,483,798 | 209,038,855 | 60.68 | 1900 | 260,293,746 | 96,982,608 | 37.25 |
| 1877 | 321,828,139 | 242,885,375 | 75.47 | 1901 | 339,884,257 | 147,486,578 | 43.39 |
| 1878 | 320,625,047 | 213,151,458 | 66.48 | 1902 | 358,173,941 | 171,869,258 | 47.98 |
| 1879 | 324,244,285 | 157,656,645 | 48.62 | 1903 | 383,173,195 | 196,429,621 | 51.26 |
| 1880 | 339,530,923 | 61,585,676 | 18.13 | 1904 | 428,886,482 | 262,141,930 | 61.12 |
| 1881 | 346,314,471 | 59,650,259 | 17.22 | 1905 | 468,285,475 | 308,298,760 | 65.84 |
| 1882 | 359,736,050 | 76,089,327 | 21.15 | 1906 | 538,065,425 | 296,292,885 | 55.07 |
| 1883 | 359,868,524 | 102,699,677 | 28.53 | 1907 | 580,445,599 | 240,314,681 | 40.77 |
| 1884 | 347,746,363 | 126,152,572 | 36.27 | 1908 | 662,473,554 | 349,634,341 | 52.78 |
| 1885 | 327,022,283 | 150,209,129 | 45.93 | 1909 | 680,666,307 | 461,522,202 | 67.80 |
| 1886 | 314,815,970 | 130,296,607 | 41.38 | 1910 | 707,919,327 | 502,498,994 | 70.98 |
| 1887 | 293,742,052 | 87,689,687 | 29.85 | 1911 | 724,911,069 | 551,531,596 | 76.08 |
| 1888 | 265,622,692 | 99,152,364 | 37.32 | 1912 | 739,940,744 | 649,954,710 | 87.84 |
| 1889 | 230,648,247 | 88,932,059 | 38.55 | 1913 | 750,906,777 | 675,889,000 | 90.01 |
| 1890 | 196,248,499 | 70,256,947 | 35.80 | 1914 | 755,598,359 | 706,756,602 | 93.54 |
| 1891 | 175,911,373 | 67,460,619 | 38.34 | 1915 | 943,887,520 | 782,633,567 | 82.92 |
| 1892 | 172,113,311 | 69,625,046 | 40.45 | 1916 | 770,598,250 | 522,923,441 | 67.86 |
| 1893 | 174,755,355 | 75,845,225 | 43.40 | 1917 | 724,305,232 | 406,462,419 | 56.12 |
| 1894 | 205,322,804 | 105,330,844 | 51.30 | 1918 | 719,159,594 | 331,507,154 | 46.10 |
| 1895 | 207,860,409 | 86,709,133 | 41.71 | 1919 | 722,275,127 | 371,361,153 | 51.42 |
| 1896 | 217,133,390 | 108,260,978 | 49.85 | 1920 | 722,934,617 | 425,741,623 | 58.89 |
| 1897 | 232,888,449 | 113,573,776 | 48.76 | 1921 | 729,728,404 | 517,041,511 | 70.85 |
| 1898 | 228,170,874 | 97,111,687 | 42.56 | 1922 | 748,385,215 | 624,341,433 | 83.43 |

No. 33.—*Federal reserve notes, canceled and uncanceled, forwarded by Federal reserve banks and branches, counted and delivered to the Comptroller of the Currency for credit of Federal reserve agents.*

Fiscal year:

| | |
|---|---|
| 1916 | $24,486,000.00 |
| 1917 | 55,042,725.00 |
| 1918 | 213,730,775.00 |
| 1919 | 701,857,330.00 |
| 1920 | 1,722,882,472.50 |
| 1921 | 1,781,861,460.00 |
| 1922 | 2,127,406,150.00 |

No. 34.—*Changes during the fiscal year 1922 in the force employed in the Treasurer's office.*

```
Total force June 30, 1921:
    Regular roll..............................................................................  685
    Postal savings roll.......................................................................   10
    Agency roll...............................................................................  471
    Bond roll.................................................................................  151
                                                                                            ——— 1,317
Decreas· in force............................................................................       137
                                                                                               ———————
    Total force June 30, 1922.................................................................     1,180
Changes during year:
    Retired...................................................................................   10
    Resigned..................................................................................   83
    Transferred from..........................................................................   99
    Died......................................................................................    5
    Discontinued..............................................................................   19
                                                                                            ———   216
    Appointed.................................................................................   19
    Reappointed...............................................................................   27
    Transferred to............................................................................   33
                                                                                            ———    79
```

# REPORT OF THE DIRECTOR OF THE MINT

TREASURY DEPARTMENT,
BUREAU OF THE MINT,
*Washington, D. C., September 23, 1922.*

SIR: In compliance with the provisions of section 345, Revised · Statutes of the United States, I have the honor to submit herewith a report covering the operations of the mints and assay offices of the United States for the fiscal year ended June 30, 1922, being the fiftieth annual report of the Director of the Mint. There is also submitted for publication in connection therewith the annual report of this bureau upon the production and consumption of the precious metals in the United States for the calendar year 1921.

## OPERATION OF THE MINTS AND ASSAY OFFICES.

### INSTITUTIONS OF THE MINT SERVICE.

The following institutions of the Mint Service continued operations during the fiscal year ended June 30, 1922: Coinage mints at Philadelphia, San Francisco, and Denver; assay office at New York, which makes large sales of fine gold bars; mints at New Orleans and Carson City conducted as assay offices; and assay offices at Seattle, Boise, Helena, Salt Lake City, and Deadwood. The seven last-named institutions are, in effect, bullion-purchasing agencies for the large institutions, and also serve the public by making, at nominal charge, assays of ores and bullion. Electrolytic refineries are operated at the New York and San Francisco institutions.

### COIN DEMAND.

The coinage of gold was resumed during the p      fiscal year, nearly $53,000,000 in value having been executed.asThis permits the issue of additional gold certificates, the issue of certificates against bullion being limited by law to two-thirds of such certificates outstanding. Over 92,000,000 silver dollars were coined during the year from bullion purchased under the terms of the Pittman Act, practically all of these dollars going into storage and being represented in circulation by silver certificates issued against them in lieu of Federal reserve bank notes retired. Retirement of the Federal reserve bank notes permits retirement of certificates of indebtedness held as security against them, thus reducing the public debt and the interest thereon. Of coins below the dollar but few were executed during the past year, those struck being confined to memorial half dollars and a small number of nickel and bronze coins for cleaning up partially completed lots. Approximately 12,000,000 pieces of coin were executed for foreign governments, making the year's aggregate number of pieces executed by the three mints

117,912,205. Working periods of 16 hours and 24 hours per day were again a feature of the year's operations, incident to the effort to reduce quickly the "dead" stock of Pittman Act silver bullion to an active asset in the form of silver dollars, against which silver certificates could be issued. Silver bullion can not be circulated as cash, nor is it available as a reserve against liabilities or paper currency. While operating on a 24-hour basis the average output reached 1,000,000 silver dollar coins per day—500,000 at the Philadelphia Mint, 280,000 at San Francisco and 220,000 at Denver.

### GOLD OPERATIONS.

Large gold receipts at the New York assay office, principally of imported refined bars, totaled some $480,000,000 as compared with $562,000,000 during the preceding year.

The value of the gold acquired by the Government at the mints and assay offices during the fiscal year 1922 was $540,629,997.69; United States coin received for recoinage was of value $2,491,089.03; transfers of gold between mint offices totaled $3,574,397.44; giving an aggregate of gold handled by the mint service during the fiscal year 1922 of $546,695,484.16.

### SILVER OPERATIONS.

Receipts of purchased silver were again very large, the total of 54,566,332.02 ounces including 52,671,710.05 ounces of Pittman Act silver costing $1 per ounce. The average cost of other purchased silver was $0.658 per fine ounce, its total cost being $1,248,-555.24; the silver received for repayment to the depositors thereof in bars bearing the Government stamp totaled 6,249,499.19 fine ounces; the United States silver coin received for recoinage totaled 1,734,695.72 fine ounces, with recoinage value of $2,398,058.70; silver deposited in trust by other Governments totaled 5,760,742.21 fine ounces; the transfers of silver between mint service offices totaled 652,533.92 fine ounces, making an aggregate quantity of silver handled by the mint service during the fiscal year 1922 of 68,963,-803.06 fine ounces.

Silver purchased under the terms of the Pittman Act, delivered to mint institutions, totaled to June 30, 1922, 117,512,000 ounces, leaving approximately 91,500,000 ounces yet to be acquired; 86,196,-979 ounces have been coined into 111,431,473 standard silver dollars, of which 86,730,000 are of the old design. Purchases under the Pittman Act during the two years since they were begun in May, 1920, have totaled somewhat more than the quantity of silver produced from domestic mines during the same period. This is due to the working up of considerable stocks of crude domestic material shown by sworn reports of reduction concerns to have been on hand at the time purchases were commenced. The New York price of silver which does not meet Pittman Act requirements averaged during the fiscal year ended June 30, 1922, $0.66821; the lowest New York price was at the opening of the fiscal year, 59⅝ cents; the highest May 22, 1922, 74$\frac{3}{16}$ cents.

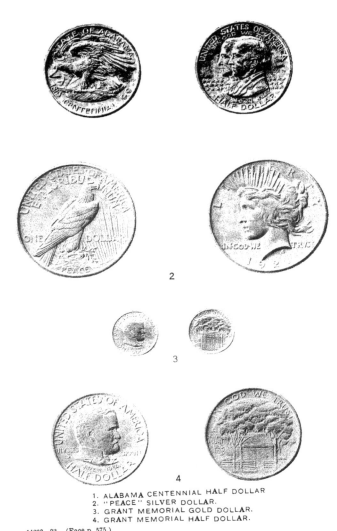

2

3

4

1. ALABAMA CENTENNIAL HALF DOLLAR
2. "PEACE" SILVER DOLLAR.
3. GRANT MEMORIAL GOLD DOLLAR.
4. GRANT MEMORIAL HALF DOLLAR.

The number of deposits received during the past fiscal year, 91,669, exceeded any prior year. Imports of gold and Pittman Act silver purchases account for the high number. Increase is noted of about 50 per cent in number of deposits received at the Boise and Helena assay offices, evidently due to greater prospecting activity; approximately 70 per cent increase at the New Orleans office is noted.

Considerably increased production of electrolytically refined gold, and reduction in silver, featured the refinery work of the past year.

Four new coins as illustrated on opposite page were issued during the past year.

The "Peace dollar' takes the place of the old design of the standard silver dollar, which was first issued in 1878. This coin commemorates the declaration of peace between the United States, Germany, and Austria, exchanges of peace treaty ratifications having been made in Berlin on November 11, 1921, and in Vienna on November 8, 1921, and peace having been proclaimed by the President of the United States on November 14 and 17, 1921, respectively. No special congressional authority was required for the change in design of the silver dollar, since the law permits changing the design of any of our coins not more frequently than once in 25 years. The design of the "Peace dollar" was selected by the Fine Arts Commission from models submitted by a number of prominent sculptors, and is the work of Anthony de Francisci. On the obverse is a female head emblematic of Liberty, wearing a tiara of light rays, and the word "Liberty"; on the reverse is an eagle perched on a mountain top, holding in its talons an olive branch, witnessing the dawn of a new day; the word "Peace" also appears. Other mottoes and inscriptions are as required by the coinage laws. The design for the silver "Peace dollar" was approved in December, 1921, and 1,006,473 pieces were executed by the close of the calendar year. Subsequent coins of this design will bear the year in which made. At the close of the fiscal year on June 30, 1922, a total of 24,701,473 of the new design coins had been struck.

The Alabama centennial half dollar bears on one side portraits of the first governor of Alabama and of the present governor of the State; also 22 stars, indicative of the twenty-second State of the Union; the reverse is an adaptation of the seal of the State, an eagle standing on the shield, holding arrows in its talons, with the motto "Here we rest," and the dates "1819–1919."

The Ulysses S. Grant centennial half dollar bears on one side a strong profile portrait of General Grant and on the other side a sketch of the historic log cabin in which he was born.

The Ulysses S. Grant centennial gold dollar is a reproduction in miniature of the half dollar, the only change being the value of the coin.

The domestic coinage of the fiscal year 1922 was of value $145,712,-742, namely, $52,990,000 in gold double eagles; $10.016 in Grant memorial gold dollars; $92,388,473 in standard silver dollars (67,687,-000 old design, 24,701,473 new design); $160,093 in subsidiary silver, consisting of $50,026.50 landing of the pilgrims tercentennial half dollars, $25,014 Missouri centennial half dollars, $35,022 in Alabama centennial half dollars, and $50,030.50 in Grant memorial half dollars; $72,350 nickel; and $91.810 bronze coin. The coinage other than domestic, totaling 11,916,030 pieces, included, at the Philadelphia Mint, 16,030 gold pieces for Costa Rica, 3,900,000 silver pieces for Venezuela, and 3,000,000 silver pieces for Colombia; at the San Francisco Mint, 5,000,000 silver pieces for Indo-China.

The seigniorage on United States coinage executed totaled $21,-088,524.79, of which $20,919,928.83 was on standard silver dollars, $40,661.82 was on subsidiary silver coins, and $127,934.14 was on nickel and bronze coins.

On June 30, 1922, the estimated stock of domestic coin in the United States was $1,515,774.608, of which $863.389,318 was gold, $381,174,404 was silver-dollar coin, and $271.210.886 was subsidiary silver coin.

The stock of gold bullion in the mints and assay offices on the same date was valued at $2,850,230,389.14, a gain over last year of $441,-548,342.54, and the stock of silver bullion was 44.334,061.59 fine ounces, a decrease over last year of 15,412,137.2 ounces.

The production of gold and silver in the United States during the calendar year 1921 was as follows: Gold, $50.067.300, a reduction from last year of $1.119.600, and silver, 53,052.441 fine ounces, a reduction from last year of 2.309,132 ounces.

The amount of gold consumed in the industrial arts during the calendar year 1921 was $50.674.270, of which $23.050,332 was new material. Silver consumed amounted to 35,867,946 fine ounces, of which 28,843,628 fine ounces were new material.

The net import of United States gold coin for the fiscal year ended June 30, 1922, was $1,774,498.

Total appropriation estimates for the mint service for the fiscal year 1924, including the office of the Director of the Mint, amount to $1,383,390. The appropriations for the year 1923 amount to $1,361,950.

## APPROPRIATIONS, EXPENSES, AND INCOME.

The appropriated amounts available for mint service uses during the fiscal year 1922 totaled $1,791,527.65: reimbursements to appropriations for services rendered amounted to $548,407.20, making an available total of $2,339,934.85.

The expenses chargeable to appropriations were $2,070,485.21; those chargeable to income, $4,120.89; total, $2,074,606.10.

The income realized by the Treasury from the mint service totaled $22,189,212.69, of which $21,088,524.79 was seigniorage. It should be noted however, that the seigniorage on the coinage of silver dollars, which amounted to $20.919,928.83 for the fiscal year 1922, merely offsets an equal loss which was incurred when silver dollars were melted and sold under the terms of the Pittman Act.

## ADDITIONS AND IMPROVEMENTS.

At the Denver Mint the inspection pit under the main storage vault was converted into a subvault, capable of holding 30,000,000 standard silver dollars, thus meeting the urgent need for additional vault space.

At the Philadelphia Mint two new rolling mills were completed in the machine shop and placed in commission in the rolling room. These additions materially add to the mint's rolling capacity. Two coining presses, as well as numerous other mechanical devices, are under way in the machine shop. It has been clearly demonstrated that the indirect arc type of electric furnace is uncertain and unsatisfactory for alloying the precious metals. Oxidation is constantly to be guarded against, and the absorption of silver by lining of hearth causes the production of a different alloy from figured standard. Alloyed metal, where fineness is so carefully checked by assay, should be melted in a crucible type of furnace free from absorption and direct effect of generated heat.

## INCOME AND EXPENSES OF THE FISCAL YEAR 1922.

### INCOME.

| Earnings: | | |
|---|---:|---:|
| Credited to appropriations— | | |
| Charges on foreign coinage executed........................ | $119,728.75 | |
| Silver dollar coinage costs, from special fund........... | 392,238.15 | |
| Charges for manufacture of special medals.............. | 13,757.37 | |
| Charges for work done for other institutions, etc.............. | 22,652.93 | |
| Total earnings credited to appropriations ........................... | | $548,407.20 |
| Credited to revenues— | | |
| Mint charges on bullion........ | 404,652.33 | |
| Proceeds of medals sold...... | 3,926.52 | |
| Receipts from special assays of bullion and ores........... | 3,525.80 | |
| Total earnings credited to revenues................................. | | 412,107.65 |
| Total earnings......................................... | | $960,514.85 |

Profits:
  Gain on bullion shipments
    to refineries..............$178.89
  Less contra losses...........  .13
                                      ――――――
                                      $178.76
  Surplus bullion recovered.... ......  87,765.28
  Proceeds of sale of by-products
    (platinum, etc.)..................  49,993.68
  Proceeds of sale of old materials....  2,067.02
  Commission on telephone calls.....    168.31

      Total profits other than seign-
        iorage...............................  $140,173.05
  Seigniorage on silver dollar coinage. 20,919,928.83
  Seigniorage on subsidiary silver
    coinage..........................   40,661.82
  Seigniorage on minor coinage—
    Nickel.......................   63,047.68
    Bronze....................... ·  64,886.46

      Total seigniorage........................... 21,088,524.79

      Total profits.............................................$21,228,697.84

      Total income............................................ 22,189,212.69

### EXPENSES.

Chargeable to appropriations:
  Compensation of employees—
    Mint Bureau, salaries appropriation.........    22,626.37
    Mint Bureau, increase of compensation ap-
      propriation.............................     2,640.00
    Mints and assay offices, salaries appropria-
      tions....................................   226,296.83
    Mints and assay offices, wages appropriations... 1,145,580.86
    Mints and assay offices, increase of compensa-
      tion appropriation.........................   190,753.98

      Total compensation of employees.......................... 1,587,898.04
  Equipment, stores, and other expenses—
    Mint Bureau, contingent appropriation........     6,155.17
    Mints and assay offices, contingent and per-
      manent appropriations (including $13,-
      624.56 wastage of gold and silver in opera-
      tive departments and $6,592.97 loss on
      assay value of sweeps sold)...............   474,167.24
    Transportation of bullion and coin between mints
      and assay offices, freight appropriation........     2,264.76

      Total miscellaneous expenses chargeable to
        appropriations........................................   482,587.17

      Total expenses chargeable to appropriations.............. 2,070,485.21
Chargeable to revenue:
  Seigniorage on minor coinage—
    Expense of distributing minor coin to Treas-
      ury offices................................     3,998.54
    Wastage of minor metals in operative depart-
      ments....................................      122.35

      Total chargeable to revenue.............................     4,120.89

Total expenses..................................................... 2,074,606.10
Net income of the Government from the Mint Service .............. 20,114,606.59

      Total....................................................... 22,189,212.69

DEPOSITS, INCOME, EXPENSES, AND EMPLOYEES, BY INSTITUTIONS, FISCAL YEAR 1922.

The number and value of deposits, the income (including seigniorage), the expenses of the fiscal year 1922, and the number of employees on June 30, 1922, at each institution, follow:

| Institution. | Deposits. | Mint Service transfers. | United States coining value of gold and silver receipts. | Income.[1] | Expenses from appropriation.[2] | Transportation of bullion and coin. | Employees June 30, 1922. |
|---|---|---|---|---|---|---|---|
| Philadelphia.... | 28,331 | 714 | $37,589,721.82 | $11,657,738.59 | $897,963.09 | $590.17 | 356 |
| San Francisco.. | 23,449 | 3,327 | 84,181,271.59 | 4,969,217.70 | 431,331.42 | 180.64 | 149 |
| Denver........ | 14,095 | 6 | 24,933,115.87 | 4,675,818.28 | 298,768.16 | 69.09 | 82 |
| New York..... | 18,748 | .......... | 481,286,684.30 | 331,321.46 | 345,875.25 | .......... | 125 |
| New Orleans... | 456 | .......... | 652,022.83 | 1,103.57 | 11,571.74 | .......... | 6 |
| Carson City.... | 241 | .......... | 61,009.29 | 454.15 | 4,461.16 | 9.78 | 3 |
| Boise.......... | 527 | .......... | 340,157.01 | 1,292.06 | 6,559.59 | 94.66 | 4 |
| Helena......... | 357 | .......... | 99,211.65 | 437.65 | 6,383.13 | 34.60 | 3 |
| Deadwood...... | 10 | .......... | 3,283.49 | 566.00 | 5,557.31 | 7.91 | 3 |
| Seattle......... | 1,302 | .......... | 3,052,812.74 | 2,448.27 | 26,461.54 | 1,256.00 | 11 |
| Salt Lake City.. | 106 | .......... | 18,819.97 | 387.89 | 4,131.28 | 21.91 | 2 |
| Total....... | 87,622 | 4,047 | 632,218,113.56 | 21,640,805.62 | 2,039,063.67 | 2,264.76 | 744 |

[1] Does not include $548,407.20 received by the Mint Service for work performed.
[2] Includes transportation of bullion and coin between mints and assay offices. Does not include $31,421.54 Mint Bureau expenses charged against appropriations or $4,121.02 Mint Service expenses paid from revenues.

## COINAGE.

Details of the coinage executed during the fiscal year ended June 30, 1922, are given in the following tables:

*Domestic coinage of the United States mints during the fiscal year 1922.*

| Denomination. | Philadelphia. | | San Francisco. | |
|---|---|---|---|---|
| | Pieces. | Value. | Pieces. | Value. |
| Double eagles.......................... | 873,000 | $17,460,000.00 | 1,776,500 | $35,530,000.00 |
| Dollars, Grant memorial...................... | 10,016 | 10,016.00 | ............ | .............. |
| Total gold............................. | 883,016 | 17,470,016.00 | 1,776,500 | 35,530,000.00 |
| Silver dollars................................. | 50,707,473 | 50,707,473.00 | 21,480,000 | 21,480,000.00 |
| Half dollars: | | | | |
| Pilgrim tercentennial..................... | 100,053 | 50,026.50 | ............ | .............. |
| Missouri centennial...................... | 50,028 | 25,014.00 | ............ | .............. |
| Alabama centennial...................... | 70,044 | 35,022.00 | ............ | .............. |
| Grant memorial.......................... | 100,061 | 50,030.50 | ............ | .............. |
| Total silver ........................... | 51,027,659 | 50,867,566.00 | 21,480,000 | 21,480,000.00 |
| 5-cent nickels................................. | 1,447,000 | 72,350.00 | ............ | .............. |
| 1-cent bronze................................. | 2,021,000 | 20,210.00 | ............ | .............. |
| Total minor........................... | 3,468,000 | 92,560.00 | ............ | .............. |
| Total coinage........................... | 55,378,675 | 68,430,142.00 | 23,256,500 | 57,010,000.00 |

*Domestic coinage of the United States mints during the fiscal year 1922*—Continued.

| Denomination. | Denver. | | Total. | |
|---|---|---|---|---|
| | Pieces. | Value. | Pieces. | Value. |
| Double eagles............................ | ................ | ................ | 2,649,500 | $52,990,000.00 |
| Dollars, Grant memorial.................. | ................ | ................ | 10,016 | 10,016.00 |
| Total gold......................... | ................ | ................ | 2,659,516 | 53,000,016.00 |
| Silver dollars......................... | 20,201,000 | $20,201,000.00 | 92,388,473 | 92,388,473.00 |
| Half dollars: | | | | |
| Pilgrim tercentennial................ | ................ | ................ | 100,053 | 50,026.50 |
| Missouri centennial.................. | ................ | ................ | 50,028 | 25,014.00 |
| Alabama centennial.................. | ................ | ................ | 70,044 | 35,022.00 |
| Grant memorial..................... | ................ | ................ | 100,061 | 50,030.50 |
| Total silver...................... | 20,201,000 | 20,201,000.00 | 92,708,659 | 92,548,566.00 |
| 5-cent nickels.......................... | ................ | ................ | 1,447,000 | 72,350.00 |
| 1-cent bronze.......................... | 7,160,000 | 71,600.00 | 9,181,000 | 91,810.00 |
| Total minor....................... | 7,160,000 | 71,600.00 | 10,628,000 | 164,160.00 |
| Total coinage..................... | 27,361,000 | 20,272,600.00 | 105,996,175 | 145,712,742.00 |

*Coinage of the United States mints for other countries during the fiscal year 1922.*

| Country and denomination. | Gold pieces. | Silver pieces. | Country and denomination. | Gold pieces. | Silver pieces. |
|---|---|---|---|---|---|
| At Philadelphia: | | | At Philadelphia—Contd. | | |
| For Costa Rico, 2 colones............... | 16,030 | ............ | For Venezuela—Contd. | | |
| For Colombia, half pesos............ | ............ | 3,000,000 | ½ bolivars.................. | ............ | 600,000 |
| For Venezuela— | | | ¼ bolivars.................. | ............ | 800,000 |
| 5 bolivars.............. | ............ | 500,000 | At San Francisco: | | |
| 2 boliva·s.............. | ............ | 1,000,000 | For Indo-China, piasters.................. | ............ | 5,000,000 |
| 1 bolivars.............. | ............ | 1,000,000 | Total number of pieces. | 16,030 | 11,900,000 |

### DEPOSITS OF FOREIGN GOLD BULLION AND COIN.

Foreign gold bullion containing 16,760,932 fine ounces, of the value of $346,479,213, and foreign gold coin containing 5,996,941 fine ounces, of the value of $123,967,772, was deposited, having been received from the following countries during the fiscal year ending June 30, 1922:

| Country. | Crude bullion. | | Refined bullion. | | Coin. | |
|---|---|---|---|---|---|---|
| | Fine ounces. | Coining value. | Fine ounces. | Coining value. | Fine ounces. | Coining value. |
| North America: | | | | | | |
| Canada.................. | 10,410 | $215,194 | 959,139 | $19,827,163 | 673 | $13,912 |
| Cuba................... | ............ | ............ | ............ | ............ | 369 | 7,628 |
| Mexico................. | 34,589 | 715,018 | 21,319 | 440,703 | 881,698 | 18,226,315 |
| Nova Scotia............. | 13 | 269 | ............ | ............ | ............ | ............ |
| Central American States and West Indies........... | 53,475 | 1,105,426 | ............ | ............ | 240 | 4,961 |
| South America............. | 319,990 | 6,614,780 | ............ | ............ | 459,701 | 9,502,863 |
| Europe: | | | | | | |
| Austria................. | ............ | ............ | ............ | ............ | 407,261 | 8,418,832 |
| Denmark............... | ............ | ............ | ............ | ............ | 199 | 4,114 |
| Finland................ | ............ | ............ | 328 | 6,780 | ............ | ............ |
| France................. | ............ | ............ | 3,450,584 | 71,329,902 | 191,536 | 3,959,401 |
| Germany............... | ............ | ............ | 14,096 | 291,390 | 1,597,184 | 33,016,724 |
| Great Britain........... | ............ | ............ | 5,769,731 | 119,270,925 | 1,313,103 | 27,144,248 |
| Holland................ | 1,517 | 31,359 | 129,278 | 2,672,413 | 115 | 2,377 |

| Country. | Crude bullion. | | Refined bullion. | | Coin. | |
|---|---|---|---|---|---|---|
| | Fine ounces. | Coining value. | Fine ounces. | Coining value. | Fine ounces. | Coining value. |
| Europe—Continued. | | | | | | |
| Italy | | | | | 2 | $41 |
| Russia (non-Bolshevik) | 39 | $806 | | | 530,473 | 10,965,850 |
| Spain | 13,998 | 289,364 | 94 | $1,943 | 863 | 17,840 |
| Sweden | 15,596 | 322,398 | 1,806,460 | 37,342,842 | 315 | 6,512 |
| Switzerland | 28,046 | 579,762 | 2,863,701 | 59,197,954 | | |
| Turkey | 2,906 | 60,072 | | | 525,657 | 10,886,294 |
| Asia: | | | | | | |
| China | 316,833 | 6,549,519 | 319 | 6,594 | | |
| India | 651,173 | 13,460,941 | 163,994 | 3,390,057 | | |
| Japan | | | | | 84,697 | 1,750,842 |
| Persia | | | | | 195 | 4,031 |
| Siberia | 2 | 41 | | | | |
| Africa: | | | | | | |
| Egypt | 4,709 | 97,344 | | | | |
| South Africa | | | | | 30 | 620 |
| Australasia, New Zealand | 73,409 | 1,517,499 | 55,184 | 1,140,755 | | |
| Mixed coin | | | | | 2,630 | 54,367 |
| | 1,526,705 | 31,559,792 | 15,234,227 | 314,919,421 | 5,996,941 | 123,967,772 |

## DEPOSITS OF FOREIGN SILVER BULLION AND COIN.

Foreign silver bullion containing 1,705,423 fine ounces, of the value of $2,357,592, and foreign silver coin containing 5,219,623 fine ounces, of the value of $7,215,653, was deposited, having been received from the following countries during the fiscal year ending June 30, 1922:

| Country. | Crude bullion. | | Refined bullion. | | Coin. | |
|---|---|---|---|---|---|---|
| | Fine ounces. | Subsidiary silver coining value. | Fine ounces. | Subsidiary silver coining value. | Fine ounces. | Subsidiary silver coining value. |
| North America: | | | | | | |
| Canada | 6,703 | $9,266 | 17,518 | $24,217 | | |
| Mexico | 1,147,171 | 1,585,859 | 37,723 | 52,149 | 26,023 | $35,974 |
| Novia Scotia | 2 | 3 | | | | |
| Central American States and West Indies | 104,814 | 144,896 | | | 11,817 | 16,336 |
| South America | 250,571 | 346,392 | | | 325,924 | 450,560 |
| Europe: | | | | | | |
| Austria | | | | | 207 | 286 |
| France | | | | | 961 | 1,329 |
| Germany | 25 | 34 | 97,040 | 134,149 | 4,397,097 | 6,078,586 |
| Holland | | | | | | |
| Norway | 5,298 | 7,324 | | | | |
| Russia (non-Bolshevik) | 5 | 7 | | | 342,949 | 474,096 |
| Spain | 750 | 1,037 | | | | |
| Sweden | 1,600 | 2,212 | | | | |
| Switzerland | 9,868 | 13,642 | | | | |
| Turkey | 3,915 | 5,412 | | | 34 | 47 |
| Asia: | | | | | | |
| China | 5,173 | 7,151 | | | | |
| India | 14,053 | 19,427 | | | | |
| Persia | | | | | 5 | 7 |
| Africa: Egypt | 380 | 525 | | | | |
| Australasia: New Zealand | 2,814 | 3,890 | | | | |
| Mixed coin | | | | | 114,606 | 158,432 |
| Total | 1,553,142 | 2,147,077 | 152,281 | 210,515 | 5,219,623 | 7,215,653 |
| Cost value | | 1,017,681 | | 100,571 | | 3,512,243 |

REFINED SILVER BULLION DEPOSITED IN TRUST FOR USE IN COINAGE FOR OTHER GOVERNMENTS.

|  | Fine ounces. |
|---|---|
| Canadian bullion | 194,532 |
| Mexican bullion | 689,862 |
| Refinery and origin unknown | 3,873,148 |
| Total | 4,757,542 |

## ISSUE OF FINE GOLD BARS FOR GOLD COIN AND GOLD BULLION.

The value of the fine gold bars issued in exchange for gold coin and bullion, monthly, by the United States mints at Philadelphia, San Francisco, and Denver, and the assay office at New York for the fiscal year 1922 was as follows:

### EXCHANGED FOR GOLD COIN.

| Month | Philadelphia. | San Francisco. | Denver. | New York. | Total. |
|---|---|---|---|---|---|
| **1921** |  |  |  |  |  |
| July | $110,652.18 | $51,065.86 | ............ | $1,010,671.50 | $1,172,389.54 |
| August | 105,668.02 | 54,086.85 | ............ | 2,890,538.17 | 3,050,293.04 |
| September | 130,809.40 | 54,431.93 | ............ | 3,575,118.44 | 3,760,359.77 |
| October | 176,187.91 | 63,325.92 | ............ | 4,014,580.85 | 4,254,094.68 |
| November | 85,687.05 | 54,390.31 | ............ | 2,988,169.04 | 3,128,246.40 |
| December | 95,995.91 | 62,533.98 | ............ | 2,309,657.81 | 2,468,187.70 |
| **1922** |  |  |  |  |  |
| January | 90,685.70 | 40,561.99 | ............ | 3,118,753.17 | 3,250,000.86 |
| February | 110,531.55 | 55,910.57 | ............ | 3,936,163.66 | 4,102,605.78 |
| March | 145,963.99 | 50,522.35 | ............ | 3,936,117.17 | 4,132,603.51 |
| April | 166,327.92 | 31,182.46 | ............ | 3,150,051.16 | 3,347,561.54 |
| May | 495,941.68 | 40,177.74 | ............ | 5,795,758.75 | 6,331,878.17 |
| June | 125,543.36 | 55,125.46 | ............ | 3,995,818.76 | 4,076,487.58 |
| Total | 1,839,994.67 | 613,315.42 | ............ | 40,621,398.48 | 43,074,708.57 |

### EXCHANGED FOR GOLD BULLION.

| Month. | Philadelphia. | San Francisco. | Denver. | New York. | Total |
|---|---|---|---|---|---|
| **1921.** |  |  |  |  |  |
| July | $37,128.56 | $3,421.71 | $4,718.55 | $565,346.04 | $610,614.86 |
| August | 36,106.29 | 9,666.65 | 2,440.78 | 377,895.37 | 426,109.09 |
| September | 46,638.03 | 11,319.59 | 5,273.27 | ............ | 63,230.89 |
| October | 47,951.74 | 5,862.11 | 5,425.28 | 538,318.69 | 597,557.82 |
| November | 51,986.52 | 6,182.34 | 3,135.66 | 364,743.06 | 426,047.58 |
| December | 45,586.16 | 6,061.86 | 2,834.20 | 419,604.62 | 474,086.84 |
| **1922.** |  |  |  |  |  |
| January | 52,575.07 | 12,132.67 | 4,437.50 | 452,755.49 | 521,900.73 |
| February | 46,641.17 | 7,749.00 | 5,806.69 | 336,428.08 | 396,624.94 |
| March | 58,585.27 | 8,319.03 | 2,854.31 | 449,174.54 | 518,933.15 |
| April | 51,322.45 | 6,965.52 | 4,478.63 | 441,018.65 | 503,785.25 |
| May | 57,908.78 | 8,539.52 | 3,899.59 | 449,303.04 | 519,650.93 |
| June | 38,114.02 | 1,600.42 | 3,532.76 | 329,123.67 | 372,370.87 |
| Total | 570,544.06 | 87,820.42 | 48,837.22 | 4,723,711.25 | 5,430,912.95 |

## BALANCES, RECEIPTS, AND DISBURSEMENTS OF GOLD BULLION.

Balances of gold bullion on hand June 30, 1921, and receipts, disbursements, and balances June 30, 1922, at the mints and assay offices, are shown in the following table:

| Institution. | Balance on June 30, 1921. | Receipts during fiscal year 1922 (details below). | Total. | Disbursements during fiscal year 1922 (details below). | Balance on June 30, 1922 |
|---|---|---|---|---|---|
| Philadelphia | $317,403,027.88 | $6,405,375.59 | $323,808,403.47 | $19,916,419.65 | $303,891,983.82 |
| San Francisco | 386,558,987.76 | 61,785,944.61 | 448,344,932.37 | 36,240,566.33 | 412,104,366.04 |
| Denver | 188,475,161.65 | 7,732,294.63 | 196,207,456.28 | 49,714.46 | 196,157,741.82 |
| New York | 1,515,983,881.79 | 466,714,163.91 | 1,982,698,045.70 | 45,381,483.04 | 1,937,316,562.66 |
| New Orleans | 126,211.75 | 528,193.31 | 654,405.06 | | 654,404.71 |
| Carson City | 17,610.46 | 58,974.68 | 76,585.14 | 72,484.88 | 4,100.26 |
| Helena | 5,615.29 | 96,271.88 | 101,887.17 | 85,801.26 | 16,085.91 |
| Boise | 14,960.37 | 333,712.10 | 348,672.47 | 336,555.57 | 12,116.90 |
| Deadwood | 1,204.63 | 2,333.68 | 3,538.31 | 2,968.17 | 570.14 |
| Seattle | 72,161.88 | 3,020,569.22 | 3,092,731.10 | 3,024,590.89 | 68,140.21 |
| Salt Lake City | 23,223.14 | 17,650.55 | 40,873.69 | 36,557.05 | 4,316.64 |
| Total | 2,408,682,046.60 | 546,695,484.16 | 2,955,377,530.76 | 105,147,141.62 | 2,850,230,389.14 |

## DETAILED RECEIPTS OF GOLD BULLION.

| Institution. | Deposits including U. S. uncurrent coin. | Surplus bullion recovered (including shipment gains). | Transfers from mints and assay offices | Total. |
|---|---|---|---|---|
| Philadelphia | $6,393,796.20 | $6,644.60 | $4,934.79 | $6,405,375.59 |
| San Francisco | 58,215,308.40 | 7,581.83 | 3,563,054.38 | 61,785,944.61 |
| Denver | 7,728,183.69 | 3,077.35 | 1,033.59 | 7,732,294.63 |
| New York | 466,685,595.73 | 23,400.22 | 5,167.96 | 466,714,163.91 |
| New Orleans | 528,021.87 | 171.44 | | 528,193.31 |
| Carson City | 58,941.69 | 32.99 | | 58,974.68 |
| Helena | 96,227.61 | 44.27 | | 96,271.88 |
| Boise | 333,431.08 | 281.02 | | 333,712.10 |
| Deadwood | 2,323.98 | 9.70 | | 2,333.68 |
| Seattle | 3,020,230.59 | 131.91 | 206.72 | 3,020,569.22 |
| Salt Lake City | 17,583.29 | 67.26 | | 17,650.55 |
| Total | 543,079,644.13 | 41,442.59 | 3,574,397.44 | 546,695,484.16 |

## DETAILED DISBURSEMENTS OF GOLD BULLION.

| Institution. | Bars paid to depositors. | Transfers to mints and assay offices. | Sold in sweeps, manufactures, etc. | Bars issued in exchange for coin. |
|---|---|---|---|---|
| Philadelphia | $570,544.06 | $11,073.42 | $8,997.19 | $1,839,994.67 |
| San Francisco | 87,820.42 | | 8,638.24 | 613,315.42 |
| Denver | 48,838.36 | | 876.10 | |
| New York | 4,721,322.27 | | 38,762.29 | 40,621,398.48 |
| Carson City | | 72,484.88 | | |
| Helena | | 85,801.26 | | |
| Boise | | 336,541.05 | | |
| Deadwood | | 2,968.17 | | |
| Seattle | | 3,024,590.87 | | |
| Salt Lake City | | 36,557.05 | | |
| Total | 5,428,525.11 | 3,570,016.70 | 57,273.82 | 43,074,708.57 |

| Institution. | Manufactured into coin.[1] | Wastage and shipment losses. | Total. |
|---|---|---|---|
| Philadelphia | $17,484,935.21 | $875.10 | $19,916,419.65 |
| San Francisco | 35,530,000.00 | 792.25 | 36,240,566.33 |
| Denver | | | 49,714.46 |
| New York | | | 45,381,483.04 |
| New Orleans | | | 32 |
| Carson City | | | 72,484.88 |
| Helena | | | 85,801.26 |
| Boise | | | 336,555.57 |
| Deadwood | | 14.52 | 2,968.17 |
| Seattle | | | 3,024,590.89 |
| Salt Lake City | | .02 | 36,557.05 |
| Total | 53,014,935.21 | 1,682.21 | 105,147,141.62 |

[1] Includes Costa Rican coinage at Philadelphia, $14,919.21.

PURCHASE OF MINOR COINAGE METAL FOR USE IN DOMESTIC COINAGE.

During the fiscal year 1922 there was purchased for delivery at the Mint at Philadelphia 584,892.37 troy ounces of minor coinage metals at a cost of $5,665.24 as follows:

| Metal. | Troy ounces. | Cost. |
|---|---|---|
| Copper, ingot | 583,333.33 | $5,650.00 |
| Mutilated bronze coin | 1,173.75 | 11.28 |
| Mutilated nickel coin | 385.29 | 3.96 |
| Total | 584,892.37 | 5,665.24 |

There were no purchases during this year of nickel and bronze blanks prepared for stamping.

DISTRIBUTION OF MINOR COINS.

The only minor coin distributed by the mints during the fiscal year 1922 was approximately $50,000, from the San Francisco Mint. Distribution costs of the year cover expenses incurred in prior years. The amounts paid were: $3,746.89 by the Philadelphia Mint and $251.65 by the Denver Mint; total, $3,998.54.

MINOR COINS OUTSTANDING.

The following statement shows the coinage of minor coins by denominations since 1793, the amount on hand, issued, melted, and outstanding June 30, 1922:

| Denomination. | Coined. | On hand. | Issued (net). | Melted. | Amount issued and outstanding June 30, 1922. |
|---|---|---|---|---|---|
| **Philadelphia:** | | | | | |
| Copper cents | $1,562,887.44 | | $1,562,887.44 | $382,267.10 | $1,180,620.34 |
| Copper half cents [1] | 39,926.11 | | 39,926.11 | | 39,926.11 |
| Copper-nickel cents | 2,007,720.00 | | 2,007,720.00 | 806,640.17 | 1,201,079.83 |
| Bronze 1-cent pieces | 36,449,066.83 | $688,196.00 | 35,760,870.83 | 714,215.25 | 35,046,655.58 |
| Bronze 2-cent pieces | 912,020.00 | | 912,020.00 | 342,111.74 | 569,908.26 |
| Nickel 3-cent pieces | 941,349.48 | | 941,349.48 | 286,041.10 | 655,308.38 |
| Nickel 5-cent pieces | 55,277,568.10 | 995,005.00 | 54,282,563.10 | 5,014,940.35 | 49,267,622.75 |
| Total | 97,190,537.96 | 1,683,201.00 | 95,507,336.96 | 7,546,215.71 | 87,961,121.25 |
| **San Francisco:** | | | | | |
| Copper cents | | | | 5.05 | |
| Bronze 1-cent pieces | 3,243,700.00 | 154,932.30 | 3,088,767.70 | 13,966.00 | 3,074,801.70 |
| Bronze 2-cent pieces | | | | 11.52 | |
| Nickel 3-cent pieces | | | | 58.80 | |
| Nickel 5-cent pieces | 2,411,450.00 | 119,441.02 | 2,292,008.98 | 44,983.60 | 2,247,025.38 |
| Total | 5,655,150.00 | 274,373.32 | 5,380,776.68 | 59,024.97 | 5,321,827.08 |
| **Denver:** | | | | | |
| Bronze 1-cent pieces | 3,146,300.00 | 202,507.00 | 2,943,793.00 | 2,919.62 | 2,940,873.38 |
| Bronze 2-cent pieces | | | | 12.32 | |
| Nickel 3-cent pieces | | | | 1.38 | |
| Nickel 5-cent pieces | 3,923,915.00 | 534,325.00 | 3,389,590.00 | 67,822.10 | 3,321,767.90 |
| Total | 7,070,215.00 | 736,832.00 | 6,333,383.00 | 70,755.42 | 6,262,641.28 |
| Grand total | 109,915,902.96 | 2,694,406.32 | 107,221,496.64 | 7,675,996.10 | [2] 99,545,589.61 |

[1] There is no record of the melting of any of the old copper half cents, but it is believed that few, if any, are now in circulation.

[2] Deduct $89.07 value of old coins melted at San Francisco and Denver Mints for the net amount issued and outstanding, $99,545,500.54. The uncurrent minor coins melted at each mint are not necessarily those of former coinage of the same mint.

## OPERATIONS OF THE ASSAY DEPARTMENTS.

The principal work of the assay department of the coinage mints and the assay office at New York during the fiscal year 1922 is summarized as follows:

| Item. | Philadelphia. | | | San Francisco. | | |
|---|---|---|---|---|---|---|
| | Samples. | Assays. | Reports. | Samples. | Assays. | Reports. |
| | *Number.* | *Number.* | *Number.* | *Number.* | *Number.* | *Number.* |
| Silver purchases (Pittman Act) | 19,933 | 20,390 | 19,933 | 22,216 | 11,766 | 11,277 |
| Deposits and other purchases | 15,399 | 59,008 | 7,240 | 25,867 | 91,476 | 12,879 |
| Redeposits | | | | 1,024 | 2,597 | 343 |
| Silver received in trust | 1,392 | 1,392 | 1,392 | 6,670 | 3,683 | 3,349 |
| Gold ingots | 1,242 | 1,731 | 451 | 1,732 | 2,429 | 63 |
| Silver ingots | 42,684 | 46,304 | 21,342 | 22,527 | 23,954 | 401 |
| Refinery | | | | 6,987 | 13,134 | 9,164 |
| Melting and refining department, miscellaneous | 192 | 437 | 86 | | | |
| Coining department | 80 | 182 | 39 | 51 | 166 | 20 |
| Mass melt | 404 | 1,385 | 115 | 222 | 726 | 13 |
| Sweeps | 113 | 60 | 13 | 44 | 172 | 141 |
| Special assays of bullion and ores | 54 | 227 | 54 | 1,468 | 3,684 | 375 |
| Miscellaneous | 365 | 648 | 309 | 263 | 1,470 | 123 |
| Total | 81,858 | 131,764 | 50,974 | 89,071 | 155,257 | 38,148 |

| Item. | Denver. | | | New York. | | |
|---|---|---|---|---|---|---|
| | Samples. | Assays. | Reports. | Samples. | Assays. | Reports. |
| | *Number.* | *Number.* | *Number.* | *Number.* | *Number.* | *Number.* |
| Silver purchases (Pittman Act) | 21,496 | 21,800 | 10,748 | | | |
| Deposits and other purchases | 6,709 | 30,861 | 3,353 | 51,473 | 147,399 | 18,396 |
| Redeposits | | | | | | |
| Silver received in trust | | | | | | |
| Gold ingots | | | | | | |
| Silver ingots | 20,141 | 42,253 | 14,390 | | | |
| Refinery | | | | 3,540 | 7,936 | 1,156 |
| Melting and refining department, miscellaneous | | | | | | |
| Coining department | 30 | 120 | 15 | | | |
| Mass melt | 36 | 144 | 12 | | | |
| Sweeps | 24 | 138 | 24 | 95 | 479 | 13 |
| Special assays of bullion and ores | 5 | 54 | 5 | 1,194 | 6,216 | 594 |
| Miscellaneous | 166 | 423 | 134 | 38 | 154 | 19 |
| Total | 48,607 | 95,793 | 28,681 | 56,340 | 162,184 | 20,178 |

### PROOF BULLION (1.000 FINE).

In order to establish uniformity in assay of bullion in the offices of the Mint Service, all proof gold and proof silver is made at the mint at Philadelphia and furnished to other offices when required.

The amount made during the fiscal year 1922 was: Gold, 749 ounces; silver, 740 ounces.

### OPERATIONS OF THE MELTING AND REFINING AND OF THE COINING DEPARTMENTS, FISCAL YEAR 1922.

The aggregate quantity of metals operated upon in the above-mentioned departments of the coinage mints and assay office at New York during the fiscal year ended June 30, 1922, was 39.86 million fine ounces of gold and 308.83 million fine ounces of silver. There were also operated upon at the coinage mints 8.7 million ounces of minor coinage metal. The figures in the table following are based on the figures obtained at the settlements of the accounts.

Legal limits of wastage on the whole amount delivered by the superintendent to operative officers, as prescribed in section 3542, Revised Statutes, are as follows: Melter and refiner—gold, 0.001; silver, 0.0015; coiner—gold, 0.0005; silver, 0.001.

## GOLD BULLION.

| Institution and department. | Amount received. | Amount returned. | Amount operated upon. | Legal allowance of wastage on amount received. | Surplus recovered. | Wasted. | Wastage per 1,000 ounces operated upon. |
|---|---|---|---|---|---|---|---|
| | *Fine ounces.* | *Fine ounces.* | *Fine ounces.* | *Fine ounces.* | *Fine ounces.* | *Fine ounces.* | *Fine ounces.* |
| Philadelphia Mint: | | | | | | | |
| Melting and refining.. | 3,883,703 | 3,883,661 | ¹ 2,651,300 | 3,884 | .......... | 42 | 0.01596 |
| Coining............... | 2,635,012 | 2,635,038 | 2,611,213 | 1,317 | 26 | .......... | .......... |
| San Francisco Mint: | | | | | | | |
| Melting and refining.. | 7,489,878 | 7,490,142 | 4,603,175 | 7,490 | 264 | .......... | 0.01007 |
| Coining............... | 4,038,996 | 4,038,958 | 3,804,071 | 2,019 | .......... | 38 | .......... |
| Denver Mint: | | | | | | | |
| Melting and refining.. | 1,522,119 | 1,522,166 | 38,770 | 1,522 | 47 | .......... | .......... |
| Coining............... | .......... | .......... | .......... | .......... | .......... | .......... | .......... |
| New York assay office: | | | | | | | |
| Melting and refining.. | 26,160,087 | 26,160,870 | 26,160,870 | 26,160 | 783 | .......... | .......... |
| Total— | | | | | | | |
| Melting and refining......... | 39,055,787 | 39,056,839 | 33,454,115 | 39,056 | 1,094 | 42 | .......... |
| Coining........ | 6,674,008 | 6,673,996 | 6,415,284 | 3,336 | 26 | 38 | .......... |
| Grand total, gold......... | 45,729,795 | 45,730,835 | 39,869,399 | 42,392 | 1,120 | 80 | .......... |

## SILVER BULLION.

| | | | | | | | |
|---|---|---|---|---|---|---|---|
| Philadelphia Mint: | | | | | | | |
| Melting and refining.. | 82,357,391 | 82,358,228 | ² 84,634,474 | 123,536 | 837 | .......... | .......... |
| Coining............... | 81,093,076 | 81,091,386 | 80,974,543 | 81,093 | .......... | 1,689 | 0.02085 |
| San Francisco Mint: | | | | | | | |
| Melting and refining.. | 56,755,915 | 56,762,869 | 43,028,839 | 85,133 | 6,954 | .......... | .......... |
| Coining............... | 42,083,070 | 42,076,702 | 40,278,350 | 42,083 | .......... | 6,368 | 0.15809 |
| Denver Mint: | | | | | | | |
| Melting and refining.. | 31,989,448 | 31,992,449 | 27,976,058 | 47,984 | 3,001 | .......... | .......... |
| Coining............... | 27,721,937 | 27,717,859 | 27,059,662 | 27,722 | .......... | 4,047 | 0.14957 |
| New York assay office: | | | | | | | |
| Melting and refining.. | 4,884,971 | 4,886,723 | 4,886,723 | 7,327 | 1,752 | .......... | .......... |
| Total— | | | | | | | |
| Melting and refining......... | 175,987,725 | 176,000,269 | 160,526,094 | 263,980 | 12,544 | .......... | .......... |
| Coining........ | 150,898,083 | 150,885,947 | 148,312,555 | 150,898 | .......... | 12,104 | .......... |
| Grand total, silver......... | 326,885,808 | 326,886,216 | 308,838,649 | 414,878 | 12,544 | 12,104 | .......... |

## NICKEL COINAGE METAL.

| | *Gross ounces.* | *Gross ounces.* | *Gross ounces.* | *Gross ounces.* | *Gross ounces.* | *Gross ounces.* | *Gross ounces.* |
|---|---|---|---|---|---|---|---|
| Philadelphia Mint: | | | | | | | |
| Melting and refining.. | 3,135,302 | 3,135,052 | 3,135,302 | .......... | .......... | 250 | 0.07974 |
| Coining............... | 2,271,556 | 2,271,556 | 237,494 | .......... | .......... | .......... | .......... |
| San Francisco Mint: | | | | | | | |
| Melting and refining.. | 2,887,373 | 2,887,373 | .......... | .......... | .......... | .......... | .......... |
| Coining............... | 161,906 | 161,906 | .......... | .......... | .......... | .......... | .......... |
| Denver Mint: | | | | | | | |
| Melting and refining.. | 1,637,056 | 1,637,056 | .......... | .......... | .......... | .......... | .......... |
| Coining............... | 580,935 | 580,935 | .......... | .......... | .......... | .......... | .......... |
| Total— | | | | | | | |
| Melting and refining......... | 7,659,731 | 7,659,481 | 3,135,302 | .......... | .......... | 250 | .......... |
| Coining........ | 3,014,397 | 3,014,397 | 237,494 | .......... | .......... | .......... | .......... |
| Grand total, nickel........ | 10,674,128 | 10,673,878 | 3,372,796 | .......... | .......... | 250 | .......... |

BRONZE COINAGE METAL.

| Institution and department | Amount received. | Amount returned. | Amount operated upon. | Legal allowance of wastage on amount received. | Surplus recovered. | Wasted. | Wastage per 1,000 ounces operated upon. |
|---|---|---|---|---|---|---|---|
| | *Fine ounces* | *Fine ounces* | *Fine ounces.* | *Fine ounces.* | *Fine ounces.* | *Fine ounces.* | *Fine ounces.* |
| Philadelphia Mint | | | | | | | |
| Melting and refining. | 3,693,065 | 3,689,812 | 3,693,065 | .......... | .......... | 3,252 | 0.88065 |
| Coining........ ..... | 1,203,253 | 1,203,064 | 203,493 | .......... | .......... | 189 | 0.93103 |
| San Francisco Mint | | | | | | | |
| Melting and refining.. | 355,643 | 355,643 | .......... | .......... | .......... | .......... | .......... |
| Coining............... | 1,062,692 | 1,062,692 | .......... | .......... | .......... | .......... | .......... |
| Denver Mint· | | | | | | | |
| Melting and refining.. | 1,966,898 | 1,966,214 | 480,068 | .......... | .......... | 684 | 1.42583 |
| Coining........ ...... | 1,001,930 | 1,000,703 | 987,905 | .......... | .......... | 1,227 | 1.24275 |
| Total— | | | | | | | |
| Melting and refining........ | 6,015,606 | 6,011,669 | 4,173,133 | .......... | .......... | 3,936 | .......... |
| Coining........ | 3,267,875 | 3,266,459 | 1,191,398 | .......... | .......... | 1,416 | .......... |
| Grand total, bronze........ | 9,283,481 | 9,278,128 | 5,364,531 | .......... | .......... | 5,352 | .......... |

¹ Includes 1,907,857 fine ounces of reworked material.
² Includes 51,818 300 fine ounces of reworked material.

REFINING OPERATIONS.

The total output of our refineries during the fiscal year 1922 of gold and silver upward of nine hundred ninety-nine thousandths fine, was 5,758,455.042 fine ounces; the net product was 5,260,562.108 fine ounces; details follow:

| Item | New York. | | San Francisco. | |
|---|---|---|---|---|
| | Gold. | Silver. | Gold. | Silver. |
| | *Fine ounces.* | *Fine ounces.* | *Fine ounces.* | *Fine ounces.* |
| Bullion placed in processes | | | | |
| Crude, with charges... ................. | 1,242,130.316 | 861,874.14 | 432,858.451 | 1,316,147.76 |
| Crude, without charges.................... | .......... | .......... | 38,901.868 | 11,059.81 |
| 0 999 and over (fire process only).......... | 912,570.538 | 29,318.01 | .......... | .......... |
| 0 900 standard (copper base, for bar making only)............................ | 651,164.799 | | | |
| 0.992 and over to aid processes.............. | 205,613.380 | 20,846.79 | 260,923.734 | 10,509.03 |
| Retreated, unrefined..................... | 640,155.452 | 239,277.32 | 162,424.850 | 87,945.60 |
| Apparent gain.. ......................... | 740.722 | 1,700.44 | 151.503 | 310.33 |
| Total....................... | 3,652,375.207 | 1,153,016.70 | 895,260.406 | 1,425,972.53 |
| Bullion obtained from processes | | | | |
| Unrefined............................. | 730,008.456 | 392,117.85 | 136,230.045 | 109,813.45 |
| Output 0.999+ fine: | | | | |
| Used to aid processes.. .............. | 205,613.380 | 20,846.79 | 260,923.734 | 10,509.03 |
| Electrolytic product................. | 1,153,399.623 | 710,734.05 | 498,106.627 | 1,305,650.05 |
| Other product...................... | 1,563,353.748 | 29,318.01 | .......... | .......... |
| Apparent loss............. ............. | | | | |
| Total.. ...... ....... ............. | 3,652,375.207 | 1,153,016.70 | 895,260.406 | 1,425,972.53 |

The following statement shows the number of melts made for domestic ingots, and the weight of metal involved, during the fiscal year 1922:

GOLD.

| Mint. | Melts. | | | Weight. | |
|---|---|---|---|---|---|
| | Passed first melting. | Re-melted. | Con-demned. | Melted. | Passed. |
| | | | | *Fineounces.* | *Fineounces.* |
| Philadelphia | 444 | 6 | 1 | 2,651,300 | 2,523,845 |
| San Francisco | 849 | ......... | 5 | 3,549,826 | 3,500,527 |
| Denver | ......... | ......... | ......... | ......... | ......... |
| Total | 1,293 | 6 | 6 | 6,201,126 | 6,024,372 |

SILVER.

| | | | | | |
|---|---|---|---|---|---|
| Philadelphia | 21,200 | 73 | 69 | 84,634,474 | 80,988,672 |
| San Francisco | 8,831 | 1 | 50 | 33,210,641 | 32,772,370 |
| Denver | 7,068 | 114 | 10 | 28,695,824 | 26,789,330 |
| Total | 37,099 | 188 | 129 | 146,540,939 | 140,550,372 |

NICKEL.

| | | | | | |
|---|---|---|---|---|---|
| | | | | *Troyounces.* | *Troyounces.* |
| Philadelphia | 3 | ......... | ......... | 64,061 | 47,600 |

BRONZE.

| | | | | | |
|---|---|---|---|---|---|
| Philadelphia | 24 | ......... | ......... | 404,396 | 399,633 |

FINENESS OF MELTS FOR GOLD AND SILVER INGOTS.

The statement following shows the number of gold and silver ingot melts made, also their reported fineness, during the fiscal year 1922:

| Gold ingots. | | | Silver ingots. | | | | | | | | |
|---|---|---|---|---|---|---|---|---|---|---|---|
| For United States coin. | | | For United States coin. | | | | For Venezuela coin. | | For Indo-China coin. | | |
| Ingot fineness. | Phila-del-phia. | San Fran-cisco. | Ingot fineness. | Phila-del-phia. | San Fran-cisco. | Den-ver. | Ingot fineness. | Phila-del-phia. | Ingot fineness. | San Fran-cisco. | |
| 899.7 | 3 | 35 | 898.00 | 100 | ......... | ......... | 835.0 | 305 | 898.6 | 332 | |
| 899.8 | 40 | 177 | 898.25 | 180 | ......... | ......... | | | 898.8 | 461 | |
| 899.9 | 118 | 376 | 898.50 | 2,882 | ......... | 5 | | | 899.1 | 761 | |
| 900.0 | 172 | 238 | 898.60 | ......... | 919 | 40 | | | 899.3 | 365 | |
| 900.1 | 88 | 20 | 898.70 | ......... | ......... | 173 | | | 899.5 | 291 | |
| 900.2 | 22 | 3 | 898.75 | 4,869 | ......... | ......... | | | 899.8 | 19 | |
| 900.3 | 1 | ......... | 898.80 | ......... | 1,464 | 602 | | | 900.0 | 1 | |
| | | | 898.90 | ......... | ......... | 1,155 | | | 900.2 | 1 | |
| | | | 899.00 | 7,736 | ......... | 1,618 | | | | | |
| | | | 899.10 | ......... | 2,475 | 1,619 | | | | | |
| | | | 899.20 | 3,824 | ......... | 931 | | | | | |
| | | | 899.25 | 3,824 | ......... | ......... | | | | | |
| | | | 899.30 | ......... | 1,974 | 625 | | | | | |
| | | | 899.40 | ......... | ......... | 215 | | | | | |
| | | | 899.50 | 871 | 1,582 | 75 | | | | | |
| | | | 899.60 | ......... | ......... | 80 | | | | | |
| | | | 899.70 | ......... | ......... | 28 | | | | | |
| | | | 899.75 | 296 | ......... | ......... | | | | | |
| | | | 899.80 | ......... | 303 | 15 | | | | | |
| | | | 899.90 | ......... | ......... | 1 | | | | | |
| | | | 900.00 | 129 | 73 | ......... | | | | | |
| | | | 900.20 | ......... | 21 | ......... | | | | | |
| | | | 900.25 | 7 | ......... | ......... | | | | | |
| | | | 900.40 | ......... | 21 | ......... | | | | | |
| | | | 900.50 | 1 | ......... | ......... | | | | | |
| Total | 444 | 849 | Total | 20,895 | 8,832 | 7,182 | Total | 305 | Total | 2,231 | |

COMMERCIAL AND CERTIFICATE BARS MANUFACTURED.

During the fiscal year 1922 the coinage mints and the assay office at New York manufactured 147,390 gold and 5,610 silver bars, valued at $511,793,767.26, as shown by the following table:

| Institution. | Gold. | | | Silver. | | |
|---|---|---|---|---|---|---|
| | Number. | Fine ounces. | Value. | Number. | Fine ounces. | Value. |
| Philadelphia | 5,201 | 124,949.779 | $2,582,941.17 | 1,595 | 308,904.51 | $399,391.60 |
| San Francisco | 5,464 | 2,196,687.399 | 45,409,558.58 | 234 | 29,751.66 | 19,636.37 |
| Denver | | | | | | |
| New York | 136,725 | 22,379,981.045 | 462,635,266.80 | 3,781 | 1,136,326.49 | 746,972.74 |
| Total | 147,390 | 24,701,618.223 | 510,627,766.55 | 5,610 | 1,474,982.66 | 1,166,000.71 |

INGOTS OPERATED UPON BY COINING DEPARTMENTS AND PERCENTAGE OF COIN PRODUCED.

FOR DOMESTIC COINAGE.

| Mint. | Gold | | Standard silver dollars. | | Subsidiary silver. | | Nickel. | |
|---|---|---|---|---|---|---|---|---|
| | Ingots operated upon. | Percentage good coin produced to ingots operated upon. | Ingots operated upon. | Percentage good coin produced to ingots operated upon. | Ingots operated upon. | Percentage good coin produced to ingots operated upon. | Ingots operated upon. | Percentage good coin produced to ingots operated upon. |
| | Ounces. | Per ct. | Ounces. | Per ct. | Ounces. | Per ct. | Ounces. | Per ct. |
| Philadelphia | 2,608,605.069 | 32.40 | 26,218,875.12 | 51.47 | 321,638.78 | 36.06 | | |
| San Francisco | 3,804,071.004 | 45.18 | 31,932,766.45 | 52.06 | | | | |
| Denver | | | 27,253,740.28 | 57.74 | | | 1,001,929.90 | 72.38 |

FOR FOREIGN COINAGE.

| Mint. | Gold. | | Silver. | |
|---|---|---|---|---|
| | Ingots operated upon. | Percentage good coin produced to ingots operated upon. | Ingots operated upon. | Percentage good coin produced to ingots operated upon. |
| | Ounces. | Per ct. | Ounces. | Per ct. |
| Philadelphia | 2,607,766 | 27.67 | 4,434,629.09 | 43.22 |
| San Francisco | | | 8,346,084.08 | 46.80 |

PERCENTAGE OF GOOD COIN PRODUCED TO PIECES STRUCK.

| Mint. | Double eagles. | | Grant gold dollars. | | Standard silver dollars. | |
|---|---|---|---|---|---|---|
| | Blanks struck. | Percentage good coin produced to blanks struck. | Blanks struck. | Percentage good coin produced to blanks struck. | Blanks struck. | Percentage good coin produced to blanks struck. |
| | *Number.* | *Per cent.* | *Number.* | *Per cent.* | *Number.* | *Per cent.* |
| Philadelphia.......... | 965,325 | 90.43 | 13,868 | 72.22 | 56,397,340 | 89.91 |
| San Francisco......... | 1,944,821 | 91.34 | | | 25,314,135 | 84.85 |
| Denver................ | | | | | 21,859,670 | 92.41 |

| Mint. | Half dollars. | | 5-cent nickels. | | 1-cent bronze. | |
|---|---|---|---|---|---|---|
| | Blanks struck. | Percentage good coin produced to blanks struck. | Blanks struck. | Percentage good coin produced to blanks struck. | Blanks struck. | Percentage good coin produced to blanks struck. |
| | *Number.* | *Per cent.* | *Number.* | *Per cent.* | *Number.* | *Per cent.* |
| Philadelphia.......... | 415,441 | 77.07 | 1,458,186 | 99.23 | 2,076,235 | 97.33 |
| San Francisco......... | | | | | | |
| Denver................ | | | | | 7,236,667 | 98.94 |

SWEEP CELLAR OPERATIONS.

| Institution. | Material. | | | | Metal content. | | | |
|---|---|---|---|---|---|---|---|---|
| | Source. | Quantity. | | | Bars recovered. | | Tailings. | |
| | | Bags. | Barrels. | Net avoirdupois pounds. | Gold. | Silver. | Gold. | Silver. |
| | | | | | *Ounces.* | *Ounces.* | *Ounces.* | *Ounces.* |
| Philadelphia.... | Melting department..... | 270 | 117 | 104,879 | 360.920 | 26,358.96 | 204.800 | 10,336.07 |
| San Francisco... | .....do................. | 703 | ...... | 48,254 | 199.976 | 6,466.85 | 94.473 | 3,687.31 |
| Denver.......... | .....do................. | 934 | ...... | 63,811 | .......... | .......... | 35.746 | 4,713.93 |
| San Francisco... | Refinery ............... | 1,081 | ...... | 86,873 | 1,160.654 | 2,848.68 | 533.591 | 3,521.34 |
| New York....... | .....do................. | 1,687 | ...... | 134,227 | 916.156 | 806.84 | 1,875.126 | 4,007.52 |
| Philadelphia.... | Coining department..... | ...... | 7 | 3,730 | .......... | 281.08 | 20.670 | 1,087.89 |
| Do.......... | Deposit receiving room.. | 16 | ...... | 2,485 | 68.160 | 107.21 | 71.752 | 119.59 |
| San Francisco... | .....do................. | 22 | ...... | 1,574 | 66.915 | 101.70 | 17.943 | 60.75 |
| Denver.......... | .....do................. | 182 | ...... | 12,440 | .......... | .......... | 117.309 | 581.63 |
| New York....... | .....do................. | 696 | ...... | 49,096 | 665.076 | 232.48 | 1,066.559 | 796.60 |

BULLION GAINS AND LOSSES.

The net gains from operations on bullion during the fiscal year 1922 amounted to $122,539.21, as follows:

| Item. | Mint at— | | | Assay office at New York. | Minor assay offices. | Total |
|---|---|---|---|---|---|---|
| | Philadel-phia. | San Fran-cisco. | Denver. | | | |
| Recovered from refining and coining operations | $5,320.35 | $12,314.54 | $3,960.46 | $17,845.39 | .......... | $39,449.74 |
| Recovered incident to receipt of deposits | 3,194.52 | 2,610.11 | 806.38 | 45,788.48 | 8645.14 | 53,044.63 |
| Net gain on shipments to Government refineries | .......... | .......... | .......... | .......... | 178.76 | 178.73 |
| Gain on light-weight and mutilated coin purchased for recoinage | 20.60 | 38.81 | .......... | 30.52 | .......... | 89.93 |
| Receipts from sale of by-products | .......... | 477.27 | .......... | 48,743.65 | 772.76 | 49,993.68 |
| Total gains | 8,535.47 | 15,440.73 | 4,775.84 | 112,408.04 | 1,596.66 | 142,756.74 |
| Wasted in refining and coining operations | 2,570.85 | 7,006.47 | 4,047.24 | .......... | .......... | 13,624.56 |
| Loss on assay value of operative sweeps sold | 2,911.24 | 1,501.94 | 853.79 | 1,326.00 | .......... | 6,592.97 |
| Total losses | 5,482.09 | 8,508.41 | 4,901.03 | 1,326.00 | .......... | 20,217.53 |
| Net gain | 3,053.38 | 6,932.32 | .......... | 111,082.04 | 1,596.66 | 122,539.21 |
| Net loss | .......... | .......... | 125.19 | .......... | .......... | .......... |

The value of metals wasted in the operative departments during the fiscal year ended June 30, 1922, was $13,746.91. A loss of $6,592.97 occurred from the difference between the assay value of the bullion contained in sweeps sold and the amount received for the same. Details are given below:

| Item. | Mint at— | | | Assay office at New York. | Total |
|---|---|---|---|---|---|
| | Philadel-phia. | San Fran-cisco. | Denver. | | |
| Gold wastage: | | | | | |
| Melting and refining department | $875.10 | .......... | .......... | .......... | $875.10 |
| Coining department | .......... | $792.25 | .......... | .......... | 792.25 |
| Silver wastage: | | | | | |
| Coining department | 1,695.75 | 6,214.22 | $4,047.24 | .......... | 11,957.21 |
| Nickel wastage: | | | | | |
| Melting and refining department | 10.04 | .......... | .......... | .......... | 10.04 |
| Bronze wastage: | | | | | |
| Melting and refining department | 87.47 | .......... | 8.90 | .......... | 96.37 |
| Coining department | .......... | .......... | 15.94 | .......... | 15.94 |
| Loss on sale of sweeps | 2,911.24 | 1,501.94 | 853.79 | $1,326.00 | 6,592.97 |
| Total wastage and loss | 5,579.60 | 8,508.41 | 4,925.87 | 1,326.00 | 20,339.88 |
| Reimbursements: | | | | | |
| Nickel and bronze wastage, from minor coinage profits | 97.51 | .......... | 24.84 | .......... | 122.35 |
| Other wastage and loss on sweeps, from contingent appropriation | 5,482.09 | 8,508.41 | 4,901.03 | 1,326.00 | 20,217.53 |
| Total reimbursements | 5,579.60 | 8,508.41 | 4,925.87 | 1,326.00 | 20,339.88 |

### ENGRAVING DEPARTMENT.

The demand for coinage dies was not so great as in former years, since but few coins below the dollar denomination were executed. However, the die department made 250 master dies and hubs for Army and Navy insignia and Marine Corps and Coast Guard Service medals. It was decided that the originals for this work should be engraved at the mint, so that a uniformity in the finished work would be assured.

The Verdun gold medal (4 inches in diameter), presented by the United States to the city of Verdun, was made in this department. The medal was cut in gold on the reproducing lathe from models supplied by the United States Fine Arts Commission.

The dies for the peace dollar were made from models approved by the same commission, and over 1,000,000 pieces were struck in 1921. Before the dies for the 1922 issue were finally ready considerable experimenting to reduce the relief was necessary because of the extreme difficulty in coinage.

DIES MANUFACTURED.

| For— | Unused. | Issued to mint at— | | | | Total prepared. |
|---|---|---|---|---|---|---|
| | | Phila-delphia. | San Francisco. | Denver. | Manila, P. I | |
| Domestic: | | | | | | |
| Regular gold coinage... ............. | 20 | 210 | 120 | ........ | ........ | 350 |
| Regular silver coinage................. | 280 | 835 | 280 | 270 | ........ | 1,665 |
| Regular minor coinage................ | 210 | 20 | 20 | 30 | ........ | 280 |
| Memorial— | | | | | | |
| Grant gold dollars and silver half dollars..... | ........ | 50 | ........ | ........ | ........ | 50 |
| Pilgrim half dollars................. | ........ | 20 | ........ | ........ | ........ | 20 |
| Missouri half dollars.............. | 15 | 20 | ........ | ........ | ........ | 35 |
| Alabama half dollars............. | 3 | 15 | ........ | ........ | ........ | 18 |
| Philippine coinage ... ............. | 50 | ........ | ........ | ........ | 144 | 194 |
| Venezuela coinage................. | 13 | 161 | ........ | ........ | ........ | 174 |
| Colombia coinage ................... | 20 | 100 | ........ | ........ | ........ | 120 |
| Costa Rica coinage................. | ........ | 20 | ........ | ........ | ........ | 20 |
| Indo-China coinage................. | ........ | ........ | 55 | ........ | ........ | 55 |
| Cuba coinage...................... | 70 | ........ | ........ | ........ | ........ | 70 |
| Salvador coinage................... | 7 | ........ | ........ | ........ | ........ | 7 |
| Peru coinage...................... | 10 | ........ | ........ | ........ | ........ | 10 |
| Total coinage working dies.......... | 698 | 1,451 | 475 | 300 | 144 | 3,068 |
| Master dies and hubs manufactured for: | | | | | | |
| United States coinage................ | ........ | ........ | ........ | ........ | ........ | 74 |
| Philippine coinage................. | ........ | ........ | ........ | ........ | ........ | 10 |
| Colombian coinage.................. | ........ | ........ | ........ | ........ | ........ | 2 |
| Other dies, hubs, etc., manufactured for: | | | | | | |
| Alabama coins....................... | ........ | ........ | ........ | ........ | ........ | 4 |
| Grant memorial coin.............. | ........ | ........ | ........ | ........ | ........ | 10 |
| Embossed stamped envelope dies..... | ........ | ........ | ........ | ........ | ........ | 54 |
| Annual assay medal................ | ........ | ........ | ........ | ........ | ........ | 4 |
| Army and Navy medals ............. | ........ | ........ | ........ | ........ | ........ | 274 |
| Miscellaneous...................... | ........ | ........ | ........ | ........ | ........ | 30 |
| Total dies and hubs............... | ........ | ........ | ........ | ........ | ........ | 462 |
| Grand total....................... | ........ | ........ | ........ | ........ | ........ | 3,530 |

MEDALS MANUFACTURED.

The medal division manufactured 30,017 medals of a national character during the year, of which bronze good-conduct medals for the Marine Corps and rifle and pistol competition medals for the Army form a large proportion. The number includes 243 gold and 671 silver medals, also 4,762 bronze medals for sale to the public at approximate cost price, at the Philadelphia Mint.

MEDALS SOLD

Medals manufactured at the mint at Philadelphia were sold during the fiscal year, as follows:

| Item. | Pieces. | Value |
|---|---|---|
| Gold medals | 179 | $6,332.94 |
| Silver medals | 439 | 980.07 |
| Bronze medals | 5,378 | 3,062.92 |
| Total | 5,996 | 10,375.93 |

### PROGRESS OF NUMISMATIC COLLECTION.

Owing to the sudden passing away on July 3, 1922, of the curator of the numismatic collection, Dr. Louis T. Comparette, definite report of the progress made in this line during the past year is not available. Accessions to the numismatic collection were not numerous, but Doctor Comparette had commenced and was far advanced in the work of collecting from all parts of the United States specimens of medals awarded to returned soldiers. It was his intention to gather as complete a collection of these medals as could be had, and it is anticipated that this work will be carried on by his successor. Doctor Comparette assumed the duties of curator in 1905, and during the 17 years of his incumbency materially improved the collection in both number of pieces and in acquisition of those having historical and numismatic value. While the numismatic collection had its inception in 1838, Doctor Comparette was its first formally recognized curator.

### EMPLOYEES.

The total number of officers and other employees of the institutions of the Mint Service on June 30, 1922, was 744, as below:

| Institution. | Departments. | | | | | Total. |
|---|---|---|---|---|---|---|
| | General. | Engraving. | Assaying. | Coining. | Melting and refining. | |
| Philadelphia | 159 | 19 | 11 | 111 | 56 | 356 |
| San Francisco | 59 | | 13 | 37 | 40 | 149 |
| Denver | 35 | | 6 | 23 | 18 | 82 |
| New York [1] | 75 | | 16 | | 34 | 125 |
| New Orleans [1] | | | | | | 6 |
| Carson [1] | | | | | | 3 |
| Boise | | | | | | 4 |
| Helena | | | | | | 3 |
| Deadwood | | | | | | 3 |
| Salt Lake City | | | | | | 2 |
| Seattle | | | | | | 11 |
| Total | 328 | 19 | 46 | 171 | 148 | 744 |

[1] Conducted as assay offices.

### VISITORS.

Visitors to the mints for the purpose of witnessing the coining processes were admitted during only a portion of the fiscal year ended June 30, 1922, those visiting the Philadelphia Mint since April 1, 1922, totaling 10,250.

### WORK OF THE MINOR ASSAY OFFICES.

The following table exhibits the principal work of the minor assay offices during the fiscal year 1922.

14263—FI 1922——38

| Item. | New Orleans. | Carson City. | Boise. | Helena. | Dead-wood. | Seattle. | Salt Lake City. |
|---|---|---|---|---|---|---|---|
| Deposits received............number.. | 456 | 241 | 527 | 357 | 10 | 1,302 | 106 |
| Fineness, average, gold..thousandths.. | 170 | 629 | 743 | 557 | 765 | 817 | 338 |
| Fineness, average, silver........do.... | 597 | 324 | 215 | 268 | 221 | 130 | 348 |
| Weight before melting........ounces.. | 158,030 | 4,991 | 22,986 | 9,143 | 846 | 180,830 | 2,598 |
| Weight after melting............do.... | 150,043 | 4,526 | 21,714 | 8,848 | 838 | 178,681 | 2,516 |
| Loss in melting.................do.... | 7,987 | 465 | 1,272 | 295 | 8 | 2,149 | 82 |
| Loss in melting.............per cent.. | 5.06 | 9.31 | 5.05 | 3.22 | .95 | 1.18 | 3.17 |
| Melts of bullion made........number.. | 449 | 247 | 527 | 357 | 32 | 1,307 | 167 |
| Melts, mass of bullion, made....do.... | | 6 | 10 | 10 | 1 | 62 | 4 |
| Melts of D. M. R. grains.........do.... | 3 | 3 | 4 | 4 | 1 | 6 | 3 |
| Melts of assayers' clips...........do.... | 1 | 3 | 4 | 8 | 2 | 55 | 2 |
| Value of deposits, gold........dollars.. | 528,193 | 58,941 | 333,431 | 96,266 | 2,334 | 3,020,553 | 17,583 |
| Value of deposits, silver, at cost..do... | 61,510 | 985 | 3,050 | 1,358 | 462 | 15,333 | 553 |
| Bullion shipped.........gross ounces.. | | 5,862 | 21,851 | 8,515 | 916 | 179,305 | 6,122 |
| Value of gold shipped.........dollars.. | | 72,485 | 336,541 | 85,801 | 2,945 | 3,024,591 | 36,502 |
| Value, cost, of silver shipped....do.... | | 1,367 | 3,056 | 1,342 | 466 | 15,416 | 2,621 |
| Quartation silver made......ounces.. | 20 | 16 | 40 | 30 | 25 | 100 | |
| Quartation silver used..........do.... | 21 | | 50 | 30 | 5 | 119 | 16 |
| Proof gold received..............do.... | | | | | | 10 | |
| Proof gold used.................do.... | 3 | 25 | 1 | 3 | .25 | 12 | 5 |
| Proof silver received............do.... | | 50 | | | | | |
| Proof silver used...............do.... | 1 | 6 | 1 | | .5 | | |
| Cupels made................number.. | 2,600 | 1,650 | 968 | 3,000 | 750 | 10,817 | 2,500 |
| Cupels used..................do.... | 2,700 | 1,300 | 1,949 | 2,257 | 750 | 10,069 | 1,500 |
| Crucibles used................do.... | 38 | 30 | 37 | 27 | 12 | | 7 |
| Assays of: | | | | | | | |
| Deposits....................do.... | 2,200 | 1,249 | 1,480 | 2,235 | 90 | 8,932 | 1,500 |
| Ore for gold and silver.......do.... | 307 | 117 | 353 | 4 | 494 | 317 | 266 |
| Ore for base metal...........do.... | 103 | 10 | 31 | | 46 | 52 | 34 |
| Ore for General Land Office.do.... | | | | | | 36 | 178 |
| Ore for Forestry Office......do.... | | | | | | | 8 |
| Mutilated coin...............do.... | | | | | | 3 | |
| Special bullion...............do.... | 12 | 10 | | | 8 | 60 | 1 |
| Slag.......................do.... | | | | | 5 | 75 | |

### ORE ASSAYS.

A comparative statement of ore assays made at the minor assay offices since 1915 shows increased use of our facilities by the mining industry as the result of reducing our charge for this service to a nominal sum. The increased number of assays in 1921 and 1922 seems to indicate revival of prospecting, doubtless incident to the slowing down of business in other lines.

| Fiscal year. | Ore assays made. | Amount of charges collected. |
|---|---|---|
| 1915 | 1,404 | $885.65 |
| 1916 | 2,318 | 1,678.00 |
| 1917 | 2,842 | 1,931.75 |
| 1918 | 2,530 | 1,644.00 |
| 1919 | 1,877 | 1,528.00 |
| 1920 | 1,938 | 1,579.00 |
| 1921 | 2,151 | 1,793.00 |
| 1922 | 2,315 | 1,912.00 |

### GOLD RECEIPTS AT SEATTLE.

Statement of gold deposits at the Seattle assay office from the opening of the institution on July 15, 1898, to the close of business June 30, 1922:

| | |
|---|---|
| Number of deposits............................... | 68,139 |
| Troy ounces...................................... | 16,034,161.12 |
| Avoirdupois tons................................. | 549.4 |
| Coining value.................................... | $274,564,803.78 |

*Origin of the foregoing*

Alaska:

| | |
|---|---:|
| Circle | $915, 411. 74 |
| Cook Inlet | 3, 335, 018. 47 |
| Copper River | 5, 700, 647. 97 |
| Eagle | 997, 075. 32 |
| Iditarod | 13, 655, 355. 49 |
| Koyukuk | 2, 013, 083. 94 |
| Kuskokwim | 168, 595. 63 |
| Nome | 67, 321, 578. 23 |
| Southeastern Alaska | 5, 911, 906. 79 |
| Tanana | 49, 950, 523. 50 |
| Unclassified | 2, 767, 506. 28 |
| | $152, 736, 703. 36 |

Canada:

| | |
|---|---:|
| British Columbia | 23, 526, 501. 79 |
| Yukon Territory | 92, 151, 983. 34 |
| All other sources | 6, 149, 615. 29 |
| Total | 274, 564, 803. 78 |

OFFICERS IN CHARGE OF MINOR ASSAY OFFICES

| Assay office | Number of employees. | Assayer in charge. | Date of oath. | Succeeded— |
|---|---|---|---|---|
| New Orleans | 6 | Leonard Magruder | Dec. 1, 1914 | W. M. Lynch. |
| Carson | 3 | Annie H. Martin | Aug 3, 1921 | W. A. Burns. |
| Boise | 4 | C. L. Longley | Sept. 17, 1921. | Curtis F. Pike. |
| Helena | 3 | W. L. Hill | Sept. 1, 1921. | Herbert Goodall. |
| Deadwood | 3 | Harry H. Stewart | July 11, 1921. | James E. Russell. |
| Seattle | 11 | T. G. Hatheway | Sept. 8, 1921. | John W. Phillips |
| Salt Lake City | 2 | John L. May | July 25, 1921. | Hugh T. Rippeto. |

## LABORATORY OF THE BUREAU OF THE MINT.

During the calendar year 1921 the assayer of this bureau tested 618 silver coins and 64 gold coins, all of which were found within the legal requirements as to weight and fineness.

The greatest deviation in fineness of silver coins above standard (the limit of tolerance being 3 above or below) was 2.4, while the greatest deviation below was 2.0.

The greatest deviation in fineness of gold coins above standard (the limit of tolerance being 1 above or below) was 0.4, while the greatest deviation below was 0.3.

The work of testing certificate bar assaying throughout the service was continued.

The following table summarizes results of domestic coin tests:

| Fineness | Number of silver coins. | | | | Fineness | Number of gold coins. | | |
|---|---|---|---|---|---|---|---|---|
| | Phila-delphia. | San Fran-cisco. | Denver. | Total. | | Phila-delphia. | San Fran-cisco. | Total |
| 898. 0 | 1 | | | 1 | 899. 7 | 7 | 3 | 10 |
| 898. 2 | 1 | | | 1 | 899. 8 | 6 | 7 | 13 |
| 898. 5 | 2 | | | 2 | 899. 9 | 14 | 4 | 18 |
| 898. 7 | 4 | | 1 | 5 | 900. 0 | 11 | | 11 |
| 898. 8 | 1 | | | 1 | 900. 1 | 6 | 2 | 8 |
| 898. 9 | 5 | 3 | 1 | 9 | 900. 2 | 3 | | 3 |
| 899. 0 | 1 | | | 1 | 900. 4 | 1 | | 1 |
| 899. 1 | 7 | 9 | 2 | 18 | | | | |
| 899. 2 | 3 | | | 3 | | | | |
| 899. 3 | 18 | 10 | 7 | 35 | | | | |
| 899. 4 | 6 | | | 6 | | | | |
| 899. 5 | 3 | | 2 | 5 | | | | |
| 899. 6 | 32 | 14 | 11 | 57 | | | | |
| 899. 7 | 4 | | | 4 | | | | |
| 899. 8 | 36 | 17 | 13 | 66 | | | | |
| 899. 9 | 2 | | | 2 | | | | |
| 900. 0 | 26 | 12 | 28 | 66 | | | | |
| 900. 1 | 1 | | | 1 | | | | |
| 900. 2 | 34 | 24 | 34 | 92 | | | | |
| 900. 3 | 3 | | | 3 | | | | |
| 900. 4 | 39 | 37 | 31 | 107 | | | | |
| 900. 5 | 1 | | | 1 | | | | |
| 900. 7 | 13 | 7 | 13 | 33 | | | | |
| 900. 9 | 7 | 7 | 16 | 30 | | | | |
| 901. 1 | 5 | 3 | 16 | 24 | | | | |
| 901. 3 | 8 | 1 | 11 | 20 | | | | |
| 901. 5 | 2 | 6 | 7 | 15 | | | | |
| 901. 8 | | 1 | 2 | 3 | | | | |
| 902. 0 | | 1 | | 4 | | | | |
| 902. 2 | 1 | | | 1 | | | | |
| 902. 4 | | | 1 | 1 | | | | |
| Total | 266 | 152 | 200 | 618 | Total | 48 | 16 | 64 |
| Average fineness | 899. 973 | 900. 136 | 900. 41 | 900. 154 | Average fineness | 899. 935 | 899. 844 | 899. 912 |

During the fiscal year a number of improvements were made in the laboratory; these included the installation of a large alberene stone worktable and a two-unit Braun electrolytic cabinet. The assay furnaces have been faced with unglazed white tile and the use of nichrome muffles adopted.

### DISEASE NOT CARRIED BY COINS.

Tests made for the purpose of determining whether coins carry disease show that, on the contrary, the coinage metals destroy the bacteria which reach them. The results of the tests are given in the following quotation from the New York Journal of Commerce of date December 29, 1921:

There seems to be little basis for the belief that coins bear any close relation to the spread of disease, according to an announcement made at the University of Illinois here by Drs. Charlotte B. Ward and Fred W. Tanner, of the university, following a series of tests made by the two.

"Coins of the lower denominations were examined for the types of bacteria which exist on them," says their report. "It has often been stated that money is a very dangerous article of commerce since it is handled by all sorts of persons and because it usually moves so quickly from one person to another. It has also been stated that cashiers and others whose vocations require them to handle money in larger quantities than the average person, might be more susceptible to disease, but this does not seem to be the case.

"It seems that the very metals from which the coins are made act to destroy the bacteria which reach the coins. In the study only the more resistant of bacteria, the spore-forming bacteria, were found. This indicates that money need not be feared, for bacteria can not live long on it."

Doctors Ward and Tanner have pointed out that postage stamps have somewhat the same relation to the public that money does, although their constitution is quite different from that of coins. Stamps are used but once and are not handled by so many individuals, although the adhesive applied to them might be a favorable abode for micro-organisms for relatively long periods of time. Nevertheless, the menace is not regarded as a threatening one, and in an investigation conducted some years ago with reference to the question here at issue, pathogenic bacteria were rarely found on stamps.

### ASSAY COMMISSION'S ANNUAL TEST OF COIN.

Section 3547 of the Revised Statutes provides for an annual test of the domestic coinage executed during the prior year, by a commission of whom part are ex officio members, the others being appointed, without compensation, by the President. The purpose is "to secure a due conformity in the gold and silver coins to their respective standards of fineness and weight." The commission, which met at the Philadelphia mint February 8 to 10, 1922, reported the following results of their examination:

Your committee on counting reports that the packages containing the pieces reserved by the several mints for the trial of coins, in accordance with section 3539 of the Revised Statutes, were delivered to us by the superintendent of the mint at Philadelphia and upon comparison with the transcripts kept by the Director of the Mint were found to be correct. Several packages were selected from the deliveries of each month from each mint of all denominations coined, and the coins contained therein were counted and found to agree with the number called for in each package. The reserved coins were then delivered to the committees on weighing and assaying.

The committee on weighing have to report that they have weighed the coins shown in an appended list and have found them to be standard within the legal tolerances. The coins were selected at random from those reserved by the mints at Philadelphia, San Francisco, and Denver. The coins were directly weighed against a set of sealed coin weights which were accompanied by a certificate signed by the Director of the Bureau of Standards, Department of Commerce, and which gave the value of the weights in terms of the United States standard. The weighings were made on a Troemner balance supplied by the Philadelphia Mint, which was tested by your committee as to the equality of the arms and as to its sensibility, which was entirely satisfactory.

The committee on assaying has completed the assays on samples taken from different lots of coin representing all denominations coined during the year 1921 by the United States mints at Philadelphia, San Francisco, and Denver. The mint at Philadelphia was the only mint to coin gold during the year 1921, double eagles being the only denomination coined. The highest assay upon the individual samples of double eagles taken was 900.5; the lowest 899.6, showing the coinage to be well within the legal limit of tolerance, which is one-thousandth for gold coin, standard being 900. The highest assays upon individual silver coins representing lots delivered by the mints during the year 1921 are Philadelphia 900, San Francisco 900.4, Denver 900.2. The lowest assays upon silver coined at the three mints during the year are Philadelphia 898 2, San Francisco 898.9, Denver 898.6. The result of the assays upon coins from the mints is very satisfactory, being well within the legal limit of tolerance, which is three one-thousandths for silver coin. The assay balances were tested and found to be in adjustment; the nitric acid used for humid assays of silver was tested and found to be free from chlorine and the silver used in parting was free from gold.

#### ASSAY OF COINS MELTED IN MASS.

Philadelphia, gold, 105 double eagles, fineness, 899.8.
Philadelphia, silver, 170 standard dollars, 14 half dollars, 50 quarter dollars and 20 dimes, fineness 899.6.
San Francisco, silver, 88 standard dollars, 8 half dollars, fineness 899.3.
Denver, silver, 100 standard dollars, 2 half dollars, 4 dimes, fineness 899.5.

The foregoing report, covering the operations of the mints and assay offices of the United States for the fiscal year ended June 30, 1922, is respectfully submitted.

F. E. SCOBEY,
*Director of the Mint.*

Hon. ANDREW W. MELLON,
*Secretary of the Treasury.*

# TABLES FROM THE REPORT OF

*Deposits and purchases of gold during*

| | Source and description. | Philadelphia. | San Francisco. | Denver. | New York. |
|---|---|---|---|---|---|
| | PURCHASED. | *Fine ounces.* | *Fine ounces.* | *Fine ounces.* | *Fine ounces.* |
| 1 | Alaska | 421.684 | 19,528.816 | 91.083 | 782.482 |
| 2 | Arizona | | 14,482.297 | 251.355 | 6.494 |
| 3 | California | 2.630 | 156,983.482 | 1.522 | |
| 4 | Colorado | 59.133 | | 43,064.262 | |
| 5 | Georgia | 67.321 | | | |
| 6 | Idaho | 7.724 | 239.339 | 705.454 | 164.879 |
| 7 | Michigan | | .063 | | 1.318 |
| 8 | Montana | 9.266 | 99.531 | 33,049.633 | 7.036 |
| 9 | Nevada | 29.123 | 36,178.028 | 201.064 | |
| 10 | New Mexico | 335.625 | 121.843 | 6,397.886 | |
| 11 | North Carolina | 70.242 | | | 54.300 |
| 12 | Oregon | | 3,952.832 | 39.937 | |
| 13 | South Carolina | 1.544 | | | |
| 14 | South Dakota | | | 15,277.944 | 311,986.369 |
| 15 | Utah | | | 342.859 | |
| 16 | Virginia | 61.116 | | | |
| 17 | Washington | | 10.859 | | |
| 18 | Wyoming | | .878 | 44.191 | |
| 19 | Philippine Islands | | 22,309.456 | | |
| 20 | Other | | | | |
| 21 | Sweeps and grains, dep. mltg. room | 104.094 | 102.842 | 10.166 | 1,130.509 |
| 22 | Total unrefined | 1,169.502 | 254,010.266 | 99,177.356 | 314,133.387 |
| | Domestic refinery bullion: | | | | |
| 22 | Less than 0.992 fine | | | 190,024.446 | 5,614.577 |
| 24 | Over 0.992 fine | 15,825.187 | 1,376,980.468 | 15.801 | 950,662.580 |
| 25 | Total domestic purchases | 16,994.689 | 1,630,990.734 | 289,517.603 | 1,270,410.544 |
| 26 | Foreign coin | 53,583.964 | 583,689.376 | 30,975.640 | 5,324,536.457 |
| 27 | Foreign bullion, crude | 1,046.406 | 435,561.263 | 14,485.256 | 1,056,082.353 |
| 28 | Foreign bullion, refined | 64,264.095 | 65,336.433 | 21,319.234 | 15,083,307.146 |
| 29 | Jewelers' bars, dental scrap, plate, etc. | 132,172.663 | 40,420.761 | 9,339.186 | 497,722.494 |
| 30 | Total deposit purchases | 268,061.817 | 2,755,998.567 | 365,636.919 | 23,232,058.994 |
| | REDEPOSITS PURCHASED. | | | | |
| 31 | Domestic coin | 77.743 | 60,009.168 | 10.179 | 12,368.323 |
| 32 | Bars stamped by U. S. Government | 242.590 | 260.655 | .055 | 4,253.079 |
| 33 | Surplus (mint recoveries) | 26.210 | 263.929 | 138.701 | [2] 1,244.042 |
| 34 | Total redeposits purchased | 346.543 | 60,533.752 | 148.935 | 17,865.444 |
| 35 | Total purchases | 268,408.360 | 2,816,532.319 | 365,785.854 | 23,249,924.438 |
| | REDEPOSITS—TRANSFERS. | | | | |
| 36 | Domestic coin from Treasury | 39,716.217 | | 7,246.400 | |
| 37 | Domestic assay coins | 238.721 | | | |
| 38 | Unrefined bars | | 172,162.757 | | |
| 39 | Proof bullion | | 200.000 | 50.000 | 250.000 |
| 40 | Total redeposits transferred | 39,954.938 | 172,362.757 | 7,296.400 | 250.000 |
| 41 | Grand total | 308,363.298 | 2,988,895.076 | 373,082.254 | 23,250,174.438 |
| | Value of— | | | | |
| 42 | Purchases | $5,548,493.26 | $58,222,890.23 | $7,561,464.67 | $480,618,593.02 |
| 43 | United States coin transfers from Treasury. | 821,007.06 | | 149,796.37 | |
| 44 | Other transfers | 4,934.80 | 3,563,054.38 | 1,083.59 | 5,167.96 |
| 45 | Total value | 6,374,435.12 | 61,785,944.61 | 7,712,294.63 | 480,623,760.98 |
| | Number of [1]— | | | | |
| 46 | Deposits, gold and silver | 26,470 | 23,082 | 14,084 | 18,724 |
| 47 | Redeposits purchased | 51 | 367 | 11 | 24 |
| 48 | Redeposits transfers | 714 | 3,327 | 6 | |
| 49 | Deposits in trust | 1,810 | | | |
| 50 | Total | 29,045 | 26,776 | 14,101 | 18,748 |

[1] By number is meant the total number of assay reports on the metal received.
[2] Includes surplus of 1921.

# THE DIRECTOR OF THE MINT.

*the fiscal year ended June 30, 1922.*

| New Orleans. | Carson. | Boise. | Helena. | Deadwood. | Seattle. | Salt Lake City. | Total. | |
|---|---|---|---|---|---|---|---|---|
| Fine ounces. | Fine ounces. | Fine ounces | Fine ounces. | Fine ounces. | Fine ounces. | Fine ounces. | Fine ounces. | |
| ......... | ......... | 3.589 | ......... | ......... | 125,358.811 | 93.836 | 146,280.301 | 1 |
| ......... | ......... | ......... | ......... | ......... | ......... | ......... | 14,740.146 | 2 |
| ......... | 371.495 | ......... | ......... | ......... | 4,424 | 49.422 | 157,412.975 | 3 |
| ......... | ......... | ......... | ......... | ......... | 4.558 | 5.069 | 43,133.022 | 4 |
| ......... | ......... | ......... | ......... | ......... | ......... | ......... | 67.321 | 5 |
| ......... | ......... | 12,117.686 | 15.681 | ......... | 220.982 | 80.560 | 13,552.305 | 6 |
| ......... | ......... | ......... | ......... | ......... | ......... | ......... | 1.381 | 7 |
| ......... | 2,442.646 | 34.680 | 4,224.095 | ......... | 2.571 | 4.003 | 37,430.815 | 8 |
| ......... | ......... | 70.017 | ......... | ......... | 1.433 | 165.339 | 39,087.650 | 9 |
| ......... | ......... | ......... | ......... | ......... | ......... | ......... | 6,855.354 | 10 |
| ......... | ......... | ......... | ......... | ......... | ......... | ......... | 124.542 | 11 |
| ......... | ......... | 3,592.345 | ......... | ......... | 397.292 | ......... | 7,982.406 | 12 |
| ......... | ......... | ......... | ......... | ......... | ......... | ......... | 1.544 | 13 |
| ......... | ......... | ......... | ......... | 92.847 | ......... | ......... | 327,357.160 | 14 |
| ......... | ......... | ......... | ......... | ......... | ......... | 49.031 | 391.890 | 15 |
| ......... | ......... | ......... | ......... | ......... | ......... | ......... | 61.116 | 16 |
| ......... | ......... | .783 | 1.194 | ......... | 3,324.618 | ......... | 3,337.454 | 17 |
| ......... | ......... | ......... | 5.833 | ......... | ......... | ......... | 50.902 | 18 |
| ......... | ......... | ......... | ......... | ......... | 6.386 | ......... | 22,315.842 | 19 |
| ......... | ......... | ......... | 38.708 | ......... | ......... | ......... | 38.708 | 20 |
| 8.294 | 1.413 | 9.683 | 1.840 | .469 | 5.598 | .583 | 1,375.491 | 21 |
| 8.294 | 2,815.554 | 15,828.783 | 4,287.351 | 93.316 | 129,326.673 | 447.843 | 821,598.325 | 22 |
| ......... | ......... | ......... | ......... | ......... | ......... | ......... | 195,639.023 | 23 |
| ......... | ......... | ......... | ......... | ......... | 13,257.241 | ......... | 2,356,741.277 | 24 |
| 8.294 | 2,815.554 | 15,828.783 | 4,287.351 | 93.316 | 142,583.914 | 447.843 | 3,373,978.625 | 25 |
| 4,126.474 | ......... | ......... | ......... | ......... | 28.657 | ......... | 5,996,940.568 | 26 |
| 18,815.328 | ......... | ......... | ......... | ......... | 714.105 | ......... | 1,526,704.711 | 27 |
| ......... | ......... | ......... | ......... | ......... | ......... | ......... | 15,234,226.908 | 28 |
| 1,769.021 | 37.164 | 310.643 | 369.506 | 19.576 | 2,568.231 | 403.343 | 685,132.588 | 29 |
| 24,719.117 | 2,852.718 | 16,139.426 | 4,656.857 | 112.892 | 145,894.907 | 851.186 | 26,816,983.400 | 30 |
| 832.188 | ......... | ......... | ......... | ......... | 7.493 | ......... | 73,305.094 | 31 |
| ......... | ......... | ......... | ......... | ......... | 206.850 | ......... | 4,963.229 | 32 |
| ......... | ......... | ......... | ......... | ......... | ......... | ......... | 1,672.882 | 33 |
| 832.188 | ......... | ......... | ......... | ......... | 214.343 | ......... | 79,941.205 | 34 |
| 25,551.305 | 2,852.718 | 16,139.426 | 4,656.857 | 112.892 | 146,109.250 | 851.186 | 26,896,924.605 | 35 |
| ......... | ......... | ......... | ......... | ......... | ......... | ......... | 46,962.617 | 36 |
| ......... | ......... | ......... | ......... | ......... | ......... | ......... | 238.721 | 37 |
| ......... | ......... | ......... | ......... | ......... | ......... | ......... | 172,162.757 | 38 |
| ......... | ......... | ......... | ......... | ......... | 10.000 | ......... | 510.000 | 39 |
| ......... | ......... | ......... | ......... | ......... | 10.000 | ......... | 219,874.095 | 40 |
| 25,551.305 | 2,852.718 | 16,139.426 | 4,656.857 | 112.892 | 146,119.250 | 851.186 | 27,116,798.700 | 41 |
| $528,193.30 | $58,970.90 | $333,631.24 | $96,265.65 | $2,333.68 | $3,020,346.31 | $17,595.34 | $556,008,777.60 | 42 |
| ......... | ......... | ......... | ......... | ......... | ......... | ......... | 970,803.43 | 43 |
| ......... | ......... | ......... | ......... | ......... | 206.72 | ......... | 3,574,397.45 | 44 |
| 528,193.30 | 58,970.90 | 333,631.24 | 96,265.65 | 2,333.68 | 3,020,553.03 | 17,595.34 | 560,553,978.48 | 45 |
| 456 | 240 | 527 | 357 | 10 | 1,288 | 106 | 85,344 | 46 |
| ......... | ......... | ......... | ......... | ......... | 14 | ......... | 467 | 47 |
| ......... | 1 | ......... | ......... | ......... | ......... | ......... | 4,048 | 48 |
| ......... | ......... | ......... | ......... | ......... | ......... | ......... | 1,810 | 49 |
| 456 | 241 | 527 | 357 | 10 | 1,302 | 106 | 91,669 | 50 |

*Deposits and purchases of silver during*

| | Source and description. | Philadelphia. | San Francisco. | Denver. | New York. |
|---|---|---|---|---|---|
| | PURCHASED. | *Fine ounces.* | *Fine ounces.* | *Fine ounces.* | *Fine ounces.* |
| 1 | Alaska | 76.17 | 2,842.34 | 17.39 | 51.13 |
| 2 | Arizona | | 51,072.51 | 5,305.38 | 12.32 |
| 3 | California | 2.18 | 46,020.50 | 1.43 | |
| 4 | Colorado | 13.20 | | 24,529.72 | |
| 5 | Georgia | 2.79 | | | |
| 6 | Idaho | .97 | 313.33 | 729.62 | 84.00 |
| 7 | Michigan | 6,589.29 | 55.07 | | 9,573.27 |
| 8 | Montana | .16 | 44.78 | 18,105.19 | 1.35 |
| 9 | Nevada | 8.36 | 1,863,043.57 | 69.68 | |
| 10 | New Mexico | 121.22 | 123.48 | 251,432.85 | |
| 11 | North Carolina | 7.08 | | | 7.13 |
| 12 | Oregon | | 1,742.72 | 11.88 | |
| 13 | South Carolina | .09 | | | |
| 14 | South Dakota | | | 22,724.74 | 91,648.47 |
| 15 | Utah | | | 463,520.55 | |
| 16 | Virginia | 13.41 | | | |
| 17 | Washington | | 1,662.35 | | |
| 18 | Wyoming | | .10 | 826.78 | |
| 19 | Philippine Islands | | 7,948.74 | | |
| 20 | Other | | | | |
| 21 | Sweeps and grains, dep. melting room | 221.23 | 157.40 | 44.02 | 1,157.01 |
| 22 | Total unrefined | 7,056.15 | 1,975,026.89 | 787,319.23 | 102,534.68 |
| | Domestic refinery bullion: | | | | |
| 23 | Less than 0.992 fine | | | 30,019.68 | 88,201.83 |
| 24 | Over 0.992 fine | 22,850,899.58 | 13,832,727.67 | 11,997,704.58 | 299,921.04 |
| 25 | Total domestic purchases | 22,857,955.73 | 15,807,754.56 | 12,815,043.49 | 490,657.55 |
| 26 | Foreign coin | 5,089,096.23 | 62,775.97 | 8,335.54 | 4,490.47 |
| 27 | Foreign bullion, crude | 412.97 | 784,305.87 | 262,918.45 | 475,138.34 |
| 28 | Foreign bullion, refined | 100,659.18 | | | 51,622.22 |
| 29 | Jewelers' bars, dental scrap, plate, etc. | 138,614.58 | 125,634.04 | 26,177.24 | 427,990.73 |
| 30 | Total deposit purchases | 28,186,738.69 | 16,780,470.44 | 13,112,474.72 | 1,449,899.31 |
| | REDEPOSITS PURCHASED. | | | | |
| 31 | Domestic coin | 2,361.47 | 344.96 | 501.39 | |
| 32 | Bars stamped by U. S. Government | 8,965.85 | 169.70 | 149.54 | 17,010.80 |
| 33 | Surplus (mint recoveries) | 837.19 | 6,953.96 | 1,041.18 | [1] 5,434.01 |
| 34 | Total redeposits purchased | 12,164.51 | 7,468.62 | 1,692.11 | 22,444.81 |
| 35 | Total purchases | 28,198,903.20 | 16,787,939.06 | 13,114,166.83 | 1,472,344.12 |
| | REDEPOSITS—TRANSFERS. | | | | |
| 36 | Domestic coin from Treasury | 1,093,216.41 | 464,119.94 | 173,128.60 | |
| 37 | Domestic assay coins | 1,022.73 | | | |
| 38 | Refined bars | 616,127.33 | | | |
| 39 | Unrefined bars | | 36,031.59 | | |
| 40 | Proof bullion | | 25.00 | 100.00 | 200.00 |
| 41 | Total redeposits transferred | 1,710,366.47 | 500,176.53 | 173,228.60 | 200.00 |
| | DEPOSITED IN TRUST. | | | | |
| 42 | U. S. Government bars | 461,275.05 | | | |
| 43 | Domestic bullion, refined | 541,925.11 | | | |
| 44 | Foreign bullion, refined | 884,293.58 | 3,873,148.47 | | |
| 45 | Total deposited in trust | 1,887,593.74 | 3,873,148.47 | | |
| 46 | Grand total, fine ounces | 31,796,863.41 | 21,161,264.06 | 13,287,395.43 | 1,472,544.12 |
| | Value: | | | | |
| 47 | Cost of purchases | $26,438,266.69 | $16,434,420.24 | $13,011,183.26 | $986,956.70 |
| 48 | Invoice value of transfers | 2,128,632.12 | 665,903.39 | 239,436.82 | 205.00 |
| 49 | Coining value of standard dollar bullion purchased | 29,556,286.38 | 20,408,208.25 | 16,565,850.16 | 118,492.41 |
| 50 | Coining value of subsidiary bullion purchased | 143,049.94 | 1,345,038.34 | 414,943.45 | 544,430.91 |
| 51 | Subsidiary coining value of purchased and transferred domestic coin | 1,515,950.38 | 642,080.39 | 240,027.63 | |

[1] Includes surplus of 1921.

*the fiscal year ended June 30, 1922.*

| New Orleans. | Carson. | Boise. | Helena. | Deadwood. | Seattle. | Salt Lake City. | Total. | |
|---|---|---|---|---|---|---|---|---|
| Fine ounces. | Fine ounces. | Fine ounces. | Fine ounces. | Fine ounces. | Fine ounces. | Fine ounces. | Fine ounces. | |
| .......... | .......... | 1.05 | .......... | .......... | 1?,217.17 | 53.59 | 18,258.84 | 1 |
| .......... | .......... | .......... | .......... | .......... | .......... | .......... | 56,390.21 | 2 |
| .......... | 27.34 | .......... | .......... | .......... | .74 | 6.72 | 46,058.91 | 3 |
| .......... | .......... | .......... | .......... | .......... | 3.70 | 1.28 | 24,547.90 | 4 |
| .......... | .......... | .......... | .......... | .......... | .......... | .......... | 2.79 | 5 |
| .......... | .......... | 3,466.82 | 2.72 | .......... | 53.25 | 33.91 | 4,684.62 | 6 |
| .......... | .......... | .......... | .......... | .......... | .......... | .......... | 16,217.63 | 7 |
| .......... | .......... | 2.26 | 1,355.55 | .......... | .29 | .99 | 19,510.57 | 8 |
| .......... | 1,424.96 | 27.59 | .......... | .......... | .86 | 93.42 | 1,864,668.44 | 9 |
| .......... | .......... | .......... | .......... | .......... | .......... | .......... | 251,677.55 | 10 |
| .......... | .......... | .......... | .......... | .......... | .......... | .......... | 14.21 | 11 |
| .......... | .......... | 972.90 | .......... | .......... | 51.48 | .......... | 2,778.98 | 12 |
| .......... | .......... | .......... | .......... | .......... | .......... | .......... | .09 | 13 |
| .......... | .......... | .......... | .......... | 7.96 | .......... | .......... | 114,381.17 | 14 |
| .......... | .......... | .......... | .......... | .......... | .......... | 252.75 | 463,773.30 | 15 |
| .......... | .......... | .......... | .......... | .......... | .......... | .......... | 13.41 | 16 |
| .......... | .......... | .17 | .23 | .......... | 237.97 | .......... | 1,900.72 | 17 |
| .......... | .......... | .......... | .42 | .......... | .......... | .......... | 827.30 | 18 |
| .......... | .......... | .......... | .......... | .......... | 4.61 | .......... | 7,953.35 | 19 |
| .......... | .......... | .......... | 47.10 | .......... | .......... | .......... | 47.10 | 20 |
| 5.28 | 4.44 | 5.31 | .97 | 1.19 | 1.23 | .72 | 1,598.80 | 21 |
| 5.28 | 1,456.74 | 4,476.10 | 1,406.99 | 9.15 | 15,571.30 | 443.38 | 2,895,305.89 | 22 |
| .......... | .......... | .......... | .......... | .......... | .......... | .......... | 118,221.51 | 23 |
| .......... | .......... | .......... | .......... | .......... | .......... | .......... | 48,981,252.87 | 24 |
| 5.28 | 1,456.74 | 4,476.10 | 1,406.99 | 9.15 | 15,571.30 | 443.38 | 51,994,780.27 | 25 |
| 54,924.93 | .......... | .......... | .......... | .......... | .......... | .......... | 5,219,623.14 | 26 |
| 30,166.66 | .......... | .......... | .......... | .......... | 199.94 | .......... | 1,553,142.23 | 27 |
| .......... | .......... | .......... | .......... | .......... | .......... | .......... | 152,281.40 | 28 |
| 4,478.32 | 16.78 | 195.68 | 695.42 | 680.09 | 7,525.29 | 433.77 | 732,441.94 | 29 |
| 89,575.19 | 1,473.52 | 4,671.78 | 2,102.41 | 689.24 | 23,296.53 | 877.15 | 59,652,268.98 | 30 |
| .......... | .......... | .......... | .......... | .......... | .22 | .......... | 3,208.04 | 31 |
| .......... | .......... | .......... | .......... | .......... | .......... | .......... | 26,295.89 | 32 |
| .......... | .......... | .......... | .......... | .......... | .......... | .......... | 14,266.34 | 33 |
| .......... | .......... | .......... | .......... | .......... | .22 | .......... | 43,770.27 | 34 |
| 89,575.19 | 1,473.52 | 4,671.78 | 2,102.41 | 689.24 | 23,296.75 | 877.15 | 59,696,039.25 | 35 |
| .......... | .......... | .......... | .......... | .......... | .......... | .......... | 1,730,464.95 | 36 |
| .......... | .......... | .......... | .......... | .......... | .......... | .......... | 1,022.73 | 37 |
| .......... | .......... | .......... | .......... | .......... | .......... | .......... | 616,127.33 | 38 |
| .......... | .......... | .......... | .......... | .......... | .......... | .......... | 36,031.59 | 39 |
| .......... | 50.00 | .......... | .......... | .......... | .......... | .......... | 375.00 | 40 |
| .......... | 50.00 | .......... | .......... | .......... | .......... | .......... | 2,384,021.60 | 41 |
| .......... | .......... | .......... | .......... | .......... | .......... | .......... | 461,275.05 | 42 |
| .......... | .......... | .......... | .......... | .......... | .......... | .......... | 541,925.11 | 43 |
| .......... | .......... | .......... | .......... | .......... | .......... | .......... | 4,757,542.05 | 44 |
| .......... | .......... | .......... | .......... | .......... | .......... | .......... | 5,760,742.21 | 45 |
| 89,575.19 | 1,523.52 | 4,671.78 | 2,102.41 | 689.24 | 23,296.75 | 877.15 | 67,840,803.06 | 46 |
| $61,510.56 | $988.90 | $3,054.13 | $1,333.43 | $461.56 | $15,333.14 | $568.24 | $56,954,076.85 | 47 |
| .......... | 50.97 | .......... | .......... | .......... | .......... | .......... | 3,034,228.30 | 48 |
| .......... | .......... | .......... | .......... | .......... | .......... | .......... | 66,648,837.20 | 49 |
| 123,829.53 | 2,038.39 | 6,525.77 | 2,946.00 | 952.81 | 32,259.41 | 1,224.63 | 2,617,239.18 | 50 |
| .......... | .......... | .......... | .......... | .......... | .30 | .......... | 2,398,058.70 | 51 |

*Deposits of gold at United States mints and assay offices since 1873.*

| Fiscal year ended June 30— | Character of gold deposited. | | | | | |
|---|---|---|---|---|---|---|
| | Domestic bullion, including domestic refinery product from foreign ores, etc. | Domestic coin. | Foreign bullion. | Foreign coin. | Surplus bullion, grains, jewelers' bars, old plate, etc. | Total. |
| 1873 | $28,868,570 | $27,116,948 | $426,108 | $518,542 | $774,218 | $57,704,386 |
| 1874 | 29,736,388 | 6,275,367 | 3,162,520 | 9,313,882 | 654,354 | 49,142,511 |
| 1875 | 34,266,125 | 1,714,311 | 739,440 | 1,111,792 | 724,626 | 38,556,294 |
| 1876 | 37,590,529 | 417,947 | 1,141,906 | 2,111,084 | 681,819 | 41,943,285 |
| 1877 | 43,478,104 | 447,340 | 1,931,163 | 2,093,261 | 837,911 | 48,787,779 |
| 1878 | 48,075,124 | 301,022 | 2,068,679 | 1,316,461 | 907,932 | 52,669,218 |
| 1879 | 38,549,706 | 198,083 | 1,069,797 | 1,498,820 | 937,751 | 42,254,157 |
| 1880 | 35,821,705 | 209,329 | 21,200,997 | 40,426,560 | 1,176,506 | 98,835,097 |
| 1881 | 35,815,037 | 440,777 | 37,771,472 | 55,462,386 | 1,343,431 | 130,833,103 |
| 1882 | 31,298,512 | 599,357 | 12,783,807 | 20,304,811 | 1,770,166 | 66,756,653 |
| 1883 | 32,481,642 | 374,129 | 4,727,143 | 6,906,084 | 1,858,108 | 46,347,106 |
| 1884 | 29,079,596 | 263,117 | 6,023,735 | 9,095,462 | 1,864,769 | 46,326,679 |
| 1885 | 31,584,437 | 325,210 | 11,221,847 | 7,893,218 | 1,869,363 | 52,894,075 |
| 1886 | 32,456,494 | 393,545 | 4,317,068 | 5,673,565 | 2,069,077 | 44,909,749 |
| 1887 | 32,973,027 | 516,985 | 22,571,329 | 9,896,512 | 2,265,220 | 68,223,073 |
| 1888 | 32,406,307 | 492,513 | 21,741,042 | 14,596,885 | 2,988,751 | 72,225,498 |
| 1889 | 31,440,779 | 585,067 | 2,136,517 | 4,447,476 | 3,526,597 | 42,136,436 |
| 1890 | 30,474,900 | 655,475 | 2,691,932 | 5,298,774 | 3,542,014 | 42,663,095 |
| 1891 | 31,555,117 | 583,847 | 4,054,823 | 8,256,304 | 4,035,710 | 48,485,801 |
| 1892 | 31,961,546 | 557,968 | 10,935,155 | 14,040,188 | 3,636,603 | 61,131,460 |
| 1893 | 33,286,168 | 792,470 | 2,247,731 | 6,293,296 | 3,830,176 | 46,449,841 |
| 1894 | 38,696,951 | 2,093,615 | 15,614,118 | 12,385,407 | 3,118,422 | 71,909,513 |
| 1895 | 44,371,950 | 1,188,258 | 14,108,436 | 2,278,614 | 3,213,809 | 65,161,067 |
| 1896 | 53,910,957 | 1,670,006 | 6,572,390 | 3,227,409 | 3,388,622 | 68,769,384 |
| 1897 | 60,618,240 | 1,015,314 | 9,371,521 | 13,183,014 | 2,810,249 | 87,003,338 |
| 1898 | 69,881,121 | 1,187,683 | 26,477,370 | 47,210,078 | 2,936,943 | 147,693,195 |
| 1899 | 78,252,487 | 1,158,308 | 30,336,560 | 32,785,152 | 2,964,684 | 143,497,191 |
| 1900 | 87,458,836 | 1,389,097 | 22,720,150 | 18,834,496 | 3,517,541 | 133,920,120 |
| 1901 | 92,929,696 | 1,116,180 | 27,189,659 | 27,906,489 | 3,959,657 | 153,101,681 |
| 1902 | 94,622,079 | 1,488,448 | 18,189,417 | 13,996,162 | 4,284,724 | 132,580,830 |
| 1903 | 96,514,298 | 960,908 | 16,331,059 | 8,950,595 | 4,247,583 | 127,004,443 |
| 1904 | 87,745,627 | 2,159,818 | 36,802,224 | 46,152,784 | 4,892,931 | 177,753,384 |
| 1905 | 101,618,315 | 3,404,967 | 17,645,527 | 15,141,678 | 5,568,483 | 143,378,970 |
| 1906 | 103,838,268 | 1,514,291 | 36,317,865 | 6,648,512 | 4,790,558 | 153,109,494 |
| 1907 | 114,217,462 | 2,754,283 | 36,656,546 | 17,221,252 | 5,731,112 | 176,580,655 |
| 1908 | 111,735,878 | 3,989,773 | 71,774,351 | 13,684,426 | 6,231,547 | 207,415,975 |
| 1909 | 119,727,439 | 3,432,288 | 16,021,521 | 1,034,378 | 5,341,604 | 145,557,230 |
| 1910 | 104,974,559 | 3,603,140 | 15,761,852 | 405,226 | 5,626,331 | 130,371,108 |
| 1911 | 120,910,247 | 2,949,199 | 35,673,116 | 10,066,643 | 5,783,886 | 175,383,091 |
| 1912 | 119,338,150 | 3,496,769 | 20,914,227 | 2,155,233 | 6,025,502 | 151,929,881 |
| 1913 | 118,504,953 | 1,846,880 | 31,985,879 | 2,732,439 | 6,061,727 | 161,131,878 |
| 1914 | 113,278,957 | 4,719,876 | 18,978,572 | 3,261,967 | 6,057,184 | 146,296,556 |
| 1915 | 119,217,239 | 4,209,612 | 22,881,854 | 15,420,256 | 5,748,959 | 167,477,920 |
| 1916 | 120,722,159 | 2,522,290 | 91,099,419 | 271,541,705 | 6,330,201 | 492,215,774 |
| 1917 | 204,355,339 | 1,906,126 | 571,448,086 | 124,111,619 | 8,046,828 | 909,867,998 |
| 1918 | 101,416,485 | 6,431,236 | 153,405,687 | 40,422,147 | 7,812,167 | 309,487,722 |
| 1919 | 83,350,336 | 24,521,645 | 34,568,599 | 15,268 | 8,907,516 | 151,363,364 |
| 1920 | 106,416,689 | 5,079,373 | 78,021,266 | 29,003,844 | 10,989,866 | 229,511,038 |
| 1921 | 72,714,480 | 1,887,929 | 509,493,374 | 76,813,705 | 12,708,620 | 673,708,108 |
| 1922 | 69,746,328 | 2,491,089 | 346,479,206 | 123,967,784 | 14,300,128 | 556,984,515 |
| Total | 3,522,285,338 | 139,449,208 | 2,507,804,062 | 1,207,119,625 | 212,782,486 | 7,589,440,719 |

*Deposits of silver at the United States mints and assay offices since 1885.*

| Fiscal year ended June 30— | Domestic bullion, including domestic refinery product from foreign ores, etc. | Character of silver deposited. | | | | | | Surplus bullion, grain, jewelers' bars, old plate, etc. | Total. |
|---|---|---|---|---|---|---|---|---|---|
| | | Domestic coin. | | Foreign bullion. | Foreign coin. | | | | |
| | | United States. | Ha-waiian. | | Philippines. | | Other. | | |
| | | | | | For recoinage. | Assay coin. | | | |
| | *Fine ounces.* | *Fine ounces.* | *Fine ounces.* | *Fine ounces.* | *Fine ounces.* | *Fine ounces.* | *Fine ounces.* | *Fine ounces.* | *Fine ounces.* |
| 1885.... | 24,943,394 | 678,741 | ........ | 1,627,619 | ............ | ........ | 867,856 | 336,981 | 28,454,591 |
| 1886.... | 25,101,639 | 216,015 | ........ | 1,145,017 | ............ | ........ | 628,545 | 361,316 | 27,452,532 |
| 1887.... | 29,293,372 | 5,848,585 | ........ | 1,127,213 | ............ | ........ | 271,166 | 396,656 | 36,936,992 |
| 1888.... | 28,921,649 | 1,202,177 | ........ | 1,290,390 | ............ | ........ | 67,549 | 485,190 | 31,966,955 |
| 1889.... | 29,606,387 | 394,346 | ........ | 1,063,900 | ............ | ........ | 328,276 | 502,223 | 31,895,132 |
| 1890.... | 29,187,135 | 466,302 | ........ | 1,852,155 | ............ | ........ | 951,162 | 526,270 | 32,983,024 |
| 1891.... | 50,667,116 | 637,652 | ........ | 1,767,908 | ............ | ........ | 1,970,912 | 633,073 | 55,676,661 |
| 1892.... | 56,817,548 | 5,036,246 | ........ | 1,556,618 | ............ | ........ | 349,652 | 572,661 | 64,332,725 |
| 1893.... | 56,976,082 | 5,346,912 | ........ | 1,738,711 | ............ | ........ | 505,171 | 582,728 | 65,149,604 |
| 1894.... | 15,296,815 | 5,012,060 | ........ | 994,901 | ............ | ........ | 522,725 | 467,958 | 22,194,459 |
| 1895.... | 6,809,626 | 3,015,905 | ........ | 1,362,141 | ............ | ........ | 15,291 | 580,125 | 11,783,088 |
| 1896.... | 4,420,770 | 3,170,768 | ........ | 680,757 | ............ | ........ | 150,942 | 604,386 | 9,027,623 |
| 1897.... | 3,914,985 | 2,208,953 | ........ | 626,085 | ............ | ........ | 101,157 | 473,755 | 7,324,935 |
| 1898.... | 2,116,690 | 1,243,050 | ........ | 209,987 | ............ | ........ | 6,808 | 249,468 | 3,826,003 |
| 1899.... | 5,584,912 | 6,060,986 | ........ | 716,077 | ............ | ........ | 19,382 | 484,751 | 12,866,108 |
| 1900.... | 4,977,978 | 3,587,992 | ........ | 1,088,019 | ............ | ........ | 44,704 | 557,831 | 10,256,524 |
| 1901.... | 2,466,749 | 2,613,570 | ........ | 1,306,149 | ............ | ........ | 4,250,196 | 567,647 | 11,204,311 |
| 1902.... | 1,425,060 | 2,275,090 | ........ | 1,152,023 | ............ | ........ | 29,265 | 575,430 | 5,456,868 |
| 1903.... | 12,523,630 | 2,050,225 | 461,686 | 1,110,463 | ............ | ........ | 21,869 | 627,108 | 16,794,981 |
| 1904.... | 9,991,187 | 1,923,609 | 148,788 | 1,361,701 | ¹2,560,236 | 6,901 | 1,471,963 | 652,015 | 18,116,400 |
| 1905.... | 4,923,655 | 1,333,595 | 3,647 | 1,906,410 | ¹7,700,310 | 3,456 | 92,995 | 739,311 | 16,703,378 |
| 1906.... | 2,398,871 | 959,568 | 3,895 | 3,162,507 | ¹ 58,670 | 2,663 | 1,287,658 | 632,544 | 8,506,377 |
| 1907.... | 20,388,163 | 770,269 | ........ | 2,552,003 | 4,680,692 | 99 | 282,612 | 636,722 | 29,310,560 |
| 1908.... | 16,114,553 | 786,085 | ........ | 2,963,399 | 8,866,622 | 3,411 | 134,974 | 648,007 | 29,517,051 |
| 1909.... | 5,375,389 | 659,935 | ........ | 2,326,847 | 7,314,573 | 5,739 | 21,917 | 520,715 | 16,225,115 |
| 1910.... | 1,547,145 | 548,821 | ........ | 1,162,240 | 1,389,545 | 2,042 | 13,295 | 460,935 | 5,124,023 |
| 1911.... | 3,220,236 | 393,906 | ........ | 799,105 | 620,964 | 836 | 6,040 | 495,013 | 5,536,100 |
| 1912.... | 5,635,513 | 458,694 | 447 | 957,233 | 227,127 | 168 | 7,934 | 540,117 | 7,827,233 |
| 1913.... | 3,104,347 | 280,688 | ........ | 624,215 | 342,053 | 236 | 17,010 | 577,423 | 4,945,972 |
| 1914.... | 9,752,614 | 580,972 | ........ | 527,233 | 143,793 | 80 | 85,141 | 572,687 | 11,671,420 |
| 1915.... | 7,250,205 | 491,028 | ........ | 2,130,138 | 136,179 | 68 | 383,439 | 536,887 | 10,927,944 |
| 1916.... | 9,346,085 | 569,510 | 99 | 1,860,420 | 138,024 | 43 | 204,470 | 698,026 | 12,816,677 |
| 1917.... | 7,556,359 | 6,240,994 | 62 | 2,327,785 | 149,129 | 69 | 816,725 | 882,893 | 17,974,016 |
| 1918.... | 21,155,924 | 8,176,334 | ........ | 6,780,011 | 1,910,998 | 378 | 7,145,336 | 964,626 | 46,133,607 |
| 1919.... | 2,669,447 | 456,283 | 100 | 1,670,071 | 617,755 | 776 | 4,801,019 | 1,145,067 | 11,360,518 |
| 1920.... | 5,336,184 | 541,117 | ........ | 2,205,066 | ............ | 225 | 4,413,248 | 1,274,743 | 13,770,583 |
| 1921.... | 63,540,055 | 507,894 | ........ | 2,158,717 | ............ | ........ | 763,075 | 830,570 | 67,800,311 |
| 1922.... | 51,994,780 | 1,734,696 | ........ | 1,705,424 | ............ | ........ | 5,219,623 | 746,708 | 61,401,231 |
| Total. | 642,352,249 | 78,488,573 | 618,724 | 61,596,658 | 36,856,670 | 27,190 | 38,171,002 | 23,140,566 | 881,251,632 |

¹ Spanish-Filipino coins.

*Coinage of the mints of the United States, authority for coinage, changes in weight and fineness, act discontinuing same, and amount coined for each denomination of coin since organization, 1792, to June 30, 1922.*

| Denomination. | Act authorizing coinage or change in weight or fineness. | Weight (grains). | Fineness. | Pieces. | Total amount coined to June 30, 1922. |
|---|---|---|---|---|---|
| **GOLD COINS.** | | | | | |
| 50-dollar piece, memorial: | | | | | |
| Panama-Pacific International Exposition— | | | | | |
| Octagonal | Jan. 16, 1915 | 1,290 | 900 | 1,509 | $75,450.00 |
| Round | ......do...... | 1,290 | 900 | 1,510 | 75,500.00 |
| Double eagle ($20) | Mar. 3, 1849 | 516 | 900 | 125,242,856 | 2,504,857,120.00 |
| Eagle ($10) | Apr. 2, 1792 | 270 | 916⅔ | 51,797,985 | 517,979,850.00 |
| | June 28, 1834 | 258 | 899.225 | | |
| | Jan. 18, 1837 | .......... | 900 | | |
| Half eagle ($5) | Apr. 2, 1792 | 135 | 916⅔ | 78,249,869 | 391,249,345.00 |
| | June 28, 1834 | 129 | 899.225 | | |
| | Jan. 18, 1837 | .......... | 900 | | |
| Quarter eagle ($2.50) | Apr. 2, 1792 | 67.5 | 916⅔ | 17,856,590 | 44,641,475.00 |
| | June 28, 1834 | 64.5 | 899.225 | | |
| | Jan. 18, 1837 | .......... | 900 | | |
| Quarter eagle ($2.50), memorial: | | | | | |
| Panama-Pacific International Exposition. | Jan. 16, 1915 | 64.5 | 900 | 10,017 | 25,042 50 |
| 3-dollar piece | Feb. 21, 1853 (act discontinuing coinage Sept. 26, 1890). | 77.4 | 900 | 539,792 | 1,619,37ɔ.00 |
| 1 dollar | Mar. 3, 1849 (act discontinuing coinage Sept. 26, 1890.) | 25.8 | 900 | 19,499,337 | 19,499,ɔɔ7.00 |
| 1 dollar, memorial: | | | | | |
| Louisiana Purchase Exposition. | June 28, 1902 | 25.8 | 900 | 250,000 | 250,000.00 |
| Lewis and Clark Exposition. | Apr. 13, 1904 | 25.8 | 900 | 60,000 | 60,000.00 |
| Panama-Pacific International Exposition. | Jan. 16, 1915 | 25.8 | 900 | 25,034 | 25,034.00 |
| McKinley | Feb. 23, 1916 | 25.8 | 900 | 30,040 | 30,040.00 |
| Grant | Feb. 2, 1922 | 25.8 | 900 | 10,016 | 10,016.00 |
| Total gold | .......... | .......... | .......... | 293,574,555 | 3,480,397,585.50 |
| **SILVER COINS.** | | | | | |
| Dollar | Apr. 2, 1792 | 4í6 | 892.4 | | |
| | Jan. 18, 1837 (act discontinuing coinage Feb. 12, 1873). | 412½ | 900 | [1]689,735,321 | 689,735,321.00 |
| | Feb. 28, 1878 | 412½ | 900 | | |
| | July 14, 1890 | 412½ | 900 | | |
| | Mar. 3, 1891 | 412½ | 900 | | |
| | Apr 23, 1918 | 412½ | 900 | | |
| Trade dollar [2] | Feb. 11, 1873 (act discontinuing coinage Mar. 3, 1887). | 420 | 900 | 35,965,924 | 35,965,924.00 |
| Dollar, memorial: | | | | | |
| Lafayette | Mar. 3, 1899 | 412½ | 900 | 50,000 | 50,000.00 |
| Half dollar | Apr. 2, 1792 | 208 | 892.4 | 443,417,312 | 221,708,656.0 |
| | Jan. 18, 1837 | 206½ | 900 | | |
| | Feb. 21, 1853 | 192 | .......... | | |
| | Feb. 12, 1873 | [3]192.9 | .......... | | |

[1] Silver dollars coined 1792 to 1805........................................................... $1,439,517
    Coined from Jan. 18, 1837, to Feb. 12, 1873................................................ 6,591,721
                                                                                                          ───────────
    Coined under acts of—                                                                                  8,031,238
      Apr. 2, 1792............................................................................
      Feb. 28, 1878...................................................... $378,166,793
      July 14, 1890...................................................... 187,027,345
      Mar 3, 1891, trade dollar conversion.............................. 5,078,472
                                                                                                          ───────────
                                                                                                          570,272,610
      Apr. 23, 1918 (Pittman Act), replacement—old design........................... 86,730,000
      Apr. 23, 1918 (Pittman Act), replacement—"Peace" dollars....................... 24,701,473
                                                                                                          ───────────
                                                                                                          689,735,321

NOTE.—Silver dollar coinage suspended 1805 to 1837 and 1874 to 1878. The bullion value of the dollar was greater than its coin value prior to 1878.

[2] Coinage limited to export demand by joint resolution July 22, 1876. Redeemed $7,689,036 at face value under act Mar. 3, 1887, which were converted into 5,078,472 standard dollars and $2,889,011 subsidiary silver coin.

[3] 12½ grams, or 192.9 grains.

*Coinage of the mints of the United States, authority for coinage, changes in weight and fineness, act discontinuing same, and amount coined for each denomination of coin since organization, 1792, to June 30, 1922*—Continued.

| Denomination. | Act authorizing coinage or change in weight or fineness. | Weight (grains). | Fineness. | Pieces. | Total amount coined to June 30, 1922. |
|---|---|---|---|---|---|
| SILVER COINS—con. | | | | | |
| Half dollar, memorial: | | | | | |
| Columbian Exposition. | Aug. 5, 1892 | 192.9 | 900 | 5,000,000 | [4] $2,500,000.00 |
| Panama-Pacific International Exposition. | Jan. 16, 1915 | 192.9 | 900 | 60,000 | 30,000.00 |
| Illinois Centennial | June 1, 1918 | 192.9 | 900 | 100,058 | 50,029.00 |
| Maine Cenntenial | May 10, 1920 | 192.9 | 900 | 50,028 | 25,014.00 |
| Landing of Pilgrims Tercentennial. | May 12, 1920 | 192.9 | 900 | 300,165 | 150,082.50 |
| Alabama Centennial | May 20, 1920 | 192.9 | 900 | 70,044 | 35,022.00 |
| Missouri Centennial | Mar. 4, 1921 | 192.9 | 900 | 50,028 | 25,014.00 |
| Grant | Feb. 2, 1922 | 192.9 | 900 | 100,061 | 50,030.50 |
| Quarter dollar | Apr. 2, 1792 | 104 | 892.4 | | |
| | Jan. 18, 1837 | 103⅛ | 900 | 551,758,558 | 137,939,639.50 |
| | Feb. 21, 1853 | 96 | | | |
| | Feb. 12, 1873 | [5] 96.45 | | | |
| Quarter dollar, memorial: | | | | | |
| Columbian Exposition. | Mar. 3, 1893 | 96.45 | 900 | 40,000 | 10,000.00 |
| 20-cent piece | Mar. 3, 1875 (act discontinuing coinage May 2, 1878). | [6] 77.16 | 900 | 1,355,000 | 271,000.00 |
| Dime | Apr. 2, 1792 | 41.6 | 892.4 | | |
| | Jan. 18, 1837 | 41¼ | 900 | 1,106,138,797 | 110,613,879.70 |
| | Feb. 21, 1853 | 38.4 | | | |
| | Feb. 12, 1873 | [7] 38.58 | | | |
| Half dime | Apr. 2, 1792 | 20.8 | 892.4 | | |
| | Jan. 18, 1837 | 20⅝ | 900 | 97,604,388 | 4,880,219.40 |
| | Feb. 21, 1853 (act discontinuing coinage Feb. 12, 1873). | 19.2 | | | |
| 3-cent piece | Mar. 3, 1851 | 12⅜ | 750 | 42,736,240 | 1,282,087.20 |
| | Mar. 3, 1853 (act discontinuing coinage Feb. 12, 1873). | 11.52 | 900 | | |
| Total silver | | | | 2,974,531,924 | 1,205,321,948.80 |
| MINOR COINS. | | | | | |
| 5-cent (nickel) | May 16, 1866 | 77.16 | (8) | 1,232,258,662 | 61,612,933.10 |
| 3-cent (nickel) | Mar. 3, 1865 (act discontinuing coinage Sept. 26, 1890). | 30 | (8) | 31,378,316 | 941,349.48 |
| 2-cent (bronze) | Apr. 22, 1864 (act discontinuing coinage Feb. 12, 1873). | 96 | (9) | 45,601,000 | 912,020.00 |
| cent (copper) | Apr. 2, 1792 | 264 | | | |
| | Jan. 14, 1793 | 208 | | 156,288,744 | 1,562,887.44 |
| | Jan. 26, 1796 [10] (act discontinuing coinage Feb. 21, 1857). | 168 | | | |
| Cent (nickel) | Feb. 21, 1857 (act discontinuing coinage Apr. 22, 1864). | 72 | (11) | 200,772,000 | 2,007,720.00 |
| Cent (bronze) | Apr. 22, 1864 | 48 | (9) | 4,283,906,683 | 42,839,066.83 |
| Half cent (copper) | Apr. 2, 1792 | 132 | | | |
| | Jan. 14, 1793 | 104 | | 7,985,222 | 39,926.11 |
| | Jan. 25, 1796 [10] (act discontinuing coinage Feb. 21, 1857). | 84 | | | |
| Total minor | | | | 5,958,190,627 | 109,915,902.96 |
| Total coinage | | | | 9,226,297,106 | 4,795,635,407.26 |

[4] Total amount coined.
[5] 6¼ grams, or 96.45 grains.
[6] 5 grams, or 77.16 grains.
[7] 2½ grams, or 38.58 grains.
[8] Composed of 75 per cent copper and 25 per cent nickel.
[9] Composed of 95 per cent copper and 5 per cent tin and zinc.
[10] By proclamation of the President, in conformity with act of Mar. 3, 1795.
[11] Composed of 88 per cent copper and 12 per cent nickel.

*Coinage of each mint of the United States since its*

[Coinage of the mint at Charlotte, N. C., from its organization, 1838, to its suspension, 1861.]

| Calendar year. | Gold. | | | Total value. |
|---|---|---|---|---|
| | Half eagles. | Quarter eagles. | Dollars. | |
| 1838 to 1861............................ | $4,405,135 | $544,915 | $109,138 | $5,059,188 |

[Coinage of the mint at Carson City from its

| Calendar year. | Gold. | | | Silver. | |
|---|---|---|---|---|---|
| | Double eagles. | Eagles. | Half eagles. | Dollars. | Trade dollars. |
| 1870 to 1893............ | $17,283,560 | $2,997,780 | $3,548,085 | $13,881,329 | $4,211,400 |

[Coinage of the mint at New Orleans from its organization, 1838,

| Calendar year. | Gold. | | | | | | Silver. |
|---|---|---|---|---|---|---|---|
| | Double eagles. | Eagles. | Half eagles. | Three dollars. | Quarter eagles. | Dollars. | Dollars. |
| 1838 to 1909........ | $16,375,500 | $23,610,890 | $4,618,625 | $72,000 | $3,023,157.50 | $1,004,000 | $187,111,529 |

[Coinage of the mint at Denver since its organization

| Calendar year. | Gold. | | | | Silver. |
|---|---|---|---|---|---|
| | Double eagles. | Eagles. | Half eagles. | Quarter eagles. | Dollars. |
| 1906 to 1910............ | $59,145,000 | $55,356,800 | $24,865,800 | .................. | .................. |
| 1911..................... | 16,930,000 | 301,000 | 362,500 | $139,200 | .................. |
| 1912..................... | .................. | .................. | .................. | .................. | .................. |
| 1913..................... | 7,870,000 | .................. | .................. | .................. | .................. |
| 1914..................... | 9,060,000 | 3,435,000 | 1,235,000 | 1,120,000 | .................. |
| 1915..................... | .................. | .................. | .................. | .................. | .................. |
| 1916..................... | .................. | .................. | .................. | .................. | .................. |
| 1917..................... | .................. | .................. | .................. | .................. | .................. |
| 1918..................... | .................. | .................. | .................. | .................. | .................. |
| 1919..................... | .................. | .................. | .................. | .................. | .................. |
| 1920..................... | .................. | .................. | .................. | .................. | .................. |
| 1921..................... | .................. | .................. | .................. | .................. | $20,345,000 |
| Total............ | 93,005,000 | 59,092,800 | 26,463,300 | 1,259,200 | 20,345,000 |

*organization; by calendar years since 1910.*

[Coinage of the mint at Dahlonega, Ga., from its organization, 1838, to its suspension, 1861.]

| Calendar year. | Gold. | | | | Total value. |
|---|---|---|---|---|---|
| | Half eagles. | Three dollars. | Quarter eagles. | Dollars. | |
| 1838 to 1861.......... | $5,536,055 | $3,360 | $494,625 | $72,529 | $6,106,569 |

organization, 1870, to its suspension, June 30, 1893.]

| Silver. | | | | Total coinage. | | Total value. |
|---|---|---|---|---|---|---|
| Half dollars. | Quarter dollars. | Twenty cents. | Dimes. | Gold. | Silver. | |
| $2,654,313.50 | $2,579,198.00 | $28,658.00 | $2,090,110.80 | $23,829,425.00 | $25,445,009.30 | $49,274,434.30 |

to its suspension, 1861, and from its reopening, 1879, to April, 1909.]

| Silver. | | | | | Total coinage. | | Total value. |
|---|---|---|---|---|---|---|---|
| Half dollars. | Quarter dollars. | Dimes. | Half dimes. | Three cents. | Gold. | Silver. | |
| $40,117,338 | $15,085,750 | $6,807,990.60 | $812,327.50 | $21,600 | $48,704,172.50 | $249,956,535.10 | $298,660,707.60 |

as a mint, February, 1906, to Dec. 31, 1921.]

| Silver. | | | Minor. | | Total coinage. | | | Total value. |
|---|---|---|---|---|---|---|---|---|
| Half dollars. | Quarter dollars. | Dimes. | Five cents. | Cents. | Gold. | Silver. | Minor. | |
| $5,582,000 | $4,541,500 | $2,007,400 | .......... | $126,720 | $139,367,600 | $12,130,900 | .......... | $151,498,500 |
| 347,540 | 233,400 | 1,120,900 | .......... | 104,110 | 17,732,700 | 1,701,840 | $126,720 | 19,561,260 |
| 1,150,400 | .......... | 1,176,000 | .......... | 158,040 | .......... | 2,326,400 | 527,810 | 2,854,210 |
| 267,000 | 362,700 | .......... | $423,700 | 11,930 | 7,870,000 | 629,700 | 632,690 | 9,132,390 |
| .......... | 761,500 | 1,190,800 | 474,650 | 220,500 | 14,850,000 | 1,952,300 | 207,530 | 17,009,830 |
| 585,200 | 923,500 | .......... | 195,600 | 369,560 | .......... | 1,508,700 | 598,975 | 2,107,675 |
| 507,200 | 1,635,200 | 26,400 | 378,475 | 551,200 | .......... | 2,168,800 | 1,026,210 | 3,195,010 |
| 1,352,700 | 1,933,400 | 940,200 | 666,650 | 478,300 | .......... | 4,226,300 | 1,046,740 | 5,273,040 |
| 1,926,520 | 1,845,000 | 2,267,410 | 495,540 | 571,540 | .......... | 6,039,000 | 896,400 | 6,935,400 |
| 582,500 | 486,000 | 993,900 | 418,100 | 492,800 | .......... | 2,062,400 | 971,840 | 3,034,240 |
| 775,500 | 896,600 | 1,917,100 | 400,300 | .......... | .......... | 3,589,200 | 963,700 | 4,552,900 |
| 104,000 | .......... | 108,000 | 470,900 | .......... | .......... | 20,557,000 | .......... | 20,557,000 |
| 13,180,560 | 13,618,800 | 11,748,180 | 3,923,915 | 3,074,700 | 179,820,300 | 58,892,540 | 6,998,615 | 245,711,455 |

REPORT ON THE FINANCES.

Coinage of each mint of the United States since its

[Coinage of the mint at San Francisco from

| Calendar year. | Gold. | | | | | | |
|---|---|---|---|---|---|---|---|
| | Fifty dollars. | Double eagles. | Eagles. | Half eagles. | Three dollars. | Quarter eagles. | Dollars. |
| 1854–1910 | | $1,386,415,520 | $135,134,060 | $125,725,040 | $186,300 | $1,861,255.00 | $90,232 |
| 1911 | | 15,515,000 | 510,000 | 7,080,000 | | | |
| 1912 | | | 3,000,000 | 1,960,000 | | | |
| 1913 | | 680,000 | 660,000 | 2,040,000 | | | |
| 1914 | | 29,960,000 | 2,080,000 | 1,315,000 | | | |
| 1915 | ¹ $150,950 | 11,350,000 | 590,000 | 820,000 | | ¹ 25,042.50 | ¹ 25,034 |
| 1916 | | 15,920,000 | 1,385,000 | 1,200,000 | | | |
| 1917 | | | | | | | |
| 1918 | | | | | | | |
| 1919 | | | | | | | |
| 1920 | | 11,160,000 | 1,265,000 | | | | |
| 1921 | | | | | | | |
| Total | 150,950 | 1,471,000,520 | 144,624,060 | 140,140,040 | 186,300 | 1,886,297.50 | 115,266 |

| Calendar year. | Minor. | | |
|---|---|---|---|
| | Five cents. | Cents. | Total. |
| 1854–1910 | | $97,780.00 | $97,780.00 |
| 1911 | | 40,260.00 | 40,260.00 |
| 1912 | $11,900.00 | 44,310.00 | 56,210.00 |
| 1913 | 165,700.00 | 61,010.00 | 226,710.00 |
| 1914 | 173,500.00 | 41,370.00 | 214,870.00 |
| 1915 | 75,250.00 | 48,330.00 | 123,580.00 |
| 1916 | 593,000.00 | 225,100.00 | 818,100.00 |
| 1917 | 209,650.00 | 326,200.00 | 535,850.00 |
| 1918 | 244,100.00 | 346,800.00 | 590,900.00 |
| 1919 | 376,050.00 | 1,397,600.00 | 1,773,650.00 |
| 1920 | 484,450.00 | 462,200.00 | 946,650.00 |
| 1921 | 77,850.00 | 152,740.00 | 230,590.00 |
| Total | 2,411,450.00 | 3,243,700.00 | 5,655,150.00 |

¹ Panama-Pacific International Exposition coins.

*organization; by calendar years since 1910*—Continued.

its organization, 1854, to Dec. 31, 1921.]

| | | Silver. | | | | |
|---|---|---|---|---|---|---|
| Dollars. | Trade dollars. | Half dollars. | Quarter dollars. | Twenty cents. | Dimes. | Half dimes. |
| $109,523,073 | $26,647,000 | $29,666,445.50 | $10,789,534.25 | $231,000 | $7,586,218.90 | $119,100 |
| .............. | .............. | 636,000.00 | 247,000.00 | .............. | 352,000.00 | .......... |
| .............. | .............. | 685,000.00 | 177,000.00 | .............. | 342,000.00 | .......... |
| .............. | .............. | 302,000.00 | 10,000.00 | .............. | 51,000.00 | .......... |
| .............. | .............. | 496,000.00 | 66,000.00 | .............. | 210,000.00 | .......... |
| .............. | .............. | ¹ 832,000.00 | 176,000.00 | .............. | 96,000.00 | .......... |
| .............. | .............. | 254,000.00 | ............ | .............. | 1,627,000.00 | .......... |
| .............. | .............. | 3,253,000.00 | 1,876,000.00 | .............. | 2,733,000.00 | .......... |
| .............. | .............. | 5,141,000.00 | 2,768,000.00 | .............. | 1,930,000.00 | .......... |
| .............. | .............. | 776,000.00 | 459,000.00 | .............. | 885,000.00 | .......... |
| .............. | .............. | 2,312,000.00 | 1,595,000.00 | .............. | 1,382,000.00 | .......... |
| 21,695,000 | .............. | 274,000.00 | | .............. | | |
| 131,218,073 | 26,647,000 | 44,627,445.50 | 18,163,534.25 | 231,000 | 17,194,218.90 | 119,100 |

| | Total coinage. | | Total value. |
|---|---|---|---|
| Gold. | Silver. | Minor. | |
| $1,649,412,407.00 | $184,562,371.65 | $97,780.00 | $1,834,072,558.65 |
| 23,105,000.00 | 1,235,000.00 | 40,260.00 | 24,380,260.00 |
| 4,960,000.00 | 1,204,000.00 | 56,210.00 | 6,220,210.00 |
| 3,380,000.00 | 363,000.00 | 226,710.00 | 3,969,710.00 |
| 33,355,000.00 | 772,000.00 | 214,870.00 | 34,341,870.00 |
| 12,961,026.50 | 1,104,000.00 | 123,580.00 | 14,188,606.50 |
| 18,505,000.00 | 1,881,000.00 | 818,100.00 | 21,204,100.00 |
| .............. | 7,862,000.00 | 535,850.00 | 8,397,850.00 |
| .............. | 9,839,000.00 | 590,900.00 | 10,429,900.00 |
| .............. | 2,120,000.00 | 1,773,650.00 | 3,893,650.00 |
| 12,425,000.00 | 5,289,000.00 | 946,650.00 | 18,660,650.00 |
| .............. | 21,969,000.00 | 230,590.00 | 22,199,590.00 |
| 1,758,103,433.50 | 238,200,371.65 | 5,655,150.00 | 2,001,958,955.15 |

¹ Includes $30,000 in Panama-Pacific International Exposition coins.

14263—FI 1922——39

*Coinage of each mint of the United States since its*

[Coinage of the mint at Philadelphia from

| Calendar year. | Gold. | | | | | |
|---|---|---|---|---|---|---|
| | Double eagles. | Eagles. | Half eagles. | Three dollars. | Quarter eagles. | Dollars. |
| 1793 to 1910 | $834,369, | $269,105,580 | $189,255,195 | $1,357,716 | $30,236,397.50 | [2]$18,533,438 |
| 1911 | 3,947, | 5,055,950 | 4,575,695 | ............ | 1,760,477.50 | ............ |
| 1912 | 2,996, | 4,050,830 | 3,950,720 | ............ | 1,540,492.50 | ............ |
| 1913 | 3,376, | 4,420,710 | 4,580,495 | ............ | 1,805,412.50 | ............ |
| 1914 | 1,906,900 | 1,510,500 | 1,235,625 | ............ | 600,292.50 | ............ |
| 1915 | 3,041,680 | 3,510,750 | 2,940,375 | ............ | 1,515,250.00 | [3] 20,026 |
| 1916 | ............ | ............ | ............ | ............ | ............ | [3] 10,014 |
| 1917 | ............ | ............ | ............ | ............ | ............ | ............ |
| 1918 | ............ | ............ | ............ | ............ | ............ | ............ |
| 1919 | ............ | ............ | ............ | ............ | ............ | ............ |
| 1920 | 4,565,000 | ............ | ............ | ............ | ............ | ............ |
| 1921 | 10,570,000 | ............ | ............ | ............ | ............ | ............ |
| Total | 864,772,540 | 287,654,320 | 206,538,105 | 1,357,716 | 37,458,322.50 | 18,563,478 |

| Calendar year. | Minor. | | |
|---|---|---|---|
| | Five cents. | Three cents. | Two cents. |
| 1793 to 1910 | $32,780,881.00 | $941,349.48 | $912,020.00 |
| 1911 | 1,977,968.60 | ............ | ............ |
| 1912 | 1,311,835.70 | ............ | ............ |
| 1913 | 3,042,611.95 | ............ | ............ |
| 1914 | 1,033,286.90 | ............ | ............ |
| 1915 | 1,049,363.50 | ............ | ............ |
| 1916 | 3,174,903.30 | ............ | ............ |
| 1917 | 2,571,201.45 | ............ | ............ |
| 1918 | 1,604,315.70 | ............ | ............ |
| 1919 | 3,043,400.00 | ............ | ............ |
| 1920 | 3,154,650.00 | ............ | ............ |
| 1921 | 533,150.00 | ............ | ............ |
| Total | 55,277,568.10 | 941,349.48 | 912,020.00 |

[1] Includes 50,000 Lafayette souvenir dollars.
[2] Includes 250,000 dollars Louisiana Purchase Exposition and 60,000 dollars Lewis and Clark Exposition.
[3] McKinley memorial dollars.

*organization; by calendar years since 1910*—Continued.

its organization, 1793, to December 31, 1921.]

| Silver. | | | | | | | |
| --- | --- | --- | --- | --- | --- | --- | --- |
| Trade dollars. | Dollars. | Half dollars. | Quarter dollars. | Twenty cents. | Dimes. | Half dimes. | Three cents. |
| $5,107,524 | $267,837,917 | $108,397,534.00 | $63,969,574.00 | $11,342 | $42,819,082.40 | $3,948,791.90 | $1,260,487.20 |
| ............ | ............ | 703,271.50 | 930,135.75 | ............ | 1,887,054.30 | ............ | ............ |
| ............ | ............ | 775,350.00 | 1,100,175.00 | ............ | 1,935,070.00 | ............ | ............ |
| ............ | ............ | 94,313.50 | 121,153.25 | ............ | 1,976,062.20 | ............ | ............ |
| ............ | ............ | 62,305.00 | 1,561,152.50 | ............ | 1,736,065.50 | ............ | ............ |
| ............ | ............ | 69,225.00 | 870,112.50 | ............ | 562,045.00 | ............ | ............ |
| ............ | ............ | 304,000.00 | 460,000.00 | ............ | 4,067,000.00 | ............ | ............ |
| ............ | ............ | 6,146,000.00 | 5,655,000.00 | ............ | 5,523,000.00 | ............ | ............ |
| ............ | ............ | 4 3,367,029.00 | 3,560,000.00 | ............ | 2,668,000.00 | ............ | ............ |
| ............ | ............ | 481,000.00 | 2,831,000.00 | ............ | 3,574,000.00 | ............ | ............ |
| ............ | ............ | 5 3,311,070.00 | 6,965,000.00 | ............ | 5,903,000.00 | ............ | ............ |
| ............ | 7 45,696,473 | 6 233,062.50 | 479,000.00 | ............ | 123,000.00 | ............ | ............ |
| 5,107,524 | 313,534,390 | 123,944,160.50 | 88,502,303.00 | 11,342 | 72,773,379.40 | 3,948,791.90 | 1,260,487.20 |

| Minor. | | Total coinage. | | | Total value. |
| --- | --- | --- | --- | --- | --- |
| Cents. | Half cents. | Gold. | Silver. | Minor. | |
| $22,940,625.80 | $39,926.11 | $1,342,858,226.50 | $493,352,252.50 | $57,614,802.39 | $1,893,825,281.39 |
| 1,011,777.87 | ............ | 15,339,122.50 | 3,520,461.55 | 2,989,746.47 | 21,849,330.52 |
| 681,530.60 | ............ | 12,538,522.50 | 3,810,595.00 | 1,993,365.30 | 18,342,483.80 |
| 765,323.52 | ............ | 14,183,377.50 | 2,191,528.95 | 3,807,935.47 | 20,182,841.92 |
| 752,384.32 | ............ | 5,252,817.50 | 3,359,523.00 | 1,785,671.22 | 10,398,011.72 |
| 290,921.20 | ............ | 11,007,375.00 | 1,501,382.50 | 1,340,284.70 | 13,849,042.20 |
| 1,318,336.77 | ............ | 20,025.00 | 4,831,000.00 | 4,493,240.07 | 9,344,266.07 |
| 1,964,297.85 | ............ | 10,014.00 | 17,324,000.00 | 4,535,499.30 | 21,869,513.30 |
| 2,881,046.34 | ............ | ............ | 9,595,029.00 | 4,485,362.04 | 14,080,391.04 |
| 3,920,210.00 | ............ | .4,565,000.00 | 6,886,000.00 | 6,963,610.00 | 13,849,610.00 |
| 3,101,650.00 | ............ | 10,570,000.00 | 16,179,070.00 | 6,256,300.00 | 27,000,370.00 |
| 391,570.00 | ............ | | 46,531,535.50 | 924,720.00 | 58,026,255.50 |
| 40,019,674.27 | 39,926.11 | 1,416,344,481.50 | 609,082,378.00 | 97,190,537.96 | 2,122,617,397.46 |

4 Includes $50,029 Illinois Centennial coins.
5 Includes $25,014 Maine Centennial and $100,056 Landing of Pilgrims coins.
6 Includes $25,014 Missouri Centennial, $35,022 Alabama Centennial, and $50,026.50 Landing of Pilgrims coins.
7 Includes 1,006,473 Peace dollars.

Combined coinage of the mints of the United States, by

| Calendar year. | Gold coinage. | | | | | | |
|---|---|---|---|---|---|---|---|
| | Fifty dollars. | Double eagles. | Eagles. | Half eagles. | Three dollars. | Quarter eagles. | Dollars. |
| 1793-95 | | | $27,950 | $43,535 | | | |
| 1796 | | | 60,800 | 16,995 | | $165.00 | |
| 1797 | | | 91,770 | 32,030 | | 4,390.00 | |
| 1798 | | | 79,740 | 124,335 | | 1,535.00 | |
| 1799 | | | 174,830 | 37,255 | | 1,200.00 | |
| 1800 | | | 259,650 | 58,110 | | | |
| 1801 | | | 292,540 | 130,030 | | | |
| 1802 | | | 150,900 | 265,880 | | 6,530.00 | |
| 1803 | | | 89,790 | 167,530 | | 1,057.50 | |
| 1804 | | | 97,950 | 152,375 | | 8,317.50 | |
| 1805 | | | | 165,915 | | 4,452.50 | |
| 1806 | | | | 320,465 | | 4,040.00 | |
| 1807 | | | | 420,465 | | 17,030.00 | |
| 1808 | | | | 277,890 | | 6,775.00 | |
| 1809 | | | | 169,375 | | | |
| 1810 | | | | 501,435 | | | |
| 1811 | | | | 497,905 | | | |
| 1812 | | | | 290,435 | | | |
| 1813 | | | | 477,140 | | | |
| 1814 | | | | 77,270 | | | |
| 1815 | | | | 3,175 | | | |
| 1816 | | | | | | | |
| 1817 | | | | | | | |
| 1818 | | | | 242,940 | | | |
| 1819 | | | | 258,615 | | | |
| 1820 | | | | 1,319,030 | | | |
| 1821 | | | | 173,205 | | 16,120.00 | |
| 1822 | | | | 88,980 | | | |
| 1823 | | | | 72,425 | | | |
| 1824 | | | | 86,700 | | 6,500.00 | |
| 1825 | | | | 145,300 | | 11,085.00 | |
| 1826 | | | | 90,345 | | 1,900.00 | |
| 1827 | | | | 124,565 | | 7,000.00 | |
| 1828 | | | | 140,145 | | | |
| 1829 | | | | 287,210 | | 8,507.50 | |
| 1830 | | | | 631,755 | | 11,350.00 | |
| 1831 | | | | 702,970 | | 11,300.00 | |
| 1832 | | | | 787,435 | | 11,000.00 | |
| 1833 | | | | 968,150 | | 10,400.00 | |
| 1834 | | | | 3,660,845 | | 293,425.00 | |
| 1835 | | | | 1,857,670 | | 328,505.00 | |
| 1836 | | | | 2,765,735 | | 1,369,965.00 | |
| 1837 | | | | 1,035,605 | | 112,700.00 | |
| 1838 | | | 72,000 | 1,600,420 | | 137,345.00 | |
| 1839 | | | 382,480 | 802,745 | | 191,622.50 | |
| 1840 | | | 473,380 | 1,048,530 | | 153,572.50 | |
| 1841 | | | 656,310 | 380,945 | | 54,602.50 | |
| 1842 | | | 1,089,070 | 655,330 | | 85,007.50 | |
| 1843 | | | 2,506,240 | 4,275,425 | | 1,327,132.50 | |
| 1844 | | | 1,250,610 | 4,087,715 | | 89,345.00 | |
| 1845 | | | 736,530 | 2,743,640 | | 276,277.50 | |
| 1846 | | | 1,018,750 | 2,736,155 | | 279,272.50 | |
| 1847 | | | 14,337,580 | 5,382,685 | | 482,060.00 | |
| 1848 | | | 1,813,340 | 1,863,560 | | 98,612.50 | |
| 1849 | | | 6,775,180 | 1,184,645 | | 111,147.50 | $936,789 |
| 1850 | | $26,225,220 | 3,489,510 | 860,160 | | 895,547.50 | 511,301 |
| 1851 | | 48,043,100 | 4,393,280 | 2,651,955 | | 3,867,337.50 | 3,658,820 |
| 1852 | | 44,860,520 | 2,811,060 | 3,689,635 | | 3,283,827.50 | 2,201,145 |
| 1853 | | 26,646,520 | 2,522,530 | 2,305,095 | | 3,519,615.00 | 4,384,149 |
| 1854 | | 18,052,340 | 2,305,760 | 1,513,235 | $491,214 | 1,896,397.50 | 1,657,016 |
| 1855 | | 25,046,820 | 1,487,010 | 1,257,090 | 171,465 | 600,700.00 | 824,883 |
| 1856 | | 30,437,560 | 1,429,900 | 1,806,665 | 181,530 | 1,213,117.50 | 1,788,996 |
| 1857 | | 28,797,500 | 481,060 | 1,232,970 | 104,673 | 796,235.00 | 801,602 |
| 1858 | | 21,873,480 | 343,210 | 439,770 | 6,399 | 144,082.50 | 131,472 |
| 1859 | | 13,782,840 | 253,930 | 361,235 | 46,914 | 142,220.00 | 193,431 |
| 1860 | | 22,594,400 | 278,830 | 352,365 | 42,465 | 164,360.00 | 51,234 |
| 1861 | | 74,989,060 | 1,287,330 | 3,332,130 | 18,216 | 3,241,295.00 | 527,499 |
| 1862 | | 18,926,120 | 234,950 | 69,825 | 17,355 | 300,882.50 | 1,326,865 |
| 1863 | | 22,187,200 | 112,480 | 97,360 | 15,117 | 27,075.00 | 6,250 |
| 1864 | | 19,958,900 | 60,800 | 40,540 | 8,040 | 7,185.00 | 5,950 |
| 1865 | | 27,874,000 | 207,050 | 144,535 | 3,495 | 62,302.50 | 3,725 |
| 1866 | | 30,820,500 | 237,800 | 253,200 | 12,090 | 105,175.00 | 7,180 |
| 1867 | | 23,436,300 | 121,400 | 179,600 | 7,950 | 78,125.00 | 5,250 |
| 1868 | | 18,722,000 | 241,550 | 288,625 | 14,625 | 94,062.50 | 10,525 |
| 1869 | | 17,238,100 | 82,850 | 163,925 | 7,575 | 84,612.50 | 5,925 |
| Carried forward | | 560,502,480 | 54,819,680 | 67,470,880 | 1,149,123 | 26,065,402.50 | 19,040,007 |

*denominations and calendar years, since their organization.*

| | | | Silver coinage. | | | | |
|---|---|---|---|---|---|---|---|
| Trade dollars. | Dollars. | Half dollars. | Quarter dollars. | Twenty cents. | Dimes. | Half dimes. | Three cents. |
| .......... | $204,791 | $161,572.00 | | | | $4,320.80 | |
| .......... | 72,920 | .......... | $1,473.50 | | $2,213.50 | 511.50 | |
| .......... | 7,776 | 1,959.00 | 63.00 | | 2,526.10 | 2,226.35 | |
| .......... | 327,536 | | | | 2,755.00 | | |
| .......... | 423,515 | | | | | | |
| .......... | 220,920 | | | | | | |
| .......... | 54,454 | 15,144.50 | | | 2,176.00 | 1,200.00 | |
| .......... | 41,650 | 14,945.00 | | | 3,464.00 | 1,695.50 | |
| .......... | 66,061 | 15,857.50 | | | 1,097.50 | 650.50 | |
| .......... | 19,570 | 78,259.50 | | | 3,304.00 | 1,892.50 | |
| .......... | 321 | 105,861.00 | 1,684.50 | | 826.50 | | |
| .......... | | 419,788.00 | 30,348.50 | | 12,078.00 | 780.00 | |
| .......... | | 525,788.00 | 51,531.00 | | | | |
| .......... | | 684,300.00 | 55,160.75 | | 16,500.00 | | |
| .......... | | 702,905.00 | | | | | |
| .......... | | 638,138.00 | | | 4,471.00 | | |
| .......... | | 601,822.00 | | | 635.50 | | |
| .......... | | 814,029.50 | | | 6,518.00 | | |
| .......... | | 620,951.50 | | | | | |
| .......... | | 519,537.50 | | 17,308.00 | 42,150.00 | | |
| .......... | | | | 5,000.75 | | | |
| .......... | | 23,575.00 | | | | | |
| .......... | | 607,783.50 | | | | | |
| .......... | | 980,161.00 | 90,293.50 | | | | |
| .......... | | 1,104,000.00 | 36,000.00 | | | | |
| .......... | | 375,561.00 | 31,861.00 | | 94,258.70 | | |
| .......... | | 652,898.50 | 54,212.75 | | 118,651.20 | | |
| .......... | | 779,786.50 | 16,020.00 | | 10,000.00 | | |
| .......... | | 847,100.00 | 4,450.00 | | 44,000.00 | | |
| .......... | | 1,752,477.00 | | | | | |
| .......... | | 1,471,583.00 | 42,000.00 | | 51,000.00 | | |
| .......... | | 2,002,090.00 | | | | | |
| .......... | | 2,746,700.00 | 1,000.00 | | 121,500.00 | | |
| .......... | | 1,537,600.00 | 25,500.00 | | 12,500.00 | | |
| .......... | | 1,856,078.00 | | | 77,000.00 | 61,500.00 | |
| .......... | | 2,382,400.00 | | | 51,000.00 | 62,000.00 | |
| .......... | | 2,936,830.00 | 99,500.00 | | 77,135.00 | 62,135.00 | |
| .......... | | 2,398,500.00 | 80,000.00 | | 52,250.00 | 48,250.00 | |
| .......... | | 2,603,000.00 | 39,000.00 | | 48,500.00 | 68,500.00 | |
| .......... | | 3,206,002.00 | 71,500.00 | | 63,500.00 | 74,000.00 | |
| .......... | | 2,676,003.00 | 488,000.00 | | 141,000.00 | 138,000.00 | |
| .......... | 1,000 | 3,273,100.00 | 118,000.00 | | 119,000.00 | 95,000.00 | |
| .......... | | 1,814,910.00 | 63,100.00 | | 104,200.00 | 113,800.00 | |
| .......... | | 1,773,000.00 | 208,000.00 | | 239,493.40 | 112,750.00 | |
| .......... | 300 | 1,748,768.00 | 122,786.50 | | 229,638.70 | 108,285.00 | |
| .......... | 61,005 | 1,145,054.00 | 153,331.75 | | 253,358.00 | 113,954.25 | |
| .......... | 173,000 | 355,500.00 | 143,000.00 | | 363,000.00 | 98,250.00 | |
| .......... | 184,618 | 1,484,882.00 | 214,250.00 | | 390,750.00 | 58,250.00 | |
| .......... | 165,100 | 3,056,000.00 | 403,400.00 | | 152,000.00 | 58,250.00 | |
| .......... | 20,000 | 1,885,500.00 | 290,300.00 | | 7,250.00 | 32,500.00 | |
| .......... | 24,500 | 1,341,500.00 | 230,500.00 | | 198,500.00 | 78,200.00 | |
| .......... | 169,600 | 2,257,000.00 | 127,500.00 | | 3,130.00 | 1,350.00 | |
| .......... | 140,750 | 1,870,000.00 | 275,500.00 | | 24,500.00 | 63,700.00 | |
| .......... | 15,000 | 1,890,000.00 | 36,500.00 | | 45,150.00 | 63,400.00 | |
| .......... | 62,600 | 1,781,000.00 | 85,000.00 | | 113,900.00 | 72,450.00 | |
| .......... | 47,500 | 1,341,500.00 | 150,700.00 | | 244,150.00 | 82,250.00 | |
| .......... | 1,300 | 301,375.00 | 62,000.00 | | 142,650.00 | 82,050.00 | $185,022.00 |
| .......... | 1,100 | 110,565.00 | 68,265.00 | | 196,550.00 | 63,025.00 | 559,905.00 |
| .......... | 46,110 | 2,430,354.00 | 4,146,555.00 | | 1,327,301.00 | 785,251.00 | 342,000.00 |
| .......... | 33,140 | 4,111,000.00 | 3,466,000.00 | | 624,000.00 | 365,000.00 | 20,130.00 |
| .......... | 26,000 | 2,288,725.00 | 857,350.00 | | 207,500.00 | 117,500.00 | 4,170.00 |
| .......... | 63,500 | 1,903,500.00 | 2,129,500.00 | | 703,000.00 | 299,000.00 | 43,740.00 |
| .......... | 94,000 | 1,482,000.00 | 2,726,500.00 | | 712,000.00 | 433,000.00 | 31,260.00 |
| .......... | | 5,998,000.00 | 2,002,250.00 | | 189,000.00 | 258,000.00 | 48,120.00 |
| .......... | 636,500 | 2,074,000.00 | 421,000.00 | | 97,000.00 | 45,000.00 | 10,950.00 |
| .......... | 733,930 | 1,032,950.00 | 312,350.00 | | 78,700.00 | 92,950.00 | 8,610.00 |
| .......... | 78,500 | 2,078,950.00 | 1,237,650.00 | | 209,650.00 | 164,050.00 | 14,940.00 |
| .......... | 12,090 | 802,175.00 | 249,887.50 | | 102,830.00 | 74,627.50 | 10,905.50 |
| .......... | 27,660 | 709,830.00 | 48,015.00 | | 17,196.00 | 5,923.00 | 643.80 |
| .......... | 31,170 | 518,785.00 | 28,517.50 | | 26,907.00 | 4,523.50 | 14.10 |
| .......... | 47,000 | 593,450.00 | 25,075.00 | | 15,550.00 | 6,675.00 | 255.00 |
| .......... | 49,625 | 899,512.50 | 11,381.25 | | 14,372.50 | 6,536.25 | 681.75 |
| .......... | 60,325 | 810,162.50 | 17,156.25 | | 14,662.50 | 6,431.25 | 138.75 |
| .......... | 182,700 | 769,100.00 | 31,500.00 | | 72,625.00 | 18,295.00 | 123.00 |
| .......... | 424,300 | 725,950.00 | 23,150.00 | | 70,660.00 | 21,930.00 | 153.00 |
| .......... | 5,053,440 | 95,509,284.50 | 21,727,878.00 | .......... | 8,376,184.10 | 4,529,818.90 | 1,281,762.90 |

*Combined coinage of the mints of the United States, by*

| Calendar year. | Gold coinage. | | | | | | |
|---|---|---|---|---|---|---|---|
| | Fifty dollars. | Double eagles. | Eagles. | Half eagles. | Three dollars. | Quarter eagles. | Dollars. |
| Brought forward.. | | $560,502,480 | $54,819,680 | $67,470,880 | $1,149,123 | $26,065,402.50 | $19,040,007 |
| 1870 | | 22,819,480 | 164,430 | 143,550 | 10,605 | 51,387.50 | 9,335 |
| 1871 | | 20,456,740 | 254,650 | 245,000 | 3,990 | 68,375.00 | 3,930 |
| 1872 | | 21,230,600 | 244,500 | 275,350 | 6,090 | 52,575.00 | 3,530 |
| 1873 | | 55,456,700 | 173,680 | 754,605 | 75 | 512,562.50 | 125,125 |
| 1874 | | 33,917,700 | 799,270 | 203,530 | 125,460 | 9,850.00 | 198,820 |
| 1875 | | 32,737,820 | 78,350 | 105,240 | 60 | 30,050.00 | 420 |
| 1876 | | 46,386,920 | 104,280 | 61,820 | 135 | 23,052.50 | 3,245 |
| 1877 | | 43,504,700 | 211,490 | 182,660 | 4,464 | 92,630.00 | 3,920 |
| 1878 | | 45,916,500 | 1,031,440 | 1,427,470 | 246,972 | 1,160,650.00 | 3,020 |
| 1879 | | 28,889,260 | 6,120,320 | 3,727,155 | 9,090 | 331,225.00 | 3,330 |
| 1880 | | 17,749,120 | 21,715,160 | 22,831,765 | 3,108 | 7,490.00 | 1,636 |
| 1881 | | 14,585,200 | 48,796,250 | 33,458,430 | 1,650 | 1,700.00 | 7,660 |
| 1882 | | 23,295,400 | 24,740,640 | 17,831,885 | 4,620 | 10,100.00 | 5,040 |
| 1883 | | 24,980,040 | 2,595,400 | 1,647,990 | 2,820 | 4,900.00 | 10,840 |
| 1884 | | 19,914,200 | 2,110,800 | 1,922,250 | 3,318 | 4,982.50 | 6,206 |
| 1885 | | 13,875,560 | 4,815,270 | 9,065,030 | 2,730 | 2,217.50 | 12,205 |
| 1886 | | 22,120 | 10,621,600 | 18,282,160 | 3,426 | 10,220.00 | 6,016 |
| 1887 | | 5,662,420 | 8,706,800 | 9,560,435 | 18,480 | 15,705.00 | 8,543 |
| 1888 | | 21,717,320 | 8,030,310 | 1,560,980 | 15,873 | 40,245.00 | 16,080 |
| 1889 | | 16,995,120 | 4,298,850 | 37,825 | 7,287 | 44,120.00 | 30,729 |
| 1890 | | 19,399,080 | 755,430 | 290,640 | | 22,032.50 | |
| 1891 | | 25,891,340 | 1,956,000 | 1,347,065 | | 27,600.00 | |
| 1892 | | 19,238,760 | 9,817,400 | 5,724,700 | | 6,362.50 | |
| 1893 | | 27,178,320 | 20,132,450 | 9,610,985 | | 75,265.00 | |
| 1894 | | 48,350,800 | 26,032,780 | 5,152,275 | | 10,305.00 | |
| 1895 | | 45,163,120 | 7,148,260 | 7,289,680 | | 15,297.50 | |
| 1896 | | 43,931,760 | 2,000,980 | 1,072,315 | | 48,005.00 | |
| 1897 | | 57,070,220 | 12,774,090 | 6,109,415 | | 74,760.00 | |
| 1898 | | 54,912,900 | 12,857,970 | 10,154,475 | | 60,412.50 | |
| 1899 | | 73,593,680 | 21,403,520 | 16,278,645 | | 68,375.00 | |
| 1900 | | 86,681,680 | 3,749,600 | 8,673,650 | | 168,012.50 | |
| 1901 | | 34,150,520 | 46,036,160 | 21,320,200 | | 228,307.50 | |
| 1902 | | 35,697,580 | 5,520,130 | 5,557,810 | | 334,332.50 | [5] $75,000 |
| 1903 | | 24,828,560 | 7,766,970 | 10,410,120 | | 503,142.50 | [5] 175,000 |
| 1904 | | 227,819,440 | 2,709,880 | 2,445,680 | | 402,400.00 | [6] 25,000 |
| 1905 | | 37,440,220 | 5,703,280 | 5,915,040 | | 544,860.00 | [6] 35,000 |
| 1906 | | 55,113,800 | 16,903,920 | 6,334,100 | | 441,225.00 | |
| 1907 | | 96,656,620 | 25,838,790 | 7,570,960 | | 841,120.00 | |
| 1908 | | 109,263,200 | 14,813,360 | 6,149,430 | | 1,412,642.50 | |
| 1909 | | 59,774,140 | 5,487,530 | 21,910,490 | | 1,104,747.50 | |
| 1910 | | 60,783,340 | 34,863,440 | 7,840,250 | | 1,231,705.00 | |
| 1911 | | 36,392,000 | 5,866,950 | 12,018,195 | | 1,899,677.50 | |
| 1912 | | 2,996,480 | 7,050,830 | 5,910,720 | | 1,540,492.50 | |
| 1913 | | 11,926,760 | 5,080,710 | 6,620,495 | | 1,805,412.50 | |
| 1914 | | 40,926,400 | 7,025,500 | 3,785,625 | | 1,720,292.50 | |
| 1915 | [7] $150,950 | 14,391,000 | 4,100,750 | 3,760,375 | | [8] 1,540,292.50 | [7] 25,034 |
| 1916 | | 15,920,000 | 1,385,000 | 1,200,000 | | | [10] 20,026 |
| 1917 | | | | | | | [10] 10,014 |
| 1918 | | | | | | | |
| 1919 | | | | | | | |
| 1920 | | 15,725,000 | 1,265,000 | | | | |
| 1921 | | 10,570,000 | | | | | |
| Total.. | 150,950 | 2,462,437,120 | 517,979,850 | 391,249,345 | 1,619,376 | 44,666,517.50 | 19,864,411 |

[1] Includes $475,000 in Columbian Exposition coins.
[2] Includes $2,025,000 in Columbian Exposition coins.
[3] Includes $10,000 in Columbian Exposition coins.
[4] Includes 50,000 Lafayette souvenir dollars.
[5] Louisiana Purchase Exposition.
[6] Lewis and Clark Exposition.
[7] Panama-Pacific International Exposition coins.

*denominations and calendar years, since their organization*—Continued.

| | | Silver coinage. | | | | | |
| Trade dollars. | Dollars. | Half dollars. | Quarter dollars. | Twenty cents. | Dimes. | Half dimes. | Three cents. |
|---|---|---|---|---|---|---|---|
| ......... | $5,053,440 | $95,509,284.50 | $21,727,878.00 | ......... | $8,376,184.10 | $4,529,818.90 | $1,281,762.90 |
| ......... | 445,462 | 829,758.50 | 23,935.00 | ......... | 52,150.00 | 26,830.00 | 120.00 |
| ......... | 1,117,136 | 1,741,655.00 | 53,255.50 | ......... | 109,371.00 | 82,493.00 | 127.80 |
| ......... | 1,118,600 | 866,775.00 | 68,762.50 | ......... | 261,045.00 | 189,247.50 | 58.50 |
| $1,225,000 | 296,600 | 1,593,780.00 | 414,190.50 | ......... | 443,329.10 | 51,830.00 | 18.00 |
| 4,910,000 | ......... | 1,406,650.00 | 215,975.00 | ......... | 319,151.70 | ......... | ......... |
| 6,279,600 | ......... | 5,117,750.00 | 1,278,375.00 | $265,598 | 2,406,570.00 | | |
| 6,192,150 | ......... | 7,451,575.00 | 7,839,287.50 | 5,180 | 3,015,115.00 | | |
| 13,092,710 | ......... | 7,540,255.00 | 6,024,927.50 | 102 | 1,735,051.00 | | |
| 4,259,900 | 22,495,550 | 726,200.00 | 849,200.00 | 120 | 187,880.00 | | |
| 1,541 | 27,560,100 | 2,950.00 | 3,675.00 | ......... | 1,510.00 | | |
| 1,987 | 27,397,355 | 4,877.50 | 3,738.75 | ......... | 3,735.50 | | |
| 960 | 27,927,975 | 5,487.50 | 3,243.75 | ......... | 3,497.50 | | |
| 1,097 | 27,574,100 | 2,750.00 | 4,075.00 | ......... | 391,110.00 | | |
| 979 | 28,470,039 | 4,519.50 | 3,859.75 | ......... | 767,571.20 | | |
| ......... | 28,136,875 | 2,637.50 | 2,218.75 | ......... | 393,134.90 | | |
| ......... | 28,697,767 | 3,085.00 | 3,632.50 | ......... | 257,711.70 | | |
| ......... | 31,423,886 | 2,943.00 | 1,471.50 | ......... | 658,409.40 | | |
| ......... | 33,611,710 | 2,855.00 | 2,677.50 | ......... | 1,573,838.90 | | |
| ......... | 31,990,833 | 6,416.50 | 306,708.25 | ......... | 721,648.70 | | |
| ......... | 34,651,811 | 6,355.50 | 3,177.75 | ......... | 835,338.90 | | |
| ......... | 38,043,004 | 6,295.00 | 20,147.50 | ......... | 1,133,461.70 | | |
| ......... | 23,562,735 | 100,300.00 | 1,551,150.00 | ......... | 2,304,671.60 | | |
| ......... | 6,333,245 | [1] 1,652,136.50 | 2,960,337.50 | ......... | 1,695,365.50 | | |
| ......... | 1,455,792 | [2] 4,002,896.00 | [3] 2,583,831.75 | ......... | 759,219.30 | | |
| ......... | 3,093,972 | 3,667,831.00 | 2,233,448.25 | ......... | 205,099.60 | | |
| ......... | 862,880 | 2,354,652.00 | 2,255,390.25 | ......... | 225,088.00 | | |
| ......... | 19,876,762 | 1,507,855.00 | 1,386,700.25 | ......... | 318,581.80 | | |
| ......... | 12,651,731 | 2,023,315.50 | 2,524,440.00 | ......... | 1,287,810.80 | | |
| ......... | 14,426,735 | 3,094,642.50 | 3,497,331.75 | ......... | 2,015,324.20 | | |
| ......... | 15,132,846 | 4,474,628.50 | 3,994,211.50 | ......... | 2,409,833.90 | | |
| ......... | [4] 25,010,912 | 5,033,617.00 | 3,822,874.25 | ......... | 2,477,918.20 | | |
| ......... | 22,566,813 | 3,119,928.50 | 2,644,369.25 | ......... | 2,507,350.00 | | |
| ......... | 18,160,777 | 4,454,723.50 | 4,617,589.00 | ......... | 2,795,077.70 | | |
| ......... | 10,343,755 | 3,149,763.50 | 3,551,516.00 | ......... | 2,829,405.50 | | |
| ......... | 8,812,650 | 2,331,654.00 | 3,011,203.25 | ......... | 1,540,102.70 | | |
| ......... | ......... | 1,830,863.50 | 2,020,562.50 | ......... | 2,480,754.90 | | |
| ......... | ......... | 5,426,414.50 | 2,248,108.75 | ......... | 2,976,504.60 | | |
| ......... | ......... | 5,825,587.50 | 3,899,143.75 | ......... | 3,453,704.50 | | |
| ......... | ......... | 5,819,686.50 | 4,262,136.25 | ......... | 2,309,954.50 | | |
| ......... | ......... | 2,529,025.00 | 4,110,662.50 | ......... | 1,448,165.00 | | |
| ......... | ......... | 1,183,275.50 | 936,137.75 | ......... | 1,625,055.10 | | |
| ......... | ......... | 1,686,811.50 | 1,410,535.75 | ......... | 3,359,954.30 | | |
| ......... | ......... | 2,610,750.00 | 1,277,175.00 | ......... | 3,453,070.00 | | |
| ......... | ......... | 663,313.50 | 493,853.25 | ......... | 2,027,062.20 | | |
| ......... | ......... | 558,305.00 | 2,388,652.50 | ......... | 3,136,865.50 | | |
| ......... | ......... | [9] 1,486,425.00 | 1,969,612.50 | ......... | 658,045.00 | | |
| ......... | ......... | 1,065,200.00 | 2,095,200.00 | ......... | 5,720,400.00 | | |
| ......... | ......... | 10,751,700.00 | 9,464,400.00 | ......... | 9,196,200.00 | | |
| ......... | ......... | [11] 10,434,549.00 | 8,173,000.00 | ......... | 6,865,480.00 | | |
| ......... | ......... | 1,839,500.00 | 3,776,000.00 | ......... | 5,452,900.00 | | |
| ......... | ......... | [12] 6,398,570.00 | 9,456,600.00 | ......... | 9,202,100.00 | | |
| ......... | [13] 87,736,473 | [14] 611,062.50 | 479,000.00 | ......... | 231,000.00 | | |
| 35,965,924 | 666,090,321 | 224,523,817.50 | 137,949,585.25 | 271,000 | 110,613,879.70 | 4,880,219.40 | 1,282,087.20 |

[8] Includes $25,042.50 in Panama-Pacific International Exposition coins.
[9] Includes $30,000 in Panama-Pacific International Exposition coins.
[10] McKinley Memorial dollars.
[11] Includes $50,029 Illinois Centennial half dollars.
[12] Includes $25,014 Maine Centennial and $100,056 Landing of Pilgrims half dollars.
[13] Includes 1,006,473 "Peace" dollars.
[14] Includes 100,053 Landing of Pilgrims, 50,028 Missouri Centennial, and 70,044 Alabama Centennial half dollars.

*Combined coinage of the mints of the United States, by*

| Calendar year. | Minor coinage. | | |
|---|---|---|---|
| | Five cents. | Three cents. | Two cents. |
| 1793–1795 | | | |
| 1796 | | | |
| 1797 | | | |
| 1798 | | | |
| 1799 | | | |
| 1800 | | | |
| 1801 | | | |
| 1802 | | | |
| 1803 | | | |
| 1804 | | | |
| 1805 | | | |
| 1806 | | | |
| 1807 | | | |
| 1808 | | | |
| 1809 | | | |
| 1810 | | | |
| 1811 | | | |
| 1812 | | | |
| 1813 | | | |
| 1814 | | | |
| 1815 | | | |
| 1816 | | | |
| 1817 | | | |
| 1818 | | | |
| 1819 | | | |
| 1820 | | | |
| 1821 | | | |
| 1822 | | | |
| 1823 | | | |
| 1824 | | | |
| 1825 | | | |
| 1826 | | | |
| 1827 | | | |
| 1828 | | | |
| 1829 | | | |
| 1830 | | | |
| 1831 | | | |
| 1832 | | | |
| 1833 | | | |
| 1834 | | | |
| 1835 | | | |
| 1836 | | | |
| 1837 | | | |
| 1838 | | | |
| 1839 | | | |
| 1840 | | | |
| 1841 | | | |
| 1842 | | | |
| 1843 | | | |
| 1844 | | | |
| 1845 | | | |
| 1846 | | | |
| 1847 | | | |
| 1848 | | | |
| 1849 | | | |
| 1850 | | | |
| 1851 | | | |
| 1852 | | | |
| 1853 | | | |
| 1854 | | | |
| 1855 | | | |
| 1856 | | | |
| 1857 | | | |
| 1858 | | | |
| 1859 | | | |
| 1860 | | | |
| 1861 | | | |
| 1862 | | | |
| 1863 | | | |
| 1864 | | | $396, 950. 00 |
| 1865 | | $341, 460. 00 | 272, 800. 00 |
| 1866 | $737, 125. 00 | 144, 030. 00 | 63, 540. 00 |
| 1867 | 1, 545, 475. 00 | 117, 450. 00 | 58, 775. 00 |
| 1868 | 1, 440, 850. 00 | 97, 560. 00 | 56, 075. 00 |
| 1869 | 819, 750. 00 | 48, 120. 00 | 30, 930. 00 |
| Carried forward | 4, 543, 200. 00 | 748, 620. 00 | 879, 070. 00 |

*denominations and calendar years, since their organization—Continued.*

| Minor coinage. | | Total coinage. | | | Total value. |
|---|---|---|---|---|---|
| Cents. | Half cents. | Gold. | Silver. | Minor. | |
| $10,660.33 | $712.67 | $71,485.00 | $370,683.80 | $11,373.00 | $453,541.80 |
| 9,747.00 | 577.40 | 77,960.00 | 77,118.50 | 10,324.40 | 165,402.90 |
| 8,975.10 | 535.24 | 128,190.00 | 14,550.45 | 9,510.34 | 152,250.79 |
| 9,797.00 | ............ | 205,610.00 | 330,291.00 | 9,797.00 | 545,698.00 |
| 9,045.85 | 60.83 | 213,285.00 | 423,515.00 | 9,106.68 | 645,906.68 |
| 28,221.75 | 1,057.65 | 317,760.00 | 224,296.00 | 29,279.40 | 571,335.40 |
| 13,628.37 | ............ | 422,570.00 | 74,758.00 | 13,628.37 | 510,956.37 |
| 34,351.00 | 71.83 | 423,310.00 | 58,343.00 | 34,422.83 | 516,075.83 |
| 24,713.53 | 489.50 | 258,377.50 | 87,118.00 | 25,203.03 | 370,698.53 |
| 7,568.38 | 5,276.56 | 258,642.50 | 100,340.50 | 12,844.94 | 371,827.94 |
| 9,411.16 | 4,072.32 | 170,367.50 | 149,388.50 | 13,483.48 | 333,232.48 |
| 3,480.00 | 1,780.00 | 324,505.00 | 471,319.00 | 5,260.00 | 801,084.00 |
| 7,272.21 | 2,380.00 | 437,495.00 | 597,448.75 | 9,652.21 | 1,044,595.96 |
| 11,090.00 | 2,000.00 | 284,665.00 | 684,300.00 | 13,090.00 | 982,055.00 |
| 2,228.67 | 5,772.86 | 169,375.00 | 707,376.00 | 8,001.53 | 884,752.53 |
| 14,585.00 | 1,075.00 | 501,435.00 | 638,773.50 | 15,660.00 | 1,155,868.50 |
| 2,180.25 | 315.70 | 497,905.00 | 608,340.00 | 2,495.95 | 1,108,740.95 |
| 10,755.00 | ............ | 290,435.00 | 814,029.50 | 10,755.00 | 1,115,219.50 |
| 4,180.00 | ............ | 477,140.00 | 620,951.50 | 4,180.00 | 1,102,271.50 |
| 3,578.30 | ............ | 77,270.00 | 561,687.50 | 3,578.30 | 642,535.80 |
| ............ | ............ | 3,175.00 | 17,308.00 | ............ | 20,483.00 |
| 28,209.82 | ............ | ............ | 28,575.75 | 28,209.82 | 56,785.57 |
| 39,484.00 | ............ | ............ | 607,783.50 | 39,484.00 | 647,267.50 |
| 31,670.00 | ............ | 242,940.00 | 1,070,454.50 | 31,670.00 | 1,345,064.50 |
| 26,710.00 | ............ | 258,615.00 | 1,140,000.00 | 26,710.00 | 1,425,325.00 |
| 44,075.50 | ............ | 1,319,030.00 | 501,680.70 | 44,075.50 | 1,864,786.20 |
| 3,890.00 | ............ | 189,365.00 | 825,762.45 | 3,890.00 | 1,018,977.45 |
| 20,723.39 | ............ | 88,980.00 | 805,806.50 | 20,723.39 | 915,509.89 |
| ............ | ............ | 72,425.00 | 895,550.00 | ............ | 967,975.00 |
| 12,620.00 | ............ | 93,200.00 | 1,752,477.00 | 12,620.00 | 1,858,297.00 |
| 14,611.00 | 315.00 | 156,385.00 | 1,564,583.00 | 14,926.00 | 1,735,894.00 |
| 15,174.25 | 1,170.00 | 92,245.00 | 2,002,090.00 | 16,344.25 | 2,110,679.25 |
| 23,577.32 | ............ | 131,565.00 | 2,869,200.00 | 23,577.32 | 3,024,342.32 |
| 22,606.24 | 3,030.00 | 140,145.00 | 1,575,600.00 | 25,636.24 | 1,741,381.24 |
| 14,145.00 | 2,435.00 | 295,717.50 | 1,994,578.00 | 16,580.00 | 2,306,875.50 |
| 17,115.00 | ............ | 643,105.00 | 2,495,400.00 | 17,115.00 | 3,155,620.00 |
| 33,592.60 | 11.00 | 714,270.00 | 3,175,600.00 | 33,603.60 | 3,923,473.60 |
| 23,620.00 | ............ | 798,435.00 | 2,579,000.00 | 23,620.00 | 3,401,055.00 |
| 27,390.00 | 770.00 | 978,550.00 | 2,759,000.00 | 28,160.00 | 3,765,710.00 |
| 18,551.00 | 600.00 | 3,954,270.00 | 3,415,002.00 | 19,151.00 | 7,388,423.00 |
| 38,784.00 | 705.00 | 2,186,175.00 | 3,443,003.00 | 39,489.00 | 5,668,667.00 |
| 21,110.00 | 1,990.00 | 4,135,700.00 | 3,606,100.00 | 23,100.00 | 7,764,900.00 |
| 55,583.00 | ............ | 1,148,305.00 | 2,096,010.00 | 55,583.00 | 3,299,898.00 |
| 63,702.00 | ............ | 1,809,765.00 | 2,333,243.40 | 63,702.00 | 4,206,710.40 |
| 31,286.61 | ............ | 1,376,847.50 | 2,209,778.20 | 31,286.61 | 3,617,912.31 |
| 24,627.00 | ............ | 1,675,482.50 | 1,726,703.00 | 24,627.00 | 3,426,812.50 |
| 15,973.67 | ............ | 1,091,857.50 | 1,132,750.00 | 15,973.67 | 2,240,581.17 |
| 23,833.90 | ............ | 1,829,407.50 | 2,332,750.00 | 23,833.90 | 4,185,991.40 |
| 24,283.20 | ............ | 8,108,797.50 | 3,834,750.00 | 24,283.20 | 11,967,830.70 |
| 23,987.52 | ............ | 5,427,670.00 | 2,235,550.00 | 23,987.52 | 7,687,207.52 |
| 38,948.04 | ............ | 3,756,447.50 | 1,873,200.00 | 38,948.04 | 5,668,595.50 |
| 41,208.00 | ............ | 4,034,177.50 | 2,558,580.00 | 41,208.00 | 6,633,965.54 |
| 61,836.69 | ............ | 20,202,325.00 | 2,374,450.00 | 61,836.69 | 22,638,611.69 |
| 64,157.99 | ............ | 3,775,512.50 | 2,040,050.00 | 64,157.99 | 5,879,720.49 |
| 41,785.00 | 199.32 | 9,007,761.50 | 2,114,950.00 | 41,984.32 | 11,164,695.82 |
| 44,268.44 | 199.06 | 31,981,738.50 | 1,866,100.00 | 44,467.50 | 33,892,306.00 |
| 98,897.07 | 738.36 | 62,614,492.50 | 774,397.00 | 99,635.43 | 63,488,524.93 |
| 50,630.94 | ............ | 56,846,187.50 | 999,410.00 | 50,630.94 | 57,896,228.44 |
| 66,411.31 | 648.47 | 39,377,909.00 | 9,077,571.00 | 67,059.78 | 48,522,539.78 |
| 42,361.56 | 276.79 | 25,915,962.50 | 8,619,270.00 | 42,638.35 | 34,577,870.85 |
| 15,748.29 | 282.50 | 29,387,968.00 | 3,501,245.00 | 16,030.79 | 32,905,243.79 |
| 26,904.63 | 202.15 | 36,857,768.50 | 5,142,240.00 | 27,106.78 | 42,027,115.28 |
| 177,834.56 | 175.90 | 32,214,040.00 | 5,478,760.00 | 178,010.46 | 37,870,810.46 |
| 246,000.00 | ............ | 22,938,413.50 | 8,495,370.00 | 246,000.00 | 31,679,783.50 |
| 364,000.00 | ............ | 14,780,570.00 | 3,284,450.00 | 364,000.00 | 18,429,020.00 |
| 205,660.00 | ............ | 23,473,654.00 | 2,259,390.00 | 205,660.00 | 25,938,704.00 |
| 101,000.00 | ............ | 83,395,530.00 | 3,783,740.00 | 101,000.00 | 87,280,270.00 |
| 280,750.00 | ............ | 20,875,997.50 | 1,252,516.50 | 280,750.00 | 22,409,264.00 |
| 498,400.00 | ............ | 22,445,482.00 | 809,267.80 | 498,400.00 | 23,753,149.80 |
| 529,737.14 | ............ | 20,081,415.00 | 609,917.10 | 926,687.14 | 21,618,019.24 |
| 354,292.86 | ............ | 28,295,107.50 | 691,005.00 | 968,552.86 | 29,954,665.36 |
| 98,265.00 | ............ | 31,435,945.00 | 982,409.25 | 1,042,960.00 | 33,461,314.25 |
| 98,210.00 | ............ | 23,823,625.00 | 908,876.25 | 1,819,910.00 | 26,557,411.25 |
| 102,665.00 | ............ | 19,371,387.50 | 1,074,343.00 | 1,697,150.00 | 22,142,880.50 |
| 64,200.00 | ............ | 17,582,987.50 | 1,266,143.00 | 963,000.00 | 19,812,130.50 |
| 4,680,577.44 | 39,926.11 | 729,047,572.50 | 136,473,368.40 | 10,891,393.55 | 876,417,334.45 |

REPORT ON THE FINANCES.

Combined coinage of the mints of the United States, by

| Calendar year. | Minor coinage. | | |
|---|---|---|---|
| | Five cents. | Three cents. | Two cents. |
| Brought forward | $4,543,200.00 | $748,620.00 | $879,070.00 |
| 1870 | 240,300.00 | 40,050.00 | 17,225.00 |
| 1871 | 28,050.00 | 18,120.00 | 14,425.90 |
| 1872 | 301,800.00 | 25,860.00 | 1,300.00 |
| 1873 | 227,500.00 | 35,190.00 | |
| 1874 | 176,900.00 | 23,700.00 | |
| 1875 | 104,850.00 | 6,840.00 | |
| 1876 | 126,500.00 | 4,860.00 | |
| 1877 | | | |
| 1878 | 117.50 | 70.50 | |
| 1879 | 1,455.00 | 1,236.00 | |
| 1880 | 997.75 | 748.65 | |
| 1881 | 3,618.75 | 32,417.25 | |
| 1882 | 573,830.00 | 759.00 | |
| 1883 | 1,148,471.05 | 318.27 | |
| 1884 | 563,697.10 | 169.26 | |
| 1885 | 73,824.50 | 143.70 | |
| 1886 | 166,514.50 | 128.70 | |
| 1887 | 763,182.60 | 238.83 | |
| 1888 | 536,024.15 | 1,232.49 | |
| 1889 | 794,068.05 | 646.83 | |
| 1890 | 812,963.60 | | |
| 1891 | 811,717.50 | | |
| 1892 | 584,982.10 | | |
| 1893 | 668,509.75 | | |
| 1894 | 270,656.60 | | |
| 1895 | 498,994.20 | | |
| 1896 | 442,146.00 | | |
| 1897 | 1,021,436.75 | | |
| 1898 | 626,604.35 | | |
| 1899 | 1,301,451.55 | | |
| 1900 | 1,362,799.75 | | |
| 1901 | 1,324,010.65 | | |
| 1902 | 1,574,028.95 | | |
| 1903 | 1,400,336.25 | | |
| 1904 | 1,070,249.20 | | |
| 1905 | 1,491,363.80 | | |
| 1906 | 1,930,686.25 | | |
| 1907 | 1,960,740.00 | | |
| 1908 | 1,134,308.85 | | |
| 1909 | 579,526.30 | | |
| 1910 | 1,508,467.65 | | |
| 1911 | 1,977,968.60 | | |
| 1912 | 1,747,435.70 | | |
| 1913 | 3,682,961.95 | | |
| 1914 | 1,402,386.90 | | |
| 1915 | 1,503,088.50 | | |
| 1916 | 4,434,553.30 | | |
| 1917 | 3,276,391.45 | | |
| 1918 | 2,266,515.70 | | |
| 1919 | 3,819,750.00 | | |
| 1920 | 4,110,000.00 | | |
| 1921 | 611,000.00 | | |
| Total | 61,612,933.10 | 941,349.48 | 912,020.00 |

*denominations and calendar years, since their organization*—Continued.

| Minor coinage. | | Total coinage. | | | Total value. |
|---|---|---|---|---|---|
| Cents. | Half cents. | Gold. | Silver. | Minor. | |
| $4,680,577.44 | $39,926.11 | $729,047,572.50 | $136,478,368.40 | $10,891,393.55 | $876,417,334.45 |
| 52,750.00 | ............... | 23,198,787.50 | 1,378,255.50 | 350,325.00 | 24,927,368.00 |
| 39,295.00 | ............... | 21,032,685.00 | 3,104,038.30 | 99,890.00 | 24,236,613.30 |
| 40,420.00 | ............... | 21,812,645.00 | 2,504,488.50 | 369,380.00 | 24,686,513.50 |
| 116,765.00 | ............... | 57,022,747.50 | 4,024,747.60 | 379,455.00 | 61,426,950.10 |
| 141,875.00 | ............... | 35,254,630.00 | 6,851,776.70 | 342,475.00 | 42,448,881.70 |
| 135,280.00 | ............... | 32,951,940.00 | 15,347,893.00 | 246,970.00 | 48,546,803.00 |
| 79,440.00 | ............... | 46,579,452.50 | 24,503,307.50 | 210,800.00 | 71,293,560.00 |
| 8,525.00 | ............... | 43,990,864.00 | 28,393,045.50 | 8,525.00 | 72,401,434.50 |
| 57,998.50 | ............... | 49,786,052.00 | 28,518,850.00 | 58,186.50 | 78,363,088.50 |
| 162,312.00 | ............... | 39,080,080.00 | 27,569,776.00 | 165,003.00 | 66,814,859.00 |
| 389,649.55 | ............... | 62,308,279.00 | 27,411,693.75 | 391,395.95 | 90,111,368.70 |
| 392,115.75 | ............... | 96,850,890.00 | 27,940,163.75 | 428,151.75 | 125,219,205.50 |
| 385,811.00 | ............... | 65,887,685.00 | 27,973,132.00 | 960,400.00 | 94,821,217.00 |
| 455,981.09 | ............... | 29,241,990.00 | 29,246,968.45 | 1,604,770.41 | 60,093,728.86 |
| 232,617.42 | ............... | 23,991,756.50 | 28,534,866.15 | 796,483.78 | 53,323,106.43 |
| 117,653.84 | ............... | 27,773,012.50 | 28,962,176.20 | 191,622.04 | 56,926,810.74 |
| 176,542.90 | ............... | 28,945,542.00 | 32,086,709.90 | 343,186.10 | 61,375,438.00 |
| 452,264.83 | ............... | 23,972,383.00 | 35,191,081.40 | 1,215,686.26 | 60,379,150.66 |
| 374,944.14 | ............... | 31,380,808.00 | 33,025,606.45 | 912,200.78 | 65,318,615.23 |
| 488,693.61 | ............... | 21,413,931.00 | 35,496,683.15 | 1,283,408.49 | 58,194,022.64 |
| 571,828.54 | ............... | 20,467,182.50 | 39,202,908.20 | 1,384,792.14 | 61,054,882.84 |
| 470,723.50 | ............... | 29,222,005.00 | 27,518,856.60 | 1,312,441.00 | 58,053,302.60 |
| 376,498.32 | ............... | 34,787,222.50 | 12,641,078.00 | 961,480.42 | 48,389,780.92 |
| 466,421.95 | ............... | 56,997,020.00 | 8,801,744.80 | 1,134,931.70 | 66,933,696.50 |
| 167,521.32 | ............... | 79,546,160.00 | 9,200,350.85 | 438,177.92 | 89,184,688.77 |
| 383,436.36 | ............... | 59,616,357.50 | 5,698,010.25 | 882,430.56 | 66,196,798.31 |
| 390,572.93 | ............... | 47,053,060.00 | 23,089,899.05 | 832,718.93 | 70,975,677.98 |
| 504,663.30 | ............... | 76,028,485.00 | 18,487,297.30 | 1,526,100.05 | 96,041,882.35 |
| 498,230.79 | ............... | 77,985,757.50 | 23,034,033.45 | 1,124,835.14 | 102,144,626.09 |
| 536,000.31 | ............... | 111,344,220.00 | 26,061,519.90 | 1,837,451.86 | 139,243,191.76 |
| 668,337.64 | ............... | 99,272,942.50 | 36,345,321.45 | 2,031,137.39 | 137,649,401.34 |
| 796,111.43 | ............... | 101,735,187.50 | 30,838,460.75 | 2,120,122.08 | 134,693,770.33 |
| 873,767.22 | ............... | 47,184,852.50 | 30,028,167.20 | 2,447,796.17 | 79,660,815.87 |
| 850,944.93 | ............... | 43,683,792.50 | 19,874,440.00 | 2,251,281.18 | 65,809,513.68 |
| 613,280.15 | ............... | 233,402,400.00 | 15,695,609.95 | 1,683,529.35 | 250,781,539.30 |
| 807,191.63 | ............... | 49,638,400.00 | 6,332,180.90 | 2,298,555.43 | 58,269,136.33 |
| 960,222.55 | ............... | 78,793,045.00 | 10,651,027.85 | 2,890,908.80 | 92,334,981.65 |
| 1,801,386.18 | ............... | 131,907,490.00 | 13,178,435.75 | 3,042,126.18 | 148,128,051.93 |
| 334,429.87 | ............... | 131,638,632.50 | 12,391,777.25 | 1,468,738.72 | 145,499,148.47 |
| 1,176,862.63 | ............... | 88,776,907.50 | 8,087,852.50 | 1,756,388.93 | 98,621,148.93 |
| 1,528,462.18 | ............... | 104,723,735.00 | 3,744,468.35 | 3,036,929.83 | 111,505,133.18 |
| 1,178,757.87 | ............... | 56,176,822.50 | 6,457,301.55 | 3,156,726.47 | 65,790,850.52 |
| 829,950.60 | ............... | 17,498,522.50 | 7,340,995.00 | 2,577,386.30 | 27,416,903.80 |
| 984,373.52 | ............... | 25,433,377.50 | 3,184,228.95 | 4,667,335.47 | 33,284,941.92 |
| 805,684.32 | ............... | 53,457,817.50 | 6,083,823.00 | 2,208,071.22 | 61,749,711.72 |
| 559,751.20 | ............... | 23,968,401.50 | 4,114,082.50 | 2,062,839.70 | 30,145,323.70 |
| 1,902,996.77 | ............... | 18,525,026.00 | 8,880,800.00 | 6,337,556.07 | 33,743,376.07 |
| 2,841,697.85 | ............... | 10,014.00 | 29,412,300.00 | 6,118,089.30 | 35,540,403.30 |
| 3,706,146.34 | ............... | ............... | 25,473,029.00 | 5,972,662.04 | 31,445,691.04 |
| 5,889,350.00 | ............... | ............... | 11,068,400.00 | 9,709,100.00 | 20,777,500.00 |
| 4,056,650.00 | ............... | 16,990,000.00 | 25,057,270.00 | 8,166,650.00 | 50,213,920.00 |
| 544,310.00 | ............... | 10,570,000.00 | 89,057,535.50 | 1,155,310.00 | 100,782,845.50 |
| 46,338,074.27 | 39,926.11 | 3,437,967,569.50 | 1,181,576,834.05 | 109,844,302.96 | 4,729,388,706.51 |

## STOCK OF MONEY IN THE UNITED STATES JUNE 30, 1922.

On June 30, 1922, the stock of domestic coin in the United States was $1,515,774,608, as shown by the following table:

*Stock of domestic coin in the United States June 30, 1922.*

| Item. | Gold. | Silver. | Total. |
|---|---|---|---|
| Estimated stock of coin in United States June 30, 1921.. | $814,616,897 | $560,102,753 | $1,374,719,650 |
| Coinage executed, fiscal year 1922......................... | 53,016,000 | 92,548,566 | 145,564,566 |
| Net imports, United States coin, fiscal year 1922........ | 1,774,498 | 2,405,319 | 4,179,817 |
| Total........................................... | 869,407,395 | 655,056,638 | 1,524,464,033 |
| Less: | | | |
| United States coin withdrawn from monetary use, face value, fiscal year 1922...................... | 2,518,077 | 2,571,348 | 5,089,425 |
| United States coin used in industrial arts, estimated, fiscal year 1922................................. | 3,500,000 | 100,000 | 3,600,000 |
| Total........................................ | 6,018,077 | 2,671,348 | 8,689,425 |
| Estimated stock of coin in United States June 30, 1922... | 863,389,318 | 652,385,290 | 1,515,774,608 |

NOTE.—The number of standard silver dollars coined to June 30, 1922, was 681,704,083, which added to the Hawaiian dollar coinage, 500,000, plus the number imported from the Philippine Islands, 150,000, and the number returned in Government transports, 496,859, equals 682,850,942. Since July 1, 1898, the number of standard silver dollars exported in transports has been 2,495,000, the net export from November, 1919, to July, 1920, in movement due to the high price of silver, was 28,287,142, those melted to June 30, 1922, under the terms of the Pittman Act of April 23, 1918, totaled 270,232,722, those melted otherwise (mutilated, etc.), since 1883 numbered 205,345, and the number of Hawaiian dollars melted to June 30, 1922, was 455,329, a total disposition of 301,676,538, leaving in the United States on June 30, 1922, 381,174,404 standard silver dollars and 271,210,886 dollars in subsidiary silver coin.

*Bullion in mints and assay offices June 30, 1922.*

| Bullion. | Value. |
|---|---|
| Gold.................................................................. | $2,850,230,389 |
| Silver................................................................. | 44,334,062 |
| Total................................................................. | 2,894,564,451 |

*Basic metallic stock June 30, 1917, 1918, 1919, 1920, 1921, and 1922.*

| Coin and bullion. | June 30, 1917. | June 30, 1918. | June 30, 1919. | June 30, 1920. | June 30, 1921. | June 30, 1922. |
|---|---|---|---|---|---|---|
| Gold.............. | $3,018,964,392 | $3,075,339,748 | $3,112,320,547 | $2,707,866,274 | $3,294,909,763 | $3,784,651,712 |
| Silver............ | 772,908,391 | 745,747,094 | 568,329,597 | 548,938,429 | 619,725,982 | 652,385,290 |
| Total....... | 3,791,872,783 | 3,821,086,842 | 3,680,650,144 | 3,256,804,703 | 3,914,635,745 | 4,437,037,002 |

Location, ownership, and per capita circulation of monetary stock, June 30, 1922.

| Kind of money. | Stock of money in the United States.[1] | Money held in the Treasury. | | | | | Money outside of the Treasury. | | | |
|---|---|---|---|---|---|---|---|---|---|---|
| | | Total. | Amount held in trust against gold and silver certificates (and Treasury notes of 1890). | Reserve against United States Treasury notes (and notes of 1890). | Held for Federal reserve banks and agents. | All other money. | Total. | Held by Federal reserve banks and agents. | In circulation. | |
| | | | | | | | | | Amount. | Per capita.[5] |
| Gold coin and bullion | $3,794,651,712 | $3,157,202,556 | $695,000,469 | $152,979,026 | $2,108,886,911 | $200,336,150 | $627,449,156 | $211,611,603 | $415,937,553 | $3.79 |
| Gold certificates | ²(695,000,469) | | | | | | 695,000,469 | 521,658,270 | 173,342,199 | 1.58 |
| Standard silver dollars | 381,174,404 | 313,504,308 | 305,577,136 | | | 7,927,172 | 67,670,096 | 9,697,027 | 57,973,069 | .53 |
| Silver certificates | ³(304,066,593) | | | | | | 304,066,593 | 38,731,219 | 265,335,374 | 2.42 |
| Treasury notes of 1890 | ⁴1,510,543 | | | | | | 1,510,543 | 1,000 | 1,509,543 | .01 |
| Subsidiary silver | 271,210,836 | 17,747,502 | | | | 17,747,502 | 253,463,384 | 24,153,011 | 229,310,373 | 2.09 |
| United States Notes | 346,681,016 | 4,145,994 | | | | 4,145,964 | 342,535,052 | 50,192,056 | 292,342,996 | 2.66 |
| Federal reserve notes | 2,555,061,660 | 2,557,722 | | | | 2,557,722 | 2,552,503,938 | 413,788,985 | 2,138,714,933 | 19.49 |
| Federal reserve bank notes | 80,495,40t | 1,030,273 | | | | 1,030,273 | 79,465,127 | 7,597,186 | 71,857,941 | .66 |
| National Bank notes | 758,202,027 | 15,774,366 | | | | 15,774,366 | 742,427,661 | 14,746,625 | 727,681,036 | 6.63 |
| Total June 30, 1922 | 8,177,477,105 | 3,511,962,691 | 1,000,577,605 | 152,979,026 | 2,108,886,911 | 249,519,149 | 5,666,092,019 | 1,292,076,982 | 4,374,015,037 | 39.88 |
| Comparative totals: | | | | | | | | | | |
| June 30, 1921 | 8,096,033,684 | 2,918,696,736 | 919,643,386 | 152,979,026 | 1,537,856,895 | 308,217,429 | 6,096,980,334 | 1,257,368,483 | 4,839,611,851 | 44.78 |
| April 1, 1917 | 5,312,109,272 | 2,942,998,527 | 2,684,800,085 | 152,979,026 | | 105,219,416 | 5,053,910,830 | 953,320,126 | 4,100,590,704 | 39.54 |
| July 1, 1914 | 3,738,288,871 | 1,843,452,323 | 1,507,178,879 | 150,000,000 | | 196,273,444 | 3,402,015,427 | | 3,402,015,427 | 34.35 |
| January 1, 1879 | 1,007,084,483 | 212,420,402 | 21,602,640 | 100,000,000 | | 90,817,702 | 816,266,721 | | 816,266,721 | 16.92 |

[1] Does not include ... bullion ... than intrinsic ... Government ... include gold bullion ... and ... units are not ...

[2] These ... bullion dollars, resp...

[4] The ... mint of money held in trust ... of the ... Treasury to arrive at the ... they in the United ... includes 189,719 of ... coin ... bank ... $47 deposited as a ...

NOTE.—Gold ... held in the ... in of ... bullion on all the ... and such discounted or ... ing the gold ... in gold or ...

... secured dollar for dollar by gold held in the ... for ... dollars, ... and a 5 per cent fund for their ... redemption. ... $14,251,012 deposited for the redemption of National ... bank ... saving deposits.

... July 1, 1917, 103,716,000; July 1, 1914, 99,027,000; Jan. 1, 1879, 48,231,000 ... and silver dollars ... are obligations of the United ... of May 6, 192,109,743,000; June 6, ... $152,979,025.63 held in the ... $178,459,108 of gold ... $5,415,374 of ...

*Estimated monetary stock of gold and silver in the United States and the amount per capita at the close of each fiscal year since 1873.*

| Fiscal year ended June 30— | Population. | Total stock of coin and bullion. | | Per capita. | | |
|---|---|---|---|---|---|---|
| | | Gold. | Silver. | Gold. | Silver. | Total metallic. |
| 1873 | 41,677,000 | $135,000,000 | $6,149,305 | $3.23 | $0.15 | $3.38 |
| 1874 | 42,796,000 | 147,379,493 | 10,355,478 | 3.44 | .24 | 3.68 |
| 1875 | 43,951,000 | 121,134,906 | 19,367,995 | 2.75 | .44 | 3.19 |
| 1876 | 45,137,000 | 130,056,907 | 36,415,992 | 2.88 | .81 | 3.69 |
| 1877 | 46,353,000 | 167,501,472 | 56,464,427 | 3.61 | 1.21 | 4.82 |
| 1878 | 47,598,000 | 213,199,977 | 88,047,907 | 4.47 | 1.85 | 6.32 |
| 1879 | 48,866,000 | 245,741,837 | 117,526,341 | 5.02 | 2.40 | 7.42 |
| 1880 | 50,155,783 | 351,841,206 | 148,522,678 | 7.01 | 2.96 | 9.97 |
| 1881 | 51,316,000 | 478,484,538 | 175,384,144 | 9.32 | 3.41 | 12.73 |
| 1882 | 52,495,000 | 506,757,715 | 203,217,124 | 9.65 | 3.87 | 13.52 |
| 1883 | 53,693,000 | 542,732,063 | 233,007,985 | 10.10 | 4.34 | 14.44 |
| 1884 | 54,911,000 | 545,500,797 | 255,568,142 | 9.93 | 4.65 | 14.58 |
| 1885 | 56,148,000 | 588,697,036 | 283,478,788 | 10.48 | 5.05 | 15.53 |
| 1886 | 57,404,000 | 590,774,461 | 312,252,844 | 10.29 | 5.44 | 15.73 |
| 1887 | 58,680,000 | 654,520,335 | 352,993,566 | 11.15 | 6.00 | 17.15 |
| 1888 | 59,974,000 | 705,818,855 | 386,611,108 | 11.76 | 6.44 | 18.20 |
| 1889 | 61,289,000 | 680,063,505 | 420,548,929 | 11.09 | 6.86 | 17.95 |
| 1890 | 62,622,250 | 695,563,029 | 463,211,919 | 11.10 | 7.39 | 18.49 |
| 1891 | 63,975,000 | 646,582,852 | 522,277,740 | 10.10 | 8.16 | 18.26 |
| 1892 | 65,520,000 | 664,275,335 | 570,313,544 | 10.15 | 8.70 | 18.85 |
| 1893 | 66,946,000 | 597,697,685 | 615,861,484 | 8.93 | 9.20 | 18.13 |
| 1894 | 68,397,000 | 627,293,201 | 624,347,757 | 9.18 | 9.13 | 18.31 |
| 1895 | 69,878,000 | 636,229,825 | 625,854,949 | 9.10 | 8.97 | 18.07 |
| 1896 | 71,390,000 | 599,597,964 | 628,728,071 | 8.40 | 8.81 | 17.21 |
| 1897 | 72,937,000 | 696,270,542 | 634,509,781 | 9.55 | 8.70 | 18.25 |
| 1898 | 74,522,000 | 861,514,780 | 637,672,743 | 11.56 | 8.56 | 20.12 |
| 1899 | 76,148,000 | 962,865,505 | 639,286,743 | 12.64 | 8.40 | 21.04 |
| 1900 | 76,891,000 | 1,034,439,264 | 647,371,030 | 13.45 | 8.42 | 21.87 |
| 1901 | 77,754,000 | 1,124,652,818 | 661,205,403 | 14.47 | 8.50 | 22.97 |
| 1902 | 79,117,000 | 1,192,395,607 | 670,540,105 | 15.07 | 8.48 | 23.55 |
| 1903 | 80,847,000 | 1,249,552,756 | 677,448,933 | 15.45 | 8.38 | 23.83 |
| 1904 | 81,867,000 | 1,327,672,672 | 682,383,277 | 16.22 | 8.33 | 24.55 |
| 1905 | 83,259,000 | 1,357,881,186 | 686,401,168 | 16.31 | 8.24 | 24.55 |
| 1906 | 84,662,000 | 1,472,995,209 | 687,958,920 | 17.40 | 8.12 | 25.52 |
| 1907 | 86,074,000 | 1,466,056,632 | 705,330,224 | 17.03 | 8.20 | 25.23 |
| 1908 | 87,496,000 | 1,615,140,575 | 723,594,595 | 18.46 | 8.27 | 26.73 |
| 1909 | 88,926,000 | 1,640,567,131 | 733,250,073 | 18.45 | 8.25 | 26.70 |
| 1910 | 90,363,000 | 1,635,424,513 | 727,078,304 | 18.10 | 8.05 | 26.15 |
| 1911 | 93,983,000 | 1,753,134,114 | 732,002,448 | 18.65 | 7.79 | 26.44 |
| 1912 | 95,656,000 | 1,812,856,241 | 741,184,095 | 18.95 | 7.75 | 26.70 |
| 1913 | 97,337,000 | 1,866,619,157 | 745,585,964 | 19.17 | 7.66 | 26.83 |
| 1914 | 99,027,000 | 1,871,611,723 | 753,563,709 | 18.90 | 7.61 | 26.51 |
| 1915 | 100,725,000 | 1,973,330,201 | 758,039,421 | 19.59 | 7.53 | 27.12 |
| 1916 | 102,431,000 | 2,450,516,328 | 763,218,469 | 23.92 | 7.45 | 31.37 |
| 1917 | 104,145,000 | 3,018,964,392 | 772,908,391 | 28.99 | 7.42 | 36.41 |
| 1918 | 105,869,000 | 3,075,339,748 | 745,747,094 | 29.05 | 7.04 | 36.09 |
| 1919 | 107,600,000 | 3,112,320,547 | 568,329,597 | 28.92 | 5.28 | 34.20 |
| 1920 | 105,768,000 | 2,707,866,274 | 548,938,429 | 25.60 | 5.19 | 30.79 |
| 1921 | 108,087,000 | 3,294,909,763 | 619,725,982 | 30.48 | 5.73 | 36.21 |
| 1922 | 109,743,000 | 3,784,651,712 | 696,719,352 | 34.49 | 6.35 | 40.84 |

## STOCK OF MONEY IN THE UNITED STATES DECEMBER 31, 1921.

On December 31, 1921, the stock of domestic coin in the United States was $1,463,804,268, as shown by the following table:

*Stock of domestic coin in the United States December 31, 1921.*

| Item. | Gold. | Silver. | Total. |
|---|---|---|---|
| Estimated stock of coin Dec. 31, 1920........................... | $800,817,098 | $548,558,259 | $1,349,375,357 |
| Coinage executed, calendar year 1921............................ | 10,570,000 | 89,057,535 | 99,627,535 |
| Net import United States coin, calendar year 1921............ | 20,045,333 | 2,027,947 | 22,073,280 |
| Total................................................. | 831,432,431 | 639,643,741 | 1,471,076,172 |
| Less— | | | |
| United States coin withdrawn from monetary use, face value, calendar year 1921............................. | 2,213,064 | 1,458,840 | 3,671,904 |
| United States coin used in industrial arts, estimated, calendar year 1921.................................. | 3,500,000 | 100,000 | 3,600,000 |
| Total................................................. | 5,713,064 | 1,558,840 | 7,271,904 |
| Estimated stock of coin in the United States Dec. 31, 1921.. | 825,719,367 | 638,084,901 | 1,463,804,268 |

NOTE.—The number of standard silver dollars coined to Dec. 31, 1921, was 658,009,083, which added to the Hawaiian dollar coinage, 500,000, plus the number imported from the Philippine Islands, 150,000, and the number returned in Government transports, 496,859, equals 659,155,942. Since July 1, 1898, the number of standard silver dollars exported in transports has been 2,495,000, the net export from November, 1919, to July, 1920, in the movement due to the high price of silver, was 28,287,142, the number melted to Dec. 31, 1921, under the terms of the Pittman Act of Apr. 23, 1918, was 270,232,722, the number otherwise melted (mutilated, etc.) since 1883 was 205,009, and the number of Hawaiian dollars melted to Dec. 31, 1921, was 455,329, a total disposition of 301,675,202, leaving in the United States on Dec. 31, 1921, 357,480,740 standard silver dollars and 280,604,161 dollars in subsidiary silver coin.

*Location of moneys of the United States December 31, 1921.*

| Money. | In Treasury. | Outside Treasury. | Total. |
|---|---|---|---|
| Metallic: | | | |
| Gold bullion........................................... | [1] $2,764,133,716 | [2] $70,715,791 | $2,834,849,507 |
| Silver bullion.......................................... | 36,889,732 | .................. | 36,889,732 |
| Gold coin.............................................. | 264,752,204 | 560,967,163 | 825,719,367 |
| Silver dollars.......................................... | 289,279,984 | 68,200,756 | 357,480,740 |
| Subsidiary silver coin............................... | 12,232,901 | 268,371,260 | 280,604,161 |
| Total metallic.................................. | 3,367,288,537 | 968,254,970 | 4,335,543,507 |
| Paper: | | | |
| United States notes (old issue)...................... | 4,836,594 | 341,844,422 | [3] 346,681,016 |
| Treasury notes (act July 14, 1890).................. | .................. | 1,545,524 | 1,545,524 |
| National bank notes [4]............................... | 19,604,084 | 847,234,240 | 866,838,324 |
| Federal reserve notes.............................. | 2,493,721 | 2,443,789,739 | 2,446,283,460 |
| Total paper.................................... | 26,934,399 | 3,634,413,925 | 3,661,348,324 |
| Gold certificates....................................... | .................. | 709,464,024 | .................. |
| Silver certificates...................................... | .................. | 279,462,163 | .................. |
| Total certificates............................... | .................. | 988,926,187 | .................. |
| Total stock of money................................ | .................. | .................. | 7,996,891,831 |

[1] In mints and assay offices.
[2] In Federal reserve banks.
[3] There is reserved $152,979,026 in gold against United States notes and Treasury notes of 1890 outstanding. Treasury notes are also secured by silver dollars in the Treasury.
[4] Includes Federal reserve bank notes.

*Monetary stock of gold in the United States since 1873.*

| End of year. | Coin in Treasury. | Bullion in Treasury.[1] | Coin in national banks, comptroller's report.[1] | Coin in circulation. | Total stock of gold. |
|---|---|---|---|---|---|
| Fiscal year June 30: | | | | | |
| 1873 | $55,518,567 | $15,669,981 | $3,818,086 | $30,000,000 | $105,006,634 |
| 1874 | 60,972,107 | 9,539,738 | 5,536,086 | 39,607,488 | 115,655,419 |
| 1875 | 45,382,484 | 8,258,706 | 3,710,682 | 31,695,660 | 89,047,532 |
| 1876 | 41,912,168 | 9,589,324 | 3,225,707 | 44,533,218 | 99,260,417 |
| 1877 | 76,661,703 | 10,962,169 | 5,306,263 | 39,058,592 | 131,988,727 |
| 1878 | 122,136,831 | 6,323,372 | 8,191,952 | 39,767,529 | 176,419,684 |
| 1879 | 129,920,099 | 5,316,376 | 21,530,846 | 53,601,228 | 210,368,549 |
| Calendar year: | | | | | |
| 1879 [2] | 95,790,430 | 61,999,892 | 98,104,792 | 46,843,424 | 302,738,538 |
| 1880 | 61,481,245 | 93,789,622 | 92,184,943 | 150,085,854 | 397,541,664 |
| 1881 | 84,639,865 | 88,726,016 | 101,115,387 | 210,775,833 | 485,257,101 |
| 1882 | 119,523,136 | 51,501,110 | 75,326,033 | 234,205,711 | 480,555,990 |
| 1883 | 152,608,393 | 65,667,190 | 73,447,061 | 228,296,821 | 526,019,465 |
| 1884 | 171,553,205 | 63,162,982 | 76,170,911 | 215,813,129 | 526,700,227 |
| 1885 | 75,434,379 | 72,938,221 | 96,741,747 | 313,346,322 | 558,460,669 |
| 1886 | 187,196,596 | 81,431,262 | 97,781,405 | 223,199,865 | 589,609,128 |
| 1887 | 182,618,963 | 123,145,136 | 99,162,377 | 245,145,579 | 650,072,055 |
| 1888 | 227,854,212 | 97,456,289 | 78,224,188 | 246,218,193 | 649,752,882 |
| 1889 | 246,401,951 | 67,265,944 | 84,416,468 | 235,434,571 | 633,518,934 |
| 1890 | 226,220,604 | 67,645,934 | 80,361,784 | 274,055,833 | 648,284,155 |
| 1891 | 196,634,061 | 83,575,643 | 91,889,590 | 253,765,288 | 625,864,582 |
| 1892 | 156,662,452 | 81,826,630 | 100,991,328 | 242,621,832 | 582,102,242 |
| 1893 | 73,624,284 | 84,631,966 | 151,233,989 | 281,940,012 | 591,430,251 |
| 1894 | 91,781,176 | 47,106,966 | 151,117,047 | 248,787,867 | 538,793,056 |
| 1895 | 83,186,960 | 29,443,955 | 147,308,401 | 242,644,697 | 502,584,013 |
| 1896 | 121,745,884 | 54,648,743 | 161,828,050 | 251,010,816 | 589,233,493 |
| 1897 | 152,488,113 | 45,279,029 | 187,608,644 | 252,419,033 | 637,794,819 |
| 1898 | 141,070,022 | 140,049,456 | 263,888,745 | 286,891,578 | 831,899,801 |
| 1899 | 257,306,366 | 143,078,146 | 203,700,570 | 293,387,672 | 897,472,754 |
| 1900 | 328,453,044 | 153,094,872 | 199,350,080 | 307,870,474 | 988,768,470 |
| 1901 | 417,343,064 | 123,735,775 | 190,172,340 | 318,388,468 | 1,049,639,647 |
| 1902 | 458,159,776 | 159,971,402 | 178,147,097 | 324,252,498 | 1,120,530,773 |
| 1903 | 478,970,232 | 209,436,811 | 170,547,258 | 332,730,989 | 1,191,685,290 |
| 1904 | 647,261,358 | 49,187,017 | 195,111,219 | 325,261,922 | 1,216,621,516 |
| 1905 | 662,153,801 | 101,183,778 | 196,680,998 | 327,549,686 | 1,287,568,263 |
| 1906 | 737,677,337 | 156,542,687 | 188,096,624 | 376,006,767 | 1,458,323,415 |
| 1907 | 788,467,689 | 162,937,136 | 203,289,045 | 457,995,462 | 1,612,689,332 |
| 1908 | 924,316,981 | 111,041,339 | 209,185,761 | 411,605,432 | 1,656,149,513 |
| 1909 | 934,803,233 | 97,347,289 | 213,990,955 | 392,507,842 | 1,638,649,319 |
| 1910 | 982,586,379 | 120,726,077 | 227,977,678 | 378,745,080 | 1,710,035,214 |
| 1911 | 1,001,413,292 | 153,088,870 | 235,184,404 | 379,941,280 | 1,799,627,846 |
| 1912 | 995,209,422 | 258,857,946 | 240,452,237 | 385,717,711 | 1,880,237,316 |
| 1913 | 987,678,101 | 303,585,254 | 232,798,904 | 380,631,886 | 1,904,694,145 |
| 1914 | 880,954,878 | 304,354,958 | 168,660,282 | 451,128,764 | 1,805,098,882 |
| 1915 | 1,042,818,106 | 643,424,187 | 118,415,762 | 494,796,127 | 2,299,454,182 |
| 1916 | 906,491,238 | 1,294,802,847 | 120,396,000 | 545,275,456 | 2,866,965,541 |
| 1917 | 697,301,630 | 1,688,745,498 | 61,560,000 | 612,913,452 | 3,042,520,580 |
| 1918 | 775,502,510 | 1,855,416,512 | 64,963,144 | 469,344,056 | 3,165,226,222 |
| 1919 | 547,210,009 | 1,810,807,589 | 69,030,951 | 281,813,828 | 2,708,862,377 |
| 1920 | 237,030,307 | 2,141,230,971 | 90,465,187 | 473,321,604 | 2,942,048,019 |
| 1921 | 264,752,204 | 2,842,042,979 | 141,259,718 | 412,513,973 | 3,660,568,874 |

[1] Includes Federal reserve bank holdings for 1918 and following years.
[2] Six months ending Dec. 31, 1879.

*Exports of refined silver bullion from the United States since 1900.*

| Calendar year. | United Kingdom. | Asia. | All other. | Total. |
|---|---|---|---|---|
| 1900 | $51,870,790 | $5,629,436 | $813,929 | $58,314,155 |
| 1901 | 44,732,679 | 4,507,540 | 2,022,053 | 51,262,272 |
| 1902 | 33,775,693 | 7,465,728 | 3,908,906 | 45,150,327 |
| 1903 | 32,809,430 | 1,654,052 | 4,202,030 | 38,665,512 |
| 1904 | 39,314,272 | 4,627,162 | 1,826,785 | 45,768,219 |
| 1905 | 42,680,190 | 6,244,301 | 1,698,489 | 50,62,080 |
| 1906 | 44,034,990 | 4,210,717 | 1,325,087 | 49,570,794 |
| 1907 | 42,692,769 | 3,003,325 | 5,798,577 | 51,494,671 |
| 1908 | 40,030,888 | 5,811,684 | 5,206,406 | 51,048,978 |
| 1909 | 44,093,497 | 7,963,217 | 4,046,639 | 56,103,353 |
| 1910 | 45,270,823 | 7,495,997 | 3,434,677 | 56,201,497 |
| 1911 | 51,143,245 | 9,370,356 | 4,019,825 | 64,533,426 |
| 1912 | 51,388,352 | 11,413,021 | 7,959,870 | 70,761,243 |
| 1913 | 41,299,073 | 12,696,925 | 7,813,558 | 61,809,556 |
| 1914 | 35,421,165 | 6,142,090 | 7,626,125 | 49,189,380 |
| 1915 | 38,564,526 | 8,361,692 | 2,971,471 | 49,897,689 |
| 1916 | 52,210,988 | 12,019,899 | 2,742,312 | 66,973,199 |
| 1917 | 27,090,143 | 50,023,842 | 2,656,203 | 79,770,188 |
| 1918 | 31,322,709 | 202,503,389 | 8,601,568 | 242,427,666 |
| 1919 | 14,440,703 | 181,671,933 | 14,066,084 | 210,178,720 |
| 1920 | 4,902,478 | 83,438,040 | 5,970,531 | 94,311,049 |
| 1921 | 4,746,869 | 15,754,664 | 2,209,990 | 22,711,523 |
| Total | 813,836,272 | 652,009,010 | 100,921,115 | 1,566,766,397 |

*Highest, lowest, and average price of silver in New York, per fine ounce, since 1874, being the asked price to and including 1917, thereafter taken at the mean of the bid and asked prices.*

| Calendar year. | Quotations. | | | Calendar year. | Quotations. | | |
|---|---|---|---|---|---|---|---|
| | Highest. | Lowest. | Average. | | Highest. | Lowest. | Average. |
| 1874 | $1.29375 | $1.25500 | $1.27195 | 1898 | $0.62250 | $0.55125 | $0.59064 |
| 1875 | 1.26125 | 1.21000 | 1.23883 | 1899 | .64750 | .58625 | .60507 |
| 1876 | 1.26000 | 1.03500 | 1.14950 | 1900 | .65750 | .59750 | .62065 |
| 1877 | 1.26000 | 1.16000 | 1.19408 | 1901 | .64500 | .54750 | .59703 |
| 1878 | 1.20750 | 1.08500 | 1.15429 | 1902 | .56875 | .47375 | .52815 |
| 1879 | 1.16750 | 1.06500 | 1.12088 | 1903 | .62375 | .47500 | .54208 |
| 1880 | 1.15000 | 1.11250 | 1.13931 | 1904 | .62500 | .53375 | .57843 |
| 1881 | 1.14500 | 1.11000 | 1.12823 | 1905 | .66500 | .55625 | .61008 |
| 1882 | 1.15000 | 1.09000 | 1.13855 | 1906 | .72375 | .63125 | .67379 |
| 1883 | 1.11750 | 1.09500 | 1.08727 | 1907 | .71000 | .52750 | .65978 |
| 1884 | 1.13250 | 1.08000 | 1.11161 | 1908 | .58875 | .48250 | .53496 |
| 1885 | 1.09500 | 1.02750 | 1.06428 | 1909 | .54500 | .50750 | .52163 |
| 1886 | 1.03500 | .92500 | .99880 | 1910 | .57625 | .50750 | .54245 |
| 1887 | 1.03500 | .95000 | .97899 | 1911 | .57500 | .52125 | .54002 |
| 1888 | .97750 | .92000 | .94300 | 1912 | .65625 | .55250 | .62006 |
| 1889 | .97250 | .92500 | .93634 | 1913 | .65125 | .58000 | .61241 |
| 1890 | 1.20500 | .95750 | 1.05329 | 1914 | .60875 | .49000 | .56331 |
| 1891 | 1.07500 | .94750 | .99033 | 1915 | .58000 | .47750 | .51062 |
| 1892 | .95250 | .83000 | .87552 | 1916 | .79125 | .57250 | .67151 |
| 1893 | .85000 | .65000 | .78219 | 1917 | 1.16500 | .73125 | .84000 |
| 1894 | .70000 | .59500 | .64043 | 1918 | 1.02500 | .89375 | .98445 |
| 1895 | .69000 | .60000 | .66268 | 1919 | 1.38750 | 1.01750 | 1.12086 |
| 1896 | .70250 | .65625 | .68195 | 1920 | 1.36750 | .60750 | 1.01940 |
| 1897 | .66125 | .52750 | .60774 | 1921 | .73813 | .53188 | .63117 |

*Highest, lowest, and average price of bar silver in London, per ounce British standard (0.925), since 1833; and the equivalent in United States gold coin, of an ounce 1.000 fine, taken at the average price and par of exchange.*

| Calendar year. | Highest quotation. | Lowest quotation. | Average quotation. | Value of a fine ounce at average quotation. |
|---|---|---|---|---|
| | Pence | Pence. | Pence. | Dollars. |
| 1833 | 59 3/8 | 58 3/4 | 59 3/16 | 1.297 |
| 1834 | 60 3/4 | 59 1/4 | 59 15/16 | 1.313 |
| 1835 | 60 | 59 1/4 | 59 11/16 | 1.308 |
| 1836 | 60 3/4 | 59 5/8 | 60 | 1.315 |
| 1837 | 60 3/8 | 59 | 59 9/16 | 1.305 |
| 1838 | 60 1/8 | 59 1/2 | 59 1/2 | 1.304 |
| 1839 | 60 5/8 | 60 | 60 3/8 | 1.323 |
| 1840 | 60 3/4 | 60 1/8 | 60 3/8 | 1.323 |
| 1841 | 60 3/8 | 59 3/4 | 60 1/16 | 1.316 |
| 1842 | 60 | 59 1/4 | 59 7/16 | 1.303 |
| 1843 | 59 3/8 | 59 | 59 3/16 | 1.297 |
| 1844 | 59 3/4 | 59 1/4 | 59 1/2 | 1.304 |
| 1845 | 59 7/8 | 58 7/8 | 59 1/4 | 1.298 |
| 1846 | 60 1/8 | 59 | 59 5/16 | 1.300 |
| 1847 | 60 3/8 | 58 7/8 | 59 11/16 | 1.308 |
| 1848 | 60 | 58 1/2 | 59 1/2 | 1.304 |
| 1849 | 60 | 59 1/2 | 59 3/4 | 1.309 |
| 1850 | 61 1/2 | 59 1/2 | 60 1/16 | 1.316 |
| 1851 | 61 5/8 | 60 | 61 | 1.337 |
| 1852 | 61 7/8 | 59 7/8 | 60 1/2 | 1.326 |
| 1853 | 61 7/8 | 60 5/8 | 61 1/2 | 1.348 |
| 1854 | 61 7/8 | 60 7/8 | 61 1/2 | 1.348 |
| 1855 | 61 5/8 | 60 | 61 5/16 | 1.344 |
| 1856 | 62 1/4 | 60 1/2 | 61 5/16 | 1.344 |
| 1857 | 62 3/8 | 61 | 61 3/4 | 1.353 |
| 1858 | 61 7/8 | 60 3/4 | 61 5/16 | 1.344 |
| 1859 | 62 3/4 | 61 3/4 | 62 1/16 | 1.360 |
| 1860 | 62 3/8 | 61 1/4 | 61 11/16 | 1.352 |
| 1861 | 61 3/8 | 60 1/8 | 60 13/16 | 1.333 |
| 1862 | 62 1/8 | 61 | 61 7/16 | 1.346 |
| 1863 | 61 3/4 | 61 | 61 3/8 | 1.345 |
| 1864 | 62 1/2 | 60 5/8 | 61 3/8 | 1.345 |
| 1865 | 61 5/8 | 60 1/2 | 61 1/16 | 1.338 |
| 1866 | 62 1/4 | 60 3/8 | 61 1/8 | 1.339 |
| 1867 | 61 1/4 | 60 3/8 | 60 9/16 | 1.328 |
| 1868 | 61 1/8 | 60 1/8 | 60 1/2 | 1.326 |
| 1869 | 61 | 60 | 60 7/16 | 1.325 |
| 1870 | 60 3/4 | 60 1/4 | 60 9/16 | 1.328 |
| 1871 | 61 | 60 3/16 | 60 1/2 | 1.326 |
| 1872 | 61 1/8 | 59 1/4 | 60 5/16 | 1.322 |
| 1873 | 59 15/16 | 57 7/8 | 59 1/4 | 1.29769 |
| 1874 | 59 1/2 | 57 1/4 | 58 5/16 | 1.27883 |
| 1875 | 57 5/8 | 55 1/2 | 56 7/8 | 1.24233 |
| 1876 | 58 1/2 | 46 3/4 | 52 3/4 | 1.16414 |
| 1877 | 58 1/4 | 53 1/4 | 54 13/16 | 1.20189 |
| 1878 | 55 1/4 | 49 1/2 | 52 9/16 | 1.15358 |
| 1879 | 53 3/4 | 58 7/8 | 51 1/4 | 1.12392 |
| 1880 | 52 13/16 | 51 5/8 | 52 1/4 | 1.14507 |
| 1881 | 52 7/8 | 50 7/8 | 51 11/16 | 1.13229 |
| 1882 | 52 3/8 | 50 | 51 5/8 | 1.13562 |
| 1883 | 51 3/16 | 50 1/16 | 50 9/16 | 1.10874 |
| 1884 | 51 3/8 | 49 1/2 | 50 11/16 | 1.11068 |
| 1885 | 50 | 46 7/8 | 48 9/16 | 1.06510 |
| 1886 | 47 | 42 | 45 3/8 | .99467 |
| 1887 | 47 1/8 | 43 1/4 | 44 11/16 | .97946 |
| 1888 | 44 9/16 | 41 5/8 | 42 7/8 | .93974 |
| 1889 | 44 3/4 | 41 15/16 | 42 11/16 | .93511 |
| 1890 | 54 5/8 | 43 5/8 | 47 3/4 | 1.04634 |
| 1891 | 48 3/4 | 43 1/2 | 45 1/16 | .98800 |
| 1892 | 43 3/4 | 37 7/8 | 39 3/4 | .87145 |
| 1893 | 38 3/4 | 30 1/2 | 35 9/16 | .78030 |
| 1894 | 31 3/4 | 27 | 28 15/16 | .63479 |
| 1895 | 31 3/8 | 27 3/16 | 29 13/16 | .65406 |
| 1896 | 31 15/16 | 29 3/4 | 30 13/16 | .67565 |
| 1897 | 29 13/16 | 23 5/8 | 27 9/16 | .60438 |
| 1898 | 28 5/8 | 25 | 26 15/16 | .59010 |
| 1899 | 29 | 26 5/8 | 27 7/16 | .60154 |
| 1900 | 30 1/4 | 27 | 28 5/16 | .62007 |
| 1901 | 29 9/16 | 24 15/16 | 27 3/16 | .59595 |
| 1902 | 26 1/16 | 21 11/16 | 24 1/16 | .52795 |
| 1903 | 28 1/2 | 21 11/16 | 24 3/4 | .54257 |
| 1904 | 28 9/16 | 24 7/16 | 26 13/32 | .57876 |
| 1905 | 30 5/16 | 25 7/16 | 27 13/16 | .61027 |
| 1906 | 33 1/8 | 29 | 30 7/8 | .67689 |
| 1907 | 32 7/16 | 24 1/4 | 30 3/16 | .66152 |
| 1908 | 27 | 22 | 24 13/32 | .53490 |
| 1909 | 24 7/8 | 23 1/16 | 23 23/32 | .52016 |
| 1910 | 26 1/4 | 23 3/16 | 24 21/32 | .54077 |
| 1911 | 26 1/8 | 23 11/16 | 24 19/32 | .53928 |
| 1912 | 29 11/16 | 25 1/8 | 28 1/32 | .61470 |
| 1913 | 29 3/8 | 26 1/16 | 27 9/16 | .60458 |
| 1914 | 27 3/4 | 22 1/8 | 25 5/16 | .55312 |
| 1915 | 27 1/4 | 22 5/16 | 23 11/16 | .51892 |
| 1916 | 37 1/8 | 26 11/16 | 31 5/16 | .68647 |
| 1917 | 55 | 35 11/16 | 40 7/8 | .89525 |
| 1918 | 49 1/2 | 42 1/2 | 47 17/32 | 1.04171 |
| 1919 | 79 1/8 | 47 3/4 | 57 1/32 | 1.25047 |
| 1920 | 89 1/2 | 38 7/8 | 61 13/32 | 1.34649 |
| 1921 | 43 3/8 | 30 5/8 | 36 23/32 | .80522 |

*Average price of an ounce of gold in London, and United States equivalent, since 1870.*

| Calendar year. | Average London price per standard ounce to 1918, inclusive, and per fine ounce thereafter.[1] | | | Equivalent in U. S. value, of London price. | | Per cent premium of average price above Bank of England's minimum buying rate. |
|---|---|---|---|---|---|---|
| | £ | s. | d. | For British standard ounce (0.916⅔). | For a fine ounce (1.000). | |
| 1870 | 3 | 17 | 9.01 | $18.9190 | $20.6389 | 0.00107 |
| 1871 | 3 | 17 | 9.01 | 18.9190 | 20.6389 | .00107 |
| 1872 | 3 | 17 | 9.24 | 18.9237 | 20.6440 | .02572 |
| 1873 | 3 | 17 | 9.28 | 18.9245 | 20.6449 | .03001 |
| 1874 | 3 | 17 | 9.00 | 18.9188 | 20.6387 | |
| 1875 | 3 | 17 | 9.23 | 18.9235 | 20.6438 | .02465 |
| 1876 | 3 | 17 | 9.30 | 18.9249 | 20.6453 | .03215 |
| 1877 | 3 | 17 | 9.42 | 18.9273 | 20.6480 | .04502 |
| 1878 | 3 | 17 | 9.41 | 18.9271 | 20.6477 | .04394 |
| 1879 | 3 | 17 | 9.11 | 18.9210 | 20.6411 | .01179 |
| 1880 | 3 | 17 | 9.15 | 18.9218 | 20.6420 | .01608 |
| 1881 | 3 | 17 | 9.35 | 18.9259 | 20.6464 | .03751 |
| 1882 | 3 | 17 | 9.43 | 18.9275 | 20.6482 | .04609 |
| 1883 | 3 | 17 | 9.18 | 18.9224 | 20.6426 | .01929 |
| 1884 | 3 | 17 | 9.32 | 18.9253 | 20.6458 | .03430 |
| 1885 | 3 | 17 | 9.17 | 18.9222 | 20.6424 | .01822 |
| 1886 | 3 | 17 | 9.10 | 18.9208 | 20.6409 | .01072 |
| 1887 | 3 | 17 | 9.01 | 18.9190 | 20.6389 | .00107 |
| 1888 | 3 | 17 | 9.21 | 18.9231 | 20.6434 | .02251 |
| 1889 | 3 | 17 | 9.04 | 18.9196 | 20.6396 | .00429 |
| 1890 | 3 | 17 | 9.44 | 18.9277 | 20.6484 | .04716 |
| 1891 | 3 | 17 | 10.29 | 18.9450 | 20.6673 | .13826 |
| 1892 | 3 | 17 | 10.17 | 18.9425 | 20.6645 | .12540 |
| 1893 | 3 | 17 | 10.57 | 18.9506 | 20.6734 | .16827 |
| 1894 | 3 | 17 | 9.33 | 18.9255 | 20.6460 | .03537 |
| 1895 | 3 | 17 | 9.03 | 18.9194 | 20.6393 | .00322 |
| 1896 | 3 | 17 | 10.16 | 18.9423 | 20.6643 | .12433 |
| 1897 | 3 | 17 | 11.23 | 18.9640 | 20.6880 | .23901 |
| 1898 | 3 | 17 | 10.46 | 18.9484 | 20.6710 | .15648 |
| 1899 | 3 | 17 | 9.27 | 18.9243 | 20.6447 | .02894 |
| 1900 | 3 | 17 | 9.91 | 18.9373 | 20.6589 | .09753 |
| 1901 | 3 | 17 | 9.83 | 18.9356 | 20.6570 | .08896 |
| 1902 | 3 | 17 | 9.55 | 18.9300 | 20.6509 | .05895 |
| 1903 | 3 | 17 | 10.06 | 18.9403 | 20.6621 | .11361 |
| 1904 | 3 | 17 | 9.94 | 18.9379 | 20.6595 | .10075 |
| 1905 | 3 | 17 | 9.42 | 18.9273 | 20.6480 | .04502 |
| 1906 | 3 | 17 | 9.82 | 18.9354 | 20.6568 | .08789 |
| 1907 | 3 | 17 | 9.95 | 18.9381 | 20.6597 | .10182 |
| 1908 | 3 | 17 | 10.19 | 18.9429 | 20.6650 | .12755 |
| 1909 | 3 | 17 | 9.18 | 18.9224 | 20.6426 | .01929 |
| 1910 | 3 | 17 | 9.03 | 18.9194 | 20.6393 | .00322 |
| 1911 | 3 | 17 | 9.00 | 18.9188 | 20.6387 | |
| 1912 | 3 | 17 | 9.00 | 18.9188 | 20.6387 | |
| 1913 | 3 | 17 | 9.00 | 18.9188 | 20.6387 | |
| 1914 | 3 | 17 | 9.04 | 18.9196 | 20.6396 | .00429 |
| 1915 | 3 | 17 | 9.00 | 18.9188 | 20.6387 | |
| 1916 | 3 | 17 | 9.00 | 18.9188 | 20.6387 | |
| 1917 | 3 | 17 | 9.00 | 18.9188 | 20.6387 | |
| 1918 | 3 | 17 | 9.00 | 18.9188 | 20.6387 | |
| 1919 | 4 | 10 | 1.03 | 20.0937 | 21.9204 | 6.21033 |
| 1920 | 5 | 12 | 11.52 | 25.1958 | 27.4863 | 33.17875 |
| 1921 | 5 | 7 | .50 | 23.8758 | 26.0463 | 26.20109 |
| Mint price per standard ounce | 3 | 17 | 10.50 | 18.9492 | 20.6718 | .16077 |
| Equivalent per fine ounce | 4 | 4 | 11.45+ | 18.9492 | 20.6718 | .16077 |
| Bank rate per standard ounce | 3 | 17 | 9.00 | 18.9188 | 20.6387 | |
| Equivalent per fine ounce | 4 | 4 | 9.82— | 18.9188 | 20.6387 | |

[1] London quotations on gold were changed in September, 1919, from the standard ounce to a fine ounce basis.

*Average commercial ratio of silver to gold each calendar year since 1687.*

[NOTE.—From 1687 to 1832 the ratios are taken from Dr. A. Soetbeer, from 1833 to 1878 from Pixley and Abell's tables, from 1879 to 1896 from daily cablegrams from London to the Bureau of the Mint, from 1897 to 1917 from daily London quotations, and since from daily New York quotations.]

| Year. | Ratio. | Year. | Ratio. | Year. | Ratio. | Year. | Ratio. | Year. | Ratio. | Year | Ratio. |
|---|---|---|---|---|---|---|---|---|---|---|---|
| 1687 | 14.94 | 1727 | 15.24 | 1766 | 14.80 | 1805 | 15.79 | 1844 | 15.85 | 1883 | 18.64 |
| 1688 | 14.94 | 1728 | 15.11 | 1767 | 14.85 | 1806 | 15.52 | 1845 | 15.92 | 1884 | 18.61 |
| 1689 | 15.02 | 1729 | 14.92 | 1768 | 14.80 | 1807 | 15.43 | 1846 | 15.90 | 1885 | 19.41 |
| 1690 | 15.02 | 1730 | 14.81 | 1769 | 14.72 | 1808 | 16.08 | 1847 | 15.80 | 1886 | 20.78 |
| 1691 | 14.98 | 1731 | 14.94 | 1770 | 14.62 | 1809 | 15.96 | 1848 | 15.85 | 1887 | 21.10 |
| 1692 | 14.92 | 1732 | 15.09 | 1771 | 14.66 | 1810 | 15.77 | 1849 | 15.78 | 1888 | 22.00 |
| 1693 | 14.83 | 1733 | 15.18 | 1772 | 14.52 | 1811 | 15.53 | 1850 | 15.70 | 1889 | 22.10 |
| 1694 | 14.87 | 1734 | 15.39 | 1773 | 14.62 | 1812 | 16.11 | 1851 | 15.46 | 1890 | 19.75 |
| 1695 | 15.02 | 1735 | 15.41 | 1774 | 14.62 | 1813 | 16.25 | 1852 | 15.59 | 1891 | 20.92 |
| 1696 | 15.00 | 1736 | 15.18 | 1775 | 14.72 | 1814 | 15.04 | 1853 | 15.33 | 1892 | 23.72 |
| 1697 | 15.20 | 1737 | 15.02 | 1776 | 14.55 | 1815 | 15.26 | 1854 | 15.33 | 1893 | 26.49 |
| 1698 | 15.07 | 1738 | 14.91 | 1777 | 14.54 | 1816 | 15.28 | 1855 | 15.38 | 1894 | 32.56 |
| 1699 | 14.94 | 1739 | 14.91 | 1778 | 14.68 | 1817 | 15.11 | 1856 | 15.38 | 1895 | 31.60 |
| 1700 | 14.81 | 1740 | 14.94 | 1779 | 14.80 | 1818 | 15.35 | 1857 | 15.27 | 1896 | 30.59 |
| 1701 | 15.07 | 1741 | 14.92 | 1780 | 14.72 | 1819 | 15.33 | 1858 | 15.38 | 1897 | 34.20 |
| 1702 | 15.52 | 1742 | 14.85 | 1781 | 14.78 | 1820 | 15.62 | 1859 | 15.19 | 1898 | 35.03 |
| 1703 | 15.17 | 1743 | 14.85 | 1782 | 14.42 | 1821 | 15.95 | 1860 | 15.29 | 1899 | 34.36 |
| 1704 | 15.22 | 1744 | 14.87 | 1783 | 14.48 | 1822 | 15.80 | 1861 | 15.50 | 1900 | 33.33 |
| 1705 | 15.11 | 1745 | 14.98 | 1784 | 14.70 | 1823 | 15.84 | 1862 | 15.35 | 1901 | 34.68 |
| 1706 | 15.27 | 1746 | 15.13 | 1785 | 14.92 | 1824 | 15.82 | 1863 | 15.37 | 1902 | 39.15 |
| 1707 | 15.44 | 1747 | 15.26 | 1786 | 14.96 | 1825 | 15.70 | 1864 | 15.37 | 1903 | 38.10 |
| 1708 | 15.41 | 1748 | 15.11 | 1787 | 14.92 | 1826 | 15.76 | 1865 | 15.44 | 1904 | 35.70 |
| 1709 | 15.31 | 1749 | 14.80 | 1788 | 14.65 | 1827 | 15.74 | 1866 | 15.43 | 1905 | 33.87 |
| 1710 | 15.22 | 1750 | 14.55 | 1789 | 14.75 | 1828 | 15.78 | 1867 | 15.57 | 1906 | 30.54 |
| 1711 | 15.29 | 1751 | 14.39 | 1790 | 15.04 | 1829 | 15.78 | 1868 | 15.59 | 1907 | 31.24 |
| 1712 | 15.31 | 1752 | 14.54 | 1791 | 15.05 | 1830 | 15.82 | 1869 | 15.60 | 1908 | 38.64 |
| 1713 | 15.24 | 1753 | 14.54 | 1792 | 15.17 | 1831 | 15.72 | 1870 | 15.57 | 1909 | 39.74 |
| 1714 | 15.13 | 1754 | 14.48 | 1793 | 15.00 | 1832 | 15.73 | 1871 | 15.57 | 1910 | 38.22 |
| 1715 | 15.11 | 1755 | 14.68 | 1794 | 15.37 | 1833 | 15.93 | 1872 | 15.63 | 1911 | 38.33 |
| 1716 | 15.09 | 1756 | 14.94 | 1795 | 15.55 | 1834 | 15.73 | 1873 | 15.93 | 1912 | 33.62 |
| 1717 | 15.13 | 1757 | 14.87 | 1796 | 15.65 | 1835 | 15.80 | 1874 | 16.16 | 1913 | 34.19 |
| 1718 | 15.11 | 1758 | 14.85 | 1797 | 15.41 | 1836 | 15.72 | 1875 | 16.64 | 1914 | 37.37 |
| 1719 | 15.09 | 1759 | 14.15 | 1798 | 15.59 | 1837 | 15.83 | 1876 | 17.75 | 1915 | 39.84 |
| 1720 | 15.04 | 1760 | 14.14 | 1799 | 15.74 | 1838 | 15.85 | 1877 | 17.20 | 1916 | 30.11 |
| 1721 | 15.05 | 1761 | 14.54 | 1800 | 15.68 | 1839 | 15.62 | 1878 | 17.92 | 1917 | 23.09 |
| 1722 | 15.17 | 1762 | 15.27 | 1801 | 15.46 | 1840 | 15.62 | 1879 | 18.39 | 1918 | 21.00 |
| 1723 | 15.20 | 1763 | 14.99 | 1802 | 15.26 | 1841 | 15.70 | 1880 | 18.05 | 1919 | 18.44 |
| 1724 | 15.11 | 1764 | 14.70 | 1803 | 15.41 | 1842 | 15.87 | 1881 | 18.25 | 1920 | 20.27 |
| 1725 | 15.11 | 1765 | 14.83 | 1804 | 15.41 | 1843 | 15.93 | 1882 | 18.20 | 1921 | 32.75 |
| 1726 | 15.15 | | | | | | | | | | |

*Bullion value of the silver dollar [371¼ grains of pure silver] at the annual average price of silver each year since 1837.*

| Year | Value. | Year. | Value. | Year. | Value. | Year. | Value. | Year. | Value. |
|---|---|---|---|---|---|---|---|---|---|
| 1837 | $1.009 | 1854 | $1.042 | 1871 | $1.025 | 1888 | $0.72683 | 1905 | $0.47200 |
| 1838 | 1.008 | 1855 | 1.039 | 1872 | 1.022 | 1889 | .72325 | 1906 | .52353 |
| 1839 | 1.023 | 1856 | 1.039 | 1873 | 1.00368 | 1890 | .80927 | 1907 | .51164 |
| 1840 | 1.023 | 1857 | 1.046 | 1874 | .98909 | 1891 | .76416 | 1908 | .41371 |
| 1841 | 1.018 | 1858 | 1.039 | 1875 | .96086 | 1892 | .67401 | 1909 | .40231 |
| 1842 | 1.007 | 1859 | 1.052 | 1876 | .90039 | 1893 | .60351 | 1910 | .41825 |
| 1843 | 1.003 | 1860 | 1.045 | 1877 | .92958 | 1894 | .49097 | 1911 | .41709 |
| 1844 | 1.008 | 1861 | 1.031 | 1878 | .89222 | 1895 | .50587 | 1912 | .47543 |
| 1845 | 1.004 | 1862 | 1.041 | 1879 | .86928 | 1896 | .52257 | 1913 | .46760 |
| 1846 | 1.005 | 1863 | 1.040 | 1880 | .88564 | 1897 | .46745 | 1914 | .42780 |
| 1847 | 1.011 | 1864 | 1.040 | 1881 | .87575 | 1898 | .45640 | 1915 | .40135 |
| 1848 | 1.008 | 1865 | 1.035 | 1882 | .87833 | 1899 | .46525 | 1916 | .53094 |
| 1849 | 1.013 | 1866 | 1.036 | 1883 | .85754 | 1900 | .47958 | 1917 | .69242 |
| 1850 | 1.018 | 1867 | 1.027 | 1884 | .85904 | 1901 | .46093 | 1918 | .76142 |
| 1851 | 1.034 | 1868 | 1.025 | 1885 | .82379 | 1902 | .40835 | 1919 | .86692 |
| 1852 | 1.025 | 1869 | 1.024 | 1886 | .76931 | 1903 | .41960 | 1920 | .78844 |
| 1853 | 1.042 | 1870 | 1.027 | 1887 | .75755 | 1904 | .44763 | 1921 | .48817 |

## VALUES OF FOREIGN COINS.

The following values, calculated by the Director of the Mint, were proclaimed by the Secretary of the Treasury under the provisions of section 25 of the act of August 27, 1894, as amended by section 403, Title IV, of the act of May 27, 1921, as the basis for estimating the value of foreign merchandise exported to the United States during the quarter beginning October 1, 1922:

| Country. | Legal standard. | Monetary unit. | Value in terms of United States money. | Remarks. |
|---|---|---|---|---|
| Argentine Republic.... | Gold...... | Peso................. | $0.9648 | Currency: Paper, normally convertible at 44 per cent of face value; now inconvertible. |
| Austria................. | ...do...... | Krone................ | .2026 | |
| Belgium................ | Gold and silver. | Franc................ | .1930 | Member Latin Union; gold is actual standard. |
| Bolivia................. | Gold...... | Boliviano............ | .3893 | 12½ bolivianos equal 1 pound sterling. |
| Brazil.................. | ...do...... | Milreis.............. | .5462 | Currency: Government paper normally convertible at 16 pence (=$0.3244) per milreis. |
| British colonies in Australasia and Africa. | ...do...... | Pound sterling....... | 4.8665 | |
| British Honduras...... | ...do...... | Dollar............... | 1.0000 | |
| Bulgaria............... | ...do...... | Lev.................. | .1930 | |
| Canada................ | ...do...... | Dollar............... | 1.0000 | |
| Chile.................. | ...do...... | Peso................. | .3650 | Currency: Inconvertible paper. |
| China................. | Silver.... | Tael: Amoy .8322; Canton .8297; Cheefoo .7960; Chin Kiang .8130; Fuchau .7698; Haikwan (customs) .8468; Hankow .7786; Kiaochow .8064; Nankin .8235; Niuchwang .7804; Ningpo .8001; Peking .8113; Shanghai .7602; Swatow .7688; Takau .8375; Tientsin .8064; Yuan .5393. Dollar: Hongkong .5474; British .5474; Mexican .5514 | The tael is a unit of weight; not a coin. The customs unit is the Haikwan tael. The values of other taels are based on their relation to the value of the Haikwan tael. The Yuan silver dollar of 100 cents is the monetary unit of the Chinese Republic; it is equivalent to 0.644+ of the Haikwan tael. Mexican silver pesos issued under Mexican decree of Nov. 13, 1918, are of silver content approximately 41 per cent less than the dollar here quoted; and those issued under decree of Oct. 27, 1919, contain about 51 per cent less silver. |
| Colombia.............. | Gold...... | Peso................. | .9733 | Currency: Government paper and gold. |
| Costa Rica............ | ...do...... | Colon............... | .4653 | |
| Cuba.................. | ...do...... | Peso................. | 1.0000 | |
| Denmark.............. | ...do...... | Krone............... | .2680 | |
| Ecuador............... | ...do...... | Sucre............... | .4867 | |
| Egypt................. | ...do...... | Pound (100 piasters).. | 4.9431 | The actual standard is the British pound sterling, which is legal tender for 97½ piasters. |
| Finland............... | ...do...... | Markka.............. | .1930 | |
| France................ | Gold and silver. | Franc................ | .1930 | Member Latin Union; gold is actual standard. |
| Germany.............. | Gold...... | Mark................ | .2382 | |
| Great Britain.......... | ...do...... | Pound sterling....... | 4.8665 | |
| Greece................ | Gold and silver. | Drachma............. | .1930 | Do. |
| Guatemala............. | Silver...... | Peso................. | .5076 | Currency: Inconvertible paper. |
| Haiti................. | Gold...... | Gourde.............. | .2000 | Do. |
| Honduras.............. | Silver...... | Peso................. | .5076 | Currency, bank notes. |
| India (British)......... | Gold...... / Silver...... | Mohur and sovereign / Rupee............... | 4.8665 / .2412 | The British sovereign and half sovereign are legal tender in India at 10 rupees per sovereign. |
| Indo-China............ | ...do...... | Piaster.............. | .5482 | |
| Italy.................. | Gold...... | Lira................. | .1930 | Member Latin Union; gold is actual standard. |
| Japan................. | ...do...... | Yen................. | .4985 | |
| Liberia................ | ...do...... | Dollar............... | 1.0000 | Currency: Depreciated silver token coins. Customs duties are collected in gold. |

| Country. | Legal standard. | Monetary unit. | Value in terms of United States money. | Remarks. |
|---|---|---|---|---|
| Mexico | Gold | Peso | $0.4985 | |
| Netherlands | ...do | Guilder (florin) | .4020 | |
| Newfoundland | ...do | Dollar | 1.0000 | |
| Nicaragua | ...do | Cordoba | 1.0000 | |
| Norway | ...do | Krone | .2680 | |
| Panama | ...do | Balboa | 1.0000 | |
| Paraguay | ...do | Peso (Argentine) | .9648 | Currency: Depreciated Paraguayan paper currency. |
| Persia | Silver | Kran | .0935 | Currency: Silver circulating above its metallic value. Gold coin is a commodity only, normally worth double the silver. |
| Peru | Gold | Libra | 4.8665 | |
| Philippine Islands | ...do | Peso | .5000 | |
| Portugal | ...do | Escudo | 1.0805 | Currency: Inconvertible paper. |
| Rumania | ...do | Leu | .1930 | |
| Russia | ...do | Ruble | .5146 | |
| Salvador | ...do | Colon | .5000 | |
| Santo Domingo | ...do | Dollar | 1.0000 | |
| Serbia | ...do | Dinar | .1930 | |
| Siam | ...do | Tical | .3709 | |
| Spain | Gold and silver. | Peseta | .1930 | Valuation is for gold peseta; currency is notes of the Bank of Spain. |
| Straits Settlements | Gold | Dollar | .5678 | |
| Sweden | ...do | Krona | .2680 | |
| Switzerland | ...do | Franc | .1930 | Member Latin Union; gold is actual standard. |
| Turkey | ...do | Piaster | .0440 | (100 piasters equal to the Turkish £.) |
| Uruguay | ...do | Peso | 1.0342 | Currency: Inconvertible paper. |
| Venezuela | ...do | Bolivar | .1930 | |

*Changes in value of foreign coins during 1922.*

| Country. | Monetary unit. | Value, 1922. | | | |
|---|---|---|---|---|---|
| | | Jan. 1. | Apr. 1. | July 1. | Oct. 1. |
| China | Silver tael, Amoy | $0.8156 | $0.7753 | $0.8318 | $0.8322 |
| Do | Silver tael, Canton | .8131 | .7728 | .8293 | .8297 |
| Do | Silver tael, Cheefoo | .7801 | .7415 | .7955 | .7960 |
| Do | Silver tael, Chinkiang | .7967 | .7573 | .8125 | .8130 |
| Do | Silver tael, Fuchau | .7544 | .7171 | .7694 | .7698 |
| Do | Silver tael, Haikwan (customs) | .8299 | .7888 | .8463 | .8468 |
| Do | Silver tael, Hankow | .7631 | .7254 | .7782 | .7786 |
| Do | Silver tael, Kiaochow | .7903 | .7509 | .8060 | .8064 |
| Do | Silver tael, Nankin | .8071 | .7672 | .8237 | .8235 |
| Do | Silver tael, Nieuchwang | .7648 | .7280 | .7800 | .7804 |
| Do | Silver tael, Ningpo | .7841 | .7454 | .7997 | .8001 |
| Do | Silver tael, Peking | .7951 | .7558 | .8109 | .8113 |
| Do | Silver tael, Shanghai | .7450 | .7082 | .7598 | .7602 |
| Do | Silver tael, Swatow | .7534 | .7162 | .7683 | .7688 |
| Do | Silver tael, Takau | .8207 | .7802 | .8370 | .8375 |
| Do | Silver tael, Tientsin | .7903 | .7509 | .8060 | .8064 |
| Do | Silver dollar (Yuan) | .5344 | .5080 | .5390 | .5393 |
| Do | Silver dollar, Hongkong | .5364 | .5099 | .5471 | .5474 |
| Do | Silver dollar, British | .5364 | .5099 | .5471 | .5474 |
| Do | Silver dollar, Mexican | .5404 | .5137 | .5511 | .5514 |
| Guatemala | Silver peso | .4975 | .4729 | .5074 | .5076 |
| Honduras | do | .4975 | .4729 | .5074 | .5076 |
| India (British) | Gold rupee | .4866 | .4866 | | |
| Do | Gold mohur and sovereign | | | 4.8665 | 4.8665 |
| Do | Silver rupee | | | .2411 | .2412 |
| Indo-China | Silver piaster | .5373 | .5107 | .5480 | .5482 |
| Persia | Silver kran | .0916 | .0871 | .0934 | .0935 |

*Mine production of gold and silver in the United States from 1792 to 1844 and annually since.*

[The estimate for 1792–1873 is by R. W. Raymond, commissioner of mining statistics, and since by Director of the Mint.]

| Calendar year. | Gold. | | Silver. | |
|---|---|---|---|---|
| | Fine ounces. | Value. | Fine ounces. | Commercial value. |
| 1792 to July 31, 1834 | 677,250 | $14,000,000 | Insignificant. | |
| July 31, 1834, to Dec. 31, 1844 | 362,812 | 7,500,000 | 193,400 | $253,400 |
| 1845 | 48,762 | 1,008,000 | 38,700 | 50,200 |
| 1846 | 55,341 | 1,140,000 | 38,700 | 50,300 |
| 1847 | 43,005 | 889,000 | 38,700 | 50,600 |
| Total | 1,187,170 | 24,537,000 | 309,500 | 404,500 |
| 1848 | 483,750 | 10,000,000 | 38,700 | 50,500 |
| 1849 | 1,935,000 | 40,000,000 | 38,700 | 50,700 |
| 1850 | 2,418,750 | 50,000,000 | 38,700 | 50,900 |
| 1851–1855 | 14,270,625 | 295,000,000 | 193,500 | 259,400 |
| 1856–1860 | 12,384,000 | 256,000,000 | 309,400 | 418,300 |
| 1861–1865 | 10,716,271 | 221,525,000 | 28,810,600 | 38,674,300 |
| 1866–1870 | 12,225,570 | 252,725,000 | 49,113,200 | 65,261,100 |
| 1871 | 2,104,312 | 43,500,000 | 17,789,100 | 23,588,300 |
| 1872 | 1,741,500 | 36,000,000 | 22,236,300 | 29,396,400 |
| Total | 58,279,778 | 1,204,750,000 | 118,568,200 | 157,749,900 |
| 1873–1875 | 4,980,631 | 102,958,800 | 81,057,900 | 103,285,000 |
| 1876–1880 | 10,300,633 | 212,933,000 | 157,680,500 | 182,506,400 |
| 1881–1885 | 7,730,372 | 159,801,000 | 182,840,700 | 202,806,600 |
| 1886–1890 | 8,077,967 | 166,984,500 | 231,819,100 | 227,495,200 |
| 1891–1895 | 9,106,834 | 188,255,000 | 287,057,000 | 227,960,100 |
| 1896–1900 | 15,728,572 | 325,138,400 | 279,544,300 | 172,688,800 |
| 1901–1905 | 19,393,722 | 400,903,800 | 278,798,400 | 159,543,400 |
| 1906 | 4,565,333 | 94,373,800 | 56,517,900 | 38,256,400 |
| 1907 | 4,374,827 | 90,435,700 | 56,514,700 | 37,299,700 |
| 1908 | 4,574,340 | 94,560,000 | 52,440,800 | 28,050,600 |
| 1909 | 4,821,701 | 99,673,400 | 54,721,500 | 28,455,200 |
| 1910 | 4,657,017 | 96,269,100 | 57,137,900 | 30,854,500 |
| 1911 | 4,687,053 | 96,890,000 | 60,399,400 | 32,615,700 |
| 1912 | 4,520,719 | 93,451,500 | 63,766,800 | 39,197,500 |
| 1913 | 4,299,784 | 88,884,400 | 66,801,500 | 40,348,100 |
| 1914 | 4,572,976 | 94,531,800 | 72,455,100 | 40,067,700 |
| 1915 | 4,887,604 | 101,035,700 | 74,961,075 | 37,397,300 |
| 1916 | 4,479,057 | 92,590,300 | 74,414,802 | 48,953,000 |
| 1917 | 4,051,440 | 83,750,700 | 71,740,362 | 59,078,100 |
| 1918 | 3,320,784 | 68,646,700 | 67,810,139 | 66,485,129 |
| 1919 | 2,918,628 | 60,333,400 | 56,682,445 | 63,533,652 |
| 1920 | 2,476,166 | 51,186,900 | 55,361,573 | 60,801,955 |
| 1921 | 2,422,006 | 50,067,300 | 53,052,441 | 53,052,441 |
| Total | 140,948,166 | 2,913,655,200 | 2,493,576,337 | 1,980,732,477 |
| Grand total | 200,415,114 | 4,142,942,200 | 2,612,454,037 | 2,138,886,877 |

*Gold furnished for use in manufactures and the arts and classification of the materials used, by calendar years, since 1880.*

| Calendar year. | New material. | | | Old material. | Grand total. |
|---|---|---|---|---|---|
| | United States coin. | Domestic and foreign bullion and foreign coin. | Total. | | |
| 1880........................... | $3,300,000 | $5,511,047 | $8,811,047 | $1,294,385 | $10,105,432 |
| 1881–1885...................... | 18,575,000 | 34,952,669 | 53,527,669 | 9,313,984 | 62,541,653 |
| 1886–18)0....................... | 17,500,000 | 42,557,772 | 60,057,772 | 20,147,122 | 80,204,894 |
| 1891–1895...................... | 17,500,000 | 39,739,298 | 57,239,298 | 25,300,282 | 82,539,580 |
| 1896–1900...................... | 17,500,000 | 46,992,508 | 64,492,508 | 20,334,856 | 84,827,364 |
| 1901–1905...................... | 17,500,000 | 91,091,680 | 108,591,680 | 33,888,252 | 142,479,932 |
| 1906–1910...................... | 17,500,000 | 134,705,630 | 152,205,630 | 38,540,215 | 190,745,845 |
| 1911........................... | 3,500,000 | 29,603,054 | 33,103,054 | 7,731,238 | 40,834,292 |
| 1912........................... | 3,500,000 | 32,370,552 | 35,870,552 | 8,106,705 | 43,977,257 |
| 1913........................... | 3,500,000 | 34,001,831 | 37,501,831 | 8,362,235 | 45,864,066 |
| 1914........................... | 3,500,000 | 33,912,758 | 37,412,758 | 8,107,274 | 45,520,032 |
| 1915........................... | 3,500,000 | 26,099,507 | 29,599,507 | 8,220,520 | 37,820,027 |
| 1916........................... | 3,500,000 | 37,620,149 | 41,120,149 | 9,941,038 | 51,061,187 |
| 1917........................... | 3,500,000 | 31,303,445 | 34,803,445 | 18,112,196 | 52,915,641 |
| 1918........................... | 3,500,000 | 29,392,395 | 32,892,395 | 19,517,345 | 52,409,740 |
| 1919........................... | 3,500,000 | 52,635,951 | 56,135,951 | 19,354,398 | 75,490,349 |
| 1920........................... | 3,500,000 | 50,509,609 | 54,009,609 | 28,205,478 | 82,215,087 |
| 1921........................... | 3,500,000 | 19,550,332 | 23,050,332 | 27,623,938 | 50,674,270 |
| Total..................... | 147,875,000 | 772,550,187 | 920,425,187 | 312,101,461 | 1,232,526,648 |

*Silver furnished for use in manufactures and the arts and classification of the materials used, by calendar years, since 1880.*

| Calendar year. | New material. | | | Old material. | Grand total. |
|---|---|---|---|---|---|
| | United States coin. | Domestic and foreign bullion and foreign coin. | Total. | | |
| | *Fine ounces.* | *Fine ounces.* | *Fine ounces.* | *Fine ounces.* | *Fine ounces.* |
| 1880.......................... | 464,063 | 2,126,326 | 2,590,389 | 203,540 | 2,793,929 |
| 1881–1885..................... | 773,435 | 18,426,369 | 19,199,804 | 1,573,954 | 20,773,758 |
| 1886–1890..................... | 773,435 | 24,155,908 | 24,929,343 | 3,378,303 | 28,307,646 |
| 1891–1895..................... | 541,406 | 34,690,186 | 35,231,592 | 4,754,381 | 39,985,973 |
| 1896–1900..................... | 386,720 | 44,685,289 | 45,072,009 | 5,998,567 | 51,070,576 |
| 1901–1905..................... | 386,720 | 82,233,057 | 82,619,777 | 15,007,946 | 97,627,723 |
| 1906–1910..................... | 386,720 | 104,035,447 | 104,422,167 | 18,342,642 | 122,764,809 |
| 1911.......................... | 77,344 | 26,210,759 | 26,288,103 | 5,725,582 | 32,013,685 |
| 1912.......................... | 77,344 | 22,567,477 | 22,644,821 | 7,291,699 | 29,936,520 |
| 1913.......................... | 77,344 | 23,051,024 | 23,128,368 | 7,864,466 | 30,992,834 |
| 1914.......................... | 77,344 | 22,474,287 | 22,551,631 | 6,758,330 | 29,309,961 |
| 1915.......................... | 77,344 | 22,888,896 | 22,966,240 | 7,001,875 | 29,968,115 |
| 1916.......................... | 77,344 | 22,126,917 | 22,204,261 | 9,899,246 | 32,103,507 |
| 1917.......................... | 77,344 | 15,921,463 | 15,998,807 | 11,041,038 | 27,039,845 |
| 1918.......................... | 77,344 | 26,644,989 | 26,722,333 | 9,530,263 | 36,252,596 |
| 1919.......................... | 77,344 | 26,160,175 | 26,237,519 | 6,463,002 | 32,700,521 |
| 1920.......................... | 77,344 | 19,202,785 | 19,280,129 | 8,694,392 | 27,974,521 |
| 1921.......................... | 77,344 | 28,766,284 | 28,843,628 | 7,024,318 | 35,867,946 |
| Total..................... | 4,563,283 | 566,367,633 | 570,930,921 | 136,553,544 | 707,484,465 |

## Monetary stock of principal countries of the world, end of calendar year 1920.

[Stated in United States dollars—(000 omitted)].

| Country | Monetary standard | Monetary unit — Name | Monetary unit — United States equivalent | Metallic stock unclassified | Gold stock — In banks and public treasuries | Gold stock — In circulation | Gold stock — Total | Silver stock | Paper circulation | Population | Per capita — Unclassified stock | Per capita — Gold | Per capita — Silver | Per capita — Paper |
|---|---|---|---|---|---|---|---|---|---|---|---|---|---|---|
| **North America:** | | | | | | | | | | | | | | |
| United States | Gold | Dollar | $1.00 | $62,552 | $2,942,048 | | $2,942,048 | $590,493 | $4,674,839 | 109,482 | $7.48 | $26.87 | $5.39 | $42.69 |
| Canada | ..do.. | ..do.. | 1.00 | 3,663 | 112,604 | | 112,604 | 28,638 | 540,473 | 8,361 | .23 | 13.46 | 3.42 | 64.42 |
| Mexico | ..do.. | Peso | .4985 | | | $125,124 | 125,124 | 25,378 | | 15,502 | | 8.07 | 1.63 | |
| British Honduras | ..do.. | Dollar | 1.00 | | 12 | 20 | 32 | 201 | 467 | 45 | | .71 | 4.47 | 10.38 |
| Costa Rica | ..do.. | ..do.. | 1.00 | | 1,188 | | 1,188 | 609 | 9,341 | 469 | | 2.53 | 1.30 | 19.92 |
| Cuba | ..do.. | Peso | 1.00 | | 5,410 | 39,590 | 45,000 | 8,500 | 150,000 | 2,899 | | 15.52 | 2.93 | 51.74 |
| Dominican Republic | ..do.. | Dollar | 1.00 | 3,000 | | | | | 7,000 | 955 | 3.10 | | | 7.32 |
| Guatemala | Silver | Peso | ([1]) | | | | | | 89,760 | 2,232 | | | | 40.21 |
| Haiti | Gold | Gourde | .20 | | 800 | | 800 | 100 | 1,960 | 2,500 | | .32 | .04 | .78 |
| Honduras | Silver | Peso | ([1]) | | 36 | | 36 | 1,131 | 1,750 | 637 | | .06 | 1.78 | 2.75 |
| Nicaragua | Gold | Cordoba | 1.00 | | | | | 315 | 2,516 | 637 | | | .49 | 3.94 |
| Newfoundland | ..do.. | Dollar | 1.00 | | [2]1,000 | | 1,000 | [2]2,000 | [2]2,000 | 265 | | 3.77 | 7.55 | 7.55 |
| British West Indies— | | | | | | | | | | | | | | |
| Barbados | ..do.. | Pound | 4.8665 | | | | | 5 | 13 | 156 | | | .03 | .08 |
| Jamaica | ..do.. | ..do.. | 4.8665 | | [2]900 | | 900 | [2]1,000 | 2,797 | 858 | | 1.05 | 1.17 | 3.26 |
| Trinidad | ..do.. | ..do.. | 4.8665 | | | | | 483 | 5,281 | 391 | | | 1.24 | 13.51 |
| Dutch West Indies | ..do.. | Guilder | .402 | | 162 | | 162 | 125 | 617 | 50 | | 3.24 | 2.50 | 12.34 |
| French West Indies— | | | | | | | | | | | | | | |
| Martinique | ..do.. | Franc | .193 | | 301 | | 301 | 119 | 4,613 | 230 | | 1.31 | .52 | 20.06 |
| Guadeloupe type | ..do.. | ..do.. | .193 | 309 | | | | | 3,873 | 240 | 1.29 | | | 16.14 |
| **South America:** | | | | | | | | | | | | | | |
| Argentina | ..do.. | Peso | .9648 | | 505,675 | | 505,675 | 1,500 | 578,425 | 8,533 | | 59.26 | .17 | 67.79 |
| Bolivia | ..do.. | Boliviano | .3893 | | 8,883 | | 8,883 | 389 | 16,383 | 2,890 | | 3.07 | | 5.67 |
| Brazil | ..do.. | Milreis | .5462 | | 33,544 | | 33,544 | | 567,199 | 30,492 | | 1.12 | | 18.60 |
| Chile | ..do.. | Peso | .365 | | [2]25,000 | | 26,000 | [2]600 | 110,530 | 3,755 | | 6.92 | 1.11 | 29.44 |
| Colombia | ..do.. | ..do.. | .9733 | | [2]23,309 | | 23,309 | 6,784 | 10,094 | 6,000 | | 3.88 | | 1.68 |
| Guiana— | | | | | | | | | | | | | | |
| British | ..do.. | Pound | 4.8665 | | | | | 1,500 | 1,600 | 298 | | | 5.03 | 5.37 |
| Dutch | ..do.. | Fler | .402 | | 96 | | 96 | 389 | 1,544 | 108 | | .89 | 3.60 | 14.30 |
| French | ..do.. | Franc | .193 | 303 | | | | | 2,605 | 49 | 6.18 | | | 63.16 |
| Paraguay | ..do.. | Peso | .9648 | | | | | | 63,542 | 1,000 | | | | 63.54 |
| Peru | ..do.. | Pound | 4.8665 | | 22,973 | 3,674 | 26,647 | [2]400 | 35,296 | 4,610 | | 5.78 | .09 | 7.65 |
| Uruguay | ..do.. | Peso | 1.0342 | | 62,203 | | 62,203 | 2,823 | 66,301 | 1,430 | | 43.50 | 1.97 | 46.36 |
| Venezuela | ..do.. | Bolivar | .193 | | 12,412 | 10,134 | 22,546 | 10,524 | 6,395 | 2,412 | | 9.35 | 4.36 | 2.65 |

Monetary stock of principal countries of the world, end of calendar year 1920—Continued.

| Country | Monetary standard | Name | U.S. equivalent | Metallic stock unclassified | Gold: In banks and public treasuries | Gold: In circulation | Gold: Total | Silver stock | Paper circulation | Population | Unclassified stock (per capita) | Per capita Gold | Per capita Silver | Per capita Paper |
|---|---|---|---|---|---|---|---|---|---|---|---|---|---|---|
| **Europe:** | | | | | | | | | | | | | | |
| Austria | Gold | Krone | $0.2026 | | $1,774 | | $1,774 | $5,289 | $6,208,810 | 6,067 | | $0.29 | $0.70 | $1,023.37 |
| Belgium | do. | Franc | .193 | | 51,428 | | 51,428 | 3,264 | 1,181,013 | 7,577 | | 6.79 | .58 | 155.87 |
| Bulgaria | do. | Lev | .193 | | 7,155 | | 7,155 | 16,370 | 647,322 | 5,598 | | 1.28 | 1.20 | 115.63 |
| Czechoslovakia | (¹) | Krone | .2026 | | 6,104 | | 6,104 | 697 | 150,047 | 13,636 | | .45 | .21 | 11.00 |
| Denmark | Gold | Krone | .268 | | 60,970 | | 60,970 | | 149,196 | 3,268 | | 18.66 | | 45.66 |
| Esthonia | (¹) | Mark | .193 | | | | | | 12,012 | 1,750 | | | | 6.87 |
| Finland | Gold | Mark | .193 | | 8,334 | $6,791 | 15,125 | 4,002 | 238,827 | 3,332 | | 4.54 | 1.38 | 77.68 |
| France | do. | Franc | .193 | | 685,517 | | 685,517 | 51,402 | 7,315,009 | 41,476 | | 11.70 | 1.24 | 176.36 |
| Germany | do. | Mark | .2382 | 14,360 | 260,028 | | 260,028 | 354,999 | 8,372,713 | 60,899 | $0.24 | 4.27 | 5.83 | 137.49 |
| Gt. Britain | do. | Pound | 4.8665 | 8,678 | 804,232 | | 804,232 | 316,323 | 2,604,950 | 47,308 | .18 | 17.00 | 6.69 | 55.06 |
| Greece | do. | Drachma | .193 | | | | | | 291,114 | 4,950 | | | | 58.81 |
| Hungary | do. | Krone | .2026 | | 7,000 | | 7,000 | 1,400 | 3,601,192 | 21,410 | | .34 | .06 | 183.61 |
| Italy | do. | Lira | .193 | | 208,968 | | 208,968 | 64,228 | 4,246,687 | 35,740 | | 5.69 | 1.75 | 116.57 |
| Latvia | do. | Ruble | .5146 | | 2,200 | | 2,200 | | | 1,728 | | 1.27 | | 488.81 |
| Lithuania | (²) | Ost mark | .2382 | | 5 | | 5 | | 414,000 | 4,651 | | | | 89.01 |
| Netherlands | do. | Gulden | .402 | | 255,729 | | 255,729 | 51,994 | 456,205 | 6,831 | | 37.44 | 7.61 | 66.78 |
| Norway | (¹) | Krone | .268 | | 39,472 | | 39,472 | 6,000 | 129,340 | 2,646 | | 14.92 | 2.27 | 48.88 |
| Poland | Gold | Mark | .2382 | | 2,958 | | 2,958 | 8,948 | 11,757,906 | 26,396 | | .11 | .34 | 445.61 |
| Portugal | Gold | Escudo | 1.0805 | | 9,266 | | 9,266 | 19,064 | 654,232 | 5,958 | | 1.55 | 3.19 | 109.83 |
| Rumania | do. | Franc | .193 | | 329 | | 329 | | 1,827,331 | 17,393 | | .02 | | 105.06 |
| Russia | do. | Ruble | .5146 | | 300,000 | | 300,000 | | | 182,183 | | 1.64 | | |
| Spain | do. | Peseta | .193 | | 473,762 | | 473,762 | 110,698 | 834,966 | 21,283 | | 22.26 | 5.20 | 39.23 |
| Sweden | do. | Krone | .268 | | 75,827 | | 75,827 | 262 | 203,647 | 5,904 | | 12.84 | .04 | 34.49 |
| Switzerland | do. | Franc | .193 | | 92,205 | | 92,205 | 23,463 | 200,483 | 3,862 | | 23.87 | 6.08 | 51.91 |
| Turkey | (¹) | £ | .044 | 294,031 | | | | | 679,930 | 21,274 | 9.60 | | | 31.95 |
| Yugoslavia | (²) | Dinar | .193 | 403 | 12,386 | | 12,386 | 2,992 | 645,417 | 13,908 | .03 | .89 | .21 | 46.41 |
| **Asia:** | | | | | | | | | | | | | | |
| British North Borneo | Gold | Dollar | .5678 | | 1,000 | | 1,000 | | 11,000 | 258 | | .22 | | 3.88 |
| Ceylon | do. | Rupee | .4866 | 19,517 | | | | 7,777 | 24,112 | 4,504 | .05 | .01 | 1.73 | 5.35 |
| China | Silver | Dollar | (¹) | | 5,000 | | 5,000 | 468,957 | 202,299 | 427,679 | | 3.83 | 1.10 | .47 |
| Cyprus Island | Gold | Pound | 4.8665 | | | 1,200 | 1,200 | 3,450 | 3,407 | 314 | | | 1.43 | 10.85 |
| Federated Malay States | do. | Dollar | .5678 | | | | | | 3,154 | 1,316 | | .36 | | 2.39 |
| India, British | do. | Rupee | .4866 | 153 | 116,261 | | 116,261 | 310,576 | 785,376 | 319,075 | .12 | .37 | .97 | 2.46 |
| Indo-China, French | do. | Rupee | .4866 | | 5,975 | | 5,975 | 15,147 | 59,942 | 16,000 | | 8.33 | .95 | 3.75 |
| Japan (including Chosen and Taiwan) | Gold | Yen | .4985 | | 645,486 | | 645,486 | 29,011 | 874,734 | 77,529 | | 1.87 | .37 | 11.28 |
| Netherlands Indies | do. | Gulder | .402 | | 83,154 | | 83,154 | 138,809 | 167,210 | 47,204 | | | 3.36 | 3.54 |
| Philippine Islands | do. | Peso | .50 | 12,372 | | | | | 49,922 | 10,779 | 1.15 | | .37 | 4.63 |

| | | | | | | | | | | | | | | | |
|---|---|---|---|---|---|---|---|---|---|---|---|---|---|---|---|
| Sarawak | do. | Dollar | .5678 | | | | | [12] 24 | [12] 61 | 600 | | | .04 | .10 |
| Siam | d. | Tical | .4054 | | | | | 10,320 | 25,908 | 8,809 | | | 1.17 | 2.94 |
| Straits Settlements | d. | Dollar | .5678 | | 1,606 | | 1,606 | 8,687 | 74,197 | 714 | | 2.25 | 12.17 | 103.92 |
| Af[illegible]: | | | | | | | | | | | | | | |
| Algeria | do. | Franc | .193 | 13,532 | | | | | 220,432 | 5,162 | 2.62 | | | 42.70 |
| Belgian Kongo | do. | do. | .193 | | | | | 4,991 | 6,755 | 15,000 | | | .33 | .45 |
| Kenya Colony | do. | Florin | .4866 | | | | | 29,052 | 14,737 | 2,529 | | | 11.49 | 5.83 |
| Egypt | do. | Pound | 4.9431 | | 3,884 | | 3,884 | 35,840 | 207,497 | 12,751 | | .30 | 2.81 | 16.27 |
| Madagascar | d. | Franc | .193 | | | | | 2,936 | 1,762 | 3,388 | | | .87 | .52 |
| Nigeria | do. | Pound | 4.8665 | | | | | 31,199 | 25,489 | 18,568 | | | 1.68 | 1.37 |
| Nyasaland | do. | do. | 4.8665 | | 584 | | 584 | 681 | | 1,377 | | .42 | .50 | |
| Reunion | do. | Franc | .193 | 580 | | | | | 5,590 | 174 | 3.33 | | | 32.13 |
| Rhodesia | d. | Pound | 4.8665 | | 942 | | 942 | 95 | 2,635 | 1,867 | | .50 | .05 | 1.41 |
| Sierra Leone | do. | do. | 4.8665 | | | | | 5 | 1,100 | 1,536 | | | | .72 |
| South Africa | d. | do. | 4.8665 | | 45,960 | | 45,960 | 3,690 | 94,225 | 6,872 | | 6.70 | .53 | 13.71 |
| West Africa, French | do. | Franc | .193 | 2,209 | | | | | 37,734 | 11,464 | .19 | | | 3.29 |
| Zanzibar | do. | Rupee | .4866 | | [3] 200 | | 200 | [3] 400 | 1,154 | 197 | | 1.02 | 2.03 | 5.86 |
| Australasia: | | | | | | | | | | | | | | |
| Australia | do. | Pound | 4.8665 | 104,541 | 115,409 | | 115,409 | 354 | 286,791 | 5,346 | 19.55 | 21.59 | .07 | 53.65 |
| New Zealand | do. | do. | 4.8665 | 37,263 | | | | | 40,160 | 1,227 | 30.37 | | | 32.73 |
| Total | | | | 487,496 | 8,155,666 | 186,533 | 8,342,199 | 2,843,113 | 64,190,688 | 1,777,744 | .27 | 4.69 | 1.60 | 36.11 |

[1] [illegible]es with the price of silver.
[2] Estimated on [illegible]sis of data considered [illegible]ly reliable.
[3] Part in circulation.
[4] In State bank.
[5] [illegible]ry standard not [illegible] s[illegible]d.
[6] [illegible]al [illegible]alue [illegible]h less; converted at gold value while original data state items as paper marks.
[7] Silver coin in circulation.
[8] Exclusive of 1 and 2 lire Government notes.
[9] Polish mark has no [illegible] [illegible]e; converted as the equivalent of the German mark.
[10] Russia's paper [illegible]n, [illegible]ed at 1,170 [illegible]ion [illegible], not [illegible]d.
[11] [illegible]mp[illegible]te.
[12] Straits Settlements [illegible] and notes in circulation not included; they predominate.

NOTE.—Figures given represent each country's stock at the end of the year, except [illegible]hen [illegible]wise indicated. Population figures are from the Statistical Abstract of the United States, [illegible]. Blanks indicate no [illegible] available, [illegible]ther than no stock. Gold held abroad as [illegible], not included in above figures (presumably reported by the country having [illegible]al possession): Argentina, $3,978,023; [illegible], $787,277; Bank of France, [illegible]; [illegible]ce, [illegible],199; Bank of Norway, $15,622,929; National Bank of Rumania, $95,294,798; [illegible]d, $12,575,880; French Indo-China, [illegible]; Japan ([illegible], 1920), $350,000,000; [illegible]ts Settlements, $3,763,687; Union of South Africa, $3,235,288; Spain, $15,929,469; Peru, 4,112,850; Yugoslavia, $67,464,875 ([illegible] and silver); Italy, $84,538,239.

Monetary stock of principal countries of the world, end of calendar year 1921.

[Stated in United States dollars—(000 omitted).]

| Country | Monetary standard | Monetary unit — Name | Monetary unit — United States equivalent | Metallic stock unclassified | Gold stock — In banks and public treasuries | Gold stock — In circulation | Gold stock — Total | Silver stock | Paper circulation | Population | Unclassified stock | Per capita — Gold | Per capita — Silver | Per capita — Paper |
|---|---|---|---|---|---|---|---|---|---|---|---|---|---|---|
| **North America:** | | | | | | | | | | | | | | |
| United States | Gold | Dollar | $1.00 | $68,102 | $3,660,569 | | $3,660,569 | $674,975 | $3,661,348 | 109,482 | $8.15 | $33.45 | $6.17 | $33.44 |
| | do | do | 1.00 | | 116,132 | | 116,132 | 129,000 | 407,591 | 8,361 | | 13.89 | 3.47 | 48.75 |
| | do | Peso | .4985 | | 22,500 | $27,500 | 50,000 | 30,000 | | 15,502 | | 3.23 | 1.94 | |
| British Honduras | do | Dollar | .4653 | | | | | 75 | 378 | 45 | | | 1.67 | 8.40 |
| Costa Rica | do | Colon | .4653 | | 11,400 | 10,000 | 11,400 | 8,737 | 113,000 | 469 | | 2.99 | | 27.71 |
| | do | Peso | 1.00 | | 7,483 | | 17,483 | 11,000 | 132,711 | 2 99 | 3.14 | 6.03 | 3.01 | 45.78 |
| Dominican Republic | do | Gourde | 1.00 | 3,000 | | | | 100 | 17,000 | 85 | | | 1.05 | 7.33 |
| Haiti | Pap. | Peso | .20 | | 800 | | 800 | | 2,900 | 2,500 | | .32 | .04 | 1.16 |
| | do | do | (?) | | | | 50 | 280 | 190,000 | 2,232 | | .08 | | 40.32 |
| Honduras | Gold | Dollar | 1.00 | | 50 | | | 85 | 2,022 | 637 | | | .44 | 3.17 |
| | do | Cordoba | 1.00 | | 1,000 | | 11,000 | 12,300 | 2,000 | 85 | | 3.77 | 8.68 | 7.55 |
| Nicaragua | do | Colon | .50 | | | | | 423 | 7,342 | 88 | | | .66 | 11.50 |
| | do | Dollar | 1.00 | | 2, 69 | | 2,039 | 28 | 3,509 | 1, 60 | | 1.36 | | 2.34 |
| Virgin Islands— | do | Pound | 4.8665 | | 83 | | 183 | | 261 | 25 | | 7.32 | 1.12 | 10.44 |
| | do | do | 4.8665 | | | | | 36 | 24 | 156 | | | .23 | .15 |
| Dutch West Indies— | do | do | 4.8665 | | | | | 1,277 | 2,061 | 858 | | | 1.49 | 2.40 |
| | do | | | | | | | 480 | 4,540 | 391 | | | 1.23 | 11.61 |
| Curacao | do | Guil dr. | .402 | | 101 | | 101 | 200 | 472 | 50 | | 2.02 | 4.00 | 9.42 |
| Guadeloupe | do | Franc | .193 | | 323 | | 323 | 78 | 6, 31 | 230 | | 1.40 | .34 | 27.41 |
| | do | | .193 | | | | | | 14,000 | 240 | | | | 16.67 |
| **South America:** | | | | | | | | | | | | | | |
| Brazil | do | Peso | .9648 | | 459,706 | | 459,706 | | 38, 98 | 8,533 | | 53.87 | | 67.78 |
| Chile | do | Milreis | .5462 | | 43,307 | | 43,307 | 839 | 616,360 | 30 492 | | 1.42 | | 20.21 |
| | do | Peso | .365 | | 40,017 | | 40,017 | 7,343 | 96,725 | 6,000 | | 10.66 | .22 | 28.42 |
| | do | do | .9733 | | 23,309 | | 23,309 | | 10,084 | | | 3.88 | 1.22 | 1.68 |
| Guiana— British | do | Pound | 4.8665 | | | | | 1,521 | 2,585 | 98 | | | 5.10 | 8.67 |
| Dutch | do | do | .402 | | | | | 300 | 1,000 | 88 | | | 2.78 | 9.26 |
| Paraguay | do | Peso | 94.8 | | 920 | | 920 | 413 | 77,158 | 1 60 | | .92 | | 77.16 |
| Peru | do | Pound | 4.8665 | | 22,432 | | 22,432 | 13,000 | 29,223 | 1 60 | | 4.87 | .09 | 6.34 |
| Uruguay | do | Peso | 1.0342 | | 56,893 | | 36,893 | 10,000 | 170,000 | 1,430 | | 39.79 | 2.10 | 48.95 |
| Venezuela | do | Bol. | .193 | | 16,405 | | 16,405 | | 7,000 | 2,412 | | 6.80 | 4.15 | 2.90 |

| Country | Standard | Monetary unit | Value in U.S. dollars |
|---|---|---|---|
| **Europe:** | | | |
| Austria | do. | Krone | .2026 |
| Belgium | do. | Franc | .193 |
| Bulgaria | do. | Lev | .2026 |
| Denmark | do. | Krone | .268 |
| Esthonia | Gold | Mark | .193 |
| | Gold | do. | .193 |
| France | do. | Franc | .193 |
| Germany | do. | Mark | .2382 |
| Great Britain | do. | Pound | 4.8665 |
| Hungary | do. | Krone | .193 |
| | do. | | .2026 |
| Italy | do. | Lira | .193 |
| Latvia | do. | Ruble | .5146 |
| | Gold | Ost mark | .2382 |
| Netherlands | do. | Krone | .402 |
| Norway | do. | Krone | .268 |
| Poland | Gold | Mark | .2382 |
| Portugal | Gold | Escudo | 1.0805 |
| Rumania | do. | Leu | .193 |
| Russia | do. | Ruble | .5146 |
| Spain | do. | Peseta | .193 |
| Sweden | do. | Krone | .268 |
| Switzerland | do. | Franc | .193 |
| Turkey | do. | Piaster | .044 |
| Yugoslavia | (?) | Dinar | .193 |
| **Asia:** | | | |
| Arabia—Oman | do. | Pound | 4.8665 |
| British North Borneo | do. | Dollar | .5678 |
| China | do. | Dollar | .860 |
| Federated Malay States | Gold | Dollar | 4.8665 |
| India, British | do. | Rupee | .5678 |
| Indo-China, French | do. | Dollar | .4866 |
| Japan (including Chosen, Kwantung, and Taiwan) | Gold | Yen | .4985 |
| Netherlands Indies | do. | Rier | .402 |
| Palestine | do. | Pound | 4.9431 |
| Philippine Islands | do. | Peso | .50 |
| Sarawak | do. | Dollar | .5678 |
| Siam | do. | Tical | .4054 |
| Straits Settlements | do. | Dollar | .5678 |
| Syria | do. | Pound | 3.860 |
| **Africa:** | | | |
| Abyssinia | Rier | Thalari | (?) |
| Algeria | Gold | Franc | .193 |
| Belgian Congo | do. | do. | .193 |
| British Somaliland | do. | Rupee | .4866 |
| Egypt | do. | Pound | 4.9431 |

*Monetary stock of principal countries of the world, end of calendar year 1921—Continued.*

| Country. | Monetary standard. | Monetary unit. Name. | Monetary unit. United States equivalent. | Metallic stock unclassified. | Gold stock. In banks and public treasuries. | Gold stock. In circulation. | Gold stock. Total. | Silver stock. | Paper circulation. | Population. | Per capita. Unclassified stock. | Per capita. Gold. | Per capita. Silver. | Per capita. Paper. |
|---|---|---|---|---|---|---|---|---|---|---|---|---|---|---|
| **Africa—Continued.** | | | | | | | | | | | | | | |
| Gambia | Gold | Pound | $4.8665 | | | | | 1 $533 | $360 | 210 | | | $0.26 | $1.71 |
| Gold Coast | do | do | 4.8665 | | | | | 1 25,000 | 22,528 | 2,078 | | | 9.89 | 10.84 |
| Kenya 2 3 | do | Shilling | .2433 | | | | | 2,355 | 1 15,000 | 2,529 | | | .80 | 5.93 |
| Madagascar 4 | do | Franc | .193 | | | | | | 15,433 | 3,288 | | | | 4.56 |
| Mo., French | do | do | .193 | | | | | | 27,071 | 6,000 | | | 1.21 | 4.51 |
| Nigeria | do | Pound | 4.8665 | | | | | 22,449 | 913 | 18,568 | | | .69 | .05 |
| Nyasaland | do | do | 4.8665 | | $567 | | $567 | 957 | 1,377 | 1,377 | | $0.41 | .05 | |
| Rhodesia | do | do | 4.8665 | $49 | 1 950 | | 950 | 1 90 | 1 2,600 | 1,867 | $0.03 | .51 | 1.41 | 1.39 |
| Senegal | do | Franc | .193 | | | | | 1,761 | 33,563 | 1,250 | | | .30 | 26.85 |
| Sierra Leone | do | Pound | 4.8665 | | | | | 458 | 450 | 1,536 | | | .51 | .29 |
| Union of South Africa 16 | do | do | 4.8665 | | 72,067 | | 72,067 | 1 3,500 | 44,689 | 6,872 | | 10.49 | 4.05 | 6.50 |
| Zanzibar | do | Rupee | .4866 | | | | | 798 | 1,299 | 197 | | | | 6.54 |
| **Australasia:** | | | | | | | | | | | | | | |
| Australia | do | Pound | 4.8665 | 106,053 | 115,533 | | 115,533 | 774 | 271,355 | 5,346 | 19.84 | 21.61 | .14 | 50.76 |
| New Zealand | do | do | 4.8665 | | 37,394 | | 37,394 | | 36,296 | 1,227 | | 30.48 | | 29.38 |
| Tahiti—Society Islands | do | Franc | .193 | | | | | 444 | 1,315 | 28 | | | 15.86 | 46.96 |
|     Total | | | | 650,743 | 8,522,912 | $39,009 | 8,561,921 | 2,170,460 | 159,543,335 | 1,787,002 | .36 | 4.79 | 1.21 | 89.28 |

1 Estimated on basis of data considered reasonably reliable.
2 Fluctuates with the price of silver.
3 Feb. 28, 1922.
4 June 30, 1921.
5 End of September, 1921, in Banco de la Republica.
6 Oct. 8.
7 State bank.
8 Five-franc pieces only.
9 Monetary standard not fixed.
10 Bank of France.
11 Germany holds $14,000 fine kilos of silver abroad (2,900 oz., valued at $16,517,719).
12 Polish mark has no par value. Converted as the weight of the German mark.
13 17,543 billions of marks.
14 In Government only.
15 Pound Le.
16 In banks.

Note.—Figures given represent each country's stock at the end of the year, except when otherwise indicated. Population figures are from the Statistical Abstract of the United States, 1921. Blanks indicate no figures available, rather than no stock. Gold held abroad as follows, not included in the above figures (presumably reported by the country having actual possession): Egypt, $15,831,811; Italy, $83,155,990; Japan, $426,217,500; Straits Settlements, $3,763,686; British Honduras, $39,000; Yugoslavia, $59,913,254 (gold and silver); Bank of France, $376,033,531; Chile, $12,511,178; Peru, $14,142,010; Honduras, $300,000; Argentina, $3,977,870; Union of South Africa, $3,500,000 (gold and silver).

## WORLD PRODUCTION OF GOLD AND SILVER, 1920 AND 1921.

The production figures given below are based upon the preceding data and that published in prior issues of the report of the Director of the Mint.

| Country | Calendar year 1920 — Gold — Kilos, fine. | Ounces, fine. | Value. | Calendar year 1920 — Silver — Kilos, fine. | Ounces, fine. | Value ($1.0194 per ounce).[1] | Calendar year 1921 — Gold — Kilos, fine. | Ounces, fine. | Value. | Calendar year 1921 — Silver — Kilos, fine. | Ounces, fine. | Value ($0.63117 per ounce).[1] |
|---|---|---|---|---|---|---|---|---|---|---|---|---|
| **North America:** | | | | | | | | | | | | |
| United States | 77,019 | 2,476,166 | $51,186,900 | 1,721,977 | 53,361,573 | $56,435,587 | 75,334 | 2,422,006 | $50,067,307 | 1,650,154 | 53,052,441 | $33,485,109 |
| Canada | 23,854 | 766,913 | 15,853,499 | 397,933 | 12,793,541 | 13,041,736 | 28,752 | 924,374 | 19,108,506 | 408,551 | 13,134,926 | 8,290,371 |
| Mexico | 22,970 | 738,485 | 15,265,550 | 2,073,476 | 66,662,253 | 67,965,501 | 21,426 | 688,846 | 14,239,711 | 2,006,642 | 64,513,540 | 40,719,011 |
| Total | 123,843 | 3,981,564 | 82,306,249 | 4,193,386 | 134,817,367 | 137,432,824 | 125,512 | 4,035,226 | 83,415,524 | 4,065,347 | 130,700,907 | 82,494,491 |
| Central America and West Indies | 4,514 | 145,125 | 3,000,000 | 83,981 | 2,700,000 | 2,752,380 | 3,762 | 120,937 | 2,500,000 | 62,208 | 2,000,000 | 1,262,340 |
| **South America:** | | | | | | | | | | | | |
| Argentina | 150 | 4,837 | 100,000 | 933 | 30,000 | 30,582 | 113 | 3,628 | 75,000 | 778 | 25,000 | 15,779 |
| Bolivia | 8 | 242 | 5,000 | 68,429 | 2,200,000 | 2,242,680 | 9 | 290 | 6,000 | 74,650 | 2,400,000 | 1,514,808 |
| Brazil | 3,912 | 125,775 | 2,600,000 | 933 | 30,000 | 30,582 | 4,183 | 134,462 | 2,780,000 | 1,027 | 33,000 | 20,829 |
| Chile | 1,354 | 43,538 | 900,000 | 81,059 | 2,604,456 | 2,654,982 | 1,204 | 38,700 | 800,000 | 68,429 | 2,200,000 | 1,388,574 |
| Colombia | 8,727 | 280,575 | 5,800,000 | 14,930 | 480,000 | 489,312 | 9,028 | 290,250 | 6,000,000 | 15,552 | 500,000 | 315,585 |
| Ecuador | 1,128 | 36,281 | 750,000 | 1,089 | 35,000 | 35,679 | 1,173 | 37,710 | 779,536 | 1,244 | 40,000 | 25,247 |
| Guiana— British | 301 | 9,675 | 200,000 | 249 | 8,000 | 8,155 | 399 | 12,828 | 265,178 | 290 | 9,000 | 5,680 |
| Dutch | 389 | 12,506 | 258,522 | | | | 376 | 12,094 | 250,000 | | | |
| French | 1,354 | 43,538 | 900,000 | | | | 1,505 | 48,375 | 1,000,000 | | | |
| Peru | 1,952 | 62,757 | 1,297,302 | 286,043 | 9,196,282 | 9,374,690 | 2,407 | 77,385 | 1,599,690 | 306,498 | 9,853,910 | 6,219,33 |
| Uruguay | 1 | 21 | 440 | 16 | 500 | 510 | 10 | 339 | 7,000 | 62 | 2,000 | 1,92 |
| Venezuela | 586 | 18,839 | 389,436 | 109 | 3,500 | 3,568 | 349 | 11,215 | 231,834 | 84 | 2,700 | 1,04 |
| Total | 19,862 | 635,584 | 13,200,700 | 453,740 | 14,587,738 | 14,870,740 | 20,756 | 667,396 | 13,794,238 | 468,604 | 15,065,610 | 9,508,961 |
| **Europe:** | | | | | | | | | | | | |
| Austria | | | | 435 | 13,965 | 14,256 | | | | 467 | 15,000 | 9,468 |
| Czechoslovakia | 272 | 8,761 | 181,106 | 21,153 | 680,069 | 693,262 | 355 | 11,413 | 235,927 | 21,868 | 703,056 | 443,748 |
| France | | | | 10,000 | 321,500 | 327,737 | | | | 10,000 | 321,500 | 202,921 |
| Germany | 138 | 4,437 | 91,715 | 102,800 | 3,305,020 | 3,369,138 | 140 | 4,501 | 93,044 | 105,000 | 3,375,750 | 2,130,672 |
| Great Britain | 1 | 32 | 661 | 2,375 | 76,356 | 77,837 | | | | 352 | 11,317 | 7,142 |
| Greece | 16 | 514 | 10,625 | 6,872 | 220,935 | 225,220 | 15 | 482 | 9,964 | 6,000 | 192,900 | 121,753 |

[1] Average price per ounce, 1,000 fine, of bar silver (other than that subject to Pittman Act price of $1 per ounce) in New York.

World production of gold and silver, 1920 and 1921—Continued.

| Country | Calendar year 1920 | | | | | | Calendar year 1921 | | | | | |
|---|---|---|---|---|---|---|---|---|---|---|---|---|
| | Gold | | | Silver | | | Gold | | | Silver | | |
| | Kilos, fine. | Ounces, fine. | Value. | Kilos, fine. | Ounces, fine. | Value ($1.0194 per ounce). | Kilos, fine. | Ounces, fine. | Value. | Kilos, fine. | Ounces, fine. | Value ($.063117 per ounce). |
| **Europe:** | | | | | | | | | | | | |
| Italy | 23 | 725 | $15,000 | 9,252 | 297,452 | $303,223 | 15 | 484 | $10,000 | 6,200 | 199,330 | $125,811 |
| Norway | | | | 10,052 | 323,172 | 329,442 | | | | 10,052 | 323,172 | 203,977 |
| Russia and Siberia | 1,789 | 57,225 | 1,182,945 | 1,555 | 50,000 | 50,970 | 1,400 | 45,000 | 930,232 | 1,244 | 40,000 | 25,247 |
| Spain | | | | 91,961 | 2,956,516 | 3,013,903 | | | | 83,339 | 2,679,349 | 1,691,124 |
| Sweden | 7 | 225 | 4,651 | 360 | 11,574 | 11,799 | 6 | 193 | 3,988 | 415 | 13,342 | 8,421 |
| Turkey | | | | 3,110 | 100,000 | 101,940 | | | | 3,110 | 100,000 | 63,117 |
| Yugoslavia | 100 | 3,215 | 66,460 | 467 | 15,000 | 15,291 | 124 | 3,986 | 82,410 | 496 | 15,946 | 10,065 |
|    Total | 2,337 | 75,134 | 1,553,163 | 260,392 | 8,371,609 | 8,534,018 | 2,055 | 66,059 | 1,365,565 | 248,543 | 7,990,662 | 5,043,468 |
| **Australasia:** | | | | | | | | | | | | |
| New South Wales | 1,521 | 48,907 | 1,010,997 | 37,195 | 1,195,821 | 1,219,020 | 1,592 | 51,173 | 1,057,840 | 258,974 | 8,326,006 | 5,255,125 |
| Northern Territory | 23 | 751 | 15,525 | | | | 15 | 490 | 10,129 | | | |
| Queensland | 3,584 | 115,290 | 2,382,016 | 8,530 | 274,235 | 279,555 | 1,256 | 40,376 | 834,646 | 6,075 | 195,328 | 123,285 |
| South Australia | 53 | 1,697 | 35,080 | 31 | 1,005 | 1,025 | 82 | 2,628 | 54,326 | 45 | 1,449 | 915 |
| Victoria | 5,256 | 168,979 | 3,493,106 | 194 | 6,231 | 6,352 | 3,251 | 104,512 | 2,160,455 | 162 | 5,204 | 3,285 |
| West Australia | 19,217 | 617,842 | 12,771,928 | 4,065 | 130,692 | 133,227 | 20,683 | 664,990 | 13,745,736 | 3,613 | 116,151 | 73,311 |
| New Zealand | 3,869 | 124,375 | 2,571,055 | 14,108 | 453,567 | 462,366 | 3,858 | 124,375 | 2,571,065 | 14,108 | 453,567 | 286,278 |
| Tasmania | 194 | 6,246 | 129,116 | 19,389 | 623,359 | 635,452 | 166 | 5,340 | 110,388 | 10,845 | 348,658 | 220,062 |
| Papua | 366 | 11,751 | 242,915 | | | | 289 | 9,289 | 192,021 | | | |
|    Total | 34,083 | 1,095,778 | 22,651,738 | 83,512 | 2,684,910 | 2,736,997 | 31,262 | 1,003,133 | 20,736,596 | 293,822 | 9,446,363 | 5,962,251 |
| **Asia:** | | | | | | | | | | | | |
| British India | 15,523 | 499,068 | 10,316,651 | 89,288 | 2,870,595 | 2,926,285 | 14,619 | 470,000 | 9,715,762 | 119,064 | 3,827,904 | 2,416,058 |
| China | 3,888 | 125,000 | 2,583,979 | 1,555 | 50,000 | 50,970 | 3,110 | 100,000 | 2,067,183 | 1,244 | 40,000 | 25,247 |
| Chosen (Korea) | 2,364 | 76,000 | 1,571,059 | 37 | 1,200 | 1,223 | 2,333 | 75,000 | 1,550,388 | 31 | 1,000 | 631 |
| East Indies— | | | | | | | | | | | | |
|   British | 903 | 29,025 | 600,000 | | | | 752 | 24,188 | 500,000 | | | |
|   Dutch | 2,828 | 90,920 | 1,879,483 | 31,973 | 1,027,983 | 1,047,874 | 2,929 | 94,168 | 1,946,625 | 31,788 | 1,021,994 | 645,052 |
| Federated Malay States | 400 | 12,853 | 265,695 | | | | 416 | 13,385 | 276,719 | | | |
| Indo-China | 5 | 160 | 3,307 | | | | 5 | 160 | 3,307 | | | |

| | | | | | | | | | | | |
|---|---|---|---|---|---|---|---|---|---|---|---|
| Japan | 7,719 | 248,181 | 5,130,357 | 152,174 | 4,892,380 | 4,987,292 | 7,144 | 229,671 | 4,747,721 | 124,220 | 3,968,981 | 2,520,881 |
| Sarawak | 509 | 16,353 | 338,047 | 161 | 5,179 | 5,279 | 532 | 17,091 | 353,302 | 107 | 3,437 | 2,169 |
| Taiwan (Formosa) | 420 | 13,500 | 279,070 | 622 | 20,000 | 20,388 | 373 | 12,000 | 348,062 | 466 | 15,000 | 9,468 |
| Total | 34,559 | 1,111,060 | 22,967,648 | 275,810 | 8,867,286 | 9,089,311 | 32,213 | 1,035,664 | 21,409,069 | 276,930 | 8,903,316 | 5,619,506 |
| Africa: | | | | | | | | | | | |
| Algeria | | | | | | | | | | | | |
| Belgian Congo | 3,011 | 96,894 | 2,001,116 | 4,666 | 150,000 | 152,910 | 559 | 18,936 | 391,442 | 4,066 | 150,000 | 94,675 |
| British West Africa (Gold Coast, Ashanti, and Nigeria) | | | | 332 | 10,673 | 10,881 | 2,044 | 65,715 | 1,358,450 | 181 | 5,819 | 3,673 |
| Egypt and Abyssinia | 7,183 | 230,948 | 4,774,119 | | | | 6,333 | 203,599 | 4,208,765 | | | |
| Eritrea | 443 | 14,232 | 294,292 | 9 | 304 | 310 | 45 | 1,451 | 30,000 | | | |
| French West Africa (Guinea, Senegal, and Ivory Coast) | 18 | 579 | 11,969 | | | | 15 | 494 | 10,000 | | | |
| Madagascar | 150 | 4,838 | 100,000 | 430 | 13,824 | 14,093 | 151 | 4,838 | 100,000 | 400 | 12,980 | 8,117 |
| Portuguese East Africa | 519 | 16,686 | 344,930 | 22 | 700 | 713 | 456 | 14,660 | 303,019 | 16 | 502 | 317 |
| Rhodesia— Northern | 226 | 7,296 | 150,000 | | | | 187 | 6,015 | 124,341 | | | |
| Southern | 18 | 569 | 11,762 | 183 | 5,583 | 5,597 | 43 | 1,383 | 28,589 | 276 | 8,867 | 5,597 |
| Transvaal, Cape Colony, and Natal | 17,185 | 552,495 | 11,421,147 | 4,945 | 158,982 | 162,066 | 18,212 | 585,525 | 12,103,876 | 4,753 | 152,989 | 96,562 |
| Total | 259,149 | 8,331,651 | 172,230,512 | 27,723 | 891,304 | 908,595 | 252,837 | 8,128,722 | 168,035,597 | 25,827 | 830,339 | 524,085 |
| Total | 287,902 | 9,256,061 | 191,839,757 | 38,310 | 1,231,670 | 1,255,565 | 280,912 | 9,031,328 | 186,694,109 | 36,124 | 1,161,376 | 733,926 |
| Total for world | 507,100 | 16,303,306 | 337,019,255 | 5,389,131 | 173,260,580 | 176,621,835 | 496,412 | 15,959,643 | 329,915,101 | 5,451,578 | 175,268,234 | 110,624,051 |

## Production of gold and silver in the world since the discovery of America.

[From 1493 to 1885 is from a table of averages for certain periods, compiled by Dr. Adolph Soetbeer; for the years since, the production is the annual estimate of the Bureau of the Mint.]

| Period. | Gold. Annual average for period. Fine ounces. | Value. | Gold. Total for period. Fine ounces. | Value. | Silver. Annual average for period. Fine ounces. | Coining value. | Silver. Total for period. Fine ounces. | Coining value in standard silver dollars. | Pct. by weight. Gold. | Pct. by weight. Silver. | Pct. by value. Gold. | Pct. by value. Silver. |
|---|---|---|---|---|---|---|---|---|---|---|---|---|
| 1493–1520 | 185,470 | $3,855,000 | 5,221,160 | $107,931,000 | 1,511,050 | $1,954,000 | 42,309,400 | $54,703,000 | 11 | 89 | 66.4 | 33.6 |
| 1521–1544 | 230,194 | 4,759,000 | 5,524,656 | 114,205,000 | 2,899,933 | 3,740,000 | 69,598,329 | 89,986,000 | 7.4 | 92.6 | 55.9 | 44.1 |
| 1545–1560 | 273,596 | 5,656,000 | 4,377,544 | 90,492,000 | 10,017,940 | 12,952,000 | 160,287,040 | 207,240,000 | 2.7 | 97.3 | 30.4 | 69.6 |
| 1561–1580 | 219,906 | 4,546,000 | 4,388,120 | 90,917,000 | 9,628,925 | 12,453,000 | 192,578,500 | 248,990,000 | 2.2 | 97.8 | 26.7 | 73.3 |
| 1581–1600 | 237,267 | 4,905,000 | 4,745,340 | 98,995,000 | 13,467,635 | 17,413,000 | 269,352,700 | 348,254,000 | 1.7 | 98.3 | 22 | 78 |
| 1601–1620 | 273,918 | 5,662,000 | 5,478,360 | 113,248,000 | 13,596,235 | 17,579,000 | 271,924,700 | 351,579,000 | 2 | 98 | 24.4 | 75.6 |
| 1621–1640 | 266,845 | 5,516,000 | 5,336,900 | 110,324,000 | 12,654,240 | 16,361,000 | 253,084,800 | 327,221,000 | 2 | 98 | 25.2 | 74.8 |
| 1641–1660 | 281,955 | 5,828,000 | 5,639,110 | 116,571,000 | 11,776,545 | 15,226,000 | 235,530,900 | 304,525,000 | 2.3 | 97.7 | 27.7 | 72.3 |
| 1661–1680 | 297,709 | 6,154,000 | 5,954,180 | 123,084,000 | 10,831,550 | 14,008,000 | 216,691,000 | 280,166,000 | 2.7 | 97.3 | 30.5 | 69.5 |
| 1681–1700 | 346,095 | 7,154,000 | 6,921,895 | 143,088,000 | 10,992,085 | 14,212,000 | 219,841,700 | 284,240,000 | 3.1 | 96.9 | 33.5 | 66.5 |
| 1701–1720 | 412,163 | 8,520,000 | 8,243,260 | 170,403,000 | 11,432,540 | 14,781,000 | 228,650,800 | 295,629,800 | 3.5 | 96.5 | 36.6 | 63.4 |
| 1721–1740 | 613,422 | 12,681,000 | 12,268,440 | 253,611,000 | 13,983,080 | 17,924,000 | 277,281,600 | 358,480,000 | 4.2 | 95.8 | 41.4 | 58.6 |
| 1741–1760 | 791,211 | 16,356,000 | 15,824,230 | 327,116,000 | 17,140,612 | 22,162,000 | 342,812,235 | 443,232,000 | 4.4 | 95.6 | 42.5 | 57.5 |
| 1761–1780 | 665,666 | 13,761,000 | 13,313,315 | 275,211,000 | 20,985,591 | 27,133,000 | 419,711,820 | 542,658,000 | 3.1 | 96.9 | 33.7 | 66.3 |
| 1781–1800 | 571,948 | 11,823,000 | 11,438,970 | 236,464,000 | 28,261,779 | 36,540,000 | 565,235,589 | 729,810,000 | 2 | 98 | 24.1 | 75.9 |
| 1801–1810 | 571,563 | 11,815,000 | 5,715,627 | 118,152,000 | 28,746,922 | 37,168,000 | 287,469,225 | 371,677,040 | 1.9 | 98.1 | 24.1 | 75.9 |
| 1811–1820 | 367,957 | 7,606,000 | 3,679,568 | 76,063,000 | 17,385,755 | 22,479,099 | 173,857,555 | 224,786,000 | 2.1 | 97.9 | 25.3 | 74.7 |
| 1821–1830 | 457,044 | 9,448,000 | 4,570,444 | 94,479,000 | 14,807,004 | 19,144,000 | 148,070,040 | 191,444,000 | 3 | 97 | 33 | 67 |
| 1831–1840 | 652,291 | 13,484,000 | 6,522,913 | 134,841,000 | 19,175,867 | 24,793,030 | 191,758,675 | 247,930,000 | 3.3 | 96.7 | 35.2 | 64.8 |
| 1841–1850 | 1,760,502 | 36,393,000 | 17,605,021 | 363,928,000 | 25,090,342 | 32,440,000 | 250,903,422 | 324,400,000 | 6.6 | 93.4 | 52.9 | 47.1 |
| 1851–1855* | 6,410,324 | 132,513,000 | 32,051,621 | 662,566,000 | 28,488,597 | 36,824,000 | 142,442,985 | 184,189,000 | 18.4 | 81.6 | 78.3 | 21.7 |
| 1856–1860 | 6,486,262 | 134,083,000 | 32,431,312 | 670,415,000 | 29,095,482 | 37,618,000 | 145,477,142 | 188,092,000 | 18.2 | 81.8 | 78.1 | 21.9 |
| 1861–1865 | 5,949,582 | 122,989,000 | 29,747,913 | 614,944,000 | 35,401,972 | 45,772,000 | 177,009,862 | 228,861,000 | 14.4 | 85.6 | 72.9 | 27.1 |
| 1866–1870 | 6,270,086 | 129,614,000 | 31,350,439 | 648,071,000 | 43,051,583 | 55,633,000 | 215,257,914 | 278,313,000 | 12.7 | 87.3 | 70 | 30 |
| 1871–1875 | 5,591,014 | 115,577,000 | 27,955,068 | 577,883,000 | 63,317,014 | 81,864,000 | 316,585,069 | 409,322,000 | 8.1 | 91.9 | 58.5 | 41.5 |
| 1876–1880 | 5,543,110 | 114,586,000 | 27,715,559 | 572,931,000 | 78,775,602 | 101,851,000 | 393,878,009 | 509,286,000 | 6.6 | 93.4 | 53 | 47 |
| 1881–1885 | 4,794,755 | 99,116,000 | 23,973,773 | 495,582,000 | 92,003,944 | 118,955,000 | 460,019,722 | 594,773,000 | 5 | 95 | 45.5 | 54.5 |
| 1886–1890 | 5,461,282 | 112,885,000 | 27,396,411 | 564,474,000 | 105,911,431 | 140,815,000 | 544,557,155 | 704,074,000 | 4.8 | 95.2 | 44.5 | 55.5 |
| 1891–1895 | 7,882,565 | 162,947,000 | 39,412,823 | 814,736,000 | 157,581,331 | 203,742,000 | 787,906,656 | 1,018,708,000 | 4.8 | 95.2 | 44.4 | 55.6 |
| 1896–1900 | 12,446,939 | 257,391,100 | 62,234,698 | 1,286,505,400 | 165,683,304 | 214,229,700 | 828,466,522 | 1,071,148,400 | 7 | 93 | 54.6 | 45.4 |
| 1901–1905 | 15,606,730 | 322,619,800 | 78,033,650 | 1,613,099,100 | 167,995,408 | 217,206,200 | 839,977,042 | 1,086,037,900 | 8.5 | 91.5 | 59.8 | 40.2 |
| 1906 | | | 19,471,080 | 402,503,000 | | | 165,054,497 | 213,403,890 | 10.5 | 89.5 | 65.3 | 34.7 |
| 1907 | | | 19,977,260 | 412,906,600 | | | 184,206,984 | 238,166,600 | 9.8 | 90.2 | 63.4 | 36.6 |
| 1908 | | | 21,922,244 | 442,837,000 | | | 203,131,404 | 262,634,500 | 9.5 | 90.5 | 62.8 | 37.2 |
| 1909 | | | 21,965,111 | 454,059,100 | | | 212,149,023 | 274,283,700 | 9.4 | 90.6 | 62.3 | 37.7 |

| Year | | | | | | | | |
|---|---|---|---|---|---|---|---|---|
| 1910 | 22,022,180 | 455,239,100 | 221,715,673 | 288,662,700 | 9 | 91 | 61.4 | 35.6 |
| 1911 | 22,348,313 | 461,980,500 | 226,192,923 | 292,451,500 | 9 | 91 | 63.3 | 36.7 |
| 1912 | 22,549,335 | 466,136,100 | 230,904,241 | 298,542,842 | 8.9 | 91.1 | 60.9 | 39.1 |
| 1913 | 22,249,596 | 459,939,900 | 208,690,446 | 289,821,982 | 9.6 | 90.4 | 63.0 | 37.0 |
| 1914 | 21,240,416 | 439,078,260 | 166,968,491 | 215,878,453 | 11.2 | 88.8 | 67.0 | 33.0 |
| 1915 | 22,674,568 | 468,724,918 | 167,544,652 | 216,623,388 | 11.9 | 88.1 | 68.3 | 31.7 |
| 1916 | 21,970,788 | 454,176,500 | 175,775,275 | 227,265,001 | 11.1 | 88.9 | 66.6 | 33.4 |
| 1917 | 20,299,546 | 419,422,100 | 181,207,464 | 234,288,438 | 10.0 | 90.0 | 64.2 | 35.8 |
| 1918 | 18,556,920 | 383,605,552 | 198,165,408 | 236,217,739 | 8.6 | 91.4 | 60 | 40 |
| 1919 | 17,695,037 | 365,788,796 | 176,459,669 | 228,149,797 | 9.1 | 90.0 | 61.5 | 38.5 |
| 1920 | 16,303,306 | 337,019,255 | 173,260,580 | 224,013,679 | 8.6 | 91.4 | 60.7 | 33.3 |
| 1921 | 15,959,643 | 329,915,101 | 173,208,234 | 226,609,434 | 8.3 | 91.7 | 59.2 | 40.8 |
| Total | 891,657,642 | 18,432,821,282 | 12,735,205,985 | 16,465,720,853 | 6.5 | 93.5 | 52.8 | 47.2 |

SURY DE 7

# REPORT OF THE REGISTER OF THE TREASURY.

TREASURY DEPARTMENT,
OFFICE OF REGISTER OF THE TREASURY,
*Washington, October 5, 1922.*

SIR: I have the honor to submit the following report of the office of the Register of the Treasury for the fiscal year ended June 30, 1922:

The retirement of public-debt securities continues in large volume, the bulk of securities retired during the fiscal year 1922 being principally due to the great amount of war savings securities and interest coupons functioned and to the heavy transactions resulting from exchange and cancellation of temporary for permanent coupon bonds. The first Liberty loan of 1932–1947, bearing interest at the rate of 3½ per cent, and the Victory notes were the only issues made in permanent form having coupons to maturity attached. As a rule the loans issued in temporary form had four coupons attached. These temporary loans were issued to meet the urgent needs resulting from the stress of war-time emergencies when the chief object was to deliver the securities in some convenient form into the hands of the public and every facility and time-saving method practical was employed with this end in view.

Appropriate statistical tables covering the work actually performed during the year have been prepared and are incorporated in this report. No mere book accounts have been tabulated and in all the tables presented the information disclosed embraces only securities actually audited and delivered to the files. These tabulations cover final audit figures and agree with the reports of the forwarding offices, except where necessary deductions have been made and securities returned for correction or repayment.

## RETIRED SECURITIES CANCELED ON ACCOUNT OF REDUCTION OF PRINCIPAL OF PUBLIC DEBT.

The securities issued by the United States and later redeemed, including bonds, notes, certificates of indebtedness, Treasury (war) savings securities, and interest coupons, are not finally paid until they reach the Register's office and receive appropriate examination. All redeemed securities, whether paid by the Treasurer of the United States direct or through Federal reserve banks, are charged against the Treasurer's account, and the amounts are included in his monthly statement, covering payments on the public debt. After examination of the securities the Register executes a certificate setting forth the classes and amounts thereof and forwards it to the Comptroller General of the United States for use in settling the Treasurer's public-debt account. Securities so retired (except interest coupons) effect a reduction in the principal of the public debt and may be divided into six general classes, viz:

(a) Those which have matured and are payable on presentation.

(b) Those which have been purchased by the Secretary of the Treasury under provisions of law for the sinking fund or other retirement account.

(c) Those received on account of estate or inheritance taxes under the provisions of the act of Congress approved September 24, 1917, as amended.

(d) Those payable before the designated maturity date at the option of the holder, as in the case of war savings certificates.

(e) Those surrendered for the benefit of the United States, as in cases where United States bonds, etc., are received by the department as donations, contributions on account of conscience, or canceled on account of forfeiture to the United States.

(f) Those called for redemption by the Secretary of the Treasury prior to maturity.

### SECURITIES RECEIVED FOR CREDIT TO FISCAL AGENCY ACCOUNT.

The Federal reserve banks, as fiscal agents of the Government, are permitted to receive and handle certain transactions as a matter of convenience to the department and the public. They receive coupon bonds of one denomination in exchange for those of another denomination and accept Liberty bonds and Victory notes for conversion purposes. They also receive and forward to the department the coupon bonds surrendered for exchange into registered bonds and registered bonds submitted to them for transfer of titles or in exchange for coupon bonds. The Division of Loans and Currency, in addition to handling transactions permitted Federal Reserve banks, makes the necessary issue in all transactions affecting registered securities, whether issued or retired. The securities surrendered in these several transactions are then forwarded to this office, where credit is made in the proper account. The total of securities surrendered in the fiscal year 1922 was considerably less than that in the year 1921. This was due in large measure to the stopping of Victory transactions owing to the redemption call on $3\frac{3}{4}$ per cent Victory notes and the diminishing of the transactions on temporary exchange or the exchange of the temporary for permanent bonds, the greater amount of the permanent bonds having been issued during the previous fiscal year. Tables have been prepared showing the above transactions as well as all other classes of securities received from the Federal reserve banks or Division of Loans and Currency for credit to their fiscal agency accounts, such as Treasury (war) savings securities, interim certificates, certificates of indebtedness, as well as interest coupons where they have been detached in transactions conducted by the banks or Division of Loans and Currency. Treasury (war) savings securities are also received from various post offices.

### DESTRUCTION OF RETIRED SECURITIES.

The work of destroying retired securities was temporarily suspended April 22, 1922. A tabulated statement in the statistical section of this report shows the total amount destroyed, after a final audit by the destruction division, within the fiscal year prior to the temporary cessation of destruction.

## INTEREST COUPONS ON FILE.

Since April 22, 1922, the date of the suspension of destruction, and up to the date of the filing of this report, the entire force of the destruction division has been engaged in the work of assorting and arranging interest coupons. This, together with the regular force of the interest coupon division and the services of the 181 clerks secured from the Division of Loans and Currency, has served to bring the work of the division of interest coupons much nearer to a current basis than it was a year ago. On October 28, 1921, the work of assorting, arranging, and recording interest coupons detached from bonds of the lower denominations was suspended. At that time there was an accumulation of approximately 269,000,000 pieces of unassorted coupons in the files of the Register's office. There was being added to this 8,000,000 or more pieces per month through receipts. Work on assorting, arranging, and registering lower denomination coupons was resumed on April 8, 1922. At the present rate of progress, with the number of employees as now engaged, it is estimated that the work in the interest coupon division will become current June 30, 1923, the end of the current fiscal year.

## SECURITIES PREPARED FOR ISSUE—REGISTERED SECURITIES ISSUED.

Although the Register's office no longer issues any securities, appropriate records are required to be kept of all securities, both coupon and registered, prepared by the Bureau of Engraving and Printing and delivered to the Division of Loans and Currency, and of registered securities issued by the Division of Loans and Currency. During the fiscal year 1922 securities were prepared and delivered, including coupon bonds, notes, certificates of indebtedness, Treasury (war) savings securities, etc., to the amount of $9,594,137,980. Of these securities $281,662,000 were in registered form, while those in bearer form amounted to $9,312,475,980. Registered securities were issued by the Division of Loans and Currency to the amount of $2,415,183,360.

## PROTECTION OF SECURITIES.

Adequate protection is given to all securities on file at the Register's annex building at 119 D Street NE. New equipment consisting of steel filing cases and shelving was installed recently, which adds to the safety of the securities. The responsibility for vault protection is held jointly by two responsible employees in each of the vaults.

## ORGANIZATION.

No material changes have been made in the organization as described in the annual report for the fiscal year 1921. The chart on page 649, based upon personnel statistics as of June 30, 1922, depicts the subdivisions of the Register's office and clearly reflects the amount of work connected with the functioning of interest coupons as hereinbefore described.

## FUNCTIONAL APPORTIONMENT.

The functions incident to securities retired are allocated to the following subdivisions:

*Chief clerk:*—Handles time reports of employees, pay rolls, requisitions for supplies, including custody thereof; prepares correspondence relating to personnel matters and keeps general correspondence files for the entire office; receives and distributes incoming mail, and collects for dispatch outgoing mail. The section of efficiency records in this division compiles all data relative to office efficiency.

*Division of accounts.*—Keeps controlling accounts of all the various securities handled by the Register's office, in addition to accounts of United States securities delivered by the Bureau of Engraving and Printing and of registered securities issued; prepares, or checks after preparation, all consolidated reports emanating from the Register's office, including semimonthly balance sheets, etc.; authorizes all adjustments in office or divisional accounts in the Register's office, consolidates and checks all statements appearing in the annual reports; makes check periodically with other Treasury bureaus having to do with the public debt. Prepares all correspondence relative to completed audits.

*Division of paid securities.*—Audits paid securities received by the department, the retirement of which effects a reduction of the public debt, such as bonds, notes, certificates of indebtedness, Treasury (war) savings securities, etc., and keeps detail records of these transactions.

*Division of canceled securities.*—Audits all securities received for credit to fiscal agency account, including bonds, notes, certificates of indebtedness, Treasury (war) savings securities, and thrift stamps, and keeps detailed records of same. Beginning July 1, 1922, this division has been authorized to audit registered securities previously handled by the division of registered files.

*Division of interest coupons.*—Audits all interest coupons whether redeemed or received for credit to fiscal agency account; keeps detail records of same.

*Division of numerical records.*—Maintains numerical records of all bearer securities retired representing the principal of the public debt, except Treasury (war) savings securities. A record is made opposite the appropriate serial number on the numerical ledgers of every bond, note, or certificate of indebtedness received. This record is coded to show the agency from which the security was received and the transaction involved, such as redemption, exchange, conversion, etc. Since the inception of this recording method more than 110,000,000 entries have been made on these records. During the 1922 fiscal year alone more than 19,000,000 pieces, representing securities, were recorded.

*Division of registered files.*—Audits and files all registered bonds retired and keeps detailed records of same. Receives, after audit, and files all other registered securities. Beginning July 1, 1922, the auditing work has been functioned by the division of canceled securities.

*Vaults and files.*—Receives all incoming securities from whatever source and delivers them to the appropriate auditing division. Receives all securities after audit except registered securities and interest coupons and is responsible for them until they are withdrawn for destruction. Keeps appropriate records of securities received, delivered, and on file.

*Division of destruction.*—Examines immediately before destruction all securities to be destroyed and delivers them to the destruction committee of the department; keeps detail records of securities destroyed.

OFFICE OF THE REGISTER

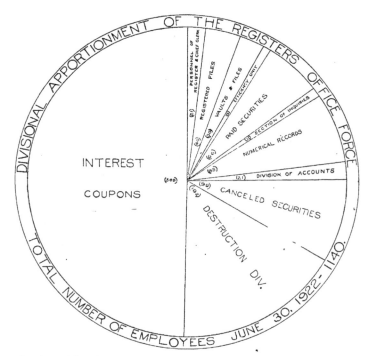

*Section of inquiries.*—Records and makes report of any available information concerning bonds and other securities which have been the subject of inquiry addressed to the department, prepares correspondence relating to retired bonds and other securities, makes and keeps a record of requisitions for securities and photostatic copies, and handles all validations. This section has received and prepared replies to more than 34,450 inquiries since its inception, March 1, 1920.

## OFFICE FORCE.

Since the establishment of the Bureau of the Budget on July 1, 1921, the office of the Register of the Treasury has made every effort to cooperate with that bureau, that expenditures be minimized as much as possible and to coordinate the functions so as to increase the general efficiency of this office. The work is now on a current basis with the exception of arranging, recording, and filing interest coupons. There has been no reduction in the personnel of this office because of the necessity of bringing all phases of the work to a current basis. On June 30, 1922, there were 959 regular clerks and 181 detail clerks, totaling 1,140, making a combined salary of $111,303.00. Every effort has been made to adjust salaries in accordance with those prescribed for the grade of work by the Bureau of Efficiency. This is not an easy task, for the need of reclassification is acute, but in every instance the chiefs of divisions and employees have cooperated with the officials in regrading positions wherever necessary.

The present incumbent assumed the duties of the office on the 25th of January, 1922. He desires to express his appreciation of the hearty cooperation which manifests itself so loyally and effectively in carrying out the work in the office of the Register of the Treasury. The employees throughout the entire office have responded most willingly to every call to duty. It is indeed a pleasure for the Register to testify to this fact.

The help given by the Assistant Register, who entered upon the discharge of his duties on June 7, 1922, has proven to be of great value. The service which he is rendering is most satisfactory.

## SUMMARY OF SECURITIES RECEIVED, EXAMINED, AND RETIRED.

The following is a summary of securities received, examined, and retired in the Register's office during the fiscal year ended June 30 1922:

| Class of securities. | Pieces. | Amount. |
|---|---|---|
| **Redeemed:** | | |
| Bearer— | | |
| Pre-war loans............................................ | 220 | $28,610.00 |
| Liberty loans........................................... | 1,206,457 | 1,884,018,300.00 |
| Certificates of indebtedness............................. | 669,511 | 2,809,044,500.00 |
| Treasury (war) savings securities....................... | 13,679,887 | 51,473,405.17 |
| Interest coupons........................................ | 91,776,882 | 776,338,623.33 |
| District of Columbia loans.............................. | 63 | 22,050.00 |
| District of Columbia interest coupons................... | 1,738 | 8,106.64½ |
| Total............................................. | 107,334,758 | 5,520,933,595.14½ |
| **Registered—** | | |
| Pre-war loans............................................ | 108 | 28,530.00 |
| Liberty loans........................................... | 45,893 | 177,571,400.00 |
| Certificates of indebtedness............................. | 397 | 1,966,829,450.00 |
| Treasury (war) savings securities....................... | 6,285,838 | 33,952,907.35 |
| Interest checks (Liberty loans)......................... | 4,711 | 153,549.76 |
| District of Columbia loans.............................. | 1,530 | 6,138,000.00 |
| District of Columbia interest checks.................... | 337 | 171,130.25 |
| Total............................................. | 6,338,814 | 2,184,844,967.36 |
| **Retired on account of exchanges for other securities, etc.:** | | |
| Bearer— | | |
| Pre-war loans............................................ | 3,628 | 2,877,730.00 |
| Liberty loans........................................... | 13,154,929 | 2,873,611,800.00 |
| Treasury notes.......................................... | 39,042 | 72,180,900.00 |
| Certificates of indebtedness............................. | 427,644 | 1,971,651,000.00 |
| Interim certificates (Liberty loans).................... | 1,031 | 105,640.00 |
| Treasury (war) savings securities....................... | 99,639,249 | 40,827,056.75 |
| Insular possessions loans............................... | 22,926 | 32,016,000.00 |
| Interest coupons........................................ | 11,503,474 | 247,201,209.11 |
| Total............................................. | 124,791,923 | 5,240,471,335.86 |
| **Registered—** | | |
| Pre-war loans............................................ | 85,429 | 170,448,090.00 |
| Liberty loans........................................... | 1,043,791 | 993,778,600.00 |
| Treasury (war) savings securities....................... | 323,146 | 26,646,300.00 |
| Insular possessions loans............................... | 12,797 | 29,867,000.00 |
| District of Columbia loans.............................. | 898 | 3,842,000.00 |
| Total............................................. | 1,466,061 | 1,224,581,990.00 |
| **Recapitulation:** | | |
| Bearer— | | |
| Pre-war loans............................................ | 3,848 | 2,906,340.00 |
| Liberty loans........................................... | 14,361,386 | 4,757,630,100.00 |
| Treasury notes.......................................... | 39,042 | 72,180,900.00 |
| Certificates of indebtedness............................. | 1,097,155 | 4,780,695,500.00 |
| Interim certificates (Liberty loans).................... | 1,031 | 105,640.00 |
| Treasury (war) savings securities....................... | 113,319,136 | 92,300,461.92 |
| Interest coupons........................................ | 103,280,356 | 1,023,539,832.44 |
| District of Columbia loans.............................. | 63 | 22,050.00 |
| District of Columbia interest coupons................... | 1,738 | 8,106.64½ |
| Insular possessions loans............................... | 22,926 | 32,016,000.00 |
| Total............................................. | 232,126,681 | 10,761,404,931.00½ |
| **Registered—** | | |
| Pre-war loans............................................ | 85,537 | 170,476,620.00 |
| Liberty loans........................................... | 1,089,684 | 1,171,350,000.00 |
| Certificates of indebtedness............................. | 397 | 1,966,829,450.00 |
| Treasury (war) savings securities....................... | 6,608,984 | 60,599,207.35 |
| Interest checks (Liberty loans)......................... | 4,711 | 153,549.76 |
| District of Columbia loans.............................. | 2,428 | 9,980,000.00 |
| Insular possessions loans............................... | 12,797 | 29,867,000.00 |
| District of Columbia interest checks.................... | 337 | 171,130.25 |
| Total............................................. | 7,804,875 | 3,409,426,957.36 |
| Grand total....................................... | 239,931,556 | 14,170,831,888.36½ |

Respectfully,

H. V. SPEELMAN,
*Register of the Treasury.*

Hon. A. W. MELLON,
*Secretary of the Treasury.*

## STATISTICAL STATEMENTS.

No. 1.—*Interest bearing debt of the United States, and debt on which interest has ceased June 30. 1922, and amount issued, retired, and outstanding at close of fiscal year 1922.*

| Title of loan. | Interest rate. | Amount issued prior to June 30, 1921. | Amount retired prior to June 30, 1921. | Amount issued during fiscal year 1922. | Amount retired during fiscal year 1922. | Total amount issued. | Total amount retired. | Amount outstanding. Matured. | Unmatured. |
|---|---|---|---|---|---|---|---|---|---|
| | *Per cent.* | | | | | | | | |
| **Pre-war das:** | | | | | | | | | |
| Stock of 1790 | 6 | $30,088,397.75 | $30,090,527.94 | | | $30,088,397.75 | $30,090,527.98 | $27,869.77 | |
| Deferred stock of 1790 | 6 | 14,649,328.76 | 14,635,393.86 | | | 14,649,328.76 | 14,635,393.86 | 13,934.90 | |
| Stock of 1790 | 3 | 19,719,237.39 | 19,705,284.26 | | | 19,719,237.39 | 19,705,284.26 | 13,953.13 | |
| Navy stock | 6 | 711,700.00 | 711,600.00 | | | 711,700.00 | 711,600.00 | 100.00 | |
| Loan of 1800 | 8 | 1,481,700.00 | 1,481,200.00 | | | 1,481,700.00 | 1,481,200.00 | 500.00 | |
| Sixteen million loan of 1813 | 8 | 18,109,377.43 | 18,109,331.04 | | | 18,109,377.43 | 18,109,331.04 | 46.39 | |
| Ten million loan of 1814 | 8 | 9,919,475.25 | 9,919,187.27 | | | 9,919,476.25 | 9,919,187.27 | 288.98 | |
| Mississippi stock | None | 4,282,035.92 | 4,281,190.11 | | | 4,282,038.92 | 4,281,190.14 | 840.78 | |
| Stock of 1815 | 7 | 9,070,386.00 | 9,070,333.48 | | | 9,070,386.00 | 9,070,333.48 | 32.52 | |
| Treasury note stock of 1815 | 6 | 1,505,352.18 | 1,505,284.65 | | | 1,505,352.18 | 1,505,284.65 | 67.53 | |
| Treasury notes prior to 1846 | 6 of 1 to 6 | 47,002,900.00 | 46,920,484.65 | | | 47,002,900.00 | 46,920,484.65 | 82,415.35 | |
| Treasury notes of 1846 | 6 of 1 to 6 | 7,687,800.00 | 7,681,900.00 | | | 7,687,800.00 | 7,681,900.00 | 5,900.00 | |
| Treasury notes of 1847 | 5½ and 6 | 26,122,100.00 | 26,121,150.00 | | | 26,122,100.00 | 26,121,150.00 | 950.00 | |
| Treasury notes of 1857 | 3 to 6 | 52,778,900.00 | 52,778,200.00 | | | 52,778,900.00 | 52,778,200.00 | 700.00 | |
| Bounty land scrip | 6 | 233,075.00 | 230,175.00 | | | 233,075.00 | 230,175.00 | 2,900.00 | |
| Mexican indemnity stock | 5 | 303,573.92 | 302,469.01 | | | 303,573.92 | 302,469.01 | 1,104.91 | |
| Loan of 1847 | 6 | 28,230,350.00 | 28,229,400.00 | | | 28,230,350.00 | 28,229,400.00 | 950.00 | |
| Texan indemnity stock | 5 | 5,000,000.00 | 4,981,000.00 | | | 5,000,000.00 | 4,981,000.00 | 19,000.00 | |
| Loan of 1858 | 5 | 20,000,000.00 | 19,998,000.00 | | | 20,000,000.00 | 19,998,000.00 | 2,000.00 | |
| Loan of February, 1861 | 6 | 18,415,000.00 | 18,410,000.00 | | | 18,415,000.00 | 18,410,000.00 | 5,000.00 | |
| Treasury notes of 1861 | 6 | 35,364,450.00 | 35,362,150.00 | | | 35,364,450.00 | 35,362,150.00 | 2,300.00 | |
| Oregon war debt | 6 | 1,090,850.00 | 1,088,600.00 | | | 1,090,850.00 | 1,088,600.00 | 2,250.00 | |
| Loan of Jly and August, 1861 | 6 | 189,321,350.00 | 189,306,300.00 | | | 189,321,350.00 | 189,306,300.00 | 15,050.00 | |
| Loan of July and August, 1861, continued | 3½, | 127,597,200.00 | 127,596,600.00 | | | 127,597,200.00 | 127,596,600.00 | 600.00 | |
| Seven-thirties of 1861 | 7 3/10 | 139,999,750.00 | 139,990,400.00 | | $50.00 | 139,999,750.00 | 139,990,450.00 | 9,300.00 | |
| Five-twenties of 1862 | 6 | 514,771,600.00 | 514,666,250.00 | | 100.00 | 514,771,600.00 | 514,666,350.00 | 105,250.00 | |
| Temporary loan of February, 1862 | 4,5,6 | 716,099,247.16 | 716,096,397.16 | | | 716,099,247.16 | 716,099,397.16 | 2,850.00 | |
| **1862-63.** Certificates of indebtedness | 6 | 561,753,241.65 | 561,750,241.65 | | | 561,753,241.65 | 561,750,241.65 | 3,000.00 | |
| Loan of 1863 | 6 | 75,000,000.00 | 74,996,900.00 | | | 75,000,000.00 | 74,996,900.00 | 3,100.00 | |
| Loan of 1863, continued | 3½ | 50,457,950.00 | 50,457,850.00 | | | 50,457,950.00 | 50,457,850.00 | 100.00 | |
| 1-year notes of 1863 | 5 | 44,520,000.00 | 44,489,860.00 | | 20.00 | 44,520,000.00 | 44,489,880.00 | 30,120.00 | |
| 2-year notes of 1863 | 5 | 166,480,000.00 | 166,455,000.00 | | | 166,480,000.00 | 166,455,000.00 | 25,000.00 | |
| Compound-interest notes | 6 | 266,595,440.00 | 266,439,110.00 | | 70.00 | 266,595,440.00 | 266,439,180.00 | 156,260.00 | |
| Ten-forties of 1864 | 5 | 196,118,300.00 | 196,099,750.00 | | | 196,118,300.00 | 196,099,750.00 | 18,560.00 | |
| Five-twenties of 1864 | 6 | 125,561,300.00 | 125,547,350.00 | | | 125,561,300.00 | 125,547,350.00 | 13,950.00 | |

| | | | | | | | | | |
|---|---|---|---|---|---|---|---|---|---|
| Seven- thirties 1864-65 | 7 3/10 | 829,992,500.00 | 829,873, 00.00 | ........ | ........ | 829,992, 0.00 | 829,873,000.00 | 119,500.00 | ........ |
| Five-twenties of 1865 | 6 | 203,327,250.00 | 93,307,400.00 | ........ | ........ | 203,327,250.00 | 203,307,400.00 | 19,850.00 | ........ |
| Consols of 1865 | 6 | 332,998,950.00 | 332,941,900.00 | ........ | ........ | 332,998,950.00 | 332,941,900.00 | 57,050.00 | ........ |
| Consols of 1867 | 6 | 379,618,000.00 | 379,524,450.00 | ........ | ........ | 379,618,000.00 | 379,524,450.00 | 93,550.00 | ........ |
| Consols of 1868 | 6 | 42,539,930.00 | 42, 50, 50.00 | ........ | ........ | 42,539,930.00 | 42,530,050.00 | 9,880.00 | ........ |
| ... ts of Mar. 2, 1867, and July 25, 1868 | 3 | 85,155,000.00 | 85,150,000.00 | ........ | ........ | 85, 55,000.00 | 85,150,000.00 | 5,000.00 | ........ |
| Funded loan of 1881 | 5 | 517,994, 10.00 | 517,971,750.00 | ........ | ........ | 517,994,150.00 | 517,971,750.00 | 22,400.00 | ........ |
| Funded loan of 1881, continued | 3½ | 401,504, 90.00 | 401,504,850.00 | ........ | ........ | 401,504,900.00 | 401, 04,850.00 | 50.00 | ........ |
| Loan of July 12, 1882 | 3 | 305,581,250.00 | 305,581,050.00 | ........ | ........ | 305,581,250.00 | 305,581,050.00 | 200.00 | ........ |
| Funded loan of 1891 | 4½ | 250,000,000.00 | 249,980,200.00 | ........ | ........ | 250,000,000.00 | 249,980,200.00 | 19,800.00 | ........ |
| Funded loan of 1891, continued | 2 | 25,364,500.00 | 25, 63,500.00 | ........ | ........ | 25, 64,500.00 | 25,363,500.00 | 1, 00.00 | ........ |
| Loan of 00 | 5 | 100,000,000.00 | 99,986,950.00 | ........ | ........ | 100, 00, 00.00 | 99,986,950.00 | 13,050.00 | ........ |
| Loan of 07 | 4 | 740,930,950.00 | 740,550,150.00 | ........ | 6,200.00 | 740,930,950.00 | 740,556,350.00 | 374,600.00 | ........ |
| Refunding certificates | 4 | 40,012,750.00 | 40,002,400.00 | ........ | 80.00 | 40,012,750.00 | 40,002,480.00 | 10,270.00 | ........ |
| Loan of 1908–1918 | 3 | 198,792,660.00 | 198,416,000.00 | ........ | 50,620.00 | 198, 92,660.00 | 198,466,620.00 | 8,040.00 | ........ |
| Loan of 1925 | 4 | 162,315,400.00 | 43,825,500.00 | ........ | ........ | 162,315,400.00 | 43,825,500.00 | ........ | $118,489, 90.00 |
| ...s of 1930 | 2 | 646,250,150.00 | 46,526,100.00 | ........ | ........ | 646,250,150.00 | 46,526,100.00 | ........ | 599,724,050.00 |
| Panama canal loan— | | | | | | | | | |
| Series of 1916–1936 | 2 | 54,631,980.00 | 5,677,800.00 | ........ | ........ | 54, 61,980.00 | 5,677,800.00 | ........ | 48,954,180.00 |
| Series of 1918–1938 | 2 | 30,000,000.00 | 4,052,600.00 | ........ | ........ | 30,000,000.00 | 4,052,600.00 | ........ | 25,947,400.00 |
| Series of 1911–1961 | 3 | 50,000,000.00 | ........ | ........ | ........ | 50,000,000.00 | ........ | ........ | 50,000,000.00 |
| Conversion bonds— | | | | | | | | | |
| Series of 1916–1946 | 3 | 15,761,000.00 | ........ | ........ | ........ | 15, 61,000.00 | ........ | ........ | 15,761,000.00 |
| Series of 1947 | 3 | 13,133,500.00 | ........ | ........ | ........ | 13,133,500.00 | ........ | ........ | 13,133,500.00 |
| Postal savings bonds— | | | | | | | | | |
| First series | 2½ | 41,900.00 | ........ | ........ | ........ | 41,900.00 | ........ | ........ | 41,900.00 |
| Second series | 2½ | 417,380.00 | ........ | ........ | ........ | 417,380.00 | ........ | ........ | 417,380.00 |
| Third series | 2½ | 854,860.00 | ........ | ........ | ........ | 854,860.00 | ........ | ........ | 854,860.00 |
| Fourth series | 2½ | 1,074,980.00 | ........ | ........ | ........ | 1,074,980.00 | ........ | ........ | 1,074,980.00 |
| Fifth series | 2½ | 1,116,880.00 | ........ | ........ | ........ | 1,116,880.00 | ........ | ........ | 1,116,880.00 |
| Sixth series | 2½ | 1,129,820.00 | ........ | ........ | ........ | 1,129,820.00 | ........ | ........ | 1,129,820.00 |
| Seventh series | 2½ | 872,240.00 | ........ | ........ | ........ | 872,240.00 | ........ | ........ | 872,240.00 |
| Eighth series | 2½ | 933,540.00 | ........ | ........ | ........ | 933,540.00 | ........ | ........ | 933,540.00 |
| Ninth series | 2½ | 865,500.00 | ........ | ........ | ........ | 865,500.00 | ........ | ........ | 865,500.00 |
| Tenth series | 2½ | 938,000.00 | ........ | ........ | ........ | 938,000.00 | ........ | ........ | 938,000.00 |
| Eleventh series | 2½ | 906,700.00 | ........ | ........ | ........ | 906,700.00 | ........ | ........ | 906,700.00 |
| Twelfth series | 2½ | 887,960.00 | ........ | ........ | ........ | 887,960.00 | ........ | ........ | 887,960.00 |
| Thirteenth series | 2½ | 718,800.00 | ........ | ........ | ........ | 718,800.00 | ........ | ........ | 718, 00.00 |
| Fourteenth series | 2½ | 302,140.00 | ........ | ........ | ........ | 302,140.00 | ........ | ........ | 302,140.00 |
| Fifteenth series | 2½ | 198,180.00 | ........ | ........ | ........ | 198,180.00 | ........ | ........ | 198,180.00 |
| Sixteenth series | 2½ | 91,080.00 | ........ | ........ | ........ | 91,080.00 | ........ | ........ | 91,080.00 |
| Seventeenth series | 2½ | 103,140.00 | ........ | ........ | ........ | 103,140.00 | ........ | ........ | 103,140.00 |
| Eighteenth series | 2½ | 86,260.00 | ........ | ........ | ........ | 86,260.00 | ........ | ........ | 86,260.00 |
| Nineteenth series | 2½ | 72,800.00 | ........ | ........ | ........ | 72,800.00 | ........ | ........ | 72,800.00 |
| Twentieth series | 2½ | 106,080.00 | ........ | ........ | ........ | 106,080.00 | ........ | ........ | 106,080.00 |
| Twenty-first series | 2½ | ........ | ........ | $55,780.00 | ........ | 55,780.00 | ........ | ........ | 55,780.00 |
| Twenty-second series | 2½ | ........ | ........ | 56,420.00 | ........ | 56,420.00 | ........ | ........ | 56,420.00 |
| Total | ........ | 8,963,664,430.41 | 8,078,240,540.15 | 112,200.00 | 57,140.00 | 8,963,776,630.41 | 8,078,297,680.15 | 1,638,480.26 | 883,840,470.00 |

No. 1.—*Interest bearing debt of the United States, and debt on which interest has ceased June 30, 1922, and amount issued, retired, and outstanding at close of fiscal year 1922*—Continued.

| Title of loan. | Interest rate. | Amount issued prior to June 30, 1921. | Amount retired prior to June 30, 1921. | Amount issued during fiscal year 1922. | Amount retired during fiscal year 1922. | Total amount issued. | Total amount retired. | Amount outstanding. | |
|---|---|---|---|---|---|---|---|---|---|
| | | | | | | | | Matured. | Unmatured. |
| Liberty loans: | | | | | | | | | |
| First, 1932–1947 | 3½ | $1,515,539,150.00 | $105,464,900.00 | | $72,200.00 | $1,515,539,150.00 | $105,537,100.00 | | $1,410,002,050.00 |
| First, converted 1932–1947 | 4 | 568,318,450.00 | 550,335,650.00 | | 5,459,300.00 | 568,318,450.00 | 555,794,950.00 | | 12,523,500.00 |
| Do | 4¼ | 542,387,650.00 | 21,678,050.00 | $5,459,000.00 | 342,550.00 | 547,846,650.00 | 22,020,600.00 | | 525,826,050.00 |
| First, second converted, 1932–1947 | 4¼ | 3,492,150.00 | | | | 3,492,150.00 | | | 3,492,150.00 |
| Second, 1927–1942 | 4 | 3,807,865,000.00 | 3,729,994,850.00 | | 23,449,350.00 | 3,807,865,000.00 | 3,753,444,200.00 | | 54,420,800.00 |
| Second, converted, 1927–1942 | 4¼ | 3,650,936,150.00 | 412,269,750.00 | 23,448,700.00 | 5,938,850.00 | 3,674,384,850.00 | 418,208,600.00 | | 3,256,176.250.00 |
| Third, 1928 | 4¼ | 4,175,650,050.00 | 564,089,750.00 | | 137,772,300.00 | 4,175,650,050.00 | 701,862,050.00 | | 3,473,788,000.00 |
| Fourth, 1933–1938 | 4¼ | 6,964,581,100.00 | 609,720,750.00 | | 9,476,600.00 | 6, 94,581,100.00 | 619,197,350.00 | | 6,345,383,750.00 |
| Victory, 1922–1923 | 4¾ | 4,115,900,450.00 | 843,048,100.00 | 211,956,350.00 | 1,493,625,300.00 | 4,327,856,800.00 | 2,336,673,400.00 | | 1,991,183,400.00 |
| Do | 3¾ | 1,078,253,250.00 | 437,325,250.00 | 18,998,600.00 | 645,317,200.00 | 1,097,251,850.00 | 1,082,642,450.00 | $14,609,400.00 | |
| Total [1] | | 26,422,923,400.00 | 7,273,927,050.00 | 259,862,650.00 | 2,321,453,650.00 | 26,682,786,050.00 | 9,595,380,700.00 | 14,609,400.00 | 17,072,795,950.00 |
| Treasury notes: | | | | | | | | | |
| Series A, 1924 | 5¾ | 311,191,600.00 | | | | 311,191,600.00 | | | 311,191,600.00 |
| Series B, 1924 | 5½ | | | 390,706,100.00 | | 390,706,100.00 | | | 390,706,100.00 |
| Series A, 1925 | 4¾ | | | 601,599,500.00 | | 601,599,500.00 | | | 601,599,500.00 |
| Series B, 1925 | 4¾ | | | 325,329,450.00 | | 325,329,450.00 | | | 325,329,450.00 |
| Series A, 1926 | 4¾ | | | 617,769,700.00 | | 617,769,700.00 | | | 617,769,700.00 |
| Total | | 311,191,600.00 | | 1,935,404,750.00 | | 2,246,596,350.00 | | | 2,246,596,350.00 |
| Certificates of indebtedness: | | | | | | | | | |
| Jan. 2, 1918 | 4 | 491,822,500.00 | 491,820,500.00 | | | 491,822,500.00 | 491,820,500.00 | 2,000.00 | |
| Mar. 20, 1918 | 4½ | 543,032,500.00 | 543,032,000.00 | | | 543,032,500.00 | 543,032,000.00 | 500.00 | |
| April 10, 1918 | 4½ | 551,226,500.00 | 551,216,500.00 | | 10,000.00 | 551,226,500.00 | 551,226,500.00 | | |
| June 25, 1918, series 4–A | 4½ | 839,646,500.00 | 839,646,000.00 | | | 839,646,500.00 | 839,646,000.00 | 500.00 | |
| July 9, 1918, series 4–B | 4½ | 753,938,000.00 | 753,936,000.00 | | | 753,938,000.00 | 753,936,000.00 | 2,000.00 | |
| July 23, 1918, series 4–C | 4½ | 584,750,500.00 | 584,745,000.00 | | | 584,750,500.00 | 584,745, 0.00 | 5,500.00 | |
| Aug. 6, 1918, series 4–D | 4½ | 575,706,500.00 | 575,703,000.00 | | | 575,706,500.00 | 575,703,000.00 | 3,500.00 | |
| Aug. 20, 1918, series T | 4 | 157,552,500.00 | 157,526,000.00 | | 5,000.00 | 157,552,500.00 | 157,531,000.00 | 21,500.00 | |
| Sept. 3, 1918, series 4–E | 4½ | 639,493,000.00 | 639,492,000.00 | | 1,000.00 | 639,493,000.00 | 639,493,000.00 | | |
| Dec. 5, 1918, series 5–A | 4½ | 613,438,000.00 | 613,436,500.00 | | 1,500.00 | 613,438,000.00 | 613,438,000.00 | | |
| Dec. 19, 1918, series 5–B | 4½ | 572,494,000.00 | 572,493,000.00 | | | 572,494,000.00 | 572,493,000.00 | 1,000.00 | |
| Jan. 16, 1919, series T–2 | 4½ | 392,381,000.00 | 392,353,500.00 | | 27,500.00 | 392,381,000.00 | 392,381,000.00 | | |
| Feb. 13, 1919, series 5–F | 4½ | 620,578,500.00 | 620,577,500.00 | | 1,000.00 | 620,578,500.00 | 620,578,500.00 | | |
| July 15, 1919, series T–8 | 4½ | 323,074,500.00 | 323,064,500.00 | | 8,000.00 | 323,074,500.00 | 323,072,500.00 | 2,000.00 | |
| Sept. 2, 1919, series C–1920 | 4½ | 573,841,500.00 | 573,838,000.00 | | 3,000.00 | 573,841,500.00 | 573,841,000.00 | 500.00 | |
| Sept. 15, 1919, series T–10 | 4½ | 657,469,000.00 | 657,435,500.00 | | 16,500.00 | 657,469,000.00 | 657,452,000.00 | 17,000.00 | |
| Dec. 1, 1919, series TM–3–1920 | 4½ | 260,322,000.00 | 260,319,000.00 | | 3,000.00 | 260,322,000.00 | 260,322,000.00 | | |
| Dec. 15, 1919, series TJ–1920 | 4½ | 728,130,000.00 | 728,088,500.00 | | 37,500.00 | 728,130,000.00 | 728,126,000.00 | 4,000.00 | |
| Jan. 2, 1920, series TD–1920 | 4¾ | 703,026,000.00 | 702,835,500.00 | | 119,000.00 | 703,026,000.00 | 70,954,500.00 | 71,500.00 | |

| | | | | | | | | |
|---|---|---|---|---|---|---|---|---|
| Feb. 2, 1920, series | 4½ | 304,877,000.00 | | | 304,872,000.00 | | 304,877,000.00 | |
| Mar. 3, 1920, series TM- | 4½ | 201,370,500.00 | | | 91, 12,500.00 | | 201,370,500.00 | |
| Apr. 1, 1920, series F-1920 | 4½ | 200,669,500.00 | | | 9, 6,500.00 | | 200,669,500.00 | |
| | 5 | 83,903,000.00 | | | 83,902,500.00 | | 83,903,000.00 | |
| Apr. 15, 1920, series G- | 5 | 170,633,500.00 | | 500.00 | 170,607,500.00 | | 170,632,500.00 | |
| May 17, 1920, series H- | 5½ | 9, 6, 00.00 | | 25,000.00 | 102,855,000.00 | | 102,894,500.00 | |
| June 1, series A-1921 | 5½ | 176,604, 00.00 | | 9,500.00 | 16, 88,500.00 | | 176,604, 00.00 | |
| June 15, series 1- | 5½ | 242,517,000.00 | | 25,500.00 | 237,117,000.00 | | 242,473,000.00 | |
| July 15, 1921, series 1- | 6 | 26,783,500.00 | 5,361,000.00 | | 125,749,500.00 | | 26,783,500.00 | 39,000.00 |
| Aug. 16, 1920, series C-1921 | 5½ | 74,278,000.00 | 34, 00.00 | | 74,129,000.00 | | 74,278,000.00 | |
| Sept. 15, 1920, series M- | 5½ | 57,654,500.00 | 133,500.00 | | 2,162,000.00 | | 57,278,000.00 | 13,500.00 |
| Sept. 15, 90, series TS-1921 | 5½ | 106,625,500.00 | 155,416,000.00 | | 106,616,500.00 | | 157,578, 00 | 76,500.00 |
| Oct. 4, 9, series 1 | 5½ | 341,969,500.00 | 9, 00.00 | | | | 106,625,500.00 | 1,000.00 |
| | 5½ | 24,252,500.00 | 341,870,000.00 | | 124,059,000.00 | | 341,870,000.00 | 99,500.00 |
| Dec. 15, 90, series 1 | 5½ | 232,124,000.00 | 83,500.00 | | 230,981,000.00 | | 24, 32, 00 | 4,000.00 |
| Dec. 15, 90, series D-1921 | 5½ | 188,123,000.00 | 1,118,500.00 | | 186,518,000.00 | | 232,124,000.00 | 24,500.00 |
| Dec. 5, 1920, series TD-1921 | 5½ | 61,557,500.00 | 1,604,000.00 | | 12,000,000.00 | | 188,123,000.00 | 1,000.00 |
| Jan. 3, series E-1921 | 5½ | 118,660,000.00 | 389,242,000.00 | | 118,584,000.00 | | 61,212,500.00 | 315,000.00 |
| Jan. 3, series F-1921 | 5½ | 192,026,500.00 | 74, 00.00 | | | | 118,658,500.00 | 1,570.00 |
| Feb. 1, series G-1921 | 5½ | 132,886,500.00 | 191,619,000.00 | | , 600.00 | | 191,619,000.00 | 407,500.00 |
| Mar. 3, 1921, series 1 | 5½ | 193,302,000.00 | 128,869,000.00 | | | | 132,989,000.00 | 17,500.00 |
| Mar. 3, 1921, series N- | 5½ | 288,501,000.00 | 193,291, 00.00 | | | | 193,294,000.00 | 8,000.00 |
| May 3, series A-1922 | 5½ | 190,511,500.00 | 287,759,000.00 | | | | 287,759,000.00 | 742,000.00 |
| June 3, series TJ-1922 | 5½ | 36, 70,000.00 | 190,472,500.00 | | | | 90, 42, 00 | 39,000.00 |
| June 3, series TJ-1922 | 5½ | 314,184,000.00 | 255,699,000.00 | | | | 255,699,000.00 | 471,000.00 |
| Aug. 1, 1921, series TM-2-1922 | 5½ | | 309,482,000.00 | | | | 309,482,000.00 | 4,702,000.00 |
| Aug. 1, 1921, series B- | 5½ | 116,891,000.00 | 116,891,000.00 | | 116,891,000.00 | | 116,801,500.00 | 89,500.00 |
| Aug. 1, 1921, series TM-3-1922 | 5½ | 259,471,500.00 | 9, 6, 00.00 | | 259,471,500.00 | | 40, 00 | |
| Sept. 15 1, series TS- | 5½ | 124,572,000.00 | 124,572,000.00 | | 124,572,000.00 | | 124,252,500.00 | 259,431,000.00 |
| Nov. 1, series | 5½ | 182,871,000.00 | 182,871,000.00 | | 182,871,000.00 | | | 309,500.00 |
| Nov. 1, 1921, series | 4½ | 179,691,500.00 | 51,796,500.00 | | 179,691,500.00 | | 51,617,500.00 | 182,871,000.00 |
| Dec. 15, 1 series TJ- | 4½ | 64,903,000.00 | 179,691,500.00 | | 51,796,500.00 | | 64,903,500.00 | 148,500.00 |
| Dec. 15, 1922, series M- | 4½ | 243,544,000.00 | 63,550,500.00 | | 179,691,500.00 | | 63,550,500.00 | 179,691,500.00 |
| Mar. 3, 1922, series 1- | 4½ | 286,250,000.00 | | | 243,544,000.00 | | 286,250,000.00 | 1,352,500.00 |
| Apr. 3, 1922 series J- | 4½ | 150,000,000.00 | | | 286,250,000.00 | | 150,000,000.00 | 83, 4, 00.00 |
| June 1 series TD-2-1922 | 3½ | 200,000,000.00 | | | 150,000,000.00 | | 200,000,000.00 | 286,250,000.00 |
| June 3 series T- 1923 | 3½ | 273,000,000.00 | | | 200,000,000.00 | | 273,000,000.00 | 90, 00, 00.00 |
| Special s— | | | | | 273,000,000.00 | | | 200,000,000.00 |
| Short-term reg. rel. | 3 | 949,000,000.00 | 946,000,000.00 | 949,000,000.00 | 949,000,000.00 | | 949,000,000.00 | 273,000,000.00 |
| Do. | 6 | 843,100,000.00 | 843,100,000.00 | 843,100,000.00 | 843,100,000.00 | | 843,100,000.00 | |
| Do. | 6 | 32,854,450.00 | 32,854,450.00 | | | | 32,854,450.00 | 74,003,000.00 |
| Pittman Act | 2 | 259,375,000.00 | 141,875,000.00 | | | | 183,375,000.00 | |
| Total | | 15,707,202,450.00 | 3,905,090,000.00 | 4,775,873,950.00 | 13,088,628,000.00 | 19,702,292,450.00 | 17,814,501,950.00 | 9,003,000.00 | 1,828,787,500.00 |
| Treasury (war) savings securities | | 1,190,675,825.42 | 70,325,767.60 | 85,415,860.52 | 496,570,415.05 | 1,261,001,593.02 | 581,986,275.57 | 25,230,880.25 | 679,015,317.45 |
| Grand total | | 52,685,657,705.83 | 6,170,795,367.60 | 7,182,800,600.52 | 28,937,366,005.20 | 58,856,653,073.43 | 36,120,166,605.72 | 25,230,880.25 | 22,711,035,557.45 |

[1] Figures on issues and retirements include securities issued and retired on conversion accounts.
[2] Includes deduction of $2,148.85 made on account of repayments by the Treasurer, United States, during the fiscal year 1922—not included in subsequent statements.
[3] Soldiers' and sailors' relief insurance bonds not included in the above: Total issue June 30, 1922, $195,500; total retired June 30, 1922, $144,600; outstanding, $50,900.

Note.—Soldiers' and sailors' relief insurance bonds not included in the above: Total issue June 30, 1922, $195,500; total retired June 30, 1922, $144,600; outstanding, $50,900.

No. 2.—*United States matured pre-war bonds and other obligations redeemed during the fiscal year ended June 30, 1922.*

| Class and title of loan. | Interest rate. | Denominations by number of pieces. | | | | | | Total. | |
|---|---|---|---|---|---|---|---|---|---|
| | | $10 | $20 | $50 | $100 | $500 | $1,000 | Pieces. | Amount. |
| | *Per cent.* | | | | | | | | |
| Coupon: | | | | | | | | | |
| Five-twenties of 1862 | 6 | | | | 1 | | | 1 | $100 |
| Seven-thirties of 1861 | 7.30 | | | 1 | | | | 1 | 50 |
| 1-year Treasury notes of 1863 | 5 | | 1 | | | | | 1 | 20 |
| Coupon interest notes | 6 | 1 | 3 | | | | | 4 | 70 |
| Loan of 1907 | 4 | | | 9 | 25 | 2 | 2 | 38 | 5,950 |
| Refunding certificates | 4 | 8 | | | | | | 8 | 80 |
| Loan of 1906-1918 | 3 | | 82 | | 57 | 26 | 2 | 167 | 22,340 |
| Total | | 9 | 86 | 10 | 83 | 28 | 4 | 220 | 28,610 |
| Registered: | | | | | | | | | |
| Loan of 1907 | 4 | | | 1 | 2 | | | 3 | 250 |
| Loan of 1908-1918 | 3 | | 39 | | 35 | 14 | 17 | 105 | 28,280 |
| Total | | | 39 | 1 | 37 | 14 | 17 | 108 | 28,530 |
| Grand total | | 9 | 125 | 11 | 120 | 42 | 21 | 328 | 57,140 |

| Class and title of loan. | Interest rate. | Denominations by number of pieces. | | | | | | | | Total. | | Principal payment. | Discount. | Accrued interest. | Total payment. |
|---|---|---|---|---|---|---|---|---|---|---|---|---|---|---|---|
| | Per ct. | $50 | $100 | $500 | $1,000 | $5,000 | $10,000 | $50,000 | $100,000 | Pieces. | Amount. | | | | |
| **Coupon:** | | | | | | | | | | | | | | | |
| First, converted, 1932–1947 | 4¼ | 1 | | | | | | | | 1 | $50.00 | $50.00 | | | $50.00 |
| Second, converted | | | | 1 | | | | | | | 700.00 | 700.00 | | | 700.00 |
| Third, permanent unit, 3¾; g- | | 1,264 | 905 | 8,728 | 34,067 | 1,954 | 4,448 | | | 51,366 | 92,834,700.00 | 92,328,333.05 | $506,371.50 | $528,136.49 | 92,856,169.54 |
| nament | 4¼ | 3 | 3 | | | | | | | 6 | 450.00 | 450.00 | | | 450.00 |
| Victory, 1922–1923 | 4¾ | 141,114 | 123,616 | 95,924 | 459,630 | 38,886 | 66,361 | | | 925,551 | 1,385,069,300.00 | 383,126,206.04 | 2,084,513.46 | 11,322,186.60 | 394,458,392.64 |
| Do | 3¾ | 56 | 28 | 492 | 40,152 | 990 | 3,864 | | | 45,582 | 83,993,600.00 | 83,493,588.46 | 518,007.03 | 537,811.64 | 84,031,860.10 |
| Total | | 142,440 | 124,553 | 105,145 | 533,869 | 41,830 | 74,673 | | | 1,022,510 | 1,561,898,800.00 | 558,949,327.55 | 3,108,891.99 | 12,358,134.73 | 1,571,347,462.28 |
| **Registered:** | | | | | | | | | | | | | | | |
| First, 1932–1947 | 3½ | | 10 | 4 | 8 | | | | | 22 | 11,000.00 | 11,000.00 | | | 11,000.00 |
| First, converted, 1932–1947 | 4¼ | 6 | 25 | 8 | 10 | | | | | 49 | 16,800.00 | 16,800.00 | | | 16,800.00 |
| Second, converted, 1927–1942 | 4¼ | 14 | 41 | 7 | 25 | 7 | 4 | | | 98 | 108,300.00 | 108,300.00 | | | 108,300.00 |
| Third, 1928 | 4¼ | 10 | 37 | 5 | 25 | 5 | 24 | 2 | 397 | 505 | 40,096,700.00 | 39,800,808.45 | 295,891.55 | 325,897.54 | 40,126,705.99 |
| Fourth, 1933–1938 | 4¼ | 6 | 24 | 3 | 16 | 4 | 10 | | 1 | 64 | 240,200.00 | 240,200.00 | | | 240,200.00 |
| Victory, 1922–1923 | 4¾ | 2,174 | 14,362 | 7,009 | 13,440 | 1,353 | 1,405 | 194 | 395 | 40,332 | 88,504,400.00 | 88,504,400.00 | | 813,224.59 | 89,317,624.59 |
| Do | 3¾ | | 2 | 1 | 21 | 3 | 6 | 4 | 12 | 49 | 1,496,700.00 | 1,496,700.00 | | 7,408.17 | 1,504,108.17 |
| Total | | 2,210 | 14,501 | 7,037 | 13,545 | 1,372 | 1,449 | 200 | 805 | 41,119 | 130,474,100.00 | 130,178,208.45 | 295,891.55 | 1,146,530.30 | 131,324,738.75 |
| Grand total | | 144,650 | 139,054 | 112,182 | 547,414 | 43,202 | 76,122 | 200 | 805 | 1,063,629 | 1,692,372,900.00 | 689,127,536.00 | 3,404,783.54 | 13,544,665.03 | 1,702,672,201.03 |

No. 4.—*United States Liberty loan bonds and Victory notes received on account of donation and forfeited recognizance in United States courts during the fiscal year ended June 30, 1922.*

| Class and title of loan. | Interest rate. | Account of— | Denominations by number of pieces. | | | | | Total pieces. | Par value (total payment). |
|---|---|---|---|---|---|---|---|---|---|
| | | | $50 | $100 | $500 | $1,000 | $5,000 | | |
| | *Per cent.* | | | | | | | | |
| Coupon: | | | | | | | | | |
| First, 1932–1947 | 3½ | Donation | 2 | 1 | 1 | | | 4 | $700 |
| First, converted, 1932–1947, permanent | 4¼ | do | 1 | | | | | 1 | 50 |
| Second, converted, 1927–1942, permanent | 4¼ | do | 1 | | | | | 1 | 50 |
| Third, 1928, permanent | 4¼ | do | 1 | | | | | 1 | 50 |
| Fourth, 1933–1938, temporary | 4¼ | do | 1 | | | | | 1 | 50 |
| Fourth, 1933–1938, permanent | 4¼ | do | 1 | | | | | 1 | 50 |
| Victory, 1922–23 | 4¾ | do | 1 | 5 | | | | 6 | 550 |
| First, 1932–1947 | 3½ | Forfeited recognizance | 2 | 9 | 81 | 19 | | 111 | 60,500 |
| First, converted, 1932–1947, temporary | 4 | do | | 3 | | | | 3 | 300 |
| Do | 4¼ | do | 1 | 1 | | | | 2 | 150 |
| First, converted, 1932–1947, permanent | 4¼ | do | | | 4 | | | 4 | 2,000 |
| Second, 1927–1942, temporary | 4 | do | 5 | 4 | | | | 9 | 650 |
| Second, converted, 1927–1942, temporary | 4¼ | do | 12 | 7 | 1 | 87 | | 107 | 88,800 |
| Second, converted, 1927–1942, permanent | 4¼ | do | 11 | 22 | 31 | 9 | 4 | 77 | 47,250 |
| Third, 1928, temporary | 4¼ | do | 13 | 7 | 1 | | | 21 | 1,850 |
| Third, 1928, permanent | 4¼ | do | 15 | 11 | 2 | 2 | | 30 | 4,850 |
| Fourth, 1933–1938, temporary | 4¼ | do | 43 | 51 | 6 | | | 100 | 10,250 |
| Fourth, 1933–1938, permanent | 4¼ | do | 6 | 24 | 5 | 3 | | 38 | 8,200 |
| Victory, 1922–23 | 4¾ | do | 7 | 8 | | 165 | | 180 | 166,150 |
| Total | | | 123 | 153 | 132 | 285 | 4 | 697 | 392,450 |
| Registered: | | | | | | | | | |
| Fourth, 1933–1938 | 4¼ | Donation | | 4 | | | | 4 | 400 |
| Grand total | | | 123 | 157 | 132 | 285 | 4 | 701 | 392,850 |

No. 5.—*United States Liberty loan bonds and Victory notes received on account of payment of estate and inheritance taxes under act of September 24, 1917, as amended by the acts approved April 4, 1918, and March 3, 1919, during the fiscal year ended June 30, 1922.*

| Class and title of loan. | Interest rate. | Denominations by number of pieces. | | | | | | | Total. | | | |
| --- | --- | --- | --- | --- | --- | --- | --- | --- | --- | --- | --- | --- |
| | | $50 | $100 | $500 | $1,000 | $5,000 | $10,000 | $50,000 | Pieces. | Amount (par value). | Accrued interest. | Total payment. |
| | Per ct. | | | | | | | | | | | |
| Coupon: | | | | | | | | | | | | |
| First, converted, 1932–1947, permanent | 4¼ | 38 | 114 | 53 | 189 | 3 | | | 397 | $243,800 | $2,117.14 | $245,917.14 |
| Second, converted, 1927–1942, permanent | 4¼ | 290 | 662 | 278 | 2,408 | 170 | 163 | | 3,941 | 5,106,200 | 51,633.88 | 5,157,833.88 |
| Third, 1928, permanent | 4¼ | 255 | 648 | 185 | 2,415 | 126 | 126 | | 3,755 | 4,475,050 | 47,398.65 | 4,522,448.65 |
| Fourth, 1933–1938, temporary | 4¼ | | | | | | | | 3 | 300 | 1.17 | 301.17 |
| Fourth, 1933–1938, permanent | 4¼ | 468 | 1,222 | 417 | 3,728 | 329 | 266 | | 6,430 | 8,357,100 | 83,811.86 | 8,470,911.86 |
| Victory, 1922–1923 | 4¾ | 69 | 138 | 49 | 423 | 14 | 22 | | 715 | 754,750 | 7,838.86 | 762,588.86 |
| Total | | 1,090 | 2,787 | 982 | 9,163 | 642 | 577 | | 15,241 | 18,867,200 | 192,821.56 | 19,160,021.56 |
| Registered: | | | | | | | | | | | | |
| First, converted, 1932–1947 | 4¼ | | 7 | 4 | 12 | 5 | 4 | | 32 | 79,700 | 363.88 | 80,063.88 |
| Second, converted, 1927–1942 | 4¼ | 7 | 42 | 30 | 73 | 21 | 29 | 2 | 204 | 587,550 | 4,838.78 | 592,388.78 |
| Third, 1928 | 4¼ | 8 | 22 | 27 | 63 | 28 | 14 | | 162 | 359,100 | 3,180.05 | 362,290.05 |
| Fourth, 1933–1938 | 4¼ | 14 | 84 | 33 | 189 | 39 | 37 | 1 | 397 | 829,600 | 5,870.86 | 835,470.86 |
| Victory, 1922–1923 | 4¾ | 1 | 15 | 19 | 24 | 1 | 3 | | 63 | 70,050 | 312.77 | 70,362.77 |
| Total | | 30 | 170 | 113 | 361 | 94 | 87 | 3 | 858 | 1,926,000 | 14,566.34 | 1,940,566.34 |
| Grand total | | 1,120 | 2,957 | 1,095 | 9,524 | 736 | 664 | 3 | 16,099 | 20,803,200 | 207,357.90 | 21,100,587.90 |

No. 6.—*United States Victory notes called for redemption by the Secretary of the Treasury on June 15 and December 15, 1922, showing presentations prior to called dates at the option of the holder and those surrendered as of June 15, 1922, and subsequent thereto, received, during fiscal year ended June 30, 1922.*

| Class and title of loan. | Interest rate. | Denominations by number of pieces. | | | | | | | | Total. | |
| --- | --- | --- | --- | --- | --- | --- | --- | --- | --- | --- | --- |
| | | $50 | $100 | $500 | $1,000 | $5,000 | $10,000 | $50,000 | $100,000 | Pieces. | Amount. |
| | Per ct. | | | | | | | | | | |
| Coupon: | | | | | | | | | | | |
| Victory, 1922–1923 | 4¾ | 312 | 198 | 13 | | 12 | | | | 535 | $53,900 |
| Do | 3¾ | 1,823 | 3,298 | 2,334 | 141,173 | 5,703 | 13,143 | | | 167,474 | 302,705,950 |
| Total | | 2,135 | 3,496 | 2,347 | 141,185 | 5,703 | 13,143 | | | 168,009 | 302,759,850 |
| Registered: | | | | | | | | | | | |
| Victory, 1922–1923 | 4¾ | 8 | 17 | 7 | 2 | | | | | 34 | 7,600 |
| Do | 3¾ | 56 | 195 | 124 | 1,329 | 678 | 1,171 | 77 | 248 | 3,878 | 45,163,300 |
| Total | | 64 | 212 | 131 | 1,331 | 678 | 1,171 | 77 | 248 | 3,912 | 45,170,900 |
| Grand total | | 2,199 | 3,708 | 2,478 | 142,516 | 6,381 | 14,314 | 77 | 248 | 171,921 | 347,930,750 |

No. 7.—*United States certificates of indebtedness, loan and tax issues, paid, canceled, and retired during the fiscal year ended June 30, 1922.*

| Class (bearer). | Series. | Date of issue. | Mo. of mty. | Interest rate. | Issued on account of— | $500 | $1,000 | $5,000 | $10,000 | $100,000 | Pieces. | Amount. |
|---|---|---|---|---|---|---|---|---|---|---|---|---|
| | | | | Per cent. | | | | | | | | |
| Loan | | 1918. Apr. 10 | Jy 9 | 4¼ | Third Liberty loan | | | | 1 | | 1 | $10,000 |
| Tax | T- | Aug. 20 | Jly 15 | 4 | Tax '99 | | 5 | | | | 5 | 5,000 |
| Loan | 4-E | Sept. 3 | Jan. | 4¼ | Bath My loan | | 1 | | | | 1 | 1,000 |
| Do | 5-A | Dec. 5 | My 6 | 4¼ | Victory loan | 1 | 1 | | | | 2 | 1,500 |
| Tax | T-2 | 1919. Jan. 16 | Jn 17 | 4¼ | K 919 | 1 | 12 | 1 | 1 | | 15 | 27,500 |
| Loan | 5-F | Feb. 13 | July 15 | 4¼ | Victory loan | | 1 | | | | 1 | 1,000 |
| Tax | F-8 | July 15 | K 15 | 4¼ | K 1920 | | 3 | 1 | | | 4 | 8,000 |
| Do | T-10 | Sept. 15 | Sept. 15 | 4¼ | do | 7 | 13 | | | | 20 | 16,500 |
| Loan | C-1920 | Sept. 2 | Feb. | 4¼ | La | 2 | 2 | | | | 4 | 3,000 |
| Tax | F- K3-1920 | Dec. 1 | K 15 | 4¼ | K 120 | | 1 | | | | 3 | 3,000 |
| Do | T-J-1920 | Dec. 15 | de 15 | 4¼ | do | 73 | 1 | | | | 74 | 37,500 |
| Do | T-D-1920 | 1920. Jan. 2 | Dec. 15 | 4¼ | do | 22 | 38 | 4 | 5 | | 69 | 119,000 |
| Do | | Feb. 2 | Mr. 15 | 4¼ | do | 2 | | | | | 2 | 1,000 |
| Do | | Mar. 15 | 29 Mr. 15 | 4¾ | Tax 1921 | 25 | 54 | 18 | 4 | | 101 | 196,500 |
| Loan | E-1920 | Apr. 1 | Jly 1 | 4¾ | Loan | 1 | 4 | | 1 | | 4 | 4,000 |
| Do | F-1920 | Apr. 15 | M 15 | 5 | do | | | | | | 1 | 500 |
| Do | 1920 | do | Q 15 | 5¾ | do | 4 | 8 | 1 | | | 14 | 25,000 |
| Do | H-1920 | Ky 17 | Nv 15 | 6 | do | 7 | 6 | | | | 13 | 9,500 |
| Do | 1921 | June 15 | de 15 | 5½ | do | 3 | 4 | 2 | 1 | | 10 | 25,500 |
| Tax | 1921 | do | de 15 | 6 | Tax | 1,968 | 1,82 | 193 | 128 | 7 | 3,728 | 5,361,000 |
| Loan | B-1921 | do | M 15 | 5½ | Loan | 10 | 14 | 3 | | | 27 | 34,00 |
| Tax | T-M-2-1921 | Aug. 6 | Ag. 15 | 5¾ | Tax | 39 | 84 | 6 | | | 129 | 133,500 |
| Loan | 1921 | Aug. 15 | Kr. 15 | 6 | Loan | 16,182 | 30,455 | 5,994 | 4,660 | 63 | 57,694 | 155,416,000 |
| Tax | 1921 | do | Kr. 15 | 5½ | Tax | 14 | 2 | | | | 16 | 9,000 |
| Do | T-S-1921 | do | Ji. 15 | 6 | do | 18,502 | 36,94 | 8,699 | 8,865 | 1,65 | 74,675 | 341,870,000 |
| Do | 1921 | Q 5 | Kr. 15 | 5½ | do | 97 | 76 | 7 | 3 | | 183 | 189,500 |
| Loan | D-1921 | Nv. 15 | Jy 16 | 5½ | Loan | 367 | 95 | 48 | 30 | | 840 | 1,118,90 |

| | | | | | | | | | | | | |
|---|---|---|---|---|---|---|---|---|---|---|---|---|
| Tax | T-J-2-1921 | Dec. 15 | June 15 | 5¾ | Tax | 750 | 389 | 94 | 37 | | 1,270 | 1,604,000 |
| Do | T-D-1921 | ...do | Dec. 15 | 6 | ...do | 19,603 | 46,491 | 11,618 | 11,356 | 1,613 | 90,681 | 389,242,500 |
| | | 1921. | | | | | | | | | | |
| Loan | E-1921 | Jan. 15 | Apr. 15 | 5½ | Loan | 29 | 25 | 3 | 2 | | 59 | 74,500 |
| Do | F-1921 | ...do | Oct. 15 | 5¾ | ...do | 11,620 | 22,604 | 5,661 | 5,300 | 819 | 46,004 | 191,619,000 |
| Do | G-1921 | Feb. 15 | July 15 | 5½ | ...do | 9,954 | 20,112 | 4,726 | 3,965 | 405 | 39,162 | 128,869,000 |
| Tax | T-S-2-1921 | Mar. 15 | Sept. 15 | 5½ | Tax | 11,492 | 16,843 | 5,043 | 5,479 | 907 | 39,764 | 193,294,000 |
| | | | 1922. | | | | | | | | | |
| Do | T-M-1922 | ...do | Mar. 15 | 5¾ | ...do | 17,942 | 36,388 | 8,306 | 7,777 | 1,231 | 71,644 | 287,759,000 |
| | | | 1921. | | | | | | | | | |
| Loan | H-1921 | Apr. 15 | Oct. 15 | 5½ | Loan | 13,981 | 23,327 | 6,067 | 5,432 | 755 | 49,562 | 190,472,500 |
| | | | 1922. | | | | | | | | | |
| Do | A-1922 | May 16 | Feb. 16 | 5½ | ...do | 13,036 | 26,791 | 8,002 | 7,648 | 1,059 | 56,536 | 255,699,000 |
| Tax | T-J-1922 | June 15 | June 15 | 5½ | Tax | 12,130 | 28,087 | 8,736 | 9,005 | 1,416 | 59,374 | 309,482,000 |
| Loan | B-1922 | Aug. 1 | Aug. 1 | 5½ | Loan | 9 | 26 | | 1 | | 36 | 40,500 |
| Tax | T-M-2-1922 | ...do | Mar. 15 | 5¼ | Tax | 5,253 | 11,775 | 3,220 | 3,580 | 505 | 24,333 | 116,801,500 |
| Do | T-M-3-1922 | Sept. 15 | ...do | 5 | ...do | 5,033 | 11,771 | 3,365 | 3,655 | 566 | 24,390 | 124,262,500 |
| Loan | C-1922 | Nov. 1 | Apr. 1 | 4¼ | Loan | 3,197 | 7,094 | 1,709 | 1,771 | 167 | 13,938 | 51,647,500 |
| Tax | T-J-2-1922 | Dec. 15 | June 15 | 4¼ | Tax | 2,927 | 7,897 | 1,970 | 2,094 | 234 | 15,122 | 63,550,500 |
| Total | | | | | | 164,283 | 329,208 | 83,497 | 80,801 | 11,722 | 669,511 | 2,809,044,500 |

No. 8.—*Special certificates of indebtedness paid, canceled, and retired during the fiscal year ended June 30, 1922.*

| Issue. | Interest rate. | Number of pieces. | Amount. |
|---|---|---|---|
| Registered: | *Per cent.* | | |
| Pittman Act.......... | 2 | 302 | $141,875,000 |
| Special, short term.... | 3 | 50 | 949,000,000 |
| Do.......... | 4 | 44 | 843,100,000 |
| Do.......... | 6 | 1 | 32,854,450 |
| Total.......... | | 397 | 1,966,829,450 |

No. 9.—*Redeemed United States war savings certificates received from the Treasurer of the United States, by months and series, during the fiscal year ended June 30, 1922.*

| Month of— | Series of 1918. | | | Series of 1919. | | | Series of 1920. | | | Series of 1921. | | | Total. | | |
|---|---|---|---|---|---|---|---|---|---|---|---|---|---|---|---|
| | Number of certificates. | Number of stamps. | Amount redemption value. | Number of certificates. | Number of stamps. | Amount redemption value. | Number of certificates. | Number of stamps. | Amount redemption value. | Number of certificates. | Number of stamps. | Amount redemption value. | Number of certificates. | Number of stamps. | Amount redemption value. |
| July, 1921.......... | 148,265 | 1,532,880 | $36,954,621.50 | 18,350 | 164,460 | $726,471.39 | 10,382 | 105,799 | $454,671.98 | 15,782 | 77,390 | $323,305.65 | 192,770 | 1,880,529 | $8,459,970.52 |
| August, 1921.......... | 145,185 | 1,537,116 | 6,989,636.21 | 17,517 | 159,539 | 706,243.11 | 9,825 | 100,518 | 432,952.82 | 15,550 | 83,994 | 351,600.36 | 188,077 | 1,881,127 | 8,480,432.50 |
| September, 1921.......... | 140,582 | 1,505,803 | 6,862,627.75 | 17,163 | 152,688 | 684,867.81 | 9,031 | 92,383 | 398,998.16 | 15,695 | 89,765 | 376,813.83 | 182,511 | 1,841,049 | 8,320,207.55 |
| October, 1921.......... | 142,364 | 1,518,101 | 6,934,115.02 | 16,836 | 152,655 | 678,897.70 | 8,590 | 87,002 | 376,541.08 | 14,693 | 82,501 | 347,134.07 | 182,483 | 1,840,259 | 8,336,687.87 |
| November, 1921.......... | 138,105 | 1,444,506 | 6,611,549.40 | 15,481 | 132,204 | 593,737.72 | 7,948 | 76,803 | 333,375.60 | 14,840 | 82,779 | 349,053.39 | 176,374 | 1,737,352 | 7,887,746.11 |
| December, 1921.......... | 152,000 | 1,416,122 | 6,496,289.22 | 17,700 | 131,102 | 585,661.66 | 9,102 | 75,686 | 329,062.14 | 20,886 | 98,520 | 416,558.25 | 199,688 | 1,721,440 | 7,827,571.27 |
| January, 1922.......... | 138,424 | 1,210,415 | 5,563,583.18 | 18,031 | 136,697 | 611,964.31 | 9,259 | 76,091 | 331,516.95 | 18,901 | 107,839 | 456,885.35 | 184,615 | 1,531,042 | 6,963,949.79 |
| February, 1922.......... | 106,242 | 942,301 | 4,340,251.02 | 14,842 | 113,757 | 510,330.33 | 7,542 | 61,819 | 269,930.20 | 8,906 | 75,157 | 319,129.46 | 137,582 | 1,193,034 | 5,439,641.01 |
| March, 1922.......... | 105,571 | 930,115 | 4,294,294.63 | 14,849 | 118,205 | 531,673.64 | 7,337 | 65,025 | 284,668.24 | 6,882 | 66,886 | 284,783.09 | 134,639 | 1,190,231 | 5,395,419.60 |
| April, 1922.......... | 85,986 | 744,490 | 3,444,019.62 | 12,488 | 94,271 | 424,719.32 | 6,404 | 56,556 | 248,146.89 | 5,424 | 55,077 | 235,054.65 | 110,302 | 930,394 | 4,351,940.48 |
| May, 1922.......... | 77,976 | 680,147 | 3,152,774.73 | 12,341 | 99,457 | 449,177.52 | 6,538 | 62,622 | 275,325.12 | 5,314 | 57,634 | 246,488.90 | 102,169 | 999,880 | 4,123,766.27 |
| June, 1922.......... | 67,183 | 566,132 | 2,630,125.70 | 11,580 | 92,833 | 420,252.62 | 5,859 | 54,822 | 241,634.92 | 4,589 | 50,531 | 216,650.11 | 89,211 | 764,318 | 3,508,663.35 |
| Total.......... | 1,447,883 | 14,028,128 | 64,273,887.98 | 187,198 | 1,549,858 | 6,920,997.13 | 97,537 | 915,196 | 3,976,724.10 | 147,462 | 928,053 | 3,923,457.11 | 1,880,380 | 17,421,235 | 79,095,066.32 |

[1] On adjustment of previous figures deduction is made of 1 stamp, $4.40.

No. 10.—*Redeemed United States war savings certificates received from the Treasurer of the United States during the fiscal year ended June 30, 1922, divided into registered and nonregistered groups.*

| Month of— | Series 1918. | | Series 1919. | | Series 1920. | | Series 1921. | | Total. | | Total. |
|---|---|---|---|---|---|---|---|---|---|---|---|
| | Registered. | Nonregistered. | Registered. | Nonregistered. | Registered. | Nonregistered. | Registered. | Nonregistered. | Registered. | Nonregistered. | |
| July, 1921 | †$2,404,680.08 | $4,549,941.42 | $286,821.96 | $469,649.43 | $207,425.42 | $247,246.56 | $96,257.16 | $227,048.49 | $2,965,184.62 | $5,493,885.90 | $8,459,070.52 |
| August, 1921 | 2,497,229.89 | 4,492,406.32 | 272,192.72 | 434,050.39 | 193,551.69 | 239,401.13 | 114,038.03 | 237,562.33 | 3,077,012.33 | 5,403,420.17 | 8,480,432.50 |
| September, 1921 | 2,483,721.95 | 4,375,905.80 | 270,344.28 | 411,523.53 | 192,035.69 | 206,862.47 | 136,742.40 | 240,071.43 | 3,087,844.32 | 5,232,363.23 | 8,320,207.55 |
| October, 1921 | 2,441,179.59 | 4,382,935.43 | 258,548.52 | 420,349.18 | 172,455.50 | 204,055.58 | 117,728.52 | 229,405.65 | 3,089,942.13 | 5,246,745.74 | 8,336,687.87 |
| November, 1921 | 2,275,422.63 | 4,336,126.77 | 222,591.88 | 371,145.84 | 145,548.83 | 187,823.77 | 117,421.98 | 231,631.41 | 2,760,985.32 | 5,126,730.79 | 7,887,716.11 |
| December, 1921 | 2,128,033.12 | 4,368,257.10 | 200,078.15 | 385,583.51 | 143,122.71 | 185,939.43 | 114,074.94 | 302,483.35 | 2,385,307.88 | 5,242,263.39 | 7,827,571.27 |
| January, 1922 | 1,854,464.31 | 3,699,118.87 | 209,735.54 | 402,228.77 | 138,290.85 | 193,226.10 | 140,805.94 | 316,079.41 | 2,353,296.64 | 4,610,653.15 | 6,963,949.79 |
| February, 1922 | 1,475,817.68 | 2,880,433.34 | 186,290.45 | 324,039.88 | 111,933.51 | 157,906.69 | 125,716.27 | 193,413.19 | 1,903,757.91 | 3,535,883.10 | 5,439,641.01 |
| March, 1922 | 1,532,655.81 | 2,701,633.82 | 215,099.28 | 316,574.36 | 335,618.46 | 149,049.78 | 124,699.98 | 160,083.11 | 2,008,073.53 | 3,387,346.07 | 5,395,419.60 |
| April, 1922 | 1,213,097.65 | 2,230,921.97 | 159,845.22 | 264,874.10 | 115,528.16 | 132,615.73 | 115,334.24 | 119,730.41 | 1,603,795.27 | 2,748,145.21 | 4,351,940.48 |
| May, 1922 | 1,083,742.79 | 2,049,051.94 | 165,612.92 | 253,584.60 | 129,583.70 | 145,476.42 | 135,214.33 | 111,274.57 | 1,514,418.74 | 2,609,347.53 | 4,123,766.27 |
| June, 1922 | 923,408.74 | 1,705,716.96 | 153,824.93 | 296,427.69 | 112,351.59 | 129,283.33 | 103,684.20 | 112,965.91 | 1,293,269.46 | 2,215,393.89 | 3,508,663.35 |
| Total | 22,432,453.24 | 41,841,434.71 | 2,570,985.85 | 4,350,011.28 | 1,797,741.11 | 2,178,982.99 | 1,441,707.95 | 2,481,749.16 | 28,242,888.15 | 50,852,178.17 | 79,095,066.32 |

† On an adjustment of previous figures, deduction is made of $1.40.

No. 11.—*United States war savings certificates redeemed during the fiscal year ended June 30, 1922, and total redeemed to June 30, 1922.*

[Reported according to the State or Territory in which originally presented for redemption.]

| State or Territory. | Population. | Amount redeemed. | |
|---|---|---|---|
| | | Fiscal year 1922. | Total to June 30, 1922. |
| Ala. | 2,38, 74 | $834,374.73 | $ .62 |
| Arizona | 34, 62 | 218,784.46 | .25 |
| Ark. | 1, 04 | 850,020.16 | 8.28 |
| Cal. | 3, 61 | 3,488,436.12 | 69.02 |
| Colorado | 9 | 1,043,621.98 | 38.95 |
| Conn. | 1, 63 | 903,743.17 | 4.55 |
| Del. | | 152,560.18 | 28.53 |
| Dist. of Col. | | 342,174.59 | 94.25 |
| Fla. | 2, 31 | 729,742.90 | 42.30 |
| Ga. | 8, 32 | 995,327.41 | 80.33 |
| Haw. | | 180,332.73 | 87.84 |
| Idaho | | 377,255.13 | 87.07 |
| Ill. | 6,485,280 | 4,931,468.68 | 28,141,497.68 |
| Ind. | 2, 90 | 2,985,069.87 | 21,531,661.90 |
| Iowa | 2, 01 | 3,232,591.81 | 09.30 |
| Kans. | 1 | 2,049,940.06 | 8.34 |
| Ky. | | 1,429,154.60 | 42.02 |
| La. | 1, 69 | 900,708.23 | .80 |
| Me. | 8, 04 | 381,998.79 | 37.82 |
| Md. | 1, 61 | 563,065.04 | 68.06 |
| Mass. | 1, 80 | 9,912.40 | .73 |
| Mich. | 3, 42 | 1,735,211.63 | 63.84 |
| Minn. | 1, 15 | 6,897.82 | .25 |
| Miss. | 1, 68 | 828,213.45 | 8.90 |
| Missouri | 3, 05 | 3,657,397.21 | 11, 992.97 |
| Mont. | 89 | 578,557.32 | .90 |
| Neb. | 1,295,372 | 2,221,780.84 | 8.78 |
| Nev. | 67 | 96,036.05 | 90.20 |
| New Hampshire | 83 | 283,301.19 | 847 |
| N. J. | 30 | 177,092.49 | 8.81 |
| N. Y. | 3, 27 | 1,351,736.16 | 8.21 |
| N. Carolina | 10, 23 | 5,540,424.77 | 6.58 |
| N. Dak. | 2, 82 | 1,712,054.00 | 3.32 |
| Ohio | 5,2, 94 | 577,305.47 | 8.64 |
| Okla. | 33 | 7,382,032.82 | 86.06 |
| Oregon | 2, 89 | 1,222,186.58 | 8.36 |
| Pa. | 2, 88 | 1,374,517.96 | 6.82 |
| R. I. | 8,720,017 | 20,296.08 | 6.46 |
| S. C. | | 4,342,425.58 | 8.17 |

No. 12.—*Redeemed United States Treasury savings certificates received, by months and series, during fiscal year ended June 30, 1922.*

| Month of— | Series 1918. | | Series 1919. | | | | | | Series 1920. | | | | | | | |
|---|---|---|---|---|---|---|---|---|---|---|---|---|---|---|---|---|
| | $100. | | $100. | | $1,000. | | Total. | | $100. | | $1,000. | | Total. | | | |
| | Pieces. | Redemption value. | Pieces. | Redemption value. | Pieces. | Redemption value. | Pieces. | Redemption value. | Pieces. | Redemption value. | Pieces. | Redemption value. | Pieces. | Redemption value. | | |
| July, 1921 | 27 | $2,451.60 | 604 | $53,374.60 | 69 | $60,996.00 | 673 | $114,370.60 | 1,747 | $150,239.40 | 40 | $34,398.80 | 1,787 | $184,638.20 | | |
| August, 1921 | 23 | 2,093.00 | 588 | 52,096.80 | 62 | 54,932.00 | 650 | 107,028.80 | 1,701 | 146,626.20 | 28 | 24,136.00 | 1,729 | 170,762.20 | | |
| September, 1921 | 69 | 6,292.80 | 598 | 53,102.40 | 67 | 59,496.00 | 665 | 112,598.40 | 1,540 | 133,056.00 | 28 | 24,192.00 | 1,568 | 157,248.00 | | |
| October, 1921 | 4 | 365.60 | 554 | 49,306.80 | 54 | 48,060.00 | 608 | 97,366.80 | 1,365 | 118,192.20 | 26 | 22,516.00 | 1,391 | 140,708.20 | | |
| November, 1921 | 8 | 732.80 | 689 | 61,458.80 | 58 | 51,736.00 | 747 | 113,194.80 | 1,365 | 118,482.00 | 25 | 21,700.00 | 1,390 | 140,182.00 | | |
| December, 1921 | 64 | 5,875.20 | 456 | 40,766.40 | 79 | 70,626.00 | 535 | 111,392.40 | 982 | 85,434.00 | 24 | 20,880.00 | 1,006 | 106,314.00 | | |
| January, 1922 | 30 | 2,760.00 | 577 | 51,699.20 | 53 | 47,488.00 | 630 | 99,187.20 | 1,019 | 88,856.80 | 31 | 27,032.00 | 1,050 | 115,888.80 | | |
| February, 1922 | 16 | 1,475.20 | 482 | 43,283.60 | 49 | 44,002.00 | 531 | 87,285.60 | 1,076 | 94,042.40 | 29 | 25,346.00 | 1,105 | 119,388.40 | | |
| March, 1922 | 7 | 646.80 | 565 | 50,850.00 | 51 | 45,900.00 | 616 | 96,750.00 | 1,096 | 96,009.60 | 26 | 22,776.00 | 1,122 | 118,785.60 | | |
| April, 1922 | 7 | 648.20 | 506 | 45,641.20 | 43 | 38,786.00 | 549 | 84,427.20 | 1,280 | 112,384.00 | 17 | 14,926.00 | 1,297 | 127,310.00 | | |
| May, 1922 | 8 | 742.40 | 379 | 34,261.60 | 38 | 34,352.00 | 417 | 68,613.60 | 990 | 87,120.00 | 12 | 10,560.00 | 1,002 | 97,680.00 | | |
| June, 1922 | 21 | 1,953.00 | 476 | 43,125.60 | 36 | 32,616.00 | 512 | 75,741.60 | 990 | 84,672.00 | 22 | 19,404.00 | 982 | 104,076.0 | | |
| Total | 284 | 26,036.60 | 6,474 | 578,966.20 | 659 | 588,990.00 | 7,133 | 1,167,956.20 | 15,121 | 1,315,114.60 | 308 | 267,866.80 | 15,429 | 1,582,981 40 | | |

Series 1921.

Series 1921 (new issue).

| Month of— | $25. | | $100. | | $1,000. | | Total. | | $25. | | $100. | | $1,000. | | | |
|---|---|---|---|---|---|---|---|---|---|---|---|---|---|---|---|---|
| | Pieces. | Redemption value. | Pieces. | Redemption value. | Pieces. | Redemption value. | Pieces. | Redemption value. | Pieces. | Sale price. | Pieces. | Sale price. | Pieces. | Sale price. | | |
| July, 1921 | 517 | $10,804.40 | 1,011 | $84,507.60 | 13 | $10,868.00 | 1,541 | $106,180.00 | | | | | | | | |
| August, 1921 | 558 | 11,687.80 | 1,124 | 94,178.40 | 15 | 12,570.00 | 1,697 | 118,436.20 | | | | | | | | |
| September, 1921 | 609 | 12,787.85 | 1,186 | 99,615.40 | 9 | 7,560.00 | 1,804 | 119,963.25 | | | | | | | | |
| October, 1921 | 650 | 13,677.80 | 1,018 | 85,703.50 | 22 | 18,514.80 | 1,690 | 117,896.10 | | | | | | | | |
| November, 1921 | 766 | 16,157.40 | 1,033 | 87,171.25 | 4 | 3,376.00 | 1,803 | 106,704.65 | | | | | | | | |
| December, 1921 | 693 | 12,541.95 | 870 | 73,601.80 | 17 | 14,382.00 | 1,490 | 100,525.75 | 9 | $180.00 | 5 | $400.00 | 7 | $5,600.00 | | |
| January, 1922 | 634 | 13,440.80 | 1,110 | 99,128.00 | 19 | 16,112.00 | 1,763 | 123,680.80 | 151 | 3,020.00 | 129 | 10,240.00 | 20 | 16,000.00 | | |
| February, 1922 | 684 | 14,535.00 | 1,165 | 99,025.00 | 21 | 17,850.00 | 1,870 | 131,410.00 | 153 | 3,028.85 | 119 | 9,571.60 | 14 | 11,200.00 | | |
| March, 1922 | 756 | 16,102.80 | 1,232 | 104,966.40 | 27 | 17,892.00 | 2,009 | 138,961.20 | 144 | 3,078.05 | 119 | 9,520.00 | 12 | 9,600.00 | | |
| April, 1922 | 708 | 15,115.80 | 1,360 | 116,144.00 | 27 | 23,058.00 | 2,095 | 154,317.80 | 144 | 2,880.00 | 184 | 14,720.00 | 18 | 14,400.00 | | |
| May, 1922 | 590 | 12,626.00 | 1,281 | 109,683.60 | 6 | 5,136.00 | 1,877 | 127,415.60 | 911 | 1,820.00 | 150 | 12,000.00 | 14 | 14,400.00 | | |
| June, 1922 | 614 | 13,170.30 | 1,069 | 91,720.20 | 20 | 17,160.00 | 1,703 | 122,050.50 | 131 | 2,620.00 | 141 | 11,280.00 | 16 | 12,800.00 | | |
| Total | 7,679 | 162,647.90 | 13,459 | 1,140,415.15 | 194 | 164,478.80 | 21,332 | 1,467,541.85 | 679 | 13,580.00 | 727 | 58,160.00 | 87 | 69,600.00 | | |

| $1,000. | | Total. | |
|---|---|---|---|
| Redemption value. | | | Redemption value. |
| | | | |
| $400.00 | | 7 | $5,600.00 |
| 10,273.50 | | 20 | 16,044.00 |
| 9,571.60 | | 14 | 11,258.00 |
| | | 12 | 9,662.00 |
| 14,840.80 | | 18 | 9,662.00 |
| 12,124.00 | | 18 | 14,558.00 |
| 11,436.20 | | 16 | 12,968.00 |
| 58,646.00 | | 87 | 70,090.00 |

| Month of— | Series 1921 (new issue). Total | | | Series 1922. $25. | | | $100. | | | $1,000. | | | Total. | | | Grand total. | |
|---|---|---|---|---|---|---|---|---|---|---|---|---|---|---|---|---|---|
| | Pieces | Sale price | Redemption value | Pieces | Sale price | Redemption value | Pieces | Sale price | Redemption value | Pieces | Sale price | Redemption value | Pieces | Sale price | Redemption value | Pieces | Redemption value |
| July, 1921 | | | | | | | | | | | | | | | | 4,028 | $407,640.40 |
| August, 1921 | | | | | | | | | | | | | | | | 4,099 | 398,320.20 |
| September, 1921 | | | | | | | | | | | | | | | | | |
| October, 1921 | | | | | | | | | | | | | | | | 4,106 | 396,102.45 |
| November, 1921 | | | | | | | | | | | | | | | | 3,683 | 356,335.90 |
| December, 1921 | | | | | | | | | | | | | | | | 3,948 | 360,814.25 |
| January, 1922 | 21 | $6,180.00 | $6,180.20 | 2 | $40.00 | $40.00 | 2 | $160.00 | $160.00 | 1 | $800.00 | $800.00 | 5 | $1,000.00 | $1,000.00 | 3,085 | 324,107.35 |
| February, 1922 | 299 | 29,260.00 | 29,346.45 | 121 | 2,420.00 | 2,424.35 | 222 | 17,760.00 | 17,796.40 | 29 | 23,200.00 | 23,246.00 | 372 | 43,380.00 | 43,466.75 | 3,499 | 348,697.00 |
| March, 1922 | 286 | 23,780.00 | 23,907.65 | 591 | 11,820.00 | 11,855.25 | 793 | 63,440.00 | 63,660.20 | 53 | 42,400.00 | 42,532.00 | 1,437 | 117,660.00 | 118,047.45 | 4,193 | 412,372.40 |
| April, 1922 | 340 | 27,200.00 | 27,405.20 | 1,151 | 23,020.00 | 23,114.45 | 1,443 | 115,440.00 | 115,988.60 | 125 | 100,000.00 | 100,438.00 | 2,719 | 238,460.00 | 239,541.05 | 5,477 | 497,098.70 |
| May, 1922 | 259 | 28,220.00 | 28,520.70 | 1,833 | 36,660.00 | 36,861.85 | 2,200 | 176,720.00 | 177,746.80 | 244 | 195,200.00 | 196,150.00 | 4,286 | 408,580.00 | 410,758.65 | 7,007 | 633,649.45 |
| June, 1922 | 288 | 26,700.00 | 27,061.65 | 2,243 | 44,860.00 | 45,148.60 | 2,654 | 212,320.00 | 213,828.80 | 312 | 249,600.00 | 251,290.00 | 5,209 | 506,780.00 | 510,267.40 | 7,849 | 733,739.95 |
| | | | | | | | | | | | | | | | | 8,715 | 841,150.15 |
| Total | 1,493 | 141,340.00 | 142,421.85 | 5,941 | 118,820.00 | 119,444.50 | 7,323 | 585,840.00 | 589,180.80 | 764 | 611,200.00 | 614,456.00 | 14,028 | 1,315,860.00 | 1,323,081.30 | 59,699 | 5,710,019.20 |

No. 13.—*Repaid United States thrift stamps received, by months, during the fiscal year ended June 30, 1922.*

| Month of— | Number of stamps. | Amount. | Month of— | Number of stamps. | Amount. |
|---|---|---|---|---|---|
| July, 1921 | 584,929 | $146,232.25 | February, 1922 | 147 | $36.75 |
| August, 1921 | 454,681 | 113,670.25 | March, 1922 | 62 | 15.50 |
| September, 1921 | 361,560 | 90,390.00 | April, 1922 | 26 | 6.50 |
| October, 1921 | 308,048 | 77,012.00 | May, 1922 | 14 | 3.50 |
| November, 1921 | 282,953 | 70,738.25 | June, 1922 | 17 | 4.25 |
| December, 1921 | | | | 22 | 5.50 |
| January, 1922 | | | Total | 123,073.25 | |
| | 2,494,752 | 621,188.00 | | 492,293 | |

No. 14.—*Repaid United States Treasury savings stamps received, by months, during the fiscal year ended June 30, 1922.*

| Month of— | Number of stamps. | Amount. |
|---|---|---|
| November, 1921 | 6 | $6.00 |
| February, 1922 | 4 | 4.00 |
| April, 1922 | 3 | 3.00 |
| May, 1922 | 26 | 26.00 |
| Total | 39 | 39.00 |

No. 15.—*Comparative statement showing all paid securities received by the Register of the Treasury, canceled on account of reduction of the public debt of United States, during the fiscal years 1919, 1920, 1921, 1922, and for the period April 6, 1917 to June 30, 1922.*

| Class of security. | 1919 | | 1920 | | 1921 | | 1922 | | Apr. 6, 1917, to June 30, 1922, | |
|---|---|---|---|---|---|---|---|---|---|---|
| | Pieces. | Amount. | Pieces. | Amount. | Pieces. | Amount. | Pieces. | Amount. | Pieces. | Amount. |
| Coupon: | | | | | | | | | | |
| Pre-war loans | 50,081 | $15,839,510.00 | 1,006 | $172,070.00 | 466 | $89,060.00 | 220 | $28,610.00 | 62,523 | $49,216,180.00 |
| Liberty loans | 541,710 | 551,021,150.00 | 1,107,571 | 1,223,731,300.00 | 305,517 | 413,073,700.00 | 1,205,457 | 1,884,018,300.00 | 3,237,195 | 4,148,485,950.00 |
| Certificates of indebtedness | 1,721,849 | 10,974,743,500.00 | 1,205,416 | 7,829,486,000.00 | 637,874 | 3,470,216,500.00 | 669,511 | 2,809,044,500.00 | 5,171,885 | 32,109,329,500.00 |
| Treasury (war) savings securities | 23,175,884 | 98,511,361.02 | 31,296,964 | 135,593,965.50 | 23,138,658 | 102,750,904.05 | 13,679,887 | 51,473,405.17 | 91,797,627 | 390,429,393.72 |
| Total | 25,489,524 | 11,643,115,521.02 | 33,610,957 | 9,188,983,335.50 | 24,082,515 | 3,986,129,864.05 | 15,556,075 | 4,744,564,815.17 | 100,269,230 | 36,697,461,023.72 |
| Registered: | | | | | | | | | | |
| Pre-war loans | 29,216 | 63,405,130.00 | 553 | 269,100.00 | 250 | 62,520.00 | 108 | 28,530.00 | 30,368 | 65,452,430.00 |
| Liberty loans | | | 170 | 323,050.00 | 1,059 | 19,138,950.00 | 45,893 | 177,571,400.00 | 47,122 | 197,033,400.00 |
| Certificates of indebtedness | 115 | 4,071,794,400.00 | 406 | 7,759,218,458.53 | 505 | 5,082,000,000.00 | 397 | 1,966,829,450.00 | 1,640 | 20,064,842,308.53 |
| Treasury (war) savings securities | 8,289,375 | 35,246,450.44 | 14,452,350 | 64,514,800.31 | 11,789,520 | 56,983,841.98 | 6,285,838 | 33,952,907.35 | 40,967,297 | 191,569,909.90 |
| Total | 8,318,706 | 4,170,445,980.44 | 14,453,479 | 7,824,325,408.84 | 11,791,334 | 5,158,185,311.98 | 6,332,236 | 2,178,382,287.35 | 41,046,427 | 20,518,898,048.43 |
| Grand total | 33,808,230 | 15,813,561,501.46 | 48,064,436 | 17,013,308,744.34 | 35,873,849 | 9,144,315,176.03 | 21,888,311 | 6,922,947,102.52 | 141,315,657 | 57,216,359,072.15 |

No. 16.—United States bonds, notes, and certificates of indebtedness in bearer form received from Federal reserve banks and the Division of Loans and Currency, audited and filed for credit to fiscal agency accounts during the fiscal year ended June 30, 1922, grouped according to accounts credited.

| Title of loan. | Interest rate. | Exchange.[1] | | Conversion.[2] | | Unissued stock.[3] | | Miscellaneous.[4] | | Total. | |
|---|---|---|---|---|---|---|---|---|---|---|---|
| | | Pieces. | Amount. | Pieces. | Amount. | Pieces. | Amount. | Pieces. | Amount. | Pieces. | Amount. |
| | Per cent. | | | | | | | | | | |
| Pre-war loans: | | | | | | | | | | | |
| Loan of 1848 | 6 | | | | | | | 17 | $21,000 | 17 | $21,000 |
| Loan of 1898 | 3 | | | | | | | 6 | 600 | 6 | 600 |
| Consols of 1930 | 2 | 218 | $115,950 | | | | | | | 218 | 115,950 |
| Loan of 1925 | 4 | 1,444 | 1,309,800 | | | | | | | 1,444 | 1,309,800 |
| Panama Canal, 1906-1936 | 2 | 2 | 40 | | | | | | | 2 | 40 |
| Panama Canal, 1918-1938 | 2 | 6 | 200 | | | | | | | 6 | 200 |
| Panama Canal, 1911- | 3 | 119 | 92,700 | | | | | 1 | 1,000 | 120 | 93,700 |
| Conversion bonds, 1946 | 3 | 200 | 200,000 | | | | | | | 200 | 200,00 |
| Conversion bonds, 1947 | 3 | 1,065 | 1,056,000 | | | | | | | 1,065 | 1,056,000 |
| Postal-savings bonds— | | | | | | | | | | | |
| First series | 2½ | 1 | 100 | | | | | | | 1 | 100 |
| Second series | 2½ | 38 | 2,360 | | | | | | | 38 | 2,360 |
| Third series | 2½ | 35 | 5,340 | | | | | | | 35 | 5,340 |
| Fourth series | 2½ | 59 | 9,020 | | | | | | | 59 | 9,020 |
| Fifth series | 2½ | 58 | 9,080 | | | | | | | 58 | 9,080 |
| Sixth series | 2½ | 44 | 7,280 | | | | | | | 44 | 7,280 |
| Seventh series | 2½ | 36 | 5,200 | | | | | | | 36 | 5,200 |
| Eighth series | 2½ | 31 | 4,540 | | | | | | | 31 | 4,540 |
| Ninth series | 2½ | 48 | 6,080 | | | | | | | 48 | 6,080 |
| Tenth series | 2½ | 24 | 4,640 | | | | | | | 24 | 4,640 |
| Eleventh series | 2½ | 23 | 3,820 | | | | | | | 23 | 3,820 |
| Twelfth series | 2½ | 48 | 5,680 | | | | | | | 48 | 5,680 |
| Thirteenth series | 2½ | 22 | 3,320 | | | | | | | 22 | 3,320 |
| Fourteenth series | 2½ | 19 | 3,740 | | | | | | | 19 | 3,740 |
| Fifteenth series | 2½ | 7 | 1,500 | | | | | | | 7 | 1,500 |
| Sixteenth series | 2½ | 21 | 2,260 | | | | | | | 21 | 2,260 |
| Seventeenth series | 2½ | 1 | 500 | | | | | | | 1 | 500 |
| Eighteenth series | 2½ | 16 | 2,960 | | | | | | | 16 | 2,960 |
| Nineteenth series | 2½ | 2 | 40 | | | | | | | 2 | 40 |
| Twentieth series | 2½ | 6 | 520 | | | | | | | 6 | 520 |
| Twenty-first series | 2½ | 7 | 460 | | | | | | | 7 | 460 |
| Twenty-second series | 2½ | 4 | 2,000 | | | | | | | 4 | 2,000 |
| Total | | 3,604 | 2,855,130 | | | | | 24 | 22,600 | 3,628 | 2,877,730 |

[1] Includes coupon exchange, denominational exchange, special denominational exchange, and temporary exchange.
[2] Includes conversion exchange.
[3] Includes unissued conversion, unissued allotment, unissued temporary exchange, and unissued stock.
[4] Includes claim issue, claim retirement, mutilated, error, securities trust fund, special deposit account, and claim registered issue.

No. 16.—*United States bonds, notes, and certificates of indebtedness in bearer form received from Federal reserve banks and the Division of Loans and Currency, audited and filed for credit to fiscal agency accounts during the fiscal year ended June 30, 1922, grouped according to accounts credited*—Continued.

| Title of loan. | Interest rate. | Exchange.[1] Pieces. | Exchange.[1] Amount. | Conversion.[2] Pieces. | Conversion.[2] Amount. | Unissued stock.[3] Pieces. | Unissued stock.[3] Amount. | Miscellaneous.[4] Pieces. | Miscellaneous.[4] Amount. | Total. Pieces. | Total. Amount. |
|---|---|---|---|---|---|---|---|---|---|---|---|
| | *Per cent.* | | | | | | | | | | |
| Liberty loans: | | | | | | | | | | | |
| First, 1932–1947 | 3½ | 333,396 | 83,361,800 | | | 1 | $500 | 129 | 69,200 | 333,526 | 83,431,500 |
| First, converted, 1932–1947, temporary | 4 | 19,798 | 1,597,550 | 22,313 | $1,841,800 | | | 24 | 2,550 | 42,135 | 3,441,900 |
| First, converted, 1932–1947, permanent | 4 | 3,519 | 422,100 | 19,592 | 2,539,700 | 4,906 | 1,540,950 | | | 28,017 | 4,502,750 |
| First, converted, 1932–1947, temporary | 4¼ | 25,542 | 3,093,350 | | | | | 1 | 50 | 25,543 | 3,093,400 |
| First, converted, 1932–1947, permanent | 4¼ | 331,096 | 54,145,800 | | | 14,356 | 6,216,350 | 62 | 21,100 | 345,514 | 60,383,250 |
| First-second, converted, 1932–1947, temporary | 4¼ | 973 | 124,700 | | | | | | | 973 | 124,700 |
| First-second, converted, 1932–1947, permanent | 4¼ | 1,304 | 150,550 | | | 29 | 10,700 | | | 1,333 | 161,250 |
| Second, 1927–1942, temporary | 4 | 88,930 | 7,014,100 | 70,724 | 5,906,600 | | | 129 | 11,350 | 159,843 | 12,932,050 |
| Second, 1927–1942, permanent | 4 | 13,519 | 1,092,550 | 86,325 | 13,520,450 | 4,527 | 1,471,300 | 3 | 250 | 104,374 | 16,084,550 |
| Second, converted, 1927–1942, temporary | 4¼ | 103,402 | 13,860,900 | | | | | 45 | 5,300 | 103,447 | 13,866,200 |
| Second, converted, 1927–1942, permanent | 4¼ | 1,290,690 | 279,684,550 | | | 14,783 | 16,005,700 | 351 | 246,850 | 1,305,824 | 295,937,100 |
| Third, 1928, temporary | 4¼ | 474,087 | 39,687,000 | | | | | 336 | 84,400 | 474,423 | 39,771,400 |
| Third, 1928, permanent | 4¼ | 2,097,738 | 334,719,750 | | | 443,801 | 34,801,250 | 386 | 426,100 | 2,541,925 | 369,947,100 |
| Fourth, 1933–1938, temporary | 4¼ | 1,602,468 | 184,159,900 | | | | | 486 | 268,450 | 1,602,954 | 184,428,350 |
| Fourth, 1933–1938, permanent | 4¼ | 2,703,926 | 562,039,350 | | | 6,578 | 8,069,200 | 587 | 214,100 | 2,711,091 | 570,322,650 |
| Victory, 1922–23 | 4¾ | 2,765,387 | 423,406,100 | 21,799 | 18,826,800 | 64,142 | 8,220,100 | 353 | 102,650 | 2,851,681 | 450,555,650 |
| Victory, 1922–23 | 3¾ | 59,652 | 66,686,250 | 99,445 | 207,124,100 | 363,229 | 490,817,650 | | | 522,326 | 764,628,000 |
| **Total** | | 11,915,487 | 2,055,246,300 | 320,198 | 249,759,450 | 916,352 | 567,153,700 | 2,892 | 1,452,350 | 13,154,929 | 2,873,611,800 |
| Treasury notes | | | | | | | | | | | |
| Series A, 1921 | 5¾ | 25,210 | 40,699,600 | | | 109 | 201,500 | | | 25,319 | 40,901,100 |
| Series B, 1924 | 5½ | 9,185 | 22,843,200 | | | | | | | 9,185 | 22,843,200 |
| Series A, 1925 | 4¾ | 2,316 | 5,781,000 | | | | | | | 2,316 | 5,781,000 |
| Series B, 1925 | 4⅞ | 31 | 90,500 | | | | | | | 34 | 90,500 |
| Series A, 1926 | 4¾ | 2,188 | 2,565,100 | | | | | | | 2,188 | 2,565,100 |
| **Total** | | 38,933 | 71,979,400 | | | 109 | 201,500 | | | 39,042 | 72,180,900 |

| Certificates of indebtedness | | | | | | | | | |
|---|---|---|---|---|---|---|---|---|---|
| June 25, 1918, IV A | .4 | | | | | | | | 5,000 |
| June 15, 1920, TJ-1921 | .6 | | | | 5,000 | 1 | | | 36,025,500 |
| Aug. 16, 1920, C-1921 | .6 | 3,859 | 26,927,000 | | 36,025,500 | 2,329 | | | 84,960,000 |
| Sept. 15, 1920, TS-1921 | .5½ | 8,699 | 31,828,500 | | 58,033,000 | 7,855 | | | 102,086,500 |
| Dec. 15, 1920, TJ2-1921 | .6 | | | | 67,267,000 | 7,285 | | | 35,334,000 |
| Dec. 15, 1920, TJD-1921 | .6 | 8,640 | 39,990,000 | | 35,334,000 | 7,723 | | | 118,536,500 |
| Jan. 15, 1921, F-1921 | .5½ | 9,251 | 33,070,000 | | 78,546,500 | 8,898 | | | 65,386,500 |
| Feb. 15, 1921, G-1921 | .5½ | 8,545 | 25,646,000 | | 32,296,500 | 9,550 | | | 90,577,500 |
| Mar. 15, 1921, TS2-1921 | .5½ | 16,002 | 32,292,000 | | 64,911,500 | 8,368 | | | 97,767,500 |
| Mar. 15, 1921, TM-1922 | .5½ | 16,534 | 40,231,500 | | 247,757,500 | 6,459 | 5,000 | | 288,044,000 |
| Apr. 15, 1921, H-1921 | .5½ | 14,239 | 34,935,500 | 5 | 67,280,000 | 16,383 | | | 102,215,500 |
| May 16, 1921, A-1922 | .5½ | 23,061 | 52,375,000 | | 131,035,000 | 15,424 | | | 183,410,000 |
| June 15, 1921, TJ-1922 | .5½ | 21,735 | 56,277,000 | | 4,500,000 | 23,920 | | | 60,777,000 |
| Aug. 1, 1921, TM2-1922 | .5½ | 20,911 | 53,199,500 | | 274,899,500 | 1,950 | | | 328,099,000 |
| Aug. 1, 1921, D-1922 | .5 | 6,279 | 28,561,000 | | | 60,660 | | | 28,301,000 |
| Sept. 15, 1921, TM3-1922 | .5½ | 18,708 | 49,798,000 | | 48,120,000 | 9,708 | | | 97,918,000 |
| Sept. 15, 1921, TS-1922 | .5½ | 3,869 | 12,277,000 | | | | | | 12,277,000 |
| Nov. 1, 1921, J-1922 | .4½ | 13,655 | 47,520,000 | | 123,174,000 | 25,319 | | | 170,694,000 |
| Nov. 1, 1921, TS2-1922 | .4½ | 5,237 | 13,189,000 | | | | | | 13,189,000 |
| Dec. 15, 1921, TJ2-1922 | .4½ | 12,204 | 44,048,500 | | | | | | 44,018,500 |
| Dec. 15, 1921, TJD-1922 | .4½ | 1,611 | 11,390,000 | | | | | | 11,390,000 |
| Mar. 15, 1922, TM-1923 | .4½ | 59 | 500,000 | | | | | | 500,000 |
| Apr. 15, 1922, D-1922 | .3½ | 26 | 205,000 | | | | | | 205,000 |
| June 1, 1922, TJ2-1922 | .3½ | 102 | 315,000 | | | 102 | | | 315,000 |
| June 15, 1922, TJ-1923 | .3½ | 1 | 100,000 | | | 1 | | | 100,000 |
| Total | | 216,197 | 637,686,500 | | 1,333,960,500 | 211,442 | 5,000 | | 1,971,651,000 |
| Grand total | | 12,174,221 | 2,767,706,330 | 320,198 | 249,759,450 | 1,901,315,700 | 1,127,903 | 2,921 | 1,479,950 | 427,641 | 13,025,243 | 4,927,821,430 |

1 Includes coupon exchange, denominational exchange, special denominational exchange, and temporary exchange.
2 Includes conversion exchange.
3 Includes unissued conversion, unissued allotment, unissued temporary exchange, and unissued stock.
4 Includes claim issue, claim retirement, mutilated, error, securities trust fund, special deposit account, and claim registered issue.

No. 17.—*United States bonds, notes, and certificates of indebtedness in bearer form received from Federal reserve banks and Division of Loans and Currency, audited and filed for credit to fiscal agency accounts during the fiscal year ended June 30, 1922, showing loans, denominations, pieces, and total amount.*

| Title of loan. | Interest rate. | Denominations by number of pieces. | | | | | | | | | Total. | |
|---|---|---|---|---|---|---|---|---|---|---|---|---|
| | | $20 | $50 | $100 | $500 | $1,000 | $3,000 | $5,000 | $10,000 | $100,000 | Pieces. | Amount. |
| | *Per cent.* | | | | | | | | | | | |
| **Pre-war loans:** | | | | | | | | | | | | |
| Loan of 1848 | 6 | | | | | 15 | 2 | | | | 17 | $21,000 |
| Loan of 1898 | 3 | | | | | | | | | | 6 | 600 |
| Cls of 1930 | 2 | | 29 | 6 | 32 | 92 | | | | | 218 | 115,950 |
| Loan of 1925 | 4 | | 16 | 65 | 112 | 1,246 | | | | | 1,444 | 1,309,800 |
| Panama Canal, 1906–1938 | 2 | 2 | | | | | | | | | 2 | 40 |
| Panama Canal, 1908–1938 | 2 | 5 | | 1 | 4 | | | | | | 6 | 200 |
| Panama Canal, 1911–1961 | 3 | | | 27 | | 89 | | | | | 120 | 93,700 |
| ...ion bonds, 1946 | 3 | | | | | 200 | | | | | 200 | 200,000 |
| ...ion bonds, 1947 | 3 | | | 10 | | 1,055 | | | | | 1,055 | 1,056,000 |
| Postal savings bonds— | | | | | | | | | | | | |
| First series | 2½ | | | 1 | | | | | | | 1 | 100 |
| Second series | 2½ | 18 | | 20 | 6 | | | | | | 38 | 2,360 |
| Third series | 2½ | 7 | | 22 | 12 | | | | | | 35 | 5,340 |
| Fourth series | 2½ | 21 | | 26 | 11 | | | | | | 59 | 9,020 |
| Fifth series | 2½ | 14 | | 33 | 11 | | | | | | 58 | 7,280 |
| Sixth series | 2½ | 10 | | 32 | 8 | | | | | | 44 | 5,200 |
| Seventh series | 2½ | 12 | | 20 | 6 | | | | | | 36 | 4,540 |
| Eighth series | 2½ | 14 | | 13 | 6 | | | | | | 31 | 6,080 |
| Ninth series | 2½ | 2 | | 28 | 6 | | | | | | 48 | 4,640 |
| Tenth series | 2½ | 6 | | 16 | 5 | | | | | | 24 | 3,520 |
| Eleventh series | 2½ | 4 | | 12 | 3 | | | | | | 23 | 5,880 |
| Twelfth series | 2½ | 6 | | 41 | 4 | | | | | | 48 | 3,320 |
| Thirteenth series | 2½ | 2 | | 12 | 5 | | | | | | 22 | 3,740 |
| Fourteenth series | 2½ | | | 12 | 2 | | | | | | 19 | 1,500 |
| Fifteenth series | 2½ | 8 | | 11 | 1 | | | | | | 7 | 2,280 |
| Sixteenth series | 2½ | | | | | | | | | | 21 | 500 |
| Seventeenth series | 2½ | | | 9 | 4 | | | | | | 1 | 2,960 |
| Eighteenth series | 2½ | 3 | | | | | | | | | 16 | 40 |
| Nineteenth series | 2½ | 2 | | 5 | | | | | | | 2 | 520 |
| Twentieth series | 2½ | 1 | | 4 | | | | | | | 6 | 460 |
| Twenty-first series | 2½ | 3 | | | 4 | | | | | | 7 | 2,000 |
| | | | | | | | | | | | 4 | |
| **Total** | | 144 | 45 | 501 | 239 | 2,697 | 2 | 2 | | | 3,628 | 2,877,730 |
| **Liberty loans:** | | | | | | | | | | | | |
| First, 1932–1947 | 3½ | | 160,200 | 100,940 | 14,117 | 58,269 | | | | | 333,526 | 83,431,500 |
| First, converted, 1932–1947, temporary | 4 | | 29,572 | 11,483 | 546 | 532 | | | | | 42,135 | 3,441,900 |
| First, converted, 1932–1947, permanent | 4 | | | 9,923 | 1,642 | 1,703 | | 2 | | | 28,017 | 4,502,750 |
| First, converted, 1932–1947, temporary | 4¼ | | 14,629 | 9,346 | 1,114 | 861 | | 27 | 3 | | 25,543 | 3,063,400 |
| First, converted, 1932–1947, permanent | 4¼ | | 14,216 | 140,717 | 21,553 | 22,038 | | 6 | | | 345,514 | 60,83,250 |
| | | | 160,441 | | | | | 435 | 330 | | | |

| | | | | | | | | | | | |
|---|---|---|---|---|---|---|---|---|---|---|---|
| First- and, converted, | 4½ | 550 | | 337 | 45 | 41 | | 22 | | | 973 | 124,700 |
| and, 1 red, 927, permanent | 4½ | 577 | | 674 | 34 | 48 | | | | | 1,333 | 161,250 |
| Second, 1927-1942, permanent | 4 | 113,063 | | 42,624 | 2,455 | 1,679 | | 114 | 142 | 150 | 159,843 | 12,932,050 |
| Second, converted | 4 | 57,611 | | 36,635 | 4,643 | 4,609 | | 116 | 41 | 69 | 104,374 | 16,084,550 |
| Second | 4 | 60,834 | | 34,245 | 3,602 | 5,229 | | | 2,873 | 3 | 103,447 | 295, 97, |
| Third, 1928, | 4¼ | 601,566 | | 494,448 | 65,930 | 137,579 | | 3,428 | 60 | | 1,305,824 | 39,771,400 |
| Third, | 4¼ | 333,054 | | 128,202 | 7,657 | 5,345 | | 105 | 2,109 | | 474,423 | 369,947,100 |
| Fourth, | 4¼ | 1,474,024 | | 842,529 | 80,256 | 141,066 | | 1,942 | 430 | 312 | 2,541,925 | 184,428,350 |
| Fourth, | 4¼ | 953,919 | | 553,314 | 45,884 | 48,219 | | 1,188 | | 518 | 1,602,954 | 570,322,650 |
| Very, 1922-23 | 4¼ | 1,220,607 | | 1,127,803 | 126,470 | 222,562 | | 5,155 | 8,494 | 315 | 2,711,091 | 450, 55, 60 |
| Very, 1 92223 | 3¾ | 1,434,717 | | 1,121,818 | 120,776 | 169,073 | | 3,155 | 2,140 | 41 | 2,851,681 | 764,625,000 |
| | | 48,766 | | 48,012 | 44,571 | 307,738 | | 61,006 | 12,284 | 743 | 522,326 | |
| **Total** | | 6,678,346 | | 4,703,060 | 541,295 | 1,126,682 | | 76,700 | 28,856 | 224 | 13,154,929 | 2, 78,611,800 |

**Treasury notes:**

| | | | | | | | | | | | |
|---|---|---|---|---|---|---|---|---|---|---|---|
| Series A–1924 | 5¼ | | | 15,206 | 2,531 | 4,810 | | 1,583 | 1,039 | | 25,319 | 40,901,100 |
| Series B–1924 | 5½ | | | 2,847 | 1,761 | 2,703 | | 1,195 | 610 | | 9,185 | 22,843,200 |
| Series A–1925 | 4¾ | | | 320 | 468 | 2,990 | | 225 | 310 | 167 | 2,316 | 3,410,000 |
| Series B–1925 | 4½ | | | 10 | 3 | 13 | | 1 | 7 | 535 | 34 | 5,781,000 |
| Series A–1926 | 4¾ | | | 871 | 346 | 795 | | 86 | 88 | 585 | 2,188 | 90,500 |
| | | | | | | | | | | 1,764 | | 2,565,100 |
| **Total** | | | | 19,254 | 5,109 | 9,311 | | 3,090 | 2,054 | 224 | 39,042 | 72,180,900 |

| | | | | | | | | | | | |
|---|---|---|---|---|---|---|---|---|---|---|---|
| June 25, 1918, IV A | 4¾ | | | | 333 | 1,019 | | 1 | 63 | 312 | 1 | 5, 00 |
| ule 15, 1920, III | 5¾ | | | | 4,380 | 2,955 | | 602 | 2,042 | 518 | 2,329 | 36,025,500 |
| Aug. 16, 1920, 921 | 6 | | | | 4,193 | 3,369 | | 1,519 | 4,949 | 315 | 11,414 | 84,960,000 |
| Sept. 15, 1920, TS–1921 | 6 | | | | 760 | 3,489 | | 3,128 | 2,040 | 41 | 15,954 | 102,96,500 |
| Dec. 15, 1920, T12–1921 | 5¾ | | | | 6,049 | 5,967 | | 1,393 | 2,360 | 743 | 7,723 | 35,334,000 |
| Dec. 15, 1920, TD– 91 | 5½ | | | | 5,177 | 5,208 | | 2,329 | 2,325 | 167 | 17,448 | 118,538,500 |
| Jan. 15, 1921, F–1921 | 5½ | | | | 5,737 | 6,208 | | 2,924 | 1,744 | 535 | 18,801 | 65,366,500 |
| Feb. 15, 1921, G-1–1921 | 5½ | | | | 5,495 | 6,929 | | 1,968 | 1,395 | 585 | 16,913 | 90,577 500 |
| Mar. 15, 1921, TM–1922 | 5½ | | | | 10,276 | 12,140 | | 1,846 | 6,972 | 1,764 | 22,461 | |
| Apr. 15, 1921, TM–1922 | 5¾ | | | | 4,969 | 16,611 | | 5,719 | 4,148 | 227 | 32,922 | 288,044,000 |
| May 16, 1921, H–1921 | 5½ | | | | 15,392 | 16,511 | | 3,808 | 4,249 | 912 | 29,663 | 102,215,500 |
| Aug. 15, 1921, A–1922 | 5½ | | | | 10,306 | 22,529 | | 3,899 | 1,958 | 113 | 46,981 | 60,777,000 |
| Aug. 1, 1921, TJ–1922 | 5½ | | | | 24,712 | 11,669 | | 2,609 | 8,419 | 1,495 | 26,685 | 328,099,000 |
| Sept. 15, 1921, 921, B–1922 | 5 | | | | 9,886 | 38,168 | | 8,777 | 1,238 | 92 | 81,571 | 28,501,000 |
| Sept. 15, 1921, TM3–1922 | 4½ | | | | 1,020 | 2,296 | | 2,625 | 2,331 | 434 | 6,279 | 97,918,000 |
| Nov. 1, 1921, TS–1922 | 4½ | | | | 1,772 | 13,140 | | 740 | 508 | 14 | 28,416 | 12,277,000 |
| Nov. 1, 1921, C–1922 | 4¼ | | | | 1,756 | 1,587 | | 4,283 | 4,223 | 833 | 3,899 | 170,684,000 |
| Dec. 15, 1921, T12–1922 | 3¾ | | | | 4,285 | 17,863 | | 740 | 355 | 13 | 38,974 | 13,139,000 |
| Mar. 15, 1922, TM–1923 | 4¼ | | | | 10 | 2,606 | | 1,087 | 1,348 | 161 | 5,237 | 44,098,500 |
| Apr. 15, 1922 D–1922 | 4¼ | | | | | 4,631 | | 1,479 | 5 | 1 | 12,204 | 500,000 |
| Dec. 15, 1922 TM2 | 3¾ | | | | 50 | 15 | | 26 | | 3 | 26 | 205,000 |
| ule 1, 1922, T12–1922 | 3¾ | | | | 2 | 5 | | 20 | | 1 | 59 | 11,390,000 |
| June 15, 19, TJ–1923 | 3¾ | | | | | 430 | | 759 | 334 | 38 | 1,611 | 315,000 |
| | | | | | | 84 | | 4 | 11 | 1 | 102 | 100,000 |
| 9H | | | | | | | | | | | 1 | |
| **Grand total** | | 6,678,391 | | 4,722,805 | 676,125 | 1,322,241 | | 132,068 | 83,017 | 9,318 | 427,644 | 1,971,651,000 |
| | | | 144 | | 129,480 | 183,551 | | 52,278 | 83,927 | 9,542 | 13,625,243 | 4,920,321,430 |

No. 18.—*United States bonds, notes, and certificates of indebtedness in bearer form received from Federal reserve banks and Division of Loans and Currency audited and filed for credit to fiscal agency accounts during the fiscal year ended June 30, 1922, grouped according to fiscal agents.*

| Federal reserve bank. | Exchange.[1] | | Conversion.[2] | | Unissued stock.[3] | | Miscellaneous.[4] | | Total. | |
|---|---|---|---|---|---|---|---|---|---|---|
| | Pieces. | Amount. | Pieces. | Amount. | Pieces. | Amount. | Pieces. | Amount. | Pieces. | Amount. |
| Boston | 595,305 | $104,493,400 | 22,765 | $5,785,000 | 317,769 | $22,718,250 | | | 935,839 | $132,996,650 |
| New York | 4,112,659 | 840,796,600 | 140,340 | 188,044,050 | 74,865 | 90,331,850 | 963 | $316,600 | 4,328,827 | 1,120,489,100 |
| Philadelphia | 562,347 | 165,883,550 | 16,868 | 9,231,950 | 3,743 | 6,249,600 | | | 582,968 | 181,365,100 |
| Cleveland | 849,194 | 265,627,550 | 21,742 | 10,578,100 | 7,446 | 9,613,350 | | | 878,382 | 285,819,000 |
| Richmond | 223,493 | 52,880,500 | 7,195 | 1,281,800 | 28,390 | 23,084,950 | | | 259,078 | 77,227,250 |
| Atlanta | 167,373 | 34,518,700 | 3,984 | 423,100 | 7,804 | 8,138,850 | | | 179,161 | 43,080,650 |
| New Orleans | 47,041 | 6,897,600 | 2,592 | 219,450 | 514 | 588,700 | | | 50,147 | 7,705,750 |
| Chicago | 2,765,257 | 478,205,250 | 48,340 | 20,980,800 | 1,012 | 1,100,750 | | | 2,814,609 | 500,286,800 |
| St. Louis | 340,487 | 83,386,000 | 5,743 | 678,900 | 3,017 | 2,013,100 | | | 349,247 | 86,578,000 |
| Minneapolis | 483,691 | 43,981,600 | 8,204 | 783,400 | 12,802 | 8,327,850 | | | 504,697 | 53,092,850 |
| Kansas City | 355,982 | 39,697,300 | 7,428 | 1,403,500 | 3,772 | 2,676,450 | | | 367,182 | 43,777,250 |
| Dallas | 147,805 | 18,599,700 | 5,742 | 700,300 | 2,120 | 707,150 | | | 155,667 | 20,007,150 |
| San Francisco | 857,038 | 188,061,800 | 20,727 | 6,586,800 | 133,815 | 18,348,650 | | | 1,011,580 | 212,997,250 |
| Loans and Currency | 666,549 | 439,256,780 | 8,528 | 2,062,300 | 530,834 | 1,707,416,200 | 1,958 | 1,163,350 | 1,207,869 | 2,149,898,630 |
| Total | 12,174,221 | 2,767,766,330 | 320,198 | 249,759,450 | 1,127,903 | 1,901,315,700 | 2,921 | 1,479,950 | 13,625,243 | 4,920,321,430 |

[1] Includes coupon exchange, denominational exchange, temporary exchange, and special denominational exchange.
[2] Includes conversion exchange.
[3] Includes unissued allotment, unissued stock, unissued conversion, and unissued temporary exchange.
[4] Includes securities trust fund, special deposit account, claim issue, mutilation, error, claim retirement, and claim registered issue.

| Federal reserve bank. | 40 per cent. | | 100 per cent. | | Total. | |
|---|---|---|---|---|---|---|
| | Pieces. | Amount. | Pieces. | Amount. | Pieces. | Amount. |
| Boston | | | [1] 120 | [1] $8,450 | 120 | $8,450 |
| New York | | | 471 | 38,950 | 471 | 38,950 |
| Philadelphia | 2 | $40 | 42 | 3,950 | 44 | 3,990 |
| Cleveland | | | 69 | 6,000 | 69 | 6,000 |
| Richmond | | | 17 | 11,400 | 17 | 11,400 |
| Atlanta | | | 13 | 1,850 | 13 | 1,850 |
| Chicago | | | 163 | 22,500 | 163 | 22,500 |
| St. Louis | | | 41 | 3,400 | 41 | 3,400 |
| Minneapolis | | | 2 | 150 | 2 | 150 |
| Kansas City | | | 11 | 1,050 | 11 | 1,050 |
| Dallas | | | 40 | 3,100 | 40 | 3,100 |
| San Francisco | | | 40 | 4,800 | 40 | 4,800 |
| Total | 2 | 40 | 1,029 | 105,600 | 1,031 | 105,640 |

[1] On adjustment, deduction is made of 1 piece, $50, previously reported.

No. 20.—*Treasury (war) savings securities received from: Federal reserve banks, postmasters, the Treasurer of the United States, and the Division of Loans and Currency for audit and credit during the fiscal year ended June 30, 1922.*

| Class of security | Received from Federal reserve banks | | Received from Third Assistant Postmaster General | | Received from Treasurer | | Received from Division of Loans and Currency | | Total received | |
|---|---|---|---|---|---|---|---|---|---|---|
| | Pieces | Amount | Pieces | Amount | Pieces | Amount | Pieces | Amount | Pieces | Amount |
| Treasury savings certificates: | | | | | | | | | | |
| Series of 1918 | 24,769 | $2,476,900 | 70 | $7,000 | | | 22 | $2,200 | 24,961 | $2,486,100 |
| Series of 1919 | 16,107 | 5,316,000 | 953 | 95,300 | | | 118 | 15,400 | 17,178 | 5,426,700 |
| Series of 1920 | 782 | 271,700 | 203 | 20,300 | | | 73 | 7,300 | 1,058 | 299,300 |
| Series of 1921 (new issue) | 66,300 | 8,802,450 | 186,762 | 8,750,325 | | | 330 | 30,225 | 254,292 | 17,704,200 |
| Series of 1921 | 15 | 10,275 | 68 | 7,250 | | | 13 | 7,450 | 96 | 24,975 |
| Series of 1922 | 292 | 104,500 | 1,880 | 417,800 | 900 | $121,200 | 189 | 66,225 | 2,361 | 588,525 |
| Total | 108,265 | 16,981,825 | 189,936 | 9,297,975 | 900 | 121,200 | 745 | 128,800 | 299,846 | 26,529,800 |
| War savings stamps: | | | | | | | | | | |
| Series of 1918 | 700 | 3,500 | 400 | 2,000 | | | 39,764 | 198,820 | 40,864 | 204,320 |
| Series of 1919 | 20 | 100 | | | | | 6,091 | 30,455 | 6,111 | 30,555 |
| Series of 1920 | 20 | 100 | 40 | 200 | | | 1,222 | 6,110 | 1,282 | 6,410 |
| Series of 1921 | 120 | 600 | 1,155 | 5,775 | 575 | 2,875 | 132 | 660 | 1,982 | 9,910 |
| Total | 860 | 4,300 | 1,595 | 7,975 | 575 | 2,875 | 47,209 | 236,045 | 50,239 | 251,195 |
| War savings stamps: | | | | | | | | | | |
| Series of 1918 | 540 | 2,700 | 1 | 5 | | | 21,076 | 105,380 | 21,617 | 108,085 |
| Series of 1919 | 104 | 520 | 45,209 | 225,045 | | | 30,868 | 154,340 | 76,181 | 380,905 |
| Series of 1920 | 36 | 180 | 4,295 | 21,475 | | | 2,289 | 11,445 | 6,620 | 33,100 |
| Series of 1921 | 569,169 | 2,845,845 | 2,625,690 | 13,128,450 | 15,955 | 79,775 | 4,400 | 22,000 | 3,215,214 | 16,076,070 |
| Total | 569,849 | 2,849,245 | 2,675,195 | 13,375,975 | 15,955 | 79,775 | 58,633 | 293,165 | 3,319,632 | 16,598,160 |
| Thrift stamps | 9,547,006 | 2,386,751.50 | 85,837,173 | 21,459,293.25 | 32,058 | 8,014.50 | 544,742 | 136,185.50 | 95,960,979 | 23,990,244.75 |
| Thrift cards | 1,424 | 336.00 | 225,746 | 56,436.50 | 75,312 | 18,823.00 | 1,174 | 293.50 | 303,656 | 75,914.00 |
| Treasury savings stamps | 829 | 829.00 | 1,774 | 1,774.00 | | | 3,218 | 3,218.00 | 5,821 | 5,821.00 |
| Treasury savings cards: | | | | | | | | | | |
| Exchange for Treasury savings certificates | 20 | 20.00 | 6,617 | 6,617.00 | 14,016 | 14,016.00 | | | 20,663 | 20,653.00 |
| Exchange for war savings certificates | | | 851 | 851.00 | 698 | 698.00 | | | 1,549 | 1,549.00 |
| Exchange for Treasury savings stamps | | | | | | | 20 | 20.00 | 20 | 20.00 |
| Grand total | 10,228,253 | 22,223,326.50 | 88,938,887 | 44,266,896.75 | 139,514 | 245,406.50 | 655,741 | 797,727.00 | 99,962,395 | 67,473,356.75 |

No. 21.—*United States securities in bearer form (interest coupons not included) received for credit to fiscal agency accounts for the fiscal year ended June 30, 1922, reported according to Federal reserve banks and other fiscal agencies.*

| Federal reserve bank or other fiscal agency | Pre-war loans. | | Liberty loans.[1] | | Liberty loan interim certificates. | | Certificates of indebtedness. | | Treasury (war) savings securities. | | Total. | | Percentage of total. |
|---|---|---|---|---|---|---|---|---|---|---|---|---|---|
| | Pieces. | Amount. | Pieces. | Amount. | Pieces. | Amount. | Pieces. | Amount. | Pieces. | Amount. | Pieces. | Amount. | |
| Boston | | | 928,003 | $105,767,150 | 120 | $8,450 | 7,836 | $27,229,500 | 1,689,516 | $461,190.00 | 2,616,475 | $133,466,290.00 | 2.69 |
| New York | | | 4,285,270 | 903,033,600 | 471 | 38,950 | 43,557 | 217,455,500 | 1,162,283 | 1,339,817.25 | 5,491,581 | 1,121,867,867.25 | 22.61 |
| Philadelphia | | | 555,944 | 104,104,100 | 44 | 3,990 | 27,014 | 77,261,000 | 1,063,509 | 539,339.50 | 1,646,511 | 181,908,429.50 | 3.67 |
| Cleveland | | | 523,575 | 170,564,000 | 69 | 6,000 | 49,807 | 115,255,000 | 1,464,720 | 426,899.25 | 2,343,171 | 286,251,899.25 | 5.77 |
| Richmond | | | 247,991 | 46,069,250 | 17 | 11,400 | 11,087 | 31,158,000 | 176,125 | 510,443.75 | 435,220 | 77,759,098.75 | 1.57 |
| Atlanta | | | 174,700 | 24,983,150 | 13 | 1,850 | 4,461 | 18,092,500 | 2,358,216 | 633,719.50 | 2,537,390 | 43,716,219.50 | .88 |
| New Orleans | | | 49,869 | 6,871,750 | | | 278 | 834,000 | 270,979 | 110,295.25 | 321,126 | 7,816,045.25 | .16 |
| Chicago | | | 2,787,385 | 379,818,500 | 163 | 22,500 | 27,224 | 120,468,000 | 60,570 | 50,226.00 | 2,875,342 | 500,359,526.50 | 10.08 |
| St. Louis | | | 330,564 | 51,017,500 | 41 | 3,400 | 18,683 | 35,560,500 | 214,905 | 111,656.50 | 564,193 | 86,693,056.50 | 1.74 |
| subs. | | | 503,095 | 52,182,350 | 2 | 150 | 1,602 | 5,910,500 | 94,283 | 31,318.00 | 598,982 | 58,124,318.00 | 1.17 |
| Kansas City | | | 365,651 | 36,949,750 | 11 | 1,050 | 531 | 6,927,500 | 422,161 | 200,602.00 | 779,354 | 43,978,902.00 | .88 |
| subs. | | | 154,536 | 16,376,150 | 40 | 3,100 | 1,131 | 3,631,000 | 58,330 | 91,570.50 | 214,037 | 21,101,820.50 | .41 |
| San ...cisco | | | 971,755 | 140,215,750 | 40 | 4,800 | 39,825 | 72,781,500 | 1,093,391 | 734,419.00 | 2,105,011 | 213,736,469.00 | 4.31 |
| Division of Loans and Currency | | | 1,089,633 | 907,934,400 | 1,031 | 105,640 | 194,608 | 1,239,086,500 | 632,421 | 556,052.00 | 1,840,290 | 2,150,454,682.00 | 43.35 |
| Treasurer United States | 3,628 | $2,877,730 | | | | | | | 138,614 | 124,206.50 | 138,614 | 124,206.50 | .01 |
| Postmasters | | | | | | | | | 88,748,226 | 34,905,296.75 | 88,748,226 | 34,905,296.75 | .70 |
| Total | 3,628 | 2,877,730 | 13,193,971 | 2,945,792,700 | 1,031 | 105,640 | 427,644 | 1,971,651,000 | 99,639,249 | 40,827,056.75 | 113,265,523 | 4,961,254,126.75 | 100.00 |

[1] Includes Treasury notes.

No. 22.—*United States registered bonds and notes received from Division of Loans and Currency, audited and filed during fiscal year ended June 30, 1922, grouped according to accounts credited.*

| Title of loan. | Interest rate. | Transfer. Pieces. | Transfer. Amount. | Conversion. Pieces. | Conversion. Amount. | Exchange. Pieces. | Exchange. Amount. | Miscellaneous. Pieces. | Miscellaneous. Amount. | Total. Pieces. | Total. Amount. |
|---|---|---|---|---|---|---|---|---|---|---|---|
| | *Per cent.* | | | | | | | | | | |
| Pre-war ▮▮: | | | | | | | | | | | |
| Loan of July and August, 1861, continued | 3¼ | | | | | | | 1 | $1,000 | 1 | $1,000 |
| Funded loan of 1891 | 4 | | | | | | | 2 | 200 | 2 | 200 |
| Loan of ▮▮ | 4 | | | | | | | 32 | 31,550 | 32 | 31,550 |
| Loan of 1908 | | | | | | | | 27 | 6,000 | 27 | 6,000 |
| ▮ ▮lls of ▮▮ | 3 | 12,799 | 80,485,950 | | | | | | | 12,799 | 80,485,950 |
| Loan of 1925 | 4 | 11,012 | 44,341,550 | | | | | 6 | 5,000 | 11,018 | 44,346,550 |
| Panama Canal, 1916–1936 | 2 | 2,979 | 13,243,080 | | | | | | | 2,979 | 13,243,080 |
| Panama Canal, 1918–1938 | 2 | 983 | 5,128,080 | | | | | | | 983 | 5,128,080 |
| Panama Canal, 19▮–1961 | 3 | 8,781 | 16,246,500 | | | | | 12 | 11,500 | 8,793 | 16,258,000 |
| ▮▮n, 1916–1946 | 3 | 551 | 3,582,700 | | | | | | | 8,551 | 3,582,700 |
| ▮▮, 1947 | 3 | 13 | 125,000 | | | | | | | 13 | 125,000 |
| Postal savings— | | | | | | | | | | | |
| First se ▮▮s | 2½ | 290 | 31,490 | | | | | | | 290 | 31,480 |
| Second series | 2½ | 2,510 | 260,120 | | | | | | | 2,510 | 260,120 |
| Third series | 2½ | 4,309 | 593,300 | | | | | | | 4,309 | 593,300 |
| Fourth series | 2½ | 5,360 | 726,760 | | | | | | 40 | 5,392 | 726,800 |
| Fifth series | 2½ | 5,388 | 754,520 | | | | | | | 5,389 | 755,620 |
| Sixth series | 2½ | 5,243 | 734,960 | | | | | 3 | 1,100 | 5,247 | 735,100 |
| Seventh ▮▮es | 2½ | 3,885 | 571,700 | | | | | 4 | 1,040 | 3,887 | 572,700 |
| Eighth ▮▮es | 2½ | 4,144 | 592,000 | | | | | 2 | 1,000 | 4,147 | 593,500 |
| ▮th series | 2½ | 3,826 | 549,800 | | | | | 3 | 1,500 | 3,826 | 549,800 |
| ▮th series | 2½ | 3,785 | 566,640 | | | | | | | 3,785 | 567,140 |
| ▮th series | 2½ | 3,349 | 556,820 | | | | | 1 | 500 | 3,356 | 558,320 |
| Twelfth series | 2½ | 3,781 | 480,980 | | | | | 7 | 1,500 | 2,637 | 480,980 |
| Thirteenth series | 2½ | 2,637 | 428,220 | | | | | | | 1,978 | 429,720 |
| Fourteenth series | 2½ | 1,975 | 157,860 | | | | | 3 | 1,500 | 682 | 158,360 |
| Fifteenth series | 2½ | 681 | 96,340 | | | | | 1 | 500 | 353 | 96,340 |
| Sixteenth series | 2½ | 353 | 37,660 | | | | | | | 151 | 37,660 |
| Seventeenth series | 2½ | 151 | 24,460 | | | | | | | 87 | 24,460 |
| Eighteenth series | 2½ | 87 | 24,440 | | | | | | | 66 | 24,440 |
| ▮th series | 2½ | 66 | 7,500 | | | | | | | 23 | 7,500 |
| ▮th series | 2½ | 23 | 26,340 | | | | | 2 | 1,000 | 95 | 22,340 |
| ▮-first se ▮▮s | 2½ | 93 | 6,500 | | | | | | | 13 | 6,500 |
| Twenty-second series | 2½ | 13 | 2,800 | | | | | | | 8 | 2,800 |
| Total | | 85,321 | 170,383,160 | | | | | 108 | 64,930 | 85,429 | 170,448,090 |

| | | | | | | | | | | |
|---|---|---|---|---|---|---|---|---|---|---|
| Liberty loans: | | | | | | | | | | |
| First, 1932–1947 | 3½ | 2,982 | 20,442,000 | ...... | $1,077,500 | 10,657 | $38,770,900 | 32 | 9,400 | 13,671 | 59,222,300 |
| First, converted, 1932–1947 | 4 | 11 | 1,400 | ...... | ...... | 3,445 | 740,100 | 85 | 16,250 | 7,060 | 1,835,250 |
| **First,** converted, 1932–1947 | 4¼ | 6,580 | 4,290,900 | 3,519 | ...... | 22,286 | 10,097,300 | 188 | 43,400 | 29,054 | 14,431,600 |
| **First,** 2nd converted, 1932–1947 | 4¼ | ³ 91 | 9,300 | ...... | ...... | 320 | 163,900 | 2 | 1,000 | 354 | 174,200 |
| Second, 1927–1942 | 4¼ | 25,119 | 25,850 | 13,228 | 4,021,650 | 17,248 | 4,296,350 | 365 | 100,550 | 30,932 | 8,444,400 |
| Second, converted, 1927–1942 | 4¼ | 48,559 | 26,633,850 | ...... | ...... | 81,457 | 67,765,300 | 767 | 216,650 | 107,343 | 94,615,800 |
| Third, 1928 | 4¼ | 91,066 | 19,117,400 | ...... | ...... | 175,652 | 110,103,950 | 2,182 | 450,150 | 226,373 | 129,671,500 |
| Fourth, 1933–1938 | 4¼ | 25,304 | 43,716,000 | 143 | 171,800 | 286,799 | 120,192,650 | 3,279 | 777,700 | 381,144 | 164,686,350 |
| Victory, 1922–1923 | 4¾ | | 13,586,750 | 295 | 4,833,550 | 173,432 | 144,421,550 | 1,593 | 515,850 | 200,472 | 158,695,950 |
| **War,** 1922–1923 | 3¾ | 67 | 1,332,200 | | | 1,040 | 19,117,500 | 16 | 1,300,300 | 1,418 | 26,583,550 |
| Total | | 199,811 | 129,155,650 | 17,185 | 10,104,500 | 772,316 | 515,669,500 | 8,509 | 3,431,250 | 997,821 | 658,360,900 |
| Grand total | | 285,132 | 299,538,810 | 17,185 | 10,104,500 | 772,316 | 515,669,500 | 8,617 | 3,496,180 | 1,083,250 | 828,808,990 |

¹ Includes conversion exchange.
² Includes claim issue, mutilated, claim retirement, and claim coupon issue.
³ On adjustment of previous figures, a deduction is made of 1 piece.

No. 23.—*United States registered bonds and notes received from Division of Loans and Currency, audited and filed during the fiscal year ended June 30, 1922, showing loans, denominations, pieces, and total amount.*

| Title of loan. | Interest rate. | Denominations by number of pieces. | | | | | | | | | Interim certificates. | | Total. | |
|---|---|---|---|---|---|---|---|---|---|---|---|---|---|---|
| | *Per cent.* | $20 | $50 | $100 | $500 | $1,000 | $5,000 | $10,000 | $50,000 | $100,000 | Pieces. | Amount. | Pieces. | Amount. |
| **Pre-war loans:** | | | | | | | | | | | | | | |
| Loan of July and August, 1861, con. | 3½ | | | | | 1 | | | | | | | 1 | $1,000 |
| Funded loan of 1891 | 4½ | | | 2 | | | | | | | | | 2 | 200 |
| Loan of 1907 | 4 | 5 | 1 | 20 | 5 | 2 | | | | | | | 32 | 31,550 |
| Loan of 1908–1918 | 3 | | | 14 | 7 | | | | | | | | 27 | 6,000 |
| Consols of 1930 | 2 | | 194 | 1,398 | 978 | 3,622 | 926 | 5,318 | 350 | | 13 | $915,450 | 12,799 | 80,485,950 |
| Loan of 1925 | 4 | | 45 | 1,143 | 926 | 4,502 | 951 | 3,451 | | | 17 | 1,804,700 | 11,018 | 44,346,550 |
| Panama Canal, 1916–1936 | 2 | 54 | | 363 | | 1,561 | | 984 | | | | | 2,979 | 13,243,080 |
| Panama Canal, 1938 | 2 | 29 | | 85 | 235 | 406 | | 461 | | | | | 983 | 5,298,080 |
| Panama Canal, 1961 | 3 | | | 305 | | 7,380 | 71 | 873 | | | 2 | 103,000 | 8,793 | 16,258,000 |
| Loan, 1917–1947 | 3 | | | 37 | | 134 | 1 | 309 | | | | | 551 | 3,582,700 |
| | | | | | | | | 12 | | | | | 13 | 125,000 |
| **Postal savings:** | | | | | | | | | | | | | | |
| First series | 2½ | 84 | | 183 | 23 | | | | | | | | 290 | 31,480 |
| Second series | 2½ | 551 | | 1,826 | 133 | | | | | | | | 2,510 | 260,120 |
| Third series | 2½ | 875 | | 2,853 | 581 | | | | | | | | 4,309 | 583,300 |
| Fourth series | 2½ | 1,175 | | 3,513 | 704 | | | | | | | | 5,392 | 728,800 |
| Fifth series | 2½ | 1,071 | | 3,562 | 756 | | | | | | | | 5,389 | 735,620 |
| Sixth series | 2½ | 1,060 | | 3,461 | 736 | | | | | | | | 5,247 | 735,100 |
| Seventh series | 2½ | | | 2,515 | 612 | | | | | | | | 3,887 | 572,700 |
| Eighth series | 2½ | 865 | | 2,662 | 620 | | | | | | | | 4,147 | 593,500 |
| Ninth series | 2½ | 760 | | 2,664 | 542 | | | | | | | | 3,826 | 549,800 |
| Tenth series | 2½ | 620 | | 2,507 | 606 | | | | | | | | 3,785 | 567,140 |
| Eleventh series | 2½ | 672 | | 2,192 | 658 | | | | | | | | 3,356 | 558,320 |
| Twelfth series | 2½ | 506 | | 1,477 | 646 | | | | | | | | 2,637 | 480,980 |
| Thirteenth series | 2½ | 514 | | 1,013 | 644 | | | | | | | | 1,978 | 429,720 |
| Fourteenth series | 2½ | 321 | | 333 | 246 | | | | | | | | 682 | 158,360 |
| Fifteenth series | 2½ | 103 | | 168 | 158 | | | | | | | | 353 | 96,340 |
| Sixteenth series | 2½ | 27 | | 43 | 65 | | | | | | | | 151 | 37,660 |
| Seventeenth series | 2½ | 43 | | 38 | 41 | | | | | | | | 87 | 24,460 |
| Eighteenth series | 2½ | 8 | | 19 | 45 | | | | | | | | 66 | 24,440 |
| Nineteenth series | 2½ | 2 | | 10 | 13 | | | | | | | | 23 | 7,500 |
| Twentieth series | 2½ | | | 42 | 46 | | | | | | | | 95 | 27,340 |
| Twenty-first series | 2½ | 7 | | | 13 | | | | | | | | 13 | 6,500 |
| Twenty-second series | 2½ | | | | 5 | | | | | | | | 8 | 2,800 |
| **Total** | | 9,342 | 240 | 34,451 | 10,044 | 17,609 | 1,952 | 11,409 | 350 | | 32 | 2,823,150 | 85,429 | 170,445,090 |

| | | | | | | | | | | | | | | |
|---|---|---|---|---|---|---|---|---|---|---|---|---|---|---|
| Liberty loans: | | | | | | | | | | | | | | |
| First, 1932–1947 | 3½ | ........ | ........ | 5,618 | 1,163 | 3,759 | 700 | 2,007 | 233 | 191 | ........ | ........ | 13,671 | 59, 2 ,300 |
| First, converted, 1932–1947 | 4 | ........ | 947 | 4,709 | 748 | 618 | 27 | 9 | 2 | ........ | ........ | ........ | 7,060 | 1,835,250 |
| Do | 4¼ | ........ | 4,930 | 14,796 | 4,135 | 4,478 | 414 | 279 | 18 | 4 | ........ | ........ | 29,054 | 14,431,600 |
| First second, converted, 1932–1947 | 4¼ | ........ | 80 | 152 | 64 | 48 | 5 | 5 | ........ | ........ | ........ | ........ | 354 | 174,200 |
| Second, 1927–1942 | 4 | ........ | 9,586 | 16,026 | [1] 2,771 | [1] 2,267 | 150 | 16 | 16 | ........ | ........ | ........ | 30,932 | 3,444,400 |
| Second, converted, 1927–1942 | 4¼ | ........ | 20,876 | 48,255 | 14,599 | 18,967 | 2,184 | 2, 91 | 129 | 242 | ........ | ........ | 107,343 | 94,615,800 |
| Third, 1928 | 4¼ | ........ | 57,680 | 115,955 | 24,370 | 23,487 | 1,854 | 2,490 | 167 | 370 | ........ | ........ | 226,373 | 129,671,500 |
| Fourth, 1933–1938 | 4¼ | ........ | 90,457 | 203,925 | 40,194 | 39,384 | 3,328 | 3,485 | 166 | 205 | ........ | ........ | 381,144 | 164,686,350 |
| Victory, 1922–1923 | 4¾ | ........ | 27,013 | 95,563 | 29,946 | 41,226 | 3,282 | 2,843 | 263 | 336 | ........ | ........ | 200,472 | 158,695,950 |
| Do | 3¾ | ........ | 27 | 82 | 32 | 408 | 150 | 480 | 66 | 173 | ........ | ........ | 1,418 | 26,583,550 |
| Total | ........ | ........ | 211,596 | 505,081 | 118,022 | 134,642 | 12,094 | 13,805 | 1,060 | 1,521 | ........ | ........ | 997,821 | 658,360,900 |
| Grand total | ........ | 9,342 | 211,836 | 539,532 | 128,066 | 152,251 | 14,046 | 25,214 | 1,410 | 1,521 | 32 | 2,823,150 | 1,083,250 | 828,808,990 |

[1] On adjustment of previous figures; addition is made of one piece at $1,000 and a deduction of two pieces at $500.

NOTE.—Although properly belonging to 1920 fiscal year, bonds amounting to $118,487,360 and interim certificates to the amount of $1,670,690 are included in the above figures on pre-war loans, inasmuch as they were received and functioned during fiscal year 1922.

No. 24.—*United States registered bonds, unissued, received from Division of Loans and Currency for audit and credit during fiscal year ended June 30, 1922.*

| Title of loan. | Interest rate. | Denominations by number of pieces. | | | | | | | | Total. | |
|---|---|---|---|---|---|---|---|---|---|---|---|
| | | $50 | $100 | $500 | $1,000 | $5,000 | $10,000 | $50,000 | $100,000 | Number of pieces. | Amount. |
| | Per cent. | | | | | | | | | | |
| First, converted, 1932–1947 | 4¼ | 179 | 524 | 214 | 263 | 32 | 42 | 11 | 10 | 1,275 | $2,561,350 |
| First second, converted, 1932–1947 | 4¼ | ........ | 4 | 1 | ........ | ........ | ........ | ........ | ........ | 5 | 900 |
| Second, converted, 1927–1942 | 4¼ | 446 | 1,415 | 375 | 895 | 136 | 173 | 34 | 44 | 3,518 | 9,756,300 |
| Third, 1928 | 4¼ | 532 | 1,267 | 394 | 659 | 91 | 118 | 15 | 21 | 3,097 | 5,494,300 |
| Fourth, 1933–1938 | 4¼ | 990 | 2,339 | 674 | 1,305 | 172 | 281 | 26 | 47 | 5,834 | 11,595,400 |
| Victory, 1922–1923 | 4¾ | 191 | 757 | 276 | 687 | 32 | 48 | 2 | 13 | 2,006 | 2,950,250 |
| Do | 3¾ | 1,010 | 1,862 | 373 | 3,361 | 11,195 | 10,525 | 1,057 | 852 | 30,235 | 303,059,200 |
| Total | ........ | 3,348 | 8,168 | 2,307 | 7,170 | 11,658 | 11,187 | 1,145 | 987 | 45,970 | 335,417,700 |

No. 25.—*Comparative statement showing United States securities (interest coupons not included) received for credit to fiscal-agency accounts for the fiscal years 1919, 1920, 1921, 1922, and totals received from April 6, 1917, to June 30, 1922.*

| Class of Securities. | 1919 | | 1920 | | 1921 | | 1922 | | Apr. 6, 1917, to June 30, 1922. | |
|---|---|---|---|---|---|---|---|---|---|---|
| | Pieces. | Amount. | Pieces. | Amount. | Pieces. | Amount. | Pieces. | Amount. | Pieces. | Amount. |
| **BEARER.** | | | | | | | | | | |
| Pre-war loans | 4,432 | $3,098,170.00 | 5,450 | $4,159,960.00 | 4,092 | $3,220,780.00 | 3,628 | $2,877,730.00 | 27,468 | $18,935,900.00 |
| Liberty loans[1] | 14,450,426 | 3,617,537,450.00 | 45,244,847 | [2]8,550,051,050.00 | 49,429,379 | 11,578,342,600.00 | 13,154,929 | 2,873,611,800.00 | 121,076,419 | 25,703,298,850.00 |
| Treasury notes | | | | | 1,141 | 2,384,500.00 | 39,042 | 72,180,900.00 | 40,183 | 74,565,400.00 |
| Certificates of indebtedness | 416,662 | 1,453,178,500.00 | 450,333 | 1,964,041,000.00 | 453,277 | 2,120,351,500.00 | 427,644 | 1,971,651,000.00 | 1,747,916 | 7,509,122,000.00 |
| Interim certificates | 4,287,833 | 2,199,342,830.00 | 7,452 | 1,080,915.00 | 3,307 | 4,560,700.00 | 1,031 | 105,640.00 | 8,402,914 | 6,969,131,800.00 |
| Treasury (war) savings securities | 69,728,131 | 348,640,655.00 | 42,331,747 | 201,495,141.00 | 20,689,074 | 70,465,235.00 | 99,639,249 | 40,827,056.75 | 232,588,437 | 714,606,787.75 |
| Total | 88,887,484 | 7,621,797,605.00 | 88,039,829 | 10,720,828,066.00 | 70,580,270 | 13,779,335,315.00 | 113,265,523 | 4,961,254,126.75 | 383,883,337 | 40,979,648,737.75 |
| **REGISTERED.** | | | | | | | | | | |
| Pre-war loans[3] | | | 2,124 | 9,470,100.00 | 16,541 | 53,179,290.00 | 85,429 | 170,448,090.00 | 104,094 | 233,097,480.00 |
| Liberty loans[4] | | | 1,357,588 | 938,834,500.00 | 840,399 | 605,365,550.00 | 1,043,791 | 903,778,500.00 | 3,271,778 | 2,590,978,650.00 |
| Certificates of indebtedness[5] | | | | | 155 | 187,838,000.00 | | | 155 | 187,838,000.00 |
| Treasury (war) savings securities[6] | | | 226,656 | 53,310,800.00 | 586,934 | 72,914,775.00 | 323,146 | 26,646,300.00 | 1,136,736 | 152,871,875.00 |
| Total | | | 1,616,368 | 1,001,615,400.00 | 1,444,029 | 972,297,615.00 | 1,452,366 | 1,190,872,990.00 | 4,512,763 | 3,164,786,005.00 |
| Grand total | 88,887,484 | 7,621,797,605.00 | 89,656,197 | 11,722,443,466.00 | 72,024,299 | 14,751,632,930.00 | 114,717,889 | 6,152,127,116.75 | 388,396,100 | 44,144,434,742.75 |

[1] Does not include uncanceled securities returned by Federal reserve banks and restored to stock.
[2] Includes 1,710,627 pieces amounting to $1,027,702,250 audited and destroyed by Division of Loans and Currency not previously reported.
[3] Includes only such securities belonging to 1919 and 1920 fiscal years as were received for audit by Register of the Treasury.
[4] Includes registered stock in blank unissued.
[5] Includes previous fiscal years audited and filed during fiscal year 1920.
[6] Includes Treasury savings certificates, in registered form, unissued and returned in blank.

No. 26.—*United States paid coupons received from the Treasurer of the United States during fiscal year ended June 30, 1922, grouped according to loans and denominations.*

Denominations of bonds, notes and certificates.

| Title of loan. | Interest rate. | $20 Coupons. | $20 Amount. | $50 Coupons. | $50 Amount. | $100 Coupons. | $100 Amount. | $500 Coupons. | $500 Amount. | $1,000 Coupons. | $1,000 Amount. |
|---|---|---|---|---|---|---|---|---|---|---|---|
| | *Per ct.* | | | | | | | | | | |
| dan of 1907 | 4 | | | 155 | $77.50 | 32 | $32.00 | 5 | $25.00 | 1 | $10.00 |
| n of 1904 | 5 | | | | | 1 | 1.25 | | | | |
| n of 1925 | 4 | 2,762 | $414.30 | 1,604 | 802.00 | 5,321 | 5,321.00 | 3,372 | 16,860.00 | 32,358 | 323,580.00 |
| of 1906–1918 | 3 | 91 | 9.10 | 422 | 105.50 | 1,812 | 1,359.00 | 416 | 1,560.00 | 35 | 282.50 |
| s of 1930 | 2 | 30 | 3.00 | | | 1,819 | 909.50 | 950 | 2,375.00 | 4,008 | 20.00 |
| 1906–1936 | 2 | | | | | 4 | 2.00 | | | 62 | 310.00 |
| | 3 | | | | | 17 | 8.50 | | | 284 | 1,420.00 |
| | 2½ | 2,640 | 660.00 | | | 2,179 | 1,634.25 | 2,552 | 9,570.00 | 21,443 | 160,822.50 |
| 196–1946 | 3 | | | | | 4,339 | 5,423.75 | 937 | 5,856.25 | 78,362 | 587,715.00 |
| | | | | | | 1,905 | 1,428.75 | | | | |
| First, 1932–1947 | 3½ | | | 1,504,304 | 1,316,170.34 | 940,591 | 1,646,034.25 | 213,066 | 1,864,327.50 | 1,919,417 | 33,9. 97.50 |
| First, 947 | 4 | | | 247,379 | 246,982.73 | 129,074 | 257,815.00 | 8, 97 | 82,499.30 | 6,609 | 31,870.31 |
| First converted, 1932–1947 | 4¼ | | | 1,490,826 | 1,551,481.15 | 1,371,530 | 2,914,981.56 | 244,967 | 2,602,762.77 | 319,633 | 6,792,201.25 |
| First | 4¼ | | | 6,404 | 6,791.24 | 5,028 | 10,679.58 | 1,137 | 12,080.50 | 2,723 | 3,983.75 |
| Second, 1927–1942 | 4¼ | | | 889,672 | 889,672.00 | 465,594 | 931,188.00 | 35,278 | 352,780.00 | 34,828 | 6,560.00 |
| Third, 1928 | 4¼ | | | 5,133,533 | 5,455,941.62 | 4,616,102 | 9, 48,351.69 | 894,230 | 9,394,840.12 | 2,071,008 | 44,008,920.00 |
| Fourth, 1922– | 4¼ | | | 10,205,077 | 10,792,927.95 | 7,724,319 | 16,392,379.81 | 1, 49, 87 | 12,419,401.31 | 2,197,213 | 46, 64,108.75 |
| Victory, 1922– | 3¾ | | | 11,263,354 | 11,935,660.20 | 10,147,491 | 21,556,359.34 | 1,621,059 | 17,221,478.65 | 3,560,584 | 75,659,130.85 |
| Do. | 4 | | | 8,476,895 | 10,104,423.65 | 6,943,910 | 16,525,778.35 | 1,066,523 | 12,678,218.88 | 1,827,824 | 43,439,808.46 |
| | 4 | | | 8,162 | 7,710.13 | 11,976 | 22,514.47 | 6,527 | 61,283.96 | 307,429 | 5,765,408.63 |
| es of indeb. | 4 | | | | | | | 5,728 | 35,331.84 | 21 | 150.89 |
| Do. | 4½ | | | | | | | 10,924 | 122,877.66 | 14,398 | 30,882.04 |
| Do. | 4½ | | | | | | | 103 | 1,207.95 | 29,477 | 663,255.10 |
| Do. | 5 | | | | | | | 4,936 | 61,700.00 | 118 | 2,779.10 |
| Do. | 5½ | | | | | | | 11,789 | 170,880.65 | 11,509 | 287,725.00 |
| Do. | 5½ | | | | | | | 95,112 | 1,199,560.58 | 27,104 | 284,484.12 |
| Do. | 6 | | | | | | | 60,719 | 792,726.80 | 192,258 | 67,382.90 |
| | 5½ | | | | | | | 73,085 | 1,096,275.00 | 118,983 | 3,107,563.34 |
| , series A, 1924 | 5½ | | | | | 33,418 | 96,039.38 | 38,690 | 556,129.86 | 139,521 | 4,185,630.00 |
| , series B, 1924 | | | | | | 11,138 | 30,629.50 | 17,298 | 237,847.50 | 96,832 | 2,783,920.00 |
| | | | | | | | | | | 45,533 | 1,252,157.50 |
| Total | | 5,523 | 1,086.40 | 39,197,787 | 42,308,746.01 | 32,417,878 | 70,208,870.93 | 5,577,007 | 61,020,427.08 | 13,039,605 | 276,106,770.39 |

No. 26.—*United States paid coupons received from the Treasurer of the United States during fiscal year ended June 30, 1922, grouped according to loans and denominations.*—Continued.

| Title of loan. | Interest rate. | Denominations of bonds, notes and certificates. | | | | | | | |
| --- | --- | --- | --- | --- | --- | --- | --- | --- | --- |
| | | $5,000 | | $10,000 | | $100,000 | | Total. | |
| | | Coupons | Amount. | Coupons. | Amount. | Coupons. | Amount. | Coupons. | Amount. |
| | *Per cent.* | | | | | | | | |
| ... of 07 | 4 | | | | | | | 193 | $144.50 |
| In of 1904 | 5 | | | | | | | 1 | 1.25 |
| ... | 4 | | | | | | | 42,655 | $6,563.00 |
| In of | 4 | | | | | | | 5,025 | 3,595.80 |
| ... of ... 1906– ... | 3 | | | | | | | 7,199 | 23,430.00 |
| ... din, 908– ... | 2 | | | | | | | 157 | 321.10 |
| ... 4, ... | 2 | | | | | | | 331 | 1,431.50 |
| ... 196 L | 3 | | | | | | | 26,174 | 172,026.75 |
| ... 4, 1916–1946 | 2½ | | | | | | | 7,916 | 11,940.00 |
| 30-year ... | 3 | | | | | | | 80,267 | 589,143.75 |
| Liberty ..., 1932–1947 | 3½ | 58 | $5,800.00 | 16 | $3,200.00 | | | 4,577,378 | 38,046,329.59 |
| ..., c...1, 1932–1947 | 4 | 11,497 | 1,221,556.25 | 8,656 | 1,889,400.00 | | | 391,393 | 728,167.34 |
| Do | 4 | 81 | 8,606.25 | 60 | 12,750.00 | | | 3,417,409 | 16,922,382.98 |
| First 4, ...–1947 | 4 | 492 | 49,200.00 | 346 | 69,300.00 | | | 15,431 | 108,771.32 |
| ..., 1927–1942 ... | 4½ | 104,575 | 11,111,083.75 | 140,993 | 29,961,012.50 | | | 1,425,210 | 2,988,600.00 |
| ..., 4, ... | 4½ | 85,840 | 9,119,890.56 | 122,840 | 26,103,118.88 | | | 12,950,441 | 109,740,159.68 |
| ..., 3–38 ... | 4½ | 198,700 | 21,111,607.25 | 293,416 | 62,350,590.11 | | | 21,504,836 | 121,511,833.26 |
| ..., 3 ... | 4½ | 68,713 | 8,161,500.47 | 85,278 | 20,255,382.24 | | | 27,085,104 | 209,834,726.40 |
| ... | 4½ | 13,399 | 1,256,437.44 | 29,147 | 5,465,169.66 | | | 18,468,423 | 11,036,622.05 |
| ... of inde... | 4 | | | | | 1 | $2,142.86 | 376,641 | 12,580,667.15 |
| | | | | | | | | 21 | 150.89 |
| Do | 4¼ | 3,495 | 341,266.15 | 3,705 | 725,176.58 | 383 | 759,224.78 | 27,709 | 61,861.39 |
| Do | 4¼ | 8,972 | 1,009,387.50 | 11,290 | 2,546,250.00 | 1,916 | 4,311,000.00 | 62,579 | 8,646,770.16 |
| Do | 4¼ | 31 | 3,657.89 | 15 | 3,445.70 | | | 267 | 11,090.64 |
| Do | 5 | 3,312 | 414,000.00 | 3,618 | 904,500.00 | 566 | 1,415,000.00 | 23,941 | 3,082,925.00 |
| Do | 5¼ | 7,948 | 1,142,770.52 | 8,547 | 2,466,148.99 | 1,308 | 3,748,217.04 | 56,696 | 8,312,471.32 |
| Do | 5¼ | 55,534 | 7,013,032.99 | 54,999 | 13,952,223.29 | 7,848 | 20,000,283.09 | 405,781 | 47,022,462.85 |
| Do | 6 | 27,910 | 3,634,117.52 | 25,966 | 6,742,897.28 | 4,045 | 10,500,937.50 | 237,623 | 24,778,242.42 |
| By ..., series A, 1924 | 5¼ | 30,842 | 4,626,300.00 | 27,729 | 8,318,700.00 | 3,911 | 11,733,000.00 | 275,088 | 29,959,905.00 |
| ..., series B, 1924 | 5¼ | 17,830 | 2,563,062.50 | 16,006 | 4,601,725.00 | 2,101 | 6,040,375.00 | 204,877 | 16,641,251.74 |
| | | 10,780 | 1,482,250.00 | 12,900 | 3,547,500.00 | 1,467 | 4,034,250.00 | 99,116 | 10,584,634.50 |
| Total | | 650,009 | 74,275,543.04 | 845,527 | 189,872,740.21 | 23,546 | 62,544,430.27 | 91,776,882 | 776,338,623.33 |

No. 27.—*Comparative statement of United States coupons redeemed during the fiscal years 1919, 1920, 1921, 1922, and total redeemed from December 15, 1917, the date of the first Liberty loan coupon, to June 30, 1922.*

| Class of securities. | 1919 | | 1920 | | 1921 | | 1922 | | December 15, 1917, to June 30, 1922. | |
|---|---|---|---|---|---|---|---|---|---|---|
| | Pieces. | Amount. | Pieces. | Amount. | Pieces. | Amount. | Pieces. | Amount. | Pieces. | Amount. |
| Pre-war loans | 430,899 | $1,888,532.84 | 220,789 | $1,450,231.68 | 197,543 | $1,299,858.73 | 169,918 | $1,148,597.65 | 1,289,569 | $7,355,739.74 |
| Liberty loans | 89,444,468 | 395,771,925.96 | 131,696,967 | 718,666,860.81 | 111,948,883 | 675,264,718.71 | 90,213,266 | 623,988,259.77 | 441,537,215 | 2,515,670,991.65 |
| Treasury notes | | | | | | | 303,993 | 27,225,886.24 | 303,993 | 27,225,886.24 |
| Certificates of indebtedness | 201,155 | 17,506,250.32 | 511,174 | 72,295,484.15 | 778,350 | 100,980,157.54 | 1,089,705 | 123,975,879.67 | 2,580,384 | 314,757,771.68 |
| Total | 90,076,522 | 415,166,709.12 | 132,428,930 | 792,412,576.64 | 112,924,776 | 777,544,734.98 | 91,776,882 | 776,338,623.33 | 445,711,161 | 2,865,010,389.31 |

No. 28.—Coupons detached from Liberty loan bonds, Victory notes, Treasury certificates of indebtedness, and Treasury notes prior to issue and forwarded to the Register of the Treasury for credit by Federal reserve banks and Division of Loans and Currency during the fiscal year ended June 30, 1922.

| Title of loan. | Interest rate. | \$50 Coupons. | \$50 Amount. | \$100 Coupons. | \$100 Amount. | \$500 Coupons. | \$500 Amount. | \$1,000 Coupons. | \$1,000 Amount. |
|---|---|---|---|---|---|---|---|---|---|
| | Per cent. | | | | | | | | |
| Liberty 3½s: | | | | | | | | | |
| First, 1932–1947 | 3½ | 31,375 | \$27,441.49 | 67,609 | \$118,315.75 | 42,458 | \$371,507.50 | 611,887 | \$10,708,022.50 |
| First, 1932–1947 | 4 | 945,839 | 945,838.87 | 387,960 | 775,919.62 | 112,422 | 1,124,220.00 | 126,793 | 2,535,860.00 |
| Do converted, 1932–1947 | 4¼ | 108,001 | 114,707.40 | 88,560 | 188,138.58 | 37,560 | 400,121.63 | 69,536 | 1,477,650.00 |
| First, converted, 1932–1947 | 4¼ | 359 | 380.54 | 457 | 1,034.06 | 252 | 2,995.90 | 348 | 7,395.00 |
| Second | 4 | 2,815,443 | 2,815,443.00 | 1,076,536 | 2,153,072.00 | 147,046 | 1,470,460.00 | 154,923 | 3,098,460.00 |
| Second, 1927–1942 | 4¼ | 374,162 | 406,374.41 | 275,550 | 592,721.44 | 79,642 | 855,249.17 | 229,789 | 4,880,916.25 |
| Third, 1928 | 4¼ | 115,651 | 122,788.85 | 193,651 | 411,627.80 | 67,559 | 717,853.03 | 291,882 | 6,202,492.50 |
| Fourth, 1933 | 4¼ | 112,213 | 118,917.83 | 187,205 | 397,535.54 | 64,481 | 684,987.15 | 244,861 | 5,202,968.90 |
| Victory, 1923 | 4¾ | 186,003 | 223,586.14 | 291,823 | 708,179.04 | 112,476 | 1,362,877.94 | 560,259 | 13,676,830.80 |
| Do, registered | 3¾ | 19,896 | 18,723.44 | 16,208 | 30,525.56 | 16,647 | 156,273.16 | 126,001 | 2,395,707.87 |
| Do | 4½ | 1,000 | 1,360.00 | 1,000 | 2,710.00 | 1,000 | 13,570.00 | 1,000 | 27,140.00 |
| Do | 3½ | 2,030 | 2,172.10 | 3,809 | 8,151.26 | 808 | 8,653.68 | 7,081 | 151,745.83 |
| **Total** | | 4,711,962 | 4,797,732.07 | 2,590,398 | 5,387,930.65 | 682,481 | 7,168,769.16 | 2,424,360 | 50,365,089.65 |
| Certificates of indebtedness: | | | | | | | | | |
| June 15, 1921, series C–1921 | 6 | | | | | 19 | 285.00 | 20 | 600.00 |
| Aug. 16, series C–1921 | 6 | | | | | 8 | 120.00 | 26 | 780.00 |
| Sept. 15, series TS–1921 | 6 | | | | | 42 | 630.00 | 977 | 29,310.00 |
| Dec. 15, 1920, series TD–1921 | 5½ | | | | | 1,732 | 25,980.00 | 6,232 | 186,960.00 |
| Dec. 15, 1920, series TJ–2–1921 | 5½ | | | | | 1,295 | 4,242.10 | 461 | 13,253.75 |
| Dec. 15, series F–19 1 | 5½ | | | | | 2,717 | 33,919.47 | 4,481 | 135,606.92 |
| Feb. 15, 1921, series G–1 | 5½ | | | | | 414 | 4,678.20 | 783 | 17,695.80 |
| Mar. 15, 1921, series TS–2–1921 | 5½ | | | | | 584 | 8,030.00 | 3,389 | 30 |
| Mar. 15, series H–1 | 5½ | | | | | 600 | 8,250.00 | 1,781 | 48,977.50 |
| May 15, series H–1922 | 5½ | | | | | 6,176 | 88,759.85 | 10,022 | 288,132.50 |
| June 15, series A–1 9 | 5½ | | | | | 10,399 | 128,526.61 | 13,871 | 345,002.58 |
| Aug. 15, series B–19 2 | 5½ | | | | | 11,868 | 163,185.00 | 12,558 | 345,345.00 |
| Sept. 15, 1921, series TS–1922 | 5½ | | | | | 5,583 | 76,766.25 | 6,295 | 173,112.50 |
| Aug. 15, 1921, series B5–1922 | 5½ | | | | | 3,519 | 46,169.28 | 9,046 | 237,457.50 |
| Sept. 15, 1921, series TM–3–1922 | 5 | | | | | 1,099 | 17,858.75 | 1,640 | 53,316.40 |
| Mar. 15, series TM–2–1922 | 4¾ | | | | | 1,096 | 12,450.00 | 968 | 24,200.00 |
| Mar. 1, series TS–2–1922 | 4¾ | | | | | 5,712 | 64,260.00 | 10,870 | 244,575.00 |
| Mar. 1, series C–1922 | 4¼ | | | | | 463 | 4,069.77 | 1,641 | 28,848.78 |

No. 28.—*Coupons detached from Liberty loan bonds, Victory notes, Treasury certificates of indebtedness, and Treasury notes prior to issue and forwarded to the Register of the Treasury for credit by Federal reserve banks and Division of Loans and Currency during the fiscal year ended June 30, 1922—Continued.*

| Title of loan. | Interest rate. | $5,000 | | $10,000 | | $50,000 | | $100,000 | | Total | |
|---|---|---|---|---|---|---|---|---|---|---|---|
| | | Coupons. | Amount. | Coupons. | Amount. | Coupons. | Amount. | Coupons. | Amount. | Coupons. | Amount. |
| | Per cent. | | | | | | | | | | |
| Liberty loans: | | | | | | | | | | | |
| First, 1932-1947 | 3½ | 4,806 | $480,600.00 | 4,697 | $939,400.00 | | | | | 753,329 | $7.24 |
| First, converted, 1932-1947 | 4 | 7,503 | 797,193.75 | 12,932 | 2,748,040.00 | | | | | 1,582,517 | 6,801,838.49 |
| Do | 4½ | 7 | 743.75 | 43 | 9,137.50 | | | | | 324,192 | 81.36 |
| First second, converted, 1932-1947 | 4 | 7,456 | 745,600.00 | 7,570 | 1,574,060.00 | | | | | 1,526 | 21,686.75 |
| Second, 1927-1942 | 4 | 21,667 | 2,302,118.75 | 67,383 | 14,320,312.50 | | | | | 4,209,274 | 87,66.00 |
| Second, converted, 1927-1942 | 4½ | 23,152 | 2,459,900.00 | 91,945 | 19,538,312.59 | | | | | 1,048,195 | 23,357,692.52 |
| Third, 1928 | 4½ | 26,245 | 2,792,734.00 | 83,336 | 17,708,762.59 | | | | | 783,840 | 2.6 |
| Fourth, 1933-1938 | 4½ | 130,804 | 15,960,061.07 | 244,889 | 59,901,543.86 | | | | | 718,381 | 26,905,806.28 |
| Victory, 1922-1923 | 4¾ | 9,105 | 858,307.03 | 19,029 | 3,673,918.74 | | | | | 1,526,264 | 91,69.75 |
| Do | 3¾ | 500 | 67,855.00 | 500 | 135,715.00 | 100 | $135,714.00 | 100 | $271,429.00 | 206,876 | 7,133,455.80 |
| Victory, 1922-1923, registered | | | | | | | | | | 5,200 | 655,493.00 |
| Do | | 22,524 | 2,413,221.36 | 21,118 | 4,525,376.22 | 2,139 | 2,291,788.77 | 1,720 | 3,685,719.20 | 61,229 | 13,086,828.42 |
| Total | | 253,869 | 28,878,335.61 | 553,754 | 125,074,519.18 | 2,239 | 2,427,502.77 | 1,820 | 3,957,148.20 | 11,220,823 | 0.29 |
| Certificates of indebtedness: | | | | | | | | | | | |
| June 3, 1 9, series T– 9i | 6 | 175 | 26,250.00 | 62 | 18,600.00 | | | 9 | 27,000.00 | 285 | 72,25.00 |
| Ag. 4, 1 9, series C–1921 | 6 | 104 | 15,600.00 | 110 | 33,000.00 | | | 14 | 42,000.00 | 262 | 91,500.00 |
| 4i, 5, 9, series B– 9i | 6 | 238 | 35,700.00 | 32 | 9,600.00 | | | 10 | 30,000.00 | 1,299 | 105,240.00 |
| 4c. 15, 9, series 9921 | 5½ | 1,002 | 150,300.00 | 805 | 241,500.00 | | | 103 | 309,000.00 | 9,874 | 913,740.00 |
| 4c. 15, 9, series 9921 | 5½ | 87 | 12,506.25 | 134 | 38,525.00 | | | 1 | 2,975.00 | 978 | 71,402.10 |
| R. 5, 9, series F–1921 | 5½ | 1,361 | 189,391.06 | 818 | 231,437.50 | | | 117 | 330,625.00 | 9,894 | 926,979.95 |
| R. 5, 9, series G–1921 | 5½ | 206 | 23,280.06 | 132 | 29,835.96 | | | 5 | 11,301.35 | 4,265 | 86,791.37 |
| Mr. 4, 9, series 9H | 5½ | 151 | 20,762.53 | 135 | 37,125.00 | | | 6 | 16,500.00 | 2,816 | 175,615.00 |
| Apr. 15, 9, series H–1921 | 5½ | 264 | 36,300.00 | 168 | 46,200.00 | | | 3 | 8,250.00 | 19,277 | 147,977.50 |
| Mar. 4, 9, series M– 92 | 5½ | 1,576 | 269,675.00 | 1,053 | 305,612.50 | | | 140 | 402,500.00 | 28,763 | 1,354,679.85 |
| My 6, 9, series A– 92 | 5½ | 2,536 | 328,880.27 | 1,862 | 491,631.78 | | | 95 | 246,375.69 | 28,400 | 1,540,426.83 |
| ule 15, 9, ries T– 92 | 5½ | 2,282 | 313,775.00 | 1,524 | 419,100.00 | | | 168 | 462,000.00 | 16,682 | 9I, 405.00 |
| 4i, 1, 9, series J– 92 | 5½ | 2,183 | 299,337.50 | 1,737 | 477,675.00 | | | 260 | 715,750.00 | 16,651 | 1,741,891.25 |
| Aug. 1, 9, es h 9I2 | 5½ | 89 | 14,465.17 | 95 | 416,062.50 | | | 311 | 834,759.00 | 2,934 | 1,820,958.03 |
| Nov. 1, 9, series TM–3–1922 | 4½ | 240 | 30,600.00 | 90 | 30,881.65 | | | 9 | 34,757.48 | 2,303 | 152,279.45 |
| Nov. 1, 9, series C–1 9 | 4½ | 3,146 | 351,675.86 | 2,164 | 22,500.00 | | | 215 | 22,500.00 | 22,087 | 11,650.00 |
| | | | 12,834.86 | 2,120 | 21,098.40 | | | 3 | 483,760.00 | 2,373 | 1,631,160.00 |
| | | | | | | | | | 5,274.66 | | 72,126.47 |

**Denominations of bonds, notes and certificates.**

| | Rate | | | | | | | | | | | |
|---|---|---|---|---|---|---|---|---|---|---|---|---|
| Dec. 15, 1921, series TD-1922 | 4½ | 1,384 | 155,700.00 | 1,020 | 229,500.00 | | | 121 | 272,250.00 | 11,555 | 811,462.50 |
| Dec. 15, 1921, series TJ-2-1922 | 4¼ | 330 | 35,062.50 | 84 | 17,850.00 | | | 19 | 40,375.00 | 2,498 | 129,437.39 |
| Total | | 19,957 | 2,608,023.92 | 13,740 | 3,604,635.29 | | | 1,627 | 4,298,084.18 | 184,106 | 13,661,457.79 |
| Treasury notes: | | | | | | | | | | | |
| A-1924 | 5¾ | 3,619 | 520,231.25 | 2,861 | 822,537.50 | | | 371 | 1,066,625.00 | 64,923 | 3,287,561.28 |
| B-1924 | 5½ | 2,476 | 340,450.00 | 2,604 | 716,100.00 | | | 267 | 734,250.00 | 33,622 | 2,195,162.75 |
| Total | | 6,095 | 860,681.25 | 5,465 | 1,538,637.50 | | | 638 | 1,800,875.00 | 98,545 | 5,482,724.03 |
| Grand total | | 279,861 | 32,347,040.78 | 572,959 | 130,217,791.97 | 2,239 | 2,427,502.77 | 4,085 | 10,056,107.38 | 11,503,474 | 247,201,209.11 |

No. 29.—*United States interest checks received from the Treasurer of the United States on account of payment of past due interest on coupon bonds during the fiscal year ended June 30, 1922.*

| Title of loan. | Interest rate. | Total pieces. | Total amount. |
|---|---|---|---|
| | *Per cent.* | | |
| First, converted, 1932–1947 | 4½ | 197 | $2,971.47 |
| First second, converted, 1932–1947 | 4½ | 7 | 20.15 |
| Second, converted, 1927–1942 | 4½ | 501 | 13,683.78 |
| Third, 1928 | 4½ | 1,475 | 42,957.44 |
| Fourth, 1933–1938 | 4½ | 2,531 | 93,916.92 |
| Total | | 4,711 | 153,549.76 |

No. 30.—*District of Columbia funded loan of 1924 (3.65 per cent).*

DEBT OUTSTANDING JUNE 30, 1922.

Amount issued prior to June 30, 1921 ............................................................ $15,000,000  
Amount retired prior to June 30, 1921 ............................................................ 10,084,250  
Amount issued during fiscal year 1922 ............................................................  
Amount retired during fiscal year 1922 ............................................................ 196,050  
Total amount issued ............................................................ 15,000,000  
Total amount retired ............................................................ 10,280,300  
Total amount outstanding ............................................................ 4,719,700  

REDEEMED DURING THE FISCAL YEAR ENDED JUNE 30, 1922.

| Class. | Denominations by number of pieces. | | | | Total. | |
|---|---|---|---|---|---|---|
| | $50 | $500 | $1,000 | $5,000 | Pieces. | Amount. |
| Coupon | 21 | 42 | | | 63 | $22,050 |
| Registered [1] | | | 378 | 1,152 | 1,530 | 6,138,000 |
| Total | 21 | 42 | 378 | 1,152 | 1,593 | 6,160,050 |

[1] Includes 1,460 pieces, $5,964,000 belonging to 1919 fiscal year, but received for audit in fiscal year 1922.

CANCELED ON ACCOUNT OF TRANSFER DURING FISCAL YEAR ENDED JUNE 30, 1922.

| Class. | Denominations by number of pieces. | | Total. | |
|---|---|---|---|---|
| | $1,000 | $5,000 | Pieces. | Amount. |
| Registered [1] | 162 | 736 | 898 | $3,842,000 |

[1] Includes bonds amounting to $3,404,000 belonging to 1920 fiscal year, but received for audit in fiscal year 1922.

INTEREST COUPONS REDEEMED DURING FISCAL YEARS 1919, 1920, 1921, AND 1922.

1919:  
    Pieces ............................................................ 1,716  
    Amount ............................................................ $9,531.97½  
1920:  
    Pieces ............................................................ 1,667  
    Amount ............................................................ $9,618.66½  
1921:  
    Pieces ............................................................ 1,892  
    Amount ............................................................ $10,431.68½  
1922: [1]  
    Pieces ............................................................ 1,738  
    Amount ............................................................ $8,106.64½  

PAID INTEREST CHECKS RECEIVED FOR FILE DURING THE FISCAL YEAR ENDED JUNE 30, 1922.

Number of pieces ............................................................ [2] 337  
Amount ............................................................ [2] $171,130.25  

[1] Includes 260 pieces amounting to $500.05 properly belonging to fiscal year 1921, but received for audit subsequent to the printing of the 1921 annual report.  
[2] Includes four pieces amounting to $766.50 properly belonging to fiscal year 1921 but received for audit subsequent to the printing of the 1921 annual report.

No. 31.—*Insular-possessions loans received on account of exchange from Division of Loans and Currency, audited and filed during fiscal year ended June 30, 1922.*

| Title of loan. | Inter-est rate. | Denominations by number of pieces. | | Total. | |
|---|---|---|---|---|---|
| | | $1,000 | $10,000 | Pieces. | Amount. |
| Government of the Philippine Islands certificates of indebtedness: | *Per ct.* | | | | |
| Apr. 1, 1919–Mar. 31, 1920, interims............... | 4 | .......... | 1,000 | 1,000 | $10,000,000 |
| Aug. 2, 1920–Aug. 2, 1921, interims............... | 4 | .......... | 10 | 10 | 100,000 |
| Aug. 1, 1921–Aug. 1, 1922, interims............... | 4 | 9,890 | .......... | 9,890 | 9,890,000 |
| Aug. 1, 1921–Aug. 1, 1922, bonds................. | 4 | 50 | .......... | 50 | 50,000 |
| Philippine Islands public-improvement loans, Aug. 1, 1921–Aug. 1, 1941, interims.................. | 5½ | 9,867 | .......... | 9,867 | 9,867,000 |
| Government of the Philippine Islands, 1922–1952, interims....................................... | 5 | 1,499 | .......... | 1,499 | 1,499,000 |
| Porto Rico public-improvement loan, 1919–1931, interims: | | | | | |
| Series J [1]........................................ | 4½ | 125 | .......... | 125 | 125,000 |
| Series K [1]........................................ | 4½ | 50 | .......... | 50 | 50,000 |
| Series L [1]........................................ | 4½ | 50 | .......... | 50 | 50,000 |
| People of Porto Rico, high-school building, loan of 1920, interims.................................. | 4½ | 27 | .......... | 27 | 27,000 |
| People of Porto Rico, workingmen's house construction of 1920: | | | | | |
| Interims— | | | | | |
| Series A........................................ | 4½ | 115 | .......... | 115 | 115,000 |
| Series B........................................ | 4½ | 217 | .......... | 217 | 217,000 |
| Bonds— | | | | | |
| Series A........................................ | 4½ | 25 | .......... | 25 | 25,000 |
| Series B........................................ | 4½ | 1 | .......... | 1 | 1,000 |
| Total....................................... | ....... | 21,916 | 1,010 | 22,926 | 32,016,000 |

[1] Belong to fiscal year of 1920, received and audited during fiscal year of 1922.

No. 32.—*Insular-possessions loans received on account of transfer from Division of Loans and Currency, audited and filed during fiscal year ended June 30, 1922.*

| Title of loan. | Interest rate, per cent. | Denominations by number of pieces. | | | Interim certificates. | | Total. | |
|---|---|---|---|---|---|---|---|---|
| | | $1,000 | $5,000 | $10,000 | Pieces. | Amount. | Pieces. | Amount. |
| Philippine loan of 1914–1934, land purchase | 4 | 1,842 | | 283 | | | 2,125 | $4,672,000 |
| Philippine loan of 1916 | 4 | 1,399 | | 352 | 1,391 | $4,545,000 | 3,142 | 9,464,000 |
| Philippine loan, public improvement: | | | | | | | | |
| First series, 1915–1935 | 4 | 310 | | 56 | | | 366 | 870,000 |
| Second series, 1916–1936 | 4 | 301 | | 41 | | | 342 | 711,000 |
| Third series, 1919–1939 | 4 | 1,626 | | | | | 1,626 | 1,626,000 |
| City of Manila, sewer and water loan: | | | | | | | | |
| First series, 1915–1935 | 4 | 757 | | 277 | | | 1,034 | 3,527,000 |
| Second series, 1917–1937 | 4 | 283 | | 87 | | | 370 | 1,153,000 |
| Third series, 1918–1938 | 4 | 235 | | | | | 235 | 235,000 |
| City of Cebu loan of 1921–1941 | 4 | 232 | | | | | 232 | 232,000 |
| Manila port works improvement loan of 1920 | 5½ | 707 | | 75 | 157 | 346,000 | 939 | 1,803,000 |
| Porto Rico gold loan of 1910 | 4 | | 3 | | | | 3 | 15,000 |
| Porto Rico gold loan of 1912 | 4 | | 1 | | | | 1 | 5,000 |
| Porto Rico gold loan of 1913 | 4 | | 42 | | | | 42 | 210,000 |
| Porto Rico irrigation loan of 1913, series A–1934 | 4 | 35 | | | | | 35 | 35,000 |
| Porto Rico irrigation loan of 1914: | | | | | | | | |
| Series A–1951 | 4 | 2 | 2 | | | | 4 | 12,000 |
| Series B–1952 | 4 | 2 | 5 | | | | 7 | 27,000 |
| Series C–1953 | 4 | 2 | 5 | | | | 7 | 27,000 |
| Porto Rico irrigation loan of 1915: | | | | | | | | |
| Series E–1955 | 4 | 3 | | | | | 3 | 3,000 |
| Series G–1957 | 4 | 18 | | | | | 18 | 18,000 |
| Series H–1958 | 4 | 1 | | | | | 1 | 1,000 |
| Porto Rico irrigation loan of 1918: | | | | | | | | |
| Series A–1958 | 4 | | 9 | | 10 | 14,000 | 19 | 59,000 |
| Series B–1959 | 4 | 15 | 10 | | 3 | 3,000 | 28 | 68,000 |
| Porto Rico public-improvement loan, 1914 | 4 | 18 | 6 | | | | 24 | 48,000 |
| Porto Rico public-improvement loan, 1916: | | | | | | | | |
| Series A–1927 | 4 | | 10 | | 10 | 50,000 | 20 | 100,000 |
| Series B–1928 | 4 | 6 | 2 | | 10 | 50,000 | 18 | 66,000 |
| Series C–1929 | 4 | 30 | 7 | | | | 37 | 65,000 |
| Series D–1930 | 4 | 1 | 3 | | | | 4 | 16,000 |
| Porto Rico public-improvement loan, 1918: | | | | | | | | |
| Series E | 4 | | 10 | | 42 | 150,000 | 52 | 200,000 |
| Series F | 4 | 50 | | | 47 | 175,000 | 97 | 225,000 |
| Series G–1929 | 4 | 26 | 8 | | 81 | 125,000 | 115 | 191,000 |
| Series H–1930 | 4 | 125 | 15 | | 96 | 220,000 | 236 | 420,000 |
| Porto Rico public-improvement loan, 1920. | | | | | | | | |
| Series A | 4½ | | 2 | | 79 | 395,000 | 81 | 405,000 |
| Series B | 4 | | 7 | | 76 | 380,000 | 83 | 415,000 |
| Series C | 4 | | 5 | | 73 | 365,000 | 78 | 390,000 |
| Series D | 4 | | 7 | | 61 | 305,000 | 68 | 340,000 |
| Porto Rico refunding loan, 1914: | | | | | | | | |
| Series I–1923 | 4 | 45 | 27 | | | | 72 | 180,000 |
| Series J–1924 | 4 | 14 | 11 | | | | 25 | 69,000 |
| Series K–1925 | 4 | 29 | 13 | | | | 42 | 94,000 |
| Series L–1926 | 4 | 1 | 6 | | | | 7 | 31,000 |
| Series M–1927 | 4 | 14 | 6 | | | | 20 | 44,000 |
| Series N–1928 | 4 | 4 | 9 | | | | 13 | 49,000 |
| Series O–1929 | 4 | 16 | 9 | | | | 25 | 61,000 |
| Series P–1930 | 4 | 18 | 2 | | | | 20 | 28,000 |
| Series Q–1931 | 4 | 8 | 4 | | | | 12 | 28,000 |
| Series R–1932 | 4 | | 6 | | | | 6 | 30,000 |
| Series S–1933 | 4 | 36 | 20 | | | | 56 | 136,000 |
| Series T–1934 | 4 | 25 | 5 | | | | 30 | 50,000 |
| Series U–1943 | 4 | 61 | 48 | | | | 109 | 301,000 |
| Series V–1953 | 4 | 69 | 35 | | | | 104 | 244,000 |
| Porto Rico refunding municipal loan, 1915: | | | | | | | | |
| Series A | 4 | 15 | | | 21 | 21,000 | 36 | 36,000 |
| Series B | 4 | 62 | | | 22 | 22,000 | 84 | 84,000 |
| Series C | 4 | 31 | | | 21 | 21,000 | 52 | 52,000 |
| Series D | 4 | 42 | | | 21 | 21,000 | 63 | 63,000 |
| Series E | 4 | 18 | | | 21 | 21,000 | 39 | 39,000 |
| Series F | 4 | 20 | | | 21 | 21,000 | 41 | 41,000 |
| Series G | 4 | 13 | | | 19 | 19,000 | 32 | 32,000 |
| Series H | 4 | 5 | | | 18 | 18,000 | 23 | 23,000 |
| Series I | 4 | 12 | | | 18 | 18,000 | 30 | 30,000 |
| Series J | 4 | 24 | | | 18 | 18,000 | 42 | 42,000 |
| Series K | 4 | 16 | | | 18 | 18,000 | 34 | 34,000 |
| Series L | 4 | 15 | | | 17 | 17,000 | 32 | 32,000 |
| Series M | 4 | 8 | | | 16 | 16,000 | 24 | 24,000 |
| Series N | 4 | 13 | | | 16 | 16,000 | 29 | 29,000 |
| Series O | 4 | 9 | | | 15 | 15,000 | 24 | 24,000 |
| Series P | 4 | 3 | | | 9 | 9,000 | 12 | 12,000 |
| Series Q | 4 | | | | 9 | 9,000 | 9 | 9,000 |

TABLE 32.—*Insular-possessions loans received on account of transfers from Division of Loans and Currency, audited and filed during fiscal year ended June 30, 1922*—Contd.

| Title of loan. | Interest rate, per cent. | Denominations by number of pieces. | | | Interim certificates. | | Total. | |
|---|---|---|---|---|---|---|---|---|
| | | $1,000 | $5,000 | $10,000 | Pieces. | Amount. | Pieces. | Amount. |
| Porto Rico refunding municipal loan, 1916: | | | | | | | | |
| Series B | 4 | ...... | 3 | ...... | ...... | ...... | 3 | 15,000 |
| Series C | 4 | ...... | 4 | ...... | ...... | ...... | 4 | 20,000 |
| Series E | 4 | ...... | 2 | ...... | ...... | ...... | 2 | 10,000 |
| Series F | 4 | ...... | 4 | ...... | ...... | ...... | 4 | 20,000 |
| Series G | 4 | ...... | 4 | ...... | ...... | ...... | 4 | 20,000 |
| Series H | 4 | ...... | 5 | 9 | ...... | ...... | 14 | 50,000 |
| Porto Rico house-construction loan, 1920, series A | 4½ | 1 | ...... | ...... | 26 | 26,000 | 27 | 27,000 |
| Porto Rico San Juan Harbor loan, 1917 | 4 | ...... | ...... | ...... | 100 | 100,000 | 100 | 100,000 |
| Total | ...... | 8,678 | 386 | 1,171 | 2,562 | 7,549,000 | 12,797 | 29,867,000 |

NOTE.—Although properly belonging to 1920 fiscal year, bonds amounting to $18,195,000 and interim certificates amounting to $5,437,000 are included in the above figures, inasmuch as they were received and functioned in fiscal year 1922.

No. 33.—*Statement showing securities destroyed during the fiscal year ended June 30, 1922.*

| Class of security. | Denominations by number of pieces. | | | | | | |
|---|---|---|---|---|---|---|---|
| | $20 | $25 | $50 | $100 | $500 | $1,000 | $5,000 |
| Coupon bonds, notes—Liberty loans | ...... | ...... | 25,406,621 | 13,620,877 | 1,582,607 | 4,932,225 | 126,457 |
| Coupon bonds, notes—Old loans | 22,478 | ...... | 9,003 | 63,891 | 43,821 | 73,372 | ...... |
| Certificates of indebtedness | ...... | ...... | ...... | ...... | 85,280 | 164,916 | 46,220 |
| War savings certificates, registered [1] | ...... | ...... | ...... | ...... | ...... | ...... | ...... |
| War savings certificates, nonregistered | ...... | ...... | ...... | ...... | ...... | ...... | ...... |
| Treasury savings certificates | ...... | 327 | ...... | 3,918 | ...... | 187 | ...... |
| Interest coupons [2] | ...... | ...... | 3,415,228 | 1,601,700 | 140,817 | 193,224 | 2,268 |
| Total | 22,478 | 327 | 28,830,852 | 15,290,386 | 1,852,525 | 5,363,924 | 174,945 |

| Class of security. | Denominations by number of pieces. | | Number of certificates. | Number of stamps. | Total. | |
|---|---|---|---|---|---|---|
| | $10,000 | $100,000 | | | Number of pieces. | Amount. |
| Coupon bonds, notes—Liberty loans | 147,574 | ...... | ...... | ...... | 45,816,361 | $10,463,972,250.00 |
| Coupon bonds, notes—Old loans | ...... | ...... | ...... | ...... | 212,565 | 102,571,310.00 |
| Certificates of indebtedness | 44,149 | 6,527 | ...... | ...... | 347,092 | 1,532,846,000.00 |
| War savings certificates, registered [1] | ...... | ...... | 4,619,390 | 26,612,091 | 26,612,091 | 116,413,486.20 |
| War savings certificates, nonregistered | ...... | ...... | 5,965,092 | 52,234,057 | 52,234,057 | 229,741,487.46 |
| Treasury savings certificates | ...... | ...... | ...... | ...... | 4,432 | 586,975.00 |
| Interest coupons [2] | 1,106 | ...... | ...... | ...... | 5,354,343 | 11,894,060.21 |
| Total | 192,829 | 6,527 | 10,584,482 | 78,846,148 | 130,580,941 | 12,458,025,568.87 |

[1] Represent two wings detached from certificates. stubs (one-third) retained in file.
[2] Represent interest coupons detached from securities of the denomination listed.

NOTE.—Does not include Treasury (war) savings securities sent to destruction committee from office of the Third Assistant Postmaster General.

# REPORT OF THE COMPTROLLER OF THE CURRENCY.

TREASURY DEPARTMENT,
OFFICE OF COMPTROLLER OF THE CURRENCY,
*Washington, December 4, 1922.*

SIR: Pursuant to section No. 333 of the Revised Statutes, I have the honor to submit the Sixtieth Annual Report of the Comptroller of the Currency, dealing with the operations of this bureau for the year ended October 31, 1922.

It is with the utmost satisfaction that I find myself able to report that although the country has been passing through a period of liquidation and deflation which was doubtless inevitable as an aftermath to the world-wide credit expansion and inflation incident to financing the World War, the national banking system of this country has splendidly justified the confidence that has been reposed in it; and, in general, the banking situation is thoroughly satisfactory.

In every section of the country there has been a decided improvement within the year covered by this report. Industrial conditions have uniformly changed for the better. Unemployment, which at the time of the last annual report was still one of the difficult and distressing features of the situation, has been reduced to a point where it may fairly be said no longer to exist. In a country of such widely variegated interests, there must always be a certain proportion of unemployment, owing to individual and economic maladjustments. This has always been true, and in our complex social organization it doubtless always will be; but the fact stands that the past year has been marked by a reduction of this proportion of unemployment to well-nigh the minimum that we can hope for under existing circumstances.

While there has been improvement throughout substantially the entire economic structure of the Nation, it must be said in all frankness that the betterment has not been equitably distributed throughout all the departments of our economic life. On the whole, industry and commerce have been advantaged very much more than has agriculture. The demand for the agricultural staples has indeed improved, but the improvement has not kept pace with the like progression in many other departments of business. To state the matter broadly, it may be said that the development of banking conditions within the year, and their present status, quite generally and accurately reflect the agricultural conditions of the country. That is, the greatest improvement in banking conditions is found in those sections where there has been most improvement in the agri-

695

cultural situation, or in those where the general business position is least dependent upon the prosperity and progress of agriculture.

The most difficult banking situations which now confront us and with which we have to deal are in those areas which have suffered agriculturally by reason of drought, of inauspicious conditions in the live-stock industry, of inadequate transportation to move products, or of other circumstances which have worked to the injury of farming communities. The areas which have been thus unfortunate constitute comparatively a small part of the entire country; while the outlook for a continuing improvement in the agricultural situation based on increased demands for the farmer's products both at home and abroad, and a consequent improvement in prices, finds immediate reflection in a more cheerful banking prospect.

It is rather a striking commentary on the unwisdom of even our most trusted economic theories, that so many of the anticipations which were almost universally entertained during the war have been proved by the events since the peace to have been startlingly erroneous. Thus, it was the well-nigh universal belief during the war that after the restoration of peace there would be found to be a vast accumulated deficit in the maritime shipping capacity of the world, partly because of the destruction of merchant ships during the war, partly because of inadequate construction, and partly because it was believed that depleted stores, empty shelves and warehouses, would constitute a vacuum to which goods would be attracted in all parts of the world. For the transportation of these goods, it was commonly assumed, a great and indeed well-nigh impossible demand would be imposed upon a depleted merchant tonnage.

We know now that these anticipations were strangely in error, and that following the industrial and merchandising boom which for a short time followed the conclusion of peace, there has been instead an almost utterly unanticipated shrinkage in the demand for seagoing tonnage. Very plainly, in this time of political, economic, and financial uncertainty, the different countries have been thrown back upon their own domestic resources to supply their various requirements, to an extent not formerly believed to be possible. There has of course been a great shrinkage in consumption, and therefore in demand; but along with this there has undoubtedly been developed in most countries a determined effort to reduce the requirement for imported articles of whatever kind, in order to bring the trade balance more nearly to a favorable basis.

It is true that if we compare the money values of imports and exports for the years since the war with corresponding figures of the years before the war, we get no adequate impression that there has been such a reduction of international exchanges. But that of course is because present-day prices are high, even in countries which have the best money; while they are still higher in countries whose currencies are inflated and where the gold standard is more or less a theory or a reminiscence. But if we will compare actual quantities of goods moved in international commerce, we will find that on the whole there has been a more unsatisfactory development.

Our own country enjoyed for a series of years an utterly unprecedented favorable balance of trade with the rest of the world, owing to war conditions. More recently we have been returning rapidly toward a more normal relationship of imports to exports, and there has of late even been intimation on high authority that in no very distant future we might actually be called upon to export gold. Whether or not that time is near, it indubitably is true that our favorable trade balance has been greatly reduced, and that we are justified in hoping for readjustments at no very distant future which will at least greatly lessen the tendency to drain the gold of the world into our coffers.

From the purely financial point of view, the cessation of gold imports would represent a long step toward the restoration of that economic equilibrium which is absolutely necessary as a prerequisite to the reestablishment of sound monetary systems throughout the world. While it is true that the paper money of some unfortunate countries has experienced disaster, it is also true that these very disasters have been a lesson to statesmen and business men everywhere, and on the whole, have emphasized in the public mind our dependence upon a sound money system, based upon gold, and enabling international commodity transactions to be conducted in confidence and security. Some of the monetary systems which have been watered down to the point of complete saturation, have begun to yield to the inevitable pressure, so that the more stable money units of other countries are being called in and utilized. All this is entirely to the good, for it testifies that in the end the gold standard will be recognized as the soundest, safest, and most reliable that fiscal and economic wisdom has yet devised.

There will hardly be serious dissent from the proposition that when social and economic balances are finally placed, throughout the world, in the way of ultimate redress, our own country must shoulder a large responsibility in connection with the reestablishment of sound conditions and relationships. One of the things which then must happen will be the disintegration, in a considerable part, of that enormous stock of gold which has been flowing to our shores since early in the European war. We hold now well-nigh half of the monetary gold stock of the world, and such a disproportionate holding is only less unfortunate for us than it is for other countries to have their gold reserves so sadly depleted. We are now well past that era of crude economic thought in which many of us quite sincerely believe that the more gold a country could accumulate, the better for it, regardless of every other consideration. We have come to understand that it is equally undesirable for a country to have either a vastly excessive or an utterly inadequate share of the monetary gold. Just in proportion as gold is liquid, free, and safe to move about the world in the process of equalizing industrial and financial requirements, so we shall have an approximation to that stability of conditions, that general level of prosperity and industrial activity, which is so greatly to be desired.

It is because we must look forward to the time when we shall have to return much of our present gold holdings to those from whom in recent years it has come to us, that we must give thought to the importance of having our financial establishment in order and prepared for the demands which will come to it. We have need to keep our stocks of gold so well in hand, our credit so sound, our banking fabric so secure, that we will be able to meet these demands without shock or jar to the industrial and business concerns of the country. It is hardly needful to say that the Federal reserve system represents that concentration of financial resource and Nation-spreading credit through which we may feel assured that we shall be able to meet all these demands.

It thus becomes important, in a very special sense, that the Federal reserve system and the national banking system upon which the Federal reserve structure is superimposed, shall be wisely fostered, promoted, and encouraged. If the Federal reserve system has been a good thing for the country in the past, if it is a good thing for the country to-day, if it is going to be a good thing for the country in the future, then it is desirable that this system be strengthened and enabled to attract to itself the backing and support of the largest possible proportion of the Nation's banking resources.

In any fair survey of the history of the Federal reserve system to this time, I think it would have to be conceded that some expectations which were entertained at the time of its establishment, have been disappointed. The system has failed to attract the participation and support of as large a proportion of the Nation's banking power as was hoped for, or as would be desirable. To say this is not to derogate from its splendid service to the country in the last eight years. That service is not likely to be overstated. But it is of the utmost importance that the service shall not be forgotten or underestimated, and that it shall be kept always in mind that such a service could not possibly have been rendered if the system had not included a sufficient proportion of the banking authority of the Nation to enable it to dominate the situation in a most difficult period. An experience of more than a year and a half in this office has convinced the present comptroller of the necessity for a continuing policy of wise liberality in dealing with the national banks and the Federal reserve system.

There is competition among banks, precisely as there is competition among other types of business enterprises, and ultimately money which seeks investment in banking will tend to enter whatever system of banking is likely to be most profitable. The States have built up great banking establishments under their own laws. These are constantly presenting their particular advantages to capital which seeks investment in banking. The laws and the administration under which the Federal reserve system is conducted must be reasonable, practical, and adapted to securing soundness in the banking structure. At the same time they must provide a fair return upon the capital investment. Only thus will this great national system always be assured a sufficient strength and substance to enable it to do its work of financial mobilization and equilibration.

These suggestions are pressed with all possible earnestness, in view of the experience resulting from service both as Comptroller of the Currency and as a member of the Federal Reserve Board. It is strongly felt that, whether in connection with legislation or administration of the national banks, or the determination of those broad policies which are intrusted to the Federal Reserve Board, these considerations ought always to be kept in the fullest view.

As one step toward the consummation of a desirable organization of the national banking system, it is recommended once more that national banks be permitted to take out perpetual charters. Within the past few months, under the act of July 1, 1922, 99-year charters have been issued to all national banks.

The present administration of the comptroller's office urged legislation reducing the minimum number of bank calls per annum from five to three; and this legislation has been enacted. On the other hand, the examining force of the bureau has for the first year in its history made two examinations of every national bank. In addition, it must be stated that many hundreds of special examinations have been made. The force of examiners, throughout a year which was marked by many difficulties and an unusual burden of exacting duties, has deserved the highest commendation for faithfulness, sound discretion, absolute reliability, and devotion to exacting duties. It is a pleasure to record this appreciation of so able and efficient an organization, and to add that the best testimony to the high quality and character of the examining force is found in the fact that the bureau has constant difficulty in retaining the services of its skilled examiners because their special qualifications constantly appeal to the best banks, which are continually drafting them away from the bureau at greatly advanced compensation.

## LEGISLATION ENACTED AND RECOMMENDED RELATING TO NATIONAL BANKS.

In connection with recommendations of the comptroller relating to amendments of the national banking law, the present Congress has passed three measures, the first, approved on March 1, 1921, relating to the qualification of directors of national banking associations, the second, on July 1, 1922, amending section 5136, Revised Statutes, to provide that national banking associations shall have succession for the period of 99 years, reference to which is made in extenso elsewhere in this report, and the third, on December 28, 1922, amending section 5211, Revised Statutes, to provide for not less than three reports each year instead of five.

It is again recommended that favorable consideration be given to further amendment of section 5136, to confer upon national banks perpetual succession in lieu of the present limitation of 99 years as was provided by the act passed by the House of Representatives and unanimously recommended by the Senate Committee on Banking and Currency at the second session of the present Congress.

To amend the act approved November 7, 1918, providing for the consolidation of national banking associations, to permit consolidation of State and national banks under the same terms and conditions as provided for the consolidation of national banks.

To amend the third paragraph of section 5134 so that it will read as follows: "Second. The place or *places within the city, town, or village in which the association is organized*, where its operations of discount and deposit are to be carried on, designating the State, Territory, or district, and the particular county and city, town or village."

To amend section 5209, prescribing penalties for embezzlement, etc., to make its provisions applicable to national bank examiners, assistants and clerks, for embezzlement, etc., of funds intrusted to or funds coming into their possession while making an examination of a bank.

To amend section 5145, relating to the election of and management by directors of national banking associations, to require directors to make written report to shareholders at annual election meetings, the report to show the assets and liabilities in detail, profit and loss, salaries paid officers and employees, together with a statement of operating expenses for the year.

To amend section 5240 to confer authority upon the Comptroller of the Currency to appoint additional examiners and assistants to examiners to be assigned to the office of the Comptroller of the Currency to aid in the examination and correspondence connected with the examination of national banks; the compensation of such employees to be defrayed from the fund provided for the compensation of national bank examiners generally.

To amend section 5138 to require an increase in capital of national banks commensurate with an increase in deposit liabilities.

To amend section 5222 so that the first sentence shall read " Within 30 days from the date of the vote to go into liquidation, the association shall deposit with the Treasurer of the United States lawful money of the United States to redeem all its outstanding circulation."

To amend section 5147 to require the oath of a director of a national bank to be taken before a notary public or other officer authorized to administer oaths, and to be filed with the comptroller within 30 days succeeding his election or appointment, and making any director who becomes disqualified by hypothecation of stock ineligible to reappointment during the remainder of the year.

To authorize the comptroller to institute proceedings through the Department of Justice against directors for losses sustained by banks through violations of the law.

The following additional amendments are recommended for the consideration of Congress:

Amend section 5169, relating to the issuance of authority to a national banking association to begin the business of banking, to provide that in case any national bank shall fail to begin business for a period of six months from date of issuance of the comptroller's authority to begin business, the comptroller may send an examiner to the bank who shall have authority to call a special meeting, upon due notice, of the shareholders for the purpose of adopting a resolution placing the bank in voluntary liquidation, and provide that if the shareholders fail to take such action or open the bank for business within 30 days after such notice, the comptroller may appoint a receiver for the purpose of winding up its affairs; the expense of the examination to be borne by the bank in question.

To amend section 5220 to provide that if any national bank shall have disposed of all its assets or closed its doors and shall refuse or neglect to formally place the association in voluntary liquidation within 30 days thereafter, the comptroller shall have authority to send an examiner to the bank with instructions to call a special meeting of shareholders, upon due notice, for the purpose of adopting a resolution placing the association in voluntary liquidation, and that if the shareholders shall refuse to adopt such resolution the comptroller may appoint a receiver for the purpose of winding up its affairs.

It is further recommended that this section be amended to provide that when any national banking association is placed in voluntary liquidation it shall continue to hold annual meetings of shareholders in the manner and on the date specified in the articles of association and to elect directors and appoint officers in the same manner as if it were in active operation. The law should also provide that the directors shall have charge of the liquidation of the bank and that the president or cashier shall act as executive officer in liquidating the affairs of the bank under the direction of the board of directors. It is also recommended that the law be amended to provide that every association placed in voluntary liquidation shall be required to render reports of condition in the manner provided by section 5211, United States Revised Statutes, and that in addition thereto the officers of such association shall file with the Comptroller of the Currency a report covering the receipts and disbursements during the preceding year, a copy of such report to be submitted to the stockholders at their annual meeting in January of each year. Upon the Comptroller of the Currency should be conferred authority to make an examination of any national bank in voluntary liquidation, the expense thereof to be paid by the liquidating bank. In the event of sale of the assets of a liquidating association to another bank, State or national, and the assumption of liabilities of the liquidating association, a contract shall be entered into between the directors of the associations interested, and a copy of such contract, duly signed by the officers of the associations and acknowledged before a notary public or other officer authorized to administer oaths, filed with the Comptroller of the Currency.

When the affairs of any liquidating national banking association are finally closed, uncollected assets shall be advertised for a period of 15 days in a local paper and sold to the highest bidder. All unclaimed dividends belonging to shareholders and unclaimed deposits shall be transmitted to the Comptroller of the Currency for deposit with the Treasurer of the United States in trust and carried as a special fund to be known as "liquidating account, national banking associations" and the claimants entitled to such dividends or deposits may subsequently receive the same upon furnishing to the Comptroller of the Currency satisfactory proof of the validity of their claim thereto.

To amend section 5138 relating to the required capital stock of a national banking association, to provide that with the approval of the Comptroller of the Currency a national bank with capital of not less than $50,000 may be organized in the suburbs of a city where the demand for banking capital would not warrant the organization of a bank with the capital required for the organization of a bank in the business section of the city.

To provide by law for the punishment of the offense of uttering false statements derogatory to the condition or standing of any national bank or any other banking institution which is subject to the supervision of the Comptroller of the Currency. On April 13, 1922, a bill, H. R. 11296, was introduced, referred to the Committee on the Judiciary, and ordered to be printed. The provisions of this bill meet with the approval of the department.

### NATIONAL BANK CHARTERS.

The act of February 25, 1863, authorizing the establishment of the national banking system, provided that every association formed pursuant to that act should "have succession" for the period named in the articles of association, not, however, exceeding 20 years from the passage of the act. This act was repealed and a revised banking law enacted June 3, 1864, providing, among other things, that every association "shall have succession for the period of 20 years from its organization."

Under the act of 1863 charters were issued to some 456 associations, of which 54 were organized for less than 20 years, and in consequence expired by limitation prior to July, 1882. Such of these banks as were in existence and desired to continue in business were compelled to reorganize, as it was not until July 12, 1882, that the act was passed authorizing extensions of charters of banks which had reached the close of their corporate existence. This act provided for the extension of the "period of succession" for a term of not more than 20 years from the expiration of the period named in the bank's articles of association.

To effect extension it was necessary for each association, first, to secure the written consent of shareholders owning two-thirds of the stock, the board of directors to cause such consent to be certified to the Comptroller of the Currency under seal of the association, by the president or cashier; second, to have a special examination to determine the condition of the bank, approval of the extension being contingent upon the bank's condition at that time; third, to permit dissenting shareholders to withdraw, and receive the value of their shares; fourth, to require that circulating notes issued subseqnent to extension should "bear such device as shall make them readily distinguishable" from circulating notes theretofore issued, and further require at the end of three years from extension a deposit of lawful money to provide for the redemption of all notes issued prior to extension and outstanding at the end of this three-year period.

In 1902 many national banks rounded out their second period of succession, and on April 12 of that year an act was approved authorizing, for an additional period of 20 years, the extension of the charters of all banks which had been extended under the act of 1882 in the same manner provided in the act granting the first extension.

Whatever may have been the motive actuating Congress in requiring that circulating notes issued by the banks subsequent to the extension of their charters (under the acts of 1882 and 1902) should be of designs distinguishing them from prior issues, experience developed the fact that this requirement resulted in an unnecessary and enormous expense both to the banks and to the Government—to the banks in the cost of new plates and to the Government in the cost of distinctive paper and in the printing of the notes. Between July 12, 1882, and June 30, 1922, the charters of 4,333 associations were extended under the act of 1882 and 1,512 were extended for the second period of 20 years under the act of 1902. The expense to the banks for the plates for the new designs of notes was approximately $1,000,000 and to the Government for paper, printing, etc., about $500,000.

At various times the Comptrollers of the Currency recommended the repeal of the law providing for new designs for the notes issued under these conditions, but no consideration was given to the question until it was formally brought to the attention of the Committees on Banking and Currency of the present Congress.

In his annual report to Congress in December, 1921, the Comptroller of the Currency submitted for consideration two bills. One provided for the extension of the charters, for an additional period of 20 years, of banks whose charters had been extended under both the act of 1882 and the act of 1902, and in the manner provided by the act of 1882, except that shareholders were to be accorded the option of giving their written consent or their vote to extend at a meeting called to consider the question. Provision was also made in the bill for the repeal of the law requiring new plates for the printing of notes after the extension of the charter.

The alternative bill and the one that was recommended by the comptroller granted national banking associations perpetual succession. This bill conferred upon the shareholders of any bank the privilege of withdrawing within 30 days after the termination of 20 years of its existence, that is, 20 years from the date of the last extension of its charter.

The House passed the bill granting banks perpetual succession, but the Senate amended the bill by fixing 99 years as the period of succession. In conference the Senate amendment was agreed to, the House accepted the report of the conferees, and the bill, as amended, was approved by the President on July 1, 1922. The act repeals all laws or parts of laws relating to extension for a period of 20 years, and amends the second section of section 5136, United States Revised Statutes, relating to the corporate powers of national banks, to read as follows:

SEC. 2. That all acts or parts of acts providing for the extension of the period of succession of national banking associations for twenty years are hereby repealed, and the provisions of paragraph second of section 5136, Revised Statutes, as herein amended shall apply to all national banking associations now organized and operating under any law of the United States.

As is apparent, the law automatically extended for 99 years the period of succession of all banks organized and operating on July 1, 1922, and granted to all banks organized after that date succession for 99 years from date of organization. It will also be noted that the act makes no provision for the withdrawal of shareholders as was provided in the extension acts of 1882 and 1902.

As national banks having the required capital and surplus located in States the laws of which permit the exercise of fiduciary powers by State financial institutions may be permitted to exercise such powers, and as trusts are often in perpetuity or for very long periods, it follows that banks having perpetual succession can most satisfactorily accept such trusts. This was the principal reason actuating the comptroller in urging favorable consideration of the bill for perpetual succession. In that connection the attention of Congress was called to the fact that the laws of some 23 States provide for or permit perpetual succession of banks or other corporations authorized to exercise fiduciary powers.

The comptroller has issued certificates, under the law which was adopted, to such banks as were organized and in operation on the date of the passage of the act, certifying to that fact and that their corporate existence was extended for a period of 99 years, unless the bank should be sooner dissolved by the act of its shareholders owning two-thirds of its stock, or unless its franchise should become forfeited by reason of violation of law, or unless it should be terminated by act of Congress hereafter enacted.

By reason of the action of the House of Representatives in passing the bill providing for perpetual succession, and in view of the unanimously favorable report of the Senate Committee on Banking and

Currency, it would appear that a reconsideration of the measure at a future session of Congress may.be reasonably anticipated and the banks accorded perpetual succession.

In the report of the Senate Committee on Banking and Currency upon the bill passed by the House of Representatives it was stated in part that:

The Committee on Banking and Currency, to whom was referred the bill (S. 3255) to amend section 5136, Revised Statutes of the United States, relating to corporate powers of associations, so as to provide succession thereof until dissolved, and to apply said section as so amended to all national banking associations, having considered the same, report favorably thereon with the recommendation that the bill do pass with amendments.

\*          \*          \*          \*          \*          \*

As the amendments proposed do not add or detract from the purposes of the bill, their adoption is recommended, particularly in view of the fact that the House Committee on Banking and Currency has reported favorably on the bill H. R. 9527 with these amendments, and if the changes suggested are made the two bills will be identical.

\*          \*          \*          \*          \*          \*

Within the next 18 months the charters of about 1,000 national banks will expire, and in the absence of some legislation authorizing the extension of these charters it will be necessary for these banks to close up their affairs and reorganize.

Under the act of 1863, national banks were to have succession for the period named in the articles of incorporation but not to exceed 20 years. In the revision and reenactment of the banking law in 1864 the period of succession was fixed at 20 years from the date of organization. Under the act of July 12, 1882, provision was made for the extension of bank charters for an additional period of 20 years. Again this 20-year period was renewed April 12, 1902. There is now need for further legislation to continue the corporate life of national banks.

Both the Comptroller of the Currency and the Federal Reserve Board have expressed themselves as favoring perpetual or indeterminate charters for national banks. The Federal Reserve Board, in a letter written to the chairman of the committee on March 20, 1922, pointed out that most of the States grant charters to banking institutions for periods in excess of 20 years, many States, including New York, granting charters which automatically continue forever unless revoked or forfeited or unless the corporation is dissolved; and the fact that it is possible to obtain charters from the States which are more favorable in this respect than the charters granted to national banks not only is a deterrent to organization under the provisions of the national bank act, but operates also as an inducement to existing national banks to convert into State institutions.

An analysis of the State statutes relating to the duration of charters of State banking institutions shows that duration of charters is unlimited in 21 States of the Union as follows: Arkansas, Connecticut, Florida, Illinois, Kentucky, Maine, Massachusetts, Minnesota, Nebraska, New Hampshire, New Jersey, New York, North Carolina, Ohio, Oregon, Rhode Island, South Carolina, Tennessee, Vermont, Virginia, and West Virginia. In Utah the duration of charters is limited to 100 years; Louisiana, 99 years; California, Idaho, Iowa (savings banks), Kansas, Mississippi, Missouri (savings banks), Montana, Nevada, New Mexico (trust companies), Oklahoma (trust companies), Texas, Washington, Wisconsin (banks and trust companies), and Wyoming, 50 years. The limitation in Maryland is 40 years; in Georgia and Michigan, 30 years; North Dakota (except trust companies) and Oklahoma, 25 years; Alabama, Colorado, Indiana, Iowa, Pennsylvania (commercial banks), and South Dakota, 20 years.

The Federal Reserve Board, in its letter to the committee, pointed out that the proposed legislation is particularly desirable from the standpoint of national banks exercising fiduciary powers granted to them under the provisions of section 11 (k) of the Federal reserve act. The fact that a national bank has to apply for periodical renewals of its charter seems to be a consideration which handicaps national banks in their competition with State institutions for fiduciary business. The Federal reserve act distinctly authorizes national banks, with the approval of the Federal Reserve Board, to exercise fiduciary powers, and the provision of the Federal reserve act has been upheld by a decision of the Supreme Court of the United States. There are numerous instances where national banks have surrendered their charters and have reorganized under State law. The committee is informed that many important national banks throughout the country are now considering the surrender of their charters, and as a concrete example mention may be made of the liquidation and reorganization of a large national bank in Cleveland recently, which reorganized under State law because of its inability to take over the trust and fiduciary relations which are so important and which are continuing and subsisting and might last 100 years.

Section 18 of the Federal reserve act contemplates the ultimate retirement of all national bank notes in circulation, which at one time yielded a substantial profit to the national banks issuing them. There is a question whether the national banking system will be perpetuated unless national banks are able to compete on more equal terms with banks and trust companies doing business under State laws. The reasons which existed in 1863 and 1864 for the limitation on the life of a national bank charter do not appear to exist at the present time. The national banking system is no longer an experiment. It has stood the test of nearly 60 years and has fully justified its existence.

The acts of 1882 and 1902 require that circulating notes issued to and by a bank subsequent to extension shall be of a design making them readily distinguishable from notes issued prior thereto. The law also requires that within three years from the date of extension a national bank shall deposit lawful money for the redemption of old issues then outstanding.

There seems to be no good reason for this requirement at the present time. The records show that compliance with the requirement has entailed unnecessary expense both to the Government and to the banks—to the Government in that it has been necessary to destroy all incomplete national bank circulating notes of the old issues in the vaults of the Treasury upon extension of charter. By reason of extensions of charter, liquidations, etc., it has been necessary to destroy since January 1, 1913, incomplete national bank currency of the face value of over $113,000,000, representing some 3,091,000 sheets of distinctive paper, costing for paper and printing alone $139,125

The Comptroller of the Currency has reported that during the existence of the national bank system destructions on these accounts have amounted to over $371,000,000, representing over 9,000,000 sheets of distinctive paper, the cost of the paper and printing paid by the Government amounting to nearly $413,000. The principal cost to the banks has been for the plates for the printing of currency on extension of charters, although there has been an incidental loss due to the necessary delay in engraving of plates and printing of currency and consequent deprivation of the use of the currency.

Other expenses incident to the handling, storing, and recording of bank currency to the amount hereinbefore indicated, it is estimated, have cost the Government about $400,000, a large portion of which could have been saved but for the law requiring the issuance of distinctive currency on extension of charter.

The proposed bill will make this expense unnecessary in future.

Your committee desires to call particular attention to the fact that this bill as reported gives national banks succession until "it shall be dissolved by the act of its shareholders owning two-thirds of its stock, unless its franchise shall become forfeited by reason of violation of law, or unless it shall be terminated by the provision of act of Congress hereinafter enacted." In other words, the national banks will have succession (unless dissolved by voluntary action of their own shareholders) during good behavior. The charters can be forfeited for noncompliance with or violation of the Federal reserve act (sec. 2, Federal reserve act) in a suit brought by the Comptroller of the Currency under the direction of the Federal Reserve Board, while section 5239 of the Revised Statutes of the United States provides for such forfeiture for the violation of the provisions of the national bank act in a suit brought by the Comptroller of the Currency in his own name. In view of these statutory provisions, it appears to your committee that ample protection is afforded against possible abuses by national banks of their franchises.

In addition to this, provision is made that an act of Congress hereinafter enacted may terminate the charter of a national bank.

In view of the foregoing and other facts considered in connection with the subject, it is the unanimous opinion of the committee that the early adoption of the bill here reported is to the best interests of the public, the national banks, and the Government of the United States.

## NATIONAL BANK EXAMINERS.

The following is a list of the examiners in the service on October 31, 1922:

### CHIEF EXAMINERS.

Federal reserve district—
  No. 1.—Herbert W. Scott, Boston, Mass.
  No. 2.—Daniel C. Borden, New York, N. Y.
  No. 3.—Stephen L. Newnham, Philadelphia, Pa.
  No. 4.—Thomas C. Thomas, Cleveland, Ohio.
  No. 5.—William J. Schechter, Washington, D. C.
  No. 6.—J. W. Pole, Atlanta, Ga.
  No. 7.—Fred Brown, Chicago, Ill.
  No. 8.—John S. Wood, St. Louis, Mo.
  No. 9.—Howard M. Sims, Minneapolis, Minn.
  No. 10.—Luther K. Roberts, Kansas City, Mo.
  No. 11.—Richard H. Collier, Dallas, Tex.
  No. 12.—Harry L. Machen, San Francisco, Calif.
Assigned as chief, examining division, comptroller's office:
  Henry B. Davenport, Washington, D. C.
Unassigned:
  John A. Best, care of First National Bank, Judsonia, Ark.
  Gail W. Crossen, Washington, D. C.
  Arthur D. Cutts, Washington, D. C.
  Robert D. Garrett, Washington, D. C.
  Robin M. Johnson, care of First National Bank, Hearne, Tex.
  Adelia M. Stewart, Washington, D. C.
  C. L Williams, care of Heard National Bank, Jacksonville, Fla.
  Charles F. Wilson, Washington, D. C.
Assigned to the War Finance Corporation:
  Reginald M. Hodgson, Washington, D. C.
  Oscar K. La Roque, Marion, S. C.
  Peter J. Lorang, Washington, D. C.
  Clarence F. Smith, Washington, D. C.
  Robert C. Williams, Washington, D. C.

### FIELD EXAMINERS.

#### FIRST DISTRICT.

Norwin S. Bean, Manchester, N. H.
Harold W. Black, Boston, Mass.
Wm. B. Carolan, Boston, Mass.
George M. Coffin, New Haven, Conn.
Thomas A. Cooper, Augusta, Me.
Michael J. Hurley, Montpelier, Vt.
Edward F. Parker, Boston, Mass.
Frank J. Ryan, Boston, Mass.

#### SECOND DISTRICT.

Russell T. August, Newark, N. J.
Oliver W. Birckhead, New York, N. Y.
Ralph W. Byers, Hillside Twp., Union County, N. J.
Frank H. Clement, Buffalo, N. Y.
Claud De Baun, New York, N. Y.
William H. Dillistin, New York, N. Y.
James B. Funsten, jr., New York, N. Y.
Richard W. Goodhart, New York, N. Y.
Charles S. Graham, New York, N. Y.
Thomas J. Harrington, New York, N. Y.
Walter B. Hilliard, Ithaca, N. Y.
Burdett Kelly, Kingston, N. Y.
Benton Klein, Albany, N. Y.
Edward J. Maguire, New York, N. Y.
Wm. W. Maloney, 3d, New York, N. Y.
Benjamin Marcuse, New York, N. Y.
Frank L. Norris, New York, N. Y.
Paul Partridge, New York, N. Y.
Ellis D. Robb, New York, N. Y.
Kenneth H. Rockey, New York, N. Y.
Edwin F. Rorebeck, Watertown, N. Y.
E. Willey Stearns, New York, N. Y.
Ernest H. Watson, New York, N. Y.
Cole J. Younger, New York, N. Y.

### THIRD DISTRICT.

Edward A. Allanson, Lancaster, Pa.
William B. Baker, Philadelphia, Pa.
John W. Barrett, Philadelphia, Pa.
Alfred Boysen, Wilkes-Barre, Pa.
Charles V. Brown, Philadelphia, Pa.
Charles H. Chapman, Philadelphia Pa.
Ralph H. Derr, Reading, Pa.
Robert W. Doty, Harrisburg, Pa.

Nathan S. Du Bois, Philadelphia, Pa.
Charles H. Hartman, Philadelphia, Pa.
Carl M. Sisk, Reading, Pa.
George F. Smith, Philadelphia, Pa.
Vernon G. Snyder, Sunbury, Pa.
Horace G. Whiteman, Altoona, Pa.
Robert W. Wylie, Williamsport, Pa.

### FOURTH DISTRICT.

John B. Chenault, Maysville. Ky.
Sidney B. Congdon, Pittsburgh, Pa.·
Leo M. Cutts, Pittsburgh, Pa.
Burton A. Faris, Cincinnati, Ohio.
Ernest M. Furbee, Pittsburgh, Pa.
William C. Griswold, Cleveland, Ohio.
Henry B. Hane, Cleveland, Ohio.

Edward C. Haneke, Lima, Ohio.
Herbert J. McKee, Cleveland, Ohio.
Joel S. McKee, Pittsburgh, Pa.
Robert Montgomery, Wheeling, W. Va.
Edwal F. Shively, Columbus, Ohio.
George H. Smith, West Newton, Pa.

### FIFTH DISTRICT.

Roger E. Brooks, Washington, D. C.
Thomas D. Carson, Washington, D. C.
William B. Cloe, Huntington, W. Va.
John W. Dalton, Charlotte, N. C.
Thomas H. Davis, Richmond, Va.
William P. Folger, Washington, D. C.
Thomas F. Kane, Washington, D. C.

John R. McMullan, Washington, D. C.
George M. Moore, Washington, D. C.
Paul C. Ramsdell, Washington, D. C.
John W. Snapp, Washington, D. C.
Charles A. Stewart, Washington, D. C.
Grattan H. Tucker, Washington, D. C.
Robertson D. Wood, Martinsburg, W. Va.

### SIXTH DISTRICT.

Albert A. Basham. Atlanta. Ga.
John C. Borden, Knoxville, Tenn.
Clyde J. Evans, Montgomery, Ala.
Thomas E. Fletcher, Cordele, Ga.
Headley B. Gilbert, Knoxville, Tenn.

W. Morris Lammond, New Orleans, La.
W. Waller McBryde, Birmingham, Ala.
V. Huborn Northcutt, Jacksonville, Fla.
Kenneth W. Thompson, Nashville, Tenn.
John R. Vann, Atlanta, Ga.

### SEVENTH DISTRICT.

Frederick J. Affeldt, jr., Lansing, Mich.
Garver J. Bly, Farmland, Ind.
Dan. H. Cooney, Milwaukee, Wis.
Claude O. Craig, Chicago, Ill.
William A. Culver, Peoria, Ill.
William P. Funsten, Evanston, Ill.
Winfield C. Gilmore, Decatur, Ill.
James B. Greenfield, Chicago, Ill.
Nels E. Haugen, Des Moines, Iowa.
Robert C. Houston, Marion, Ind.
Carl E. H. Johnson, Chicago, Ill.
Edward M. Joseph, Danville. Ill.
John C. McGrath, Indianapolis, Ind.

William G. Minor, Cannelton, Ind.
Earl W. Moon, Rock Island, Ill.
Bert K. Patterson, Chicago, Ill.
Fulton F. Potter, Mason City, Iowa.
Robert E. Power, Chicago, Ill.
E. Robert Robinson, Grand Rapids, Mich.
John T. Sawyer, jr., Milwaukee, Wis.
Robert K. Stuart, Sheldon, Iowa.
Harry W. Walker, Chicago, Ill.
Edward B. Wilson, Des Moines, Iowa.
Robert F. Wilson, Waterloo, Iowa.

### EIGHTH DISTRICT.

Samuel W. Dye, St. Louis, Mo.
Joseph L. Kennedy, Memphis, Tenn.
Stuart H. Mann, St. Louis, Mo.
Samuel T. Millard, St. Louis, Mo.
William M. Morgan, Louisville, Ky.

Benj. M. McPike, Boonville, Ind.
Herbert Pearson, St. Louis, Mo.
John C. Peightel, Springfield, Mo.
Carl. A. Reinholdt, St. Louis, Mo.
William R. Young, Hot Springs, Ark.

### NINTH DISTRICT.

William H. Baldridge, Billings, Mont.
Bernard E. Boldin, Minneapolis, Minn.
Thos. R. Dwyer, Minneapolis, Minn.
Charles F. Fiman, Minneapolis, Minn.
John P. Hughes, Fargo, N. Dak.
Alfred P. Leyburn, Minneapolis, Minn.
Leland L. Madland, Minneapolis, Minn.
William A. Regan, Minneapolis, Minn.

William F. Sheehan, Fargo, N. Dak.
Mervale D. Smiley, Minneapolis, Minn.
Arthur B. Smith, Minneapolis, Minn.
John H. Smith, Minneapolis, Minn.
Charles C. Storing, Sioux Falls, S. Dak.
F. D. Williams, Helena, Mont.
Laurence H. Williams, Aberdeen, S. Dak.
Irwin D. Wright, Minneapolis, Minn.

### TENTH DISTRICT.

Archie S. Allsup, Kansas City, Mo.
George E. Armstrong, Denver, Colo.
Henry C. Bergman, jr., Coffeyville, Kans.
Arthur R. Bradley, Kansas City, Mo.
Roland F. Brock, Hutchinson, Kans.
Edward L. Chapman, Kansas City, Mo.
Roy A. Cooper, Muskogee, Okla.
Warren W. Dunaway, Cheyenne, Wyo.
Charles H. Filson, Guthrie, Okla.
John O. Fredlund, Kansas City, Mo.
George W. Goodell, Denver, Colo.
Orville A. Griffey, Kansas City, Mo.

William N. Hackney, Norfolk, Nebr.
Harry N. Horner, Davis, Okla.
Leon G. Kennedy, Hobart, Okla.
Howard S. Lahman, Kansas City, Mo.
Arthur M. Mueller, Kansas City, Mo.
Dennis L. Noone, Salina, Kans.
Raymond F. Peterson, Kansas City, Mo.
William H. Reed, Kansas City, Mo.
Albert L. Ritt, Kansas City, Mo.
J. Oscar Roots, Kansas City, Mo.
Roy E. Smith, Hastings, Nebr.
Sam. F. Sullenberger, Kansas City, Mo.

### ELEVENTH DISTRICT.

John C. Alvey, Dallas, Tex.
James S. Bartee, Dallas, Tex.
Henry F. Brewer, jr., El Paso, Tex.
Jacob Embry, Houston, Tex.
William C. Evans, Amarillo, Tex.
William B. Hamilton, Brownwood, Tex.
Gilbar C. Hedrick, Dallas, Tex.
James B. Herndon, jr., Dallas, Tex.
William E. Hutt, Sherman, Tex.
Marvin J. Knight, Dallas, Tex.

Ernest Lamb, Dallas, Tex.
Stanley A. Longmoor, Dallas, Tex.
Alexander B. McCans, Dallas, Tex.
Fred S. Mansfield, Dallas, Tex.
Jesse L. Penix, Waco, Tex.
Allison D. Thompson, San Antonio, Tex.
Leslie D. Thorn, Mineola, Tex.
Earle V. K. Willson, Amarillo, Tex.
William P. Wilson, Dallas, Tex.
John K. Woods, Dallas, Tex.

### TWELFTH DISTRICT.

Christopher H. Anheier, San Francisco, Calif.
Ira I. Chorpening, Los Angeles, Calif.
Gilbert S. Coffin, Spokane, Wash.
William C. Crawley, San Francisco, Calif.
Eugene H. Gough, Seattle, Wash.
William M. Gray, Ocean Park, Calif.
Thomas E. Harris, San Francisco, Calif.
Marshall Hooper, San Francisco, Calif.
Arthur L. James, Sacramento, Calif.
Gustave W. Jorres, Los Angeles, Calif.
R. Foster Lamm, Boise, Idaho.

Joseph M. Logan, Los Angeles, Calif.
Charles S. McLean, Portland, Oreg.
Leo. H. Martin, San Francisco, Calif.
Charles T. Maxey, Portland, Oreg.
Charles C. Otto, San Francisco, Calif.
John L. Proctor, Pocatello, Idaho.
Lewis M. Sawyer, jr., Los Angeles, Calif.
Norman D. Vaughan, Fresno, Calif.
Walter J. Waldron, San Francisco, Calif.
Max C. Wilde, Portland, Oreg.
Thomas M. Williams, San Francisco, Calif.

### FOR THE TERRITORY OF HAWAII.

C. F. Sutton, Honolulu, T. H.

*Assessments on national banks to pay salaries and expenses of national bank examiners year ended October 1, 1922.*

| | |
|---|---|
| Amount on hand Nov. 1, 1921................................... | $56,009.02 |
| Receipts from Nov. 1, 1921, to Oct. 31, 1922............... | 2,159,509.99 |
| | $2,215,519.10 |
| Expenses Nov. 1, 1921, to Oct. 31, 1922................................. | 2,031,286.20 |
| Balance on hand Nov. 1, 1922................................. | 184,232.81 |

BANK OFFICERS AND EMPLOYEES CONVICTED OF CRIMINAL VIOLATIO
OF LAW DURING THE YEAR ENDED OCTOBER 31, 1922.

The following statement, prepared from data furnished by t Department of Justice, shows the names of officers or employees national banks convicted during the year ended October 31, 19' of violations of the national banking laws, with the occupation employees affected, the title and location of the bank, the offen the sentence, and the date of sentence:

Criminal cases under the national banking laws resulting in conviction during the year ended Oct. 31, 1922.

| Name of officer or employee. | Position. | Title and location of the bank. | Offense | Sentence. | Date of sentence. |
|---|---|---|---|---|---|
| | | | | | 1921 |
| William Hyde Taylor | Teller | Penns Grove National Bank, Penns Grove, N. J. | Misapplication | 3 to 6 mths | Nov. 1 |
| A. V. Co | Assistant cashier | First National Bank of Douglas County, Castle Rock, Colo | Abstraction | 5 years | Nov. 2 |
| Otto Bothin | Teller | Farmers' National Bank of Pekin, Ill. | Embezzlement and abstraction. | 1 year and 1 day | Nov. 14 |
| Ira McCormick | Employee | Hudson County National Bank, Jersey City, N. J. | False entries | ...do... | Nov. 17 |
| Ray Williams | ...do... | Stock Growers National Bank, Rawlins, Wyo. | Abstraction | 6 months | Nov. 23 |
| H. D. Johnston | Head bookkeeper | First National Bank, El Dorado, Ark. | False entries | $100 fine and costs. | Nov. 5 |
| Herbert M. Price | Paying teller | Grand Rapids National City Bank, Grand Rapids, Mich. | Embezzlement | 5 years | Dec. 5 |
| Wr C. Martz | Teller | Lebanon National Bank, Lebanon, Pa. | ...do... | 1 year and $100 fine. | Dec. 6 |
| Isac L. Price | Cashier | Peoples National Bank, Salisbury, Md. | Embezzlement and misapplication. | 18 months. | Dec. 9 |
| Markley Gilston | Discount and collection clerk | National Security Bank, Philadelphia, Pa. | Embezzlement and abstraction. | 2 months | Dec. 21 |
| Robert L. Bean | Cashier | Megunticook National Bank, Camden, Me. | Embezzlement and misapplication. | 18 mths | Dec. 27 |
| | | | | | 1922. |
| Otto L. Schriever | Bookkeeper | First National Bank of Springfield, Springfield, Ill. | Embezzlement | 2 years | Jan. 17 |
| Richard Slaughter | Teller | Huntington National Bank, Columbus, Ohio | tion and misapplication. | 5 years | Jan. 21 |
| Bert V. Whittaker | Bookkeeper | City National Bank, San Antonio, Tex. | | 1 year and 1 day | Do. |
| J. H. Grant | Cashier | Farmers National Bank, Okla. | Embezzlement | 6 years and 1 day | Jan. 25 |
| Wilton G. Rucker | ...do... | First National ank, Schwertner, Tex. | ...do... | 6 months | Jan. 31 |
| C. M. Charters | ...do... | ens National Bank, Peru, Ind. | ...do... | 4 years | Feb. 10 |
| T. S. Le Me | Collection teller | al National Bank, Shreveport, La. | ...ags... | 1 year and 1 day | Feb. 11 |
| B. L. Barker | Teller | al Bank of El Paso, El Paso, Tex. | Misapplication | 3 years | Feb. 25 |
| George A. Horal | ce president and director. | First National Bank, Fairfield, Idaho | False report to ...ller | | Feb. 25 |
| E. L. Mayo | Head paying teller | Stockmen's National al, N mpo, Idaho | Embezzlement. | 5 years | Mar. 6 |
| John Keishgens | Employee | Fort Worth al Bank, Fort Worth, Tex. Manufacturers and al Bank, Buffalo, N. Y. | ...on and ...e entries. | 1 year and 6 mths | Mar. 7 |
| T. C. Jenson | Vice al | First National Bank of Crawford, Crawford, Tex. | Embezzlement. | 2 years and $500 fine. | Mar. 13 |
| Loren Felts | Cashier | First National Bank, Harrisburg, Ill. | ...do... | 30 months. | Mar. 23 |
| James R. Wilson | ...do... | al Bank, Scotland, S. Dak. Corn Belt | Embezzlement and false entries. | 8 months. | Apr. 8 |
| Sam C. Sharp | ...do... | First National Bank, Campbell, Mo. | Embezzlement. | 1 month and $100 fine and costs. | Apr. 10 |
| Alfred H. Raymond | Teller | First National Bank, New Canaan, Conn. | ...do... | $300 fine. | Apr. 11 |
| R. R. Conroy | Cashier | First National Bank, Hammond, N. Y. | Embezzlement and false entries. | 8 years | Apr. 12 |

| Name | Office | Bank and location | Offense | Sentence | Date |
|---|---|---|---|---|---|
| M. Margaret B. Hunter | Assistant cashier | do | do | R... | Do |
| Harry C. ... | Cashier | Boone National Bank, Boone, Iowa | Misapplication and false entries. | $7,500 fine | Apr. 27 |
| John H. Harkin | do | First National Bank, Lepanto, Ark | Misapplication and false entries. | $1,000 ... | May 3 |
| F. R. Powers | | Farmers National Bank, Rome, Pa | Abstraction and misapplication. | 2 months and $500 fine. | Do. |
| C. C. Robinson | Teller | First National Bank, Globe, Ariz | Misapplication and false entries. | 4 months. | Do. |
| Dudley Humphrey | Cashier | First National Bank, Galeton, Pa. | Misapplication. | 6 months and $500 fine. | May 15 |
| R. B. ...rd | Note teller | Chatham and Phoenix National Bank, New York City, N. Y. | Abstraction and embezzlement. | $500 fine. | May 16 |
| J. J. Knodel | Paying teller | First National Bank, Arlington, N. J. | Embezzlement and false entries. | 1 day in custody of United States marshal. | May 22 |
| Samuel Rosenberger | Bookkeeper | do | do | do | May 23 |
| A. R. Suter | Assistant cashier | Peoples National Bank, Sistersville, W. Va. | Abstraction and embezzlement. | 2 years and 6 mths. | June 20 |
| ...lbon E. Cook | President | Corydon National Bank, Corydon, Ind. | Misapplication and false entries. | 3 yrs. | June 21 |
| George W. Applegate | Ke... | do | do | do | Do. |
| Ben S. Applegate | do | do | do | do | Do. |
| ...ce Wampner | Employee | Indiana National Bank of Indianapolis, Indianapolis, Ind. | Embezzlement | 18 mths. | June 23 |
| ...nes Knight | do | do | do | do | Do. |
| Naomi Cochrane | do | do | do | 1 year and 1 day. | Do. |
| ...ild P. ...er | do | do | do | 6 ...hs. | Do. |
| ...ird F. Olmstead | Cashier | First National Bank, Union Bridge, Md. | Abstraction and embezzlement. | 4½ yrs... nearrently on each of 6 ...nts. | June 30 |
| C. E. Phillips | do | Peoples National Bank, Rowlesburg, W. Va. | Embezzlement. | 6 months and $1,000 fine; to remain in jail until fine and costs are pd. | July 8 |
| O. H. Wilson | do | First National Bank, Albright, W. Va. | False entries. | do | Do. |
| ...ard Zacher | Bookkeeper | La Salle National Bank, La Salle, Ill. | Abstraction. | 1 day in custody of United States marshal | July 11 |
| S. L. Reece | President | Bannock National Bank, Pocatello, Idaho. | False entries. | 3 yrs and $5,000 fine. | July 21 |
| R. Hale | Cashier | First National Bank, Morris, Okla. | Embezzlement and false entries. | 2 years. | July 28 |
| Mark J. ... | Collection teller | First National Bank, San Francisco, Calif. | Abstraction and embezzlement. | $1,000... | Sept. 19 |

CONDITION OF NATIONAL BANKS AT DATE OF EACH CALL DURING REPORT YEAR.

During the year ended October 31, 1922, national banks were called upon to submit as of various dates, in accordance with the provisions of section 5211, United States Revised Statutes, five reports of condition. These reports show in detail the resources and liabilities of reporting banks and such other information in the form of schedules as is necessary for the information of the comptroller and, with examiners' reports of semiannual examinations, prescribed by section 5240, United States Revised Statutes, are examined to determine the true condition of each association.

The consolidated returns of reporting national banks at dates of the several calls during the year are shown in the following table:

*Abstract of reports of condition of national banks in the United States on December 31, 1921, March 10, May 5, June 30, and September 15, 1922.*

[In thousands of dollars.]

| | Dec. 31, 1921—8,169 banks. | Mar. 10, 1922—8,197 banks. | May 5, 1922—8,230 banks. | June 30, 1922—8,249 banks. | Sept. 15, 1922—8,240 banks. |
|---|---|---|---|---|---|
| **RESOURCES.** | | | | | |
| Loans and discounts [1],[2] | 10,981,783 | [2]11,282,579 | [2]11,184,116 | [2]11,248,214 | [2]11,236,025 |
| Overdrafts | 9,949 | 11,295 | 10,227 | 9,198 | 12,141 |
| Customers' liability account of acceptances. | 200,663 | 169,887 | 168,935 | 176,238 | 171,190 |
| United States Government securities owned | 1,975,898 | 2,031,564 | 2,124,691 | 2,285,459 | 2,402,492 |
| Other bonds, stocks, securities, etc | 2,081,442 | 2,086,596 | 2,162,587 | 2,277,866 | 2,289,782 |
| Banking house, furniture and fixtures | 429,929 | 440,296 | 444,368 | 452,434 | 459,020 |
| Other real estate owned | 54,368 | 57,598 | 62,531 | 64,383 | 67,789 |
| Lawful reserve with Federal reserve banks. | 1,143,259 | 1,124,707 | 1,150,885 | 1,151,605 | 1,232,104 |
| Items with Federal reserve banks in process of collection | 349,911 | 312,900 | 330,917 | 355,666 | 418,923 |
| Cash in vault | 341,811 | 336,065 | 334,504 | 326,181 | 331,951 |
| Amount due from national banks | 863,508 | 987,816 | 974,375 | 974,975 | 1,063,695 |
| Amount due from other banks, bankers, and trust companies | 228,802 | 248,578 | 244,707 | 267,050 | 299,541 |
| Exchanges for clearing house | 437,750 | 481,368 | 681,269 | 767,096 | 614,771 |
| Checks on other banks in the same place | 69,236 | 38,207 | 45,215 | 63,394 | 54,623 |
| Outside checks and other cash items | 62,209 | 41,205 | 44,053 | 64,928 | 63,112 |
| Redemption fund and due from U. S. Treasurer | 36,697 | 36,507 | 36,823 | 36,767 | 36,656 |
| Other assets | 132,921 | 163,234 | 176,445 | 184,556 | 172,284 |
| Total | 19,420,136 | [2]19,850,402 | [2]20,176,648 | [2]20,706,010 | [2]20,926,099 |
| **LIABILITIES.** | | | | | |
| Capital stock paid in | 1,282,432 | 1,289,528 | 1,296,220 | 1,307,216 | 1,307,122 |
| Surplus fund | 1,033,406 | 1,036,184 | 1,040,249 | 1,048,806 | 1,042,197 |
| Undivided profits, less expenses and taxes paid | 464,782 | 508,560 | 522,658 | 492,434 | 539,047 |
| National bank notes outstanding | 717,473 | 719,570 | 720,984 | 725,748 | 726,789 |
| Due to Federal reserve banks | 18,882 | 17,641 | 21,213 | 19,852 | 26,472 |
| Amount due to national banks | 779,783 | 962,140 | 936,399 | 916,740 | 1,031,648 |
| Amount due to other banks, bankers, and trust companies | 1,467,221 | 1,560,920 | 1,657,409 | 1,565,459 | 1,582,444 |
| Certified checks outstanding | 56,061 | 174,469 | 190,877 | 205,682 | 164,427 |
| Cashier's checks outstanding | 208,795 | 175,632 | 193,763 | 245,091 | 208,991 |
| Demand deposits | 8,606,943 | 8,446,530 | 8,707,201 | 9,152,415 | 9,270,378 |
| Time deposits (including postal savings) | 3,749,328 | 3,837,759 | 3,918,282 | 4,111,951 | 4,169,220 |
| United States deposits | 188,089 | 215,347 | 141,844 | 103,374 | 145,182 |
| Total deposits | 15,075,102 | 15,390,438 | 15,766,988 | 16,320,564 | 16,598,762 |
| United States Government securities borrowed | 66,923 | 53,722 | 46,225 | 42,475 | 38,104 |
| Bonds and securities (other than United States) borrowed | 5,740 | 6,103 | 3,058 | 2,897 | 2,990 |

[1] Includes customers' liability under letters of credit.
[2] Beginning Mar. 10, 1922, rediscounts are included in loans and discounts and totals of resources and liabilities.

*Abstract of reports of condition of national banks in the United States on December 31, 1921, March 10, May 5, June 30, and September 15, 1922*—Continued.

| | Dec. 31, 1921—8,169 banks. | Mar. 10, 1922—8,197 banks. | May 5, 1922—8,230 banks. | June 30, 1922—8,249 banks. | Sept. 15, 1922—8,240 banks. |
|---|---|---|---|---|---|
| LIABILITIES—continued. | | | | | |
| Bills payable (including all obligations representing borrowed money other than rediscounts).......................... | 496,323 | 275,089 | 248,681 | 228,481 | 181,765 |
| Notes and bills rediscounted (including acceptances of other banks and foreign bills of exchange or drafts sold with indorsement)................................... | .......... | 323,737 | 285,940 | 280,271 | 247,559 |
| Letters of credit and travelers' checks outstanding................................ | 3,951 | 4,719 | 5,030 | 8,256 | 6,639 |
| Acceptances executed for customers and to furnish dollar exchange less those purchased or discounted................... | 202,378 | 171,332 | 170,132 | 172,887 | 165,715 |
| Acceptances executed by other banks..... | 16,558 | 13,869 | 14,748 | 16,494 | 17,654 |
| Liabilities other than those stated above.. | 55,068 | 57,551 | 55,715 | 59,481 | 51,756 |
| Total²........................... | 19,420,136 | ²19,850,402 | ²20,176,648 | ²20,706,010 | ²20,926,099 |
| Liabilities for rediscounts, including those with Federal reserve banks²............ | 523,606 | (²) | (²) | (²) | (²) |

² Beginning Mar. 10, 1922, rediscounts are included in loans and discounts and total of resources and liabilities.

## CONDITION OF NATIONAL BANKS SEPTEMBER 15, 1922.

Analyses in detail with respect to the combined resources and liabilities of reporting national banks in the United States and Territories as of September 15, 1922, follow:

### RESOURCES.

#### LOANS AND DISCOUNTS.

The loans and discounts, including rediscounts, of national banks were reduced during the intervals between the dates of each call subsequent to September 6, 1921, and on September 15, 1922, amounted to $11,236,025,000. The reduction since September 6, 1921, was $446,667,000, and the reduction since date of preceding call, June 30, 1922, was $12,189,000.

The percentage of loans and discounts to aggregate deposits, September 15, 1922, was 67.69, compared with 80.23 per cent September 6, 1921.

#### OVERDRAFTS.

The amount of overdrafts reported September 15, 1922, was $12,141,000, or $2,943,000 more than reported June 30, 1922, but a reduction since September 6, 1921, of $214,000.

#### CUSTOMERS' LIABILITY ON ACCOUNT OF ACCEPTANCES.

The acceptance liability of customers of national banks on September 15, 1922, was $171,190,000, showing a decrease since June 30, 1922, of $5,048,000, and a reduction since September 6, 1921, of $31,164,000.

## UNITED STATES GOVERNMENT SECURITIES.

National-bank holdings of United States Government securities September 15, 1922, amounted to $2,402,492,000, which was the greatest amount reported at date of any call during the year, the increase since June 30, 1922, was $117,033,000 and the increase during the year amounted to $540,515,000. Approximately $736,000,000 of these securities were United States bonds deposited with Treasurer of the United States to secure national-bank circulation.

## OTHER BONDS, STOCKS, SECURITIES, ETC.

The investments of national banks September 15, 1922, in miscellaneous bonds, stocks, securities, etc., amounting to $2,289,782,000, likewise was the largest amount reported during the year, the increase since June 30, 1922, being $11,916,000, while the increase for the year was $316,033,000.

## BANK PREMISES AND OTHER REAL ESTATE OWNED.

The book value of banking houses, furniture, and fixtures owned by national banks September 15, 1922, was $459,020,000, an increase over June 30, 1922, of $6,586,000 and an increase since September 6, 1921, of $37,993,000.

The amount of other real estate owned by these banks September 15, 1922, was $67,789,000, an increase since June 30, 1922, of $3,406,000 and an increase during the year of $14,850,000. The increase in the volume of other real estate owned is apparently due to the fact that during the process of liquidation of loans and discounts, it has been necessary for these banks to acquire title to real estate as additional protection to secure debts previously contracted, in accordance with the provision of section 5137, United States Revised Statutes, as under no other conditions is a national bank permitted to own real estate other than that necessary for occupation incident to the transaction of its business. The increase in the items, banking houses, furniture, and fixtures, is due principally to the increase in the number of reporting banks during the year.

## LAWFUL RESERVE.

In accordance with the provision of section 19 of the Federal reserve act, national banks in central reserve cities, reserve cities, and country banks (banks situated elsewhere than in cities designated as central reserve or reserve cities) are required to maintain balances with Federal reserve banks in the several reserve districts equivalent to 13, 10, and 7 per cent, respectively, of demand deposits and 3 per cent, regardless of situation of the bank, of time deposits.

The lawful reserve of national banks with Federal reserve banks September 15, 1922, was $1,232,104,000, some $80,499,000 in excess of the amount reported June 30, 1922, and $202,126,000 in excess of amount reported September 6, 1921. Reference to the returns at date of each call during the year with respect to the amount of reserve required and the amount held with Federal reserve banks, published in the appendix of this report, shows excess reserve held at date of each report, the amount of excess September 15, 1922, being $96,081,000. The increase in reserve is due to substantial increases in demand and time deposits during the past year.

### CASH IN VAULT.

The tendency of national banks to carry less actual cash in vaults is noted by reference to the returns at date of each call subsequent to September 6, 1921, which show substantial reductions up to June 30, 1922, when the amount was reported at $326,181,000, compared with $331,951,000 September 15, 1922, the increase between the latter two dates being $5,770,000. The decrease in cash on hand between September 6, 1921, and September 15, 1922, was $25,847,000.

### DUE FROM BANKS AND BANKERS.

Debit balances with correspondent banks reported by national banks, including balances due from Federal reserve banks incident to items sent for collection, to the amount of $418,923,000, aggregated $1,782,159,000, an increase over the amount reported June 30, 1922, of $184,468,000 and an increase over the amount reported September 6, 1921, of $437,027,000. Of these balances the greater portion, or $1,063,695,000, was due from national banks.

### EXCHANGES FOR CLEARING HOUSE.

The amount of exchanges for clearing house was $614,771,000, a reduction since June 30, 1922, of $152,325,000, but an increase since September 6, 1921, of $146,926,000.

### ALL OTHER ASSETS.

Other miscellaneous assets, consisting of checks and cash items and redemption fund, etc., amounted to $326,675,000, a reduction of $22,970,000 since June 30, 1922, and an increase over September 6, 1921, of $15,341,000.

### LIABILITIES.

### CAPITAL STOCK, SURPLUS, AND UNDIVIDED PROFITS.

Incident to the issuance of new charters and increases in the capital of existing banks, the paid-in capital stock of national banks was increased between September 6, 1921, and September 15, 1922, from $1,276,177,000 to $1,307,122,000.

The surplus of these banks was likewise increased in the period indicated from $1,027,373,000 to $1,042,197,000, while undivided profits (less deductions incident to expenses and taxes paid), were increased from $538,784,000 to $539,047,000.

### NATIONAL BANK NOTES OUTSTANDING.

The volume of national bank notes in circulation was far in excess of any amount previously reported, with exception of the period during the latter part of 1914 and the early part of 1915, when emergency currency was issued in accordance with the provisions of the act of May 30, 1908, and amounted to $726,789,000, which was

$1,041,000 greater than the amount outstanding June 30, 1922, and $22,121,000 in excess of the amount reported September 6, 1921.

## ALL DEPOSITS.

The deposit liability of national banks September 15, 1922, was $16,598,762,000, and was greater than at the date of any previous call during the year, the increase over June 30, 1922, being $278,198,000, while the increase over September 6, 1921, was $2,037,910,000. Of the total deposits September 15, 1922, $3,013,982,000 was due to other banks and bankers and Federal reserve banks, while demand deposits, including United States deposits of $145,182,000, amounted to $9,415,560,000, and time deposits, including postal savings deposits, were $4,169,220,000. Noticeable increases are reflected in the returns during the year with respect to demand and time deposits, the latter item showing an increase at the date of each call subsequent to September 6, 1921, while demand deposits, with exception of the period between December 31, 1921, and March 10, 1922, when a reduction of $133,155,000 was registered, were substantially increased.

## BONDS AND BORROWED MONEY.

The liability of national banks for Government securities borrowed was $38,104,000, a reduction of $4,371,000 since June 30, 1922, and a reduction since September 6, 1921, of $46,743,000. Other bonds and securities were borrowed to the extent of $2,990,000, an increase over June 30, 1922, of $93,000, but a reduction since September 6, 1921, of $240,000.

Decided reductions on account of bills payable and notes and bills rediscounted are shown by the returns at date of each call subsequent to September 6, 1921. The reduction on account of bills payable during the year was $369,930,000, the amount reported September 15, 1922, being $181,765,000, or $46,716,000 less than on June 30, 1922, while notes and bills rediscounted were reduced during the year to the extent of $457,519,000, or to $247,559,000. The reduction in notes and bills rediscounted between June 30 and September 15, 1922, was $32,712,000. Of the total bills payable September 15, 1922, $103,747,000, represented liabilities to Federal reserve banks, and on the same date $182,061,000 of the total notes and bills rediscounted were with these banks.

## BANK ACCEPTANCES AND OTHER LIABILITIES.

The aggregate of acceptances executed for customers and by other banks for account of reporting banks was $183,369,000, a reduction during the year of $34,811,000, while all other liabilities, amounting to $58,395,000, show an increase over September 6, 1921, of $10,099,000.

## AGGREGATE RESOURCES AND LIABILITIES.

An analysis of the returns from the 8,240 reporting national banks, with aggregate resources and liabilities September 15, 1922, of $20,926,099,000, an increase of $1,206,919,000 during the past year, and an increase of $220,089,000 since the midsummer call of June

30 of the present year, warrants the conclusion that our national banks with resources representative of 41.50 per cent of the aggregate resources of all banks in the United States as late as June 30, 1922, constitute the keystone of American banking institutions.

The principal items of resources and liabilities of these banks September 15, 1922, the date of the last call during this report year, are shown in the following statement by States and geographical divisions:

*Principal items of resources and liabilities of national banks September 15, 1922.*

[In thousands of dollars.]

| | Number of banks. | Loans, including overdrafts. | United States securities. | Other bonds, stocks, etc. | Cash in vault. | Due from banks and other cash items. | Capital. | Surplus. | Profits. | Circulation outstanding. | Total deposits. | Bills payable. | Rediscounts. | Total assets. |
|---|---|---|---|---|---|---|---|---|---|---|---|---|---|---|
| Maine | 60 | 53,535 | 13,849 | 33,965 | 1,937 | 11,765 | 7,245 | 4,696 | 3,891 | 5,590 | 94,813 | 326 | 899 | 117,488 |
| New Hampshire | 56 | 31,326 | 11,349 | 10,170 | 1,557 | 9,397 | 5,365 | 4,291 | 2,539 | 5,073 | 47,404 | 801 | 205 | 65,740 |
| Vermont | 49 | 28,417 | 6,888 | 13,488 | 971 | 4,943 | 5,410 | 2,462 | 2,127 | 4,401 | 39,671 | 862 | 711 | 56,079 |
| Mass. | 158 | 564,560 | 99,972 | 120,045 | 13,492 | 149,620 | 63,693 | 58,198 | 31,100 | 20,292 | 810,278 | 3,008 | 16,342 | 1,035,307 |
| Rhode Island | 17 | 36,314 | 8,978 | 12,292 | 1,622 | 8,126 | 5,570 | 4,795 | 4,967 | 4,713 | 47,917 | 80 | 171 | 68,897 |
| Conn. | 64 | 125,641 | 32,369 | 29,405 | 5,410 | 31,785 | 21,607 | 15,009 | 10,761 | 12,980 | 171,880 | 1,411 | 658 | 235,150 |
| Total New England States | 404 | 859,793 | 173,405 | 219,365 | 24,989 | 215,636 | 108,890 | 89,441 | 55,385 | 53,049 | 1,211,973 | 6,488 | 18,967 | 1,578,571 |
| New York | 504 | 2,400,546 | 646,875 | 518,618 | 55,871 | 1,063,897 | 228,474 | 255,507 | 141,928 | 76,039 | 4,063,894 | 15,393 | 43,492 | 4,946,492 |
| New Jersey | 228 | 281,982 | 71,729 | 168,965 | 12,438 | 67,613 | 29,762 | 28,063 | 15,925 | 16,179 | 323,447 | 5,583 | 2,473 | 623,002 |
| Pennsylvania | 867 | 1,170,202 | 306,283 | 497,458 | 38,638 | 360,630 | 138,988 | 179,535 | 72,561 | 95,374 | 1,918,362 | 38,995 | 7,677 | 2,406,734 |
| Delaware | 18 | 9,329 | 2,460 | 5,313 | 413 | 1,800 | 1,660 | 1,942 | 775 | 1,091 | 14,142 | 273 | 203 | 20,111 |
| Maryland | 86 | 139,124 | 25,896 | 42,232 | 3,948 | 42,549 | 17,929 | 16,070 | 6,967 | 1,435 | 204,044 | 4,193 | 1,017 | 261,256 |
| District of Columbia | 15 | 62,351 | 17,160 | 13,043 | 2,990 | 17,764 | 7,677 | 5,898 | 2,341 | 5,04 | 97,435 | 1,389 | 698 | 121,563 |
| Total Eastern States | 1,718 | 4,063,534 | 1,070,403 | 1,245,629 | 114,318 | 1,554,363 | 422,490 | 487,015 | 240,497 | 203,822 | 6,821,224 | 65,826 | 55,560 | 8,439,188 |
| Virginia | 177 | 237,774 | 37,853 | 20,501 | 5,567 | 46,343 | 28,168 | 22,192 | 3,675 | 21,275 | 263,192 | 5,362 | 8,394 | 360,105 |
| West Virginia | 121 | 114,875 | 21,508 | 14,768 | 3,101 | 21,952 | 12,281 | 9,484 | 4,747 | 10,388 | 140,567 | 3,131 | 1,741 | 183,039 |
| North Carolina | 87 | 113,846 | 15,499 | 4,461 | 3,337 | 26,224 | 13,340 | 8,414 | 4,034 | 8,384 | 125,793 | 3,310 | 6,779 | 170,685 |
| South Carolina | 83 | 76,831 | 15,268 | 5,173 | 1,655 | 15,568 | 12,305 | 8,451 | 4,974 | 8,451 | 82,113 | 1,998 | 5,241 | 120,696 |
| Georgia | 99 | 111,474 | 19,756 | 3,293 | 3,294 | 29,203 | 15,230 | 12,006 | 4,974 | 11,163 | 121,518 | 1,920 | 6,154 | 173,381 |
| Florida | 61 | 64,163 | 20,603 | 12,974 | 2,719 | 20,347 | 7,695 | 4,533 | 2,608 | 5,781 | 103,227 | 454 | 1,024 | 126,076 |
| Alabama | 107 | 83,288 | 16,476 | 9,010 | 3,398 | 23,321 | 12,800 | 7,933 | 4,056 | 10,367 | 99,721 | 619 | 4,106 | 140,243 |
| Mississippi | 32 | 34,473 | 5,490 | 5,463 | 959 | 8,479 | 4,535 | 2,699 | 1,057 | 2,906 | 41,987 | 1,356 | 1,884 | 56,635 |
| Louisiana | 34 | 71,976 | 10,369 | 4,496 | 1,812 | 19,190 | 8,700 | 5,249 | 1,995 | 4,328 | 89,374 | 433 | 3,566 | 116,403 |
| Texas | 559 | 461,997 | 84,349 | 18,033 | 16,144 | 96,472 | 69,300 | 34,196 | 18,688 | 45,033 | 603,813 | 10,539 | 19,386 | 808,547 |
| Arkansas | 85 | 47,303 | 9,018 | 2,870 | 1,661 | 14,018 | 7,573 | 3,343 | 1,776 | 4,251 | 55,746 | 1,630 | 3,153 | 72,516 |
| Kentucky | 136 | 136,132 | 35,200 | 19,751 | 3,917 | 32,204 | 18,191 | 12,369 | 5,688 | 15,925 | 172,711 | 3,775 | 1,533 | 232,596 |
| Tennessee | 101 | 121,244 | 19,482 | 9,256 | 3,049 | 34,602 | 15,659 | 9,016 | 5,804 | 12,976 | 148,125 | 1,557 | 3,175 | 185,218 |
| Total Southern States | 1,682 | 1,675,376 | 314,871 | 130,049 | 50,613 | 477,813 | 225,847 | 141,765 | 65,050 | 161,248 | 2,047,770 | 36,084 | 68,256 | 2,761,140 |
| Ohio | 372 | 468,024 | 111,465 | 126,723 | 17,336 | 132,444 | 63,425 | 46,054 | 26,464 | 47,388 | 675,731 | 6,541 | 6,994 | 884,322 |
| Indiana | 251 | 207,109 | 14,948 | 43,497 | 11,645 | 53,257 | 30,712 | 13,694 | 8,782 | 27,738 | 290,590 | 5,047 | 2,606 | 384,590 |
| Illinois | 501 | 885,939 | 140,438 | 116,785 | 26,653 | 296,360 | 90,680 | 68,710 | 37,622 | 30,937 | 1,225,670 | 6,815 | 9,061 | 1,505,871 |
| Michigan | 119 | 216,726 | 43,175 | 60,568 | 6,951 | 81,509 | 23,625 | 14,911 | 9,956 | 12,813 | 363,894 | 2,009 | 1,796 | 430,516 |

| | | | | | | | | | | | | | |
|---|---|---|---|---|---|---|---|---|---|---|---|---|---|
| Wisconsin | 135 | 214,732 | 31,135 | 33,261 | 6,250 | 52,748 | 24,835 | 12,851 | 9,851 | 15,068 | 283,344 | 1,508 | 3,387 | 852,295 |
| Minnesota | 342 | 356,894 | 56,834 | 39,708 | 7,883 | 101,558 | 37,436 | 23,048 | 14,681 | 15,506 | 478,893 | 5,216 | 5,182 | 588,921 |
| Iowa | 351 | 243,406 | 35,636 | 16,194 | 6,326 | 47,980 | 26,100 | 15,365 | 6,538 | 20,228 | 274,101 | 4,431 | 14,586 | 173,747 |
| Missouri | 134 | 325,844 | 53,911 | 34,894 | 5,615 | 128,412 | 42,775 | 16,618 | 13,083 | 15,345 | 461,762 | 1,249 | 2,196 | 362,469 |
| **Total Middle Western States** | 2,225 | 2,901,674 | 531,842 | 471,620 | 88,719 | 888,268 | 339,638 | 215,061 | 126,977 | 188,073 | 4,053,985 | 32,816 | 45,811 | 5,066,737 |
| North Dakota | 123 | 67,789 | 6,903 | 5,448 | 1,616 | 10,799 | 7,245 | 3,499 | 883 | 4,569 | 71,703 | 5,755 | 4,087 | 97,877 |
| South Dakota | 133 | 66,021 | 6,681 | 3,688 | 1,316 | 12,860 | 6,215 | 3,028 | 801 | 4,222 | 73,363 | 2,759 | 4,851 | 95,272 |
| Nebraska | 182 | 152,520 | 19,494 | 8,482 | 3,550 | 54,188 | 17,245 | 10,048 | 5,324 | 9,519 | 200,008 | 1,455 | 3,229 | 247,331 |
| Kansas | 267 | 133,801 | 22,348 | 11,930 | 4,467 | 45,957 | 17,923 | 9,752 | 4,651 | 11,181 | 179,773 | 1,452 | 3,081 | 228,633 |
| Montana | 131 | 60,553 | 6,729 | 6,877 | 1,877 | 14,372 | 7,990 | 3,899 | 1,514 | 4,097 | 67,645 | 4,063 | 5,843 | 95,094 |
| Wyoming | 47 | 38,296 | 3,657 | 2,744 | 1,267 | 8,896 | 3,195 | 2,703 | 781 | 2,391 | 45,063 | 398 | 1,987 | 56,693 |
| Colorado | 144 | 125,247 | 27,654 | 26,537 | 5,627 | 54,539 | 12,375 | 9,528 | 3,799 | 6,872 | 208,487 | 1,631 | 2,856 | 245,765 |
| New Mexico | 45 | 29,210 | 3,326 | 1,296 | 659 | 5,201 | 3,210 | 1,757 | 356 | 2,291 | 30,166 | 571 | 3,013 | 41,536 |
| Oklahoma | 449 | 209,629 | 28,756 | 23,480 | 6,695 | 94,596 | 29,010 | 9,379 | 3,386 | 11,834 | 310,133 | 2,783 | 9,218 | 377,105 |
| **Total Western States** | 1,581 | 883,066 | 125,538 | 90,452 | 27,074 | 301,338 | 101,408 | 53,593 | 20,895 | 56,996 | 1,186,343 | 20,857 | 38,165 | 1,485,306 |
| Washington | 111 | 136,240 | 33,683 | 28,299 | 4,925 | 52,997 | 16,380 | 7,077 | 3,615 | 7,396 | 226,354 | 2,218 | 2,016 | 296,588 |
| Oregon | 97 | 90,917 | 24,009 | 16,272 | 3,173 | 32,118 | 12,364 | 5,814 | 2,327 | 6,037 | 142,413 | 2,473 | 1,538 | 173,855 |
| California | 281 | 539,784 | 107,476 | 78,679 | 14,770 | 196,426 | 63,455 | 36,020 | 21,876 | 40,396 | 783,829 | 6,641 | 12,504 | 985,809 |
| Idaho | 79 | 40,858 | 6,092 | 3,686 | 1,023 | 9,438 | 5,340 | 2,185 | 731 | 3,369 | 44,746 | 6,682 | 1,698 | 64,874 |
| Utah | 24 | 28,115 | 6,153 | 2,222 | 583 | 9,372 | 4,200 | 2,114 | 891 | 3,463 | 36,351 | 700 | 1,614 | 49,699 |
| Nevada | 11 | 9,082 | 2,236 | 1,039 | 388 | 2,514 | 1,460 | 598 | 243 | 1,221 | 12,199 | 195 | | 15,927 |
| Arizona | 22 | 17,665 | 3,466 | 1,294 | 906 | 4,388 | 1,900 | 984 | 414 | 1,218 | 22,290 | 785 | 1,440 | 29,165 |
| **Total Pacific States** | 625 | 862,661 | 183,205 | 131,491 | 25,768 | 307,253 | 105,099 | 54,792 | 30,097 | 63,100 | 1,270,181 | 19,694 | 20,810 | 1,585,917 |
| Alaska (nonmember banks) | 3 | 650 | 826 | 89 | 141 | 631 | 150 | 80 | 63 | 59 | 2,071 | | | 2,423 |
| Hawaii (nonmember banks) | 2 | 1,412 | 2,402 | 1,087 | 329 | 1,467 | 600 | 450 | 83 | 442 | 5,215 | | | 6,817 |
| **Total (nonmember banks)** | 5 | 2,062 | 3,228 | 1,176 | 470 | 2,098 | 730 | 530 | 146 | 501 | 7,296 | | | 9,240 |
| **Total United States** | 8,240 | 11,248,166 | 2,402,492 | 2,289,782 | 331,951 | 3,746,769 | 1,307,122 | 1,042,197 | 539,047 | 726,789 | 16,598,762 | 181,765 | 247,559 | 20,926,099 |

## NONBORROWING NATIONAL BANKS, SEPTEMBER 15, 1922.

In connection with the preceding statement, showing principal items of resources and liabilities of national banks in each State and geographical division, September 15, 1922, the following statement with respect to the principal items of resources and liabilities of non-borrowing national banks on the same date, shows that of the 8,240 banks reporting, 56.72 per cent had no outstanding obligations for borrowed money. The loans and discounts of these banks, amounting to $5,379,886,000, equaled 47.83 per cent of the total loans and discounts of all national banks. Investments in United States Government and other bonds and securities were 56.79 per cent of the total investments of national banks and amounted to $2,664,609,000. Cash in vaults of nonborrowing banks was 59.63 per cent of total cash in vault. Balances due reporting banks from other banks and bankers, including miscellaneous cash items amounting to $1,907,-669,000 represented 50.92 per cent of the total of all reporting banks, and their aggregate resources were 50.13 per cent of total resources of all reporting banks, and amounted to $10,489,400,000.

The capital, surplus, and profits of nonborrowing national banks were 50.14 per cent of the aggregate for all reporting banks, and amounted to $1,448,163,000, while the liability for $420,079,000 circulating notes outstanding was 57.80 per cent of the total amount outstanding and the total deposits of nonborrowing banks amounted to $8,569,884,000, or 51.63 per cent of total deposits of all national banks.

The fact that more than one-half of the national banks reporting were not borrowing from any source, is additional evidence of the stability of the national banking system.

On April 28, 1921, the latest prior date for which similar information with reference to borrowing and nonborrowing national banks is available for comparative purposes, the percentage of nonborrowing banks to the number of all reporting banks was 39.78. The percentage of loans and discounts of nonborrowing banks to the loans and discounts of all national banks was 26.48. The percentage of cash in vault of nonborrowing banks to the total cash in vault of all national banks was 37 and the percentage of total deposits of non-borrowing banks to total deposits of all national banks was 30.50.

Statement showing the number and the principal items of resources and liabilities of national banks in each State (including city banks) that were not borrowing money, either by bills payable or rediscounts September 15, 1922.

[In thousands of dollars.]

| | Number of banks. | Loans, discounts, and overdrafts. | United States Government securities, and other bonds, stocks, securities, etc. | Cash in vault | Due from banks and other cash items. | Aggregate resources | Capital, surplus, and profits. | Circulation outstanding. | Deposits |
|---|---|---|---|---|---|---|---|---|---|
| Maine | 44 | 35,577 | 36,319 | 1,482 | 9,179 | 84,323 | 11,955 | 4,405 | 67,899 |
| New Hampshire | 37 | 20,832 | 14,708 | 1,208 | 7,291 | 45,342 | 8,188 | 3,378 | 33,714 |
| Vermont | 31 | 13,922 | 11,977 | 615 | 3,116 | 30,314 | 5,400 | 2,576 | 22,232 |
| Massachusetts | 102 | 150,124 | 84,536 | 5,861 | 31,367 | 278,918 | 42,781 | 11,168 | 224,489 |
| Rhode Island | 13 | 30,348 | 17,730 | 1,400 | 7,121 | 57,853 | 12,185 | 3,570 | 41,606 |
| Connecticut | 47 | 94,319 | 48,762 | 4,085 | 25,361 | 180,582 | 35,312 | 9,709 | 134,903 |
| Total New England States | 274 | 345,122 | 214,032 | 14,651 | 83,435 | 677,332 | 115,821 | 34,806 | 524,843 |
| New York | 375 | 716,690 | 448,520 | 28,783 | 284,413 | 1,521,665 | 182,784 | 39,324 | 1,286,411 |
| New Jersey | 159 | 181,328 | 176,970 | 8,636 | 45,786 | 428,881 | 49,231 | 10,958 | 367,699 |
| Pennsylvania | 523 | 633,607 | 515,854 | 24,002 | 209,845 | 1,428,067 | 228,435 | 62,205 | 1,139,107 |
| Delaware | 11 | 6,651 | 4,897 | 325 | 1,599 | 13,984 | 3,212 | 775 | 9,986 |
| Maryland | 47 | 81,028 | 34,720 | 2,034 | 25,037 | 148,116 | 20,988 | 5,309 | 120,587 |
| District of Columbia | 9 | 30,511 | 13,554 | 1,426 | 9,113 | 58,192 | 7,971 | 3,366 | 46,748 |
| Total Eastern States | 1,124 | 1,649,815 | 1,194,515 | 65,206 | 576,796 | 3,598,905 | 492,621 | 121,937 | 2,970,536 |
| Virginia | 71 | 119,739 | 30,346 | 2,889 | 31,714 | 189,134 | 28,628 | 7,988 | 148,334 |
| West Virginia | 62 | 54,873 | 17,484 | 1,796 | 12,380 | 90,008 | 13,128 | 4,953 | 71,637 |
| North Carolina | 36 | 48,697 | 8,343 | 1,507 | 13,779 | 75,409 | 12,800 | 3,732 | 58,511 |
| South Carolina | 26 | 28,215 | 11,554 | 774 | 6,548 | 49,266 | 9,529 | 3,372 | 35,357 |
| Georgia | 45 | 76,873 | 16,020 | 2,393 | 23,834 | 122,648 | 21,509 | 6,972 | 94,075 |
| Florida | 39 | 54,452 | 27,874 | 2,240 | 18,164 | 107,072 | 12,525 | 4,683 | 89,505 |
| Alabama | 58 | 39,870 | 16,399 | 2,203 | 12,782 | 73,978 | 13,424 | 5,638 | 54,736 |
| Mississippi | 19 | 18,363 | 7,019 | 684 | 5,791 | 32,637 | 4,898 | 1,790 | 25,850 |
| Louisiana | 21 | 51,511 | 13,192 | 1,322 | 16,802 | 89,024 | 11,848 | 3,518 | 72,914 |
| Texas | 266 | 273,198 | 74,266 | 11,028 | 138,845 | 519,199 | 77,501 | 27,301 | 411,780 |
| Arkansas | 38 | 23,609 | 6,514 | 975 | 9,515 | 41,498 | 6,415 | 2,341 | 32,683 |
| Kentucky | 83 | 47,997 | 17,657 | 1,707 | 10,595 | 80,127 | 14,205 | 5,923 | 60,801 |
| Tennessee | 59 | 71,122 | 17,554 | 2,055 | 23,689 | 118,603 | 17,462 | 7,656 | 93,231 |
| Total Southern States | 823 | 908,519 | 264,222 | 31,573 | 324,438 | 1,588,603 | 243,872 | 85,867 | 1,249,414 |
| Ohio | 219 | 267,046 | 153,861 | 11,519 | 91,174 | 540,091 | 81,500 | 26,080 | 425,656 |
| Indiana | 171 | 108,416 | 59,773 | 6,096 | 30,514 | 213,016 | 30,386 | 15,102 | 166,554 |
| Illinois | 311 | 292,499 | 142,507 | 10,861 | 93,939 | 554,712 | 79,879 | 20,706 | 450,778 |
| Michigan | 77 | 134,682 | 73,404 | 5,074 | 54,126 | 275,894 | 31,073 | 8,838 | 235,164 |
| Wisconsin | 101 | 100,210 | 45,614 | 4,026 | 26,247 | 182,461 | 24,943 | 8,127 | 148,740 |
| Minnesota | 210 | 278,334 | 76,855 | 6,336 | 90,491 | 467,634 | 61,405 | 10,383 | 392,480 |
| Iowa | 148 | 121,272 | 32,087 | 3,909 | 33,093 | 196,281 | 25,800 | 10,243 | 159,486 |
| Missouri | 92 | 202,089 | 62,201 | 4,212 | 95,503 | 373,146 | 49,974 | 14,833 | 305,308 |
| Total Middle Western States | 1,320 | 1,504,548 | 646,302 | 52,033 | 515,087 | 2,803,235 | 384,960 | 114,312 | 2,284,166 |
| North Dakota | 49 | 22,522 | 5,550 | 766 | 5,780 | 35,981 | 4,373 | 1,621 | 29,976 |
| South Dakota | 59 | 31,409 | 6,749 | 802 | 8,796 | 49,487 | 5,277 | 2,008 | 42,179 |
| Nebraska | 105 | 108,222 | 22,711 | 2,807 | 46,099 | 186,307 | 23,729 | 6,048 | 156,235 |
| Kansas | 186 | 91,437 | 26,705 | 3,382 | 36,161 | 164,475 | 22,654 | 8,022 | 132,765 |
| Montana | 29 | 24,429 | 8,982 | 1,199 | 9,879 | 46,243 | 6,170 | 1,949 | 38,121 |
| Wyoming | 20 | 17,490 | 3,405 | 759 | 4,946 | 27,314 | 3,139 | 1,137 | 23,030 |
| Colorado | 74 | 97,176 | 49,689 | 4,856 | 49,750 | 205,197 | 19,654 | 4,683 | 181,692 |
| New Mexico | 14 | 7,542 | 1,709 | 239 | 1,654 | 11,565 | 1,438 | 648 | 9,475 |
| Oklahoma | 248 | 152,346 | 42,239 | 5,155 | 84,470 | 293,137 | 30,799 | 8,097 | 253,693 |
| Total Western States | 784 | 552,573 | 167,739 | 19,965 | 247,535 | 1,019,706 | 117,233 | 34,213 | 867,166 |

14263—FI 1922——46

*Statement showing the number and the principal items of resources and liabilities of national banks in each State (including city banks) that were not borrowing money, either by bills payable or rediscounts September 15, 1922—Continued.*

| | Number of banks. | Loans, discounts, and overdrafts | United States Government securities, and other bonds, stocks, securities, etc. | Cash in vault. | Due from banks and other cash items. | Aggregate resources. | Capital, surplus, and profits. | Circulation outstanding. | Deposits. |
|---|---|---|---|---|---|---|---|---|---|
| Washington | 63 | 97,119 | 49,905 | 3,680 | 42,870 | 200,797 | 19,331 | 5,509 | 174,737 |
| Oregon | 61 | 57,849 | 31,885 | 2,074 | 24,231 | 121,400 | 13,327 | 4,203 | 103,306 |
| California | 163 | 224,662 | 79,400 | 6,875 | 77,788 | 402,720 | 50,517 | 14,436 | 334,489 |
| Idaho | 24 | 16,011 | 5,364 | 485 | 5,501 | 28,424 | 3,249 | 1,450 | 23,623 |
| Utah | 9 | 10,198 | 2,726 | 245 | 3,946 | 18,133 | 3,031 | 1,472 | 13,598 |
| Nevada | 9 | 6,583 | 3,084 | 319 | 2,210 | 12,814 | 1,891 | 1,108 | 9,804 |
| Arizona | 6 | 4,825 | 1,031 | 371 | 1,734 | 8,091 | 884 | 265 | 6,914 |
| Total Pacific States | 335 | 417,247 | 173,395 | 14,049 | 158,280 | 792,379 | 92,230 | 28,443 | 666,471 |
| Alaska (nonmember banks) | 3 | 650 | 915 | 141 | 631 | 2,423 | 293 | 59 | 2,071 |
| Hawaii (nonmember banks) | 2 | 1,412 | 3,489 | 329 | 1,467 | 6,817 | 1,133 | 442 | 5,215 |
| Total (nonmember banks) | 5 | 2,062 | 4,404 | 470 | 2,098 | 9,240 | 1,426 | 501 | 7,286 |
| Total United States | 4,674 | 5,379,886 | 2,664,609 | 197,947 | 1,907,669 | 10,489,400 | 1,448,163 | 420,079 | 8,509,884 |
| Total principal items, all national banks | 8,240 | 11,248,166 | 4,692,274 | 331,951 | 3,746,769 | 20,926,099 | 2,888,366 | 726,789 | 16,598,762 |
| Percentage of principal items of nonborrowing national banks to total all banks | 56.72 | 47.83 | 56.79 | 59.63 | 50.92 | 50.13 | 50.14 | 57.80 | 51.63 |

## BORROWINGS OF NATIONAL BANKS ON ACCOUNT OF BILLS PAYABLE AND REDISCOUNTS.

On September 15, 1922, the total borrowings of national banks on account of bills payable and incident to the rediscount of notes and bills, amounted to $429,324,000. compared with $1,019,929,000, December 31, 1921, the date of the first call during the year covered by this report.

The liquidation of liabilities on account of bills payable and rediscounts of national banks, indicated by the returns at date of each call during the report year, shows that our national banks are rapidly getting back to normal condition, and are very largely able to meet the demands from their customers without the necessity of resorting to borrowing.

The following statement shows the amount of bills payable and rediscounts of national banks in each of the 12 Federal reserve districts at date of each call since September 6, 1921:

*Total borrowings of national banks on account of bills payable and rediscounts in each Federal reserve district at date of each call during year ended September 15, 1922.*

[In thousands of dollars.]

| | District No. 1. | District No. 2. | District No. 3. | District No. 4. | District No 5. | District No. 6. | District No. 7. |
|---|---|---|---|---|---|---|---|
| **Dec. 31, 1921:** | | | | | | | |
| Bills payable................. | 16,563 | 141,036 | 61,436 | 34,416 | 49,415 | 32,517 | 43,663 |
| Rediscounts................. | 31,381 | 51,660 | 21,663 | 32,465 | 50,648 | 42,558 | 97,888 |
| Total.................... | 47,944 | 192,696 | 83,099 | 66,881 | 100,063 | 75,075 | 141,551 |
| **Mar. 10. 1922.** | | | | | | | |
| Bills payable................. | 11,825 | 32,913 | 45,231 | 19,525 | 38,675 | 15,176 | 25,423 |
| Rediscounts................. | 19,650 | 44,603 | 14,229 | 17,654 | 38,377 | 25,967 | 41,217 |
| Total.................... | 31,475 | 77,516 | 59,460 | 37,179 | 77,052 | 41,143 | 66,640 |
| **May 5, 1922:** | | | | | | | |
| Bills payable................. | 9,420 | 45,176 | 39,731 | 17,239 | 29,550 | 9,009 | 23,728 |
| Rediscounts................. | 16,846 | 41,994 | 10,628 | 16,484 | 34,325 | 23,757 | 39,316 |
| Total.................... | 26,266 | 87,170 | 50,359 | 33,723 | 63,875 | 32,766 | 63,044 |
| **June 30, 1922:** | | | | | | | |
| Bills payable................. | 11,168 | 42,399 | 37,972 | 22,657 | 21,705 | 6,464 | 15,467 |
| Rediscounts................. | 27,642 | 47,395 | 9,031 | 12,622 | 26,467 | 19,954 | 38,064 |
| Total.................... | 38,810 | 89,794 | 47,003 | 35,279 | 48,172 | 26,418 | 53,531 |
| **Sept. 15, 1922:** | | | | | | | |
| Bills payable................. | 6,488 | 18,886 | 34,763 | 15,193 | 19,174 | 4,890 | 15,886 |
| Rediscounts................. | 18,957 | 45,615 | 6,334 | 9,936 | 23,870 | 19,456 | 29,079 |
| Total.................... | 25,445 | 64,501 | 41,097 | 25,129 | 43,044 | 24,346 | 44,965 |

| | District No. 8. | District No. 9. | District No. 10. | District No. 11. | District No. 12. | Total. |
|---|---|---|---|---|---|---|
| **Dec. 31, 1921:** | | | | | | |
| Bills payable..................... | 17,102 | 22,305 | 26,791 | 21,822 | 29,257 | 496,323 |
| Rediscounts..................... | 24,903 | 39,376 | 54,797 | 34,942 | 41,325 | 523,606 |
| Total........................... | 42,005 | 61,681 | 81,588 | 56,764 | 70,582 | 1,019,929 |
| **Mar. 10, 1922:** | | | | | | |
| Bills payable..................... | 10,358 | 18,906 | 15,513 | 13,325 | 28,219 | 275,089 |
| Rediscounts..................... | 12,814 | 24,662 | 30,893 | 26,475 | 27,196 | 323,737 |
| Total........................... | 23,172 | 43,568 | 46,406 | 39,800 | 55,415 | 598,826 |
| **May 5, 1922** | | | | | | |
| Bills payable..................... | 9,555 | 18,784 | 12,646 | 11,821 | 22,022 | 248,681 |
| Rediscounts..................... | 7,444 | 22,116 | 25,327 | 25,168 | 22,535 | 285,940 |
| Total........................... | 16,999 | 40,900 | 37,973 | 36,989 | 44,557 | 534,621 |
| **June 30, 1922** | | | | | | |
| Bills payable..................... | 9,877 | 19,410 | 9,707 | 9,864 | 21,791 | 228,481 |
| Rediscounts..................... | 6,390 | 22,440 | 19,881 | 26,103 | 24,282 | 280,271 |
| Total........................... | 16,267 | 41,850 | 29,588 | 35,967 | 46,073 | 508,752 |
| **Sept. 15, 1922:** | | | | | | |
| Bills payable..................... | 8,316 | 18,749 | 8,022 | 11,813 | 19,585 | 181,765 |
| Rediscounts..................... | 8,466 | 20,783 | 17,963 | 26,998 | 20,102 | 247,559 |
| Total........................... | 16,782 | 39,532 | 25,985 | 38,811 | 39,687 | 429,324 |

CLASSIFICATION OF LOANS AND DISCOUNTS OF NATIONAL BANKS, IN
CITIES AND STATES, JUNE 30, 1922.

Of the total loans and discounts of reporting national banks June 30, 1922, amounting to $11,248,214,000, approximately 50 per cent, or $5,818,207,000 were made on time paper with one or more individual or firm names not secured by collateral. The next largest amount in the classification of loans and discounts was on time paper, secured by stocks and bonds, aggregating $1,499,092,000, while loans on demand secured by stocks and bonds amounted to $1,408,369,000. Loans on other time paper, secured by personal securities, including merchandise and warehouse receipts, etc., amounted to $1,112,434,000.

A classification of the loans and discounts of national banks in central reserve and reserve cities and elsewhere in each State June 30, 1922, is shown in the following statement:

Loans and discounts by national banks, June 30, 1922 (including all loans and discounts on which officers and directors are liable, all loans and discounts rediscounted or hypothecated for bills payable, and acceptances of other banks and foreign bills of exchange or drafts sold with indorsement).

[In thousands of dollars.]

| Cities, States, and Territories. | On demand — Paper with one or more individual or firm names (not secured by collateral). | On demand — Secured by stocks and bonds. | On demand — Secured by other personal securities, including merchandise, warehouse receipts, etc. | On time — Paper with one or more individual or firm names (not secured by collateral). | On time — Secured by stocks and bonds. | On time — Secured by other personal securities, including merchandise, warehouse receipts, etc. | Secured by improved real estate under authority of sec. 24, Federal reserve act, as amended — Farm lands. | Other real estate. | Secured by real estate mortgages... 1. For debts previously contracted (sec. 5137, R. S. U. S.) — Farm lands. | Other real estate. | 2. All other real estate loans — Farm lands. | Other real estate. | Acceptances of other banks discounted. | Acceptances of reporting banks purchased or discounted. | Customers' liability on account of drafts paid under letters of credit. | Total. |
|---|---|---|---|---|---|---|---|---|---|---|---|---|---|---|---|---|
| **CENTRAL RESERVE CITIES.** | | | | | | | | | | | | | | | | |
| New York | 52,635 | 488,014 | 58,280 | 929,342 | 366,111 | 95,994 | | | 121 | 966 | | 793 | 41,024 | 25,856 | 1,248 | 2,062,213 |
| Chicago | 42,764 | 92,570 | 33,544 | 242,614 | 63,551 | 54,779 | | | | 251 | | | 730 | 337 | 38 | 531,599 |
| St. Louis | 12,736 | 26,375 | 6,702 | 66,400 | 29,321 | 15,717 | | | 207 | 61 | 83 | 2,120 | 1,036 | 481 | 14 | 161,253 |
| Total | 108,135 | 606,959 | 98,476 | 1,238,356 | 461,283 | 166,490 | | | 328 | 1,278 | 83 | 2,913 | 42,790 | 26,674 | 1,300 | 2,755,065 |
| **ALL OTHER RESERVE CITIES.** | | | | | | | | | | | | | | | | |
| Boston | 26,754 | 48,217 | 10,807 | 203,297 | 49,509 | 94 | | 286 | | 178 | | 97 | 13,987 | 446 | 555 | 359,037 |
| Albany | 2,089 | 16,552 | 1,099 | 17,504 | 2,938 | 65 | | 51 | | 69 | | | | | | 40,097 |
| Brooklyn and Bronx | 204 | 4,960 | 305 | 20,197 | 2,919 | 481 | | 4 | | 79 | | 5 | | 24 | | 29,049 |
| Buffalo | 2,255 | 12,348 | 267 | 17,192 | 1,919 | 15 | | 109 | | 326 | 2 | 117 | | | | 34,562 |
| Philadelphia | 19,467 | 79,872 | 10,237 | 220,109 | 46,988 | 9,301 | | 268 | | 1,675 | | 41 | 1,452 | 583 | 525 | 390,084 |
| Pittsburgh | 12,012 | 56,524 | 1,944 | 86,210 | 21,652 | 1,550 | | 436 | 5 | 347 | | 12 | 14 | 333 | 9 | 181,127 |
| Baltimore | 3,514 | 19,455 | 1,533 | 60,854 | 6,074 | 1,121 | 48 | 137 | | 175 | | 200 | 69 | 101 | 517 | 96,952 |
|  | 2,472 | 13,455 | 1,623 | 20,971 | 6,695 | 4,908 | 137 | 465 | 25 | 323 | | 4 | | | | 58,019 |
| Richmond | 2,694 | 3,574 | 1,281 | 44,082 | 10,394 | 5,898 | 14 | 155 | | 185 | | | | | | 68,094 |
| Charleston | 489 | 3,695 | 1,727 | 26,736 | 1,908 | 1,418 | 3 | 12 | | 504 | | | | 93 | | 11,222 |
| Atlanta | 1,510 | 5,018 | 1,549 | 5,692 | 6,842 | 5,315 | 75 | | 251 | 185 | | | | | | 47,800 |
| Savannah | 36 | 7 | 18 | 1,090 | 28 | 47 | | 5 | | 569 | | | | | | 1,231 |
| Jacksonville | 622 | 2,226 | 868 | 12,465 | 4,827 | 4,557 | 1 | 117 | | 50 | | | | | | 26,260 |
| Birmingham | 138 | 73 | 567 | 16,933 | 1,587 | 1,571 | 192 | 97 | 3 | 8 | | | | | | 21,211 |
| New Orleans | 1,975 | 4,197 | 2,476 | 11,934 | 1,075 | 1,129 | | 9 | | | | | 553 | 46 | | 23,402 |
| Dallas | 681 | 9,813 | 1,413 | 23,085 | 8,038 | 9,179 | 22 | 88 | 87 | 571 | 138 | 168 | 836 | 250 | | 54,479 |

Loans and discounts by national banks, June 30, 1922 (including all loans and discounts on which officers and directors are liable, all loans and discounts rediscounted or hypothecated for bills payable, and acceptances of other banks and foreign bills of exchange or drafts sold with indorsement)—Continued.

| Cities, States, and Territories. | On demand. | | | On time. | | | Secured by improved real estate under authority of sec. 24, Federal reserve act, as amended. | | Secured by real estate mortgages or other liens on realty not in accordance with sec. 24, Federal reserve act, as amended. | | | | Acceptances of other banks discounted. | Acceptances of reporting banks purchased or discounted. | Customers' liability on account of drafts paid under letters of credit. | Total. |
|---|---|---|---|---|---|---|---|---|---|---|---|---|---|---|---|---|
| | Paper with one or more individual or firm names (not secured by col.). | Secured by stocks and bonds. | Secured by other personal securities, including merchandise, warehouse receipts, etc. | Paper with one or more individual or firm names (not secured by collateral). | Secured by stocks and bonds. | Secured by other personal securities, including merchandise, warehouse receipts, etc. | Farm lands. | Other real estate. | 1. For debts previously contracted (sec. 5137, R. S. U. S.). | | 2. All other real estate loans. | | | | | |
| | | | | | | | | | Farm lands. | Other real estate. | Farm lands. | Other real estate. | | | | |
| El Paso | 471 | 80 | 49 | 12,989 | 1,541 | 3,720 | 66 | 2 | 186 | 46 | 156 | 128 | 127 | 55 | | 19,431 |
| Fort ⬛ | 815 | 1,625 | 614 | 12,983 | 4,560 | 6,042 | 49 | 85 | 156 | 740 | | 8 | 216 | | | 27,859 |
| ⬛ton | 242 | 1,833 | 1,117 | 1,598 | 401 | 314 | 9 | | 6 | 6 | | 44 | 124 | | 3 | 5,842 |
| Houston | 1,253 | 4,556 | 1,931 | 25,864 | 12,370 | 9,402 | 99 | 76 | 281 | 450 | 35 | 136 | | | | 56,577 |
| San ⬛io | 1,004 | 59 | 216 | 12,174 | 2,692 | 5,497 | 1 | 7 | 549 | 568 | 9 | | | 200 | | 22,444 |
| ⬛a | | 571 | 1,082 | 5,272 | 97 | 1,238 | | 5 | 413 | 143 | | | | | | 10,876 |
| ⬛lle Rock | 71 | | 151 | 2,569 | 377 | 837 | 37 | 23 | | | | | | | | 4,065 |
| ⬛ville | 1,391 | 4,950 | 530 | 26,037 | 8,141 | 4,270 | | 19 | | 88 | | | 28 | | 3 | 46,457 |
| Chattanooga | 290 | 135 | 28 | 12,163 | 5,337 | 1,545 | 43 | 55 | 71 | 215 | | 5 | 25 | | | 19,907 |
| Memphis | 127 | 28 | 1,061 | 4,917 | 5,238 | 1,739 | 10 | 11 | 393 | 178 | | | | | | 10,075 |
| Nashville | 552 | 346 | 356 | 17,039 | 4,881 | 3,441 | 66 | 40 | 174 | 215 | | | | | | 28,209 |
| ⬛t | 4,567 | 1,416 | 1,425 | 32,815 | 15,644 | 3,672 | 6 | 148 | | 2 | | 763 | 421 | 5 | | 74,495 |
| ⬛nd | 3,806 | 13,215 | 1,016 | 22,478 | 15,537 | 6,672 | 10 | 3,752 | 7 | 396 | | | | | | 48,701 |
| Columbus | 2,841 | 9,286 | 178 | 18,853 | 9,099 | 1,014 | 9 | 39 | 303 | 71 | | | | | | 41,587 |
| Toledo | | 7,790 | 202 | 18,455 | 8,577 | 1,811 | 23 | 234 | 12 | 113 | | | 52 | 10 | | 20,472 |
| Indianapolis | 862 | 6,425 | 1,149 | 27,155 | 3,122 | 45 | 45 | 51 | 6 | 19 | | | 48 | | | 46,407 |
| Chicago | 1,586 | 1,675 | 350 | 11,160 | 8,577 | 4,730 | | 1 | 79 | 134 | | 2 | | 50 | | 21,711 |
| Peoria | 666 | 1,456 | 79 | 7,739 | 6,298 | 1,510 | 93 | 26 | | 216 | 7 | 44 | | | | 17,136 |
| Detroit | 317 | 2,566 | 1,421 | 46,477 | 27,161 | 3,288 | 46 | 1,652 | | 93 | | 298 | 1,120 | | | 98,462 |
| Grand Rapids | 480 | 2,341 | 1,521 | 10,845 | 8,708 | 4,719 | 40 | 146 | 198 | 24 | | | | | 2 | 17,900 |
| Milwaukee | 8,770 | 6,165 | 1,521 | 45,530 | 7,827 | 7,517 | 587 | 17 | | 285 | | | 492 | 121 | | 78,297 |
| Minneapolis | 6,538 | 8,950 | 783 | 43,890 | 7,183 | 24,202 | 370 | | 49 | | | | | | | 100,538 |
| St. Paul | 1,691 | 7,892 | 95 | 27,042 | 4,649 | 12,096 | 717 | | 51 | 18 | 23 | | | | | 57,004 |
| ⬛dar Rapids | | | 873 | 4,332 | 3,505 | 1,304 | | 17 | 143 | 238 | | | | | | 11,999 |
| Des ⬛ | 1,437 | 7,602 | 57 | 8,719 | 722 | 4,761 | 66 | 3 | | 10 | | | | | | 23,021 |
| Dubuque | 1,299 | 1,411 | | 1,255 | | 612 | | 113 | | | | | | | | 3,299 |

| | | | | | | | | | | | | | | | | Total |
|---|---|---|---|---|---|---|---|---|---|---|---|---|---|---|---|---|
| Sioux City, Mo | 749 | 298 | 422 | 9,963 | 1,680 | 4,390 | 112 | | 564 | 339 | | | | | | 18,537 |
| Kansas City, Mo | 3,961 | 2,464 | 6,907 | 27,599 | 12,073 | 32,333 | 244 | 59 | 909 | 256 | 3 | | | 5 | | 87,203 |
| St. Joseph | 750 | 238 | 445 | 10,836 | 1,461 | 1,533 | 72 | | | | | | | | | 15,340 |
| Lincoln | 158 | 132 | 233 | 6,482 | 2,223 | 3,366 | | | | | | | | | | 12,837 |
| Omaha | 2,162 | 3,983 | 2,088 | 27,411 | 7,105 | 21,820 | 518 | 25 | 135 | 111 | 17 | 5 | | | | 66,840 |
| Kansas City, Kans | 54 | 98 | 54 | 1,679 | 708 | 2,904 | 66 | 16 | | 16 | 186 | | | | | 5,731 |
| Topeka | 281 | 70 | 33 | 3,091 | 988 | 322 | 36 | 8 | 1,053 | 14 | | | | | | 4,890 |
| Helena | 123 | 1,093 | 715 | 6,027 | 227 | 8,685 | 29 | 20 | 46 | 13 | | | | 11 | | 17,528 |
| Denver | 301 | 127 | 226 | 2,660 | 227 | 334 | 61 | | 17 | 10 | | 114 | | | | 3,946 |
| Pueblo | 375 | 3,745 | 639 | 18,199 | 13,357 | 18,197 | 618 | 363 | 489 | 270 | 33 | | | | | 56,450 |
| | 23 | | | 509 | 1,078 | 1,190 | | | 21 | 6 | 3 | 96 | | | | 4,828 |
| Oklahoma City | 239 | 143 | 228 | 3,818 | 1,477 | 2,826 | 261 | 44 | 114 | 33 | | 57 | | 36 | | 9,308 |
| Muskogee | 869 | 913 | 511 | 10,172 | 5,564 | 6,687 | 53 | 38 | 290 | 201 | 2 | | | 1 | | 27,393 |
| Tulsa | 1,355 | 925 | 493 | 20,689 | 9,597 | 5,215 | 98 | 364 | 411 | 1,049 | | | | | 1 | 40,165 |
| Seattle | 2,651 | 5,425 | 3,456 | 26,092 | 3,436 | 6,193 | 29 | 518 | 195 | | 11 | 28 | 218 | | | 52,394 |
| Spokane | 212 | 42 | 92 | 15,198 | 3,294 | 3,697 | 33 | | 348 | 284 | | 50 | 410 | | | 23,813 |
| Tacoma | 421 | 2,171 | 446 | 3,041 | 256 | 1,256 | 4 | | | 138 | | 368 | | | | 9,139 |
| Portland | 402 | 5,505 | 2,130 | 26,624 | 5,372 | 7,253 | 30 | 141 | 210 | 1,268 | | | 544 | 509 | 6 | 49,853 |
| Los Angeles | 4,890 | 7,102 | 3,338 | 73,703 | 21,673 | 9,839 | 23 | 6 | 1,112 | 1,138 | | | 1,203 | 184 | 37 | 124,398 |
| Oakland | 3,200 | 2,479 | 2,137 | 7,794 | 4,262 | 313 | 281 | 59 | 337 | 375 | 11 | 28 | 112 | | | 17,296 |
| San Francisco | 22,727 | 31,757 | 5,281 | 99,931 | 23,875 | 16,731 | 17 | 17 | 351 | 696 | | | 2,955 | 384 | 48 | 204,785 |
| Ogden | 98 | 150 | 63 | 2,831 | 1,467 | 763 | | 46 | 191 | 112 | | | | | | 5,712 |
| Salt Lake City | 1,189 | 1,561 | 705 | 6,586 | 3,020 | 3,053 | | | 352 | 75 | | 3 | | | | 16,587 |
| Total all other reserve cities | 169,824 | 438,640 | 93,052 | 1,660,593 | 461,143 | 322,168 | 5,477 | 10,833 | 10,581 | 16,944 | 625 | 2,800 | 25,056 | 3,497 | 1,706 | 3,222,921 |
| Total all reserve cities | 277,959 | 1,045,599 | 191,508 | 2,898,949 | 922,426 | 488,658 | 5,477 | 10,835 | 10,909 | 18,222 | 708 | 5,713 | 67,846 | 30,171 | 3,006 | 5,977,986 |
| COUNTRY BANKS. | | | | | | | | | | | | | | | | |
| Maine | 5,664 | 7,470 | 597 | 29,653 | 6,603 | 1,749 | 390 | 641 | 99 | 617 | 19 | 55 | 17 | 31 | | 53,637 |
| New Hampshire | 4,961 | 7,105 | 691 | 13,810 | 3,195 | 704 | 126 | 138 | 35 | 194 | 9 | 57 | | | | 31,025 |
| Vermont | 4,522 | 2,264 | 706 | 14,918 | 3,043 | 1,404 | 670 | 369 | 48 | 254 | 33 | 6 | 28 | 221 | 2 | 28,265 |
| Rhode Island | 10,157 | 20,591 | 5,913 | 132,445 | 42,760 | 5,278 | 174 | 16 | 82 | 1,087 | | 754 | 1,319 | | | 222,906 |
| Connecticut | 10,706 | 19,906 | 1,338 | 24,656 | 5,568 | 1,109 | | 16 | 20 | 22 | | | 30 | | | 38,209 |
| | | | 1,192 | 65,591 | 20,407 | 1,989 | 145 | 1,316 | 215 | 1,197 | | 338 | 467 | | | 123,460 |
| Total New England States | 37,062 | 59,764 | 10,437 | 281,103 | 81,576 | 12,233 | 1,505 | 4,575 | 499 | 3,371 | 61 | 1,210 | 1,861 | 252 | 2 | 495,511 |
| New York | 34,196 | 47,096 | 4,087 | 232,012 | 39,890 | 9,642 | 1,633 | 3,623 | 1,212 | 4,209 | 364 | 789 | 2,430 | 64 | | 381,187 |
| New Jersey | 23,252 | 50,181 | 1,934 | 158,909 | 24,186 | 2,145 | 391 | 391 | 486 | 2,058 | 70 | 1,279 | 547 | 34 | | 272,614 |
| Pennsylvania | 72,857 | 89,303 | 4,073 | 302,355 | 81,636 | 6,694 | 2,516 | 13,543 | 615 | 3,405 | 305 | 1,148 | 589 | 136 | 11 | 578,755 |
| Delaware | 1,267 | 2,241 | 127 | 5,230 | 638 | 74 | 243 | 82 | 67 | 53 | 5 | 44 | | | | 10,011 |
| Maryland | 5,702 | 4,177 | 363 | 23,831 | 5,666 | 1,590 | 984 | 796 | 269 | 154 | 234 | 142 | 11 | | | 45,919 |
| Total Eastern States | 137,184 | 192,968 | 10,584 | 724,337 | 151,686 | 20,055 | 5,767 | 25,175 | 2,649 | 9,579 | 978 | 3,402 | 3,577 | 234 | 11 | 1,288,486 |

Loans and discounts by national banks, June 30, 1922 (including all loans and discounts on which officers and directors are liable, all loans and discounts rediscounted or hypothecated for bills payable, and acceptances of other banks and foreign bills of exchange or drafts sold with indorsement)—Continued.

| Cities, States, and Territories. | On demand — Paper with one or more individual or firm names (not secured by collateral). | On demand — Secured by stocks and bonds. | On demand — Secured by other personal securities, including merchandise, warehouse receipts, etc. | On time — Paper with one or more individual or firm names (not secured by collateral). | On time — Secured by stocks and bonds. | On time — Secured by other personal securities, including merchandise, warehouse receipts, etc. | Secured by improved real estate under authority of sec. 24, Federal reserve act, as amended — Farm lands. | Secured by improved real estate under authority of sec. 24, Federal reserve act, as amended — Other real estate. | Secured by real estate mortgages or other liens on realty not in accordance with sec. 24, Federal reserve act, as amended. 1. For debts previously contracted (sec. 5137, R. S. U. S.) — Farm lands. | 1. For debts previously contracted — Other real estate. | 2. All other real estate loans — Farm lands. | 2. All other real estate loans — Other real estate. | Acceptances of other banks discounted. | Acceptances of reporting banks purchased or discounted. | Customers' liability on account of drafts paid under letters of credit. | Total. |
|---|---|---|---|---|---|---|---|---|---|---|---|---|---|---|---|---|
| **COUNTRY BANKS—contd.** | | | | | | | | | | | | | | | | |
| Virginia | 5,261 | 3,273 | 1,689 | 116,822 | 30,188 | 10,261 | 2,516 | 2,819 | 770 | 1,006 | 32 | 246 | 18 | | | 174,973 |
| West Virginia | 4,110 | 6,776 | 1,189 | 69,544 | 27,324 | 2,109 | 541 | 2,080 | 110 | 785 | 21 | 203 | | 5 | | 114,765 |
| North Carolina | 1,842 | 1,166 | 879 | 72,094 | 19,963 | 11,163 | 1,555 | 1,149 | 900 | 683 | 8 | 115 | 56 | | | 110,820 |
| South Carolina | 1,238 | 894 | 974 | 28,365 | 10,116 | 19,676 | 1,487 | 537 | 835 | 539 | 99 | 81 | 20 | | | 64,897 |
| Georgia | 1,875 | 700 | 2,040 | 33,003 | 5,293 | 10,894 | 1,709 | 641 | 2,951 | 1,234 | 113 | 115 | | 63 | 9 | 64,660 |
| Florida | 1,015 | 542 | 527 | 24,469 | 4,553 | 5,865 | 720 | 916 | 334 | 423 | 59 | 273 | 28 | 3 | 10 | 39,737 |
| Alabama | 1,711 | 1,882 | 2,531 | 27,210 | 4,825 | 16,317 | 1,364 | 745 | 1,811 | 752 | 31 | 71 | | 11 | | 59,261 |
| Mississippi | 490 | 410 | 887 | 16,857 | 3,394 | 7,227 | 669 | 424 | 912 | 403 | 366 | 56 | 97 | | | 32,207 |
| Louisiana | 859 | 592 | 1,676 | 28,394 | 5,152 | 7,054 | 720 | 392 | 1,273 | 386 | 432 | 345 | 1 | | | 46,557 |
| Texas | 9,797 | 8,243 | 6,717 | 105,505 | 13,436 | 79,671 | 2,277 | 1,064 | 8,737 | 3,697 | 19 | 49 | 439 | 205 | 13 | 240,555 |
| Arkansas | 684 | 90 | 1,161 | 22,660 | 3,364 | 10,412 | 1,237 | 422 | 1,158 | 422 | 101 | 87 | | 9 | | 41,703 |
| Kentucky | 5,478 | 4,030 | 577 | 58,583 | 12,651 | 5,267 | 2,697 | 825 | 1,209 | 459 | 44 | 122 | | 138 | | 90,937 |
| Tennessee | 1,813 | 365 | 693 | 42,744 | 8,660 | 4,038 | 734 | 565 | 566 | 266 | 2 | 81 | 35 | | 13 | 60,610 |
| **Total Southern States** | 36,163 | 28,963 | 21,540 | 646,250 | 147,919 | 189,954 | 17,629 | 12,522 | 21,266 | 11,145 | 1,327 | 1,844 | 694 | 434 | 32 | 1,137,682 |
| Ohio | 41,539 | 35,751 | 4,528 | 138,175 | 34,483 | 5,100 | 6,339 | 7,943 | 2,499 | 2,120 | 214 | 568 | 40 | | | 277,312 |
| Indiana | 7,741 | 2,988 | 840 | 107,450 | 19,454 | 5,925 | 6,691 | 3,483 | 2,701 | 1,423 | 262 | 160 | 147 | 53 | | 159,263 |
| Illinois | 25,942 | 7,718 | 3,195 | 177,029 | 24,154 | 17,672 | 8,741 | 1,966 | 3,280 | 1,210 | 376 | 230 | 96 | | | 271,562 |
| Michigan | 3,316 | 2,912 | 715 | 64,433 | 20,608 | 3,809 | 4,218 | 5,049 | 317 | 423 | 72 | 171 | 168 | 53 | | 110,211 |
| Wisconsin | 5,860 | 3,219 | 1,541 | 89,367 | 17,032 | 9,711 | 4,668 | 2,222 | 771 | 847 | 245 | 171 | 26 | | | 135,690 |
| Minnesota | 10,850 | 6,655 | 4,501 | 88,116 | 14,405 | 35,940 | 11,281 | 3,781 | 6,996 | 1,395 | 393 | 109 | 252 | | | 184,061 |

| | | | | | | | | | | | | | | | | |
|---|---|---|---|---|---|---|---|---|---|---|---|---|---|---|---|---|
| Iowa | 9,216 | 1,059 | 1,350 | 131,191 | 9,094 | 18,225 | 3,798 | 834 | 9,778 | 2,000 | 241 | 79 | 93 | 65 | 19 | 187,064 |
| Missouri | 5,210 | 1,163 | 878 | 26,210 | 2,359 | 6,466 | 1,067 | 395 | 1,254 | 280 | 40 | 35 | 12 | | | 45,388 |
| Total Middle Western States | 109,724 | 65,454 | 17,548 | 819,971 | 141,579 | 102,848 | 46,803 | 25,020 | 27,496 | 9,648 | 1,843 | 1,523 | 834 | 171 | 19 | 1,370,531 |
| North Dakota | 2,479 | 161 | 975 | 24,450 | 1,464 | 26,789 | 3,168 | 898 | 5,230 | 464 | 222 | 78 | 7 | | | 66,402 |
| South Dakota | 953 | 171 | 389 | 32,239 | 2,619 | 22,510 | 1,851 | 461 | 3,120 | 531 | 26 | 140 | 11 | 17 | | 65,021 |
| Nebraska | 1,959 | 136 | 523 | 42,947 | 2,304 | 19,104 | 1,068 | 141 | 2,653 | 508 | 64 | 27 | | 170 | 11 | 71,604 |
| Kansas | 5,498 | 1,914 | 1,505 | 51,145 | 5,331 | 32,951 | 1,825 | 623 | 2,605 | 512 | 57 | 31 | 117 | 6 | | 104,131 |
| Montana | 3,934 | 792 | 1,305 | 19,515 | 2,726 | 20,198 | 1,832 | 374 | 3,695 | 749 | 120 | 39 | 3 | 130 | 3 | 56,515 |
| Wyoming | 262 | 255 | 238 | 13,706 | 4,039 | 15,867 | 1,010 | 279 | 1,926 | 305 | 40 | 15 | | 1 | | 37,963 |
| Colorado | 1,577 | 959 | 954 | 26,325 | 3,784 | 20,858 | 1,081 | 257 | 2,350 | 422 | 57 | 71 | 8 | | | 58,703 |
| New Mexico | 1,606 | 426 | 303 | 10,837 | 2,017 | 13,092 | 349 | 221 | 388 | 190 | 10 | 21 | 67 | | | 29,516 |
| Oklahoma | 4,362 | 328 | 1,874 | 43,200 | 6,726 | 64,833 | 1,498 | 987 | 4,631 | 1,770 | 529 | 107 | 1 | 162 | 8 | 131,016 |
| Total Western States | 22,629 | 6,142 | 8,066 | 264,364 | 31,030 | 237,202 | 13,782 | 4,241 | 26,598 | 5,441 | 1,125 | 529 | 214 | 486 | 22 | 621,871 |
| Washington | 2,713 | 481 | 1,811 | 27,690 | 2,318 | 9,142 | 1,557 | 348 | 1,473 | 272 | 211 | 65 | 127 | 2 | | 48,210 |
| Oregon | 6,225 | 625 | 2,633 | 19,299 | 1,190 | 9,504 | 743 | 255 | 1,722 | 428 | 42 | 38 | 226 | 10 | 13 | 42,953 |
| California | 23,738 | 6,373 | 5,026 | 101,064 | 15,832 | 22,506 | 6,510 | 3,430 | 2,703 | 1,229 | 143 | 373 | 501 | 151 | | 189,587 |
| Idaho | 742 | 77 | 372 | 19,816 | 1,472 | 13,619 | 943 | 239 | 3,803 | 287 | 26 | 37 | | | 18 | 41,433 |
| Utah | 53 | 55 | 12 | 2,882 | 901 | 692 | 253 | 54 | 375 | 93 | 3 | 23 | | | | 5,396 |
| Nevada | 2,202 | 744 | 825 | 2,584 | 423 | 742 | 594 | 135 | 323 | 116 | 52 | 38 | | | | 8,778 |
| Arizona | 510 | 186 | 163 | 9,459 | 656 | 5,173 | 218 | 99 | 968 | 170 | 3 | 9 | 26 | | | 17,640 |
| Total Pacific States | 36,183 | 8,541 | 10,842 | 182,784 | 22,792 | 61,378 | 10,818 | 4,560 | 11,367 | 2,595 | 480 | 583 | 890 | 163 | 31 | 353,997 |
| Alaska (nonmember banks) | 191 | 24 | 23 | 366 | 21 | 17 | 1 | 79 | | | | | | | | 722 |
| Hawaii (nonmember banks) | 203 | 914 | 35 | 83 | 63 | 89 | 13 | 28 | | | | | | | | 1,428 |
| Total (nonmember banks) | 394 | 938 | 58 | 449 | 84 | 106 | 14 | 107 | | | | | | | 117 | 2,150 |
| Total country banks | 379,339 | 362,770 | 79,075 | 2,919,258 | 576,666 | 623,776 | 96,318 | 76,200 | 89,875 | 42,129 | 5,814 | 9,091 | 8,060 | 1,740 | 3,123 | 5,270,228 |
| Total United States | 657,298 | 1,408,369 | 270,583 | 5,818,207 | 1,499,092 | 1,112,434 | 101,795 | 87,035 | 100,784 | 60,351 | 6,522 | 14,804 | 75,906 | 31,911 | 3,123 | 11,248,214 |

The amount and character of loans and discounts of national banks with the percentage of each class of loans to total loans and discounts, is shown in the following statement for the last three fiscal years:

[In thousands of dollars.]

| Class. | June 30, 1920. | | June 30, 1921. | | June 30, 1922. | |
|---|---|---|---|---|---|---|
| | Amount. | Per cent. | Amount. | Per cent. | Amount. | Per cent. |
| On demand, paper with one or more individual or firm names (not secured by collateral)........................... | 707,229 | 5.20 | 679,704 | 5.66 | 657,298 | 5.84 |
| On demand, secured by stocks and bonds... | 1,261,984 | 9.27 | 1,151,114 | 9.59 | 1,408,369 | 12.52 |
| On demand, secured by other personal securities, including merchandise, warehouse receipts, etc...................... | 392,277 | 2.88 | 312,394 | 2.85 | 270,583 | 2.41 |
| On time, paper with one or more individual or firm names (not secured by collateral)........................... | 7,601,971 | 55.87 | 6,564,444 | 54.68 | 5,818,207 | 51.73 |
| On time, secured by stocks and bonds..... | 1,855,906 | 13.64 | 1,548,055 | 12.90 | 1,499,092 | 13.33 |
| On time, secured by other personal securities, including merchandise, warehouse receipts, etc........................... | 1,390,122 | 10.21 | 1,320,323 | 11.00 | 1,112,434 | 9.89 |
| Secured by improved real estate under authority of section 24, Federal reserve act, as amended: | | | | | | |
| 1. On farm land.................... | (1) | ........ | 93,042 | .77 | 101,795 | .90 |
| 2. On other real estate............... | 135,902 | 1.00 | 60,024 | .50 | 87,035 | .77 |
| Secured by real-estate mortgages or other liens on realty not in accordance with section 24, Federal reserve act, as amended: | | | | | | |
| 1. For debts previously contracted (sec. 5137, R. S. U. S.)— | | | | | | |
| (a) Farm lands.................. | ............ | ........ | 60,895 | .51 | 100,784 | .90 |
| (b) Other real estate............. | ............ | ........ | 45,695 | .38 | 60,351 | .54 |
| 2. All other real-estate loans— | | | | | | |
| (a) Farm lands.................. | (1) | ........ | 7,724 | .06 | 6,522 | .06 |
| (b) Other real estate............. | 93,927 | .69 | 12,857 | .11 | 14,804 | .13 |
| Acceptances of other banks discounted.... | 146,838 | 1.08 | 94,470 | .79 | 75,906 | .67 |
| Acceptances of this bank purchased or discounted............................ | 22,260 | .16 | 16,429 | .14 | 31,911 | .28 |
| Customers' liability on account of drafts paid under letters of credit and for which this bank has not been reimbursed...... | ............ | ........ | 7,347 | .06 | 3,123 | .03 |
| Total..................... | 13,611,416 | 100.00 | 12,004,515 | 100.00 | 11,248,214 | 100.00 |

[1] No information.

COMPARATIVE STATEMENT OF LOANS AND DISCOUNTS, INCLUDING REDISCOUNTS MADE BY NATIONAL BANKS DURING PAST THREE FISCAL YEARS.

A comparison of the loans and discounts, including rediscounts, of national banks in the central reserve cities of New York, Chicago, and St. Louis, in other reserve cities of country banks, and total for United States are shown in the following statement as of June 30 for years 1920 to 1922, inclusive:

[In thousands of dollars]

| Banks in— | Loans. | | | | | |
|---|---|---|---|---|---|---|
| | June 30, 1920. | | June 30, 1921 | | June 30, 1922 | |
| | Amount. | Per cent. | Amount. | Per cent. | Amount. | Per cent. |
| New York | 2,744,244 | 20.16 | 2,202,265 | 18.35 | 2,062,213 | 18.33 |
| Do. | | | | | | |
| Chicago | 3,687,702 | 27.09 | 2,996,346 | 24.96 | 2,755,065 | 24.49 |
| St. Louis | | | | | | |
| Other reserve cities | 4,170,946 | 30.64 | 3,523,178 | 29.35 | 3,222,921 | 28.65 |
| All reserve cities | 7,858,648 | 57.73 | 6,519,524 | 54.31 | 5,977,986 | 53.15 |
| Country | 5,752,768 | 42.27 | 5,484,991 | 45.69 | 5,270,228 | 46.85 |
| Total United States | 13,611,416 | 100.00 | 12,004,515 | 100.00 | 11,248,214 | 100.00 |

## NATIONAL BANKS IN AGRICULTURAL, SEMIAGRICULTURAL, AND NON-AGRICULTURAL COUNTIES.

On March 10, 1922, 61.67 per cent of the total number of reporting national banks in continental United States were in agricultural counties, 11.21 per cent in semiagricultural counties, and 27.12 per cent in nonagricultural counties.

The loans and discounts of banks in agricultural counties were 21.34 per cent of the aggregate loans and discounts of all national banks and amounted to $2,407,436,000; loans and discounts of banks in semiagricultural counties were $1,094,819,000, or 9.71 per cent of the aggregate; and the loans and discounts of national banks in non-agricultural counties were 68.95 per cent of the total, and amounted to $7,778,085,000.

The resources of national banks in agricultural counties were $4,014,-701,000, or 20.23 per cent of the resources of all national banks; the resources of banks in semiagricultural counties were 9.84 per cent and amounted to $1,952,962,000; while the resources of banks in nonagricultural counties were $13,873,919,000, or 69.93 per cent of the total.

The total deposits of banks in agricultural counties were $3,-298,961,000, or 21.45 per cent of the total deposits of all national banks; the deposits of banks in semiagricultural counties were $1,480,183,000, or 9.62 per cent of the total; and the deposits of banks in nonagricultural counties were $10,604,364,000, or 68.93 per cent of the deposits of all national banks.

Information with respect to the principal items of resources and liabilities and the classification of loans and discounts of national banks in agricultural, semiagricultural, and nonagricultural counties in each State and Federal reserve district March 10, 1922, is published in the appendix to the report of the Comptroller of the Currency, a summary of which follows:

[In thousands of dollars.]

| | Per cent of number of banks to total number of banks. | Loans and discounts. | | Aggregate resources. | | Aggregate deposits. | |
|---|---|---|---|---|---|---|---|
| | | Amount. | Per cent. | Amount. | Per cent. | Amount. | Per cent. |
| Agricultural counties | 61.67 | 2,407,436 | 21.34 | 4,014,701 | 20.23 | 3,298,961 | 21.45 |
| Semiagricultural counties | 11.21 | 1,094,819 | 9.71 | 1,952,962 | 9.84 | 1,480,183 | 9.62 |
| Nonagricultural counties | 27.12 | 7,778,085 | 68.95 | 13,873,919 | 69.93 | 10,604,364 | 68.93 |
| Total United States | 100.00 | 11,280,340 | 100.00 | 19,841,582 | 100.00 | 15,383,508 | 100.00 |

INVESTMENTS OF NATIONAL BANKS JUNE 30, 1922.

On June 30, 1922, the total investments of national banks in United States Government securities and other miscellaneous bonds, stocks, and securities, amounted to $4,563,325,000, or 22.04 per cent of total resources, which amounted to $20,706,010,000. The total investment in miscellaneous bonds, stocks, and securities, as will be noted by reference to the following statement, which shows a comparison for years ended June 30, 1921 and 1922, was $2,277,-866,000 compared with $2,005,584,000 June 30, 1921, while the total investment in United States Government securities was $2,-285,459,000 compared with $2,019,497,000 June 30, 1921.

[In thousands of dollars.]

|  | June 30, 1921. | June 30, 1922. |
|---|---|---|
| Domestic securities: |  |  |
| State, county, or other municipal bonds | 393,682 | 414,414 |
| Railroad bonds | 404,936 | 486,453 |
| Other public-service corporation bonds | 277,205 | 318,456 |
| All other bonds (domestic) | 352,405 | 423,040 |
| Claims, warrants, judgments, etc | 82,586 | 87,727 |
| Collateral trust and other corporation notes issued for not more than one year nor less than three years' time | 159,766 | 168,082 |
| Foreign Government bonds | 140,226 | 162,054 |
| Other foreign bonds and securities | 63,513 | 87,895 |
| Stocks, Federal reserve bank | 68,724 | 70,575 |
| Stocks, all other | 62,541 | 59,170 |
| Total | 2,005,584 | 2,277,866 |
| United States Government securities | 2,019,497 | 2,285,459 |
| Total bonds of all classes | 4,025,081 | 4,563,325 |

UNITED STATES, DOMESTIC, FOREIGN BONDS, SECURITIES, ETC., HELD BY NATIONAL BANKS IN RESERVE CITIES AND STATES.

A classification of the holdings of national banks in central reserve and reserve cities and elsewhere in each State of domestic and foreign bonds, securities, etc., and the total only of United States Government securities are shown in the following statement as of June 30, 1922:

United States Government, domestic, and foreign bonds, securities, etc., owned by national banks June 30, 1922.

[In thousands of dollars.]

| Cities, States, and Territories. | United States Government securities. | State, county, or municipal bonds. | Railroad bonds. | Other public service corporation bonds. | All other bonds. | Stock of Federal reserve bank. | Stock of other corporations. | Claims, warrants, etc. | Judgments. | Collateral trust and other corporation notes. | Bonds of the Russian, German, or Austrian Governments. | Bonds of other foreign governments. | Other foreign bonds and securities. | Total bonds, stocks, securities, etc., other than United States. | Total all bonds and securities. |
|---|---|---|---|---|---|---|---|---|---|---|---|---|---|---|---|
| **CENTRAL RESERVE CITIES.** | | | | | | | | | | | | | | | |
| New York | 503,893 | 49,247 | 92,644 | 23,916 | 49,463 | 12,054 | 16,314 | 1,655 | | 37,378 | 786 | 15,902 | 8,463 | 308,721 | 812,614 |
| Chicago | 46,560 | 11,263 | 3,021 | 2,776 | 5,355 | 2,720 | 1,004 | 1,259 | | 6,224 | 14 | 1,719 | 314 | 36,256 | 82,816 |
| St. Louis | 20,538 | 6,560 | 4,598 | 2,403 | 1,803 | 1,069 | 1,427 | 729 | 376 | 110 | | 1,546 | 527 | 21,231 | 41,769 |
| Total | 570,991 | 67,079 | 100,263 | 29,095 | 56,682 | 15,843 | 19,345 | 3,643 | 376 | 43,712 | 800 | 20,067 | 9,303 | 366,208 | 937,199 |
| **ALL OTHER RESERVE CITIES.** | | | | | | | | | | | | | | | |
| Boston | 41,539 | 1,267 | 5,239 | 8,330 | 6,993 | 2,255 | 5,418 | 76 | | 7,595 | 88 | 3,630 | 1,531 | 42,442 | 83,981 |
| Albany | 3,055 | 2,000 | 1,611 | 1,852 | 3,375 | 187 | 179 | 93 | | 1,390 | 28 | 697 | 677 | 12,089 | 20,144 |
| Brooklyn and Bronx | 4,121 | 818 | 964 | 44 | 3,702 | 120 | 16 | 2 | | 873 | 4 | 337 | 322 | 4,612 | 8,733 |
| Buffalo | 5,484 | 756 | 1,390 | 1,449 | 1,978 | 153 | 20 | 23 | | 272 | 34 | 710 | 462 | 7,252 | 12,736 |
| Philadelphia | 50,205 | 9,115 | 18,621 | 10,057 | 11,311 | 2,597 | 1,749 | 188 | | 15,127 | 57 | 4,354 | 2,419 | 76,557 | 126,762 |
| Pittsburgh | 71,206 | 2,136 | 14,732 | 4,438 | 15,969 | 1,601 | 1,827 | 63 | 2 | 2,145 | 184 | 3,094 | 858 | 55,655 | 126,861 |
| Baltimore | 13,898 | 3,750 | 3,343 | 1,427 | 3,814 | 1,758 | 356 | | 2 | 10,751 | | 1,215 | 228 | 17,041 | 30,939 |
| Washington | 16,705 | 1,538 | 4,102 | 2,635 | 1,897 | 405 | 227 | 361 | 1 | 792 | 2 | 604 | 640 | 13,204 | 30,909 |
| [illegible] | 6,987 | 540 | 728 | 124 | 1,116 | 390 | 511 | 12 | | 957 | | 100 | 188 | 4,666 | 11,653 |
| [illegible] | 5,416 | 1,000 | 405 | 63 | 369 | 103 | 157 | 85 | | 19 | 2 | 177 | 9 | 2,487 | 7,903 |
| [illegible] | 8,517 | 168 | 10 | 45 | 150 | 255 | 229 | | | 23 | | | | 880 | 9,397 |
| Savannah | 77 | | | | 965 | 10 | 3 | | | | | | | 13 | 90 |
| Jacksonville | 6,478 | 1,623 | 783 | 114 | 1,021 | 88 | 49 | 20 | 18 | 439 | 3 | 151 | 49 | 4,304 | 10,782 |
| Birmingham | 2,990 | 167 | 250 | 103 | 242 | 99 | 95 | 15 | | | | 160 | 61 | 1,971 | 4,961 |
| New Orleans | 4,355 | 438 | 26 | 1 | 445 | 44 | 127 | | | 7 | | | | 1,034 | 5,389 |
| Dallas | 16,048 | | | | 127 | 314 | 195 | 1,322 | | | | 24 | | 2,301 | 18,349 |
| El Paso | 2,615 | 6 | 139 | | 23 | 73 | 174 | 816 | 18 | | | | | 1,353 | 3,968 |
| Fort Worth | 3,802 | 1,886 | | 20 | 230 | 161 | 125 | 229 | 66 | | | | | 2,490 | 6,292 |
| [illegible] | 848 | 99 | 6 | 51 | 388 | 24 | 20 | 49 | | | | | 20 | 468 | 1,316 |
| Houston | 13,551 | 152 | 14 | 68 | 65 | 293 | 400 | 182 | | 59 | | 59 | 24 | 1,563 | 15,114 |
| San Antonio | 5,367 | 44 | | | 91 | 91 | 43 | 140 | | | | | | 551 | 5,918 |
| Waco | 1,934 | | | 5 | 1 | 78 | 36 | 18 | | | | | | 138 | 2,072 |

*United States Government, domestic, and foreign bonds, securities, etc., owned by national banks June 30, 1922—Continued.*

| Cities, States, and Territories. | United States Government securities. | Domestic securities. | | | | | | | | | Foreign government bonds. | | | Total bonds, stocks, securities, etc., other than United States. | Total all bonds and securities. |
|---|---|---|---|---|---|---|---|---|---|---|---|---|---|---|---|
| | | State, county, or municipal bonds. | Railroad bonds. | Other public service corporation bonds. | All other bonds. | Stock of Federal reserve bank. | Stock of other corporations. | Claims, warrants, etc. | Judgments. | Collateral trust and other corporation notes. | Bonds of the Russian, German, or Austrian Governments. | Bonds of other foreign governments. | Other foreign bonds and securities. | | |
| **ALL OTHER RESERVE CITIES—continued.** | | | | | | | | | | | | | | | |
| Little Rock | 685 | 75 | 4,041 | 1,617 | 585 | 26 | 11 | 7 | | 313 | | 411 | | 119 | 894 |
| Louisville | 16,246 | 621 | 183 | 106 | 129 | 264 | 55 | 1,357 | 4 | | | 15 | 320 | 9,644 | 25,890 |
| Chattanooga | 2,828 | 25 | 51 | 6 | 58 | 120 | 112 | 9 | 2 | 11 | | | | 703 | 3,531 |
| Memphis | 2,365 | 208 | 197 | 402 | 424 | 72 | 34 | 2 | 8 | 112 | | 257 | 264 | 444 | 2,809 |
| Nashville | 6,431 | 761 | 2,680 | 1,364 | 1,523 | 161 | 67 | 114 | | | 16 | 958 | 403 | 2,783 | 9,214 |
| Cincinnati | 23,440 | 6,402 | 5 | 651 | 2,253 | 624 | 362 | 38 | | 1,980 | | 757 | 1,459 | 16,234 | 39,774 |
| Cleveland | 10,072 | 1,695 | 1,693 | 919 | 858 | 232 | 319 | 55 | | 329 | | 784 | 140 | 8,785 | 17,857 |
| | 11,640 | 3,393 | 1,124 | 205 | 1,054 | 289 | 60 | 81 | | 758 | | 128 | 462 | | 20,595 |
| Toledo | 5,431 | 3,384 | 1,294 | 1,026 | 1,521 | 180 | | 180 | 49 | 1,291 | 9 | 367 | 99 | 5,512 | 11,439 |
| Indianapolis | 12,366 | 427 | 255 | 2,478 | 1,521 | 303 | 587 | 612 | 39 | 247 | | 485 | 356 | 13,741 | 17,878 |
| Chicago | 9,658 | 4,894 | 255 | 445 | 3,263 | 122 | 10 | 46 | | 754 | | 221 | 80 | 2,150 | 23,399 |
| Peoria | 4,459 | 265 | 744 | 1,217 | 407 | 146 | | 24 | | 13 | | 514 | 1,251 | 3,036 | 6,609 |
| Detroit | 19,738 | 2,529 | 305 | 623 | 287 | 403 | 485 | 88 | 13 | 551 | 4 | 582 | 230 | 8,105 | 27,883 |
| Grand Rapids | 3,476 | 2,331 | 439 | 1,252 | 612 | 101 | 110 | 28 | | 90 | 9 | 86 | 352 | 3,050 | 6,512 |
| Milwaukee | 5,534 | 1,295 | 777 | 324 | 413 | 384 | 122 | 163 | | 534 | | 283 | 32 | 5,142 | 10,584 |
| Minneapolis | 12,380 | 2,523 | 2,315 | 315 | 236 | 399 | 100 | 147 | 2 | 119 | | 198 | 180 | 5,478 | 17,522 |
| St. Paul | 22,119 | 819 | 45 | 72 | 939 | 325 | 8 | 336 | | 43 | | 40 | 16 | 885 | 27,597 |
| Cedar Rapids | 2,004 | 119 | 42 | 25 | 388 | 45 | | | 5 | 160 | | 19 | | 1,646 | 2,889 |
| Des Moines | 2,616 | 706 | 137 | 378 | 137 | 117 | 453 | 142 | | | | 34 | | 1,624 | 4,262 |
| Dubuque | 1,175 | 700 | | 65 | 218 | 73 | | 133 | | 25 | | 5 | 41 | 1,460 | 2,799 |
| Sioux City | 3,185 | 621 | 795 | 266 | 177 | 389 | 28 | 466 | 1 | 17 | 5 | 225 | 94 | 6,545 | 4,645 |
| Kansas City, Mo. | 10,317 | 2,967 | 209 | 58 | 760 | 60 | 140 | 939 | | | | | | | 16,862 |
| St. Joseph | 2,498 | 52 | | 13 | 41 | 68 | | 11 | 4 | 109 | | 12 | 23 | 325 | 3,023 |
| Lincoln | 875 | 87 | | | 96 | 64 | | 64 | 76 | 65 | | 4.4 | 161 | 476 | 1,351 |
| Omaha | 6,874 | 1,342 | 1,091 | 508 | 1,092 | 320 | 68 | 299 | 43 | 5 | | 5 | 15 | 5,466 | 12,340 |
| Kansas City, Kans | 997 | 301 | 87 | | 57 | 36 | | | | 6 | | 10 | 12 | 536 | 1,533 |
| Topeka | 60 | 1,080 | 30 | | 22 | 34 | 1 | | | | | | | 460 | 2,929 |
| Helena | 1,934 | 2,403 | 44 | | 53 | 161 | | 266 | | | | | | 2,832 | 5,766 |
| Denver | 2,500 | 10 | 19 | | 2 | 23 | | 206 | | | | | | 54 | 644 |
| | 15,191 | 3,751 | 1,965 | 1,808 | 1,670 | 240 | 1,401 | 631 | 5 | 691 | 7 | 269 | 737 | 13,138 | 28,329 |

| | C1 | C2 | C3 | C4 | C5 | C6 | C7 | C8 | C9 | C10 | C11 | C12 | C13 | C14 | C15 |
|---|---|---|---|---|---|---|---|---|---|---|---|---|---|---|---|
| .......... | 1,776 | 1,104 | 563 | 551 | 236 | 51 | | 350 | | 31 | 1 | 88 | 69 | 3,044 | 4,820 |
| Muskogee | 2,021 | 176 | | 313 | 43 | 48 | 34 | 257 | 19 | | 2 | 10 | | 590 | 2,611 |
| Oklahoma City | 4,350 | 6,980 | 139 | 161 | 200 | 149 | 79 | 830 | 159 | 52 | 47 | 89 | 173 | 8,852 | 13,202 |
| ............ | 6,903 | 537 | 180 | 805 | 271 | 178 | 332 | 821 | 141 | 31 | | 199 | 933 | 2,761 | 5,664 |
| Seattle | 16,531 | 5,409 | 1,264 | 245 | 1,673 | 259 | | 1,338 | 55 | 72 | 24 | 1,376 | | 13,604 | 30,125 |
| Spokane | 3,308 | 420 | 9 | 17 | 137 | 140 | 230 | 178 | 3 | | | 85 | 215 | 1,218 | 4,586 |
| Tacoma | 1,421 | 960 | 2 | 258 | 1,252 | 38 | 1,030 | 222 | | 223 | 10 | 30 | 53 | 1,331 | 2,952 |
| Portland | 11,883 | 2,006 | 777 | 356 | 2,311 | 217 | 15 | 880 | 4 | 83 | 1 | 364 | | 7,040 | 18,923 |
| Los Angeles | 18,180 | 1,578 | 102 | 137 | 569 | 427 | 3,017 | 121 | 100 | 5 | | 282 | 3 | 8,289 | 25,469 |
| Oakland | 3,794 | 8,184 | 2,634 | 1,961 | 4,839 | 88 | 44 | 107 | | 4 | 82 | 271 | | 2,895 | 6,689 |
| San Francisco | 39,914 | 91 | 194 | | 46 | 1,401 | 147 | 2,900 | 4 | | | 795 | 6 | 25,972 | 65,886 |
| Ogden | 1,370 | | | | | 46 | 44 | 80 | 24 | 5 | | | | 530 | 1,900 |
| Salt Lake City | 3,252 | 278 | 329 | 67 | 260 | 116 | 147 | 65 | 13 | 4 | | 30 | | 1,315 | 4,567 |
| All other reserve cities | 620,364 | 100,943 | 79,620 | 53,604 | 82,599 | 19,320 | 21,447 | 18,313 | 882 | 49,142 | 651 | 26,120 | 15,677 | 468,348 | 1,088,912 |
| Total all reserve cities | 1,191,555 | 168,022 | 179,913 | 82,699 | 139,281 | 35,163 | 40,702 | 21,956 | 1,258 | 92,854 | 1,451 | 46,187 | 24,960 | 834,556 | 2,026,111 |
| **COUNTRY BANKS.** | | | | | | | | | | | | | | | |
| Maine | 12,719 | 1,374 | 4,890 | 12,034 | 6,379 | 340 | 234 | 30 | | 2,649 | | 2,978 | 2,173 | 33,094 | 45,813 |
| New Hampshire | 10,976 | 612 | 1,748 | 3,054 | 1,744 | 284 | 110 | 43 | 10 | 445 | | 1,047 | 595 | 9,751 | 20,727 |
| Vermont | 6,847 | 358 | 2,291 | 3,929 | 2,612 | 238 | 167 | 133 | | 771 | | 2,047 | 712 | 13,072 | 19,919 |
| Massachusetts | 50,571 | 3,075 | 11,434 | 21,317 | 17,511 | 1,401 | 1,277 | 249 | 22 | 7,383 | | 6,474 | 4,509 | 74,743 | 125,311 |
| Rhode Island | 8,582 | 1,206 | 1,879 | 4,008 | 1,454 | 311 | 72 | 13 | | 1,611 | | 704 | 850 | 12,110 | 20,692 |
| Connecticut | 30,530 | 1,581 | 7,879 | 6,332 | 3,473 | 1,068 | 663 | 332 | | 1,518 | | 3,232 | 1,176 | 27,268 | 57,798 |
| Total New England States | 120,215 | 8,206 | 30,114 | 50,371 | 33,173 | 3,642 | 2,523 | 850 | 32 | 14,377 | 250 | 16,482 | 10,015 | 170,038 | 290,253 |
| New York | 94,747 | 18,123 | 62,845 | 33,573 | 43,549 | 2,452 | 1,938 | 686 | 91 | 10,771 | 412 | 23,407 | 13,815 | 211,968 | 306,715 |
| New Jersey | 70,547 | 23,296 | 50,669 | 26,839 | 27,653 | 1,689 | 1,323 | 685 | | 9,335 | 112 | 12,743 | 5,254 | 158,998 | 229,545 |
| Pennsylvania | 177,568 | 26,556 | 113,430 | 63,534 | 85,039 | 5,103 | 4,235 | 1,409 | 1,627 | 19,764 | 373 | 27,362 | 13,888 | 362,320 | 539,898 |
| Delaware | 2,371 | 391 | 988 | 1,456 | 635 | 108 | 19 | | 6 | 771 | 3 | 343 | 253 | 4,973 | 7,344 |
| Maryland | 9,685 | 1,993 | 5,886 | 6,291 | 5,320 | 296 | 196 | 108 | 111 | 1,322 | 10 | 1,966 | 926 | 24,128 | 33,813 |
| Total Eastern States | 354,918 | 70,662 | 233,516 | 131,701 | 161,396 | 9,648 | 7,711 | 2,888 | 1,835 | 41,963 | 910 | 65,821 | 34,136 | 762,387 | 1,117,305 |
| Virginia | 30,055 | 2,928 | 1,984 | 1,977 | 3,326 | 1,130 | 667 | 518 | 21 | 570 | 56 | 811 | 591 | 11,807 | 44,962 |
| West Virginia | 21,430 | 2,472 | 2,266 | 2,484 | 4,836 | 635 | 376 | 105 | 145 | 544 | 38 | 1,750 | 345 | 13,016 | 36,446 |
| North Carolina | 14,811 | 1,796 | 147 | 112 | 546 | 650 | 519 | 31 | 49 | | | 33 | 181 | 4,694 | 18,935 |
| South Carolina | 10,361 | 513 | 239 | 295 | 526 | 451 | 186 | 52 | 18 | 19 | 68 | 51 | | 2,421 | 12,782 |
| Georgia | 10,773 | 236 | 156 | 69 | 252 | 544 | 306 | 529 | 12 | 5 | 7 | 124 | 4 | 2,244 | 13,017 |
| Florida | 12,181 | 2,954 | 613 | 446 | 776 | 286 | 231 | 711 | 97 | 484 | | 1,613 | 616 | 2,807 | 20,988 |
| Alabama | 13,481 | 1,728 | 365 | 223 | 715 | 526 | 235 | 526 | 77 | 1,380 | | 284 | 102 | 6,441 | 19,922 |
| Mississippi | 5,423 | 3,303 | 293 | 188 | 783 | 218 | 64 | 148 | | 31 | | 330 | 58 | 3,305 | 10,840 |
| Louisiana | 5,669 | 982 | 110 | 121 | 585 | 275 | 119 | 984 | 1 | 77 | 7 | 19 | 11 | 89 | 8,974 |
| Texas | 30,168 | 1,787 | 318 | 227 | 1,326 | 2,074 | 461 | 2,227 | 127 | 255 | | 33 | 31 | | 49,027 |
| Arkansas | 7,874 | 1,123 | 21 | 59 | 270 | 300 | 98 | 777 | 226 | | | | | | 10,786 |
| Kentucky | 21,254 | 1,569 | 1,895 | 1,304 | 1,500 | 632 | 84 | 1,004 | 57 | 605 | | 405 | 192 | 9,247 | 30,301 |
| Tennessee | 9,746 | 640 | 347 | 361 | 1,179 | 377 | 179 | 651 | 43 | 389 | | 702 | 192 | 5,060 | 14,805 |
| Total Southern States | 203,256 | 21,009 | 8,754 | 7,866 | 16,840 | 8,101 | 3,515 | 8,643 | 821 | 4,359 | 176 | 6,188 | 2,328 | 88,630 | 291,886 |

*United States Government, domestic, and foreign bonds, securities, etc., owned by national banks June 30, 1922—Continued.*

| Cities, States, and Territories | United States Government securities | Domestic securities — State, county, or municipal bonds | Railroad bonds | Other public service corporation bonds | All other bonds | Stock of Federal reserve bank | Stock of other corporations | Claims, warrants, etc. | Judgments | Collateral trust and other corporation notes | Bonds of the Russian, German, or Austrian Governments | Bonds of other foreign governments | Other foreign bonds and securities | Total bonds, stocks, securities, etc., other than United States | Total all bonds and securities |
|---|---|---|---|---|---|---|---|---|---|---|---|---|---|---|---|
| **COUNTRY BANKS—continued.** | | | | | | | | | | | | | | | |
| Ohio | 53,772 | 31,394 | 9,405 | 6,000 | 18,083 | 1,971 | 690 | 544 | 153 | 4,249 | 93 | 6,071 | 4,396 | 85,058 | 138,830 |
| Indiana | 40,005 | 7,942 | 5,307 | 5,930 | 7,356 | 1,092 | 408 | 266 | 122 | 2,110 | 3 | 2,645 | 2,070 | 35,251 | 75,256 |
| Illinois | 61,960 | 19,900 | 5,999 | 10,320 | 11,881 | 1,780 | 522 | 4,847 | 477 | 3,885 | 3 | 3,242 | 1,257 | 64,131 | 126,091 |
| Michigan | 20,450 | 17,896 | 4,170 | 5,490 | 8,108 | 606 | 284 | 607 | 24 | 771 | 45 | 3,194 | 1,058 | 45,033 | 65,483 |
| Wisconsin | 24,428 | 8,291 | 2,396 | 5,635 | 6,017 | 730 | 176 | 724 | 65 | 1,494 | 4 | 1,634 | 939 | 28,095 | 52,523 |
| Minnesota | 21,994 | 8,374 | 1,831 | 1,964 | 4,288 | 905 | 135 | 7,526 | 228 | 438 | 32 | 1,662 | 894 | 27,439 | 49,433 |
| Iowa | 25,293 | 3,201 | 683 | 964 | 4,080 | 991 | 613 | 2,735 | 262 | 111 | | 332 | 174 | 9,146 | 34,439 |
| Missouri | 10,744 | 1,965 | 304 | 301 | 556 | 324 | 13 | 513 | 33 | 200 | | 161 | 53 | 4,413 | 15,157 |
| Total Middle Western States | 258,646 | 98,953 | 29,785 | 38,056 | 57,339 | 8,399 | 2,821 | 17,762 | 1,364 | 13,258 | 198 | 18,941 | 13,740 | 298,566 | 557,212 |
| North Dakota | 6,913 | 680 | 65 | 108 | 157 | 322 | 51 | 3,434 | 110 | 18 | | 235 | 3 | 5,183 | 12,090 |
| South Dakota | 6,008 | 288 | 135 | 44 | 753 | 276 | 26 | 1,659 | 99 | 137 | 1 | 103 | 30 | 3,551 | 9,649 |
| Nebraska | 9,979 | 384 | 123 | 37 | 235 | 430 | 17 | 941 | 169 | 19 | | 240 | 72 | 2,667 | 12,646 |
| Kansas | 16,279 | 3,768 | 242 | 234 | 494 | 643 | 24 | 1,504 | 87 | 9 | 3 | 203 | 51 | 7,262 | 23,541 |
| Montana | 6,385 | 1,650 | 20 | 254 | 810 | 342 | 73 | 2,413 | 104 | 7 | | 333 | 67 | 6,073 | 12,458 |
| Wyoming | 3,738 | 172 | 159 | 168 | 617 | 178 | 67 | 394 | 13 | 5 | 12 | 94 | 7 | 2,386 | 6,124 |
| Colorado | 8,508 | 2,718 | 545 | 1,216 | 1,343 | 367 | 415 | 1,816 | 93 | 248 | 2 | 122 | 221 | 9,106 | 17,614 |
| New Mexico | 3,314 | 255 | 86 | 98 | 186 | 134 | 81 | 313 | 51 | 51 | 1 | 25 | 5 | 1,297 | 4,611 |
| Oklahoma | 17,312 | 3,963 | 11 | 129 | 516 | 776 | 33 | 7,303 | 326 | 101 | 3 | 16 | 214 | 13,411 | 30,723 |
| Total Western States | 78,526 | 13,898 | 1,386 | 2,288 | 5,111 | 3,468 | 787 | 20,277 | 1,063 | 595 | 22 | 1,371 | 670 | 50,936 | 129,462 |
| Washington | 11,171 | 4,188 | 521 | 743 | 1,502 | 296 | 89 | 1,611 | 75 | 259 | 3 | 1,331 | 602 | 11,220 | 22,391 |
| Oregon | 9,582 | 3,850 | 342 | 349 | 583 | 294 | 69 | 2,116 | 80 | 33 | 1 | 395 | 411 | 8,523 | 18,106 |
| California | 41,806 | 22,881 | 1,957 | 6,154 | 6,811 | 1,151 | 541 | 1,890 | 82 | 380 | 9 | 2,300 | 942 | 45,108 | 86,914 |
| Idaho | 5,683 | 760 | 37 | 87 | 254 | 229 | 134 | 2,565 | 167 | 4 | 5 | 78 | 37 | 4,357 | 10,050 |
| Utah | 1,227 | 180 | 11 | 17 | 33 | 35 | 13 | 48 | 13 | | | 10 | 24 | 394 | 1,611 |

| | | | | | | | | | | | | | | | |
|---|---|---|---|---|---|---|---|---|---|---|---|---|---|---|---|
| Nevada | 2,167 | 635 | 73 | 69 | 76 | 59 | 34 | 21 | 23 | | | 23 | 10 | 1,023 | 3,18, |
| Arizona | 3,539 | 621 | 5 | 34 | 180 | 90 | 111 | 258 | 25 | | 18 | | | 1,324 | 4,863 |
| Total Pacific States | 75,185 | 33,115 | 2,956 | 7,453 | 9,439 | 2,154 | 991 | 8,509 | 465 | 676 | | 4,137 | 2,026 | 71,939 | 147,124 |
| Alaska (nonmember banks) | 758 | 25 | | 19 | 12 | | | | | | 2 | | | 87 | 845 |
| Hawaii (nonmember banks) | 2,400 | 524 | | | 199 | | 4 | | | | | | | 727 | 3,127 |
| Total (nonmember banks) | 3,158 | 549 | | 19 | 211 | | 4 | | | | 2 | | | 814 | 3,972 |
| Total country banks | 1,093,904 | 246,392 | 306,540 | 235,757 | 283,759 | 35,412 | 18,378 | 58,933 | 5,580 | 75,228 | 1,576 | 112,840 | 62,915 | 1,443,310 | 2,537,214 |
| Total United States | 2,285,459 | 414,414 | 498,453 | 318,456 | 423,040 | 70,575 | 69,170 | 80,889 | 6,838 | 168,082 | 3,027 | 159,027 | 87,895 | 2,277,866 | 4,563,325 |

## UNITED STATES GOVERNMENT SECURITIES OWNED BY NATIONAL BANKS IN RESERVE CITIES AND STATES.

A classification of holdings of national banks in central reserve cities, reserve cities, and elsewhere in each State of United States Government securities is shown in the following statement as of June 30, 1922:

*United States Government securities owned by national banks, June 30, 1922.*

[In thousands of dollars.]

| Cities, States, and Territories. | Liberty loan bonds, all issues. | Victory notes. | War savings certificates and thrift stamps. | United States certificates of indebtedness. | Short-term Treasury notes. | All other issues of United States bonds. | Total. |
|---|---|---|---|---|---|---|---|
| **CENTRAL RESERVE CITIES.** | | | | | | | |
| New York | 191,875 | 1,908 | 1 | 57,018 | 211,949 | 41,142 | 503,893 |
| Chicago | 10,965 | 903 | 5 | 11,699 | 21,153 | 1,835 | 46,560 |
| St. Louis | 2,358 | 738 | 5 | 3,691 | 3,965 | 9,781 | 20,538 |
| Total | 205,198 | 3,549 | 11 | 72,408 | 237,067 | 52,758 | 570,991 |
| **ALL OTHER RESERVE CITIES.** | | | | | | | |
| Boston | 22,644 | 5 | | 6,161 | 10,225 | 2,504 | 41,539 |
| Albany | 3,670 | 2 | 3 | 1,084 | 1,442 | 1,854 | 8,055 |
| Brooklyn and Bronx | 2,704 | | 3 | 110 | 430 | 874 | 4,121 |
| Buffalo | 1,784 | 17 | 2 | 790 | 85 | 2,806 | 5,484 |
| Philadelphia | 22,024 | 7,353 | 26 | 7,043 | 6,319 | 7,440 | 50,205 |
| Pittsburgh | 34,763 | 184 | 1 | 1,797 | 11,217 | 23,244 | 71,206 |
| Baltimore | 5,065 | 133 | | 2,237 | 213 | 6,220 | 13,898 |
| Washington | 8,437 | 161 | 6 | 855 | 1,382 | 5,864 | 16,705 |
| Richmond | 3,253 | 11 | 2 | 756 | 101 | 2,864 | 6,987 |
| Charleston | 2,585 | 154 | | 200 | 545 | 1,932 | 5,416 |
| Atlanta | 890 | | | 3,028 | 660 | 3,939 | 8,517 |
| Savannah | 76 | | 1 | | | 1,411 | 77 |
| Jacksonville | 2,412 | 1,413 | 1 | 586 | 655 | 1,411 | 6,478 |
| Birmingham | 878 | 49 | 4 | 256 | 50 | 1,753 | 2,990 |
| New Orleans | 1,708 | 25 | 2 | 1,044 | | 1,576 | 4,355 |
| Dallas | 3,902 | 3 | | 3,653 | 3,657 | 4,833 | 16,048 |
| El Paso | 958 | 40 | 2 | | | 1,615 | 2,615 |
| Fort Worth | 1,142 | 30 | | 859 | 171 | 1,600 | 3,802 |
| Galveston | 350 | 27 | 2 | 55 | 9 | 405 | 848 |
| Houston | 4,649 | 359 | 3 | 217 | 3,228 | 5,095 | 13,551 |
| San Antonio | 1,497 | 18 | 3 | 75 | | 3,774 | 5,367 |
| Waco | 74 | 5 | 3 | | 52 | 1,800 | 1,934 |
| Little Rock | 298 | 2 | | | | 385 | 685 |
| Louisville | 4,008 | 147 | 4 | 748 | 7,020 | 4,319 | 16,246 |
| Chattanooga | 66 | 1 | | 130 | | 2,631 | 2,828 |
| Memphis | 1,273 | 131 | | 101 | | 860 | 2,365 |
| Nashville | 3,744 | 164 | 2 | 176 | 10 | 2,335 | 6,431 |
| Cincinnati | 8,154 | 149 | | 2,286 | 4,945 | 7,906 | 23,440 |
| Cleveland | 4,648 | 129 | 1 | 143 | 581 | 4,570 | 10,072 |
| Columbus | 5,103 | 231 | 3 | 850 | 2,219 | 3,234 | 11,640 |
| Toledo | 2,421 | | 1 | 9 | 500 | 2,500 | 5,431 |
| Indianapolis | 3,524 | 83 | 6 | 850 | 2,334 | 5,569 | 12,366 |
| Chicago | 4,159 | 408 | 8 | 1,154 | 2,363 | 1,566 | 9,658 |
| Peoria | 1,160 | 1 | 8 | 143 | 574 | 2,573 | 4,459 |
| Detroit | 12,775 | | 3 | 1,774 | 2,940 | 2,266 | 19,758 |
| Grand Rapids | 1,080 | 10 | 1 | 3 | 365 | 2,017 | 3,476 |
| Milwaukee | 701 | | | 307 | 743 | 3,783 | 5,534 |
| Minneapolis | 3,912 | 164 | | 3,922 | 1,586 | 2,796 | 12,380 |
| St. Paul | 11,881 | 9 | | 2,284 | 6,660 | 1,285 | 22,119 |
| Cedar Rapids | 656 | 13 | | 253 | 532 | 550 | 2,004 |
| Des Moines | 785 | 11 | | 1 | 254 | 1,565 | 2,616 |
| Dubuque | 545 | 7 | | | 231 | 392 | 1,175 |
| Sioux City | 1,682 | 96 | 4 | 369 | 54 | 981 | 3,185 |
| Kansas City, Mo | 3,616 | 111 | | 1,934 | 2,533 | 2,123 | 10,317 |
| St. Joseph | 714 | | | 154 | 743 | 887 | 2,498 |
| Lincoln | 187 | | | 100 | | 588 | 875 |
| Omaha | 1,905 | 426 | | 2,107 | 100 | 2,336 | 6,874 |
| Kansas City, Kans | 360 | 16 | 2 | 83 | 32 | 504 | 997 |
| Topeka | 297 | 24 | | 170 | 54 | 924 | 1,469 |
| Wichita | 2,424 | 255 | 1 | 4 | 150 | 100 | 2,934 |
| Helena | 165 | 7 | | | 62 | 356 | 590 |
| Denver | 7,354 | 12 | 1 | 1,541 | 4,299 | 1,984 | 15,191 |
| Pueblo | 1,242 | 133 | 1 | | | 400 | 1,776 |
| Muskogee | 531 | 82 | | 90 | 46 | 1,272 | 2,021 |
| Oklahoma City | 2,904 | 72 | 1 | 60 | 227 | 1,086 | 4,350 |
| Tulsa | 1,410 | 141 | | 376 | | 976 | 2,903 |

*United States Government securities owned by national banks, June 30, 1922*—Continued.

| Cities, States, and Territories. | Liberty loan bonds, all issues. | Victory notes. | War savings certificates and thrift stamps. | United States certificates of indebtedness. | Short-term Treasury notes. | All other issues of United States bonds. | Total. |
|---|---|---|---|---|---|---|---|
| ALL OTHER RESERVE CITIES—con. | | | | | | | |
| Seattle | 6,167 | 1,163 | 3 | 5,004 | 2,646 | 1,538 | 16,521 |
| Spokane | 707 | 8 | | 202 | | 2,451 | 3,368 |
| Tacoma | 315 | 9 | | 107 | 290 | 700 | 1,421 |
| Portland | 5,977 | 86 | | 1,260 | 2,435 | 2,125 | 11,883 |
| Los Angeles | 5,324 | 521 | 3 | 5,868 | 1,403 | 5,061 | 18,180 |
| Oakland | 1,827 | 100 | | 76 | 161 | 1,630 | 3,794 |
| San Francisco | 15,686 | 1,013 | 3 | 2,468 | 3,210 | 17,534 | 39,914 |
| Ogden | 414 | | 1 | 1 | | 954 | 1,370 |
| Salt Lake City | 918 | 5 | 1 | 10 | 206 | 2,112 | 3,252 |
| Total all other reserve cities | 258,484 | 15,928 | 122 | 67,924 | 92,979 | 185,127 | 620,564 |
| Total all reserve cities | 463,682 | 19,477 | 133 | 140,332 | 330,046 | 237,885 | 1,191,555 |
| COUNTRY BANKS. | | | | | | | |
| Maine | 5,382 | 187 | 14 | 515 | 888 | 5,733 | 12,719 |
| New Hampshire | 4,495 | 85 | 8 | 631 | 665 | 5,092 | 10,976 |
| Vermont | 1,921 | 135 | 10 | 43 | 273 | 4,465 | 6,847 |
| Massachusetts | 21,474 | 623 | 2 | 3,819 | 6,680 | 17,973 | 50,571 |
| Rhode Island | 2,981 | 106 | 5 | 35 | 682 | 4,773 | 8,582 |
| Connecticut | 13,166 | 586 | 16 | 989 | 2,528 | 13,235 | 30,520 |
| Total New England States | 49,419 | 1,722 | 55 | 6,032 | 11,716 | 51,271 | 120,215 |
| New York | 46,462 | 3,142 | 111 | 4,279 | 6,334 | 34,419 | 94,747 |
| New Jersey | 39,100 | 2,957 | 245 | 4,582 | 6,851 | 16,812 | 70,547 |
| Pennsylvania | 84,221 | 5,836 | 147 | 7,828 | 13,274 | 66,262 | 177,568 |
| Delaware | 1,116 | 47 | 3 | 49 | 23 | 1,133 | 2,371 |
| Maryland | 5,187 | 98 | 10 | 270 | 172 | 3,948 | 9,685 |
| Total Eastern States | 176,086 | 12,080 | 516 | 17,008 | 26,654 | 122,574 | 354,918 |
| Virginia | 9,565 | 403 | 30 | 228 | 279 | 19,550 | 30,055 |
| West Virginia | 8,289 | 473 | 22 | 600 | 1,375 | 10,671 | 21,430 |
| North Carolina | 5,536 | 335 | 9 | 246 | 124 | 8,591 | 14,841 |
| South Carolina | 3,145 | 353 | 5 | 74 | | 6,784 | 10,361 |
| Georgia | 2,526 | 139 | 18 | 341 | 61 | 7,688 | 10,773 |
| Florida | 5,613 | 316 | 49 | 1,167 | 151 | 4,885 | 12,181 |
| Alabama | 3,169 | 175 | 19 | 803 | 296 | 9,019 | 13,481 |
| Mississippi | 2,033 | 146 | 13 | 148 | | 3,083 | 5,423 |
| Louisiana | 2,232 | 235 | 12 | 324 | 26 | 2,840 | 5,669 |
| Texas | 7,079 | 1,770 | 103 | 3,131 | 1,843 | 26,242 | 40,168 |
| Arkansas | 2,867 | 137 | 10 | 810 | 78 | 3,972 | 7,874 |
| Kentucky | 7,137 | 425 | 17 | 1,041 | 460 | 12,174 | 21,254 |
| Tennessee | 1,587 | 342 | 31 | 179 | 51 | 7,556 | 9,746 |
| Total Southern States | 60,778 | 5,249 | 338 | 9,092 | 4,744 | 123,055 | 203,256 |
| Ohio | 18,837 | 1,383 | 75 | 2,428 | 1,449 | 29,600 | 53,772 |
| Indiana | 14,833 | 718 | 31 | 1,420 | 1,013 | 21,990 | 40,005 |
| Illinois | 26,031 | 1,972 | 240 | 3,402 | 2,744 | 27,571 | 61,960 |
| Michigan | 8,458 | 629 | 32 | 1,158 | 945 | 9,228 | 20,450 |
| Wisconsin | 7,306 | 635 | 21 | 3,273 | 1,465 | 11,728 | 24,428 |
| Minnesota | 6,015 | 457 | 14 | 2,173 | 1,407 | 11,928 | 21,994 |
| Iowa | 7,301 | 456 | 117 | 525 | 164 | 16,730 | 25,293 |
| Missouri | 3,430 | 172 | 13 | 1,216 | 244 | 5,669 | 10,744 |
| Total Middle Western States | 92,211 | 6,422 | 543 | 15,595 | 9,431 | 134,444 | 258,646 |
| North Dakota | 1,947 | 176 | 6 | 105 | 5 | 4,674 | 6,913 |
| South Dakota | 1,411 | 98 | 6 | 181 | 29 | 4,373 | 6,098 |
| Nebraska | 2,221 | 319 | 3 | 40 | 159 | 7,237 | 9,979 |
| Kansas | 4,601 | 533 | 18 | 697 | 312 | 10,118 | 16,279 |
| Montana | 1,994 | 74 | 6 | 253 | 27 | 4,031 | 6,385 |
| Wyoming | 904 | 109 | 3 | 161 | | 2,561 | 3,738 |
| Colorado | 2,982 | 158 | 19 | 141 | 46 | 5,162 | 8,508 |
| New Mexico | 866 | 47 | 7 | | 39 | 2,355 | 3,314 |
| Oklahoma | 7,180 | 606 | 27 | 488 | 62 | 8,949 | 17,312 |
| Total Western States | 24,106 | 2,120 | 95 | 2,066 | 679 | 49,460 | 78,526 |

*United States Government securities owned by national banks, June 30, 1922—Continued.*

| Cities, States, and Territories. | Liberty loan bonds, all issues. | Victory notes. | War savings certificates and thrift stamps. | United States certificates of indebtedness. | Short-term Treasury notes. | All other issues of United States bonds. | Total. |
|---|---|---|---|---|---|---|---|
| COUNTRY BANKS—continued. | | | | | | | |
| Washington.................... | 5,806 | 534 | 17 | 514 | 1,110 | 3,190 | 11,171 |
| Oregon........................ | 4,295 | 624 | 22 | 232 | 174 | 4,235 | 9,582 |
| California..................... | 19,114 | 1,960 | 64 | 1,921 | 840 | 17,907 | 41,806 |
| Idaho......................... | 1,832 | 183 | 3 | 83 | 45 | 3,547 | 5,693 |
| Utah.......................... | 517 | 71 | 3 | 40 | .......... | 596 | 1,227 |
| Nevada........................ | 742 | 76 | 5 | 55 | 50 | 1,239 | 2,167 |
| Arizona....................... | 1,992 | 123 | 4 | 25 | .......... | 1,395 | 3,539 |
| Total Pacific States....... | 34,298 | 3,571 | 118 | 2,870 | 2,219 | 32,109 | 75,185 |
| Alaska (nonmember banks).... | 378 | 38 | .......... | 50 | .......... | 292 | 758 |
| Hawaii (nonmember banks).... | 1,195 | 21 | 2 | .......... | 732 | 450 | 2,400 |
| Total (nonmember banks). | 1,573 | 59 | 2 | 50 | 732 | 742 | 3,158 |
| Total country banks...... | 438,471 | 31,223 | 1,667 | 52,713 | 56,175 | 513,655 | 1,093,904 |
| Total United States...... | 902,153 | 50,700 | 1,800 | 193,045 | 386,221 | 751,540 | 2,285,459 |

SAVINGS DEPOSITORS AND DEPOSITS IN NATIONAL BANKS.

On June 30, 1922, the returns from 5,785 national banks operating savings departments or carrying savings accounts showed savings depositors to the number of 8,875,088, with credit balances of $3,046,647,000.

By reference to the following statement showing information with respect to savings depositors and deposits, by central reserve cities, reserve cities, and States, it is noted that banks in the Eastern States report the greatest number of depositors and largest volume of deposits. The Middle Western States are credited with the next largest number of depositors and amount of deposits, while the Southern States come next in order and the New England States, the Pacific States, and the Western States rank in the order indicated with respect to the number of depositors, but the banks in the New England States are credited with the next largest volume of deposits, the Pacific States banks coming next, the banks in the Western States reporting the smallest amount of savings deposits in any geographical section. The average rate of interest credited to savings deposits by national banks according to the tabulation is 3.71 per cent.

Although national banks were requested to include in the classification of savings deposits only those deposits subject to 30 days or more notice before withdrawal, it will be noted from the following statements that the aggregate of deposits includes approximately $85,353,000 certificates of deposit.

Savings depositors and deposits in national banks June 30, 1922.

| Cities, States, and Territories. | Number of banks reporting savings deposits. | Number of savings depositors. | Amount of savings deposits. | Average rate of interest paid. |
|---|---|---|---|---|
| CENTRAL RESERVE CITIES. | | | | |
| | | | | Per cent. |
| New York | 16 | 187,346 | $71,826,000 | 3.50 |
| Chicago | 6 | 74,158 | 15,269,000 | 3.00 |
| St. Louis | 8 | 117,482 | 27,730,000 | 3.00 |
| Total | 30 | 378,986 | 114,825,000 | 3.25 |
| ALL OTHER RESERVE CITIES. | | | | |
| Boston | 10 | 32,801 | 25,828,000 | 4.50 |
| Albany | 3 | 7,727 | 8,618,000 | 3.50 |
| Buffalo | 4 | 10,162 | 7,137,000 | 4.00 |
| Philadelphia | 18 | 55,123 | 20,946,000 | 3.25 |
| Pittsburgh | 10 | 52,044 | 27,453,000 | 3.75 |
| Baltimore | 9 | 20,040 | 11,915,000 | 4.00 |
| Washington | 14 | 73,332 | 21,394,000 | 3.25 |
| Richmond | 7 | 62,236 | 19,144,000 | 3.00 |
| Charleston | 4 | 10,237 | 9,538,000 | 4.00 |
| Atlanta | 4 | 77,270 | 15,982,000 | 3.50 |
| Savannah | 1 | 2,500 | 372,000 | 4.00 |
| Jacksonville | 3 | 34,482 | 15,243,000 | 4.00 |
| Birmingham | 2 | 27,476 | 11,162,000 | 4.00 |
| Dallas | 5 | 17,133 | 7,095,000 | 4.00 |
| El Paso | 4 | 20,323 | 6,664,000 | 4.00 |
| Fort Worth | 4 | 16,616 | 5,698,000 | 4.00 |
| Galveston | 2 | 6,838 | 3,787,000 | 4.00 |
| Houston | 9 | 37,584 | 16,178,000 | 4.00 |
| San Antonio | 2 | 1,655 | 1,020,000 | 4.00 |
| Waco | 6 | 5,901 | 2,427,000 | 4.06 |
| Little Rock | 2 | 1,984 | 768,000 | 4.00 |
| Louisville | 4 | 31,712 | 9,030,000 | 3.25 |
| Chattanooga | 2 | 18,251 | 10,623,000 | 4.00 |
| Memphis | 3 | 14,232 | 3,088,000 | 3.00 |
| Nashville | 4 | 26,322 | 8,886,000 | 4.00 |
| Cincinnati | 7 | 28,655 | 11,305,000 | 3.00 |
| Cleveland | 3 | 30,447 | 17,394,000 | 4.00 |
| Columbus | 6 | 30,795 | 5,301,000 | 3.00 |
| Toledo | 3 | 23,525 | 7,289,000 | 3.00 |
| Indianapolis | 5 | 5,604 | 1,209,000 | 3.00 |
| Chicago | 18 | 124,307 | 28,597,000 | 3.00 |
| Peoria | 4 | 20,619 | 6,727,000 | 3.00 |
| Detroit | 3 | 4,094 | 16,566,000 | 3.00 |
| Grand Rapids | 3 | 23,931 | 10,608,000 | 3.25 |
| Milwaukee | 4 | 58,551 | 17,693,000 | 3.00 |
| Minneapolis | 7 | 57,640 | 15,216,000 | 4.00 |
| St. Paul | 5 | 29,386 | 13,098,000 | 3.25 |
| Cedar Rapids | 2 | 12,400 | 3,806,000 | 4.00 |
| Des Moines | 3 | 8,850 | 3,016,000 | 4.00 |
| Dubuque | 3 | 6,065 | 1,945,000 | 4.00 |
| Sioux City | 5 | 18,944 | 4,978,000 | 3.00 |
| Kansas City, Mo | 7 | 21,442 | 3,114,000 | 3.00 |
| St. Joseph | 4 | 7,192 | 4,380,000 | 4.00 |
| Lincoln | 3 | 4,616 | 789,000 | 4.00 |
| Omaha | 8 | 39,561 | 7,056,000 | 3.25 |
| Kansas City, Kans | 1 | 1,850 | 370,000 | 3.00 |
| Topeka | 2 | 2,088 | 96,000 | 3.00 |
| Wichita | 3 | 15,628 | 3,475,000 | 4.00 |
| Helena | 1 | 1,996 | 1,029,000 | 4.00 |
| Denver | 8 | 33,788 | 28,808,000 | 4.00 |
| Pueblo | 2 | 3,184 | 1,960,000 | 3.00 |
| Muskogee | 4 | 4,828 | 1,350,000 | 4.00 |
| Oklahoma City | 9 | 16,286 | 5,572,000 | 4.00 |
| Tulsa | 7 | 18,242 | 6,085,000 | 4.00 |
| Seattle | 9 | 64,478 | 22,198,000 | 3.00 |
| Spokane | 3 | 29,376 | 11,378,000 | 3.50 |
| Tacoma | 1 | 10,253 | 4,631,000 | 3.00 |
| Portland | 3 | 65,305 | 24,876,000 | 3.00 |
| Los Angeles | 7 | 35,930 | 37,667,000 | 3.75 |
| Oakland | 2 | 2,419 | 3,105,000 | 3.50 |
| San Francisco | 4 | 34,671 | 21,721,000 | 3.75 |
| Ogden | 4 | 5,375 | 2,306,000 | 4.00 |
| Salt Lake City | 5 | 12,958 | 3,356,000 | 4.00 |
| Total all other reserve cities | 314 | 1,585,260 | 630,066,000 | 3.50 |
| Total all reserve cities | 344 | 1,964,246 | 744,891,000 | 3.50 |

*Savings depositors and deposits in national banks June 30, 1922—Continued.*

| Cities, States, and Territories. | Number of banks reporting savings deposits. | Number of savings depositors. | Amount of savings deposits. | Average rate of interest paid. |
|---|---|---|---|---|
| COUNTRY BANKS. | | | | *Per cent.* |
| Maine................................ | 41 | 135, 692 | $56, 718, 000 | 4. 00 |
| New Hampshire...................... | 19 | 35, 448 | 9, 054, 000 | 3. 50 |
| Vermont............................. | 39 | 54, 867 | 21, 613, 000 | 4. 00 |
| Massachusetts....................... | 105 | 345, 886 | 115, 656, 000 | 4. 50 |
| Rhode Island........................ | 4 | 10, 085 | 9, 917, 000 | 4. 00 |
| Connecticut......................... | 33 | 90, 370 | 34, 467, 000 | 4. 00 |
| Total New England States......... | 241 | 672, 348 | 247, 425, 000 | 4. 00 |
| New York............................ | 398 | 730, 105 | 301, 134, 000 | 3. 75 |
| New Jersey.......................... | 208 | 469, 196 | 198, 450, 000 | 3. 50 |
| Pennsylvania........................ | 751 | 1, 522, 092 | 474, 408, 000 | 3. 50 |
| Delaware............................ | 15 | 8, 823 | 4, 849, 000 | 4. 00 |
| Maryland............................ | 73 | 93, 518 | 48, 170, 000 | 3. 75 |
| Total Eastern States............. | 1, 445 | 2, 823, 734 | 1, 027, 011, 000 | 3. 75 |
| Virginia............................. | 154 | 229, 940 | 81, 492, 000 | 3. 75 |
| West Virginia....................... | 108 | 136, 411 | 47, 687, 000 | 3. 50 |
| North Carolina...................... | 76 | 120, 740 | 34, 467, 000 | 4. 00 |
| South Carolina...................... | 72 | 65, 138 | 30, 208, 000 | 4. 50 |
| Georgia............................. | 61 | 45, 610 | 14, 333, 000 | 4. 00 |
| Florida.............................. | 56 | 60, 295 | 21, 400, 000 | 4. 00 |
| Alabama............................ | 66 | 48, 467 | 17, 773, 000 | 4. 00 |
| Mississippi.......................... | 16 | 17, 819 | 7, 820, 000 | 4. 00 |
| Louisiana........................... | 20 | 26, 894 | 10, 336, 000 | 4. 00 |
| Texas............................... | 89 | 42, 429 | 16, 821, 000 | 4. 00 |
| Arkansas............................ | 40 | 21, 602 | 7, 613, 000 | 4. 00 |
| Kentucky............................ | 58 | 46, 521 | 17, 836, 000 | 3. 50 |
| Tennessee........................... | 49 | 57, 771 | 15, 003, 000 | 3. 50 |
| Total Southern States............. | 865 | 919, 637 | 322, 789, 000 | 4. 00 |
| Ohio................................ | 258 | 416, 456 | 107, 119, 000 | 4. 00 |
| Indiana............................. | 160 | 184, 473 | 52, 118, 000 | 3. 75 |
| Illinois.............................. | 375 | 366, 234 | 106, 537, 000 | 3. 50 |
| Michigan............................ | 110 | 287, 709 | 96, 247, 000 | 3. 25 |
| Wisconsin........................... | 142 | 271, 467 | 65, 426, 000 | 3. 50 |
| Minnesota........................... | 288 | 214, 039 | 52, 170, 000 | 4. 50 |
| Iowa................................ | 232 | 143, 381 | 33, 806, 000 | 4. 25 |
| Missouri............................ | 49 | 25, 564 | 5, 209, 000 | 3. 50 |
| Total Middle Western States...... | 1, 614 | 1, 909, 323 | 518, 632, 000 | 3. 75 |
| North Dakota........................ | 115 | 36, 530 | 7, 834, 000 | 5. 00 |
| South Dakota........................ | 99 | 35, 465 | 7, 307, 000 | 4. 95 |
| Nebraska............................ | 70 | 22, 752 | 3, 218, 000 | 4. 25 |
| Kansas.............................. | 121 | 50, 673 | 6, 386, 000 | 3. 25 |
| Montana............................ | 83 | 33, 661 | 12, 782, 000 | 4. 25 |
| Wyoming............................ | 41 | 25, 332 | 7, 428, 000 | 4. 25 |
| Colorado............................ | 93 | 43, 034 | 12, 999, 000 | 4. 00 |
| New Mexico.......................... | 28 | 11, 719 | 2, 701, 000 | 4. 00 |
| Oklahoma........................... | 141 | 41, 487 | 6, 570, 000 | 4. 00 |
| Total Western States............. | 791 | 300, 653 | 67, 225, 000 | 4. 22 |
| Washington......................... | 90 | 60, 990 | 22, 353, 000 | 4. 00 |
| Oregon.............................. | 67 | 31, 925 | 8, 117, 000 | 3. 75 |
| California........................... | 210 | 140, 502 | 69, 809, 000 | 4. 00 |
| Idaho............................... | 71 | 27, 894 | 7, 219, 000 | 4. 50 |
| Utah................................ | 15 | 8, 586 | 2, 389, 000 | 4. 00 |
| Nevada............................. | 9 | 4, 975 | 3, 627, 000 | 4. 00 |
| Arizona............................. | 20 | 8, 514 | 4, 567, 000 | 4. 00 |
| Total Pacific States.............. | 482 | 283, 386 | 118, 081, 000 | 4. 00 |
| Alaska (nonmember banks)........... | 2 | 590 | 334, 000 | 3. 50 |
| Hawaii (nonmember banks)........... | 1 | 1, 171 | 259, 000 | 4. 00 |
| Total (nonmember banks).......... | 3 | 1, 761 | 593, 000 | 3. 75 |
| Total country banks.............. | 5, 441 | 6, 910, 842 | 2, 301, 756, 000 | 3. 93 |
| Total United States.............. | 5, 785 | 8, 875, 088 | [1] 3, 046, 647, 000 | 3. 71 |

[1] Includes approximately $85,353,000 certificates of deposit.

SAVINGS DEPOSITORS AND DEPOSITS IN NATIONAL BANKS IN EACH
STATE (INCLUDING RESERVE CITIES), JUNE 30, 1922.

| States and Territories. | Number of banks reporting savings deposits. | Number of savings depositors. | Amount of savings deposits. | Average rate of interest paid. |
|---|---|---|---|---|
| | | | | Per cent. |
| Maine......................................... | 41 | 135,692 | $56,718,000 | 4.00 |
| New Hampshire.................................. | 19 | 35,448 | 9,054,000 | 3.50 |
| Vermont........................................ | 39 | 54,867 | 21,613,000 | 4.00 |
| Massachusetts.................................. | 115 | 378,687 | 141,484,000 | 4.50 |
| Rhode Island................................... | 4 | 10,085 | 9,917,000 | 4.00 |
| Connecticut.................................... | 33 | 90,370 | 34,467,000 | 4.00 |
| Total New England States............... | 251 | 705,149 | 273,253,000 | 4.00 |
| New York....................................... | 421 | 935,340 | 388,715,000 | 3.75 |
| New Jersey..................................... | 208 | 469,196 | 198,450,000 | 3.50 |
| Pennsylvania................................... | 779 | 1,629,259 | 522,807,000 | 3.50 |
| Delaware....................................... | 15 | 8,823 | 4,849,000 | 4.00 |
| Maryland....................................... | 82 | 113,558 | 60,085,000 | 4.00 |
| Washington, D. C............................... | 14 | 73,332 | 21,394,000 | 3.25 |
| Total Eastern States................... | 1,519 | 3,229,508 | 1,196,300,000 | 3.75 |
| Virginia....................................... | 161 | 292,176 | 100,636,000 | 3.50 |
| West Virginia.................................. | 108 | 136,411 | 47,687,000 | 3.50 |
| North Carolina................................. | 76 | 120,740 | 34,467,000 | 4.00 |
| South Carolina................................. | 76 | 75,375 | 39,746,000 | 4.25 |
| Georgia........................................ | 66 | 125,380 | 30,687,000 | 4.00 |
| Florida........................................ | 59 | 94,777 | 36,643,000 | 4.00 |
| Alabama........................................ | 68 | 75,943 | 28,935,000 | 4.00 |
| Mississippi.................................... | 16 | 17,819 | 7,820,000 | 4.00 |
| Louisiana...................................... | 20 | 26,894 | 10,336,000 | 4.00 |
| Texas.......................................... | 121 | 148,479 | 59,690,000 | 4.00 |
| Arkansas....................................... | 42 | 23,586 | 8,381,000 | 4.00 |
| Kentucky....................................... | 62 | 78,233 | 26,866,000 | 3.50 |
| Tennessee...................................... | 58 | 116,576 | 37,600,000 | 3.75 |
| Total Southern States.................. | 933 | 1,332,389 | 469,494,000 | 4.00 |
| Ohio........................................... | 277 | 535,878 | 148,408,000 | 3.50 |
| Indiana........................................ | 165 | 190,077 | 53,327,000 | 3.50 |
| Illinois....................................... | 403 | 585,318 | 157,130,000 | 3.00 |
| Michigan....................................... | 116 | 315,734 | 123,421,000 | 3.25 |
| Wisconsin...................................... | 146 | 330,018 | 83,119,000 | 3.25 |
| Minnesota...................................... | 300 | 301,065 | 80,484,000 | 4.00 |
| Iowa........................................... | 245 | 189,640 | 47,551,000 | 3.75 |
| Missouri....................................... | 68 | 171,680 | 40,433,000 | 3.50 |
| Total Middle Western States............ | 1,720 | 2,619,410 | 733,873,000 | 3.50 |
| North Dakota................................... | 115 | 36,530 | 7,834,000 | 5.00 |
| South Dakota................................... | 99 | 35,465 | 7,307,000 | 4.95 |
| Nebraska....................................... | 81 | 66,929 | 11,063,000 | 3.75 |
| Kansas......................................... | 127 | 70,239 | 10,327,000 | 3.25 |
| Montana........................................ | 84 | 35,657 | 13,811,000 | 4.50 |
| Wyoming........................................ | 41 | 25,332 | 7,428,000 | 4.25 |
| Colorado....................................... | 103 | 80,006 | 43,767,000 | 3.75 |
| New Mexico..................................... | 28 | 11,719 | 2,701,000 | 4.00 |
| Oklahoma....................................... | 161 | 80,843 | 19,577,000 | 4.00 |
| Total Western States................... | 839 | 442,720 | 123,815,000 | 4.16 |
| Washington..................................... | 103 | 165,097 | 60,560,000 | 3.25 |
| Oregon......................................... | 70 | 97,230 | 32,993,000 | 3.25 |
| California...................................... | 223 | 213,522 | 132,302,000 | 3.75 |
| Idaho.......................................... | 71 | 27,894 | 7,219,000 | 4.50 |
| Utah........................................... | 24 | 26,919 | 8,051,000 | 4.00 |
| Nevada......................................... | 9 | 4,975 | 3,627,000 | 4.00 |
| Arizona........................................ | 20 | 8,514 | 4,567,000 | 4.00 |
| Total Pacific States................... | 520 | 544,151 | 249,319,000 | 3.75 |
| Alaska (nonmember banks)....................... | 2 | 590 | 334,000 | 3.50 |
| Hawaii (nonmember banks)....................... | 1 | 1,171 | 259,000 | 4.00 |
| Total (nonmember banks)................ | 3 | 1,761 | 593,000 | 3.75 |
| Total United States.................... | 5,785 | 8,875,088 | [1] 3,046,647,000 | 3.71 |

[1] Includes approximately $85,353,000 certificates of deposit.

## RELATION OF CAPITAL OF NATIONAL BANKS TO DEPOSITS, ETC.

The variation in the proportion of the (a) capital of national banks to individual deposits; (b) capital to loans; (c) capital to aggregate resources; (d) capital, surplus, and profits to deposits; and (e) cash on hand and amounts due from Federal reserve banks to individual deposits from 1916 to 1922, as of the date of the call immediately following the midsummer call for reports of condition from national banks, is shown in the following table:

| Item. | Sept. 12, 1916. | Sept. 11, 1917. | Aug. 31, 1918. | Sept. 12, 1919. | Sept. 8, 1920. | Sept. 6, 1921. | Sept. 15, 1922. |
|---|---|---|---|---|---|---|---|
| Capital to individual deposits | $1.00–$7.66 | $1.00–$8.96 | $1.00–$9.41 | $1.00–$11.14 | $1.00–$10.89 | $1.00–$9.43 | $1.00–$10.28 |
| Capital to loans | 1.00– 7.49 | 1.00– 8.49 | 1.00– 9.18 | 1.00– 10.13 | 1.00– 10.99 | 1.00– 9.15 | 1.00– 8.60 |
| Capital to aggregate resources | 1.00–13.55 | 1.00–15.33 | 1.00–16.92 | 1.00– 19.38 | 1.00– 18.57 | 1.00–15.45 | 1.00– 16.01 |
| Capital and surplus and other profits to individual deposits | 1.00– 3.83 | 1.00– 4.87 | 1.00– 4.47 | 1.00– 5.07 | 1.00– 4.90 | 1.00– 4.23 | 1.00– 4.65 |
| Cash on hand and balances with Federal reserve bank to individual deposits | 1.00– 5.94 | 1.00– 5.86 | 1.00– 6.20 | 1.00– 6.20 | 1.00– 6.19 | 1.00– 7.11 | 1.00– 6.78 |

## PERCENTAGE OF THE PRINCIPAL ITEMS OF ASSETS AND LIABILITIES OF NATIONAL BANKS.

The percentages of loans and discounts of national banks, of United States Government securities, capital, surplus and profits, and individual deposits, to aggregate resources (including rediscounts), are shown in the following statement, as of the date of fall reports of national banks for years 1914 to 1922, inclusive:

| Item. | 1914 | 1915 | 1916 | 1917 | 1918 | 1919 | 1920 | 1921 | 1922 |
|---|---|---|---|---|---|---|---|---|---|
| Loans and discounts, including rediscounts | 55.7 | 55.5 | 55.2 | 55.4 | 54.2 | 52.3 | 59.2 | 59.2 | 53.7 |
| United States Government securities | 6.9 | 6.4 | 5.0 | 6.9 | 13.2 | 14.9 | 9.4 | 9.4 | 11.5 |
| Total | 62.6 | 61.9 | 60.2 | 62.3 | 67.4 | 67.2 | 68.6 | 68.6 | 65.2 |
| Capital | 9.2 | 8.7 | 7.4 | 6.5 | 5.9 | 5.2 | 5.4 | 6.5 | 6.2 |
| Surplus and profits | 8.8 | 8.3 | 7.4 | 6.8 | 6.5 | 6.2 | 6.6 | 7.9 | 7.6 |
| Deposits (individual) | 53.2 | 53.4 | 56.5 | 58.4 | 55.6 | 57.4 | 58.7 | 61.0 | 64.2 |
| Total | 71.2 | 70.4 | 71.3 | 71.7 | 68.0 | 68.8 | 70.7 | 75.4 | 78.0 |

## PROGRESS OF NATIONAL BANKS SINCE PASSAGE OF THE FEDERAL RESERVE ACT.

The principal items of resources and liabilities of national banks in central reserve cities, other reserve cities and banks outside of reserve cities, commonly referred to as country banks, as of the date of the call in the fall of each year, from 1913 to 1922, are shown in the statement following.

*Principal items of assets and liabilities of national banks, 1913-1922.*

[In thousands of dollars.]

| Date. | Central reserve city banks. | Other reserve city banks. | Country banks. | Aggregate. |
|---|---|---|---|---|
| **LOANS AND DISCOUNTS.** | | | | |
| [Including overdrafts and rediscounts.] | | | | |
| Oct. 21, 1913 | 1,348,251 | 1,649,905 | 3,290,182 | 6,288,338 |
| Dec. 31, 1914 | 1,453,275 | 1,702,882 | 3,207,278 | 6,363,435 |
| Nov. 10, 1915 | 2,060,444 | 1,870,810 | 3,309,886 | 7,241,140 |
| Nov. 17, 1916 | 2,343,162 | 2,383,982 | 3,676,511 | 8,403,655 |
| Nov. 20, 1917 | 2,649,534 | 2,871,016 | 4,277,234 | 9,797,784 |
| Aug. 31, 1918 | 2,883,871 | 3,127,062 | 4,100,180 | 10,111,113 |
| Sept. 12, 1919 | 3,144,150 | 3,637,689 | 4,759,664 | 11,541,503 |
| Sept. 8, 1920 | 3,695,463 | 4,174,877 | 5,853,271 | 13,723,611 |
| Sept. 6, 1921 | 2,866,210 | 3,418,497 | 5,410,340 | 11,695,047 |
| Sept. 15, 1922 | 2,469,124 | 3,453,410 | 5,325,632 | 11,248,166 |
| **UNITED STATES GOVERNMENT SECURITIES.** | | | | |
| Oct. 21, 1913 | 85,478 | 187,783 | 527,264 | 800,525 |
| Dec. 31, 1914 | 81,802 | 196,955 | 516,321 | 795,078 |
| Nov. 10, 1915 | 76,510 | 193,328 | 507,927 | 777,765 |
| Nov. 17, 1916 | 53,953 | 175,530 | 494,990 | 724,473 |
| Nov. 20, 1917 | 873,431 | 521,248 | 959,504 | 2,354,183 |
| Aug. 31, 1918 | 572,660 | 629,870 | 1,263,738 | 2,466,268 |
| Sept. 12, 1919 | 727,609 | 966,506 | 1,602,478 | 3,296,593 |
| Sept. 8, 1920 | 339,433 | 553,343 | 1,282,243 | 2,175,019 |
| Sept. 6, 1921 | 216,687 | 451,130 | 1,194,160 | 1,861,977 |
| Sept. 15, 1922 | 588,318 | 689,652 | 1,124,522 | 2,402,492 |
| **OTHER BONDS.[1]** | | | | |
| Oct. 21, 1913 | 207,335 | 251,802 | 647,950 | 1,107,087 |
| Dec. 31, 1914 | 230,281 | 317,478 | 722,164 | 1,270,443 |
| Nov. 10, 1915 | 285,736 | 324,254 | 733,832 | 1,343,822 |
| Nov. 17, 1916 | 345,693 | 402,420 | 961,843 | 1,709,956 |
| Nov. 20, 1917 | 405,830 | 427,400 | 1,073,552 | 1,906,782 |
| Aug. 31, 1918 | 311,025 | 410,632 | 973,413 | 1,695,070 |
| Sept. 12, 1919 | 313,161 | 411,046 | 1,082,388 | 1,806,595 |
| Sept. 8, 1920 | 284,125 | 374,574 | 1,146,880 | 1,805,579 |
| Sept. 6, 1921 | 274,638 | 405,057 | 1,294,054 | 1,973,749 |
| Sept. 15, 1922 | 299,641 | 496,010 | 1,494,131 | 2,289,782 |
| **STOCK IN FEDERAL RESERVE BANKS.** | | | | |
| Nov. 10, 1915 | 10,178 | 14,139 | 29,200 | 53,517 |
| Nov. 17, 1916 | 10,507 | 14,367 | 29,252 | 54,126 |
| Nov. 20, 1917 | 10,941 | 15,210 | 29,547 | 55,698 |
| Aug. 31, 1918 | 11,519 | 16,690 | 29,050 | 57,259 |
| Sept. 12, 1919 | 12,763 | 17,472 | 30,238 | 60,473 |
| Sept. 8, 1920 | 14,362 | 19,198 | 33,290 | 66,850 |
| **DUE FROM FEDERAL RESERVE BANKS.[2]** | | | | |
| Dec. 31, 1914 | 133,560 | 59,992 | 67,908 | 261,460 |
| Nov. 10, 1915 | 211,776 | 73,459 | 80,951 | 366,186 |
| Nov. 17, 1916 | 234,067 | 194,654 | 220,450 | 649,171 |
| Nov. 20, 1917 | 488,006 | 389,899 | 364,914 | 1,242,819 |
| Aug. 31, 1918 | 515,948 | 441,465 | 350,334 | 1,307,747 |
| Sept. 12, 1919 | 576,944 | 600,488 | 427,770 | 1,605,202 |
| Sept. 8, 1920 | 554,140 | 679,147 | 490,210 | 1,723,497 |
| Sept. 6, 1921 | 447,110 | 479,841 | 408,496 | 1,335,447 |
| Sept. 15, 1922 | 561,773 | 624,568 | 464,686 | 1,651,027 |
| **DUE FROM ALL OTHER BANKS.** | | | | |
| Oct. 21, 1913 | 242,575 | 586,462 | 710,834 | 1,539,871 |
| Dec. 31, 1914 | 185,319 | 444,400 | 529,271 | 1,158,990 |
| Nov. 10, 1915 | 210,470 | 708,259 | 684,494 | 1,603,223 |
| Nov. 17, 1916 | 285,619 | 788,380 | 944,767 | 2,018,766 |
| Nov. 20, 1917 | 247,365 | 685,801 | 837,018 | 1,770,184 |
| Aug. 31, 1918 | 213,861 | 601,253 | 712,682 | 1,527,796 |
| Sept. 12, 1919 | 230,307 | 667,586 | 809,783 | 1,707,676 |
| Sept. 8, 1920 | 137,864 | 519,208 | 767,151 | 1,424,223 |
| Sept. 6, 1921 | 94,954 | 387,007 | 557,702 | 1,039,663 |
| Sept. 15, 1922 | 105,371 | 566,520 | 691,345 | 1,363,236 |

[1] Includes all stocks, and securities, etc., commencing Sept. 6, 1921.
[2] Includes items with Federal reserve bank in process of collection.

*Principal items of assets and liabilities of national banks, 1913-1922*—Continued.

| Date. | Central reserve city banks. | Other reserve city banks. | Country banks. | Aggregate. |
|---|---|---|---|---|
| **TOTAL CASH.** | | | | |
| Oct. 21, 1913.......................... | 380,796 | 256,236 | 304,374 | 941,408 |
| Dec. 31, 1914.......................... | 264,340 | 203,357 | 267,010 | 734,706 |
| Nov. 10, 1915.......................... | 445,632 | 204,843 | 269,905 | 920,380 |
| Nov. 17, 1916.......................... | 358,231 | 217,978 | 282,064 | 858,273 |
| Nov. 20, 1917.......................... | 118,588 | 148,695 | 248,837 | 516,120 |
| Aug. 31, 1918.......................... | 87,693 | 99,677 | 176,676 | 364,136 |
| Sept. 12, 1919......................... | 97,231 | 116,355 | 225,625 | 439,211 |
| Sept. 8, 1920.......................... | 98,073 | 121,555 | 251,918 | 471,546 |
| Sept. 6, 1921.......................... | 64,232 | 87,544 | 206,022 | 357,798 |
| Sept. 15, 1922......................... | 52,262 | 81,585 | 198,104 | 331,951 |
| **AGGREGATE ASSETS (INCLUDING REDISCOUNTS).** | | | | |
| Oct. 21, 1913.......................... | 2,485,195 | 3,102,543 | 5,713,820 | 11,301,558 |
| Dec. 31, 1914.......................... | 2,599,688 | 3,154,413 | 5,602,985 | 11,357,086 |
| Nov. 10, 1915.......................... | 3,684,992 | 3,644,370 | 5,906,969 | 13,236,331 |
| Nov. 17, 1916.......................... | 4,176,733 | 4,469,025 | 6,923,002 | 15,568,759 |
| Nov. 20, 1917.......................... | 5,247,833 | 5,419,224 | 8,133,353 | 18,800,410 |
| Aug. 31, 1918.......................... | 4,995,053 | 5,728,724 | 7,922,969 | 18,646,746 |
| Sept. 12, 1919......................... | 5,844,951 | 6,912,648 | 9,298,727 | 22,056,326 |
| Sept. 8, 1920.......................... | 5,965,698 | 6,983,850 | 10,226,236 | 23,175,784 |
| Sept. 6, 1921.......................... | 4,638,167 | 5,621,379 | 9,459,634 | 19,719,180 |
| Sept. 15, 1922......................... | 4,853,988 | 6,354,978 | 9,717,133 | 20,926,099 |
| **CAPITAL STOCK.** | | | | |
| Oct. 21, 1913.......................... | 182,650 | 263,018 | 613,735 | 1,059,403 |
| Dec. 31, 1914.......................... | 175,900 | 280,963 | 609,088 | 1,065,951 |
| Nov. 10, 1915.......................... | 177,290 | 283,311 | 608,048 | 1,068,649 |
| Nov. 17, 1916.......................... | 182,650 | 281,736 | 606,730 | 1,071,116 |
| Nov. 20, 1917.......................... | 188,200 | 293,686 | 610,321 | 1,092,207 |
| Aug. 31, 1918.......................... | 189,850 | 315,763 | 596,226 | 1,101,839 |
| Sept. 12, 1919......................... | 200,550 | 324,328 | 613,092 | 1,137,970 |
| Sept. 8, 1920.......................... | 228,170 | 353,543 | 666,558 | 1,248,271 |
| Sept. 6, 1921.......................... | 246,760 | 345,107 | 684,310 | 1,276,177 |
| Sept. 15, 1922......................... | 223,055 | 378,532 | 705,535 | 1,307,122 |
| **SURPLUS AND OTHER PROFITS.** | | | | |
| Oct. 21, 1913.......................... | 225,640 | 254,142 | 527,796 | 1,007,578 |
| Dec. 31, 1914.......................... | 225,359 | 262,985 | 520,517 | 1,008,861 |
| Nov. 10, 1915.......................... | 234,091 | 268,115 | 537,908 | 1,040,114 |
| Nov. 17, 1916.......................... | 252,157 | 279,097 | 559,520 | 1,090,774 |
| Nov. 20, 1917.......................... | 293,167 | 315,246 | 603,456 | 1,211,869 |
| Aug. 31, 1918.......................... | 323,358 | 354,422 | 565,321 | 1,243,101 |
| Sept. 12, 1919......................... | 381,633 | 396,672 | 641,973 | 1,420,278 |
| Sept. 8, 1920.......................... | 436,133 | 453,979 | 709,567 | 1,599,679 |
| Sept. 6, 1921.......................... | 422,087 | 441,308 | 702,762 | 1,566,157 |
| Sept. 15, 1922......................... | 391,510 | 454,148 | 735,586 | 1,581,244 |
| **CIRCULATION OUTSTANDING.** | | | | |
| Oct. 21, 1913.......................... | 76,978 | 163,959 | 486,142 | 727,079 |
| Dec. 31, 1914.......................... | 87,844 | 222,655 | 538,308 | 848,807 |
| Nov. 10, 1915.......................... | 63,634 | 172,078 | 477,754 | 713,466 |
| Nov. 17, 1916.......................... | 46,995 | 157,166 | 461,098 | 665,259 |
| Nov. 20, 1917.......................... | 46,542 | 159,986 | 463,134 | 669,662 |
| Aug. 31, 1918.......................... | 49,630 | 172,766 | 451,805 | 674,201 |
| Sept. 12, 1919......................... | 48,751 | 172,791 | 460,047 | 681,589 |
| Sept. 8, 1920.......................... | 47,751 | 170,609 | 474,910 | 693,270 |
| Sept. 6, 1921.......................... | 46,680 | 169,323 | 488,665 | 704,668 |
| Sept. 15, 1922......................... | 38,050 | 185,853 | 502,886 | 726,789 |
| **DUE TO ALL BANKS.[3]** | | | | |
| Oct. 21, 1913.......................... | 965,229 | 918,624 | 297,183 | 2,181,036 |
| Dec. 31, 1914.......................... | 878,377 | 755,368 | 236,026 | 1,869,771 |
| Nov. 10, 1915.......................... | 1,467,834 | 972,339 | 269,501 | 2,709,674 |
| Nov. 17, 1916.......................... | 1,553,234 | 1,363,209 | 432,312 | 3,348,755 |
| Nov. 20, 1917.......................... | 1,373,243 | 1,298,390 | 435,884 | 3,107,517 |
| Aug. 31, 1918.......................... | 1,349,552 | 1,214,721 | 321,663 | 2,885,936 |
| Sept. 12, 1919......................... | 1,600,195 | 1,455,080 | 434,862 | 3,490,137 |
| Sept. 8, 1920.......................... | 1,361,572 | 1,342,989 | 398,008 | 3,102,569 |
| Sept. 6, 1921.......................... | 1,158,076 | 967,524 | 291,811 | 2,417,411 |
| Sept. 15, 1922......................... | 1,355,766 | 1,282,239 | 375,977 | 3,013,982 |

[3] Beginning Sept. 12, 1919, includes certified checks and cashiers' checks outstanding heretofore included in individual demand deposits.

*Principal items of assets and liabilities of national banks, 1913-1922*—Continued.

| Date. | Central reserve city banks. | Other reserve city banks. | Country banks. | Aggregate. |
|---|---|---|---|---|
| **DEMAND DEPOSITS.** | | | | |
| [Including U. S. deposits.] | | | | |
| Oct. 21, 1913 | 992,365 | 1,304,136 | 2,683,682 | 4,980,183 |
| Dec. 31, 1914 | 1,175,524 | 1,415,490 | 2,604,461 | 5,195,475 |
| Nov. 10, 1915 | 1,618,422 | 1,660,375 | 2,793,046 | 6,071,843 |
| Nov. 17, 1916 | 1,960,715 | 2,015,366 | 3,347,997 | 7,324,078 |
| Nov. 20, 1917 | 2,789,524 | 2,646,858 | 3,972,572 | 9,358,954 |
| Aug. 31, 1918 | 2,290,436 | 2,646,452 | 3,665,444 | 8,602,332 |
| Sept. 12, 1919 | 2,695,597 | 3,203,295 | 4,371,544 | 10,270,468 |
| Sept. 8, 1920 | 2,508,519 | 3,002,659 | 4,577,911 | 10,089,039 |
| Sept. 6, 1921 | 2,174,616 | 2,498,477 | 3,789,644 | 8,462,737 |
| Sept. 15, 1922 | 2,367,231 | 3,047,596 | 4,000,733 | 9,415,560 |
| **TIME DEPOSITS.[4]** | | | | |
| Oct. 21, 1913 | 15,113 | 157,588 | 1,012,091 | 1,184,792 |
| Dec. 31, 1914 | 17,922 | 171,037 | 982,263 | 1,171,222 |
| Nov. 10, 1915 | 39,781 | 215,739 | 1,120,436 | 1,375,956 |
| Nov. 17, 1916 | 76,272 | 287,922 | 1,452,252 | 1,816,446 |
| Nov. 20, 1917 | 121,917 | 362,742 | 1,797,206 | 2,281,865 |
| Aug. 31, 1918 | 133,055 | 409,557 | 1,854,879 | 2,397,491 |
| Sept. 12, 1919 | 172,993 | 502,924 | 2,245,117 | 2,921,034 |
| Sept. 8, 1920 | 192,969 | 620,606 | 2,746,723 | 3,560,298 |
| Sept. 6, 1921 | 159,104 | 659,461 | 2,862,139 | 3,680,704 |
| Sept. 15, 1922 | 271,214 | 822,519 | 3,075,487 | 4,169,220 |
| **TOTAL DEPOSITS.** | | | | |
| Oct. 21, 1913 | 1,972,707 | 2,380,348 | 3,992,956 | 8,346,011 |
| Dec. 31, 1914 | 2,071,823 | 2,341,895 | 3,822,750 | 8,236,468 |
| Nov. 10, 1915 | 3,126,037 | 2,848,453 | 4,182,983 | 10,157,473 |
| Nov. 17, 1916 | 3,590,221 | 3,666,497 | 5,232,561 | 12,489,279 |
| Nov. 20, 1917 | 4,284,684 | 4,307,990 | 6,205,662 | 14,798,336 |
| Aug. 31, 1918 | 3,773,043 | 4,270,730 | 5,841,986 | 13,885,759 |
| Sept. 12, 1919 | 4,468,785 | 5,161,299 | 7,051,498 | 16,681,582 |
| Sept. 8, 1920 | 4,063,060 | 4,966,254 | 7,722,642 | 16,751,956 |
| Sept. 6, 1921 | 3,491,796 | 4,125,462 | 6,943,594 | 14,560,852 |
| Sept. 15, 1922 | 3,994,211 | 5,152,354 | 7,452,197 | 16,598,762 |
| **BILLS PAYABLE.** | | | | |
| Oct. 21, 1913 | 7,249 | 14,315 | 62,380 | 83,944 |
| Dec. 31, 1914 | 5,860 | 15,374 | 75,622 | 96,856 |
| Nov. 10, 1915 | 3,407 | 5,424 | 51,736 | 60,576 |
| Nov. 17, 1916 | 336 | 2,383 | 22,398 | 25,117 |
| Nov. 20, 1917 | 174,188 | 94,791 | 83,753 | 352,732 |
| Aug. 31, 1918 | 272,923 | 195,752 | 222,189 | 690,864 |
| Sept. 12, 1919 | 348,283 | 409,980 | 306,343 | 1,064,606 |
| Sept. 8, 1920 | 401,614 | 280,322 | 327,400 | 1,009,336 |
| Sept. 6, 1921 | 113,353 | 147,296 | 291,046 | 551,695 |
| Sept. 15, 1922 | 10,290 | 36,412 | 135,063 | 181,765 |
| **LETTERS OF CREDIT.** | | | | |
| Oct. 21, 1913 | | | | |
| Dec. 31, 1914 | | | | |
| Nov. 10, 1915 | 40,208 | 34,611 | 592 | 75,741 |
| Nov. 17, 1916 | 14,837 | 15,283 | 1,252 | 31,372 |
| Nov. 20, 1917 | 17,866 | 20,583 | 1,239 | 39,688 |
| Aug. 31, 1918 | 11,486 | 12,647 | 652 | 24,785 |
| Sept. 12, 1919 | 8,262 | 1,186 | 463 | 9,911 |
| Sept. 8, 1920 | 6,370 | 1,652 | 580 | 8,602 |
| Sept. 6, 1921 | 3,482 | 1,129 | 365 | 4,976 |
| Sept. 15, 1922 | 4,855 | 1,427 | 357 | 6,639 |
| **ACCEPTANCES.** | | | | |
| Oct. 21, 1913 | | | | |
| Dec. 31, 1914 | | | | |
| Nov. 10, 1915 | 16,634 | 10,004 | 170 | 26,808 |
| Nov. 17, 1916 | 57,171 | 35,393 | 5,667 | 98,231 |
| Nov. 20, 1917 | 76,373 | 66,241 | 11,031 | 153,645 |
| Aug. 31, 1918 | 125,347 | 109,947 | 8,478 | 243,772 |
| Sept. 12, 1919 | 160,864 | 150,046 | 12,316 | 323,228 |
| Sept. 8, 1920 | 242,313 | 159,649 | 12,621 | 414,583 |
| Sept. 6, 1921 | 147,236 | 64,725 | 6,219 | 218,180 |
| Sept. 15, 1922 | 114,022 | 65,159 | 4,188 | 183,369 |

[4] Beginning Sept. 11, 1917, includes postal savings deposits.

In the fiscal year ended June 30, 1922, the gross earnings of national banks amounted to $1,067,268,000, or a reduction compared with the gross earnings for the fiscal year ended June 30, 1921, of $134,651,000. This reduction is accounted for principally by reason of the curtailment of the loans and discounts of these banks, the amount of interest and discount collected being reduced between these dates from $1,105,832,000 to $955,451,000. Exchange and collection charges amounted to $15,546,000, compared with $20,439,000 June 30, 1921, and foreign exchange profits dropped from $21,472,000 June.30, 1921, to $15,868,000. Very little change is noted in the amount of collections incident to commissions and earnings from insurance premiums and the negotiation of real estate loans authorized by section 13 of the Federal reserve act, the respective amounts for the two periods indicated being $1,191,000 and $1,169,000. Other miscellaneous earnings during the year aggregated $79,234,000, compared with $52,985,000 during the prior year.

The expenses paid by national banks in the last fiscal year amounted to $732,990,000, of which amount the principal item was on account of interest paid on deposits, which totaled $294,076,000. The next largest item of expense was on account of salaries and wages, aggregating $198,404,000, while interest and discount on borrowed money amounted to $47,685,000, and the amount paid on account of taxes was $79,376,000. The total of other miscellaneous expenses was $113,449,000, leaving the net earnings of these banks, with the addition of $41,782,000, which was recovered on account of charged-off assets, at $376,060,000, compared with $395,991,000 during the previous year.

During the current year it was necessary for national banks to charge off $135,208,000, losses on account of loans and discounts, compared with $76,210,000 charged off during 1921. It was also necessary to charge off on account of bonds, securities, etc., $33,444,000, compared with $76,179,000 during the prior year, and other losses charged off, including $2,073,000 on foreign exchange, amounted to $23,738,000, compared with $27,496,000 during 1921.

The net addition to profits, after deducting the losses referred to in the preceding paragraph, amounted to $183,670,000, which was $32,436,000 less than the amount added to profits during the preceding year. Dividends were declared to the amount of $165,884,000, compared with $158,158,000 in 1921. The per cent rate of dividends to paid-in capital stock was 12.69, compared with 12.42 for 1921, and the amount of net addition to profits during the current year was equal to 14.05 per cent of capital, compared with 16.97 per cent during the previous fiscal year. Including surplus and undivided profits with capital, the per cent rate of dividends paid during the fiscal year ended June 30, 1922, was 5.82, compared with 5.66 for 1921, and on this basis the net addition to profits was equal to 6.45 per cent, compared with 7.73 during the preceding fiscal year.

The comparison of earnings, expenses, and dividends of national banks for the fiscal years ended June 30, 1921 and 1922, is shown in the statement following.

*Earnings, expenses, and dividends of national banks' for the fiscal years ended June 30, 1921 and 1922.*

[In thousands of dollars.]

|  | June 30, 1921—8,147 banks. | June 30, 1922—8,246 banks. |
|---|---|---|
| Capital stock | 1,273,237 | 1,307,199 |
| Total surplus fund | 1,026,270 | 1,049,228 |
| Dividends declared | 158,158 | 165,884 |
| **Gross earnings:** |  |  |
| (a) Interest and discount | 1,105,832 | 955,451 |
| (b) Exchange and collection charges | 20,439 | 15,546 |
| (c) Foreign exchange profits | 21,472 | 15,868 |
| (d) Commissions and earnings from insurance premiums and the negotiation of real estate loans | 1,191 | 1,169 |
| (e) Other earnings | 52,985 | 79,234 |
| Total | 1,201,919 | 1,067,268 |
| **Expenses paid:** |  |  |
| (a) Salaries and wages | 202,726 | 198,404 |
| (b) Interest and discount on borrowed money | 119,396 | 47,685 |
| (c) Interest on deposits | 291,828 | 294,076 |
| (d) Taxes | 87,398 | 79,376 |
| (e) Contributions to American National Red Cross | 187 | ......... |
| (f) Other expenses | 128,371 | 113,449 |
| Total | 829,906 | 732,990 |
| Net earnings during the year | 372,013 | 334,278 |
| Recoveries on charged-off assets | 23,978 | 41,782 |
| Total | 395,991 | 376,060 |
| **Losses charged off:** |  |  |
| (a) On loans and discounts | 76,210 | 135,208 |
| (b) On bonds, securities, etc | 76,179 | 33,444 |
| (c) Other losses | 16,868 | 21,665 |
| (d) On foreign exchange | 10,628 | 2,073 |
| Total | 179,885 | 192,390 |
| Net addition to profits during the year | 216,106 | 183,670 |

## EARNINGS, EXPENSES, AND DIVIDENDS OF NATIONAL BANKS IN RESERVE CITIES AND STATES.

The earnings, expenses, and dividends of national banks in reserve cities and States and in Federal reserve districts are shown in the following statements for the fiscal year ended June 30, 1922:

Abstract of reports of earnings, expenses, and dividends of national banks for year ended June 30, 1922.

[In thousands of dollars.]

| Cities, States, and Territories | Number of banks | Capital | Surplus | Capital and surplus | Gross earnings | | | | | | Expenses | | | | | |
|---|---|---|---|---|---|---|---|---|---|---|---|---|---|---|---|---|
| | | | | | Interest and discount | Exchange and collection charges | Foreign exchange profits | Commissions and earnings from insurance premiums and the negotiation of real-estate loans | Other earnings | Total gross earnings | Salaries and wages | Interest and discount on borrowed money | Interest on deposits | Taxes | Other expenses | Total expenses paid |
| Maine | 60 | 7,045 | 4,561 | 11,606 | 5,458 | 45 | 10 | | 473 | 6,016 | 814 | 106 | 2,457 | 240 | 523 | 4,140 |
| New Hampshire | 56 | 5,365 | 4,288 | 9,653 | 2,922 | 51 | 7 | | 221 | 3,201 | 705 | 175 | 545 | 141 | 481 | 2,047 |
| Vermont | 49 | 5,410 | 2,463 | 7,873 | 2,699 | 29 | 10 | | 158 | 2,896 | 537 | 124 | 912 | 200 | 280 | 2,053 |
| Massachusetts | 147 | 27,049 | 19,863 | 46,912 | 19,272 | 153 | 33 | 8 | 1,916 | 21,382 | 3,648 | 395 | 7,224 | 1,704 | 2,387 | 15,358 |
| Boston | 13 | 36,600 | 38,550 | 75,150 | 23,963 | 373 | 748 | | 2,818 | 27,907 | 4,043 | 551 | 7,845 | 3,491 | 2,454 | 18,384 |
| Rhode Island | 17 | 5,570 | 4,795 | 10,365 | 3,204 | 18 | 9 | 2 | 230 | 3,463 | 483 | 23 | 1,114 | 223 | 369 | 2,212 |
| Connecticut | 64 | 21,607 | 14,959 | 36,566 | 10,200 | 95 | 39 | | 1,031 | 11,365 | 2,255 | 398 | 2,749 | 806 | 1,236 | 7,444 |
| New England States | 406 | 108,646 | 89,479 | 198,125 | 67,748 | 769 | 856 | 10 | 6,847 | 76,230 | 12,485 | 1,772 | 22,846 | 6,805 | 7,730 | 51,638 |
| New York | 464 | 46,117 | 34,562 | 80,679 | 33,129 | 376 | 29 | 6 | 3,482 | 42,022 | 7,040 | 1,044 | 14,786 | 2,073 | 4,204 | 29,147 |
| Albany | 3 | 2,850 | 3,400 | 6,250 | 3,347 | 48 | 2 | | 320 | 3,717 | 480 | 54 | 1,316 | 159 | 385 | 2,404 |
| Brooklyn and Bronx | 5 | 2,100 | 1,905 | 4,005 | 2,166 | 13 | | | 166 | 2,353 | 479 | 31 | 572 | 116 | 276 | 1,474 |
| Buffalo | 4 | 3,350 | 1,913 | 5,263 | 2,924 | 38 | 25 | | 155 | 3,142 | 544 | 88 | 1,223 | 211 | 285 | 2,351 |
| New York | 31 | 179,060 | 220,903 | 399,963 | 133,004 | 2,429 | 9,511 | | 17,923 | 182,867 | 28,888 | 4,656 | 50,763 | 11,535 | 16,409 | 112,251 |
| New Jersey | 229 | 29,949 | 28,426 | 58,375 | 27,104 | 127 | 85 | 13 | 2,548 | 29,877 | 5,177 | 971 | 9,900 | 1,253 | 3,045 | 20,346 |
| Pennsylvania | 819 | 76,694 | 94,973 | 171,667 | 63,797 | 491 | 166 | 16 | 5,649 | 70,119 | 10,918 | 2,177 | 22,273 | 3,003 | 5,972 | 44,873 |
| Philadelphia | 33 | 29,405 | 27,855 | 57,260 | 28,705 | 255 | 994 | | 2,707 | 32,661 | 4,958 | 675 | 7,884 | 1,917 | 3,223 | 19,759 |
| Pittsburgh | 14 | 23,650 | 24,600 | 33,250 | 17,609 | 107 | 335 | | 2,579 | 20,630 | 3,079 | 57 | 6,244 | 1,361 | 2,476 | 13,815 |
| Delaware | 18 | 1,660 | 1,924 | 3,584 | 983 | 6 | | | 37 | 1,038 | 311 | 174 | 297 | 49 | 75 | 689 |
| Maryland | 75 | 6,029 | 4,969 | 9,998 | 4,733 | 23 | 38 | | 193 | 4,949 | 808 | 674 | 1,952 | 265 | 409 | 3,608 |
| Baltimore | 12 | 13,400 | 12,075 | 25,475 | 7,572 | 131 | 30 | | 492 | 8,231 | 1,346 | 176 | 1,698 | 640 | 811 | 5,169 |
| Washington, D. C. | 15 | 13,677 | 5,883 | 13,560 | 4,885 | 43 | | | 477 | 5,435 | 1,220 | | 1,225 | 496 | 585 | 3,705 |
| Eastern States | 1,722 | 425,941 | 493,388 | 919,329 | 354,967 | 4,087 | 11,222 | 35 | 36,728 | 407,039 | 65,148 | 12,494 | 120,136 | 23,148 | 38,165 | 259,091 |
| Virginia | 171 | 22,468 | 15,572 | 38,040 | 13,234 | 171 | 21 | 7 | 752 | 14,185 | 2,532 | 1,382 | 3,803 | 776 | 1,447 | 9,940 |
| Richmond | 7 | 6,100 | 6,900 | 13,000 | 4,846 | 97 | 4 | | 268 | 5,315 | 965 | 394 | 1,371 | 365 | 1,520 | 3,615 |
| West Virginia | 122 | 12,092 | 9,427 | 21,519 | 8,858 | 67 | 20 | 3 | 644 | 9,592 | 1,643 | 374 | 2,962 | 801 | 1,000 | 6,785 |
| North Carolina | 86 | 13,290 | 8,415 | 21,705 | 8,078 | 266 | | 4 | 323 | 8,671 | 1,702 | 1,160 | 2,057 | 592 | 980 | 6,501 |

| | | | | | | | | | | | | | | | | | | | | | |
|---|---|---|---|---|---|---|---|---|---|---|---|---|---|---|---|---|---|---|---|---|---|
| South —. | 78 | 10,240 | 4,788 | 15,028 | 5,872 | 110 | 9 | | | 333 | 6,324 | 1,137 | 993 | 1,425 | 527 | 653 | 4,735 |
| Charleston | 4 | 1,900 | 1,540 | 3,440 | 1,308 | 231 | 5 | | | 121 | 1,565 | 203 | 263 | 429 | 105 | 113 | 1,113 |
| Georgia —. | 92 | 10,548 | 4,398 | 17,945 | 5,508 | 169 | 1 | | 4 | 193 | 5,875 | 1,256 | 916 | 1,041 | 526 | 616 | 4,355 |
| Savannah | 1 | 3,850 | 4,550 | 8,500 | 5,429 | 207 | | | | 288 | 3,924 | 925 | 90 | 946 | 375 | 628 | 2,994 |
| Florida | 4 | 3,300 | 47 | 347 | 88 | 1 | | | | 7 | 94 | 15 | 24 | 11 | 9 | 12 | 71 |
| Jacksonville | 59 | 6,195 | 3,464 | 9,659 | 4,429 | 144 | 8 | | 3 | 321 | 4,905 | 1,094 | 223 | 1,156 | 438 | 662 | 3,583 |
| Alabama | 3 | 1,600 | 1,100 | 2,700 | 2,222 | 183 | | | | 116 | 2,521 | 531 | 59 | 822 | 159 | 357 | 1,928 |
| Birmingham | 105 | 11,750 | 6,416 | 17,566 | 5,594 | 188 | 7 | | | 233 | 6,022 | 1,388 | 533 | 1,070 | 543 | 679 | 4,213 |
| Mississippi | 2 | 1,750 | 1,550 | 3,300 | 1,589 | 6 | | | | 178 | 1,773 | 313 | 6 | 532 | 192 | 214 | 1,257 |
| Louisiana | 31 | 4,035 | 2,649 | 6,684 | 3,031 | 148 | | | | 158 | 3,337 | 699 | 253 | 1,009 | 432 | 429 | 2,450 |
| New Orleans | 33 | 5,900 | 3,250 | 9,150 | 3,189 | 88 | 70 | | 6 | 278 | 4,555 | 1,000 | 501 | 323 | 375 | 558 | 3,443 |
| Texas | 516 | 42,392 | 25,802 | 68,194 | 1,717 | 81 | 26 | | | 435 | 24,984 | 6,343 | 203 | 637 | 343 | 278 | 17,892 |
| Dallas | 6 | 2,150 | 3,890 | 6,040 | 23,305 | 612 | | | 6 | 1,035 | 4,670 | 1,149 | 2,071 | 4,066 | 2,299 | 3,113 | 3,211 |
| El Paso | 4 | 2,000 | 437 | 2,437 | 4,295 | 223 | | | | 342 | 4,871 | 1,494 | 238 | 928 | 403 | 507 | 1,507 |
| Fort Worth | 5 | 3,050 | 2,300 | 5,350 | 2,593 | 102 | 13 | | 8 | 122 | 1,854 | 618 | 224 | 466 | 78 | 241 | 2,113 |
| Galveston | 2 | 400 | 400 | 800 | 496 | 53 | 7 | | | 146 | 557 | 95 | 112 | 741 | 262 | 380 | 464 |
| Houston | 9 | 6,450 | 3,300 | 9,750 | 4,374 | 120 | | | | 556 | 5,059 | 1,010 | 104 | 1,220 | 39 | 796 | 3,585 |
| San Antonio | 8 | 4,750 | 1,660 | 6,410 | 979 | 42 | | | 10 | 210 | 2,231 | 564 | 373 | 1,205 | 205 | 283 | 3,498 |
| Waco | 6 | 2,050 | 565 | 2,615 | 979 | 69 | | | | 24 | 1,072 | 141 | 71 | 205 | 132 | 120 | 764 |
| Ohio | 82 | 6,948 | 3,085 | 10,033 | 4,096 | 112 | 7 | | | 151 | 4,376 | 213 | 94 | 205 | 238 | 612 | 129 |
| Little Rock | | 600 | 290 | 860 | 443 | 12 | 16 | | 2 | 11 | 482 | 122 | 373 | 95 | 45 | 55 | 388 |
| Kentucky | 132 | 13,358 | 8,025 | 21,383 | 7,265 | 31 | 3 | | 17 | 370 | 7,871 | 1,614 | 393 | 1,436 | 858 | 792 | 5,093 |
| Louisville | 6 | 4,500 | 4,300 | 8,800 | 4,116 | 24 | | | 2 | 125 | 4,283 | 1,141 | 311 | 1,023 | 474 | 383 | 2,894 |
| Tennessee | 92 | 8,409 | 4,289 | 12,678 | 1,755 | 107 | | | | 276 | 5,486 | 297 | 414 | 1,400 | 422 | 597 | 3,974 |
| Chattanooga | 2 | 2,500 | 1,500 | 4,000 | 994 | 28 | | | | 120 | 1,903 | 220 | 176 | 581 | 120 | 179 | 1,353 |
| Memphis | 3 | 1,400 | 1,000 | 2,400 | 994 | 70 | 3 | | | 109 | 1,173 | 220 | 114 | 227 | 116 | 128 | 805 |
| Nashville | 4 | 3,100 | 2,270 | 5,370 | 2,824 | 126 | | | | 104 | 3,054 | 440 | 303 | 728 | 201 | 272 | 1,944 |
| **Southern States** | 1,676 | 223,315 | 142,069 | 365,384 | 140,230 | 3,910 | 221 | 66 | | 8,450 | 152,877 | 31,936 | 12,589 | 34,190 | 12,845 | 17,655 | 109,215 |
| Ohio | 353 | 38,050 | 27,686 | 65,736 | 25,858 | 217 | 48 | 2 | | 1,484 | 27,609 | 5,164 | 680 | 8,749 | 2,295 | 2,872 | 19,760 |
| Cincinnati | 7 | 13,400 | 7,400 | 20,800 | 6,202 | 100 | 35 | | | 1,226 | 7,563 | 1,315 | 130 | 1,792 | 684 | 498 | 4,419 |
| Cleveland | 3 | 4,800 | 2,935 | 7,735 | 3,528 | 9 | 50 | | | 739 | 4,326 | 639 | 268 | 1,420 | 356 | 413 | 3,096 |
| Columbus | 7 | 4,460 | 4,660 | 9,000 | 3,334 | 32 | 1 | | | 694 | 4,061 | 743 | 87 | 1,072 | 306 | 591 | 2,799 |
| Toledo | 3 | 2,500 | 3,500 | 6,000 | 2,053 | 35 | 4 | | | 193 | 2,285 | 327 | 18 | 734 | 253 | 252 | 1,584 |
| Indiana | 245 | 24,013 | 12,391 | 36,404 | 14,519 | 187 | 32 | 11 | | 972 | 15,721 | 3,225 | 518 | 4,354 | 1,490 | 1,584 | 11,171 |
| Indianapolis | 6 | 6,710 | 3,220 | 9,930 | 3,634 | 61 | 23 | | | 406 | 4,124 | 386 | 136 | 713 | 532 | 445 | 2,712 |
| Illinois | 409 | 35,790 | 23,834 | 59,624 | 24,397 | 275 | 23 | | 34 | 1,329 | 26,058 | 5,713 | 985 | 6,595 | 2,178 | 2,866 | 18,337 |
| Chicago, central reserve | 9 | 49,550 | 41,100 | 90,650 | 36,809 | 1,231 | 875 | | | 2,935 | 41,851 | 5,921 | 643 | 10,460 | 5,336 | 3,788 | 26,148 |
| Chicago, other reserve | 18 | 3,175 | 938 | 4,113 | 2,390 | 30 | 24 | | | 323 | 767 | 671 | 21 | 813 | 155 | 464 | 2,124 |
| Peoria | 4 | 3,100 | 1,750 | 4,850 | 357 | 33 | | | | 42 | 1,432 | 251 | | 339 | 159 | 99 | 848 |
| Michigan | 113 | 12,475 | 8,107 | 20,582 | 10,902 | 149 | 43 | 4 | | 820 | 11,014 | 2,106 | 328 | 2,331 | 787 | 1,385 | 8,738 |
| Detroit | 3 | 8,500 | 5,000 | 13,500 | 6,568 | 15 | 102 | | | 329 | 1,085 | 289 | 321 | 455 | 585 | 320 | 5,142 |
| Grand Rapids | 3 | 2,100 | 1,275 | 3,375 | 1,519 | 39 | 6 | | | 85 | 1,649 | | 83 | 3,780 | 112 | 312 | 1,151 |
| Wisconsin | 151 | 16,885 | 4,800 | 24,910 | 1,789 | 144 | 8 | 51 | | 674 | 12,666 | 2,450 | 537 | 1,682 | 1,121 | 1,429 | 9,317 |
| Milwaukee | 4 | 8,000 | 4,800 | 12,800 | 6,363 | 72 | 61 | | | 583 | 7,079 | 1,147 | 825 | 6,863 | 1,394 | 744 | 4,554 |
| Minnesota | 330 | 19,001 | 11,228 | 30,229 | 16,454 | 315 | 11 | 285 | | 777 | 17,842 | 3,558 | 602 | 2,059 | 1,298 | 1,537 | 14,481 |
| Minneapolis | 7 | 12,000 | 7,950 | 19,950 | 7,880 | 435 | 18 | 7 | | 137 | 8,477 | 1,795 | | | 800 | 1,011 | 6,267 |
| St. Paul | 6 | 12,900 | 3,918 | 10,818 | 5,469 | 129 | 56 | | | 635 | 6,299 | 1,020 | 242 | 1,650 | 430 | 698 | 4,040 |

Abstract of reports of earnings, expenses, and dividends of national banks for year ended June 30, 1922—Continued.

| Cities, States, and Territories. | Number of banks. | Capital. | Surplus. | Capital and surplus. | Gross earnings. | | | | | | Expenses. | | | | | |
|---|---|---|---|---|---|---|---|---|---|---|---|---|---|---|---|---|
| | | | | | Interest and discount. | Exchange and collection charges. | Foreign exchange profits. | Commissions and earnings from insurance premiums and the negotiation of real-estate loans. | Other earnings. | Total gross earnings. | Salaries and wages. | Interest and discount on borrowed money. | Interest on deposits. | Taxes. | Other expenses. | Total expenses paid. |
| Iowa | 336 | 20,700 | 11,991 | 32,691 | 16,461 | 160 | 12 | 158 | 555 | 17,346 | 3,500 | 1,861 | 5,260 | 1,074 | 1,766 | 13,461 |
| Cedar Rapids | 2 | 800 | 700 | 1,500 | 1,211 | 10 | | | 81 | 1,302 | 181 | 232 | 375 | 66 | 113 | 967 |
| Des Moines | 3 | 2,500 | 1,400 | 3,900 | 2,108 | 20 | | | 57 | 2,185 | 367 | 130 | 700 | 109 | 302 | 1,500 |
| Dubuque | 3 | 525 | 255 | 780 | 365 | 6 | 1 | | 27 | 398 | 70 | 6 | 154 | 41 | 40 | 311 |
| Sioux City | 5 | 1,500 | 945 | 2,445 | 1,736 | 36 | | 5 | 111 | 1,884 | 419 | 209 | 485 | 73 | 304 | 1,490 |
| Missouri | 110 | 6,950 | 3,846 | 10,796 | 4,100 | 25 | 1 | 5 | 67 | 4,197 | 1,026 | 235 | 1,001 | 361 | 505 | 3,128 |
| Kansas City | 12 | 8,400 | 4,530 | 12,920 | 7,138 | 143 | 7 | | 494 | 4,772 | 1,638 | 561 | 1,973 | 792 | 948 | 5,912 |
| St. Joseph | 4 | 1,100 | 900 | 2,000 | 1,257 | 48 | | | 40 | 1,575 | 316 | 56 | 466 | 92 | 199 | 1,129 |
| St. Louis | 8 | 26,150 | 9,275 | 35,425 | 11,681 | 326 | 73 | | 728 | 12,808 | 2,549 | 331 | 3,357 | 1,387 | 1,278 | 8,882 |
| Middle Western States | 2,224 | 338,964 | 214,499 | 553,463 | 237,112 | 4,282 | 1,513 | 557 | 16,534 | 259,998 | 48,370 | 10,632 | 73,765 | 23,246 | 27,555 | 183,568 |
| North Dakota | 182 | 7,220 | 3,504 | 10,724 | 6,137 | 101 | 3 | 79 | 231 | 6,551 | 1,552 | 614 | 2,610 | 328 | 888 | 5,992 |
| South Dakota | 134 | 6,265 | 3,037 | 9,302 | 5,901 | 66 | 4 | 92 | 230 | 6,293 | 1,465 | 630 | 2,365 | 408 | 802 | 5,670 |
| Nebraska | 168 | 8,945 | 5,541 | 14,486 | 6,598 | 68 | 12 | 40 | 205 | 6,923 | 1,612 | 493 | 2,088 | 657 | 777 | 5,627 |
| Omaha | 4 | 1,425 | 825 | 2,250 | 930 | 6 | | | 48 | 984 | 1,222 | 86 | 227 | 83 | 120 | 738 |
| Kansas | 10 | 6,950 | 3,700 | 10,650 | 5,784 | 91 | 11 | 57 | 244 | 6,187 | 1,317 | 473 | 1,478 | 471 | 851 | 4,590 |
| Kansas City | 258 | 13,947 | 7,808 | 21,755 | 9,444 | 85 | 4 | 27 | 411 | 9,971 | 2,545 | 433 | 2,338 | 1,002 | 1,298 | 7,616 |
| Topeka | 2 | 800 | 500 | 1,300 | 530 | 2 | 1 | | 48 | 552 | 113 | 18 | 137 | 43 | 68 | 379 |
| Wichita | 3 | 900 | 245 | 1,436 | 530 | 7 | | | 36 | 573 | 137 | | 158 | 44 | 68 | 407 |
| Montana | 130 | 2,200 | 1,225 | 3,425 | 3,425 | 50 | 4 | 55 | 193 | 5,606 | 320 | 66 | 415 | 149 | 242 | 1,192 |
| Helena | 2 | 7,840 | 3,596 | 11,436 | 5,514 | 69 | | | 315 | 5,957 | 1,862 | 645 | 1,691 | 388 | 814 | 4,900 |
| Wyoming | 47 | 450 | 325 | 775 | 353 | 6 | | | 18 | 377 | 89 | 7 | 101 | 23 | 35 | 255 |
| Colorado | 133 | 3,195 | 2,853 | 6,048 | 3,512 | 32 | 5 | 6 | 119 | 3,674 | 784 | 169 | 1,078 | 283 | 509 | 2,823 |
| Denver | 8 | 7,525 | 4,554 | 12,109 | 6,194 | 54 | 5 | 7 | 302 | 6,562 | 1,698 | 526 | 1,366 | 661 | 846 | 5,097 |
| New Mexico | 2 | 4,150 | 3,839 | 7,989 | 5,059 | 104 | 14 | 1 | 330 | 5,508 | 1,043 | 159 | 1,964 | 292 | 650 | 4,108 |
| | | 600 | 1,110 | 1,710 | 667 | 4 | | | 84 | 755 | 119 | 23 | 137 | 80 | 73 | 432 |
| New Mexico | 47 | 3,285 | 1,793 | 5,078 | 2,823 | 19 | 9 | 9 | 112 | 2,963 | 666 | 353 | 670 | 291 | 371 | 2,351 |

| | 1 | 2 | 3 | 4 | 5 | 6 | 7 | 8 | 9 | 10 | 11 | 12 | 13 | 14 | 15 | 16 |
|---|---|---|---|---|---|---|---|---|---|---|---|---|---|---|---|---|
| Oklahoma | 423 | 19,685 | 5,834 | 25,519 | 12,740 | 239 | | 10 | 513 | 13,503 | 3,832 | 1,110 | 2,921 | 1,261 | 2,303 | 11,427 |
| Muskogee | 4 | 1,250 | 370 | 1,620 | 901 | 36 | | | 78 | 1,015 | 205 | 34 | 257 | 119 | 139 | 754 |
| Oklahoma City | 9 | 3,300 | 1,690 | 4,990 | 2,590 | 84 | | | 524 | 1,198 | 741 | 195 | 735 | 142 | 569 | 2,383 |
| Tulsa | 7 | 4,400 | 1,530 | 5,930 | 3,068 | 26 | | | 136 | 3,220 | 834 | 212 | 877 | 280 | 511 | 2,704 |
| Western States | 1,577 | 104,332 | 53,909 | 158,241 | 80,609 | 1,149 | 64 | 353 | 4,177 | 86,382 | 20,646 | 6,246 | 23,613 | 7,005 | 11,934 | 69,444 |
| Washington | 94 | 6,330 | 3,502 | 9,832 | 4,742 | 90 | 13 | 26 | 358 | 5,229 | 1,326 | 179 | 1,285 | 416 | 759 | 3,965 |
| Seattle | 10 | 6,100 | 2,555 | 8,655 | 4,933 | 316 | 61 | | 542 | 5,852 | 1,519 | 13 | 1,479 | 378 | 856 | 4,245 |
| Spokane | 3 | 2,600 | 600 | 3,200 | 1,928 | 75 | 22 | | 114 | 2,139 | 445 | 65 | 513 | 161 | 316 | 1,500 |
| Tacoma | 1 | 1,000 | 250 | 1,250 | 707 | 28 | | | 27 | 762 | 184 | | 210 | 51 | 83 | 528 |
| Oregon | 93 | 6,315 | 3,420 | 9,735 | 4,281 | 68 | 4 | 5 | 235 | 4,593 | 1,196 | 331 | 911 | 478 | 610 | 3,528 |
| Portland | 3 | 5,000 | 2,250 | 7,250 | 3,967 | 153 | 66 | 67 | 139 | 4,335 | 1,066 | 22 | 1,169 | 392 | 550 | 3,199 |
| California | 280 | 26,276 | 11,933 | 38,209 | 18,274 | 274 | 43 | | 1,806 | 20,464 | 5,372 | 832 | 4,180 | 1,245 | 2,905 | 14,434 |
| Los Angeles | 7 | 9,300 | 4,947 | 14,247 | 8,719 | 48 | 101 | | 614 | 9,482 | 2,162 | 112 | 2,550 | 614 | 1,046 | 6,484 |
| Oakland | 2 | 1,600 | 1,320 | 2,920 | 1,318 | 7 | | | 178 | 1,507 | 362 | 68 | 334 | 93 | 195 | 1,052 |
| San Francisco | 7 | 28,000 | 18,700 | 46,700 | 15,868 | 129 | 1,645 | | 1,853 | 19,495 | 3,532 | 1,063 | 4,754 | 1,553 | 1,718 | 12,620 |
| Idaho | 79 | 5,240 | 2,179 | 7,419 | 4,108 | 45 | 4 | 4 | 178 | 613 | 1,073 | 637 | 817 | 369 | 616 | 3,512 |
| Utah | 15 | 780 | 373 | 1,153 | 573 | 3 | 2 | 3 | 32 | 658 | 130 | 44 | 185 | 49 | 80 | 488 |
| Ogden | 4 | 1,000 | 500 | 1,500 | 612 | 7 | 1 | | 38 | | 160 | 66 | 154 | 63 | 75 | 518 |
| Salt Lake City | 5 | 2,350 | 1,290 | 3,610 | 1,690 | 21 | 5 | | 140 | 1,856 | 364 | 263 | 339 | 175 | 182 | 1,323 |
| Nevada | 11 | 2,460 | 590 | 3,050 | 861 | 9 | 16 | 7 | 61 | 954 | 173 | 5 | 211 | 94 | 105 | 588 |
| Arizona | 22 | 1,900 | 985 | 2,885 | 1,859 | 50 | 1 | 4 | 134 | 2,048 | 628 | 252 | 354 | 178 | 352 | 1,764 |
| Pacific States | 636 | 105,251 | 55,364 | 160,615 | 74,440 | 1,323 | 1,968 | 116 | 6,449 | 84,316 | 19,692 | 3,952 | 19,445 | 6,309 | 10,348 | 59,746 |
| Alaska-nonmember | 3 | 150 | 80 | 230 | 83 | 9 | 4 | | 28 | 120 | 39 | | 19 | 5 | 21 | 84 |
| Hawaii-nonmember | 3 | 600 | 440 | 1,040 | 262 | 17 | | 2 | 21 | 306 | 88 | | 62 | 13 | 41 | 204 |
| Total nonmember banks | 5 | 750 | 520 | 1,270 | 345 | 26 | 4 | 2 | 49 | 426 | 127 | | 81 | 18 | 62 | 288 |
| Total United States | 8,246 | 1,307,199 | 1,049,228 | 2,356,427 | 955,451 | 15,546 | 15,808 | 1,169 | 79,234 | 1,067,288 | 198,404 | 47,685 | 294,076 | 79,376 | 113,449 | 732,990 |

Abstract of reports of earnings, expenses, and dividends of national banks for year ended June 30, 1922—Continued.

[In thousands of dollars.]

| Cities, States, and Territories. | Net earnings since last report. | Recoveries on charged off assets. | Total net earnings and recoveries on charged off assets. | Losses charged off. | | | | | Net addition to profits. | Dividends. | Ratios. | | | |
|---|---|---|---|---|---|---|---|---|---|---|---|---|---|---|
| | | | | On loans and discounts. | On bonds, securities, etc. | Other losses. | On foreign exchange. | Total losses charged off. | | | Dividends to capital. | Dividends to capital and surplus. | Net addition to profits to capital and surplus. | Net addition to profits to capital. |
| | | | | | | | | | | | Per cent. | Per cent. | Per cent. | Per cent. |
| Maine | 1,876 | 108 | 1,984 | 222 | 465 | 135 | 8 | 830 | 1,154 | 671 | 9.52 | 5.78 | 9.94 | 16.38 |
| New Hampshire | 1,154 | 56 | 1,210 | 124 | 139 | 41 | 1 | 305 | 905 | 551 | 10.27 | 5.71 | 9.38 | 16.87 |
| Vermont | 843 | 142 | 985 | 172 | 92 | 27 | 8 | 309 | 676 | 531 | 9.82 | 6.74 | 8.59 | 12.50 |
| Massachusetts | 6,024 | 593 | 6,617 | 1,958 | 774 | 262 | 42 | 3,036 | 3,581 | 2,531 | 9.36 | 5.40 | 7.63 | 13.24 |
| Boston | 9,523 | 457 | 9,980 | 4,913 | 2,293 | 53 | 31 | 7,290 | 2,690 | 5,205 | 14.22 | 6.93 | 3.58 | 7.35 |
| Rhode Island | 1,251 | 68 | 1,319 | 120 | 132 | 65 | | 317 | 1,002 | 562 | 10.09 | 5.42 | 9.67 | 17.99 |
| Connecticut | 3,921 | 762 | 4,683 | 906 | 465 | 136 | 25 | 1,532 | 3,151 | 4,223 | 19.54 | 11.55 | 8.62 | 14.58 |
| New England States | 24,592 | 2,186 | 26,778 | 8,415 | 4,360 | 729 | 115 | 13,619 | 13,159 | 14,274 | 13.14 | 7.20 | 6.64 | 12.11 |
| New York | 12,875 | 1,397 | 14,272 | 2,289 | 2,181 | 1,046 | 16 | 5,532 | 8,740 | 5,569 | 12.08 | 6.90 | 10.83 | 18.95 |
| Albany | 1,313 | 263 | 1,576 | 349 | 448 | 148 | | 946 | 630 | 418 | 14.67 | 6.69 | 10.08 | 22.11 |
| Brooklyn and Bronx | 879 | 340 | 1,219 | 526 | 155 | 47 | 1 | 729 | 490 | 244 | 11.62 | 6.09 | 12.23 | 23.33 |
| New Yk | 791 | 22 | 813 | 148 | 265 | 15 | | 428 | 385 | 438 | 13.07 | 8.33 | 7.32 | 11.49 |
| New Yk | 70,616 | 11,584 | 82,200 | 35,532 | 3,812 | 5,909 | 543 | 45,796 | 36,404 | 34,117 | 19.05 | 8.53 | 9.10 | 20.33 |
| New Jersey | 9,531 | 1,613 | 11,144 | 1,135 | 1,721 | 439 | 101 | 3,396 | 7,748 | 4,082 | 13.63 | 5.99 | 13.27 | 25.87 |
| Pennsylvania | 25,746 | 1,900 | 27,646 | 1,970 | 5,414 | 1,226 | 43 | 8,653 | 18,993 | 9,827 | 12.81 | 5.72 | 11.06 | 24.76 |
| Philadelphia | 12,902 | 491 | 13,393 | 3,913 | 1,300 | 363 | 439 | 6,015 | 7,378 | 6,140 | 20.88 | 7.04 | 8.46 | 25.09 |
| Pittsburgh | 6,815 | 430 | 7,245 | 1,256 | 1,119 | 326 | 48 | 2,749 | 4,496 | 4,299 | 15.01 | 8.07 | 8.44 | 15.69 |
| Delaware | 347 | 24 | 371 | 13 | 100 | 3 | 2 | 118 | 253 | 203 | 12.23 | 5.66 | 7.06 | 15.24 |
| Maryland | 1,341 | 52 | 1,393 | 94 | 246 | 47 | 14 | 401 | 992 | 644 | 12.81 | 6.44 | 9.92 | 19.73 |
| Baltimore | 3,062 | 183 | 3,245 | 633 | 67 | 22 | | 742 | 2,503 | 1,617 | 12.07 | 6.35 | 9.83 | 18.66 |
| ..., D. C. | 1,730 | 660 | 2,390 | 515 | 181 | 250 | | 946 | 1,444 | 854 | 11.12 | 6.30 | 10.65 | 18.81 |
| Eastern States | 147,948 | 18,959 | 166,907 | 48,393 | 17,010 | 9,841 | 1,207 | 76,651 | 90,456 | 68,452 | 16.07 | 7.45 | 9.84 | 21.24 |
| Virginia | 4,245 | 274 | 4,519 | 752 | 104 | 152 | 14 | 1,022 | 3,497 | 2,323 | 10.34 | 6.11 | 9.19 | 15.56 |
| Richmond | 1,700 | 207 | 1,907 | 384 | 125 | 60 | 29 | 598 | 1,309 | 846 | 13.87 | 6.51 | 10.07 | 21.46 |
| West Virginia | 2,807 | 148 | 2,955 | 220 | 362 | 149 | 12 | 743 | 2,212 | 1,560 | 12.90 | 7.25 | 10.28 | 18.29 |
| North Carolina | 2,170 | 61 | 2,231 | 450 | 30 | 84 | 8 | 572 | 1,659 | 1,294 | 9.51 | 5.82 | 7.64 | 12.48 |
| South Carolina | 1,589 | 128 | 1,717 | 1,069 | 104 | 82 | 4 | 1,259 | 468 | 774 | 7.56 | 5.15 | 3.05 | 4.47 |
| Charleston | 552 | 243 | 795 | 616 | 74 | 10 | | 700 | 95 | 289 | 15.21 | 8.40 | 2.76 | 5.00 |
| Georgia | 1,520 | 215 | 1,735 | 1,015 | 69 | 115 | 5 | 1,204 | 531 | 822 | 7.79 | 4.58 | 2.96 | 5.03 |
| Atlanta | 960 | 63 | 1,023 | 253 | 3 | 69 | | 325 | 698 | 518 | 13.11 | 6.09 | 8.21 | 17.67 |
| Savannah | 23 | | 23 | 1 | | | | 1 | 22 | 22 | 7.33 | 6.34 | 6.34 | 7.33 |

| | | | | | | | | | | | | | | | |
|---|---|---|---|---|---|---|---|---|---|---|---|---|---|---|---|
| Florida | 1,322 | 118 | 1,440 | 382 | 108 | 118 | | | 609 | 531 | 611 | 9.96 | 6.33 | 8.60 | 13.41 |
| Jacksonville | 563 | 48 | 641 | 231 | 70 | 77 | 1 | | 378 | 263 | 254 | 15.88 | 9.41 | 9.74 | 16.44 |
| Alabama | 1,809 | 212 | 2,021 | 509 | 74 | 80 | | | 723 | 1,298 | 1,164 | 14.06 | 6.65 | 7.41 | 11.70 |
| Birmingham | 516 | 132 | 648 | 155 | | 5 | | | 160 | 438 | 246 | 14.06 | 6.01 | 11.79 | 27.89 |
| Mississippi | 887 | 162 | 1,049 | 445 | 52 | 54 | | | 551 | 498 | 402 | 8.05 | 5.19 | 7.45 | 12.34 |
| Louisiana | 1,112 | 129 | 1,241 | 484 | 131 | 88 | 68 | | 1,703 | 462 | 475 | 8.03 | 11.67 | 5.05 | 7.83 |
| New Orleans | 635 | 118 | 773 | 319 | | 11 | 21 | | 330 | 443 | 560 | 20.00 | 7.37 | 9.23 | 15.82 |
| Texas | 7,092 | 1,244 | 8,336 | 7,766 | 178 | 650 | | | 8,662 | 1,336 | 5,021 | 11.84 | 11.91 | 10.48 | 0.77 |
| Dallas | 1,559 | 114 | 1,673 | 373 | 13 | 64 | | | 471 | 1,202 | 1,318 | 11.97 | 7.93 | 10.92 | 16.81 |
| El Paso | 364 | 17 | 381 | 91 | | 65 | 24 | | 176 | 265 | 206 | 8.45 | 5.70 | 8.41 | 10.25 |
| Fort Worth | 741 | 93 | 834 | 521 | | 45 | | | 566 | 268 | 324 | 10.38 | 7.14 | 5.01 | 8.79 |
| Galveston | 93 | 3 | 96 | 33 | 11 | 17 | | | 85 | 11 | 58 | 10.62 | 6.08 | 1.38 | 2.75 |
| Houston | 1,465 | 273 | 1,738 | 684 | 155 | 143 | 24 | | 982 | 756 | 539 | 22.00 | 8.40 | 5.73 | 11.72 |
| San Antonio | 733 | 33 | 766 | 164 | 32 | 299 | | | 495 | 271 | 527 | 8.67 | 4.25 | 4.23 | 5.71 |
| Waco | 308 | 11 | 319 | 108 | 7 | 21 | 1 | | 136 | 183 | 223 | 11.09 | 6.59 | 7.00 | 5.93 |
| Arkansas | 1,247 | 96 | 1,343 | 543 | 32 | 74 | | | 650 | 693 | 690 | 10.88 | 6.40 | 6.91 | 9.97 |
| Isle Rock | 94 | 2 | 96 | 6 | | 1 | | | 7 | 89 | 51 | 9.50 | 7.57 | 10.35 | 14.83 |
| Kentucky | 2,578 | 138 | 2,716 | 430 | 108 | 97 | 3 | | 633 | 2,078 | 1,472 | 11.02 | 7.09 | 9.72 | 15.56 |
| Louisville | 1,388 | 200 | 1,588 | 503 | 100 | 115 | | | 718 | 870 | 830 | 18.44 | 5.57 | 9.89 | 19.33 |
| Tennessee | 1,512 | 74 | 1,586 | 337 | 44 | 46 | | | 427 | 1,159 | 953 | 11.33 | 6.70 | 9.14 | 13.78 |
| Chattanooga | 550 | 16 | 566 | 117 | 69 | 36 | | | 222 | 344 | 270 | 10.66 | 6.39 | 8.04 | 13.76 |
| Memphis | 368 | 35 | 403 | 155 | 10 | 21 | | | 196 | 217 | 179 | 10.01 | 6.47 | 8.60 | 13.50 |
| Nashville | 1,110 | 88 | 1,198 | 278 | 77 | 43 | | | 398 | 800 | 349 | 11.26 | 6.42 | 14.90 | 25.81 |
| Southern States | 43,662 | 4,695 | 48,357 | 20,434 | 2,142 | 2,911 | 190 | | 25,697 | 22,660 | 25,187 | 11.28 | 6.89 | 6.20 | 10.15 |
| Ohio | 7,849 | 649 | 8,498 | 1,568 | 778 | 483 | 29 | | 2,878 | 5,620 | 4,372 | 11.49 | 6.65 | 8.55 | 14.77 |
| Cincinnati | 3,144 | 186 | 3,330 | 663 | 292 | 231 | 2 | | 2,188 | 2,142 | 1,094 | 8.09 | 5.21 | 10.30 | 15.99 |
| Cleveland | 1,230 | 7 | 1,237 | 179 | 73 | 22 | 1 | | 275 | 962 | 503 | 10.43 | 6.50 | 12.44 | 20.04 |
| Columbus | 1,262 | 144 | 1,406 | 467 | 90 | 27 | | | 584 | 822 | 468 | 10.64 | 5.21 | 9.13 | 18.68 |
| Toledo | 701 | 253 | 951 | 380 | 71 | 25 | 14 | | 476 | 478 | 310 | 12.40 | 5.17 | 9.13 | 19.12 |
| Indiana | 4,550 | 433 | 4,983 | 1,001 | 517 | 321 | | | 1,383 | 3,130 | 2,896 | 12.40 | 7.93 | 7.97 | 13.03 |
| Indianapolis | 1,412 | 726 | 2,138 | 960 | 121 | 272 | 20 | | 1,383 | 755 | 566 | 8.45 | 5.70 | 8.60 | 11.27 |
| Illinois | 7,721 | 465 | 8,186 | 319 | 566 | 343 | 29 | | 2,448 | 5,738 | 4,199 | 11.73 | 7.04 | 7.60 | 16.03 |
| Chicago, central reserve | 15,705 | 51 | 17,851 | 9,385 | 1,150 | 332 | 13 | | 10,906 | 6,545 | 6,474 | 13.07 | 7.14 | 7.22 | 13.21 |
| Chicago, other exe. | 643 | 48 | 694 | 51 | 36 | 75 | | | 178 | 516 | 250 | 7.87 | 6.08 | 12.55 | 16.25 |
| Peoria | 584 | 255 | 632 | 132 | 45 | 24 | 20 | | 221 | 411 | 206 | 9.81 | 8.40 | 8.47 | 19.57 |
| Michigan | 3,180 | 215 | 3,435 | 423 | 380 | 193 | | | 1,016 | 1,729 | 1,009 | 13.96 | 6.40 | 11.75 | 19.39 |
| Detroit | 1,872 | 585 | 3,087 | 562 | 203 | 22 | 23 | | 787 | 1,300 | 890 | 10.47 | 6.59 | 9.63 | 15.29 |
| Grand Rapids | 398 | 88 | 486 | 97 | 76 | 162 | 14 | | 357 | 129 | 216 | 11.17 | 7.57 | 3.82 | 6.14 |
| ... | 3,349 | 240 | 3,589 | 812 | 224 | 237 | 11 | | 1,287 | 2,302 | 1,888 | 11.35 | 7.09 | 9.24 | 13.63 |
| Milwaukee | 3,525 | 27 | 3,552 | 1,013 | 503 | 198 | 9 | | 1,545 | 1,007 | 908 | 11.35 | 5.57 | 7.87 | 12.59 |
| Minnesota | 3,361 | 338 | 3,699 | 1,637 | 97 | 35 | 1 | | 1,939 | 1,760 | 2,025 | 10.66 | 6.70 | 5.82 | 9.26 |
| Minneapolis | 2,210 | 239 | 2,449 | 1,249 | 164 | 196 | | | 1,428 | 971 | 1,311 | 10.93 | 5.57 | 5.11 | 8.50 |
| St. Paul | 2,219 | 87 | 2,306 | 779 | 253 | 245 | 5 | | 971 | 1,035 | 691 | 10.01 | 6.39 | 12.34 | 19.35 |
| Iowa | 3,885 | 590 | 4,475 | 2,966 | 17 | 13 | | | 3,449 | 1,026 | 397 | 9.84 | 6.23 | 3.14 | 4.96 |
| Cedar Rapids | 335 | 22 | 357 | 229 | 18 | 7 | | | 259 | 98 | 37 | 12.13 | 6.47 | 6.53 | 12.25 |
| Des Mes. | 635 | 52 | 737 | 306 | 27 | 16 | | | 331 | 406 | 354 | 12.16 | 9.18 | 10.41 | 16.24 |
| Dubuque | 87 | 15 | 102 | | | 1 | | | 34 | 62 | 62 | 14.16 | 9.84 | 8.72 | 12.95 |
| Sioux City | 94 | 109 | 503 | | | | | | 312 | 191 | 157 | 10.47 | 6.42 | 7.81 | 12.73 |

1 Deficit.

Abstract of reports of earnings, expenses, and dividends of national banks for year ended June 30, 1922—Continued.

| Cities, States, and Territories. | Net earnings since last report. | Recoveries on charged off assets. | Total net earnings and recoveries on charged-off assets. | Losses charged off. On loans and discounts. | On bonds, securities, etc. | Other losses. | On foreign exchange. | Total losses charged off. | Net addition to profits. | Dividends. | Ratios. Dividends to capital. | Dividends to capital and surplus. | Net addition to profits to capital and surplus. | Net addition to profits to capital. |
|---|---|---|---|---|---|---|---|---|---|---|---|---|---|---|
| | | | | | | | | | | | Per cent. | Per cent. | Per cent. | Per cent. |
| Missouri— | 1,069 | 78 | 1,147 | 419 | 20 | 210 | 7 | 656 | 491 | 720 | 10.36 | 6.67 | 4.55 | 7.06 |
| Kansas City | 1,860 | 349 | 2,209 | 1,409 | 110 | 106 | 5 | 1,630 | 579 | 1,030 | 12.28 | 7.97 | 4.48 | 6.99 |
| St. Joseph | 246 | 77 | 323 | 228 | 7 | 17 | | 252 | 71 | 148 | 13.45 | 7.40 | 3.55 | 6.45 |
| St. Louis | 3,926 | 624 | 4,550 | 1,566 | 330 | 80 | 2 | 1,978 | 2,572 | 2,481 | 9.49 | 7.00 | 7.26 | 9.84 |
| Middle Western States | 76,430 | 7,985 | 84,415 | 30,078 | 6,304 | 3,933 | 207 | 40,522 | 43,893 | 38,060 | 11.23 | 6.88 | 7.93 | 12.95 |
| North Dakota | 539 | 166 | 725 | 499 | 48 | 98 | 1 | 646 | 79 | 450 | 6.23 | 4.20 | .74 | 1.09 |
| South Dakota | 623 | 231 | 854 | 739 | 39 | 76 | | 854 | | 422 | 6.74 | 4.54 | | |
| Nebraska— | 1,296 | 154 | 1,450 | 897 | 45 | 71 | | 1,013 | 437 | 908 | 9.03 | 5.58 | 3.02 | 4.89 |
| Lincoln | 246 | 126 | 372 | 152 | 16 | 100 | | 298 | 104 | 133 | 9.33 | 5.91 | 4.62 | 7.30 |
| Omaha | 1,597 | 339 | 1,936 | 1,307 | 133 | 42 | | 1,432 | 454 | 604 | 9.99 | 6.92 | 4.26 | 6.53 |
| Kansas— | 2,355 | 300 | 2,655 | 1,091 | 76 | 202 | | 1,369 | 1,286 | 1,505 | 10.79 | 6.84 | 5.91 | 9.22 |
| Kansas City | 173 | 16 | 189 | 66 | 11 | 11 | | 88 | 101 | 370 | 46.25 | 22.27 | 7.77 | 12.63 |
| Topeka | 166 | 9 | 175 | 32 | 8 | 10 | | 50 | 125 | 255 | 28.33 | 6.42 | 10.92 | 13.89 |
| Wichita | 414 | 50 | 464 | 257 | 2 | 80 | 11 | 350 | 114 | 220 | 20.00 | 3.00 | 3.33 | 5.18 |
| Montana— | 1,057 | 433 | 1,490 | 1,433 | 69 | 96 | | 1,599 | 109 | 353 | 4.50 | 9.81 | 1.95 | 1.39 |
| Helena | 1,122 | 6 | 128 | 49 | 1 | 1 | | 51 | 77 | 76 | 16.89 | 7.21 | 9.94 | 17.11 |
| Wyoming | 851 | 106 | 957 | 565 | 37 | 56 | 8 | 666 | 291 | 436 | 13.65 | 6.80 | 4.81 | 9.11 |
| Colorado— | 1,465 | 523 | 1,988 | 1,342 | 103 | 129 | | 1,684 | 304 | 823 | 10.94 | 7.55 | 2.51 | 4.04 |
| Denver | 1,400 | 169 | 1,569 | 666 | 208 | 56 | 110 | 930 | 639 | 603 | 14.53 | 9.06 | 8.00 | 15.40 |
| Pueblo | 233 | 8 | 331 | 84 | 202 | 15 | | 301 | 30 | 155 | 25.83 | 5.00 | 1.75 | 5.00 |
| New Mexico | 612 | 89 | 701 | 508 | 116 | 66 | | 597 | 104 | 254 | 7.73 | 3.73 | 2.05 | 3.17 |
| Oklahoma— | 2,076 | 559 | 2,635 | 2,627 | 4 | 260 | 1 | 3,004 | 369 | 951 | 4.83 | 7.72 | 1.45 | 1.87 |
| Muskogee | 261 | 58 | 319 | 171 | 83 | 51 | | 236 | 93 | 125 | 10.00 | 5.43 | 5.74 | 7.44 |
| Oklahoma City | 816 | 156 | 972 | 571 | 29 | 67 | | 721 | 251 | 271 | 8.21 | 6.91 | 5.03 | 7.61 |
| Tulsa | 526 | 251 | 777 | 950 | | 28 | | 1,005 | 228 | 410 | 9.32 | | 3.84 | 5.18 |
| Western States | 16,938 | 3,749 | 20,687 | 14,006 | 1,253 | 1,513 | 132 | 16,904 | 3,783 | 9,314 | 8.93 | 5.89 | 2.39 | 3.63 |
| Washington— | 1,264 | 217 | 1,481 | 623 | 85 | 117 | 177 | 1,002 | 479 | 710 | 11.22 | 7.22 | 4.87 | 7.57 |
| Seattle | 1,607 | 240 | 1,847 | 857 | 33 | 154 | | 1,044 | 803 | 773 | 12.67 | 8.93 | 9.28 | 13.16 |
| Spokane | 639 | 206 | 846 | 318 | 54 | 106 | | 478 | 367 | 224 | 8.62 | 7.00 | 11.47 | 14.12 |
| Tacoma | 234 | 23 | 257 | 209 | 28 | 90 | | 325 | 53 | 80 | 8.00 | 6.40 | 5.44 | 6.80 |

Earnings, expenses, and dividends of national banks by Federal reserve districts, year ended June 30, 1922.

[In thousands of dollars.]

| | District No. 1, 394 banks. | District No. 2, 669 banks. | District No. 3, 655 banks. | District No. 4, 768 banks. | District No. 5, 558 banks. | District No. 6, 389 banks. | District No. 7, 1,061 banks. | District No. 8, 494 banks. | District No. 9, 877 banks. | District No. 10, 1,099 banks. | District No. 11, 659 banks. | District No. 12, 628 banks. | Non-member, 5 banks. | Grand total, 8,246 banks. |
|---|---|---|---|---|---|---|---|---|---|---|---|---|---|---|
| Capital | 103,863 | 260,737 | 90,941 | 126,127 | 90,541 | 56,403 | 172,128 | 67,948 | 66,521 | 89,567 | 77,097 | 104,576 | 750 | 1,307,199 |
| Surplus | 85,432 | 285,360 | 132,451 | 108,040 | 68,310 | 38,136 | 113,993 | 33,388 | 37,521 | 48,172 | 42,105 | 54,800 | 520 | 1,049,228 |
| Capital and surplus | 190,295 | 546,097 | 223,392 | 234,167 | 158,851 | 94,539 | 286,121 | 101,336 | 104,042 | 137,739 | 119,202 | 159,376 | 1,270 | 2,356,427 |
| **Gross earnings:** | | | | | | | | | | | | | | |
| Loans and discount | 65,366 | 221,652 | 78,014 | 86,791 | 58,337 | 38,098 | 125,508 | 39,790 | 53,059 | 68,946 | 45,900 | 73,645 | 345 | 935,451 |
| Domestic exchange and collection charges | 757 | 3,014 | 621 | 635 | 1,133 | 1,363 | 2,266 | 753 | 1,198 | 1,076 | 1,367 | 1,287 | 26 | 15,546 |
| Foreign exchange profits | 851 | 9,660 | 1,069 | 581 | 126 | 89 | 1,193 | 104 | 106 | 60 | 47 | 1,988 | 4 | 15,868 |
| Commission and fees from insurance premiums and negotiation of real estate, authorized by act of September 7, 1916, in towns of 5,000 population or less | 10 | 16 | 12 | 12 | 11 | 9 | 245 | 37 | 528 | 156 | 17 | 114 | 2 | 1,169 |
| Other earnings | 6,552 | 24,246 | 6,965 | 9,266 | 3,635 | 2,412 | 8,552 | 1,944 | 2,567 | 3,818 | 2,842 | 6,386 | 49 | 79,234 |
| Total | 73,536 | 258,578 | 86,681 | 97,335 | 63,242 | 41,971 | 137,764 | 42,628 | 57,458 | 74,056 | 50,173 | 83,420 | 426 | 1,067,268 |
| **Expenses paid:** | | | | | | | | | | | | | | |
| Salaries and wages | 12,002 | 41,727 | 13,350 | 16,459 | 11,410 | 8,772 | 24,721 | 8,651 | 12,004 | 17,615 | 12,154 | 19,412 | 127 | 198,404 |
| Interest and discount on borrowed money | 4,658 | 8,180 | 3,710 | 2,687 | 5,552 | 3,418 | 6,050 | 2,038 | 3,777 | 1,441 | 3,829 | 3,887 | 81 | 47,685 |
| Interest on deposits | 22,165 | 76,991 | 24,193 | 29,702 | 16,523 | 9,400 | 37,178 | 10,916 | 19,130 | 18,820 | 9,743 | 19,224 | 18 | 294,076 |
| Taxes | 6,640 | 15,135 | 4,286 | 7,000 | 4,480 | 3,770 | 12,752 | 3,901 | 4,866 | 6,508 | 4,429 | 6,248 | 18 | 79,376 |
| Other expenses | 7,444 | 24,049 | 7,840 | 9,944 | 6,427 | 5,023 | 14,458 | 4,506 | 6,866 | 10,167 | 6,453 | 10,210 | 62 | 113,449 |
| Total | 49,889 | 164,560 | 53,379 | 65,792 | 44,392 | 30,283 | 95,159 | 30,012 | 45,986 | 57,551 | 36,608 | 58,991 | 288 | 732,990 |
| Net earnings during year | 23,647 | 94,018 | 33,302 | 31,543 | 18,850 | 11,588 | 42,605 | 12,616 | 11,472 | 16,505 | 13,565 | 24,429 | 138 | 334,278 |
| Recoveries on charged-off assets | 2,121 | 15,014 | 1,880 | 2,593 | 1,942 | 1,278 | 4,592 | 1,421 | 1,566 | 3,229 | 1,991 | 4,168 | 7 | 41,782 |
| Total | 25,768 | 109,032 | 35,162 | 34,136 | 20,792 | 12,866 | 47,197 | 14,037 | 13,038 | 19,734 | 15,556 | 28,597 | 145 | 376,060 |
| **Losses charged off:** | | | | | | | | | | | | | | |
| On loans and discounts | 8,191 | 39,880 | 5,416 | 5,592 | 4,750 | 4,128 | 18,539 | 4,163 | 6,659 | 12,304 | 11,893 | 13,662 | 31 | 135,208 |
| On bonds, securities, etc | 4,104 | 8,180 | 5,594 | 4,553 | 1,199 | 612 | 3,784 | 807 | 648 | 1,188 | 498 | 2,367 | | 33,444 |
| Other losses | 698 | 7,505 | 1,258 | 1,644 | 833 | 671 | 2,193 | 616 | 561 | 1,498 | 1,472 | 2,711 | 5 | 21,665 |
| On foreign exchange | 110 | 656 | 471 | 114 | 73 | 6 | 133 | 23 | 17 | 135 | 122 | 213 | | 2,073 |
| Total | 13,103 | 56,221 | 12,649 | 11,903 | 6,855 | 5,417 | 24,649 | 5,609 | 7,885 | 15,125 | 13,985 | 18,953 | 36 | 192,390 |
| Net addition to profits from operations during year | 12,665 | 52,811 | 22,513 | 22,233 | 13,937 | 7,449 | 22,548 | 8,428 | 5,153 | 4,609 | 1,571 | 9,644 | 109 | 183,670 |
| Total dividends declared since June 30, 1921 | 13,913 | 43,904 | 13,970 | 15,682 | 9,999 | 6,253 | 20,228 | 7,272 | 5,136 | 9,259 | 8,699 | 10,506 | 63 | 165,894 |
| **Ratio:** | | | | | | | | | | | | | | |
| Dividends to capital...per cent | 13.40 | 16.84 | 15.36 | 12.43 | 11.04 | 11.09 | 11.75 | 10.70 | 9.22 | 10.34 | 11.28 | 10.05 | 8.40 | 12.69 |
| Dividends to capital and surplus...do | 7.31 | 8.04 | 6.25 | 6.70 | 6.29 | 6.61 | 7.07 | 7.18 | 5.90 | 6.72 | 7.30 | 6.59 | 4.96 | 7.04 |
| Net addition to profits, to capital, and surplus...per cent | 6.66 | 9.67 | 10.08 | 9.49 | 8.77 | 7.88 | 7.88 | 8.32 | 4.95 | 3.35 | 1.32 | 6.05 | 8.58 | 7.79 |

*National-bank investments in United States Government securities and other bonds and securities, etc., loans and discounts (including rediscounts), and losses charged off on account of bonds and securities, etc., and loans and discounts, years ended June 30, 1918 to 1922, inclusive.*

[In thousands of dollars.]

| Year ended June 30— | United States Government securities. | Other bonds and securities. | Total bonds and securities, etc. | Loans and discounts including rediscounts. | Losses charged off on loans and discounts. | Losses charged off on bonds and securities, etc. | Percentage of losses charged off on account loans and discounts to total loans and discounts. | Percentage of losses charged off on bonds and securities to total bonds and securities. |
|---|---|---|---|---|---|---|---|---|
| 1918........ | 2,129,283 | 1,840,487 | 3,969,770 | 10,135,842 | 33,964 | 44,350 | 0.34 | 1.12 |
| 1919........ | 3,176,314 | 1,875,609 | 5,051,923 | 11,010,206 | 35,440 | 27,819 | .32 | .55 |
| 1920........ | 2,269,575 | 1,916,890 | 4,186,465 | 13,611,416 | 31,284 | 61,790 | .23 | 1.48 |
| 1921........ | 2,019,497 | 2,005,584 | 4,025,081 | 12,004,515 | 76,210 | 76,179 | .63 | 1.89 |
| 1922........ | 2,285,459 | 2,277,866 | 4,563,325 | 11,248,214 | 135,208 | 33,444 | 1.20 | .73 |

*Number of national banks, capital, surplus, dividends, net addition to profits, and ratios, years ended June 30, 1914 to 1922.*

| Year ended June 30— | Number of banks. | Capital. | Surplus. | Dividends. | Net addition to profits. | Percentages. | | |
|---|---|---|---|---|---|---|---|---|
| | | | | | | Dividends to capital. | Dividends to capital and surplus. | Net addition to profits to capital and surplus. |
| 1914........ | 7,453 | $1,063,978,175 | $714,117,131 | $120,947,096 | $149,270,171 | 11.37 | 6.80 | 8.39 |
| 1915........ | 7,560 | 1,068,577,080 | 726,620,202 | 113,707,065 | 127,094,709 | 10.63 | 6.33 | 7.08 |
| 1916........ | 7,571 | 1,066,208,875 | 731,820,365 | 114,724,594 | 157,543,547 | 10.76 | 6.38 | 8.76 |
| 1917........ | 7,589 | 1,081,670,000 | 765,918,000 | 125,538,000 | 194,321,000 | 11.61 | 6.79 | 10.52 |
| 1918........ | 7,691 | 1,098,264,000 | 816,801,000 | 129,778,000 | 212,332,000 | 11.82 | 6.78 | 11.09 |
| 1919........ | 7,762 | 1,115,507,000 | 869,457,000 | 135,588,000 | 240,366,000 | 12.15 | 6.83 | 12.11 |
| 1920........ | 8,019 | 1,221,453,000 | 984,977,000 | 147,793,000 | 282,083,000 | 12.10 | 6.70 | 12.78 |
| 1921........ | 8,147 | 1,273,237,000 | 1,026,270,000 | 158,158,000 | 216,106,000 | 12.42 | 6.88 | 9.40 |
| 1922........ | 8,246 | 1,307,199,000 | 1,049,228,000 | 165,884,000 | 183,670,000 | 12.69 | 7.04 | 7.79 |

NATIONAL BANKS CLASSIFIED ACCORDING TO CAPITAL STOCK.

On September 15, 1922, there were 2,142 national banks operating in accordance with the provision of section 5138, United States Revised Statutes, with minimum capital of $25,000. The loans and discounts of these banks amounted to $418,754,000, their total resources were $734,522,000, and aggregate capital and deposits were $53,529,000 and $565,796,000, respectively.

There were 2,459 banks with individual capital stock of over $25,000 but not over $50,000 with combined capital of $116,007,000, aggregate resources of $1,630,333,000, loans and discounts of $893,-227,000, and total deposits of $1,250,095,000.

The largest number of banks in any class were those having capital in excess of $50,000 but not over $200,000. In this class there were 2,801 banks with loans and discounts of $2,417,571,000, total resources of $4,523,833,000, capital stock of $323,812,000, and total deposits of $3,483,594,000.

There were 534 banks with loans and discounts of $1,562,985,000, total resources of $2,858,511,000, capital stock of $189,819,000, and total deposits of $2,232,850,000, in the class of banks with capital in excess of $200,000 but not over $500,000.

The number of banks with capital in excess of $500,000 but not over $1,000,000 was 171; their loans and discounts were $1,228,778,000, total resources $2,196,900,000, capital stock $147,425,000, and total deposits $1,743,491,000; while in the class with capital in excess of $1,000,000 but not over $5,000,000 there were 113 banks with loans and discounts of $2,251,797,000, total resources of $4,162,345,000, capital stock of $216,030,000, and aggregate deposits of $3,389,441,000. There were 20 banks with capital stock in excess of $5,000,000. Eight of these banks are in New York, 2 in Chicago, 2 in Boston, 2 in Pittsburgh, 1 in Cincinnati, 1 in Milwaukee, 2 in St. Louis, and 2 in San Francisco. The combined loans and discounts of these 20 banks were $2,462,913,000, their total resources $4,819,655,000, or 23.03 per cent of the total resources of all reporting banks, capital $260,500,000, and total deposits $3,933,495,000.

A classification of national banks by cities and States according to capital stock is published in the appendix to the report of the Comptroller of the Currency, of which the following is a summary:

| | Number of banks. | Loans and discounts. | Aggregate resources. | Capital. | Total deposits. |
|---|---|---|---|---|---|
| Capital of $25,000............. | 2,142 | $418,754,000 | $734,522,000 | $53,529,000 | $565,796,000 |
| Capital over $25,000 but not over $50,000................ | 2,459 | 893,227,000 | 1,630,333,000 | 116,007,000 | 1,250,095,000 |
| Capital over $50,000 but not over $200,000................. | 2,801 | 2,417,571,000 | 4,523,833,000 | 323,812,000 | 3,483,594,000 |
| Capital over $200,000 but not over $500,000................. | 534 | 1,562,985,000 | 2,858,511,000 | 189,819,000 | 2,232,850,000 |
| Capital over $500,000 but not over $1,000,000................. | 171 | 1,228,778,000 | 2,196,900,000 | 147,425,000 | 1,743,491,000 |
| Capital over $1,000,000, but not over $5,000,000............... | 113 | 2,251,797,000 | 4,162,345,000 | 216,030,000 | 3,389,441,000 |
| Capital over $5,000,000......... | 20 | 2,462,913,000 | 4,819,655,000 | 260,500,000 | 3,933,495,000 |
| Total United States..... | 8,240 | 11,236,025,000 | 20,926,099,000 | 1,307,122,000 | 16,598,762,000 |

## NATIONAL BANK FAILURES.

Thirty-one national banks, with aggregate capital of $2,015,000, were placed in charge of receivers during the year ended October 31, 1922. The date that each bank was authorized to commence business, date of appointment of the receiver, the capital stock, and the circulation outstanding at date of failure are shown in the appendix to the report of the Comptroller of the Currency.

The first failure of a national bank took place in 1865; from that date until the close of business on October 31, 1922, the number of banks placed in charge of receivers was 659. Of this number, however, 47 were subsequently restored to solvency and permitted to resume business. The total capital of these failed banks at date of failure was $99,560,920, while the book or nominal value of the assets administered by receivers under the supervision of the comptroller aggregated $443,197,772, and the total cash thus far realized from the liquidation of these assets amounted to $221,170,213. In addition to this amount, however, there has been realized from assessments levied against shareholders the sum of $25,688,666, making the total cash collections from all sources $246,858,879, which have been disbursed as follows:

| | |
|---|---:|
| In dividends to creditors on claims proved, amounting to $228,869,734, the sum of......................................................... | $167,291,006 |
| In payment of loans and other disbursements discharging liabilities of the bank other than those of the general creditors.................... | 55,309,379 |
| In payment of legal expenses incurred in the administration of such receiverships......................................................... | 6,265,539 |
| In payment of receivers' salaries and other expenses of receiverships... | 11,414,302 |
| There has been returned to shareholders in cash....................... | 4,139,078 |
| Leaving a balance with the comptroller and the receivers of........... | 2,439,575 |
| Total...................................................... | 246,858,879 |

In addition to the funds thus distributed there has been returned to agents for shareholders, to be liquidated for their benefit, assets having a nominal value of $15,818,008.

The book or nominal value of the assets of the 83 national banks that are still in charge of receivers amount to $77,334,921. The receivers had realized from these assets at the close of business on October 31, 1922, the sum of $35,031,386 and had collected from the shareholders on account of assessments levied against them to cover deficiencies in assets the further sum of $2,596,307, making the total collections from all sources in the liquidation of active receiverships the sum of $37,627,693, which amount has been distributed as follows:

| | |
|---|---:|
| Dividends to creditors (to Sept. 30, 1922)............................. | $20,511,703 |
| Loans paid and other disbursements discharging liabilities of the bank other than those to the general creditors........................... | 12,278,312 |
| Legal expenses...................................................... | 586,253 |
| Receivers' salaries and all other expenses of administration............ | 1,482,095 |
| Amount returned to shareholders in cash............................ | 354,245 |
| Leaving a balance with the comptroller and the receivers of........... | 2,415,085 |
| Total...................................................... | 37,627,693 |

The receiverships of five national banks which had failed in previous years were finally closed during the year ended October 31, 1922, making a total of 576 closed receiverships.

The collections from the assets of the 576 national banks, the affairs of which have been finally closed, amounted to $186,138,827, and, together with the collections of $23,092,359 from assessments levied against the shareholders, make a total of $209,231,186, from which on claims aggregating $190,080,923 dividends were paid amounting to $146,779,303.

The average rate of dividends paid on claims proved was 77.21 per cent, but including offsets allowed, loans paid, and other disbursements with dividends, creditors received on an average 83.72 per cent.

The expenses incident to the administration of these 576 trusts—that is, receivers' salaries and legal and other expenses—amounted to $15,611,493, or 4.26 per cent of the nominal value of the assets and 7.46 per cent of the collections from assets and from shareholders. The outstanding circulation of these banks at the date of failure was $28,966,801, which was secured by United States bonds on deposit in the Treasury of the face value of $31,223,550. The assessments against shareholders averaged 51.43 per cent of their holdings, while the collections from the assessments levied were 48.55 per cent of the amount assessed. The total amount disbursed in dividends during the current year to the creditors of insolvent banks was $2,439,692.

In the table following is summarized the condition of all insolvent national banks, the closed and active receiverships being shown separately:

| Item. | Closed receiverships, 576.[1] | Active receiverships, 83. | Total, 659.[1] |
|---|---|---|---|
| Total assets taken charge of by receivers | $365,862,851 | $77,334,921 | $443,197,772 |
| Disposition of assets: | | | |
| Collected from assets | 186,138,827 | 35,031,386 | 221,170,213 |
| Offsets allowed and settled | 33,031,764 | 6,818,514 | 39,850,278 |
| Loss on assets compounded or sold under order of court | 126,669,476 | 8,062,761 | 134,732,237 |
| Nominal value of assets returned to stockholders | 15,818,008 | | 15,818,008 |
| Nominal value of remaining assets | 4,204,776 | 27,422,260 | 31,627,036 |
| Total | 365,862,851 | 77,334,921 | 443,197,772 |
| Collected from assets as above | 186,138,827 | 35,031,386 | 221,170,213 |
| Collected from assessments upon shareholders | 23,092,359 | 2,596,307 | 25,688,666 |
| Total collections | 209,231,186 | 37,627,693 | 246,858,879 |
| Disposition of collections: | | | |
| Loans paid and other disbursements | 43,031,067 | 12,278,312 | 55,309,379 |
| Dividends paid | 146,779,303 | 20,511,703 | 167,291,006 |
| Legal expenses | 5,679,286 | 586,253 | 6,265,539 |
| Receivers' salary and other expenses | 9,932,207 | 1,482,095 | 11,414,302 |
| Amount returned to shareholders in cash | 3,784,833 | 354,245 | 4,139,078 |
| Balance with comptroller or receiver | 24,490 | 2,415,085 | 2,439,575 |
| Total | 209,231,186 | 37,627,693 | 246,858,879 |
| Capital stock at date of failure | [2] 92,470,920 | 7,090,000 | 99,560,920 |
| United States bonds held at failure to secure circulating notes | 31,223,550 | 5,051,300 | 36,274,850 |
| Amount realized from sale of United States bonds held to secure circulating notes | 32,978,652 | 2,739,035 | 35,717,687 |
| Circulation outstanding at failure | 28,966,801 | 4,478,777 | 33,445,578 |
| Amount of assessment upon shareholders | 47,563,240 | 6,131,000 | 53,694,240 |
| Claims proved | 190,080,923 | 38,788,811 | 228,869,734 |

[1] Includes 47 banks restored to solvency.
[2] Includes capital stock of 47 banks restored to solvency.

Information relative to the capital, date of appointment of receiver, and per cent of dividends paid to creditors of five insolvent national banks, the affairs of which were closed during the year ended October 31, 1922, appears in the following table:

| Title. | Location. | Date receiver appointed. | Capital. | Per cent dividends paid to creditors. |
|---|---|---|---|---|
| First National Bank | Bayonne, N. J | Dec. 8, 1913 | $100,000 | 76.333 |
| Do | London, Ky | Apr. 9, 1914 | 50,000 | 95.5 |
| United States National Bank | Centralia, Wash | Sept. 21, 1914 | 100,000 | 66.67 |
| First National Bank | Clarkfield, Minn | Sept. 25, 1917 | 25,000 | 93 |
| Idaho National Bank | Boise, Idaho [1] | Sept. 15, 1921 | 100,000 | |

[1] After sale of assets, stockholders failed to vote for liquidation; bank placed in hand of receiver to wind up affairs.

Of the 31 banks placed in charge of receivers since October 31, 1921, 8 were closed on account of the inability to realize on loans; 2, defalcation of officers; 1, fraudulent management and injudicious banking; 7, deficient reserve and inability to realize on loans; 7, injudicious banking; 2, inability to meet demands; 3 by reason of "runs"; and 1 on account of injudicious banking and depreciation of securities.

## NATIONAL BANK CHARTERS APPLIED FOR, GRANTED, AND REFUSED.

,⁻ Applications for charters for 272 national banking associations, with capital of $25,490,800, were made during the 12 months ended October 31, 1922, as compared with 206 applications and capital of $25,370,000 during the previous year. Of the applications received, 210, with capital of $23,700,800, were approved, as against 153 and capital of $17,595,000 in 1921.

In the last year 25 applications, with capital of $1,205,000, were rejected, and 22, with capital of $1,610,000, were abandoned or action thereon indefinitely deferred. The principal causes of rejection were lack of demand for additional banking facilities in the various communities or the reported unsatisfactory financial standing or character of the applicants.

National banking associations to the number of 232, with capital of $24,890,800, were chartered in the year ended October 31, 1922, as compared with 169 associations, with capital of $20,005,000, chartered in 1921. Of the national banks chartered during the year just closed, only 53 became banks of issue, and of this latter number 27 were converted from or succeeded State banks, 3 were reorganized national banks, and 23 were banks of primary organization.

### INCREASES AND REDUCTIONS OF CAPITAL STOCK OF NATIONAL BANKS.

In order to meet the constantly increasing demands for additional capital, there was an increase in the capital stock of national banks of $35,027,350 on the part of 229 national banks during the year. The increases of 73 of these banks were effected partially or entirely by the declaration of stock dividends from the undivided profits of the banks. The aggregate amount of stock dividends was $10,790,800. In the previous year the increase in capital of existing banks was $27,835,800, the number of banks concerned in this increase being 259.

In 1922 there were but 15 banks which effected a reduction in their capital stock, the aggregate being $1,145,000; there were also 9 reductions in capital, aggregating $3,275,000, incident to consolidations of national banks under the act of November 7, 1918. In 1921 the number of reductions of capital was 3 and the aggregate amount of the reductions was $200,000; there were also 3 reductions, aggregating $850,000, under the consolidation act of November 7, 1918.

### LIQUIDATION OF NATIONAL BANKS.

Exclusive of 25 banks, with capital of $6,295,000, liquidated and absorbed by other national banks, 78 national banking associations, with capital of $12,615,000, were placed in voluntary liquidation, or the corporate existence expired during the past year, of which 61 were absorbed by State banks, 16 reorganized as State banks, and 1 quit business. Of the 103 liquidations for the past year, advice has been received from 25 that their affairs have been entirely closed. The year before there were 93 liquidations, with $37,075,000 capital. The number of receiverships was 31, and the capital involved was only $2,015,000.

## CONSOLIDATION OF NATIONAL BANKS.

Under the provisions of the act of Congress approved November 7, 1918, providing for the consolidation of national banking associations, 170 national banks have consolidated into 84 associations. During the last year 21 consolidations were effected, with capital of $46,425,000, surplus $42,833,404, and other undivided profits of $21,494,383, the number of banks concerned being 42 and their capital $46,750,000. There was therefore a reduction as a result of these consolidations of $325,000 in aggregate capital stock. The total assets of the 21 consolidated banks amounted at the date of consolidation to $997,328,244.

In the following table the capital, surplus, undivided profits, and aggregate assets and date of consolidation of each of the 21 consolidated banks are shown.

*National banks consolidated under act of November 7, 1918, their capital, surplus, undivided profits, and aggregate assets, year ended October 31, 1922.*

| Consolidation No. | Charter No. | Title and location of bank. | State. | Date of consolidation. | Capital. | Surplus. | Undivided profits. | Aggregate assets. |
|---|---|---|---|---|---|---|---|---|
| | | | | *1921.* | | | | |
| 64 | 2370 | The Chase National Bank of the City of New York. | N. Y.. | Nov. 22 | $20,000,000 | $15,000,000 | $8,331,602 | $454,737,100 |
| 65 | 2996 | The Owego National Bank | N. Y.. | Dec. 31 | 150,000 | 30,000 | 13,820 | 1,247,203 |
| | | | | *1922.* | | | | |
| 66 | 3721 | Alliance First National Bank. | Ohio.. | Jan. 3 | 300,000 | 300,000 | 58,260 | 6,209,867 |
| 67 | 10112 | American Exchange National Bank of Greensboro. | N. C.. | Feb. 21 | 750,000 | 250,000 | 209,220 | 8,776,441 |
| 68 | 219 | The First National Bank of Greencastle. | Ind... | Feb. 27 | 100,000 | 20,000 | .......... | 1,187,630 |
| 69 | 3293 | Grand Rapids National Bank. | Mich.. | Mar. 13 | 1,000,000 | 200,000 | 295,010 | 12,875,956 |
| 70 | 12123 | The Seaboard National Bank of the City of New York. | N. Y.. | Mar. 31 | 4,000,000 | 6,378,404 | 797,142 | 91,581,213 |
| 71 | 542 | Corn Exchange National Bank of Philadelphia. | Pa.... | Apr. 25 | 2,200,000 | 4,000,000 | 1,070,958 | 58,818,679 |
| 72 | 7779 | The First National Bank of Lemoore. | Calif.. | Apr. 26 | 150,000 | 30,000 | 3,412 | 1,404,538 |
| 73 | 10194 | The Seaboard National Bank of Norfolk. | Va.... | May 6 | 800,000 | 400,000 | 273,796 | 9,086,163 |
| 74 | 5046 | The Riggs National Bank of Washington, D. C. | D. C.. | June 10 | 1,000,000 | 2,000,000 | 608,135 | 29,867,258 |
| 75 | 9852 | The Farmers and First National Bank of New Castle. | Ind... | June 21 | 200,000 | 100,000 | 30,454 | 1,637,878 |
| 76 | 12205 | Passaic National Bank & Trust Company. | N. J... | June 22 | 1,150,000 | 800,000 | 649,135 | 17,353,523 |
| 77 | 1209 | The First National State Bank of Camden. | N. J... | June 30 | 850,000 | 750,000 | 104,841 | 16,501,872 |
| 78 | 5028 | The Union National Bank of Sistersville. | W. Va. | July 3 | 175,000 | 75,000 | 21,446 | 2,129,411 |
| 79 | 1250 | The Mechanics & Metals National Bank of the City of New York. | N. Y.. | July 22 | 10,000,000 | 10,000,000 | 7,891,998 | 224,885,592 |
| 80 | 3917 | The Peoples National Bank of Leesburg. | Va.... | Aug. 1 | 100,000 | 100,000 | 68,991 | 2,352,690 |
| 81 | 9403 | The Continental National Bank of Salt Lake City. | Utah.. | Sept. 30 | 600,000 | 100,000 | 98 | 8,338,520 |
| 82 | 5045 | The Fourth National Bank of Atlanta. | Ga..... | ...do.... | 1,200,000 | 1,800,000 | 555,254 | 28,942,223 |
| 83 | 2597 | The First & Utah National Bank of Ogden. | Utah.. | Oct. 2 | 500,000 | 100,000 | 208,111 | 5,523,303 |
| 84 | 10316 | Federal-American National Bank of Washington. | D. C.. | Oct. 31 | 1,200,000 | 400,000 | 302,700 | 13,871,184 |
| | | Total (21 banks).... | ........ | .......... | 46,425,000 | 42,833,404 | 21,494,383 | 997,328,244 |

## GROWTH IN NUMBER AND CAPITAL OF NATIONAL BANKS.

Notwithstanding the liquidations and the consolidations which took place there was a net increase in the year ended October 31, 1922, of 83 in the number of national banking associations and of $34,973,150 in capital. The authorized capital stock of the 8,262 national banks in existence at the close of the year was $1,316,968,715.

### NATIONAL BANKS' CAPITAL STOCK CHANGES, 1914–1922.

During the period covered by the existence of the Federal reserve system, years ended October 31, 1914, to October 31, 1922, applications to the number of 2,710 were received for the organization of national banking associations, with aggregate capital of $169,500,000; of this number, 1,972 were approved. The number of banks chartered was 1,808, with combined capital of $157,700,000. In this period 2,063 banks effected increases in their capital stock to the amount of $298,700,000. As a result of voluntary liquidations to the number of 870 and 119 failures, there was a loss of capital aggregating $182,900,000. Banks to the number of 95 reduced their capital to the extent of $11,890,000. There was no material increase in capital resulting from the consolidation of banks under act November 7, 1918; but the various changes referred to occasioned a net increase of national bank capital of approximately $250,000,000 during the period covered by this survey.

From the inauguration of the national banking system in 1863 to October 31, 1922, national banking associations to the number of 12,265 were chartered, the capital stock at organization being $1,245,109,282. The total loss to the system in the number of banks during this period was 4,003, of which 3,391 were closed by voluntary liquidation or by consolidation with other national banks and 612 were liquidated through receivers.

### ORGANIZATION AND LIQUIDATION OF NATIONAL BANKS.

The statistical or report year of the Comptroller of the Currency terminates on October 31, and the following table contains a statistical annual history from 1914 to 1922, inclusive, of the number of banks organized each year, and their capital at date of organization, together with the number and capital of banks closed voluntarily or by reason of failure, together with the yearly net increase or decrease in the number of banks and original capital. In the table the increases and reductions of capital of existing banks are not taken into account.

*Number and authorized capital of national banks chartered and the number and capital stock of banks closed in each year ended October 31, since 1913, with the yearly increase or decrease.*

| Year. | Chartered. | | Closed. | | | | | | Net yearly increase (exclusive of existing banks increasing their capital). | | Net yearly decrease (exclusive of existing banks decreasing their capital). | |
| | | | Consolidated under act Nov. 7, 1918. | | In voluntary liquidation. | | Insolvent. | | | | | |
| | No. | Capital. | No. | Loss to capital. | No. | Capital. | No. | Capital. | No. | Capital. | No. | Capital. |
|---|---|---|---|---|---|---|---|---|---|---|---|---|
| 1914.. | 195 | $18,675,000 | .... | ............ | 113 | $26,487,000 | 21 | $1,810,000 | 61 | ............ | .... | $9,622,000 |
| 1915.. | 144 | 9,689,500 | .... | ............ | 82 | 13,795,000 | 14 | 1,830,000 | 48 | ............ | .... | 5,935,500 |
| 1916.. | 122 | 6,630,000 | .... | ............ | 135 | 14,828,500 | 13 | 805,000 | .... | ............ | 26 | 9,003,000 |
| 1917.. | 176 | 11,590,000 | .... | ............ | 107 | 14,367,500 | 7 | 1,230,000 | 62 | ............ | .... | 4,007,500 |
| 1918.. | 164 | 13,400,000 | .... | ............ | 68 | 16,165,000 | 2 | 250,000 | 94 | ............ | .... | 3,015,000 |
| 1919.. | 245 | 21,780,000 | 26 | 1 $3,220,000 | 83 | 16,380,000 | 1 | 25,000 | 135 | $2,155,000 | .... | ............ |
| 1920.. | 361 | 31,077,500 | 15 | 1 1,650,000 | 84 | 14,730,000 | 5 | 205,000 | 257 | 14,492,500 | .... | ............ |
| 1921.. | 169 | 20,005,000 | 24 | 1 850,000 | 93 | 37,075,000 | 34 | 1,370,000 | 18 | ............ | .... | 19,790,000 |
| 1922.. | 232 | 24,890,800 | 21 | 1 3,275,000 | 103 | 18,910,000 | 2 31 | 2,015,000 | 3 77 | 690,800 | .... | ............ |

[1] Amount of capital stock reductions incident to consolidations.
[2] Includes 5 banks with capital of $375,000 restored to solvency. There was also one bank restored with capital of $25,000 for which a receiver had been appointed the previous year.
[3] The net gain was 83 banks.

*Number of national banks organized, consolidated under act November 7, 1918, insolvent, in voluntary liquidation, and in operation on October 31, 1922.*

| State or Territory. | Organized. | Consolidated under act Nov. 7, 1918. | Insolvent. | In liquidation. | In operation. |
|---|---|---|---|---|---|
| Maine | 113 | ............ | ............ | 53 | 60 |
| New Hampshire | 72 | ............ | 4 | 12 | 56 |
| Vermont | 76 | ............ | 7 | 20 | 49 |
| Massachusetts | 333 | 1 | 15 | 158 | 159 |
| Rhode Island | 65 | ............ | 1 | 47 | 17 |
| Connecticut | 111 | 2 | 5 | 41 | 63 |
| Total New England States | 770 | 3 | 32 | 331 | 404 |
| New York | 806 | 12 | 50 | 238 | 506 |
| New Jersey | 282 | 4 | 10 | 38 | 230 |
| Pennsylvania | 1,077 | 3 | 45 | 161 | 868 |
| Delaware | 28 | ............ | ............ | 10 | 18 |
| Maryland | 125 | ............ | 2 | 37 | 86 |
| District of Columbia | 29 | 2 | 3 | 10 | 14 |
| Total Eastern States | 2,347 | 21 | 110 | 494 | 1,722 |
| Virginia | 226 | 4 | 7 | 36 | 179 |
| West Virginia | 156 | 1 | 5 | 28 | 122 |
| North Carolina | 121 | 2 | 6 | 25 | 88 |
| South Carolina | 105 | 1 | 1 | 19 | 84 |
| Georgia | 161 | 2 | 10 | 50 | 99 |
| Florida | 91 | ............ | 13 | 17 | 61 |
| Alabama | 153 | ............ | 9 | 37 | 107 |
| Mississippi | 61 | ............ | 2 | 27 | 32 |
| Louisiana | 80 | 2 | 8 | 36 | 34 |
| Texas | 884 | 6 | 44 | 274 | 560 |
| Arkansas | 112 | 1 | 8 | 18 | 85 |
| Kentucky | 223 | 5 | 6 | 75 | 137 |
| Tennessee | 180 | 1 | 8 | 68 | 103 |
| Total Southern States | 2,553 | 25 | 127 | 710 | 1,691 |
| Ohio | 624 | 4 | 32 | 217 | 371 |
| Indiana | 390 | 5 | 17 | 117 | 251 |
| Illinois | 675 | 1 | 22 | 150 | 502 |
| Michigan | 245 | 1 | 16 | 109 | 119 |
| Wisconsin | 226 | 2 | 6 | 63 | 155 |
| Minnesota | 419 | 2 | 10 | 64 | 343 |
| Iowa | 483 | 2 | 18 | 112 | 351 |
| Missouri | 250 | 4 | 12 | 99 | 135 |
| Total Middle Western States | 3,312 | 21 | 133 | 931 | 2,227 |

*Number of national banks organized, consolidated under act November 7, 1918, insolvent, in voluntary liquidation, and in operation on October 31, 1922—Continued.*

| State or Territory. | Organ-ized. | Consoli-dated under act Nov. 7, 1918. | Insol-vent. | In liqui-dation. | In opera-tion. |
|---|---|---|---|---|---|
| North Dakota | 231 | .......... | 18 | 30 | 183 |
| South Dakota | 183 | .......... | 14 | 36 | 133 |
| Nebraska | 338 | .......... | 27 | 129 | 182 |
| Kansas | 419 | 2 | 37 | 112 | 268 |
| Montana | 182 | 2 | 21 | 29 | 130 |
| Wyoming | 55 | .......... | 2 | 6 | 47 |
| Colorado | 199 | .......... | 13 | 42 | 144 |
| New Mexico | 71 | .......... | 6 | 20 | 45 |
| Oklahoma | 678 | 1 | 11 | 214 | 452 |
| Total Western States | 2,356 | 5 | 149 | 618 | 1,584 |
| Washington | 189 | 1 | 24 | 53 | 111 |
| Oregon | 129 | .......... | 9 | 22 | 98 |
| California | 412 | 8 | 13 | 106 | 285 |
| Idaho | 104 | .......... | 9 | 15 | 80 |
| Utah | 38 | 2 | 3 | 11 | 22 |
| Nevada | 16 | .......... | 2 | 3 | 11 |
| Arizona | 28 | .......... | 1 | 5 | 22 |
| Alaska | 4 | .......... | .......... | 1 | 3 |
| Total Pacific States | 920 | 11 | 61 | 216 | 632 |
| Hawaii | 6 | .......... | .......... | 4 | 2 |
| Porto Rico | 1 | .......... | .......... | 1 | .......... |
| Total island possessions | 7 | .......... | .......... | 5 | 2 |
| Total United States | 12,265 | 86 | 612 | 3,305 | 8,262 |

*National banks chartered during the year ended October 31, 1922.*

| Charter No. | Title. | Capital. |
|---|---|---|
| | ALASKA. | |
| 12072 | First National Bank of Anchorage | $50,000 |
| | ARIZONA. | |
| 12198 | First National Bank of Holbrook | 25,000 |
| | ARKANSAS. | |
| 12083 | Planters National Bank of Walnut Ridge | 25,000 |
| 12156 | Peoples National Bank of Stuttgart | 50,000 |
| 12219 | Farmers National Bank of Cotton Plant | 25,000 |
| 12238 | First National Bank of Lamar | 25,000 |
| | Total (4 banks) | 125,000 |
| | CALIFORNIA. | |
| 12056 | Placerville National Bank, Placerville | 50,000 |
| 12061 | First National Bank of Monterey Park | 25,000 |
| 12112 | Citizens National Bank of Lodi | 200,000 |
| 12127 | National Bank of Lemoore [1] | 100,000 |
| 12160 | National Bank of Dinuba [2] | 50,000 |
| 12172 | Paso Robles National Bank, Paso Robles | 50,000 |
| 12201 | American National Bank of Santa Rosa | 100,000 |
| 12209 | First National Bank of Hermosa Beach | 50,000 |
| 12210 | First National Bank of Watts | 50,000 |
| 12226 | United States National Bank of Sawtelle | 50,000 |
| 12253 | First National Bank of East San Gabriel | 50,000 |
| | Total (11 banks) | 775,000 |

[1] With branch at Stratford, Calif. Consolidated on Apr. 26, 1922, with The First National Bank of Lemoore, Calif., under act Nov. 7, 1918.
[2] Placed in voluntary liquidation June 21, 1922, and absorbed by First National Bank of Dinuba, Calif.

*National banks chartered during the year ended October 31, 1922*—Continued.

| Charter No. | Title. | Capital. |
|---|---|---|
| | COLORADO. | |
| 12250 | Broadway National Bank of Denver............................................. | $200,000 |
| | DISTRICT OF COLUMBIA. | |
| 12139 | Standard National Bank of Washington............................................. | 200,000 |
| 12194 | Hamilton National Bank of Washington [2]............................................. | 200,000 |
| | Total (2 banks)............................................. | 400,000 |
| | FLORIDA. | |
| 12047 | Miami Beach First National Bank, Miami Beach............................................. | 50,000 |
| 12057 | American National Bank of West Palm Beach............................................. | 100,000 |
| 12090 | First National Bank of Sebring............................................. | 50,000 |
| 12100 | National Bank of Winter Haven............................................. | 75,000 |
| | Total (4 banks)............................................. | 275,000 |
| | GEORGIA. | |
| 12105 | First National Bank of Dallas............................................. | 25,000 |
| 12232 | Citizens National Bank of Marietta............................................. | 100,000 |
| 12249 | Ninth National Bank of Atlanta [4]............................................. | 325,000 |
| 12254 | National Bank of Lumpkin, Lumpkin............................................. | 25,000 |
| | Total (4 banks)............................................. | 475,000 |
| | IDAHO. | |
| 12256 | Cassia National Bank of Burley............................................. | 50,000 |
| | ILLINOIS. | |
| 12096 | First National Bank of Xenia............................................. | 25,000 |
| 12097 | First National Bank of Zeigler............................................. | 35,000 |
| 12178 | Security National Bank of East St. Louis............................................. | 300,000 |
| 12227 | Douglass National Bank of Chicago............................................. | 200,000 |
| | Total (4 banks)............................................. | 560,000 |
| | INDIANA. | |
| 12058 | United States National Bank of Indiana Harbor at East Chicago.................... | 100,000 |
| 12132 | National City Bank of Evansville............................................. | 500,000 |
| | Total (2 banks)............................................. | 600,000 |
| | IOWA. | |
| 12248 | First National Bank of Lorimor............................................. | 35,000 |
| | KANSAS. | |
| 12168 | First National Bank of Tribune............................................. | 25,000 |
| 12191 | First National Bank of McCune............................................. | 25,000 |
| | Total (2 banks)............................................. | 50,000 |
| | KENTUCKY. | |
| 12202 | Wallins National Bank of Wallins Creek............................................. | 25,000 |
| 12243 | Citizens National Bank of Harlan............................................. | 100,000 |
| | Total (2 banks)............................................. | 125,000 |
| | MICHIGAN. | |
| 12084 | First National Bank of Lawton............................................. | 25,000 |
| 12108 | City National Bank of Grand Rapids [5]............................................. | 200,000 |
| | Total (2 banks)............................................. | 225,000 |
| | MINNESOTA. | |
| 12115 | Richfield National Bank, Richfield............................................. | 25,000 |
| 12140 | Duluth National Bank, Duluth............................................. | 200,000 |
| | Total (2 banks)............................................. | 225,000 |
| | MISSISSIPPI. | |
| 12073 | Rosedale National Bank, Rosedale............................................. | 85,000 |
| 12222 | Planters National Bank of Clarksdale............................................. | 500,000 |
| | Total (2 banks)............................................. | 585,000 |

[2] With 3 branches in Washington, D. C. Consolidated on June 10, 1922, with The Riggs National Bank of Washington, D. C., under act of Nov. 7, 1918.
[4] With 4 branches in Atlanta and one at Decatur, Ga. Consolidated on Sept. 30, 1922, with The Fourth National Bank of Atlanta, under act Nov. 7, 1918.
[5] With 9 branches in Grand Rapids, Mich. Consolidated on Mar. 13, 1922, with Grand Rapids National Bank, under act Nov. 7, 1918.

*National banks chartered during the year ended October 31, 1922*—Continued.

| Charter No. | Title. | Capital. |
|---|---|---|
| | MISSOURI. | |
| 12066 | Security National Bank Savings & Trust Co. of St. Louis | $250,000 |
| 12216 | St. Louis National Bank, St. Louis | 200,000 |
| 12220 | Missouri National Bank of St. Louis | 200,000 |
| 12260 | Continental National Bank & Trust Co. of Kansas City | 500,000 |
| | Total (4 banks) | 1,150,000 |
| | NEBRASKA. | |
| 12225 | First National Bank of Unadilla | 25,000 |
| | NEW JERSEY. | |
| 12037 | Ridgefield National Bank, Ridgefield | 25,000 |
| 12064 | First National Bank of West New York [6] | 100,000 |
| 12145 | First National Bank of Newfield | 25,000 |
| 12167 | Totowa National Bank of Paterson | 200,000 |
| 12195 | First National Bank of Park Ridge | 25,000 |
| 12205 | Passaic National Bank & Trust Co, Passaic | 650,000 |
| 12223 | First National Bank of East Rutherford | 50,000 |
| 12255 | Bergen National Bank of Jersey City | 250,000 |
| 12263 | First National Bank of Cranford | 100,000 |
| | Total (9 banks) | 1,425,000 |
| | NEW YORK. | |
| 12071 | Atlanta National Bank, Atlanta | 25,000 |
| 12122 | Liberty National Bank of Syracuse | 200,000 |
| 12123 | Mercantile National Bank in New York [7] | 1,000,000 |
| 12164 | First National Bank of Windham | 25,000 |
| 12174 | First National Bank of Greene | 50,000 |
| 12208 | First National Bank of Kenmore | 65,000 |
| 12213 | Capitol National Bank of New York | 2,000,000 |
| 12214 | Lebanon National Bank of New York | 250,000 |
| 12224 | Lincoln National Bank of New York [8] | 2,000,000 |
| 12242 | Germantown National Bank, Germantown | 50,000 |
| 12252 | Rockaway Beach National Bank of New York | 200,000 |
| | Total (11 banks) | 5,865,000 |
| | NORTH CAROLINA. | |
| 12176 | Commercial National Bank of Wilmington | 200,000 |
| 12244 | National Bank of Commerce, Asheville | 100,000 |
| 12259 | First National Bank of Leaksville | 40,000 |
| | Total (3 banks) | 340,000 |
| | NORTH DAKOTA. | |
| 12046 | Merchants National Bank of Cavalier | 25,000 |
| 12258 | First National Bank of Donnybrook | 25,000 |
| | Total (2 banks) | 50,000 |
| | OHIO. | |
| 12034 | Alliance National Bank, Alliance [9] | 150,000 |
| 12196 | Old National Bank of Delphos | 75,000 |
| | Total (2 banks) | 225,000 |
| | OKLAHOMA. | |
| 12035 | First National Bank of Moore | 25,000 |
| 12036 | Security National Bank of Norman | 50,000 |
| 12038 | Blackwell National Bank, Blackwell | 100,000 |
| 12039 | Garfield National Bank of Enid | 100,000 |
| 12040 | Security National Bank of Blackwell | 100,000 |
| 12041 | First National Bank in Billings | 40,000 |
| 12042 | Producers National Bank of Tulsa | 250,000 |
| 12043 | Security National Bank of Tulsa | 200,000 |
| 12044 | Central National Bank of Enid | 130,000 |
| 12045 | Billings National Bank, Billings | 30,000 |
| 12048 | American National Bank of Okmulgee | 200,000 |
| 12049 | Cherokee National Bank, Cherokee | 30,000 |
| 12050 | Security National Bank of Clinton | 50,000 |
| 12051 | Oklahoma National Bank of Duncan | 100,000 |
| 12052 | Wynona National Bank, Wynona | 100,000 |
| 12053 | American National Bank of Ardmore | 200,000 |
| 12054 | Oklahoma National Bank of Cushing | 50,000 |
| 12059 | Farmers National Bank of Carnegie | 25,000 |
| 12060 | Farmers National Bank of Chandler | 25,000 |
| 12065 | Security National Bank of Duncan | 50,000 |

[6] P. O. Weehawken.
[7] With 2 branches in New York City. Mar 31, 1922, under act Nov. 7, 1918, title was changed to The Seaboard National Bank of The City of New York.
[8] With 3 branches in New York City. Consolidated July 22, 1922, with The Mechanics & Metals National Bank of the City of New York, under act Nov 7, 1918.
[9] Consolidated on Jan. 3, 1922, with Alliance First National Bank under act Nov. 7, 1918.

*National banks chartered during the year ended October 31, 1922*—Continued.

| Charter No. | Title. | Capital. |
|---|---|---|
| | OKLAHOMA—continued. | |
| 12067 | American National Bank of Lawton | $100,000 |
| 12068 | Citizens National Bank of Kingfisher | 50,000 |
| 12069 | Hominy National Bank, Hominy | 25,000 |
| 12074 | State National Bank of Weleetka | 25,000 |
| 12076 | Barnsdall National Bank, Barnsdall | 50,000 |
| 12078 | Wellston National Bank, Wellston | 25,000 |
| 12079 | First National Bank of Sand Springs | 50,000 |
| 12081 | Helena National Bank, Helena | 25,000 |
| 12082 | American National Bank of Stillwater | 50,000 |
| 12086 | First National Bank of Putnam | 25,000 |
| 12087 | American National Bank of Holdenville | 75,000 |
| 12088 | First National Bank of Hitchcock | 25,000 |
| 12089 | Liberty National Bank of Tahlequah | 50,000 |
| 12093 | Farmers National Bank of Elk City | 50,000 |
| 12094 | Farmers National Bank of Waurika | 25,000 |
| 12095 | State National Bank of Stroud | 25,000 |
| 12099 | National Bank of Commerce of Wetumka | 30,000 |
| 12102 | First National Bank in Kenefick [10] | 25,000 |
| 12103 | First National Bank of Locust Grove | 25,000 |
| 12104 | State National Bank of Depew | 25,000 |
| 12106 | State National Bank of Idabel | 50,000 |
| 12107 | First National Bank of Hinton | 25,000 |
| 12109 | First National Bank of Leedey | 25,000 |
| 12111 | Security National Bank of Coweta | 30,000 |
| 12113 | Clarks National Bank of Aline | 25,000 |
| 12116 | First National Bank of Centrahoma | 25,000 |
| 12117 | American National Bank of Pryor Creek [11] | 25,000 |
| 12118 | American National Bank of Walters | 30,000 |
| 12120 | American National Bank of Apache | 25,000 |
| 12125 | Farmers National Bank of Texhoma | 25,000 |
| 12126 | American National Bank of Durant | 100,000 |
| 12128 | Farmers & Merchants National Bank of Hooker | 40,000 |
| 12129 | First National Bank in Marlow | 25,000 |
| 12130 | First National Bank in Blair | 25,000 |
| 12131 | First National Bank of Brinkman | 25,000 |
| 12133 | First National Bank of Binger | 25,000 |
| 12134 | McClain County National Bank of Purcell | 30,000 |
| 12135 | Le Flore County National Bank of Poteau | 25,000 |
| 12136 | City National Bank of Hugo | 100,000 |
| 12141 | First National Bank of Fletcher | 25,000 |
| 12142 | First National Bank in Granite | 25,000 |
| 12144 | Security National Bank of Ada | 100,000 |
| 12147 | First National Bank of Carter | 25,000 |
| 12148 | First National Bank of Coyle | 25,000 |
| 12149 | City National Bank of Davis | 25,000 |
| 12150 | Oklahoma National Bank of Hastings | 25,000 |
| 12152 | Central National Bank of Alva | 50,000 |
| 12155 | Altus National Bank, Altus | 50,000 |
| 12157 | City National Bank in Norman | 50,000 |
| 12158 | Central National Bank of Poteau | 25,000 |
| 12161 | First National Bank of Kemp City [12] | 25,000 |
| 12163 | Farmers National Bank of Tyrone | 25,000 |
| 12165 | First National Bank of Shidler | 25,000 |
| 12169 | First National Bank of Wheatland | 25,000 |
| 12171 | First National Bank in Dustin | 25,000 |
| 12173 | First National Bank of Ninnekah | 25,000 |
| 12177 | Shidler National Bank, Shidler | 25,000 |
| 12179 | Texas County National Bank of Guymon | 25,000 |
| 12185 | Peoples National Bank of Custer City | 25,000 |
| 12188 | Mill Creek National Bank, Mill Creek | 25,000 |
| 12200 | First National Bank of Calumet | 25,000 |
| 12203 | American National Bank of Beggs | 50,000 |
| 12206 | Security National Bank of Newkirk | 30,000 |
| 12207 | Farmers National Bank of Erick | 25,000 |
| 12211 | First National Bank in Bokchito | 25,000 |
| 12212 | National Bank of Commerce of Pawhuska | 50,000 |
| 12215 | Exchange National Bank of Pauls Valley | 50,000 |
| 12218 | Kiowa National Bank in Snyder | 25,000 |
| 12221 | First National Bank of Loco | 25,000 |
| 12223 | First National Bank of Britton | 25,000 |
| 12230 | Farmers National Bank of Chickasha | 100,000 |
| 12237 | Farmers National Bank of Hollis | 25,000 |
| 12239 | First National Bank in Kiefer | 25,000 |
| 12245 | First National Bank of Cheyenne | 25,000 |
| 12265 | American National Bank of Boynton | 25,000 |
| | Total (95 banks) | 4,540,000 |

[10] P. O. Kenefic
[11] P. O. Pryor
[12] P. O. Hendrix.

*National banks chartered during the year ended October 31, 1922—*Continued.

| Charter No. | Title. | Capital. |
|---|---|---|
| | OREGON. | |
| 12077 | Coos Bay National Bank of Marshfield | $50,000 |
| 12193 | First National Bank of Mount Angel | 30,000 |
| 12262 | Vale National Bank, Vale | 50,000 |
| | Total (3 banks) | 130,000 |
| | PENNSYLVANIA. | |
| 12063 | First National Bank of Windsor | 25,000 |
| 12098 | Moxham National Bank of Johnstown | 200,000 |
| 12137 | Rittenhouse National Bank of Philadelphia [13] | 500,000 |
| 12159 | Nescopeck National Bank, Nescopeck | 25,000 |
| 12189 | First National Bank in Conneautville | 50,000 |
| 12192 | First National Bank of Center Hall | 25,000 |
| 12197 | National Bank of Penbrook | 25,000 |
| 12261 | Peoples National Bank of State College | 50,000 |
| | Total (8 banks) | 900,000 |
| | SOUTH CAROLINA. | |
| 12146 | Carolina National Bank of Spartanburg | 200,000 |
| 12175 | Carolina National Bank of Anderson | 200,000 |
| 12233 | First National Bank of St. George | 50,000 |
| | Total (3 banks) | 450,000 |
| | TENNESSEE. | |
| 12080 | First National Bank of Loudon | 50,000 |
| 12257 | Rockwood National Bank, Rockwood | 50,000 |
| 12264 | City National Bank of Rockwood | 50,000 |
| | Total (3 banks) | 150,000 |
| | TEXAS. | |
| 12055 | Public National Bank of Houston | 300,000 |
| 12062 | Guaranty National Bank of Houston | 200,000 |
| 12070 | State National Bank of Houston | 200,000 |
| 12091 | Merchants National Bank of Port Arthur | 100,000 |
| 12101 | Follett National Bank, Follett | 25,000 |
| 12110 | First National Bank of Ennis | 200,000 |
| 12119 | Security National Bank of Harlinger [14] | 25,000 |
| 12138 | Texas National Bank of Beaumont | 250,000 |
| 12162 | Commercial National Bank of San Antonio | 200,000 |
| 12166 | City National Bank in Wellington | 100,000 |
| 12182 | First National Bank of Kenedy | 50,000 |
| 12186 | Republic National Bank of Dallas | 1,000,000 |
| 12187 | Nichols National Bank of Kenedy | 60,000 |
| 12190 | Prendergast-Smith National Bank of Mexia | 100,000 |
| 12199 | City National Bank of Beaumont | 100,000 |
| 12235 | State National Bank of Corpus Christi | 100,000 |
| 12236 | State National Bank of Brownsville | 100,000 |
| 12241 | Farmers National Bank of Buda | 30,000 |
| 12247 | Corrigan National Bank, Corrigan | 25,000 |
| | Total (19 banks) | 3,165,000 |
| | VIRGINIA. | |
| 12092 | First National Bank of Poquoson [15] | 25,000 |
| 12151 | Continental National Bank of Norfolk [16] | 350,000 |
| 12183 | First National Bank of Victoria | 25,000 |
| 12204 | Leesburg Upperville National Bank of Leesburg [17] | 25,000 |
| 12229 | National Bank of Blacksburg | 75,000 |
| 12240 | Citizens National Bank of Emporia | 180,000 |
| 12251 | First National Bank of Kenbridge | 45,800 |
| | Total (7 banks) | 725,800 |

[13] Consolidated on Apr. 25, 1922, with Corn Exchange National Bank of Philadelphia under act Nov. 7, 1918.

[14] Title changed on Apr. 17, 1922, to The First National Bank in Harlingen.

[15] P. O. Odd.

[16] With one branch in Norfolk. Consolidated on May 6, 1922, with The Seaboard National Bank of Norfolk, under act Nov. 7, 1918.

[17] With one branch at Upperville, Va., Consolidated on Aug. 1, 1922, with The Peoples National Bank of Leesburg under act Nov. 7, 1918.

*National banks chartered during the year ended October 31, 1922*—Continued.

| Charter No. | Title. | Capital. |
|---|---|---|
| | **WASHINGTON.** | |
| 12085 | Auburn National Bank, Auburn | $50,000 |
| 12114 | First National Bank of Enumclaw | 60,000 |
| 12121 | First National Bank of Redmond | 25,000 |
| 12143 | Enumclaw National Bank, Enumclaw | 50,000 |
| 12153 | University National Bank of Seattle | 200,000 |
| 12154 | Skagit National Bank of Mount Vernon | 50,000 |
| 12170 | First National Bank in Odessa | 40,000 |
| 12180 | First National Bank in Sprague | 30,000 |
| 12181 | Sunnyside National Bank, Sunnyside | 50,000 |
| 12184 | Security National Bank of Palouse | 50,000 |
| 12217 | Kent National Bank, Kent | 40,000 |
| 12231 | State National Bank of Garfield | 50,000 |
| 12234 | American National Bank of Bellingham | 100,000 |
| 12246 | West Side National Bank of Yakima | 100,000 |
| | Total (14 banks) | 895,000 |
| | **WEST VIRGINIA.** | |
| 12075 | Oak Hill National Bank, Oak Hill | 50,000 |
| | **WISCONSIN.** | |
| 12124 | First National Bank of Eagle River | 25,000 |
| | Total United States (232 banks) | 24,800,800 |

*National banks organized, failed, and reported in voluntary liquidation during the year ended October 31, 1922.*

| State. | Organized. | | Failed. | | | Voluntary liquidations. | | |
|---|---|---|---|---|---|---|---|---|
| | Number. | Authorized capital. | Number. | Capital. | Gross assets. | Number. | Capital. | Gross assets. |
| Massachusetts | | | | | | 3 | $550,000 | $3,534,181.38 |
| Connecticut | | | | | | 1 | 200,000 | 1,306,700.35 |
| Total New England States | | | | | | 4 | 750,000 | 4,840,881.73 |
| New York | 11 | $5,865,000 | | | | 9 | 6,650,000 | 173,303,483.40 |
| New Jersey | 9 | 1,425,000 | | | | 2 | 250,000 | 4,781,073.84 |
| Pennsylvania | 8 | 900,000 | | | | 3 | 575,000 | 6,879,974.73 |
| Maryland | | | 1 | $50,000 | $425,931 | 3 | 550,000 | 6,576,316.90 |
| District of Columbia | 2 | 400,000 | | | | 1 | 200,000 | 2,720,757.81 |
| Total Eastern States | 30 | 8,590,000 | 1 | 50,000 | 425,931 | 18 | 8,225,000 | 194,261,606.68 |
| Virginia | 7 | 725,800 | | | | 1 | 1,000,000 | 15,853,976.61 |
| West Virginia | 1 | 50,000 | | | | | | |
| North Carolina | 3 | 340,000 | | | | 1 | 50,000 | 372,386.72 |
| South Carolina | 3 | 450,000 | | | | 1 | 50,000 | 304,749.55 |
| Georgia | 4 | 475,000 | | | | | | |
| Florida | 4 | 275,000 | | | | 1 | 200,000 | 1,949,396.24 |
| Alabama | | | | | | 1 | 200,000 | 1,823,009.89 |
| Mississippi | 2 | 585,000 | 1 | 25,000 | 303,932 | 2 | 175,000 | 1,516,754.11 |
| Louisiana | | | 1 | 50,000 | 134,854 | 1 | 50,000 | 212,709.23 |
| Texas | 19 | 3,165,000 | 2 | 50,000 | 327,620 | 9 | 895,000 | 8,903,623.07 |
| Arkansas | 4 | 125,000 | 1 | 60,000 | 851,274 | 1 | 40,000 | 358,811.61 |
| Kentucky | 2 | 125,000 | | | | | | |
| Tennessee | 3 | 150,000 | | | | | | |
| Total Southern States | 52 | 6,465,800 | 5 | 185,000 | 1,617,680 | 18 | 2,660,000 | 31,295,417.06 |

*National banks organized, failed, and reported in voluntary liquidation during the year ended October 31, 1922—Continued.*

| State. | Organized. | | Failed. | | | Voluntary liquidations. | | |
|---|---|---|---|---|---|---|---|---|
| | Num-ber. | Authorized capital. | Num-ber. | Capital. | Gross assets. | Num-ber. | Capital. | Gross assets. |
| Ohio | 2 | 225,000 | | | | 5 | 650,000 | 13,018,785.40 |
| Indiana | 2 | 600,000 | 1 | 125,000 | 1,677,159 | 1 | 350,000 | 7,335,178.78 |
| Illinois | 4 | 560,000 | | | | | | |
| Michigan | 2 | 225,000 | | | | | | |
| Wisconsin | 1 | 25,000 | | | | | | |
| Minnesota | 2 | 225,000 | | | | 1 | 500,000 | 3,839,676.22 |
| Iowa | 1 | 35,000 | | | | 3 | 410,000 | 2,556,928.56 |
| Missouri | 4 | 1,150,000 | | | | 1 | 25,000 | 396,094.55 |
| Total Middle West'n States | 18 | 3,045,000 | 1 | 125,000 | 1,677,159 | 11 | 1,935,000 | 27,140,663.51 |
| North Dakota | 2 | 50,000 | 2 2 | 50,000 | 492,065 | | | |
| South Dakota | | | | | | 3 | 100,000 | 357,959.58 |
| Nebraska | 1 | 25,000 | 2 | 250,000 | 2,388,766 | 3 | 150,000 | 1,515,676.93 |
| Kansas | 2 | 50,000 | | | | 1 | 60,000 | 234,934.41 |
| Montana | | | 7 | 300,000 | 2,058,811 | 4 | 290,000 | 2,516,180.77 |
| Colorado | 1 | 200,000 | | | | | | |
| New Mexico | | | 1 | 25,000 | 95,576 | 4 | 200,000 | 1,176,346.82 |
| Oklahoma | 95 | 4,540,000 | 3 4 | 525,000 | 4,145,649 | 2 | 110,000 | 1,130,118.79 |
| Total Western States | 101 | 4,865,000 | 16 | 1,150,000 | 9,180,867 | 17 | 910,000 | 6,931,227.30 |
| Washington | 14 | 895,000 | | | | | | |
| Oregon | 3 | 130,000 | 2 | 125,000 | 1,322,869 | | | |
| California | 11 | 775,000 | 2 | 50,000 | 575,676 | 32 | 4,350,000 | 59,422,261.58 |
| Idaho | 1 | 50,000 | 2 | 55,000 | 1,293,010 | 1 | 25,000 | 233,071.16 |
| Utah | | | 2 | 275,000 | 3,691,427 | 2 | 55,000 | 460,260.91 |
| Arizona | 1 | 25,000 | | | | | | |
| Alaska | 1 | 50,000 | | | | | | |
| Total Pacific States | 31 | 1,925,000 | 8 | 505,000 | 6,882,982 | 35 | 4,430,000 | 60,115,593.65 |
| Total of United States | 232 | 24,890,800 | 31 | 2,015,000 | 19,784,619 | 103 | 18,910,000 | 324,391,389.93 |

[1] Afterwards restored to solvency.
[2] One bank was restored to solvency.
[3] Three banks were restored to solvency with aggregate capital of $325,000.

*Number and classification of national banks chartered during the year ended October 31, 1922.*

| Month. | Conversions. | | Reorganizations. | | Primary organizations. | | Total. | |
|---|---|---|---|---|---|---|---|---|
| | Num-ber. | Capital. | Num-ber. | Capital. | Num-ber. | Capital. | Num-ber. | Capital. |
| November | 8 | $975,000 | 1 | $25,000 | 5 | $325,000 | 14 | $1,525,000 |
| December | 19 | 1,200,000 | 7 | 785,000 | 9 | 675,000 | 35 | 2,660,000 |
| January | 17 | 680,000 | 2 | 225,000 | 6 | 210,000 | 25 | 1,115,000 |
| February | 12 | 1,570,000 | 2 | 50,000 | 5 | 650,000 | 19 | 2,270,000 |
| March | 20 | 2,170,000 | 5 | 775,000 | 1 | 25,000 | 26 | 2,970,000 |
| April | 23 | 2,380,000 | 2 | 50,000 | 10 | 950,000 | 35 | 3,380,000 |
| May | 7 | 1,155,000 | 4 | 175,000 | 11 | 420,000 | 22 | 1,750,000 |
| June | 8 | 2,515,000 | 4 | 275,000 | 9 | 3,175,000 | 21 | 5,965,000 |
| July | 9 | 660,000 | | | 3 | 175,000 | 12 | 835,000 |
| August | 3 | 375,000 | 2 | 235,000 | 3 | 300,000 | 8 | 910,000 |
| September | 1 | 45,800 | | | 5 | 575,000 | 6 | 620,800 |
| October | 2 | 90,000 | 2 | 525,000 | 5 | 275,000 | 9 | 890,000 |
| Total | 129 | 13,815,800 | 31 | 3,120,000 | 72 | 7,955,000 | 232 | 24,890,800 |

CONVERSIONS OF STATE BANKS AND PRIMARY ORGANIZATIONS AS
NATIONAL BANKS SINCE 1900.

The number and capital, by classes, of conversions, reorganizations, and primary organizations of national banks, are shown in the following table:

*Summary, by classes, of national banks chartered from March 14, 1900, to October 31, 1922.*

| Classification. | Conversions of State banks. | | Reorganizations from State and private banks and National banks. | | Primary organizations. | | Total. | |
|---|---|---|---|---|---|---|---|---|
| | Number. | Capital. | Number. | Capital. | Number. | Capital. | Number. | Capital. |
| Capital less than $50,000.. | 785 | $20,825,800 | 1,113 | $29,492,000 | 2,437 | $62,750,500 | 4,335 | $113,068,300 |
| Capital $50,000 or over.... | 603 | 98,607,800 | 680 | 105,935,000 | 1,383 | 171,065,000 | 2,666 | 375,607,800 |
| Total.................. | 1,388 | 119,433,600 | 1,793 | 135,427,000 | 3,820 | 233,815,500 | 7,001 | 488,676,100 |

*Number and capital of State banks converted into national banking associations in each State and Territory from 1863 to October 31, 1922.*

| State or Territory. | Number of banks. | Capital. | State or Territory. | Number of banks. | Capital. |
|---|---|---|---|---|---|
| Maine........................ | 34 | $4,605,000 | Ohio...................... | 23 | $2,840,000 |
| New Hampshire.............. | 28 | 2,595,000 | Indiana................... | 25 | 1,608,000 |
| Vermont.................... | 22 | 2,029,990 | Illinois.................. | 32 | 3,455,000 |
| Massachusetts.............. | 182 | 65,641,200 | Michigan.................. | 21 | 2,495,000 |
| Rhode Island............... | 52 | 16,717,550 | Wisconsin................. | 31 | 2,295,000 |
| Connecticut................ | 65 | 18,932,770 | Minnesota................. | 104 | 6,666,000 |
| | | | Iowa...................... | 41 | 1,895,000 |
| New England States..... | 383 | 110,521,510 | Missouri.................. | 42 | 14,814,300 |
| New York................... | 223 | 105,906,291 | Middle Western States.. | 319 | 36,068,300 |
| New Jersey................. | 46 | 8,620,450 | | | |
| Pennsylvania............... | 109 | 31,894,095 | North Dakota.............. | 79 | 2,610,000 |
| Delaware................... | 6 | 585,010 | South Dakota.............. | 47 | 1,625,000 |
| Maryland................... | 35 | 10,224,372 | Nebraska.................. | 71 | 3,400,000 |
| District of Columbia......... | 5 | 880,000 | Kansas.................... | 73 | 3,152,000 |
| | | | Montana................... | 37 | 1,485,000 |
| Eastern States.......... | 424 | 158,110,218 | Wyoming................... | 9 | 320,000 |
| | | | Colorado.................. | 32 | 2,130,000 |
| Virginia................... | 63 | 5,797,100 | New Mexico................ | 7 | 400,000 |
| West Virginia.............. | 32 | 2,183,900 | Oklahoma.................. | 180 | 7,510,000 |
| North Carolina............. | 35 | 3,111,000 | | | |
| South Carolina............. | 45 | 3,912,000 | Western States.......... | 535 | 22,632,000 |
| Georgia.................... | 25 | 2,587,000 | | | |
| Florida.................... | 18 | 1,815,000 | Washington................ | 55 | 5,125,000 |
| Alabama.................... | 27 | 2,760,000 | Oregon.................... | 26 | 1,576,000 |
| Mississippi................ | 10 | 640,000 | California................ | 102 | 20,822,800 |
| Louisiana.................. | 12 | 3,575,000 | Idaho..................... | 26 | 1,080,000 |
| Texas...................... | 46 | 4,257,500 | Nevada.................... | 1 | 50,000 |
| Arkansas................... | 37 | 2,232,500 | Arizona................... | 4 | 250,000 |
| Kentucky................... | 37 | 5,581,900 | | | |
| Tennessee.................. | 45 | 3,965,000 | Pacific States.......... | 214 | 28,903,800 |
| Southern States......... | 432 | 42,417,900 | United States............ | 2,307 | 398,653,728 |

EXPIRATIONS AND EXTENSIONS OF CHARTERS OF NATIONAL BANKS.

Charters were granted to national banks for a period of 20 years from the date of the execution of the organization certificate. In the eight months ended July 1 last, the effective date of the act conferring upon all national banks in existence on that date a corporate existence of 99 years, regardless of prior extensions, 236 banks, with capital of $24,332,500, reached the termination of their existence, and their charters were extended for an additional period of 20 years under authority of the act of July 12, 1882. In the same period charters of 97 banks, with capital of $40,670,000, extended under the act of 1882, were extended for a further period of 20 years under the act of April 12, 1902. The total number of extensions of charters under the act of 1882 is 4,336 and under the act of 1902, 1,512.

*Number of national banks in each State the charters of which were extended under the act of July 12, 1882, to July 1, 1922.*

| State or Territory. | Number of banks. | State or Territory. | Number of banks. | State or Territory. | Number of banks. |
|---|---|---|---|---|---|
| Maine | 85 | Alabama | 31 | Nebraska | 109 |
| New Hampshire | 60 | Mississippi | 12 | Kansas | 126 |
| Vermont | 51 | Louisiana | 20 | Montana | 22 |
| Massachusetts | 273 | Texas | 275 | Wyoming | 14 |
| Rhode Island | 61 | Arkansas | 10 | Colorado | 45 |
| Connecticut | 88 | Kentucky | 93 | New Mexico | 13 |
| | | Tennessee | 49 | Oklahoma | 87 |
| New England States | 618 | Southern States | 702 | Western States | 504 |
| New York | 371 | Ohio | 268 | Washington | 28 |
| New Jersey | 122 | Indiana | 137 | Oregon | 27 |
| Pennsylvania | 530 | Illinois | 264 | California | 45 |
| Delaware | 19 | Michigan | 86 | Idaho | 11 |
| Maryland | 77 | Wisconsin | 88 | Utah | 11 |
| District of Columbia | 11 | Minnesota | 116 | Nevada | 1 |
| | | Iowa | 215 | Arizona | 7 |
| Eastern States | 1,130 | Missouri | 76 | Alaska | 1 |
| Virginia | 55 | Middle Western States | 1,250 | Pacific States | 131 |
| West Virginia | 51 | | | | |
| North Carolina | 35 | | | Hawaii | 1 |
| South Carolina | 17 | North Dakota | 47 | | |
| Georgia | 37 | South Dakota | 41 | United States | 4,336 |
| Florida | 17 | | | | |

### REEXTENSION OF NATIONAL BANK CHARTERS.

*Number of national banks in each State the charters of which were reextended under the act of July 12, 1882, as amended April 12, 1902, to July 1, 1922.*

| State. | Number of banks. | State. | Number of banks. | State. | Number of banks. |
|---|---|---|---|---|---|
| Maine | 55 | South Carolina | 8 | North Dakota | 6 |
| New Hampshire | 40 | Georgia | 9 | South Dakota | 4 |
| Vermont | 35 | Alabama | 4 | Nebraska | 13 |
| Massachusetts | 164 | Louisiana | 1 | Kansas | 8 |
| Rhode Island | 24 | Texas | 13 | Montana | 3 |
| Connecticut | 68 | Arkansas | 1 | Wyoming | 2 |
| | | Kentucky | 29 | Colorado | 13 |
| New England States | 386 | Tennessee | 17 | New Mexico | 4 |
| New York | 211 | Southern States | 118 | Western States | 53 |
| New Jersey | 59 | Ohio | 113 | Washington | 1 |
| Pennsylvania | 202 | Indiana | 54 | Oregon | 2 |
| Delaware | 14 | Illinois | 96 | California | 9 |
| Maryland | 35 | Michigan | 25 | Utah | 2 |
| District of Columbia | 3 | Wisconsin | 27 | | |
| | | Minnesota | 24 | Pacific States | 14 |
| Eastern States | 524 | Iowa | 66 | | |
| | | Missouri | 12 | United States | 1,512 |
| Virginia | 18 | | | | |
| West Virginia | 12 | Middle Western States | 417 | | |
| North Carolina | 6 | | | | |

### CHANGES OF TITLE OF NATIONAL BANKS.

During the last year 35 national banking associations were authorized to change their corporate titles, or titles and locations under the act of May 1, 1886.

The following is a list of the banks involved in the changes with date of approval indicated:

Changes of corporate title of national banks, year ended October 31, 1922.

| No. | Title and location. | Date. |
|---|---|---|
| 3188 | The Farmers and Merchants National Bank of Fremont, Nebr..to "The Union National Bank of Fremont". | 1921. Dec. 8 |
| 2495 | The Citizens National Bank of Cincinnati, Ohio, to" The Citizens National Bank & Trust Co. of Cincinnati". | Dec. 10 |
| 10005 | Farmers National Bank of Pond Creek, Okla., to "First National Bank in Pond Creek". | Dec. 19 |
| 8510 | The Exchange National Bank of Long Beach, Calif., to "The Long Beach National Bank". | Dec. 21 |
| | | 1922. |
| 11384 | The Security National Bank of Temple, Okla., to "First National Bank in Temple".... | Jan. 4 |
| 1788 | The Merchants National Bank of Dayton, Ohio, to "The Merchants National Bank and Trust Co. of Dayton". | Jan. 16 |
| 6794 | The First National Bank of Wilson, I'a., to "The First National Bank of Clairton" (change in title of location). | Jan. 16 |
| 7649 | The National Bank of Logan, Ohio, to "First National Bank in Logan". | Jan. 16 |
| 7796 | The Central National Bank of St. Petersburg, Fla , to "The Central National Bank and Trust Co. of St. Petersburg". | Jan. 16 |
| 11929 | The National Bank of Iron Mountain, Mich., to "The United States National Bank of Iron Mountain". | Jan. 17 |
| 11 | The First and Hamilton National Bank of Fort Wayne, Ind., to "First National Bank of Fort Wayne". | Jan. 19 |
| 10527 | The First and Old Detroit National Bank, Detroit, Mich., to "First National Bank in Detroit". | Jan. 19 |
| 11550 | The First National Bank of Motordale, Minn., to "First National Bank of New Germany" (to conform to change of name of place of location). | Feb. 3 |
| 10801 | The Peoples National Bank of Harrison, Ark., to "First National Bank in Harrison". | Feb. 4 |
| 11329 | The First National Bank of Willard, N. Mex., to "The First National Bank of Mountainair" (change of location). | Feb. 7 |
| 6974 | The Deming National Bank, Deming, N. Mex., to "First National Bank in Deming"... | Feb. 15 |
| 11492 | The Security National Bank of Lima, Mont., to "The First National Bank of Lima". | Feb. 23 |
| 11460 | The First National Bank of Bigheart, Okla., to "The First National Bank of Barnsdall" (to conform to change of name of place of location). | Mar. 6 |
| 7125 | The Moffet Bros.' National Bank of Larned, Kans., to "First National Bank in Larned". | Mar. 21 |
| 5512 | Albany National Bank, Albany, Ga., to "Albany Exchange National Bank". | Apr. 11 |
| 12119 | The Security National Bank of Harlingen, Tex., to "The First National Bank of Harlingen". | Apr. 17 |
| 1997 | The Clinton County National Bank of Wilmington, Ohio, to "The Clinton County National Bank and Trust Co. of Wilmington". | May 9 |
| 66 | The First National Bank of Lyons, Iowa, to "First National Bank of Lyons at Clinton" (to conform to change of name of place of location). | June 6 |
| 11861 | The Payday National Bank of Minneapolis, Minn., to "The Marquette National Bank of Minneapolis". | June 26 |
| 7121 | The First National Bank of White Hall, Ill., to "Peoples-First National Bank of White Hall". | June 30 |
| 1011 | The Ocean National Bank of Newburyport, Mass., to "First and Ocean National Bank of Newburyport". | July 1 |
| 2360 | The Lebanon National Bank, Lebanon, Ohio, to "Lebanon National Bank & Trust Co.". | July 5 |
| 2160 | The National Exchange Bank of Steubenville, Ohio, to "The National Exchange Bank and Trust Co. of Steubenville". | July 17 |
| 3052 | The Phoenix and Third National Bank of Lexington, Ky., to "Phoenix National Bank and Trust Co. of Lexington". | July 17 |
| 11436 | The Citizens National Bank of Lenapah, Okla., to "The First National Bank of Lenapah". | Aug. 22 |
| 9626 | The First National Bank of Fort Bragg, Calif., to "The Coast National Bank of Fort Bragg". | Sept. 5 |
| 1790 | The Madison National Bank of Richmond, Ky., to "The Madison National Bank & Trust Co. of Richmond". | Sept. 6 |
| 11900 | The National Bank of Gallup, N. Mex., to "The First National Bank in Gallup". | Oct. 13 |
| 11853 | American National Bank of Modesto, Calif., to "First National Bank in Modesto". | Oct. 20 |
| 10094 | The National Bank of Hastings, Okla., to "First National Bank in Hastings". | Oct. 30 |

## CHANGES OF TITLE INCIDENT TO CONSOLIDATIONS OF NATIONAL BANKS.

In the consolidation of national banks under the act of November 7, 1918, a number of changes resulted in the corporate title of banks under the charter of which consolidations were effected.

In the following statement the titles of the banks consolidating and also the new titles of the consolidated banks are given:

The Alliance National Bank, Alliance, Ohio (12034), and The First National Bank of Alliance (3721), consolidated under the charter of the latter, with title: Alliance First National Bank.

The Greensboro National Bank, Greensboro, N. C. (5031), and The American Exchange National Bank of Greensboro (10112), consolidated under the charter of the latter, with title: American Exchange National Bank of Greensboro.

The City National Bank of Grand Rapids, Mich. (12108), and The Grand Rapids ational City Bank (3293), consolidated under the charter of the latter, with title· Grand Rapids National Bank.

The Seaboard National Bank of the City of New York (3415) and Mercantile National Bank in New York (12123), consolidated under the charter of the latter, with title: The Seaboard National Bank of the City of New York.

The Rittenhouse National Bank of Philadelphia, Pa. (12137), and The Corn Exchange National Bank of Philadelphia (542), consolidated under the charter of the latter, with title: Corn Exchange National Bank of Philadelphia.

The First National Bank of New Castle, Ind. (804), and The Farmers National Bank of New Castle (9852), consolidated under the charter of the latter, with title: The Farmers and First National Bank of New Castle.

The First National Bank of Camden, N. J. (431), and The National State Bank of Camden (1209), consolidated under the charter of the latter, with title: The First National State Bank of Camden.

The People's National Bank of Sistersville, W. Va. (6548), and The Farmers and Producers National Bank of Sistersville (5028), consolidated under the charter of the latter, with title: The Union National Bank of Sistersville.

The Utah National Bank of Ogden, Utah (2880), and The First National Bank of Ogden (2597), consolidated under the charter of the latter, with title: The First & Utah National Bank of Ogden.

American National Bank of Washington, D. C. (6716), and the Federal National Bank of Washington (10316), consolidated under the charter of the latter, with title: Federal-American National Bank of Washington. ʼ

*Number of national banks increasing their capital, together with the amount of increase monthly for the years ended October 31, 1920, 1921, and 1922.*

| Month. | 1920 | | 1921 | | 1922 | |
|---|---|---|---|---|---|---|
| | Number. | Capital. | Number. | Capital. | Number. | Capital. |
| November | 28 | $3,270,000 | 22 | $985,000 | 7 | $2,690,000 |
| December | 24 | 2,015,000 | 22 | 1,580,000 | 7 | 425,000 |
| January | 107 | 15,805,000 | 65 | 5,605,800 | 24 | 3,320,000 |
| February | 50 | 5,900,000 | 38 | 4,575,000 | 25 | 7,420,000 |
| March | 77 | 8,615,000 | 23 | 1,495,000 | 16 | 1,288,000 |
| April | 69 | 19,030,100 | 26 | 5,700,000 | 23 | 3,030,000 |
| May | 49 | 4,084,000 | 9 | 1,090,000 | 17 | 2,055,000 |
| June | 53 | 4,694,000 | 16 | 2,765,000 | 23 | 4,040,000 |
| July | 75 | 13,695,000 | 15 | 1,760,000 | 39 | 6,074,850 |
| August | 36 | 8,515,000 | 6 | 295,000 | 21 | 1,821,500 |
| September | 19 | 1,485,000 | 10 | 1,510,000 | 12 | 1,200,000 |
| October | 21 | 17,510,000 | 7 | 475,000 | 15 | 1,665,000 |
| Total | 608 | 104,618,100· | 259 | 27,835,800 | 229 | 35,027,350 |

### DOMESTIC BRANCHES OF NATIONAL BANKS.

Under authority of section 5155, of the Revised Statutes of the United States, the following national banks, formerly State banks, continue to operate the branches indicated:

California:
    Bank of California, National Association, San Francisco; capital, $8,500,000.
        Branch at Portland. Oreg.; capital, $300,000.
        Branch at Seattle, Wash.; capital, $200,000.
        Branch at Tacoma, Wash.; capital, $200,000.
Louisiana:
    Calcasieu National Bank of Southwestern Louisiana, Lake Charles; capital, $750,000.
        Branch at De Quincy; capital, $21,000.
        Branch at Jennings; capital, $105,000.
        Branch at Kinder; capital, $30,000.
        Branch at Lake Arthur; capital, $33,000.
        Branch at Oakdale; capital, $60,000.
        Branch at Sulphur; capital, $21,000.
        Branch at Vinton; capital, $45,000.
        Branch at Welsh; capital, $60,000.

Michigan:
    City National Bank of Battle Creek; capital, $350,000.
        Branch in Battle Creek; capital, $25,000.
    National Union Bank of Jackson; capital, $400,000.
        Branch in Jackson; capital, $100,000.
Mississippi:
    Pascagoula National Bank of Moss Point; capital, $75,000.
        Branch in Pascagoula; capital, $25,000.
New York:
    Chatham & Phoenix National Bank of New York; capital, $10,500,000.
        Twelve branches in the city of New York, with capital of $100,000 assigned to
            each.
    Public National Bank of New York; capital, $3,000,000.
        Five branches in the city of New York, with capital of $100,000 assigned to each.
    Seaboard National Bank of the City of New York; capital, $4,000,000.
        Two branches in the city of New York, with capital of $100,000 assigned to each.
North Carolina:
    American Exchange National Bank of Greensboro; capital, $750,000.
        Branch in Greensboro; capital, $150,000.
Oregon:
    First National Bank of Milton; capital, $50,000.
        Branch at Freewater; capital, $10,000.
Washington:
    Union National Bank of Seattle; capital, $600,000.
        Branch at Ballard; capital, $50,000.
        Branch at Georgetown; capital, $50,000.

Under the consolidation act of November 7, 1918, converted State
banks having branches were consolidated with the following banks
and the branches continued:

California:
    The First National Bank of Lemoore; capital, $150,000.
        Branch at Stratford; capital, $25,000.
District of Columbia:
    The Riggs National Bank of Washington, D. C.; capital, $1,000,000.
        Three branches in the city of Washington, with capital of $10,000 assigned
            to each.
Georgia:
    The Fourth National Bank of Atlanta; capital, $1,200,000.
        Four branches in the city of Atlanta, with capital of $50,000 assigned to each.
        Branch at Decatur; capital, $25,000.
Michigan:
    Grand Rapids National Bank of Grand Rapids; capital, $1,000,000.
        Nine branches in the city of Grand Rapids with capital of $10,000 assigned
            to each.
New York:
    Chase National Bank of New York; capital, $20,000,000.
        Seven branches in the city of New York, with capital of $100,000 assigned
            to each.
    Irving National Bank of New York; capital, $12,500,000.
        Eight branches in the city of New York, with capital of $100,000 assigned
            to each.
    Mechanics & Metals National Bank, New York; capital, $10,000,000.
        Twelve branches in the city of New York, to which is assigned $50,000 capital
            each to eight, and $100,000 each to four of the branches.
    National City Bank of New York; capital, $40,000,000.
        Three branches in the city of New York, with capital of $100,000 assigned
            to each.
    National Commercial Bank & Trust Company of Albany; capital, $1,250,000.
        Branch in Albany; capital, $100,000.
Virginia:
    First National Bank of Abingdon; capital, $200,000.
        Branch in Abingdon; capital, $25,000.
    Peoples National Bank of Leesburg; capital, $100,000.
        Branch at Upperville; capital, $10,000.
    Seaboard National Bank of Norfolk; capital, $800,000.
        Branch in Norfolk; capital, $50,000.

List of national banks, with number of additional local offices and dates of approval of their establishment, year ended October 31, 1922.

| Location. | Title of bank. | Number of additional offices. | Date of approval of establishment of additional offices. | |
|---|---|---|---|---|
| California: | | | 1922. | |
| Long Beach.................. | Long Beach National Bank...................... | 2 | Oct. | 11 |
| | | | Oct. | 27 |
| Los Angeles................. | Commercial National Bank..................... | 3 | June | 13 |
| Do..................... | First National Bank........................... | 1 | July | 1 |
| Do..................... | Merchants National Bank...................... | 2 | Aug. | 1 |
| | | | Oct. | 11 |
| Oakland..................... | Central National Bank...................... | 1 | Aug. | 2 |
| Sacramento................. | California National Bank...................... | 1 | Sept. | 6 |
| District of Columbia: Washington | Riggs National Bank........................... | 1 | Sept. | 8 |
| Georgia: Atlanta.............. | Atlanta National Bank......................... | 1 | Sept. | 22 |
| Kentucky: Louisville ........... | Louisville National Bank...................... | 4 | July | 20 |
| | | | Aug. | 15 |
| Maryland: | | | | |
| Baltimore.................. | Merchants National Bank...................... | 2 | Aug. | 1 |
| Do..................... | Farmers & Merchants National Bank........... | 1 | Aug. | 18 |
| Massachusetts: Boston.......... | Fourth Atlantic National Bank.................. | 1 | Aug. | 23 |
| Michigan: | | | | |
| Detroit.................... | National Bank of Commerce.................... | 1 | July | 19 |
| Ludington................. | First National Bank........................... | 1 | Sept. | 8 |
| New York: | | | | |
| Buffalo.................... | Community National Bank..................... | 1 | Aug. | 18 |
| New York.................. | Public National Bank.......................... | 3 | July | 18 |
| | | | Aug. | 29 |
| Do..................... | Richmond Hill National Bank of N. Y........... | 1 | Aug. | 1 |
| Watertown................. | Jefferson County National Bank................. | 1 | Oct. | 13 |
| Yonkers................... | Yonkers National Bank........................ | 1 | Oct. | 24 |
| North Carolina: Greensboro..... | American Exchange National Bank............... | 1 | July | 24 |
| Ohio: Cleveland.............. | Brotherhood of Locomotive Engineers Cooperative National Bank. | 2 | Sept. | 8 |
| Pennsylvania: | | | | |
| Chester.................... | First National Bank........................... | 2 | Sept. | 22 |
| McKees Rocks.............. | .....do....................................... | 1 | Oct. | 24 |
| Philadelphia................ | Corn Exchange National Bank................... | [1] 2 | July | 18 |
| Do..................... | Central National Bank......................... | 1 | July | 24 |
| Do..................... | First National Bank........................... | 1 | July | 25 |
| Do..................... | Fourth Street National Bank................... | 1 | Aug. | 17 |
| Reading.................... | Reading National Bank........................ | 1 | Aug. | 24 |
| Williamsport............... | West Branch National Bank.................... | 1 | Aug. | 31 |
| South Carolina: Charleston...... | Bank of Charleston National Banking Association. | 2 | Aug. | 30 |
| Virginia: | | | | |
| Richmond.................. | Planters National Bank........................ | 1 | July | 19 |
| Do..................... | American National Bank....................... | 4 | July | 20 |
| Do..................... | Merchants National Bank...................... | 1 | July | 21 |
| | Total..................................... | 51 | | |

[1] Sites of offices of trust company converted and consolidated with this bank.

## FOREIGN BRANCHES OF NATIONAL BANKS.

In accordance with the provision of section 25 of the Federal reserve act, "any national banking association possessing a capital and surplus of $1,000,000 or more may, with the approval of the Federal Reserve Board, establish branches in foreign countries or dependencies or insular possessions of the United States for the furtherance of the foreign commerce of the United States, and to act, if required to do so, as fiscal agents of the United States."

Only two national banks, however, have taken advantage of this provision of the law, namely, the First National Bank of Boston and the National City Bank of New York.

The location and the condition of each foreign branch of the banks referred to is shown in the following statement as of June 30, 1922:

Condition of foreign branches of National City Bank, New York, N. Y., and First National Bank, Boston, Mass., June 30, 1922.

RESOURCES.

[In thousands of dollars.]

| Country and city. | Loans and discounts including overdrafts and re-discounts. | Letters of credit and acceptances. | Bonds. | Furniture and fixtures and real estate owned. | Due from home office. | Due from branches. | Due from other banks. | Checks and cash items. | Cash. | Other assets. | Aggregate. |
|---|---|---|---|---|---|---|---|---|---|---|---|
| Cuba: | | | | | | | | | | | |
| Artemisa | 160 | | | | | | 1 | 20 | 37 | 1 | 219 |
| Bayamo | 1,096 | | 18 | | | | | 47 | 41 | | 1,202 |
| Caibarian | 819 | | | | | | | 30 | 185 | 17 | 1,051 |
| Camaguey | 661 | | | | | | | 59 | 967 | 1 | 1,702 |
| Cardenas | 128 | | | | | 124 | | 13 | 154 | 1 | 420 |
| Ciego de Avila | 761 | | | | | | | 73 | 152 | 37 | 1,023 |
| Cienfuegos | 1,022 | 302 | | | | 292 | 4 | 86 | 607 | 1 | 2,314 |
| Colon | 491 | | | | | 45 | | 7 | 38 | 1 | 582 |
| Cruces | 14 | | | | | 45 | | 26 | 30 | | 115 |
| Cuatro Caminos | 172 | | | | | 725 | 3 | 128 | 161 | | 1,189 |
| Guantanamo | 195 | | | | | | 66 | 24 | 151 | | 436 |
| Havana | 44,175 | 1,311 | 3,658 | 3,790 | | 1,644 | 231 | 2,277 | 3,233 | 61 | 60,380 |
| Havana, (Galiano Street Branch) | 163 | | | | | 935 | | 101 | 224 | | 1,414 |
| Manzanillo | 362 | | | | | | 26 | 13 | 183 | 1 | 585 |
| Matanzas | 637 | | | | | | | 113 | 171 | 4 | 925 |
| Moron | 133 | | | | | 55 | | 18 | 116 | 4 | 326 |
| Pinar del Rio | 55 | | | | | 48 | | 23 | 25 | | 151 |
| Placetas del Norte | 98 | | | | | 7 | 10 | 9 | 76 | | 200 |
| Remedios | 135 | | | | | 90 | | 12 | 93 | | 330 |
| Sagua la Grande | 384 | | | | | | 5 | 29 | 116 | | 534 |
| Sancti Spiritus | 240 | | | | | 7 | | 28 | 137 | 5 | 417 |
| Santa Clara | 85 | | | | | 260 | | 21 | 348 | | 714 |
| Santiago de Cuba | 670 | | | | | | 118 | 80 | 1,250 | 14 | 2,132 |
| Union de Reyes | 572 | | | | | | | 12 | 68 | | 652 |
| Yaguajay | 834 | | | | | | | 19 | 63 | 1 | 917 |
| Brazil: | | | | | | | | | | | |
| Recife Pernambuco | 912 | | | | | | 115 | 18 | 407 | | 1,452 |
| Rio de Janeiro | 10,033 | | 112 | | | 490 | 962 | 258 | 3,476 | 9 | 15,370 |
| Sao Paulo | 5,687 | | | | | | 858 | 67 | 1,919 | 2 | 8,583 |
| Argentina: | | | | | | | | | | | |
| Buenos Aires | 16,801 | | | | | | 6,424 | 206 | 320 | 6 | 23,757 |
| Rosario | 1,748 | | | | | 302 | 243 | 9 | 93 | 4 | 2,399 |
| Belgium: | | | | | | | | | | | |
| Antwerp | 878 | 3 | 1,060 | | | | 322 | 29 | 12 | 5 | 2,309 |
| Brussels | 511 | | 3,068 | | | | 393 | 53 | 8 | 3 | 4,241 |

| | | | | | | | | | | | |
|---|---|---|---|---|---|---|---|---|---|---|---|
| Chile: | | | | | | | | | | | |
| Santiago | 2,998 | | 250 | | 225 | 417 | 130 | 87 | 87 | 15 | 4,299 |
| Valparaiso | 2,144 | | | | 264 | 26 | 886 | 67 | 86 | 8 | 3,481 |
| Porto Rico: | | | | | | | | | | | |
| Ponce | 302 | | | | 23 | | 19 | 31 | 42 | | 474 |
| San Juan | 1,325 | | | | 1,086 | 57 | 403 | 75 | 291 | | 3,180 |
| Colombia: | | | | | | | | | | | |
| Barranquilla | | | | | 1 | | | | | | 1 |
| England: | | | | | | | | | | | |
| London | 17,947 | 1,119 | 2,547 | | | 1,918 | 2,864 | 77 | 20 | 15 | 26,307 |
| France: | | | | | | | | | | | |
| Paris | 497 | 70 | 9,260 | | 185 | | 1,502 | 29 | 56 | 4 | 11,603 |
| Italy: | | | | | | | | | | | |
| Genoa | 98 | 369 | 1,623 | | 697 | | 571 | 3 | 8 | | 3,309 |
| Peru: | | | | | | | | | | | |
| Lima | 2,004 | | 206 | | 125 | | 46 | 27 | 1,421 | 4 | 3,833 |
| Uruguay: | | | | | | | | | | | |
| Montevideo | 2,001 | | | | | | 247 | 1 | 146 | | 2,396 |
| Venezuela: | | | | | | | | | | | |
| Caracas | 990 | 27 | 47 | 63 | 61 | 181 | 224 | 77 | 782 | 4 | 2,457 |
| Total | 120,931 | 3,291 | 21,882 | 3,853 | 2,607 | 7,623 | 16,675 | 4,384 | 17,848 | 238 | 199,302 |
| First National Bank of Boston, Mass.: | | | | | | | | | | | |
| Argentina, Buenos Aires | 21,624 | 157 | 735 | 1,652 | 1 | | 6,190 | 170 | 423 | | 38,972 |

Condition of foreign branches of National City Bank, New York, N. Y., and First National Bank, Boston, Mass., June 30, 1922.

LIABILITIES.

[In thousands of dollars.]

| | Capital | Profits, including amount reserved for taxes and interest accrued | Due to home office | Due to branches | Due to other banks | Individual deposits | Rediscounts | Letters of credit and acceptances executed by reporting bank | Acceptances executed by other banks | Other liabilities |
|---|---|---|---|---|---|---|---|---|---|---|
| **Cuba:** | | | | | | | | | | |
| Bayamo | | 1 | | 31 | 2 | 183 | | | | 2 |
| Caibarien | | 3 | | 1,051 | 1 | 45 | | | | 102 |
| Camaguey | | | | 631 | 6 | 348 | | | | 68 |
| Cardenas | | 2 | | 362 | 71 | 1,247 | | | | 16 |
| Clego de Avila | | 1 | | | 15 | 403 | | 4 | | 1 |
| Cienfuegos | | 2 | | 529 | 4 | 446 | | | | 42 |
| Colon | | 2 | | | 20 | 1,839 | | 310 | | 143 |
| Cruces | | | | | 5 | 149 | | | | 4 |
| Cuatro Caminos | | 1 | | 124 | 34 | 110 | | | | 1 |
| Guanabacoa | | | | | 10 | 1,150 | | | | 2 |
| Guantanamo | | | | 40 | | 423 | | 2 | | 3 |
| Havana | 1,000 | 121 | 41,633 | | 697 | 13,645 | 717 | 1,475 | | 1,062 |
| Havana-Galiana Street Branch | | | | 160 | 36 | 1,360 | | 14 | | 3 |
| Manzanillo | | 14 | | 336 | 13 | 394 | | | | 18 |
| Matanzas | | | | | 20 | 469 | | 2 | | 84 |
| Nuevitas | | | | | 10 | 311 | | | | 5 |
| Pinar del Rio | | | | | 12 | 147 | | | | 3 |
| Placetas del Norte | | | | | 4 | 170 | | | | 18 |
| Remedios | | 1 | | | 3 | 317 | | | | 8 |
| Sagua la | | | | 71 | 18 | 434 | | 9 | | 17 |
| Sancti Spiritus | | | | | 4 | 396 | | | | 3 |
| Santa Clara | | | | | 20 | 706 | | | | 4 |
| Santiago de Cuba | | 4 | | 168 | 2 | 1,852 | | 34 | | 54 |
| Union de Reyes | | | | 530 | 1 | 70 | | | | 50 |
| Yaguajay | | 1 | | 752 | | 127 | | | | 36 |
| **Brazil:** | | | | | | | | | | |
| Recife Pernambuco | | 11 | 173 | 120 | 102 | 626 | *418 | | | 2 |
| Rio de Janeiro | 545 | 161 | 2,534 | | 1 185 | 5,709 | 3,579 | 1,650 | | 7 |
| Sao Paulo | | 75 | 2,247 | 1,089 | 160 | 2,773 | 1,567 | 4 | 612 | 6 |
| **Argentina:** | | | | | | | | | | |
| Buenos Aires | 844 | 501 | 3,079 | | 3,255 | 13,280 | | 29 | | 1,039 |
| Rosario | 212 | 32 | 36 | 518 | 72 | 2,038 | 1,212 | 2 | | 7 |

| | | | | | | | | | | |
|---|--:|--:|--:|--:|--:|--:|--:|--:|--:|--:|
| Belgium: | | | | | | | | | | |
| Antwerp | | 52 | | 397 | 239 | 1,495 | | 4 | | 9 |
| Brussels | | 30 | | 647 | 1,950 | 1,541 | | 13 | | 40 |
| Chile: | | | | | | | | | | |
| Santiago | 625 | 19 | 113 | | 1,002 | 2,028 | 1,134 | 20 | | 6 |
| Valparaiso | | 178 | | | 1,591 | 1,632 | 55 | | | |
| Porto Rico: | | | | | | | | | | |
| Ponce | | 7 | | | 13 | 451 | | | | 3 |
| San Juan | | 136 | | 19 | 224 | 2,781 | | 15 | | 5 |
| Colombia: | | | | | | | | | | |
| Barranquilla | | | | | | | | 1 | | |
| England: | | | | | | | | | | |
| London | 1,000 | 94 | 3,573 | 1,055 | 3,725 | 7,895 | 7,089 | 1,005 | 176 | 2,750 |
| France: | | | | | | | | | | |
| Paris | | 14 | | 427 | 2,765 | 7,345 | 36 | 165 | | 223 |
| Italy: | | | | | | | | | | |
| Genoa | | 22 | | | 547 | 975 | | 371 | | 27 |
| Peru: | | | | | | | | | | |
| Lima | 208 | 9 | | 77 | 1,081 | 1,882 | 567 | 12 | | 2 |
| Uruguay: | | | | | | | | | | |
| Montevideo | 303 | 51 | 232 | 2 | 48 | 1,659 | | 5 | | 5 |
| Venezuela: | | | | | | | | | | |
| Caracas | | 53 | | | 91 | 2,274 | | 39 | | |
| Total | 4,822 | 1,599 | 53,620 | 9,456 | 19,063 | 82,525 | 16,374 | 5,185 | 788 | 5,870 |
| First National Bank of Boston, Mass.: Argentina, | | | | | | | | | | |
| Buenos Aires | 2,000 | 228 | 3,042 | | 4,157 | ¹ 12,468 | ² 7,330 | 92 | 1,655 | |

¹ Includes $188,000 of United States deposits.  ² Includes bills payable.

UNITED STATES BONDS AND OTHER INTEREST-BEARING OBLIGATIONS.

The public debt of the United States at close of the current fiscal year was $22,963,381,708, of which $22,710,338,105 is interest bearing. In the obligations classed as bonds, aggregating $15,965,451,970, are the following:

Available as security for national-bank circulation................ $793,115,530
Panama Canal 3 per cent bonds........ ......................... 50,000,000
Conversion bonds......................... ...................... 28,894,500
Postal savings bonds..................... ..................... 11,830,440

Other interest-bearing obligations—notes, certificates and war savings securities—are as follows:

Liberty loan bonds.............................................. $15,081,611,500
Victory Liberty loan notes........................................ 1,991,183,400
Treasury notes................................................... 2,246,596,350
Treasury certificates............................................,.. 1,828,787,500
War savings securities........................................... 619,371,842
Treasury savings securities.....................· .................... 58,947,043

Of the bonds available as security for national bank circulation, aggregating $793,115,530, the Treasurer of the United States holds in trust for national and Federal reserve banks, and to secure public deposits, $746,651,500. As will be noted by reference to the table following, over 98 per cent of the Treasurer's holdings of these securities is held as security for national bank circulation. It further appears that of the total of these securities, the national banks have on deposit an amount representing over 92 per cent.

As the paid-in capital of the national banks on June 30, 1922, was roundly $1,307,000,000 (the measure of the amount of national bank currency issuable), it is evident that the volume of eligible bonds is only 60 per cent of the amount necessary to permit the maximum issue of national bank circulation.

In the following statement is shown the amount of United States bonds outstanding, eligible as security for national bank circulation, together with the amount of each class held by the Treasurer of the United States as security for national bank circulation, Federal reserve bank notes, and United States deposits.

| Class. | Interest rate. | Outstanding. | To secure national-bank circulation. | To secure Federal reserve bank notes. | To secure deposits. of public moneys. | Total. |
|---|---|---|---|---|---|---|
| Loan of 1925................... | 4 | $118,489,900 | $81,548,400 | $1,768,000 | $171,500 | $83,487,900 |
| Consols, 1930.................. | 2 | 599,724,050 | 579,642,200 | 8,063,400 | 1,249,000 | 588,954,600 |
| Panama....................... | 2 | 74,901,580 | 73,625,700 | 387,300 | 196,000 | 74,209,000 |
| Total...................... | | 793,115,530 | 734,816,300 | 10,218,700 | 1,616,500 | 746,651,500 |

BANKS' INVESTMENTS IN UNITED STATES BONDS, ETC.

By reference to banks' statements on or about June 30, 1922, it appears that their investments in United States interest-bearing obligations amounted to $4,124,463,000, approximately one-fifth of the aggregate, as follows:

National banks................................................ $2,285,459,000
State banks and trust companies.............................. 1,214,708,000
Federal reserve banks........................................ 556,607,000
Federal land banks [1]....................................... 67,689,000

4,124,463,000

*United States bonds deposited as security for circulation by banks chartered and by those increasing their circulation, together with the amount withdrawn by banks reducing their circulation, and by those closed, during each month, year ended October 31, 1922.*

| Date. | Bonds deposited by all banks chartered and those increasing circulation during the year.[1] | Bonds withdrawn by banks reducing circulation. | Bonds withdrawn by banks in liquidation. | Bonds withdrawn by banks in insolvency. |
|---|---|---|---|---|
| **1921.** | | | | |
| November.............. | $1,356,750 | $255,000 | $263,000 | ............ |
| December.............. | 1,553,250 | 725,000 | 656,250 | ............ |
| **1922.** | | | | |
| January............... | 2,102,500 | 140,000 | 910,000 | $150,000 |
| February.............. | 1,328,250 | 103,000 | 750,000 | 198,750 |
| March................. | 3,145,500 | 1,120,750 | 1,687,750 | 22,300 |
| April................. | 3,183,000 | 1,210,000 | 296,250 | ............ |
| May................... | 4,199,900 | 786,250 | 1,230,750 | ............ |
| June.................. | 1,735,710 | 941,000 | 125,000 | ............ |
| July.................. | 1,758,140 | 1,093,750 | 50,000 | ............ |
| August................ | 1,750,000 | 400,000 | 1,050,000 | ............ |
| September............. | 3,182,500 | 285,000 | 856,250 | ............ |
| October............... | 2,353,750 | 555,000 | 1,670,000 | ............ |
| Total................. | 27,679,250 | 7,614,750 | 9,545,250 | 371,050 |

[1] Includes $4,042,750 deposited by banks chartered during the year.

*United States bonds and special certificates of indebtedness for account of Federal reserve banks, withdrawn during each month, together with the amount on deposit, October 31, 1921–October 31, 1922.*

| Date. | Bonds withdrawn by banks reducing circulation. | Special certificates of indebtedness withdrawn by banks reducing circulation. |
|---|---|---|
| **1921.** | | |
| November.............. | ............ | $20,375,000 |
| December.............. | ............ | 13,000,000 |
| **1922.** | | |
| January............... | | |
| February.............. | | 16,034,000 |
| March................. | | 7,986,000 |
| April................. | $825,000 | 6,000,000 |
| May................... | 2,350,000 | 6,000,000 |
| June.................. | | 3,000,000 |
| July.................. | 200,000 | 3,500,000 |
| August................ | 500,000 | 12,500,000 |
| September............. | 750,000 | 10,000,000 |
| October............... | 300,000 | 10,000,000 |
| Total................. | 4,925,000 | 108,375,000 |

Bonds on deposit Oct. 31, 1921............................... $13,006,400
Special certificates of indebtedness on deposit Oct. 31, 1921. 146,375,000

$159,381,400

Bonds on deposit Oct. 31, 1922............................... 8,081,400
Special certificates of indebtedness on deposit Oct. 31, 1922. 38,000,000

46,081,400

Balance on deposit Oct. 31, 1922............................. 113,300,000

[1] Oct. 31, 1922.

14263—FI 1922——50

## PROFIT ON NATIONAL BANK CIRCULATION.

In computations made by the Actuary of the Treasury Department, the profit on the issuance of national-bank circulation is stated to be measured by the difference between interest at the rate of 6 per cent on the amount invested in the bonds and the net receipt from interest on the bonds and interest on 95 per cent of the circulation loaned at the rate of 6 per cent. The maintenance of the 5 per cent redemption fund depletes to that extent the volume of loanable funds.

Investment of $100,000 in 4 per cent bonds of 1925 at the market price in October last would amount to $104,068. The interest on bonds deposited would be $4,000; interest on circulation, less 5 per cent redemption fund, at 6 per cent, $5,700; total receipts, $9,700. Deducting from this amount the circulation tax, expenses for redemption and sinking fund, aggregating $2,731.65, would leave net receipts of $6,968.35. The difference between the latter amount and interest at 6 per cent on the cost of the bonds, $6,244.08, represents the measure of profit on the circulation; that is, $724.27, or 0.696 of 1 per cent.

With the deposit of $100,000 2 per cent consols at cost in October last of $102,858, the profit on circulation would be $761.59, or 0.74 of 1 per cent.

Upon deposit of $100,000 2 per cent Panama Canal bonds of 1916–1936 at a cost in October last of $102,918 the profit on circulation would be $824.95, or 0.802 of 1 per cent.

In the appendix of this report will be found tables compiled by the actuary, showing the profit on circulation secured by the classes of bonds mentioned, based upon the average net price monthly from November, 1921, to October, 1922; the investment value of United States bonds, eligible as security for national-bank circulation, quarterly to October, 1922, and also the monthly range of prices in New York for these bonds, both coupon and registered, from November, 1921 to October, 1922.

## REDEMPTION OF NATIONAL BANK AND FEDERAL RESERVE CURRENCY.

The amount of currency received for redemption, by months, from November 1, 1921, to October 31, 1922, and counted into the cash of the National Bank Redemption Agency, was as follows:

| Date. | National bank notes. | Federal reserve bank notes. | Federal reserve notes. | Total. |
|---|---|---|---|---|
| **1921** | | | | |
| November | $52,046,578.45 | $13,326,082.50 | $5,674,035.00 | $71,046,695.95 |
| December | 54,285,859.49 | 13,072,562.00 | 5,864,457.50 | 73,222,878.99 |
| **1922** | | | | |
| January | 67,065,105.78 | 12,707,349.00 | 5,705,220.00 | 85,477,674.78 |
| February | 47,224,565.57 | 10,699,458.00 | 4,551,655.00 | 62,475,678.57 |
| March | 51,617,817.30 | 11,034,037.50 | 4,884,037.50 | 67,535,892.30 |
| April | 47,386,649.93 | 9,322,223.50 | 4,244,657.50 | 60,953,530.93 |
| May | 46,273,481.39 | 9,232,277.50 | 4,813,302.50 | 60,319,061.39 |
| June | 43,425,003.01 | 9,305,956.00 | 5,496,377.50 | 58,227,336.51 |
| July | 37,828,872.45 | 7,488,969.00 | 4,553,582.50 | 49,871,423.95 |
| August | 27,843,225.40 | 6,037,074.00 | 4,394,735.00 | 38,275,034.40 |
| September | 38,641,956.64 | 7,407,472.00 | 4,581,235.00 | 50,630,663.64 |
| October | 53,935,199.67 | 8,621,150.00 | 5,407,607.50 | 67,963,957.17 |
| Total | 567,574,315.08 | 118,254,611.00 | 60,170,902.50 | 745,999,828.58 |

The amount of currency received for redemption from the following cities was:

| | | | |
|---|---|---|---|
| Boston | $49,760,950 | Kansas City | $10,851,000 |
| New York | 140,596,525 | Dallas | 21,882,700 |
| Philadelphia | 57,094,250 | San Francisco | 21,232,900 |
| Cleveland | 23,954,700 | Cincinnati | 17,568,000 |
| Richmond | 19,527,250 | Baltimore | 10,932,300 |
| Atlanta | 19,954,500 | New Orleans | 9,672,895 |
| Chicago | 60,841,284 | Other sources | 233,726,850 |
| St. Louis | 25,627,900 | | |
| Minneapolis | 16,349,500 | Total | 748,573,504 |

The difference between the totals in the foregoing tables is accounted for by the inclusion of a relatively small amount of United States currency in remittances.

The average cost per $1,000 for all notes redeemed through cash was $0.91. The average rates by classes were as follows:

| | |
|---|---|
| National-bank notes | $0.95 |
| Federal reserve bank notes | .92 |
| Federal reserve notes | .45 |

There were also received direct from Federal reserve banks and their branches canceled Federal reserve notes amounting to $2,127,406,150, which were not counted into cash and therefore are not included in the foregoing figures. The average rate per $1,000 for expenses of redemption of this class was $0.10.

The amount of national-bank notes fit for circulation received and returned to banks during the year ended October 31, 1922, was $9,554,320.

The total cost of redemption of Federal reserve and national currency for the fiscal year 1922 was $985,255.83, in accordance with the following statement:

| | | | | |
|---|---|---|---|---|
| Charges for transportation, including postage, insurance, and express charges | | | | $265,809.00 |
| Cost for assorting: | | | | |
| Office Treasurer United States, National Bank Redemption Agency, salaries | | $567,518.28 | | |
| Printing, binding, and stationery | | 17,569.68 | | |
| Contingent expenses | | 14,117.68 | | |
| | | | $599,205.64 | |
| Office, Comptroller of the Currency, Redemption Division: | | | | |
| Salaries | | 117,129.58 | | |
| Printing, binding, and stationery | | 2,343.80 | | |
| Contingent expenses | | 767.81 | | |
| | | | 120,241.19 | |
| | | | | 719,446.83 |
| Total | | | | 985,255.83 |

The following statement indicates the classification of redemptions, the amount of each class redeemed, the rate per $1,000, and the amount of expenses assessed thereon:

| Class. | Amount redeemed. | Rate per $1,000. | Amount of expense. |
|---|---|---|---|
| Federal reserve notes: | | | |
| Redeemed in regular course of business................ | $63,679,100.00 | $0.45312981 | $31,120.55 |
| Received from Federal reserve banks—canceled and uncanceled............................................ | 2,127,406,150.00 | .10062773 | 214,076.05 |
| Federal reserve bank notes: | | | |
| Redeemed out of 5 per cent fund...................... | 68,273,000.00 | .91759090 | 62,646.68 |
| Redeemed on retirement account...................... | 90,720,090.00 | .91759090 | 83,243.85 |
| National bank notes | | | |
| Redeemed out of 5 per cent fund— | | | |
| Fit for use............................................ | 8,006,740.00 | .78670470 | 6,298.94 |
| Unfit for use. ...................................... | 597,684,942.50 | .96382853 | 576,065.80 |
| Redeemed on retirement account...................... | 16,568,350.00 | .71244028 | 11,803.96 |
| Total............................................ | 2,977,338,282.50 | .33091833 | 985,255.83 |

Based upon the records of the office of the Comptroller of the Currency and of the Federal reserve banks, it appears that the average amount of bank circulation outstanding during the year was some $3,052,600,000, and that from the foregoing figures it would appear that an amount exceeding 94 per cent of the average issues was redeemed. The average amount of national-bank circulation outstanding was $754,700,000 and the amount received for redemption was over 75 per cent. During the last year over $50,000,000 of Federal reserve bank notes have been retired, leaving the amount outstanding on November 1, 1922, $35,500,000. As a result of the retirements the average amount of these notes outstanding during the year appears to have been approximately $70,000,000. The amount of this class of notes received for redemption from the National Bank Redemption Agency during the last year reached $118,254,000. The redemptions of all Federal reserve issues through Federal reserve banks and the National Bank Redemption Agency during the last year aggregated $2,305,000,000, a fraction over 100 per cent of the average amount in circulation.

### NATIONAL-BANK CIRCULATION.

At the close of business October 31, 1922, the aggregate amount of national-bank circulation outstanding was $760,679,187. With the exception of a small amount of $1 and $2 notes issued under the act of 1864 and prior to 1879 the principal denominations of these notes were $5, $10, $20, $50, and $100, as shown by the following statement:

*National-bank notes outstanding October 31, 1922.*

| Denomination. | Amount. | Denomination. | Amount. |
|---|---|---|---|
| One dollar............................ | $341,844 | One thousand dollars................ | $21,000 |
| Two dollars........................... | 163,190 | Fractional parts...................... | 60,738 |
| Five dollars........................... | 140,181,445 | | |
| Ten dollars............................ | 322,938,620 | Total.......................... | 766,211,037 |
| Twenty dollars........................ | 248,991,650 | Less.................................. | [1] 5,531,850 |
| Fifty dollars........................... | 26,728,350 | | |
| One hundred dollars.................. | 26,696,700 | Total.......................... | 760,679,187 |
| Five hundred dollars................. | 87,500 | | |

[1] Notes redeemed but not assorted by denominations.

NATIONAL BANK CIRCULATION IN VAULTS OF CURRENCY BUREAU.

During the year ended October 31, 1922, national bank notes were received from the Bureau of Engraving and Printing to the amount of $527,981,000, which amount, with the balance of $351,-412,930 in the vaults of this bureau at close of business October 31, 1921, makes a total to be accounted for at close of business October 31, 1922, of $879,393,930. During the year ended October 31, 1922, notes were issued to replace notes of existing banks redeemed and destroyed, to new banks chartered, and on account of banks increasing their circulation to the amount of $569,444,140, while the amount of notes withdrawn and destroyed on account of liquidations and expirations of charter amounted to $6,720,160, making aggregate withdrawals during this period of $576,164,300, leaving a balance of currency in the vaults at close of business October 31, 1922, of $303,229,630, or $48,183,300 less than the balance at close of business October 31, 1921.

The amount of national bank circulation issued and the total amount outstanding each month during the year ended October 31, 1922, together with the amount received from the Bureau of Engraving and Printing, the cost of paper, the cost of printing, etc., and the total cost, is shown in the following statements:

*Statement of national bank currency issued to banks from November 1, 1921, to October 31, 1922.*

| | Issued on account of redemption. | Issued on bonds. | Total issue. | Grand total issued. |
|---|---|---|---|---|
| **1921.** | | | | |
| November | $52,981,510 | $1,407,570 | $54,389,080 | $9,983,398,125 |
| December | 53,144,730 | 1,446,750 | 54,591,480 | 10,037,989,605 |
| **1922.** | | | | |
| January | 63,482,920 | 1,503,130 | 64,986,050 | 10,102,975,655 |
| February | 51,675,680 | 661,100 | 52,336,780 | 10,155,312,435 |
| March | 48,348,880 | 1,798,210 | 50,147,090 | 10,205,459,525 |
| April | 43,569,010 | 3,103,000 | 46,672,010 | 10,252,131,535 |
| May | 43,610,630 | 3,129,640 | 46,740,270 | 10,298,871,805 |
| June | 43,225,170 | 2,773,180 | 45,998,350 | 10,344,870,155 |
| July | 34,589,960 | 1,554,720 | 36,144,680 | 10,381,014,835 |
| August | 30,982,820 | 2,035,210 | 33,018,030 | 10,414,032,865 |
| September | 31,630,720 | 2,355,340 | 33,986,060 | 10,448,018,925 |
| October | 48,040,700 | 2,393,560 | 50,434,260 | 10,498,453,185 |
| Total | 545,282,730 | 24,161,410 | 569,444,140 | .............. |

RECEIVED FROM BUREAU OF ENGRAVING AND PRINTING.

| Denomination. | Number of sheets. | Number of notes. | Amount. | Cost of paper. | Cost of printing, etc. | Total cost. |
|---|---|---|---|---|---|---|
| 5, 5, 5, 5 | 6,953,060 | 27,812,240 | 139,061,200 | $47,280.81 | $361,559.12 | $408,839.93 |
| 10, 10, 10, 10 | 774,245 | 3,096,980 | 30,969,800 | 5,264.87 | 40,260.74 | 45,525.61 |
| 10, 10, 10, 20 | 6,872,900 | 27,491,600 | 343,645,000 | 46,735.72 | 357,390.80 | 404,126.52 |
| 50, 50, 50, 100 | 57,220 | 228,880 | 14,305,000 | 389.09 | 2,975.44 | 3,364.53 |
| Total | 14,657,425 | 58,629,700 | 527,981,000 | 99,670.49 | 762,186.10 | 861,856.59 |

ISSUED TO BANKS.

| 5, 5, 5, 5 | 7,707,598 | 30,830,392 | 154,151,960 | $52,411.67 | $400,795.10 | $453,206.77 |
|---|---|---|---|---|---|---|
| 10, 10, 10, 10 | 876,687 | 3,506,748 | 35,067,480 | 5,961.47 | 45,587.72 | 51,549.19 |
| 10, 10, 10, 20 | 7,280,084 | 29,120,336 | 364,004,200 | 49,504.57 | 378,564.37 | 428,068.94 |
| 50, 100 | 2,030 | 4,060 | 304,500 | 6.90 | 105.56 | 112.46 |
| 50, 50, 50, 100 | 63,664 | 251,656 | 15,916,000 | 432.91 | 3,310.53 | 3,743.44 |
| Total | 15,930,063 | 63,713,192 | 569,444,140 | 108,317.52 | 828,363.28 | 936,680.80 |

The amount of national bank circulation issued and retired for years ended October 31, from 1914 to 1921, and the amount issued and retired quarterly during the year ended October 31, 1922, with the grand total issued and retired during this period, is shown in the following statement:

*Yearly increase or decrease in national-bank circulation from Nov. 1, 1913, to Oct. 31, 1921, and quarterly increase or decrease for the year ended Oct. 31, 1922.*

| Date. | Issued. | Retired. | Increase. | Decrease. |
|---|---|---|---|---|
| 1914 | $387,763,860 | $20,246,418 | $367,517,442 | |
| 1915 | 27,484,675 | 342,807,533 | | $315,322,858 |
| 1916 | 10,593,700 | 59,026,803 | | 48,433,103 |
| 1917 | 22,749,150 | 37,211,370 | | 14,462,220 |
| 1918 | 26,227,740 | 18,781,552 | 7,446,188 | |
| 1919 | 29,660,850 | 24,864,635 | 4,796,215 | |
| 1920 | 29,057,140 | 19,794,540 | 9,262,600 | |
| 1921 | 36,461,040 | 20,417,025 | 16,044,015 | |
| From Nov. 1, 1921, to Jan. 31, 1922 | 4,357,450 | 4,079,480 | 277,970 | |
| From Feb. 1 to April 30, 1922 | 5,562,310 | 3,075,500 | 2,486,810 | |
| From May 1 to July 31, 1922 | 7,457,540 | 3,377,650 | 4,079,890 | |
| From Aug. 1 to Oct. 31, 1922 | 6,784,110 | 3,156,000 | 3,628,110 | |
| Total (1922) | 24,161,410 | 13,688,630 | 10,472,780 | |
| Surrendered to this office and retired, from Nov. 1, 1913, to Oct. 31, 1922 | | 33,136,197 | | 33,136,197 |
| Grand total | 594,159,565 | 589,974,703 | 415,539,240 | 411,354,378 |

## FEDERAL RESERVE SYSTEM.

The development of the Federal reserve system since its inauguration in 1914 is shown by reference to the following statements issued by the Federal Reserve Board during the latter part of November of each year from 1914 to 1920 and during the latter part of October for the years 1921 and 1922:

[In thousands of dollars.]

| | Nov. 27, 1914. | Nov. 26, 1915. | Nov. 24, 1916. | Nov. 16, 1917. | Nov. 22, 1918. | Nov. 28, 1919. | Nov. 26, 1920. | Oct. 26, 1921. | Oct. 25, 1922. |
|---|---|---|---|---|---|---|---|---|---|
| **ASSETS.** | | | | | | | | | |
| Gold | 227,840 | 321,068 | 459,935 | 1,584,325 | 2,060,265 | 2,093,641 | 2,023,916 | 2,786,239 | 3,085,083 |
| Other lawful money | 34,630 | 37,212 | 17,974 | 52,525 | 55,992 | 66,025 | 171,364 | 150,909 | 126,835 |
| Bills discounted and bought | 7,383 | 48,973 | 122,863 | 681,719 | 2,078,219 | 2,709,804 | 2,983,133 | 1,371,075 | 727,090 |
| United States securities | | 12,919 | 50,594 | 241,906 | 177,314 | 314,937 | 320,614 | 190,946 | 405,636 |
| Municipal warrants | | 27,308 | 22,166 | 1,273 | 27 | | | | 27 |
| Federal reserve notes—net | | 19,176 | 15,414 | | | | | | |
| Due from Federal reserve banks—net | | 14,053 | 43,263 | | | | | | |
| Uncollected items | | | | 428,544 | 819,010 | 1,013,426 | 709,401 | 540,067 | 633,493 |
| All other assets | 165 | 4,633 | 3,121 | 22,111 | 28,700 | 32,208 | 36,152 | 55,679 | 63,931 |
| Total | 270,018 | 485,342 | 735,060 | 3,012,406 | 5,219,527 | 6,230,041 | 6,244,580 | 5,091,915 | 5,065,095 |
| **LIABILITIES.** | | | | | | | | | |
| Capital paid in | 18,050 | 54,846 | 55,711 | 66,691 | 80,025 | 87,001 | 99,020 | 103,007 | 106,277 |
| Surplus | | | | | | | | | |
| Government deposits | | 15,000 | 26,319 | 218,887 | 1,134 | 81,087 | 164,745 | 213,824 | 215,398 |
| Member bank deposits—net | 249,268 | 397,962 | 637,072 | 1,501,423 | 113,174 | 98,157 | 15,909 | 46,624 | 23,659 |
| Due to member and nonmember banks | | | | | 1,718,000 | 1,943,232 | 1,734,691 | 1,669,059 | 1,799,931 |
| All other deposits | | | | | | | | 22,573 | 18,180 |
| Federal reserve notes—net | 2,700 | 13,385 | 14,296 | 1,972,585 | 2,565,215 | [1]2,852,277 | [1]3,325,629 | [1]2,408,779 | [1]2,298,536 |
| Federal reserve bank notes in circulation | | | 1,028 | 8,000 | 80,504 | 256,793 | 214,610 | 88,024 | 37,995 |
| Collection items | | | | 240,437 | 620,608 | 561,436 | 582,442 | 466,044 | 539,773 |
| All other liabilities | | 4,169 | 634 | 4,383 | 50,867 | 50,058 | 107,534 | 76,681 | 25,346 |
| Total | 270,018 | 485,342 | 735,060 | 3,012,406 | 5,219,527 | 6,230,041 | 6,244,580 | 5,091,915 | 5,065,095 |

[1] In actual circulation.

The condition of the 12 Federal reserve banks at close of each month from January 25, 1918, to October 25, 1922, is shown in the following statement:

[In millions of dollars.]

| Year. | Assets. | | | | | Liabilities. | | | |
|---|---|---|---|---|---|---|---|---|---|
| | Gold. | Other currency. | Bills discounted and bought. | United States securities. | Aggregate assets. | Capital. | Surplus. | Gross deposits. | Circulation. |
| **1918.** | | | | | | | | | |
| Jan. 25 | 1,727 | 56 | 902 | 123 | 3,169 | 72 | 1 | 1,849 | 1,243 |
| Feb. 21 | 1,772 | 60 | 806 | 222 | 3,176 | 73 | 1 | 1,773 | 1,323 |
| Mar. 29 | 1,816 | 58 | 887 | 311 | 3,446 | 74 | 1 | 1,901 | 1,461 |
| Apr. 26 | 1,827 | 64 | 1,205 | 79 | 3,567 | 75 | 1 | 1,945 | 1,534 |
| May 31 | 1,918 | 58 | 1,154 | 147 | 3,686 | 75 | 1 | 1,995 | 1,609 |
| June 28 | 1,949 | 57 | 1,086 | 259 | 3,872 | 76 | 1 | 2,050 | 1,733 |
| July 26 | 1,974 | 55 | 1,507 | 57 | 4,165 | 76 | 1 | 2,181 | 1,882 |
| Aug. 30 | 2,014 | 53 | 1,661 | 58 | 4,366 | 78 | 1 | 2,142 | 2,113 |
| Sept. 27 | 2,021 | 51 | 2,002 | 79 | 4,817 | 79 | 1 | 2,317 | 2,385 |
| Oct. 25 | 2,045 | 53 | 1,945 | 350 | 5,271 | 79 | 1 | 2,581 | 2,567 |
| Nov. 29 | 2,065 | 55 | 2,191 | 122 | 5,195 | 80 | 1 | 2,405 | 2,655 |
| Dec. 27 | 2,090 | 56 | 2,007 | 312 | 5,252 | 81 | 1 | 2,313 | 2,802 |
| **1919.** | | | | | | | | | |
| Jan. 31 | 2,112 | 68 | 1,882 | 295 | 5,075 | 81 | 23 | 2,351 | 2,580 |
| Feb. 28 | 2,123 | 66 | 2,157 | 183 | 5,207 | 81 | 23 | 2,450 | 2,606 |
| Mar. 28 | 2,142 | 68 | 2,134 | 201 | 5,230 | 81 | 49 | 2,401 | 2,667 |
| Apr. 25 | 2,169 | 71 | 2,136 | 219 | 5,253 | 82 | 49 | 2,383 | 2,708 |
| May 29 | 2,187 | 67 | 2,173 | 229 | 5,322 | 83 | 49 | 2,466 | 2,688 |
| June 27 | 2,148 | 68 | 2,123 | 232 | 5,288 | 83 | 49 | 2,437 | 2,676 |
| July 25 | 2,095 | 66 | 2,243 | 239 | 5,366 | 83 | 81 | 2,487 | 2,698 |
| Aug. 29 | 2,067 | 69 | 2,178 | 271 | 5,436 | 85 | 81 | 2,446 | 2,800 |
| Sept. 26 | 2,118 | 70 | 2,225 | 278 | 5,632 | 85 | 81 | 2,542 | 2,895 |
| Oct. 31 | 2,138 | 68 | 2,523 | 301 | 5,939 | 86 | 81 | 2,726 | 3,008 |
| Nov. 28 | 2,094 | 66 | 2,710 | 315 | 6,230 | 87 | 81 | 2,903 | 3,109 |
| Dec. 26 | 2,078 | 57 | 2,780 | 300 | 6,325 | 87 | 81 | 2,780 | 3,319 |
| **1920.** | | | | | | | | | |
| Jan. 30 | 2,013 | 61 | 2,736 | 304 | 6,074 | 88 | 120 | 2,740 | 3,101 |
| Feb. 27 | 1,967 | 116 | 2,985 | 294 | 6,416 | 91 | 120 | 2,911 | 3,257 |
| Mar. 26 | 1,935 | 122 | 2,901 | 290 | 6,048 | 91 | 120 | 2,542 | 3,249 |
| Apr. 30 | 1,937 | 134 | 2,942 | 294 | 6,050 | 92 | 120 | 2,526 | 3,252 |
| May 28 | 1,953 | 139 | 2,933 | 306 | 6,114 | 94 | 120 | 2,542 | 3,286 |
| June 25 | 1,969 | 139 | 2,831 | 352 | 6,075 | 95 | 120 | 2,473 | 3,302 |
| July 30 | 1,978 | 151 | 2,837 | 325 | 6,033 | 95 | 165 | 2,408 | 3,312 |
| Aug. 27 | 1,972 | 156 | 2,989 | 301 | 6,179 | 97 | 165 | 2,448 | 3,404 |
| Sept. 24 | 1,990 | 162 | 3,012 | 298 | 6,312 | 97 | 165 | 2,477 | 3,494 |
| Oct. 29 | 2,003 | 165 | 3,100 | 296 | 6,342 | 98 | 165 | 2,418 | 3,566 |
| Nov. 26 | 2,024 | 171 | 2,983 | 321 | 6,245 | 99 | 165 | 2,333 | 3,648 |
| Dec. 30 | 2,059 | 190 | 2,975 | 288 | 6,270 | 100 | 165 | 2,321 | 3,562 |
| **1921.** | | | | | | | | | |
| Jan. 28 | 2,106 | 214 | 2,622 | 287 | 5,862 | 100 | 202 | 2,239 | 3,293 |
| Feb. 25 | 2,140 | 217 | 2,567 | 287 | 5,861 | 101 | 202 | 2,279 | 3,241 |
| Mar. 25 | 2,211 | 211 | 2,410 | 283 | 5,753 | 101 | 202 | 2,295 | 3,106 |
| Apr. 27 | 2,318 | 187 | 2,167 | 268 | 5,504 | 101 | 202 | 2,157 | 2,986 |
| May 25 | 2,393 | 165 | 1,957 | 306 | 5,380 | 102 | 202 | 2,131 | 2,880 |
| June 29 | 2,462 | 164 | 1,803 | 257 | 5,242 | 102 | 202 | 2,098 | 2,767 |
| July 27 | 2,531 | 154 | 1,670 | 249 | 5,150 | 102 | 214 | 2,108 | 2,663 |
| Aug. 24 | 2,619 | 147 | 1,531 | 239 | 5,053 | 103 | 214 | 2,071 | 2,599 |
| Sept. 28 | 2,726 | 153 | 1,442 | 224 | 5,107 | 103 | 214 | 2,159 | 2,559 |
| Oct. 26 | 2,786 | 151 | 1,371 | 191 | 5,095 | 103 | 214 | 2,205 | 2,497 |
| Nov. 30 | 2,849 | 140 | 1,255 | 205 | 5,044 | 103 | 214 | 2,206 | 2,442 |
| Dec. 28 | 2,870 | 123 | 1,294 | 241 | 5,151 | 103 | 214 | 2,223 | 2,528 |
| **1922.** | | | | | | | | | |
| Jan. 25 | 2,904 | 155 | 933 | 250 | 4,781 | 103 | 215 | 2,177 | 2,269 |
| Feb. 21 | 2,947 | 134 | 804 | 355 | 4,789 | 104 | 215 | 2,198 | 2,255 |
| Mar. 29 | 2,975 | 128 | 739 | 441 | 4,816 | 104 | 215 | 2,214 | 2,262 |
| Apr. 26 | 2,995 | 130 | 583 | 567 | 4,860 | 104 | 215 | 2,333 | 2,237 |
| May 31 | 3,008 | 123 | 590 | 603 | 4,847 | 105 | 215 | 2,293 | 2,212 |
| June 28 | 3,021 | 127 | 623 | 557 | 4,905 | 105 | 215 | 2,370 | 2,192 |
| July 26 | 3,055 | 127 | 536 | 541 | 4,863 | 105 | 215 | 2,331 | 2,190 |
| Aug. 30 | 3,063 | 132 | 576 | 498 | 4,849 | 106 | 215 | 2,297 | 2,207 |
| Sept. 27 | 3,077 | 126 | 658 | 451 | 4,970 | 106 | 215 | 2,336 | 2,289 |
| Oct. 25 | 3,085 | 127 | 727 | 409 | 5,065 | 10? | 215 | 2,382 | 2,337 |

*Percentage of bills discounted secured by United States Government obligations to the total bills discounted and purchased by the Federal reserve banks at the end of each month, year ended October 31, 1922.*

[In thousands of dollars.]

| Date. | Bills discounted secured by United States Government obligations. | Total holdings of bills discounted and purchased. | Percentage of bills discounted secured by Government obligations to total bills discounted and purchased. | Date. | Bills discounted secured by United States Government obligations. | Total holdings of bills discounted and purchased. | Percentage of bills discounted secured by Government obligations to total bills discounted and purchased. |
|---|---|---|---|---|---|---|---|
| **1921.** | | | | **1922.** | | | |
| Nov. 30...... | 476,360 | 1,255,255 | 37.9 | Apr. 30...... | 185,743 | 600,781 | 30.9 |
| Dec. 31...... | 485,233 | 1,289,609 | 37.6 | May 31...... | 171,106 | 589,672 | 29.0 |
| **1922.** | | | | June 30...... | 167,241 | 622,530 | 26.9 |
| Jan. 31...... | 363,586 | 913,820 | 39.8 | July 31...... | 132,390 | 546,289 | 24.2 |
| Feb. 28...... | 284,614 | 806,035 | 35.3 | Aug. 31...... | 126,113 | 577,624 | 21.8 |
| Mar. 31...... | 260,781 | 785,737 | 33.2 | Sept. 30...... | 162,780 | 708,071 | 23.0 |
| | | | | Oct. 31...... | 269,040 | 834,598 | 32.2 |

### FEDERAL RESERVE BANK DISCOUNT RATES.

The discount rates of Federal reserve banks, approved by the Federal Reserve Board, and in effect October 31, 1922, with respect to each class of paper, are shown in the following statement:

*Discount rates of Federal reserve banks in effect October 31, 1922.*

| Federal reserve bank. | Paper maturing within 90 days. | | | | Bankers' acceptances maturing within 3 months. | Agricultural and live-stock paper maturing after 90 days, but within 6 months. |
|---|---|---|---|---|---|---|
| | Secured by— | | Trade acceptances. | Commercial, agricultural, and live-stock paper, n. e. s. | | |
| | Treasury notes and certificates of indebtedness. | Liberty bonds and Victory notes. | | | | |
| Boston...................... | 4 | 4 | 4 | 4 | ............ | 4 |
| New York................... | 4 | 4 | 4 | 4 | 4 | 4 |
| Philadelphia................ | 4½ | 4½ | 4½ | 4½ | 4½ | 4½ |
| Cleveland................... | 4½ | 4½ | 4½ | 4½ | 4½ | 4½ |
| Richmond................... | 4½ | 4½ | 4½ | 4½ | 4½ | 4½ |
| Atlanta..................... | 4½ | 4½ | 4½ | 4½ | 4½ | 4½ |
| Chicago..................... | 4½ | 4½ | 4½ | 4½ | 4½ | 4½ |
| St. Louis................... | 4½ | 4½ | 4½ | 4½ | 4½ | 4½ |
| Minneapolis................. | 4½ | 4½ | 4½ | 4½ | 4½ | 4½ |
| Kansas City................. | 4½ | 4½ | 4½ | 4½ | 4½ | 4½ |
| Dallas...................... | 4½ | 4½ | 4½ | 4½ | 4½ | 4½ |
| San Francisco............... | 4 | 4 | 4 | 4 | 4 | 4 |

### FEDERAL RESERVE NOTES.

Weekly statements issued by the Federal Reserve Board with respect to the amount of Federal reserve notes outstanding, based upon reports of Federal reserve agents, show a reduction during the past year, or between November 2, 1921, and October 25, 1922, of $26,784,000. The amount of Federal reserve notes outstanding October 25, 1922, was $2,688,822,000, $2,124,432,000 of which was secured by gold and the balance by commercial or other eligible paper. In the period indicated the ratio of notes secured by gold was increased from $1,708,670,000 to $2,124,432,000, while the amount of notes secured by commercial and other eligible paper was reduced from $1,006,936,000 to $564,390,000.

The amount of notes outstanding at the close of each week, the amount secured by gold, and the amount secured by commercial or other eligible paper, is shown in the following statement for the period November 2, 1921, to October 25, 1922:

*Weekly statement of Federal reserve notes outstanding (amount issued by Federal reserve agents to the banks, less "unfit" notes returned for redemption), amount secured by gold and amount secured by commercial and other eligible paper, from November 2, 1921, to October 25, 1922.*

[In thousands of dollars.]

| Date. | Federal reserve notes outstanding. | Amounts secured by gold. | Amounts secured by commercial and other eligible paper. | Date. | Federal reserve notes outstanding. | Amounts secured by gold. | Amounts secured by commercial and other eligible paper. |
|---|---|---|---|---|---|---|---|
| **1921.** | | | | **1922.** | | | |
| Nov. 2.... | 2,715,606 | 1,708,670 | 1,006,936 | May 3...... | 2,537,262 | 2,169,736 | 367,526 |
| 9...... | 2,708,845 | 1,723,523 | 985,322 | 10...... | 2,541,503 | 2,172,052 | 369,451 |
| 16...... | 2,716,943 | 1,810,060 | 906,883 | 17...... | 2,527,081 | 2,140,192 | 386,889 |
| 23...... | 2,704,639 | 1,811,316 | 893,323 | 24...... | 2,509,652 | 2,141,120 | 368,532 |
| 30...... | 2,698,682 | 1,779,605 | 919,077 | 31...... | 2,511,810 | 2,140,891 | 370,919 |
| Dec. 7...... | 2,691,689 | 1,787,724 | 903,965 | June 7...... | 2,526,949 | 2,128,242 | 398,707 |
| 14...... | 2,726,175 | 1,813,422 | 912,753 | 14...... | 2,518,799 | 2,142,118 | 376,681 |
| 21...... | 2,772,812 | 1,833,108 | 939,704 | 21...... | 2,522,750 | 2,121,680 | 401,070 |
| 28...... | 2,796,540 | 1,846,369 | 950,171 | 28...... | 2,537,485 | 2,123,373 | 414,112 |
| **1922.** | | | | July 5...... | 2,561,837 | 2,123,816 | 438,021 |
| Jan. 4...... | 2,786,114 | 1,902,912 | 883,202 | 12...... | 2,589,509 | 2,161,560 | 427,949 |
| 11...... | 2,732,861 | 1,910,561 | 822,300 | 19...... | 2,583,868 | 2,195,062 | 388,806 |
| 18...... | 2,666,397 | 1,948,657 | 717,740 | 26...... | 2,571,963 | 2,197,645 | 374,318 |
| 25...... | 2,604,957 | 1,939,792 | 665,165 | Aug. 2...... | 2,572,297 | 2,223,384 | 348,913 |
| Feb. 1...... | 2,559,656 | 1,928,419 | 631,237 | 9...... | 2,581,583 | 2,233,430 | 348,153 |
| 8...... | 2,525,009 | 1,942,725 | 582,284 | 16...... | 2,590,069 | 2,238,893 | 351,176 |
| 15...... | 2,506,972 | 1,940,665 | 566,307 | 23...... | 2,601,281 | 2,197,316 | 403,965 |
| 21...... | 2,510,576 | 1,977,602 | 532,974 | 30...... | 2,603,919 | 2,197,658 | 406,261 |
| Mar. 1...... | 2,526,660 | 1,982,061 | 544,599 | Sept. 6...... | 2,639,293 | 2,206,468 | 432,825 |
| 8...... | 2,540,443 | 2,030,161 | 510,282 | 13...... | 2,652,313 | 2,219,162 | 433,151 |
| 15...... | 2,527,772 | 2,090,124 | 437,648 | 20...... | 2,636,112 | 2,202,258 | 433,854 |
| 22...... | 2,523,374 | 2,061,361 | 462,013 | 27...... | 2,653,544 | 2,160,522 | 493,022 |
| 29...... | 2,518,516 | 2,065,992 | 452,524 | Oct. 4...... | 2,682,940 | 2,194,932 | 488,008 |
| Apr. 5...... | 2,529,602 | 2,046,479 | 483,123 | 11...... | 2,708,014 | 2,192,940 | 515,074 |
| 12...... | 2,532,853 | 2,091,844 | 441,009 | 18...... | 2,722,446 | 2,163,465 | 558,981 |
| 19...... | 2,534,997 | 2,094,362 | 440,635 | 25...... | 2,688,822 | 2,124,432 | 564,390 |
| 26...... | 2,536,895 | 2,154,510 | 382,385 | | | | |

The amount and denominations of Federal reserve notes printed and retired, and the amount of these notes received from Federal reserve banks for destruction during the year ended October 31, 1922, with the balances on hand, are shown in the following statement:

*Federal reserve notes.*

VAULT BALANCE, OCTOBER 31, 1922.

| | Fives. | Tens. | Twenties. | Fifties. | One hundreds. | Five hundreds. | One thousands. | Five thousands. | Ten thousands. | Total. |
|---|---|---|---|---|---|---|---|---|---|---|
| Total printed | $2,811,800,000 | $3,978,120,000 | $4,270,560,000 | $900,600,000 | $750,800,000 | $155,800,000 | $311,200,000 | $108,000,000 | $184,000,000 | $13,470,880,000 |
| Total shipped | 2,470,000,000 | 3,517,160,000 | 3,707,920,000 | 747,000,000 | 610,000,000 | 85,200,000 | 179,600,000 | 34,000,000 | 56,000,000 | 11,406,880,000 |
| Total on hand | 341,800,000 | 460,960,000 | 562,640,000 | 153,600,000 | 140,800,000 | 70,600,000 | 131,600,000 | 74,000,000 | 128,000,000 | 2,064,000,000 |

ISSUED, RETIRED, AND OUTSTANDING, OCTOBER 31, 1922.

| | Fives. | Tens. | Twenties. | Fifties. | One hundreds. | Five hundreds. | One thousands. | Five thousands. | Ten thousands. | Total. |
|---|---|---|---|---|---|---|---|---|---|---|
| Total issued | $2,562,356,000 | $3,689,605,540 | $4,003,107,040 | $777,989,550 | $635,353,800 | $79,912,500 | $204,416,000 | $32,375,000 | $45,640,000 | $12,030,755,430 |
| Total retired | 2,095,661,160 | 2,977,779,770 | 3,105,212,840 | 554,949,650 | 401,341,600 | 39,887,500 | 116,709,000 | 20,395,000 | 29,880,000 | 9,341,816,520 |
| Total outstanding | 466,694,840 | 711,825,770 | 897,894,200 | 223,039,900 | 234,012,200 | 40,025,000 | 87,707,000 | 11,980,000 | 15,760,000 | 2,688,988,910 |

*Mutilated Federal reserve notes, by denominations, received and destroyed since organization of banks and on hand in vault, October 31, 1922.*

RECEIVED FOR DESTRUCTION.

| | Fives. | Tens. | Twenties. | Fifties. | One hundreds. | Five hundreds. | One thousands. | Five thousands. | Ten thousands. | Total. |
|---|---|---|---|---|---|---|---|---|---|---|
| Boston | $155,562,355 | $285,288,480 | $194,854,360 | $19,991,450 | $20,385,300 | $906,000 | $6,120,000 | $80,000 | $130,000 | $683,327,945 |
| New York | 461,919,900 | 829,292,580 | 575,108,520 | 122,194,850 | 122,299,800 | 13,402,000 | 33,652,000 | 70,000 | 1,040,000 | 2,158,980,050 |
| Phila | 164,259,075 | 222,953,490 | 269,741,420 | 46,895,350 | 21,919,800 | 539,000 | 2,395,000 | | | 728,613,135 |
| Cl | 109,951,240 | 159,175,250 | 283,154,560 | 95,380,650 | 17,531,200 | 631,000 | 754,000 | 15,000 | 40,000 | 666,632,900 |
| Rich | 107,599,660 | 125,732,390 | 150,531,140 | 35,999,900 | 16,749,000 | 146,500 | 2,752,000 | 10,000 | 20,000 | 439,540,590 |
| atla | 94,786,375 | 115,160,570 | 132,813,300 | 9,097,450 | 6,821,500 | 298,500 | 690,000 | | | 359,669,695 |
| Chicago | 250,502,145 | 379,350,960 | 427,716,200 | 74,597,850 | 24,216,300 | 1,773,500 | 2,481,000 | 15,000 | 230,000 | 1,160,652,945 |
| St. Louis | 117,188,465 | 129,632,600 | 120,026,040 | 12,277,750 | 5,054,000 | 413,000 | 745,000 | 5,000 | | 385,571,855 |
| Minneapolis | 59,480,960 | 62,395,280 | 48,089,520 | 1,748,000 | 2,405,200 | 122,000 | 272,000 | | | 174,512,960 |
| Kansas City | 89,577,870 | 78,386,370 | 82,235,380 | 4,015,100 | 4,595,300 | 292,000 | 327,000 | | | 259,429,020 |
| allas | 48,326,710 | 59,228,380 | 59,411,440 | 4,813,800 | 3,569,900 | 135,000 | 334,000 | | | 175,819,230 |
| San | 162,536,255 | 132,142,640 | 259,225,120 | 24,769,450 | 31,619,100 | 1,691,500 | 3,399,000 | 30,000 | 50,000 | 635,663,065 |
| Total issued | 1,821,693,010 | 2,598,738,980 | 2,602,907,400 | 451,691,600 | 277,166,400 | 20,350,000 | 54,131,000 | 225,000 | 1,510,000 | 7,828,413,300 |
| Total destroyed | 1,819,910,560 | 2,596,618,780 | 2,599,819,500 | 451,237,700 | 276,981,300 | 20,343,500 | 54,110,000 | 225,000 | 1,510,000 | 7,820,756,340 |
| balance on hand | 1,782,450 | 2,120,200 | 3,087,900 | 453,900 | 185,100 | 6,500 | 21,000 | | | 7,657,050 |

NOTE.—During the year, burned, badly mutilated, and fractional parts of Federal reserve notes, amounting to $67,175, have been identified, valued, and the bank of issue determined.

## FEDERAL RESERVE BANK NOTES.

Federal reserve bank notes are secured by the deposit of United States bonds with the Treasurer of the United States, or in accordance with the provisions of the act of April 23, 1918, known as the Pittman Act, by United States certificates of indebtedness.

The following statements show the denominations and the aggregate amount of Federal reserve bank notes printed, issued, and redeemed during the year ended October 31, 1922, and the balance on hand on that date:

*Federal reserve bank notes.*

### VAULT BALANCE OCTOBER 31, 1922.

| · | Ones. | Twos. | Fives. | Tens. | Twenties. | Fifties. | Total. |
|---|---|---|---|---|---|---|---|
| Total printed......... | $478,892,000 | $136,232,000 | $132,500,000 | $24,040,000 | $14,080,000 | $2,600,000 | $788,344,000 |
| Total issued.......... | 478,412,000 | 135,040,000 | 121,200,000 | 16,440,000 | 9,760,000 | 200,000 | 761,052,000 |
| Total on hand.. | 480,000 | 1,192,000 | 11,300,000 | 7,600,000 | 4,320,000 | 2,400,000 | 27,292,000 |

### ISSUED, REDEEMED, AND OUTSTANDING OCTOBER 31, 1922.

| | Ones. | Twos. | Fives. | Tens. | Twenties. | Fifties. | Total. |
|---|---|---|---|---|---|---|---|
| Total issued.......... | $478,412,000 | $135,040,000 | $121,200,000 | $16,440,000 | $9,760,000 | $200,000 | $761,052,000 |
| Total redeemed....... | 449,927,164 | 122,198,636 | 111,184,140 | 14,219,200 | 7,196,560 | 121,900 | 704,847,600 |
| Total outstanding........... | 28,484,836 | 12,841,364 | 10,015,860 | 2,220,800 | 2,563,440 | 78,100 | 56,204,400 |

## BANKING POWER OF THE UNITED STATES.

The banking power of the United States, June 30, 1922, measured by the capital, surplus and profits, deposits and circulation of all reporting banks, including national banks and Federal reserve banks, and estimated figures for nonreporting private banks, aggregated $50,175,300,000, which was $1,955,400,000 greater than the total banking power June 30, 1921.

The number of banks and the proportion of the aggregate banking power contributed by each class of institutions is shown in the following statement as of June 30, 1922, with the amount of increase since June 30, 1921:

*Banking power of the United States June 30, 1922.*

[Money columns in millions.]

| | Number of banks. | Capital paid in. | Surplus and profits. | Deposits [1] | National bank circulation, Federal reserve notes and Federal reserve bank notes. | Total, June, 1922. | Total, June, 1921. | Increase over 1921. |
|---|---|---|---|---|---|---|---|---|
| National banks............. | 8,249 | 1,307.2 | 1,541.2 | 13,818.5 | 725.7 | 17,392.6 | 16,491.6 | 901.0 |
| Reporting State banks, savings banks, trust companies, and private banks. | 22,140 | 1,636.7 | 2,090.0 | 24,057.2 | ......... | 27,783.9 | 26,418.3 | 1,365.6 |
| Nonreporting private banks (estimated)................ | 445 | 6.8 | 11.6 | 96.3 | ......... | 114.7 | 100.2 | 14.5 |
| Total.................. | 30,834 | 2,950.7 | 3,642.8 | 37,972.0 | 725.7 | 45,291.2 | 43,010.1 | 2,281.1 |
| Federal reserve banks....... | [2] 12 | 105.1 | 217.7 | 2,369.6 | 2,191.7 | 4,884.1 | 5,209.8 | [3] 325.7 |
| Grand total........... | 30,846 | 3,055.8 | 3,860.5 | 40,341.6 | 2,917.4 | 50,175.3 | 48,219.9 | 1,955.4 |

[1] Includes dividends unpaid, postal savings and United States deposits, certified checks and cashiers' checks outstanding, but not amounts due to other banks, except deposits of Federal reserve banks, which are reported gross.
[2] June 28.
[3] Decrease.

NOTE.—Information for nonreporting private banks has been estimated by using as a basis for the calculation statements of reporting private banks. Only such institutions as are performing the functions of a bank are included in the total number of private banks. Concerns whose business is confined to the selling of investments are not included in the list of private bankers.

## MONEY IN THE UNITED STATES.

From July 1, 1914, to July 1, 1922, the stock of money increased from $3,738,000,000 to $8,177,000,000; the amount in circulation per capita, from $34.35 to $39.86, and the population from 99,000,000 to 109,700,000.

Incidentally it is interesting to note that between January 1, 1914, and August 31, 1922, the importations of gold and silver amounted to $3,684,700,000, the exports to $2,507,979,000, resulting in an excess of imports of these metals of $1,176,721,000.

The statements following prepared by the Division of Loans and Currency, Treasury Department, and compiled from information furnished by the Department of Commerce, Bureau of Foreign and Domestic Commerce, respectively, show the general stock of money in the United States July 1, 1922, and the amount of imports and exports of merchandise, gold and silver, for calendar years 1914 to 1921, and the eight months ended August 31, 1922, respectively.

United States Treasury Department circulation statement, July 1, 1922. [1]

| Kind of money. | Stock of money in the United States. | Money held in the Treasury. | | | | | Money outside of the Treasury. | | | | Population of continental United States (estimated). |
|---|---|---|---|---|---|---|---|---|---|---|---|
| | | Total. | That held in trust against gold and silver certificates (and Treasury notes of 1890). | Reserve against United States notes (and Treasury notes of 1890). | Held for Federal reserve banks and agents. | All other money. | Total. | Held by Federal reserve banks and agents. | In circulation. | | |
| | | | | | | | | | Amount. | Per capita. | |
| Gold coin and bullion | [2] $3,784,651,712 | $3,157,202,556 | $695,000,469 | $152,979,026 | $2,108,886,911 | $200,336,159 | $627,449,156 | $211,511,603 | $415,937,553 | $3.79 | .......... |
| Gold certificates | [2] 695,000,469 | 313,504,308 | 305,577,136 | .......... | .......... | 7,927,172 | 695,000,469 | 531,658,270 | 173,342,199 | 1.58 | .......... |
| Standard silver dollars | [3] 381,174,404 | .......... | .......... | .......... | .......... | .......... | 67,670,096 | 9,697,027 | 57,973,069 | .53 | .......... |
| Silver certificates | [3] 304,965,583 | .......... | .......... | .......... | .......... | .......... | 304,966,583 | 38,731,219 | 265,335,374 | 2.42 | .......... |
| Treasury notes of 1890 | 1,510,543 | .......... | .......... | .......... | .......... | .......... | 1,510,543 | .......... | 1,509,543 | .01 | .......... |
| Subsidiary silver | 271,210,886 | 17,747,502 | .......... | .......... | .......... | 17,747,502 | 253,463,384 | 24,153,011 | 229,310,373 | 2.09 | .......... |
| United States notes | 346,681,016 | 4,145,964 | .......... | .......... | .......... | 4,145,964 | 342,535,052 | 50,192,056 | 292,342,996 | 2.66 | .......... |
| Federal reserve notes | 2,355,461,600 | 2,557,722 | .......... | .......... | .......... | 2,557,722 | 2,552,903,938 | 413,788,985 | 2,138,714,953 | 19.49 | .......... |
| Federal reserve bank notes | 80,495,400 | 1,030,273 | .......... | .......... | .......... | 1,030,273 | 79,465,127 | 7,897,186 | 71,567,941 | .66 | .......... |
| National bank notes | 738,302,027 | 15,774,366 | .......... | .......... | .......... | 15,774,366 | 742,427,661 | 14,746,625 | 727,681,036 | 6.63 | .......... |
| Total July 1, 1922 | 8,177,377,105 | 3,511,962,691 | 1,000,577,605 | 152,979,026 | 2,108,886,911 | 249,519,149 | 5,666,092,019 | 1,292,076,982 | 4,374,015,037 | [1] 39.86 | 109,743,000 |
| Comparative totals: | | | | | | | | | | | |
| June 1, 1922 | 8,126,500,982 | 3,495,160,979 | 994,959,698 | 152,979,026 | 2,082,738,419 | 264,483,836 | 5,626,299,701 | 1,255,829,710 | 4,370,469,991 | [1] 39.87 | 109,605,000 |
| July 1, 1921 | 8,096,033,684 | 2,918,696,736 | 919,643,396 | 152,979,026 | 1,537,856,893 | 308,217,429 | 6,096,980,334 | 1,257,368,483 | 4,839,611,851 | [1] 44.78 | 108,087,000 |
| Apr. 1, 1917 | 5,312,109,272 | 2,942,998,527 | 2,654,800,083 | 152,979,026 | .......... | 105,219,416 | 5,053,910,830 | 953,220,126 | 4,100,590,704 | [1] 39.54 | 103,716,000 |
| July 1, 1914 | 3,738,288,871 | 1,843,462,323 | 1,507,178,879 | 150,000,000 | .......... | 186,273,444 | 3,402,015,427 | .......... | 3,402,015,427 | 34.35 | 99,027,000 |
| Jan. 1, 1879 | 1,007,684,483 | [4] 212,420,402 | 21,602,640 | 100,000,000 | .......... | 90,817,762 | 816,266,721 | .......... | 816,266,721 | 16.92 | 48,231,000 |

[1] The form of ... the Federal reserve ... a per capita circulation on July 1, 1922, June 1, 1922, July 1, 1921, and Apr. 1, 1917, of $39.86, ...

[2] Does not include gold bullion or foreign coin ...

[3] These are ... held in the ... since the ..., respectively.

[4] ... held in trust ... against ... National bank notes ... United States in gold or ...

*Imports and exports of merchandise, calendar years 1914, 1915, 1916, 1917, 1918, 1919, 1920, 1921, and from January to August 31, 1922.*

| | Imports of merchandise. | Exports of merchandise. | Excess of exports over imports. |
|---|---|---|---|
| 1914 | $1,789,276,001 | $3,113,624,050 | $1,324,348,049 |
| 1915 | 1,778,596,695 | 3,554,670,847 | 1,776,074,152 |
| 1916 | 2,391,635,335 | 5,482,641,101 | 3,091,005,766 |
| 1917 | 2,952,465,955 | 6,226,255,654 | 3,273,789,699 |
| 1918 | 3,031,304,721 | 6,149,241,951 | 3,117,937,230 |
| 1919 | 3,904,364,932 | 7,920,425,990 | 4,016,061,058 |
| 1920 | 5,278,481,490 | 8,228,016,307 | 2,949,534,817 |
| 1921 | 2,509,147,570 | 4,485,031,356 | ·1,975,883,786 |
| 1922 (8 months) | 1,952,956,596 | 2,423,787,872 | 470,831,276 |
| Total, 8 years and 8 months | 25,588,229,295 | 47,583,695,128 | 21,995,465,833 |

*Gold and silver imports and exports in period indicated.*

GOLD.

| | Imports. | Exports. | Excess of exports over imports. | Excess of imports over exports. |
|---|---|---|---|---|
| 1914 | $57,387,741 | $222,616,156 | $165,228,415 | |
| 1915 | 451,954,590 | 31,425,918 | | $420,528,672 |
| 1916 | 685,990,234 | 155,792,927 | | 530,197,307 |
| 1917 | 552,454,374 | 371,883,884 | | 180,570,490 |
| 1918 | 62,042,748 | 41,069,818 | | 20,972,930 |
| 1919 | 76,534,046 | 368,185,248 | 291,651,202 | |
| 1920 | 417,068,273 | 322,091,208 | | · 94,977,065 |
| 1921 | 691,248,297 | 23,891,377 | | 667,356,920 |
| 1922 (8 months) | 185,091,630 | 11,744,036 | | 173,347,594 |
| Total, 8 years and 8 months | 3,179,771,933 | 1,548,700,572 | 456,879,617 | 2,087,950,978 |

SILVER.

| | Imports. | Exports. | Excess of exports over imports. | Excess of imports over exports. |
|---|---|---|---|---|
| 1914 | $25,959,187 | $51,603,060 | $25,643,873 · | |
| 1915 | 34,483,954 | 53,598,884 | 19,114,930 | |
| 1916 | 32,263,289 | 70,595,037 | 38,331,748 | |
| 1917 | 53,340,477 | 84,130,876 | 30,790,399 | |
| 1918 | 71,375,699 | 252,846,464 | 181,470,765 | |
| 1919 | 89,410,018 | 239,021,051 | 149,611,033 | |
| 1920 | 88,060,041 | 113,616,224 | 25,556,183 | |
| 1921 | 63,242,671 | .51,575,399 | | $11,667,272 |
| 1922 (8 months) | 46,793,050 | 42,291,006 | | 4,502,044 |
| Total, 8 years and 8 months | 504,928,386 | 959,278,001 | 479,518,931 | 16,169,316 |

*Stock of money in the United States, in the Treasury, in reporting banks, Federal reserve banks and in general circulation years ended June 30, 1914 to 1922.*

| Year ending June 30— | Coin and other money in the United States. | Coin and other money in Treasury as assets.[1] | | Coin and other money in reporting banks.[2] | | Held by or for Federal reserve banks and agents.[3] | | In general circulation, exclusive of amounts held by reporting banks and Federal reserve banks. | | |
|---|---|---|---|---|---|---|---|---|---|---|
| | | Amount. | Per cent. | Amount. | Per cent. | Amount. | Per cent. | Amount. | Per cent. | Per capita. |
| | *Millions.* | *Millions.* | | *Millions.* | | *Millions.* | | *Millions.* | | |
| 1914 | 3,738.3 | 336.3 | 9.00 | 1,630.0 | 43.60 | | | 1,772.0 | 47.40 | $17.89 |
| 1915 | 3,989.4 | ·345.4 | 8.66 | 1,447.9 | 36.29 | 386.2 | 9.68 | 1,809.9 | 45.37 | 17.97 |
| 1916 | 4,482.9 | 298.2 | 6.65 | 1,472.2 | 32.84 | 592.7 | 13.22 | 2,119.8 | 47.29 | 20.69 |
| 1917 | 5,408.0 | 268.4 | 4.96 | 1,487.3 | 27.50 | 1,280.9 | 23.69 | 2,371.4 | 43.85 | 22.77 |
| 1918 | 6,741.0 | 360.3 | 5.34 | 882.7 | 13.10 | 2,018.4 | 29.94 | 3,479.6 | 51.62 | 32.87 |
| 1919 | 7,518.8 | 584.2 | 7.77 | 981.3 | 13.05 | 2,167.3 | 28.83 | 3,786.0 | 50.35 | 35.67 |
| 1920 | 7,894.5 | 489.7 | 6.20 | 1,047.3 | 13.27 | 2,021.3 | 25.60 | 4,336.2 | .54.93 | 40.47 |
| 1921 | 8,096.0 | 461.2 | 5.70 | 926.3 | 11.44 | 2,795.2 | 34.52 | 3,913.3 | 48.34 | 36.21 |
| 1922 | 8,177.5 | 402.5 | 4.92 | 814.0 | 9.95 | 3,401.0 | 41.59 | 3,560.0 | 43.54 | 32.44 |

[1] Public money in national-bank depositories to the credit of the Treasurer of the United States not included.

[2] Includes national banks and all reporting State banks with exception of banks in island possessions.

[3] Includes gold reserve held by banks against issues and gold or other funds deposited by banks with agents to retire Federal reserve notes in circulation and own Federal reserve notes held by Federal reserve banks.

[4] Population estimated at 105,869,000 in 1918, 106,136,000 in 1919, 107,155,000 in 1920, 108,087,000 in 1921, and 109,743,000 in 1922

## RATES FOR MONEY IN NEW YORK.

The following table, compiled by the Commercial and Financial Chronicle, shows the range of rates for money on the New York market for the year ended October 31, 1921. Call loans on the stock exchange ranged from 4½ to 6 per cent in November, 1921; three and one-half to 5 per cent in the following April; dropped to 2¾ to 5 per cent in July, and ranged from 4 to 6 per cent in October.

Time loans, 60 and 90 day paper, at the beginning of the year ranged from 5 to 5½ per cent; in April quotations were 4¼ to 4½ per cent; in July, 3¾ to 4¼; and in October, 4½ to 5 per cent.

Time loans, 4 to 6 months paper, ranged from 5 to 5½ in November, 1921; 4¼ to 4¾ per cent in April, 1922; 4 to 4¼ in July; and 4¾ to 5 per cent in October, 1922.

Commercial paper, 60 to 90 days, double name, and single name prime, 4 to 6 months, ranged from 5 to 5¾ per cent, November, 1921; 4½ to 4¾ per cent in April; 3¾ to 4 per cent in July; and 4¼ to 4½ in October, 1922.

*Range of rates for money in the New York market, year ended October 31, 1922.*

| | 1921 | | 1922 | | | |
|---|---|---|---|---|---|---|
| | November. | December. | January. | February. | March. | April. |
| Call loans, stock exchange: | | | | | | |
| Range | 4½-6 | 4½-6 | 3 -6 | 4 -6 | 2 -5½ | 3½-5 |
| Time loans: [1] | | | | | | |
| 60 days | 5 -5¼ | 5 -5¼ | 4½-5¼ | 4½-5 | 4½-5 | 4¼-4½ |
| 90 days | 5 -5½ | 5 -5¼ | 4½-5¼ | 4½-5 | 4½-5 | 4¼-4½ |
| 4 months | 5 -5½ | 5 -5¼ | 4½-5¼ | 4½-5 | 4½-5 | 4¼-4½ |
| 5 months | 5 -5½ | 5 -5¼ | 4½-5¼ | 4½-5 | 4½-5 | 4¼-4¾ |
| 6 months | 5 -5½ | 5 -5¼ | 4½-5¼ | 4½-5 | 4½-5 | 4¼-4¾ |
| Commercial paper: | | | | | | |
| Double names— | | | | | | |
| Choice 60 to 90 days | 5 -5¾ | 5 -5¼ | 4¾-5¼ | 4¾-5 | 4½-5 | 4½-4¾ |
| Single names— | | | | | | |
| Prime, 4 to 6 months | 5 -5¾ | 5 -5¼ | 4¾-5¼ | 4¾-5 | 4½-5 | 4½-4¾ |
| Good, 4 to 6 months | 5¼-6 | 5¼-5½ | 4¾-5¼ | 5 -5¼ | 4¾-5¼ | 4¾-5 |

| | 1922 | | | | | |
|---|---|---|---|---|---|---|
| | May. | June. | July. | August. | September. | October. |
| Call loans, stock exchange: | | | | | | |
| Range | 3 -5 | 2¾-5½ | 2¾-5 | 3 -5 | 3½-6 | 4 -6 |
| Time loans: [1] | | | | | | |
| 60 days | 4 -4¼ | 4 -4¼ | 3¾-4¼ | 3¾-4¼ | 4¼-4¾ | 4½-5 |
| 90 days | 4 -4¼ | 4 -4¼ | 3¾-4¼ | 3¾-4¼ | 4¼-4¾ | 4½-5 |
| 4 months | 4 -4½ | 4 -4½ | 4 -4¼ | 4 -4½ | 4½-5 | 4¾-5 |
| 5 months | 4 -4½ | 4 -4½ | 4 -4¼ | 4 -4½ | 4½-5 | 4¾-5 |
| 6 months | 4 -4½ | 4¼-4½ | 4¼ | 4¼-4½ | 4½-5 | 4¾-5 |
| Commercial paper: | | | | | | |
| Double names— | | | | | | |
| Choice 60 to 90 days | 4¼-4½ | 4 -4¼ | 3¾-4 | 3¾-4 | 3¾-4½ | 4¼-4½ |
| Single names— | | | | | | |
| Prime, 4 to 6 months | 4¼-4½ | 4 -4¼ | 3¾-4 | 3¾-4 | 3¾-4½ | 4¼-4½ |
| Good, 4 to 6 months | 4½-4¾ | 4¼-4½ | 4¼ | 4 -4¼ | 4¼-4½ | 4½-4¾ |

[1] These rates are for loans on mixed collateral. Loans against exclusively industrial collateral usually range at about one-fourth of 1 per cent higher.

Fluctuations in the rates for bankers' sterling bills, monthly from November, 1921, to October 31, 1922, inclusive, are shown in the following statement, also furnished by the Commercial and Financial Chronicle.

*Rates for sterling bills.*

| Date. | 60-day. | Sight. | Cable transfers. | Date. | 60-day. | Sight. | Cable transfers. |
|---|---|---|---|---|---|---|---|
| 1921. | | | | 1922. | | | |
| November... | 384 3/4-398 9/16 | 390 3/8-400 9/16 | 391 1/8-401 1/16 | April.......... | 435 1/4-440 7/8 | 437 1/4-442 7/8 | 437 5/8-442 3/4 |
| December.... | 399 3/4-422 1/4 | 401 3/4-424 1/4 | 402 1/4-424 1/4 | May.......... | 440-441 3/4 | 442-444 7/8 | 442 3/8-445 1/4 |
| | | | | June.......... | 434 1/4-449 1/16 | 437 1/2-451 1/16 | 437 7/8-451 7/16 |
| 1922. | | | | July.......... | 438 1/4-444 3/8 | 441 1/4-446 1/8 | 441 5/8-446 1/2 |
| January...... | 415-425 13/16 | 417-427 13/16 | 417 1/2-428 3/8 | August........ | 442 1/4-447 15/16 | 443 7/8-449 3/16 | 444 1/4-449 7/16 |
| February.... | 425 1/4-441 3/4 | 427 1/4-443 7/8 | 427 3/4-444 1/4 | September... | 434 1/2-445 1/4 | 436 1/8-447 3/8 | 436 3/8-447 5/8 |
| March........ | 424 1/4-442 1/2 | 426 13/16-444 1/2 | 427 1/16-444 7/8 | October...... | 436 11/16-446 3/8 | 438 3/16-447 7/8 | 438 7/16-448 1/8 |

A comparison of the range of rates for call loans, 60-day time loans, and two-name commercial paper loans in New York, annually from 1913 to 1922, is shown in the statement following.

*Range of rates for money in New York annually, 1913 to 1922.*

| | 1913 | | | | 1914 | | | | 1915 | | | | 1916 | | | | 1917 | | | |
|---|---|---|---|---|---|---|---|---|---|---|---|---|---|---|---|---|---|---|---|---|
| | Range for January. | High. | Low. | Range for December. | Range for January. | High. | Low. | Range for December. | Range for January. | High. | Low. | Range for December. | Range for January. | High. | Low. | Range for December. | Range for January. | High. | Low. | Range for December. |
| Call loans | 2½-6 | 10 | 1 | 2½-8 | 1½-10 | 10 | 1½ | 2½-5 | 1½-3 | 3 | 1 | 1½-2½ | 1½-3 | 15 | 1½ | 2¼-15 | 1½-3 | 10 | 1¼ | 3-6 |
| Time loans (60 days) | 3¼-5¼ | 6 | 2¾ | 4¾-5½ | 2½-5 | 8 | 2 | 3½-4¼ | 2½-3½ | 3½ | 2¼ | 2¼-2½ | 2½-2¾ | 4½ | 2½ | 4-4½ | 2½-4 | 5¾ | 2½ | 5¼-5½ |
| Commercial (2-name) | 4¼-6 | 6½ | 4¼ | 5¼-6 | 4-5¾ | 7 | 3¼ | 4-5 | 3½-4 | 4 | 2¾ | 3-3¼ | 3-3¼ | 4¼ | 3 | 3¾-4¼ | 3¼-4¼ | 5¾ | 3¼ | 5¼-5¾ |

| | 1918 | | | | 1919 | | | | 1920 | | | | 1921 | | | | 1922 | | | |
|---|---|---|---|---|---|---|---|---|---|---|---|---|---|---|---|---|---|---|---|---|
| | Range for January. | High. | Low. | Range for December. | Range for January. | High. | Low. | Range for December. | Range for January. | High. | Low. | Range for December. | Range for January. | High. | Low. | Range for December. | Range for January. | High. | Low. | Range (to Oct.). |
| Call loans | 2½-6 | 6 | 2 | 3½-6 | 3¾-6 | 30 | 2 | 5½-25 | 6-20 | 25 | 5 | 6-7 | 6-8 | 9 | 3½ | 4½-6 | 3-6 | 6 | 2¾ | 4-6 |
| Time loans (60 days) | 5-6 | 6 | 5 | 5½-6 | 5-5½ | 7 | 5 | 6-7 | 7-8 | 8¾ | 7 | 7-7½ | 6-7½ | 7½ | 5 | 5-5¼ | 4½-5¼ | 5¼ | 3¾ | 4½-5 |
| Commercial 2-name) | 5¼-5¾ | 6 | 5¼ | 5½-6 | 5-5¾ | 6 | 5 | 5¾-6 | 6 | 8 | 6 | 7¾-8 | 7½-8 | 8 | 5 | 5-5½ | 3¾-4 | 5¼ | 3¾ | 4¼-4½ |

## DISCOUNT AND INTEREST RATES.

In the table following, appearing in the Federal Reserve Board Bulletin of October, are presented actual discount and interest rates prevailing during the 30-day period ended September 15, 1922, in the various cities in which the several Federal reserve banks and their branches are located.

Discount and interest rates prevailing in various centers during 30-day period ended September 15, 1922 [1].

| District No. | City | Prime commercial paper — Customers' 30 to 60 days. H. L. C. | Customers' 4 to 6 months. H. L. C. | Open market. 30 to 60 days. H. L. C. | Open market. 4 to 6 months. H. L. C. | Interbank loans. H. L. C. | Bankers' acceptances 60 to 90 days. Indorsed. H. L. C. | Unindorsed. H. L. C. | Collateral loans—stock exchange. Demand. H. L. C. | 3 months. H. L. C. | 3 to 6 months. H. L. C. | Cattle loans. H. L. C. | Secured by warehouse receipts. H. L. C. | Ordinary loans to customers secured by Liberty bonds. H. L. C. |
|---|---|---|---|---|---|---|---|---|---|---|---|---|---|---|
| 1 | Boston | | | | | | | | | | | | | |
| 2 | New York [2] | | | | | | | | | | | | | |
| | Buffalo | | | | | | | | | | | | | |
| 3 | Philadelphia | | | | | | | | | | | | | |
| 4 | Cleveland | | | | | | | | | | | | | |
| | Pittsburgh | | | | | | | | | | | | | |
| | Cincinnati | | | | | | | | | | | | | |
| 5 | Richmond | | | | | | | | | | | | | |
| | Baltimore | | | | | | | | | | | | | |
| 6 | Atlanta | | | | | | | | | | | | | |
| | Birmingham | | | | | | | | | | | | | |
| | Jacksonville | | | | | | | | | | | | | |
| | New Orleans | | | | | | | | | | | | | |
| | Nashville | | | | | | | | | | | | | |
| 7 | Chicago | | | | | | | | | | | | | |
| | Detroit | | | | | | | | | | | | | |
| 8 | St. Louis | | | | | | | | | | | | | |
| | Louisville | | | | | | | | | | | | | |
| | Memphis | | | | | | | | | | | | | |
| | Little Rock | | | | | | | | | | | | | |
| 9 | Minneapolis | | | | | | | | | | | | | |
| | Helena | | | | | | | | | | | | | |
| 10 | Kansas City | | | | | | | | | | | | | |
| | Omaha | | | | | | | | | | | | | |
| | Denver | | | | | | | | | | | | | |
| | Oklahoma City | | | | | | | | | | | | | |
| 11 | Dallas | | | | | | | | | | | | | |
| | El Paso | | | | | | | | | | | | | |
| | Houston | | | | | | | | | | | | | |
| 12 | San Francisco | | | | | | | | | | | | | |
| | Portland | | | | | | | | | | | | | |
| | Seattle | | | | | | | | | | | | | |
| | Spokane | | | | | | | | | | | | | |
| | Salt Lake City | | | | | | | | | | | | | |
| | Los Angeles | | | | | | | | | | | | | |

[1] A comparison of discount and interest rates prevailing during the 30-day period ended September 15 and the 30-day period ended August 15, shows very little change. The only declines of any importance are in prime commercial paper to customers, interbank loans, and indorsed bankers' acceptances. Compared with the corresponding period last year, all rates continue to be lower.

[2] Rates for demand paper secured by prime bankers' acceptances, high 4½, low 3, customary 3½-4.

MONETARY STOCKS IN THE PRINCIPAL COUNTRIES OF THE WORLD.

[Omitted here, but to be found on p. 636 of this volume.]

## NEW YORK CLEARING HOUSE.

The transactions of the New York Clearing House for the year ended September 30, 1922, which comprises a membership of 43 banks with capital of $288,100,000, show an increase in the amount of clearings, although nine banks withdrew from membership during the year. The total clearings for the year ended September 30, 1922, were $213,326,385,752, compared with $204,082,339,000 for the year ended September 30, 1921. The average daily clearings during the year ended September 30, 1922, were $706,378,761, compared with $673,539,074 during the year ended September 30, 1921, while the average daily balances for the years 1922 and 1921 were $69,644,619 and $68,845,693, respectively. The percentage of balances to clearings for the year 1922 was 9.86 compared with 10.22 for 1921.

The clearing-house transactions of the Federal Reserve Bank of New York for the year ended September 30, 1922, are shown in the following statement, and in the appendix to the report of the Comptroller of the Currency volume, statements showing the exchanges of the clearing houses of the United States for years ended September 30, 1921 and 1922, and the transactions of the New York Clearing House Association for a period of 69 years, or since 1854, furnished through the courtesy of Manager W. J. Gilpin of the New York Clearing House Association, appear:

*Clearing-house transactions of the Federal Reserve Bank of New York for the year ended September 30, 1922.*

Debit exchanges............................................. $2,933,962,838.99
Credit exchanges............................................. 18,839,142,319.91
Credit balances............................................. 15,905,179,480.92

### CLEARING-HOUSE ASSOCIATIONS IN THE UNITED STATES.

Evidence of increased activities in connection with the enormous business transacted by the clearing houses of the United States is shown by the comparative statement of the exchanges of these clearing houses for the years ended September 30, 1921 and 1922, referred to in the preceding paragraph.

Although the number of associations was decreased from 216 in 1921 to 204 in 1922, the aggregate clearings during the year ended September 30, 1922, were $380,492,992,000, or an increase of $5,667,611,000 over the clearings for the year ended September 30, 1921.

In connection with the activities of the clearing houses throughout the United States for the year ended September 30, 1922, it is interesting to note, by reference to the following statement, the volume of transactions of the clearing houses in the 12 Federal reserve bank cities, and in other principal cities throughout the country where the transactions amounted to one billion dollars or more, that the net increase in the clearings of associations in the 12 Federal reserve bank cities for the year ended September 30, 1922, over September 30, 1921, was $7,012,825,000, while the reduction in the transactions of associations in 16 other principal cities was $1,391,287,000. The transactions of associations in 176 other cities, however, were increased during the year ended September 30, 1922, $46,073,000.

*Comparisons of the transactions of clearing house associations in the 12 Federal reserve bank cities and in other cities with transactions of $1,000,000,000 in the years ended Sept. 30, 1921 and 1922.*

[In thousands of dollars.]

| Clearing house at— | 1921 | 1922 | Increase. | Decrease. |
|---|---|---|---|---|
| Boston, Mass. | 14,932,519 | 15,630,440 | 697,921 | |
| New York, N. Y. | 204,082,339 | 213,326,386 | 9,244,047 | |
| Philadelphia, Pa. | 21,392,098 | 21,514,198 | 122,100 | |
| Cleveland, Ohio. | 5,329,087 | 4,732,214 | | 596,873 |
| Richmond, Va. | 2,224,552 | 2,214,589 | | 9,963 |
| Atlanta, Ga. | 2,305,292 | 2,101,402 | | 203,890 |
| Chicago, Ill. | 27,399,814 | 27,102,207 | | 297,607 |
| St. Louis, Mo. | 6,494,752 | 6,587,896 | 93,144 | |
| Minneapolis, Minn. | 3,858,960 | 3,266,626 | | 592,334 |
| Kansas City, Mo. | 8,274,866 | 6,728,345 | | 1,546,521 |
| Dallas, Tex. | 1,344,714 | 1,300,253 | | 44,461 |
| San Francisco, Calif. | 6,909,332 | 7,056,594 | 147,262 | |
| Total 12 Federal reserve bank cities | 304,548,325 | 311,561,150 | 10,304,474 | 3,291,649 |
| Other cities: | | | | |
| Pittsburgh, Pa. | 7,685,979 | 6,538,949 | | 1,147,030 |
| Detroit, Mich. | 4,887,555 | 5,074,622 | 187,067 | |
| Los Angeles, Calif. | 4,152,228 | 4,850,147 | 697,919 | |
| Baltimore, Md. | 4,074,724 | 3,830,961 | | 243,763 |
| Cincinnati, Ohio. | 2,974,869 | 2,888,682 | | 86,187 |
| New Orleans, La. | 2,391,297 | 2,266,898 | | 124,399 |
| Omaha, Nebr. | 2,094,297 | 1,897,986 | | 196,311 |
| Buffalo, N. Y. | 1,916,450 | 1,908,737 | | 7,713 |
| St. Paul, Minn. | 1,843,739 | 1,586,498 | | 257,241 |
| Portland, Oreg. | 1,599,518 | 1,563,491 | | 36,027 |
| Seattle, Wash. | 1,577,323 | 1,750,315 | 172,992 | |
| Milwaukee, Wis. | 1,500,031 | 1,512,244 | 12,213 | |
| Denver, Colo. | 1,623,221 | 1,523,239 | | 99,982 |
| Oklahoma City, Okla. | 1,288,165 | 1,083,736 | | 204,429 |
| Houston, Tex. | 1,287,500 | 1,200,712 | | 86,788 |
| Louisville, Ky. | 1,249,357 | 1,277,749 | 28,392 | |
| Total of 16 other principal cities | 42,146,253 | 40,754,966 | 1,098,583 | 2,489,870 |
| Total | 346,694,578 | 352,316,116 | 11,403,057 | 5,781,519 |
| Total all other cities (176) | 28,130,803 | 28,176,876 | 2,041,230 | 1,995,157 |
| Grand total of all cities (204) | 374,825,381 | 380,492,992 | 13,444,287 | 7,776,676 |

## BANKS IN THE DISTRICT OF COLUMBIA.

On June 30, 1922, there were 72 banks or institutions doing a banking business in the District of Columbia, under the supervision of the Comptroller of the Currency. The aggregate capital of these institutions was $21,614,000, the total individual deposits $200,567,075, and aggregate resources $268,376,755. The increase in the capital of these institutions during the fiscal year was $649,000, the increase in individual deposits $15,916,075, and the increase in resources $21,055,755.

Information referred to with respect to each class of institutions s shown in the following statement:

|  | Num-ber. | Capital. | Individual deposits.[1] | Aggregate resources. |
|---|---|---|---|---|
| National banks | 15 | $7,677,000 | $82,166,000 | $118,249,000 |
| Loan and trust companies | 6 | 10,400,000 | 56,74,000 | 77,566,000 |
| Savings banks | 29 | 3,537,000 | 30,972,000 | 37,683,000 |
| Building and loan associations | 22 | | [2] 30,555,075 | 34,878,755 |
| Total | 72 | 21,614,000 | 200,567,075 | 268,376,755 |

[1] Amount due to banks not included.          [2] Share payments mainly.

## EARNINGS, EXPENSES, AND DIVIDENDS OF SAVINGS BANKS AND TRUST COMPANIES IN THE DISTRICT OF COLUMBIA.

Evidence of a prosperous year for savings banks and trust companies in the District of Columbia is manifested by a comparison of the earnings, expenses, and dividends of these banks, shown in the following statement for fiscal years ended June 30, 1921 and 1922.

In the fiscal year ended June 30, 1922, the gross earnings of these banks amounted to $6,754,000, and show an increase of $312,000 over gross earnings for the prior year. Interest and discount collected amounted to $5,272,000, as compared with $5,258,000 for the previous year. Profit on foreign exchange, commissions, and earnings from insurance premiums, etc., amounted to $169,000, compared with $98,000 for 1921, while exchange and collection charges were $4,000 in excess of the amount earned in the previous year, and amounted to $25,000.

The expenses of these banks during the year amounted to $4,783,000, an increase of $346,000 over the previous year. The largest item charged against expense was on account of interest on deposits, amounting to $1,695,000, and the next largest item was incident to salaries and wages paid, to the amount of $1,514,000. Interest and discount on borrowed money amounted to $63,000. Taxes were paid to the amount of $623,000 and other miscellaneous expenses totaled $888,000. Net earnings for the year, with the addition of $110,000 recovered on charged off assets amounted to $2,081,000, compared with $2,050,000 for the previous fiscal year.

During the last year $155,000 was charged off by these banks on account of loans and discounts, $135,000 on account of bonds and securities, $7,000 on account of foreign exchange and other losses to the amount of $136,000, making a total of $433,000, which amount deducted from the net earnings of $2,081,000 leaves a net addition to the profits of these banks of $1,648,000, or $207,000 in excess of the net addition to profits during the prior year.

The amount of dividends declared during the fiscal year ended June 30, 1922, was $1,092,000, compared with $1,037,000 for the fiscal year ended June 30, 1921.

[In thousands of dollars.]

| | June 30, 1921, 33 banks. | June 30, 1922, 35 banks. |
|---|---|---|
| Capital stock | 13,372 | 13,937 |
| Total surplus fund | 6,108 | 6,507 |
| Dividends declared | 1,037 | 1,092 |
| Gross earnings: | | |
| (a) Interest and discount | 5,258 | 5,272 |
| (b) Exchange and collection charges | 21 | 25 |
| (c) Foreign exchange profits | 14 | 39 |
| (d) Commissions and earnings from insurance premiums and the negotiation of real estate loans | 84 | 130 |
| (e) Other earnings | 1,065 | 1,288 |
| Total | 6,442 | 6,754 |
| Expenses paid: | | |
| (a) Salaries and wages | 1,411 | 1,514 |
| (b) Interest and discount on borrowed money | 101 | 63 |
| (c) Interest on deposits | 1,644 | 1,695 |
| (d) Taxes | 597 | 623 |
| (e) Contributions to American National Red Cross | | |
| (f) Other expenses | 684 | 888 |
| Total | 4,437 | 4,783 |
| Net earnings during the year | 2,005 | 1,971 |
| Recoveries on charged-off assets | 45 | 110 |
| Total | 2,050 | 2,081 |
| Losses charged off: | | |
| (a) On loans and discounts | 83 | 155 |
| (b) On bonds, securities, etc | 425 | 135 |
| (c) Other losses | 97 | 136 |
| (d) On foreign exchange | 1 | 7 |
| Total | 609 | 433 |
| Net addition to profits during the year | 1,441 | 1,648 |

BUILDING AND LOAN ASSOCIATIONS IN THE DISTRICT OF COLUMBIA.

On June 30, 1922, there were 22 building and loan associations in the District of Columbia, with aggregate resources of $34,879,000, the activities of which are under the supervision of the Comptroller of the Currency, in accordance with the provisions of the act of March 4, 1909.

Reports for the 6 months period ended June 30, 1922, show that these associations had borrowing members to the number of 13,501, compared with 12,786 for the six months ended June 30, 1921, and nonborrowing members to the number of 35,754, compared with 34,873 last year. The rate of interest paid by borrowing members for accommodations extended was 6 per cent. The total operating expenses for the six months ended June 30, 1922, were $185,200.89, of which amount $110,973.25 was on account of salaries paid officers and other employees. These items of expense compare with $182,162.46 and $103,598.24, respectively, for the 6 months period ended June 30, 1921. Fifteen associations operate on the permanent plan, 6 on the serial plan, and 1 operates on the terminating plan. Nineteen associations require installment payments of $1, two associations, $2, and one association, $2.50.

Supplementary reports received from these associations show that during the year ended June 30, 1922, loans to the amount of $1,434,000 were made in connection with 279 transactions incident to the building of homes; 2,508 loans amounting to $8,610,000 were made for the purpose of purchasing homes already built; and 525 loans, amounting to $387,000, were made for the purpose of enabling persons accommodated to make improvements on real estate already acquired.

By reference to the following statement it will be noted that the loans of these associations have increased since June 30, 1909, from $13,511,587 to $33,233,000 June 30, 1922; installments on shares have increased in this period from $11,996,357 to $30,506,000 and aggregate resources from $14,393,927 to $34,879,000:

| Year. | Number of associations. | Loans. | Installments on shares. | Aggregate resources. |
|---|---|---|---|---|
| June 30— | | | | |
| 1909 | 22 | $13,511,587 | $11,996,357 | $14,393,927 |
| 1910 | 19 | 14,415,832 | 13,213,644 | 15,250,731 |
| 1911 | 19 | 14,965,220 | 13,324,217 | 16,017,405 |
| 1912 | 20 | 16,004,700 | 14,529,977 | 17,100,293 |
| 1913 | 20 | 17,398,010 | 16,453,044 | 18,438,294 |
| 1914 | 20 | 18,582,156 | 17,113,899 | 19,029,260 |
| 1915 | 20 | 19,524,065 | 17,866,337 | 20,655,614 |
| 1916 | 19 | 20,186,662 | 18,668,808 | 21,611,007 |
| 1917 | 19 | 20,951,089 | 19,413,266 | 22,264,005 |
| 1918 | 20 | 21,567,904 | 20,252,005 | 23,215,027 |
| 1919 | 20 | 23,654,000 | 22,463,000 | 25,699,000 |
| 1920 | 21 | 27,398,000 | 25,373,000 | 29,322,000 |
| 1921 | 24 | 29,520,000 | 27,593,000 | 31,683,000 |
| 1922 | 22 | 33,233,000 | 30,506,000 | 34,879,000 |

## BANKS OTHER THAN NATIONAL.

### STATE (COMMERCIAL) BANKS.

The returns with respect to the condition of State (commercial) banks as of June 30, 1922, show a reduction in the number of reporting banks during the year, or since June 30, 1921, of 643 banks with an incident reduction of $1,134,693,000 in aggregate resources.

Loans and discounts declined during the year to $7,934,123,000, the decrease since June 30, 1921, amounting to $1,136,835,000. Overdrafts were reduced by $8,018,000 and amounted to $60,225,000. Investments were reduced from $2,438,057,000 June 30, 1921, to $2,304,891,000 June 30, 1922.

Banking houses, furniture, and fixtures amounted to $328,767,000, compared with $330,005,000 June 30, 1921, while other real estate owned was reported to the amount of $72,761,000, the increase for the year being $17,417,000. The amount due these banks from other banks and bankers, including lawful reserve with Federal reserve banks, of member banks, and from so-called "reserve agents" of banks not members of the Federal reserve system, was $1,443,117,000, showing an increase over the amount due June 30, 1921, of $49,334,000. Checks and other miscellaneous cash items, including exchanges for clearing house, amounted to $354,874,000, showing an increase over the total of these items June 30, 1921, of $76,581,000. Total cash on hand was reduced during the year $37,005,000 and amounted to $309,584,000.

Miscellaneous assets were reported to the amount of $256,064,000, or $38,237,000 more than on June 30, 1921.

Total resources amounted to $13,064,406,000, compared with $14,199,099,000 June 30, 1921.

Capital stock of these banks was $1,014,248,000 and showed a reduction since 1921 of $48,797,000. Surplus was likewise reduced to the extent of $18,699,000 and amounted to $561,131,000. Undivided profits were reported at $210,536,000, compared with $211,-882,000 in 1921.

The deposit liability of State (commercial) banks to other banks and bankers was $387,657,000, compared with $337,373,000 in 1921. The liability incident to certified checks and cashiers' checks outstanding was $69,803,000, the reduction during the year amounting to $64,518,000. Individual deposits declined to $10,107,597,000 and were $567,870,000 less than last year. United States deposits amounted to only $7,734,000 and showed a reduction during the year of $32,285,000.

The liability of these banks on account of borrowed money represented by notes and bills rediscounted and bills payable was considerably reduced during the year. Notes and bills rediscounted were reported at $111,651,000, compared with $257,450,000 in 1921, and bills payable were reduced from $560,839,000 to $311,149,000.

Other liabilities amounted to $282,900,000 and showed a reduction of $55,973,000 during the year.

The following summary shows resources and liabilities June 30, 1922, with classifications of loans and discounts, investments, cash on hand, and deposits:

*Summary of reports of condition of 18,232 State (commercial) banks in the United States and island possessions at the close of business June 30, 1922.*

[In thousands of dollars]

### RESOURCES.

| | | |
|---|---:|---:|
| Loans and discounts (including rediscounts): | | |
| On demand (secured by collateral other than real estate). | 729, 207 | |
| On demand (not secured by collateral)................... | 95, 157 | |
| On time (secured by collateral other than real estate).... | 523, 225 | |
| On time (not secured by collateral)..................... | 556, 269 | |
| Secured by farm land.................................. | 133, 061 | |
| Secured by other real estate........................... | 967, 865 | |
| Not classified........................................ | 4, 929, 339 | |
| Total.......................................... | | 7, 934, 123 |
| Overdrafts.................................................... | | 60, 225 |
| Investments (including premiums on bonds): | | |
| United States Government securities..................... | 390, 929 | |
| State, county, and municipal bonds..................... | 220, 551 | |
| Railroad bonds........................................ | 66, 649 | |
| Bonds of other public service corporations (including street and interurban railway bonds)................. | 56, 783 | |
| Other bonds, stocks, warrants, etc..................... | 1, 569, 979 | |
| Total......................................... | | 2, 304, 891 |
| Banking house (including furniture and fixtures)........................ | | 328, 767 |
| Other real estate owned................................................. | | 72, 761 |
| Due from banks......................................................... | | 862, 051 |
| Lawful reserve with Federal reserve banks or other reserve agents........ | | 581, 066 |
| Checks and other cash items............................................ | | 231, 013 |
| Exchanges for clearing house........................................... | | 123, 861 |

Cash on hand:
 Gold coin.............................................. 12, 939
 Silver coin............................................ 12, 608
 Paper currency........................................ 120, 704
 Nickels and cents..................................... 1, 583
 Not classified........................................ 161, 750

  Total........................................ 309, 584
Other resources............................................ 256, 064

  Total resources.............................. 13, 064, 406

LIABILITIES.

Capital stock paid in...................................... 1, 014, 248
Surplus................................................... 561, 131
Undivided profits (less expenses and taxes paid)........... 210, 536
Due to all banks.......................................... 387, 657
Certified checks and cashiers' checks...................... 69, 803
Individual deposits (including dividends unpaid and postal savings):
 Demand deposits—
  Individual deposits subject to check............... 3, 669, 927
  Demand certificates of deposit..................... 237, 352
  Dividends unpaid................................. 9, 744
 Time deposits—
  Savings deposits, or deposits in interest or savings de-
   partment...................................... 2, 649, 660
  Time certificates of deposit...................... 1, 177, 442
 Postal savings deposits............................... 4, 367
 Not classified........................................ 2, 359, 105

  Total........................................ 10, 107, 597
United States deposits (exclusive of postal savings)....... 7, 734
Notes and bills rediscounted.............................. 111, 651
Bills payable (including advances received from War Finance Corporation
 and certificates of deposit representing money borrowed)............. 311, 149
Other liabilities.......................................... 282, 900

  Total........................................ 13, 064, 406

LOAN AND TRUST COMPANIES.

The returns from loan and trust companies for the current year show an increase of 76 in the number reporting over last year. The resources of these companies, amounting to $8,533,850,000, likewise show an increase over the aggregate for 1921 of $352,758,000. The returns from loan and trust companies for the current year, however, are more complete than heretofore, which fact is accountable to a certain extent for the increases referred to.

Loans and discounts were increased from $4,274,581,000 June 30, 1921, to $4,342,895,000. Overdrafts amounted to $2,603,000, compared with $2,541,000 in 1921. Investments in United States Government securities and other miscellaneous bonds, stocks, and securities were increased during the year from $1,942,676,000 to $2,311,101,000.

Banking houses, furniture, and fixtures were carried at $198,-267,000, showing an increase over the amount re orted in 1921 of $9,394,000, while other real estate owned was carriedpat $38,424,000, compared with $26,163,000 in 1921.

Balances due from correspondent banks and bankers were increased from $780,214,000 to $895,922,000 June 30, 1922. Checks and other miscellaneous cash items, including exchanges for clearing house, were increased $84,616,000 during the year and amounted to $315,381,000.

Cash in vaults of these companies was less by $55,638,000 than a year ago and totaled $117,079,000.

Other miscellaneous assets aggregated $312 178,000, compared with $562,562,000 in 1921.

Capital stock was increased from $515,533,000 in 1921 to $532,-316,000, while in this period surplus was increased from $537,947,000 to $562,731,000 and undivided profits from $111,614,000 to $117,513,000.

The deposit liability of these companies to other banks and bankers was $351,547,000, an increase over 1921 of $32,387,000. The liability on account of certified checks and cashiers' checks outstandingywas $31,109,000 and showed a reduction during the year of $112,035,000. A decided increase in the amount of individual deposits, which rose from $5,611,787.000 in 1921 to $6,495,-928,000, is noted. United States deposits declined during the year from $100,951,000 to $13,800,000.

The liability for borrowings incident to the rediscount of notes and bills and bills payable shows considerable reductions. Notes and bills reported June 30, 1921, at $132,778,000 were reduced to $42,237,000 and bills payable were reduced in this period from $173,186,000 to $61,333,000. Other liabilities amounted to $325,-336,000, compared with $534,992,000 in 1921.

The following statement shows the resources and liabilities of loan and trust companies June 30, 1922, with classifications of loans and discounts, investments, cash on hand, and deposits:

*Summary of reports of condition of 1,550 loan and trust companies in the United States at the close of business June 30, 1922.*

[In thousand-dollars.]

RESOURCES.

| | | |
|---|---:|---:|
| Loans and discounts (including rediscounts): | | |
| On demand (secured by collateral other than real estate)... | 659,047 | |
| On demand (not secured by collateral)................... | 126,372 | |
| On time (secured by collateral other than real estate)..... | 288,544 | |
| On time (not secured by collateral)........:............ | 597,816 | |
| Secured by farm land....................................... | 19,804 | |
| Secured by other real estate............................. | 474,120 | |
| Not classified.......................................... | 2,177,192 | |
| Total......................................... | | 4,342,895 |
| Overdrafts...................................... | | 2,603 |
| Investments (including premiums on bonds): | | |
| United States Government securities...................... | 318,498 | |
| State, county, and municipal bonds...................... | 87,161 | |
| Railroad bonds......................................... | 248,165 | |
| Bonds of other public service corporations (including street and interurban railway bonds)........................ | 168,545 | |
| Other bonds, stocks, warrants, etc...................... | 1,488,732 | |
| Total...........:.................................. | | 2,311,101 |
| Banking house (including furniture and fixtures)....................... | | 198,267 |
| Other real estate owned...., ............................. | | 38,424 |
| Due from banks....:.....,.................................. | | 327,886 |
| Lawful reserve with Federal reserve bank or other reserve agents........ | | 568,036 |
| Checks and other cash items.,............................. | | 278,377 |
| Exchanges for clearing house............................. | | 37,004 |

Cash on hand:
```
Gold coin................................................   5,576
Silver coin..............................................   4,498
Paper currency...........................................  54,577
Nickels and cents........................................   4,861
Not classified...........................................  47,567
```

```
Total...............................................  117,079
Other resources..........................................  312,178
```

```
Total resources.....................................  8,533,850
```

### LIABILITIES.

```
Capital stock paid in....................................  532,316
Surplus..................................................  562,731
Undivided profits (less expenses and taxes paid).........  117,513
Due to all banks.........................................  351,547
Certified checks and cashiers' checks....................   31,109
Individual deposits (including dividends unpaid and postal savings):
  Demand deposits—
    Individual deposits subject to check.........  2,053,254
    Demand certificates of deposit...............     72,927
    Dividends unpaid.............................      5,448
  Time deposits—
    Savings deposits, or deposits in interest or savings
      department.............................  1,382,748
    Time certificates of deposit...............    136,768
    Postal savings deposits....................      6,041
    Not classified.............................  2,838,742
```

```
Total...............................................  6,495,928
United States deposits (exclusive of postal savings).....   13,800
Notes and bills rediscounted.............................   42,237
Bills payable (including advances received from War Finance Corporation
  and certificates of deposit representing money borrowed)  61,333
Other liabilities........................................  325,336
```

```
Total liabilities...................................  8,533,850
```

### PRINCIPAL ITEMS OF RESOURCES AND LIABILITIES OF LOAN AND TRUST COMPANIES IN JUNE OF EACH YEAR, 1914 TO 1922.

The following table shows the number of trust companies and principal items of resources and liabilities on or about June 30 of each year from 1914 to 1922, inclusive.

[In millions of dollars.]

| Year. | Number. | Loans.[1] | Investments. | Capital. | Surplus and profits. | All deposits. | Aggregate resources. |
|---|---|---|---|---|---|---|---|
| 1914 | 1,564 | 2,905.7 | 1,261.3 | 462.2 | 564.4 | 4,289.1 | 5,489.5 |
| 1915 | 1,664 | 3,048.6 | 1,349.6 | 476.8 | 577.4 | 4,604.0 | 5,873.1 |
| 1916 | 1,606 | 3,704.3 | 1,605.4 | 475.8 | 605.5 | 5,732.4 | 7,028.2 |
| 1917 | 1,608 | 4,311.7 | 1,789.7 | 505.5 | 641.8 | 6,413.1 | 7,899.8 |
| 1918 | 1,669 | 4,403.8 | 2,115.6 | 525.2 | 646.9 | 6,493.3 | 8,317.4 |
| 1919 | 1,377 | 4,091.0 | 2,069.9 | 450.4 | 588.6 | 6,157.2 | 7,959.9 |
| 1920 | 1,408 | 4,601.5 | 1,902.1 | 475.7 | 612.1 | 6,518.0 | 8,320.0 |
| 1921 | 1,474 | 4,277.1 | 1,942.6 | 515.5 | 649.5 | 6,175.0 | 8,181.0 |
| 1922 | 1,550 | 4,345.4 | 2,311.1 | 532.3 | 680.2 | 6,861.2 | 8,533.8 |

[1] Includes overdrafts.

## STOCK SAVINGS BANKS.

Information relative to stock savings banks is more complete for the current year than that heretofore received, the number of these banks, according to the returns, being increased from 978, with resources of $557,910.000 June 30, 1921, to 1,066, with resources of $1,583,922,000 June 30, 1922.

Loans and discounts were increased during the year $621,723,000 and amounted to $1,051,310,000. Overdrafts were increased from $361,000 to $498,000.

Investments of these banks, amounting to $325,687,000, show an increase of $267,910,000 over the amount reported in 1921. Banking houses, furniture, and fixtures carried at $14,611,000, June 30, 1921, were reported at $43,770,000 June 30, 1922, while other real estate owned was increased from $1,500,000 to $6,837,000. Balances on the books of other banks and bankers to the credit of stock savings banks were greater by $74,237,000 than a year ago, and amounted to $116,382,000. Checks and other miscellaneous cash items, including exchanges for clearing house, amounted to $6,576,000, compared with $391,000 in 1921. Cash in the vaults of these banks was increased from $11,013,000 in 1921 to $28,001,000.

Other resources show an increase during the year of $4,336,000 and amounted to $4,861,000.

Capital stock was $79, 850,000, or $39,948,000 greater than in 1921. Surplus funds amounted to $41,180,000 compared with $19,210,000 a year ago, and undivided profits of $18,995,000 show an increase in this period of $9,779,000.

Balances due to other banks and bankers were increased from $393,000 to $1,336,000, and the liability for certified checks and cashiers' checks outstanding was increased from $226,000 to $557,000 during the year. Individual deposits were increased from $442,851,000 in 1921 to $1,401,742,000, while United States deposits show an increase of $3,626,000 over the amount reported in 1921.

Notes and bills rediscounted show a reduction of $25,000 during the year, and amounted to $61,000, and the liability for bills payable was reduced from $40,411,000 to $29,355,000. Other liabilities amounted to $7,110,000, and were $1,605,000 greater than on June 30, 1921.

The resources and liabilities of stock savings banks, with classifications of loans and discounts, investments, cash and deposits, June 30, 1922, also a comparative statement of the number of stock savings banks in each State, the number of depositors, the amount of individual deposits, the average amount due each depositor, and the per cent rate of interest paid for years ended June 30, 1921 and 1922, are shown in the following statements:

*Summary of reports of condition of 1,066 stock savings banks in the United States at the close of business June 30, 1922.*

[In thousands of dollars.]

## RESOURCES.

Loans and discounts (including rediscounts):

| | |
|---|---:|
| On demand (secured by collateral other than real estate) | 9,884 |
| On demand (not secured by collateral) | 1,153 |
| On time (secured by collateral other than real estate) | 3,958 |
| On time (not secured by collateral) | 18,049 |
| Secured by farm land | 2,920 |
| Secured by other real estate | 573,667 |
| Not classified | 441,679 |
| Total | 1,051,310 |
| Overdrafts | 498 |

Investments (including premiums on bonds):

| | |
|---|---:|
| United States Government securities | 21,414 |
| State, county, and municipal bonds | 5,106 |
| Railroad bonds | 12,518 |
| Bonds of other public service corporations (including street and interurban railway bonds) | 3,116 |
| Other bonds, stocks, warrants, etc | 283,533 |
| Total | 325,687 |
| Banking house (including furniture and fixtures) | 43,770 |
| Other real estate owned | 6,837 |
| Due from banks | 98,188 |
| Lawful reserve with Federal reserve bank or other reserve agents | 18,194 |
| Checks and other cash items | 4,184 |
| Exchanges for clearing house | 2,392 |

Cash on hand:

| | |
|---|---:|
| Gold coin | 111 |
| Silver coin | 80 |
| Paper currency | 1,000 |
| Nickels and cents | |
| Not classified | 26,810 |
| Total | 28,001 |
| Other resources | 4,861 |
| Total resources | 1,583,922 |

## LIABILITIES.

| | |
|---|---:|
| Capital stock paid in | 79,850 |
| Surplus | 41,180 |
| Undivided profits (less expenses and taxes paid) | 18,995 |
| Due to all banks | 1,336 |
| Certified checks and cashiers' checks | 557 |

Individual deposits (including dividends unpaid and postal savings):

Demand deposits—

| | |
|---|---:|
| Individual deposits subject to check | 17,167 |
| Demand certificates of deposit | 495 |
| Dividends unpaid | 55 |

Time deposits—

| | |
|---|---:|
| Savings deposits, or deposits in interest or savings department | 439,016 |
| Time certificates of deposit | 2,950 |
| Postal savings deposits | 4 |
| Not classified | 942,055 |
| Total | 1,401,742 |
| United States deposits (exclusive of postal savings) | 3,736 |
| Notes and bills rediscounted | 61 |
| Bills payable (including advances received from War Finance Corporation and certificates of deposit representing money borrowed) | 29,355 |
| Other liabilities | 7,110 |
| Total liabilities | 1,583,922 |

Number of stock savings banks, number of depositors, individual deposits, and average deposit account, by States, June 30, 1921 and 1922.

[In thousands of dollars.]

| State.[1] | 1921 | | | | | 1922 | | | | |
|---|---|---|---|---|---|---|---|---|---|---|
| | Number of banks. | Depositors. | Deposits. | Average due each depositor. | Per cent rate of interest paid. | Number of banks. | Depositors. | Deposits. | Average due each depositor. | Per cent rate of interest paid. |
| New Hampshire | 11 | 32,993 | 13,499 | 409.15 | [2] 4.00 | 11 | 33,448 | 14,030 | 419.46 | [2] 4.00 |
| New Jersey | 1 | 42,729 | 20,905 | 459.25 | 3.50 | 1 | 43,900 | 21,118 | 481.05 | 3.50 |
| Pennsylvania | | | | | | 1 | 3,714 | 2,012 | 541.73 | 3.00 |
| District of Columbia | 26 | 88,568 | 27,102 | 306.00 | [2] 3.00 | 29 | 90,305 | 30,972 | 342.97 | 3.31 |
| Michigan | | | | | | 4 | 37,887 | 9,236 | 243.78 | 4.00 |
| Iowa | 928 | 893,664 | 358,951 | 401.66 | 4.00 | [2] 908 | 874,384 | 358,328 | 409.81 | 4.00 |
| Wyoming | 3 | 4,087 | 1,706 | 417.42 | 4.00 | 3 | 2,494 | 1,665 | 647.60 | 4.00 |
| Oregon | 5 | 8,422 | 3,781 | 448.94 | 3.60 | 6 | 9,180 | 3,792 | 413.07 | 3.75 |
| California | | | | | | [4] 98 | 1,736,285 | 940,833 | 541.87 | [6] 4.00 |
| Utah | 3 | 45,806 | 15,669 | 342.71 | 3.72 | 3 | 46,292 | 15,758 | 541.87 | 3.75 |
| Nevada | | | | | | 1 | 3,050 | 2,793 | 915.74 | 4.00 |
| Arizona | 1 | 2,312 | 1,208 | 522.49 | 4.00 | 1 | [5] 2,197 | [5] 1,205 | 548.48 | 4.00 |
| Total, United States | 978 | 1,118,583 | 442,851 | 395.90 | | 1,066 | 2,883,136 | 1,401,742 | 486.19 | |

[1] No separate returns received from stock savings banks in any other States.
[2] Generally.
[3] Returns as of June 10, 1922.
[4] Includes business of branches.
[5] Estimated.
[6] Includes due to banks.

## MUTUAL SAVINGS BANKS.

Returns were received from 619 mutual savings banks June 30, 1922, with resources of $6,351,648,000, showing an increase in the number of reporting banks of 4 since June 30, 1921, and an increase in resources of $311,527,000.

Loans and discounts, including overdrafts, were increased from $2,809,805,000 to $3,002,746,000. The investments of these banks amounted to $3,007,293,000 and showed an increase over the amount reported in 1921 of $118,322,000.

Banking houses, furniture, and fixtures were reported at $49,084,000, compared with $46,171,000 in 1921, and other real estate owned showed a reduction in this period of $1,070,000, the amount June 30, 1922, being $10,630,000.

Balances due from other banks and bankers amounted to $185,903,000, the increase during the year amounting to $14,161,000. Checks and other miscellaneous cash items, including exchanges for clearing house, totaled $1,353,000, and were reduced during the year to the amount of $1,346,000.

Cash on hand was $7,454,000 greater than on June 30, 1921, and amounted to $44,883,000. Other miscellaneous assets show a reduction during the year of $21,848,000 and amounted to $49,756,000.

The surplus funds of these banks, reported at $366,420,000 in 1921, were increased to $468,193,000, and undivided profits were increased during this period from $79,920,000 to $92,196,000.

The aggregate deposits of these banks, consisting principally of savings deposits, were $5,779,795,000, the amount of increase during the year being $204,477,000.

Liabilities incident to notes and bills rediscounted and bills payable show a reduction of $101,000 during the year, and amounted to $754,000.

Other liabilities were $10,710,000, compared with $17,608,000 in 1921.

The resources and liabilities of these banks June 30, 1922, are shown in the following statement, with classifications of loans and discounts, investments, cash and deposits:

*Summary of reports of condition of 619 mutual savings banks in the United States at the close of business June 30, 1922.*

[In thousands of dollars.]

### RESOURCES.

Loans and discounts (including rediscounts):

| | |
|---|---|
| On demand (secured by collateral other than real estate)... | 21,181 |
| On demand (not secured by collateral)...................... | 4,827 |
| On time (secured by collateral other than real estate)...... | 98,296 |
| On time (not secured by collateral)........................ | 51,603 |
| Secured by farm land...................................... | 40,232 |
| Secured by other real estate.............................. | 905,313 |
| Not classified............................................ | 1,879,973 |
|     Total................................................. | 3,001,425 |
| Overdrafts................................................... | 1,321 |

Investments (including premiums on bonds):
   United States Government securities......................... 477,421
   State, county, and municipal bonds......................... 252,382
   Railroad bonds............................................. 604,223
   Bonds of other public-service corporations (including street
     and interurban railway bonds).......................... 140,554
   Other bonds, stocks, warrants, etc........................ 1,532,713

     Total............................................................. 3,007,293
Banking house (including furniture and fixtures)........................ 49,084
Other real estate owned................................................. 10,630
Due from banks......................................................... 171,639
Lawful reserve with Federal reserve bank or other reserve agents......... 14,264
Checks and other cash items............................................. 1,274
Exchanges for clearing house............................................ 79
Cash on hand:
   Gold coin................................................. 929
   Silver coin............................................... 118
   Paper currency........................................... 14,077
   Nickels and cents......................................... 16
   Not classified........................................... 29,743

     Total............................................................ 44,883
Other resources........................................................ 49,756

     Total resources.................................................. 6,351,648

### LIABILITIES.

Surplus................................................................ [1] 468,193
Undivided profits (less expenses and taxes paid)........................ 92,196
Due to all banks........................................................ 264
Certified checks and cashiers' checks................................... 24
Individual deposits (including dividends unpaid and postal
 savings):
  Demand deposits—
    Individual deposits subject to check................... 41,549
    Demand certificates of deposit.......................
    Dividends unpaid...................................... 653
  Time deposits—
    Savings deposits, or deposits in interest or savings
     department........................................ 5,686,603
    Time certificates of deposit.......................... 117
  Postal savings deposits.............................................
  Not classified....................................... 50,584

     Total....................................................... 5,779,506
United States deposits (exclusive of postal savings)..................... 1
Notes and bills rediscounted........................................... 107
Bills payable (including advances received from War Finance Corporation
 and certificates of deposit representing money borrowed)................ 647
Other liabilities....................................................... 10,710

     Total liabilities................................................ 6,351,648

### DEPOSITORS AND DEPOSITS IN MUTUAL SAVINGS BANKS.

An analysis of the following comparative statement, showing the
number of mutual savings banks in each State, the number of depositors, the amount of individual deposits, the average amount due each
depositor, and the rate of interest paid June 30, 1921 and 1922, dis-
closes a notable increase in the number of depositors and deposits in
these banks during the past year. Mutual savings banks are oper-

---

[1] Includes $350,000 stock of two stock savings banks.

ted principally in the New England States, the largest number eing in the State of Massachusetts, the returns from which State how a marked increase, both in the number of depositors and in he amount of deposits. The next largest number of banks is cred-ed to the State of New York, the returns from which State likewise how increases in the number of depositors and the amount of eposits.

From the statement referred to it will be noted the total number f depositors in this class of banks, including returns from two stock avings banks in the State of Minnesota, June 30, 1922, was 9,655,861, r 36,101 more than on June 30, 1921, while the amount of deposits as increased from $5,575,147,000 to $5,779,506,000; the average mount due each depositor was $598.55, compared with $579.58 in 921. The general interest rate paid these banks on deposits is 4 per ent.

**Number of mutual savings banks, number of depositors, individual deposits, and average deposit account, by States, June 30, 1921, and 1922.**

[In thousands of dollars.]

| State | 1921 | | | | | 1922 | | | | |
|---|---|---|---|---|---|---|---|---|---|---|
| | Number of banks | Depositors | Deposits | Average due each depositor | Per cent rate of interest paid | Number of banks | Depositors | Deposits | Average due each depositor | Per cent rate of interest paid |
| Maine | 42 | 237,556 | 106,603 | 448.75 | 3.96 | 43 | [1] 237,531 | 105,324 | 443.41 | 4.00 |
| New Hampshire | 45 | 230,534 | 120,157 | 521.21 | 4.00 | 45 | 233,374 | 123,340 | 528.68 | [2] 4.00 |
| Vermont | 20 | 122,627 | 46,648 | 543.50 | 4.26 | 20 | 122,176 | 68,082 | 557.25 | 4.375 |
| Massachusetts | 197 | 2,574,169 | 1,235,847 | 480.10 | 4.54 | 195 | 2,611,057 | 1,274,594 | 488.15 | 4.405 |
| Rhode Island | 15 | 182,195 | 118,051 | 647.94 | 4.00 | [3] 14 | 182,706 | 120,843 | 661.41 | 4.00 |
| Connecticut | 80 | 787,013 | 419,753 | 533.35 | 4.00 | 79 | 733,961 | 418,980 | 570.85 | 4.18 |
| Total New England States | 399 | 4,134,094 | 2,067,059 | 500.00 | | 396 | 4,120,805 | 2,111,203 | 512.33 | |
| New York | 143 | 3,854,090 | 2,648,251 | 687.13 | [2] 4.00 | 144 | 3,915,912 | 2,791,353 | 712.82 | [2] 4.00 |
| New Jersey | 26 | 357,541 | 183,254 | 512.54 | 3.75 | 26 | 360,911 | 185,111 | 512.90 | 3.77 |
| Pennsylvania | 10 | 559,025 | 307,241 | 549.60 | 3.00 to 4.00 | 9 | 320,535 | 306,739 | 580.28 | 3.00 to 4.25 |
| Delaware | 2 | 43,416 | 19,238 | 443.11 | 4.00 | 2 | 42,561 | 19,031 | 447.14 | 4.00 |
| Maryland | 17 | 278,259 | 126,686 | 455.28 | 3.50 | 17 | 279,311 | 129,811 | 454.75 | 3.75 |
| Total Eastern States | 198 | 5,092,331 | 3,284,670 | 645.02 | 4.50 | 198 | 5,119,230 | 3,432,045 | 670.42 | |
| West Virginia (total Southern States) | [1] 1 | 7,052 | 2,209 | 321.75 | | | | | | |
| Ohio | 3 | 106,090 | 68,450 | 645.21 | 3.83 | 3 | 101,467 | 65,539 | 645.91 | 4.00 |
| Indiana | 5 | [4] 33,897 | 16,455 | 483.44 | 4.00 | 5 | 32,459 | 16,121 | 496.66 | 4.00 |
| Wisconsin | 7 | 13,176 | 4,377 | 332.17 | [2] 4.00 | 6 | 12,725 | 3,979 | 312.09 | 4.30 |
| Minnesota | 9 | 153,638 | 58,654 | 381.77 | 4.25 | [3] 9 | 159,205 | 59,817 | 375.72 | 4.00 |
| Total Middle Western States | 24 | 306,801 | 147,936 | 482.19 | | 23 | 305,836 | 145,456 | 475.57 | |
| Washington | 1 | 78,982 | 73,213 | 926.96 | 4.00 | 1 | 34,714 | 17,184 | 495.02 | 5.00 |
| California | | | | | | 1 | 75,256 | 73,618 | 978.23 | [7] 4.00 |
| Total Pacific States | 1 | 78,982 | 73,213 | 926.96 | | 2 | 109,970 | 90,802 | 825.70 | |
| Total United States | 623 | 9,619,260 | 5,575,147 | 579.53 | | 619 | 9,655,801 | 5,779,506 | 598.55 | |

[1] As of Sept., 1921.
[2] Generally.
[3] Includes business of branches.
[4] Bank dissolved, 1922.
[5] Jan. 1, 1921.
[6] Includes stock savings banks.
[7] Approximately.

## MUTUAL AND STOCK SAVINGS BANKS.

The number of mutual and stock savings banks, the number of depositors, the amount of individual deposits, and the average amount due each depositor for years ended June 30, 1914 to 1922, inclusive, are shown in the following statement:

*Number of savings banks (mutual and stock) in the United States, number of depositors, amount of individual deposits, and average amount due each depositor in years ended June 30, 1914 to 1922, inclusive.*

| Year. | Banks. | Depositors | Deposits.[1] | Average due each depositor. |
|---|---|---|---|---|
| 1914 {Mutual savings banks | 634 | 8,277,359 | $3,915,555,286 | $473.04 |
| Stock savings banks | 1,466 | 2,832,140 | 1,018,330,071 | 359.56 |
| 1915 {Mutual savings banks | 630 | 8,307,787 | 3,950,585,631 | 475.53 |
| Stock savings banks | 1,529 | 2,977,968 | 1,046,096,917 | 351.28 |
| 1916 {Mutual savings banks | 622 | 8,592,271 | 4,187,916,941 | 487.40 |
| Stock savings banks | 1,242 | 2,556,121 | 901,936,188 | 352.85 |
| 1917 {Mutual savings banks | 622 | 8,935,055 | 4,422,489,344 | 494.96 |
| Stock savings banks | 1,185 | 2,431,958 | 996,165,631 | 409.61 |
| 1918 {Mutual savings banks | 625 | 9,011,464 | 4,422,092,991 | 490.72 |
| Stock savings banks | 1,194 | 2,368,089 | 1,049,694,890 | 443.27 |
| 1919 {Mutual savings banks | 622 | 8,948,808 | 4,751,300,000 | 530.94 |
| Stock savings banks | 1,097 | 2,486,073 | 1,152,127,000 | 463.43 |
| 1920 {Mutual savings banks | 620 | 9,445,327 | 5,186,952,000 | 549.16 |
| Stock savings banks | 1,087 | 1,982,229 | 1,351,242,000 | 681.68 |
| 1921 {Mutual savings banks | 623 | 9,619,230 | 5,575,147,000 | 579.58 |
| Stock savings banks | 978 | 1,118,583 | 442,851,000 | 395.90 |
| 1922 {Mutual savings banks | 619 | 9,655,891 | 5,779,506,000 | 598.55 |
| Stock savings banks | 1,066 | 2,883,136 | 1,401,742,000 | 486.19 |

[1] Dividends unpaid included.

## PRIVATE BANKS.

Information was received as of June 30, 1922, showing the condition of 673 private banks with aggregate resources of $185,331,000. Due to the fact that private banks in the States of Connecticut, Texas, Michigan, and Iowa are not under the supervision of the State banking departments, and are under no obligation to furnish the Comptroller's office with statements of condition, the returns from this class of banks, which are estimated to number 1,200 throughout the United States, are incomplete. The returns show a reduction since 1921 of 35 banks, although resources were increased $10,225,000.

Loans and discounts amounted to $106,238,000, compared with $104,285,000 in 1921. Overdrafts were increased during the year from $727,000 to $755,000.

Investments, amounting to $35,270,000, show an increase over June 30, 1921, of $5,909,000. Banking houses, furniture, and fixtures, valued at $5,852,000, show an increase of $2,006,000 in the year, and other real estate owned was reduced from $7,174,000 to $5,422,000. Balances due from other banks and bankers aggregated $23,621,000, compared with $21,597,000 in 1921. Checks and other cash items, including exchanges for clearing house, were increased from $710,000 to $1,006,000 during the year. Cash in bank was reduced from $4,470,000 to $4,164,000, while other miscellaneous assets amounting to $3,203,000 show an increase over 1921 of $67,000.

Capital stock was reduced to the extent of $1,281,000 in the year and amounted to $10,320,000. Surplus was increased by $2,999,000 and amounted to $15,368,000, and undivided profits were increased from $1,956,000 in 1921 to $2,169,000.

Aggregate deposits, amounting to $147,191,000, show an increase of $11,843,000 during the year. Notes and bills rediscounted and bills payable show reductions of $479,000 and $3,229,000, respectively, the amount of notes and bills rediscounted being $1,384,000, while the amount of bills payable was $4,599,000. Other liabilities, amounting to $4,500,000, were $159,000 greater than in 1921.

The condition of reporting private banks, June 30, 1922, is shown in the following statement:

*Summary of reports of condition of 673 private banks in the United States at the close of business June 30, 1922.*

[In thousands of dollars.]

### RESOURCES.

| | | |
|---|---:|---:|
| Loans and discounts (including rediscounts): | | |
| On demand (secured by collateral other than real estate) | 1,768 | |
| On demand (not secured by collateral) | 1,120 | |
| On time (secured by collateral other than real estate) | 8,923 | |
| On time (not secured by collateral) | 9,905 | |
| Secured by farm land | 4,798 | |
| Secured by other real estate | 17,938 | |
| Not classified | 61,786 | |
| Total | | 106,238 |
| Overdrafts | | 755 |
| Investments (including premiums on bonds): | | |
| United States Government securities | 6,446 | |
| State, county, and municipal bonds | 1,761 | |
| Railroad bonds | 2,455 | |
| Bonds of other public service corporations (including street and interurban railway bonds) | 946 | |
| Other bonds, stocks, warrants, etc | 23,662 | |
| Total | | 35,270 |
| Banking house (including furniture and fixtures) | | 5,852 |
| Other real estate owned | | 5,422 |
| Due from banks | | 15,989 |
| Lawful reserve with Federal reserve bank or other reserve agents | | 7,632 |
| Checks and other cash items | | 844 |
| Exchanges for clearing house | | 162 |
| Cash on hand: | | |
| Gold coin | 223 | |
| Silver coin | 258 | |
| Paper currency | 1,731 | |
| Nickels and cents | 36 | |
| Not classified | 1,916 | |
| Total | | 4,164 |
| Other resources | | 3,203 |
| Total resources | | 185,531 |

### LIABILITIES.

| | | |
|---|---:|---:|
| Capital stock paid in | | 10,320 |
| Surplus | | 15,368 |
| Undivided profits (less expenses and taxes paid) | | 2,169 |
| Due to all banks | | 1,531 |
| Certified checks and cashiers' checks | | 239 |
| Individual deposits (including dividends unpaid and postal savings): | | |
| Demand deposits— | | |
| Individual deposits subject to check | 48,121 | |
| Demand certificates of deposit | 14,396 | |
| Dividends unpaid | 12 | |

Individual deposits—Continued.
Time deposits—

| | |
|---|---:|
| Savings deposits, or deposits in interest of savings department | 32,733 |
| Time certificates of deposit | 20,001 |
| Postal savings deposits | 313 |
| Not classified | 29,603 |
| | |
| Total | 145,179 |
| United States deposits (exclusive of postal savings) | 242 |
| Notes and bills rediscounted | 1,384 |
| Bills payable (including advances received from War Finance Corporation and certificates of deposit representing money borrowed) | 4,599 |
| Other liabilities | 4,500 |
| | |
| Total liabilities | 185,531 |

## ALL REPORTING BANKS OTHER THAN NATIONAL, STATE (COMMERCIAL), SAVINGS, PRIVATE BANKS, AND LOAN AND TRUST COMPANIES.

The returns relative to the condition of all reporting banks other than national in the continental United States, referred to in preceding paragraphs, with respect to each class of institutions, were received from the State banking department officials of the several States, who responded generously to the comptroller's requests for this information, and data with reference to banks in the insular possessions and Territories, was supplied through the cooperation of the Bureau of Insular Affairs, War Department, and the office of the Secretary of the Interior.

The combined data as of June 30, 1922, represent the returns from 22,140 reporting banks with aggregate resources of $29,719,357,000. This shows a reduction of 518 in the number of reporting banks, but an increase in aggregate resources of $565,829,000.

The reduction in the number of reporting banks is due to the fact that during the last fiscal year, as shown by information at command, there were 364 failures of banks other than national, while of the 245 charters issued to national banking associations during the year, 128 were conversions of State banks. The failure of the guaranty deposit system law in some States to meet the demands made upon it was responsible to some extent for the number of conversions of State banking institutions.

The loans and discounts of all reporting banks other than national totaled $16,435,991,000, and show a reduction of $253,218,000 during the year. Overdrafts were reduced from $71,879,000 in 1921, to $65,402,000.

The investments of these banks amounted to $7,984,242,000 and were $627,400,000 more than in 1921.

Banking houses, furniture, and fixtures, reported at $625,740,000, show an increase of $42,234,000 during the year, and other real estate owned was increased from $101,881,000 in 1921 to $134,074,000.

Balances on the books of other banks and bankers to the credit of reporting banks were $2,664,945,000, compared with $2,409,481,000 in 1921.

Checks and other miscellaneous cash items, including exchanges for clearing house, were $166,332.000 greater than in 1921, and amounted to $679,190,000.

The total cash in the vaults of these banks was $503,711,000 and was $68,507,000 below the amount reported a year ago. Other miscellaneous assets. reported at $626,062,000 showed a reduction of $229,592,000.

Capital stock, reported at $1,636,734,000, was $6,663,000 greater than in 1921; surplus funds were $1,648,603,000, compared with $1,515,776,000. a year ago, while undivided profits were increased to the extent of $26,821,000 during the year, and amounted to $441,409,000.

The liability of these banks on account of balances to the credit of correspondent banks was $742,335,000, showing an increase of $83,932,000 since 1921, and the liability for certified checks and cashiers' checks outstanding, amounting to $101,732,000, was $176,201,000 less than a year ago. Individual deposits to the amount of $23,929,952,000 show an increase of $1,491,011,000 since 1921. United States deposits decreased $115,678,000 during the year and amounted to $25,513,000.

Liabilities for borrowed money represented by the rediscount of notes and bills and by bills payable were considerably liquidated during the year, the amount of notes and bills rediscounted being only $155,440,000, compared with $392,268,000 a year ago, while in this period bills payable were reduced from $783,028,000 to $407,083,000.

Other liabilities, amounting to $630,556,000, were $270,763,000 less than a year ago.

The following summary shows the combined returns of all reporting banks other than national in the United States and island possessions, June 30, 1922, with classifications of loans, investments, cash, and deposits:

*Summary of reports of condition of 22,140 State, savings, private banks, and loan and trust companies in the United States and island possessions at the close of business June 30, 1922.*

[In thousands of dollars ]

RESOURCES.

| | | |
|---|---:|---:|
| Loans and discounts (including rediscounts): | | |
| On demand (secured by collateral other than real estate). | 1,421,087 | |
| On demand (not secured by collateral) | 228,629 | |
| On time (secured by collateral other than real estate)... | 922,946 | |
| On time (not secured by collateral) | 1,233,642 | |
| Secured by farm land | 200,815 | |
| Secured by other real estate | 2,938,903 | |
| Not classified | 9,489,969 | |
| Total | | 16,435,991 |
| Overdrafts | | 65,402 |
| Investments (including premiums on bonds): | | |
| United States Government securities | 1,214,708 | |
| State, county, and municipal bonds | 566,961 | |
| Railroad bonds | 934,010 | |
| Bonds of other public service corporations (including street and interurban railway bonds) | 369,944 | |
| Other bonds, stocks, warrants, etc. | 4,898,619 | |
| Total | | 7,984,242 |
| Banking house (including furniture and fixtures) | | 625,740 |
| Other real estate owned | | 134,074 |
| Due from banks | | 1,475,753 |
| Lawful reserve with Federal reserve bank or other reserve agents | | 1,189,192 |

| | | |
|---|---|---:|
| Checks and other cash items............................................... | | 515, 692 |
| Exchanges for clearing house............................................. | | 163, 498 |
| Cash on hand: | | |
|     Gold coin............................................... | 19, 778 | |
|     Silver coin............................................. | 17, 562 | |
|     Paper currency......................................... | 192, 089 | |
|     Nickels and cents...................................... | 6, 496 | |
|     Not classified......................................... | 267, 786 | |
|       Total............................................ | | 503, 711 |
| Other resources......................................................... | | 626, 062 |
|       Total resources.................................... | | 29, 719, 357 |

### LIABILITIES.

| | | |
|---|---|---:|
| Capital stock paid in................................................... | | 1, 636, 734 |
| Surplus................................................................ | | 1, 648, 603 |
| Undivided profits (less expenses and taxes paid)......................... | | 441, 409 |
| Due to all banks....................................................... | | 742, 335 |
| Certified checks and cashiers' checks.................................... | | 101, 732 |
| Individual deposits (including dividends unpaid and postal savings: | | |
|   Demand deposits— | | |
|     Individual deposits subject to check................ | 5, 830, 018 | |
|     Demand certificates of deposit...................... | 325, 170 | |
|     Dividends unpaid.................................... | 15, 912 | |
|   Time deposits— | | |
|     Savings deposits, or deposits in interest or savings | | |
|       department..................................... | 10, 190, 760 | |
|     Time certificates of deposit........................ | 1, 337, 278 | |
|     Postal savings deposits............................. | 10, 725 | |
|     Not classified...................................... | 6, 220, 089 | |
|       Total.......................................... | | 23, 929, 952 |
| United States deposits (exclusive of postal savings).................... | | 25, 513 |
| Notes and bills rediscounted........................................... | | 155, 440 |
| Bills payable (including advances received from War Finance Corpora- | | |
|   tion and certificates of deposit representing money borrowed)........ | | 407, 083 |
| Other liabilities....................................................... | | 630, 556 |
|       Total liabilities.................................. | | 29, 719, 357 |

The resources and liabilities of each class of reporting banks other than national, June 30, 1922, are shown in the following statement:

*Resources and liabilities of 22,140 State (commercial) banks, loan and trust companies, savings and private banks, June 30, 1922.*

[In thousands of dollars.]

| | 18,232 State (commercial) banks. | 1,550 loan and trust companies. | 1,066 stock savings banks. | 619 mutual savings banks. | 673 private banks. | 22,140 total banks. |
|---|---:|---:|---:|---:|---:|---:|
| **RESOURCES.** | | | | | | |
| Loans and discounts................ | 7, 934, 123 | 4, 342, 895 | 1, 051, 310 | 3, 001, 425 | 106, 238 | 16, 435, 991 |
| Overdrafts......................... | 60, 225 | 2, 603 | 498 | 1, 321 | 755 | 65, 402 |
| Investments (including premiums on | | | | | | |
|   bonds)......................... | 2, 304, 891 | 2, 311, 101 | 325, 687 | 3, 007, 293 | 35, 270 | 7, 984, 242 |
| Banking house (including furniture | | | | | | |
|   and fixtures)................... | 328, 767 | 198, 267 | 43, 770 | 49, 084 | 5, 852 | 625, 740 |
| Other real estate owned............ | 72, 761 | 38, 424 | 6, 837 | 10, 630 | 5, 422 | 134, 074 |
| Due from banks.................... | 862, 051 | 327, 886 | 98, 188 | 171, 639 | 15, 989 | 1, 475, 753 |
| Lawful reserve with Federal reserve | | | | | | |
|   bank or other reserve agents...... | 581, 056 | 568, 036 | 18, 194 | 14, 264 | 7, 632 | 1, 189, 192 |
| Checks and other cash items........ | 231, 013 | 278, 377 | 4, 184 | 1, 274 | 844 | 515, 692 |
| Exchanges for clearing house....... | 123, 861 | 37, 004 | 2, 392 | 79 | 162 | 163, 498 |
| Cash on hand...................... | 309, 584 | 117, 079 | 28, 001 | 44, 883 | 4, 164 | 503, 711 |
| Other resources.................... | 256, 064 | 312, 178 | 4, 861 | 49, 756 | 3, 203 | 626, 062 |
|   Total resources............... | 13, 064, 406 | 8, 533, 850 | 1, 583, 922 | 6, 351, 648 | 185, 531 | 29, 719, 357 |

*Resources and liabilities of 22,140 State (commercial) banks, loan and trust companies, savings and private banks, June 30, 1922—Continued.*

| | 18,232 State (commercial) banks. | 1,550 loan and trust companies. | 1,066 stock savings banks. | 619 mutual savings banks. | 673 private banks. | 22,140 total bank. |
|---|---|---|---|---|---|---|
| **LIABILITIES.** | | | | | | |
| Capital stock paid in............... | 1,014,248 | 532,316 | 79,850 | .......... | 10,320 | 1,636,734 |
| Surplus...................... | 561,131 | 562,731 | 41,180 | [1] 468,193 | 15,368 | 1,648,603 |
| Undivided profits (less expenses and taxes paid)...................... | 210,536 | 117,513 | 18,995 | 92,196 | 2,169 | 441,409 |
| Due to all banks.................... | 387,657 | 351,547 | 1,336 | 264 | 1,531 | 742,335 |
| Certified checks and cashiers' checks.. | 69,803 | 31,109 | 557 | 24 | 239 | 101,732 |
| Individual deposits (including dividends unpaid and postal savings).. | 10,107,597 | 6,495,928 | 1,401,742 | 5,779,506 | 145,179 | 23,929,952 |
| United States deposits (exclusive of postal savings).................... | 7,734 | 13,800 | 3,736 | 1 | 242 | 25,513 |
| Notes and bills rediscounted......... | 111,651 | 42,237 | 61 | 107 | 1,384 | 155,440 |
| Bills payable (including advances received from War Finance Corporation and certificates of deposit representing money borrowed)........ | 311,149 | 61,333 | 29,355 | 647 | 4,599 | 407,083 |
| Other liabilities..................... | 282,900 | 325,336 | 7,110 | 10,710 | 4,500 | 630,556 |
| Total liabilities................ | 13,064,406 | 8,533,850 | 1,583,922 | 6,351,648 | 185,531 | 29,719,357 |

[1] Includes $350,000 stock of 2 stock savings banks.

## PRINCIPAL ITEMS OF RESOURCES AND LIABILITIES OF ALL REPORTING BANKS OTHER THAN NATIONAL, ON OR ABOUT JUNE 30, 1917–1922.

The principal items of resources and liabilities of all reporting banks other than national, are shown in the following statement for years ended on or about June 30, for the past six years:

*Consolidated returns from State, savings, private banks, and loan and trust companies.*

[In thousands of dollars.]

| Item. | 1917 | 1918 | 1919 | 1920 | 1921 | 1922 |
|---|---|---|---|---|---|---|
| Loans [1]...................... | 11,674,130 | 12,426,598 | 14,061,698 | 17,263,796 | 16,761,088 | 16,501,393 |
| Bonds......................... | 4,990,752 | 5,784,381 | 7,177,605 | 7,201,060 | 7,356,842 | 7,984,242 |
| Cash.......................... | 749,791 | 513,869 | 572,898 | 626,027 | 572,218 | 503,711 |
| Capital....................... | 1,191,421 | 1,253,032 | 1,318,762 | 1,478,473 | 1,630,081 | 1,636,734 |
| Surplus and undivided profits. | 1,484,875 | 1,509,328 | 1,653,440 | 1,853,435 | 1,930,364 | 2,090,012 |
| Deposits (individual).......... | 16,739,573 | 17,719,043 | 20,774,154 | 23,609,798 | 22,438,941 | 23,929,952 |
| Resources..................... | 20,836,357 | 22,371,497 | 26,380,529 | 29,667,855 | 29,153,528 | 29,719,357 |

[1] Including overdrafts.

## RESOURCES AND LIABILITIES OF ALL REPORTING BANKS IN EACH STATE AND ISLAND POSSESSIONS.

The returns from all reporting banks June 30, 1922, including national, State (commercial), loan and trust companies, stock savings, mutual savings, and private banks, show the condition of 30,389 banks with aggregate resources of $50,425,367,000. The reduction in the number of reporting banks during the fiscal year was 423, but resources were increased $753,977,000.

The loans and discounts of these banks were $27,860,443,000 and show a reduction of $1,071,568,000 since June 30, 1921. Overdrafts were reduced during the year $7,249,000 and amounted to $74,600,000.

Investments in bonds and other securities amounted to $12,547,-567,000 compared with $11,381,923,000 a year ago.

Banking houses, furniture, and fixtures were carried at $1,078,-174,000, or $84,276,000 in excess of the amount in 1921. Other real estate owned was increased $44,834,000 during the year and amounted to $198,457,000.

Balances due from other banks and bankers to reporting banks, including lawful reserve and items in process of collection with Federal reserve banks to the credit of national banks and member State banks, aggregated $5,414,241,000, showing an increase of $620,036,000 over the aggregate of these balances in 1921. Checks and other miscellaneous cash items, including exchanges for clearing house, were $1,574,608,000 compared with $1,290,667,000 a year ago.

The returns from all classes of banking institutions indicate a tendency to carry less cash on hand, the reduction during the past fiscal year amounting to $116,675,000. The total cash on hand June 30, 1922, was $829,892,000.

Other miscellaneous assets show a reduction during the year of $249,262,000, and amounted to $847,385,000.

Capital stock was increased during the year $39,989,000 and amounted to $2,943,950,000. Surplus funds were also increased $155,377,000 in this period and amounted to $2,697,409,000, while undivided profits of $933,843,000 show an increase of $23,100,000 during the year.

The liability of national banks for circulating notes outstanding June 30, 1922, was $725,748,000, compared with $704,147,000 June 30, 1921.

The deposit liability of all reporting banks to correspondent banks and bankers, including the Federal reserve banks, was $3,244,386,000, or $434,972,000 in excess of the amount of these balances June 30, 1921.

The liability of all reporting banks incident to the issuance of certified checks and cashiers' checks was $62,078,000 less than a year ago, and amounted to $552,505,000.

Individual deposits show an increase of $2,349,746,000 during the year, the amount reported being $37,194,318,000. United States deposits were decreased from $390,230,000 June 30, 1921, to $128,887,000.

The liabilities of reporting banks for money borrowed, arising from the rediscount of notes and bills and bills payable, show decided reductions during the year. Notes and bills rediscounted were reduced from $1,271,684,000 to $435,711,000, and bills payable from $1,375,591,000 to $635,564,000.

Other liabilities were $933,046,000, and show a reduction of $371,387,000 during the year.

The resources and liabilities of all reporting banks in each State and the island possessions, with the estimated population as of June 30, 1922, and a recapitulation of the aggregate resources and liabilities of each class of banks are shown in the following statement:

Condensed statement, by States, of assets and liabilities of all reporting banks in the United States and island possessions, June, 1922.

[Includes national, State (commercial) banks, loan and trust companies, savings, and private banks.]

Resources (in thousands of dollars).

| States and Territories, etc. | Population (approximate). | Number of banks. | Loans and discounts.[1] | Overdrafts. | Investments. | Banking house, furniture, and fixtures. | Other real estate owned. | Due from banks. | Lawful reserve with Federal Reserve Bank or other reserve agents. | Checks and other cash items. | Exchanges for clearing house. | Cash on hand. | Other resources. | Aggregate resources. |
|---|---|---|---|---|---|---|---|---|---|---|---|---|---|---|
| Maine | 770,000 | 158 | 141,296 | 90 | 184,305 | 3,696 | 1,756 | 13,451 | 4,256 | 414 | 514 | 4,810 | 18,082 | 372,640 |
| New Hampshire | 448,000 | 126 | 101,158 | 40 | 111,826 | 2,724 | 257 | 7,484 | 2,840 | 555 | 86 | 2,132 | 286 | 231,388 |
| Vermont | 353,000 | 108 | 129,917 | 93 | 50,925 | 1,979 | 327 | 7,461 | 1,948 | 461 |  | 1,883 | 3,325 | 198,321 |
| Massachusetts | 4,005,000 | 459 | 1,927,646 | 308 | 911,998 | 43,471 | 12,066 | 123,541 | 97,988 | 11,188 | 42,301 | 27,816 | 26,433 | 3,224,654 |
| Rhode Island | 622,000 | 46 | 189,550 | 19 | 192,301 | 5,119 | 563 | 23,112 | 2,727 | 207 | 2,843 | 7,714 | 1,701 | 416,858 |
| Connecticut | 1,432,000 | 221 | 416,232 | 156 | 378,622 | 15,976 | 2,176 | 18,508 | 19,959 | 3,459 | 2,058 | 20,525 | 2,225 | 879,896 |
| Total New England States | 7,660,000 | 1,118 | 2,808,769 | 706 | 1,829,979 | 72,965 | 17,145 | 193,557 | 129,718 | 16,282 | 47,702 | 64,882 | 52,052 | 5,323,757 |
| New York | 10,950,000 | 1,084 | 6,595,643 | 1,390 | 3,718,943 | 165,272 | 7,570 | 368,244 | 827,225 | 470,405 | 571,012 | 137,149 | 391,443 | 13,254,296 |
| New Jersey | 3,540,000 | 434 | 719,535 | 103 | 623,246 | 34,952 | 4,827 | 66,720 | 49,762 | 6,237 | 5,797 | 25,803 | 9,827 | 1,546,811 |
| Pennsylvania | 9,000,000 | 1,620 | 2,084,383 | 674 | 1,750,290 | 128,136 | 32,450 | 204,073 | 266,077 | 18,164 | 52,681 | 76,172 | 37,629 | 4,658,719 |
| Delaware | 225,000 | 57 | 45,311 | 1,457 | 40,449 | 3,279 | 885 | 2,834 | 5,357 | 157 | 659 | 1,437 | 382 | 102,107 |
| Maryland | 1,540,000 | 247 | 336,785 | 131 | 261,696 | 14,513 | 2,224 | 42,578 | 46,371 | 3,071 | 8,850 | 8,559 | 2,956 | 717,675 |
| District of Columbia | 453,000 | 50 | 122,502 | 92 | 56,679 | 17,056 | 1,192 | 16,475 | 7,896 | 2,240 | 3,081 | 5,130 | 970 | 233,283 |
| Total Eastern States | 25,675,000 | 3,492 | 9,903,160 | 3,749 | 6,450,193 | 363,198 | 49,148 | 700,924 | 1,202,658 | 500,274 | 642,090 | 254,280 | 443,207 | 20,512,881 |
| Virginia | 2,362,000 | 509 | 385,531 | 340 | 72,414 | 14,954 | 2,444 | 42,549 | 15,579 | 3,054 | 2,802 | 9,404 | 3,371 | 553,502 |
| West Virginia | 1,500,000 | 347 | 261,332 | 517 | 63,953 | 12,754 | 1,792 | 32,716 | 6,816 | 942 | 1,391 | 8,230 | 1,379 | 391,822 |
| North Carolina | 2,690,000 | 582 | 295,273 | 617 | 31,696 | 13,285 | 1,747 | 43,075 | 6,543 | 1,644 | 2,337 | 8,444 | 2,465 | 407,127 |
| South Carolina | 1,760,000 | 454 | 192,298 | 942 | 29,542 | 7,497 | 2,111 | 23,267 | 4,423 | 1,455 | 1,197 | 3,863 | 3,135 | 269,730 |
| Georgia | 2,990,000 | 693 | 295,991 | 327 | 36,516 | 12,370 | 3,198 | 23,493 | 31,812 | 1,243 | 4,047 | 7,507 | 4,078 | 420,582 |
| Florida | 1,015,000 | 280 | 132,686 | 109 | 47,112 | 8,614 | 2,606 | 37,195 | 6,065 | 1,226 | 510 | 6,487 | 1,157 | 242,460 |
| Alabama | 2,385,000 | 356 | 159,655 | 1,202 | 31,953 | 6,586 | 1,299 | 23,206 | 6,173 | 1,780 | 1,095 | 6,884 | 1,949 | 244,156 |
| Mississippi | 1,799,000 | 351 | 123,302 | 880 | 28,631 | 4,174 | 1,071 | 6,499 | 27,773 | 380 | 455 | 4,000 | 3,740 | 201,197 |
| Louisiana | 1,843,000 | 264 | 268,890 | 2,124 | 43,604 | 21,022 | 2,674 | 54,644 | 13,347 | 3,127 | 7,111 | 8,062 | 4,685 | 428,016 |
| Texas | 4,840,000 | 1,563 | 658,632 | 336 | 115,072 | 36,680 | 11,354 | 137,829 | 37,301 | 4,898 | 4,078 | 22,836 | 13,462 | 1,046,966 |
| Arkansas | 1,815,000 | 486 | 146,800 | 909 | 19,757 | 6,279 | 1,930 | 29,532 | 5,387 | 1,235 | 2,415 | 4,896 | 1,587 | 220,424 |
| Kentucky | 2,468,000 | 601 | 290,081 | 706 | 89,191 | 8,888 | 924 | 42,691 | 10,691 | 1,272 | 1,946 | 10,823 | 3,163 | 460,502 |
| Tennessee | 2,375,000 | 571 | 272,407 |  | 45,829 | 12,703 | 2,373 | 51,160 | 8,402 | 5,109 | 1,639 | 8,517 | 11,439 | 420,284 |
| Total Southern States | 29,803,000 | 7,050 | 3,483,848 | 9,198 | 658,253 | 165,806 | 35,523 | 547,427 | 183,512 | 27,365 | 31,103 | 109,923 | 54,810 | 5,306,768 |

| | | | | | | | | | | | | | | |
|---|---:|---:|---:|---:|---:|---:|---:|---:|---:|---:|---:|---:|---:|---:|
| Ohio | 5,960,000 | 1,123 | 1,400,231 | 796 | 513,199 | 61,483 | 14,517 | 99,349 | 140,982 | 4,212 | 38,240 | 46,589 | 19,733 | 2,39,81 |
| Indiana | 3,000,000 | 1,094 | 1,534,105 | 902 | 168,402 | 27,003 | 4,164 | 86,532 | 16,798 | 6,308 | 2,751 | 23,752 | 51,799 | 92,86 |
| Illinois | 6,700,000 | 1,906 | 2,040,096 | 2,094 | 662,844 | 63,224 | 8,284 | 327,541 | 179,35 | 12,258 | 75,953 | 66,524 | 53,174 | 3,491,527 |
| Michigan | 3,830,000 | 745 | 596,144 | 515 | 558,731 | 40,016 | 2,415 | 41,453 | 1,0 | 4,275 | 7,145 | 27,202 | 26,073 | 1,46,74 |
| Wisconsin | 2,770,000 | 1,002 | 541,760 | 775 | 145,402 | 23,024 | 2,890 | 32,143 | 59,810 | 4,249 | 5,234 | 15,961 | 2,277 | 1,83,96 |
| Minnesota | 2,480,000 | 1,517 | 685,497 | 1,413 | 186,582 | 23,076 | 7,398 | 104,203 | 28,689 | 847 | 5,397 | 20,950 | 9,362 | 60,61 |
| Iowa | 2,445,000 | 1,772 | 890,490 | 1,637 | 80,944 | 28,017 | 7,771 | 102,914 | 15,999 | 1,647 | 5,397 | 21,274 | 3,589 | 1,3,86 |
| Missouri | 3,412,000 | 1,651 | 854,024 | 1,195 | 193,542 | 29,005 | 6,232 | 189,683 | 29,754 | 15,109 | 11,858 | 22,107 | 28,653 | 1,380,562 |
| **Total Middle Western States** | 30,620,000 | 10,810 | 7,512,247 | 9,317 | 2,509,646 | 294,848 | 53,671 | 983,798 | 572,966 | 59,028 | 155,993 | 244,359 | 194,360 | 12,590,333 |
| North Dakota | 664,000 | 846 | 171,483 | 335 | 17,323 | 6,960 | 5,163 | 5,656 | 10,326 | 697 | 91 | 2,904 | 1,731 | 222,773 |
| South Dakota | 652,000 | 695 | 208,337 | 1,106 | 12,336 | 7,822 | 3,539 | 36,357 | 3,544 | 554 | 63 | 4,487 | 6,388 | 285,673 |
| Nebraska | 1,319,000 | 1,153 | 360,674 | 1,395 | 36,482 | 13,962 | 3,965 | 80,315 | 12,312 | 2,053 | 3,42 | 12,984 | 7,224 | 534,648 |
| Kansas | 1,806,000 | 1,384 | 334,474 | 1,098 | 63,919 | 15,035 | 3,427 | 74,689 | 10,786 | 2,249 | 2 | 11,823 | 3,296 | 533,396 |
| Montana | 595,000 | 400 | 132,843 | 393 | 22,635 | 6,547 | 3,750 | 8,618 | 15,706 | 847 | 90 | 4,512 | 1,566 | 197,631 |
| Wyoming | 204,000 | 146 | 57,529 | 158 | 7,263 | 2,100 | 502 | 9,185 | 2,547 | 438 | 15 | 2,189 | 699 | 82,765 |
| Colorado | 964,000 | 381 | 181,111 | 282 | 74,944 | 7,532 | 1,371 | 29,209 | 24,978 | 2,933 | 82 | 9,178 | 1,037 | 335,207 |
| New Mexico | 368,000 | 110 | 46,220 | 83 | 6,157 | 1,629 | 812 | 6,112 | 1,918 | 437 | 24 | 1,284 | 445 | 65,221 |
| Oklahoma | 2,118,000 | 933 | 276,834 | 733 | 61,979 | 12,969 | 2,641 | 88,718 | 19,866 | 2,416 | 67 | 9,200 | 1,040 | 473,073 |
| **Total Western States** | 8,690,000 | 6,028 | 1,789,517 | 5,583 | 293,038 | 74,556 | 25,470 | 338,839 | 101,983 | 12,624 | 12,596 | 58,431 | 23,428 | 2,736,387 |
| Washington | 1,420,000 | 392 | 223,858 | 279 | 91,641 | 13,539 | 2,638 | 25,059 | 32,729 | 1,566 | 4,344 | 9,875 | 3,508 | 412,336 |
| Oregon | 818,000 | 277 | 160,106 | 221 | 58,865 | 7,218 | 1,912 | 19,904 | 19,424 | 1,135 | 2,645 | 7,296 | 2,359 | 281,085 |
| California | 3,680,000 | 724 | 1,523,512 | 1,490 | 580,757 | 71,000 | 7,796 | 198,035 | 87,755 | 22,678 | 30,686 | 52,793 | 37,438 | 2,611,840 |
| Idaho | 454,000 | 198 | 68,457 | 147 | 14,177 | 3,583 | 1,782 | 11,234 | 3,277 | 361 | 515 | 1,825 | 837 | 106,610 |
| Utah | 470,000 | 121 | 87,505 | 289 | 20,200 | 4,884 | 1,651 | 15,302 | 4,572 | 404 | 1,081 | 1,379 | 1,052 | 138,765 |
| Nevada | 78,000 | 35 | 23,078 | 191 | 5,179 | 1,038 | 152 | 5,790 | 727 | 183 | | 185 | 185 | 38,031 |
| Arizona | 365,000 | 80 | 50,178 | 63 | 13,061 | 2,928 | 307 | 11,468 | 1,447 | 248 | 69 | 128 | 128 | 85,720 |
| Alaska | 90,000 | 18 | 3,795 | 31 | 2,386 | 296 | 176 | 1,126 | | 81 | 183 | 51 | 51 | 8,833 |
| **Total Pacific States** | 7,385,000 | 1,845 | 2,140,489 | 2,711 | 786,256 | 104,546 | 16,414 | 291,878 | 149,931 | 26,656 | 39,323 | 82,148 | 45,858 | 3,636,220 |
| Hawaii | 265,000 | 18 | 31,803 | 1,183 | 13,658 | 757 | 365 | 6,309 | | 524 | 1,014 | 4,014 | 2,552 | 62,209 |
| Porto Rico | 1,310,000 | 17 | 23,980 | 185 | 3,627 | 693 | 63 | 3,246 | | 941 | 420 | 4,076 | 887 | 38,118 |
| Philippines | 10,700,000 | 11 | 76,530 | 41,968 | 2,907 | 775 | 658 | 7,446 | 29 | 320 | 51 | 7,779 | 30,231 | 168,69 |
| **Total island possessions** | 12,275,000 | 46 | 132,313 | 43,336 | 20,192 | 2,255 | 1,086 | 17,001 | 29 | 1,785 | 1,485 | 15,889 | 33,670 | 209,021 |
| **Total United States** | 122,108,000 | 30,389 | 27,860,443 | 74,600 | 12,547,567 | 1,078,174 | 198,457 | 3,073,444 | 2,340,797 | 644,014 | 930,504 | 829,592 | 847,385 | 50,425,367 |

Condensed statement, by States, of assets and liabilities of all reporting banks in the United States and island possessions, June, 1922—Continued.

RECAPITULATION.

| States and Territories, etc. | Population (approximate). | Number of banks. | Loans and discounts.[1] | Overdrafts. | Investments. | Banking house, furniture, and fixtures. | Other real estate owned. | Due from banks. | Lawful reserve with Federal Reserve Bank or other reserve agents. | Checks and other cash items. | Exchanges for clearing house. | Cash on hand. | Other resources. | Aggregate resources. |
|---|---|---|---|---|---|---|---|---|---|---|---|---|---|---|
| Nal | | 8,249 | 11,424,452 | 9,198 | 4,563,325 | 452,434 | 64,383 | 1,597,691 | 1,151,605 | 128,322 | 767,096 | 326,181 | 221,323 | 20,706,010 |
| State (mial) banks | | 18,232 | 7,934,123 | 60,225 | 2,304,891 | 328,767 | 72,761 | 862,051 | 581,066 | 231,013 | 123,861 | 309,584 | 256,064 | 13,064,406 |
| ...s | | 619 | 3,001,425 | 1,321 | 3,007,293 | 49,084 | 10,630 | 171,639 | 14,264 | 1,274 | 79 | 44,883 | 49,756 | 6,351,648 |
| Stock ...gs | | 1,066 | 1,051,310 | 498 | 325,687 | 43,770 | 6,837 | 98,188 | 18,194 | 4,184 | 2,392 | 28,001 | 4,861 | 1,683,922 |
| ...t... c...s | | 1,550 | 4,342,895 | 2,603 | 2,311,101 | 198,267 | 38,424 | 327,886 | 568,036 | 278,377 | 37,004 | 117,079 | 312,178 | 8,533,850 |
| Pvate banks | | 673 | 106,238 | 755 | 35,270 | 5,852 | 5,422 | 15,989 | 7,632 | 844 | 162 | 4,164 | 3,203 | 185,531 |
| tal total | | 30,389 | 27,860,443 | 74,600 | 12,547,567 | 1,078,174 | 198,457 | 3,073,444 | 2,340,797 | 644,014 | 930,594 | 829,892 | 847,385 | 50,425,367 |

[1] Includes acceptances and rediscounts.

Condensed statement, by States, of assets and liabilities of all reporting banks in the United States and island possessions, June, 1922—Continued.

Liabilities (in thousands of dollars).

| States and Territories, etc. | Capital stock paid in. | Surplus. | Undivided profits (less expenses and taxes paid). | National-bank circulation. | Due to all banks. | Certified checks and cashiers' checks. | Individual deposits. | United States deposits. | Notes and bills re-discounted. | Bills payable. | Other liabilities. |
|---|---|---|---|---|---|---|---|---|---|---|---|
| Maine | 12,210 | 14,728 | 11,523 | 5,561 | 3,163 | 727 | 500,030 | 290 | 1,502 | 4,879 | 17,964 |
| New Hampshire | 7,473 | 12,688 | 5,322 | 5,069 | 3,078 | 490 | 191,510 | 278 | 609 | 1,797 | 1,181 |
| Vermont | 7,626 | 10,623 | 6,209 | 4,424 | 1,648 | 354 | 162,546 | 51 | 792 | 2,852 | 1,196 |
| Massachusetts | 105,183 | 170,299 | 87,983 | 20,003 | 129,304 | 18,293 | 2,388,880 | 12,208 | 33,021 | 9,391 | 53,504 |
| Rhode Island | 15,180 | 20,143 | 17,771 | 4,727 | 4,630 | 1,432 | 348,935 | 830 | 1,320 | 325 | 1,572 |
| Connecticut | 35,342 | 44,437 | 31,939 | 12,936 | 10,018 | 4,407 | 731,212 | 950 | 2,372 | 3,964 | 2,378 |
| Total New England States | 183,216 | 272,728 | 162,741 | 52,723 | 151,831 | 25,676 | 4,319,543 | 14,577 | 39,706 | 23,208 | 77,798 |
| New York | 453,491 | 864,291 | 129,699 | 78,263 | 1,098,720 | 314,114 | 9,859,446 | 25,518 | 53,031 | 50,087 | 357,623 |
| New Jersey | 66,349 | 75,118 | 28,130 | 16,137 | 21,094 | 8,906 | 1,299,238 | 2,589 | 4,296 | 16,602 | 8,312 |
| Pennsylvania | 281,708 | 402,337 | 120,603 | 94,144 | 284,708 | 31,954 | 3,275,906 | 19,632 | 14,334 | 74,126 | 38,827 |
| Delaware | 7,104 | 7,393 | 3,120 | 1,090 | 1,302 | 390 | 78,611 | 573 | 264 | 1,011 | 1,219 |
| Maryland | 37,993 | 44,388 | 17,568 | 9,912 | 39,201 | 1,896 | 554,994 | 1,766 | 1,541 | 5,291 | 3,125 |
| District of Columbia | 21,614 | 12,450 | 5,629 | 5,691 | 8,575 | 2,310 | 170,012 | 894 | 1,021 | 3,811 | 1,363 |
| Total Eastern States | 865,849 | 1,406,190 | 301,839 | 205,240 | 1,453,600 | 359,570 | 15,238,207 | 50,832 | 74,487 | 151,048 | 400,469 |
| Virginia | 52,563 | 35,454 | 13,062 | 21,069 | 35,722 | 3,813 | 359,157 | 2,781 | 11,302 | 10,996 | 7,583 |
| West Virginia | 29,952 | 21,082 | 7,916 | 10,351 | 10,380 | 2,112 | 292,464 | 453 | 1,888 | 4,838 | 3,356 |
| South Carolina | 36,882 | 18,719 | 8,372 | 8,296 | 21,274 | 3,964 | 275,631 | 432 | 9,855 | 18,295 | 5,427 |
| Georgia | 29,440 | 14,601 | 5,763 | 8,529 | 7,306 | 1,146 | 172,781 | 658 | 8,078 | 13,820 | 8,208 |
| Florida | 47,785 | 29,078 | 12,199 | 11,172 | 26,590 | 1,702 | 253,514 | 1,178 | 14,070 | 17,415 | 5,879 |
| Alabama | 18,045 | 7,885 | 3,974 | 5,906 | 15,348 | 1,676 | 184,955 | 554 | 1,034 | 1,599 | 1,524 |
| Mississippi | 24,329 | 14,200 | 6,678 | 10,450 | 8,252 | 792 | 166,040 | 624 | 5,885 | 5,848 | 1,018 |
| Louisiana | 17,000 | 8,693 | 3,236 | 2,960 | 7,577 | 618 | 148,788 | 301 | 2,799 | 6,309 | 2,906 |
| Texas | 31,687 | 17,432 | 7,014 | 4,291 | 42,210 | 2,051 | 301,519 | 340 | 5,251 | 6,971 | 6,228 |
| | 113,914 | 32,401 | 22,207 | 44,123 | 77,863 | 9,337 | 602,609 | 4,477 | 19,058 | 31,492 | 9,482 |
| Arkansas | 23,825 | 9,573 | 4,369 | 4,245 | 12,178 | 1,146 | 147,256 | 279 | 5,682 | 10,039 | 1,832 |
| | 39,446 | 25,092 | 7,597 | 15,962 | 24,776 | 2,418 | 317,991 | 1,519 | 2,446 | 10,558 | 12,067 |
| Tennessee | 38,188 | 22,046 | 3,369 | 12,866 | 19,107 | 1,060 | 294,086 | 451 | 4,022 | 12,192 | 12,897 |
| Total Southern States | 501,016 | 275,679 | 105,746 | 160,222 | 308,583 | 31,835 | 3,579,721 | 14,077 | 94,380 | 154,372 | 79,137 |
| Ohio | 160,363 | 111,427 | 45,764 | 46,749 | 109,502 | 14,500 | 1,787,646 | 6,563 | 13,967 | 20,152 | 31,548 |
| Indiana | 75,362 | 34,428 | 16,892 | 27,467 | 39,564 | 3,653 | 633,302 | 1,207 | 7,838 | 11,056 | 51,332 |
| Illinois | 283,027 | 151,597 | 91,630 | 30,580 | 373,564 | 32,882 | 2,439,943 | 7,050 | 22,336 | 29,043 | 79,455 |
| Michigan | 86,559 | 59,482 | 22,390 | 12,694 | 37,308 | 7,988 | 1,124,009 | 3,636 | 7,998 | 13,959 | 40,771 |

*Condensed statement, by States, of assets and liabilities of all reporting banks in the United States and island possessions, June, 1922—Continued.*

Liabilities (in thousands of dollars).

| States and Territories, etc. | Capital stock paid in. | Surplus. | Undivided profits (less expenses and taxes paid). | National-bank circulation. | Due to all banks. | Certified checks and cashiers' checks. | Individual deposits. | United States deposits. | Notes and bills rediscounted. | Bills payable. | Other liabilities. |
|---|---|---|---|---|---|---|---|---|---|---|---|
| Wisconsin | 59,613 | 26,087 | 17,863 | 15,059 | 37,756 | 4,156 | 641,854 | 1,659 | 8,953 | 14,817 | 5,260 |
| Minnesota | 73,506 | 38,788 | 18,423 | 15,565 | 82,167 | 11,584 | 797,943 | 3,022 | 26,919 | 4,838 | 5,946 |
| Iowa | 83,701 | 43,190 | 20,376 | 20,144 | 46,718 | 2,472 | 821,799 | 1,040 | 16,060 | 57,818 | 12,465 |
| Missouri | 115,351 | 60,018 | 24,830 | 18,337 | 196,856 | 5,565 | 892,479 | 2,700 | 2,564 | 22,600 | 39,212 |
| Total Middle Western States | 887,485 | 525,387 | 258,167 | 196,535 | 911,835 | 83,085 | 9,158,975 | 28,877 | 106,605 | 174,283 | 266,009 |
| North Dakota | 18,527 | 7,595 | 982 | 4,557 | 3,632 | 1,662 | 148,769 | 135 | 4,467 | 31,888 | 559 |
| South Dakota | 19,195 | 7,373 | 5,519 | 4,221 | 16,492 | 2,164 | 199,712 | 483 | 8,528 | 20,037 | 1,951 |
| Nebraska | 42,600 | 17,661 | 13,092 | 9,608 | 55,773 | 3,070 | 371,561 | 566 | 3,776 | 14,262 | 2,679 |
| Kansas | 46,388 | 25,006 | 8,899 | 11,156 | 33,207 | 3,839 | 377,085 | 1,145 | 13,278 | 3,270 | 10,143 |
| Montana | 19,710 | 7,412 | 2,991 | 4,102 | 5,662 | 1,734 | 130,619 | 150 | 21,411 | 3,890 | 360 |
| Wyoming | 6,148 | 4,021 | 1,489 | 2,381 | 3,796 | 517 | 60,742 | 137 | 1,801 | 1,672 | 31 |
| Colorado | 21,842 | 13,840 | 5,071 | 6,851 | 21,187 | 4,270 | 252,370 | 706 | 3,464 | 4,479 | 1,127 |
| New Mexico | 6,135 | 2,598 | 439 | 2,320 | 2,366 | 743 | 45,391 | 368 | 3,299 | 1,315 | 254 |
| Oklahoma | 38,610 | 11,531 | 3,453 | 11,790 | 36,999 | 9,891 | 340,885 | 1,344 | 18,483 | 4,524 | 1,563 |
| Total Western States | 219,155 | 97,037 | 41,505 | 56,986 | 179,114 | 27,920 | 1,927,137 | 5,034 | 78,505 | 85,327 | 18,667 |
| Washington | 29,477 | 11,734 | 4,411 | 7,417 | 23,185 | 3,591 | 318,687 | 1,427 | 3,506 | 3,746 | 5,150 |
| Oregon | 20,944 | 9,912 | 4,492 | 6,129 | 14,586 | 3,211 | 212,376 | 274 | 3,562 | 3,415 | 2,991 |
| California | 165,190 | 80,007 | 40,305 | 40,774 | 156,436 | 13,580 | 2,036,313 | 11,080 | 22,502 | 16,134 | 32,699 |
| Idaho | 9,425 | 3,559 | 881 | 3,363 | 2,631 | 963 | 69,919 | 95 | 3,720 | 11,466 | 478 |
| Utah | 11,908 | 5,711 | 2,127 | 3,445 | 9,138 | 1,080 | 92,882 | 51 | 3,627 | 2,553 | 7,153 |
| Nevada | 3,221 | 1,140 | 602 | 1,211 | 1,974 | 373 | 22,536 | 87 | 2,269 | 367 | 251 |
| Arizona | 6,460 | 2,924 | 1,248 | 1,210 | 2,572 | 426 | 64,927 | 183 | 2,541 | 2,850 | 379 |
| Alaska | 805 | 260 | 250 | 44 | 248 | 46 | 6,846 | 244 | 80 | | 10 |
| Total Pacific States | 247,420 | 114,547 | 54,409 | 63,593 | 210,770 | 23,273 | 2,830,306 | 13,441 | 38,816 | 40,531 | 49,114 |
| Hawaii | 5,221 | 2,991 | 1,170 | 439 | 603 | 258 | 46,674 | 1,154 | 87 | 975 | 2,637 |
| Porto Rico | 5,750 | 1,252 | 844 | | 1,534 | 247 | 23,519 | 835 | 1,436 | 821 | 1,790 |
| Philippines | 24,338 | 1,608 | 4,422 | | 23,516 | 641 | 70,146 | | 1,599 | 4,999 | 37,425 |
| Total island possessions | 35,309 | 5,851 | 6,436 | 439 | 25,653 | 1,146 | 140,369 | 2,019 | 3,122 | 6,705 | 41,852 |
| Total United States | 2,943,950 | 2,697,409 | 933,843 | 725,748 | 3,244,386 | 552,505 | 37,194,318 | 128,887 | 435,711 | 635,564 | 933,016 |

RECAPITULATION.

| | | | | | | | | | | | |
|---|---:|---:|---:|---:|---:|---:|---:|---:|---:|---:|---:|
| National banks | 1,307,216 | 1,048,806 | 492,434 | 725,748 | 2,502,051 | 450,773 | 13,254,366 | 103,374 | 280,271 | 228,481 | 302,490 |
| State (commercial) banks | 1,014,248 | 561,131 | 210,536 | ........ | 387,657 | 69,803 | 10,107,597 | 7,731 | 111,651 | 311,149 | 282,900 |
| Mutual savings banks | ........ | 468,193 | 92,196 | ........ | 264 | 24 | 5,779,506 | 1 | 107 | 647 | 10,710 |
| Stock savings banks | 79,850 | 41,180 | 18,995 | ........ | 1,336 | 557 | 1,401,712 | 3,736 | 61 | 29,355 | 7,110 |
| Trust companies | 532,316 | 562,731 | 117,513 | ........ | 351,517 | 31,109 | 6,495,928 | 13,800 | 42,237 | 61,333 | 325,336 |
| Private banks | 10,320 | 15,368 | 2,169 | ........ | 1,531 | 239 | 145,179 | 242 | 1,384 | 4,599 | 4,500 |
| Grand total | 2,943,950 | 2,697,409 | 933,843 | 725,748 | 3,244,386 | 552,505 | 37,194,318 | 128,887 | 435,711 | 635,564 | 933,016 |

The resources and liabilities of all reporting banks in the United
States and island possessions, June 30, 1922, are shown in the following statement, with classifications of loans and discounts, investments, cash and deposits:

*Summary of reports of condition of 30,389 reporting banks in the United States and
island possessions at the close of business June 30, 1922.*

[In thousands of dollars.]

RESOURCES.

| | | |
|---|---:|---:|
| Loans and discounts (including rediscounts): | | |
| On demand (secured by collateral other than real estate).. | 3,100,039 | |
| On demand (not secured by collateral). | 885,927 | |
| On time (secured by collateral other than real estate)..... | 3,534,472 | |
| On time (not secured by collateral) | 7,051,849 | |
| Secured by farm land | 409,916 | |
| Secured by other real estate | 3,101,093 | |
| Not classified | 9,777,147 | |
| Total | | 27,860,443 |
| Overdrafts | | 74,600 |
| Investments (including premiums on bonds): | | |
| United States Government securities | 3,500,167 | |
| State, county, and municipal bonds | 981,375 | |
| Railroad bonds | 1,420,463 | |
| Bonds of other public service corporations (including street and interurban railway bonds) | 688,400 | |
| Other bonds, stocks, warrants, etc | 5,957,162 | |
| Total | | 12,547,567 |
| Banking house (including furniture and fixtures) | | 1,078,174 |
| Other real estate owned | | 198,457 |
| Due from banks | | 3,073,444 |
| Lawful reserve with Federal reserve bank or other reserve agents | | 2,340,797 |
| Checks and other cash items | | 644,014 |
| Exchanges for clearing house | | 930,594 |
| Cash on hand: | | |
| Gold coin | 40,216 | |
| Silver coin | ¹ 52,452 | |
| Paper currency | ² 462,942 | |
| Nickels and cents | 6,496 | |
| Not classified | 267,786 | |
| Total | | 829,892 |
| Other resources | | 847,385 |
| Total resources | | 50,425,367 |

LIABILITIES.

| | | |
|---|---:|---:|
| Capital stock paid in | | 2,943,950 |
| Surplus | | 2,697,409 |
| Undivided profits (less expenses and taxes paid) | | 933,843 |
| National bank circulation | | 725,748 |
| Due to all banks | | 3,244,386 |
| Certified checks and cashiers' checks | | 552,505 |
| Individual deposits: | | |
| Demand deposits— | | |
| Individual deposits subject to check | 14,334,122 | |
| Demand certificates of deposit | 600,257 | |
| Dividends unpaid | 50,848 | |

Individual deposits—Continued.
  Time deposits—
    Savings deposits, or deposits in interest or savings
      department..................................... 13, 237, 407
    Time certificates of deposit........................ 2, 332, 753
    Postal savings deposits............................. 43, 668
    Deposits not classified............................. 6, 505, 263

      Total...................................................... 37, 194, 318
United States deposits (exclusive of postal savings)................... 128, 887
Notes and bills rediscounted......................................... 435, 711
Bills payable (including advances received from War Finance Corpora-
  tion and certificates of deposit representing money borrowed)........ 635, 564
Other liabilities.................................................... 933, 046

      Total liabilities............................................. 50, 425, 367

[1] National bank figures include nickels and cents.
[2] National bank figures include gold certificates and clearing-house certificates.

-COMPARISON OF PRINCIPAL ITEMS OF RESOURCES AND LIABILITIES
OF ALL REPORTING BANKS IN THE UNITED STATES AND ISLAND
POSSESSIONS IN JUNE, 1921 AND 1922.

The following statement shows the changes in the principal items
of resources and liabilities of reporting banks, other than national
banks, national banks, and the aggregates for all reporting banks in
the fiscal years 1921 and 1922.

The loans and discounts of all reporting banks were reduced
$1,071,568,000 during the fiscal year, or 3.70 per cent. Cash in
vault and balances due from Federal reserve banks were increased
$138,349,000, or 4.58 per cent. Aggregate deposits were increased
$2,461,297,000, or 6.37 per cent, and total resources were increased
$753,977,000, or 1.52 per cent. The percentage of cash in vault
and due from Federal reserve banks to total deposits for the fiscal
year ended June 30, 1922, was 7.68 per cent, compared with 7.81
per cent for the fiscal year ended June 30, 1921. The number of
reporting banks other than national June 30, 1922, was 518 less
than a year ago, while the number of national banks was increased
by 95.

*Comparative statement of the number of banks reporting, loans, cash in vault,
total deposits, and aggregate resources of all banks in the United States and island
possessions, on dates nearest to June 30, for the years 1921 and 1922.*

STATE, SAVINGS, AND PRIVATE BANKS, AND LOAN AND TRUST COMPANIES.

[In thousands of dollars.]

| Year. | Number of banks. | Loans.[1] | Cash in vault and due from Federal reserve banks.[2] | All deposits. | Aggregate resources. |
|---|---|---|---|---|---|
| 1922................................. | 22, 140 | 16, 435, 991 | 1, 324, 891 | 24, 799, 532 | 29, 719, 357 |
| 1921................................. | 22, 658 | 16, 689, 209 | 1, 277, 438 | 23, 516, 468 | 29, 153, 528 |
| Decrease........................... | 518 | · 253, 218 | .......... | .......... | .......... |
| Increase............................ | .......... | .......... | 47, 453 | 1, 283, 064 | 565, 829 |
| Per cent of decrease................ | 2. 29 | 1. 52 | .......... | .......... | .......... |
| Per cent of increase................ | .......... | .......... | 3. 71 | 5. 46 | 1. 94 |

Per cent of "Cash in vault and due from Federal reserve banks" to "All deposits":
  1922.................................................................................... 5. 34
  1921.................................................................................... 5. 43

*Comparative statement of the number of banks reporting, loans, cash in vault. total deposits, and aggregate resources of all banks in the United States and island possessions, on dates nearest to June 30, for the years 1921 and 1922—Continued.*

### NATIONAL BANKS.

[In thousands of dollars.]

| Year. | Number of banks. | Loans.[1] | Cash in vault and due from Federal reserve banks.[2] | All deposits. | Aggregate resources. |
|---|---|---|---|---|---|
| 1922 | 8,249 | 11,424,452 | 1,833,452 | 16,320,564 | 20,706,010 |
| 1921 | 8,154 | 12,242,802 | 1,742,556 | 15,142,331 | 20,517,862 |
| Decrease | | 818,350 | | | |
| Increase | 95 | | 90,896 | 1,178,233 | 188,148 |
| Per cent of decrease | | 6.68 | | | |
| Per cent of increase | 1.17 | | 5.22 | 7.78 | .92 |

Per cent of "Cash in vault and due from Federal reserve banks" to "All deposits":
1922.....................................................................................................................11.23
1921......................................................................................................................11.51

### TOTAL NATIONAL, STATE, SAVINGS, AND PRIVATE BANKS, AND LOAN AND TRUST COMPANIES.

| Year. | Number of banks. | Loans.[1] | Cash in vault and due from Federal reserve banks.[2] | All deposits. | Aggregate resources. |
|---|---|---|---|---|---|
| 1922 | 30,389 | 27,860,443 | 3,158,343 | 41,120,096 | 50,425,367 |
| 1921 | 30,812 | 28,932,011 | 3,019,994 | 38,658,799 | 49,671,390 |
| Decrease | 423 | 1,071,568 | | | |
| Increase | | | 138,349 | 2,461,297 | 753,977 |
| Per cent of decrease | 1.37 | 3.70 | | | |
| Per cent of increase | | | 4.58 | 6.37 | 1.52 |

Per cent of "Cash in vault and due from Federal reserve banks" to "All deposits":
1922......................................................................................................................7.68
1921......................................................................................................................7.81

[1] Acceptances, customers' liability under letters of credit, and rediscounts included.
[2] Includes balances due from Federal reserve banks to State banks and trust companies, members of Federal Reserve System.

### INDIVIDUAL DEPOSITS IN ALL REPORTING BANKS.

Individual deposits in all reporting banks in the United States and island possessions June 30, 1922, consisting of time and demand deposits and including postal savings deposits, aggregated $37,194,-318,000 and showed an increase of $2,349,746,000 over the amount reported June 30, 1921.

A classification of these deposits shown by the returns from State (commercial) banks, stock savings banks, mutual savings banks, loan and trust companies, private banks, and national banks, is shown in the following statement.

Individual deposits subject to check show a reduction in the year of $1,740,003,000; demand certificates of deposit, a reduction of $94,524,000; dividends unpaid, a reduction of $2,853,000; time certificates of deposit, an increase of $331,870,000; postal savings deposits, a reduction of $24,892,000; while savings deposits show an increase of $95,272,000, and deposits not classified an increase of $3,784,876,000.

*Individual deposits in each class of banks June 30, 1922.*

[In thousands of dollars.]

|  | Number of banks. | Individual deposits subject to check without notice. | Demand certificates of deposit. | Dividends unpaid. | Savings deposits. |
|---|---|---|---|---|---|
| State banks | 18,232 | 3,666,927 | 237,352 | 9,744 | 2,649,660 |
| Stock savings banks | 1,066 | 17,167 | 495 | 55 | 439,016 |
| Mutual savings banks | 619 | 41,549 | | 653 | 5,686,603 |
| Loan and trust companies | 1,550 | 2,053,254 | 72,927 | 5,448 | 1,382,748 |
| Private banks | 673 | 48,121 | 14,396 | 12 | 32,733 |
| Total | 22,140 | 5,830,018 | 325,170 | 15,912 | 10,190,760 |
| National banks | 8,249 | 8,504,104 | 275,087 | 34,936 | [1] 3,046,647 |
| Grand total | 30,389 | 14,334,122 | 600,257 | 50,848 | 13,237,407 |

|  | Time certificates of deposit. | Postal savings deposits. | Deposits not classified. | Total. |
|---|---|---|---|---|
| State banks | 1,177,442 | 4,367 | 2,359,105 | 10,107,597 |
| Stock savings banks | 2,950 | 4 | 942,055 | 1,401,742 |
| Mutual savings banks | 117 | | 50,524 | 5,779,506 |
| Loan and trust companies | 136,768 | 6,041 | 2,838,742 | 6,495,928 |
| Private banks | 20,001 | 313 | 29,603 | 145,179 |
| Total | 1,337,278 | 10,725 | 6,220,089 | 23,929,952 |
| National banks | 995,475 | 32,943 | 375,174 | 13,264,366 |
| Grand total | 2,332,753 | 43,668 | 6,595,263 | 37,194,318 |

[1] Includes approximately $85,353,000 certificates of deposit.

### CASH IN ALL REPORTING BANKS.

The cash in the vaults of all reporting banks June 30, 1922, amounted to $829,892,000, which, with the addition of the cash holdings of the 12 Federal reserve banks, aggregating $3,148,366,000, made total cash in all banks $3,978,258,000, an increase over the amount held June 30, 1921, of $406,233,000.

Of the total cash in vaults of reporting banks June 30, 1922, $503,711,000 was held by banks other than national and $326,181,000 by national banks.

The following statement shows a classification of cash holdings on date indicated:

REPORT ON THE FINANCES.

*Cash in all banks June 30, 1922.*

[In thousands of dollars.]

| Classification. | 8,249 national banks. | 22,140 State, etc., banks. | Total, 30,401 banks.[1] |
|---|---|---|---|
| Gold coin | 20,438 | 19,778 | 40,216 |
| Gold certificates | [2] 18,364 | | 18,364 |
| Silver coin | [3] 34,885 | 17,562 | 52,447 |
| Silver certificates | 23,012 | | 23,012 |
| Legal-tender notes | 24,421 | | 24,421 |
| National-bank notes | 61,015 | [4] 192,089 | 253,104 |
| Federal reserve notes [5] | 144,046 | | 144,046 |
| Nickels and cents | | 6,496 | 6,496 |
| Cash not classified | | 267,786 | 267,786 |
| Total | 326,181 | 503,711 | 829,892 |
| Cash in Federal reserve banks June 28, 1922: | | | |
| Gold coin and certificates (reserve) | | | 3,020,868 |
| Legal-tender notes, silver, etc. (reserve) | | | 127,498 |
| Grand total | | | 3,978,258 |

[1] Number of banks includes 12 Federal reserve banks.
[2] Includes clearing-house certificates.
[3] Includes nickels and cents.
[4] Includes all paper currency.
[5] Includes Federal reserve bank notes.

SAVINGS DEPOSITS IN ALL REPORTING BANKS, INCLUDING POSTAL SAVINGS AND SCHOOL SAVINGS DEPOSITS, JUNE, 1922.

The following statement shows the amount of deposits classified as savings in the returns of all reporting banks, including the postal savings and school savings systems, information with respect to the latter having been furnished by the savings bank section of the American Bankers' Association, in each State and the insular possessions in June, 1922:

Deposits classified as savings, in all reporting banks, including postal savings and school savings deposits, June, 1922.

[In thousands of dollars.]

| States, Territories, etc. | National banks. | State (commercial) banks. | Stock savings banks. | Mutual savings banks. | Loan and trust companies. | Private banks. | Postal Savings System. | School savings banks. | Total savings deposits. |
|---|---|---|---|---|---|---|---|---|---|
| Maine | 56,718 | | | 105,324 | 69,325 | | 276 | 5 | 231,648 |
| New Hampshire | 9,054 | | 14,030 | 123,380 | 12,164 | | 527 | 2 | 159,157 |
| Vermont | 21,613 | | | 67,878 | 49,892 | | 140 | | 139,523 |
| Massachusetts | 141,484 | 293 | | 1,187,039 | 149,504 | | 8,371 | 162 | 1,486,833 |
| Rhode Island | 9,917 | 1,457 | | 120,843 | 91,480 | | 967 | | 224,664 |
| Connecticut | 34,467 | | | 418,980 | 64,013 | | 2,260 | 101 | 519,821 |
| Total New England States | 273,253 | 1,750 | 14,030 | 2,023,444 | 436,378 | | 12,541 | 270 | 2,761,666 |
| New York | 388,715 | | | 2,791,353 | | | 61,312 | 1,319 | 3,242,729 |
| New Jersey | 198,450 | 23,962 | 20,845 | 184,297 | 293,444 | 978 | 4,699 | 153 | 726,828 |
| Pennsylvania | 522,807 | 197,223 | 2,012 | 302,751 | 363,527 | 1,494 | 11,948 | 1,580 | 1,403,342 |
| Delaware | 4,849 | 5,293 | | 19,031 | 9,471 | | 216 | 1 | 38,561 |
| Maryland | 60,085 | 55,069 | | 129,811 | 53,482 | | 237 | | 298,685 |
| Washington, D. C. | 21,394 | | 13,970 | | 18,400 | | 351 | | 54,115 |
| Total Eastern States | 1,196,300 | 281,547 | 36,827 | 3,427,243 | 738,324 | 2,472 | 78,793 | 3,054 | 5,764,560 |
| Virginia | 100,636 | 42,164 | | | | | 323 | 60 | 143,183 |
| West Virginia | 47,687 | 21,889 | | | 20,947 | | 315 | 67 | 90,905 |
| North Carolina | 34,467 | 70,498 | | | | | 40 | 14 | 105,019 |
| South Carolina | 39,746 | 36,400 | | | | | 61 | | 76,207 |
| Georgia | 30,687 | 46,001 | | | | | 267 | 15 | 76,970 |
| Florida | 36,643 | 29,185 | | | | | 324 | 1 | 66,633 |
| Alabama | 28,955 | 23,037 | | | | | 374 | | 52,346 |
| Mississippi | 7,829 | 23,042 | | | | | 72 | | 30,935 |
| Louisiana | 10,336 | 67,579 | | | | | 392 | 86 | 78,333 |
| Texas | 59,690 | 2,988 | | | 7,113 | | 867 | | 70,660 |
| Arkansas | 8,381 | 14,459 | | | | | 176 | | 23,016 |
| Kentucky | 26,866 | 30,664 | | | | | 373 | 137 | 58,040 |
| Tennessee | 37,600 | | | | | 2 | 231 | 85 | 37,916 |
| Total Southern States | 469,494 | 407,906 | | | 28,060 | 2 | 4,315 | 466 | 910,243 |
| Ohio | 148,408 | 507,257 | | 65,537 | | 3,435 | 4,168 | 708 | 729,573 |
| Indiana | 53,327 | 32,740 | | 15,811 | 68,882 | 1,354 | 1,024 | 167 | 173,305 |
| Illinois | 157,130 | 614,729 | | | | | 8,551 | 216 | 780,617 |
| Michigan | 123,421 | 450,155 | 8,779 | | | 1,761 | 3,247 | 235 | 587,598 |
| Wisconsin | 83,119 | 110,552 | | 3,979 | 2,737 | | 1,375 | 106 | 201,868 |
| Minnesota | 80,484 | 56,201 | | 59,787 | 10,900 | | 1,457 | 188 | 209,017 |
| Iowa | 47,551 | | 358,328 | | | 20,542 | 412 | 128 | 426,961 |
| Missouri | 40,433 | 39,371 | | | 58,338 | | 2,678 | 8 | 140,828 |
| Total Middle Western States | 733,873 | 1,810,996 | 367,107 | 145,114 | 140,857 | 27,092 | 22,912 | 1,816 | 3,249,757 |

Deposits classified as savings, in all reporting banks, including postal savings and school savings deposits, June, 1922—Continued.

[In thousands of dollars.]

| States, Territories, etc. | National banks. | State (commercial) banks. | Stock savings banks. | Mutual savings banks. | Loan and trust companies. | Private banks. | Postal Savings System. | School savings banks. | Total savings deposits. |
|---|---|---|---|---|---|---|---|---|---|
| North Dakota | 7,834 | 1,963 | | | 405 | 3 | 20 | | 10,225 |
| South Dakota | 7,307 | 6,347 | | | 708 | | 23 | | 14,385 |
| Nebraska | 11,063 | | | | | | 373 | 172 | 11,608 |
| Kansas | 10,327 | | | | | | 614 | 2 | 10,943 |
| Montana | 13,811 | 3,063 | | | 8,581 | 3,086 | 923 | | 29,464 |
| Wyoming | 7,428 | | | | | | 205 | | 7,633 |
| Colorado | 43,767 | 8,060 | | | 26,272 | | 1,431 | | 79,598 |
| New Mexico | 2,701 | 1,860 | | | 1,564 | 78 | 39 | 2 | 6,166 |
| Oklahoma | 19,577 | 20,607 | | | | | 514 | 4 | 40,702 |
| Total Western States | 123,815 | 41,880 | | | 37,530 | 3,167 | 4,142 | 180 | 210,724 |
| Washington | 60,560 | 30,219 | | 17,184 | | | 7,312 | 21 | 115,296 |
| Oregon | 32,993 | 21,874 | 2,823 | | | | 1,954 | | 59,644 |
| California | 132,302 | | | 73,618 | | | 3,109 | 711 | 209,740 |
| Idaho | 7,219 | 3,250 | | | | | 576 | | 11,045 |
| Utah | 8,051 | 16,716 | 15,458 | | 349 | | 473 | | 41,047 |
| Nevada | 3,627 | 5,068 | 2,771 | | | | 289 | | 11,755 |
| Arizona | 4,567 | | | | | | 349 | | 4,916 |
| Total Pacific States | 249,319 | 77,127 | 21,052 | 90,852 | 349 | | 14,062 | 732 | 453,443 |
| Alaska | 334 | 1,828 | | | | | 784 | | 2,946 |
| Hawaii | 259 | 13,272 | | | 1,250 | | 28 | | 14,809 |
| Porto Rico | | 7,424 | | | | | 155 | | 7,579 |
| Philippines | | 5,920 | | | | | | | 5,920 |
| Virgin Islands | | | | | | | 4 | | 4 |
| Total foreign possessions | 593 | 28,444 | | | 1,250 | | 971 | | 31,258 |
| Total United States | ¹13,046,647 | 2,649,660 | 439,016 | 5,686,603 | 1,382,748 | 32,733 | 137,736 | 6,518 | 13,351,661 |

¹ Includes approximately $85,353,000 certificates of deposit.

## DEVELOPMENT OF BANKING INSTITUTIONS IN THE UNITED STATES AND ISLAND POSSESSIONS SINCE JUNE 30, 1914.

The remarkable expansion of banking business in the United States and island possessions since June 30, 1914, a few months prior to the opening of the 12 Federal reserve banks, to June 30, 1922, is reflected in a compilation of returns with respect to the condition of all reporting banks on the two dates named.

In the 8-year period referred to the number of reporting institutions has grown from 26,765 to 30,389, and resources have been increased from $26,971,398,000 to $50,425,367,000.

Loans and discounts were increased from $15,288,357,000 to $27,860,443,000, and overdrafts from $51,121,000 to $74,600,000 in this period.

Investments of these banks were increased more than 100 per cent, or from $5,584,925,000 to $12,547,567,000.

Banking houses, furniture, and fixtures show an increase of $468,478,000, the amount June 30, 1922, being $1,078,174,000. Other real estate owned was increased from $129,983,000 to $198,457,000.

On June 30, 1914, the balances due reporting banks from other banks and bankers were $2,872,698,000, compared with $5,414,241,000 June 30, 1922, while miscellaneous checks and other cash items, including exchanges for clearing house, rose from $520,995,000 to $1,574,608,000 in this period.

By reason of the provision of the Federal reserve act, which requires national banks and member State banks and trust companies to maintain lawful reserve with Federal reserve banks against demand and time deposits, which became effective subsequent to June 30, 1914, the cash in vaults of these banks was decreased from $1,639,219,000 on that date to $829,892,000 June 30, 1922.

Other miscellaneous assets were $274,404,000 in 1914, compared with $847,385,000 in 1922.

Capital stock of $2,943,950,000 was $811,876,000 in excess of the amount in 1914, and surplus funds amounting to $2,697,409,000 show an increase of $982,923,000 over the 1914 returns. Undivided profits in this period were increased from $562,032,000 to $933,843,000.

Balances on the books of reporting banks to the credit of correspondent banks and bankers June 30, 1914, amounted to $2,705,076,000, compared with $3,244,386,000 June 30, 1922, and the liability for certified checks and cashiers' checks outstanding was increased from $270,500,000 to $552,505,000 between the two dates. Individual deposits show an increase in this period of more than 100 per cent, the amount June 30, 1922, being $37,194,318,000, an increase of $18,876,707,000.

National bank circulation was increased from $722,555,000 to $725,748,000, while United States deposits increased from $66,655,000 to $128,887,000.

The liabilities for notes and bills rediscounted and bills payable were increased from $38,130,000 to $435,711,000, and from $194,431,000 to $635,564,000, respectively, in this period.

Other liabilities were increased $685,198,000 and amounted to $933,046,000.

The percentage of loans and discounts of all reporting banks June 30, 1914, to total deposits was 71.58, compared with 67.75 per cent June 30, 1922.

### RESOURCES AND LIABILITIES OF ALL REPORTING BANKS, 1917–1922.

The principal items of resources and liabilities of all banks, other than Federal reserve banks, for the six years 1917 to 1922 are shown in the following statement:

[In thousands of dollars.]

| Classification. | 1917 (27,923 banks). | 1918 (28,880 banks). | 1919 (29,123 banks). | 1920 (30,139 banks). | 1921 (30,812 banks). | 1922 (30,389 banks). |
|---|---|---|---|---|---|---|
| **RESOURCES.** | | | | | | |
| Loans and discounts (including rediscounts)[1] | 20,594,228 | 22,514,602 | 25,255,171 | 31,208,142 | 28,932,011 | 27,860,443 |
| Overdrafts | 47,199 | 60,335 | 94,293 | 109,186 | 81,849 | 74,600 |
| Bonds, stocks, and other securities | 8,003,820 | 9,741,653 | 12,229,528 | 11,387,525 | 11,381,923 | 12,547,567 |
| Due from other banks and bankers | 4,793,167 | 5,136,604 | 5,865,414 | 5,833,241 | 4,794,205 | 5,414,241 |
| Real estate, furniture, etc.[2] | 862,967 | 909,183 | 936,707 | 1,000,976 | 1,147,521 | 1,276,631 |
| Checks and other cash items[3] | 758,692 | 683,078 | 1,420,809 | 1,457,773 | 1,290,667 | 1,574,608 |
| Cash on hand | 1,502,502 | 896,571 | 997,353 | 1,079,378 | 946,567 | 829,892 |
| Other resources | 564,188 | 784,413 | 816,172 | 1,005,882 | 1,096,647 | 847,385 |
| Total | 37,126,763 | 40,726,439 | 47,615,447 | 53,079,108 | 49,671,390 | 50,425,367 |
| **LIABILITIES.** | | | | | | |
| Capital stock paid in | 2,274,200 | 2,351,588 | 2,437,365 | 2,702,639 | 2,903,961 | 2,943,950 |
| Surplus fund | 1,945,544 | 2,034,764 | 2,181,994 | 2,410,346 | 2,542,032 | 2,697,409 |
| Other undivided profits | 674,191 | 684,260 | 825,889 | 976,261 | 910,743 | 933,843 |
| Circulation (national banks) | 660,431 | 681,631 | 677,162 | 688,178 | 704,147 | 725,748 |
| Certified checks and cashiers' checks | 333,181 | 207,907 | 546,345 | 514,862 | 614,583 | 552,505 |
| Individual deposits | 26,062,986 | 27,748,471 | 32,665,286 | 37,315,123 | 34,844,572 | 37,194,318 |
| United States deposits | 132,965 | 1,037,787 | 566,793 | 175,788 | 390,230 | 128,887 |
| Due to other banks and bankers | 3,913,944 | 3,595,062 | 3,890,487 | 3,708,302 | 2,809,414 | 3,244,386 |
| Other liabilities | 1,129,321 | 2,384,969 | 3,824,126 | 4,587,609 | 3,951,708 | 2,004,321 |
| Total | 37,126,763 | 40,726,439 | 47,615,447 | 53,079,108 | 49,671,390 | 50,425,367 |

[1] Includes acceptances reported by national banks.
[2] Includes real estate owned other than banking house.
[3] Includes exchanges for clearing house.

### NATIONAL BANKS, FEDERAL RESERVE AND STATE (COMMERCIAL), LOAN AND TRUST COMPANIES, SAVINGS AND PRIVATE BANKS.

In the fiscal year ended June 30, 1922, the aggregate resources of all reporting banks, including the twelve Federal reserve banks, show a gain of $416,784,000 over the returns for June 30, 1921. Loans and discounts show a reduction of $2,251,570,000 during the year, the aggregate for June 30, 1922, being $28,483,604,000.

The investments of these banks were increased during the year $1,464,919,000, and amounted to $13,104,174,000. Cash on hand, amounting to $3,978,258,000, shows an increase over 1921 of $406,233,000.

Capital stock was increased during the year from $3,006,145,000 to $3,049,028,000; surplus funds show an increase of $168,739,000 and undivided profits a reduction of $15,529,000. The latter reduction, however, is largely accounted for by reason of the fact that the item of reserve for Government franchise tax, in the Federal Reserve

Board statement of condition of the twelve Federal reserve banks for the latter part of June, was reduced between 1921 and 1922 from $40,910,000 to $2,281,000.

The items of resources and liabilities of reporting banks, and the 12 Federal reserve banks, are shown in the following statement with the aggregate for all banks as of June, 1922:

*Statement of the principal items of resources and liabilities of 30,401 reporting banks, including the Federal reserve banks, in the United States and island possessions, June, 1922.*

[In thousands of dollars ]

| | 30,389 reporting banks, June 30, 1922. | 12 Federal reserve banks, June 28, 1922. | Total, 30,401 banks. |
|---|---|---|---|
| **RESOURCES.** | | | |
| Loans and discounts, including rediscounts.................. | [1] 27,860,443 | 623,161 | 28,483,604 |
| Overdrafts........................................ | 74,600 | | 74,600 |
| Investments...................................... | 12,547,567 | 556,607 | 13,104,174 |
| Banking house (including furniture and fixtures)........... | 1,078,174 | 41,568 | 1,119,742 |
| Other real estate owned............................ | 198,457 | | 198,457 |
| Due from banks................................... | 3,073,444 | [2] 511,571 | 3,585,015 |
| Lawful reserve with Federal reserve bank or other reserve agents.......................................... | 2,340,797 | | 2,340,797 |
| Checks and other cash items........................ | 644,014 | | 644,014 |
| Exchanges for clearing house....................... | 930,594 | | 930,594 |
| Cash on hand..................................... | 829,892 | 3,148,366 | 3,978,258 |
| Other resources................................... | 847,385 | 23,575 | 870,960 |
| Total resources............................... | 50,425,367 | 4,904,848 | 55,330,215 |
| **LIABILITIES.** | | | |
| Capital stock paid in....... ..................... | 2,943,950 | 105,078 | 3,049,028 |
| Surplus.......................................... | 2,697,409 | 215,398 | 2,912,807 |
| Undivided profits (less expenses and taxes paid)............ | 933,843 | [3] 2,281 | 936,124 |
| National bank circulation...... ................... | 725,748 | | 725,748 |
| Federal reserve note circulation.................... | | 2,191,681 | 2,191,681 |
| Due to all banks................................. | 3,244,386 | [4] 2,295,513 | 5,539,899 |
| Certified checks and cashiers' checks................ | 552,505 | | 552,505 |
| Individual deposits............................... | 37,194,318 | 30,297 | 37,224,615 |
| United States deposits (exclusive of postal savings).......... | 128,887 | 43,780 | 172,667 |
| Notes and bills rediscounted....................... | 435,711 | | 435,711 |
| Bills payable (including all obligations representing money borrowed)..................................... | 635,564 | | 635,564 |
| Other liabilities................................. | 933,046 | 20,820 | 953,866 |
| Total liabilities.............................. | 50,425,367 | 4,904,848 | 55,330,215 |

[1] Includes acceptances of national banks.
[2] Uncollected items.
[3] Represents reserve for Government franchise tax.
[4] Due to members, reserve account, and deferred availability items.

## BUILDING AND LOAN ASSOCIATIONS.

"The notable feature of the continued development of building and loan associations last year was the large increase in membership—the greatest ever recorded in a single year," states Secretary H. F. Cellarius, of the United States League of Local Building and Loan Associations in the annual report of the proceedings of the thirtieth annual convention of these institutions. Mr Cellarius further states that—

Eight hundred and forty-seven thousand new members were enrolled in the 9,255 associations actually engaged in business in the United States last year, an increase of over 17 per cent; the total members now number 5,809,888. The resources of these associations are $2,890,764,621, or net increase for the year of $370,849,650, or nearly 15 per cent. These results clearly show that the true value of building and loan associations and the real benefits which they confer on their respective communities in encouraging saving and home owning are being recognized and appreciated by the public to a fuller extent than ever before.

Building and loan associations are the only financial institutions which loan practically all their funds available for investment on mortgage security to those desiring to either build or buy homes  The housing shortage, which became acute during the war, has not yet been relieved to any great extent, although building associations have been drawn upon to the fullest for loans for these purposes.  Unfortunately the unemployment resulting from industrial conditions last year caused a greater volume of withdrawals than ordinary. and this reduced the amount applicable for mortgage loans.  During 1920 the building associations loaned $770,000,000 for home buying or home owning purposes, but last year only about $693,000,000 of their funds could be thus invested.  As unemployment decreases and the wage earners are again able to save, building associations will be able to correspondingly increase the making of mortgage loans.  The current year is showing a substantial improvement in this regard, but it is, in part only, taking care of the pronounced increases in dwelling-house construction now under way.

The more important increases in assets of the several States for 1921 are as follows: Pennsylvania, $71,884,501;  Ohio, $62,905,954;  New Jersey, $46,106,480;  Illinois, $37,390,342; Massachusetts, $22,152,397; New York, $15,490,292; Indiana, $11,874,043; Oklahoma, $10,757,888;  Louisiana, $9,728,387;  Wisconsin, $9,358,858;  Missouri, $8,905,302;  California, $8,645,254;  Kansas, $7,720,132;  Nebraska, $6,131,676: and Kentucky, $5,000,000.

The average amount due each member is $497.56, as against $507.75, the amount shown last year.

## STATISTICS FOR 1921-22.

The following table shows, by States, the number of associations, total membership, and total assets for States in which accurate statistics are compiled by State supervisors:

| | State. | Number of associations. | Total membership. | Total assets. | Increase in assets. | Increase in membership. |
|---|---|---|---|---|---|---|
| 1 | Pennsylvania | 2,997 | 1,193,372 | $546,884,501 | $71,884,501 | 193,372 |
| 2 | Ohio | 787 | 1,152,123 | 525,696,242 | 62,905,954 | 178,953 |
| 3 | New Jersey | 986 | 536,391 | 285,014,487 | 46,106,480 | 110,127 |
| 4 | Massachusetts | 206 | 308,791 | 196,195,049 | 22,152,397 | 12,380 |
| 5 | Illinois | 709 | 348,000 | 174,360,342 | 37,360,342 | 79,000 |
| 6 | New York | 280 | 279,749 | 131,270,691 | 15,490,292 | 30,575 |
| 7 | Indiana | 364 | 245,983 | 121,595,380 | 11,874,043 | 33,683 |
| 8 | Nebraska | 76 | 133,782 | 84,071,013 | 6,131,676 | 14,651 |
| 9 | Maryland | 777 | 161,045 | 80,522,440 | (²) | (²) |
| 10 | California | 96 | 54,102 | 56,496,548 | 8,645,254 | 11,682 |
| 11 | Louisiana | 67 | 90,000 | 55,911,982 | 9,728,387 | 10,000 |
| 12 | Michigan | 78 | 106,250 | 54,306,848 | 3,330,053 | 6,485 |
| 13 | Wisconsin [1] | 105 | 105,000 | 53,000,000 | 9,358,858 | 18,000 |
| 14 | Missouri | 190 | 94,882 | 49,768,530 | 8,905,362 | 23,388 |
| 15 | Kansas | 110 | 103,575 | 46,820,132 | 7,720,132 | 21,075 |
| 16 | Kentucky | 117 | 95,000 | 40,000,000 | 5,000,000 | 20,000 |
| 17 | Oklahoma | 73 | 66,684 | 39,348,311 | 10,757,888 | 20,341 |
| 18 | District of Columbia | 24 | 48,569 | 33,261,000 | 2,135,375 | 3,044 |
| 19 | North Carolina [1] | 219 | 65,000 | 29,500,000 | 3,500,000 | 7,000 |
| 20 | Washington | 48 | 59,459 | 23,950,160 | 3,774,997 | 4,105 |
| 21 | Iowa [1] | 70 | 52,800 | 19,000,000 | 1,345,610 | 3,800 |
| 22 | Arkansas | 54 | 28,225 | 17,997,261 | 110,473 | 225 |
| 23 | Minnesota [1] | 75 | 26,000 | 12,400,000 | 1,045,507 | 2,096 |
| 24 | Utah | 16 | 24,570 | 12,284,112 | (²) | (²) |
| 25 | West Virginia | 44 | 30,000 | 11,644,805 | 944,805 | 2,300 |
| 26 | Colorado | 42 | 22,000 | 10,986,445 | ............ | ............ |
| 27 | Maine | 39 | 18,200 | 10,176,958 | 927,998 | 652 |
| 28 | Connecticut | 32 | 25,000 | 9,383,012 | 2,285,730 | 6,385 |
| 29 | Rhode Island | 8 | 18,398 | 9,275,587 | 1,148,631 | 3,718 |
| 30 | South Carolina | 139 | 18,315 | 6,975,583 | 1,198,131 | 2,395 |
| 31 | Oregon | 12 | 18,626 | 6,816,954 | 1,616,497 | 1,015 |
| 32 | New Hampshire | 25 | 14,458 | 5,255,668 | 555,139 | 3,391 |
| 33 | Texas | 40 | 12,420 | 4,464,056 | 1,212,165 | 3,060 |
| 34 | Montana [1] | 21 | 17,000 | 4,050,000 | 382,514 | 844 |
| 35 | North Dakota | 13 | 8,100 | 4,041,443 | 384,648 | 775 |
| 36 | South Dakota | 16 | 6,515 | 4,006,312 | ............ | ............ |
| 37 | Delaware | 24 | 8,000 | 3,945,522 | (²) | (²) |
| 38 | Tennessee [1] | 11 | 5,800 | 3,500,000 | ............ | ............ |
| 39 | New Mexico | 13 | 4,700 | 1,937,744 | 230,544 | 600 |
| 40 | Arizona | 4 | 3,500 | 1,315,782 | 141,970 | 400 |
| 41 | Vermont | 8 | 1,601 | 658,360 | 109,742 | 102 |
| | Other States [1] | 240 | 197,905 | 102,675,981 | 9,447,055 | 17,350 |
| | Total | 9,255 | 5,809,888 | 2,890,764,621 | 370,849,650 | 846,969 |

[1] Estimated.　　　　[2] Included in "Other States."

The secretary also says that—

Attention should be called to a class of associations that have been promoted in the West and Southwest which are claiming to do business in a manner similar to building and loan associations. Their promoters promise to make loans to members at 3 or 4 per cent, and at the same time hold out the hope of a dividend return of from 10 to 12 per cent to their investing members. These companies are not building and loan associations and are not organized as such, but they are seeking to capitalize on their good name. The public should be warned against them. They are organized on fundamentally unsound principles, and it is only a question of time until they will come to grief. A number of State departments supervising building and loan associations have already given attention to these promotions and where State laws permitted have put them out of business. In some States, however, additional legislation will be required to properly protect the public.

## UNITED STATES POSTAL SAVINGS SYSTEM.

Through the courtesy of the Third Assistant Postmaster General, Post Office Department, under whose supervision the Postal Savings System is operated, this bureau is enabled to present the following information, showing the resources and liabilities of the postal savings on June 30, 1922, and June 30, 1921, together with the increase or decrease in the various items entering into the service during the period covered by the report, as well as related data.

A comparison of the report for the years 1921 and 1922 shows a decrease of $13,973,263.76 in the resources and liabilities for the last fiscal year, or a reduction of 8.76 per cent.

There was a decrease in each of the following funds in the amounts shown: Working cash deposited with banks and postmasters, $4,522,240; special funds deposited with the Treasurer of the United States on account of returnable deposits fund and bond investment fund, $89,674.16; accounts receivable, being accrued interest on bond investments and amounts due from late postmasters, including credits temporarily withheld, $151,390.78; investments, carried at cost price, in United States 4¼ per cent third and fourth Liberty loan bonds, $13,082,357.14, or a total gross decrease of $17,845,662.08.

The funds in which there were increases are as follows: Special reserve fund, $3,063,177.30; accounts receivable, being amounts due from discontinued depositary banks, $1.02; investments, carried at cost prices, in 2½ per cent postal savings certificates, $809,220, making a total gross increase of $3,872,398.32, or, as stated, a net decrease of $13,973,263.76.

There was, incidentally, a corresponding decrease of $13,973,263.76, in the liabilities, or a reduction of 8.76 per cent. There was a decrease of $14,653,464 in the amount due depositors on account of outstanding principal, represented by certificates of deposit, while the decrease of surplus funds, being the interest and profits (undistributed earnings) subject to future allocation of maturing interest charges, was $3,141,738.32, or a gross decrease of $17,795,202.32. There were increased liabilities on account of interest payable on certificates of deposit and outstanding savings stamps amounting to $76,088.28, while the accounts payable showed an increase represented by interest and profits due postal service in the sum of $3,745,850.28, making a total increase of $3,821,938.56, hence a net decrease of $13,973,263.76.

There was a decrease in the interest-bearing resources of
$4,489,641.38 on account of a reduction in the working cash in de-
pository banks, and $12,273,137.14 because of a reduction in invest-
ments, carried at cost, or a total decrease of $16,762,778.52. There
was a corresponding decrease in the liabilities, $14,653,464 of which
being represented by the outstanding principal due depositors,
while the difference between the excess of resources in 1921 and the
excess of liabilities for 1922 amounted to $2,109,314.52, or a total
decrease of $16,762,778.52.

The interest and profits for the fiscal year ended June 30, 1922,
show a very gratifying increase. While there was a decrease of
$935,239.22 on account of interest on bank deposits, the interest on
bond investments increased $1,296,815.53, miscellaneous receipts
$316.19, and profits realized on sale of investments $389,550.30,
total gross increase of $1,686,682.02, or an apparent net increase of
$751,442.80. There was, however, an increase in the debits of
$32,573.98 on account of interest credited to depositors, and allow-
ances to postmasters because of losses by fire, burglary, etc., erroneous
payments, uncollectible items, etc., and miscellaneous losses amounting to $1,009.70, making a total increase of $33,583.68, or a gross
profit of $717,859.12.

The following comparative tables show in detail the various items
entering into the operation of the Postal Savings System, together
with the changes that have occurred during the last fiscal year.

| Item. | Par value (U. S. bonds). | June 30, 1922. | June 30, 1921. | Increase. | Decrease. |
|---|---|---|---|---|---|
| **RESOURCES.** | | | | | |
| **Working cash:** | | | | | |
| Depository banks | | $43,989,257.90 | $48,478,899.28 | | $4,489,641.38 |
| Postmasters | | 77,460.38 | 110,059.03 | | 32,598.62 |
| | | $44,066,718.28 | $48,588,958.28 | | 4,522,240.00 |
| **Special funds:** | | | | | |
| Treasurer of the United States—Reserve fund | | 7,047,167.74 | 3,953,990.44 | $3,063,177.30 | |
| Treasurer of the United States—Returnable deposits fund | | 7,006.24 | 67,094.21 | | 60,087.97 |
| Treasurer of the United States—Bond investment fund | | 100.85 | 29,687.04 | | 29,586.19 |
| | | 7,064,274.83 | 4,090,771.69 | 2,973,503.14 | |
| **Accounts receivable:** | | | | | |
| Accrued interest on bond investments | | 922,441.84 | 1,071,701.59 | | 149,259.75 |
| Due from discontinued depository banks | | 2.57 | 1.55 | 1.02 | |
| Due from late postmasters, including credits temporarily withheld | | 101,755.68 | 103,886.71 | | 2,131.03 |
| | | 1,024,200.09 | 1,175,559.83 | | 151,389.76 |
| **Investments, carried at cost price (U. S. bonds):** | | | | | |
| Postal Savings 2½'s | $8,278,800 | 8,278,800.00 | 7,469,580.00 | 809,220.00 | |
| First Liberty 4¼'s | 375,000 | 323,925.82 | 323,925.52 | | |
| Second Liberty 4¼'s | 15,237,000 | 13,338,829.12 | 13,338,829.12 | | |
| Third Liberty 4¼'s | 4,000,000 | 3,840,142.86 | 13,440,500.00 | | 9,600,357.14 |
| Fourth Liberty 4¼'s | 77,676,750 | 67,613,969.68 | 71,055,969.68 | | 3,442,000.00 |
| | 105,567,550 | 93,395,667.48 | 105,668,804.62 | | 12,273,137.14 |
| | | 145,540,860.68 | 159,514,124.44 | | 13,973,263.76 |
| **LIABILITIES.** | | | | | |
| **Due depositors:** | | | | | |
| Outstanding principal, represented by certificates of deposit | | 137,736,439.00 | 152,389,903.00 | | 14,653,464.00 |
| Interest payable on certificates of deposit | | 2,632,024.73 | 2,561,420.15 | 70,604.58 | |
| Outstanding savings stamps | | 61,704.20 | 36,220.50 | 5,483.70 | |
| | | 140,430,167.93 | 155,007,543.65 | | 14,577,375.72 |
| **Accounts payable:** | | | | | |
| Due the Postal Service—Interest and profits | | 3,981,217.32 | 235,367.04 | 3,745,850.28 | |
| **Surplus funds:** | | | | | |
| Interest and profits (undistributed earnings) subject to future allocation of maturing interest charges | | 1,129,475.43 | 4,271,213.75 | | 3,141,738.32 |
| | | 145,540,860.68 | 159,514,124.44 | | 13,973,263.76 |

Statement of interest-earning resources and liabilities June 30, 1922, compared with June 30, 1921.

| Item. | June 30, 1922. | June 30, 1921. | Increase. | Decrease. |
|---|---|---|---|---|
| RESOURCES. | | | | |
| Working cash: | | | | |
| Depository banks | $43,989,257.90 | $48,478,899.28 | | $4,489,641.38 |
| Investments, carried at cost price | 93,395,667.48 | 105,668,804.62 | | 12,273,137.14 |
| | $137,384,925.38 | $154,147,703.90 | | 16,762,778.52 |
| LIABILITIES. | | | | |
| Due depositors: | | | | |
| Outstanding principal, represented by certificates of deposit | 137,735,439.00 | 152,389,903.00 | | 14,653,464.00 |
| Excess of resources | | | | |
| Excess of liabilities | 351,513.62 | 1,757,800.90 | | 2,109,314.52 |

Statement of interest and profits for fiscal year ending June 30, 1922, compared with fiscal year ending June 30, 1921.

| Item. | Fiscal year 1922. | Fiscal year 1921. | Increase. | Decrease. |
|---|---|---|---|---|
| Credits: | | | | |
| Interest on bank deposits | $1,136,622.79 | $2,071,862.01 | | $935,239.22 |
| Interest on bond investments | 4,698,301.58 | 3,401,489.05 | $1,296,815.53 | |
| Miscellaneous receipts | 604.71 | 288.52 | 316.19 | |
| Profit realized on sale of investments | 389,550.30 | | 389,550.30 | |
| | $6,225,082.38 | $5,473,639.58 | 751,442.80 | |
| Debits: | | | | |
| Interest credited to depositors | 2,267,579.16 | 2,235,005.18 | 32,573.98 | |
| Allowances to postmasters: | | | | |
| Losses by fire, burglary, etc. | 1,738.40 | 747.02 | 991.38 | |
| Erroneous payments, uncollectible items, etc. | 270.00 | 266.40 | 3.60 | |
| Miscellaneous losses | 15.82 | 1.10 | 14.72 | |
| | 2,269,603.38 | 2,236,019.70 | 33,583.68 | |
| Gross profit | 3,955,479.00 | 3,237,619.88 | 717,859.12 | |

| State | Balance to the credit of depositors June 30, 1921. | Deposits.[1] | Withdrawals.[1] | Balance to the credit of depositors June 30, 1922. | Increase in balance to the credit of depositors.[2] | Saving stamps. Sold.[3] | Saving stamps. Redeemed. | Amount at interest in banks June 30, 1922, including outstanding items. | Interest received from banks. | Interest paid depositors. | Amount of deposits surrendered for bonds. |
|---|---|---|---|---|---|---|---|---|---|---|---|
| United States | $152,389,903 | $98,137,620 | $112,791,084 | $137,736,439 | −$14,653,464 | $73,671.70 | $68,188 | $44,160,416.74 | $1,136,622.79 | $2,196,974.58 | $112,200 |
| Ala. | 481,659 | 291,624 | 399,456 | 373,827 | −107,832 | 44.40 | 38 | 96,698.68 | 2,056.41 | 6,605.08 | |
| Alaska | 685,131 | 733,687 | 634,967 | 783,851 | 98,720 | | | 535,536.23 | 12,520.85 | 7,613.73 | |
| Ariz. | 579,229 | 283,775 | 513,541 | 349,463 | −229,766 | 14.10 | 14 | 138,385.53 | 5,808.37 | 8,502.89 | |
| Arkansas | 201,265 | 98,760 | 119,264 | 175,761 | −25,504 | 17.20 | 13 | 80,662.18 | 2,020.69 | 3,346.18 | |
| California | 3,558,471 | 2,789,133 | 3,238,498 | 3,109,106 | −449,365 | 518.80 | 511 | 808,583.96 | 22,877.54 | 53,512.91 | 2,080 |
| Colo. | 1,712,562 | 783,469 | 1,064,490 | 1,431,541 | −281,021 | 185.30 | 159 | 309,357.61 | 12,421.77 | 28,081.28 | 500 |
| Connecticut | 2,743,969 | 1,359,399 | 1,843,682 | 2,259,716 | −484,283 | 1,643.40 | 1,344 | 512,752.16 | 7,054.73 | 41,176.50 | 100 |
| Delaware | 318,870 | 129,447 | 232,257 | 216,060 | −102,810 | 45.80 | 51 | 73,428.49 | 1,976.25 | 4,407.22 | |
| District of Columbia | 413,996 | 290,910 | 353,531 | 351,075 | −62,921 | 161.70 | 142 | 709,433.10 | 8,632.01 | 6,731.98 | 2,560 |
| Fla. | 910,776 | 879,264 | 965,650 | 824,390 | −86,386 | 85.30 | 82 | 283,826.38 | 3,332.77 | 10,516.81 | |
| Georgia | 172,973 | 306,588 | 212,687 | 266,874 | 93,901 | 34.30 | 33 | 174,405.90 | 251.17 | 2,403.63 | |
| Hawaii | 28,999 | 51,384 | 52,358 | 28,025 | −974 | 1.80 | | 11,599.14 | | 264.08 | |
| Idaho | 432,537 | 689,619 | 546,468 | 575,688 | 143,151 | 31.80 | | 403,680.98 | 8,832.95 | 5,146.61 | |
| Ill. | 9,544,875 | 4,816,338 | 5,809,766 | 8,551,447 | −993,428 | 1,593.30 | 28 | 2,058,201.00 | 59,569.94 | 155,381.94 | 1,500 |
| Indiana | 1,426,511 | 487,128 | 890,017 | 1,023,662 | −402,889 | 153.70 | 1,311 | 285,679.31 | 7,634.36 | 23,511.56 | 580 |
| Iowa | 391,567 | 297,170 | 276,429 | 412,308 | 20,741 | 41.50 | 127 | 181,940.70 | 4,671.54 | 13,663.64 | 500 |
| Kansas | 753,714 | 280,858 | 420,678 | 613,894 | −139,820 | 72.10 | 63 | 178,598.76 | 5,563.86 | 7,308.53 | 700 |
| Kentucky | 444,095 | 238,558 | 309,760 | 372,893 | −71,202 | 56.40 | 46 | 111,948.99 | 2,537.19 | 6,465.57 | 2,000 |
| Louisiana | 451,669 | 253,760 | 313,054 | 392,275 | −59,294 | 7.50 | 50 | 121,321.56 | 3,544.04 | 5,199.40 | |
| Maine | 322,677 | 182,290 | 228,772 | 276,195 | −46,482 | 124.70 | 8 | 60,999.96 | 1,800.13 | 4,582.18 | |
| Maryland | 303,879 | 200,115 | 266,753 | 237,241 | −66,638 | 62.80 | 58 | 68,190.22 | 1,362.17 | | |
| Massachusetts | 6,398,732 | 7,474,389 | 6,062,709 | 8,371,412 | 1,411,680 | 4,262.80 | 3,881 | 4,090,474.92 | 92,883.85 | 78,484.48 | 3,100 |
| Michigan | 4,393,041 | 2,257,884 | 3,466,565 | 3,247,360 | −1,145,681 | 213.50 | 223 | 548,029.43 | 23,018.26 | 70,453.83 | 3,700 |
| Minnesota | 1,634,128 | 685,585 | 1,173,203 | 1,457,510 | −477,618 | 162.30 | 133 | 322,132.40 | 8,784.96 | 35,227.01 | 2,000 |
| Mississippi | 101,633 | 30,055 | 69,841 | 71,847 | −29,786 | 23.60 | 12 | 46,766.64 | 1,339.06 | 1,791.90 | 6,800 |
| Missouri | 3,022,388 | 1,675,582 | 2,023,910 | 2,678,060 | −345,328 | 255.60 | 204 | 807,029.15 | 20,394.96 | 47,261.62 | 7,060 |
| Montana | 900,983 | 680,096 | 658,950 | 922,729 | 21,936 | 28.30 | 19 | 375,517.14 | 7,532.55 | 15,237.90 | 7,500 |
| Nebraska | 390,996 | 255,961 | 254,335 | 373,045 | 1,626 | 70.30 | 53 | 119,041.53 | 3,433.89 | 5,630.39 | |
| Nevada | 353,142 | 135,951 | | 288,758 | −14,384 | 3.10 | 5 | 81,670.49 | 1,717.89 | 5,638.62 | 520 |
| New Hampshire | 557,762 | 282,255 | 313,244 | 526,773 | −30,989 | 368.10 | 335 | 142,681.87 | 3,933.69 | 8,722.52 | |
| New Jersey | 5,607,629 | 3,124,122 | 4,029,180 | 4,698,571 | −905,088 | 6,525.80 | 5,263 | 947,881.65 | 23,707.25 | 82,696.61 | |
| New Mexico | 72,028 | 25,851 | 58,370 | 39,509 | −32,519 | 4.80 | 3 | 16,051.66 | 643.18 | | |
| New York | 60,607,073 | 45,006,225 | 50,271,506 | 61,341,792 | −5,265,281 | 38,002.90 | 35,240 | 19,592,047.87 | 499,093.65 | 890,092.20 | 25,700 |
| North Carolina | 44,106 | 31,755 | 36,227 | 39,634 | −4,472 | 11.00 | 9 | 14,482.17 | 339.67 | 811.13 | |
| North Dakota | 20,627 | 20,173 | 20,410 | 20,390 | −237 | 5.80 | 7 | 13,928.47 | 319.26 | 178.80 | |
| Ohio | 5,506,038 | 2,029,630 | 3,368,113 | 4,167,555 | −1,338,483 | 432.20 | 389 | 961,213.27 | 26,935.98 | 91,925.24 | 24,140 |
| Oklahoma | 311,709 | 584,622 | 382,472 | 513,859 | 202,150 | 44.70 | 51 | 331,160.14 | 5,039.45 | 4,795.45 | 500 |
| Oregon | 2,146,794 | 1,381,147 | 1,573,921 | 1,954,020 | −192,774 | 34.50 | 35 | 541,324.73 | 15,905.80 | 32,823.50 | 1,540 |

Summary of postal savings business for the fiscal year ended June 30, 1922, by States—Continued.

| State. | Balance to the credit of depositors June 30, 1921. | Deposits.[1] | Withdrawals.[1] | Balance to the credit of depositors June 30, 1922. | Increase in balance to the credit of depositors.[2] | Saving stamps. | | Amount at interest in banks June 30, 1922, including outstanding items. | Interest received from banks. | Interest paid depositors. | Amount of deposits surrendered for bonds. |
|---|---|---|---|---|---|---|---|---|---|---|---|
| | | | | | | Sold. | Redeemed. | | | | |
| Pennsylvania | 15,570,044 | 6,202,170 | 9,824,375 | 11,947,839 | -3,622,205 | 3,714.40 | 3,601 | 2,119,857.66 | 70,194.28 | 244,075.19 | 11,780 |
| Porto Rico | 168,089 | 217,936 | 231,176 | 154,849 | -13,240 | 11,411.10 | 11,829 | 121,478.68 | 2,957.71 | 1,223.85 | |
| Rhode Island | 1,131,285 | 715,541 | 879,975 | 966,851 | -164,434 | 2,545.80 | 2,136 | 235,107.15 | 4,354.12 | 16,341.74 | |
| South Carolina | 47,881 | 72,056 | 59,364 | 60,573 | 12,692 | 24.00 | 19 | 32,890.50 | 565.44 | 782.92 | |
| South Dakota | 33,590 | 10,357 | 20,399 | 23,548 | -10,042 | 3.60 | 4 | 10,711.86 | 313.96 | 663.54 | 1,000 |
| Tennessee | 282,238 | 142,692 | 194,130 | 230,800 | -51,438 | 84.50 | 76 | 57,522.16 | 1,870.69 | 4,477.55 | |
| Texas | 867,744 | 752,791 | 753,450 | 867,085 | -659 | 76.70 | 80 | 375,633.51 | 8,961.83 | 12,960.22 | |
| Utah | 548,654 | 360,251 | 435,402 | 473,503 | -75,151 | 18.70 | | 77,524.38 | 2,523.39 | 8,018.51 | |
| Vermont | 91,180 | 119,678 | 71,241 | 139,617 | 48,437 | 45.40 | 4 | 112,103.07 | 2,296.02 | 1,106.82 | 4,840 |
| Virginia | 476,080 | 285,010 | 421,474 | 322,616 | -153,464 | 228.40 | 22 | 131,358.88 | 3,967.16 | 8,358.63 | |
| Virgin Islds | 2,416 | 5,654 | 4,450 | 3,620 | 1,204 | | 244 | | | 15.78 | |
| Washington | 5,740,472 | 7,068,491 | 5,496,665 | 7,312,298 | 1,571,826 | 110.40 | 87 | 4,213,997.33 | 109,048.41 | 79,983.65 | 1,500 |
| West Virginia | 435,914 | 254,159 | 374,706 | 315,367 | -120,547 | 17.30 | 16 | 53,035.33 | 2,669.67 | 6,249.51 | |
| Wisconsin | 1,967,666 | 573,138 | 1,166,091 | 1,374,713 | -592,953 | 32.70 | 39 | 339,633.22 | 6,164.52 | 35,231.40 | |
| Wyoming | 219,537 | 188,142 | 202,635 | 205,044 | -14,493 | 13.50 | 9 | 83,531.60 | 2,216.64 | 3,201.58 | |

[1] These totals include the amount of $1,629,874 transferred between depository offices.
[2] A minus (—) sign denotes decrease.

## SCHOOL SAVINGS BANKS.

In 1885 Prof. J. H. Thiry introduced the school savings system in this country, Long Island City, N. Y., being the location of his initial efforts. His interest in the work was continued until his death in 1911 and thereafter was carried on by Mrs. Sarah S. Oberholtzer, of Philadelphia, until taken up by the savings bank division of the American Bankers' Association.

In 1910, according to Mr. Thiry's last report, there were in operation school savings banks in 530 schoolhouses, with 16,488 depositing pupils having $721,732.18 to their credit.

Notable development of the system is evident from the data appearing in the third annual report, 1921–22, of the American Bankers' Association.

It appears that school savings banks have been established in about 5,000 school buildings in towns and cities throughout the country. The enrollment in these schools aggregated 2,206,132 and the number of participants (depositors) 1,295,607, or.60 per cent of the enrollment. Deposits during the last year exceeded five and one-half millions of dollars and the balance. due on June 30, 1922, was $6,518,171, with interest credited to the amount of $145,554. Development of the activities of the school savings system from 1919–20 to 1921-22 is shown in the following table.:

| Year. | Partici-pants. | Bank balances. |
|-------|------|------|
| 1919–20 | 462,651 | $3,891,495 |
| 1920–21 | 802,906 | 4,434,875 |
| 1921–22 | 1,295,607 | 6,518,171 |

In lieu of a staff of officers—tellers, bookkeepers, and cashiers—having charge of the work, there has been installed in some city schools a metal mechanical device, on the order of the cash register, in which there are slots for the reception of each denomination of coins. As a coin is dropped in, there is an automatic release of an adhesive stamp representing the value of the coin. The pupil affixes the stamp to a folder which is retained by him, until his credits on the folder equal $1. In the meantime arrangements have been made with a local savings or commercial bank to collect daily, or as often as may be deemed advisable,. the contents of the receptacle, which are credited on the books of the bank to the particular school or ·mechanical device whence taken until the pupil presents his folder with the dollar credit, when a personal account is opened with him. It is claimed that the necessary safeguards are provided for the receptacles and their use.

The following table compiled from information furnished by the savings bank division of the American Bankers' Association, shows the activities in connection with the school savings banking in the several States:

## School savings banking, for the school year of 1921 and 1922.

[Compiled by savings bank division, American Bankers' Association.]

| State | Number | | | | Changes during year | | | Balance in bank | |
|---|---|---|---|---|---|---|---|---|---|
| | Towns | School buildings | Enrollment | Participating | Collections | Interest | Withdrawals | June 30, 1921 | June 30, 1922 |
| Maine | 2 | 20 | 3,521 | 1,185 | $2,951.34 | $31.51 | (¹)$10,609.28 | (¹)$3,306.60 | $5,098.85 |
| New Hampshire | | 44 | 15,309 | 7,638 | 9,313.29 | | 5,678.70 | 2,378.70 | 2,010.61 |
| Vermont | 1 | 3 | 750 | 531 | 3,300.00 | | | | |
| Massachusetts | | 470 | 159,399 | 69,191 | 295,648.59 | 3,806.63 | 335,319.17 | 107,472.35 | 161,608.40 |
| Rhode Island | 33 | | | | | | 9,358.91 | 9,358.91 | |
| Connecticut | 16 | 294 | 87,456 | 46,083 | 190,143.94 | 31.14 | 126,994.92 | 37,955.96 | 101,136.12 |
| Total New England States | 54 | 831 | 266,435 | 124,628 | 501,357.16 | 3,869.28 | 487,960.98 | 250,472.52 | 269,853.98 |
| New York | 27 | 481 | 311,376 | 218,635 | 720,777.01 | 31,988.98 | 526,455.72 | 1,092,874.37 | 1,319,184.64 |
| New Jersey | 14 | 148 | 95,323 | 48,833 | 245,408.24 | 5,104.75 | 292,922.50 | 195,153.91 | 152,744.40 |
| Pennsylvania | 60 | 637 | 287,301 | 198,196 | 1,343,501.10 | 18,918.33 | 657,156.43 | 874,924.83 | 1,580,187.83 |
| Delaware | 1 | 6 | 558 | 113 | 857.00 | 138.00 | 1,385.56 | 1,749.56 | 1,359.00 |
| Maryland | 2 | 1 | 1,670 | 646 | 12,831.76 | | 11,631.76 | | 900.00 |
| District of Columbia | 1 | 33 | 16,962 | 8,257 | 9,006.31 | | 17,785.58 | 8,779.27 | |
| Total Eastern States | 105 | 1,306 | 713,190 | 474,670 | 2,332,081.42 | 56,150.06 | 1,507,337.55 | 2,173,481.94 | 3,054,375.87 |
| Virginia | 7 | 97 | 54,582 | 28,816 | 110,940.41 | 1,898.25 | 105,372.29 | 53,562.55 | 60,128.92 |
| West Virginia | 15 | 82 | 28,312 | 16,293 | 96,457.89 | 91.50 | 33,674.37 | 4,078.38 | 66,561.41 |
| North Ⅰ. | 8 | 34 | 16,417 | 12,118 | 13,357.26 | | 14.81 | 380.66 | 13,633.10 |
| Georgia | 2 | 15 | 7,563 | 4,183 | 19,901.35 | 230.60 | 15,844.52 | 11,220.45 | 15,507.88 |
| Florida | | | 434 | 131 | 1,425.47 | | 390.28 | | 1,038.19 |
| Alabama | | 2 | 701 | 380 | 687.22 | | 687.22 | | |
| Mississippi | 3 | 15 | 5,392 | 2,191 | 3,893.21 | | 5,131.03 | 2,604.85 | 1,343.13 |
| Louisiana | 4 | 84 | 44,330 | 28,922 | 82,494.93 | 12.30 | 11,324.73 | 14,687.73 | 85,770.23 |
| Texas | 1 | 12 | 3,513 | 628 | 1,266.92 | | 888.87 | | 377.05 |
| Kentucky | 5 | 95 | 40,662 | 33,092 | 106,950.11 | 259.20 | 78,922.80 | 108,685.29 | 136,971.80 |
| Tennessee | 1 | 39 | 23,500 | 19,992 | 70,654.16 | 738.91 | 35,426.78 | 43,598.56 | 84,965.85 |
| Total Southern States | 49 | 494 | 235,634 | 146,746 | 513,549.81 | 3,239.76 | 294,590.48 | 244,098.47 | 466,297.56 |
| Ohio | 42 | 460 | 235,221 | 148,049 | 712,417.76 | 7,748.56 | 493,962.78 | 542,146.13 | 768,319.67 |
| Indiana | 10 | 115 | 122,559 | 35,980 | 140,182.96 | 1,063.81 | 75,034.60 | 100,465.26 | 166,717.43 |
| Illinois | 19 | 129 | 78,074 | 56,491 | 202,029.78 | 792.13 | 75,011.29 | 87,131.07 | 215,541.69 |
| Michigan | 29 | 254 | 77,713 | 49,266 | 171,991.50 | 2,439.49 | 138,078.13 | 198,635.73 | 234,988.59 |
| Wisconsin | 18 | 124 | 57,223 | 41,784 | 123,139.42 | 373.45 | 42,633.77 | 25,310.21 | 106,189.31 |
| Minnesota | 5 | 195 | 102,280 | 82,215 | 255,577.44 | 24,421.99 | 304,953.21 | 213,360.30 | 188,406.52 |

| | | | | | | | | | |
|---|---|---|---|---|---|---|---|---|---|
| Iowa | 11 | 108 | 50,207 | 28,380 | 142,003.14 | 578.22 | 93,149.86 | 78,416.87 | 127,848.37 |
| Missouri | 2 | 60 | 35,611 | 15,916 | 62,317.30 | 571.56 | 99,965.82 | 44,624.97 | 7,548.01 |
| Total Middle Western States | 136 | 1,445 | 758,888 | 458,061 | 1,810,269.30 | 37,929.21 | 1,322,789.46 | 1,290,160.54 | 1,815,559.59 |
| Nebraska | 3 | 62 | 34,315 | 20,384 | 147,088.32 | 3,687.33 | 74,850.11 | 96,249.39 | 172,174.93 |
| Kansas | 1 | 7 | 2,457 | 1,805 | 2,726.62 | | 756.47 | | 1,970.15 |
| Wyoming | 3 | | 450 | 82 | 1,066.28 | 18.64 | 1,084.92 | | |
| Colorado | 1 | 1 | 687 | 487 | 1,443.85 | | 1,443.85 | | |
| New Mexico | 1 | 18 | 2,390 | 697 | 2,042.38 | 1.38 | 63.11 | | 1,980.65 |
| Oklahoma | 3 | 25 | 14,186 | 6,191 | 10,668.85 | 209.03 | 13,805.09 | 7,045.65 | 4,118.44 |
| Total Western States | 12 | 113 | 54,515 | 29,646 | 165,036.30 | 3,916.38 | 92,003.55 | 103,295.04 | 180,244.17 |
| Washington | 1 | 14 | 6,479 | 3,738 | | 261.00 | (¹) | (¹) | 21,147.00 |
| California | 13 | 582 | 171,103 | 53,118 | 412,032.11 | 40,188.73 | 847,212.21 | 1,105,683.86 | 710,692.49 |
| Total Pacific States | 14 | 596 | 177,582 | 61,856 | 412,032.11 | 40,449.73 | 847,212.21 | 1,105,683.86 | 731,839.49 |
| Total all United States | 370 | 4,785 | 2,206,144 | 1,295,607 | 5,734,316.10 | 145,554.42 | 4,551,894.23 | 5,167,192.37 | 6,518,170.66 |

¹ Not reported.

## FEDERAL FARM LOAN SYSTEM.

At the close of business October 31, 1922, the aggregate assets of the 12 Federal land banks amounted to $702,649,882.46, an increase over the amount on October 31, 1921, of $258,435,410.46. In the past year the net mortgage loans of these banks were increased from $400,985,000 to $605,987,000, and investments in United States Government securities were increased from $30,226,000 to $67,689,000. Cash on hand and in banks was reduced from $18,917,000, to $11,672,-000. Banking houses, furniture, and fixtures were increased from $304,000 to $656,000 during the year.

The capital stock of these banks was increased $8,170,463, and amounted to $35,256,730. In capitalizing these banks, national farm loan associations subscribed for $30,866,995, United States Government $4,264,880, and the agents of borrowers and individual subscribers, $124,855. The undivided profits of these banks were $4,471,000 compared with $2,165,000 in 1921. A special reserve from the earnings amounted to $2,533,000 compared with $1,515,000 in 1921, and the amount of surplus was $300,000.

The obligations of these banks incident to the issuance of farm loan bonds, on October 31, 1922, amounted to $641,208,000, and the amount of accrued interest on farm loan bonds was $14,328,000. In addition to these liabilities the banks had notes payable aggregating $2,200,000. Other liabilities amounted to $918,000 compared with $416,000 a year ago.

The net earnings of these banks since organization have amounted to $11,787,000, out of which dividends have been paid to the amount of $4,022,000; $380,000 has been carried to suspense account and other miscellaneous charges have amounted to $81,000, leaving surplus reserve and undivided profits accounts referred to, aggregating $7,304,000.

It appears that the original subscription to capital by the United States Government was $8,892,000, of which amount $4,627,000 had been retired.

*Consolidated statement of condition of the twelve Federal land banks at the close of business October 31, 1922.*

### ASSETS.

| | |
|---|---:|
| Net mortgage loans | $605,987,214.04 |
| Accrued interest on mortgage loans (not matured) | 10,921,559.80 |
| United States Government bonds and securities | 67,688,829.51 |
| Accrued interest on bonds and securities (not matured) | 523,720.54 |
| Farm loan bonds on hand (unsold) | 2,595,925.00 |
| Accrued interest on farm loan bonds on hand (not matured) | 26,511.18 |
| Other accrued interest (uncollected) | 12,840.64 |
| Notes receivable, acceptances, etc | 373,719.03 |
| Cash on hand and in banks | 11,672,006.39 |
| Accounts receivable | 86,726.21 |
| Installments matured (in process of collection) | 1,049,351.43 |
| Banking houses | 489,393.63 |
| Furniture and fixtures | 166,733.50 |
| Other assets | 1,055,351.56 |
| Total assets | 702,649,882.46 |

*Consolidated statement of the twelve Federal land banks at the close of business October 31, 1922—Continued.*

## LIABILITIES.

Capital stock:

| | |
|---|---|
| United States Government................... | $4, 264, 880. 00 |
| National farm loan associations............... | 30, 866, 995. 00 |
| Borrowers through agents.................... | 119, 965. 00 |
| Individual subscribers...................... | 4, 890. 00 |

| | |
|---|---|
| Total capital stock........................................ | $35, 256, 730. 00 |
| Reserve (from earnings)......................................... | 2, 532, 500. 00 |
| Surplus (from earnings)........................................ | 300, 000. 00 |
| Farm loan bonds authorized and issued........'................. | 641, 208, 375. 00 |
| Accrued interest on farm loan bonds (not matured).............. | 14, 328, 140. 69 |
| Notes payable................................................. | 2, 200, 000. 00 |
| Due borrowers on uncompleted loans........................... | 311, 202. 95 |
| Amortization installments paid in advance...................... | 896, 977. 20 |
| Matured interest on farm loan bonds (coupons not presented)....... | 139, 783. 07 |
| Reserved for dividends unpaid................................. | 86, 877. 53 |
| Other liabilities.............................................. | 918, 417. 62 |
| Undivided profits............................................. | 4, 470, 878. 40 |
| Total liabilities........................................ | 702, 649, 882. 46 |

## MEMORANDA.

| | | |
|---|---|---|
| Net earnings to Oct. 31, 1922.................................... | | 11, 786, 591. 94 |
| Less: | | |
| Dividends paid to Oct. 31, 1922................ | $4, 022, 141. 74 | |
| Carried to suspense account to Oct. 31.......... | 379, 790. 27 | |
| Other charges to Oct. 31, 1922................. | 81, 281. 53 | |
| | | 4, 483, 213. 54 |
| Carried to surplus account to Oct. 31............ | 300, 000. 00 | |
| Carried to reserve account to Oct. 31............. | 2, 532, 500. 00 | |
| Undivided profits Oct. 31, 1922................. | 4, 470, 878. 40 | |
| Total reserve and undivided profits Oct. 31, 1922............ | | 7, 303, 378. 40 |
| Capital stock originally subscribed by United States Government.. | | 8, 892, 130. 00 |
| Amount of Government stock retired to Oct. 31, 1922............. | | 4, 627, 250. 00 |
| Capital stock held by United States Government Oct. 31, 1922..... | | 4, 264, 880. 00 |

NOTE.—Unpledged mortages (gross) $13,316,762.62.

## RESOURCES OF CENTRAL BANKS IN FOREIGN COUNTRIES.

The resources of 21 principal central banks in foreign countries, on or about July 1, 1922, are shown in the following statement, prepared by the Federal Reserve Board, in the local currencies of the several countries, as well as converted at the rate of exchange on given dates.

The total assets of these banks, converted at rates of exchange on given dates, amounted to $10,947,335,000, or 21.71 per cent of the aggregate resources of all reporting banks in the United States and insular possessions June 30, 1922.

*Total assets of principal central banks about July 1, 1922.*

[In thousands of local currency and dollars.]

| Bank. | Date. | Local currency. | Total assets. | Par of exchange. | Total assets converted at par of exchange. | Rate of exchange on given date. | Total assets converted at rate of exchange on given date. |
|---|---|---|---|---|---|---|---|
| | 1922. | | | *Cents.* | | *Cents.* | |
| Austro-Hungarian Bank—Austrian Department. | June 30 | Kronen....... | 639,581,191 | 20.26 | 129,579,149 | 0.0054 | 34,537 |
| Bank of Belgium....... | June 29 | Francs........ | 7,175,983 | 19.30 | 1,384,965 | 7.9400 | 569,773 |
| Czechoslovakian Banking Office. | June 30 | Kronen....... | 14,508,931 | 20.26 | 2,939,509 | 1.9114 | 277,324 |
| Bank of Denmark...... | ...do..... | ....do........ | 674,145 | 26.80 | 180,671 | 21.4000 | 144,267 |
| Bank of England....... | June 28 | Pounds....... | 272,343 | 486.65 | 1,325,357 | 440.1100 | 1,198,609 |
| Bank of Finland........ | June 30 | Marks......... | 1,755,621 | 19.30 | 338,835 | 2.2763 | 39,963 |
| Bank of France......... | June 29 | Francs........ | 41,014,036 | 19.30 | 7,915,709 | 8.3500 | 3,424,672 |
| German Reichsbank.... | June 30 | Reichsmarks.. | 210,486,144 | 23.82 | 50,137,800 | .2645 | 556,736 |
| Bank of Greece......... | ...do..... | Drachmas..... | 5,034,590 | 19.30 | 971,676 | 3.0300 | 152,548 |
| Hungarian Office of Note Issue. | ...do..... | Kronen....... | 39,487,928 | 20.26 | 8,000,254 | .1003 | 39,606 |
| Banks of Italy, Naples, and Sicily. | ...do..... | Lire.......... | 23,936,444 | 19.30 | 4,619,734 | 4.6900 | 1,122,619 |
| Bank of Netherlands... | July 3 | Florins........ | 1,094,507 | 40.20 | 439,992 | 38.5000 | 421,385 |
| Bank of Norway........ | June 30 | Kroner....... | 663,453 | 26.80 | 177,805 | 16.4400 | 109,072 |
| Bank of Rumania...... | July 8 | Lei............ | 20,287,644 | 19.30 | 3,915,515 | .5629 | 114,199 |
| Bank of Spain.......... | July 1 | Pesetas........ | 5,927,463 | 19.30 | 1,144,000 | 15.5900 | 924,091 |
| Bank of Sweden........ | June 30 | Kronor....... | 932,113 | 26.80 | 249,806 | 25.7200 | 239,739 |
| Bank of Switzerland.... | ...do..... | Francs........ | 1,040,168 | 19.30 | 200,752 | 18.9700 | 197,320 |
| Bank of Yugoslavia..... | ...do..... | Dinars........ | 5,738,329 | 19.30 | 1,107,497 | 1.2675 | 72,733 |
| Reserve Bank of Peru.. | ...do..... | Pounds....... | 8,172 | 486.65 | 39,769 | 412.0000 | 33,669 |
| Bank of Japan.......... | July 1 | Yen........... | 2,356,450 | 49.85 | 1,174,690 | 47.7300 | 1,124,734 |
| Bank of Java........... | ...do..... | Florins........ | 392,758 | 40.20 | 157,889 | 38.125 | 149,739 |
| Total.............. | .......... | ............... | ............. | ........ | 216,001,374 | .......... | 10,947,335 |

## SAVINGS BANKS IN THE PRINCIPAL COUNTRIES OF THE WORLD.

The following statement, prepared by the Bureau of Foreign and Domestic Commerce, Department of Commerce, shows the number of depositors, amount of deposits, average deposit account, and the average deposit per inhabitant with respect to savings banks in principal countries of the world, supplemented by similar data relative to savings institutions in the United States and Philippine Islands, on specified dates:

[Compiled by the Bureau of Foreign and Domestic Commerce, Department of Commerce, from official reports of the respective countries.]

| Country. | Population.[1] | Date of report. | Form of organization. | Number of depositors. | Deposits. | Average deposit account. | Average deposit per inhabitant. |
|---|---|---|---|---|---|---|---|
| Argentina | 8,533,000 | Dec. 31, 1921 | Postal savings banks | 473,782 | $10,968,398 | $21.88 | $1.22 |
| Chile | 3,755,000 | Mar. 31, 1922 | Public savings banks | 1,050,912 | 26,264,314 | 24.99 | 6.99 |
| Denmark | 3,268,000 | Mar. 31, 1920 | usual and corporate savings banks | 1,552,959 | 266,201,423 | 171.42 | 81.46 |
| Egypt | 12,751,000 | Dec. 31, 1919 | Postal savings banks | 224,759 | 3,998,569 | 17.79 | .31 |
| Finland | 3,335,000 | Dec. 31, 1930 | Private savings banks | 521,124 | 32,225,123 | 61.84 | 9.66 |
|  |  | ...do... | Postal savings banks | 113,962 | 1,930,369 | 16.92 | .58 |
| France | 39,210,000 | ...do... | Private savings banks | 8,755,000 | 344,802,500 | 39.38 | 8.79 |
|  |  | ...do... | Postal savings banks | 6,982,684 | 140,040,792 | 20.06 | 3.57 |
| Algeria | 5,564,000 | Dec. 31, 1918 | Postal savings banks | 20,511 | 885,945 | 43.19 | .16 |
| Tunis | 1,953,000 | Dec. 31, 1920 | Postal savings banks | 3,919 | 930,948 | 237.55 | .47 |
| Germany [2] | 59,378,000 | Dec. 31, 1919 | Public and corp rate savings banks | 33,506,915 | 750,592,409 | 22.40 | 12.64 |
| Italy | 36,710,000 | Dec. 31, 1917 | Postal and corp rate savings banks | 2,639,201 | 410,338,435 | 149.80 | 11.17 |
|  |  | Dec. 31, 1918 | Postal savings banks | 6,273,500 | 547,211,842 | 87.23 | 14.89 |
| Japan | 55,963,000 | Dec. 31, 1919 | Private savings banks | 12,041,213 | 215,723,496 | 17.92 | 3.86 |
|  |  | Mar. 31, 1920 | Postal savings banks | 20,679,910 | 335,085,525 | 16.20 | 5.99 |
| Formosa | 3,654,000 | ...do... |  | 1,386,578 | 2,966,707 | 7.43 | .81 |
| Chosen | 17,284,000 | Mar. 31, 1921 | Private savings banks | 603,133 | 8,399,014 | 5.98 | .43 |
| Netherlands | 6,841,000 | Dec. 31, 1929 | Postal savings banks | 1,908,305 | 76,965,000 | 127.61 | 11.25 |
|  |  | Dec. 31, 1929 | Private savings banks | 57,345,290 |  | 45.77 | 12.77 |
| Dutch East Indies | 47,204,000 | Dec. 31, 1918 | Private savings banks | 8,473 | 2,050,642 | 242.02 | .05 |
|  |  | ...do... | Postal savings banks | 182,348 | 5,225,950 | 28.66 | .11 |
| Dutch Guiana | 95,000 | ...do... |  | 12,805 | 411,550 | 32.14 | 4.33 |
| Dutch West Indies | 56,000 | ...do... |  | 4,896 | 88,920 | 18.16 | 1.59 |
| Norway | 2,632,000 | Dec. 31, 1920 | Communal and private savings banks | 1,697,048 | 326,411,770 | 192.34 | 121.02 |
| Poland | 26,386,000 | Nov. 30, 1921 | Postal savings banks | 42,794 | 3,546,600 | 82.88 | .13 |
| Spain | 21,347,000 | Dec. 31, 1920 | Private savings banks | 1,001,379 | 93,057,846 | 92.93 | 4.36 |
|  |  | ...do... | Postal savings banks | 305,239 | 8,925,757 | 29.25 | .42 |
| Sweden | 5,904,000 | ...do... | Communal and private savings banks | 2,270,318 | 101,197,660 | 44.57 | 17.14 |
|  |  | Dec. 31, 1921 | Postal savings banks | 672,901 | 25,289,722 | 37.58 | 4.28 |
| Switzerland | 3,970,000 | Dec. 31, 1918 | Communal and private savings banks | 2,397,947 | 496,732,891 | 191.20 | 125.12 |
| United Kingdom | 46,156,000 | Nov. 20, 1919 | Trustee savings banks | 2,220,373 | 289,471,427 | 130.37 | 6.27 |
|  |  | Dec. 31, 1918 | Postal savings banks | 15,998,375 | 1,118,215,491 | 69.90 | 24.23 |
| British India [3] | 244,268,000 | ...do... |  | 1,877,957 | 59,441,646 | 31.65 | .24 |
| Australia | 5,510,000 | Dec. 31, 1921 | Government and private savings banks | 3,327,456 | 650,962,486 | 195.45 | 118.03 |
|  |  | Mar. 31, 1921 | Postal savings banks | 664,819 | 171,240,522 | 257.58 | 138.10 |
| New Zealand | 1,240,000 | Mar. 31, 1922 | Private savings banks | 104,395 | 17,150,896 | 164.29 | 13.83 |

[1] The figures for population are for the nearest date to which the statistics of savings banks relate.
[2] Exclusive of Brunswick.
[3] Exclusive of the population of the feudatory States.

*Savings banks, including postal savings banks, number of depositors, amount of deposits, average deposits per deposit account and per inhabitant, by specified countries—Continued.*

[Compiled by the Bureau of Foreign and Domestic Commerce, Department of Commerce, from official reports of the respective countries.]

| Country. | Population | Date of report. | Form of organization. | Number of depositors. | Deposits. | Average deposit account. | Average deposit per inhabitant. |
|---|---|---|---|---|---|---|---|
| Canada | 9,030,000 | Mar. 31, 1920 | Postal savings banks | 97,154 | $28,761,090 | $296.04 | $3.19 |
| Union of South Africa | 6,941,000 | Mar. 31, 1919 | Dominion Government savings banks | 26,728 | 11,402,098 | 426.60 | 1.26 |
| British West Indies | 1,867,000 | Mar. 31, 1921 | Postal savings banks | 308,140 | 26,964,037 | 87.51 | 3.88 |
| British colonies, n. e. s. | 39,412,000 | 1919–20 | Government and post-office savings banks | 99,386 | 5,476,855 | 55.11 | 2.93 |
|  |  | 1919–20 | do | 292,180 | 13,681,398 | 46.83 | .35 |
| Total, foreign countries | 720,247,000 |  |  | 132,914,566 | 6,717,257,335 | 50.53 | 9.33 |
| United States | [4]109,833,000 | June 30, 1922 | Postal savings system | 420,242 | 137,736,439 | 327.76 | 1.25 |
|  |  | do | Mutual and stock savings banks | 12,538,997 | 7,181,248,000 | 572.71 | 65.38 |
| Philippines [5] | [4]110,700,000 | do | Postal savings bank | 151,076 | 2,882,976 | 19.08 | .27 |
| Grand total | 840,780,000 |  |  | 146,054,881 | 14,039,124,750 | 96.12 | 96.12 |

[4] Estimated by Government actuary.
[5] Information from Bureau of Insular Affairs, War Department.

NOTE.—The foreign currencies have been converted at their approximate exchange value on the date of the report.

EXPENSES INCIDENT TO MAINTENANCE OF CURRENCY BUREAU AND NET PROFIT DERIVED BY GOVERNMENT FROM TAXES ON NATIONAL AND FEDERAL RESERVE BANK NOTES, FISCAL YEAR ENDED JUNE 30, 1922.

The total expense incident to maintenance of the Currency Bureau during the fiscal year ended June 30, 1922, was $6,418,861.76, of which amount $4,698,746.77 was reimbursed to the Government by national banks and Federal reserve banks, and the difference of $1,720,114.99 was expended from appropriations made by Congress.

That the Currency Bureau is self-sustaining and an excellent revenue producer is evidenced by the fact that during the fiscal year ended June 30, 1922, national banks paid to the Treasurer of the United States, as a tax on circulating notes, $3,941,461.17, and Federal reserve banks paid $445,944.01 as a tax on Federal reserve bank notes, making total payments of $4,387,405.18, or a net profit to the United States Government of $2,667,290.19 after deducting expenses paid from appropriations by Congress.

The records show that considerable saving was effected during the past fiscal year incident to the ordinary expenses of the bureau. The item of printing and binding was reduced from $41,768.54 for the fiscal year 1921 to $21,247.22 for the current year. The expenditure on account of stationery was reduced in this period from $27,744.61 to $15,723.77 and expense on account of furniture and labor-saving machines was reduced from $8,005.91 to $5,337.29.

An itemized statement of expenses incident to maintenance of Currency Bureau for fiscal year ended June 30, 1922, follows:

*Expenses incident to maintenance of Currency Bureau and net profit derived by Government from taxes on national and Federal reserve bank notes, fiscal year ended June 30, 1922.*

| | Expenses paid from appropriation. | Expenses reimbursed by banks. | Total expenses. |
|---|---|---|---|
| Salaries: | | | |
| Regular roll, including bonus and $5,036 for retirement fund | $236,509.02 | | |
| National currency reimbursable roll, including bonus and $2,044.21 for retirement fund | | $100,390.32 | |
| Federal Reserve Issue and Redemption Division, and Redemption Division. Comptroller of the Currency (paid by Federal Reserve Board) | | 96,035.14 | |
| Total salaries | | | $432,934.48 |
| General expenses: | | | |
| Printing and binding | 21,247.22 | 1,412.14 | |
| Stationery | 15,723.77 | 1,139.07 | |
| Amount expended for light, heat, telephone, telegraph, furniture, labor-saving machines, etc., partially estimated | 5,337.29 | | |
| Special examination of national banks, repairs to macerator, etc. | 1,581.45 | | |
| Contingent expenses, Redemption Division, for light, heat, furniture, etc. (reimbursable) | | 767.81 | |
| Total general expenses | | | • 47,208.75 |
| Currency issues: | | | |
| National-bank notes— | | | |
| Paper | 131,803.22 | | |
| Printing, etc. | 1,017,598.42 | | |
| Plates (reimbursed) | | 88,250.00 | |
| Federal reserve bank notes— | | | |
| Paper | 43,880.00 | | |
| Printing, etc. | 246,434.60 | | |
| Plates (reimbursed) | | 2,140.00 | |

*Expenses incident to maintenance of Currency Bureau and net profit derived by Government from tax on national and Federal reserve bank notes, fiscal year ended June 30, 1922*—Continued.

| | Expenses paid from appropriation. | Expenses reimbursed by banks. | Total expenses. |
|---|---|---|---|
| Currency issues—Continued. | | | |
| Federal reserve notes— | | | |
| Paper........................ | .............. | $316,780.04 | |
| Plates, printing, etc.............. | .............. | 1,992,919.13 | |
| Total currency issues............. | .............. | .............. | $3,839,805.41 |
| Expenses on account of national bank examining service paid by banks................ | .............. | 1,945,156.41 | 1,945,156.41 |
| Postage on shipments of national-bank notes.............. | .............. | 97,150.76 | 97,150.76 |
| Insurance on shipments of national-bank notes.............. | .............. | 56,655.95 | 56,655.95 |
| Total expenses paid from appropriations............. | $1,720,114.99 | .............. | |
| Total expenses reimbursed by banks............. | .............. | 4,698,796.77 | |
| Total expenses............. | .............. | .............. | 6,418,911.76 |
| | | | |
| Tax paid by national banks on circulating notes............. | | | $3,941,461.17 |
| Tax paid by Federal reserve banks on Federal reserve bank notes............. | | | 445,944.01 |
| Total............. | | | 4,387,405.18 |
| Total expenses of Currency Bureau paid from congressional appropriations......... | | | 1,720,114.99 |
| Net profit to Government from taxes on circulation............. | | | 2,667,290.19 |

## CONCLUSION.

No other activity of the Government more directly concerns the interests of the people than the national banking system, representing as it does approximately 35 per cent of the banking power of the United States.

Our national banks are the bulwark of America's financial establishment. Their resources June 30, 1922, the latest date for which comparable figures with other banks are available, were $20,706,010,-000, or 41.06 per cent of the total resources of all reporting banks; and their total deposits were 39.69 per cent of the total deposits of all banks.

The success of the national banks is due mainly to the management of their affairs by competent officers and directors who have generally displayed a desire to comply with the law and to cooperate with the comptroller. It must be remembered, however, that general economic conditions have had their effect on national banks as well as all other financial institutions, necessitating the exercise of great care and prudence in their management. Responsibility, therefore, to a great extent, devolves upon the corps of national bank examiners, and in turn upon administrative officers of the Currency Bureau. That national banks have been well managed is evidenced by the fact that during the fiscal year ended June 30, 1922, the number of failures was only forty one-hundredths of 1 per cent of the total number of reporting banks, and the nominal value of assets of banks placed in charge of receivers was only one-tenth of 1 per cent of the total assets of all reporting banks.

In my last annual report, I called attention to the meager salaries paid officers of this bureau, with particular reference to Deputy Comptrollers Thomas P. Kane and Willis J. Fowler, and recommended increases in their salaries. In renewing this recommendation, the attention of the Congress is called to the provision of section 5173 Revised Statutes, as follows:

The plates and special dies to be procured by the Comptroller of the Currency fo the printing of such circulating notes shall remain under his control and direction, an the expenses necessarily incurred in executing the laws respecting the procuring c such notes, *and all other expenses of the Bureau of the Currency, shall be paid out of th proceeds of the taxes or duties assessed and collected on the circulation of national bankin associations under this title.*

In view of this provision of the law, it is respectfully suggested tha to increase the salaries to be paid deputy comptrollers will place n additional burden on the Treasury. The net profit to the Govern ment from taxes on national and Federal reserve bank circulation after meeting all expenses of the bureau for the fiscal year ende June 30, 1922, was $2,667,290.19. This bureau pays its expenses earns a large profit to the Government, and ought to be allowed t pay reasonable salaries.

In the appendix to the report to the Comptroller of the Currenc will be found condensed statements of the condition of each nationa bank in the United States at the close of business September 15, 1922 statistics relating in detail to the assets and liabilities of nationa banks; data relative to the affairs of national banks in charge o receivers; information with reference to the condition of banks unde the supervision of the banking departments of the several States clearing house transactions; and digest of decisions relating t national banks.

Respectfully submitted.

D. R. CRISSINGER,
*Comptroller of the Currency.*

To the SPEAKER OF THE HOUSE OF REPRESENTATIVES.

# REPORT OF THE COMMISSIONER OF INTERNAL REVENUE.

TREASURY DEPARTMENT,
OFFICE OF COMMISSIONER OF INTERNAL REVENUE,
*Washington, October 1, 1922.*

SIR: I have the honor to submit the following report of the work of the Bureau of Internal Revenue for the fiscal year ended June 30, 1922.

## COLLECTIONS.

The operations of the Internal Revenue Bureau during the fiscal year 1922 under the revenue acts of 1918 and 1921, and other internal-revenue tax legislation resulted in the collection of $3,197,451,083 compared with $4,595,357,061.95 in the fiscal year ended June 30, 1921, a decrease of $1,397,905,978.95, or 30 per cent.

The income and profits tax collections for the fiscal year 1922 amounted to $2,086,918,464.85 compared with $3,228,137,673.75 for the fiscal year 1921, a decrease of $1,141,219,208.90, or 35 per cent. The collections made during the first six months of the fiscal year 1922 embraced the third and fourth installments of the income and profits taxes due on incomes in the calendar year 1920, together with additional collections on assessments made for prior years, while the collections made during the last six months of the fiscal year embraced the first and second installments of the income and profits taxes on incomes in the calendar year 1921, together with additional collections made on assessments for prior years.

The profits tax rates in the calendar year 1921 were the same as those in effect for the calendar years 1919 and 1920, the rates in the first and second brackets being 20 and 40 per cent, respectively.

The normal tax on corporations in the calendar year 1921 was 10 per cent of the net income after deduction of allowable credits, as was also the case in the calendar years 1919 and 1920. In 1921, however, the specific credit of $2,000 to a domestic corporation was allowed only where its net income was $25,000 or less, while in the two previous calendar years this specific credit was $2,000 irrespective of the amount of the net income.

The normal tax rate for individuals in 1921 as provided in the revenue act of 1921 was 4 per cent upon the first $4,000 of net income subject to the normal tax and 8 per cent upon the excess over that amount. The same rates were in effect during the calendar years 1919 and 1920 under the revenue act of 1918. In 1921, for the purpose of the normal tax, there was allowed as a credit in the case of a head of a family or a married person a personal exemption of $2,500 unless the net income was in excess of $5,000, in which case the personal exemption was $2,000, and there was also allowed a credit of $400 for each person dependent upon and receiving his chief support from the taxpayer. In the calendar years 1919 and 1920 this personal exemption was $2,000 regardless of the amount of the net income, and the credit for a dependent was $200.

The miscellaneous collections arising from objects of taxation other than income and profits taxes amounted to $1,110,532,618.15 for the fiscal year 1922, compared with $1,367,219,388.20 for the fiscal year 1921, a decrease of $256,686,770.05, or 19 per cent, which is mostly accounted for by the repeal or reduction in rates of various taxes provided for in the revenue act of 1921, effective January 1, 1922. The principal decreases in miscellaneous taxes for 1922 were as follows: Estates, $14,624,414.35; distilled spirits, $37,034,714.54; transportation, $102,814,685.58; insurance, $8,136,690.64; excise taxes, $55,003,803.12; stamp taxes, $13,668,528.08; nonalcoholic beverages, $25,171,688.85; and admissions to theaters, etc., $15,890,-061.10. The total decrease from these several sources was offset to the extent of $15,539,998.95 by the increase in collections from tobacco manufactures.

The collection of internal-revenue taxes for the fiscal year 1922 and the last seven preceding years are summarized in the following table:

| Source. | 1922 | 1921 | 1920 | 1919 |
|---|---|---|---|---|
| Distilled spirits, including wines, etc | $45,563,350.47 | $82,598,065.01 | $97,905,275.71 | $365,211,232.26 |
| Fermented liquors | 46,086.00 | 25,363.82 | 41,965,874.09 | 117,839,602.21 |
| Tobacco manufactures | 270,759,384.44 | 255,219,385.49 | 295,809,355.44 | 206,003,091.84 |
| Oleomargarine | 2,121,079.68 | 2,986,465.35 | 3,728,276.05 | 2,791,831.08 |
| Capital-stock tax, including other special taxes | 90,544,039.59 | 91,281,484.31 | 102,933,701.35 | 33,497,047.82 |
| Miscellaneous, including war excise taxes, etc., since 1917 | 686,881,719.92 | 914,227,755.36 | 883,863,871.82 | 513,823,884.14 |
| Sales of internal-revenue stamps by postmasters | 14,616,958.05 | 20,880,868.86 | 24,437,893.75 | 10,199,466.51 |
| Total receipts from other than income and profits taxes | 1,110,532,618.15 | 1,367,219,388.20 | 1,450,644,248.21 | 1,249,366,175.86 |
| Income and profits taxes | 2,086,918,464.85 | 3,228,137,673.75 | 3,956,936,003.60 | 2,600,783,902.70 |
| Total receipts [1] | 3,197,451,083.00 | 4,595,357,061.95 | 5,407,580,251.81 | 3,850,150,078.56 |

| Source. | 1918 | 1917 | 1916 | 1915 |
|---|---|---|---|---|
| Distilled spirits, including wines, etc | $317,553,687.33 | $192,111,318.81 | $158,682,439.53 | $144,619,699.37 |
| Fermented liquors | 126,285,857.65 | 91,897,193.81 | 88,771,103.99 | 79,328,946.72 |
| Tobacco manufactures | 156,188,659.90 | 103,201,592.16 | 88,063,947.51 | 79,957,373.54 |
| Oleomargarine | 2,336,907.00 | 1,995,720.02 | 1,485,970.72 | 1,695,256.95 |
| Capital-stock tax, including other special taxes | 27,281,269.12 | 15,708,732.87 | 6,908,108.21 | 4,967,179.18 |
| Miscellaneous, including war excise taxes, etc., since 1917 | 225,973,363.44 | 44,760,678.44 | 43,874,465.20 | 24,910,809.24 |
| Sales of internal-revenue stamps by postmasters | 4,336,182.21 | | | |
| Total receipts from other than income and profits taxes | 859,955,926.65 | 449,675,236.11 | 387,786,035.16 | 335,479,265.00 |
| Income and profits taxes | 2,838,999,894.28 | 359,718,404.33 | 124,937,252.61 | 80,201,758.86 |
| Total receipts [1] | 3,698,955,820.93 | 809,393,640.44 | 512,723,287.77 | 415,681,023.86 |

[1] The figures concerning internal-revenue receipts as given in this statement differ from the figures carried in other Treasury statements showing the financial condition of the Government, because the former represent collections by internal-revenue officers throughout the country, including deposits by postmasters of amounts received from sale of internal-revenue stamps and deposits of internal revenue collected through customs offices, while the latter represent the deposits of these collections in the Treasury or depositaries during the fiscal year concerned, the differences being due to the fact that some of the collections in the latter part of the fiscal year can not be deposited, or are not reported to the Treasury as deposited until after June 30, thus carrying them into the following fiscal year as recorded in the statements showing the condition of the Treasury.

## COST OF ADMINISTRATION.

The cost of administering the internal revenue laws for the fiscal ear 1922 was $41,577,374.49. This does not include expenditures rom the appropriations for refunding internal-revenue collections and for refunding taxes illegally collected, which are in no sense administrative expenses but are properly deductions from the gross receipts. The cost of operation for the year on this basis was $1.30 or each $100 collected, compared with 87 cents for the preceding ear. Included in these expenditures, however, was $7,202,723.07 or the administration of the prohibition and narcotic laws (of which amount $658,728.77 was for the enforcement of the narcotic law) and $88,000 for the enforcement of the child-labor section of the revenue act of 1918. Deducting these amounts from the total eaves $34,286,651.42 as the expenditure for collecting the internal-revenue taxes for the fiscal year 1922, which is equivalent to $1.07 or each $100 collected. The cost of collection on a similar basis or the fiscal year 1921 was 72 cents for each $100 collected.

The difference in the relative cost of collection for the fiscal years .921 and 1922 is due mainly to the large reduction in the revenues or 1922 incident to the shrinkage in business and incomes, the repeal of certain miscellaneous war taxes, and various provisions of law such as the amortization of war-time facilities and the increase in individual exemptions contained in the revenue act of 1921, with the consequent reduction in the income-tax liability of corporations and individuals.

## INADEQUATE HOUSING OF BUREAU.

The unsatisfactory housing conditions mentioned in the annual report for the fiscal year 1921 have been accentuated. One more building, making eight in all, has been added to the number in which the bureau is functioning. The Income Tax Unit alone is quartered in five buildings, viz, Annex No. 1 at Pennsylvania Avenue and Madison Place NW.; Annex No. 2 at Fourteenth and B Streets NW.; Building C at Sixth and B Streets SW.; Building No. 5 at Twentieth and B Streets NW.; and the Interior Department Building at Eighteenth and F Streets NW. There are also located in Building C the Miscellaneous Division and the Tobacco Division, of the Miscellaneous Unit, the Sales Tax Unit, and the Capital Stock Tax and Estate Tax Unit. A part of the Accounts and Collections Unit is housed in Building No. 5 and a part in the Treasury Department Building. The Prohibition Unit occupies the Hooe Building at 1330 F Street NW. The solicitor's office and the Committee on Appeals and Review are located in the Interior Department Building. The Stamp Division is in the Auditors' Building at Fourteenth and B Streets SW. The office of the Commissioner and of two Deputy Commissioners, the Special Intelligence Unit, the Division of Supplies and Equipment, the Appointment Division, and the chemical laboratory are in the Treasury Building.

Annex No. 2, Building C, and No. 5 are temporary war structures. They are rapidly deteriorating and are not only flimsily constructed but are otherwise illy adapted to the work of the bureau. The fire hazard is very great. Thousands of income-tax returns and other valuable papers are held in these buildings, while the returns are in process of audit, among them documents covering hundreds of millions of dollars in increased assessments, many of which could not be replaced should they be destroyed.

This condition not only seriously interferes with proper administrative control and conduct of the bureau, but causes much inconvenience to taxpayers.

If the bureau were housed in a building adapted to the purpose, it would be possible to handle the work much more expeditiously, efficiently, and economically. Also danger from loss by fire and misplacement would be reduced to a minimum. It is, therefore, again recommended that immediate steps be taken to provide a suitable fireproof building that will adequately care for the needs of the entire bureau and thus permit of a more efficient and economical administration of the internal revenue laws.

## INCOME TAX UNIT.

### WORK ACCOMPLISHED.

*Audit of returns.*—During the fiscal year 954,731 income and excess-profits returns were audited. Of these 717,879 were individual and partnership returns and 236,852 were corporation returns. On office audits (those made without field examination) $22,736,236. 26 additional tax was assessed on individual and partnership returns, and $56,943,624. 71 on corporation returns, a total $79,679,860. 97.

*Revenue agents' reports.*—Revenue agents' reports on individual and partnership returns to the number of 24,868 were reviewed in Washington, and as a result $28,885,736.49 in additional tax was assessed. Corporation reports reviewed numbered 14,088 resulting in an additional assessment of $78,717,066. 69. The total additional tax assessed as a result of the audit of revenue agents' reports was $107,-602,803. 18.

During the fiscal year transcripts of 249,018 returns were sent to the field, compared with 285,427 transcripts investigated and returned.

*Adjustment of claims.*—The number of claims adjusted during the year was 167,405 involving $332,479,050. 60. Of these 139,631 involving $182,371,597. 88 were allowed and 27,774 involving $150,107,-452.72 were rejected. During the year 135,637 claims involving $467,829,361.91 were received.

*Administrative and statistical service.*—Approximately 1,250,000 income tax returns are received in Washington annually. These returns are checked with the assessment lists, and computations proved in the proving section; coded for industry in the statistical division, where the necessary statistical information is compiled, coded for filing, control cards typed in the registration section, and filed by districts in the unaudited returns section. The records subdivision, of which the unaudited returns section is a part, is called upon to maintain a control of all these returns for the years 1914 to date, furnish a flow of work to the audit sections, and maintain a file of revenue agents' reports and correspondence in regard to returns. Some of the items of work in this connection are—returns coded, 1,463,007; cards typed, 1,643,632; returns filed, 4,123,328; returns transferred, 425,000; and requisitions searched, 1,047,371.

The records subdivision also maintains a control of claims, receiving, coding, carding and assembling them with related papers, and, after adjustment, scheduling them for payment or rejection. During the fiscal year 135,367 claims were received, 160,000 carded, 162,700 assembled, and 167,405 scheduled.

The mail section during the year handled 3,863,962 pieces of mail. The sorting section sorted 31,009,241 certificates of information and adjusted 50,231 withholding returns. The stenographic section typed 5,473,173 pages. The duplicating section made 22,249,270 multigraph and mimeograph copies.

The statistical division, in addition to coding for industry all incoming returns, transcribed statistics from the returns, and issued the completed report for Statistics of Income for 1919 and the preliminary report for the Statistics of Income for 1920. In addition to its regular work the statistical division has compiled many special and valuable reports for administrative and legislative use.

*Information service.*—The rules and regulations section has carried on the important work of answering inquiries of taxpayers on technical and administrative questions and of preparing and issuing weekly, bimonthly, and semiannual bulletins and digests of income tax rulings. During the year 53,393 inquiries of taxpayers were answered.

*Recruitment and training of personnel.*—In December, 1921, Congress made a sufficient additional appropriation to enable the bureau to recruit 300 auditors for the consolidated returns subdivision; 75 engineers for the natural resources division and the amortization section, and 300 bureau clerks. Authorization was also made for the recruitment of 600 additional field auditors and 120 field clerks. The staff division, through rosters of eligibles established by the civil-service examinations prepared by the training section, began recruitment and training of auditors in February, 1922. Since that time 173 auditors have been assigned to the consolidated returns subdivision. Of these auditors however, 111 were recruited from other sections of the unit and assigned to consolidated returns after training, thereby creating vacancies in other sections of the unit necessary to be refilled. On the authorization for engineers a net recruitment of 68 was made. The turnover among clerks has been so great that despite the appointment of 422 clerks the net increase in the number of bureau clerks was but 58. Of the 600 field auditors 469 have been appointed, and of the field clerks 60 of the 120 authorized were employed.

In addition to the recruitment and training of the new personnel, the personnel section made replacements to the regular force. A total of 1,150 appointments was made compared with 1,087 separations, a net increase in personnel of 63.

The training section conducted, in addition to the field and consolidated returns training classes, regular classes for employees of the unit in tax law and accountancy, and also a correspondence course for field employees. Twenty-eight hundred and seventy-two employees of the unit were enrolled in the classes in tax law and accountancy and 1,700 field employees were enrolled in the correspondence course.

CHANGES AND IMPROVEMENTS IN POLICY, ORGANIZATION, AND
PROCEDURE.

A survey of the work of the unit last fall resulted in several
important changes in policy, necessitating many changes in organization and procedure.

The prompt audit of returns was delayed by claims accumulating
in the bureau, which for the most part offset the audit of returns and
the assessment of additional taxes, for the reason that in practically
all cases an assessment resulted in a claim which had to be adjusted
before the tax was collectible. The decision was therefore reached
that the prompt collection of additional taxes due, and effective
audit progress, were dependent primarily on the immediate adjustment of the 163,000 claims then pending.

Precedence was given to claims work, the decentralization of that
work was carried to completion, duplication of review was eliminated,
and a number of minor changes in the procedure were made. As a
result, the number of returns audited was reduced materially. On
the other hand, the number of claims adjusted more than offset this
loss in production, by making available for collection the additional
tax held up by claims in abatement and claims for credit. Once the
accumulation of claims is disposed of progress on the audit will be
comparatively rapid. The number of claims on hand was reduced
from 163,000 in October to 106,000 on June 30, 1922. During this
period 130,000 claims were adjusted, compared with 73,000 received.
During the quarter ending June 30, 1922, 56,236 claims involving
$96,757,574.63 were scheduled, as compared with 51,318 involving
$67,157,098.70 for the preceding quarter. This is the largest number
of claims scheduled by the bureau in any similar period in its history.
Of these 56,236 claims, 3,659 were rejected claims in abatement.
The amount involved in these rejected claims was $15,438,873.69,
which amount is now available for collection as additional tax due.

To eliminate unnecessary reviewing and recording and to place
the responsibility for producing results of standard quantity and
quality on the official directly in charge of the work it was decided
to abolish the review division. Separate review sections were created
under the supervision of a head of each audit division, who is now
solely responsible for the proper audit and review of cases handled in
his division. A large part of the review work has been eliminated,
particularly in certain classes of small and unimportant cases. In
addition to the eliminations of unnecessary review, the constant
fear on the part of the auditor that his work would be returned for
trivial error has also been eliminated. As an indication of the effect
of these changes in organization, procedure, and records on work in
process, the number of cases held for review during the last quarter
of the fiscal year decreased from 116,000 to 73,000, and the number
of letters mailed decreased from 161,049 to 151,649, despite the large
increase in the number of personal returns audited during that
period. Three of the four technical divisions showed a substantial
decrease in the number of letters mailed. Personal division showed
an increase from 69,000 to 78,000 on an increase in production of 100
per cent for the quarter.

Letter-critic work was abolished throughout the unit and the
auditors who prepare the letters review them on their return from

the stenographic section. Letters are only criticized for form when they require the signature of the higher officials of the bureau. This change has resulted in a material increase in the speed in which letters are dictated, signed, and mailed, and has made available for more productive work about 100 clerks. Form letters have been introduced in thousands of cases where letters were formerly dictated.

The former general audit division was reorganized into two divisions, the personal audit division and the corporation audit division. The personal audit division is comprised of what was formerly the personal section, together with the personal subsection of the field audit review section. There are now six sections auditing personal returns according to districts, and one section, the field review section, auditing revenue agents reports of individuals and partnership returns. The corporation audit division is now comprised of five sections, namely, manufacturers, trading, finance, public utilities, and personal service, and miscellaneous sections. The public utilities and personal service section includes the former transportation and public utilities section, together with the personal service subsection of the old personal service section. The miscellaneous section is comprised of the former miscellaneous subsection of the personal service section. The field audit review section was disbanded, the personal subsection being transferred to the personal divison and the corporation subsection being apportioned to the various corporation sections. Revenue agents' reports of corporations hereafter will be handled by sections according to industries, as returns have been handled in the past.

The natural resources division was created from the former subdivision of that name of the special audit division. Its establishment marks a departure from the functional organization of the unit, but it was deemed expedient, because of the specialized problems involved therein, to constitute it an entity so far as practicable. To the work of the former subdivision has been added the natural resource audits formerly carried on in the consolidated returns subdivison and the special assessment section.

In the consolidated returns subdivision, sections A to E, the old section unit organization has been abandoned in favor of a division into senior and junior audit groups under a group head with review made independently.

The inventory section of the special audit division was discontinued and its functions distributed to the various audit sections who would, in the ordinary course of events, audit the complete return.

In the administration division the returns control and files sections were combined and their functions transferred to the newly created records subdivision. This subdivision is comprised of five sections— the registration section, which receives and codes returns and types control cards; the unaudited returns section, which maintains files of returns for 1918 and subsequent years and 1917 corporation returns and a complete control record of all returns in the unit; the correspondence section, which maintains the files of correspondence, closed revenue agents' reports, 1917 individual, and all returns for prior years; the distribution section, which controls the flow of work and is responsible for its prompt transfer from place to place; and the claims control section, which receives, records, assembles, and routes claims to the proper sections.   A control of all claims in the unit is kept by this section.

In the unaudited returns section a district filing system has been introduced, centering in one file all of the returns for each year for each district.   Starting with the 1920 returns, returns will be delivered to the personal division by districts, eliminating much of the recording and delay in securing papers in the past.

A production office was created with the Assistant Deputy Commissioner as production manager.   The personnel research section of the staff division was abolished, and that part of its functions relating to production statistics was transferred to the production office.

The staff division was placed directly under the supervision of the Assistant Deputy Commissioner, and he, as production manager, was given final authority in personnel matters.

Special attention is being directed toward insuring the completion of the 1917 returns before the statute of limitations runs on March 15, 1923.   Precedence in both field and departmental offices has been given these cases with a view to completing the audits by December 1.   While the smaller cases will, no doubt, be entirely disposed of, a stupendous effort will be necessary in order to complete the audit of the large 1917 cases in the allotted time.

CONDITIONS OF THE WORK AND PROSPECTS FOR THE COMING FISCAL YEAR.

Audit of the 1920 personal returns has begun and should be completed by March 1, 1923.   The corporation audit division by the close of the fiscal year 1923 should be practically through its 1920 returns.   In the special audit and natural resources division there is approximately three years' work on hand for the present force. The work of these two divisions comprises the larger cases which are contested to the end by the taxpayer.   However, once the 1917 returns, which involve the settlement of certain primary questions, are completed, a much greater rate of speed will be possible on the returns of later years.   Every effort is being made to secure from the outside and by training from within the unit as many auditors for this grade of work as the appropriations will permit.

Progress during the past six months on the adjustment of claims encourages the belief that the unit will be near currency in the handling of claims toward the end of the fiscal year.

On June 30, 1922, there were in the field awaiting investigation 275,485 transcripts; during the last two quarters substantial reductions in the number of transcripts outstanding were made.   Indications at the close of the fiscal year were that less than a year's work remains to be done by the field force.   Considerable effort has been directed toward reducing the number of transcripts sent to the field for investigation on minor points, and 25,000 cases were recalled from the field to be audited in the office without investigation.   The drive on 1917 cases has somewhat retarded the production of the various field divisions but will assure the completion of at least all of the smaller cases by December 1, 1922, centering the work between that time and March, 1923, on the large cases located for the most part in the big cities.

## COMMITTEE ON APPEALS AND REVIEW.

In the annual report for the fiscal year 1920 reference was made to the creation on October 1, 1919, from the personnel of the bureau, of the Committee on Appeals and Review to serve entirely independent of the Income Tax Unit in an advisory capacity to the Commissioner in connection with the income and profits tax provisions of the law.

The personnel of the committee, consisting of five members during the fiscal year ended June 30, 1921, was increased during the current fiscal year to 10 members, all of whom have had valuable experience in the Income Tax Unit. This increase was made necessary by the rapidly increasing volume of work.

The members of the committee give their entire time and attention to the hearing and consideration of cases that have been appealed by taxpayers, and to questions upon which the advice of the committee is requested by the Income Tax Unit or the Commissioner.

The conclusions of the individual members of the committee, after being formulated and reduced to writing, are referred to an executive conference of the entire committee, and when agreed to, are sub- -mitted to the Commissioner in the form of recommendations. When approved by the Commissioner, these decisions are accepted by the Income Tax Unit as final conclusions of the Bureau and action is taken accordingly.

During the year the committee received 1,148 appeals from taxpayers and 70 requests for advice from the Income Tax Unit. It also received for criticism or approval 347 important letters making new rulings or new applications of old rulings submitted by the Income Tax Unit, 124 Treasury decisions, and 46 law opinions and solicitor's memoranda. In addition, 482 committee recommendations and 39 formal memoranda were submitted to and approved by the Commissioner for the guidance of the Income Tax Unit, 17 informal memoranda were prepared for officers of the bureau, 124 appeals and 8 requests for advice were closed by cancellation at request of the Income Tax Unit or the taxpayer; 525 oral hearings on appeals were given to taxpayers or their representatives and 43 executive conferences were held for the consideration and approval of decisions rendered by the committee. In addition, the committee held many informal conferences with taxpayers and with officers of the department upon questions of interpretation, policy, or procedure.

## ESTATE TAX AND CAPITAL-STOCK TAX UNIT.

This unit is charged with the administration of the tax on the transfer of estates of decedents and the annual excise tax and is measured by the fair value of the capital stock of corporations and certain associations "carrying on or doing business." These taxes are administered by two divisions—the Estate Tax Division and the Capital-Stock Tax Division. A third division (the Child-Labor Tax Division) was formerly a part of this unit. On May 15, 1922, the child-labor tax law was declared unconstitutional by the Supreme Court of the United States, and the division went out of existence.

In the administration of these two taxes, it is the policy of the bureau to afford taxpayers or their representatives full opportunity to be heard in personal conference upon all disputed questions that arise in connection with any particular case. Hearings are granted either in advance of the assessment of additional tax or in connection with claims for abatement and refund filed after such assessment has been made. As a result of these conferences, the bureau has disposed of many important and complicated cases on a basis satisfactory to the Government and without the necessity of resorting to litigation.

### PERSONNEL.

This unit has a total personnel of 607, as follows:

| | Officers. | Technicians. | Clerks. | Field. |
|---|---|---|---|---|
| Executive section | 2 | | 4 | |
| Estate Tax Division | 2 | 67 | 68 | 326 |
| Capital-Stock Tax Division | 2 | 33 | 88 | 15 |
| Total | 6 | 100 | 160 | 341 |

On June 30, 1922, there were 137 employees in the office of the Estate Tax Division and 326 in the field, compared with 100 in the office and 271 in the field at the end of the fiscal year 1921. This increase in the force was necessary in order to place the work on a current basis, and to comply with section 407, revenue act of 1921, requiring investigation within one year. The total number of employees in the Capital-Stock Tax Division was the same on June 30, 1922, as at the end of the fiscal year 1921.

### ESTATE AND CAPITAL-STOCK TAXES COLLECTED.

The collections of estate and capital-stock taxes for each of the fiscal years 1919, 1920, 1921, and 1922 are shown in the following table:

| | 1919 | 1920 | 1921 | 1922 |
|---|---|---|---|---|
| Estate tax | $82,029,983.13 | $103,635,563.24 | $154,043,260.39 | $139,418,846.04 |
| Capital-stock tax | 28,775,749.66 | 93,020,420.50 | 81,525,652.88 | 80,612,239.80 |
| Total | 110,805,732.79 | 196,655,983.74 | 235,568,913.27 | 220,031,085.84 |

The total collections for the fiscal year 1922 compared with those for 1921 show a decrease of $15,537,827.43. The decrease in collections of estate taxes is not due to a falling off in the number of returns or of tax shown on original returns, which have increased, as shown below, but to the fact that during the fiscal year 1921 special payment drives were instituted and in addition the bureau changed its former practice of permitting estates to make payment within a year and 180 days from date of death of decedent and instead insisted on payment at the expiration of one year, so that there was an acceleration of six months resulting from this change.

There was also a decrease in the amount of capital-stock tax collected. This tax is imposed upon corporations for the privilege of doing business and is measured by the fair average value for the year preceding the taxable year, and valuations fluctuate with conditions in business from year to year.

## ESTATE TAX DIVISION.

The Federal estate tax is imposed upon the transfer of the net estate occurring by reason of the death of a person. The basis of the tax is the value at the time of death of all property belonging to the gross estate, less a specific exemption of $50,000 in the case of an estate of a resident of the United States and certain other allowable deductions. On nonresident estates the basis for the tax differs from that of the resident, as only that part of the estate is taxed which at the time of death was situated in the United States, and the specific exemption of $50,000 is not allowed.

The most important part of the work of this division is of a legal nature, requiring consideration of nearly every branch of substantive law, knowledge of State statutes, and at times a study of laws of foreign nations, especially those applicable to the administration of estates and the descent and distribution of property. Examiners and field agents not only must qualify under a civil-service examination but must take a course of study and instruction and pass a subsequent examination on the laws and regulations governing the Federal estate tax before being assigned to duty. This procedure tends to avoid errors in the final assessment of the tax and lessens claims for abatement and refund, thus resulting in a saving to the Government.

During the last quarter of the year the plan of training new field appointees in the bureau was discontinued and they are now instructed to report to the office of the nearest internal revenue agent in charge for training and examination. This plan has resulted in the saving of considerable expense to the Government.

The total number of estate-tax returns filed in 1922 was 13,192, showing a tax liability of $114,614,189.56. As the result of field examinations and division audit, additional tax in the sum of $13,645,598.29 was disclosed. The total number of estate-tax returns filed during the fiscal year ended June 30, 1921, was 11,833, showing tax liability of $103,057,273.83.

An analysis of all estate tax returns filed up to January 15, 1922, shows that as of January 15 the following returns had been filed:

| Estates. | Number. | Tax collected. |
|---|---|---|
| Resident | 42,230 | $351,138,323 |
| Nonresident | 2,896 | 5,377,928 |
| Total | 45,126 | 356,516,251 |

The decision of the Supreme Court holding that the act of September 8, 1916, was not retroactive in the matter of transfers will result in a large increase in the amount to be abated and refunded in the current year. Under this decision where a decedent who died prior to the act of 1918 had made a transfer prior to September 8, 1916, the transfer could not be taxed, even though made in contemplation of death or intended to take effect at or after death.

Of greatest interest so far as the administration of the act of 1921 is concerned is the new provision under which, if an executor files a complete return and makes written request, the amount of tax due must be determined within one year and the executor is thereafter discharged from personal liability.

## CAPITAL-STOCK TAX DIVISION.

The capital-stock tax is an excise tax imposed upon domestic corporations, associations, and joint-stock companies for the privilege of doing business in an organized capacity; and upon like foreign organizations for the privilege of doing business within the United States.

In the case of the former, the measure of the tax is the fair average value of the capital-stock for the year preceding the taxable year, the rate being $1 for each full $1,000 of fair value in excess of the $5,000 exemption allowed by law. With the latter, the rate is $1 for each full $1,000 of the average capital employed in the transaction of the organization's business in the United States.

Form 707 for domestic concerns and Form 708 for foreign have proved satisfactory. They do not require a voluminous amount of data and are used by approximately 325,000 establishments in all lines of business with greatly varying fair values of their capital stoc .

Section 1000, Title X, of the revenue act of 1921, which imposes the capital-stock tax, is similar to the sections of the acts of 1916 and 1918 except that domestic and foreign insurance companies of either stock or mutual character are exempt, whereas they were formerly liable for the tax; and the so-called personal service corporations, which were formerly exempt, are liable to tax under existing law.

The administrative provisions were modified, permitting claims for refund to be filed within four years instead of two years from date of payment, and the assessment of the tax within four years instead of fifteen months under the former law. Provision is also made for payment of interest on refund claims under certain conditions.

The work of the division is divided in the following manner: Administrative, audit, claims, assessment, stenographic, mail review, and mail and file—the designation denoting the character of the work of each section.

In the audit a trained personnel has been developed and advantage taken of every opportunity to reach a higher degree of efficiency each year.

The additional capital-stock tax assessed and collected as a result of the audit for the fiscal year was $9,258,697.72, compared with $7,761,988.85 for the fiscal year 1921.

The work of the field force of 15 deputy collectors assigned to capital-stock tax investigation has proved wholly satisfactory, especially as regards cases that the office has been unable to dispose of through correspondence or where suit is contemplated. These deputy collectors also instruct employees in the various collectors' offices who handle capital-stock tax work.

The capital-stock tax has been in effect since January, 1917, with only slight modifications in the law, and is an important revenue producer at a small cost of collection.

## SALES TAX UNIT.

The Sales Tax Unit is charged with the interpretation and administration of Title V (sec. 500) of the revenue act of 1921, covering the tax on telegraph and telephone messages; Title VI (sec. 602) relating to the tax on beverages and the constituent parts thereof; Title VIII (secs. 800–801) regarding tax on admissions and dues; and Title IX (secs. 900, 902, 904, and 905) pertaining to the excise taxes.

At the beginning of the year there were approximately 10,100 abatement and refund claims on hand, while during the year 88,600 claims were received, making a total of 98,700 to be accounted for. Due to the transfer to the Miscellaneous Unit of special taxes upon businesses and occupations and upon the use of boats and documentary stamp taxes, 1,300 claims were transferred to that office for disposition, and about 62,700 claims were adjudicated, or a total of 64,000 disposed of, leaving a balance of 34,700 on hand at the close of the year. The excessive number of claims received during the year is ascribed to the repeal of the proprietary stamp tax, the repeal of the transportation tax, and a provision of the revenue act of 1921 that refund shall be made of the proportionate part of the tax collected on tickets or mileage books purchased and only partially used before January 1, 1922, the date of the repeal.

The passage of the revenue act of 1921 necessitated the revision and preparation of many regulations and forms and the promulgation of information in regard to its application.

It has not been deemed necessary to increase the personnel to meet the abnormal inflow of claims, as it is anticipated that there will be a gradual decrease in the number received, and those undisposed of will consequently in a little while materially decline.

During the year 29,433 offers in compromise were received, of which 14,872, representing $471,757.86, were accepted. In 751 cases it was found that no violation of the law had occurred, and the amounts paid, aggregating $40,950.03, were refunded to the taxpayers. At the close of the year 16,109 compromise cases were on hand, of which 4,383 had been acted upon but not completed.

During the first six months of the fiscal year, when the taxes imposed by the revenue act of 1918 were in effect, an average of 366,000 returns were received monthly. Since January 1, 1922, when sections of the revenue act of 1921, administered by the Sales Tax Unit, became effective, the average number of returns received monthly has been 240,000.

At the beginning of the fiscal year there were 6,836 credit cases on hand, while during the year approximately 27,437 cases were received and approximately 28,307 were disposed of, leaving 5,966 on hand on June 30, 1922. Improper credits totaling $321,408.86 were rejected and assessments made. The repeal of certain taxes on January 1, 1922, has caused a decrease in the number of credit cases of from approximately 2,400 to 1,900 for each month.

The following statement shows the various taxes which have been included in the general classification of sales taxes. The date on which each tax became effective is shown, as well as the number of the return form used and the number of the regulations relating to each tax.

| Section of law. | Class of taxes. | Effective date | Return forms. | Regulations No. |
|---|---|---|---|---|
| 500 | Telegraph and telephone............................. | Jan. 1, 1922 | 727 | 57. |
| 602 | Beverages and constituent parts thereof................ | .....do........ | 726 | 52. |
| 800 | Admissions........................................ | .....do........ | 729–729A | 43, Part 1. |
| 801 | Dues............................................. | .....do........ | 729 | 43, Part 2. |
| 900–4 | Manufacturers' excise taxes......................... | .....do........ | 728 | 47. |
| 902–5 | Works of art and jewelry........................... | .....do........ | 728A | 48. |

For the fiscal year, the total amount of taxes collected from these sources amounted to approximately $497,385,838.13.

The last issue of the Sales Tax Bulletin was that for December, 1921. In January, 1922, the Internal Revenue Bureau began the publication of a weekly bulletin containing rulings pertaining to the several units of the bureau. This bulletin is issued on a subscription basis and is sold by the Superintendent of Documents, Government Printing Office.

## TOBACCO DIVISION.

The Tobacco Division is charged with the administration of the internal revenue laws imposing taxes on tobacco products and cigarette papers and tubes and governing the purchase and sale of leaf tobacco. The revenue act of 1921, approved November 23, 1921, reenacted without change the rates of taxes imposed by the revenue act of 1918. The regulations (No. 8) relating to the taxes on tobacco, snuff, cigars, and cigarettes and purchase and sale of leaf tobacco were revised and promulgated in February, 1922.

The total receipts from all tobacco taxes during the fiscal year were $270,759,384.44, an increase of $15,539,998.95, or 6.09 per cent, compared with the preceding year. These receipts represent 8.46 per cent of the total internal-revenue receipts from all sources, compared with 5.5 per cent for the preceding year. The tobacco taxes collected during the past fiscal year were 162 per cent greater than during 1917, the fiscal year preceding that in which the increased war taxes first imposed under the revenue act of 1917 became effective.

The items of tobacco products showing increases in receipts as compared with the preceding year were: Cigarettes weighing not more than 3 pounds per thousand $15,074,145.19, or 11.2 per cent; manufactured chewing and smoking tobacco, $7,011,211 80, or 11.8 per cent; and snuff, $1,152,229.19, or 19.9 per cent.

The taxes on cigars weighing more than 3 pounds per thousand decreased $6,892,987.90, or 13.5 per cent; on cigars weighing not more than 3 pounds per thousand, $44,983.36, or 4.4 per cent; on cigarettes weighing more than 3 pounds per thousand, $237,780.19, or 66.7 per cent; and on cigarette papers and tubes, $182,676.28, or 15.4 per cent.

The receipts from special taxes imposed on manufacturerers of cigars, cigarettes, and tobacco amounted to $988,274.81, a decrease of $241,011.56, or 19.6 per cent. This decrease was due to the fact that there was a decrease in sales of tobacco manufactures during the preceding fiscal year, upon which basis the special taxes were computed as provided by law.

The total tax collected during the year on cigarette papers and tubes amounted to $1,001,509.93. Of this amount, $90,073.12 was paid on 9,006,968 packages of cigarette papers of domestic manufacture and $899,334.54 on 69,543,559 packages imported.

Stamps to the value of $12,102.27 were affixed to packages of cigarette tubes.

There were removed for consumption or use 309,559,077 packages, each containing not more than 25 cigarette papers, exempt from tax, and there were released tax free for use of cigarette manufacturers 26,196,627 tubes.

The taxes collected on the following products constitute 98.8 per cent of the total receipts from tobacco taxes: Cigarettes weighing not more than 3 pounds per thousand, 55.4 per cent; manufactured smoking and chewing tobacco, 24.5 per cent; cigars weighing more than 3 pounds per thousand, 16.3 per cent; and snuff, 2.6 per cent.

The following seven States furnished 83.6 per cent of the total receipts from tobacco manufactures: North Carolina, $93,189,086.02; New York, $45,314,839.78; New Jersey, $23,257,628.83; Pennsylvania, $21,993,634.54; Virginia, $19,697,056.40; Ohio, $12,542,432.37; Missouri, $10,725,986.79; total, $226,720,664.73.

The number of cigars of each class weighing more than 3 pounds per thousand tax paid during the fiscal year, as indicated by sales of stamps, and the percentages of increase or decrease as compared with the previous year, were as follows: Class A, 2,285,333,690, an increase of 29 per cent; class B, 1,660,764,580, a decrease of 22 per cent; class C, 2,525,740,254, a decrease of 17 per cent; class D, 116,815,008, a decrease of 29 per cent; class E, 32,530,808, a decrese of 29 per cent.

The leading States in the manufacture of tobacco products are as follows, in the order named: In the manufacture of cigars weighing more than 3 pounds per thousand, Pennsylvania, New York, Ohio, New Jersey, Virginia, Florida, and Michigan; in the manufacture of cigars weighing not more than 3 pounds per thousand, Maryland, Pennsylvania, New York, New Jersey, Virginia, and West Virginia; in the manufacture of cigarettes weighing not more than 3 pounds per thousand, North Carolina, New York, Virginia, New Jersey, and Pennsylvania; in the manufacture of cigarettes weighing more than 3 pounds per thousand, New York, which accounts for 74.65 per cent of the total manufactured; in the manufacture of plug tobacco, Missouri and North Carolina; twist, Missouri, Tennessee, and Kentucky; fine cut, Kentucky, Illinois, and New Jersey; smoking tobacco, North Carolina, Ohio, New Jersey, Kentucky, Illinois, and Virginia; snuff, Tennessee, New Jersey, and Illinois.

There was a small increase in the number of manufacturers of tobacco, snuff, cigars, and cigarettes, and a decrease in the number of dealers in leaf tobacco. The following table gives the number in each class of business on December 31 of each year, 1914 to 1921, inclusive:

| Dec. 31— | Manufacturers of— | | | | Dealers in leaf tobacco. |
|---|---|---|---|---|---|
| | Cigars. | Cigarettes. | Tobacco. | Snuff. | |
| | *Number.* | *Number.* | *Number.* | *Number.* | *Number.* |
| 1914 | 16,754 | 381 | 2,364 | 68 | 3,164 |
| 1915 | 15,732 | 367 | 2,214 | 71 | 3,497 |
| 1916 | 14,576 | 311 | 2,085 | 67 | 4,139 |
| 1917 | 13,217 | 311 | 1,915 | 61 | 3,668 |
| 1918 | 11,291 | 263 | 1,803 | 60 | 3,092 |
| 1919 | 11,483 | 237 | 1,814 | 57 | 3,424 |
| 1920 | 11,110 | 213 | 1,810 | 35 | 3,662 |
| 1921 | 12,105 | 225 | 1,817 | 39 | 3,619 |

Growers of and dealers in perique tobacco numbered 54 during the calendar year 1921. This class of tobacco, which is raised principally in St. James Parish, La., is so prepared and cured as to require growers and dealers to report their transactions as manufacturers of tobacco. Their operations during the calendar year 1921 were as follows:

| | Pounds. | | Pounds. |
|---|---|---|---|
| On hand Jan. 1, 1921 | 290,373 | Tax paid | 1,548 |
| Grown | 419,154 | Exported in bond | 173,199 |
| Purchased | 458,000 | Sold | 564,517 |
| | | On hand Jan. 1, 1922 | 428,263 |
| Total | 1,167,527 | Total | 1,167,527 |

During the fiscal year 306 reports of violations of tobacco laws were received and handled in the division, and in 274 of these cases offers in compromise, totaling $3,400 were tendered and accepted.

## MISCELLANEOUS TAXES.

### OLEOMARGARINE.

During the fiscal year there were 72 oleomargarine factories in operation. Nine factories closed during the year, leaving 63 in business on June 30, 1922. The 72 factories produced 6,603,981 pounds of colored and 184,346,392 pounds of uncolored oleomargarine, compared with 11,600,319 pounds of colored and 269,481,195 pounds of uncolored oleomargarine in the fiscal year 1921, a decrease of 43.1 and 31.6 per cent, respectively.

The following comparative data for the years 1921 and 1922 indicate the trend of the industry.

| | Colored oleomargarine. | | Uncolored oleomargarine. | |
|---|---|---|---|---|
| | 1921 | 1922 | 1921 | 1922 |
| | *Pounds.* | *Pounds.* | *Pounds.* | *Pounds.* |
| Produced | 11,600,319 | 6,603,981 | 269,481,195 | 184,346,392 |
| Withdrawn tax paid for domestic use | 9,214,650 | 5,159,236 | 269,734,142 | 183,670,536 |
| Withdrawn free of tax for export | 1,826,703 | 687,969 | 1,667,980 | 378,220 |
| Withdrawn free of tax for United States | 668,623 | 713,439 | 3,000 | |

The receipts from stamp tax on oleomargarine and the special taxes imposed upon those engaging in the manufacture and sale of this product amounted to $2,121,079.68, which is $865,385.67 less than was collected from the same source in 1921, a decrease of 29 per cent. The receipts for 1921 and 1922 were as follows:

| Receipts from— | 1921 | 1922 | Increase (+) or decrease (−). | |
| --- | --- | --- | --- | --- |
| | | | Amount. | Per cent. |
| Oleomargarine taxed at 10 cents a pound....... | $921,192.25 | $494,005.50 | −$427,186.75 | 46.3 |
| Oleomargarine taxed at ¼ cent a pound......... | 655,427.08 | 452,774.47 | −202,652.61 | 30.9 |
| Manufacturers' special tax..................... | 52,478.94 | 40,028.95 | − 12.449.99 | 23.7 |
| Wholesale dealers' special tax................. | 450,986.44 | 347,403.23 | −103,583.21 | 23.0 |
| Retail dealers' special tax.................... | 906,380.64 | 786,867,53 | −119,513 11 | 13.2 |
| Total................................. | 2,986,465.35 | 2,121,079.68 | −865,385.67 | 29.0 |

## ADULTERATED BUTTER.

Collections under the adulterated butter law aggregated $17,871.84 for the year. This amount is $16,368.12 less than was collected from the same source last year, a decrease of 47.8 per cent. There are still only three manufacturers of adulterated butter regularly engaged in the business and their entire output is withdrawn tax free for export to foreign countries. The bulk of the collections under the act result from creamery butter found on the market containing 16 per cent or more of moisture which brings it within the classification of adulterated butter.

## RENOVATED BUTTER.

There were 5,355,816 pounds of renovated butter produced during the year, compared with 6,099,110 pounds produced in 1921, a decrease of 743,294 pounds. The tax of one-fourth cent a pound on renovated butter and the special tax of $50 per annum imposed on manufacturers thereof yielded $14,416.27 during the year, compared with $15,511.56 collected from this source in 1921, a decrease of 7.1 per cent.

## MIXED FLOUR.

There were 3,101,720 pounds of mixed flour manufactured during the year, compared with 3,500,209 pounds produced in 1921, a decrease of 398,489 pounds. Receipts from special and stamp taxes on mixed flour amounted to $1,167.45 in 1922, compared with $1,225.85 in 1921, a decrease of $58.40, or .5 per cent.

## CLAIMS.

On August 8, 1921, when the organization of the Miscellaneous Division was completed, there were transferred to it 1,757 refund claims, involving $1,152,594.52; 138 abatement claims, involving $1,070,074.65; and 48 uncollectible claims, involving $739.99. In addition to these there were received during the fiscal year 8,086 refund claims, involving $1,362,372.54; 2,528 abatement claims, involving $1,967,946.11; and 2,179 uncollectible claims, involving $55,899.79.

During the year there were disposed of 7,178 refund claims (6,159 by allowance and 1,019 by rejection), involving $1,947,406.59; 1,818 abatement claims (1,572 by allowance and 246 by rejection), involving $160,145.37; 1,437 uncollectible claims (1,390 by allowance and 47 by rejection), involving $21,822.06. On June 30, 1922, there were on hand 2,665 refund claims, involving $567,560.47; 848 abatement claims, involving $2,876,875.39; and 690 uncollectible claims, involving $34,817.72.

The receipts of claims for the last half of the year increased 51 per cent over those for the first half, due largely to discontinuance of certain stamp taxes and an increase in the number of claims for abatement filed to clear collectors' accounts.

### ACCOUNTS AND COLLECTIONS UNIT.

#### ORGANIZATION.

In conformity with a recommendation of the Tax Simplification Board, approved by the Secretary of the Treasury, the Accounts Unit and the office of the supervisor of collectors' offices were abolished, effective May 23, 1922, and the duties formerly performed in those units are now administered in a new unit known as the "Accounts and Collections Unit." This consolidation has resulted in reduction in personnel cost, as well as increased efficiency.

For purposes of effective administration, the Accounts and Collections Unit is divided into five divisions.

#### DIVISION OF FIELD ALLOWANCES.

This division is in charge of the administration of the granting of allowances for all requirements of collection districts.

During the fiscal year a total of 5,966 forms AP–100 (recommendation of collectors for personnel changes), including 2,865 new appointments, were reviewed and acted upon.

On June 30, 1921, there were in this service 4,548 office employees and 2,235 field deputy collectors, or a total of 6,783, compared with 4,617 office employees and 2,854 field deputy collectors, or a total of 7,471, on June 30, 1922, or a net increase of 688. Of the 688 additional employees, 619 were designated field deputy collectors. The wisdom of increasing the number of field deputies is reflected in the increase in delinquent and additional taxes collected. During the fiscal year 1922 $120,000 was expended for temporary clerical assistance, compared with $232,000 for the fiscal year 1921.

Prior to November 1, 1921, the only means of determining the efficiency of employees in the various collection districts was through the medium of reports received from assistant supervisors. On that date an efficiency rating system was inaugurated for the collection service. As a result of the adoption of this system the bureau is assisted in acting intelligently upon collectors' recommendations for promotions, and is in possession of information which may be utilized in considering the reduction in salary or dismissal of an employee who is not rendering maximum service. With the establishment of this system, a new scale of entrance salaries for employees was adopted covering the seven classes of work within a collection district. This plan also provided for the filling of a vacancy by appointment at the entrance salary established for the particular grade, the difference in salary between the retiring employee and the new appointee reverting to the Treasury.

Every effort has been made to effect economies in the rental of office space, and on June 30, 1922, the annual rental rate had been reduced by $19,836.95.

A committee on mechanical office appliances, consisting of representatives of this bureau and a representative of the Bureau of Efficiency, considered the method of preparing assessment lists, bills, and other accounting records in collectors' offices with a view to adopting an improved procedure. A billing machine carbon system was installed which has already resulted in an approximate net saving of $23,500. In view of the fact that this economy was effected notwithstanding the entire cost of installation is chargeable during this period, it is believed that a greater economy for the following fiscal year will be effected.

Due to the many new appointments made throughout the field collection service and because of the enactment of the revenue act of 1921, it was found desirable to continue the correspondence study courses for the benefit of collectors' employees. These courses cover individual income tax, corporation income and profits tax, sales taxes, miscellaneous taxes, bookkeeping, elements of accounts, and elementary law. On June 30, 1922, a total of 58 courses had been prepared and were being studied by collectors' employees, in comparison with 42 courses available June 30, 1921, and 24 courses available June 30, 1920. It is a requirement of employment in a collection district that the employees enroll for certain courses. On June 30, 1922, a total of 4,988 students were enrolled, compared with 2,189 on June 30, 1921.

### FIELD PROCEDURE DIVISION.

This division has charge of the direction of the collection field forces, the planning of delinquent drives, and the organization of division, subdivision, and stamp offices.

Constant endeavor is being made to afford taxpayers the best possible facilities in the transaction of their business with the Internal Revenue Service. On June 30, 1922, there were open 183 division headquarters offices, 27 subdivision offices, and 18 offices at which stamps only were sold, in addition to the 64 collectors' offices, a total of 292 offices and branch offices.

Collectors were instructed to give special attention to the serving of warrants for distraint, the verifying of returns showing additional tax due, and the conduct of delinquent drives. A total of 211,635 warrants for distraint were served, which involved the collection of $9,902,306, compared with 169,409 warrants served during the fiscal year 1921, involving the collection of $7,034,335. A total of 789,384 revenue-producing investigations were made by collectors' field forces, compared with 769,065 investigations during the previous fiscal year. The total amount collected and reported for assessment as the result of such investigations aggregated $56,791,914 in 1922, compared with $39,976,126 for the fiscal year 1921. The average number of investigations per deputy increased from 301 in 1921 to 332 in 1922, with an increase in the average amount collected and reported for assessment per deputy from $15,634 in 1921 to $23,901 in 1922. Taking into consideration the average salary and traveling expenses of a field deputy collector, the net annual return to the Government for each deputy so employed was in excess of $21,000.

The bureau at all times maintains a complete record of the accomplishments of field deputy collectors, which information is prepared from reports received monthly from the 64 collectors of internal revenue.

### DISBURSEMENT DIVISION.

This division supervises the administrative audit of the disbursing accounts of all collectors, revenue agents in charge, and other special disbursing agents of the Internal Revenue Bureau and Service. All miscellaneous bills for transportation, equipment, telephone service, rental, etc., paid from internal-revenue appropriations by the disbursing clerk of the Treasury Department are examined in this division before payment is made, and all amounts allowed for the refund of taxes illegally collected, redemption of stamps, abatement of claims, etc., are recorded.

For the fiscal year 1922 the Disbursement Division examined and recorded 1,876 monthly accounts of collectors of internal revenue, internal-revenue agents in charge, and Federal prohibition directors, together with 179,853 supporting vouchers; 14,126 salary and expense vouchers of employees paid by the disbursing clerk of the Treasury Department; 1,400 bills of special employees, informers, etc.; and 10,250 bills for miscellaneous expenses.

### OFFICE ACCOUNTS AND PROCEDURE DIVISION.

This division has charge of the office procedure and accounting methods in collectors' offices, as well as the auditing of all revenue accounts of collectors.

One of the outstanding accomplishments of this division during the fiscal year was the transfer of collection districts from outgoing to incoming collectors. From April 1 to July 1, 1921, 13 new collectors were inducted into office, while during the fiscal year ended June 30, 1922, 49 new collectors were installed, making a total of 62 new collectors inducted into office in a period of 15 months.

An inventory of claims for abatement, credit, and refund was taken September 1, 1921, and 60,362 claims were found to be on hand in collectors' offices upon which there had been no action. Steps were taken to remedy this condition, and on June 30, 1922, there were but 15,764 claims in collectors' offices, a reduction of 44,598, notwithstanding that during this period collectors received 238,257 claims. From September 1, 1921, to June 30, 1922, 282,855 claims were actually transmitted to the bureau by collectors.

The prompt deposit of collections with Federal reserve banks and other Government depositories has received careful attention and tax collections have been made immediately available to meet outstanding certificates of indebtedness. When necessary, the accounting system has been modified so as to meet existing conditions and the fiscal transactions of collectors' offices are being handled in an efficient and business-like manner. The examining and auditing work in the bureau incident to collectors' revenue accounts has been kept current, and every account has been referred to the Comptroller General within the required time.

Because of the abolishment of the office of the supervisor of collectors' offices, and the creation of the new unit known as the "Accounts and Collections Unit," those field employees formerly designated as "assistant supervisors of collectors' offices" are now designated "supervisors of accounts and collections." This mobile force is constantly visiting collectors' offices and assisting in problems of office management and accounting. Their services have been utilized particularly in examining accounts in order that there may be complete reconciliation between the accounts of the collectors and their liability as reflected by the bureau's records. The need of a force of mobile employees thoroughly familiar with the work and needs of a collection district has been satisfactorily demonstrated during the past fiscal year, when so many new collectors were inducted into office.

### STAMP DIVISION.

The Stamp Division is charged with the responsibilities incident to the receipt and distribution of internal-revenue stamps. Approximately seven hundred different kinds and denominations comprising upward of 1,300,000,000 stamps is an average current stock supply. During the fiscal year a total of 6,264,697,607 stamps of an aggregate money value of $413,864,005.13 were issued for sale to the public through collectors of internal revenue and the Post Office Department.

During the year stamps were returned by collectors and the Postmaster General and credited in their accounts to the value of $50,992,-154.83. These were of various kinds and denominations, including partly used books from outgoing collectors and stamps made obsolete by legislation.

### CONCLUSION.

Since the consolidation of the Office of the Supervisor of Collectors Offices and Accounts Unit, there has been effected a saving of $48,710 in the annual salary rate of this unit. It is believed that further economy in the matter of personnel may be effected. Notwithstanding this reduction in personnel, and resultant saving in salary cost, the work of the unit is practically current.

### PROHIBITION UNIT.

During the fiscal year ended June 30, 1922, a complete reorganization of the activities of the Prohibition Unit was effected, which has resulted in handling the work of the unit more efficiently and expeditiously.

The office of the head of the executive division has been discontinued, also the office of field supervisor, and the duties of these positions assumed by the Assistant Prohibition Commissioner.

The position of supervising Federal prohibition agent has been abolished, and permissive and enforcement work under the national prohibition act has been combined in the offices of State prohibition directors. The supervising Federal prohibition agents formerly had charge of enforcement work, leaving the permissive features to be supervised by the State prohibition directors. This change has eliminated duplication of work and has simplified greatly the carrying into effect of the provisions of the national prohibition act.

The law forces of the unit have been combined in the office of the counsel for the Prohibition Unit, which office has two branches, the division of interpretation and the division of litigation.

A mobile force of general prohibition agents working under the immediate supervision of 18 divisional chiefs and directed from Washington through the chief, general prohibition agents, has been established and has proved a valuable factor in suppressing violations of the law. These general prohibition agents work independently of the State prohibition directors and are assigned to important special cases.

The audit and statistics division has been reorganized and is known as the audit division, to which has been transferred the assessment section, the claims section, and the compromise section of the former legal division.

A narcotic division as an entity has been established to handle all phases of the enforcement of the Harrison Narcotic Act, this division being in lieu of the narcotic section of the former legal division, the narcotic returns section of the former audit and statistics division, and the office of the narcotic field supervisor.

The divisions comprising the Prohibition Unit are now as follows:

Office of the Federal Prohibition Commissioner.
Office of the Assistant Prohibition Commissioner.
Office of counsel.
    Division of interpretation.
    Division of litigation.
Office of chief, general prohibition agents.
Narcotic division.
Permit division.
Industrial alcohol and chemical division.
Audit division.

Every effort has been made to reduce the number of counterfeit and forged withdrawal permits and physicians' prescription blanks. A new withdrawal permit and a new physicians' prescription blank have been designed and put into use.

A requirement has been put into effect that permits to purchase covering interstate shipments of intoxicating liquor, including alcohol, shall be countersigned by the prohibition director of the State in which the distillery or warehouse from which such shipments are removed is located, thus furnishing a director full knowledge of all liquor transactions within his State.

A campaign has been conducted to discourage transportation of intoxicating liquor by automobile truck. Regulations have been issued to the effect that all shipments of liquor, both interstate and intrastate, shall be, as far as practicable, by railroad, express, or boat, rather than by truck, the means of transportation being specified on the withdrawal permit. The regulations provide that shipment by truck shall ordinarily be permitted only where the vendor and vendee are in reasonably close proximity and the facilities for transportation by railroad, express, or boat are inadequate. The vendor or other person authorized to furnish the liquor is required to make delivery only to a carrier of the character indicated by the permit.

The Virgin Islands have been added to the territory under the jurisdiction of the Federal prohibition director for Porto Rico. There is now a Federal prohibition director for each State in the Union, one for Alaska, one for Hawaii, and one for Porto Rico and the Virgin Islands.

There has been a reduction of $170,000 in the amount paid for rent of offices and storage space during the fiscal year just ended. This has been accomplished through securing more reasonable rates of rental and the moving of seized property from commercial warehouses to Government warehouses, and through the destruction and disposition of seized liquors

The number of employees in the unit in Washington increased from 503 at the beginning of the fiscal year to 596 at the close of the year. In the field during that time the force has increased from 1,818 to 2,881. The total force of the unit has, therefore, increased from 2,321 to 3,477 in the past fiscal year. The total pay roll of the unit on June 30, 1922, was $6,045,073, an increase of $2,015,943 over that of June 30, 1921.

During the year 3,332,271 pieces of mail passed through the section of mail control.

### OFFICE OF COUNSEL OF PROHIBITION UNIT.

*Division of interpretation.*—This division advises the Prohibition Commissioner and the Assistant Prohibition Commissioner and the various divisions of the unit in matters referred to it and conducts the library of the unit. Written opinions have been rendered on numerous questions formally referred with request for ruling, and informal opinions have also been rendered in conferences at which representatives of the division have been present. The miscellaneous correspondence of the unit on matters involving interpretation of the liquor and narcotic laws and regulations has also been handled in this division. The majority of the Treasury decisions, mimeographs, and circulars issued by the unit have been prepared in this division and such regulations as have been prepared in other divisions have been reviewed here. The compilation of prohibition and internal-revenue laws affecting liquor has been revised. Several bills and amendments to bills have been prepared at the request of members and committees of Congress, and other assistance has been rendered legislative committees considering various bills, particularly the Willis-Campbell Act, the revenue act of 1921, and the tariff bill. All claims and offers in compromise have been reviewed in this division.

*Division of litigation.*—This division handles, in conjunction with the proper court officials, all matters relating to the prosecution of criminal and civil cases arising under the national prohibition act. A policy of closer cooperation with the various United States attorneys throughout the country was established during the year. Numerous criminal informations and indictments, briefs, bills in equity, and search warrants have been drawn and letters written requesting the institution of proceedings on bonds, all with a view of aiding United States attorneys and assuring speedy and successful prosecution in the more important cases. Attorneys from this division have visited the offices of United States attorneys in various districts and assisted in the preparation and trial of numerous cases involving violations of the national prohibition act upon the request of the United States attorneys and with the consent and approval of the Department of Justice.

On November 23, 1921, the Willis-Campbell Act was approved supplementing the national prohibition act. This new act prohibits the dispensing of malt liquors on physicians' prescriptions and prohibits the further importation and manufacture of distilled spirits, except alcohol, until the quantities in this country are reduced to an amount which, in the opinion of the Commissioner, is insufficient for any but lawful uses. Importations not already in transit by November 23, 1921, have been prohibited by this act.

Suits were instituted by the following named companies to test the constitutionality of the Willis-Campbell Act:

The Falstaff Corporation v. Wm. H. Allen, Federal prohibition director, in the District Court of the United States for the Eastern District of Missouri.

Piel Brothers v. Ralph A. Day, Federal prohibition director, in the District Court of the United States for the Eastern District of New York.

Everards Brewing Company v. Ralph A. Day, Federal prohibition director, in the District Court of the United States for the Southern District of New York.

In each of the above-mentioned cases the contention of the Government was sustained and the constitutionality of the Willis-Campbell Act upheld. Briefs on all of these cases, upon which the United States attorneys based their argument, were prepared in this division.

The number of nonbeverage cases involving permit violations has materially increased during the past year, and criminal prosecutions have been successfully maintained against numerous permit holders. This is a result of a more rigid enforcement rather than increased violations on the part of permit holders.

Initial steps have been taken to recover on forfeited bonds of permittees to the extent of $3,500,000.

Upon the issuance of Prohibition Mimeograph 201, dated August 9, 1921, a decided improvement in the brewery situation was brought about. Since that date criminal informations, indictments, injunctions, libels, and search warrants in brewery cases, with all the necessary supporting affidavits, are prepared in this unit and filed through the Department of Justice. This policy has proved invaluable as a weapon in the proper enforcement of the law. By means of this active assistance and cooperation the various United States attorneys are enabled to make much progress in the trials of cases, with a resulting decrease in the number of cases on their overcrowded court dockets, as such procedure eliminates the gathering of evidence and the preparing of the necessary legal papers by them. Before the adoption of the policy above mentioned at least 40 per cent of the brewers who were detected violating the law were reported for a second offense. In approximately 50 cases handled under the new policy only 2 companies have violated the law a second time.

While the number of reports in brewery cases have also increased during the past year, this does not indicate a disregard of the law, but a more vigorous investigation of the activities of violators. There are also several large wine cases pending.

There are approximately 500 cereal-beverage manufacturing plants in the United States. Over 200 of these plants have been reported during the past 12 months for violations of law. Approximately 125 of them have been placed under seizure. Approximately 75 of such companies have settled their civil liabilities by compromise where the case arose prior to August 8, 1921. Those arising subsequent to said date were settled by a compromise of their civil liabilities after a plea' of guilty to the criminal information filed against them. The unit has refused to issue permits to some 48 brewers who have violated the law under permits previously issued.

Approximately $500,000 have been submitted as offers in compromise of civil liabilities in brewery cases, and that amount has been paid into the Treasury. Some 38 of the largest companies have entered pleas of guilty to the criminal charges. There are now pending in the courts cases against approximately 30 brewers.

During the year the beverage section, which handles all cases involving the illicit manufacture, sale, and use of intoxicating liquors, has devoted much time to working out legal questions and questions of policy in the type of cases enumerated, presented by prohibition directors and United States attorneys throughout the country.

In several jurisdictions where the question of the disposal of seized property was a serious one libels have been prepared' and forwarded to the United States attorneys for filing. In this manner the unit has succeeded in disposing of great quantities of contraband liquor. Proceeds of the sale of liquor fit for medicinal purposes has, in the majority of the States, been more than ample to defray all storage expenses.

### OFFICE OF CHIEF, GENERAL PROHIBITION AGENTS.

At the end of the fiscal year 299 agents were assigned to duty on the force of general prohibition agents. During the year 2,036 cases were reported by the general prohibition agents, covering violations of every nature. Taxes in the amount of $19,716,440.98 were reported for assessment. The cases covered investigation of breweries, distilleries, holders of the various kinds of permits, as well as violations by the illegal manufacture, sale, transportation, importation, and exportation of intoxicating liquors.

During the year a prohibition patrol service was organized consisting of six boats of the submarine chaser type, assigned at various points along the Atlantic coast. These boats have proved very effective in the suppression of smuggling.

In addition, there were placed on the Great Lakes five motor patrol boats which are capable of making 33 miles per hour. These boats have proved very effective in apprehending liquor smuggled from Canada.

### NARCOTIC DIVISION.

On June 30, 1922, 516 persons were registered under the Harrison narcotic law, as amended, as importers and manufacturers, 2,467 as wholesale dealers, 42,942 as retail dealers, 147,677 as practitioners, and 74,656 as dealers in and manufacturers of untaxed narcotic preparations, the latter number including registrants not required to pay special tax by reason of paying another tax under the act, or a total of 268,258 registrations.

At the beginning of the year a total of 868,662 ounces of imported taxable narcotic drugs of all kinds was in customs custody, and 2,699,876 ounces were imported during the year, making a total available quantity of 3,568,538 ounces. Of this, 2,629,269 ounces were withdrawn during the year for domestic consumption, and 540,287 ounces were withdrawn for export, leaving a total of 392,163 ounces in customs custody at the close of the year. There was an aggregate of 5,016,808 ounces of narcotic drugs, both in pure form and as part content of compounds and preparations, in the possession of manufacturers on July 1, 1921. Imports amounting to 3,169,556 ounces were withdrawn and added to this quantity during the year, making a total of 8,168,364 ounces. During the year manufacturers exported 25,575 ounces of this supply or of the drugs derived therefrom through manufacturing, and 1,419,044 ounces of like description were sold by them to domestic purchasers, leaving a total of 2,312,014 ounces in the possession of manufacturers on June 30, 1922. A mathematical balance can not be produced from the foregoing statement, as an alkaloid or derivative is not the equivalent in weight of the drug from which it is obtained through a manufacturing process.

During the year ended June 30, 1921, a total of 6,951,677 ounces of narcotic drugs of all kinds was imported, while during the year ended June 30, 1922, an aggregate of 2,699,876 ounces was imported, a decrease of 4,251,801 ounces. During the same periods 59,955 ounces and 40,113 ounces, respectively, were exported, showing a decrease of 19,842 ounces. The net aggregate quantity of pure drugs of all kinds contained in products sold by manufacturers to domestic purchasers during the fiscal year 1921 amounted to 856,437 ounces, and domestic sales of this description for the fiscal year 1922 involve 1,419,044 ounces, or an increase of 562,607 ounces. The drugs exported involved 587,312 taxable ounces of products and those sold to domestic purchasers 6,316,774 taxable ounces. (Tax is paid by stamps at the rate of 1 cent per ounce or fraction thereof for the entire contents of each package or bottle. A compound or preparation containing a narcotic drug in a quantity exceeding the statutory exemption is taxed the same as the pure drug.)

Manufacturers of exempt (nontaxable) narcotic preparations purchased 8,617 ounces of narcotic drugs, involving a total of 19,727 taxable ounces.

Officials of the Federal and of State, county, and municipal governments and institutions, who, as such, are exempt from registration and payment of tax under the Harrison Narcotic Act, purchased during the year a total of 7,569 ounces of narcotic drugs contained in stamped packages, amounting to 66,931 taxable ounces.

During the year a total of 71,151 ounces of narcotic drugs and preparations came into the possession of the Government through nforcing the internal revenue narcotic laws, an increase of 37,082 ounces over the previous year, during which 34,069 ounces were acquired.

At the beginning of the year 1,740 violations of the Harrison Narcotic Act were pending against persons not entitled to registration under the law, and a total of 5,168 violations against such persons was reported during the year. At the beginning of the year 1,381 violations of the law were pending against registered persons. During the year penalties, imposed by section 3176 of the Revised Statutes, as amended, were assessed against 40,055 registered persons on account of failure to register and pay special tax as required under the act, and 1,483 violations of the law were reported during the year which involved other charges of greater significance. Accordingly, a total of 6,908 violations accrued during the year against unregistered persons and 42,919 violations of all kinds against registered persons.

Of the unregistered persons charged with violations of the law, 2,945 were convicted, 199 were acquitted, 17 submitted acceptable offers in compromise of their liability, 693 cases were dropped, and 3,054 cases were pending at the close of the year. Of the cases accruing against registered persons, collection of specific penalty was made in 40,055 cases, 159 persons were convicted, 33 were acquitted, 498 submitted acceptable offers in compromise of their liability, 254 cases were dropped, and 1,920 cases were pending at the close of the year.

At the beginning of the year 124 cases of violations of the act of January 17, 1914, regulating the manufacture of smoking opium, were pending and 50 cases were reported during the year, or a total of 174 violations. During the year 27 persons were convicted, 1 was acquitted, 32 cases were dropped, and 114 violations were pending at the close of the fiscal year.

A total of 3,104 convictions under the internal revenue narcotic laws was had for which the courts imposed sentences aggregating 2,814 years, 3 months, and 20 days, and fines amounting to $204,059. A total of 515 cases was compromised, the aggregate amount collected being $55,640.

At the beginning of the year the narcotic field force consisted of 157 agents and inspectors, which number was increased to 176 agents and inspectors in the service on June 30, 1922.

During the year ended June 30, 1921, a total of 4,014 cases of criminal character were reported, whereas during the last fiscal year 6,651 such cases were reported. An increase of 2,637 cases over the previous year is to be noted, indicating a more effective operation of the field force and more efficient means for disclosing violations of the law.

Monthly returns of sales, etc., rendered by importers, manufacturers, and wholesale dealers afford means not only for controlling the manufacture and sale of narcotics but also for a systematic scrutinizing of all purchases. In so far as possible with the present force, every person, the aggregate of whose purchases has appeared excessive, has been investigated. An abstract system arranged in connection with the audit of the monthly returns for apprehending such purchasers has been installed which results in directing the inspections and investigations of registered persons most essential to that aspect of the enforcement of the law. Greater economy in the operation of the field force in making inspections is also thereby afforded. Although the great increase in the number of cases reported is largely due to increased activity of field officers, it is the unanimous opinion of these officers that the quantity of drugs smuggled into the United States during the past year was largely in excess of the illegal importation during the previous year.

The general attitude of the courts toward violators of the narcotic laws is reflected in the fact that 3,104 convictions were had during the year ended June 30, 1922, whereas only 1,583 convictions were obtained during the fiscal year 1921.

The collections under the narcotic laws for the fiscal year ended June 30, 1922, were $1,269,039.90, an increase of $98,748.58 over the collections for the previous year, which were $1,170,291.32.

### PERMIT DIVISION.

The functions of the permit division are as follows: The issuance of permits for use of intoxicating liquor under the national prohibition act, including the importation and exportation of the same (the division does not issue permits to transport liquor or to prescribe liquor); the passing upon all nonbeverage bonds submitted in support of nonbeverage permits under the national prohibition act to ascertain whether bonds are properly executed; the renewal of all nonbeverage permits which have been outstanding for one year; establishing standards for medicinal preparations, toilet preparations and extracts.

A new section was created in this division in January, 1922, for the purpose of checking the withdrawals, as shown on Forms 1410–A, with the amount allowed on the basic permits. Any irregularities found by such checking are immediately taken up with the proper authorities.

Special hearings in numerous revocation proceedings in Illinois, Ohio, and New York, and investigations of applicants for basic permits, were conducted by this division during the year. The number of bonds executed during the year was 60,147.

The following table shows the number and classes of permits issued during the fiscal year:

| | Renewals. | New. |
|---|---|---|
| A permits, to manufacture. | 493 | 551 |
| B permits, wholesale druggists, bonded warehouses, free warehouses, storage warehouses. | 259 | 427 |
| C permits, to transport (issued and renewed by State prohibition directors). | 1,314 | |
| Special transport. | | 35 |
| D permits, to import and use. | 2 | 4 |
| E permits, to import and sell. | 20 | 31 |
| F permits, to export. | 32 | 50 |
| G permits, to export and sell. | | |
| H permits, to use (intoxicating liquors for manufacturing purposes). | 43,092 | 21,247 |
| I permits, to use and sell. | 12,401 | 6,097 |
| J permits, to prescribe (issued and renewed by State prohibition directors). | 44,346 | |
| K permits, to manufacture vinegar and to produce intoxicating liquor for conversion into same. | 277 | 192 |
| L permits, to operate dealcoholizing plants. | 245 | 177 |
| N permits, to procure alcoholic preparations. | 63 | 37 |
| R permits, to produce mash for the purpose of producing yeast, after which residue is to be destroyed. | | 2 |

Permits revoked............................................................... 159
Renewal applications disapproved........................................... 2,061
New applications disapproved.............................................. 2,018
Permits canceled, superseded, surrendered, and recalled.................. 3,673
Active permits issued in Washington, D. C................................. 85,734
Total outstanding permits, including those issued by State prohibition
    directors............................................................. 131,394

## INDUSTRIAL ALCOHOL AND CHEMICAL DIVISION.

This division conducts the chemical work of the Bureau of Internal Revenue in Washington and in the field and administers the provisions of Title III of the national prohibition act. It also administers certain features of the general internal revenue laws relating to bonded warehouses, storekeeper-gauger assignments, and other miscellaneous items, under Regulations Nos. 7 and 30.

*Chemical section.*—During the past year the chemist stationed at Denver, Colo., was transferred to San Francisco on account of additional work at the last-named point. A laboratory has been installed in the Federal Building at Buffalo, N. Y., and steps have been taken to establish laboratories at Philadelphia, Pa., and Boston, Mass., on account of the steadily increasing field work in connection with the administration of the national prohibition act. Increased activity of the field officers of the bureau has reflected itself in the increased number of samples examined in the laboratories during the fiscal year. In the Washington laboratory 29,320 samples were analyzed, an increase of 9,639 over the number analyzed during the preceding year; in the branch laboratories 34,387 samples were analyzed during the fiscal year 1922, an increase of 14,593 over the number analyzed during 1921.

There has been a considerable increase in the attendance of chemists at court, a total of 1,946 days having been spent by members of this division in attendance at court as expert witnesses and in special field investigations where a technical assistant was needed.

The Washington laboratory has worked under a decided handicap during the last six months on account of the alterations being made on the fourth floor of the Treasury Building, but in spite of this handicap the entire chemical work is current.

*Industrial alcohol section.*—The work of this section, which administers Regulations No. 61, drawn under Title III of the national prohibition act, has changed very little in character during the year, with the exception of the work pertaining to the transfer of the 90-day tax-paid alcohol permits to the Permit Division.

At the close of the last fiscal year there were 73 industrial alcohol plants, 78 bonded warehouses, and 74 denaturing plants qualified to operate for the production, storage, and denaturation of alcohol, respectively, under Title III of the national prohibition act. During the year 9 industrial alcohol plants, 10 bonded warehouses, and 12 denaturing plants were established, while 6 industrial alcohol plants, 8 bonded warehouses, and 3 denaturing plants were discontinued, resulting in a comparatively small net increase over the number qualified on June 30, 1921. For the production of distilled spirits for nonbeverage purposes, other than alcohol, there were operated during the year 2 grain distilleries, 2 rum distilleries, and 33 fruit distilleries.

Under Title III of the national prohibition act 3,297 permits for withdrawal of tax-free alcohol were issued during the fiscal year ended June 30, 1922, compared with 3,053 such permits issued during the fiscal year ended June 30, 1921.   There were also issued 26 permits covering tax-free withdrawals of spirits, other than alcohol, by the United States under section 3464 of the Revised Statutes.

The number of bonded manufacturers using specially denatured alcohol at the end of the fiscal year 1922 was 3,287, compared with 1,761 such manufacturers at the end of the fiscal year 1921.   The increase of 1,526 was due to the qualification of many permittees heretofore using pure alcohol.   During the same period of time 67 permits to use specially denatured alcohol were revoked.

A number of changes have occurred during the year with respect to distillery bonded warehouses, general bonded warehouses, and special bonded warehouses, such as discontinuances in whole or in part due to the gradual reduction of the quantities of distilled spirits stored in warehouses of these classes.   These changes have resulted in some reduction in the number of storekeeper-gaugers assigned.

### AUDIT DIVISION.

The audit division is charged with the recording and the consideration of field officers' reports concerning violations of the national prohibition act, the Harrison Narcotic Act, and the internal revenue laws involving both civil and criminal liabilities.   In this division all civil liabilities are determined in connection with cases involving violations; assessments are made and assessment lists prepared; and all prohibition claims and compromises are handled.   In the division are examined and audited all reports and accounts which relate to distilleries; general and special bonded warehouses; industrial and denatured alcohol plants; dealers in and manufacturers using denatured alcohol; wineries, breweries, dealcoholizing plants; liquor dispensed on physicians' prescriptions; wines for sacramental purposes; liquors used in manufacturing and compounding; and liquors received by physicians, hospitals, etc.

At the beginning of the fiscal year there were 5,175 reports from field officers which had not been examined.   During the year 44,356 reports were received, 34,944 were examined showing assessable liabilities and 11,598 showing no assessable liabilities.   During the fiscal year 3,451 offers in compromise were accepted and 2,179 offers rejected.

*Claims.*—On July 1, 1921, there were 8,728 claims pending, amounting to $20,415,129.33.   During the year 21,060 claims were received, amounting to $40,802,576.63.   Of the total on hand and received during the year 22,332 were disposed of in the following manner:

|  | Claims. | Amount. |
|---|---|---|
| Refunds | 1,566 | $1,772,014.66 |
| Abatements | 6,682 | 13,258,317.85 |
| Uncollectibles | 14,084 | 25,918,948.85 |
| Total | 22,332 | 40,949,281.36 |

At the end of the fiscal year there were 7,456 claims on hand, mounting to $20,268,424.60.

*Distilled spirits.*—During the fiscal year ended June 30, 1922, there were produced 79,906,101.51 proof gallons of alcohol, a decrease of 5,162,674.82 proof gallons compared with the quantity produced during the preceding fiscal year.

There were withdrawn from warehouse on payment of tax 16,363,301.85 proof gallons of alcohol, and there were withdrawn for tax-free purposes, including withdrawals for denaturation, for export, and for use of the United States, hospitals, laboratories, colleges, and other educational institutions, a total of 63,147,767.22 proof gallons of alcohol.

There were withdrawn, tax paid, from distillery, general and special bonded warehouses 2,724,363.4 taxable gallons of distilled spirits (including brandy) other than alcohol, a decrease of 6,352,782.1 gallons compared with the quantity withdrawn tax paid during the preceding year.

The act making appropriations for the Treasury Department for the fiscal year ending June 30, 1923, contains a provision giving the Commissioner of Internal Revenue authority to concentrate into a small number of warehouses all distilled spirits at present stored in distillery, general and special bonded warehouses, and provides that distilled spirits may be bottled in bond in any internal-revenue bonded warehouse before tax payment as well as after tax payment. Regulations have been issued pursuant to this provision of law which will effect a large saving in money and render the spirits more secure from loss by theft, casualty, leakage, and evaporation, and will materially assist the department in preventing withdrawals on fraudulent permits.

Effective July 1, 1922, only one set of reports and accounts were required for distillery, general and special bonded warehouses, instead of three sets as heretofore required. This will effect a large saving in the number of forms to be handled and will cause a corresponding reduction in the number of clerks.

*Cereal beverages.*—During the fiscal year ended June 30, 1922, there were 550 dealcoholizing plants in operation, compared with 454 such plants in operation during the preceding year. There were 196,781,781 gallons of cereal beverages produced during the past year, a decrease of 89,044,049 gallons under the quantity produced during the preceding year.

*Denatured alcohol.*—During the fiscal year 1922 there were withdrawn from bond, free of tax, for denaturation 59,549,919.6 proof gallons of alcohol and rum, against 38,812,138.7 proof gallons withdrawn for this purpose during the previous year.

There were 33,345,747.91 wine gallons of denatured alcohol produced during the past fiscal year, of which 16,193,523.60 wine gallons were completely denatured and 17,152,224.31 wine gallons were specially denatured, compared with 22,388,824.92 wine gallons of denatured alcohol produced during the previous fiscal year, of which 12,392,-595.02 wine gallons were completely denatured and 9,996,229.90 wine gallons were specially denatured.

*Wines and cordials.*—Revenue from taxes on wines and cordials during the fiscal year 1922 amounted to $1,306,249.72 compared with

$2,001,779.87 in 1921, $4,017,596.82 in 1920, $10,521,609.14 in 1919, $9,124,368.56 in 1918, and $5,164,075.03 in 1917.

The total production of wine amounted to 5,827,917.90 gallons during the fiscal year ended June 30, 1922. Of this quantity of wine 2,791,971.50 gallons, having not over 14 per cent alcoholic content, were fortified with brandy, and 3,194,516.81 gallons of sweet wines were produced therefrom, of which 5,127.18 gallons had not over 14 per cent, 3,127,395.75 had over 14 but not over 21 per cent, and 61,993.88 gallons over 21 but not over 24 per cent alcoholic content. The quantity of wines removed on payment of tax for medicinal and sacramental purposes during the fiscal year amounted to 3,014,364.88 gallons, of which 1,170,164.13 gallons had not over 14 per cent and 1,844,200.75 gallons had over 14 but not over 21 per cent alcoholic content.

On June 30, 1922, there were 27,069,539.90 gallons of wine on hand at bonded wineries and storerooms, of which 19,105,926.30 gallons had not over 14 per cent, 7,941,364.60 gallons had over 14 but not over 21 per cent, and 22,249 gallons had over 21 but not over 24 per cent alcoholic content, compared with 27,604,898.76 gallons on hand June 30, 1921, of which 20,278,912.60 gallons had not over 14 per cent, 7,075,966.80 gallons had over 14 but not over 21 per cent, and 250,019.36 gallons had over 21 but not over 24 per cent alcoholic content.

## SOLICITOR OF INTERNAL REVENUE.

The work of the solicitor's office embraces the whole field of Federal taxation and may be summarized as cases in suit (criminal and civil); income and profits tax cases from the Income Tax Unit; memoranda from the Committee on Appeals and Review; estate; capital-stock and child-labor tax questions; documentary, public utilities, insurance, sales, occupational, beverage, luxury, tobacco, oleomargarine, and special taxes; the more important prohibition questions; distilled spirits and narcotics; accounts, supplies, equipment, leases, etc.; matters referred by the commissioner; and the consideration, preparation, and revision of Treasury Decisions, and of regulations, mimeographs, and other formal compilations.

### CONFERENCE COMMITTEE.

The conference committee, composed of the assistant solicitors, has continued to function with marked success. Six hundred and eighty-nine cases of considerable importance were disposed of by this committee during the fiscal year ended June 30, 1922. In addition oral hearings were granted in 64 instances, wherein taxpayers and their attorneys appeared in person before the committee to argue the merits of their respective cases.

### INTERPRETATIVE DIVISION I.

The work of Interpretative Division I may be separated into three general classes. The first embraces the preparation and revision of regulations and Treasury Decisions relating to income, excess-profits, and estate taxes; the second comprises the preparation of law opinions, solicitor's opinions, and informal memoranda, and a review of such recommendations and memoranda of the Committee on Appeals and Review as are submitted to the solicitor, and of letters prepared by the Income Tax Unit and Estate Tax Division in which information is furnished taxpayers with respect to income, excess-profits, and estate tax returns; the third relates to suggestions and technical assistance in the drafting of contemplated revenue legislation. The Weekly Bulletin of Internal Revenue Rulings is submitted to this division for review and approval.

During the past year the division assisted in revising the internal revenue laws and in the technical drafting of the revenue act of 1921. It also offered suggestions and rendered assistance in the technical drafting of the provisions of the China trade act, 1922, with reference to income taxation, and the provisions of the proposed merchant marine act, 1922, dealing with taxation.

The most extensive work undertaken during the year in connection with the regulations was the preparation of Regulations 62 under the income and excess-profits tax provisions of the revenue act of 1921 and of Regulations 63 under the estate-tax provisions of the act. Due to the many changes that were made in the income, excess-profits, and estate tax provisions of existing law by the revenue act of 1921 the preparation of regulations under the new act involved exhaustive work with reference to the interpretation of the many new sections.

Extensive researches have been made with reference to the following: The proper treatment from the standpoint both of the employee and the corporation of stock of the corporation given to employees as a bonus; the application of the decision in the case of Eisner v. Macomber to various problems arising in connection with stock dividends; the interpretation of the provisions of the revenue act requiring consolidated returns in the case of affiliated corporations, and the determination of the elements necessary to constitute affiliation; the determination of consolidated invested capital of affiliated corporations; the consideration of the taxability of the income of a revocable trust; the differentiation between trusts and associations in view of the case of Crocker v. Malley (249 U. S. 223); the realization of taxable income when stock or securities are exchanged for other stock or securities in connection with the reorganization, consolidation, or merger of a corporation; the taxability of trustees and receivers in dissolution; the effect upon invested capital of the reorganization, consolidation, or merger of a corporation before or after March 3, 1917; the revision of regulations under section 23 of the merchant marine act, 1920, and the determination of the incidence of State inheritance, succession, and legacy taxes for the purpose of ascertaining by whom such taxes are deductible under the decision of the Supreme Court in the case of United States v. Woodward (256 U. S. 632).

### INTERPRETATIVE DIVISION II.

Interpretative Division II passes on questions of an interpretative nature arising under the internal revenue laws other than the laws relating to income and estate taxes, and on administrative matters of a legal nature other than litigation, distraints, and penalties. This division also passes on all compromise cases, and reviews claims for abatement, refund, and credit and certificates of overassessment in certain cases. In the case of income taxes, only certificates of overassessment and claims involving more than.$50,000 are reviewed, unless the opinion of the solicitor has been requested upon a certificate or a claim involving a less amount, the limit upon such matters having been increased from $5,000 to $50,000 during the year. In the case of taxes other than income taxes, all claims involving amounts in excess of $500 are reviewed.

The work of the division steadily increased during the year. Despite the fact that the limit in the case of income-tax claims was raised from $5,000 to $50,000, the work of reviewing the certificates of overassessment and claims became greater. A smaller number of claims was received under the new procedure, but those that were received involved such large amounts and were of such complexity that a greater amount of time was required for their review than was required for the review of those cases which were received prior to the establishment of the new claims procedure.

During the year the division assisted in the preparation and revision of Regulations Nos. 8, 40, 43, 47, 48, 52, 55, 57, 59, and 64.

### CIVIL DIVISION.

The Civil Division, in cooperation with the Department of Justice and United States attorneys' offices, handles all civil internal-revenue cases pending in the various Federal courts. The cases include the prosecution of suits by the United States to recover unpaid taxes, where the period for assessment has expired, and the defense of suits brought by taxpayers against collectors of internal revenue or the United States to recover taxes paid under protest and duress. While the United States attorneys are charged with the responsibility for these cases, the attorneys of the Civil Division prepare the cases for trial both as to the facts and the law. They assemble the necessary evidence and forward it to the United States attorneys, procure the attendance of witnesses, prepare and forward to the United States attorney a brief upon the law of the case, and an attorney of the division is present at the actual trial to render any necessary assistance. In many instances the trial of the case is, at the suggestion of the United States attorney, handled by the attorney of the solicitor's office. In addition to these cases the Civil Division handles all claims for unpaid taxes where the taxpayer is in bankruptcy or receivership proceedings have been instituted.

On July 1, 1921, there were pending in the Federal courts 915 civil internal-revenue cases (including bankruptcy and receiverships). During the fiscal year over 2,000 new cases were received and 841 pending cases were closed. Therefore, during the fiscal year the work of the division more than doubled, and on June 30, 1922, there was a total of 2,400 pending cases, as follows: Civil cases, 1,014; bankruptcy, 1,249; receiverships, 137.

The civil cases, numbering 1,014, were divided as follows: Suits to be instituted by the United States for the recovery of unpaid taxes, the period for assessment having expired, 67; cases pending in the district courts, 531; cases pending in the circuit courts of appeal, 35; cases pending in the Court of Claims, 215; cases pending in the Supreme Court, 7; cases pending in court in which a settlement may be effected, 99; cases in which judgment has been entered, pending filing of judgment claim for refund, 29; cases in which judgment has been entered, judgment claim forwarded to the claims section for allowance and payment, 27; miscellaneous cases, 4.

During the year civil internal-revenue cases decided by the courts were as follows: Court of Claims, 1; district courts, 61; circuit courts of appeal, 27; Supreme Court, 16; total 105. Of these the following were decided for the Government: District courts, 41; circuit courts of appeal, 15; Supreme Court, 9; total 65; and the following were lost: District courts, 20; circuit courts of appeal, 12; Court of Claims, 1; Supreme Court, 7; total 40.

The important centers of litigation in the order of number of cases pending and amounts involved are New York, Philadelphia, Boston, Chicago, Pittsburgh, San Francisco, Cleveland, and Baltimore. The States with the larger number of bankruptcy and receivership proceedings are, in the order named, New York, Illinois, Pennsylvania, Massachusetts, Texas, New Jersey, Michigan, Alabama, Tennessee, Missouri, Wisconsin, Virginia, Indiana, and Oregon.

Among the important decisions of the Supreme Court of the United States were those holding that the distribution made by the Ohio Oil Co. and the Prairie Oil & Gas Co. in the year 1915 was taxable as income to the stockholders; that the reorganization and distribution during the year 1915 made by the E. I. du Pont de Nemours Powder Co. in stock of the E. I. du Pont de Nemours & Co. was taxable as income to the stockholders; that under the estate-tax provisions of the revenue act of 1916 bonds issued by a political subdivision of a State may be included in the gross estate of a decedent without violating the Federal Constitution; that the special tax on bankers imposed by the act of June 13, 1898, includes the capital, surplus, and undivided profits used in the banking business, and where a trust company is engaged in several businesses the burden of proof is upon it to show a segregation and separation of assets not used in the banking business in order to avoid taxation upon its entire assets; that a suit against a collector to recover taxes alleged to have been erroneously assessed and collected must be brought against the collector to whom the tax was paid and not his successor in office at the time suit was brought; that the estate tax, Title II of the revenue act of 1916, is prospective and not retroactive in operation, and a transfer in contemplation of death made prior to the passage of the act can not be included in the gross estate of a decedent nor can a trust created prior to the passage of the act be included as a gift to take effect in possession or enjoyment at or after the death of the creator; that a trust estate is not taxable as an entity, and income held and accumulated by a trustee for the benefit of unborn or unascertained beneficiaries is not subject to the income tax imposed by the act of 1913, although such income is expressly subject to tax under later income-tax acts; that the child-labor tax imposed by the revenue act of 1918 is unconstitutional; that injunction will lie against the enforcement of the collection of the trading in future tax, which was also declared unconstitutional; that the acquisition of a right to subscribe for stock is not income, but the sale of a right to subscribe to additional stock at an advance over and above the cost is taxable income, as in the case of the sales of a capital asset at a gain.

Among the important decisions of the circuit courts of appeal are the following: That the munitions manufacturers' tax is imposed upon the business of manufacturing and is measured by the profits received from the "sale or disposition" of munitions or parts of munitions, and covers the profits received from work and labor performed under a subletting contract upon uncompleted "parts" of shells, which parts were subsequently completed and assembled; that injunction will not lie against a collector to restrain the collection of an estate tax within the 180-day period after the due date where the commissioner has not extended the time for payment as provided in section 406 of the revenue act of 1918; that certain business organizations commonly known as "Massachusetts trusts" are subject to capital-stock tax as "associations" under the provisions of the revenue acts of 1916 and 1918; that a mutual insurance association is taxable as an insurance company and not entitled to exemption under paragraph (d) of section 504 of the revenue act of 1917, since the plaintiff was not a fraternal beneficiary society, was not organized or operated exclusively for religious, charitable, scientific, or educational purposes, and was not a "like organization of a purely local character, the income of which consists solely of assessments, dues, and fees collected from members for the sole purpose of meeting expenses"; that "sweet chocolate" is taxable as "candy" under the provisions of Title IX, section 900, of the revenue act of 1918; that the State soldiers' bonus tax imposed by the Laws of Wisconsin, 1919, "accrued" and was deductible for Federal income-tax purposes in the year 1919 and did not "accrue" in the year 1918, although 1918 income was the basis for computing the amount of the tax payable; that expenses incurred in the care, feeding, breeding, and marketing of blooded horses, and transportation charges to various racing centers were deductible business expenses under the provisions of the income tax act of 1913; that a lawyer who acted in one instance as an executor is not subject to the excess-profits tax imposed by the revenue act of 1917 upon commissions received as such executor, since a single isolated activity of the character of an executorship does not constitute a trade, business, profession, or vocation within the meaning of the act; that a dividend declared prior to March 1, 1913, but paid thereafter is not taxable income of the stockholder under the provisions of the income tax of 1913.

Among the important cases decided by the district courts are the following: The proper rule for determining the profit on the sale of stock which includes in part stock received as a stock dividend; that under Title XII, section 1205, subdivision (c), of the revenue act of 1917, taxes on bonds of a corporation containing covenants agreeing to pay to bondholders interest at a prescribed rate without deduction of taxes constitute income to the individual to the extent of the taxes paid by the corporation; that a tobacco warehouseman, to whose place of business tobacco planters bring their product to be sold at auction and tobacco buyers attend to bid for tobacco, is a broker within the meaning of section 1001 of the revenue act of 1918; that a New York corporation doing business in and deriving its income from Porto Rico is subject to the income and excess-profits taxes imposed by the revenue acts of 1917 and 1918; that a finding of fact by a former Commissioner of Internal Revenue in assessing income tax is final but not conclusive where a different question is involved; that section 250 (d) of the revenue act of 1918, providing that no suit or proceeding for the collection of any income tax shall be begun after the expiration of five years from the date when the return was due or was made, has no application in an action to recover back a tax paid under protest; that a building and loan association organized under the laws of Ohio is not exempt from taxation under the provisions of section 231 (4) of the revenue act of 1918 where it makes loans to nonmembers, borrows from nonmembers, receives deposits to be withdrawn on demand or in time, and lacks the essential characteristic of "mutuality," since under these conditions it is not a true building and loan association but performs the functions of an ordinary savings bank; that the principle of construing taxing acts in favor of the taxpayer and against the Government does not apply where exemption from taxation is claimed, and a health and accident insurance company doing business throughout a State is not a "like organization of a purely local character" within the meaning of paragraph 10 of section 11 of the revenue act of 1916 and paragraph 10 of section 231 of the revenue act of 1918; that under the excess-profits tax a corporation which traded substantially on its own account and required capital in the conduct of its business is not entitled to assessment under the provisions of section 209 of the revenue act of 1917 which applied to businesses having "no invested capital or not more than a nominal capital," although the corporation did a large business by buying and selling on commission; that a corporation organized to purchase land, construct a hotel, and to operate, manage, lease, mortgage, or sell the same, which bought land, built a hotel, and leased it to an operating corporation, received rents, added five stories to the hotel, negotiated loans to pay for the improvement, was carrying on or doing business within the meaning of section 38 of the corporation excise tax of 1909; that the Federal estate tax is constitutional and where a widow elects to accept a provision made in lieu of dower property passing under such provision should be included in the gross estate of the decedent; that under the Federal estate tax act the New York transfer tax can not be taken as a deduction from the gross estate in determining the net estate subject to tax; that a voluntary payment of internal-revenue taxes without protest precludes a suit for recovery, section 252 of the revenue act of 1918 not changing or modifying the established principle; that the capital-stock tax is not a property tax but an excise tax imposed upon the privilege of doing business in corporate form as a going concern, and the value of this privilege includes franchises, good will, existing contracts, and established business as well as the value of all tangible property, less debts, thus in estimating the value of "capital stock" elements of intangible value should be considered; that a decedent, who is liable for an income tax to the date of death, and his estate, which pays an income tax upon income received by the estate and also an estate tax, are two separate entities and different taxpayers, although all three taxes are paid by the executor out of the estate, therefore the estate tax paid could not be deducted from the gross income of the decedent for the period prior to death; that a belt which carries the ammunition used in connection with a machine gun is taxable as a "part" or "appendage" under the munitions manufacturers' tax imposed by Title III of the revenue act of 1916; that where a dealer purchases a truck chassis, paying the excise tax of 3 per cent thereon, and secures the manufacture of a body by another concern, paying a tax of 5 per cent thereon as a "part" of an automobile, the two component parts being assembled and sold by the dealer as a whole, he is not a "dealer" but a "producer or manufacturer" within the meaning of section 900 of the revenue act of 1918, and must pay an excise tax upon the sales price of the completed automobile, but may take a credit for the tax paid on the chassis and the body before the two were assembled; that under section 3466 of the Revised Statutes, the claim of the United States against an insolvent corporation for unpaid taxes takes priority over claims for taxes due a State, county, or municipality.

### PENAL DIVISION.

To the Penal Division falls the responsibility of recommending the assessment of fraud penalties and criminal prosecutions under the tax laws. In addition this division has been called upon to review and make recommendations in pardon and parole cases arising from liquor, narcotic, and internal-revenue statutes generally.

During the past fiscal year, after review by this office, there were many prosecutions of individuals and corporations charged with the violation of tax laws, and this division assisted United States attorneys in many convictions of offenders under these statutes.

It is the practice to have special attorneys who are assigned to the Penal Division go into the field and investigate important cases pending in the solicitor's office, and when prosecution is contemplated these attorneys act as special advisers to the proper officials charged with the duty of representing the Government in court. Thus, frequent convictions have been secured against persons who have fraudulently attempted to evade their tax liabilities. Special attorneys were stationed in New York and Chicago during the year.

A large amount of work in the office grows out of the preparation of opinions requested by the Commissioner of Internal Revenue as to whether or not penalties should be asserted against persons and corporations who have intentionally failed regularly to account to the Government for the proper tax due, and to pay the tax, when the amount has been determined, within the time prescribed by law.

There were pending July 1, 1922, 383 cases involving alleged fraud in connection with the internal revenue laws. Of this number criminal proceedings have been instituted in 255. Two hundred and seventy-three cases of this nature were disposed of during the year, in 126 of which criminal action had been brought. In addition to the cases referred to, numerous requests for opinions as to the interpretation of penal sections of the law have been received and answered, and advice has been given covering the collection of the tax by distraint and otherwise.

Two attorneys of this division represent the commissioner on the department committee on enrollment and disbarment. Approximately 4,300 applications were filed with the committee during the fiscal year, of which number 2,850 were assigned to the commissioner's representatives for examination and recommendation.

Field investigations were made of the eligibility of these applicants, upon which the recommendations to the Secretary were based.

As a result of these investigations more than 100 special cases arose involving reports on the eligibility of the applicants adverse to their enrollment. Of this number approximately 81 applications were disapproved by the Secretary and 1 suspension resulted. Two disbarments were had during the year.

Early in 1922 a subcommittee composed of three was appointed by the chairman to draft and submit a revision of Department Circular 230, which contains the laws and regulations governing the practice of agents and attorneys before the department. The principal additions to the practice regulations are those prohibiting a corporation or its officers or employees from representing claimants before the Treasury Department; those, prohibiting advertising for and the solicitation of claims or other business before the department, and several provisions fixing a generally higher standard of ethics in the practice of agents and attorneys than was theretofore required. A provision was finally inserted by the Secretary's office asserting that the department looks with disfavor upon contingent fees, and regulating this practice for the protection of taxpayers and other claimants.

Under the act of Congress to parole United States prisoners, and for other purposes, approved June 25, 1910, such prisoners become eligible for release on parole when they shall have served one-third of the terms of imprisonment to which they were sentenced by the court. One hundred and fourteen parole cases arising under the internal revenue and national prohibition laws were pending July 1, 1921, and 1,407 cases were received during the fiscal year. The cases disposed of during the year numbered 1,223, leaving 298 cases pending July 1, 1922. In 33 cases this office recommended that the prisoners be given the benefit of parole; in 1,088 cases the recommendations were adverse; in 102 cases no recommendations were submitted by this bureau for the reason that the cases in question were not made by its field officers.

On July 1, 1921, 15 pardon cases arising under the internal revenue and prohibition laws were pending, and 158 such cases were received during the fiscal year. One hundred and seventy-three cases were disposed of during the year and there were no cases pending July 1, 1922. In 42 cases the bureau expressed favorable opinion upon the extension of Executive clemency to the applicants; in 111 such cases the recommendation was adverse, and in 20 such cases no expression of opinion was submitted to the attorney in charge of pardons for the reason that investigations disclosed that such cases did not originate and were not adopted by officers of the bureau in the field service.

Claims for reward for information relative to violations of the internal revenue laws, submitted under the provisions of Circular 99, revised, were presented and disposed of during the year, as follows: Pending July 1, 1921, 10; presented during the year, 7; disposed of during the year, 7; pending July 1, 1922, 10. A majority of the pending claims are indefinite and incomplete and final action thereon is awaiting receipt of further evidence.

Two claims were allowed during the fiscal year wherein the informants received the sums of $12,000 and $18,000, respectively, and the Government recovered, largely as the result of the information given by said informants, the sum of $1,600,000.

### ADMINISTRATIVE DIVISION.

The Administrative Division is charged with the supervision of the library, the mails and files, the supplies and equipment, personnel, and editorial matters arising in and affecting the work of the office. The support and cooperation rendered by this division have proved of benefit to attorneys assigned to the other divisions and have afforded them great assistance in the dispatch of matters handled by them.

A compilation of decisions of the courts in internal-revenue cases during the fiscal year ended June 30, 1922, is printed on pages 911 to 938 of this report.

*Summary of work in the office of the Solicitor of Internal Revenue, year ended June 30, 1922.*

|  | First quarter. | Second quarter. | Third quarter. | Fourth quarter. | Total. |
|---|---|---|---|---|---|
| Letters prepared | 1,731 | 2,574 | 2,701 | 3,288 | 10,294 |
| Letters approved | 1,706 | 1,419 | 1,090 | 920 | 5,135 |
| Opinions prepared | 15 | 21 | 21 | 14 | 71 |
| Opinions approved (A. R. R. and A. R. M.) | 19 | 45 | 54 | 90 | 208 |
| Treasury decisions prepared | 23 | 15 | 38 | 39 | 115 |
| Treasury decisions approved | 9 | 11 | 8 | 11 | 39 |
| Memorandums prepared | 959 | 1,215 | 2,532 | 2,528 | 7,234 |
| Telegrams (prepared and approved) | 69 | 141 | 145 | 149 | 504 |
| Mimeographs | 6 | 4 | 2 | 4 | 16 |
| Miscellaneous (forms, regulations, etc.) | | 3 | 21 | 26 | 50 |
| Total | 4,537 | 5,448 | 6,612 | 7,069 | 23,666 |

*Claims for abatement and refund.[1]*

| Kind of tax involved. | On hand July 1, 1921. | Received during year. | Disposed of during year. | On hand June 30, 1922. |
|---|---|---|---|---|
| Income and excess profits | 56 | 4,315 | 4,097 | 274 |
| Legacy | | 99 | 99 | |
| Prohibition | 153 | 17,608 | 17,559 | 202 |
| Capital stock | 4 | 912 | 911 | 5 |
| Estate | 8 | 1,021 | 1,020 | 9 |
| Beverage | 1 | 242 | 240 | 3 |
| Admissions and dues | 9 | 357 | 361 | 5 |
| Excise | 12 | 1,096 | 1,083 | 25 |
| Transportation | 2 | 474 | 474 | 2 |
| Stamp | 4 | 342 | 343 | 3 |
| Tobacco | 1 | 78 | 79 | |
| Special | | 15 | 15 | |
| Insurance | 3 | 259 | 255 | 7 |
| Child labor | | 32 | 32 | |
| Miscellaneous | | 71 | 71 | |
| Total | 253 | 26,921 | 26,639 | 545 |

[1] Prior to Aug. 29, 1921, all claims involving $500 and more were sent to this office for review. On that date the standard on income-tax claims was raised to $5,000, and again on Jan. 17, 1922, it was raised to $50,000.

*Compromises.*

IN SUIT.

On hand July 1, 1921:
Not acted upon................................................... 31
Rejected....................................................... 14
Received during year........................................... 104

    Total to be accounted for....................................... 149

Accepted:
Corporation income tax......................................... 51
Individual income tax.......................................... 11
Miscellaneous income tax....................................... 13

    Total accepted.................................................. 75
Otherwise disposed of.............................................. 12
                                                   87

On hand June 30, 1922, under consideration:
Income tax..................................................... 40
Sales tax...................................................... 10
Capital-stock tax.............................................. 8
Estate tax..................................................... 4
                                                   62

    Total accounted for............................................. 149

Amounts accepted:
Corporation income tax......................................... \$1, 970, 956. 76
Individual income tax.......................................... 111, 513. 01
Miscellaneous.................................................. 32, 816. 00

    Total........................................................ 2, 115, 285. 77

NOT IN SUIT.

| Kind of compromise. | On hand July 1, 1921. | Received during year. | Total to be accounted for. | Accepted. | Rejected. | Total handled. | On hand June 30, 1922. | Total of amounts accepted. |
|---|---|---|---|---|---|---|---|---|
| Income tax................ | 16,718 | 172,707 | 189,425 | 168,863 | 1,458 | 170,321 | 19,104 | \$1,262,800.59 |
| Estate tax................ | 120 | 2,455 | 2,575 | 2,133 | 1 | 2,134 | 441 | 26,121.00 |
| Capital stock tax.......... | 1,803 | 13,034 | 14,837 | 5,374 | 730 | 6,104 | 8,733 | 53,541.50 |
| Sales tax.................. | 2,299 | 29,433 | 31,732 | 14,872 | 751 | 15,623 | 16,109 | 471,757.86 |
| Prohibition and narcotic... | 5,493 | 9,035 | 14,528. | 5,580 | 2,292 | 7,872 | 6,656 | 1,676,197.99 |
|     Total.............. | 26,433 | 226,664 | 253,097 | 196,822 | 5,232 | 202,054 | 51,043 | 3,490,418.94 |

## SUITS AND PROSECUTIONS.

The following is a statement of internal-revenue and prohibition cases handled by the district courts of the United States during the fiscal year ended June 30, 1922, as furnished this office by the Department of Justice:

| | Internal revenue suits. | | Prohibition suits. | |
|---|---|---|---|---|
| | Civil. | Criminal. | Civil. | Criminal. |
| Cases pending July 1, 1921........................... | 1,238 | 4,841 | 2,074 | 10,472 |
| Cases commenced during fiscal year ended June 30, 1922........ | 1,232 | 275 | 2,157 | 34,984 |
| Cases terminated during same period........................ | 709 | 1,866 | 1,537 | 28,743 |
| Cases pending at close of business on June 30, 1922.............. | 1,761 | 3,250 | 2,694 | 16,713 |

## BUREAU AND FIELD PERSONNEL.

The following statement shows the number of employees in the Internal Revenue Service on June 30, 1921, and the number in the service on June 30, 1922. A net increase in personnel of 1,795 is shown.

| | June 30, 1921. | June 30, 1922. | Increase (+) or decrease. (−). | | June 30, 1921. | June 30, 1922. | Increase (+) or decrease (−). |
|---|---|---|---|---|---|---|---|
| Employees in Washington | 7,052 | 7,275 | +223 | Assistant supervisors of collectors | 48 | 51 | +3 |
| Collectors' offices | 6,783 | 7,110 | +327 | Special agents (Special Intelligence Unit) | 36 | 52 | +16 |
| Internal revenue agents' force | 2,737 | 3,251 | +514 | Storekeeper-gaugers | 769 | 575 | −194 |
| Prohibition field service (including narcotic officers) | 2,168 | 3,074 | +906 | Total | 19,593 | 21,388 | +1,795 |

A total of 1,078 resignations was accepted from employees in the bureau at Washington during the past year, a decrease of 608 in comparison with the number reported during the previous fiscal year.

Under the provisions of the retirement act, 12 classified employees were retained in the service after reaching the age of 70; 24 were retired, 2 of the latter being retired on account of total disability.

Respectfully,

D. H. BLAIR,
*Commissioner of Internal Revenue.*

HON. A. W. MELLON,
*Secretary of the Treasury.*

NOTE.—For statistical details of the Report of the Commissioner of Internal Revenue, see annual report.

## FROM TABLES ACCOMPANYING THE REPORT OF THE COMMISSIONER OF INTERNAL REVENUE.

SUMMARY OF INTERNAL-REVENUE RECEIPTS, YEARS ENDED JUNE 30, 1921 AND 1922, BY SOURCES.

| Source. | 1921 | 1922 | Increase (+) or decrease (−). |
|---|---|---|---|
| Income and profits: | | | |
| Individuals, partnerships, and corporations. | [1] $3,228,137,673.75 | [2] $2,086,918,464 85 | −$1,141,219,208.90 |
| Estates: | | | |
| Transfer of estates of decedents............ | 154,043,260.39 | 139,418,846.04 | −14,624,414.35 |
| Distilled spirits: | | | |
| Distilled spirits (nonbeverage)............. | 78,097,756.93 | 42,259,351.63 | −35,838,405.30 |
| Distilled spirits (beverage)................ | 373,736.33 | 113,103.61 | −260,632.72 |
| Rectified spirits or wine.................. | 28,587.14 | 19,192.52 | −9,394.62 |
| Still or sparkling wines, cordials, etc....... | 2,001,779.87 | 1,306,249.72 | −695,530.15 |
| Grape brandy used in fortifying sweet wines | 578,628.32 | 1,115,646.83 | +537,018.51 |
| Rectifiers, retail and wholesale dealers, manufacturers of stills, etc. (special taxes).... | 687,519.30 | 543,248.66 | −144,270.64 |
| Stamps for distilled spirits intended for export................................. | 7,566.89 | 2,049.45 | −5,517.44 |
| Case stamps for distilled spirits bottled in bond.................................. | 209,368.25 | 68,856.00 | −140,512.25 |
| Miscellaneous collections relating to distilled spirits......................... | 613,121.98 | 135,652.05 | −477,469.93 |
| Total.................. | 82,598,065.01 | 45,563,350.47 | −37,034,714.54 |
| Fermented liquors: | | | |
| Fermented liquors (barrel tax)........... | 17,133.65 | 35,239.63 | +18,105.98 |
| Brewers; retail and wholesale dealers in malt liquors (special taxes).............. | 8,230.17 | 10,846.37 | +2,616.20 |
| Total.................. | 25,363.82 | 46,086.00 | +20,722.18 |
| Tobacco: | | | |
| Cigars (large)...:.......................... | 51,076,563.24 | 44,183,575.34 | −6,892,987.90 |
| Cigars (small)............................. | 1,013,510.07 | 968,526.71 | −44,983.36 |
| Cigarettes (large)......................... | 356,258.38 | 118,478.19 | −237,780.19 |
| Cigarettes (small)........................ | 135,053,369.43 | 150,127,514.62 | +15,074,145.19 |
| Snuff of all descriptions................... | 5,795,401.75 | 6,947,630.94 | +1,152,229.19 |
| Tobacco, chewing and smoking............ | 59,330,627.08 | 66,341,838.88 | +7,011,211.80 |
| Cigarette papers and tubes............... | 1,184,186.21 | 1,001,509.93 | −182,676.28 |
| Manufacturers of cigars, cigarettes, and tobacco (special taxes)..................... | 1,229,286.37 | 988,274.81 | −241,011.56 |
| Miscellaneous collections relating to tobacco | 180,182.96 | 82,035.02 | −98,147.94 |
| Total.................. | 255,219,385.49 | 270,759,384.44 | +15,539,998.95 |
| Revenue acts 1918 and 1921: | | | |
| Stamps, documentary, etc.— | | | |
| Sales by postmasters................ | 20,880,868.86 | 14,616,958.05 | −6,263,910.81 |
| Bonds, capital-stock issues, conveyances, etc...................... | 32,670,622.32 | 26,730,794.37 | −5,939,827.95 |
| Capital-stock transfers............. | 8,790,905.49 | 9,012,702.29 | +221,796.80 |
| Sales of produce (future deliveries).... | 7,521,675.44 | 5,558,589.09 | −1,963,086.35 |
| Playing cards...................... | 2,603,941.42 | 2,880,441.65 | +276,500.23 |
| Transportation of freight.............. | 140,019,200.14 | 85,292,665.34 | −54,726,534.80 |
| Transportation of express.............. | 17,093,935.58 | 12,475,870.18 | −4,618,065.40 |
| Transportation of persons.............. | 97,481,976.35 | 58,042,230.71 | −39,439,745.64 |
| Seats, berths, and staterooms.......... | 8,485,015.59 | 5,991,623.63 | −2,493,391.96 |
| Oil by pipe lines...................... | 9,989,873.62 | 7,623,816.51 | −2,366,057.11 |
| Telegraph, telephone, and radio messages.. | 27,360,361.00 | 28,086,886.47 | +726,525.47 |
| Leased wires or talking circuits......... | 1,082,051.46 | 1,184,635.32 | +102,583.86 |
| Insurance (life, marine, inland, and casualty) | 18,992,094.45 | 10,855,403.81 | −8,136,690.64 |
| Manufacturers' excise tax— | | | |
| Automobile trucks and automobile wagons......................... | 11,640,055.92 | 8,404,557.85 | −3,235,498.07 |
| Other automobiles and motor cycles.... | 64,388,184.22 | 56,684,540.30 | −7,703,643.92 |
| Tires, parts, or accessories for automobiles, etc....................... | 39,518,009.17 | 39,344,664.60 | −173,344.57 |
| Pianos, organs, etc................. | 11,568,034.90 | 4,951,752.13 | −6,616,282.77 |
| Tennis rackets and sporting goods, etc.. | 4,283,902.31 | 2,215,607.05 | −2,068,295.26 |
| Chewing gum....................... | 1,332,267.44 | 742,870.69 | −589,396.75 |
| Cameras............................ | 849,940.06 | 681,546.34 | −168,393.72 |
| Photographic films, etc.............. | 1,045,430.01 | 743,670.05 | −301,759.96 |
| Candy............................. | 20,436,700.35 | 13,593,754.39 | −6,842,945.96 |
| Firearms, shells, etc................ | 3,702,642.93 | 3,374,921.49 | −327,721.44 |
| Hunting and bowie knives............ | 33,971.36 | 21,748.02 | −12,223.34 |
| Dirk knives, daggers, etc............ | 2,328.22 | 6,526.70 | +4,198.48 |
| Portable electric fans................ | 297,583.14 | 125,015.38 | −172,567.76 |
| Thermos bottles.................... | 175,862.18 | 88,891.90 | −86,970.28 |
| Cigar holders, pipes, etc............. | 151,702.35 | 165,453.74 | +13,751.39 |
| Automatic slot device machines........ | 100,504.85 | 88,888.22 | −11,616.63 |
| Liveries, livery boots, etc............ | 150,732.25 | 112,380.67 | −38,351.58 |

[1] Includes $31,835.22 income tax on Alaska railroads (act of July 18, 1914).
[2] Includes $14,395.31 income tax on Alaska railroads (act of July 18, 1914).

SUMMARY OF INTERNAL-REVENUE RECEIPTS, YEARS ENDED JUNE 30,1921 AND 1922, BY SOURCES—Continued.

| Source. | 1921 | 1922 | Increase (+) or decrease (−). |
|---|---|---|---|
| Revenue acts 1918 and 1921—Continued. | | | |
| Manufacturers' excise tax—Continued. | | | |
| Hunting garments, etc.............. | $182,816.32 | $230,535.40 | +$47,719.08 |
| Articles made of fur................. | 9,081,238.55 | 6,523,971.03 | −2,557,267.52 |
| Yachts, motor boats, etc............ | 553,201.63 | 406,867.90 | −146,333.73 |
| Toilet soap and toilet soap powders.... | 2,223,773.99 | 1,324,600.55 | −899,173.44 |
| Motion-picture films leased........... | 6,008,108.18 | 3,678,868.17 | −2,329,240.01 |
| Child-labor tax.................... | 24,223.67 | 15,224.99 | −8,998.68 |
| Consumers' or dealers' excise tax— | | | |
| Sculpture, paintings, statuary, etc..... | 1,116,337.02 | 582,800.03 | −533,536.99 |
| Carpets and rugs, picture frames, trunks, wearing apparel, etc......... | 20,374,604.39 | 1 8,413,452.76 | −11,961,151.63 |
| Jewelry, watches, clocks, opera glasses, etc...... | 24,303,936.91 | 19,514,465.01 | −4,789,471.90 |
| Perfumes, cosmetics, and medicinal articles........ | 5,800,768.41 | 2,305,482.25 | −3,495,286.16 |
| Beverages (nonalcoholic), including soft drinks, mineral waters, etc...... | 58,675,972.86 | 2 33,504,284.01 | −25,171,688.85 |
| Opium, coca leaves, including special taxes, etc......................... | 1,170,291.32 | 1,269,039.90 | +98,748.58 |
| Corporations, on value of capital stock..... | 81,525,652.88 | 80,612,239.80 | −913,413.08 |
| Brokers, stock, etc................... | 1,966,312.35 | 1,934,179.88 | −32,132.47 |
| Theaters, museums, circuses, etc....... | 1,703,380.26 | 1,863,252.26 | +159,872.00 |
| Bowling alleys, billiard and pool tables.... | 2,368,007.65 | 2,499,831.81 | +131,824.16 |
| Shooting galleries........................ | 23,313.63 | 21,366.81 | −1,946.82 |
| Riding academies........................ | 16,939.88 | 12,667.80 | −4,272.08 |
| Passenger automobiles for hire........ | 1,776,493.88 | 1,785,619.89 | +9,126.01 |
| Yachts, pleasure boats, power boats, etc... | 731,092.46 | 545,841.44 | −185,251.02 |
| Admissions to theaters, concerts, cabarets, etc... | 89,730,832.94 | 73,384,955.61 | −16,345,877.33 |
| Dues of clubs (athletic, social, and sporting) | 6,159,817.69 | 6,615,633.92 | +455,816.23 |
| Total................... | 868,167,490.25 | 646,744,588.16 | −221,422,902.09 |
| Miscellaneous: | | | |
| Adulterated and process or renovated butter, and mixed flour.................. | 50,977.37 | 33,455.56 | −17,521.81 |
| Oleomargarine, colored................. | 921,192.25 | 494,005.50 | −427,186.75 |
| Oleomargarine, uncolored............. | 655,427.08 | 452,774.47 | −202,652.61 |
| Oleomargarine, manufacturers and dealers (special taxes)................. | 1,409,846.02 | 1,174,299.71 | −235,546.31 |
| Opium manufactured for smoking purposes. | 25.00 | 50.00 | +25.00 |
| Collections under provisions of the national prohibition act...................... | 2,152,387.45 | 1,979,586.94 | −172,800.51 |
| Internal revenue collected through customs offices...................... | 356,296.21 | 495,559.43 | +139,263.22 |
| Other receipts, including unidentified collections.................... | 1,619,671.86 | 3 3,370,631.43 | +1,750,959.57 |
| Total................... | 7,165,823.24 | 8,000,363.04 | +834,539.80 |
| Grand total.................... | 4,593,357,061.95 | 3,197,451,083.00 | −1,397,905,978.95 |

1 Includes $381,998.53 from manufacturers' excise tax collected after Jan. 1, 1922, under sec. 904, revenue act of 1921.
2 Includes $16,523,761 52 collected under sec. 628, $14,051,050.66 under sec. 630, revenue act of 1918, and $2,929,471.83 under sec. 602, revenue act of 1921.
3 The unidentified collections are now in process of classification in collectors' offices.

SUMMARY OF INTERNAL-REVENUE RECEIPTS, YEARS ENDED JUNE 30, 1921 AND 1922, BY COLLECTION DISTRICTS—Continued.

| District. | Location of collector's office. | 1921 | 1922 1 | Per cent of decrease. |
|---|---|---|---|---|
| Alabama...................... | Birmingham, Ala...... | $18,429,531.41 | $11,464,180.76 | 38 |
| Arizona...................... | Phoenix, Ariz........... | 4,202,663.42 | 2,141,234.92 | 49 |
| Arkansas.................... | Little Rock, Ark....... | 10,564,467.99 | 6,979,045.06 | 34 |
| 1st California................ | San Francisco, Calif..... | 125,376,149.19 | 81,686,526.04 | 35 |
| 6th California................ | Los Angeles, Calif..... | 56,873,190.15 | 49,966,329.85 | 12 |
| Colorado..................... | Denver, Colo.......... | 34,214,963.26 | 19,956,650.68 | 42 |
| Connecticut.................. | Hartford, Conn......... | 71,603,071.55 | 50,224,645.95 | 30 |
| Delaware..................... | Wilmington, Del........ | 11,848,203.14 | 5,889,266.17 | 50 |

1 The collections for 1922 from sale of stamps affixed to products from Porto Rico are included as follows: 1st New York, $18,220.40; 2d New York, $32.33. In addition to these amounts there was also collected $866,949.87, which was deposited at San Juan, P. R., to the credit of the treasurer of Porto Rico, and is not included in above statement. The collections for 1922 on account of products from the Virgin Islands are included as follows: 1st Illinois, $204.49; and 2d New York, $1,743.90. There are also included in the collections for the 2d New York the following internal revenue stamp sales by postmasters, namely, $2.71 on account of Porto Rico and $3.51 on account of the Virgin Islands.

SUMMARY OF INTERNAL-REVENUE RECEIPTS, YEARS ENDED JUNE 30, 1921 AND 1922, BY COLLECTION DISTRICTS—Continued.

| District. | Location of collector's office. | 1921 | 1922 | Per cent of decrease. |
|---|---|---|---|---|
| Florida | Jacksonville, Fla | $16,476,054.09 | $14,319,857.28 | 13 |
| Georgia | Atlanta, Ga | 37,231,770.85 | 20,988,703.60 | 44 |
| Hawaii | Honolulu, Hawaii | 20,680,103.23 | 15,515,063.03 | 25 |
| Idaho | Boise, Idaho | 4,617,761.92 | 2,111,891.01 | 54 |
| 1st Illinois | Chicago, Ill | 353,079,926.71 | 245,880,134.57 | 30 |
| 8th Illinois | Springfield, Ill | 35,845,028.04 | 24,452,433.16 | 32 |
| Indiana | Indianapolis, Ind | 78,158,446.40 | 53,032,399.55 | 32 |
| Iowa | Dubuque, Iowa | 37,745,745.99 | 23,658,789.19 | 37 |
| Kansas | Wichita, Kans | 38,689,551.68 | 30,379,621.69 | 21 |
| Kentucky | Louisville, Ky | 50,696,269.84 | 33,122,196.21 | 35 |
| Louisiana | New Orleans, La | 40,121,096.58 | 22,753,957.90 | 43 |
| Maine | Augusta, Me | 18,038,864.09 | 14,804,208.07 | 18 |
| Maryland | Baltimore, Md | 91,206,513.83 | 63,826,622.72 | 30 |
| Massachusetts | Boston, Mass | 259,865,213.85 | 169,813,493.51 | 35 |
| 1st Michigan | Detroit, Mich | 245,198,048.80 | 182,102,205.01 | 26 |
| 4th Michigan | Grand Rapids, Mich | 27,196,235.91 | 19,771,979.49 | 27 |
| Minnesota | St. Paul, Minn | 77,722,157.80 | 46,253,942.88 | 40 |
| Mississippi | Jackson, Miss | 8,998,571.95 | 4,640,497.50 | 49 |
| 1st Missouri | St. Louis, Mo | 90,658,133.35 | 63,816,622.41 | 30 |
| 6th Missouri | Kansas City, Mo | 35,475,533.25 | 23,639,865.69 | 33 |
| Montana | Helena, Mont | 5,446,565.52 | 3,432,162.06 | 37 |
| Nebraska | Omaha, Nebr | 23,683,008.72 | 15,261,390.75 | 36 |
| Nevada | Reno, Nev | 1,207,832.91 | 837,546.39 | 31 |
| New Hampshire | Portsmouth, N. H | 10,321,265.97 | 5,909,990.22 | 43 |
| 1st New Jersey | Camden, N. J | 28,752,918.16 | 21,244,233.36 | 26 |
| 5th New Jersey | Newark, N. J | 114,658,718.59 | 85,905,105.65 | 25 |
| New Mexico | Albuquerque, N. Mex | 1,774,171.86 | 1,230,700.50 | 31 |
| 1st New York | Brooklyn, N. Y | 95,624,118.53 | 69,790,338.24 | 27 |
| 2d New York | New York, N. Y | 859,851,705.63 | 587,442,366.07 | 32 |
| 14th New York | Albany, N. Y | 61,114,993.00 | 47,149,084.39 | 23 |
| 21st New York | Syracuse, N. Y | 36,988,349.88 | 24,616,757.67 | 33 |
| 28th New York | Buffalo, N. Y | 71,893,607.10 | 50,774,201.07 | 29 |
| North Carolina | Raleigh, N. C | 124,890,499.06 | 122,413,329.34 | 2 |
| North Dakota | Fargo, N. Dak | 3,043,905.73 | 1,911,739.38 | 37 |
| 1st Ohio | Cincinnati, Ohio | 77,547,445.20 | 54,622,623.69 | 30 |
| 10th Ohio | Toledo, Ohio | 39,870,208.74 | 27,621,179.08 | 31 |
| 11th Ohio | Columbus, Ohio | 26,899,619.37 | 20,702,529.70 | 23 |
| 18th Ohio | Cleveland, Ohio | 141,351,260.14 | 89,355,347.49 | 37 |
| Oklahoma | Oklahoma, Okla | 27,569,643.12 | 18,402,452.57 | 33 |
| Oregon | Portland, Oreg | 28,135,975.16 | 18,792,189.26 | 33 |
| 1st Pennsylvania | Philadelphia, Pa | 265,725,367.78 | 189,059,715.49 | 29 |
| 12th Pennsylvania | Scranton, Pa | 29,837,654.91 | 23,627,414.38 | 21 |
| 23d Pennsylvania | Pittsburgh, Pa | 193,495,077.74 | 124,020,912.71 | 36 |
| Rhode Island | Providence, R. I | 42,259,894.81 | 35,743,706.98 | 15 |
| South Carolina | Columbia, S. C | 28,610,623.37 | 11,447,385.27 | 60 |
| South Dakota | Aberdeen, S. Dak | 5,049,101.71 | 2,565,444.05 | 49 |
| Tennessee | Nashville, Tenn | 34,369,120.71 | 21,794,676.93 | 37 |
| 1st Texas | Austin, Tex | 35,586,495.64 | 27,859,142.37 | 22 |
| 2d Texas | Dallas, Tex | 42,639,778.49 | 24,488,533.36 | 43 |
| Utah | Salt Lake City, Utah | 10,574,849.13 | 5,130,487.26 | 51 |
| Vermont | Burlington, Vt | 6,358,196.04 | 4,157,296.23 | 35 |
| Virginia | Richmond, Va | 61,854,341.11 | 46,595,648.69 | 25 |
| Washington | Tacoma, Wash | 36,815,140.71 | [1] 23,875,014.29 | 35 |
| West Virginia | Parkersburg, W. Va | 41,878,872.96 | 33,452,437.59 | 20 |
| Wisconsin | Milwaukee, Wis | 74,309,939.20 | 50,488,606.16 | 32 |
| Wyoming | Cheyenne, Wyo | 3,250,361.11 | 2,079,558.17 | 36 |
| Philippine Islands | Manila, P. I | 945,859.66 | [2] 457,430.29 | 52 |
| Total | | 4,595,000,765.74 | 3,197,451,083.00 | 30.41 |
| Internal revenue collected through customs offices [3] | | 356,296.21 | | |
| Grand total | | 4,595,357,061.95 | [4] 3,197,451,083.00 | 30.42 |

[1] Includes $14,395.31 income tax on Alaska railroads (act of July 18, 1914).
[2] In addition to this amount reported by the United States internal-revenue stamp agent, collections from sale of stamps affixed to products from the Philippine Islands are included as follows: 1st California, $1,883.65; 6th California, $14.11, Hawaii, $669.92; and 1st Illinois, $45.47.
[3] These receipts for 1922 amounting to $495,559.43 are included in the totals by districts, while for 1921 they are shown in total for the United States only.
[4] The figures concerning internal-revenue receipts as given in this statement differ from such figures carried in other Treasury statements showing the financial condition of the Government, because the former represent collections by internal-revenue officers throughout the country,·including deposits by postmasters of amounts received from sale of internal-revenue stamps and deposits of internal revenue collected through customs offices, while the latter represent the deposits of these collections in the Treasury or depositaries during the fiscal year concerned, the differences being due to the fact that some of the collections in the latter part of the fiscal year can not be deposited, or are not reported to the Treasury as deposited until after June 30, thus carrying them into the following fiscal year as recorded in the statements showing the condition of the Treasury.

SUMMARY OF INTERNAL-REVENUE RECEIPTS, YEAR ENDED JUNE 30, 1922, BY STATES.

| State.[1] | Income and profits tax. | Miscellaneous taxes. | Total. |
|---|---|---|---|
| Alabama | $9,009,980.66 | $2,454,200.10 | $11,464,180.76 |
| Alaska | 173,787.12 | 90,444.90 | 264,232.02 |
| Arizona | 1,427,375.40 | 713,859.52 | 2,141,234.92 |
| Arkansas | 5,336,259.50 | 1,642,785.56 | 6,979,045.06 |
| California | 92,251,113.85 | 39,401,742.04 | 131,652,855.89 |
| Colorado | 14,545,632.75 | 5,411,017.93 | 19,956,650.68 |
| Connecticut | 27,245,128.42 | 22,979,517.53 | 50,224,645.95 |
| Delaware | 3,986,808.83 | 1,902,457.34 | 5,889,266.17 |
| District of Columbia | 10,521,286.04 | 7,333,400.12 | 17,854,686.16 |
| Florida | 8,433,602.21 | 5,886,255.07 | 14,319,857.28 |
| Georgia | 14,270,049.82 | 6,718,656.78 | 20,988,706.60 |
| Hawaii | 14,632,590.97 | 882,472.06 | 15,515,063.03 |
| Idaho | 1,372,658.22 | 739,232.79 | 2,111,891.01 |
| Illinois | 179,633,973.81 | 90,698,593.92 | 270,332,567.73 |
| Indiana | 30,715,323.47 | 22,317,076.08 | 53,032,399.55 |
| Iowa | 17,046,762.88 | 6,612,026.31 | 23,658,789.19 |
| Kansas | 22,242,152.01 | 8,137,469.68 | 30,379,621.69 |
| Kentucky | 16,285,993.78 | 16,836,202.43 | 33,122,196.21 |
| Louisiana | 15,477,826.58 | 7,276,131.32 | 22,753,957.90 |
| Maine | 10,989,939.85 | 3,814,268.22 | 14,804,208.07 |
| Maryland | 29,070,268.90 | 16,901,667.66 | 45,971,936.56 |
| Massachusetts | 130,180,292.05 | 39,633,201.46 | 169,813,493.51 |
| Michigan | 112,258,181.64 | 89,616,002.86 | 201,874,184.50 |
| Minnesota | 30,297,828.71 | 15,956,114.17 | 46,253,942.88 |
| Mississippi | 3,405,262.01 | 1,235,235.49 | 4,640,497.50 |
| Missouri | 55,035,012.61 | 32,421,475.49 | 87,456,488.10 |
| Montana | 2,302,331.74 | 1,129,830.32 | 3,432,162.06 |
| Nebraska | 9,215,553.66 | 6,045,837.09 | 15,261,390.75 |
| Nevada | 564,023.45 | 273,522.94 | 837,546.39 |
| New Hampshire | 4,311,758.90 | 1,598,240.32 | 5,909,999.22 |
| New Jersey | 67,766,027.83 | 39,383,311.18 | 107,149,339.01 |
| New Mexico | 811,595.86 | 419,104.64 | 1,230,700.50 |
| New York | 527,695,268.75 | 252,077,508.69 | 779,772,777.44 |
| North Carolina | 23,179,559.81 | 99,233,769.53 | 122,413,329.34 |
| North Dakota | 1,163,686.83 | 748,052.55 | 1,911,730.38 |
| Ohio | 128,898,272.31 | 63,403,407.65 | 192,301,679.96 |
| Oklahoma | 14,276,549.14 | 4,125,903.43 | 18,402,452.57 |
| Oregon | 14,934,997.18 | 3,857,192.08 | 18,792,189.26 |
| Pennsylvania | 245,798,087.82 | 90,909,954.76 | 336,708,042.58 |
| Rhode Island | 19,992,123.36 | 15,751,583.62 | 35,743,706.98 |
| South Carolina | 9,699,041.79 | 1,745,343.48 | 11,447,385.27 |
| South Dakota | 1,643,613.83 | 921,830.22 | 2,565,444.05 |
| Tennessee | 14,174,092.51 | 7,620,584.42 | 21,794,676.93 |
| Texas | 34,978,009.92 | 17,369,665.81 | 52,347,675.73 |
| Utah | 2,971,391.01 | 2,159,096.25 | 5,130,487.26 |
| Vermont | 2,997,106.08 | 1,160,190.15 | 4,157,296.23 |
| Virginia | 18,577,380.51 | 28,018,268.18 | 46,595,648.69 |
| Washington | 18,733,630.39 | 4,877,151.88 | 23,610,782.27 |
| West Virginia | 27,961,834.15 | 5,490,603.44 | 33,452,437.59 |
| Wisconsin | 36,879,538.91 | 13,609,067.25 | 50,488,606.16 |
| Wyoming | 1,547,897.02 | 531,661.15 | 2,079,558.17 |
| Philippine Islands | | 457,430.29 | 457,430.29 |
| Total | 2,086,918,464.85 | 1,110,532,618.15 | 3,197,451,083.00 |

[1] Maryland and the District of Columbia comprise the district of Maryland, and Washington and the Territory of Alaska the district of Washington.

SUMMARY OF RECEIPTS FROM INCOME AND PROFITS TAXES, YEARS ENDED JUNE 30, 1920, 1921, AND 1922, BY STATES; WITH PER CENT OF INCREASE OR DECREASE IN 1922, COMPARED WITH 1921.

| States and Territories. | 1920 [1] | 1921 [2] | 1922 [3] | Per cent 1921-22 increase (+) or decrease (−). |
|---|---|---|---|---|
| Alabama | $14,413,217.67 | $14,222,196.12 | $9,009,980.66 | −37 |
| Alaska | 372,949.02 | 279,821.67 | 173,787.12 | −38 |
| Arizona | 2,685,349.24 | 2,784,941.73 | 1,427,375.40 | −49 |
| Arkansas | 9,928,798.46 | 8,228,525.73 | 5,336,259.50 | −35 |
| California | 129,858,256.29 | 129,170,961.21 | 92,251,113.85 | −29 |
| Colorado | 28,116,321.15 | 25,085,242.95 | 14,545,632.75 | −42 |
| Connecticut | 75,958,692.37 | 49,208,464.34 | 27,245,128.42 | −45 |
| Delaware | 18,606,049.42 | 9,848,404.28 | 3,986,808.83 | −60 |
| District of Columbia | 8,928,755.77 | 8,054,914.26 | 10,521,286.04 | +31 |
| Florida | 8,027,614.62 | 10,108,053.94 | 8,433,602.21 | −17 |
| Georgia | 33,731,763.14 | 28,792,002.73 | 14,270,049.82 | −50 |
| Hawaii | 10,737,113.35 | 18,859,082.76 | 14,632,590.97 | −22 |
| Idaho | 3,730,432.25 | 3,495,317.45 | 1,372,658.22 | −61 |
| Illinois | 310,793,183.68 | 260,944,632.48 | 179,633,973.81 | −31 |
| Indiana | 49,691,162.26 | 49,809,541.01 | 30,715,323.47 | −38 |
| Iowa | 30,352,715.68 | 28,893,632.48 | 17,046,762.88 | −41 |
| Kansas | 29,147,067.71 | 26,873,549.31 | 22,242,152.01 | −17 |
| Kentucky | 27,003,508.96 | 25,091,391.06 | 16,285,993.78 | −35 |
| Louisiana | 31,973,161.51 | 29,242,438.18 | 15,477,826.58 | −47 |
| Maine | 16,091,951.59 | 14,459,568.04 | 10,989,939.85 | −24 |
| Maryland | 49,905,750.90 | 44,948,063.92 | 29,070,268.90 | −35 |
| Massachusetts | 302,205,596.50 | 214,058,413.88 | 130,180,292.05 | −39 |
| Michigan | 187,521,362.04 | 184,494,520.82 | 112,258,181.64 | −39 |
| Minnesota | 53,405,882.23 | 53,886,224.54 | 30,297,828.71 | −44 |
| Mississippi | 9,741,970.10 | 7,244,977.45 | 3,405,262.01 | −53 |
| Missouri | 101,963,031.86 | 86,121,595.25 | 55,035,012.61 | −36 |
| Montana | 4,830,980.75 | 3,925,062.65 | 2,302,331.74 | −41 |
| Nebraska | 16,293,174.65 | 15,828,609.66 | 9,215,553.66 | −42 |
| Nevada | 849,759.29 | 718,136.11 | 564,023.45 | −21 |
| New Hampshire | 12,579,024.13 | 8,304,563.93 | 4,311,758.90 | −48 |
| New Jersey | 109,908,678.42 | 97,391,062.92 | 67,766,027.83 | −30 |
| New Mexico | 3,672,720.76 | 1,306,243.22 | 811,595.86 | −38 |
| New York | 1,109,802,448.70 | 814,736,708.37 | 527,695,268.75 | −35 |
| North Carolina | 44,982,859.99 | 38,664,722.96 | 23,179,559.81 | −40 |
| North Dakota | 2,418,932.45 | 2,072,432.20 | 1,163,686.83 | −44 |
| Ohio | 279,754,263.17 | 203,847,472.40 | 128,898,272.31 | −37 |
| Oklahoma | 20,039,573.97 | 21,637,304.77 | 14,276,549.14 | −34 |
| Oregon | 21,994,587.22 | 21,973,313.00 | 14,934,997.18 | −32 |
| Pennsylvania | 429,930,354.00 | 351,737,751.22 | 245,798,087.82 | −30 |
| Rhode Island | 40,139,827.10 | 36,086,774.07 | 19,992,122.36 | −45 |
| South Carolina | 23,943,518.47 | 26,032,367.96 | 9,699,041.79 | −63 |
| South Dakota | 4,829,056.81 | 3,648,484.22 | 1,643,613.83 | −55 |
| Tennessee | 26,295,058.15 | 25,606,805.43 | 14,174,092.51 | −45 |
| Texas | 76,216,882.75 | 52,190,451.75 | 34,978,009.92 | −33 |
| Utah | 5,545,632.00 | 7,116,197.70 | 2,971,391.01 | −58 |
| Vermont | 5,431,701.59 | 4,803,370.92 | 2,997,106.08 | −38 |
| Virginia | 37,447,725.14 | 31,594,403.02 | 18,577,380.51 | −41 |
| Washington | 34,755,730.83 | 29,221,005.72 | [4] 18,733,630.39 | −36 |
| West Virginia | 27,671,888.57 | 35,819,846.89 | 27,961,834.15 | −22 |
| Wisconsin | 69,522,627.13 | 57,131,042.40 | 36,879,538.91 | −35 |
| Wyoming | 3,207,279.76 | 2,537,062.67 | 1,547,897.02 | −39 |
| Total | 3,956,936,003.60 | 3,228,137,673.75 | 2,086,918,464.85 | −35 |

[1] Includes the third and fourth installments of the 1918 and the first and second installments of the 1919 income and profits tax.
[2] Includes the third and fourth installments of the 1919 and the first and second installments of the 1920 income and profits tax.
[3] Includes the third and fourth installments of the 1920 and the first and second installments of the 1921 income and profits tax.
[4] Includes $14,395.31 income tax on Alaska railroads (act of July 18, 1914).

## TOTAL INTERNAL-REVENUE RECEIPTS, YEARS ENDED JUNE 30, 1863-1922.[1]

| | | | |
|---|---|---|---|
| 1863 [2] | $41,003,192.93 | 1894 | $147,168,449.70 |
| 1864 | 116,965,578.26 | 1895 | 143,246,077.75 |
| 1865 | 210,855,864.53 | 1896 | 146,830,615.66 |
| 1866 | 310,120,448.13 | 1897 | 146,619,593.47 |
| 1867 | 265,064,938.43 | 1898 | 170,866,819.36 |
| 1868 | 190,374,925.59 | 1899 | 273,484,573.44 |
| 1869 | 159,124,126.86 | 1900 | 295,316,107.57 |
| 1870 | 184,302,828.34 | 1901 | 306,871,669.42 |
| 1871 | 143,198,322.10 | 1902 | 271,867,990.25 |
| 1872 | 130,890,096.90 | 1903 | 230,740,925.22 |
| 1873 | 113,504,012.80 | 1904 | 232,903,781.06 |
| 1874 | 102,191,016.98 | 1905 | 234,187,976.37 |
| 1875 | 110,071,515.00 | 1906 | 249,102,738.00 |
| 1876 | 116,768,096.22 | 1907 | 269,664,022.85 |
| 1877 | 118,549,230.25 | 1908 | 251,665,950.04 |
| 1878 | 110,654,163.37 | 1909 | 246,212,719.22 |
| 1879 | 113,449,621.38 | 1910 | 289,957,220.16 |
| 1880 | 123,981,916.10 | 1911 | 322,526,299.73 |
| 1881 | 135,229,912.30 | 1912 | 321,615,894.69 |
| 1882 | 146,523,273.72 | 1913 | 344,424,453.85 |
| 1883 | 144,553,344.86 | 1914 | 380,008,893.96 |
| 1884 | 121,590,039.83 | 1915 | 415,681,023.86 |
| 1885 | 112,421,121.07 | 1916 | 512,723,287.77 |
| 1886 | 116,902,869.44 | 1917 | 809,393,640.44 |
| 1887 | 118,837,301.06 | 1918 | 3,698,955,820.93 |
| 1888 | 124,326,475.32 | 1919 | 3,850,150,078.56 |
| 1889 | 130,894,434.20 | 1920 | 5,407,580,251.81 |
| 1890 | 142,594,696.57 | 1921 | 4,595,357,061.95 |
| 1891 | 146,035,415.97 | 1922 | 3,197,451,083.00 |
| 1892 | 153,857,544.35 | | |
| 1893 | 161,004,989.67 | Total | 32,178,416,332.62 |

[1] Internal revenue collected through customs offices, which amounted to $356,296.21 for 1921 and $495,559.43 for 1922, are not included for years prior to 1921.
[2] Nine months only.

## INTERNAL-REVENUE TAX ON PRODUCTS FROM PHILIPPINE ISLANDS, YEARS ENDED JUNE 30, 1921 AND 1922, BY ARTICLES TAXED.[1]

| Articles taxed. | 1921 | 1922 | Increase (+) or decrease (−). |
|---|---|---|---|
| Cigars (large) | $985,119.22 | $455,740.45 | −$529,378.77 |
| Cigars (small) | 9.00 | | −9.00 |
| Cigarettes (large) | 19.44 | 77.04 | +57.60 |
| Cigarettes (small) | 5,833.31 | 2,097.36 | −3,735.95 |
| Manufactured tobacco | 490.33 | 432.59 | −57.74 |
| Miscellaneous collections relating to tobacco | 11.98 | | −11.98 |
| Stamp sales (documentary) | | 1,696.00 | +1,696.00 |
| Total | 991,483.28 | 460,043.44 | −531,439.84 |

[1] With the exception of the internal revenue collected from sale of documentary stamps, these receipts were covered into the Treasury of the United States to the credit of the treasurer of the Philippine Islands.

## INTERNAL-REVENUE TAX ON PRODUCTS FROM PORTO RICO, YEARS ENDED JUNE 30, 1921 AND 1922, BY ARTICLES TAXED.[1]

| Articles taxed. | 1921 | 1922 | Increase (+) or decrease (−). |
|---|---|---|---|
| Distilled spirits (nonbeverage) | $81,414.08 | $18,224.58 | −$63,189.50 |
| Cigars (large) | 1,023,753.99 | 844,878.82 | −178,875.17 |
| Cigars (small) | 9,690.00 | 18,613.65 | +8,923.65 |
| Cigarettes (large) | 864.00 | 1,944.00 | +1,080.00 |
| Cigarettes (small) | 1,218.00 | 1,110.00 | −108.00 |
| Stamp sales (documentary) | 544.47 | 431.55 | −112.92 |
| Total | 1,117,484.54 | 885,202.60 | −232,281.94 |

[1] Includes $790,158.27 for 1921 and $866,949.87 for 1922, internal revenue collected, which was deposited at San Juan, P. R., to the credit of the treasurer of Porto Rico. These amounts are not included in the internal-revenue collections shown in other statements herein.

Important Decisions of the Courts in Internal-Revenue Cases During the Fiscal Year Ended June 30, 1922.

BANKERS' SPECIAL TAX.

*Fidelity & Deposit Co. of Maryland* v. *United States.*—Supreme Court of the United States (42 Sup. Ct. Rep. 511; T. D. 3356).

Where a company, in additionpto a banking business, engages in the surety business, the safe-deposit business, and the business of acting as trustee, to the successful conduct of each of which credit is necessary, and the company's capital supplies such credit to each, the whole of the common capital can not be deemed capital of a single department; hence, the special tax imposed by section 2 of the act of June 13, 1898, on bankers using or employing a capital, should not be computed on the total capital of such company, but only on that proportion thereof shown to have been used specifically in the banking operations.

Money derived from the sale of capital stock and all the money of the surplus of a company engaged in the banking, surety, and safe-deposit businesses, and the business of acting as trustee, were invested in real estate (including office building in which the company's business was done) and in securities, designated on its books as "Capital Stock Investments," the papers representing same being segregated in the company's vault in separate envelopes earmarked as capital stock; the banking business was likewise kept separate, physically and as matter of accounting, from other business of the company, and money received from deposits was invested in securities which were kept in separate envelopes earmarked as such; expense of each business of the company was charged to the separate account of that business payable out of its earnings, but physically expenses of the several businesses may have been paid from a common fund; part of the income from each business was maintained as cash and remained uninvested, part of the money being carried as counter cash and the balance being deposited in the company's depositaries, the money so deposited not being segregated according to source from which it came, though source of items comprising its total amount was recorded in the respective books of each business; earnings of each business were carried to undivided profits account at end of each year; a portion of the office building was occupied by the banking business. *Held*, that it could not be said as a matter of law that all the capital of the company was used in the banking business, nor that at least the amount upon which the special tax imposed by section 2 of the act of June 13, 1898, was assessed (which in no year was as much as one-half the company's capital) was so used; therefore a request for findings of fact whether the banking business used only the funds of its depositors in the conduct of such business, whether any capital or surplus was actually used or employed in such business, and, if so, what amount, and what was the net income of the surety or bonding business, should be granted.

Capital may be employed in banking although it is not used strictly as working capital and none of it is used in making loans or directly in other banking transactions.

Money of a banker held in the vault or with depositaries as a reserve is employed in banking as much as money loaned to customers.

Capital invested in securities may be employed in banking even if
its sole use is to give to the banker the credit which attracts depositors
or to make it possible for him otherwise to raise money with which
banking operations are conducted; and if such securities serve to give
credit, they will continue, also in the legal sense, to be capital used in
the banking business, even if they are designated by the company as
assets of another department and physically segregated as such.

Where claim for the refund of tax assessed and paid under section 2
of the act of June 13, 1898, imposing a special tax on bankers using
or employing a capital, was made November 22, 1913, and claim was
rejected by the Secretary of the Treasury on April 19, 1917, suit
brought in the Court of Claims on July 25, 1918, under the act of
July 27, 1912, chapter 256, was not barred by limitations, the six-
year statute (sec. 1069, R. S.) applying.

*Fidelity Title & Trust Company of Pittsburgh* v. *United States.*—
Supreme Court of the United States (42 Sup. Ct. Rep. 514; T. D.
3353).

Suit brought in the Court of Claims in July, 1918, under the act
of July 27, 1912, c. 256, to recover tax assessed and paid under the
provisions of section 2 of the act of June 13, 1898, imposing a special
tax on bankers using or employing a capital, was not barred by
limitations, where claim for refund was rejected in November, 1913,
as such suit was governed by the six-year statute (Sec. 1069, R. S.).

A company which, in addition to a banking business, engages in
four other classes of business, has the burden of proving, in a suit
to recover back the special tax assessed and paid under section 2 of
the act of June 13, 1898, imposing a special tax on bankers using or
employing a capital, that none of its capital, or that less of it than
the amount for which it was assessed, had been used or employed
in the banking business.

A company which carried on five classes of business, one of which
was banking, permanently invested an amount in excess of its
capital in bonds and real estate, the latter including its office building (used by all the several departments of business), a schedule of
which investments was carried on its books designated "Schedule
of investments of the capital stock of one million dollars," but there
was no physical segregation of such assets from others of the company, nor was there segregation of money received from capital
stock or from investments made therewith from money derived
from earnings of the several businesses; all moneys received, including bank deposits, were commingled and from such general
funds all investments were made and all expenses and losses paid;
all earnings of the several departments were pooled and went into
the profit and loss account, in which there was carried a credit
representing undivided profits which were not set apart as a separate fund, but were at all times subject to distribution as dividends
and available for any of the several departments; additional stock
was sold, at a date subsequent to the period here in question, above
par to form a surplus fund. Held, that it could not be said as a
matter of law that the "undivided profits" were not assessable as
capital, under the provisions of section 2 of the act of June 13,
1898, imposing a special tax on bankers using or employing a capital.
Therefore, in the absence of evidence establishing or of a request for

a finding of the proportions of capital and accumulated profits used in the respective departments, recovery of any part of the tax paid was properly denied.

Congress did not, by declaring in section 2 of the act of June 13, 1898, imposing a special tax on bankers employing a capital, that "in estimating capital, surplus shall be included" and that the "annual tax shall in all cases be computed on the basis of the capital and surplus for the preceding fiscal year," intend to draw a distinction between surplus and undivided profits, but intended that all capital actually used in banking should be taxed, whether it was strictly capital stock, or surplus, or undivided profits.

*Mayes v. United States Trust Co.*—United States Circuit Court of Appeals, Sixth Circuit (280 Fed. 25).

A company, which was incorporated to carry on a general trust and financial business and also to receive money on deposit and pay interest thereon and to loan money upon such securities as it might approve, carried on a general trust business but received deposits subject to check and made loans secured by collateral. *Held*, the company had some capital employed in the banking business which was subject to the bankers' special tax imposed by the act of October 22, 1914. The amount of capital used in the banking business should be measured, at least in the absence of a more satisfactory method, by the ratio which the assets employed in the banking business bear to the assets employed in the aggregate business.

## CAPITAL-STOCK TAX.

*Central Union Trust Co. v. Edwards.*—United States District Court, Southern District of New York (T. D. 3359).

The capital stock tax imposed by section 407 of the revenue act of 1916 is not a property tax, but is an excise tax imposed upon the privilege of doing business in corporate form, as a going concern, and the value of this privilege is the obvious way to measure the tax.

The meaning of the words "capital stock" is to be determined by the character of the particular statute in which used, the context and the language. As employed in section 407 of the revenue act of 1916, the words indicate an appraisal of the value of the capital stock arrived at by considering various factors of value, by the exercise of judgment, rather than an auditor's exact determination of the value of the net worth of tangible assets, taken from the corporate books of account.

The purpose of the use of the words "in estimating the value of capital stock the surplus and undivided profits shall be included," in section 407, was to make certain that these two factors should be considered, but not to eliminate other factors equally as important, and the words do not restrict the computation to the par value of the capital stock plus surplus and undivided profits.

In computing the value of capital stock, there should be considered in addition to the net worth of the corporate assets, including surplus and undivided profits, as shown by the books, the franchises, good will, outstanding contracts, earning capacity of the corporation and the market value of its share stock over the preceding year. If such intangibles were eliminated as factors of value, the computation of value would in no sense be an estimation, but the value would be the exact value rather than the fair value, and it would be made determinable as of the end of the fiscal year, rather than by "the fair average value of the capital stock for the preceding year."

*Malley* v. *Howard; Casey* v. *Howard; Malley* v. *Crocker; Malley* v. *Hecht.*—United States Circuit Court of Appeals, First Circuit (281 Fed. 363; T. D. 3368).

While, in applying tax statutes, reasonable doubts must be resolved in favor of the taxpayer, revenue acts are not penal statutes; the Government is not to be crippled by strained and unnatural construction of tax statutes fairly plain.

When language used in an earlier statute has in application received judicial construction, change in language in later analogous legislation imports legislative purpose to attain a different result.

The contrast between the language used in the act of August 5, 1909, imposing a tax on every joint-stock company or association "organized *under the laws of the United States*," etc., and in the revenue acts of 1916 and 1918, which imposed a capital stock tax upon associations "organized *in* the United States," shows that Congress intended to avoid the effect of the holding in *Elliott* v. *Freeman* (220 U. S. 178), that the 1909 act did not cover certain Massachusetts trusts because limited to organizations deriving some power or benefit from statute. Therefore, nonstatutory associations are subject to the capital stock taxes imposed by the revenue acts of 1916 and 1918.

Section 407 of the revenue act of 1916 and section 1000 (a) of the revenue act of 1918, imposing an excise tax measured by the value of the capital stock of associations, include business organizations known as Massachusetts trusts, where the shareholders or beneficiaries have power to control the trustees.

Whether the stock of a corporation, of an association, or of a joint-stock company, has or has not par value is immaterial in determining liability for the capital stock tax imposed by the revenue acts of 1916 and 1918, since stockholders own beneficially the net value of the corporation's assets, whether a definite value is or is not attributed to their shares, severally or in mass.

The manifest general purpose of Congress, in imposing a capital stock tax by the revenue acts of 1916 and 1918, was to tax business deriving powers and making profits from association, particularly business done by organizations getting all or a substantial part of their capital on transferable shares, such as are commonly sold to the investing public.

The Massachusetts Legislature, by acts passed prior to the passage of the revenue acts of 1916 and 1918, expressly recognized Massachusetts trusts as associations, not as trusts or partnerships; Congress must be held to have used the word "association" as the Massachusetts Legislature had previously defined and used it.

By act of 1916, c. 184, the Massachusetts Legislature made Massachusetts trusts liable to creditors in like manner as if corporations; by analogy they have similar liability to the Federal Government for taxes.

*Malley* v. *Bowditch* (259 Fed. 809), followed, and *Crocker* v. *Malley* (249 U. S. 223), distinguished.

CHILD-LABOR TAX.

*Bailey* v. *The Drexel Furniture Co.*—Supreme Court of the United tates (42 Sup. Ct. Rep. 449; T. D. 3346).

Where the sovereign enacting a law has power to impose both tax and penalty the difference between revenue production and mere regulation may be immaterial; but not so when one sovereign can impose a tax only and the power of regulation rests in another.

Taxes imposed in the discretion of the legislature on proper subjects with the primary motive of obtaining revenue from them and with the incidental motive of discouraging them by making their continuance onerous do not lose their character as taxes because of the incidental motive; but there comes a time in the extension of the penalizing features of the so-called tax when it loses its character as such and becomes a mere penalty with the characteristics of regulation and punishment.

Revenue act of 1918, Title XII, provides, in section 1200, that with certain exceptions every person operating any mine or quarry in which children under the age of 16 years have been employed or permitted to work during any portion of the taxable year, or any mill, cannery, workshop, factory, or manufacturing establishment in which children under the age of 14 years have been employed or permitted to work, or children between the ages of 14 and 16 have been employed or permitted to work more than eight hours in any day, or more than six days in any week, or after the hour of 7 o'clock postmeridian, or before the hour of 6 o'clock antemeridian, during any portion of the taxable year, shall pay for each taxable year an excise tax equivalent to 10 per cent of the entire net profits received or accrued for such year from the sale or disposition of the product of such mine, mill, factory, etc. Section 1203 relieves from liability where the employer did not know that the child was within the named age limit, and section 1206 subjects the employer's factory to inspection not only by Treasury Department officials but by the Secretary of Labor and his subordinates. *Held*, that the so-called tax is in fact a penalty, and hence Title XII is unconstitutional as a regulation of the employment of child labor in the States, an exclusively State function under the Federal Constitution and within the reservation of the tenth amendment.

*Bailey* v. *George (Vivian Cotton Mills).*—Supreme Court of the United States (42 Sup. Ct. Rep. 419; T. D. 3347).

Complainants brought a bill in equity to enjoin the collector of internal revenue from collecting the child-labor tax by distraint, averring that claim for abatement of the tax had been filed and rejected; that they had exhausted all legal remedies; and that the act was invalid and unconstitutional. *Held*, that in the absence of extraordinary and exceptional circumstances not averred in the bill or shown to exist, and in the absence of specific facts supporting the legal conclusion, the averment that a taxing statute is unconstitutional does not take the case out of section 3224, Revised Statutes, which provides "that no suit for the purpose of restraining the assessment or collection of any tax shall be maintained in any court."

Complainants could have paid the tax under protest and then rought suit against the collector of internal revenue to recover the mount paid with interest; not having done so, they did not exhaust all their legal remedies, and no fact having been alleged which would prevent them from availing themselves of this form of remedy, the decree of the district court in granting the injunction is reversed with directions to dismiss the bill.

*Atherton Mills* v. *Johnson et al.*—Supreme Court of the United States (42 Sup. Ct. Rep. 422).

This action was brought to restrain a corporation from dismissing a child employee under authority of the child labor tax act. It was contended that since the act was unconstitutional the dismissal of the child was wrongful. The case was dismissed on the ground that the lapse of time since the case was heard and decided in the district court had brought the minor whose employment was the subject of the suit to an age not within the ages affected by the act, so that, even if valid, it could not affect him.

## CORPORATION EXCISE TAX.

*Detroit Hotel Co.* v. *Brady.*—United States District Court, Eastern District of Michigan (275 Fed. 995; T. D. 3314).

Action to recover internal-revenue taxes illegally collected does not lie against successor of the collector to whom the taxes were paid, the successor not having received the taxes, so as to be liable under section 3220, United States Revised Statutes (sec. 5944, U. S. Comp. Stats.).

A corporation organized under act 232 of the Michigan public acts of 1903 to purchase land and "construct thereon a modern fireproof hotel, and to operate, manage or lease, mortgage, or sell the same," immediately after its organization acquired land and constructed a hotel which it leased to an operating corporation for an annual rental dependent upon the lessee's profits from operating the hotel. The lease gave the lessor the right to "inspect the books and accounts of the lessee at all reasonable times." The lessor added five stories to the hotel, negotiating loans for this purpose secured by mortgages on the property, and thereupon entered into a new lease with the operating company at an increased rental. The lessor filed annual reports required by the Michigan statutes. *Held*, that the foregoing acts and activities constituted "carrying on or doing business" by the lessor corporation within the meaning of section 38 of the corporation excise tax act of 1909.

*United States* v. *Philadelphia Knitting Mills Co.*—United States Circuit Court of Appeals, Third Circuit (273 Fed. 657; T. D. 3203).

The Government may attack the action of the board of directors of a corporation and show by evidence, not that a given salary is too much, but that, in the circumstances, the whole or some part of it is not salary at all but is profits diverted to a stockholding officer under the guise of salary and as such is subject to taxation.

Where there was evidence that the activities of the president of a corporation in the business decreased as he advanced in years, that the vice president's duties and interests correspondingly increased, until, at the time in question, the president did almost nothing and the vice president did almost everything in the management of the corporation's affairs, and that a large increase in the salary of the president was voted by a board of directors wholly controlled by his dominating stock ownership, for the sole reason, stated by him, that the vice president's salary had been similarly increased and that he thought his salary should be the same as that of the vice president, a jury could find that the amount paid him was not all for services rendered, but was in part a distribution of profits, and a nonsuit was improper.

## ESTATE TAX.

*Shwab* v. *Doyle.*—Supreme Court of the United States (42 Sup. Ct. Rep. 391; T. D. 3339).

Statutes will not be construed as retroactive unless that intention is clearly declared and the language makes such operation imperative.

Act of September 8, 1916, Title II, is prospective and not retroactive in operation, and section 202 (b) thereof is therefore not applicable to transfers made or trusts created in contemplation of death prior to the passage of· the act, though the maker of the transfer or the creator of the trust died subsequently thereto.

The provision of section 402 of the revenue act of 1918, which reenacted section 202 of the act of September 8, 1916, that the transfer or trust should be taxed whether "made or created before or after the passage of the act," was not an elucidation of the act of September 8, 1916, but was the declaration of a new purpose, not the explanation of an old one.

*Union Trust Co.* v. *Wardell.*—Supreme Court of the United States (42 Sup. Ct. Rep. 393; T. D. 3338).

Act of September 8, 1916, Title II, is prospective and not retroactive in operation, and section 202 (b) thereof is therefore not applicable to a trust created prior to the passage of the act, but intended to take effect in possession or enjoyment at or after the death of the creator of the trust who died subsequently to the· passage of such act.

Suit may not be brought against a collector of internal revenue for the recovery of a tax, in the collection and disbursement of which such officer had no agency; therefore the substitution of the successor to a collector who collected a tax as defendant on the resignation of such collector was error, and a defense of nonliability set up by such successor is sufficient.

*Levy* v. *Wardell.*—Supreme Court of the United States (42 Sup. Ct. Rep. 395).

Where a decedent, prior to the passage of the 1916 revenue act, made an absolute transfer of certain shares of stock; reserving the dividends thereon to herself for life and died after the passage of the act the value of the shares of stock so transferred should not be included in the gross estate of the decedent, as section 202 (b), 1916 revenue act, is prospective and not retroactive in its operation.

*McElligott* v. *Kissam et al.*—Supreme Court of the United States (42 Sup. Ct. Rep. 396).

Section 202 (c) of the revenue act of 1916 is not retroactive in operation, and joint estates created prior to the passage of the act can not be included in the gross estates of decedents for purposes of the Federal estate tax.

*New York Trust Co. et al.* v. *Eisner.*—Supreme Court of the United States (41 Sup. Ct. Rep. 506; 256 U. S. 345; T. D. 3267).

Title II, act of September 8, 1916, is not unconstitutional as ·an interference with the rights of the States to regulate descent and distribution as unequal or as a direct tax not apportioned as the Constitution requires.

State inheritance and succession taxes paid to New York and other States are not deductible under section 203 as "charges against the estate," for the purpose of determining the net estate subject to tax.

*Greiner* v. *Lewellyn.*—Supreme Court of the United States (42 Sup. Ct. Rep. 324; T. D. 3326).

Bonds issued by political subdivisions of a State may be included in determining the net estate of a decedent for purposes of the estate tax imposed by the revenue act of 1916; to do so does not in effect amount to taxation of such bonds in violation of the Federal Constitution.

*Wardell* v. *Blum.*—United States Circuit Court of Appeals, Ninth Circuit (276 Fed. 226). Writ of certiorari denied. Motion to reconsider filed. Mandate stayed.

All inheritance taxes are imposed on the transfer of the net estate of the deceased, and the property upon which such a tax is imposed must, in truth, be the property of the deceased, under revenue act of 1916, sections 201–203.

The interest of a decedent subject to inheritance tax under revenue act of 1916, sections 201–203, providing that the tax be upon the transfer of the net estate of the decedent "to the extent of the interest therein of the decedent," etc., is to be determined by the law of the State where the property is situated.

Only one-half of community property is subject to Federal inheritance tax under revenue act of 1916, sections 201–203, in view of Civ. Code Cal., sec. 1402, and St. Cal. 1917, p. 880.

*Nichols* v. *Gaston.*—United States Circuit Court of Appeals, First Circuit (281 Fed. 67; T. D. 3325).

A suit in equity by the executors of an estate against a collector of internal revenue individually and as collector to restrain him from collecting a tax assessed against the estate under Title IV of the revenue act of 1918 is one involving a controversy arising under the laws of the United States, and hence the United States district court as a Federal court had jurisdiction thereof.

Section 3220, Revised Statutes, as amended by section 1316 (*a*) of the revenue act of 1918, authorizes the Commissioner of Internal Revenue to remit, refund, and pay back all taxes erroneously or illegally assessed or collected, and also all damages and costs recovered against any collector in any suit brought against him by reason of anything done in due performance of his official duty. Complainants, as executors of an estate, brought suit against a collector of internal revenue to restrain collection of an estate tax on the ground that under section 408 of the revenue act of 1918 they had until the expiration of 180 days after such tax became due to pay same, and alleged that they were without adequate remedy at law. *Held,* that had complainants paid the tax under protest when demanded, they could have recovered judgment against the collector for damages sustained, if collection was premature and they were thereby damaged; that in view thereof and the further facts that under the law they would have been entitled to interest on such damages down to entry of final judgment, and that, upon a certificate of probable cause, under section 989 of Revised Statutes, the liability of the Government to pay the judgment would attach, complainants had a legal remedy, and, irrespective of the inhibition in section 3224 of the Revised Statutes against suits to restrain assessment or collection of any tax in any court, injunction would not lie to restrain the collection of the tax, though interest on the judgment, after it became final, would not run against the Government.

The inhibition in section 3224, Revised Statutes, against suits to restrain assessment or collection of any tax in any court, applies to all assessments or collections of internal-revenue taxes made or attempted to be made under color of office by internal-revenue officers charged .with general jurisdiction over assessment and collection of such taxes, and, if the Commissioner of Internal Revenue, in assessing a tax or the collector, in collecting it, acts under color of office, such section applies and no suit to restrain the assessment or collection of the tax can be maintained.

In view of the provisions of sections 404, 1305, and 1307 of the revenue act of 1918, and sections 3182, 3183, 3184, and 3187 of the Revised Statutes, it was the duty of a collector of internal revenue to whom the Commissioner of Internal Revenue certified an estate tax in his list for collection, to proceed to collect the tax, and such collector in demanding payment of the tax, and, on nonpayment thereof, in issuing a distraint warrant and enforcing collection, acted under color of office and his acts were not purely ministerial.

*Page* v. *Polk.*—United States Circuit Court of Appeals, First Circuit (281 Fed. 74; T. D. 3348).

Injunction will not issue to restrain a collector of internal revenue from collecting an estate tax imposed by the revenue act of 1918, Title IV, on the ground that under section 408 of such act the executors of the estate had until the expiration of one year and 180 days after decedent's death in which to pay the tax, and that such executors were without adequate remedy at law. (*Nichols* v. *Gaston*, T. D. 3325, followed.)

Where costs have been decreed against a collector in the district court in a suit enjoining collection of a tax from which he would be relieved if the decree should be reversed, motion to affirm the decree or dismiss the appeal on the ground that, in view of the payment of the tax before hearing in the circuit court of appeals, the questions presented by the appeal were academic, will be denied, and the case will be considered on its merits.

*Smietanka* v. *Ullman.*—United States Circuit Court of Appeals, Seventh Circuit (275 Fed. 814; T. D. 3227).

Where a decedent converted second Liberty 4 per cent bonds into third Liberty 4¼ per cent bonds three weeks prior to his death, the latter bonds are not receivable for estate or inheritance taxes under the provisions of section 14, act of April 4, 1918 (40 Stat. 503, 505), as they were not held by him for at least six months prior to his death, and as the time that the 4 per cent bonds were held can not be tacked onto the period of holding the 4¼ per cent bonds.

Section 14, so construed, does not work such unwarranted discrimination against that class of holders whose death occurred within the six months period after the issue of the bonds as to render unconstitutional so much of section 14 as makes possible such result, as the classification is reasonable and proper and treats all persons alike.

*Congdon* v. *Lynch.*—United States District Court, District of Minne
sota (T. D. 3324).

Title II, act of September 8, 1916, imposing an estate tax, is constitutional. Decision of the United States Supreme Court in New
York Trust Co. *v.* Eisner (41 Sup. Ct. Rep. 506) held controlling.

Section 202 (*b*) of the revenue act of 1916 is retroactive and applies
to a trust executed prior to the passage of the act, to take effect in
possession or enjoyment at or after the death of the donor, who dies
after the passage of the act.

On August 3, 1916, decedent placed certain securities in trust by
an instrument in writing appointing trustees who accepted the trust
and distributed the income to the beneficiaries named. Decedent
did not change the terms of the trust prior to his death on November
21, 1916. The trust did not expressly provide that it was to take
effect in possession or enjoyment at or after the donor's death. The
donor reserved neither income, a life estate, nor the right to revoke,
but did reserve (1) the right to change the beneficiaries and their
respective interests, and the income therefrom; (2) the right to change
the trustees and the number of the trustees (the trustees being the
donor, his wife, and his children); (3) the right to modify the period
of the trust; (4) the right to change the disposition of the trust fund
at the expiration of the trust period; (5) the right to compel the trustees to pay out of the income or principal of the trust premiums
on any insurance policies on the donor's life which were payable to
any beneficiary or to the other trustees and the beneficiaries; (6) the
right to terminate the trust at any time within five years—the property then to revert to the donor; (7) the power to prevent the sale,
disposition, pledge, or incumbrance of certain specified securities, his
written consent being requisite; (8) the right, in case the trust should
end during the donor's life, to secure the reversion to the donor
*Held*, that the management, control, and disposition retained by the
donor was complete, except that he could not make himself a beneficiary of the trust and under certain circumstances could not secure
the reversion to himself; until his death, when the reserved rights
would cease, the trust could not take full effect in complete possession
or in complete enjoyment, and there could be "no element of finality"
about the trust. Although donor did not reserve a life estate in
himself or in a third person during his life, he did reserve the power
to defeat the substantial rights of the beneficiaries, and, as far as the
beneficiaries were concerned, the reserved rights were tantamount to
a power of revocation. In conclusion the court held that the trust
was intended to take possession in effect or enjoyment at or after the
death of the donor, and was within the provisions of section 202 (*b*)
of the revenue act of 1916. The trust property was, therefore, properly included in the gross estate.

Sums paid as inheritance or succession taxes in the States of Arizona,
Michigan, Minnesota, New York, and Washington may not be deducted
from the gross estate as charges against the estate under the provisions
of section 203 of the revenue act of 1916. Decision of United States
Supreme Court in New York Trust Co. *v.* Eisner (41 Sup. Ct. 506)
held controlling.

*Curley et al.* v. *Tait.*—United States District Court, District of
Maryland (276 Fed. 840, 845).

A decedent, several years before his death, made an absolute transfer of certain securities, the transferee by a contemporaneous agreement binding itself to pay the net income to the wife of the transferor during her lifetime, and after her death, in case he survived her, to him during his lifetime. *Held*, that the estate was not subject to tax on the value of the securities themselves, under act September 8, 1916, section 202, but at most on the value of the reserved contingent interest of decedent therein.

Act September 8, 1916, section 202(b), providing for a tax with respect to property of which a decedent has at any time made a transfer, is not retroactive, and does not apply to transfers made prior to its enactment; the words "at any time" being limited to a time subsequent thereto.

The Maryland collateral inheritance tax is imposed upon the estate before distribution and consequently deductible before ascertaining the amount of the Federal estate tax imposed by act of September 8, 1916.

*Dugan et al.* v. *Miles.*—United States District Court, District of Maryland (276 Fed. 401).

Where, under a will, an estate was left during the life of decedent's widow, to trustees who were to accumulate the income thereon and pay to her a specified annuity during her life and at her death after applying a specified sum to such uses as she might by will appoint were to turn over all the rest of the estate to three corporations, legacies and devises to each of which are exempt from estate tax; the amount which is liable to estate tax is the amount over which the widow has the power of appointment plus the present worth of that part of the annuity which would not be provided by the income from the said amount over which she has this power of appointment and which must come from other sources.

*Kearns* v. *Dunbar.*—United States District Court, District of Utah (unreported to date).

The inheritance tax imposed by the State of Utah under section 3185, compiled laws of Utah, 1917, is a tax against the estate as distinguished from a tax against the inheritance and amounts paid thereunder are deductible from the gross estate in computing the amount of the Federal estate tax under section 203, revenue act, September 8, 1916.

*Liebman* v. *Fontenot.*—United States District Court, District of Louisiana (275 Fed. 688; T. D. 3222).

The value of the life usufruct in favor of a widow under section 916 of the Louisiana civil code is not deductible from the half of the community property going to the heirs of the deceased spouse, for the purpose of computing the estate tax imposed by act of September 8, 1916.

*Title Guarantee & Trust Co. et al.* v. *Edwards.*—United States District Court, Southern District of New York (T. D. 3319).

Title II, act of September 8, 1916, imposing an estate tax, is constitutional. Decision of the United States Supreme Court in New York Trust Co. v. Eisner (41 Sup. Ct. Rep. 506) held controlling.

The New York State transfer tax is not a charge that affects "the estate as a whole." It diminishes each legacy bequeathed by decedent, and is therefore not "a charge against the estate" and may not be deducted from the gross estate under the provisions of section 203 of the revenue act of 1916. Decision of the United States Supreme Court in New York Trust Co. *v.* Eisner (41 Sup. Ct. Rep. 506) held controlling.

If a widow accepts a provision made in lieu of dower, the value of the property thus bequeathed or devised must be included in the gross estate, as defined in section 203 of the revenue act of 1916, and the amount so included may not be diminished by deducting the value of the widow's dower in decedent's realty.

## EXCESS-PROFITS TAX.

*Cartier & Holland* v. *Doyle.*—United States Circuit Court of Appeals, Sixth Circuit (277 Fed. 150).

A partnership doing business on borrowed capital is taxable as a trade or business having no invested capital or not more than a nominal capital.

Collateral deposited by partners with a bank to secure partnership notes, indorsed by the partners, for the purpose of financing partnership business does not constitute tangible property, other than cash paid in for stock or shares in such partnership, for the purpose of ascertaining invested capital.

Money borrowed from a bank on notes of a partnership, indorsed by the partners, secured by collateral deposited by the partners does not constitute actual cash paid in, for purposes of ascertaining invested capital.

Withdrawals by partners against anticipated profits are not used in the partnership business and do not constitute earned surplus and undivided profits used or employed in the business, exclusive of undivided profits earned during the taxable year.

*Lederer* v. *Cadwalader.*—United States Circuit Court of Appeals, Third Circuit (274 Fed. 753).

A lawyer who acted in one instance as an executor is not subject to excess-profits tax under the revenue act of 1917 upon commissions received as such executor, since a single isolated activity of the character of an executorship does not constitute a trade, business, profession, or vocation within the meaning of the act.

*Castner, Curran & Bullitt* v. *Lederer.*—United States District Court, Eastern District of Pennsylvania (275 Fed. 221).

The invested capital of a corporation formed by the combination of two business concerns for the purpose of excess-profits tax under act February 24, 1919, section 326 (Comp. St. Ann. Supp. 1919, sec. 6336 7/16 i), held to be the value of the property as agreed upon by the parties at the time of the combination and for which stock was issued to each party.

"Actual cash value" and "value in actual cash" and other like expressions convey the thought of the sum which can be obtained at a fair sale—i. e., the market value.

*Ehret Magnesia Manufacturing Co.* v. *Lederer.*—United States District Court, Eastern District of Pennsylvania (273 Fed. 689; T. D. 3200).

"The amount of the net income in excess of the deduction," as used in section 201, means that, where the deduction does not exceed 15 per cent of the invested capital, the first of the graduated percentages of tax is to be 20 per cent of the difference between the deduction and 15 per cent of the invested capital.

The construction placed on section 201 by the regulations of the Commissioner of Internal Revenue does not render the law unconstitutional as preventing uniformity and equality in the application of the tax.

*R. H. Martin (Inc.)* v. *Edwards.*—United States District Court, Southern District of New York (T. D. 3334).

Plaintiff corporation acted as sole agent for a mining company under an arrangement contemplating that it should discount drafts in the case of foreign shipments and pay the amount of the invoices in the case of domestic shipments, retaining in both cases only commissions and interest, so that the principal was constantly in the corporation's debt for advances. The corporation was incorporated for $25,000, and in 1917 had capital, at the beginning of the year, of $51,074, and income of $26,890.34 from commissions from selling for account of its principal, $22,133.25 profits from buying and selling on its own account, and $5,851.90 from interest. In 1915 the proportion of gross profits from trading on its own account was 23 per cent; in 1916, 9.8 per cent, and in 1917, 45 per cent. Its profits during 1917 were retained, and not distributed as dividends, and its officers made substantial advances to aid it in financing the business. The capital of the corporation was not used merely to pay ordinary expenses, but to assist in paying advances to its principal, as well as to trade on its own account. During 1917 its capital was engaged in its business and was being turned over in connection with sales, its advances including capital available or capital repaid from advances. On December 31, 1917, when its bank balance was larger than in any other month of the year, it was only $16,501.67, while its capital and surplus amounted to $78,330. *Held,* that such corporation did not merely buy and sell on commission but traded substantially on its own account, and had a substantial invested capital which was employed in making advances to or on account of its principal, and also in buying merchandise on its own account for profitable sale, and hence it was not entitled to assessment under section 209 of the revenue act of 1917, which applies only to businesses having no invested capital or not more than a nominal capital.

### INCOME TAXES.

*Miles* v. *Safe Deposit & Trust Co. of Baltimore.*—Supreme Court of the United States (42 Sup. Ct. Rep. 483; T. D. 3365).

The acquisition of a new share by the exercise of a right to subscribe is merely an exercise of one of the rights of stock ownership, and until the new share has been sold no profit has been realized, and there is no taxable income.

A stockholder's privilege of subscribing to new shares of stock before they are offered to the public is an incident of his stock ownership, and the acquisition of that privilege, while it may increase the value of the stockholder's interest in the corporation, does not constitute a segregation of the profits of the corporation, and is not gain, profit, or income to the stockholder.

A stockholder of a corporation who receives the right to subscribe for shares of a new issue of stock is, on sale of such right, liable to income tax on so much of the proceeds as exceeds the cost of the right (citing Merchants Loan & Trust Co. v. Smietanka, T. D. 3173).

The new shares, if and when issued, are indistinguishable from the old shares, and as they are received by reason of the ownership of the old shares, the average of the price paid for the old shares and of the subscribing price for the new shares constitutes cost for either an old share or a new share in computing taxable gain, following the analogy of the computation employed in the case of the sale of stock dividend shares. On the sale of stock rights cost and selling price are determined by assuming that the stockholder, instead of selling his rights, subscribed for new shares and sold them, and the gain taxable to a stockholder who sells his rights is equal to the gain taxable to a stockholder who subscribes for a new share and sells his new share. In ascertaining the selling price it is assumed that the stockholder, if he had subscribed, would have refused to sell his new share for any amount less than the sum of the subscribing figure and the prevailing price offered for the rights, and the sum of these two amounts is assumed to represent the selling price of the stock rights. The taxable gain, therefore, is found by taking the sum of the subscribing price and the market value of the rights and subtracting from that sum the average of (1) the cost of one old share and (2) the subscribing price of one new share.

*Rockefeller* v. *United States; New York Trust Co.* v. *Edwards.*—Supreme Court of the United States (42 Sup. Ct. Rep. 68; T. D. 3271).

Where the stockholders of an oil company owning pipe-line and oil properties caused the organization of a pipe-line company to which it contracted to convey its pipe-line property, on consideration of which the pipe-line company agreed to distribute its stock to the stockholders of the oil company in the same proportion as their existing holdings, the pipe-line property representing a surplus above the par value of the oil company's stock, the shares of the pipe-line company received by the oil company stockholders in carrying out the contract constituted income to such stockholders under the revenue act of October 3, 1913.

Under the circumstances cited above the effect was the same whether the stock was distributed directly by the new corporation to the stockholders of the old corporation or transferred from the new corporation to the old corporation, and by the latter distributed to its stockholders.

Where a corporation having a surplus of accumulated profits exchanged a part of its assets for the common stock of a new corporation, organized by the stockholders of said corporation to take over a part of the business and business assets of the old corporation, and then distributed said shares of common stock to its stockholders, the distribution, whatever its effect upon the aggregate interests of the mass of stockholders, constituted in the case of each individual a gain in the form of actual exchangeable assets transferred to him from the old corporation for his separate use in partial realization of his former indivisible and contingent interest in the corporate surplus. It was in substance and effect, not merely in form, a dividend of profits by the corporation, an individual income to the stockholder. United States v. Phellis (decided at the same time) followed.

Where a new corporation was formed by the stockholders of an old corporation to take over a part of the business and a part of the business assets of the old corporation, with the same officers and stockholders for the time being having the same proportionate holdings of common stock of the new company that they had of the old company, *held* that the new corporation was not identical with the old, but was a separate and distinct corporate entity.

*Smietanka* v. *First Trust & Savings Bank.*—Supreme Court of the United States (42 Sup. Ct. Rep. 223; T. D. 3321).

Income held and accumulated by a trustee for the benefit of unborn or unascertained beneficiaries is not subject to the income tax imposed by the revenue act of 1913, although such income is expressly subjected to tax under all later income-tax acts.

Under the provisions of the revenue act of 1913 a trust estate is not taxable as an entity. The act requires the fiduciary to withhold and pay the normal tax upon the income of the estate or trust property distributed, but the trustee is not liable for the surtax which is payable by the beneficiary.

*United States* v. *Phellis.*—Supreme Court of the United States (42 Sup. Ct. Rep. 63; T. D. 3270).

Under Section II (*b*) of the act of October 3, 1913, declaring that income shall include, among other things, gains derived "from interest, rent, dividends, securities, * * * or gains or profits and income derived from any source whatever," not everything in the form of a dividend must be treated as income, but income *in the way* of dividends shall be taxed.

Where a stockholder, as the result of a reorganization and financial readjustment of the business of the corporation, received as a dividend on each share of common stock held by him two shares of the common stock of a new corporation, the dividend so received representing the surplus of accumulated profits of the first corporation, and the shares so received having a market value separate and distinct from the original share, such dividend was a gain, a profit, derived from his capital interest in the old company, and constituted individual income to the stockholder within the meaning of the income tax law of 1913. The rule laid down in Peabody *v.* Eisner (247 U. S. 347) followed; Eisner *v.* Macomber (252 U. S. 189) distinguished.

That a comparison of the market value of the stockholder's shares in the old corporation immediately before, with the aggregate market value of those shares plus the dividend shares immediately after the dividend, showed no change in the aggregate, is immaterial and is not a proper test for determining whether individual income, taxable against the stockholder, has been received by means of the dividend.

The question whether a dividend made out of company profits constitutes income of the stockholder is not affected by antecedent transfers of the stock from hand to hand.

Where a new corporation was formed under the laws of another State, to take over the business and business assets of an old corporation, having authorized capital amounting to nearly four times the aggregate stock issues and funded debt of the old company, of which less than one-half was to be issued at once to the old company or its stockholders, held that the new corporation was not indentical with the old, but was a separate and distinct corporate entity, despite the fact that both corporations had for the time being the same personnel of officers and stockholders, having the same proportionate holdings of stock in both companies.

The question whether an individual stockholder derived income in the true and substantial sense through receiving a part in the distribution of the new shares can not be tested by regarding alone the general effect of the reorganization upon the aggregate body of stockholders; the liability of a stockholder to pay an individual income tax must be tested by the effect of the transaction upon the individual.

*Ed. Schuster & Co. (Inc.)* v. *Williams.*—United States Circuit Court of Appeals, Seventh Circuit (T. D. 3330).

The plaintiff was a corporation, keeping its accounts and filing returns upon an accrual basis, and annually set up upon its books a "reserve" for income taxes due the State of Wisconsin, under the laws of which it was organized. Under the provisions of section 234 (a) (3), revenue act of 1918, the company deducted from its Federal income-tax return for the year 1918 the "reserve" for income taxes due the State at the rate in effect on December 31, 1918. On July 30, 1919, the Wisconsin Legislature passed a "soldiers' bonus" act, which provided for the raising of the money by a single tax levy of one mill on all assessed property for the year 1919, and a surtax over the normal tax on the incomes of corporations upon the basis of the 1918 State income-tax returns. After the ratification of the soldiers' bonus act on October 10, 1919, the plaintiff filed an amended Federal income-tax return for the year 1918 and sought to deduct therein as taxes accrued for the year 1918 the amount of additional taxes due the State under the soldiers' bonus act. *Held*, that the basis of the levy of the soldiers' bonus tax was 1918 incomes, but there is no relation between the basis for the State levy and the time of the accrual of the tax for Federal tax purposes.

A tax does not "accrue" until it becomes a liability of the taxpayer, and a tax can not be "accrued" and deducted for Federal income-tax purposes in the year 1918 where the State act creating the tax liability was not passed until the year 1919.

*United States* v. *Guinzburg.*—United States Circuit Court of Appeals, Second Circuit (278 Fed. 363).

Under income tax act October 3, 1913, section 2, A, subdivision 1, which took effect from March 1, 1913, and imposed an annual tax on the entire net income of citizens and residents "arising or accruing from all sources in the preceding calendar year," a dividend declared by a corporation prior to March 1, 1913, though not paid until after that date, held to have been capital of the stockholder at the time the act took effect, and not taxable as income arising or accruing thereafter.

*Wilson* v. *Eisner.*—United States Circuit Court of Appeals, Second Circuit (unreported to date).

A taxpayer engaged in business as a horse breeder and stock raiser may deduct as business expenses amount spent in caring for, feeding, breeding, and marketing blooded horses and for transportation charges in taking the horses to various racing centers. The fact that the taxpayer was a sportsman in the sense that he was fond of racing horses did not change the character of the undertaking if he was engaged in business for profit.

In determining the deductibility of certain business expenses, here the undisputed proof leaves only the question of whether the axpayer was or was not engaged in business as a horse breeder and tock raiser within the meaning of the taxing act, such question is ne of law for the court and not a question of fact for the jury.

*Catherwood* v. *United States.*—United States District Court, Eastrn District of Pennsylvania (280 Fed. 241).

A decedent who is liable for an income tax to the date of his death, nd his estate, which pays an income tax upon income received by he estate during the period of administration and also an estate tax, re two separate entities and different taxpayers, although all three axes are paid by the executor out of the estate. The estate tax paid s therefore not a proper deduction from the gross income of the decelent for the period prior to her death, notwithstanding there was no axable net income to the estate during the period of administration rom which this deduction could be taken under the authority of the ase of *United States* v. *Woodward* (256 U. S. 632; T. D. 3195).

*Commercial Health & Accident Co.* v. *Pickering.*—United States istrict Court, Southern District of Illinois (281 Fed. 539; T. D. 3313).

A general life, health, and accident insurance company organized mder a general law and doing a general business throughout an ntire State is not "a like organization of a purely local character" nd is, therefore, not an exempt organization within the meaning of ection 11, paragraph 10, of the revenue act of 1916, and section 231, aragraph 10, of the revenne act of 1918.

Section 11, paragraph 10, of the revenue act 1916, and section 231, aragraph 10, of the revenue act of 1918, being exemption provisos, are construed strictly and take no case out of the enacting clause of the statutes which does not fall fairly within their terms.

The words "of a purly local character" in section 11, paragraph 10, of the revenue act of 1916, and section 231 (10) of the revenue act of 1918 are words of limitation upon all of the organizations named in the paragraph and do not apply solely to "like organizations."

*Fox* v. *Edwards.*—United States District Court, Southern District of New York (280 Fed. 413; T. D. 3308).

Where a taxpayer voluntarily files a return and pays the tax due thereunder without protest or complaint, but later determines that he has overpaid his tax, due to failure to take deductions to which he believes he was entitled, there can be no recovery against the collector to whom the taxes were paid at common law or under the statute relating to him or his office.

Any rights which may be granted by section 252 of the revenue act of 1918 can not be asserted in a suit against a collector for the recovery of taxes voluntarily paid; nor does that section relieve a taxpayer from the obligation of establishing payment under protest in a suit against a collector.

*Lilley Building & Loan Co.* v. *Miller.*—United States District Court, Southern District of Ohio (280 Fed. 143; T. D. 3355).

Mutuality is the essential principle of a building and loan association. Its object is to raise a fund to be loaned among its members or such as may desire to avail themselves of the privilege. Its business is confined to its members.

When a building and loan association ceases to be substantially mutual and adopts as its chief business dealing for profit with the general public by the methods of an ordinary savings bank, it is no longer entitled to exemption under section 231, paragraph 4, of the revenue act of 1918.

The making of loans to nonmembers or borrowing from nonmembers does not defeat exemption under section 231, paragraph 4, of the revenue act of 1918, if such transactions are simply incidental to the primary business of operating a building and loan association.

*Massey* v. *Lederer.*—United States District Court, Eastern District of Pennsylvania (277 Fed. 123; T. D. 3315).

Under Title XII, section 1205, subdivision (*c*) of act of October 3, 1917, amending subdivision (*c*) of section 9 of act of September 8, 1916, taxes on bonds of a corporation, containing covenants agreeing to pay to bondholders interest at a prescribed rate without deduction of taxes, is income to the individual to the extent of the tax thus paid by the corporation.

The normal tax of 2 per cent, while paid at the source by the corporation, is not a tax on the corporation but a tax on the individual.

The taxes so paid by a corporation for and on behalf of the individual bondholder come within the definition of income as "gains, profits, and income derived from any source whatever" in section 1200 of the act of 1917.

The tax-free covenant in the bonds is equivalent to an agreement of the obligors to pay the owners the agreed rate of interest plus the taxes, and it is immaterial whether the taxes are paid by the owners of the bonds to the Government and the amount thereof refunded by the obligors to the owners, or whether under the covenant and the statute the taxes are paid direct to the Government by the obligors, since the tax is on the individual but collectible from the corporation, the corporation paying the tax because of its contract with the bondholder.

*Park* v. *Gilligan.*—United States District Court, Southern District of Ohio (unreported to date).

An amount received by a corporation in 1916, in settlement of litigation begun prior to March 1, 1913, under the antitrust laws, which amount was apportioned among the stockholders and credited to them on the books of the corporation, did not constitute income of the stockholders in 1916. The amount on March 1, 1913, was accrued capital represented by a chose in action which was reduced to cash in 1916. It was not a distribution from profits accumulated within the taxable period; therefore it was not taxable to the distributees as income.

*Penrose* v. *Skinner.*—United States District Court, District of Colorado (278 Fed. 284).

Where a taxpayer's income-tax return was false, in that he had not sustained the losses deducted therein, the tax subsequently collected on the amount of such deduction was justly exacted, whether an assessment had or had not been made, and could not be recovered, there being no implied promise for its return.

Act February 24, 1919, section 250 (*d*) (Comp. St. Ann. Supp. 1919, sec. 6336 ⅛tt), providing that no suit or proceeding for the collection if any income tax shall be begun after the expiration of five years from the date when the return was due or was made, has no application in an action to recover back a tax paid under protest.

No authority has been vested in the Commissioner of Internal Revenue to overrule and reverse the action of his predecessor in office, and where a former commissioner heard and determined a question of fact necessary to enable him to act intelligently in determining the amount of plaintiff's net income on which he would be required to make a levy and assessment, and his finding on that issue has not been impeached, it should be regarded as final.

Where the only question of fact under consideration on plaintiff's application to a former Commissioner of Internal Revenue for remission of an income tax assessed against him was whether he was within the class of persons entitled to deduct losses sustained in buying and selling stocks and securities, the commissioner's decision is not conclusive on the present commissioner, where it now appears that plaintiff did not during the tax period sustain any such losses as those claimed.

*Plant* v. *Walsh.*—United States District Court, District of Connecticut (280 Fed. 722).

Corporate dividends declared prior to March 1, 1913, and payable subsequent to that date to stockholders of record at dates prior to that time are not liable to tax under the 1913 income tax act.

Bookkeeping entries are at least prima facie evidence of the actual value of bonds owned by a corporation for the purpose of ascertaining deductions allowable for bad debts.

Interest due and accrued for six months ending February 28, 1913, but paid after March 1, 1913, is not taxable as income.

Excess of expenditures over receipts is not conclusive evidence that a farm is not conducted as a business enterprise. The court finds upon the evidence that the plaintiff's farm "was conducted as a business enterprise and with the expectation that it would eventually become profitable" and holds that the mere fact that a heavy loss was incurred in the initial stages of so large an enterprise does not necessarily show the contrary.

*Porto Rico Coal Co.* v. *Edwards.*—United States District Court, Southern District of New York (275 Fed. 104).

That under act March 2, 1917, section 9, internal revenue laws are not effective in Porto Rico, does not affect the liability of a State corporation for an income tax because it conducts its business in and derives its income from Porto Rico.

The subjection of a State corporation deriving its income from Porto Rico to an income tax for the benefit of the National Government and also by revenue act 1918, section 261, to a similar tax as a foreign corporation for the benefit of Porto Rico, does not constitute a double taxation.

A New York corporation doing business in and deriving its income from Porto Rico subject to the income and excess-profits taxes imposed by revenue act of 1918, sections 230 (a), 301(a).

A corporation of New York can not invoke a supposed immunity from Federal taxation granted by the bill of rights of Porto Rico (act Mar. 2, 1917, sec. 2) merely because it derives its income from that island.

A statute imposing internal revenue taxes is not in violation of the fifth amendment to the Constitution, as taking the property of those taxes without due process of law, because it is not made applicable to citizens of Porto Rico.

The fact that a New York corporation derives its income from business in Porto Rico not to exempt it from the excess-profits tax imposed by act October 3, 1917, section 201.

*Towne* v. *McElligott.*—United States District Court, Southern District of New York (274 Fed. 960; T. D. 3252).

A graduated income tax which applies at a rate of 72 per cent on a portion of a taxpayer's net income and at an average rate of 50 per cent on his entire net income is not confiscatory within the meaning of the fifth amendment to the Constitution.

Where a taxpayer received a 50 per cent stock dividend upon shares of stock, part of which were purchased prior to March 1, 1913, and part subsequent thereto, and in 1918 sold the orginal certificates held on March 1, 1913, part of the stock purchased after March 1, 1913, and part of the stock received as the 50 per cent stock dividend, the basis for computing the profit from such sale shall be as follows: For each certificate held on March 1, 1913, two-thirds of its value on that date; for each certificate acquired thereafter, two-thirds of its purchase price; and upon each certificate for stock dividend shares if identified as issued against a specified earlier certificate, one-third of the value on March 1, 1913, of the stock upon which the dividend was declared or one-third of the purchase price of the stock upon which the dividend was declared, as the case may be. If the stock received as a dividend can not be identified as having been declared upon any specific lot of the old stock, the sales of the dividend stock should be applied against the dividend stock chargeable to the first purchase remaining unsold when the stock dividend was declared.

### INSURANCE TAX.

*Bankers & Planters Mutual Insurance Co.* v. *Walker.*—United States Circuit Court of Appeals, Eighth Circuit (279 Fed. 53; T. D. 3318).

Plaintiff association, comprised of members brought together without regard to locality of place for the sole purpose of insuring the lives of such members, under a business plan which divided the members into "circles" of 1,000 members each, charged a small entrance fee and paid losses by graduated, limited assessments, collected at time of losses upon the surviving members of that particular "circle." The assessments also provided for the maintenance of the business organization and operation, but no reserve, surplus, or other fund was provided, and no dividends or profits could be earned. The amount of insurance of each member was at entrance $100, which amount increased after the first six months at the rate of $12.50 per month to a maximum of $1,000, provided that all dues and assessments were promptly paid, and provided that the value of any certificate should not exceed the net proceeds of a regular assessment of the surviving members of that "circle." *Held,* that the association was not merely a mutual aid society but was a life insurance company, within the meaning of section 504 of the revenue act of 1917, imposing a tax on each $100 or fractional part thereof of the amount for which ny life is insured under any policy of insurance or other instrument, y whatever name the same is called, said section not requiring rofits or dividends as a prerequisite to the tax.

Said association is not exempt under subdivision (d) of section 504 of he revenue act of 1917, which exempts policies issued by associations rhose income is exempt from taxation under Title I of the revenue ct of 1916, the association not coming within the meaning of either he third, sixth, or tenth paragraphs of section 11 (a) of said latter ct, which, respectively, limit the exemption to fraternal beneficiary ocieties operating under the lodge system, to nonprofit organizations rhich are organized and operated exclusively for religious, charitable, cientific, or educational purposes, and to farmers' or other mutual ail, cyclone, or fire insurance company, mutual ditch or irrigation ompany, mutual or cooperative telephone company, or like organiza- ion of a purely local character, the income of which consists solely f assessments, dues, and fees collected from members for the sole urpose of meeting its expenses.

A life insurance company is not a "like organization" to those numerated in subdivision "tenth" of section 11 (a), revenue act of 916, such organizations being "farmers' or other mutual hail, yclone, or fire insurance company, mutual ditch or irrigation com- any, mutual or cooperative telephone company."

Assessment and collection of the tax not alone on the initial cer- ificate value of $100 but also upon the accrued increased valuation asis of $12.50 monthly after the first six months, was proper, such otal sum representing the "amount of insurance" intended by sec- ion 504 (a) of the revenue act of 1917.

## LEGACY TAXES.

*Kahn v. United States.*—Supreme Court of the United States (42 Sup. Ct. Rep. 85; T. D. 3311).

The test to be applied in ascertaining whether legacies were, on July 1, 1902, still contingent, so as to determine whether taxes assessed thereon under the provisions of section 29 of the act of June 13, 1898, may be recovered under the act of June 27, 1902, directing a refund of any tax that may have been collected on contingent bene- ficial interests which shall not have become vested prior to July 1, 1902, is a practical, not a technical one; the beneficial interests were contingent unless the legatees were then in actual possession or enjoy- ment, or were entitled to immediate possession or enjoyment.

A gift to a trustee of a fund, the income of which is to be paid over periodically during life, is, at least after the payments have com- menced, a life estate, not a contingent beneficial interest.

The mere failure of executors to establish the trust fund will not prevent the investing of the legacy, if under the State law the time 'or payment has come, the right thereto is uncontroverted, and it is :lear that the money will not be needed to satisfy outstanding claims.

Where, on July 1, 1902, trustees were entitled to possession of trust unds and all of the beneficiaries to the immediate enjoyment of the ncome thereof, with the exception of an amount involved in contro- versies over taxes, and, under the State law, the executors of the will which created the trust might then have paid over the balance of :he estate in their hands to the trustees, retaining funds sufficient to satisfy the disputed claims for taxes, failure of the trustees to retain such funds did not prevent the beneficial interests from vesting, it not appearing that the amount on which the taxes in question were assessed exceeded the amount of such balance.

## MUNITIONS MANUFACTURERS' TAX.

*Dayton Brass Castings Co.* v. *Gilligan.*—United States Circuit Court of Appeals, Sixth Circuit (277 Fed. 227; T. D. 3274).

"A" company had a contract for the sale of shrapnel shells to the Russian Government and sublet to "B" company a contract for making the shell fuses. "B" company entered into a contract with "D" company whereby "B" company agreed to furnish "D" company certain brass ingots, and the latter agreed to mold the metal into small castings which were to be united by "B" company with other parts to make a complete fuse, the materials and castings molded therefrom to remain the property of "B" company at all times. For this service "D" company was to be paid a specified price per pound. Pursuant to the contract, "D" company molded and delivered to "B" company a large number of castings. *Held,* that the "D" company was a manufacturer of munitions and its conduct constituted a "sale or disposition" of munitions within the meaning of Title III of the revenue act of 1916, imposing a tax upon the net profits received or accrued from the sale or disposition of "any part" of fuses by any person manufacturing the same.

The tax is imposed upon the business of manufacturing and is measured by the profits received upon the sale or disposition of the munitions manufactured.

*Mills Woven Cartridge Belt Co.* v. *Malley.*—United States District Court, District of Massachusetts (unreported to date).

The cartridge belt which carries the ammunition used in connection with the Vickers machine gun is taxable under act of September 8, 1916, Title III, as a "part" or "appendage."

## NARCOTICS.

*Pierriero* v. *United States.*—United States Circuit Court of Appeals Fourth Circuit (271 Fed. 912; T. D. 3218).

The mere possession of narcotic drugs is prima facie evidence of purchase, sale, dispensing, or distribution of narcotic drugs in violation of the Harrison Narcotic Act, section 1, as amended by the revenue act of 1918, section 1006, and places upon defendant the burden of proving that his possession was not unlawful.

An allegation in the indictment that defendant sold, dispensed, and distributed narcotics implies that he was within the class required to register by Harrison Narcotic Act, section 1, as amended by revenue act of 1918, section 1006, and with proof that narcotics were found in his possession, is sufficient, allegation and proof that he was required to register to place on him the burden of showing that he was not in the class required to register and that his possession was not unlawful.

In a prosecution for violating Harrison Narcotic Act, section 1, as amended by revenue act of 1918, section 1006, where it was undisputed that narcotics were found in defendant's room, but he denied any knowledge of them, and offered evidence that others had access to his room, a charge that if the narcotics were found in defendant's possession—that is, in the room occupied by him—such possession was prima facie evidence of purchase and sale by him, was not errone-ous, as declaring the finding of the narcotics in the room established his possession, where immediately after that paragraph the court directly charged that, in determining whether the narcotics were found in defendant's possession, the jury should consider all the circumstances in the case, including the fact, if so found, that other persons had access to the room.

## OCCUPATIONAL TAX.

*Cothran & Connally* v. *United States.*—United States District Court, Western District of Virginia (276 Fed. 48; T. D. 3244).

A tobacco warehouseman whose business is to arrange that tobacco planters shall bring their produce to the warehouse to be sold at auction, and that tobacco buyers shall attend such auction sales and bid for the tobacco, is a broker within the meaning of subsection 1 of section 1001 of the revenue act of 1918, and subject to the special tax imposed thereby.

## PROHIBITION.

*Lewinsohn* v. *United States.*—United States Circuit Court of Appeals, Seventh Circuit (278 Fed. 421; T. D. 3303). Certiorari denied by Supreme Court (42 Sup. Ct. Rep. 463).

A finding that a room or building is a common nuisance within the meaning of section 21 of the national prohibition act may properly be made upon evidence of a single sale, provided the facts surrounding such sale warranted the inference that it was one of the ordinary and usual incidents of the business there conducted.

On a charge of contempt for violation of an injunction the right of trial by jury was not violated.

Neither a court rule nor a general statute can overthrow the specific provisions of section 22, Title II, of the national prohibition act, providing for a temporary injunction until the conclusion of the trial. A temporary injunctional order does not expire in 10 days from its entry because granted ex parte.

Congress, by sections 21–24 of the national prohibition act, intended to supply a more prompt, effective, and efficient means of abating nuisances than the institution of criminal actions and it is unnecessary to allege that defendant had been prosecuted and convicted of a similar criminal offense in order to invoke the jurisdiction of a court of equity to secure an injunction under these sections.

*Lipke* v. *Lederer.*—Supreme Court of the United States (42 Sup. Ct. Rep. 549; T. D. 3354).

In March, 1921, an assessment of double tax and penalty was made under section 35, Title II, national prohibition act. While a criminal charge under the act was still pending the collector of internal revenue attempted to collect the assessment by distraint as taxes are collected under the internal-revenue laws. *Held,* That naming a penalty a "tax" does not make it such in fact and, Congress not having declared in language admitting of no other construction its intention that such assessments should be collected in such manner, a temporary injunction should have been granted.

*Baltimore Talking Board Co. (Inc.)* v. *Miles.*--United States Circuit Court of Appeals, Fourth Circuit (T. D. 3312). Certiorari denied by Supreme Court (42 Sup. Ct. Rep. 590).

The scope of the sales tax is comprehensive and not limited to the articles named in section 900, subdivision 5 of the revenue act of 1918.

In its broadest sense a game is "a play or sport for amusement." In its restricted and more generally applied sense it is "a contest for success or superiority in a trial of chance, skill, or endurance, or any two or all of the three combined." (Century Dictionary.)

The word "games" as used in section 900, subdivision 5, of the revenue act of 1918, does not mean the games themselves but the instrumentalities used in playing them, and includes ouija boards, the purpose of which is to supply amusement and diversion.

Size alone does not make a game a child's toy and a ."wee" ouija board is not exempt from taxation as a child's toy.

The rule that taxing acts are to be construed most strongly against the Government only applies in cases where doubt remains after all recognized rules for ascertaining a statute's meaning have been tried. Doubt as to the meaning of a word is often removed by consideration of the legislative intent, as shown by the entire statute. Gould v. Gould (245 U. S. 151), and other cases distinguished.

The findings and practice of the administrative officers of the Government are presumed to be based on fair conclusions as the result of investigation required of them by sections 3165 and 3172, Revised Statutes, as amended by the revenue act of 1918.

*Malley* v. *Walter Baker & Co. (Ltd.).*—United States Circuit Court of Appeals, First Circuit (281 Fed. 41; T. D. 3344).

Revenue laws are not penal laws in the sense that requires them to be construed with great strictness in favor of the taxpayer, but are remedial in character and should be so construed as to carry out the intention of the legislature.

Sweet chocolate consisting more than half of sugar, manufactured in cakes and bars, adapted for consumption as candy, packed in convenient cartons for sale as candy, advertised as "delicious for eating," or "excellent as a confection," and sold in large quantities over candy counters, and consumed, at least in substantial part, in the form put out by the manufacturer for such consumption, is not a food, but is taxable as candy under Title IX, section 900 of the revenue act of 1918.

Where ambiguity is found in a statute or when it is necessary to determine a fact upon which the operation of a statute is made to depend, the regulations made by the department charged with the administration of the act are to be given great, sometimes practically controlling, weight.

The distinction undertaken in article 22 of Regulations No. 47 made by the Commissioner of Internal Revenue that sweet chocolate should be taxed when put up and sold in such form as to indicate that it was to be consumed as candy is consumed, and not taxed when it is obvious from the packing or other circumstances surrounding the transaction that it was to be merely an ingredient for further manufacture, is a sound distinction, and such regulation is not invalid as an attempt to extend the natural meaning of the language of the statute.

The burden of proof is on the taxpayer, suing to recover taxes paid, to show that the taxes collected were illegal or the assessments excessive.

It was error, in a suit to recover taxes paid on sweet chocolate as candy under the provisions of section 900 of the revenue act of 1918, to refuse to submit to the jury the question of what proportion of such chocolate was used for cooking or domestic purposes.

*Klepper* v. *Carter.*—United States District Court, Southern District of California (unreported to date).

Where a dealer purchased a truck chassis, paying the excise tax of 3 per cent thereon, and secures the manufacture of a body of another concern, paying a tax of 5 per cent thereon as a part of any automobile, the two component parts being assembled and sold by the dealer as a whole, he is not a dealer but a "producer or manufacturer" within the meaning of section 900 of the revenue act of 1918 and must pay an excise tax upon the sales price of the completed automobile truck. The dealer may in such case take a credit for the tax paid on the chassis and the body before the two were assembled.

### STAMP TAXES.

*Fidelity Trust Co.* v. *Edwards.*—United States District Court Southern District of New York (276 Fed. 51; T. D. 3233).

So-called "car-trust certificates" are taxable as corporate securities under the revenue act of 1918 (subdiv. 1, Sched. A, Title XI).

*Marconi Wireless Telegraph Co. of America* v. *Duffy.*—United States District Court, District of New Jersey (273 Fed. 197; T. D. 3219).

Where one corporation sold to another corporation certain property in consideration of the issuance to it of a fixed number of shares of the capital stock of the purchasing corporation, and thereafter, prior to the actual issuance of the stock certificates, the vendor corporation authorized the vendee corporation to issue the shares direct to the stockholders of the vendor corporation, the resolution of the board of directors of the vendor corporation conveying the authority is a transfer of the right to receive such shares, and the transaction is subject to the stamp tax imposed by subdivision 4, Schedule A, revenue act of 1918.

The substantial difference between a corporation and its stockholders may not be disregarded.

### TAX ON TRANSPORTATION AND OTHER FACILITIES.

*Meischke-Smith et al.* v. *Wardell.*—United States District Court, Northern District of California (unreported to date).

Where a corporation owning oil wells and refineries organized a pipe-line company and conveyed to it all the stock owned by said parent company and this pipe-line company transported oil solely for the parent company, collecting no tax or charge, but entering such charges on its books, the subsidiary is liable to tax under Title V, act of October 3, 1917, as one transporting oil by pipe line for another.

The question of the separate legal entity of a corporation as affected by ownership of its stock by another company at the time taxes accrued is considered in a memorandum opinion and the case is decided on the authority of 115 U. S. 587; 205 U. S. 364; 269 Fed. 885.

*Western Union Telegraph Co.* v. *The Delaware, Lackawanna & Western Railroad Co.*—United States District Court, Southern District of New York (T. D. 3369).

. Where a telegraph company paid the tax imposed on telegraph messages by section 500(f) of the revenue act of 1918, as construed and applied by article 9 of regulations No. 57, on messages transmitted by it without charge for a railroad company under a contract providing for the mutual interchange of services between such companies, the validity of such tax should be raised by a proceeding to recover the taxes back, and the legality of the regulations could not be tested in any manner convenient to such companies, as in a friendly suit to which the Government was not a party.

Section 500(f) of the revenue act of 1918, levying a tax on telegraphic messages, must be construed to cover all messages transmitted for an economic consideration—money or money's worth—and no differentiation can be made between exchanges and cash-paid services; therefore, the tax attaches to messages transmitted by a telegraph company without charge for a railroad company under a contract providing for the mutual interchange of services between such companies, and article 9 of regulations No. 57 (providing that where a telegraph company agrees, in consideration of the payment of a lump sum or of the performance of services, to transmit messages on frank, such messages are subject to the tax) is not invalid as being without the scope of the statute.

### TRADING IN FUTURES.

*Hill et al.* v. *Wallace et al.*—Supreme Court of the United States (42 Sup. Ct. Rep. 453; T. D. 3345).

A bill filed by several members in good standing of a board of trade, suing in behalf of other members, averred that complainants applied to the directors of such board to institute a suit to have the future trading act of August 24, 1921, adjudged unconstitutional before they could comply with it, but that the directors refused to take any steps because they feared to antagonize public officials charged with the duty of construing and enforcing the act. The establishment and organization of said board were set out and its methods of doing business stated, and it was shown that the act, if enforced, would seriously injure the value of the board of trade to its members, and the pecuniary value of their memberships. *Held,* that, assuming the act to be invalid, the bill stated sufficient equitable grounds to justify the granting of an injunction restraining the board of trade and each of its officers and directors from applying to the Secretary of Agriculture to have such board designated as a contract market under the act, and from admitting to membership into such board any representative or any cooperative association of producers in compliance with section 5 of the act, or from taking any other steps to comply with the act.

Section 3224, Revised Statutes, providing that no suit to restrain he assessment or collection of any tax shall be maintained, does not rohibit the maintenance of a suit by members of a board of trade to ⏄njoin a collector of internal revenue and United States district attorney from attempting to collect any tax, penalty, or fine, under the futures trading act of August 24, 1921, as under such act a sale of grain for future delivery without paying the tax will subject one to heavy criminal penalties, and to pay the heavy tax on each of many daily transactions which occur in the ordinary business of a member of an exchange, and then sue to recover it back, would necessitate a multiplicity of suits, and as refusal of the board to apply for designation as a contract market in order to test the validity of the act would stop its 1,600 members in a branch of their business most important to themselves and to the country; the right to sue for an injunction against the taxing officials is not, however, necessary to give the court jurisdiction, as, if they were to be dismissed under section 3224, Revised Statutes, the bill would still raise the question against the board of trade and its directors.

The futures trading act of August 24, 1921, entitled "An act taxing contracts for the sale of grain for future delivery, and options for such contracts, and providing for the regulation of boards of trade, and for other purposes," imposing a tax of 20 cents a bushel on all contracts for the sale of grain for future delivery, but excepting from its application sales on boards of trades designated as contract markets by the Secretary of Agriculture, on fulfillment by such boards of certain conditions and requirements, is in essence and on its face a complete regulation of boards of trade, with a penalty of 20 cents a bushel on all "futures" to coerce boards of trade and their members in compliance, and it can not be sustained as an exercise of the taxing power of Congress conferred by section 8, Article I, of the Federal Constitution.

Regulations of boards of trade by Congress, attempted by the futures trading act of August 24, 1921, can not be sustained under the commerce clause of the Constitution, since sales for future delivery on boards of trade are not in and of themselves interstate commerce; therefore, section 4 and those parts of the act which are regulations affected by the so-called tax imposed by section 4 are unenforceable.

Section 4 of the futures trading act of August 24, 1921, with its penalty to secure compliance with the regulations of boards of trade is so interwoven with those regulations that they can not be separated, and none of them can stand, though section 11 of such act directs that if any provision of the act or the application thereof to any person or circumstances is held invalid, the validity of the remainder of the act and of the application of such provision to other persons and circumstances shall not be affected thereby; section 11 did not intend the court to dissect an unconstitutional measure and reframe a valid one out of it by inserting limitations it does not contain, this being legislative work beyond the power and function of the court.

## MISCELLANEOUS.

*In re Anderson: Ex Parte Edwards.*—United States District Court, Southern District of New York (275 Fed. 397).

Under bankruptcy act, section 64a (Comp. St. sec. 9648), providing that the court shall order the trustee to pay all taxes legally due and owing by the bankrupt to the United States, etc., in advance of payment of dividends, "and in case any question arises as to the amount or legality of any such tax the same shall be heard and determined by the court," while the United States is not required to file a claim for taxes, in the absence of any action on its part, the court has jurisdiction to proceed in invitum to liquidate any such tax, and notice to the collector of internal revenue for the district is sufficient as a condition precedent to such proceedings.

*In re Anderson: United States v. Lyttle.*—United States Circuit Court of Appeals, Second Circuit (279 Fed. 525).

The United States is subject to the terms of the bankruptcy act and must file its claim for taxes like any other creditor if it desires to share in the estate. Any other procedure would prevent the winding up of bankruptcy proceedings and the distribution of the assets, since the trustee may only pay out assets under an order of the referee or of the court and without such order he could not pay income taxes owing to the Government.

The Circuit Court of Appeals has jurisdiction to review questions of jurisdiction of claims for Federal taxes against bankrupt estates.

The collector of internal revenue is the proper party defendant and the proper party upon whom the trustee in bankruptcy should serve notice in order that the United States may have an opportunity to establish its claim for taxes due from a bankrupt estate.

*Hurst v. Lederer.*—United States Circuit Court of Appeals, Third Circuit (273 Fed. 174; T. D. 3221).

Under act of March 1, 1879 (ch. 125, sec. 2), providing that "each deputy collector shall have like authority in every respect to collect the taxes levied or assessed within the portion of the district assigned to him which is by law vested in the collector himself," payment of money to a deputy collector other than the one authorized to receive it is not a satisfaction of the tax liability, and does not bind the collector.

*Smietanka v. Indiana Steel Co.*—Supreme Court of the United States (42 Sup. Ct. Rep. 1; T. D. 3304).

An action against an internal revenue collector to recover internal revenue taxes paid is personal, and can not be brought and maintained against the successor in office of the collector collecting them, when the successor did not participate in the collection, receipt, or disbursement of such taxes.

Act of February 8, 1899 (ch. 121, 30 Stat., 822), providing that a suit by or against an officer of the United States in his official capacity shall not abate by reason of his death, or the expiration of his term of office, etc., but that the court upon motion within 12 months showing the necessity for the survival of the suit to obtain a settlement of the question involved, may allow the same to be maintained by or against his successor in office, does not affect the above conclusion, the act being applicable, if at all, only where suit has already been begun against the predecessor in office in his lifetime.

*United States v. San Juan County et al.*—United States District Court, Northern District of Washington (280 Fed. 120; T. D. 3298).

Under the provisions of section 3466, Revised Statutes, the claim of the United States against an insolvent corporation for unpaid taxes takes priority over claims for taxes due a State, county, or municipality.

# INDEX.

## A.

## B.